Principles of External Auditing

Fourth Edition

Brenda Porter
Jon Simon
David Hatherly

Contents

About the Authors

Brenda Porter is a Visiting Professor, teaching auditing, at Exeter University (UK) and Chulalongkorn University (Bangkok). She recently retired as Professor and Head of the School of Accounting and Commercial Law at Victoria University, New Zealand. She is a Fellow of the Institute of Chartered Accountants of New Zealand and a member of the Institute of Chartered Accountants of Scotland. Her main research interests are the role of auditing in society, the audit expectation gap and the role of the tripartite audit function (external and internal auditors and audit committees) in securing responsible corporate governance. She has published widely on auditing issues in academic, business and professional journals.

Jon Simon is Senior Lecturer in Accounting at Hull University Business School. He teaches financial reporting, auditing and business research methods. His primary research interests are in these areas as well as in accounting and business education (with a focus on concept mapping). He has published in a range of academic and professional journals on accounting and auditing issues.

David Hatherly is Professor Emeritus of Accounting at the University of Edinburgh Business School having previously been Head of the Accounting and Finance Group at the School. He was for ten years a member of the Auditing Practices Board for the UK and Ireland where he worked on the Board's papers on the future development of auditing. He is a member of both the Institute of Chartered Accountants in England and Wales and the Institute of Chartered Accountants of Scotland where he has served on numerous committees. He has published widely on auditing in the professional and academic journals.

Preface

The fourth edition of *Principles of External Auditing* follows the first three editions, published in 1996, 2002 and 2008, respectively. Like its predecessors, this edition describes and explains, in readily comprehensible, non-technical language, the role of the auditor in society, the nature of the audit function and the principles of the audit process. The book is designed for *anyone* who is interested in understanding the principles that underlie external auditing. It also provides an ideal foundation for all those studying auditing, and is particularly suitable as a text for introductory courses in universities and for professional examinations such as the ACCA's *Audit and Assurance* and *Advanced Audit and Assurance*. For more advanced auditing courses, the book may usefully be supplemented by articles and other reading material drawn from professional and academic journals. Some suitable references are indicated in the 'Additional Reading' provided at the end of each chapter.

Since 2008, numerous changes have affected the auditing environment and the audit process. Some of these have been effected through legislative changes, such as the raising of the audit exemption threshold and the restructuring of the Financial Reporting Council (FRC) – the United Kingdom's (UK) independent regulator for corporate reporting and governance which oversees, inter alia, the auditing profession, ethical and technical auditing standards and the monitoring of auditors' performance.[1] Other changes have resulted from the International Audit and Assurance Standards Board's (IAASB) 'clarity project' which was completed in 2009 and introduced one new and 16 revised International Standards on Auditing (ISAs); further changes for UK auditors have been introduced by the FRC's revisions of the UK and Ireland's versions of ISAs in the wake of the 2008 global financial crisis.

Notwithstanding the extent and significance of changes which have been implemented in the auditing arena since 2008, probably those most widely discussed and hotly debated are yet to have a direct impact. These are the numerous reforms which have been proposed, primarily, as an outcome of the extensive investigations of the audit function which followed the 2008 global financial crisis; for example, those of the European Commission and European Parliament (and relevant committees thereof) and, in the UK, Select Committees of the House of Commons and House of Lords, the Office of Fair Trading and

---

[1] We provide a diagrammatic representation of the former and current structure of the FRC on page xix.

the Competition Commission. We explore many of the proposed reforms in the final chapter of this book.

Although change has been a characteristic feature of the audit environment, the audit function and the audit process, for the past couple of decades, the basic principles of auditing have remained unchanged. Nevertheless, this fourth edition of the book has been extensively revised and incorporates important recent developments. These include:

- the strengthening of requirements in respect of auditors' independence – in particular, those in the revised Ethical Standards (ES), especially, ES 5: *Non-audit Services Provided to Audited Entities*;
- the marked increase in the corporate governance requirements that apply to listed companies and to auditors' responsibilities in relation thereto;
- enhanced requirements (for both companies and auditors) resulting from the Sharman Inquiry into *Going Concern and Liquidity Risks* (which was itself instigated as an outcome of the House of Lords *Inquiry into Auditors: Market Concentration and Their Role* which was launched in the aftermath of the 2008 global financial crisis);
- changes to the standard auditor's report prepared in accordance with ISA (UK and Ireland) 700: *The Independent Auditor's Report on Financial Statements* (FRC, 2013);
- enhanced responsibilities for external auditors in relation to communicating with those charged with audit clients' governance;
- developments in respect of limiting auditors' liability to their clients and to third parties;
- developments in the realm of corporate responsibility reporting and the independent assurance of such reports;
- the findings of research into the audit expectation-performance gap in the UK and New Zealand;
- the numerous (largely controversial) audit-related reforms proposed in the wake of the 2008 global financial crisis.

This book commences with six chapters which form the 'backdrop' for understanding the audit process. The first two chapters discuss the role of auditing in society and the next two explain the conceptual underpinnings of the audit process. Given the importance of auditors' independence to the audit function, one chapter (Chapter 4) is devoted to this issue. Chapters 5 and 6 are concerned with auditors' responsibilities: while Chapter 5 describes the legal and regulatory requirements which govern the reporting responsibilities of companies, the appointment, payment and removal of auditors and their rights and responsibilities, Chapter 6 examines the somewhat controversial issue of auditors' responsibility for detecting and reporting corporate fraud and other illegal acts.

Chapter 7 constitutes an introduction to auditing practice in that it provides an overview of the audit process and its staffing, documentation and administration. This is followed by seven chapters (Chapters 8 to 14) which take the reader, step by step, through the audit process – from conducting pre-engagement procedures through to issuing reports to users of financial statements and to those charged with the entity's governance.

After exploring the audit process, we devote two chapters to the importance of securing high quality audits. More specifically, in Chapter 15 we discuss the issue of auditors' liability – in particular, how auditors' duty of care to third parties has evolved up to, and since, the landmark *Caparo* case – and in Chapter 16 we describe measures implemented by the profession and by regulators to ensure high quality audits are conducted – thereby helping auditors to avoid exposure to liability. This chapter includes an analysis of findings of the monitoring of auditors' performance in the UK since 1991 and also includes measures that have been proposed or adopted to limit auditors' liability.

The final two chapters of the book are devoted to topical and emerging issues. In Chapter 17 we examine corporate responsibility (CR) reporting and the independent assurance of CR reports and in Chapter 18 we explore the reforms that have been proposed (and, in a few cases, implemented) in the aftermath of the 2008 global financial crisis.

The fundamental principles of auditing, as set out in *The Auditors' Code*, have been incorporated in the FRC's *Scope and Authority of Audit and Assurance Pronouncements* (revised in 2013). As in the earlier editions, they are reproduced on the inside cover of this book. These fundamental principles are all pervasive but we have identified the chapter where each principle seems to have greatest application and have highlighted the principle within that chapter. Inevitably in a technical book of this nature, we make fairly extensive use of abbreviations. Each abbreviation used is defined in the chapter where it is used. However, to assist readers, we have provided a list of abbreviations we use in this book.[2] This list is provided on page xxi. A further important point to note is that legally a company's board of directors (comprising both executive and non-executive directors) is responsible for the company's governance. However, the board relies on senior executives (who may or may not be directors) to implement its strategy and policies and to ensure the smooth running of the company on a day-to-day basis. In this book we use the term 'management' to embrace executive and non-executive directors and non-director senior executives (that is, all directors and senior executives).

---

[2] We confine this list to abbreviations we use more than once in the book.

As with earlier editions of this book, we have been greatly assisted in the preparation of this fourth edition by members of the profession (in particular, Steven Leonard and Jon Hooper of the Financial Reporting Council, Warren Allen, the 2013–14 President of the International Federation of Accountants, and Wim Bartels of KPMG, the Netherlands), an anonymous person in FTSE-4Good who kindly provided up-to-date data on FTSE4Good companies, and numerous colleagues and students who have provided helpful feedback on earlier editions of the book. We are exceptionally grateful to all of these people. We are also grateful to colleagues, family and friends whose patience, understanding and support during the preparation of this edition of the book has been truly remarkable.

Brenda Porter
Jon Simon
David Hatherly

Structure of the Financial Reporting Council

BETWEEN 2004 AND 2012

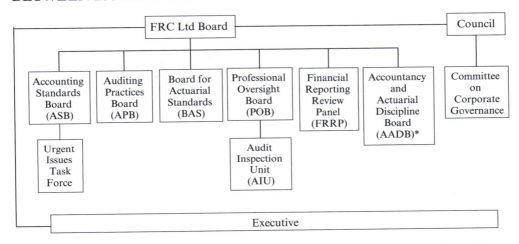

*The AADB replaced the earlier Accountancy Investigation and Discipline Board (AIDB) in 2007 when the Board became responsible for actuarial as well as accountancy disciplinary cases

SINCE JULY 2012

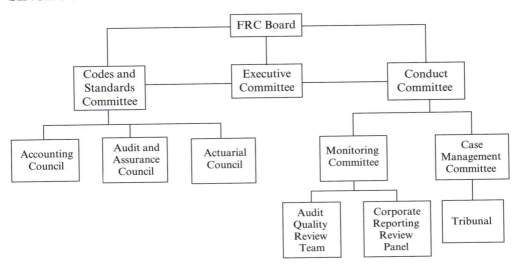

Glossary of Terms

Acronym	Meaning
AADB	Accountancy and Actuarial Discipline Board (replaced the AIDB in 2007)
AAPA	Association of Authorised Public Accountants
ABI	Association of British Insurers
ACCA	Association of Chartered Certified Accountants
AICPA	American Institute of Certified Public Accountants
AIDB	Accountancy Investigation and Disciplinary Board (replaced by the AADB in 2007 when it became responsible for Actuarial as well as Accountancy disciplinary cases)
AIU	Audit Inspection Unit (since 2012, known as the Audit Quality Review team)
APB	Audit Practices Board (replaced by the FRC's Audit and Assurance Council in 2012)
AQR	Audit Quality Review (the AQR team replaced the AIU in 2012)
BCCI	Bank of Credit and Commercial International
CA	Companies Act
CARB	Chartered Accountants Regulatory Board (responsible for regulating ICAI registered auditors)
CC	Competition Commission
CR	Corporate responsibility
E&Y	Ernst & Young
EC	European Commission
ES	Ethical Standards
EU	European Union
FCA	Financial Conduct Authority (assumed same of the former FSA's functions in 2013)
FRC	Financial Reporting Council
FSA	Financial Services Authority (disbanded in 2013 when its functions were transferred to the FCA and PRA)
IAASA	Irish Auditing & Accounting Supervisory Authority
ICAEW	Institute of Chartered Accountants in England and Wales
ICAI	Institute of Chartered Accountants in Ireland
ICAS	Institute of Chartered Accountants of Scotland
ICPAI	Institute of Certified Public Accountants in Ireland
IESBA	International Ethics Standards Board for Accountants
IIPA	Institute of Incorporated Public Accountants

ISA	International Standard on Auditing
JDS	Joint Disciplinary Scheme (replaced in 2004 by the AIDB)
JMU	Joint Monitoring Unit (monitored the performance of ICAEW, ICAS and ICAI registered auditors between 1991 and 2004)
LLC	Limited Liability Company
LLP	Limited Liability Partnership
NAPF	National Association of Pension Funds
NZICA	New Zealand Institute of Chartered Accountants
PIRC	Pensions Investment Research Company
POB	Professional Oversight Board (an operating body of the FRC between 2004 and 2012)
PRA	Prudential Regulation Authority (assumed same of the former FSA's functions in 2013)
PwC	PricewaterhouseCoopers
QAD	Quality Assurance Directorate of the ICAEW
RSB	Recognised Supervisory Body
SI	Statutory Instrument
SOX	Sarbanes-Oxley Act 2002
UKLA	United Kingdom Listing Authority (Since 2013 this has been the responsibility of the FCA)

1   What Is Auditing?

LEARNING OBJECTIVES

After studying the material in this chapter you should be able to:
- explain the key features of the audit function;
- distinguish between financial statement audits, compliance audits and operational audits;
- distinguish between external and internal audits;
- describe how auditing differs from accounting;
- explain why financial statement audits are necessary;
- discuss the benefits of financial statement audits for
  - users of financial statements,
  - the auditee (the entity whose financial statements are audited),
  - society as a whole;
- explain why the benefits to be gained from financial statement audits are sometimes not obtained.

1.1   INTRODUCTION

In general, United Kingdom (UK) legislation requires all but small companies, and virtually all public sector entities, to produce audited financial statements annually. The audits of these financial statements require time, effort and resources. As shown in Figure 1.1, in 2012 the audit fees of the 10 largest companies listed on the London Stock Exchange alone amounted to £148.5 million.[1] From this it is evident that the audits of the financial statements of UK corporate entities as a whole consume a considerable amount of the nation's resources. But, what is an audit? Why are they needed? Indeed, why are financial statement audits so important that they are required by law? Do they provide benefits which are commensurate with their cost?

In this chapter we address the questions posed above. More specifically, we examine the nature of the audit function and distinguish between financial statement audits, compliance audits and operational audits, and also between external and internal audits. We also consider the factors which make financial statement audits necessary and explain their value for financial statement

---

[1] The ten largest companies by market capitalisation on 31 March 2013. The financial year for Vodafone ended on 31 March 2012, for Diageo on 30 June 2012 and for all other companies on 31 December 2012.

Figure 1.1: Audit and non-audit fees paid to the auditors of the 10 largest (by market capitalisation) companies listed on the London Stock Exchange in March 2013[2]

| Company | Audit fees | Non-audit fees paid to auditors | | Auditor |
		Audit related[‡]	Other services[¥]	
	£million	£million	£million	
Royal Dutch Shell plc*	29.5	0.6	0.6	PricewaterhouseCoopers
HSBC Holdings plc*	29.9	14.5	6.0	KPMG
BP plc*	20.3	8.0	4.3	Ernst & Young
Vodafone Group plc	14.0	1.0	1.0	Deloitte
GlaxoSmithKline plc	14.6	3.3	5.9	PricewaterhouseCoopers
British American Tobacco	10.5	1.0	4.1	PricewaterhouseCoopers
SABMiller	7.4	11.1	22.8	PricewaterhouseCoopers
Diageo	5.8	1.6	4.0	KPMG
BG Group*	4.0	0.0	0.2	
Rio Tinto plc*	12.4	3.3	48.0	
Total	**£148.5**	**£44.4**	**£96.9**	

*Figures in these annual reports are in $US. Converted at the rate on 31 December 2012: US$1 = £0.6165
‡ Examples of 'audit related' service are reviews of interim financial information, filings pursuant to legislation and reporting on internal controls
¥ Examples of 'other services' are tax compliance, internal audit and information technology services

Source: Relevant companies' annual reports

users, auditees (that is, the entities whose financial statements are audited) and society as a whole. Before concluding the chapter we discuss why the benefits which should be provided by financial statement audits are sometimes not obtained.

1.2 WHAT IS AN AUDIT?

Anderson (1977) captured the essence of auditing when he stated:

> The practice of auditing commenced on the day that one individual assumed stewardship over another's property. In reporting on his stewardship, the accuracy and reliability of that information would have been subjected to some sort of critical review [i.e., an audit]. (p. 6)

The term 'audit' is derived from the Latin word meaning 'a hearing'. Auditing originated over 2,000 years ago when, firstly in Egypt and later in Greece, Rome and elsewhere, citizens (or sometimes slaves) who were entrusted with the collection and disbursement of public funds were required to give an

---

[2] The fees shown include the worldwide audit and non-audit services fees paid to the auditor by the relevant company (or group).

oral account of their handling of those funds, in public, to a responsible official (an auditor).[3]

In order to understand what an audit is, and how it is conducted in the modern context, we need a definition. A comprehensive definition of auditing with general application is as follows:

> Auditing is a systematic process of objectively gathering and evaluating evidence relating to 2assertions about economic actions and events in which the individual or organisation making the assertions has been engaged, to ascertain the degree of correspondence between those assertions and established criteria, and communicating the results to users of the reports in which the assertions are made.[4]

This definition conveys that:
- auditing proceeds by means of an ordered series of steps (a systematic process);
- auditing primarily involves gathering and evaluating evidence;
- in pursuing this activity the auditor maintains an objective unbiased attitude of mind;
- the auditor critically examines assertions (statements implied to be true) made by an individual or organisation about economic activities in which they have been engaged;
- the auditor assesses how closely these assertions conform to the 'set of rules' which govern how the individual or organisation is to report to others about the economic activities and events that have occurred. This 'set of rules' comprises the established criteria which enable the auditor to evaluate whether the assertions fairly represent the underlying events;
- the auditor communicates the results of this evaluation in a written report. The report is available to all users of the document(s) in which the assertions are made.

The major features of an audit are presented diagrammatically in Figure 1.2.

1.3 TYPES OF AUDIT

Audits may be classified in various ways. They may, for instance, be classified according to:
- the primary objective of the audit, or
- the primary beneficiaries of the audit.

---

[3] It should be remembered that, at the time, very few people could write or read, thus the account of public funds collected and disbursed needed to be given orally and in public.

[4] Adapted from the definition provided by the Committee on Basic Auditing Concepts (1973, p. 8).

Figure 1.2: Major features of an audit

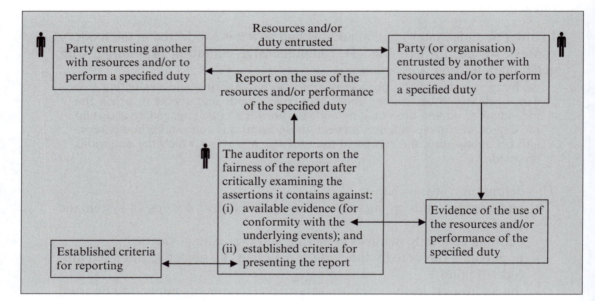

1.3.1 Classification by primary audit objective

Based on the primary audit objective, three main categories of audits may be recognised:

(i) financial statement audits,
(ii) compliance audits, and
(iii) operational audits.

(i) Financial statement audits

A financial statement audit is an examination of an entity's financial statements, which have been prepared by its management/directors[5] for shareholders and other interested parties outside the entity, and of the evidence supporting the information contained in those financial statements. It is conducted by a qualified, experienced professional[6] who is independent of the entity, for the purpose of expressing an opinion on whether or not the financial statements provide a true and fair view of the entity's financial performance and financial position

---

[5] In the Preface to this book we note that the term 'management' is defined to mean a company's executive directors, non-executive directors and non-director executives (that is, all executives and directors). Under the Companies Act 2006 (s. 394), a company's directors are responsible for the preparation of its annual financial statements.

[6] The term 'an auditor' usually refers to an audit firm. Although one person in the firm (referred to in the Companies Act 2006, s. 504, as 'the senior statutory auditor') is responsible for an individual audit engagement (the audit of a client's financial statements for a single year) and signs the audit report, the audit is usually conducted by an audit team. We explain this further in Chapter 7.

Figure 1.3: Major features of a financial statement audit

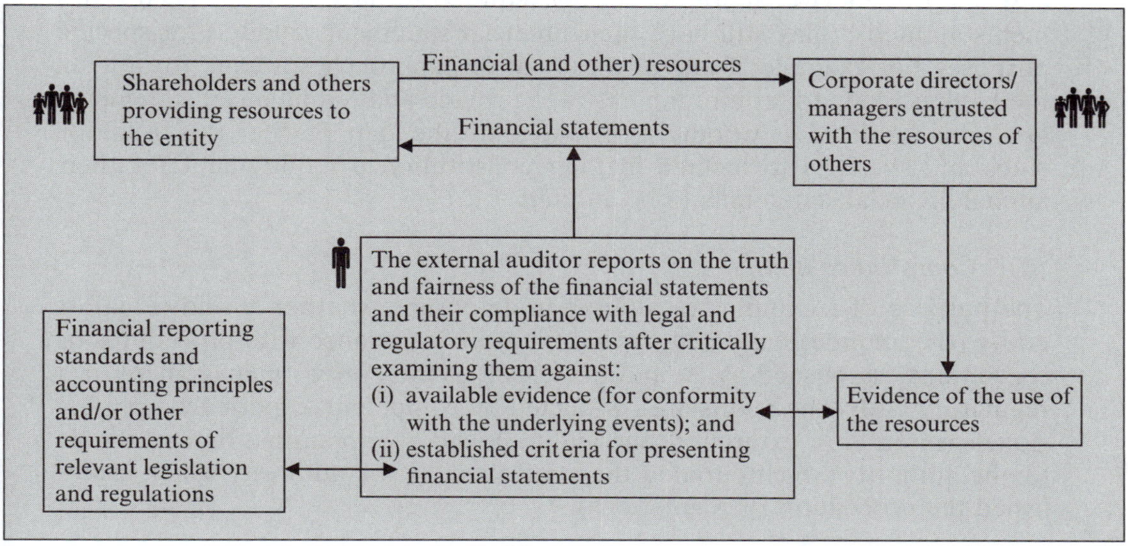

and comply with relevant legal and/or other regulatory requirements. The major features of a financial statement audit are presented in Figure 1.3.

The Companies Act (CA) 2006 (ss. 396, 404) requires the directors of all companies to prepare annually financial statements which include:
- a balance sheet showing a true and fair view of the company's 'state of affairs' (or financial position) as at the last day of the financial year; and
- a profit and loss statement showing a true and fair view of the company's profit or loss for the financial year.[7]

CA 2006, s. 495, also requires auditors to report on these financial statements. Thus, *prima facie*, all companies must, by law, have their financial statements audited. However, companies which are not public companies and which qualify as small [that is, companies which meet two of the following three criteria: turnover of no more than £6.5 million, balance sheet total (total assets) of no more than £3.26 million and no more than 50 employees during the financial year] are generally exempt from a statutory audit (CA 2006, s. 477).[8]

---

[7] Accounting standards also require all but small companies to provide a cash flow statement showing the company's cash flows during the financial year. It should also be noted that International Financial Reporting Standards use the terms 'statement of financial position' and 'income statement' in place of 'balance sheet' and 'profit and loss statement', respectively.

[8] Until October 2012, non-public companies could qualify for exemption from an audit if they met the turnover and total assets criteria. In October 2012, 'no more than 50 employees' was added as a criterion, and non-public companies could be exempted from having an audit if they met any two of the three criteria. The statutory and regulatory requirements applying to the audits of companies' financial statements are explained in Chapter 5, section 5.2.1.

Companies taking advantage of the audit exemption, and also partnerships and sole traders (which are not legally required to have their financial statements audited),[9] may still have their financial statements audited for specific purposes. For example, if one of these entities approaches a bank for a loan, the bank is likely to require the entity to provide audited financial statements as a basis for deciding whether or not to grant the loan. Further, it is usual for clubs and societies to include in their constitution a requirement for their annual financial statements to be audited.

(ii) Compliance audits

The purpose of a compliance audit is to determine whether an individual or entity (the auditee) has acted (or is acting) in accordance with procedures or regulations established by an authority, such as the entity's management or a regulatory body. The audits are conducted by competent, experienced professionals (internal or external to the auditee) who are appointed by, and report to, the authority which initiated the audit (usually the authority which established the procedures or regulations).

Examples of compliance audits include audits conducted by HM Revenue & Customs which are designed to ascertain whether individuals or organisations have complied with tax legislation or legislation governing duties or taxes levied on imports and exports. They also include audits conducted within companies or other entities to ascertain whether the entity's employees are complying with the system of internal control established by management.[10]

(iii) Operational audits

An operational audit involves a systematic examination and evaluation of an entity's operations which is conducted with a view to improving the efficiency and/or effectiveness of the entity. Such audits are usually initiated by the entity's management or, sometimes, if there is one, by its audit committee.[11] They are conducted by competent, experienced professionals (internal or external to the organisation) who report their findings to the party which initiated the audit. An operational audit may apply to the organisation as a whole or to an identified segment thereof such as a subsidiary, division or department. The objectives of the audit may be broad, for example, to improve the overall

---

[9] Limited liability partnerships, but not ordinary partnerships, are legally required to have their annual financial statements audited unless they meet two of the following criteria to qualify as 'small': turnover of no more than £6.5 million, balance sheet total of no more than £3.26 milion, and no more than 50 employees. We explain this in relation to audit firms in Chapter 16, section 16.5.3.

[10] Internal control is discussed in Chapter 10.

[11] An audit committee is a subcommittee of the board of directors (or its equivalent).

efficiency of the entity, or narrow and designed, for example, to solve a specific problem such as excessive staff turnover.[12]

1.3.2 Classification by primary audit beneficiaries

Based on the primary audit beneficiaries (that is, those for whom the audit is conducted), audits may be classified as:
  (i) external audits, or
  (ii) internal audits.

(i) External audits

An external audit is an audit performed for parties external to the auditee and it is these parties to whom the auditor reports the audit findings or conclusions. Competent, experienced professionals, independent of the auditee and its personnel, conduct these audits in accordance with requirements which are defined by, or on behalf of, the parties for whose benefit the audit is conducted. Probably the best-known and most frequently performed external audits are the statutory audits of the financial statements of companies and public sector entities (that is, financial statement audits). However, compliance audits conducted by HM Revenue & Customs are also examples of external audits.

(ii) Internal audits

In contrast to external audits, internal audits are performed for a party (usually management or, if it has one, the entity's audit committee) internal to the entity. They may be performed by employees of the entity (internal auditors) or by personnel from an outside source (such as an accounting firm or, for example, environmental or other specialists). In either case, the audit is conducted in accordance with the requirements of the party which initiated the audit and it is this party to whom the auditor reports his/her audit findings. Internal audits may be wide-ranging or narrowly-focused, and they may be continuous (on-going) or one-off in nature. They may, for example, be as broad as investigating the appropriateness of, and level of compliance with, the organisation's system of internal control, or as narrow as examining the entity's policies and procedures for ensuring compliance with health and safety or environmental regulations.

1.3.3 Common characteristics of audits

It should be noted that, although different categories and types of audit may be recognised, all audits possess the same general characteristics. Whether they

---

[12] In public sector entities, broadly-based operational audits (value for money audits) are generally required as part of the statutory audit (that is, the audit required by law). However, additional more specific operational audits may also be initiated by the entity's management and conducted along the lines of those undertaken in companies.

are financial statement, compliance or operational audits, and whether they are conducted for parties external or internal to the entity, they all involve:

- the systematic collection and evaluation of evidence which is undertaken to ascertain whether assertions by individuals or organisations fairly represent the underlying facts and comply with established criteria; and
- communication of the results of the examination, usually in a written report, to the party by whom, or on whose behalf, the auditor was appointed to conduct the audit.

1.4 AUDITING vs ACCOUNTING

This book is primarily concerned with the external financial statement audits of companies which issue shares and/or debt instruments to the public and, unless we indicate otherwise, the terms 'audit' and 'auditor' should be understood in that context. However, before focusing attention on these audits we need to distinguish between auditing and accounting.

Accounting data, and the accounting systems which capture and process the data, provide the raw materials with which financial statement auditors work. In order to understand these systems, and the data they process, a financial statement auditor must first be a qualified accountant. However, the processes involved in auditing and accounting are rather different. Accounting is primarily *a creative* process which involves identifying, collecting, organising, summarising and communicating information about economic events. Auditing, on the other hand, is primarily an *evaluative* process. It involves gathering and evaluating audit evidence from which conclusions may be drawn about the fairness with which the communication resulting from the accounting process (that is, the financial statements) reflects the underlying economic events and communicating those conclusions to the users of the financial statements.

1.5 WHY ARE EXTERNAL FINANCIAL STATEMENT AUDITS NEEDED?

1.5.1 The need to communicate financial information

Since the Industrial Revolution (the late eighteenth century), 'large' business organisations have changed from being owner-operated entities with a small number of employees, many of whom were family members, to vast multinational companies staffed by many thousands of employees. The growth of such organisations has been made possible by the channelling of financial resources from numerous investors, through financial markets and credit-granting institutions, to the growing companies.

As companies have grown in size, their management has passed from shareholder-owners to small groups of professional managers. Thus, company growth has been accompanied by the increasing separation of ownership interests and management functions. As a consequence, a need has arisen for company managers to report to the entity's owners, and other providers of funds such as banks and other lenders, on the financial outcomes of their activities. Those receiving these reports (external financial statements) need assurance that they are reliable. Therefore, they wish to have the information in the reports 'checked out' or audited.

1.5.2 The need to have the communication examined

Three questions arise in relation to 'checking out' the reports provided by management to the entity's owners and other interested parties external to the entity:
1. Why might the information in the reports not be reliable?
2. Why is it important to receivers of the reports that the information is reliable?
3. Why do receivers of the reports not audit the information for themselves?

The answers to these questions lie in four main factors:
(i)   conflict of interests,
(ii) consequences of error,
(iii) practicality and remoteness, and
(iv) complexity.
We discuss each of these factors below.

(i) Conflict of interests

We noted earlier that a company's directors are legally responsible for preparing its financial statements; these directors are essentially reporting on their own performance. Users of the financial statements want the statements to portray the company's financial position and performance as accurately as possible but they perceive it is in the directors' personal interests to bias their report so that it reflects favourably on their management of the company's financial affairs. Thus, there is a potential conflict of interest between the preparers and users of the financial statements. The audit plays a vital role in helping to ensure that directors provide, and users are confident in receiving, information which fairly reflects the company's financial affairs.[13]

---

[13] Some commentators apply agency theory to explain the existence of financial statement audits. They view the company's owners (shareholders) as 'the principal' and its directors as 'the agent'. In brief, agency theorists maintain that the agent is aware that the principal will perceive the agent has an incentive and opportunity (for example, by taking unauthorised perquisites) to act in his/her personal interests rather than in

(ii) Consequences of error

If users of a company's financial statements base decisions (such as whether to invest in, buy from, supply to, or accept employment with the company) on unreliable information, they may suffer serious financial loss as a result. Therefore, before basing decisions on financial statement information, they wish to be assured that the information is reliable and 'safe' to act upon.

(iii) Practicality and remoteness

In general, as a consequence of practical, legal, physical and economic factors, users of a company's external financial statements are not able to verify the reliability of information in the financial statements for themselves. In the modern environment, it is common for public companies to have hundreds of thousands of shareholders and it is clearly not practical for such a large number of shareholders to verify the financial statements for themselves. Further, even if a person is a major shareholder in a company, that person has no legal right of access to the company's records (such access is limited to the company's directors and other authorised personnel within the entity). Additionally, shareholders may live many miles away from the company whose financial statements they would like to examine, and/or they may not be able to afford the time and expense which would be involved in travelling to the company and checking the information personally, should they have the legal right to do so.[14] Thus, as a result of practical, legal, physical and economic factors, which prevent users of financial statements from personally examining the information provided by a company's directors in its financial statements, an independent party is needed to assess the reliability of the information on their behalf.

---

the best interests of the principal. The agent believes the principal will introduce costly measures to monitor his/her (the agent's) activities in order to prevent him/her from acting in his/her own interests to the detriment of the principal. The agent also believes the principal will impose the costs of the monitoring activities on the agent by reducing the agent's rewards. In an attempt to minimise the monitoring costs, the agent offers to provide the principal with financial statements that are examined by an independent expert who is able to verify their 'correctness'. Thus, to agency theorists, a financial statement audit is the least cost option for agents to have their performance monitored by the principal (for example, Wallace, 1985).

In the modern corporate environment, in which public companies frequently have many hundreds of thousands of shareholders, and company directors are accountable to a wide range of stakeholders in addition to shareholders, it is difficult to conceive of a direct agency relationship existing between companies' owners (shareholders) and agents (directors) such as that envisaged by agency theorists. In our view, agency theory does not adequately explain the role of financial statement audits in holding company directors accountable to all of those whose well-being is affected by their decisions and actions (i.e., to a broad range of stakeholders). In our opinion, accountability theory, as reflected in section 1.6.3, provides a more satisfactory explanation of the role of financial statement audits in modern society.

[14] However, it should be noted that the senior executives of many financial institutions (including pension funds, insurance companies, and unit and investment trusts) which have significant shareholdings in major UK companies visit companies in which the institution has, or is considering, investment and question their directors/senior executives. These institutions have considerable influence over the investee companies especially if, in the view of the relevant financial institution(s), they are under-performing.

(iv) Complexity

As companies grow in size, the number of their transactions increases. Further, especially in recent years, economic transactions, the accounting systems which capture and process them, and the 'rules' governing their measurement and disclosure (that is, financial reporting standards) have become very complex. As a result, errors are more likely to occur in financial statements. Additionally, with the increasing complexity of economic transactions, accounting systems and financial reporting standards, users of companies' financial statements are less able to evaluate the quality of the information for themselves. The financial statements need to be examined by an independent qualified auditor who has the necessary competence and expertise to understand the entity's business, its transactions, its accounting system and the 'rules' which govern external financial reporting.

1.6 BENEFITS DERIVED FROM EXTERNAL FINANCIAL STATEMENT AUDITS

In section 1.5 we explained why external financial statement audits are necessary. We now consider the benefits these audits provide for financial statement users, auditees and society as a whole. These benefits are reflected in the fundamental principle of external auditing – *Providing value*:

> Auditors add to the reliability and quality of financial reporting [to external parties]; they [also] provide to directors and officers [of the auditee] constructive observations arising from the audit process; and thereby contribute to the effective operation of business, capital markets and the public sector. (Financial Reporting Council, 2013, Appendix 2)

1.6.1 Financial statement users

The value of an external audit for financial statement users lies in the credibility it gives to the financial information provided by the reporting entity. This credibility arises from three forms of control which an audit provides:

(i) *Preventive control*: Employees involved in the capture and processing of accounting data and in the preparation of the entity's financial statements, who know their work will be subject to the scrutiny of an auditor, are likely to work more carefully than they would in the absence of an audit. It is probable that the extra care taken by employees prevents at least some errors from occurring in the financial statements.

(ii) *Detective control*: Even if employees in the reporting entity process the accounting data and prepare the financial statements carefully, errors may still occur. The auditor may detect these errors during the audit and draw them to management's attention. They may then be corrected prior to publication of the financial statements.

(iii) *Reporting control*: If the auditor detects material errors in the financial statements and refers them to management, but management refuses to correct them, the auditor draws attention to the errors by modifying the audit report (that is, the auditor states that all is not well with the financial statements, giving reasons for this conclusion). In this way, users of the financial statements are made aware that, in the auditor's opinion, at least some of the information provided is not reliable.

It is interesting to note that the UK's Companies Act 2006 is silent on the qualifications of those who may prepare a company's financial statements but it specifies (in section 1212) that the auditor of these statements must be a member of a Recognised Supervisory Body (RSB). To become a member, an individual (or firm) must be appropriately qualified and be subject to the rules of the RSB – including those governing "the conduct of statutory audit work" (s. 1217).[15] Thus, although the preparer of the financial statements need not be a qualified accountant, the auditor must be a well-qualified, competent and experienced professional. It seems that Parliament looks to auditors to protect the interests of financial statement users by providing assurance that the financial statements are reliable or giving a warning that they are not.

1.6.2 Auditees

During the course of a financial statement audit, the auditor becomes very familiar with the reporting entity, its business, its accounting system and all aspects of its financial affairs. Added to this, the auditor is a qualified and experienced professional who comes to the auditee as an independent objective outsider, divorced from the day-to-day operation of the entity.

These factors place the auditor in an ideal position to observe where improvements can be made. The auditor is able to advise the auditee on, for example, strengthening its internal controls, the development of its accounting and/or other management information systems, and on tax, investment and financial planning matters. In addition, the auditor is able to provide advice on issues (in cases where they arise for the auditee) such as how to proceed with a share float, business acquisition or divestment, or liquidation. The provision of these 'additional services' by the auditor is very valuable for the auditee. Indeed, as Anderson (1977) pointed out:

---

[15] The required qualifications and supervision of auditors are discussed in Chapter 5, section 5.3.1.

In many cases, it is the presence of these collateral services which makes the audit an economical package from management's point of view. The professional auditor must always be alert for opportunities to be of service to his or her client while at the same time discharging conscientiously his or her responsibilities to the users of the audited financial statements. (p. 6)

Notwithstanding the value of these advisory services for the auditee, largely as a result of investigations following audit failures[16] in the early 2000s at Enron, WorldCom and Xerox (amongst others) in the United States of America (USA), Equitable Life in the UK, Parmalat in Italy, HIH in Australia, and similar failures elsewhere, serious disquiet was expressed by politicians, regulators and investors about the extent of non-audit services provided by auditors to their audit clients. Indeed, at the turn of the twenty-first century, fees paid by audit clients to their auditors for non-audit services had grown to such an extent that, in many instances, they exceeded the audit fee by a significant margin.[17] This led to concerns that the provision of such services results in auditors compromising their independence; in order to avoid upsetting the entity's management, and thus losing lucrative non-audit as well as audit work, auditors are not sufficiently sceptical or rigorous when performing their auditing duties. As a consequence, laws and regulations have been enacted in many parts of the world to prohibit or curtail the provision of non-audit services by auditors to their audit clients. Probably the most far-reaching and stringent restrictions have been enacted in the USA in the Sarbanes-Oxley Act of 2002.[18]

1.6.3 Society as a whole

The benefits flowing from financial statement audits for society as a whole fall into two broad groups, namely those relating to:
   (i) the smooth functioning of financial markets; and
   (ii) securing the accountability of corporate managements.

---

[16] An audit failure occurs when the auditor expresses an unmodified ('clean') opinion on financial statements that are materially misstated.

[17] For example, in 2001 in the USA, Enron paid Arthur Andersen $25 (£17.9) million in audit fees and a further $27 (£19.3) million in non-audit fees; similarly, Disney paid PricewaterhouseCoopers $8.7 (£6.2) million in audit fees and a staggering $32 (£22.9) million for non-audit services. In 2001 in the UK, BP paid Ernst & Young £16.7 million in audit fees and an additional £41 million for non-audit services; and Vodafone paid Deloitte & Touche £3 million in audit fees and a further £22 million for non-audit work.

[18] Notwithstanding the sharp curtailment since the turn of the twenty-first century in the non-audit services that UK auditors can offer their audit clients, it may be seen from Figure 1.1 that the fees paid to PricewaterhouseCoopers by both Rio Tinto and SABMiller for non-audit services exceeded the fees they paid for audit services. The dangers to auditors' independence of providing non-audit services to audit clients, and measures taken in recent years to reduce those dangers, are discussed in Chapter 4.

(i) Smooth functioning of financial markets

The benefits – and importance – of financial statement audits in helping to ensure the smooth functioning of financial markets was aptly conveyed by Turner (2001) when he was Chief Accountant of the Securities and Exchange Commission (SEC) in the USA. He stated:

> The enduring confidence of the investing public in the integrity of our capital markets is vital. In America today, approximately one out of every two adults has invested their savings in the securities markets, either [directly] through the purchase of individual stocks or [indirectly through investment] in a mutual fund or . . . pension plan. . . . These investments have provided trillions of dollars in capital for companies in the United States and around the globe. That capital is providing the fuel for our economic engine, funding for the growth of new businesses, and providing . . . job opportunities for tens of millions of workers. But . . . the willingness of investors to continue to invest their money in the markets cannot be taken for granted. . . . Public trust begins, and ends, with the integrity of the numbers the public uses to form the basis for making their investment decisions. . . . Accordingly, investors in the U.S. capital markets have depended for over a hundred years on an independent third party, an external auditor, to examine the books and financial reports prepared by management. (pp. 1–2)

Along similar lines, the UK's House of Lords' Select Committee on Economic Affairs[19] stated:

> . . . investors, regulators and commentators regard rigorous and reliable external audit as an essential underpinning of business and the capital markets which finance it, in Britain and elsewhere. . . . Audit and accountancy are absolutely fundamental to the integrity of our capital markets. . . . (House of Lords, 2011, Abstract, para 2)

It is evident that continued investment in capital markets is essential to the well-being of the economy – and to the financial well-being of those who invest directly or indirectly in those markets. However, continued investment rests on investors having confidence in the financial information on which they base their investment decisions – and hence in the external audit function. Although not referred to by Turner, indirect investment includes investment by the Government, local authorities and other public sector bodies of funds provided by the vast majority of the public in the form of taxes of one type or another. Therefore, most members of society – directly or indirectly – benefit from external financial statement audits.

(ii) Securing the accountability of corporate managements

Since the late eighteenth century, as financial and non-financial resources have been channelled by individuals and groups in society to companies, so these

---

[19] The House of Lords' Select Committee conducted an eight-month inquiry into the part played by auditors in the 2007–9 financial crisis (House of Lords, 2011).

entities have been able to grow. As they have become larger, they have gained significant social, economic and political power. Today, large national and multinational companies dominate the lives, and affect the well-being, of whole communities and have a major impact on society in general. However, in a democratic society, power is not absolute. Mindful of Lord Acton's dictum that "power corrupts and absolute power corrupts absolutely", society has established checks and balances designed to prevent possible abuse of power. One of the checks designed to ensure that company managements do not abuse the power bestowed upon them through the provision of resources is holding them accountable for the responsible use of the resources entrusted to them. This accountability is secured primarily by requiring company directors:

- to provide publicly available annual reports (which include financial statements) that report, among other things, on their use of resources and the outcomes thereof; and
- to submit the financial statements (and some other information in their annual reports) to a critical examination by an independent expert (that is, to an audit).[20]

Thus, auditors are a key element in the process of securing the accountability of company managements who control and use the financial and non-financial resources of various groups in society such as shareholders, debtholders, creditors, employees, suppliers, customers and the general public. In the UK, a company's auditor is legally appointed by, and reports to, the shareholders. However, all those who provide resources to company managements, or who are otherwise affected by company managements' decisions or actions, have an interest in the accountability process of which auditing is a part.

Therefore, in addition to benefitting financial statement users and auditees, by helping to ensure the smooth functioning of financial markets and by functioning as an element of social control within the corporate accountability process, external audits are also of value to society as a whole.

1.6.4 Failure to secure the potential benefits of the audit function

While the external audit function can – and does – provide important benefits for financial statement users, auditees and society as a whole, the manner in which auditors have performed their function has, on occasion, been subject to criticism – and, in some cases, the criticism has been justifiably scathing. Indeed,

---

[20] As we will see in Chapter 5, the audited information companies are required to provide in their annual reports has increased markedly during the past couple of decades.

some critics go so far as to argue that the 'Big' accounting firms[21] use their extensive power and knowledge to facilitate doubtful financial practices which help a few wealthy clients, who can afford to pay "exorbitant consultancy fees" (Mitchell & Sikka, 2002, p. 50), to exploit the capital system for their own benefit. They assert that these firms are at the centre of a web of conspiracies to "operate cartels, launder money, facilitate tax avoidance/evasion, [engage in] bribery and obstruct enquiries into frauds and deliver shoddy audits" (Mitchell & Sikka, 2002, p. 50).

While few would adopt such an extreme view, many observers have commented on the failings of auditors; others have noted the reluctance of audit firms and/or the profession to acknowledge that they might be at fault and to recognise the need for improvement. For example, in 1994 Shields noted:

> The Big Six firms have been key players in a recent spate of audit failures around the world which are beginning to undermine the internal system of accountability on which the business world relies. But instead of focusing on improving their practices and regaining the public's trust, the Big Six have launched a full-scale campaign to reduce their liability for failed audits. (Shields, 1994, p. 1)

A decade later, Sarup (2004) observed:

> [T]he audit profession . . . is increasingly under attack as the profession attracts, fairly or unfairly, some of the blame for the recent corporate failures and the consequent losses to the investing public, the thousands of innocent employees and suppliers, and a multitude of other stakeholders. At Enron . . . the profession tried, unsuccessfully, to rationalize the patently failed audit. . . . [T]he circumstances of the multibillion-dollar fraud at WorldCom are hard to even attempt to rationalize. . . . People are asking, given [the] basic nature [of the fraud] and its magnitude, how could it have been missed. The alleged frauds at Tyco International, Adelphia Communications, HealthSouth Corp, and Dutch retailing giant Ahold NV all beg the same questions: What were the auditors doing? Is the audit approach fundamentally flawed? (pp. 1–2)

Similar questions have been raised in relation to auditors' failure to alert investors (and others) to the undue risks investment banks around the globe were increasingly accepting during the first half of the 2000s – risks that resulted in the 2008 financial crisis. The House of Lords' Select Committee which enquired into the part auditors played in the crisis noted:

───────────────

[21] During the 1980s there were 'the Big 8' global accounting firms – Arthur Andersen, Arthur Young, Coopers & Lybrand, Deloitte Haskins & Sells, Ernst & Whinney, Peat Marwick, Price Waterhouse and Touche Ross. During the 1990s, 'the Big 8' first became 'the Big 6' – Arthur Andersen, Coopers & Lybrand, Deloitte & Touche, Ernst & Young, KPMG and Price Waterhouse – then, with the merger of Coopers & Lybrand and Price Waterhouse, they were reduced to 'the Big 5'. With the demise of Arthur Andersen in 2002, 'the Big 5' became 'the Big 4' accounting firms.

> The Big Four [accountancy firms] expressed the general view that in auditing banks before and during the crisis they had carried out their duties properly. . . . We [the Committee] do not accept the defence that bank auditors did all that was required of them . . . that defence appears disconcertingly complacent. It may be that the Big Four carried out their duties properly in the strict legal sense, but we have to conclude that, in the wider sense, they did not do so. (House of Lords, 2011, para 142)

As we will see when we discuss audit quality in Chapter 16, in general, audit failures result from two key causes – auditors' not being sufficiently independent of their audit clients and not applying the required level of competence. As a consequence of one or both of these underlying causes, auditors may not adhere to auditing and/or ethical standards, employ an appropriate level of scepticism and/or exercise due professional skill and care appropriate to the circumstances. Whatever the reason for an audit failure, when it occurs, the auditee, financial statement users and society as a whole are deprived of the benefits they should have gained as an outcome of the audit. Further, as we explain in Chapter 16, the culpable auditors also suffer. A significant number who have performed defective audits have faced court action and hefty financial penalties; others have had their audit activities curtailed and, in a few extreme cases, the adverse consequences of poor quality auditing have been so severe that the audit firm concerned has been unable to survive (as was the case with Arthur Andersen in 2002).

Notwithstanding that some auditors have attracted criticism – and sanctions – as a result of shoddy audit work, and the reputation of, and the public's confidence in, the auditing profession has suffered as a consequence, it should be remembered that:

> Commentary in the media tends to focus on the few, high profile audit failures, rather than the huge number of successful audits. . . . The overwhelming majority of audits conducted by the major accounting firms are highly professional, effective and valuable. (Accountancy Age, 2005, p. 1)

This conclusion is supported by the findings of Francis (2004) who reviewed empirical research which investigated audit quality during the last quarter of the twentieth century. His findings suggest that, although there is some indication of a decline in audit quality during the 1990s, audit failure is infrequent.

When considering the failings of auditors, it should be noted that the deficiencies relate, not to the audit function *per se*, but to how that function is fulfilled by sub-standard auditors. In Chapter 16 we explore the steps the profession and regulators have taken to ensure that auditors perform their audits to the highest standard thus enabling the audit function to deliver its potential benefits to the users of audited financial statements, auditees and society as a whole.

1.7 SUMMARY

In this chapter we have considered the nature of the audit function and distinguished between financial statement audits, compliance audits and operational audits, and also between external and internal audits. Additionally, we have noted the difference between accounting and auditing and discussed why external financial statement audits are needed. In the final section of the chapter we have examined some of the benefits provided by these audits for financial statement users, auditees and society as a whole – and explained why these benefits may not always be obtained.

In the next chapter we trace the development of auditing noting, in particular, how auditing has responded over time to changes in its socio-economic environment.

SELF-REVIEW QUESTIONS

1.1 Explain briefly the following phrases included in the definition of auditing given in this chapter:
   (i) systematic process
   (ii) objectively gathering and evaluating evidence
   (iii) assertions about economic actions and events
   (iv) the degree of correspondence between the assertions and established criteria.

1.2 List the major elements (or features) which are present in all audits.

1.3 Explain briefly the key differences between the following types of audits:
   (i) financial statement audits
   (ii) compliance audits
   (iii) operational audits.
   For each type of audit you need to mention who appoints the auditor, the purpose of the audit and to whom the auditor reports his/her audit findings.

1.4 Distinguish between:
   (i) auditing and accounting;
   (ii) internal and external audits.

1.5   Explain briefly why external financial statement audits are needed.

1.6   Explain briefly why the users of a company's financial statement cannot examine those financial statements (and the supporting evidence) for themselves to determine whether or not the financial statements can be relied on.

1.7   The value of an audit for financial statement users lies primarily in the credibility it gives to the financial statements which are prepared by management. Explain briefly the three types of control which help an audit to make audited financial statements credible.

1.8   Explain briefly the benefits which an external financial statement audit provides for an auditee. Also explain any dangers which may result from auditors providing additional (non-audit) services to auditees.

1.9   Explain briefly the value of external financial statement audits for society as a whole. (Your answer should identify two sources of benefits an audit can provide.)

1.10   Explain briefly why the beneficiaries of a financial statement audit (financial statement users, the auditee and society as a whole) may not obtain the benefits the audit should provide.

REFERENCES

Accountancy Age (2005, 5 August). *Audit Failure? Don't Blame Us*, www.accountancy age.com/aa/opinion/1787180/audit-failure-dont-blame, accessed 7 May 2013.

Anderson, R.J. (1977). *The External Audit*. Toronto: Cropp Clark Pitman.

Committee on Basic Auditing Concepts. (1973). *A Statement of Basic Auditing Concepts*. Sarasota, FL: American Accounting Association.

Financial Reporting Council (FRC). (2013). *Scope and Authority of Audit and Assurance Pronouncements*. London: FRC.

Francis, J. (2004). What do we know about audit quality? *British Accounting Review*, *36*, 345–368.

House of Lords Select Committee on Economic Affairs (House of Lords). (2011, 30 March). *2nd report of Session 2010–11 Auditors: Market Concentration and Their Role*. Volume 1: Report. London: The Stationery Office.

Mitchell, A., & Sikka, P. (2002). *Dirty Business: The Unchecked Power of Major Accountancy Firms*. Basildon: Association for Accountancy and Business Affairs.

Sarup, D. (2004). The watchdog or bloodhound? The push and pull toward a new audit model. *Information Systems Control Journal*, *1*, 1–2.

Shields, J. (1994). *A Worldwide Trail of Failures*, www.multinationalmonitor.org/hyper/issues/1994/12/mm1294_09.html, accessed 7 May 2013.

Turner, L.E. (2001, 28 June). *Independence: A Covenant for the Ages*. Speech at the International Organisation of Securities Commissions, Stockholm, Sweden.

Wallace, W.A. (1985). *Auditing Monographs 1: The Economic Role of the Audit in Free and Regulated Markets*. London: Macmillan.

ADDITIONAL READING

Asthana, S.C., Balsam, S., & Krishnon, J. (2010). Corporate governance, audit firm reputation, auditor switches, and client stock price reactions: The Andersen experience. *International Journal of Auditing*, *14*(3), 274–293.

Bagley, P.L. (2010). Negative affect: A consequence of multiple accountabilities in auditing. *Auditing: A Journal of Practice & Theory*, *29*(2), 141–157.

Benston, G. (1985). The market for public accounting services: Demand, supply and regulation. *Journal of Accounting and Public Policy*, *4*, 33–79.

Cassell, C.A., Giroux, G.A., Myers, L.A., & Omer, T.C. (2012). The effect of corporate governance on auditor–client realignment. *Auditing: A Journal of Practice & Theory*, *31*(2), 167–188.

Chahine, S., & Filatotchev, I. (2011). The effects of corporate governance and audit and non-audit fees on IPO value. *British Accounting Review*, *43*(3), 155–172.

Collis, J. (2010). Audit exemption and the demand for voluntary audit: A comparative study of UK and Denmark. *International Journal of Auditing*, *14*(2), 211–231.

Collis, J. (2012). Determinants of voluntary audit and voluntary full accounts in micro- and non-micro small firms in the UK. *Accounting and Business Research*, *42*(4), 441–468.

Cousins, J., Mitchell, A., & Sikka, P. (2004). *Race to the Bottom: The Case of the Accountancy Firms*. Basildon: Association for Accountancy and Business Affairs.

Davis, J.S. (2011). Insights from assurance analogs. *Accounting, Organizations and Society*, *36*, 313–317.

Dean, D. (2009). Auditing Santa. *Accounting, Auditing & Accountability Journal*, *22*(8), 1311–1314.

Dedman, E., & Asad, K. (2012). The impact of voluntary audit on credit ratings: Evidence from UK private firms. *Accounting and Business Research*, *42*(4), 397–418.

Francis, J.R. (2011). Auditing without borders. *Accounting, Organizations and Society*, *36*(4–5), 318–323.

Hoopes, J.L., Mescall, D., & Pittman, J.A. (2012). Do IRS audits deter corporate tax avoidance? *Accounting Review*, *87*(5), 1603–1639.

Hope, O-K., Langli, J.C., & Thomas, W.B. (2012) Agency conflicts and auditing in private firms. *Accounting, Organizations and Society*, *37*(7), 500–517.

Lennox, C.S., & Pittman, J.A. (2011). Voluntary audits verses mandatory audits. *Accounting Review*, *86*(5), 1655–1678.

Malsch, B., & Gendron, Y. (2009). Mythical representations of trust in auditors and the preservation of social order in the financial community. *Critical Perspectives on Accounting*, *20*(6), 735–750.

Newman, D. (2005). The role of auditing in investor protection. *Accounting Review*, *80*(1), 289–314.

2 The Development of Auditing and Its Objectives

LEARNING OBJECTIVES

After studying the material in this chapter you should be able to:

- **describe and explain the changes in audit objectives which have taken place during the last 170 or so years;**
- **explain the relationship between changes in the external audit function and changes in the socio-economic environment of the Anglo-American world over the last 170 or so years;**
- **discuss the difference between the audit risk and business risk approach to auditing;**
- **describe, and explain reasons for, the significant legal and regulatory changes that have affected external auditing in the twenty-first century.**

2.1 INTRODUCTION

In this chapter we examine the evolution of the objectives of company audits and explore the ways in which the external audit function has responded to changes in its socio-economic environment. We also discuss recent changes in the regulatory framework which governs external auditing.

2.2 OVERVIEW OF THE DEVELOPMENT OF COMPANY AUDITING

Auditing, like all professions, exists to satisfy an identified need in society. It is therefore to be expected that auditing changes as the needs and demands of society change. Figure 2.1 shows the close link between auditing and the socio-economic environment it serves in the Anglo-American context. In particular, it shows:

- how audit objectives have changed in response to changes in the socio-economic environment (in particular, to changes in the characteristics, and the accountability expected, of business enterprises);
- that the main centre of auditing development shifted from the United Kingdom (UK) to the United States of America (USA) as the centre of economic development moved across the Atlantic and that, during the past couple of decades, auditing development has become more global in nature;
- how the procedures adopted by auditors accord with the objectives auditing is trying to meet.

Figure 2.1:   The inter-relationships of external auditing

Period	Centre of audit developmt	Main characteristics of business enterprises and audit environment	Accountability of business enterprises	
			To Whom	For What?
Medieval times to 1844	United Kingdom	• Cottage Industries • Individual trading ventures • End of 18th century, Industrial Revolution and emergence of indurial organisations	• Owners (Shareholders)	Honest authorised use of funds
1844–1920s	United Kingdom	• Growth in the number and size of companies • Separation of ownership and management • Emergence and increasing number of professional accountants and auditors	• Shareholders • Debtholders	Honest, authorised use of funds
1920s–1960s	Shift from United Kingdom to United States of America in early 1920s	• Wall Street Crash (1929) and the Great Depression • Increasing concentration of capital in, and growth of, large companies • Increased separation of ownership and professional managers • Emergence and growing importance of institutional investors • Emergence of a few (simple) auditing standards	• Shareholders • Debtholders • Creditors • Investors in general	• Honest, authorised use of funds • Profitable use of resources
1960s–1990s	United States of America	• Continued growth of large corporations (with many takeovers and mergers) • Companies increasingly multinational in nature • Dominance of professional management divorced from ownership interests • Increasing importance of taxation • Dominance of institutional investors • Increasing competition between businesses and between audit firms • Development of more numerous and more stringent auditing standards • Stock Market Crash (1987)	• Shareholders • Debtholders • Creditors • Investors • Customers • Suppliers • Society in general	• Honest, authorised use of funds • Profitable use of resources • Increasing social and environmental responsibilities (e.g. pollution, reduction, product and employee safety)
1990s–2002	Primarily United States of America but increasingly global in focus	• Dominance of global businesses and audit firms • Technological advances affect all aspects of the corporate/business environment • Regulatory action to secure responsible corporate governance • Increased societal pressure for companies to be socially responsible • Reduction of 'Big 8' audit firms to the 'Big 5'	• Shareholders • Debtholders • Creditors • Investors • Customers • Suppliers • Society in general	• Honest, authorised use of funds • Profitable use of resources • Responsible corporate governance • Broad social, environmental and ethical responsibilities
Post 2002	Global	• Increased importance of China, India, Russia and Brazil in the global economy • Emergence of stockmarket indices of socially responsibly companies • Reduction of 'Big 5' to 'Big 4' audit firms • Almost universal adoption of international accounting and auditing standards (other than by the USA) • Increased regulation of external auditing in virtually all countries in the world • 2008-9 Financial crisis and 2011- ? Eurozone crisis		

Audit objectives	Major characteristics of auditing techniques
Detection of fraud (Little auditing conducted prior to 1844 and limited to Balance Sheet)	• Detailed checking of transactions and account entries • Concern for arithmetical accuracy and agreement between account balances and Balance Sheet
• Detection of fraud • Detection of errors • Determination of solvency/insolvency (Compulsory auditing of companies introduced in the UK in 1844. Only Balance Sheet of importance)	• Detailed checking of transactions and account entries • Emergence of physical observation of assets and use of external evidence • Concern for arithmetical accuracy and agreement between account balances and Balance Sheet
• Lending credibility to financial statements prepared by management • Fraud detection of minor importance as an audit objective (Emphasis gradually shifted to Profit and Loss Statement but Balance Sheet also important)	• Gradual change to reliance on internal controls combined with test checking of samples of evidence • Increasing emphasis given to physical observation of external and other evidence outside the 'books of account' • Concern for the truth and fairness of financial information provided by management

• Providing credibility to financial statements prepared by management
• Provision of management advisory services
• Gradual increase in importance of detecting and reporting corporate fraud and other illegal acts
	• Examination of evidence from a wide variety of sources internal and external to the entity
	• Emergence of computer-based accounting systems and auditing techniques
	• Emergence and reliance on statistical sampling
	• Audit risk approach to auditing – based on:
	   - thorough understanding of the client, its business and its industry
	   - identification of likely material misstatements in the financial statements through analytical review
	   - assessment of reliance that can be placed on auditees' internal controls

• Lending credibility to financial and non-financial information provided by management in annual reports • Provision of management advisory services (largely removed as an audit objective since 2002) • Increased responsibility for detecting, and reporting fraud and other illegal acts • Increased emphasis on reporting doubts about an auditee's status as a 'going concern' • Reviewing corporate governance statements in auditees' annual reports • Some assurance of corporate responsibility reports • Increasing expectation by regulatory authorities that auditors will report to them matters of concern	• 1990s: Adoption of audit methodologies focusing on clients' business risks and measures taken to mitigate those risks (business risk approach – risk of auditees not meeting their objectives) • Increased reliance on computerised accounting systems and computer techniques - • Post-2002: Move back to audit risk approach but with enhanced requirements in respect of understanding the client and its external and internal environment • Auditing procedures more strictly prescribed by auditing standards • Dominance of information technology in auditees' accounting systems and in the audit process • Adaptation of auditing to the e-commerce/e-business environment

Figure 2.1 also shows that the development of auditing can be considered conveniently in five phases:

- period up to 1844
- 1844–1920s
- 1920s–1960s
- 1960s–1990s
- 1990s–present (subdivided in some respects into the periods before and after 2002).

2.3 DEVELOPMENT OF AUDITING IN THE PERIOD UP TO 1844

During this earliest and longest phase in its development, auditing was primarily concerned with public accounts. Evidence, mainly in the form of markings on tablets and buildings, shows that over 2000 years ago the Egyptians, Greeks and Romans all used systems to check the accounting of officials entrusted with public funds. In the old Greek and Roman Empires, those responsible for public funds (who were generally unable to read or write) were required to appear periodically before a government official to give an oral presentation of their accounts. As noted in Chapter 1, the word 'audit' (derived from the Latin for 'a hearing') dates from these times.

Similarly, in medieval times in England, government officials visited the various manors and estates to check the accounts (now in written form) to ensure that the funds collected and disbursed on behalf of the Crown were properly accounted for. Interestingly, as the following quotation reveals, the information collected for the Domesday Book in 1085 (which formed the initial basis for assessing the amounts due to the Crown from the manors and estates) was subject to audit.

> The *Saxon Chronicle* records that in 1085 at Gloucester,
> . . . at midwinter . . . the King [William the Conqueror] . . . sent men all over England
> to each shire [or county] . . . to find out . . . what or how much each landowner held
> . . . in land and livestock, and what it was worth. The returns were brought to him.
> William was thorough. . . . [H]e also sent a second set of Commissioners to shires
> they did not know, where they themselves were unknown, to check their predecessors' survey, and report culprits to the King. (Reported and cited by Morris, 1977, p. 1, from the Domesday Book, 20 Bedfordshire)

Prior to the industrial revolution (which began in the late eighteenth century), auditing had little commercial application. Industry was principally based in cottages and small mills, located where water power was available. Individuals both owned and managed these small businesses and therefore there was no need for the business managers to report to the owners on their management of resources – and no need for such reports to be audited.

However, especially during the eighteenth century, overseas trading ventures became important. The captains of the ships engaged in these commercial ventures were required to account for the funds and cargos entrusted to their care, to those who had financed the undertaking. These accounts were subject to audit. Indeed, private commercial venture audits originate in the audits of the accounts of trading ships returning to Britain from the East and the New World.

During this pre-1844 period, concern centred on the honest authorised use of funds by those to whom the funds had been entrusted. Correspondingly, the main audit objective was the detection of fraud. In order to meet this objective, the accounts under audit were subjected to a detailed and thorough examination, with special emphasis on arithmetical accuracy and compliance with the authority given to the custodian of the funds.

2.4 DEVELOPMENT OF COMPANY AUDITING 1844–1920s

2.4.1 Socio-economic developments 1844–1920s

Between 1844 and the 1920s, as in the latter stages of the pre-1844 period, economic and auditing development was centred in the UK. This period, which followed the industrial revolution, saw far-reaching changes in the socio-economic environment. In particular, it witnessed the emergence of large-scale industrial and commercial enterprises and the displacement of individual (one-off) trading ventures by continuing corporations. Accompanying these changes, the period also witnessed a significant advancement in auditing.

In the late eighteenth century, the industrial revolution, with its associated large factories and machine-based production, led to a demand for large amounts of capital. At the same time, a new 'middle class' emerged, with small amounts of surplus funds available for investment. As a result, small amounts of capital were contributed by many people to financial entrepreneurs who channelled the funds to the growing industrial and commercial undertakings. However, in the eighteenth and early nineteenth centuries, the share market was unregulated and highly speculative, and the rate of financial failure was high. At this time, an individual's liability was not limited and the treatment of debtors, including innocent investors who became debtors when the business venture in which they had invested failed, was very harsh. Given this environment, it was clear that the growing number of small investors needed some protection.

2.4.2 Statutory developments 1844–1920s

As a result of these socio-economic developments, the Joint Stock Companies Act was passed in the UK in 1844. This Act enabled companies to be formed and officially recognised merely by registration. Previously, companies could only become recognised as such by means of a Royal Charter or a special Act of Parliament. The first option was very expensive; the latter very slow.

In return for gaining legal status by means of registration, companies had to comply with certain regulations. Among other things:

- each company's directors had to provide annually to their shareholders a balance sheet[1] setting out the state of affairs (in particular, the assets and liabilities) of the company; and
- an auditor had to be appointed by the company's shareholders. The auditor was empowered to examine the company's records at reasonable intervals throughout the year and was required to report to the company's shareholders whether, in his opinion, the balance sheet gave a 'full and fair' view of the company's state of affairs. Unlike today, the auditor was not required to be independent of the company's management or a qualified accountant. In practice, a shareholder was usually appointed as auditor by his fellow members.

In 1856, the statutory provisions requiring companies' balance sheets to be audited were repealed. Subsequent events proved this move to be ill-advised: of 88,000 companies registered between 1862 and 1904, more than 50,000 had come to an end by 1904 (Brown, 1905, p. 325). Not surprisingly, compulsory audits were re-introduced in the Companies Act of 1900. Under the auditing provisions of this Act, an auditor was still not required to be a qualified accountant, but the need for auditors to be independent of the company's management was recognised. The Act provided that neither a director nor an officer of the company (that is, any of the company's management) could be appointed as the company's auditor. The Act also provided that:

- auditors were to be given access to all of the company's books and records they required to enable them to perform their duties as auditors. This included access to documents such as contracts and minutes of directors' meetings;
- auditors were to append a certificate to the foot of the audited balance sheet stating that all of their requirements as auditors had been met;
- in addition to the above certificate, auditors were to report to the auditees' shareholders on the balance sheet stating whether, in their

---

[1] Today, International Financial Reporting Standards use the term 'statement of financial position' in place of 'balance sheet'.

opinion, it conveyed a 'true and correct' view of the state of affairs of the company.

The Institute of Chartered Accountants in England and Wales (ICAEW) sought legal advice on the form the required certificate and report should take. This resulted in the adoption of a standard form of certificate and audit report; they were reported in an Editorial in *The Accountant's Magazine* (1901, p. 47) as follows:

Auditor's Certificate

In accordance with the provisions of the Companies Act 1900, I certify that all my requirements as auditor have been complied with.

Auditor's Report

I have audited the above balance sheet and, in my opinion, such a balance sheet is properly drawn up, so as to exhibit a true and correct view of the state of affairs of the company, as shown by the books of the company.

The Companies Act 1900 was a prominent milestone in the history of company auditing; it established a requirement for companies' balance sheets to be audited, auditor independence from company managements and a standard form of audit report.

2.4.3 Corporate accountability and audit objectives 1844–1920s

During the period from 1844 to the 1920s, companies remained relatively small and their directors/managers were generally regarded as accountable only for the safe custody and honest, authorised use of the funds entrusted to them. In accordance with society's needs and expectations of the time, audit objectives were designed to protect primarily shareholders, but secondarily lenders/bankers, from unscrupulous acts by company managers who had custody of their funds. Hence, the main audit objectives were:
- the detection of fraud and error; and
- the proper portrayal of the company's solvency (or insolvency) in the balance sheet.

During most of this period, company managers were usually considered to be accountable only to the company's shareholders although, after the turn of the century, their accountability to debtholders also came to be recognised. The primacy of managers' accountability to shareholders is reflected in the fact that the balance sheet was regarded as a private communication between the company's management and its shareholders. Indeed, there was much debate in accounting circles about the auditor's report on the balance sheet. The Act only required the report to be read at the shareholders' annual general meeting and, according to Lee (1970, p. 366), many professional accountants thought it was wrong also to attach it to the published balance sheet. They feared that the auditor might have something to say in the report which, should it become public knowledge, might be injurious to the company; for example, comments which might cause debtholders to panic and to demand that their claims be met immediately, causing the company to collapse. Others considered that, logically, the report should be combined and published with the auditor's certificate. In the event, the Companies Act 1908 settled the debate by supporting the latter view and requiring the auditor to provide just one (combined) report.

2.4.4   Development of auditors' duties 1844–1920s

The decisions of the courts during the period from 1844 to 1920 served to clarify auditors' duties. The two most notable cases are those of *London and General Bank* (1895) and *Kingston Cotton Mill* (1896).

- In the case of *Re London and General Bank (No. 2)* [1895] 2 Ch. 673, the auditor discovered errors in the balance sheet which he reported to the directors but failed to report to the shareholders. In his summing up, Lindley L J stated that it was not the duty of the auditor to see that the company and its directors acted prudently or imprudently, profitably or unprofitably, in performing their business activities, but it was the auditor's duty to report to shareholders any dishonest acts which had occurred and which affected the propriety of the information contained in the balance sheet. However, he also noted that the auditor could not be expected to find every fraud and error within the company. That would be asking too much; the auditor is not an insurer or guarantor. What is expected of him is the exercise of reasonable skill and care in the circumstances.

- In *Re Kingston Cotton Mill Co Ltd (No. 2)* [1896] 2 Ch. 279, Lopes, L J elaborated on the remarks of Lindley L J (above). He stated:

  It is the duty of an auditor to bring to bear on the work he has to perform that skill, care and caution which a reasonably competent, careful and cautious auditor would use. What is reasonable skill, care and caution must depend on the particular circumstances of each case. An auditor is not bound to be a detective or . . . to approach his work with suspicion or with a foregone conclusion that there is something wrong. He is a watchdog not

> a bloodhound. If there is anything to excite suspicion he should probe it to the bottom; but in the absence of anything of that kind he is only bound to be reasonably cautious and careful.

These two cases reinforced the audit objectives of detecting fraud and error and established the general standard of work expected of auditors. They established that auditors are not expected to ferret out every fraud but they are required to use reasonable skill and care in examining the company's accounting records.

Corresponding with the primary audit objective of detecting fraud and error, from 1844 to the 1920s, auditing procedures involved close examination of the company's accounting entries and related documents combined with detailed checking of the arithmetical accuracy of the accounting records. However, towards the end of the period, judgments by the courts made it clear that auditors were required to do more than merely check the company's records. In the case of *London Oil Storage Co Ltd* v *Seear, Hasluck & Co*. [1904] 31 Acct. LR 1, the cash balance shown in the balance sheet did not agree with the cash the company owned (most of which was held by a bank). The judge held that an auditor is liable for damage sustained by a company which results from his omission to verify the existence of assets stated in the balance sheet. It was established that the auditor, in ensuring that the information given in the audited balance sheet corresponds with the company's accounting records, is not merely required to check the arithmetical accuracy of the entries. He is also required to ensure that the data in the company's records represent fact rather than fiction. This case made it clear, for the first time, that an auditor is required to go beyond the auditee's internal records for evidence to support his audit opinion.

This position was confirmed and extended in *Arthur E. Green & Co.* v *The Central Advance and Discount Corporation Ltd* [1920] 63 Acct LR 1. In this case the court held that the auditor was negligent in accepting a schedule of bad debts provided by a responsible officer of the company when it was apparent that other debts, not included in the schedule, were also irrecoverable. The case established that the auditor is required not only to go beyond the company's internal documentary evidence but is also required to relate evidence obtained from different sources.

These cases indicate that, by the 1920s, auditing was rapidly developing into a technical process, requiring the skills of qualified accountants. However, many auditors were still laymen: frequently, they were merely shareholders chosen to be auditors by their fellow members. This reflects the key to this early period in the development of company audits. Company managers were regarded as accountable for the safe custody and honest, authorised use of the funds entrusted to them, primarily by shareholders. Audits were required to protect the interests of, and secure managers' accountability to, the company's shareholders.[2]

2.5 DEVELOPMENT OF COMPANY AUDITING 1920s–1960s

2.5.1 Socio-economic developments 1920s–1960s

During this period the centre of economic and auditing development shifted from the UK to the USA. The period is characterised by the continued growth in the size of companies and the development of sophisticated securities markets and credit-granting institutions, designed to serve the financial needs of the growing economic entities.

Particularly in the years of recovery following the 1929 Wall Street Crash and ensuing depression, investment in business entities grew rapidly. Company ownership became highly diffused and a new class of small investors emerged. Unlike the shareholders of earlier years, who were relatively few in number but closely bound to the companies they partially owned, the new breed of investors were little interested in the management or fortunes of 'their' companies *per se*. They were primarily concerned with the return they could earn on their investment and, if they perceived better returns could be earned elsewhere, they readily switched their allegiance to another company.

Accompanying the growth in the size of companies and the changing attitudes of investors, ownership interests and management functions of companies

---

[2] Chandler, Edwards and Anderson (1993) present a contrary view of audit objectives for the period from 1844 to the 1920s. They provide evidence to support the notion that verifying financial statements prepared by company managements, rather than fraud detection, was the chief audit objective during the second and third quarters of the nineteenth century. However, they limit this suggestion to banking, railway and insurance companies which:

> were generally much larger and possessed a much more widely dispersed shareholder group than the majority of industrial and manufacturing companies. [These] shareholders . . . tended to view themselves not so much as owners but as investors looking for the best return . . . For the generality of companies, which remained relatively small, it was the auditor's fraud detection role which remained predominant. (Chandler *et al.*, 1993, pp. 444–445)

It seems that between 1844 and the 1870s, the shareholders of banking, railway and insurance companies were similar to the typical investors of the 1920s to 1960s period – investors who required reliable (verified) information for their investment decisions. However, Chandler *et al.* (1993) note that during the latter part of the nineteenth century the primary audit objective, even for "sectors of the economy where large (usually quoted) companies predominated" (p. 445), became fraud detection. They suggest the change can be traced to leading professional accountant-auditors (who were beginning to replace the amateur shareholder-auditors) becoming obsessed with fraud detection as a consequence of the frequency of corporate bankruptcy in the 1860s and 1870s – bankruptcies largely caused by fraud (p. 447). Professional accountants at this time were heavily involved in bankruptcy and insolvency work and thus many gained insight into the causes and adverse effects of fraud. The dominance of fraud detection as the chief audit objective at the turn of the century is reflected in Spicer and Pegler's (1911) textbook:

> In the minds of the public at large, and of the majority of clients, the discovery of fraud is so far the principal function of the Auditor as to overshadow his other duties entirely, and there can be no question that it is of primary importance. (p. 5)

became increasingly separated. The management and control of companies gradually passed to small groups of well-qualified, professional managers (directors and executives) who frequently owned no shares in the companies they managed (Porter, 1989). In this new economic environment, the accountability of company managers was extended from the honest, authorised use of shareholders' funds to include the profitable use of those funds; business managers became accountable for generating a reasonable return on the financial resources entrusted to them.

At the same time as companies grew in size and shareholders became divorced from the companies in which they invested, it came to be recognised that the survival and growth of companies rested not only on the financial resources provided by shareholders but on the joint contribution of all stakeholders, that is, all those with a particular 'stake' or interest in the company – shareholders, debtholders, employees, suppliers, customers and the government. As a consequence, many in society came to regard company managements as accountable to all of their company's stakeholders, and as having an obligation to ensure that each stakeholder group was sufficiently rewarded for its contribution so as to ensure it maintained its 'stake' in the company.

The trend towards society expecting increased accountability from company managements was reinforced by events such as the 1929 Wall Street Crash and the questionable or downright dishonest acts of company directors which resulted in cases such as the *Royal Mail* case (1932) in the UK (discussed in the next sub-section) and the *McKesson & Robbins* case (1938) in the USA (see Chapter 5, section 5.5.3).

2.5.2 Developments in company auditing 1920s–1960s

Between the 1920s and 1960s, in response to changes in the socio-economic environment such as those outlined above, auditing changed in four main ways. These are as follows.

(a) *Evaluation of internal control and development of sampling techniques:* As companies grew in size, the increasing volume of transactions in which they engaged made it progressively less feasible for auditors to check all of the entries in the accounting records. At the same time, as companies grew larger, their managers found it necessary to delegate accounting and other duties to employees. With the growth in the volume of transactions and the need to delegate responsibilities, errors in the company's records (as well as fraud) became more likely. In order to prevent and/or detect errors and fraud, and to ensure delegated responsibilities were properly performed, managements introduced systems of internal control.[3] As a result of these changes, auditing procedures changed from meticulous checking of accounting records to testing samples of transactions and accounting entries, combined with an evaluation of the company's system of internal control.

(b) *Increased emphasis on external audit evidence:* As a result of judges' decisions in cases such as *London Oil Storage Co. Ltd* v *Seear Hasluck and Co.* (1904) mentioned above and the *McKesson & Robbins* case (1938), emphasis was placed on auditors physically observing assets such as cash and inventory and using evidence obtained from outside the auditee (for example, confirmation of accounts receivable). These duties came to be recognised as equally important as auditors' traditional task of examining the company's internal accounting records and other documents.

(c) *Auditing the profit and loss statement:*[4] As the return on their investment became the factor of prime importance for companies' shareholders and other investors, so the emphasis of financial statement users shifted away from the balance sheet and ideas of solvency, towards the profit and loss statement and ideas of earning power. This shift in emphasis was led from the USA but was dramatically reinforced in the UK by the *Royal Mail* case (*Rex* v *Kyslant* [1932] I KB 442; [1931] All ER 179) which, in the words of De Paula, "fell like an atom bomb and changed the face of the world of accounting" (as reported in Johnston, Edgar & Hays, 1982, p. 9). Chandler *et al.* (1993) similarly refer to it as: "perhaps the single most significant twentieth century case in terms of its impact on the development of accounting thought and practice" (p. 454). They also attribute "the transition [in the 1930s] from fraud detection to [financial] statement verification" as the primary audit objective "mainly to the effects of the Royal Mail case" (p. 457).

The case principally revolved around publication by the Royal Mail Steam Packet Company, between 1921 and 1928, of profit and loss statements which failed to show whether profits had or had not been earned. During these years, the company paid dividends amounting to £5 million, funded largely from undisclosed transfers from secret reserves. Additionally, in 1928, the company published:

> a prospectus inviting the public to subscribe to the issue of debenture stock . . . which . . . concealed the true position of the company, with intent to induce persons to entrust or advance property to the company. (Mr Justice Wright, presiding Judge)

───────────────────────────

[3] Systems of internal control are discussed in Chapter 10.

[4] International Financial Reporting Standards use the term 'income statement' in place of 'profit and loss statement'.

The profit and loss statements and prospectus disclosed 'surpluses' for the years 1921 to 1928, ranging from £628,535 to £779,114 – implying that the company was profitable and provided a sound investment opportunity. In fact, the company made significant losses in each of these years, ranging from £95,614 to £779,153.

The *Royal Mail* case highlighted the need for companies' profit and loss statements to be audited and, not surprisingly, such a requirement was introduced in the Securities and Exchange Commission Act 1934 in the USA and in the Companies Act 1948 in the UK. Since the time the requirement was enacted, auditors in the USA and UK have been required to report to audit clients' shareholders on the truth and fairness[5] of the company's profit and loss statement as well as of its balance sheet.

(d) *Change in audit objectives:* Although the other changes which occurred in auditing between the 1920s and 1960s were significant, the greatest single change was that in audit objectives. The focus of auditing shifted away from preventing and detecting fraud and error towards assessing the truth and fairness of the information presented in companies' financial statements.

As we noted earlier, as companies grew larger, their ownership and management functions became separated. In order to ensure that financial markets functioned smoothly, and that funds continued to flow from investors to companies, it was essential that participants in the financial markets were confident that companies' financial statements provided a true and fair portrayal of their financial position and performance. Responding to these needs, auditors accepted as their primary audit objective providing credibility to the financial statements prepared by a company's management[6] for its shareholders which essentially reported on its own (that is, management's) performance.

At the same time as providing credibility to externally reported financial information emerged as the primary audit objective, that of detecting fraud and error declined in importance. As Spicer and Pegler (1936) observed:

> The main object of an audit is the verification of accounts and statements prepared by a client or client's staff. Although of great importance the detection of fraud and error must be regarded as incidental to such main object. (p. 5)

---

[5] In the USA, the term 'fair presentation' is used in place of 'truth and fairness'.

[6] Readers are reminded that in this book we use the term 'management' to mean a company's executive directors, non-executive directors and non-director executives (that is, all executives and directors). In the UK, a company's directors are legally responsible for the preparation of its annual financial statements.

The displacement of detecting fraud and error as the primary audit objective corresponded with the fact that, as companies grew in size:

- their managements established systems of internal control designed, *inter alia*, to prevent and detect fraud and error; and
- auditing procedures changed from detailed checking of the company's accounting records to testing samples of transactions and accounting entries, combined with an evaluation of the company's system of internal control. This change reduced the likelihood of discovering fraud during an audit.

The changes indicated above also provided new opportunities for auditors. Through their review of audit clients' accounting systems and related internal controls, and through the in-depth knowledge of client entities which auditors acquire during the course of their audits, they are ideally placed to offer advisory services to their audit clients. They are, for example, in an ideal position to suggest ways in which the efficiency and effectiveness of the accounting system and/or internal controls might be improved, and to offer assistance in areas such as financial and tax planning. During the 1920s to 1960s period, auditors began to provide non-audit services to their audit clients but, as we shall see, the provision of such services gained ground between the 1960s and 1990s and became extremely important (and lucrative) for auditors during the 1990s.

By the mid-1960s, companies had become a very influential element in society and their managements were regarded as accountable to a wide range of interested parties, not only for the honest, authorised use of resources entrusted to their care but also for the profitable use of those resources. Auditing had become well established as a profession and auditors' rights and duties were embodied in statute and case law. Nevertheless, since the 1960s further notable changes have occurred in the audit environment, audit objectives and auditing techniques.

2.6 DEVELOPMENT OF COMPANY AUDITING 1960s–1990s

2.6.1 Socio-economic developments 1960s–1990s

Between the 1960s and 1990s, aided – and accelerated – by technological advances and by mergers and takeovers, 'large' companies continued to grow in size and, particularly in the case of national and multinational companies, became extremely powerful and influential forces in society. The extent of the power held by companies during this period is reflected in the enormous share of the nation's financial and non-financial resources which they owned or controlled.

The social and economic influence of companies is also reflected in the effect they had in their local communities. This was not restricted to providing employment and generating a flow of funds in their neighbourhood. They also had an impact through the presence and appearance of their grounds and buildings; they used the local transport network and affected traffic volumes and flows; they produced goods and services desired by consumers and they purchased goods and services from suppliers. Many provided sporting and cultural facilities, and many helped to beautify, or to exploit and pollute, the local environment. When these and other factors are taken into consideration, it is clear that even a moderately sized company could have a significant influence on the economic and social life of the community of which it is a part. Taken as a whole, the corporate sector had an enormous impact on the well-being of society in general. Given this level of power and influence in society, it came to be argued that company managements should be held accountable for behaving in a socially responsible manner. A significant – and increasing – number of commentators advanced the notion that company managers had an obligation to consider the impact of their decisions and actions on those who would be affected thereby at the same time as they sought to accomplish their traditional economic goals of profit-making, growth and long term survival (see, for example, Davis, 1976; Demers & Wayland, 1982).

By the late-1980s, companies' wider obligation to society was fairly well established. Their managers were, for example, considered to have an obligation to prevent environmental pollution, to ensure employee and product safety, to adopt equal employment opportunities, and to protect consumers. Parliament had introduced a considerable volume of laws and regulations covering these and similar issues with which company managements were required to comply. The necessary compliance auditing was not, however, the responsibility of the company's financial statement auditors; instead, it was usually undertaken by inspectors from a State agency.

Notwithstanding the extension of the accountability expected of company managers since the 1960s, legislation governing external reporting by companies in the UK (as elsewhere) continued to focus on company managements' accountability to shareholders for financial performance. Nevertheless, the legislators recognised that corporate managers were also accountable to their company's debenture-holders as, under the Companies Act 1985, s. 238, companies were required to provide their debenture-holders, as well as their shareholders, with a copy of their annual audited financial statements, directors' report and auditor's report.

2.6.2 Developments in company auditing 1960s–1990s

As shown in Figure 2.1, four significant developments in auditing techniques occurred during the 1960s–1990s period. These are as follows:

- increased emphasis was placed on examining audit evidence obtained from a wide variety of sources, both internal and external to the auditee. (This is a continuation of the trend noted in the earlier phases of auditing's development);
- computers emerged and became increasingly significant both as an audit tool and as an element in auditees' operations and information (including accounting) systems;
- statistical sampling techniques were adopted as an aid to making difficult audit judgments and, to an extent, to place those judgments on a 'scientific' basis which could be justified and defended should they be challenged subsequently – for example, in a court of law;[7]
- a risk-based approach to auditing was widely adopted. In essence, this involves assessing the likelihood of material misstatements being present in the financial statements, identifying the areas where such misstatements appear most likely, and focusing audit effort on those areas. This 'audit risk' approach was designed to reduce to an acceptable level the risk of the auditor expressing an unmodified (i.e., 'clean') audit opinion on materially misstated financial statements – and to achieve this at minimum cost (an important consideration at a time when audit fees were under severe downward pressure – a point we explain below).

The adoption of risk-based auditing resulted in auditors needing to gain a thorough understanding of their audit clients' organisation, key personnel, policies, procedures, etc., their business operations and their industries. It also involved auditors understanding their clients' systems of internal financial controls and the extent to which these could be relied upon to prevent misstatements from occurring in the financial statements. Additionally, during the 1980s and 1990s, virtually all companies introduced computer systems to process their financial and other data, and to perform, monitor and/or control many (if not most) of their operational and administrative processes. These changes provided auditors with new opportunities to identify areas within their client companies where improvements could be made and, thus, where they could offer advice – for example, in their accounting, management information and internal control systems, in their tax and financial planning, and in aspects of their operations.

---

[7] Statistical sampling is discussed in Chapter 12. In respect of the adoption of such techniques, Bell, Peecher and Solomon (2005) explain:

> During the 1980s some [audit] firms . . . developed and implemented a suite of sophisticated mathematical tools. . . . Auditors used these state-of-the-art statistical sampling and mathematical decision aids to help make difficult audit judgments, including judgments about audit scope, planning materiality, evaluations of internal control and assessment of control risk, and judgments about sample size for tests of details. . . . The high level of structure [of audits, including the adoption of statistical sampling,] was an attempt to reduce variation across audits and thereby promote consistently high audit quality. (p. 10)

At the same time as changes in the auditing domain generated opportunities for auditors to provide advisory services to their clients, fierce competition developed between businesses and between audit firms. This largely resulted from advances in information technology and the phenomenal increase in the speed of information transfer, which meant companies' (and audit firms') products and services, prices, processes, etc. were quickly known by their competitors and others. In the case of audit firms, increased competition also resulted from company mergers and acquisitions which reduced the number of potential audit clients. As a consequence of the competition – combined with a view held by many company managements that financial statement audits are a commodity and, therefore, should be obtained at minimum cost – audit fees came under severe downward pressure. Auditors seeking to maintain (or increase) their fees emphasised to auditees' managements that, rather than being viewed as 'a costly evil required by law', an audit should be viewed as a value-adding activity: valuable advisory services could be provided as an outcome of the audit. As a result, the provision of advisory services for management emerged as a secondary audit objective.

2.7 DEVELOPMENT OF COMPANY AUDITING 1990s–PRESENT

2.7.1 Socio-economic developments 1990s–present

Since 1990, the socio-economic developments which typified the 1960s–1990s period have continued – at an accelerating pace. Today, huge multinational companies dominate the developed, and many developing, economies, many other businesses are global in nature, and technology (and technical advances) pervades all aspects of the commercial environment. The size of some companies is reflected in an observation by Turley, Chairman and Chief Executive Officer of Ernst & Young: "We live in a world where scores of individual corporations boast revenue figures that exceed the GDP of whole nations" (Turley, 2004, p. 18).

The growth of major companies into huge business enterprises has been accompanied by a commensurate increase in their power and influence in society. However, this power and influence has not remained unfettered. As we saw in Chapter 1, as a check on the misuse of their power, the directors of companies are required to publish annual reports (which include the company's audited financial statements) that report on the company's activities during the previous financial year. However, the 1987 stock market crash, together with well-publicised company failures such as those of Polly Peck in 1990[8] and the Bank

---

[8] During the 1980s, Polly Peck grew into a major electronics, food and leisure company; in 1989 it was among the UK's largest 100 listed companies. In 1990 it collapsed amid charges against Nadir, its Chief Executive Officer, of fraudulent financial reporting and theft of company assets (Wikipedia, 2011a).

of Credit and Commerce International (BCCI) in 1991,[9] and misconduct by senior company officials which came to light during investigations of the failed companies by agencies such as the Department of Trade and Industry (DTI)[10] in the UK and the Securities and Exchange Commission (SEC) in the USA, clearly demonstrated that more was needed. In the UK, in 1991, the Financial Reporting Council (FRC), the London Stock Exchange and the accountancy profession established the Committee on the Financial Aspects of Corporate Governance (CFACG; Cadbury Committee). In December 1992, the committee published its report and a *Code of Best Practice* (CFACG, 1992).[11] Since then, regulators around the world have introduced corporate governance require-ments, designed to ensure that companies are governed properly. In many countries (including the UK), listed companies are required to comply with the requirements and to report (in their annual reports) that they have done so.[12]

During and since the 1990s, in addition to being subject to corporate gover-nance requirements, large companies have come under increasing societal, political and media pressure to conduct their business in a socially and envi-ronmentally responsible manner. This is reflected, for example, in the introduc-tion in the UK's Companies Act (CA) 2006 (s. 417) of a requirement for the directors of all quoted companies[13] to include in the business review section of their directors' report:

> ... to the extent necessary for an understanding of the development, performance or position of the company's business, ... information about –
>> (i) environmental matters (including the impact of the company's business on the environment),
>> (ii) the company's employees, and
>> (iii) social and community issues,
> including information about any policies of the company in relation to those matters and the effectiveness of those policies; ...

---

[9] In the mid-1980s, BCCI was a major international bank which operated in 78 countries and had more than 400 branches. It engaged in a variety of financial crimes, including fraud and money laundering and, in 1991, it collapsed when its offices in five countries were raided by regulators and customs officers (Wikipedia, 2011b).

[10] In 2007, the DTI was replaced by the Department for Business, Enterprise and Regulatory Reform (DBERR); in 2009 the latter was replaced by the Department for Business, Innovation & Skills (BIS).

[11] This Code was the forerunner of the *Combined Code on Corporate Governance* (Committee on Corporate Governance, 1998), its subsequent versions (FRC, 2003, 2006a and 2008) and its successors, *The UK Corporate Governance Code* (FRC 2010, 2012).

[12] Or, as in the UK, if they do not comply, to disclose the respects in which they have not done so and explain the reasons for the non-compliance. We explain the corporate governance requirements which apply to listed companies in the UK in Chapter 5, section 5.2.2.

[13] A quoted company is a company whose equity shares are traded on a regulated market in any Member State of the European Economic Area (EEA; that is, Member States of the European Union, other than Croatia, together with Norway, Iceland and Liechtenstein), or on the New York Stock Exchange or NASDAQ (CA 2006, s. 385).

Auditors are not specifically required to audit this information but they are required to state in their audit reports whether, in their opinion, the information given in the directors' report is consistent with the financial statements (CA 2006 s. 496).[14]

Notwithstanding this and other changes which have been introduced in CA 2006, companies are not (as yet) required to report to stakeholders other than their shareholders and debenture-holders, nor are they required to report fully on their environmental impact or social activities.[15] Nevertheless, many companies report on their environmental and social performance voluntarily and submit at least part of this information to audit (or, more correctly, assurance).[16] The essence of the present position is reflected in the fundamental principle of external auditing – *Accountability*:[17]

> Auditors act in the interests of primary stakeholders, whilst having regard to the wider public interest. The identity of primary stakeholders is determined by reference to the statute or agreement requiring an audit: in the case of companies, the primary stakeholder is the general body of shareholders. (FRC, 2013, Appendix 2)

2.7.2 Developments in company auditing 1990s–present

As in the earlier periods of auditing's development, during and since the 1990s auditing has adapted and responded to changes in its environment. However, unlike the earlier phases, the post-1990 period can be divided into two distinct parts:

(i) 1990s–2002 – a period characterised by adoption of the business (rather than audit) risk approach to auditing, and

(ii) 2002–present – a period characterised by increased regulation of auditing.

---

[14] Since 1 October 2013, when ss. 414A, 414B, 414C and 414D were inserted in, and s. 417 was removed from, CA 2006, the requirement for the directors of quoted companies to provide a business review in their directors' report has been replaced by a requirement for the directors of all but small companies (see Chapter 5, Figure 5.2) to provide a strategic report. For quoted companies, this is to provide, *inter alia*, the information indicated above that was formerly required to be included in the business review. Since 1 October 2013, CA 2006, s. 496, has required the auditors of all but small companies to state in their audit reports whether, in their opinion, the information provided in the client's strategic and directors' reports is consistent with its financial statements. We consider the requirements relating to the strategic report in greater detail in Chapter 5, section 5.2.2.

[15] The statutory duties of companies with respect to external reporting are discussed in Chapter 5, section 5.2.

[16] Environmental and social reporting by companies – and the assurance thereof – is discussed in Chapter 17.

[17] The fundamental principles which constitute *The Auditors' Code* are reproduced on the inside front cover of this book.

(i)   1990s–2002: Adoption of the business risk approach to auditing

During the 1990s, trends evident in the 1980s continued and culminated in adoption of the business risk approach to auditing. As we noted previously, during the 1960s–1990s period, auditors experienced serious downward pressure on their audit fees. This was exacerbated in 1994 by the introduction of an exemption from audit for many small companies. Faced by increased competition in the audit market, auditors sought a means to:

(a) conduct effective audits (that is, those that result in the auditor expressing an appropriate opinion on the financial statements) more efficiently (that is, at lower cost); and

(b) increase their revenue through the provision of non-audit services.

The business risk approach to auditing provided the means for auditors to meet both of these goals. The objective of the audit remains that of forming and expressing an opinion on the truth and fairness of the auditee's financial statements. However, while the audit risk approach seeks to achieve this by focusing on the financial statements (assessing the likelihood of material misstatements and identifying the areas where errors seem most likely), the business risk approach adopts a holistic, business-wide perspective.

The business risk approach rests on the notion that many of a client's business risks (operational, financial, compliance and other risks), if not controlled, will eventually affect the financial statements. Its proponents maintain that by understanding the full range (and potential impact and likelihood of occurrence) of the client's risks – and measures the entity has put in place to manage them – the auditor is better able to identify significant matters of relevance to the audit.

Supporters of the approach point out that, as a result of computer technology, the processing of auditees' routine transactions and accounting records are inherently less prone to error than formerly. As a consequence, there is scope for less audit effort to be devoted to detailed checking of 'lower level' accounting information and correspondingly more effort to be applied to 'higher-level' (less detailed, business- and financial statement-wide) analysis and assessment. This higher-level assessment of the client and its risks generates more broadly-based evidence about the auditee and this, in turn, provides the auditor with a broader, more soundly based context for evaluating the significance and veracity of other evidence gathered during the audit and for making judgments about the truth and fairness of the financial statements.

Along related lines, analysis of the causes of audit failure (that is, expressing a 'clean' audit opinion on financial statements that are materially misstated) by academics and audit firms revealed that such failure does not generally stem from auditors' failure to detect errors in the recording or processing of account-ing data. Instead, it tends to result from matters associated with how the busi-ness is managed. As Defliese, Jaenicke, Sullivan and Gnospelius (1985) observe:

> Analyses of past alleged audit failures indicate that such . . . factors as failure to understand business situations or risks, errors in interpreting accounting princi-ples, mistakes in interpreting and implementing standards, and misstatements caused by client fraud are among the most significant audit risk factors and sources of auditor liability. (p. 248)

Following such reasoning, audit firms which adopted the business risk approach concluded that: "effective auditing requires greater attention to be paid to understanding the risks of the business" (Lemon, Tatum & Turley, 2000, p. 12).

In addition to claims that the business risk approach enhances the effectiveness and efficiency of audits, its proponents observe that, by adopting a business-wide approach and considering a broad range of issues associated with the risks faced by their auditees, auditors have a greater opportunity to assist their clients avoid problems which would, if not addressed, threaten achievement of their (the clients') objectives – or even their survival. Their stance is explained by Lemon *et al.* (2000) as follows:

> Rather than an ex-post exercise to detect misstatement in financial statements, the audit is viewed as a means of influencing the conduct and control of business such that problems with financial statement information are less likely to arise. There is therefore an added-value or client service dimension to . . . the business risk audit approaches . . . [that is] consistent with a desire to ensure that the audit provides insights and information which is valued by the entity's management and contributes to the enterprise in some positive way. (pp. 10, 12)

Based on such reasoning, the provision of non-audit services became an impor-tant secondary audit object. By the end of the 1990s, the revenue some audit firms derived from the provision of non-audit services to their audit clients far exceeded their audit fee income.[18]

Another benefit identified for the business risk approach to auditing is the assistance it provides for auditors in detecting fraud[19] and forming an opinion on the ability of the auditee to continue as a going concern.[20] Since the early 1990s, in line with society's and regulators' increasing concern about corporate

---

[18] Hermes (2002) reports that a study of the largest 100 companies listed on the London Stock Exchange by the *Financial Director* magazine, published in January 2002, found that the average audit fee for these companies was £2.21 million but they also paid their auditors an average in excess of £6.5 million for non-audit services. In a number of cases, the ratio of non-audit to audit fees was 12:1 and in two extreme cases was 48:1 and 78:1, respectively. We discuss this issue in greater detail in Chapter 4.

[19] Auditors' responsibilities for detecting and reporting fraud are discussed in Chapter 6.

[20] Auditors' responsibilities for assessing, and reporting on, an auditee's status as a going concern are dis-cussed in Chapter 13, section 13.4.

governance issues, auditors have come under pressure to accept greater responsibility in these regards.

Despite the advantages claimed for the business risk approach, it was not
without its critics. Perhaps most prominent among these are Turner and Levitt,
former Chief Accountant and Chairman, respectively, of the SEC in the USA.[21]
Turner (1999), for example, observed:

> Recent events[22] have caused the Commission and other securities regulators
> around the world to raise questions about the effectiveness of audits and the
> audit process, in particular, the perceived strengths and weaknesses of a [busi-
> ness] risk-based audit approach. . . . This approach requires an assessment of
> business risks within the [entity] . . . [S]ome have argued that this approach . . .
> has resulted in less verification of account balances by examining documenta-
> tion from independent sources . . . Instead, the firms are relying on analytical
> analysis, inquiries of company personnel, and when appropriate control testing.
> . . . While some auditors have asserted that changes to their audit processes are
> responsive to the increased use of technology in financial reporting and account-
> ing, other market participants have indicated a belief that the accounting profes-
> sion is discarding the techniques that, in the past, made the financial statement
> audit a tool that enhances the reliability of information provided to investors.
> (pp. 3–6)

Along similar lines, Levitt observed:

> In an era that calls for greater risk management the [audit] industry has migrated
> to what they call the '[business] risk-based' model. It sounds right on target . . .
> [R]ecent headlines of accounting failures have led some people to question the
> thoroughness of audits. . . . We rely on auditors to put something like the good
> housekeeping seal of approval on the information investors receive. The integrity
> of that information must take priority over a desire for cost efficiencies or com-
> petitive advantage in the audit process. . . . We cannot permit thorough audits to
> be sacrificed for re-engineered approaches that are efficient but less effective.
> (Levitt, 1999, p. 2; 1998, p. 6)

By the turn of the twenty-first century, partly as a result of criticism of the
business risk approach by influential regulators such as the SEC, and partly in
response to doubts being expressed within the auditing profession about its
effectiveness as an audit approach, in both the UK and the USA some of the
larger firms were beginning to retreat from its wholesale adoption. Some of

---

[21] It should be noted that the propriety of the business risk approach to auditing was being questioned by
commentators such as Turner and Levitt before the collapse of Enron in November 2001.

[22] "Recent events" referred, in particular, to some well-publicised audit failures such as Andersen's audit of
Waste Management's 1992–1996 financial statements. In June 2001, the SEC settled enforcement actions
against Arthur Andersen in respect of its audits of Waste Management amounting to $7 million. The SEC
found that "Arthur Andersen's reports on the financial statements for Waste Management Inc were
materially false and misleading and that Andersen engaged in improper professional conduct" (SEC Press
Release, 19 June 2001).

these firms were also beginning to question the efficiency gains claimed for the approach, in particular, those arising from assessing and evaluating business risks that have no direct relationship with the financial statements.[23] Thus, the efficiency and effectiveness factors motivating adoption of the business risk approach were already being questioned when Enron and Arthur Andersen collapsed in 2001 and 2002, respectively – events that were to trigger a new (regulated) phase in the development of auditing, and a sharp curtailment of the provision of non-audit services by auditors to their audit clients.

(ii) 2002–present: Increased regulation of auditing

Since the early 2000s, auditing has been subject to increasingly wide-ranging and stringent regulation which, to a significant extent, has reversed the trends of the 1990s. Bell, Peecher and Solomon (2005) provide a succinct account of events at the turn of the twenty-first century and the regulatory action which followed:

> The NASDAQ market index reached its all-time high in March of 2000 and then begun a precipitous slide. . . . As has been the case many times before, when the economy turned down, indications of business improprieties came to light. Some of the alleged improprieties were of enormous scale, appeared to involve the highest levels of business management, and were perpetuated or facilitated, at least in part, by materially misstated financial statements. Quickly, the cry went out – *Where were the auditors*? One of the Big Five [audit] firms,[24] Arthur Andersen LLP was the auditor . . . for several of these high-profile cases, including Enron and WorldCom. . . . Andersen was charged with several crimes, convicted of obstructing justice, and ultimately had to discontinue operations.[25] . . . Sweeping standard-setting and regulatory changes followed these and related events. The International Auditing and Assurance Standards Board (IAASB)[26] developed an ambitious action plan and issued several new International Standards on Auditing (ISAs). The U.S. Congress passed . . . the *Corporate and Auditing Accountability, Responsibility, and Transparency Act of 2002*, commonly called the Sarbanes-Oxley (SOX) Act. . . . [R]egulators from across the globe are contemplating or already have introduced legislation, regulations, and/or authoritative auditing guidance that, collectively, represent some of the most significant reforms in 70 years for public company auditing . . . [which are] intended to enhance public company financial reporting and thereby elevate investors' confidence. (Preface and pp. 1–2)

---

[23] These assertions are based on discussions between one of the authors and senior audit partners in some of the large accounting firms in the UK.

[24] Arthur Andersen, Deloitte, Ernst & Young, KPMG and PricewaterhouseCoopers.

[25] In May 2005 the US Supreme Court announced its unanimous decision to reverse the 2002 criminal conviction of Andersen (Bell *et al.*, 2005, p. 1).

[26] The IAASB replaced the International Auditing Practices Committee of the International Federation of Accountants (IFAC) in 2002. It is an independent standard-setting body established by, and operating under the auspices of, IFAC. Its goal is to "serve the public interest by setting high-quality international standards for auditing, quality control, review, other assurance, and related services . . ." (IAASB, 2011a).

The IAASB's "ambitious action plan" mentioned by Bell *et al*. (2005) refers to its 'clarity project', which commenced in 2004 and was completed in 2009. The IAASB, noting that standards need to be understandable, clear and capable of consistent application, explains that the aim of the project was to "enhance the clarity of its International Standards on Auditing (ISAs)" in order to "enhance the quality and uniformity of [auditing] practice worldwide" (IAASB, 2011b). The 'clarified' ISAs include one new standard on the communication of deficiencies in internal control, 16 standards containing new and revised requirements, and 20 standards that have been redrafted. There is also one 'clarified' International Standard on Quality Control (ISQC 1) (IAASB, 2011c). The IAASB has taken the opportunity provided by the project to extend and strengthen auditors' responsibilities and to specify more explicitly the requirements auditors are to fulfil in each stage of the audit process.

Enactment of the Sarbanes-Oxley Act of 2002 (SOX) is also highlighted by Bell *et al*. (2005) as a response to the demise of companies like Enron and WorldCom and the improprieties which came to light in the early 2000s. To a significant extent, SOX has served as an exemplar for legislation and regulations that have been enacted in many parts of the world since 2002, including the UK and the European Union (EU) more generally.[27] It is likely that this has resulted, in no small measure, from the fact that the SOX provisions relate not only to the audits (and auditors) of public companies registered in the USA but to those of all companies listed on the USA's stock exchanges (irrespective of where they are registered) and, also, to those of all significant subsidiaries of companies registered or listed in the USA, irrespective of where those subsidiaries are located. As a result, the tentacles of SOX have extended into many parts of the world and have a significant effect in the UK. Likewise, the EU's *Statutory Audit Directive* (EU, 2006) has tentacles that extend beyond the boundaries of the EU. Its provisions apply to "third country auditors and audit firms" (including those in the USA) that provide audits for companies incorporated outside the EU but whose transferable securities are traded on a regulated market of a Member State. Indeed, the *Statutory Audit Directive* has been described as the European equivalent of SOX (for example, Turley, 2004; Woolf, 2006).[28]

Key elements of SOX that are reflected, to an extent, in legislation and/or regulations in the UK and EU include the following:
   (i)   the establishment of an authority to oversee and regulate the auditors of public companies;

---

[27] Relevant UK and EU legislation and regulations are discussed in detail in Chapter 5.

[28] It should be noted that, under EU law, the provisions of EU Directives are required to be enacted in the national legislation of all EU Member States.

(ii) restrictions on auditors providing non-audit services to their audit clients;

(iii) reporting on the effectiveness of audit clients' systems of internal control.

We discuss each of these below.

(i) Authority to oversee and regulate public company auditors

SOX established a Public Company Accounting Oversight Board (PCAOB) in the USA:

> to oversee the audit of public companies that are subject to the securities laws . . . in order to protect the interests of investors and further the public interest in the preparation of informative, accurate and independent audit reports . . .
>
> The Board shall . . .
> (1) register public accounting firms that prepare audit reports for issuers [that is, audit firms that audit public companies] . . .
> (2) establish . . . auditing, quality control, ethics, independence, and other standards relating to the preparation of audit reports for issuers . . .
> (3) conduct inspections of registered public accounting firms . . .
> (4) conduct investigations and disciplinary proceedings concerning, and impose appropriate sanctions where justified upon, registered public accounting firms and associated persons of such firms . . . (sec. 101)

Along similar lines, the *Statutory Audit Directive* (EU, 2006) requires EU Member States to appoint "one or more competent authorities . . . [to be] in charge of the regulation and/or oversight of statutory auditors and audit firms"[29] (art. 2). The responsibilities of a competent authority include:

- approving and registering statutory auditors and audit firms;
- ensuring approved statutory auditors and audit firms:
    - meet the standards of education, training and continuing education required by the *Statutory Audit Directive*;[30]
    - are subject to principles of professional ethics (including their public interest function, integrity, objectivity, professional competence and due care) and are independent of their audit clients;
    - conduct statutory audits in compliance with international standards on auditing adopted by the European Commission;
    - are subject to a system of quality assurance which meets specified minimum requirements and to a system of public oversight;
- ensuring there are effective systems of investigations and penalties to detect, correct and prevent inadequate performance of statutory audits.

---

[29] A statutory auditor is a natural person, and an audit firm is an entity, approved in accordance with the *Statutory Audit Directive* by the competent authority of a Member State to carry out audits that are required by statute (i.e., laws enacted by Parliament) (art. 2).

[30] We explain these standards in Chapter 3 (section 3.3.2) in relation to the concept of 'competence'.

In the UK, the FRC fulfils the function of a 'competent authority'. In 2004, the UK Government extended the FRC's responsibilities to create: "a unified regulator with a wide range of functions . . . [whose objective is] to promote confidence in corporate reporting and governance" (FRC, 2006b, pp. 1, 3). Like the PCAOB in the USA, the FRC is "an independent regulator . . . [with] . . . statutory powers derived from Parliament". Its functions include:

- the oversight and regulation of auditing and external financial reporting;
- setting, monitoring and enforcing accounting and auditing standards;
- establishing ethical standards in relation to the independence, objectivity and integrity of external auditors;
- operating an independent investigation and discipline scheme for matters which raise, or appear to raise, important issues affecting the public interest;
- overseeing the regulatory activities of the accountancy profession (FRC, 2006b, pp. 2, 11, 14).

(ii)   *Restrictions on auditors providing non-audit services to audit clients*

Many commentators attribute much, if not most, of Arthur Andersen's apparent failure to conduct proper audits of Enron's financial statements to the absence of the required degree of independence and, more particularly, to the extent of its provision of non-audit services to its audit client.[31] Reflecting this view, SOX (sec. 201) prohibits auditors from providing a wide range of non-audit services to their audit clients.[32] Services that are not explicitly prohibited may be provided but they must be pre-approved by the company's audit committee and disclosed in the company's annual report (sec. 202).

Unlike SOX, the *Statutory Audit Directive* does not prohibit auditors in EU Member States from providing particular non-audit services to their audit clients but they are prohibited from involvement in their audit clients' decision-making. They are also prohibited from carrying out a statutory audit for a client if there is any financial, business, employment or other relationship (including the provision of non-audit services) with the client from which an objective, reasonable and informed third party would conclude that the auditor's independence is compromised (art. 22). Additionally, the Directive requires the

---

[31] In 2000, Enron paid Arthur Andersen $25 million for the audit of its financial statements and a further $27 million for non-audit services (Hirsch, 2002). Not only was the fee for non-audit work exceptionally high, but so too was the audit fee. As Hirsch (2002, p. 1) reported:

   Andersen's [exceptionally high audit] fee was a red flag to some experts and critics who say it could have clouded the [firm's] judgment as it examined Enron's tangled financial structure. . . . Indeed, Andersen executives debated internally whether the audit and other fees would be perceived as a breach of the firm's independence.

[32] Auditors' provision of non-audit services to audit clients – and the SOX prohibitions – are discussed in detail in Chapter 4, section 4.3.3.

audit committee of all public interest entities (which includes all companies whose tradable securities are listed on a stock exchange in any EU Member State) to review and monitor the independence of the entity's auditor and, in particular, the provision of non-audit services provided to the entity by its auditor (art. 41).

In the UK, the *Statutory Audit Directive's* provisions are reflected in Ethical Standard (ES) 1: *Integrity, Objectivity and Independence* [Auditing Practices Board (APB), 2011] and *The UK Corporate Governance Code* (Governance Code: FRC, 2012). ES1 specifies that auditors are to avoid:

> . . . situations and relationships which make it probable that a reasonable and informed third party would conclude that objectivity either is impaired or could be impaired. . . . For example, if a third party were aware that the auditor had certain financial, employment, business or personal relationships with the audited entity, that individual might reasonably conclude that the auditor could be subject to undue influence from the directors or would not be impartial or unbiased. (paras 13, 14)

The *Governance Code* requires the audit committee of any company listed on the London Stock Exchange which engages its auditor to provide non-audit services, to develop and implement policy regarding the provision of such services by the auditor. The Committee is also required to report, and make recommendations, to the board of directors if it considers that changes in respect of the company's auditor providing non-audit services are needed (prov. C.3.2). Additionally, if a listed company obtains non-audit services from its auditor, it must include in its annual report an explanation of how the auditor's objectivity and independence have been safeguarded (prov. C.3.8).

Similar to SOX, the *Statutory Audit Directive* requires companies listed on a stock exchange in the EU to disclose in the notes to their audited financial statements the total fees paid to their auditor for each of the following: (i) the statutory audit, (ii) other assurance services, (iii) tax advisory services, and (iv) other non-audit services (art. 49).[33] Such disclosure enables users of a company's financial statements to judge for themselves whether, and if so the extent to which, the auditor's independence may have been compromised through the provision of non-audit services.

(iii) *Reporting on the effectiveness of audit clients' systems of internal control*

The issue of auditors reporting on the effectiveness of auditees' systems of internal control was first raised in the UK by the Cadbury Committee (CFACG,

---

[33] In the UK, more detailed disclosures are required by *The Companies (Disclosure of Auditor Remuneration and Liability Limitation Agreements) Regulations 2008* [Statutory Instrument (SI), 2008] as amended by SI 2011. These are explained in Chapter 4, section 4.3.1.

1992) and was examined in some detail by the Working Party on Internal Control (1999; Turnbull Committee). Since then, it has been a hotly debated issue in auditing circles. Enactment of SOX largely resolved the issue in the USA as it requires the annual report of all public companies registered or listed in the USA (and significant subsidiaries of such companies) to contain a report that sets out management's responsibility for, and its assessment of, the effectiveness of the company's internal control structure and procedures for financial reporting (sec. 404). It also requires the auditors of these companies to "attest to, and report on, the assessment made by the management" (sec. 404).

In the UK, the requirements have not gone as far as those in the USA, but significant steps in that direction have been taken. The United Kingdom Listing Authority (UKLA)[34] requires companies listed on the London Stock Exchange to include a corporate governance statement in their annual report.[35] The *Governance Code* (FRC, 2012; prov. C.2.1) requires the board of directors of these companies to undertake, at least annually, a review of the effectiveness of their company's financial, operational and compliance internal controls and to report to the shareholders (in the corporate governance statement) that they have done so. The UKLA's Listing Rules additionally require listed companies to include in their corporate governance statement a description of the main features of their internal control and risk management systems insofar as they relate to the financial reporting process. Auditors are not specifically required to report on the directors' statements relating to their company's internal control and risks management systems. However, they are required to state in their audit reports whether, in their opinion, the information given in the company's corporate governance statement is consistent with the financial statements (CA 2006, ss. 465, 497A). The UKLA's Listing Rules also require auditors to review the directors' statement on the board's review of the effectiveness of the company's internal controls in order to verify that the company has complied with the *Governance Code's* provision C.2.1 (see above).[36] However, notwithstanding this requirement, as auditors in the UK (other than those who are subject to the SOX provisions) explain in their audit reports, they:

---

[34] Regulatory responsibility for companies listed on the London Stock Exchange passed from the London Stock Exchange to the Financial Services Authority (FSA) in 2001. From 2001 until 2013, one of the functions of the FSA was to act as the UKLA. In 2013, when the FSA was disbanded, responsibility for the UKLA passed to the Financial Conduct Authority (FCA). We discuss auditors' responsibilities in relation to the UKLA's Listing Rules in Chapter 5, section 5.5.5.

[35] By virtue of EU Directive 2006/46 (para 10), the same rule applies to all companies which are listed on a stock exchange in any EU Member State and have their registered office within the EU. The corporate governance statement may be included in the company's annual report as a separate section in the directors' report or as a separate statement.

[36] Or disclosed that it has not so complied and explained the reasons for the non-compliance.

are not required to consider whether the board's statements on internal control cover all risks and controls, or form an opinion on the effectiveness of the company's corporate governance procedures or its risk and control procedures. (APB, 2006, para 37)

2.7.3 Where are we now?

As noted earlier, by 2002 the effectiveness and efficiency arguments for adopting the business risk approach to auditing were already being challenged. With the subsequent curtailment of auditors' provision of non-audit services to their audit clients, the 'added value' motivation was also undermined. This, combined with the new regulatory regime and the promulgation of more prescriptive ISAs, has resulted in auditors moving back towards the audit risk approach to auditing that typified the 1980s. Nevertheless, the business risk approach's emphasis on auditors gaining an in-depth understanding of their audit clients (their business, industry, key personnel, etc.) and on identifying and assessing relevant risks has remained – and, indeed, has been enshrined in ISA 315: *Identifying and Assessing the Risks of Material Misstatement through Understanding the Entity and Its Environment* (IAASB, 2012).

Given the extent and nature of the legal and regulatory changes to the audit environment since 2002, it might be expected that further changes in the near future are unlikely. Such might have been the case were it not for the 2008 global financial crisis. The collapse of Enron and WorldCom – together with other well-publicised corporate debacles in the USA, UK, Europe and elsewhere – resulted in a plethora of reviews of, and reports on, the role and responsibilities of external auditors and their independence and competence, followed by the introduction of far-reaching and stringent regulation. Similarly, the 2008 global financial crisis has resulted in a flurry of reviews, reports and proposed audit regulations. We examine these developments in Chapter 18 and consider the regulatory changes to external auditing that seem likely to result.

2.8 SUMMARY

In this chapter we have reviewed the development of auditing and highlighted the close link between changes in the socio-economic environment and changes in audit objectives and techniques. We have noted that auditing continually evolves as it responds to, and utilises opportunities provided by, changes in its environment.

We have also highlighted the relationship between auditing and the accountability expected of company managements. We have observed that current legislation, which governs the preparation and audit of companies' financial statements and other reports, may not be attuned to the level of accountability now expected of corporate managers. However, particularly since 2002, new reporting and auditing requirements have been introduced and it seems likely that in the future large national and multinational companies, at least, will be required to produce, and external auditors will be required to audit, more comprehensive accountability (i.e., annual) reports.

We have explained the essence of, and difference between, the audit risk and business risk approaches to auditing. It seemed that the business risk approach might provide auditors with a cost-effective means of fulfilling a wider set of responsibilities. However, critics noted – and well-publicised audit failures seem to confirm – that it carried the risk that its adoption may result in compromising the quality of financial statement audits, which remain the essence of auditors' role in society.

Following the well-publicised corporate and audit failures around the turn of the twenty-first century, auditing has become highly regulated and auditors have moved back towards the audit risk approach to auditing. Nevertheless, a fundamental attribute of the business risk approach has been retained – that of gaining a thorough understanding of the auditee and its internal control and risk management systems. Given the extensive regulatory changes introduced since 2002, it might be thought that further significant changes in the auditing arena in the near future are unlikely. However, as we explain in Chapter 18, with proposals for further change already in the pipeline, it seems probable that the 2008 global financial crisis will be the catalyst for a further tightening of auditing regulation.

SELF-REVIEW QUESTIONS

2.1   Briefly describe key features of the socio-economic environment in each of the following periods:
- (i)   pre-1844
- (ii) 1844–1920s
- (iii) 1920s–1960s
- (iv) 1960s–1990s
- (v) 1990s–present

2.2   Outline the major audit objectives in each of the following periods:
- (i)   pre–1844
- (ii) 1844–1920s
- (iii) 1920s–1960s
- (iv) 1960s–1990s
- (v) 1990s–present

2.3   Explain briefly how auditing techniques have been affected by:
       (i) growth in the size of companies
       (ii) changes in technology.

2.4   Explain briefly the significance of the Joint Stock Companies Act 1844
       to the development of auditing.

2.5   The Companies Act 1900 has been referred to as "a prominent milestone
       in the history of company auditing". List reasons which help to explain
       why this Act has been given this title.

2.6   Explain briefly the importance of the following cases to the development
       of auditors' responsibilities:
       (i)   Re *London and General Bank (No. 2)* [1895];
       (ii) Re *Kingston Cotton Mill Co. Ltd (No. 2)* [1896].

2.7   "Changes in auditing reflect, and represent a response to, changes in the
       socio-economic environment." Using an example to illustrate your
       answer, explain briefly the link between changes in auditing and changes
       in the socio-economic environment.

2.8   Outline key differences between the audit risk and business risk
       approaches to auditing.

2.9   Explain briefly why auditing firms have tended to return to the audit risk
       approach since 2002.

2.10   Outline the key legislative and regulatory changes that have affected
       auditing since 2002.

REFERENCES

Auditing Practices Board (APB). (2006). *The Combined Code on Corporate Governance: Requirements of Auditors under the Listing Rules of the Financial Services Authority and the Irish Stock Exchange. Bulletin 2006/5*. London: Financial Reporting Council.

Auditing Practices Board (APB). (2011). APB Ethical Standard (ES) 1: *Integrity, Objectivity and Independence*. London: Financial Reporting Council.

Bell, T.B., Peecher, M.E., & Solomon, I. (2005). *The 21st Public Company Audit: Conceptual Elements of KPMG's Global Audit Methodology*. KPMG International.

Brown, R. (1905). *History of Accounting and Accountants*. London: Jack.

Chandler, R.A., Edwards, J.R., & Anderson, M. (1993). Changing perceptions of the role of the company auditor, 1840–1940. *Accounting and Business Research*, *23*(92), 443–459.

Committee on Corporate Governance. (1998). *The Combined Code*. London: The London Stock Exchange.

Committee on the Financial Aspects of Corporate Governance (CFACG; Cadbury Committee). (1992). *Report of the Committee on the Financial Aspects of Corporate Governance*. London: Gee.

Davis, K. (1976). Social responsibility is inevitable. *California Management Review*, *XIX*(Fall), 14–20.

Defliese, P.L., Jaenicke, H.R., Sullivan, J.D., & Gnospelius, R.A. (1985). *Montgomery's Auditing*, 10th ed. (College version). United States of America: Coopers & Lybrand.

Demers, L., & Wayland, D. (1982). Corporate social responsibility: Is no news good news? *CA Magazine*, *115* (January), 42–46; *115* (February), 56–60.

European Union (EU). (2006). *Directive 2006/43/EC of the European Parliament and of the Council on the Statutory Audits of Annual Accounts and Consolidated Accounts (Statutory Audit Directive)*. Brussels: European Parliament and Council.

Financial Reporting Council (FRC). (2003, 2006a, 2008). *The Combined Code on Corporate Governance*. London: FRC.

Financial Reporting Council (FRC). (2006b). *Regulatory Strategy (Version 2.1)*. London: FRC.

Financial Reporting Council (FRC). (2010, 2012). *The UK Corporate Governance Code*. London: FRC.

Financial Reporting Council (FRC). (2013). *Scope and Authority of Audit and Assurance Pronouncements*. London: FRC.

Johnston, T.R., Edgar, G.C., & Hays, P.L. (1982). *The Law and Practice of Company Accounting*, 6th ed. Wellington: Butterworths.

Hermes. (2002). *Auditor Independence*, www.hermes.co.uk/pdf/corporate_governance/ commentary/comment_on_auditorindependence, accessed 28 October 2011.

Hirsch, J. (2002, 23 January). Enron audit fee raises some brows. *Los Angeles Times*. Los Angeles.

International Auditing and Assurance Board (IAASB). (2011a). *International Auditing and Assurance Standards Board*, www.ifac.org/auditing-assurance/clarity-center, accessed 9 May 2013.

International Auditing and Assurance Board (IAASB). (2011b). *IAASB Clarity Center: Clarity Project Overview*, www.ifac.org/clarity-center/index, accessed 25 November 2011.

International Auditing and Assurance Board (IAASB). (2011c). *The Clarified Standards*, www.ifac.org/auditing-assurance/clarity-center/clarified-standards, accessed 9 May 2013.

International Auditing and Assurance Board (IAASB). (2012). International Auditing Standard (ISA) 315: *Identifying and Assessing the Risks of Material Misstatement through Understanding the Entity and Its Environment*. New York: International Federation of Accountants.

Lee, T.A. (1970). A brief history of company audits: 1840–1940. *Accountant's Magazine, 74*(782), 363–368.

Lemon, W.M., Tatum, K.W., & Turley, W.S. (2000). *Developments in the Audit Methodologies of Large Accounting Firms*. London: Auditing Practices Board.

Levitt, A. (1998, 28 September). *The Numbers Game*. Remarks at the NYU Center for Law and Business, New York.

Levitt, A. (1999, 7 October). Remarks to the Panel on Audit Effectiveness of the Public Oversight Board. Public Oversight Hearings, New York.

Morris, J. (1977). *Domesday Book 20 Bedfordshire*. Chichester: Philimore & Co. Ltd.

Porter, B.A. (1989). *The Development of Corporate Accountability and the Role of the External Auditor*. Palmerston North: Massey University, Accountancy Department, Discussion Paper Series, No. 92.

Securities & Exchange Commission (SEC). (2001, 19 June). *Arthur Andersen LLP agrees to Settlement Resulting in First Anti-Fraud Injunction in More than 20 Years*. SEC Press Release 2001–62.

Spicer, E.E., & Pegler, E.C. (1911). *Practical Auditing*. London: U.F.L.

Spicer, E.E., & Pegler, E.C. (1936). *Practical Auditing*, 7th ed., edited by Bigg, W.W. London: U.F.L.

Statutory Instrument (SI) (2008) No. 489: *The Companies (Disclosure of Auditor Remuneration and Liability Limitation Agreements) Regulations 2008*.

Statutory Instrument (SI) (2011) No. 2198: *The Companies (Disclosure of Auditor Remuneration and Liability Limitation Agreements) Regulations 2011*.

The Accountant's Magazine. (1901, January). *Editorial*.

Turley, J.S. (2004, June). Get ready for the EU's 8th Directive. *Directorship*, 18–21.

Turner, L.E. (1999, 7 October). Speech to the Panel on Audit Effectiveness. New York.

Wikipedia. (2011a). *Polly Peck*, en.wikipedia.org/wiki/Polly_Peck, accessed 9 May 2013.

Wikipedia. (2011b). *Bank of Credit and Commercial International*, en.wikipedia.org/wiki/Bank_of_Credit_and_Commerce_International, accessed 8 May 2013.

Woolf, E. (2006). Sarbox in Europe. *Accountancy, 138*(1357), 24.

Working Party on Internal Control (Turnbull Committee). (1999). *Internal Control: Guidance for Directors on the Combined Code*. London: ICAEW.

ADDITIONAL READING

Chandler, R.A. (1997). Taking responsibility: The early demand for institutional action to define an auditor's duties. *International Journal of Auditing, 1*(3), 165–174.

Chandler, R.A., & Edwards, J.R. (1996). Recurring issues in auditing: Back to the future. *Accounting, Auditing & Accountability Journal, 9*(2), 4–29.

Curtis, E., & Turley, S. (2007). The business risk audit: A longitudinal case study of an audit engagement. *Accounting, Organizations and Society*, *32*(4–5), 439–461.

Edwards, R.J., Anderson, M., & Matthews, D. (1997). Accountability in a free-market economy: The British company audit, 1886. *Abacus*, *33*(1), 1–25.

Flesher, D.L., Previts, G.J., & Samson, W.D. (2005). Auditing in the United States: A historical perspective. *Abacus*, *41*(1), 21–39.

Flint, D. (1971). The role of the auditor in modern society: An exploratory essay. *Accounting and Business Research*, *1*(4), 287–293.

Knechel, W.R. (2007). The business risk audit: Origins, obstacles and opportunities. *Accounting, Organizations and Society*, *32*(3–4), 383–408.

Mennicken, A. (2010). From inspection to auditing: Audit and markets as linked ecologies. *Accounting, Organizations and Society*, *35*(3), 334–359.

Power, M. (1994). *The Audit Explosion*. London: Demos.

Robson, K., Humphrey, C., Khalifa, R., & Jones, J. (2007). Transforming audit technologies: Business risk audit methodologies and the audit field. *Accounting, Organizations and Society*, *32*(4–5), 409–438.

3 A Framework of Auditing Concepts

LEARNING OBJECTIVES

After studying the material in this chapter you should be able to:
- explain the meaning of, and relationship between, the social purpose of auditing, postulates (or basic assumptions) of auditing, and key concepts of auditing;
- state seven postulates of auditing;
- explain and discuss the importance of the concepts relating to:
  - the credibility of auditors' work (i.e., Independence, Competence and Ethical Conduct),
  - the audit process (i.e., Evidence, Materiality, Audit Risk, Judgment and Scepticism),
  - auditors' communication (i.e., Reporting),
  - the standard of auditors' work (i.e., Due Care and Quality Control).

3.1 INTRODUCTION

During auditing's long history and, more particularly, during the last 170 or so years which witnessed its very rapid development,[1] auditing has developed in a very practical way. Perhaps surprisingly, given the effort devoted to developing a coherent theory (or conceptual framework) of *accounting* over the past four decades, relatively little attention has been given to developing a theory of *auditing*. Three notable exceptions are the classical works of Mautz and Sharaf (1961), the Committee on Basic Auditing Concepts (1973), and Flint (1988).

Why is a theory of auditing important? It is because a theory (which embodies the principles of philosophy) helps us to:
- identify (and be cognisant of) basic assumptions which underpin auditing practice;
- organise auditing knowledge so that it is useful and internally consistent; and
- understand the social role and context of the audit function.

---

[1] The historical development of auditing is the topic of Chapter 2.

As Mautz and Sharaf (1961) explain:

1. Philosophy gets back to first principles, to the rationale behind the actions and thoughts which tend to be taken for granted.
2. Philosophy is concerned with the systematic organisation of knowledge in such a way that it becomes at once more useful and less likely to be self-contradictory.
3. Philosophy provides a basis whereby social relationships may be molded and understood. (p. 8)

Flint (1988) shed more light on the issue when he stated:

The purpose of theory in relation to auditing is to provide a coherent set of propositions about the activity which explains its social purpose and objectives, which furnishes a rational foundation and justification for its practices and procedures, relating them to the purposes and objectives, and which explains the place of the activity in the context of the institutions of society and the social, economic and political environment. (p. 9)

From this a three-tier hierarchy of notions may be distilled. At the top is a statement of the social purpose and objectives of auditing. This is followed by the basic assumptions (or postulates) which underpin the social purpose of the audit function on the one hand and auditing practice on the other. At the bottom we have a coherent set of concepts which underlie auditing practice. This 'hierarchy of notions' is presented in outline form in Figure 3.1 and discussed below.

Figure 3.1: Hierarchy of notions underpinning a theory of auditing

Social purpose of auditing						
Auditors are agents of social control in the process of corporate accountability						

Postulates of auditing						
(Fundamental assumptions which underpin the social purpose of auditing and audit practice)						
An accountability relationship exists such that an audit of information is needed	The subject matter is remote, complex, and significant	Auditors are independent and have investigatory and reporting freedom	The subject matter is capable of verification	Standards of accountability can be set, measured and compared with known criteria	The credibility given to financial and other information can be communicated	Auditing provides an economic or social benefit

Key concepts of auditing										
Credibility of work performed			Audit process					Commun -ication	Standard of performance	
Independence, Objectivity	Competence	Ethical conduct, Integrity	Evidence	Materiality	Audit risk	Judgment	Scepticism	Reporting	Due care	Quality control

Source: Adapted from Flint (1988)

In this chapter we do not attempt to provide a comprehensive theory of auditing. For this, reference may be made to the three 'classics' noted above. Rather, our purpose is to provide a basic framework for, and to discuss, the key concepts which underpin auditing practice. First, we outline the social purpose and postulates of auditing, and identify a framework for the auditing concepts. We then discuss the meaning and relevance to auditing of the 11 concepts shown in Figure 3.1. Most of the concepts have particular significance for material presented in subsequent chapters and these are cross-referenced to, and further developed in, the relevant later chapter.

3.2 SOCIAL PURPOSE, POSTULATES AND FRAMEWORK FOR CONCEPTS OF AUDITING

3.2.1 Social purpose of the audit function

The primary objective of company audits is to provide credibility to the accountability reports (principally the financial statements) prepared by the company's directors for use by parties external to the entity. As we explain in Chapter 1, in performing this function, auditors are one of the checks and balances imposed by society (through legislation) on company directors as a counter to the power and influence they wield in society. Thus, auditors' social purpose is to act as agents of social control in the process of corporate accountability.

3.2.2 Postulates of auditing

A postulate is a basic (or fundamental) assumption. According to Mautz and Sharaf (1961, p. 37), they have the following five general attributes.
Postulates are:
1. Essential to the development of any intellectual discipline.
2. Assumptions that do not lend themselves to direct verification.
3. A basis for inference.
4. A foundation for erection of any theoretical structure.
5. Susceptible to challenge in the light of later advancement of knowledge.

In the context of auditing, postulates may be defined as fundamental principles, assumed to be truths, which help to explain the social purpose of auditing and auditing practice. Flint (1988, pp. 21–23) identifies seven basic postulates. These are as follows:
1. The primary condition for an audit is that there is either:
   (a) a relationship of accountability between two or more parties in the sense that there is a duty of acceptable conduct or performance owed by one party to the other party or parties;
   (b) a need by some party to establish the reliability and credibility of information for which they are responsible which is expected to be used and relied

       on by a specified group or groups . . . producing constructively a relation-
       ship of accountability . . .

2. The subject matter of accountability is too remote, too complex and/or of too great a significance for the discharge of the duty to be demonstrated without the process of audit.
3. Essential distinguishing characteristics of audit are the independence of its status and its freedom from investigatory and reporting constraints.
4. The subject matter of audit . . . is susceptible to verification by evidence.
5. Standards of accountability, for example of conduct, performance, achievement and quality of information, can be set for those who are accountable; actual conduct, performance, achievement, quality and so on can be measured and compared with those standards by reference to known criteria; and the process of measurement and comparison requires special skill and the exercise of judgement.
6. The meaning, significance and intention of financial and other statements and data which are audited are sufficiently clear that the credibility which is given thereto as a result of audit can be clearly expressed and communicated.
7. An audit produces an economic or social benefit.

Reviewing these postulates, it may be seen that postulates 1, 2, 5 and 7 correspond with material presented in Chapter 1. The fundamental truth of the other postulates underpins, and should become evident as we discuss, the concepts of independence, evidence and reporting later in this chapter.

3.2.3 Framework for key concepts of auditing

Concepts of auditing are general notions (or sets of ideas) that underlie audit practice. As indicated in Figure 3.1, they can usefully be categorised into four groups, namely, those relating to:
- the credibility of auditors' work [auditors' independence and objectivity, competence and ethical conduct (including integrity)];
- the audit process (evidence, materiality, audit risk, judgment and scepticism);
- the communication of audit conclusions (reporting);
- the standard of auditors' work (due care and quality control).

We discuss each of these concepts below.

3.3 CONCEPTS RELATING TO THE CREDIBILITY OF AUDITORS' WORK

3.3.1 Concept of independence and objectivity

3.3.1a Independence: The cornerstone of auditing

As may be seen from Figure 3.1, independence has a unique status within auditing. It figures among the postulates: it is a fundamental assumption that the audit function is independent. It is also a key concept – a characteristic that is essential for ensuring the credibility of auditors' work. Indeed, independence has been referred to as "the cornerstone [the very heart] of auditing" (Stewart, 1977; Levitt, 2000; Haber, 2005): without independence an audit is virtually worthless.

Let us examine this more closely. Auditors are intermediaries between the management[2] of an entity and external parties interested in the entity. They have a duty to form and express an opinion on, *inter alia*, whether the entity's financial statements (prepared by management for use by shareholders and others outside the entity) provide a true and fair view of the entity's financial position and performance. If users of the financial statements are to believe and rely on the auditor's opinion, it is essential that the auditor is, and is perceived to be, independent of the entity, its management and all other influences. This is reflected in the fundamental principle of external auditing – *Objectivity and independence*[3], which states:

> Auditors are objective and provide impartial opinions unaffected by bias, prejudice, compromise and conflicts of interest. Auditors are also independent, this requires them to be free from situations and relationships which would make it probable that a reasonable and informed third party would conclude that the auditors' objectivity either is impaired or could be impaired. [Financial Reporting Council (FRC), 2013, Appendix 2]

If auditors are considered not to be independent of the client entity and its management, their opinion will carry little credibility and users of the financial statements will gain little, if any, assurance from the auditor's report about the truth and fairness (or otherwise) of the financial statements. As a consequence, the audit will have little purpose or value.

The importance of auditors' independence – to both investors and the wider economy – was conveyed succinctly by Turner (2001), former Chief Accountant of the Securities and Exchange Commission (SEC) in the United States of America (USA), when he stated:

> The enduring confidence of the investing public in the integrity of our capital markets is vital. . . . [The capital they invest provides] the fuel for our economic engine, funding for the growth of new businesses, . . . and job opportunities for tens of millions of workers. But . . . the willingness of investors to continue to invest their money in the markets cannot be taken for granted. . . . Public trust begins, and ends, with the integrity of the numbers the public uses to form the basis for making their investment decisions. . . . [I]t is the report of the independent auditor that provides investors with the critical assurance that the numbers in the financial statements have been subjected to an impartial, unbiased, and rigorous examination by a skilled professional. But in order for that report to

---

[2] Readers are reminded that in this book we use the term 'management' to mean a company's executive directors, non-executive directors and non-director executives (that is, all executives and directors). In the UK, a company's directors are legally responsible for the preparation of its annual financial statements.

[3] The fundamental principles of external auditing constitute *The Auditors' Code* which is reproduced on the inside front cover of this book.

have credibility with investors, to add value to the process and investors, it must be issued by a person or firm that *the investor* perceives is free of all conflicts – conflicts that may or will in part, weight on or impair the auditor's judgments about the accuracy of the numbers. (pp. 1–2; emphasis in original)

3.3.1b   Meaning of independence in the auditing context

Given the importance of independence to the audit function, it is clearly important to examine what the concept means. However, as will be seen below, the auditing profession has been grappling with finding appropriate terms to explain the concept.

It is well accepted that independence, in the sense of being self-reliant and not subordinating one's professional judgment to the opinions of others, is a fundamental hallmark of all professions (including auditing). However, in auditing the term means more than this. As indicated in the fundamental principle cited above, in addition to maintaining an independent attitude of mind, it means avoiding situations which could impair, or might be perceived as likely to impair, the auditor's objectivity or to create personal bias. Until recent years, these two forms of independence were usually referred to as 'independence in fact (or of mind)' and 'independence in appearance'. The International Ethics Standards Board for Accountants (IESBA)[4] continues to define the term with this dual meaning. In its *Code of Ethics for Professional Accountants* (*IESBA Code*; IESBA, 2009, Definitions), it defines independence as follows:

Independence is:
(a) Independence of mind – the state of mind that permits the expression of a conclusion without being affected by influences that compromise professional judgment, thereby allowing an individual to act with integrity, and exercise objectivity and professional skepticism.
(b) Independence in appearance – the avoidance of facts and circumstances that are so significant that a reasonable and informed third party would be likely to conclude, weighing all the specific facts and circumstances, that a firm's, or a member of the audit or assurance team's, integrity, objectivity or professional skepticism has been compromised.

In Ethical Standard (ES) 1: *Integrity, Objectivity and Independence* [Auditing Practices Board (APB), 2011a], the APB distinguishes between the two forms of independence; it adopts the terms 'objectivity' for 'independence of mind' and 'independence' for 'independence in appearance'.[5] It explains:

---

[4] The IESBA is an independent standard-setting body established by, and operating under the auspices of, the International Federation of Accountants (IFAC) (IFAC, 2010).

[5] The *IESBA Code* (which we discuss in section 3.3.3) distinguishes between objectivity and the two forms of independence. It recognises 'objectivity' as a fundamental principle and defines it as: "to not allow bias, conflict of interest or undue influence of others to override professional or business judgments" (IESBA, 2009, para 100.5b).

- Objectivity is a state of mind that excludes bias, prejudice and compromise and that gives fair and impartial consideration to all matters that are relevant to the task in hand, disregarding those that are not. Like integrity, objectivity is a fundamental ethical principle and requires that the auditor's judgment is not affected by conflicts of interest. (para 10)
- Independence is freedom from situations and relationships which make it probable that a reasonable and informed third party would conclude that objectivity either is impaired or could be impaired. Independence is related to and underpins objectivity. However, whereas objectivity is a personal behavioural characteristic concerning the auditor's state of mind, independence relates to the circumstances surrounding the audit, including the financial, employment, business and personal relationships between the auditor and the audited entity. (para 13)

If interested parties are to rely on the auditor's opinion, it is clearly essential that the auditor is both independent in mind (objective) and independent in appearance (independent) when conducting the audit and expressing an opinion in the audit report. Indeed, to stipulate that auditors must be independent in both mind and appearance (objective and independent) may seem to be an obvious requirement. However, in practice, such independence may be difficult to achieve and easy to compromise. This issue is explored in detail in Chapter 4.

3.3.2 Concept of competence

If auditors' opinions are to have credibility and be relied upon by users of financial statements, auditors must be regarded as competent. According to Flint (1988), "Audit competence requires both knowledge and skill, which are the products of education, training and experience" (p. 48). The fundamental principle of external auditing – *Competence* – conveys similar ideas but goes a little further in explaining the requirements of auditors' competence. It states:

> Auditors act with professional skill, derived from their qualification, training and practical experience. This demands an understanding of financial reporting and business issues, together with expertise in accumulating and assessing the evidence necessary to form an opinion. (FRC, 2013, Appendix 2)

From Flint's assertion and the fundamental principle cited above it may be discerned that 'competence' involves both *acquiring* and *applying* "knowledge and skill" (Flint) or "professional skills" (fundamental principle). International Education Standard (IES) 8: *Competence Requirements for Audit Professionals*[6]

---

[6] IES 8 defines an audit professional as:
> a professional accountant who has responsibility, or has been delegated responsibility, for significant judgments in an audit of historical financial information. (para 9)

It therefore includes the audit engagement partner (the individual responsible for the audit) and senior members of the audit team.

[International Accounting Education Standards Board (IAESB),[7] 2006] makes this two-fold notion explicit. It distinguishes between 'capabilities' and 'competence', defining them as follows:

- **Capabilities:** The professional knowledge; professional skills; and professional values, ethics, and attitudes required to demonstrate competence.
- **Competence:** Being able to perform a work role to a defined standard, with reference to real working environments. (para 8)

From these definitions it is evident that acquiring capabilities is a necessary prerequisite of, and integral to, auditors performing their work competently.

IES 8 expands on its definition of capabilities by outlining the components of the 'knowledge', 'skills', and 'values, ethics and attitudes' required by audit professionals.

- With respect to knowledge, it notes (paras 32–40) that auditors need to be informed about matters such as:
  - (i)   best practices employed in the audits of historical financial information;
  - (ii)   financial accounting and reporting processes and practices;
  - (iii) relevant current issues and developments in audit practices and financial accounting and reporting;
  - (iv) International Standards on Auditing (ISAs), the International Standard on Quality Control (ISQC) 1, International Auditing Practice Statements (IAPS), and International Financial Reporting Standards (IFRS);
  - (v)   other applicable auditing and accounting standards or laws;
  - (vi) information technology (IT) systems for financial accounting and reporting, and related current issues and developments;
  - (vii) IT frameworks for evaluating controls and assessing risks in accounting and reporting systems which are relevant to the audit of historical financial information.
- As regards professional skills, IES 8 (para 42) specifies that, in the context of the audit environment, audit professionals need to be able, *inter alia*, to:
  - (i)   identify and solve problems;
  - (ii)   work effectively in teams;
  - (iv) gather and evaluate evidence;
  - (v)   apply relevant auditing standards and guidance;
  - (vi) demonstrate a capacity for enquiry, abstract logical thought and critical analysis;
  - (vii) apply professional scepticism and professional judgment;
  - (viii) withstand and resolve conflict.

---

[7] Like the IESBA, the IAESB is an independent standard-setting body established by, and operating under the auspices of, IFAC (IFAC, 2010).

- In terms of professional values, ethics and attitudes, IES 8 (paras 47–53) requires auditors to be able to:
    (i)   act ethically in the best interests of both society and the profession;
    (ii) apply the fundamental principles of the *IESBA Code* (we explain these principles in section 3.3.3 below);
    (iii) act independently of their clients;
    (iv) understand the consequences of unethical behaviour and how to resolve ethical dilemmas;
    (v)   be aware of potential new ethical dimensions and conflicts in their work.
  In relation to this component of auditors' capabilities (that is, professional values, ethics and attitudes), IES 8 notes:

> The fundamental ethical principles that apply to all professional accountants [those contained in the *IESBA Code*] have an added dimension in the audit domain, because of the heavy public reliance on and public interest in this aspect of the profession worldwide. (para 50)

It can be seen that the capabilities audit professionals are required to possess in order to be considered competent are wide-ranging and demanding. But the question arises: how do they acquire these capabilities? Broadly, they are acquired through a combination of general and technical accounting education, on-the-job training and work experience. Flint (1988), observing that "auditing is intellectually demanding, requiring a trained mind and the capacity for exercise of judgement" (p. 48), gives particular emphasis to the contribution of general education to auditors' competence. He notes:

> A broad general education cultivating the habit of systematic thinking and mental discipline, combined with a basic understanding of the principal fields of knowledge and ability for expression and communication orally and in writing, are an essential foundation. . . . [A]uditing requires much more than a knowledge of its own theory or philosophy and the principles of its peculiar investigative process: it requires an understanding of the nature, structure, institutions and law of the society in which it is applied. (pp. 48–49)

Further guidance on how capabilities and competence are acquired is provided by ISQC 1: *Quality Control for Firms that Perform Audits and Reviews of Financial Statements, and Other Assurance and Related Services Engagements* [International Auditing and Assurance Standards Board (IAASB),[8] 2009a]. It explains that they are developed through a variety of means including professional education, continuing professional development and training, work

---

[8] Like the IESBA and the IAESB, the IAASB is an independent standard-setting body established by, and operating under the auspices of, IFAC (IFAC, 2010).

experience, and coaching by more experienced members of the engagement team (para A25).

As we observed earlier, it is not merely a case of *acquiring* the requisite capabilities; auditors must also be able to *apply* their knowledge and skills in the context of each audit engagement. Thus, they also require adequate practical experience. In this regard IES 8 specifies:

> Professional accountants should complete a period of relevant practical experience before taking on the role of an audit professional. This period should be long enough and intensive enough to permit them to demonstrate that they have acquired the necessary professional knowledge; professional skills; and professional values, ethics, and attitudes.[9] . . . The required audit experience should be obtained with an organisation that can provide suitable audit experience under the guidance of an [audit] engagement partner. (paras 54, 59)

Although auditors acquire their capabilities and competence in a variety of ways, the process is not haphazard. As Flint (1988, p. 51) points out, if auditors are to gain the public's confidence in the credibility of their work, they must be able to demonstrate that they have obtained a recognised reputable qualification – one that requires them to successfully complete a formal programme of education, training and experience. Flint further notes:

> Audit is a matter of such social importance that the state has a responsibility to be satisfied in the public interest that appropriate standards of knowledge, training and experience are prescribed and that an adequate standard of proficiency is achieved. (p. 51)

In the United Kingdom (UK) (as in most other countries) the State achieves this through legislation which requires the auditors of companies to be members of a Recognised Supervisory Body[10] and specifies, among other things, that they must be "properly supervised and appropriately qualified" [Companies Act (CA) 2006, s. 1209]. In order to be "appropriately qualified", auditors must hold a "recognised professional qualification" (CA 2006, s. 1219). In order to hold such a qualification, an auditor must have, *inter alia*:

- attained university entrance (or the equivalent);
- completed a course of theoretical instruction in a wide range of subjects including accounting, finance, financial reporting, auditing and profes-

---

[9] The period of "relevant practical experience" is to be at least three years, two of which are to be spent in the area of auditing financial statements (IES 8, para 58).

[10] In some countries the relevant legislation requires auditors to be licensed or approved rather than members of a regulatory body. As we explain in Chapter 5, in general, the Companies Act 2006 requires the auditors of UK companies to be members of one of five Recognised Supervisory Bodies (RSBs) – the Institute of Chartered Accountants in England and Wales (ICAEW), of Scotland (ICAS), or in Ireland (ICAI), or the Association of Chartered Certified Accountants (ACCA) or of Authorised Public Accountants (AAPA).

sional skills, risk management and internal control, legal requirements and professional standards relating to the audit of companies' financial statements, and professional ethics. (The required subjects reflect those specified in IES 8, paras 32–40, noted above);

- passed an examination which tests the theoretical knowledge and the ability to apply that knowledge;
- completed a period of at least seven years' experience in a professional capacity in the fields of finance, law and accountancy (CA 2006, Schedule 11).[11]

Acquiring capabilities and competence is not the end of the story for auditors (or indeed for other professional accountants). The *IESBA Code* requires all professional accountants "to maintain professional knowledge and skill at the level required to ensure that a client or employer receives competent professional services based on current developments in practice . . ." (para 100.5c). In order to maintain their professional knowledge and skill at the required level, professional accountants need to engage in continuing professional development.

ISQC 1, which relates to audit firms rather than professional accountants, similarly underlines the importance of maintaining professional competence. It also expands on how this may be achieved. It explains:

> The continuing competence of the [audit] firm's personnel depends to a significant extent on an appropriate level of continuing professional development so that personnel maintain their knowledge and capabilities. Effective policies and procedures emphasize the need for continuing training for all levels of firm personnel, and provide the necessary training resources and assistance to enable personnel to develop and maintain the required capabilities and competence. (para A26)

---

[11] These provisions enact the requirements of the European Union's (EU) *Statutory Audit Directive* (EU, 2006). Under EU law, the provisions of EU Directives are required to be enacted in the national legislation of all EU Member States. In the UK, the provisions of the *Statutory Audit Directive* are enacted in the Companies Act 2006. The Directive states:

> [A] natural person may be approved to carry out a statutory audit only after having attained university entrance or equivalent level, then completed a course of theoretical instruction, undergone practical training and passed an examination of professional competence. (art. 6)

> The examination of professional competence . . . shall guarantee the necessary level of theoretical knowledge of subjects relevant to statutory audit [which are listed in Article 8 and reflect those specified in IES 8] and the ability to apply such knowledge in practice. (art. 7)

> In order to ensure the ability to apply theoretical knowledge in practice . . . a trainee shall complete a minimum of three years' practical training in, *inter alia*, the auditing of annual accounts, consolidated accounts or similar financial statements. (art. 10)

We discuss the qualification and registration of auditors in the UK in detail in Chapter 5, section 5.3.1.

It should be noted that for company auditors in the European Union (EU) continuing professional education is a compulsory requirement. The *Statutory Audit Directive* (EU, 2006) states:

> Member States shall ensure that statutory [company] auditors are required to take part in appropriate programmes of continuing education in order to maintain their theoretical knowledge, professional skills and values at a sufficiently high level, and that failure to respect the continuing education requirements is subject to appropriate penalties. (art. 13)

In the UK, as in most other countries, the professional accounting bodies require their members to undertake continuing professional development as a condition of membership.

The concept of competence is particularly relevant to the topics of 'staffing an audit' and 'controlling the quality of audit work'. These are discussed in Chapters 7 and 16, respectively.

3.3.3 Concept of ethical conduct and integrity

As shown in Figure 3.1, the credibility of auditors' work rests on auditors being regarded as independent, competent and adhering to ethical conduct. But what is meant by 'ethical conduct' – and how does it impact on the credibility of auditors' work?

Flint (1988) provides an answer when he observes:

> Public trust and confidence in auditors are dependent on a continuing belief in their unqualified integrity, objectivity, and . . . acceptance of a duty to the public interest, with a consequential subordination of self-interest. (p. 87)

In order to retain the public's trust and confidence in their work, auditors must adhere to standards of ethical conduct: standards of conduct that embody and demonstrate integrity, objectivity, and concern for the public (rather than self-) interest.

As for all other professions, the conduct expected of members of the auditing profession is set out in a Code of Ethics.[12] IFAC published its first *Code of Ethics for Professional Accountants* in 1996; since then it has been revised a number of times. In the Preface to its *Handbook of the Code of Ethics for Professional Accountants* (IFAC, 2010), IFAC explains:

---

[12] A Code of Ethics may have various titles, for example, a Guide to Ethical Conduct, Code of Professional Conduct, Guide to Professional Ethics, etc. but, in essence, the content is the same. It sets out the conduct expected of members of the profession (or of the professional body) in question.

[its] mission is to serve the public interest [and] continue to strengthen the accountancy profession worldwide . . . by establishing and promoting adherence to high-quality professional standards. . . . In pursuing this mission, the IFAC Board has established the International Ethics Standards Board for Accountants (IESBA) to develop and issue, under its own authority, high quality ethical standards. . . . [The] *Code of Ethics for Professional Accountants* (IESBA Code) establishes ethical requirements for professional accountants. . . . A member body of IFAC or firm shall not apply less stringent standards than those stated in this Code.[13]

Central to the *IESBA Code* are five fundamental principles of professional ethics with which professional accountants are required to comply, namely: integrity, objectivity, professional competence and due care, confidentiality, and professional behaviour. The Code defines these principles as follows (para 100.5):

(a) Integrity – to be straightforward and honest in all professional and business relationships.

(b) Objectivity – to not allow bias, conflict of interest or undue influence of others to override professional or business judgments.

(c) Professional Competence and Due Care – to maintain professional knowledge and skill at the level required to ensure that a client or employer receives competent professional services based on current developments in practice, legislation and techniques and act diligently and in accordance with applicable technical and professional standards.

(d) Confidentiality – to respect the confidentiality of information acquired as a result of professional and business relationships and, therefore, not disclose any such information to third parties without proper and specific authority, unless there is a legal or professional right or duty to disclose, nor use the information for the personal advantage of the professional accountant or third parties.

(e) Professional Behavior – to comply with relevant laws and regulations and avoid any action that discredits the profession.

In relation to the principle of integrity, the Code explains: "Integrity also implies fair dealing and truthfulness" (para 110.1).

The principles of objectivity and professional competence were discussed earlier in sections 3.3.1b and 3.3.2, respectively; the principle of due care

---

[13] In the UK, the Institutes of Chartered Accountants in England and Wales and of Scotland, and the Association of Chartered Certified Accountants (all of which are member bodies of IFAC) has each issued its own Code of Ethics (with varying titles) based on the *IESBA Code*. However, in January 2003, following the Enron, WorldCom and similar debacles, the UK Government, as part of its reform of the regulations governing the accounting profession, determined that the APB should take over responsibility for setting standards for the independence, objectivity and integrity of auditors. To date, the APB has issued five Ethical Standards (ES1 to ES5) in relation to these matters. (ES1 to ES5 are discussed in detail in Chapter 4.) The APB explains that, in developing these standards, it "has sought to ensure that the APB Ethical Standards for Auditors . . . adhere to the principles of the IFAC Code" (APB, 2009, para 12). Ethical issues other than those covered by ES1 to ES5 remain the responsibility of the individual professional bodies (ES1, para 5).

(which, as may be seen from above, the IESBA combines with professional competence) is discussed in section 3.6.1 below; and the principle of confidentiality is discussed in Chapter 6, section 6.7.

Although the *IESBA Code* applies to all professional accountants, the essence of its principles of integrity and confidentiality are embodied in the fundamental principle of external auditing – *Integrity*. This states:

> Auditors act with integrity, fulfilling their responsibilities with honesty, fairness, candour, courage and confidentiality. Confidential information obtained in the course of the audit is disclosed only when required in the public interest, or by operation of law. (FRC, 2013, Appendix 2)

In addition to specifying the five fundamental principles of professional ethics, the *IESBA Code* provides a conceptual framework for applying the principles. It recognises the impossibility of trying to define every situation in which accountants might find themselves which poses a threat to their compliance with one or more of the principles and, similarly, the impossibility of identifying appropriate measures to mitigate all possible threats. Instead of trying to achieve the impossible, the Code provides a conceptual framework "that requires a professional accountant to identify, evaluate and address threats to compliance with the fundamental principles" (para 100.6). It explains the framework as follows:

> When a professional accountant identifies threats to compliance with the fundamental principles and, based on an evaluation of those threats, determines that they are not at an acceptable level, the professional accountant shall determine whether appropriate safeguards are available and can be applied to eliminate the threats or reduce them to an acceptable level. In making that determination, the professional accountant shall exercise professional judgment and take into account whether a reasonable and informed third party, weighing all the specific facts and circumstances . . . would be likely to conclude that the threats would be eliminated or reduced to an acceptable level by the application of the safeguards, such that compliance with the fundamental principles is not compromised. (para 100.7)

We explore this framework in greater detail in Chapter 4 in the context of auditors' independence.

3.4 CONCEPTS RELATING TO THE AUDIT PROCESS

3.4.1 Concept of evidence

3.4.1a Need for sufficient appropriate evidence

As we have previously noted, the primary objective of an audit is to provide credibility to an auditee's financial statements through the expression of the auditor's opinion on the truth and fairness (or otherwise) of the financial statements. Auditors can only express such an opinion if they are able to examine sufficient appropriate evidence to form an opinion. If no evidence exists in relation to the subject matter on which an auditor is to express an opinion, there can be no audit. The fundamental necessity of the existence of evidence for an audit to take place is reflected in postulate 4 cited in section 3.2.2 above: "The subject matter of audit . . . is susceptible to verification by evidence".

The key task of the auditor is to obtain sufficient appropriate audit evidence on which to base an audit opinion. ISA 500: *Audit Evidence* (IAASB, 2009g) defines the terms 'sufficient' and 'appropriate' as follows:

> Sufficiency (of audit evidence) – The measure of the quantity of audit evidence. The quantity of the audit evidence needed is affected by the auditor's assessment of the risks of material misstatement[14] and also by the quality of such audit evidence. (para 5e)
>
> Appropriateness (of audit evidence) – The measure of the quality of audit evidence; that is, its relevance and its reliability in providing support for the conclusions on which the auditor's opinion is based. (para 5b)

From these definitions it is clear that the sufficiency and appropriateness of audit evidence are interrelated. All other things being equal, the more appropriate the audit evidence, the less that is required (and *vice versa*).[15]

But the question arises: What is meant by 'audit evidence' and what are its characteristics?

3.4.1b Definition of audit evidence

ISA 500 defines audit evidence as:

> Information used by the auditor in arriving at the conclusions on which the audit opinion is based. Audit evidence includes both information contained in the accounting records underlying the financial statements and other information. (para 5c)

The second part of this definition seems limited in scope and, as a result, it does not convey the all-embracing nature of audit evidence. A rather more useful definition has been provided by Anderson (1977). To him, audit evidence is:

> any perceived object, action or condition relevant to the formation of a knowledgeable opinion on the financial statements. Perceived objects may include certain tangible assets (such as cash funds, inventories and fixed assets), various documents, accounting records and reports, and written representations. Perceived actions generally consist of certain procedures performed by the client's employees. Perceived conditions may include the observed quality of assets, the apparent competence of employees met, the care with which procedures were

---

[14] "Risks of material misstatement" refers to the likelihood of material errors or omissions being present in the financial statements prior to the audit. The concept of materiality is discussed in section 3.4.2.

[15] The relationship between the sufficiency and appropriateness of audit evidence is discussed in detail in Chapter 7, section 7.4.3.

seen to be performed, or an identified logical relationship with other facts known to the auditor. (p. 251)

Thus, in auditing, 'evidence' means all of the facts, information and impressions auditors acquire which help them to form an opinion about the truth and fairness of the financial statements under review and their compliance (or otherwise) with the applicable financial reporting framework.

3.4.1c Characteristics of audit evidence

Unlike scientific evidence, audit evidence does not consist of hard facts which prove or disprove the accuracy of financial statements. Instead, it comprises pieces of information and impressions which are gradually accumulated during the course of an audit and which, taken together, persuade the auditor about the truth and fairness (or otherwise) of the financial statements under consideration. Thus, audit evidence is generally persuasive rather than conclusive in nature.

Furthermore, not all of the available evidence is examined by an auditor. The purpose of an audit is not to *prove* or *disprove* the accuracy of the financial statements. If it were, auditors would have to collect and evaluate as much evidence as possible. Instead, the objective is to form an *opinion* about the truth and fairness of the financial statements under review. To accomplish this, auditors need only gather sufficient appropriate evidence to enable them to form an opinion about the financial statements. Thus, for example, rather than examining all of – say – the client's purchase invoices, auditors usually test only a sample of the invoices.

Although only part, rather than all, of the available evidence is examined, when evidence derived from different sources is consistent, it has a reinforcing effect; conversely, when evidence is inconsistent, it has an undermining effect. An auditor may, for example, wish to reach a conclusion about a particular financial statement assertion (for example, about the ownership or value of an asset) using evidence from different sources and/or of different types. When such evidence is consistent, the auditor gains cumulative assurance about the assertion in question; the assurance the auditor gains about the assertion is greater than that obtained from the individual pieces of evidence by themselves. However, when evidence from different sources or of different types is inconsistent, further evidence usually needs to be obtained in order to resolve the inconsistency.

The procedures used to gather audit evidence, and the various types and sources of evidence available to auditors, are discussed in detail in Chapter 7, section 7.4.

3.4.2   Concept of materiality

3.4.2a   *Importance and meaning of materiality in the auditing context*

ISA 200: *Overall Objectives of the Independent Auditor and the Conduct of an Audit in Accordance with International Standards on Auditing* (IAASB, 2009b) states:

> The purpose of an audit is to enhance the degree of confidence of intended users in the financial statements. This is achieved by the expression of an opinion by the auditor on whether the financial statements are prepared, in all *material* respects, in accordance with an applicable financial reporting framework.[16] (para 3, emphasis added)

From this statement it is clear that the term 'material' is of critical importance in the auditing context. But, what does the term mean?

ISA 320: *Materiality in Planning and Performing an Audit* (IAASB, 2009f) explains:
- Misstatements, including omissions, are considered to be material if they, individually or in the aggregate, could reasonably be expected to influence the economic decisions of users taken on the basis of the financial statements;
- Judgments about materiality are made in light of surrounding circumstances, and are affected by the size or nature of a misstatement, or a combination of both; and
- Judgments about matters that are material to users of the financial statements are based on a consideration of the common financial information needs of users as a group. The possible effect of misstatements on specific individual users, whose needs may vary widely, is not considered. (para 2)

This explanation makes it clear that the term 'materiality' needs to be understood in the context of users of the financial statements as a group. However, it is also helpful to identify some of the characteristics that auditors may assume the users possess. According to ISA 320 (para 4), they may assume users:
- (a) Have a reasonable knowledge of business and economic activities and accounting and a willingness to study the information in the financial statements with reasonable diligence;
- (b) Understand that financial statements are prepared, presented and audited to levels of materiality;
- (c) Recognize the uncertainties inherent in the measurement of [financial statement] amounts based on the use of estimates, judgment and the consideration of future events; and
- (d) Make reasonable economic decisions on the basis of the information in the financial statements.

---

[16] In the UK (as in all EU Member States and countries such as New Zealand and Australia), companies' financial statements must provide a true and fair view of their financial position and performance as well as complying with an applicable financial reporting framework (CA 2006, s. 393).

3.4.2b   *Characteristics of materiality*

Although it is helpful to recognise that 'materiality' must be understood in the context of the economic decisions of users of the financial statements (users who possess the characteristics outlined above), the question remains as to how auditors determine what is to qualify as a *material* misstatement. In order to address this question, it is useful to identify some characteristic features of the concept, in particular:

(i)   deciding what is, and what is not, material in any given circumstance is a matter of professional judgment;

(ii)   an item may be material by virtue of its size or its nature;

(iii)   materiality needs to be considered at both the financial statement level and at the level of individual account balances and other financial statement disclosures.

We examine each of these characteristics below.

(i)   A matter of professional judgment

ISA 320 (para A3) states: "Determining materiality involves the exercise of professional judgment". In order to help auditors identify an appropriate amount (or limit) to distinguish between what is, and what is not, to be considered a *material* misstatement in the financial statements as a whole, they usually apply a selected percentage (frequently in the region of a half to five per cent) to a selected benchmark (that is, a significant financial statement total). ISA 320 (para A3) indicates that the benchmark chosen by auditors is influenced by factors such as:

• the components in the financial statements. (In the financial statements of companies, these include assets, liabilities, equity, income and expenses);

• whether there are items on which users of the reporting entity's financial statements are likely to focus. (In profit-oriented companies this is likely to be net profit or revenue; if the entity is displaying signs of financial difficulty, it is also likely to be net assets);

• the relative importance of debt in the entity's financial structure. (If debt is unusually significant relative to equity, financial statement users may focus on net assets rather than on profit measures); and

• the relative volatility of potential benchmarks.

As we shall see when we discuss materiality in greater detail in Chapter 9, the benchmarks selected by different audit firms, and the percentages applied to the benchmarks, vary quite widely. However, those most frequently chosen include profit before tax, total revenue, gross profit, total equity and net assets. But, whatever the benchmarks and percentages used, it is important to recognise that determining an amount (or upper limit) for materiality in this way does not generate a 'magic number' such that any errors or omissions larger than this will be adjudged 'material' and those smaller will be considered 'immaterial'. In every case, auditors must exercise their professional judgment:

(a) to establish a materiality limit to apply in the audit of the entity's financial statements;

(b) when deciding whether, in the particular circumstances, an omission or misstatement is material. The question the auditor must consider is: Is the omission or misstatement likely to affect the economic decisions of users of the entity's financial statements?

(ii)   Size vs nature of an omission or misstatement

When determining whether an omission or misstatement is material, it is not only its size which is relevant; its nature is also significant. This is reflected in ISA 320 (para 6) which states:

> Although it is not practicable to design audit procedures to detect misstatements that could be material solely because of their nature, the auditor considers not only the size but also the nature of uncorrected misstatements, and the particular circumstances of their occurrence, when evaluating their effect on the financial statements.

A number of factors relating to the nature of items may affect the auditor's judgment regarding their materiality. These include:

(a) Whether the item is required to be disclosed in the financial statements by law, regulations or the applicable financial reporting framework. For example, the *Companies (Disclosure of Auditor Remuneration and Liability Limitation Agreements) Regulations 2008* [Statutory Instrument, (SI) 2008, as amended by SI 2011] require large companies to disclose in their financial statements the fees paid to the auditor for audit and non-audit services. Similarly, International Accounting Standard (IAS) 17: *Leases* (International Accounting Standards Board, 2011) (para 31) requires lessees to disclose in the notes to their financial statements finance lease liabilities, classified into the amounts of minimum lease payments at the date of the financial statements and the present value thereof (i) for the next year, (ii) years two to five inclusive (as a combined total), and (iii) beyond five years. In most cases, failure to disclose required items such as these will be regarded by the auditor as a material omission. Along similar lines, if an accounting policy or other financial statement disclosure is described so inadequately or inaccurately that it is likely that financial statement users could be misled by the description, the auditor would judge this to be a material misstatement.

(b) Whether the item is particularly relevant to the industry in which the entity operates. For example, because of the importance of research and development to the future of a pharmaceutical company, the omission or a misstatement of research and development costs by such a company is likely to be considered material by the auditor.

(c) Whether the item is related to a particularly sensitive issue. For example, the amount paid to the directors of public listed companies is a sensitive issue; many in society believe their remuneration is excessive. As a consequence, the amounts disclosed for directors' remuneration are likely to be of importance to the users of listed companies' financial statements and, therefore, even a small misstatement of the amounts may be judged to be material by the auditor.

(iii)   Materiality for the financial statements as a whole and for account balances and disclosures

Materiality for the financial statements as a whole (or overall materiality) refers to the maximum amount of error (whether through omission and/or error) the auditor is prepared to accept in the financial statements as a whole while still concluding that they provide a true and fair view of the auditee's financial performance and financial position. It is the amount of misstatement the auditor considers may be present in the financial statements without affecting the economic decisions of reasonable users of those financial statements. This level of materiality is frequently referred to as 'planning materiality'.[17]

Materiality for account balances or other disclosures refers to the maximum amount of error an auditor will accept in a particular class of transactions, account balance or financial statement disclosure before concluding that the relevant financial statement account balance or disclosure may mislead reasonable users of the financial statements. In this book, we adopt the term 'tolerable error' to denote this level of materiality. The means by which auditors determine an appropriate limit for tolerable error is explained in Chapter 9. However, at this point it is useful to note that the tolerable error determined for one account balance or disclosure may differ quite markedly from that determined for another. In general, the greater the amount of judgment or estimation involved in arriving at the account balance or disclosure, the higher the tolerable error. For example, the tolerable error determined for the cash account balance is likely to be significantly smaller than that for – say – allowance for bad debts or accumulated depreciation.

Before we leave the concept of materiality, we need to emphasise that the materiality limits established for overall materiality and tolerable error are only a starting point. Even where omissions and/or errors are less than the

---

[17] Although the term 'planning materiality' is frequently used for overall materiality, the materiality of account balances and other disclosures, like overall materiality, is set during the planning stage of the audit.

applicable materiality limit, the auditor must consider their nature, the circumstances surrounding their occurrence, the characteristics of the reporting entity and the likely users of the entity's financial statements. These issues are discussed in greater detail in Chapter 9.

3.4.3 Concept of audit risk

3.4.3a *Definition of audit risk*

The International Federation of Accountants' (IFAC's) *Glossary of Terms* (2009) defines audit risk as:

> The risk that the auditor expresses an inappropriate audit opinion when the financial statements are materially misstated. Audit risk is a function of the risks of material misstatement and detection risk.

Technically speaking, the IFAC definition conveys only half of the story. Audit risk is more correctly defined as 'the risk that the auditor issues an inappropriate opinion on the financial statements examined'. Expressed in this way, it is evident that audit risk has two forms:

- α risk: the risk that the auditor expresses a *modified* opinion[18] (says something is amiss) on financial statements that are *not* materially misstated; and
- β risk: the risk that the auditor expresses an *unmodified* ('clean') opinion on financial statements that *are* materially misstated.

The risk of an auditor expressing a modified opinion on financial statements that are not materially misstated is very unlikely. Before modifying the audit report, the auditor will need good reasons for so doing, and such reasons will need to be justified to the relevant company's directors. If the auditor has drawn invalid conclusions about the financial statements, these are likely to come to light during this 'justification process'. Thus, as reflected in the IAASB's definition cited above, the term 'audit risk' is commonly used to mean β risk. Ultimately, to the auditor, audit risk amounts to exposure to legal liability if, as a result of issuing a 'clean' audit report on financial statements which are materially misstated, users of the financial statements are misled and suffer loss as a consequence. However, as we noted in relation to audit evidence above, auditors are required to *express an opinion* on the financial statements, not to *certify* their truth and fairness. As a result, some degree of

---

[18] The Companies Act 2006 refers to the auditor's opinion being qualified or unqualified. In International Standard on Auditing (ISA) 700: *Forming an Opinion and Reporting on Financial Statements* (IAASB, 2009h) the term 'modified' has been adopted to refer to any audit report which does not contain an unmodified opinion. The term 'qualified' has been used to signify an audit opinion which conveys that the auditor has reservations about one or more particular aspects of the financial statements. We discuss the different types of audit opinion in Chapter 14.

audit risk is always present. Consequently, legal action against an auditor is likely to succeed only if the auditor deliberately or negligently accepts an unreasonably high level of audit risk (that is, the auditor fails to conduct an adequate audit before issuing a 'clean' audit report on materially misstated financial statements).

3.4.3b   Components of audit risk

As indicated in the IAASB's definition of audit risk, it has two main components, namely:

(i)   the risk that, prior to the audit, the financial statements are materially misstated. This risk results from inherent risk and internal control risk;

(ii)   the risk that the auditor fails to detect material misstatement(s) in the financial statements. This component is referred to as detection risk and comprises sampling risk and quality control risk.[19]

These components of audit risk are shown in Figure 3.2 and discussed below.

Figure 3.2:   The components of audit risk

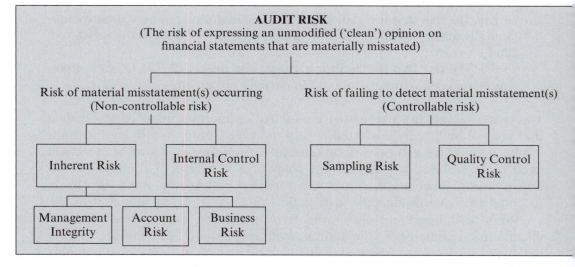

(i)   Risk of misstatement(s) occurring in the financial statements

The likelihood of material misstatement(s) occurring in the financial statements prior to the audit is, for the most part, beyond the auditor's control. This component of audit risk results from two factors: inherent risk and internal control risk.

---

[19] IFAC's *Glossary of Terms* (2009) recognises as separate audit risk components inherent risk, control risk and detection risk. Control risk, as defined in the *Glossary*, equates with what we term internal control risk, and detection risk embraces both sampling risk and quality control risk.

- **Inherent risk:** This is the risk or likelihood of material misstatement(s) being present in the financial statements in the absence of internal controls (that is, controls designed to prevent misstatements from occurring). As may be seen from Figure 3.2, inherent risk derives from three main sources:

  1. Management integrity: The likelihood of material misstatement(s) occurring in the financial statements is strongly influenced by the integrity of the auditee's management. This integrity has two aspects:
     (a) *inherent integrity*, that is, management's moral and ethical stance; its 'natural' tendency towards being honest or dishonest; and
     (b) *situational integrity*, that is, management's ability to withstand temptation to misrepresent the company's financial position or profitability in situations of pressure. For example, when the entity has failed to meet profit forecasts, or when there are plans to float new shares and the year's profit has been small, management may be tempted to 'artificially improve' the entity's reported profit.

  If a company's management lacks integrity, the information presented in its financial statements may well be manipulated to the extent necessary to portray the company's financial position or profitability as desired by management.

  2. Account risk: Material misstatement(s) may also occur in the financial statements as a result of account balances being susceptible to misstatement. In general, these are account balances which involve significant judgment (such as the allowance for bad debts) or those where values are uncertain (for example, stands of unsold timber in plantations for which market demand is uncertain).

  3. Business risk: The likelihood of material misstatement(s) occurring in the financial statements is also affected by the nature of the auditee's business. While some businesses are not particularly vulnerable to changes in the state of the economy, competition and/or technological advances, the reverse is true for others. For example, jewellery outlets are affected by changes in consumer wealth; fashion-wear businesses are susceptible to changes in customer 'fads'; businesses in the electronics industry are prone to changes in technology; and those in the oil industry are exposed to rapid and large changes in oil prices in world markets. In each case, a high risk attaches to the entity's inventory valuation and net profit and, possibly, also to its ability to sustain operating cash flow at a level necessary to meet its debt obligations. In the latter case, business risk may generate a situation in which management's integrity is put under pressure.

- **Internal control risk:**[20] This is the risk that material misstatement(s) will occur in the auditee's accounting data (and, hence, in its financial statements) because it is not prevented or detected by the company's internal controls. Some internal control risk will always be present because every internal control system has some inherent limitations.[21] However, the more effective a company's internal controls, the less the likelihood of material misstatement(s) being present in its financial statements.

In relation to the risk of material misstatement occurring in an auditee's pre-audited financial statements, it is pertinent to note that, although auditors have little or no direct control over inherent risk and internal control risk, they can and should be aware of the circumstances in which these risks are likely to be high. They can perform procedures to ascertain whether these circumstances are present in any given audit and adjust their audit effort and techniques accordingly. (Evaluating the integrity of the client's management and evaluating internal control risk are discussed in Chapters 8 and 10, respectively).

(ii)   The risk that material misstatement(s) will not be detected (detection risk)

Unlike the risk of material misstatement(s) occurring in the financial statements, the risk of auditors failing to detect such misstatement(s) is subject to their direct control. As shown in Figure 3.2, this component of audit risk derives from sampling risk and quality control risk.

- **Sampling risk:** This is the risk that the auditor may fail to detect material misstatement(s) because not all of the available evidence is examined; transactions or account balances which contain a material misstatement, or indicate such a misstatement is present, may not be included in the sample of transactions or account balances examined during the audit. Alternatively stated, sampling risk is:

   [t]he risk that the auditor's conclusion based on a sample may be different from the conclusion [the auditor would reach] if the entire population were subjected to the same audit procedure. (IFAC, 2009)

When statistical sampling techniques are used, sampling risk is quantifiable and controllable. As explained in Chapter 12, statistical sampling techniques enable auditors to adjust their sample sizes so they can attain the level of audit (sampling) risk they are willing to accept.

---

[20] As noted in footnote 19, IFAC's *Glossary of Terms* refers to this type of risk as 'control risk'.

[21] The inherent limitations of internal control systems are discussed in Chapter 10, section 10.3.6.

- **Quality control risk:** This is the risk that the auditor will fail to detect material misstatement(s) because sufficient appropriate audit evidence is not collected and/or is not evaluated properly. IFAC (2009) terms this 'non-sampling risk' and defines it as: "[t]he risk that the auditor reaches an erroneous conclusion for any reason not related to sampling risk".[22]

  As with internal control risk, some quality control risk will always be present in an audit simply because audits are conducted by humans (who are fallible) and they involve a considerable amount of judgment. Audit staff cannot be expected to make optimal judgments, to select the appropriate audit procedure, and to reach appropriate conclusions, on *every* occasion throughout an audit. Some human error is inevitable![23]

As noted above, the risk of auditors failing to detect material misstatement(s) in the financial statements is under their direct control. They should therefore seek to reduce sampling risk and quality control risk (that is, detection risk) to the level it is economically feasible to do so. As explained in Chapter 9, this level varies inversely with the auditor's assessment of inherent risk and internal control risk and affects the nature, timing and extent of audit procedures performed.

3.4.4 Concept of judgment

Judgment is a fundamental characteristic of all professions – including auditing. The concept encapsulates the notion of applying knowledge and experience to evaluate the circumstances, and/or available evidence, relevant to a known objective and forming an opinion based on that evaluation. It contrasts with achieving an objective by means of following an established set of rules or procedures.

In order for a professional judgment to be sound, it is essential that the person exercising it (for example, an auditor) has integrity, is competent and maintains an objective, unbiased attitude of mind – concepts that, as we have already seen, are central to the credibility of auditors' work.

---

[22] Although IFAC's *Glossary of Terms* uses the term 'non-sampling risk', as the latter is directly affected by the standard of quality control applied during an audit, in our view, the title 'quality control risk' affords a better description of this component of detection risk.

[23] In relation to quality control risk, Bell, Peecher & Solomon (2005) state:

In our view, given today's complex business environment as well as the subjectivity both featured in applicable financial reporting frameworks and associated with the assessment of audit risk components, non-sampling risk is a significant, if not the major, source of DR [detection risk]. Further, the auditor cannot accurately assess and manage sampling risk (e.g. determine a sufficient sample size and draw implications from sample findings to the population of interest) unless he or she properly assesses and manages non-sampling risk. (p. 10)

Judgment pervades every stage of the audit process. As Bell, Peecher and Solomon (2005) observe: "Professional judgment is the very essence of auditing; it pervasively influences audit quality from beginning to end . . ." (p. 18). The auditor must exercise judgment, for example, in relation to questions such as:

- what is the likelihood that the financial statements are materially misstated?
- how much effort (time and expertise) should be devoted to the audit?
- who should constitute the audit team (in terms of the number of staff and their level of competence and experience)?
- in which areas of the financial statements should audit effort be focused?
- what is an appropriate limit for materiality in the financial statements as a whole and for each class of transactions, account balance and other financial statement disclosure?
- how much, what, from where, when and by whom should audit evidence be gathered?
- what conclusions about the truth and fairness of the financial statements (and each segment thereof) are supported by the evidence gathered?
- in preparing the financial statements, has management applied appropriately the applicable financial reporting framework, including accounting policies?
- are estimates made by management in the preparation of the financial statements reasonable?
- has sufficient appropriate audit evidence been collected and evaluated to form an opinion on the financial statements?

These, and numerous other questions that arise in any audit, do not have clear-cut answers that apply routinely in a given situation. Each audit is unique, and the circumstances of the particular audit must be considered when auditors exercise their judgment. However, one general factor that impacts on and, to some extent, limits the exercise of auditors' judgment in each audit is the materiality of the matter in question. As the fundamental principle of external auditing – *Judgment* explains:

> Auditors apply professional judgment taking account of materiality in the context of the matter on which they are reporting. (FRC, 2013, Appendix 2)

Whether or not an error or omission is material is itself a matter for the auditor's judgment and, as we have seen, varies according to the circumstances of the error or omission, characteristics of the auditee and likely users of its financial statements.

The exercise of auditors' judgment is not only unique to the circumstances of each audit; it is also unique to each auditor. The ability of auditors to arrive at professional decisions and opinions, and the cognitive process by which they do so, varies according to a wide range of environmental and personal factors. These include such things as:

- the social, cultural and political environment in which the auditor (and auditee) operates;
- the auditor's general and professional education, professional training and experience, and his or her problem-solving ability;
- the extent and detail of guidance provided by auditing standards and other professional promulgations; and
- the policies and culture of the auditor's firm.

However, because the same minimum competence (knowledge, skills and experience) requirements apply to all audit professionals (as outlined in IES 8 and discussed in section 3.3.2), it can be expected that the judgments they make in a given set of circumstances will be reasonably similar.

3.4.5 Concept of scepticism

The APB (2011b) states: "The application of an appropriate degree of professional scepticism is a crucial skill for auditors" (para 1). Along related lines, the first part of the fundamental principle of external auditing – *Rigour* notes:

> Auditors approach their work with thoroughness and with an attitude of professional scepticism. (FRC, 2013, Appendix 2)

Although these statements convey the importance of auditors maintaining a sceptical attitude when performing an audit, they do not explain what the term 'professional scepticism' means.

The concept is defined in ISA 200 (para 13) as:

> An attitude that includes a questioning mind, being alert to conditions which may indicate possible misstatement due to error or fraud, and a critical assessment of audit evidence. (IAASB, 2009b)

The APB (1998) provides further insight into what the concept entails. It observes: "scepticism is a personal quality that relates to the attitude of individual auditors: it is characterised by a questioning, probing – almost suspicious – approach being applied throughout the audit" (para 3.7).

It should be noted that the APB refers to an *almost* suspicious approach: there is a fine but clear line between auditors adopting a 'suspicious' rather than 'sceptical' approach to an audit. As indicated by Lopes, L J in the *Kingston Cotton Mill* case [1896] 2 Ch. 279,[24] auditors are not required to "approach [their] work with suspicion or with a foregone conclusion that there is something wrong". This is beyond the concept of professional scepticism. Auditors

---

[24] This case was referred to in Chapter 2, section 2.4.4 and is discussed further in Chapter 5, section 5.5.3.

should not assume the auditee's directors, executives and other employees are dishonest, nor should they assume unquestioned honesty – even if they have found them to be honest and possessing integrity in the past. Professional scepticism requires auditors to be alert to the possibility that circumstances have changed, to instances of audit evidence being inconsistent, to information that raises questions about the reliability of documents or management's responses to their enquiries, and to conditions that indicate that fraud may exist in the reporting entity. They need to critically evaluate (rather than merely accept) information and explanations obtained from auditee personnel, and other audit evidence gathered, with an objective, unbiased attitude of mind. They need to ask themselves: "Given my knowledge of this auditee, its business, its circumstances and its operations, does the evidence (or information or explanations) obtained make sense?" If not, they should ask probing questions and/or seek further audit evidence to satisfy themselves as to the validity or otherwise of the information, explanations and other evidence obtained.

In recent years, auditors (at least in the UK) have not, apparently, been exercising sufficient professional scepticism in their audits. This is reflected, for example, in the Audit Inspection Unit's (AIU)[25] 2010/11 annual report which states:

> The AIU continued to identify cases where . . . insufficient professional scepticism had been exercised in key areas of judgment. . . . [Audit] firms . . . are . . . undertaking a number of initiatives to reinforce the importance of exercising professional scepticism in the conduct of their audit work. These include additional training and specific communications to staff from key management personnel. . . . Some firms have more work to do than others to demonstrate that professional scepticism is appropriately embedded in their processes and culture. (AIU, 2011, pp. 21–22)

The APB (2011b) has also expressed concern about the lack of consensus about the meaning of the term 'professional scepticism' within the accountancy profession. While some members of the profession consider it requires auditors to adopt a neutral position (neither assuming the entity's management is honest or dishonest, nor that the financial statements are, or are not, materially misstated), others believe it involves a more questioning approach

---

[25] Until July 2012, the AIU operated independently of, but was overseen by, the Professional Oversight Board (POB) – one of the former operating bodies of the FRC. The FRC was established as the independent regulator of the accountancy profession in the UK in 2004 following the UK Government's post-Enron review of the regulation of the UK's accountancy profession. In 2012, the AIU was renamed the Audit Quality Review (AQR) team and, since then, has been overseen by the FRC's Monitoring Committee. (The former and current structure of the FRC is presented diagrammatically at the front of this book on page xix). The remit of the AQR team is to inspect the audits of public interest entities (which includes all public listed companies). We discuss the role and responsibilities of the AQR team in Chapter 16, section 16.4.3.

which may be referred to as 'presumptive doubt' (APB, 2011b, paras 23, 24). It seems that, in the post-2002, closely regulated era of auditing's development (discussed in Chapter 2, section 2.7.2), the concept of professional scepticism has moved a notch or two along the continuum from neutrality towards presumptive doubt (Bell *et al.*, 2005, p. 18). This is reflected, for example, in the APB questioning whether a neutral position (or even an 'inquiring mind') is an appropriate position for an auditor to adopt and pointing to "an element of 'doubt' [underlying] a number of requirements in Auditing Standards" (APB, 2011, para 27). It cites as examples extracts from ISA 200: *Overall Objectives of the Independent Auditor and the Conduct of an Audit in Accordance with International Standards on Auditing* (IAASB, 2009b) and ISA 240: *The Auditor's Responsibilities Relating to Fraud in an Audit of Financial Statements* (IAASB, 2009d). These state, respectively:

- The auditor shall plan and perform an audit with professional skepticism recognizing that circumstances may exist that cause the financial statements to be materially misstated. (ISA 200, para 15)
- [T]he auditor shall maintain professional skepticism throughout the audit, recognizing the possibility that a material misstatement due to fraud could exist, notwithstanding the auditor's past experience of the honesty and integrity of the entity's management and those charged with governance. (ISA 240, para 12)

In 2012, in an attempt to establish a common understanding of the concept of professional scepticism, the APB undertook a detailed investigation of its origin, development and importance. The APB concluded:

> ... the appropriate application of professional scepticism in the audit requires a mindset which rigorously questions and challenges management's assertions with a degree of doubt that reflects the expectations of shareholders (and other stakeholders) for whose benefit it is performed. (APB, 2012, p. 12)

This seems to reaffirm the APB's view that the concept incorporates a measure of 'presumptive doubt'. Nevertheless, it is important that auditors maintain a balance in their application of the concept. Too little scepticism may result in an ineffective audit – something being missed and an inappropriate opinion being expressed in the audit report. However, too much scepticism (challenging the validity of documents and management's responses unnecessarily) may result in an inefficient audit – the incurrence of unnecessary costs.

It is clear that, in order to conduct an effective audit, auditors must exercise an appropriate degree of professional scepticism. However, auditors' ability and propensity to critically evaluate evidence gathered and information provided, and to ask probing questions, is affected by a variety of environmental and personal factors. These factors tend to coincide with those (noted in section 3.4.4 above) that impact auditors' ability to, and the manner in which they, exercise judgment.

3.5 CONCEPT RELATING TO AUDITORS' COMMUNICATION: REPORTING

Given that the key objective of an audit is to form and express an opinion (in an audit report) on the truth and fairness of the auditee's financial statements, reporting is clearly a concept that goes to the very heart of the audit function. However, it is not just a case of auditors completing their audit and issuing a report without regard to the readers of that report. Rather, it involves *communicating* essential information to users of the audited financial statements. As the first part of the fundamental principle of external auditing – *Clear, complete and effective communication* explains:

> Auditors' reports contain clear expressions of opinion and set out information necessary for a proper understanding of the opinion. (FRC, 2013, Appendix 2)

When preparing their reports on financial statements, auditors need to bear in mind that the users of those financial statements, unlike themselves, do not have access to the auditee's data, records, documents and other information, and, frequently, they have little technical accounting or auditing knowledge. Thus, they rely on auditors not only to report their opinion on the financial statements in which they are interested but to do so in a manner that enables them to comprehend the opinion expressed and the level of assurance it provides.

Flint (1988, p. 117) explains the importance of auditors' reports:

> The inadequacy of [an audit] report and the failure to communicate successfully could result in consequences which were not justified by the facts, with injustice and damage to the interests of the parties.

If users of audited financial statements rely on the auditor's report and make investment or other decisions based on their understanding of the message it contains, should their understanding be erroneous, their decisions could be unwise and they could suffer serious adverse financial consequences as a result.

It may be deduced from Flint's statement (cited above) that, in order to be effective, auditors' reports need to meet two important criteria: they need to (a) be adequate in content and (b) communicate successfully with users of the audited financial statements. We examine each of these criteria a little more closely.

(i) *Adequacy:* To be of value, audit reports must contain sufficient information for users of the financial statements to be left in no doubt about the opinion (and any reservations) the auditor is expressing. Audit reports must be explicit and complete. As Flint (1988, p. 117–118) observes:

> Auditors are rarely in a position to engage in a dialogue with the parties who will use their report, and once released the report is frequently

public information. . . . An audit report must be complete and explicit so that the reader . . . knows fully and exactly what the auditors had to communicate as the outcome of the audit. It must be complete within itself, not requiring the reader to refer to any other document to understand its terms.

(ii) *Successful communication:* In order to communicate a message to financial statement users, audit reports need to be precise and comprehensible. However, meeting these requirements is no easy task. The subject matter of an audit is frequently complex and technical in nature yet auditors need to communicate their opinion on the financial statements to persons with limited understanding of technical accounting and/or auditing matters. Moreover, their communication must be sufficiently precise to convey the limits of an audit and the level of assurance they are providing on the financial statements. As Flint (1988) points out, although it is unrealistic to expect an audit report to be understandable by the least knowledgeable of its recipients:

> [it] must be in terms which enable the knowledgeable[26] to be informed . . . whether or not accounts, reports or other statements provide the information which they should, and in what respects, if any, there have been failures or defaults . . . in relation to matters with which the recipients of the audit report are concerned. (pp. 118–119)

Since 1988 (when the 'extended' audit report was first adopted in the USA; it was adopted in the UK in 1993), the auditing profession has made efforts to ensure that audit reports are complete, explicit and comprehensible. As we explain in Chapter 14, ISA 700: *Forming an Opinion and Reporting on Financial Statements* (IAASB, 2009h) has been revised on a number of occasions since the early 1990s with this objective in view. Today, auditors' reports, amongst other things:

- identify the financial statements which have been audited and about which the auditor is expressing an opinion;
- explain the respective responsibilities of the auditee's directors and auditors for the financial statements;
- outline the audit process which forms the basis for the opinion expressed;
- express an opinion about the truth and fairness (or otherwise) of the financial statements and their compliance (or otherwise) with legal requirements and the applicable financial reporting framework.[27]

---

[26] As noted in section 3.4.2 above, the IAASB assumes financial statement users "[h]ave a reasonable knowledge of business and economic activities and accounting and a willingness to study the information in the financial statements with reasonable diligence" (ISA 320, para 4).

[27] For all listed companies in the EU (including the UK), as in most other countries in the world, the International Financial Reporting Standards (IFRS) constitute the applicable financial reporting framework.

Notwithstanding that ISA 700 has been revised a number of times, in recent years the style and content of auditors' reports have been severely criticised; financial statement users claim the reports do not meet the necessary criteria of adequacy and successful communication (see, for example, Audit Quality Forum, 2007). We examine the criticism in some detail in Chapter 14, section 14.7.

In addition to reporting to users of the audited financial statements, ISA 260: *Communication with Those Charged with Governance* (IAASB, 2009e) requires auditors to provide to the company's directors: "timely observations arising from the audit that are significant and relevant to their responsibility to oversee the financial reporting process" (para 5c). This responsibility of auditors is also conveyed in the second part of the fundamental principle of external auditing – *Clear, complete and effective communication*, which states:

> Auditors communicate audit matters of governance interest arising from the audit of financial statements with those charged with governance of an entity. (FRC, 2013, Appendix 2)

ISA 260 (paras 10–13) details the matters auditors are to communicate to those charged with governance. They include:
- the auditor's responsibilities in relation to the financial statement audit;
- an overview of the scope and timing of the audit;
- significant findings from the audit, including:
    - the auditor's views about significant qualitative aspects of the entity's accounting practices including the accounting policies and estimates applied in the preparation of the financial statements;
    - significant difficulties encountered during the audit (such as executives not making available information requested by the auditor, or attempting to limit the scope of the auditor's work);
    - internal control deficiencies; and
    - misstatements in the financial statements that have not been adjusted by management;
- in the case of listed entities, assurance regarding the audit firm's and audit team's independence.[28]

As might be expected, the key principles of the concept of reporting which underpin auditors' communication with users of financial statements also apply to their communication with those charged with governance. To be effective, these communications must be complete, explicit and comprehensible. Also like auditors' reports on financial statements, unless their reports to auditees' directors meet these criteria, the directors might be misled and, as a result, make

---

[28] These, and other matters auditors are required to report to those charged with governance, are discussed in detail in Chapter 14, section 14.8.

erroneous decisions. These, in turn, could cause serious adverse consequences for the reporting entity. If, for example, the auditor of a bank encounters serious deficiencies in the internal controls relating to foreign exchange dealing and does not communicate his or her findings in an unequivocal and comprehensible manner to the board of directors (or, possibly, the audit committee),[29] a dealer may exploit the internal control deficiencies and engage in unauthorised trading activities undetected for an extended period of time. This (as the collapse of Barings Bank in 1995[30] and the unauthorised dealing by an UBS bank employee in 2011 testify) can result in disastrous financial consequences.

Notwithstanding the similarities in the concept of reporting in the context of auditors' reports to users of audited financial statements and to those charged with governance, there are two important differences. One relates to dialogue; the other to knowledge.

(i) *Dialogue:* It was noted above (when quoting Flint, 1988) that "auditors are rarely in a position to engage in a dialogue with the parties who will use their report". While this is generally true of auditors reporting to users of the audited financial statements,[31] it does (or should!) not apply to auditors reporting to those charged with the entity's governance. It is normal practice for an auditor to meet with the auditee's audit committee (or board of directors) at the conclusion of the audit to discuss any matters relating to the auditor's findings.[32] This provides an opportunity for those charged with the entity's governance to ask the auditor probing questions about a wide range of issues; for example, the adequacy of the entity's system of internal control, errors the auditor detected in the financial statements, and any disagreements with management about, for instance, the choice of accounting policies or the reasonableness of accounting estimates included in the financial statements.

(ii) *Knowledge:* Also unlike the users of audited financial statements, those charged with governance have access to their company's internal

---

[29] Audit committees are discussed in Chapter 4, section 4.5.

[30] This case is discussed in Chapter 15, section 15.4.3.

[31] A limited opportunity for communication between a company's auditor and its shareholders is provided by CA 2006, s. 502. This gives auditors the right to attend any general meeting of the company's shareholders and to speak on any matter discussed at the meeting that concerns them as auditor. In general, auditors attend meetings where the audited financial statements are presented to the company's shareholders. They are, therefore, available to answer questions relating to the audit of the financial statements. The issue of seeking ways to increase auditors' interaction with shareholders is a matter of considerable discussion. We examine the issue, and the current discussion, in Chapter 18, section 18.4.

[32] Such meetings are recommended in the FRC's *Guidance on Audit Committees* (FRC, 2012a). This Guidance is intended to assist Boards of Directors implement the provisions of *The UK Corporate Governance Code* (FRC, 2012b) insofar as they relate to audit committees (FRC, 2012a, para 1.1).

information – its financial and non-financial data, accounting and other records, minutes of meetings, correspondence, and so on. Thus, although the auditor's communication with the company's directors (or audit committee) is very important, it is only one source of information available to them. Equally important, in terms of assisting the board fulfil its governance responsibilities, is the communication between the directors (or audit committee) and the entity's internal auditors (or those who fulfil the internal audit function).[33]

3.6 CONCEPTS RELATING TO THE STANDARD OF AUDITORS' PERFORMANCE

3.6.1 Concept of due care

In order for an auditor's opinion to be respected and valued, those relying on that opinion must be able to assume it has been formed by an auditor who has conducted the audit diligently, competently and with due care. But what does the term 'due care' mean in the context of an audit?

Court decisions in the nineteenth and twentieth centuries shed some light on the issue. In *Re Kingston Cotton Mill (No. 2)* [1896] 2 Ch 279, Lopes L J explained:

> It is the duty of an auditor to bring to bear on the work he has to perform, that skill, care and caution which a reasonably competent, careful and cautious auditor would use. What is reasonable skill, care and caution must depend on the particular circumstances of each case.

Some 70 years later, Pennycuick, J, in the case of *Re Thomas Gerrard & Son Ltd.*, [1967] 2 All ER 525, observed:

> I am not clear that the quality of the auditor's duty has changed in any relevant respect since 1896. Basically that duty has always been to audit the company's accounts with reasonable care and skill. The real ground on which Re Kingston Cotton Mill Co. (No. 2) is I think capable of being distinguished, is that the standards of reasonable care and skill are . . . more exacting today than those which prevailed in 1896.

Similar ideas were expressed by Moffitt, J in *Pacific Acceptance Corporation Ltd.* v *Forsyth and Others* (1970) 92 WN (NSW) 29:[34]

> It is beyond question that when an auditor . . . enters into a contract to perform certain tasks as auditor, he promises to perform such tasks using that degree of skill and care as is reasonable in the circumstances as they then exist. . . . The

---

[33] Audit committee communications with internal auditors is discussed in Chapter 4, section 4.5.

[34] Key findings of this case are reported in Chapter 5, section 5.5.3.

legal duty, namely, to audit the accounts with reasonable skill and care remains the same, but . . . reasonable skill and care calls for changed standards to meet changed conditions or changed understanding of dangers and in this sense standards are more exacting today than in 1896.

Moffitt, J goes on to note that the auditing profession, by changing the guidance it provides for auditors in auditing standards, recognises that changed conditions call for changed audit practices. However, he also warns:

> [The] standards and practices adopted by the profession to meet current circumstances provide a sound guide to the court in determining what is reasonable. . . . [However] when the conduct of an auditor is in question in legal proceedings it is not the province of the audit profession itself [but of the court] to determine . . . what reasonable skill and care require to be done in a particular case.

So, what can we distil from the Judges' statements in the cases cited above about the concept of due care? It may be seen that it has four key characteristics, namely:

(i) It embodies the notion of auditors exercising reasonable skill, care and caution.

(ii) What qualifies as 'reasonable skill, care and caution' in any audit depends on the particular circumstances of the case.

(iii) The standard of 'reasonable skill, care and caution' has become more exacting since 1896, as society and, more particularly, the financial, commercial and corporate worlds have become more complex and dynamic.

(iv) Although Auditing Standards and other professional promulgations provide guidance to the court on what may reasonably be expected of auditors, it is up to the court, not the auditing profession, to determine whether an auditor has exercised due care in any audit where the standard of the auditor's work has been questioned.

This concept is discussed further in Chapter 15 in the context of auditors' legal liability.

3.6.2 Concept of quality control

If financial statement users are to have confidence in auditors' opinions, it is essential that measures (or controls) are in place to ensure that high quality audits are performed. Flint (1988) conveys the importance of high quality audit work:

> In a profession [that is, auditing] whose authority is dependent among other things on public confidence . . . a demonstrable concern, individually and collectively on the part of the members of the profession, to control and maintain the highest quality in its work, is a matter of basic principle. The basis of continuing public confidence and trust in professional competence is a belief that the standards of the members of the profession will be maintained and can be relied on. (pp. 159, 161)

Two main measures have been adopted by the auditing profession to secure consistently high quality audit work, namely:

(i) embodying quality control requirements in two professional standards – ISQC 1: *Quality Controls for Firms that Perform Audits and Reviews of Financial Statements, and Other Assurance and Related Services Engagements* (IAASB 2009a), and ISA 220: *Quality Control for an Audit of Financial Statements* (IAASB, 2009c);

(ii) implementing external monitoring (or inspection) of auditors' compliance with legal, regulatory and professional requirements.

(i) Quality control standards

ISQC 1 and ISA 220 recognise that responsibility for securing high quality audit work lies at all levels of audit firms. While ISQC 1 relates to quality control at audit firm level, ISA 220 addresses quality control at audit engagement (individual audit) level. The need for controls at both firm and engagement level derives from the fact that audit firms frequently have many offices and each office has a number of audit engagement partners. Further, audits are generally conducted by audit teams ranging from two or three members for fairly small auditees to some 20 or more members for large clients. It is only by implementing quality controls at both firm and engagement level that the auditing profession can ensure the quality of audit work is at a consistently high level.

Important elements in securing high quality audit work at audit firm level are embedding quality in the firm's policies and procedures, and monitoring the result of audit work. Thus, ISQC 1 (para 11) requires each audit firm to establish a system of quality control designed to provide it with reasonable assurance that:

(a) The firm and its personnel comply with professional standards and regulatory and legal requirements; and

(b) Reports issued by the firm or engagement partners are appropriate in the circumstances.

According to ISQC 1 (para 15), such a system of quality control includes policies and procedures that address issues related to:

(a) Leadership responsibilities for quality within the firm.

(b) Relevant ethical requirements.

(c) Acceptance and continuance of client relationships and specific engagements.

(d) Human resources.

(e) Engagement performance.

(f) Monitoring.[35]

---

[35] Each of these elements of audit firms' quality control systems is discussed in Chapter 16, section 16.3.2.

In order to be effective, the firm's quality control policies and procedures need to be documented and communicated to the firm's personnel. The firm's personnel need to recognise and accept that each individual in the firm has a personal responsibility for quality and is expected to comply with the firm's policies and procedures.

Although maintaining an effective system of quality controls at the audit firm level is a necessary element of the auditing profession's measures for ensuring that audit work is consistently of a high quality, it is not sufficient. Audits are conducted by audit teams and, therefore, quality controls are also needed at the audit engagement level. ISA 220 places primary responsibility on the audit engagement partner (the partner responsible for the particular audit)[36] for engendering a quality culture within the audit team and for ensuring that audit team members adhere to the firm's quality control policies and procedures. More specifically, the engagement partner has responsibility for matters such as:

- ensuring the audit engagement complies with legal and professional requirements relating to independence, and that members of the engagement team comply with the profession's ethical requirements;
- ensuring the audit team has the appropriate capabilities, competence and time to perform the audit in accordance with professional standards and regulatory and legal requirements;
- assigning, directing, supervising and reviewing the audit work performed;
- ensuring the audit team undertakes appropriate consultation during the audit, especially where difficult or contentious matters are encountered;
- ensuring that, by the conclusion of the audit, sufficient appropriate evidence has been collected and evaluated, that it supports the conclusions reached, and is adequate for the auditor to form and express the appropriate opinion on the financial statements.

(ii) External monitoring/inspection of company auditors

Not only has the profession sought to ensure that all audits are performed to a high standard, Parliament too, recognising the importance of the audit function to society, has taken steps in this direction. As noted in relation to the concept of competence discussed in section 3.3.2 above, in order to be appointed as the auditor of a UK company, in general, an auditor must be a member of a Recognised Supervisory Body (RSB). Each RSB is required to have procedures in place which enable it to monitor the performance of its members.

---

[36] CA 2006, s. 504, uses the term 'senior statutory auditor' for the engagement partner for a statutory audit (i.e., an audit required by statute, or Act of Parliament; in this case the Companies Act 2006).

Since 1992, monitoring units established by the RSBs have been responsible for monitoring auditors' compliance with the legal, regulatory and professional requirements – including their compliance with Auditing and Ethical Standards. The monitoring activities of the RSBs are overseen and reviewed by the Conduct Committee of the FRC.

Since June 2004, in accordance with the Companies (Audit, Investigations and Community Enterprise) Act 2004, the audits of all public listed companies, and those of other entities considered to be of major public interest, have been subject to inspection by an independent Audit Inspection Unit (AIU).[37] The AIU was established as a unit of, and reported to, the Professional Oversight Board (POB), a former operating body of the FRC. In addition to conducting inspections, the AIU (and its successor, the Audit Quality Review team) issues formal reports to the RSBs on the results of its inspection of audits conducted by auditors who are members of the RSB in question. If auditors are found not to be complying with all of the RSB's requirements, they are subject to sanction – including the ultimate sanction of loss of membership of the RSB – and, hence, loss of eligibility for appointment as a company auditor.

We discuss the requirements of ISQC 1, ISA 220 and the monitoring of auditors' work in detail in Chapter 16.

3.7 SUMMARY

In this chapter we have laid the theoretical foundation for our study of the practice of auditing. We have noted the interrelationship between the social purpose, the postulates and the concepts of auditing. We have also described seven postulates and examined the meaning and importance to auditing of 11 concepts. We have seen that these concepts fall into four groups – the credibility of auditors' work (independence, competence and ethical conduct), the audit process (evidence, materiality, audit risk, judgment and scepticism), communication (reporting) and the standard of performance of audit work (due care and quality control) – and that each is of fundamental importance to the audit function. We will study most of these concepts in greater detail in subsequent chapters. However, we devote all of the next chapter to the critically important issue of auditors' independence.

---

[37] As noted in footnote 25, in July 2012, the AIU was renamed the Audit Quality Review (AQR) team; since that time, it has been overseen by the FRC's Monitoring Committee.

SELF-REVIEW QUESTIONS

3.1   State the social purpose of auditing and explain how this relates to the postulates and concepts of auditing.

3.2   (a) Explain briefly what is meant by a 'postulate'.
      (b) List four postulates of auditing.

3.3   Define and explain the importance of the concept of 'independence' as it relates to auditing. (Your definition should refer to both independence in mind and independence in appearance.)

3.4   Explain briefly the meaning and importance to auditing of the concept of competence.

3.5   Explain briefly the meaning and importance to auditing of the concept of evidence.

3.6   Explain briefly the meaning and importance to auditing of the concept of materiality.

3.7   Explain briefly the meaning and importance to auditing of the concept of audit risk.

3.8   Explain briefly the meaning and importance to auditing of the concept of scepticism.

3.9   (a) Explain briefly the importance to the concept of reporting of:
          (i) the adequacy of reporting; and
          (ii) successful communication.
      (b) Identify two important differences between auditors' reports to:
          (i) financial statement users; and
          (ii) those charged with the entity's governance.

3.10 Explain briefly the meaning and importance to auditing of the concept of due care.

REFERENCES

Anderson, R.J. (1977). *The External Audit.* Toronto: Cropp Clark Pitman.

Audit Inspection Unit (AIU). (2011). *Annual Report 2010/11.* London: Financial Reporting Council.

Auditing Practices Board (APB). (1998). *Fraud and Audit: Choices for Society*. Consultation Paper. London: APB.

Auditing Practices Board (APB). (2009). *The Auditing Practices Board: Scope and Authority of Pronouncements*. London: Financial Reporting Council.

Auditing Practices Board (APB). (2011a). APB Ethical Standard (ES) 1: *Integrity, Objectivity and Independence*. London: Financial Reporting Council.

Auditing Practices Board (APB). (2011b). *Auditor Scepticism: Raising the Bar* (Feedback paper). London: Financial Reporting Council.

Auditing Practices Board (APB). (2012). *Professional Scepticism: Establishing a Common Understanding and Reaffirming its Central Role in Delivering Audit Quality*. London: Financial Reporting Council.

Audit Quality Forum (AQF). (2007). *Fundamentals: Auditor Reporting* (Report of the Working Group on Auditor Reporting). London: Institute of Chartered Accountants in England and Wales (ICAEW).

Bell, T.B., Peecher, M.E., & Solomon, I. (2005). *The 21st Public Company Audit: Conceptual Elements of KPMG's Global Audit Methodology*. KPMG International.

Committee on Basic Auditing Concepts. (1973). *A Statement of Basic Auditing Concepts*. Sarasota, FL: American Accounting Association.

European Union (EU). (2006). *Directive 2006/43/EC of the European Parliament and of the Council on the Statutory Audits of Annual Accounts and Consolidated Accounts (Statutory Audit Directive)*. Brussels: European Parliament and Council.

Financial Reporting Council (FRC). (2012a). *Guidance on Audit Committees*. London: FRC.

Financial Reporting Council (FRC). (2012b). *The UK Corporate Governance Code*. London: FRC.

Financial Reporting Council (FRC). (2013). *Scope and Authority of Audit and Assurance Pronouncements*. London: FRC.

Flint, D. (1988). *Philosophy and Principles of Auditing: An Introduction*. Basingstoke: MacMillan Education Ltd.

Haber, J.R. (2005). Does being the auditor impair independence? *CPA Journal, LXXV*(6), 12.

International Auditing and Assurance Standards Board (IAASB). (2009a). International Standard on Quality Control (ISQC) 1: *Quality Controls for Firms that Perform Audits and Reviews of Financial Statements, and Other Assurance and Related Services Engagements*. New York: International Federation of Accountants.

International Auditing and Assurance Standards Board (IAASB). (2009b). International Standard on Auditing (ISA) 200: *Overall Objectives of the Independent Auditor and the Conduct of an Audit in Accordance with International Standards on Auditing*. New York: International Federation of Accountants.

International Auditing and Assurance Standards Board (IAASB). (2009c). International Standard on Auditing (ISA) 220: *Quality Control for an Audit of Financial Statements*. New York: International Federation of Accountants.

International Auditing and Assurance Standards Board (IAASB). (2009d). International Standard on Auditing (ISA) 240: *The Auditor's Responsibilities Relating to Fraud in an Audit of Financial Statements*. New York: International Federation of Accountants.

International Auditing and Assurance Standards Board (IAASB). (2009e). International Standard on Auditing (ISA) 260: *Communication with Those Charged with Governance*. New York: International Federation of Accountants.

International Auditing and Assurance Standards Board (IAASB). (2009f). International Standard on Auditing (ISA) 320: *Materiality in Planning and Performing an Audit*. New York: International Federation of Accountants.

International Auditing and Assurance Standards Board (IAASB). (2009g). International Standard on Auditing (ISA) 500: *Audit Evidence*. New York: International Federation of Accountants.

International Auditing and Assurance Standards Board (IAASB). (2009h). International Standard on Auditing (ISA) 700: *Forming an Opinion and Reporting on Financial Statements*. New York: International Federation of Accountants.

International Accounting Education Standards Board (IAESB). (2006). International Education Standard (IES) 8: *Competence Requirements for Audit Professionals*. New York: International Federation of Accountants.

International Accounting Standards Board (IASB). (2011). International Accounting Standard (IAS) 17: *Leases*. London: International Financial Reporting Standards Foundation.

International Ethics Standards Board for Accountants (IESBA). (2009). *Code of Ethics for Professional Accountants (IESBA Code)*. New York: International Federation of Accountants.

International Federation of Accountants (IFAC). (2009). *Glossary of Terms,* included in *Handbook of International Quality Control, Auditing, Review, Other Assurance and Related Services Pronouncements: 2010 edition*. New York: IFAC.

International Federation of Accountants (IFAC). (2010). *Handbook of the Code of Ethics for Professional Accountants*. New York: IFAC.

Levitt, A. (2000, 18 September). *A Profession at the Crossroads*. Speech by SEC Chairman to National Association of State Boards of Accountancy, Boston.

Mautz, R.K., & Sharaf, H.A. (1961). *The Philosophy of Auditing*. New York: AAA.

Statutory Instrument (SI). (2008). No. 489: *The Companies (Disclosure of Auditor Remuneration and Liability Limitation Agreements) Regulations 2008*.

Statutory Instrument (SI). (2011). No. 2198: *The Companies (Disclosure of Auditor Remuneration and Liability Limitation Agreements) Regulations 2011*.

Stewart, R.E. (1977). Independence: The auditor's cornerstone. *Accountants' Journal*, 56(9), 333–337.

Turner, L.E. (2001, 28 June). *Independence: A Covenant for the Ages*. Speech by SEC Chief Accountant to International Organization of Securities Commissions, Stockholm.

ADDITIONAL READING

Cianci, A.M., & Bierstaker, J.L. (2009). The impact of positive and negative mood on the hypothesis generation and ethical judgement of auditors. *Auditing: A Journal of Practice & Theory*, 28(2), 119–144.

Dennis, I. (2010). Clarity' begins at home: An examination of the conceptual underpinnings of the IAASB's clarity project. *International Journal of Auditing*, 14(3), 294–319.

Fédération des Experts Comptables Européens (FEE). (2007). *Selected Issues Relating to Financial Statement Audits: Inherent Limitations, Reasonable Assurance, Professional Judgement and its Documentation and Enforceability of Auditing Standards.* Brussels: FEE.

Feldmann, D.A., & Read, W.J. (2010). Auditor conservatism after Enron, *Auditing: A Journal of Practice & Theory*, 29(1), 267–278.

Hayward, J. (2003). *Thinking not Ticking: Bringing Competition to the Public Interest Audit.* London: Centre for the Study of Financial Innovation (CSFI).

Hurtt, R.K. (2010). Development of a scale to measure professional scepticism. *Auditing: A Journal of Practice & Theory*, 29(1), 149–171.

Iselin, E.R., & Iskandar, T.M. (2000). Auditors' recognition and disclosure materiality thresholds: Their magnitude and the effects of industry. *British Accounting Review*, 32, 289–309.

Nelson, M.W. (2009). A model and literature review of professional skepticism in auditing. *Auditing: A Journal of Practice & Theory* 28(2), 1–34.

O'Sullivan, H. (2007). A question of ethics. *Accountancy*, 140(1372), 86–87.

Peytcheva, M., & Gillett, P.R. (2011). How partners' views influence auditor judgment. *Auditing: A Journal of Practice & Theory*, 30(4), 285–301.

Shafer, W.E. (2009). Ethical climate, organizational-professional conflict and organizational commitment: A study of Chinese auditors. *Accounting, Auditing & Accountability Journal*, 22(7), 1087–1110.

Velayutham, S. (2003). The accounting profession's code of ethics: Is it a code of ethics or a code of quality assurance? *Critical Perspectives on Accounting*, 14(4), 483–503.

4 Threats to, and Safeguarding of, Auditors' Independence

LEARNING OBJECTIVES

After studying the material in this chapter you should be able to:

- explain the importance of auditors being independent of mind and independent in appearance;
- describe the circumstances in which auditors' independence may appear to be compromised;
- discuss measures introduced by legislation and regulation which are designed to ensure that auditors are independent;
- distinguish between two forms of auditor rotation;
- discuss the effectiveness of each form of auditor rotation as a means of strengthening auditors' independence;
- outline arguments for and against auditors being appointed by (i) a State agency and (ii) a shareholder or stakeholder panel as means of strengthening their independence;
- explain the importance and principal responsibilities of audit committees with particular reference to auditors' independence.

4.1 INTRODUCTION

The fundamental principle of external auditing – *Objectivity and independence*[1], explains:

> Auditors are objective and provide impartial opinions unaffected by bias, prejudice, compromise and conflicts of interest. Auditors are also independent, this requires them to be free from situations and relationships which would make it probable that a reasonable and informed third party would conclude that the auditors' objectivity either is impaired or could be impaired. [Financial Reporting Council (FRC), 2013a, Appendix 2][2]

If auditors are not, and are not perceived by financial statement users to be, objective and impartial when they conduct their audits and express their opinion on the audited financial statements, their opinion will lack credibility. As a result, audits will have little or no value.

---

[1] The fundamental principles of external auditing constitute *The Auditors' Code* which is reproduced on the inside of the front cover of this book.

[2] As noted in Chapter 3 (section 3.3.1b), the two forms of independence required of auditors were, until recently, referred to as 'independence of mind' and 'independence in appearance'. The International Ethics Standards Board for Accountants continues to use these two terms but the UK's APB has adopted the terms 'objectivity' for 'independence of mind' and 'independence' for 'independence in appearance'.

The critical importance to the audit function of auditors maintaining their independence may seem obvious. However, as Enron, WorldCom, Tyco and similar debacles in the early years of the twenty-first century bear witness, auditors' independence may be compromised all too readily. Although the subsequent court cases revealed that the unexpected corporate failures resulted from a number of factors, lack of independence was highlighted as a key reason for the auditors concerned not providing warning of falsified financial statements and impending financial disaster.

Cognisant of the importance of investors having confidence in the integrity of the audit function to the smooth functioning of capital markets, governments in the United Kingdom (UK), the United States of America (USA) and elsewhere have enacted legislative provisions to ensure that auditors are independent of their audit clients. Regulatory and professional bodies such as the Auditing Practices Board (APB) and the International Ethics Standards Board for Accountants (IESBA)[3] have also promulgated standards or other 'rules' with the same objective.

In this chapter we examine factors that might cause auditors' independence to be compromised (that is, 'threats' to their independence) and steps taken, or proposed, to mitigate those threats and to strengthen their independence.

4.2 THREATS TO AUDITORS' INDEPENDENCE

For many years, politicians (such as Congressman Dingell in the USA and Austin Mitchell, Member of Parliament in the UK), regulators [such as the Department of Trade and Industry (DTI)[4] in the UK and the Securities and Exchange Commission (SEC) in the USA] and various commentators (such as Briloff, 1986; Mitchell & Sikka, 1993; Jeppesen, 1998) have raised questions about auditors' ability to remain independent of their audit clients. They observe that, although under the provisions of the Companies Act 2006, s. 489, auditors are appointed by the company's shareholders, in practice, auditors are hired, fired and paid by their clients' managements;[5,6] they work closely with their clients' managements as they conduct their audits and, after a

---

[3] The IESBA is an independent standard-setting body established by, and operating under the auspices of, the International Federation of Accountants (IFAC) (IFAC, 2010).

[4] In 2007 the DTI was replaced by the Department for Business, Enterprise and Regulatory Reform (DBERR); in 2009 the latter was replaced by the Department for Business, Innovation & Skills (BIS).

[5] Readers are reminded that in this book we use the term 'management' to mean a company's executive directors, non-executive directors and non-director executives (that is, all executives and directors).

[6] The statutory provisions relating to the appointment, remuneration and resignation of auditors in the UK are explained in Chapter 5, section 5.3.

number of years of acting as auditor for a client, they become very familiar with the client and its management. Additionally, as we note in Chapter 2, from the 1960s until the turn of the century, auditors frequently (and increasingly) provided non-audit, as well as audit, services to their clients. They often still provide such services but, particularly in the USA since enactment in 2002 of the Sarbanes-Oxley Act, to a far more limited extent than formerly.

During the 1990s, the SEC, in particular, grew very concerned about the possible impairment of auditors' independence as a consequence of auditors providing non-audit services to their audit clients. In its Proposed Rule on Auditor Independence (SEC, 2000a), the SEC noted:

> We have become increasingly concerned that the dramatic increase in the nature, number, and monetary value of non-audit services that accounting firms provide to audit clients may affect their independence. (p. 3)

It reported that, in 1999, the Big Five audit firms[7] earned revenues from non-audit services of more than $15 billion in the USA alone and, between 1993 and 1999, the average annual growth rate in revenues from these services was 26 per cent, compared with nine per cent for audit, and 13 per cent for tax, services (SEC, 2000a, p. 9). Levitt (2000), former Chairman of the SEC, also observed:

> [A]uditors who also provide consulting services for their audit clients must now serve two masters: a public obligation to shareholders, and a professional duty to management. And when the *two* come into conflict, the independent audit – dwarfed by the more lucrative consulting businesses – too often may be compromised. (p. 2, emphasis in original)

Given the story of Enron's demise – and the extent of the non-audit services provided to the company by its auditor, Arthur Andersen – it seems that the SEC's and Levitt's fears were not unfounded.[8]

---

[7] Arthur Andersen, Deloitte & Touche, Ernst & Young, KPMG, PricewaterhouseCoopers.

[8] In 2000, Enron paid Andersen $25 million for the audit of its financial statements and a further $27 million for non-audit services (Hirsch, 2002). Not only was the fee for non-audit work exceptionally high, so too was the audit fee. As Hirsch (2002, p. 1) reported:

> The average charge [audit fee] among the blue chips was just $9 million . . . [Enron's audit fee] was also large compared with the fees other energy companies paid their accountants, even Andersen. In a review of fees listed in Securities and Exchange Commission filings, The Times found that audit contracts averaged $3 million at nine large energy companies, including Andersen clients Mirant Corp., UtiliCorp United Inc., Dynegy Inc. and Calpine Corp. Andersen's fee was a red flag to some experts and critics who say it could have clouded the company's judgment as it examined Enron's tangled financial structure. . . . Indeed, Andersen executives debated internally whether the audit and other fees would be perceived as a breach of the firm's independence.

However, the extent of the provision of non-audit services to Enron was not the only problematic element of Andersen maintaining its independence from this audit client. Enron Watchdog (2002, p. 2) observed that Andersen's audit and other accounting staff

> had permanent offices in Enron's building. Its staff wore Enron golf shirts, attended Enron parties and ski trips and generally were difficult to tell from Enron staff. Enron's Chief Accounting Officer and Chief Financial Officer were both Andersen alums (i.e., former Andersen partners).

Squires, Smith, McDougall and Yeack (2003) further noted that Duncan (Andersen's engagement partner for the Enron audit) and Causey (Enron's Chief Financial Officer) "were virtually inseparable. They worked together, went to lunch together, and played golf together. Their families even went on vacations together" (p. 2).

The provision of non-audit services by auditors to their audit clients is clearly a circumstance which may result in impairment of auditors' independence. A useful way to examine such circumstances, and to assess their likely impact on auditors' independence, is to consider different types of threats to auditors' independence which may be present. The APB, in Ethical Standard (ES) 1: *Integrity, Objectivity and Independence* (APB, 2011a, para 35), identifies the following six types of threats.

(i) *Self-interest threat* – this arises when the auditor (or another person in a position to influence the conduct or outcome of the audit[9]) has a financial, business, personal or other interest in the client (or with a director, senior executive or major shareholder of the client) which might cause the auditor not to act in the best interests of users of the auditee's financial statements, the audit firm or the public. This threat may arise, for example, if the auditor:
   • has some financial involvement with the client as a shareholder, debtholder or creditor;[10]
   • has a close family or personal relationship with a director or senior executive of the client;[11]
   • receives favourable treatment from the client in the form of goods, services or hospitality;[12]
   • depends on the client for a substantial portion of total fee income; this may be derived from the provision of non-audit as well as audit services.[13]

(ii) *Self-review threat* – this arises when the auditor (or other members of the audit firm) provides non-audit services to the audit client and

---

[9] This includes anyone who is directly involved in the audit engagement – all members of the audit engagement team, other professional personnel who assist with the audit (for example, actuaries, lawyers, and IT, tax and treasury management specialists) and those responsible for the quality control of the audit (ES1, para 17).

[10] An example of such involvement is provided by KPMG in the USA. An SEC (2002) Press Release reported that it had:

> censured KPMG . . . for engaging in improper professional conduct because it purported to serve as an independent accounting firm for an audit client at the same time that it had made substantial financial investments in the client. . . . [F]rom May through December 2000, KPMG held a substantial investment in the Short-Term Investment Trust ("STIT"), a money market fund. . . . KPMG opened the money market account with an initial deposit of $25 million on May 5, 2000, and at one point the account balance constituted approximately 15% of the fund's net assets. . . . [T]he SEC found that KPMG audited the financial statements of STIT at a time when the firm's independence was impaired, and that STIT included KPMG's audit report in 16 separate filings it made with the SEC on November 9, 2000. (p. 1)

[11] As illustrated by the relationship between Duncan (Andersen's audit engagement partner) and Causey (Enron's Chief Financial Officer) (see footnote 8).

[12] For example, when arriving to conduct the audit of a ski company client just before the start of the skiing season, one of the authors was offered (and declined!) a free ski pass for the entire season.

[13] In 2000, Enron's audit fee accounted for 27 per cent of the audit fees earned from the audits of public company clients by Arthur Andersen's Houston Office (Healy & Palepu, 2003).

those services impact the client's accounting system, accounting records and/or the amounts or disclosures in its financial statements. By providing such services, the audit firm is associated with aspects of the preparation of the financial statements. When conducting a subsequent audit, the auditor may be (or may appear to be) unable to maintain an objective and impartial attitude when reviewing these aspects of the financial statements.

(iii) *Management threat* – this arises when the auditor, a member of the audit team or others in the audit firm make judgments or decisions which should be those of the client's management. For example:
  - the audit firm might be engaged to design, select and/or implement a new information technology system for the client. In undertaking such work, members of the audit firm may become closely aligned with the interests of management. As a consequence, when performing the audit for this client, the auditor may not (or may be perceived as unlikely to) maintain his/her objectivity and impartiality;
  - the auditor may offer advice to the auditee's management on matters such as improvements in the company's system of internal control or in its financial planning. In so doing, the auditor may cross the line between giving advice to, and making decisions for, management.

A management threat also arises if the auditor (or a member of the audit team) participates in the affairs of a client other than as auditor – for example, as a director of, or consultant to, the client. In such circumstances, the auditor (or audit team member) would be (or would appear to be) too closely aligned with management and its decision-making to remain objective and impartial.

(iv) *Advocacy threat* – this arises when the auditor (or the audit firm) acts as an advocate for the audit client (or its management) in an adversarial context. The auditor (or audit firm) may, for example, act as an advocate for (or supporter of) the client in legal proceedings brought against it by the tax authorities. By acting as an advocate, the auditor (or firm) is too closely aligned with management's interests for the auditor's independence (of mind and in appearance) not to be put under threat. Along similar lines, if the auditor (or audit firm) is embroiled in litigation against the client (for example, to recover unpaid audit fees), it is unlikely that the auditor will be (or will appear to be) objective and impartial when conducting the audit.

(v) *Familiarity (or trust) threat* – this arises when the auditor is too ready to accept, or is insufficiently sceptical about, information and/or documents and records provided by the audit client and its personnel. This may occur, for example, if the auditor (or audit firm) has had a long association with the audit client and, as a result, a close personal relationship has developed and/or, based on past audits when nothing untoward has been encountered, the auditor becomes too trusting and makes unjustified assumptions that 'all is well' instead of exercising an appropriate degree of scepticism.

(vi) *Intimidation threat* – this arises when the auditor's conduct is influenced by fear or threats from the client (an aggressive and dominating director or senior executive) or some other influential party. This may occur, for example, if the auditor challenges some significant aspect(s) of the client's financial statements and an influential director or senior executive threatens to ensure the auditor is replaced as the company's auditor.

Although identification of these six threats to auditors' independence provides a useful tool for analysing circumstances which may result in impairment of their independence, it should be recognised that some circumstances may give rise to more than one type of threat. For example, if a significant proportion of a firm's fee income is derived from a particular audit client, and the client's Managing Director is aggressive and dominating, this may give rise to a self-interest and an intimidation threat. Similarly, the provision of non-audit services to an audit client may generate a self-interest, a self-review and a management threat.

In its *Code of Ethics for Professional Accountants* (*IESBA Code*; 2009, para 100.12), the IESBA recognises five of the six threats to auditors' independence identified by the APB, namely, the self-interest, self-review, advocacy, familiarity or trust, and intimidation threats.[14] However, although the essence of the 'threats' is the same as those in the APB's ES1, the IESBA sets them in a broader context: they are signalled as threats, not just to auditors' independence but to professional accountants' compliance with the five fundamental principles of professional ethics – integrity, objectivity, professional competence and due care, confidentiality, and professional behaviour.[15]

4.3 STEPS TAKEN BY PARLIAMENT AND REGULATORS TO SAFEGUARD AUDITORS' INDEPENDENCE

4.3.1 Overview of measures introduced by Parliament and regulators

From the above, it is evident that a wide range of circumstances may cause auditors' independence to be impaired. However, Parliament and regulators

---

[14] Unlike the APB, the IESBA does not recognise management threat as a separate threat.

[15] These five fundamental principles of professional ethics for professional accountants are discussed in Chapter 3, sections 3.3.1 to 3.3.3.

(such as the FRC) have established measures designed to ensure that auditors are, and remain, independent of their clients. For example, the Companies Act (CA) 2006, s. 1214, stipulates that a person may not be the auditor of a company if that person is:

(i) an officer or employee of the company, or of a parent or subsidiary undertaking of the company, or of another subsidiary of the parent undertaking; or

(ii) a partner or employee of such a person as in (i) above, or a partnership in which such a person is a partner.

These provisions are designed to ensure that the auditor is not exposed to a conflict of interest as a result of having a direct or indirect relationship with the auditee company in a capacity other than that of auditor.

CA 2006 (s. 1212) also specifies that, in order to be eligible for appointment as a company auditor, an individual or firm must be a member of a Recognised Supervisory Body (RSB)[16] and eligible for appointment under the rules of that body. To qualify as such, an RSB must, *inter alia*, have rules and practices designed to ensure that all of its member auditors:

- conduct their audit work properly and with integrity;
- are not appointed as a company's auditor in circumstances where they have an interest which is likely to conflict with the proper conduct of the audit;
- take steps to safeguard their independence from any significant threats (CA 2006, Schedule 10, para 9).

These provisions are designed to ensure that auditors maintain their integrity and independence when conducting their audits.

In addition to the above measure, CA 2006 (s. 494) empowers the Secretary of State to make regulations which require companies to disclose the remuneration paid to their auditors. In accordance with these powers, *The Companies (Disclosure of Auditor Remuneration and Liability Limitation Agreements) Regulations 2008* [Statutory Instrument (SI), 2008] as amended by SI 2011,[17]

---

[16] There are, in effect, four RSBs of which UK company auditors may be members, namely, the Institutes of Chartered Accountants in England and Wales (ICAEW), of Scotland (ICAS), and in Ireland (ICAI), and the Association of Chartered Certified Accountants (ACCA). The requirements relating to (i) eligibility for appointment as company auditors and (ii) the RSBs are discussed in Chapter 5, section 5.3.1.

[17] Regulations requiring disclosure of auditors' remuneration were originally made by the Secretary of State in accordance with powers conferred on him by CA 1985, s. 390B, as amended by the Companies (Audit, Investigations and Community Enterprise) Act 2004, s. 7. These regulations, entitled *The Companies (Disclosure of Auditor Remuneration) Regulations 2005* (SI 2005), came into force on 1 October 2005. CA 1985, s. 390B (as amended) was incorporated in CA 2006, s. 494, and new regulations were promulgated in February 2008 in *The Companies (Disclosure of Auditor Remuneration and Liability Limitation Agreements) Regulations 2008* (SI 2008). These came into force on 6 April 2008. *The Companies (Disclosure of Auditor Remuneration and Liability Limitation Agreements) (Amendment) Regulations 2011* (SI 2011), which amended SI 2008, came into force on 1 October 2011. The key change was to substitute Schedule 2A in place of Schedule 2 (i.e., it updated the services, and associated remuneration, provided to audit clients by auditors which are required to be disclosed).

have been promulgated. These require all but small and medium sized companies (i.e., all companies which do not meet at least two of the following criteria: turnover of not more than £25.9 million, balance sheet total of not more than £12.9 million, and not more than 250 employees: CA 2006, s. 465) to disclose in the notes to their audited financial statements the amount receivable by the auditor (and any associates of the auditor) for:

(i) the audit of the company's financial statements, and

(ii) all other services provided to the company, its subsidiaries and its associated pension funds.[18]

In respect of the 'other services', each type of service specified in Schedule 2A to the 2011 Regulations, together with the associated remuneration,[19] must be disclosed separately. These services are as follows:

1. The auditing of accounts of any associate of the company.
2. Audit-related assurance services.
3. Taxation compliance services.
4. All taxation advisory services not falling within paragraph 3.
5. Internal audit services.
6. All assurance services not falling within paragraphs 1 to 5.
7. All services relating to corporate finance transactions entered into, or proposed to be entered into, by or on behalf of the company and any of its associates not falling within paragraphs 1 to 6.
8. All non-audit services not falling within paragraphs 2 to 7.

Services to the company and its subsidiaries on the one hand, and to associated pension schemes on the other, must be disclosed separately (SI 2008; Reg. 5).[20] These disclosure requirements ensure that financial statement users are provided with information which enables them to assess the likelihood of the auditor's independence being compromised through too great an involvement with the audit client through the provision of non-audit services.

Notwithstanding the importance of the measures outlined above, probably the most significant and far-reaching steps the UK Government has taken which impact auditors' independence involve a change in the status and responsibilities of the APB and FRC. Following the Enron, WorldCom and similar debacles, and enactment of the Sarbanes-Oxley Act of 2002 (SOX) in the USA,

---

[18] Small and medium-sized companies (those that meet at least two of the criteria indicated above) are only required to disclose in the notes to their financial statements the remuneration receivable by the auditor for the audit of the company's financial statements (Reg. 4).

[19] 'Remuneration' is defined to include: "payments in respect of expenses and benefits in kind" (Reg. 3). Reg. 5 explains that: "where the remuneration includes benefits in kind, the nature and estimated money-value of those benefits must also be disclosed in a note [to the financial statements]."

[20] Individual companies within a group need not make these disclosures providing the group financial statements disclose the information for the group as a whole (SI 2008; Reg. 6).

the UK Government sought to enhance the regulation of auditors in the UK. To this end, in January 2003, it determined that the APB (which was then a professional body responsible for setting auditing standards) should also be responsible for setting standards governing the independence, objectivity and integrity of auditors. Additionally, in April 2004, the Government extended the responsibilities of the FRC; it appointed the FRC as "the United Kingdom's independent regulator for corporate reporting and governance in the UK" (FRC, 2004, p. 1). It was made responsible for, among other things, setting, monitoring and enforcing auditing standards and oversight and regulation of auditors (p. 2). To assist it discharge its responsibilities, the APB was transferred to the FRC to become one of its 'operating bodies'.[21]

As noted in Chapter 3 (section 3.3.3), the APB has issued five Ethical Standards (ES1 to ES5) and, in developing these standards, it sought to ensure they adhere to the principles of the *IESBA Code* (IESBA, 2009). Like the IESBA, the APB adopted a conceptual framework approach to secure compliance with its ethical principles. This requires auditors to:

- identify circumstances that may threaten their objectivity and independence;
- evaluate those threats to determine whether they are at an acceptable level;[22]
- if the threats are not at an acceptable level, to determine whether safeguards are available that can be applied to eliminate the threats or reduce them to an acceptable level.

ES1 to ES5 detail 'safeguards' – measures (similar in nature to rules) that are able to eliminate threats to auditors' independence or reduce them to an acceptable level. The safeguards are of two types, namely, those that relate to:

- the audit environment and audit engagements;
- specific situations where auditors' independence may be at risk.

---

[21] As may be seen from the diagrammatic presentation of the former and current structure of the FRC presented in the front of this book (p. xix), until 2012, the FRC had six operating bodies: the Accounting Standards Boards, APB, Board for Actuarial Standards, Professional Oversight Board (POB), Financial Reporting Review Panel and Accountancy and Actuarial Disciplinary Board (AADB). Since July 2012, the FRC Board has been supported by three committees – Codes and Standards Committee, Conduct Committee and Executive Committee. The former Accounting Standards Board (renamed Accounting Council), APB (renamed Audit and Assurance Council) and Board of Actuarial Standards (renamed Actuarial Council) are advisory committees of the Codes and Standards Committee. Along similar lines, the POB (now part of the Monitoring Committee) and the AADB (now part of the Case Management Committee) are advisory committees of the Conduct Committee (FRC, 2012b).

[22] An 'acceptable level' in this context is "a level at which it is not probable that a reasonable and informed third party would conclude that the auditor's objectivity is impaired or is likely to be impaired" (ES1, APB 2011a, para 30).

4.3.2   Safeguards relating to the audit environment and audit engagements

ES1: *Integrity, Objectivity and Independence* (APB, 2011a) sets out requirements that seek to ensure the audit environment is conducive to auditors
maintaining their independence. In some cases responsibility is assigned to the
audit firm; in others to the audit engagement partner.[23]

(a)   Audit firm responsibilities

Audit firms are required to establish, document and communicate to members of their firm, policies and procedures designed to ensure, for each audit
engagement, that the audit firm and all those in a position to influence the
conduct and outcome of the audit:[24]
  – act with objectivity and independence,
  – are constantly alert to circumstances that might reasonably be considered
    to be threats to their objectivity or independence, and
  – where such circumstances are identified, report them to the audit engage-
    ment partner or ethics partner, as appropriate (ES1, paras 16, 31).
The ethics partner is a senior and experienced partner in the audit firm who is
responsible for:
  – the adequacy of the firm's policies and procedures relating to objectivity
    and independence, the firm's compliance with the APB's Ethical Stand-
    ards, and the effectiveness of the firm's communications to partners and
    staff on ethical issues;
  – providing guidance to individual partners with a view to ensuring that
    members of the firm adopt a consistent approach to applying the Ethical
    Standards (ES1, para 22).

Audit firms are also required to promote a strong control environment within
the firm that places adherence to ethical principles and compliance with the
Ethical Standards above commercial considerations. More particularly, they
are required to establish policies and procedures that include:
  – requiring audit partners and staff to report matters that affect their objec-
    tivity or independence in respect of any particular audit client. (This
    includes reporting past, present or planned personal, family, financial or
    employment relationships with the client, its directors or its senior
    executives);
  – monitoring compliance with the firm's independence policies and
    procedures;

---

[23] The audit engagement partner is the partner who is responsible for the particular audit engagement and
who signs the audit report on behalf of the firm. CA 2006 uses the term 'statutory auditor' in place of
audit engagement partner.

[24] See footnote 9.

- requiring prompt communication of possible or actual breaches of the firm's independence policies and procedures to the relevant audit engagement partner;
- requiring audit engagement partners to evaluate the implications of possible or actual breaches of the firm's policies and procedures that are reported to them;
- empowering and encouraging staff members to communicate to senior levels within the firm any issue which concerns them relating to objectivity or independence (ES1, paras 19, 21).

(b) Engagement partner responsibilities

Audit engagement partners (rather than the audit firm) are responsible for, *inter alia*, identifying and assessing the significance of threats (individually and cumulatively) to the audit firm's, their own, or members of the audit engagement team's objectivity and independence, especially when:

- considering whether to accept or retain an audit engagement;
- planning the audit;
- forming an opinion on the financial statements;
- considering whether to accept an invitation to provide non-audit services to the audit client;
- potential threats to independence are reported to them.

When identifying and assessing the significance of threats to objectivity or independence, an engagement partner is to consider the firm's, and members of the audit engagement team's, current, past and likely future relationships with the audit client (including the provision of non-audit services) (ES1, paras 38, 40).

Having identified threats to the independence of the audit engagement, the audit engagement partner is required to identify and assess the effectiveness of available safeguards, and to apply sufficient safeguards to eliminate the identified threat(s) or reduce them to an acceptable level. If the threats cannot be reduced to this level, the engagement partner is not to accept, or continue with, the engagement (as applicable). Additionally, at the end of the audit, when forming an opinion on the financial statements but before issuing the audit report, the engagement partner is to review the objectivity and independence of the audit engagement and be able to conclude that any threats to objectivity and independence have been properly addressed. If the engagement partner cannot reach such a conclusion, s/he is not to issue the audit report and the audit firm is to resign from the engagement (ES1, paras 43, 49, 54).

A further responsibility of the audit engagement partner is that of ensuring the company's directors (or more usually, its audit committee) are appropriately informed, on a timely basis, of all significant matters relating to the audit

firm's and the audit engagement team's objectivity and independence. The matters to be communicated include:
- the principal threats (if any) to objectivity and independence of which the engagement partner is aware, including any relevant relationships between the audit firm or engagement team members on the one hand and the audit client, its affiliates[25] and its management on the other;
- any safeguards applied to mitigate the identified threats and the reasons why the audit engagement partner considers they are effective;
- the engagement partner's overall assessment of the identified threats and safeguards applied;
- information about the general policies and processes within the audit firm for maintaining objectivity and independence (ES1, paras 63, 65).

Audit engagement partners are additionally required to ensure that their consideration of the firm's, their own, and members of the audit engagement team's, objectivity and independence is appropriately documented on a timely basis. They are to document all of the key elements of the assessment process and any significant judgments concerning:
- the threats to objectivity and independence which have been identified and the process used to identify them;
- the safeguards adopted and the reasons why they are considered to be effective;
- the partner's overall assessment of the threats and safeguards;
- communication of the identified threats and related safeguards to the client's directors (or audit committee) (ES1, paras 64, 66).

For listed company clients, audit engagement partners have two additional responsibilities:
1. They must ensure that an engagement quality control reviewer:[26]
   • is appointed for the audit, and
   • is involved in ensuring the objectivity and independence of the audit engagement.

   More specifically, the quality control reviewer is to:

---

[25] An affiliate is an entity that has direct or indirect control over, or a material financial interest in, the auditee, an entity over which the auditee has direct or indirect control or in which it has a material financial interest, or an entity under common control with the auditee (APB, 2010a). It may be thought of as any other company within a group of companies – a parent, subsidiary or a 'sister' company.

[26] An 'engagement quality control reviewer' is:

A partner or other person in the firm or a suitably qualified external person, with sufficient and appropriate experience and authority to objectively evaluate, before the auditor's report is issued, the significant judgments which the engagement team has made and the conclusions reached in formulating the auditor's report. (APB, 2010a)

The role and responsibilities of an engagement quality control reviewer are discussed in detail in Chapter 16.

- consider the audit firm's compliance with the APB's Ethical Standards in relation to the audit engagement;
- form an independent opinion on the appropriateness and adequacy of any safeguards applied to mitigate identified threats to the objectivity and independence of the audit engagement;
- consider the adequacy of the documentation of the engagement partner's consideration of the objectivity and independence of the audit engagement (ES1, para 51).

2. They must disclose, in writing, to the company's audit committee:
- details of all relationships (including the provision of non-audit services) between the audit firm, associates of the audit firm, or members of the audit engagement team on the one hand and the client, its affiliates, its directors or senior executives on the other, which the engagement partner considers may have a bearing on the objectivity and independence of the audit engagement;
- any threats to independence and objectivity such relationships create and the related safeguards that have been applied;
- details of non-audit services provided by the audit firm and the fees charged in relation thereto;
- the total amount of fees the audit firm (and its related firms) have charged the client and its affiliates for the provision of services during the reporting period, grouped into appropriate categories; for example, statutory audit services for (i) the company and (ii) any subsidiaries, tax compliance services, tax advisory services, services related to corporate finance transactions, and other non-audit services;
- a statement that the audit firm and all those involved in the audit have complied with the APB's Ethical Standards and that, in the engagement partner's opinion, they are independent and their objectivity has not been impaired (ES1, paras 67–71).

4.3.3 Safeguards relating to specific situations where independence may be at risk

While ES1 sets out measures designed to ensure the audit environment is conducive to auditors maintaining their independence, ES2 to ES5 address specific circumstances that may create threats to auditors' independence and provide safeguards to eliminate such threats or reduce them to an acceptable level.

The specific circumstances which may impair auditors' independence can be considered conveniently under the following headings:
(i)   financial involvement with an audit client;
(ii) business, employment or personal relationships with an audit client;

    (iii) undue dependence on an audit client for fee income;
    (iv) threatened or actual litigation;
    (v) gifts and hospitality from an audit client;
    (vi) long association with an audit client;
    (vii) provision of non-audit services to an audit client.
We discuss each of these circumstances below.

(i) Financial involvement with an audit client

Financial involvement with an audit client may arise through holding shares or debentures in, or granting a loan to or receiving a loan from, an audit client or one of its affiliates (such as a subsidiary or parent company within the same group), or through other direct or indirect financial interests in the client or its affiliates: this includes a financial interest arising through a trust or a pension scheme which has the audit client among its investments.

ES2: *Financial, Business, Employment and Personal Relationships* (APB, 2010a) provides a number of measures that seek to prevent auditors' independence from being compromised as a result of financial involvement with an audit client. These include the following:

1. Prohibiting audit firms, partners in audit firms, anyone in a position to influence the conduct and outcome of the audit, or an immediate family member[27] of such persons who is able to control the investment concerned, from holding in an audit client or its affiliates:
    (a) any direct financial interest;
    (b) any indirect financial interest (that is, a financial interest owned through an intermediary such as a pension scheme) if:
        – the investment is material to the audit firm, the owner of the financial interest or the intermediary; or
        – the financial interest owner has both the ability to influence the investment decisions of the intermediary and knowledge of the investment in the audit client (ES2, para 7).
    In such circumstances, no safeguards can eliminate the threat to auditors' independence or reduce it to an acceptable level. Thus, such financial interests in an audit client are prohibited (ES2, para 8).

    If a financial interest (similar to those outlined above) is acquired unintentionally (for example, through inheritance, a gift, or a merger of audit firms or companies), the interest is to be disposed of as soon as possible after the person becomes aware of it and has the right to dispose of it. Until the interest is disposed of, appropriate safeguards are to be applied.

---

[27] An 'immediate family member' is "a spouse (or equivalent) or dependent" (APB, 2010a).

If someone in a position to influence the conduct and outcome of the audit, or any partner in the audit firm, becomes aware that a close family member[28] holds a direct or indirect financial interest in an audit client, the individual concerned is to report the matter to the relevant audit engagement partner so that appropriate safeguards can be applied. If the family member is that of the audit engagement partner, or the audit engagement partner is unsure about the safeguards to be applied, s/he is to consult the firm's ethics partner about the action to be taken (ES2, paras 14, 15, 18).

2. Prohibiting all partners in audit firms, anyone in a position to influence the conduct and outcome of the audit, and any immediate family member thereof, from holding a direct or indirect financial interest in an audit client or its affiliates as a trustee unless all of the following conditions are met:
   – the person concerned is not an identified potential beneficiary of the trust;
   – the trust's financial interest in the audit client is not material to the trust;
   – the trust is not able to exercise significant influence over the audit client or any of its affiliates;
   – the person concerned cannot significantly influence the investment decisions of the trust which relate to the financial interest in the audit client.

If these conditions are not met, the trustee interest may influence the conduct of the audit or the trust may influence the actions of the audit client. In either case, a self-interest threat may impair the auditor's independence (ES2, para 19).

3. Prohibiting audit firms from having as an audit client any organisation in which the firm's pension scheme has a financial interest and the firm is able to influence the investment decisions of the pension scheme's trustees. In such a case, no safeguards can eliminate the self-interest threat to auditors' independence or reduce it to an acceptable level. However, where the relationship between the firm's pension scheme and the audit client is less direct (for example, where the pension fund is invested through a collective investment scheme and the firm's influence is limited to investment policy decisions, such as the allocation of the pension fund between – say – debt and equity investments), the firm's ethics partner is to determine whether the indirect investment in the audit client or its affiliates is acceptable having regard to the materiality of the financial interest in the client to the pension scheme (ES2, para 22).

---

[28] A 'close family member' is "a non-dependent parent, child or sibling" (APB, 2010a).

4. Prohibiting audit firms, anyone in a position to influence the conduct and outcome of the audit, and any immediate family member thereof, from:
   (a) making a loan to, or guaranteeing the borrowings of, an audit client or its affiliates, or
   (b) accepting a loan from, or having borrowings guaranteed by, an audit client or its affiliates,
   unless three conditions are met:
   (i) the audit client is a bank or similar deposit-taking institution,
   (ii) the loan or guarantee is made in the ordinary course of business on normal business terms, and
   (iii) the loan or guarantee is not material to either the audit client or the audit firm (ES2, paras 24–26).

(ii)   Business, employment and personal relationships with an audit client

A business relationship between an audit firm, persons in a position to influence the conduct and outcome of the audit or their immediate family members, on the one hand and the audit client, its affiliates, or its management, on the other, may, like financial involvement, impair auditors' independence. Ernst & Young's profit-sharing agreement with the travel unit of its audit client, American Express Company, in the 1990s affords an example of such an interest. During 2004, the SEC investigated this apparent breach of auditor independence and, as a result, in November 2004, American Express appointed PricewaterhouseCoopers as its auditor in place of Ernst & Young (a position Ernst & Young, and its predecessor firm Arthur Young, had held since 1975) (Raiborn, Schorg & Massoud, 2006). Other examples of business relationships with audit clients include arrangements whereby:
   (i) an audit firm combines its products or services with those of an audit client and the 'package' is marketed on behalf of both parties;
   (ii) the audit firm or the audit client acts as a distributor or marketer of the products or services of the other;
   (iii) an audit firm leases office space from (or to) an audit client (ES2, para 28).

To counter the self-interest, advocacy or intimidation threat to auditors' independence that may arise from such arrangements, ES2 prohibits audit firms, and persons in a position to influence the conduct and outcome of the audit and their immediate family members, from entering into a business relationship with an audit client or its affiliates. An exception to this is the purchase of goods and services from the audit firm or the audit client (as applicable) in the ordinary course of business on an arm's length basis where the value involved is clearly inconsequential to both parties (ES2, para 29).

Like business relationships, family, personal and employment relationships between audit firm members and the audit client (or the audit firm and audit client members) can endanger auditors' independence through, in particular, self-interest, self-review, familiarity and intimidation threats. Pertinent examples include the infamous personal and employment relationships between Arthur Andersen's audit staff, partners, and former partners, and its audit client, Enron, cited in section 4.2 above (see footnote 8); and the 'personal-service' agreement between an independent director of Best Buy Company in the USA and the company's auditor, Ernst & Young. The latter relationship resulted in the company replacing Ernst & Young (Best Buy's auditor since 1994) with Deloitte & Touche in December 2004 (Raiborn *et al*, 2006).

In order to eliminate, or reduce to an acceptable level, threats to auditors' independence resulting from family, personal and employment relationships, ES2 provides safeguards which include the following:

1. Requiring audit firms to establish policies and procedures that ensure:
   (a) the firm is notified of potential employment:
      – by any partner within the firm with any of the firm's audit clients;
      – by any member of the audit engagement team which is assigned to the client concerned;
   (b) where such notice is given, the person concerned is to be excluded from the relevant audit engagement team and their work on the current and, if appropriate, the most recent, audit is to be reviewed;
   (c) any partner or professional staff member in the audit firm who has an immediate or close family member in, or other personal relationships with, an audit client, which the partner or staff member considers might create a threat to the auditor's independence, is to report this fact to the audit firm;
   (d) relevant audit engagement partners are notified promptly of any such reported relationships. The audit engagement partner is to assess the resulting threat(s) to independence and apply appropriate safeguards to eliminate or reduce the threat(s) to an acceptable level. If the partner is unsure of the appropriate action s/he is to consult the firm's ethics partner (paras 45, 63, 64).

2. Requiring audit firms to take prompt action (before any further audit work is performed for the client) if a former partner of the firm joins an audit client to ensure that no significant connections remain between the firm and the individual. If the former partner joins the client as a director or senior executive and, at any time during the previous two years the partner played a significant role in that client's audit (for example, as the engagement partner or quality control reviewer), the firm is to resign as auditor and not accept re-appointment for a period of two years following the former partner's involvement with the client's audit or, if sooner, until the person concerned ceases to be employed by the client (paras 43, 49).

3. Requiring audit firms to ensure that, if a former director or employee of an audit client, who was in a position to exert significant influence over the preparation of the financial statements, joins the audit firm, the person concerned is not assigned to a position where they are able to influence the conduct and outcome of the audit for that client or its affiliates for a period of at least two years after leaving the client (para 58).

4. Limiting the circumstances in which an audit firm may agree to a partner or employee of the firm working temporarily for an audit client or one of its affiliates. Audit firms can only enter into such arrangements if the client agrees:
   - the arrangement is only for a short period of time;
   - the individual concerned will not hold a management position or be involved in performing non-audit services that would not be permitted under ES5 (we discuss these later in this chapter);
   - the client is responsible for directing and supervising the work the individual is to perform;
   - the work performed will not involve the individual in making management decisions or exercising discretionary authority which commits the client to a particular accounting treatment.

   Upon returning to the audit firm, the individual concerned is not to be given a role in the audit of the client that involves any work undertaken for the client (paras 38, 41).

5. Prohibiting partners and employees of the audit firm from accepting appointment as a director of:
   (i) any entity for which the partner or employee undertakes audit work;
   (ii) any entity which holds more than 20 per cent of the voting rights in an audit client for which the partner or employee undertakes audit work, or in which the audit client holds more than 20 per cent of the voting rights.

   If an immediate or close family member of anyone in a position to influence the conduct and outcome of an audit holds a directorship in such an entity, the person concerned is to be removed from a position in which they can influence the conduct or outcome of the audit. In other cases where a partner or employee of the audit firm has an immediate or close family member who is director of such an entity, they are to inform the relevant audit engagement partner. The engagement partner is to determine whether the circumstance is likely to compromise the firm's independence and, if so, to consult the firm's ethics partner regarding appropriate safeguards. If such safeguards are not available, the firm is to withdraw from the audit engagement (paras 54–56).

(iii) Undue dependence on an audit client for fee income

As in circumstances where the audit firm or a member of the audit team has a financial, personal or business relationship with an audit client, a self-interest threat to auditors' objectivity and independence arises if the audit firm is economically dependent on an audit client. In this situation, the audit engagement partner may be unwilling to express a modified opinion on the financial statements (where such is appropriate) for fear of losing the entity as a client. ES4: *Fees, Remuneration and Evaluation Policies, Litigation, Gifts and Hospitality* (APB, 2010b) deems an audit firm to be economically dependent on a client if the total fees derived from that client and its subsidiaries (for audit and non-audit services) represent 10 per cent of the audit firm's total annual fee income if it is a listed client, or 15 per cent if it is a non-listed client (para 37). An example where this limit was exceeded is provided by the UK firm of Jasini & Co. In 2011 it conducted audits for a non-listed company client which represented 25 per cent of its annual fee income (Reed, 2011).

As a safeguard against this threat to independence, ES4 prohibits audit firms from acting as the auditor for a client if they expect the total fees for audit and non-audit services from that client and its subsidiaries to regularly exceed 10 per cent of the firm's annual fee income if it is a listed client, or 15 per cent if a non-listed client.[29] If necessary, the firm is to resign from the audit or not seek re-appointment, as applicable (paras 31, 32).

Where the regularly expected total fee income from a listed client and its subsidiaries is between five and 10 per cent of the firm's annual fee income (or between 10 and 15 per cent for a non-listed client):
(a) the audit engagement partner is to disclose that expectation to both the firm's ethics partner and the client's directors (or audit committee); and
(b) (i) for a listed company client, the engagement partner is to consider whether appropriate safeguards (such as reducing the non-audit work or applying independent quality control reviews) need to be applied so as to eliminate, or reduce to an acceptable level, the threat to auditors' objectivity and independence;
(ii) for a non-listed client, the audit firm is to arrange for an external independent quality control review of the audit engagement to be conducted before the audit report is finalised (paras 35–39).

---

[29] If a firm's profits are not shared on a firm-wide basis, the 10 per cent and 15 per cent of fees from a listed or non-listed client, respectively, is to be calculated by reference to the part of the firm on which the audit engagement partner's profit share is calculated. (For example, for an international firm, this may be the portion of the firm in a particular country). ES4, para 33, notes that, if a client is expected to contribute more than 10 or 15 per cent (as applicable) of the annual fee income by reference to which the audit engagement partner's profit share is calculated, it may be possible to reassign the client to another part of the firm.

ES4 (para 40) explains:

> A quality control review involves discussion with the audit engagement partner, a review of the financial statements and the auditor's report, and consideration of whether the report is appropriate. It also involves a review of selected working papers relating to the significant judgments the engagement team has made and the conclusions they have reached.[30]

As for economic dependence on an audit client, overdue fees may create a self-interest threat to auditors' objectivity and independence. If a client has not paid a significant portion of the previous year's fee before the audit report on the current year's financial statements is due to be issued, a firm may lean towards issuing an unmodified (i.e., a 'clean') audit report as this may enhance its prospects of receiving the overdue fees. To guard against such an eventuality, ES4 requires audit firms to agree the fee for the previous year's audit and the arrangements for its payment with the client before formally accepting appointment as auditor for the following year. ES4 also notes that, ordinarily, any outstanding fees for the previous audit period should be paid before the firm commences any new audit work (paras 24, 25).

According to ES4 (para 28), if overdue fees from an audit client are in dispute and the amount involved is significant, the threat to auditor's objectivity and independence may be such that no safeguards can reduce it to an acceptable level. In this circumstance, the engagement partner needs to consider whether it is necessary to resign from the audit. If the audit firm does not resign, the engagement partner is to apply appropriate safeguards (such as arranging for an independent internal review of the engagement) and to inform the firm's ethics partner about the overdue fees (ES4, para 30).

Economic dependence on an audit client (or group of related clients) and overdue fees, although serious, are not the only threats to auditors' independence arising from audit fees. The Companies Act 2006, s. 492, provides for the remuneration of a company's auditor to be determined by the company's shareholders. However, in practice, the fees are normally settled through direct negotiation between the audit firm and the client's management, and it is a widely held view that, while this situation continues, auditors are unlikely to be truly independent of their clients. They are perceived as unlikely to bite the hand that feeds them!

A significant proposal designed to divorce company managements from negotiating the audit fee with their company's auditor is that of having audit fees determined according to a fixed scale. The main difficulty with this proposal is identifying a suitable base for developing a scale of fees. The most common

---

[30] Quality control reviews are discussed in greater detail in Chapter 16, section 16.3.2.

suggestion is that of the size of the audit client. However, there is no consensus as to the appropriate indicator of size. Should it be, for example, total assets? total revenue? total profits? – and, if so, before or after exceptional items? before or after tax? etc.

Even if agreement could be reached on the 'best' indicator of size, this may not be an appropriate basis for determining audit fees. The time, effort and skills required for an audit frequently depend on factors other than size; for example, whether the audit is an initial or subsequent engagement (an initial audit requires additional time to become familiar with the client, its business, its accounting system, and so on); the complexity (or simplicity) of the client's organisational structure, business operations and industry; the quality of the client's internal controls; the expertise of the client's accountancy staff; and the presence (or absence) of circumstances which might motivate client-personnel to manipulate the financial statements (for example, plans to float shares during the ensuing accounting period, or managers' bonuses being linked to reported profits).

Further, even if a satisfactory scale of fees could be developed which accommodated factors recognised as affecting the time and skills needed for different audits, there is a danger that auditors would be tempted to 'tailor' their audits to the set fees rather than to the particular circumstances of the audit. In some cases, this could result in over-auditing: that is, auditors conducting audit tests beyond those which are necessary for them to form an opinion on the financial statements because additional time is 'available' under the set fee. In other cases, under-auditing may result: auditors failing to perform tests which are required because the fee is insufficient to cover the time needed.

Direct negotiation of audit fees between auditors and audit-client managements is a serious obstacle to securing and maintaining auditors' objectivity and independence and is an obstacle that is difficult to overcome. However, a mechanism that ensures executives who are responsible for the day-to-day management of the entity are not involved in negotiating the audit fee with the auditor is that of assigning this responsibility to the audit committee (where the reporting entity has one). Audit committees are discussed in section 4.5 below.

(iv) Threatened or actual litigation

Where litigation between an auditor and audit client is in progress, or is likely to take place, it seems most unlikely that the auditor will be able to maintain an independent attitude of mind when evaluating the client's financial statements and supporting evidence. Even if the auditor is, in fact, able to maintain his/her objectivity, independence in appearance will almost certainly be impaired. This applies whether the client has sued the auditor (for example, for negligence) or the auditor has brought a case against the client for matters such as deceit or overdue fees.

ES4 explains that where litigation (in relation to audit or non-audit services) takes place between the audit client and audit firm (or any person able to influence the conduct and outcome of the audit), or where litigation is threatened and is likely to proceed, self-interest, advocacy and intimidation threats to the auditor's independence are created and the auditor should resign from, or not accept, the audit engagement. In such circumstances the audit firm will be (or will be perceived to be) concerned with achieving a favourable outcome to the litigation rather than conducting the audit with an objective, unbiased attitude of mind. Additionally, with the audit team and the audit client on opposing adversarial sides, it seems unlikely that the client's management will feel disposed to make full and frank disclosure to the audit team – a necessary requirement for an effective audit to be performed (ES4, paras 48, 49).

(v)   Gifts and hospitality received from or offered to the audit client

A self-interest and familiarity (or trust) threat to auditors' independence may arise if gifts or hospitality are received from, or offered to, an audit client. ES4 (para 57) observes that the relevant test is not whether auditors believe that accepting or offering gifts or hospitality impairs their independence but whether a reasonable and informed third party is likely to conclude that it is impaired.

In order to avoid such an eventuality, ES4 (para 56) requires audit firms to establish policies on the nature and value of gifts and hospitality that may be accepted from, or offered to, audit clients. It also prohibits audit firms, and those in a position to influence the conduct and outcome of the audit and their immediate family members, from accepting from an audit client:
- gifts, unless the value is clearly insignificant; and
- hospitality, unless it is reasonable in terms of its frequency, nature and cost.

Nevertheless, ES4 is fairly permissive in respect of the hospitality auditors may receive from audit clients. It observes:

> Hospitality is a component of many business relationships and can provide valuable opportunities for developing an understanding of the audited entity's business and for gaining the insight on which an effective and successful working relationship depends. Therefore, the auditors' objectivity and independence is not necessarily impaired as a result of accepting hospitality from the audited entity, provided it is reasonable in terms of its frequency, its nature and its cost. (para 55)

However, the Standard does not explain what is to qualify as "reasonable in terms of its frequency, its nature and its cost" nor does it explain what amounts to "clearly insignificant" in relation to gifts. Nevertheless, it states that, where there is doubt, members of an audit engagement team should consult the engagement partner and, if the latter is in doubt, s/he should consult the firm's ethics partner (ES4, para 58).

In the circumstances described above, the safeguards to be applied by auditors to ensure their independence is not compromised are relatively straightforward and non-controversial. As will be seen from the discussion below, this is not the case in respect of the remaining two situations which threaten auditors' independence, that is:

- a long association between auditors and their clients, and
- the provision of non-audit services by auditors to their audit clients.

(vi) Long association with an audit client

For more than three decades, politicians, the media and regulatory and professional committees have been concerned about the serious threats to auditors' independence which result from audit firms having a long association with their audit clients – the familiarity (or trust), self-interest and self-review threats. Arel, Brody and Pany (2005), for example, report:

> In 1985, Congressman Richard Shelby asked on the floor of the House of Representatives, "How can an audit firm remain independent . . . when it has established long-term personal and professional relationships with a company by auditing that company for many years, some 10, 20 or 30 years?" (p. 2)

Arel *et al.* (2005) also note that a study by the Fulcrum Financial Group in 2003 "found that the average auditor tenure for Fortune 1000 companies is 22 years . . . [and that] 10% of the companies in the study were found to have had the same auditor for 50 years, with the average tenure of this group being 75 years" (p. 2).

In 1976, a Senate Subcommittee in the USA, chaired by Metcalf, proposed mandatory (i.e., compulsory) auditor rotation as a possible solution to the threat to auditors' independence that may result from a long association between auditors and their audit clients (Metcalf, 1976).[31] Since then, two forms of rotating auditors away from their audit clients after a number of years have been hotly debated in professional and regulatory circles, namely:

- the rotation of senior audit engagement team members while retaining the audit within the audit firm; and
- rotating audit firms.

Arguments for and against both forms of rotation are summarised below.

---

[31] The Committee was highly critical of the accounting profession and, in a 1,769-page report, made numerous recommendations on how the accounting (including auditing) profession should be regulated (see, for example, Arens & Loebbecke, 1980, p. 26). It is interesting to note that many of the Metcalf Committee's recommendations were enacted, nearly three decades later, in the Sarbanes-Oxley Act of 2002.

(a) Arguments in favour of mandatory auditor rotation

(i) The quality and competence of auditors' work tends to decline over time as auditors become over-familiar with their audit clients and, as a consequence, do not maintain an appropriate level of professional scepticism and make unjustified assumptions. An auditor may, for example, make assumptions about the effectiveness of certain internal controls and the reliability of management's representations based on the findings of previous audits, rather than objectively evaluating current evidence. As Arel *et al.* (2005) explain:

> Auditors may become stale and view the audit as a simple repetition of earlier engagements. This staleness fosters a tendency to anticipate results rather than keeping alert to . . . changes in circumstances . . . (p. 37)

Mandatory auditor rotation limits the time auditors audit a particular client and thus reduces the risk of them becoming complacent; it ensures a 'fresh view' is introduced to the audit every – say – five or so years.

(ii) A long term relationship with an audit client may result in the development of a close personal relationship between the auditor and the client's management. This may result in the auditor identifying too closely with management and reducing his/her objectivity and impartial attitude when conducting the client's audits. Mandatory auditor rotation prevents long term relationships with audit clients from developing.

(iii) As a consequence of the financial rewards associated with maintaining a long term relationship with an audit client (in particular, those arising from opportunities to provide non-audit services), auditors might be tempted to 'overlook' or to 'accommodate' management's viewpoint on financial reporting issues. As Bazerman, Loewenstein and Moore (2002) observe: "auditors have strong business reasons to remain in clients' good graces and are thus highly motivated to approve their clients' accounts" (p. 99). Audit firm rotation nullifies auditors' desire to "remain in clients' good graces" and 'frees them' to challenge questionable client practices. As the auditee will be a client for only a limited period, the audit firm does not risk future revenue streams if it challenges aggressive accounting practices, dubious judgments or unorthodox recording of business transactions.

(iv) Auditor rotation ensures that a successor engagement partner or firm will, at some future time, review the financial statement judgments made by the current engagement partner or firm. The successor auditor will bring 'fresh eyes' to the engagement and any financial statement errors or irregularities that may have been overlooked by the predecessor auditor, or to which the predecessor acquiesced, are likely to come to light. Awareness of this eventuality reduces the likelihood of the current auditor overlooking accounting irregularities or signing off on controversial accounting practices.

(v) The costs associated with mandatory rotation are significantly less than the costs associated with audit failure. Healey (2004) notes, for example, that Morgan Stanley estimated the loss in market capitalisation which resulted from the failure, in the early 2000s, of WorldCom, Tyco, Qwest, Enron and Computer Associates alone to be about $460 billion. He compares this with his estimate of the annual cost of rotation by the Big 4 accounting firms, assuming rotation occurs every five years, of approximately $1.2 billion.

(vi) Mandatory audit firm rotation promotes greater competition among audit firms and thereby promotes better audit quality and reduced audit fees. As Raiborn *et al.* (2006) explain: "[M]andatory rotation puts all audit firms on some degree of level footing and could encourage smaller firms to grow and develop niche specializations that would allow greater competition with the Big Four" (p. 40). Support for this viewpoint is provided by Arrunada and Paz-Ares (1995) who note that, following the introduction of mandatory rotation in Spain in 1988, the non-Big 6[32] audit firms' share of the statutory audit market increased from 28 per cent to 40 per cent [as reported, Institute of Chartered Accountants in England and Wales (ICAEW), 2002, p. 18).

(vii) Mandatory audit firm rotation increases the public's perception of auditors' independence as it implies a distancing between audit firms and their audit clients.

Reviewing the arguments advanced in favour of mandatory auditor rotation, it can be seen that some apply equally to the rotation of senior audit team personnel (while retaining the audit within the firm) and to the rotation of audit firms. The benefits to be derived from the mandatory rotation of audit firms, but not from the rotation of senior audit team personnel, are the removal of the lure of continued financial rewards flowing to the audit firm, increased competition amongst audit firms and the public's perception of increased independence [(iii), (vi) and (vii) above].

Although the arguments in favour of mandatory auditor rotation may seem compelling, opponents support their position with equally strong contrary arguments.

---

[32] In 1995 the Big 6 firms were Arthur Andersen, Coopers & Lybrand, Ernst & Young, Deloitte, KPMG and Price Waterhouse. By 2006 (when Raiborn *et al.* were writing), Coopers & Lybrand had merged with Price Waterhouse and Arthur Andersen had collapsed.

(b) *Arguments against mandatory audit firm rotation*

(i)   During the course of an audit, the audit team gains an in-depth knowledge of the client's industry, business, policies, operations, accounting system, internal controls, key personnel, and so on – an essential requirement for an effective audit in today's environment. However, as a consequence of the increasing complexity and size of many modern businesses in terms of their organisational structure, business processes, financial controls, technology and geographical spread, it takes auditors an increasing amount of time to thoroughly understand a client and its operations. Additionally, as a result of the continued development of financial reporting standards, auditors need to gain an in-depth understanding of their clients' businesses to enable them to assess the impact of changes in financial reporting requirements on a client's financial statements. The American Institute of Certified Public Accountants (AICPA; 1992) observed that newly appointed auditors have to climb a steep learning curve in order to become deeply knowledgeable about the client's operating environment, risks, and technical accounting policies and procedures. It estimated that, for complex clients, auditors require two to three years of audit engagements before they fully understand the client's business, procedures and structure.

Under a system of mandatory auditor rotation, knowledge of the audit client is lost with each change of auditor. Following from this, opponents of mandatory rotation assert that a new auditor's lack of knowledge of the client's operations, financial information systems and financial reporting practices dramatically reduces audit quality.

(ii) In order to perform an effective audit, auditors must build a co-operative relationship with the client regardless of the period of the auditor–client relationship. As Arel *et al.* (2005) explain:

> [A] client must feel comfortable with an auditor and be willing to share information and discuss problems when they exist. . . . An auditor must be able to gauge when the client is not revealing all available information, and this often comes from knowing the client and its management. . . . The familiarity the auditor has with [a client] provides a better understanding of the issues and a better appreciation of the changes that have taken place from one year to the next. (p. 37)

(iii) Audit failure rates are higher during the first few years of an engagement when the auditor has yet to develop the institutional and personnel knowledge of the client necessary for the discovery of audit problems. Supporting evidence for this assertion is provided by, for example, George (2004) who studied audit failures between 1996 and 2001. He found that audit failures occur most often in the first three years, and in seven years or more, of auditor tenure. He concluded that the risk of audit failure increases with each change of audit firm and that a reduction in audit quality results when a new auditor is unfamiliar with the client's business and operations. It follows from George's findings that mandatory rotation of audit firms increases the risk of audit failure – at least in the early years following a change of auditor.[33]

(iv) Auditor rotation significantly increases audit costs for both audit firms and their clients. During the initial years of any audit, auditors must devote considerable time and effort to becoming familiar with the client, its business and its systems. Research by the SDA Università Bocconi in Italy (2002) found that more qualified audit staff, and up to 40 per cent more man-hours, are required in the first year of an audit and that the "'training period' is never less than two to three years for complex international groups" (as reported, ICAEW, 2002, p. 19).

There are also additional costs for the client in selecting a new auditor and familiarising the new auditor with the company's business, operations and systems. The SDA Università Bocconi researchers (2002) found that an auditor change results in an "increased burden on managers, personnel and internal auditors in supplying necessary information about corporate governance, internal control systems, organizational structure, market relations, and so on" (as cited, ICAEW, 2002, p. 20). Further, should the end of a rotation period occur when the client is involved in a major transaction or restructuring, the need to change auditors will cause unwelcome, additional, disruption.

(v) Mandatory audit firm rotation results in lower audit quality as audit firms, aware that a particular audit engagement will be terminated after a limited number of years, have little incentive to invest in the development of audit processes to achieve increased effectiveness and efficiency. Arrunada and Paz-Ares (1995) contend that, where audit firms are subject to mandatory rotation, they are unlikely to invest either in new audit technologies or in training audit staff. The lack of investment in audit staff results in lower-quality auditors and this, combined with reduced investment in new technologies, results in lower-quality audits (as reported, ICAEW, 2002, p. 21).

A further adverse impact on audit quality from mandatory audit firm rotation results from audit firms transferring audit partners and staff from one client to another as a rotation period nears its end. Respondents to a survey in the USA by the General Accounting Office

---

[33] However, George's (2004) finding that audit failures increase in the seventh and subsequent years of audit tenure seems to provide evidence which supports the mandatory rotation of auditors after a period of seven years.

(GAO), which investigated the potential effects of audit firm rotation, indicated that they would shift their most knowledgeable and experienced audit personnel from the current engagement to another audit client towards the end of the rotation period even though they believed re-assigning these individuals would increase the risk of audit failure (GAO, 2003).

(vi) Companies in specialised industries, such as banking, insurance and mining, are particularly vulnerable to a reduction in audit quality as a result of mandatory audit firm rotation. Only a small number of firms are likely to have the required complement of audit personnel with specialist knowledge and expertise in these industries. One of these firms may provide non-audit services to a company in a specialised industry – services that are considered incompatible with the provision of audit services (as specified by, for example, SOX, the APB's Ethical Standards, or the *IESBA Code*). When the company is forced to change its auditors as a result of mandatory audit firm rotation, it may be forced to appoint an audit firm that lacks the desired depth of industry expertise. This is likely to increase the risk of audit failure and potentially harm the company and its shareholders.[34]

(vii) Mandatory rotation of audit firms may result in an inadequate supply of competent firms, not just in the specialised industries, but in the audit market generally. Raiborn *et al.* (2006), for instance, point out that, in the USA, there is a limited "number of audit firms that have the quantity of personnel, depth and breadth of industry expertise, or the name recognition to satisfy large domestic and international client companies" (p. 41). They note that, in 2001, there were approximately 18,000 domestic and foreign entities registered with the SEC, 10,500 of which were audited by the Big 4 auditing firms (an average of 2,625 companies per firm). The remaining 7,500 companies were audited by about 700 other accounting firms (an average of fewer than 11 companies per firm). Therefore, if a public company, currently audited by a Big 4 firm, wishes to continue to be audited by a Big 4 firm but engages another Big 4 firm to provide non-audit services that are incompatible with the provision of audit services, the choice of a new firm, required by mandatory audit firm rotation, is extremely limited. The situation applies equally in the UK, where 98 per cent of the 350 largest companies listed on the London Stock Exchange (the FTSE 350) are audited by the Big 4 audit firms (Financial Director, 2010).

---

[34] The 'new' audit firm may, however, be able to overcome its lack of industry expertise by recruiting knowledgeable audit staff from the outgoing audit firm – an occurrence which, anecdotal evidence suggests, is fairly common in countries such as Italy, where mandatory rotation of audit firms has been required for public listed companies since 1974.

Further, since the demise of Enron and Arthur Andersen, the Big 4 firms' engagement procedures have become far more stringent and, according to Raiborn *et al.* (2006), between 2003 and 2005, these firms were "shedding clients at almost three times the rate they did in 2002" – in general "shedding" clients that are "too small to be worth the extra work and those judged too risky to work with under the new accounting rules" (p. 42).[35] Given this scenario, there might be a shortage of firms willing to accept some audit engagements when they become available at the end of the rotation period.

(viii) Audit firm rotation negates the signalling effect of auditor switches. Without mandatory rotation, a change of auditors tends to be an unusual event and suggests there are reasons worth probing that have prompted the change. Mandatory audit firm rotation renders auditor switches a usual occurrence and thus masks the valuable information a change of auditor signals to the market.

Reviewing the arguments against mandatory rotation, it may be seen that, at least to some extent, those relating to decreased quality and increased audit costs resulting from a lack of knowledge about the client and the absence of a personal relationship between senior audit personnel and the audit client [(i), (ii), (iii) and (iv) above] apply to both the rotation of senior audit personnel and to the rotation of audit firms. However, with the rotation of senior audit personnel, the institutional and personnel knowledge of the client is available within the audit firm and therefore the impact on audit quality and cost is likely to be significantly less than that resulting from the rotation of audit firms.

(c)   Arguments contending that mandatory auditor rotation is unnecessary

Although mandatory auditor rotation has attracted significant support as a means of strengthening auditors' independence, a number of commentators, audit firms and professional bodies maintain that it is unnecessary because client managements and audit personnel change naturally over time. The AICPA (1992), for example, reported that a review of executives of the largest 100 industrial concerns in the 1991 Fortune 500 companies, and the 50 largest bank holding companies in the USA at 31 December 1990, showed that the turnover of executives is sufficiently high to ensure the relationship between client managements and audit personnel is continually changing without mandatory rotation (as reported, ICAEW, 2002, p. 21). Similarly, Larkin (2004),

---

[35] During interviews with senior audit partners of the Big 4 firms in both the UK and New Zealand in 2004 and 2005, one of the authors of this textbook was informed that the strengthening of audit engagement procedures and the "shedding of clients that are no longer considered acceptable" (i.e., that pose a high audit risk) is a global phenomenon for each Big 4 audit firm.

focusing on audit firms rather than their clients, observed: "slow rotation occurs naturally within a firm as staff members are promoted, retire, change assignments, etc., thus bringing new personnel to every audit over time".

Others contend that mandatory rotation is not necessary as more effective, less costly alternative ways of ensuring that auditors' maintain their independence are available. PricewaterhouseCoopers (2002) and the SDA Università Bocconi study (2002), for example, point to the importance in this regard of:
  (i)   independent quality control reviews of audit firms' and audit team members' independence,
  (ii) audit firms' quality controls and governance mechanisms, and
  (iii) effective oversight (or inspections) of auditors' performance and independence by regulatory bodies.[36,37]

Another significant mechanism that helps to ensure the maintenance of auditors' independence and one which, according to some commentators, renders mandatory rotation unnecessary is that of the audit committee. As the GAO (2003) observed:

> [I]f audit committees . . . are actively involved in helping to ensure audit independence and audit quality, many of the intended benefits of audit firm rotation could be realized at the initiative of the audit committee rather than through a mandatory requirement. (p. 52)

As noted earlier, audit committees are discussed in section 4.5 below.

Notwithstanding the arguments opposing the adoption of mandatory auditor rotation, the APB in ES3: *Long Association with the Audit Engagement* (APB, 2009) [like the *IESBA Code* and the Sarbanes-Oxley Act of 2002 (SOX)] has adopted the rotation of senior audit team members as a 'safeguard' to the threat to auditors' independence resulting from a long association between auditors and their clients. However, it distinguishes between the audits of listed companies and those of other reporting entities.

For listed companies, ES3 requires audit firms to establish policies and procedures that ensure:
  (a)   in the absence of special circumstances, no one acts as the audit engagement partner for the audit of a particular company for a period of more

---

[36] These three mechanisms for securing auditor independence and audit quality are discussed in detail in Chapter 16. It is also pertinent to note that, although these mechanisms help to ensure that auditors are objective and unbiased when they conduct their audits, they do not affect auditors' independence in appearance.

[37] The European Union's *Statutory Audit Directive* (EU, 2006) made external inspection of listed company auditors' performance a requirement throughout the EU. As explained in Chapter 16, such monitoring of company auditors' performance has been in effect in the UK since 1991.

than five years,[38] and does not participate in the audit of this company for at least the following five years (para 12);

(b) no one acts as the engagement quality control reviewer,[39] a key partner involved in the audit,[40] or as a combination of quality control reviewer, key audit partner and engagement partner, for more than seven years, and does not participate in the audit of the company for at least the following five years (para 19);[41]

(c) where partners (other than key partners) or staff have been involved in the audit of a company in senior positions for a continuous period of more than seven years, the audit engagement partner is to review the safeguards put in place to address the resulting threats to auditors' independence and to discuss those situations with the engagement quality control reviewer. If issues remain unresolved, these are referred to the firm's ethics partner (para 20).

For reporting entities other than listed companies, ES3 is rather less restrictive. It requires audit firms who have audit engagement partners, key partners and other partners and staff in senior positions in the audit engagement team who have a long association with an audit client, to assess the resulting threats to auditors' independence and to apply safeguards to reduce the threats to an acceptable level. The safeguards may include:

– rotating audit partners and other senior members of the engagement team away from the audit client in question after a pre-determined number of years;

– appointing an additional partner who is not, and has not recently been, a member of the audit engagement team, to review the work of the audit partner(s) and other senior members of the engagement team and to advise them as necessary;

– applying independent internal quality reviews to the engagement in question.

---

[38] Should an audit committee decide that a degree of flexibility over the timing of the engagement partner's rotation is necessary to safeguard the quality of the audit, the engagement partner is permitted to remain in that position for up to two further years (a total of seven years). Such a situation may arise if, for example, there are unexpected changes in the client's senior management or substantial changes have recently been, or are soon to be, made to the company's nature or structure (ES3, para 16).

[39] See footnote 26.

[40] A 'key partner involved in the audit' is defined by the APB (2010a) as:

A partner, or other person in the engagement team (other than the audit engagement partner or engagement quality control reviewer), who either:
• is involved at the group level and is responsible for key decisions or judgments on significant matters or risk factors that relate to the audit of that audited entity, or
• is primarily responsible for the audit of a significant affiliate or division of the audited entity.

[41] Someone who has only been a key partner (but not the engagement partner) involved in the audit of a particular company for a period of seven years is not able to participate in that company's audit for a period of two (rather than five) years following the seven years (ES3, para 19).

If appropriate safeguards cannot be found to reduce the threat to auditors' independence to an acceptable level, the firm is to resign or not seek reappointment, as applicable (paras 6, 8).

ES3 (para 9) also notes that, if an individual has been the engagement partner for a non-listed company audit client for a continuous period of ten years, careful consideration needs to be given to the likely conclusion a reasonable and informed third party would reach about impairment of the audit firm's independence. Further, in any case where an audit engagement partner is not rotated after ten years, appropriate safeguards are to be applied and reasons for the individual remaining as the audit engagement partner are to be documented and communicated to the company's directors (or, if it has one, its audit committee).

Provisions like those in ES3 are contained in the EU Commission's *Recommendation: Statutory Auditors' Independence in the EU: A Set of Fundamental Principles* (EU, 2002) and IFAC's *Code of Ethics for Professional Accountants* (IFAC, 2002) – a predecessor of the *IESBA Code* (IESBA, 2009). Similarly, in the USA, SOX, sec. 203, prohibits "the lead (or coordinating) audit partner (having primary responsibility for the audit), or the audit partner responsible for reviewing the audit" (equivalent to the audit engagement partner and engagement quality reviewer in the UK) from providing audit services to a public company for more than five years.

Given their timing, the requirement for senior audit team personnel to be rotated after a specified number of years may appear to be a reaction by regulators to the audit failures associated with the Enron, WorldCom, Tyco, Parmalat and similar debacles. However, in reality, they are a formalisation and extension of measures previously introduced by the professional accounting bodies. For example, in 1985, the AICPA required all firms joining its SEC Practice Section[42] to rotate the audit engagement partner of an SEC-registered audit client every seven years. Similarly, in 1994, the Institutes of Chartered Accountants in England and Wales (ICAEW), of Scotland (ICAS) and in Ireland (ICAI) introduced a requirement for the engagement partner responsible for the audit of a public listed company to be rotated every seven years. Indeed, by the turn of the twenty-first century, the rotation of audit engagement partners (if not of other senior audit personnel) was generally accepted as a concept, and in practice, in many parts of the world.

The same is not true of the rotation of audit firms. Nevertheless, according to Pajuelo (2003), the Brazilian securities regulator (CVM)

---

[42] Firms joining the AICPA's SEC Practice Section audit companies registered with the SEC; that is, in essence, all public companies registered or listed in the USA and their significant subsidiaries.

believes that audit firm rotation would provide a better safeguard against improper accounting than mere rotation of the engagement partners. An auditor may be less likely to go easy on a client's audit for the sake of retaining the relationship if the engagement will end after several years.

His belief was given effect in Brazil in 1999 "following the bankruptcy of two major banks" (ICAEW, 2002 p. 10). In that year a five-year mandatory audit firm rotation requirement for all listed companies was introduced, with the first mandated rotation of audit firms commencing in May 2004 (Pajuelo, 2003). Other countries have also mandated the rotation of audit firms. For example, in Italy, a three-year mandatory rotation of audit firms (with a maximum of two re-appointments, i.e., a total of nine years) has applied to firms auditing public listed companies since 1974. In Spain, mandatory audit firm rotation for firms auditing listed clients was introduced in 1988 (with a minimum period of appointment of three years and a maximum of nine years). However, it was abolished in 1995 by the Limited Liability Partnership Act. The Czech Republic introduced mandatory audit firm rotation (with a four-year maximum period of appointment) in 1989 but abolished it in 1992. In 1996, the system was introduced in the Slovak Republic for the audits of all companies (with a maximum period of appointment of three years) but was abolished in 2000. Latvia briefly introduced a two-year audit firm rotation for banks but the requirement was dropped in 2001 "following complaints from two of the country's largest banks that they were unable to find an international accounting firm prepared to undertake the audit" [Fédération des Experts Comptables Européens (FEE), 2004, p. 6]. In 2002, Singapore introduced a five-year mandatory audit firm rotation for banking engagements as "part of an ongoing effort to enhance the independence and effectiveness of external auditors" (Harian, 2002).

The experience of a significant number of countries which have introduced and subsequently abolished the mandatory rotation of audit firms indicates that such a system is generally considered not to be cost-effective. However, the issue remains the subject of vigorous debate and, as we explain in Chapter 18 (section 18.5.1), in 2011, new proposals were advanced for the introduction of audit firm rotation for public interest entities throughout the European Union (EU, 2011).

Although falling well short of mandatory audit firm rotation, in 2012 the FRC took steps to ensure that large listed companies in the UK at least consider changing their auditor every ten years. It introduced a requirement in *The UK Corporate Governance Code* (FRC, 2012a) for all FTSE 350 companies (the largest 350 companies listed on the London Stock Exchange) to "put the external audit contract out to tender at least every ten years" (prov. C.3.7). In its *Guidance on Audit Committees* (2012c), the FRC explains that this will "enable the audit committee to compare the quality and effectiveness of the services provided by the incumbent auditor with those of other audit firms" (para 4.23). From the number of FTSE 350 companies which, according to the media, have changed their auditor during 2013, it seems that the FRC's measure is an effective means of prompting large companies in the UK to change their auditor periodically.

(vii) Provision of non-audit services by auditors to their audit clients

The possible impairment of auditors' independence as a result of providing non-audit services to audit clients, like that arising from a long association between auditors and their clients, has been a highly contentious issue for many years. The Commission on Auditors' Responsibilities (1978), commentators such as Cowen (1980) and organisations like Hermes (2002) have asserted that there is little or no empirical evidence to suggest that the provision of non-audit services by auditors to their clients impairs their independence. However, others from both inside the auditing profession, such as Briloff (1986), and from outside, such as Congressman Dingell (a vocal critic of auditors in the USA) and Austin Mitchell MP (a vocal critic of auditors in the UK), are adamant that such an activity must, and does, impair auditors' independence. The latter view now generally prevails but the issue attracts opposing arguments: some commentators focus on the benefits to be gained from auditors providing non-audit services to their audit clients; others highlight the dangers to their independence from them doing so.

(a) Benefits of auditors providing non-audit services to their audit clients

As explained in Chapter 2, as auditors conduct their audits they become familiar with all aspects of their clients – their industry, business operations, organisation, accounting system, internal controls, significant risks, key personnel, etc. This familiarity places them in an ideal position to provide financial and management advice to their clients. Auditors, unlike other outside consultants, do not have to spend time getting to know the client. This clearly reduces the costs involved. Furthermore, because auditors are familiar with all aspects of their clients, they are able to anticipate the likely impact of any advice given to the client's management, on all parts of the organisation. An outside consultant is likely to become familiar only with the aspect of the entity related to the particular task in hand. This consultant may not, therefore, appreciate wider ramifications within the organisation of advice given to the entity's management. A further benefit to be derived from auditors providing non-audit services to their audit clients is that, during the process of providing those services, auditors gain greater insight into aspects of their clients (their business, risk exposures, operations, etc.) than they would acquire through the audit process – knowledge that assists them perform effective audits.[43]

---

[43] The importance of auditors gaining an in-depth knowledge of their clients is discussed in detail in Chapter 8, section 8.4.1.

(b)   Dangers to auditors' independence from the provision of non-audit services

While it is generally agreed that auditors are well placed to provide financial and management advice to their audit clients more efficiently and effectively than other outside consultants, and frequently there is a beneficial 'spill-over' to the audit from the provision of non-audit services, providing these services is likely to be at the cost of at least some of the auditor's objectivity and independence. The threat to independence comes from four main sources – the self-interest, self-review, management and advocacy threats. We examine each of these below.

- *Self-interest threat:* ES5: *Non-audit Services Provided to Audited Entities* (APB, 2011b) asserts: "In relation to non-audit services, the main self-interest threat concerns fees and economic dependence" (para 26). If the provision of non-audit services is lucrative, the auditor may be tempted to bias the audit opinion in the client's favour rather than risk losing the client – and associated lucrative non-audit services work. The limitation imposed by ES4 on the proportion of the firm's annual fee income that may be derived from any one client and its subsidiaries (noted earlier) has, to an extent, limited this danger. However, ES5 (para 27) notes that where an audit firm regularly earns substantial fees from a client for non-audit services, and these fees exceed the client's audit fees, the audit engagement partner needs to consider whether this results in a perceived loss of independence. If after considering, in particular, the nature of the non-audit services provided and the size and nature of the related fee, the engagement partner concludes that the threat to independence is at an acceptable level (or can be reduced to such a level by applying appropriate safeguards), s/he is to inform those charged with the client's governance (or, more usually, the audit committee) of the position on a timely basis. However, if the audit client is a listed company and the fees from non-audit services exceed the audit fee, the engagement partner is also to inform the firm's Ethics Partner. ES5 explains: "Discussing the level of fees for non-audit services with the Ethics Partner ensures that appropriate attention is paid to the issue by the audit firm" (para 28).

- *Self-review threat:* If an auditor (or audit firm) advises an audit client on – say – a new accounting system and the client, acting on that advice, installs the new system, in any subsequent audit the auditor (or members of the audit firm) will review the outcome of their own (or their firm's) advice. In this circumstance, it is difficult to believe the auditor will evaluate the system with the same level of objectivity that s/he would apply if the advice had come from an outside consultant. Even if the auditor is, in fact, able to maintain an objective and unbiased attitude of mind, it may be difficult for a reasonable and informed outside observer to accept that this is the case and so, as a minimum, independence in appearance will be impaired.

A similar situation exists when the results of a non-audit service provided by the auditor impact on the client's financial statements. An extreme example is afforded by an auditor (or audit firm) both preparing and auditing a set of financial statements.[44] Even if the auditor manages to maintain an impartial attitude of mind whilst performing the audit, it seems unlikely that a reasonable and informed third party would conclude that this is the case. Other examples include the auditor providing valuation or tax advisory services to an audit client, where the valuation amounts or tax calculations have a material effect on the financial statements.[45] A further example is that of an auditor (or audit firm) providing internal audit services to a client, where the auditor subsequently places reliance on the internal audit work performed.[46] In each of these circumstances it is difficult to conceive of safeguards that could be applied that would reduce the self-review threat to an acceptable level. The situation might be helped if some other person or group within the audit firm compiles the financial statements or provides the advisory service. However, independence in appearance, if not in fact, is still at a lower level than it would have been had the audit firm not been involved in providing the service.

_____

[44] In 2007/8, the Audit Inspection Unit (AIU) found that an audit firm had assisted all of the subsidiaries of its listed company audit client with the preparation of their financial statements (AIU, 2008). Along similar lines, in 2009/10, the AIU found that an audit firm had assisted its listed company client compile its financial policies and procedures manuals – policies and procedures that impact on the client's financial statements (AIU, 2010). The AIU (which was renamed the Audit Quality Review team in 2012) is a component of the FRC and is responsible for inspecting the audits of companies listed on the London Stock Exchange and other 'public interest entities'. Audit Quality Review team inspections are explained in Chapter 16, section 16.4.

[45] Valuation services require the provider to make assumptions about future events and/or to apply appropriate methodologies and techniques to arrive at a value (or range of values) for an asset, liability or the business as a whole (ES5, para 76). In 2009/10, the AIU found that an audit firm had provided actuarial valuation services to a listed company audit client. It also found that a major audit firm had been involved in the preparation of calculations for the purpose of determining the tax amounts which appeared in the listed company client's financial statements (AIU, 2010).

[46] In 2009, KPMG was appointed as auditor of Rentokil Initial plc after "promoting an audit package which promised to cut costs and integrate the internal and external audit functions" (Christodoulou, 2009). In response to this development, Boyle (2009), then Chief Executive of the FRC, observed:

> audit firms and their clients . . . may want to be cautious before entering into arrangements which stretch the internal/ external audit boundary, not least because it could prove to be inconvenient and/or costly to change such arrangements should . . . the Ethical Standards [be] changed in a way that affects the provision of such services.

The revision of ES5 in 2010, which clarified and curtailed the internal audit services auditors can provide to their audit clients, suggests Boyle's warning was well founded. In 2013, the FRC complemented the limitation on the internal audit services auditors can provide to audit clients by introducing, in ISA (UK and Ireland) 610: *Using the Work of Internal Auditors* (FRC, 2013b, para 5-1), a prohibition on the use of "direct assistance" from the client's internal auditors on the external audit; that is, using internal audit staff as members of the audit team (FRC, 2013b, paras 5-1, 14). The FRC explained that the intent of this prohibition is to further "ensure the independence of the external auditor and promote greater confidence in the integrity of the audit for investors" (FRC, 2013c).

- *Management threat:* If an auditor provides non-audit services to an audit client which involve making judgments or decisions that are properly the responsibility of management, then the distinction between the auditor and the client becomes blurred. ES5 (para 36) warns that, if auditors become closely aligned with the views and interests of management, this may impair or call into question their ability to apply a proper degree of professional scepticism when auditing the client's financial statements. This may occur, for example, if an auditor (or audit firm) designs and implements an information technology system for an audit client and the client's management lacks the expertise to take responsibility for the system concerned. In this situation, the auditor is relied upon to make significant decisions in respect of the system and, in essence, acts in the role of management. In such circumstances, it is unlikely that any safeguards can eliminate the management threat or reduce it to an acceptable level (ES5, para 74).

- *Advocacy threat:* If an auditor agrees to provide non-audit services which involve him/her adopting an advocacy role for an audit client, s/he will, of necessity, support a position aligned to that of the client. This could make it difficult for the auditor to adopt an objective, unbiased attitude of mind when conducting the audit – or, at the very least, it would be difficult for a reasonable and informed third party to conclude that the auditor can, and will, adopt such an attitude. For example, if the auditor agrees to provide tax advice to an audit client and this involves (or results in) him/her acting as an advocate for the client before Commissioners of HM Revenue & Customs (or another tax tribunal), it is likely that the auditor's objectivity and independence will be impaired. ES5 (para 41) notes that, if a non-audit service requires an auditor to act as an advocate for an audit client in relation to matters that are material to the financial statements, it is unlikely that any safeguards can eliminate the advocacy threat or reduce it to an acceptable level.

While not ignoring the benefits that may accrue from auditors providing non-audit services to their audit clients, during the 1990s the SEC in the USA became so concerned about the extent and growth of this practice, and the resulting impairment to auditors' independence, that it introduced strict new independence rules (SEC, 2000b). These limited the services auditors could provide to their SEC registrant audit clients (essentially, all US public companies). The SEC's Chief Accountant, Turner (2001), explained that, in formulating the rules, the SEC was guided by four principles which indicate a likely breach of auditors' independence:

The four principles specify an auditor would not be considered independent when the auditor:

1. Has a mutual or conflicting interest with the audit client.
2. Is placed in the position of auditing his or her own work.

3. Acts as management or an employee of the audit client; or
4. Is in the position of being an advocate for the client. (p. 5)

These principles coincide with the threats to auditors' independence identified in ES5 (outlined above). They also underlie the services that SOX prohibits auditors from providing to audit clients that are public companies registered or listed in the USA or significant components thereof.[47] The prohibited services specified in SOX (sec. 201) are as follows:

(1) bookkeeping or other services related to the accounting records or financial statements of the audit client;
(2) financial information systems design and implementation;
(3) appraisal or valuation services, fairness opinions, or contribution-in-kind reports;[48]
(4) actuarial services;
(5) internal audit outsourcing services;
(6) management functions or human resources;
(7) broker or dealer, investment adviser, or investment banking services;
(8) legal services and expert services unrelated to the audit; and
(9) any other service that the [Public Company Accounting Oversight] Board determines, by regulation, is impermissible.

Auditors may provide any non-prohibited non-audit service to their audit clients, including tax services, but before doing so the client's audit committee must approve the auditor's provision of the service in question (SOX, sec. 201).[49]

Unlike SOX, ES5 specifies general safeguards that audit firms or engagement partners are required to apply in order to eliminate, or reduce to an acceptable level, threats to auditors' independence resulting from the provision of non-audit services to audit clients. However, it also identifies particular non-audit services which, according to ES5, present such a serious threat to auditors' independence that it is unlikely that safeguards are able to reduce the threat(s) they pose to auditors' independence to an acceptable level. Audit firms are

---

[47] It should be recalled from Chapter 2 (section 2.7.2) that the SOX provisions relate not only to the audits (and auditors) of public companies registered in the USA but to those of all companies listed on a stock exchange in the USA (irrespective of where they are registered) and, also, to those of all significant subsidiaries of companies registered or listed in the USA, irrespective of where those subsidiaries are located.

[48] The SEC (2000b) explains:

Appraisal and valuation services include any process of valuing assets, both tangible and intangible, or liabilities. Fairness opinions are opinions that an accounting firm provides on the adequacy of consideration in a transaction. . . . [I]f an audit firm provides these services to an audit client, when it is time to audit the financial statements the accountant could well end up reviewing his or her own work. . . . (p. 55)

[49] In April 2008, the Public Company Accounting Oversight Board (PCAOB) adopted a rule which requires the auditors of public companies listed or registered in the USA (or subsidiaries thereof), before accepting a new or continuing audit engagement, to describe in writing to the audit committee all relationships between the audit firm (and its affiliates) and the company (or persons in a financial reporting oversight role in the company) that may reasonably be thought to bear on the audit firm's independence. The audit firm is also required to hold discussions with the audit committee about the potential effects of any such relationships on the audit firm's independence (PCAOB, 2008).

prohibited from providing these services to their audit clients. We first describe some of the general safeguards identified by ES5 and then provide examples of non-audit services audit firms are not permitted to supply to their audit clients.

(a) General safeguards

1. Audit firms are to establish policies and procedures that require partners or staff within the firm, when considering whether to accept a proposed engagement to provide a non-audit service to an audit client (or to any of its subsidiaries or other affiliates), to communicate details of the proposed engagement to the audit engagement partner (ES5, para 14).[50]

2. Before an audit firm accepts a proposed engagement to provide a non-audit service to an audit client, the audit engagement partner is to:
   - consider whether a reasonable and informed third party is likely to regard the objectives of the proposed engagement to be inconsistent with those of the audit of the financial statements;
   - identify and assess the significance of any related threat(s) to auditors' objectivity and independence; and
   - identify and assess the effectiveness of available safeguards to eliminate or reduce the identified threat(s) to an acceptable level (ES5, para 17).

   If the audit engagement partner concludes that:
   - (i) a reasonable and informed third party is likely to regard the objectives of the proposed non-audit service engagement as inconsistent with those of the financial statement audit; or
   - (ii) no appropriate safeguards are available to eliminate or reduce the related threat(s) to auditors' independence to an acceptable level,

   the audit firm is to decline the non-audit work or not accept, or resign from (as applicable), the audit engagement (ES5, para 22).

3. If an audit firm decides to accept an engagement to provide non-audit services to an audit client, the audit engagement partner is to ensure the reasoning underlying the decision is appropriately documented. The matters to be documented include:
   - (a) any identified threats to the auditor's objectivity and independence;

---

[50] *The UK Corporate Governance Code* (FRC, 2012a) requires the audit committee of companies listed on the London Stock Exchange to develop their company's policy with regard to engaging the company's external auditor to provide non-audit services. ES5 (para 16) specifies that, in the case of a listed company, the group audit engagement partner is to establish that the company has communicated its policy on the provision of non-audit services by the company's external auditor to its subsidiaries and other affiliates, and to obtain confirmation that the auditors of the affiliates will comply with this policy.

(b) the safeguards adopted and the reasons why they are considered to be effective;

(c) the communication of these matters to those charged with the client's governance (ES5, paras 51, 52).

4. The audit engagement partner is also to ensure that those charged with the audit client's governance (or, in most cases, its audit committee) are appropriately informed on a timely basis of:

- all significant matters relating to the provision of non-audit services that impact on the auditors' objectivity and independence, and the safeguards the audit firm has applied; and

- for listed companies, any inconsistencies between the APB's Ethical Standards and the company's policy on the provision of non-audit services by the audit firm, and any apparent breach of that policy (ES5, para 48).

ES5 (para 49) explains the importance of this communication. It states:

> Transparency is a key element in addressing the issues raised by the provision of non-audit services by audit firms to the entities audited by them. This can be facilitated by timely communication with those charged with governance of the audited entity.

However, it is pertinent to note that, unless the information is also placed in the public domain (for example, by including it in the company's annual report or publishing it on the company's website), it will not allay the concerns of those outside the entity who may perceive a breach of the auditor's independence resulting from the auditor (or audit firm) providing non-audit services to the company concerned.

(b)   Non-audit services audit firms are not permitted to provide to their audit clients

As we noted earlier, in addition to specifying general safeguards to auditors' independence, ES5 identifies certain non-audit services which pose particularly serious threats to auditors' independence. These are services that are likely to:

(i) have a significant impact on the audit client's financial statements and thus result in the auditor reviewing his/her own (or their firm's) work (i.e., services that pose a particularly serious self-review threat); and/or

(ii) result in the auditor:

- making decisions that should be made by the client's management (i.e., services that pose a particularly serious management threat); or

- acting as an advocate for the client (i.e., services that pose a particularly serious advocacy threat).

Figure 4.1:   Non-audit services UK auditors may not provide to their audit clients

Non-audit services	Threats to independence		
	Self-review	Manage-ment	Advo-cacy
	√	√	
Internal Audit services especially where these involve outsourcing substantially all of the internal audit function to the audit firm or the audit cannot be performed without placing significant reliance on the internal audit work performed	√	√	
Services involving the design, provision or implementation of information technology systems which are important to any significant part of the accounting system or preparation of the financial statements	√	√	
Valuation (including actuarial) services where the resulting valuations have a material effect on the financial statements	√	√	
Tax services in cases where the audit firm provides a significant portion of the client's tax planning and compliance work, or tax work that results in calculations likely to be used in the preparation of accounting entries that are material to the financial statements	√	√	
Tax services that result in the auditor (or firm) acting as an advocate for the client in an appeals court or tribunal in relation to a matter that is material to the financial statements or an audit judgment	√		√
Corporate finance services (including taking responsibility for dealing in, underwriting or promoting shares) and other transaction-related services (such as due diligence investigations, and investigations of the tax affairs of possible acquisitions or disposals)	√	√	√
Recruitment and remuneration services where such services involve the audit firm taking responsibility for appointing a director or employee, for recruiting a person to a key management position, or providing advice on the remuneration of a director or key management position of the client		√	
Litigation support services that involve the audit firm estimating the likely outcome of a pending legal matter that could be material to an amount or other disclosure in the financial statements	√		
Legal services that involve the audit firm acting as the client's solicitor, representing the client in the resolution of a dispute or litigation which is material to an amount or other disclosure in the financial statements	√		√

We provide examples of such services in Figure 4.1. ES5 notes that, for these services, no safeguards are available to reduce the threat they pose to auditors' independence to an acceptable level; thus, auditors may not provide them to their audit clients. Comparing the services ES5 prohibits auditors in the UK from providing to their audit clients with those prohibited by SOX, sec. 201 (outlined above), it may be seen that they are remarkably similar.

4.4 OTHER PROPOSALS TO STRENGTHEN AUDITORS' INDEPENDENCE

4.4.1 Key objectives of other proposals

We noted earlier in this chapter that many politicians, investors and other commentators have drawn attention to the dangers posed to auditors' independence from auditors being dependent on their clients' managements for their continued appointment. From the measures discussed in section 4.3, it is clear that, especially since the turn of the twenty-first century, significant legislative and regulatory changes have been introduced to try to ensure that auditors avoid situations where threats to their independence cannot be eliminated or reduced to an acceptable level. Nevertheless, since the mid-1980s, concern about the apparent impairment of auditors' independence in high profile cases such as Johnson Matthey Bankers, Ferranti, Bank of Credit & Commerce International (BCCI), and Barings Bank in the UK; Enron, World-Com, Tyco, Xerox, and Lehman Brothers in the USA; Parmalat in Italy; and HIH in Australia, has resulted in a number of proposals which are designed, in particular, to prevent audit client managements from being involved in the appointment of their company's auditor. We examine two such proposals below, namely:

* the appointment of auditors by the State or a State agency;
* the appointment of auditors by a shareholder or stakeholder panel.

A further development designed to divorce those responsible for the day-to-day management of companies from the appointment of their company's auditor is that of enhancing the role of audit committees in the auditor appointment process. We discuss the role and responsibilities of audit committees in section 4.5.

4.4.2 Appointment of company auditors by the State or a State agency

Although the Companies Act 2006 (s. 489) places responsibility on shareholders to appoint their company's auditor and determine the associated remuneration, the shareholders generally delegate this responsibility to the company's management. This is regrettable as it seems unlikely that auditors will be truly independent of their clients while their appointment, dismissal and remuneration depends on (or is significantly influenced by) their clients' managements – those who prepare the financial statements the auditor is to examine. This has given rise to the suggestion that auditors' independence would be strengthened if company auditors were appointed by the State, a State agency or an independent oversight body. Haber (2005), for example, notes:

> Discussion of the Enron scandal tends to focus on the length of the relationship between Andersen and Enron and the additional services rendered by Andersen to Enron . . . [however] Andersen's independence would be questioned simply because . . . the client paid a fee to the auditor. . . . Auditors are hired and paid

by the client, but their product is really for use by the public . . . Having the stock exchanges (or the SEC or another oversight body) be responsible for hiring and paying the auditors would remove the potential for independence impairment. If the goal is to increase the public's perception of auditor independence, then the company being audited can no longer be the client. Another party must contract for the audit, pay the auditor, and become the client. . . . All other solutions . . . leave open the potential for questioning independence, and therefore for undermining the usefulness of the audit process.

However, this 'solution' to the auditor independence problem is not without significant difficulties. For example, if the State, a State agency, or a regulatory oversight body such as the Public Company Accounting Oversight Board (PCAOB) in the USA or the FRC in the UK were to be responsible for auditors' appointment and remuneration, then the State could also exert influence over the audit function. This would introduce the possibility of auditors becoming susceptible to the political agenda of the day and of the audit profession losing its political and professional independence. Further, the body responsible for appointing auditors would face the difficulty of deciding a basis for assigning particular auditors to particular companies. Each company would need to be assigned an audit firm with the knowledge and skills, and complement of suitably qualified and experienced staff, appropriate to its circumstances; equally, the audits would need to be assigned equitably among the available audit firms.

4.4.3   Shareholder or stakeholder panel

An alternative proposal, which overcomes the difficulties attaching to auditors being appointed by the State, a State agency or a regulatory oversight body, is that of auditors being appointed by an independent panel of the relevant company's shareholders. Rather than the company's shareholders as a body being legally responsible for appointing the auditor and, for pragmatic reasons, delegating this responsibility to the company's management, the shareholders could appoint a panel (which would exclude the company's directors) to represent their interests in appointing, and determining the remuneration of, the company's auditor and overseeing the external audit function.

The idea of a shareholder panel was mooted by the APB (1992, 1994) and it was also suggested that, in time, it might develop into a stakeholder panel. Such a panel would represent a wider group of interests – those of the company's stakeholders (including the shareholders) – rather than those of the shareholders alone (Hatherly, 1995).[51] From the perspective of strengthening

---

[51] The notion of auditors' appointment by a panel of the relevant company's stakeholders accords with the idea discussed in Chapter 1 (section 1.6.3) and the social purpose of auditing identified in Chapter 3 (section 3.1), namely, that the audit is an integral element of securing corporate accountability.

auditors' independence, the shareholder/stakeholder panel is conceptually superior to the notion of auditors being appointed by the company's audit committee which is discussed below. This is because, unlike stakeholders (or shareholders) who are outside – and independent of – the auditee's governance structure, the audit committee is a committee of the company's board of directors and it cannot therefore support the auditor independently of the board. Although the audit committee should consist of mainly (or wholly) non-executive directors (who are independent of the day-to-day management of the company), it is the board as a whole (including non-executive as well as executive directors) which is legally responsible for the preparation of the company's financial statements.

Although the shareholder/stakeholder panel idea may have conceptual superiority over alternative proposals for securing auditors' independence, its implementation faces serious obstacles. For example, if the shareholder or stakeholder panel is to be responsible for the appointment and oversight of the company's auditor, its members would gain detailed knowledge of the company, its financial performance and its prospects that would not be available (at least at the same time) to all other shareholders and investors. As a consequence, there is a danger that, if some members of the panel traded in the company's shares, they would be open to allegations of insider trading.

There is also the difficulty of appointing the shareholder or stakeholder panel. Should, for example, the shareholder panel comprise (or be elected or appointed by) only shareholders who intend, or guarantee, to hold their shares in the company for – say – the next 12 months? Should the panel comprise (or be elected or appointed by) only those who have been shareholders in the company for a specified number of years? If so, what period should be specified? and so on. The appointment criteria are even more problematic for a stakeholder panel. For example, how should the stakeholder groups to be represented on the panel be identified? How should the representatives of disparate groups such as customers, suppliers and the local community be selected? How large should the panel be? How should the places on the panel be allocated to the various stakeholder groups, each of which has a distinct relationship with the company?

Notwithstanding its conceptual merit, largely as a consequence of implementation difficulties, to date the idea of shareholder/stakeholder panels has not attracted much support as a mechanism for divorcing company managements from the auditor appointment process. Instead, the attention of regulators around the world has focused on the role audit committees can play in ensuring their company's auditor is properly independent.

4.5   ROLE AND RESPONSIBILITIES OF AUDIT COMMITTEES

4.5.1   Reasons for establishing audit committees

An audit committee is a committee of the board of directors which has delegated responsibility from the board for, *inter alia*, overseeing the external financial reporting process and the external audit.

Over the past four or so decades, the value of audit committees as a means of enhancing external financial reporting, and ensuring the independence of external auditors, has been increasingly recognised and these committees have become a normal feature of corporate life, especially of public companies, in many parts of the world. Their development has varied from country to country but, interestingly, in each case it has been stimulated by unexpected corporate failure and/or reports of misconduct by senior executives or directors. It seems that politicians, regulators and the public believe that, had the auditors been properly independent of their audit clients' managements and performed their duties with due skill and care, they would have sounded warning bells in at least some of the cases. Following on from this, it is generally reasoned that if audit committees, consisting of independent non-executive directors, are established to oversee the appointment of external auditors and the external audit function, then unexpected corporate failure and undetected misconduct by senior officials will be significantly reduced if not eliminated. In the next two sections we outline (a) the development and (b) the responsibilities of audit committees.

4.5.2   Development of audit committees

The first significant appearance of audit committees was in Canada and the USA. During the 1970s, audit committees were established in these countries largely as a result of "several well-publicised instances of corporate wrongdoing and questionable conduct that severely tarnished the image of big business in North America" (CICA, 1981, p. 1). In 1971, prompted by the collapse of Atlantic Acceptance Corporation Ltd in Canada in 1965, audit committees became a legal requirement for public companies incorporated in Ontario. In 1973, a similar requirement became effective for public companies incorporated in British Columbia and, in 1975, for federally incorporated public companies. Thus, Canada became the first country to introduce a legal requirement for public companies to establish audit committees.

In the USA, audit committees received their first major endorsement, from both the New York Stock Exchange (NYSE) and the SEC, in the late 1930s as a result of the infamous *McKesson & Robbins* case. However, few companies established audit committees until the 1970s when interest in them was revived as a result of several factors, including a number of legal decisions (including the *BarChris Construction Corporation* case) which emphasised that executive and non-executive directors are equally responsible for their company's affairs, and equally liable for misleading financial statements. Other factors included the unexpected collapse of Penn Central Company, the notorious Equity Funding fraud, and the widespread instances of corporate misconduct which came to light during the enquiries which led to enactment of the Foreign Corrupt Practices Act in 1977 (CICA, 1981, pp. 98–99).

In 1978, primarily as a result of pressure from politicians and the SEC for public companies to be required to establish audit committees, the NYSE introduced a requirement for companies listed on the exchange to establish an audit committee. The adoption of these committees was further encouraged in 1987 when the National Commission on Fraudulent Financial Reporting (1987; the Treadway Commission) recommended that they be established by all public companies. Since enactment of SOX in 2002, all companies registered with the SEC (virtually all public companies registered or listed in the USA and their significant subsidiaries) have been required to establish an audit committee comprised solely of independent directors.[52]

In the UK, adoption of audit committees did not begin in earnest until the late 1980s. Indeed, until 1987, neither the professional accountancy bodies nor regulatory agencies such as the Bank of England and the DTI[53] seemed to give these committees serious consideration. However, in 1987, stimulated by the serious and growing size and incidence of corporate fraud, the ICAEW recommended that public companies be required to establish audit committees, and the Bank of England and PRO-NED[54] urged these companies to adopt such committees. Pressure on public companies to establish audit committees was boosted in 1992 when the Committee on the Financial Aspects of Corporate Governance (CFACG; the Cadbury Committee) included the establishment of an audit committee, composed of at least three non-executive directors, in its *Code of Best Practice* (CFACG, 1992, clause 4.3).[55] Today, the

---

[52] SOX, sec. 301, provides that, in order to be considered independent, audit committee members may not, other than in their capacity as directors:
    (i) accept any consulting, advisory, or other compensatory fee from the company;
    (ii) be an affiliated person of the company or any subsidiary thereof.

[53] See footnote 4.

[54] An organisation established in 1982 by the Stock Exchange, the Confederation of British Industry, the Bank of England and other financial institutions to promote the appointment of non-executive directors to Boards of Directors.

[55] In April 1993, the London Stock Exchange made it a requirement for companies listed on the Stock Exchange to include in their annual reports a statement on whether or not they had complied with the Cadbury Committee's *Code of Best Practice* during the reporting period and, if not, to identify and provide reasons for their non-compliance.

UK Listing Authority (UKLA)[56] requires all companies listed on the London Stock Exchange to comply with *The UK Corporate Governance Code* (FRC, 2012a) or to disclose the respects in which they have not done so and to provide reasons for their non-compliance. The Code requires listed companies to establish an audit committee of at least three (or, in the case of smaller companies, two[57]) independent non-executive directors[58] one of whom possesses "recent and relevant financial experience" (Code provision C.3.1).

Today, audit committees are a normal feature of corporate life in most parts of the world. However, although there has been a trend in recent years towards regulators requiring audit committees to comprise, or include, independent non-executive directors, regulations governing the composition of audit committees vary between countries. This may be illustrated by reference to the EU *Statutory Audit Directive* (EU, 2006; EU Audit Directive) which states:

> Each public-interest entity[59] shall have an audit committee. The Member State shall determine whether audit committees are to be composed of non-executive members of the administrative body [i.e., Board of Directors] and/or members of the supervisory body [in States, such as Germany, which have a two-tier board structure] of the audited entity and/or members appointed by the general meeting

---

[56] In 2001, responsibility for the UKLA (and hence for the listing rules) passed from the London Stock Exchange to the Financial Services Authority (FSA). The FSA delegated responsibility for *The UK Corporate Governance Code* to the FRC. In April 2013, the FSA was disbanded and its functions were transferred to the Financial Conduct Authority (FCA) and the Prudential Regulation Authority (PRA) (both of which are overseen by the Policy Committee of the Bank of England). Responsibility for the UKLA passed to the FCA but that for *The UK Corporate Governance Code* remained with the FRC.

[57] Smaller companies are defined as those below the FTSE 350 (*The UK Corporate Governance Code*, footnote 6).

[58] Non-executive directors are directors who are not involved in the day-to-day management of the company. According to *The UK Corporate Governance Code* (provision B.1.1), it is a matter for the Board of Directors to determine whether a director:

is independent in character and judgement and whether there are relationships or circumstances which are likely to affect, or could appear to affect, the director's judgement. The Board should state its reasons if it determines that a director is independent notwithstanding the existence of relationships or circumstances which may appear relevant to its determination, including if the director:

- has been an employee of the company or group within the last five years;
- has, or has had within the last three years, a material business relationship with the company either directly, or as a partner, shareholder, director or senior employee of a body that has such a relationship with the company;
- has received or receives additional remuneration from the company apart from a director's fee, participates in the company's share option or a performance-related pay scheme, or is a member of the company's pension scheme;
- has close family ties with any of the company's advisers, directors or senior employees;
- holds cross-directorships or has significant links with other directors through involvement in other companies or bodies;
- represents a significant shareholder; or
- has served on the board for more than nine years from the date of their first election.

[59] 'Public-interest entities' are defined in Article 2(13) as:

entities governed by the law of a Member State whose transferable securities are admitted to trading on a regulated market of any Member State . . ., credit institutions . . . and insurance undertakings . . . Member States may also designate other entities as public-interest entities, for instance entities that are of significant public relevance because of the nature of their business, their size or the number of their employees.

of shareholders of the audited entity. At least one member of the audit committee shall be independent and shall have competence in accounting and/or auditing. [art. 41(1)]

4.5.3 Responsibilities of audit committees

Until the mid-1970s, the principal responsibilities of audit committees were confined to matters related to external financial reporting and the external audit. In general, audit committees were expected to do little more than:

- select (and recommend to the shareholders for approval) the company's external auditor;
- oversee the external financial reporting process – including the external audit; and
- review the external financial statements prior to their submission to the full board of directors for approval.

Since the mid-1970s, the value of audit committees to fulfil a much broader function has been recognised – that of securing responsible corporate governance.[60] This broader function is reflected in the duties audit committees are now typically expected to perform. These include, for example:

- helping to establish an environment in which the company's internal controls can operate effectively;
- ensuring the maintenance of an effective accounting system (with effective internal financial controls);
- reviewing the company's accounting policies and external reporting requirements;
- selecting, and recommending for appointment, the company's external auditor and recommending the auditor's remuneration;
- appointing the company's chief internal auditor;
- discussing with the chief internal auditor and external audit engagement partner, the intended scope of the internal and external audit, respectively, and satisfying itself that no unjustified restrictions on internal or external audit activities have been imposed by the company's senior managers;
- reviewing the findings and recommendations of the internal and external auditors;
- reviewing implementation of the auditors' recommendations;
- reviewing the company's annual report (including its financial statements) prior to its submission to the full board of directors;
- reviewing public announcements relating to financial matters prior to their release;

---

[60] For a full discussion of the development of audit committees and the change in their role in the mid-1970s see Porter and Gendall (1997).

- reviewing, and monitoring compliance with, the company's code of conduct;
- reviewing the company's compliance with legal and regulatory requirements.

As audit committees have become more commonplace, and their value in fulfilling a broad corporate governance role has come to be recognised, so regulators have sought to specify not only the requirements of audit committees' composition but also their role and responsibilities. A significant early step in this direction was taken in 1998 in the USA when the Blue Ribbon Committee on *Improving the Effectiveness of Corporate Audit Committees* was established by the NYSE and the National Association of Securities Dealers (NASD). The Committee's Report and Recommendations (Blue Ribbon Report, 1999, pp. 37–44) set out five Guiding Principles for audit committees' best practice. These may be summarised as follows:

- *Principle 1*: a company's audit committee plays a pivotal role in monitoring the other components of the audit function. In particular, the audit committee should oversee:
    - (i) the company's management, which has primary responsibility for preparing the financial statements,
    - (ii) the external auditor, on whom investors rely to provide an impartial, robust examination of the financial statements to ensure their credibility, and
    - (iii) where they exist, internal auditors, who provide information and advice on the company's financial reporting processes and the safeguards that exist.
- *Principle 2*: independent communication and information flow between the audit committee and the company's internal auditors is extremely important.
- *Principle 3*: independent communication and information flow between the audit committee and the external auditor is extremely important.[61]
- *Principle 4*: candid discussions between the audit committee and, respectively, management, the internal auditors and the external auditor regarding issues concerned with judgments used in, and the quality of, the company's financial statements are extremely important.
- *Principle 5*: the existence of an effective audit committee, comprised of diligent and knowledgeable members, is extremely important for all public companies.

---

[61] External auditors' communication with companies' directors (or, more usually, their audit committees) is discussed in Chapter 14, section 14.8.

In 2000, building on the work and recommendations of the Blue Ribbon Committee, the Panel on Audit Effectiveness [established in the USA in 1998 by the Public Oversight Board (POB)[62] in response to a request by the SEC] published its Final Report (Panel on Audit Effectiveness, 2000). This recommended, *inter alia*, that audit committees:

- obtain annually from management a written report on the effectiveness of the company's internal controls;
- review annually the performance of the company's external and internal auditors;
- be advised of plans to appoint personnel from the external audit firm to high level positions within the company;
- be proactive in ensuring factors such as time pressures on internal and external auditors are addressed so they do not impact negatively on the credibility of the audits performed;
- pre-approve any non-audit services, above a specified threshold, that are to be provided by the company's external auditor.

In 2002, SOX adopted and extended the recommendations of the Blue Ribbon Committee and Panel on Audit Effectiveness and enshrined some audit committee responsibilities in legislation. SOX, sec. 301, for example, specifies that the audit committee of each public company registered or listed in the USA is to:

- be directly responsible for the appointment, remuneration, and oversight of the work performed by the company's external auditor and for resolving any disagreements between the company's management and external auditor regarding financial reporting matters;
- establish procedures for
  - the receipt, retention and treatment of complaints received by the company regarding accounting, internal accounting controls or auditing matters; and
  - the confidential, anonymous submission by company employees of concerns regarding questionable accounting or auditing matters;
- have the authority to engage independent solicitors or other advisers as the committee considers necessary to carry out its duties;
- be provided with the funding the audit committee considers appropriate to pay for the services received from:
  - the external auditor, and
  - advisers employed by the audit committee.

---

[62] The POB was created as an independent, autonomous body in 1977 by the AICPA. Its primary role was to oversee and report on the programmes of the SEC Practice Section of the AICPA. (This Practice Section oversaw the auditors and audits of companies registered with the SEC.) In 2002, SOX, sec. 101, created the Public Company Accounting Oversight Board which, in effect, replaced the POB.

SOX, sec. 204, requires the company's auditor to report in a timely manner to the audit committee:

- all significant accounting policies and practices used in the preparation of the company's financial statements;
- all alternative treatments of financial information within generally accepted accounting principles the auditor has discussed with management, ramifications of adopting the alternative disclosures and treatments, and the treatment preferred by the auditor; and
- other material written communications between the auditor and management, such as any management letter or schedule of unadjusted differences.[63]

Additionally, in accordance with SOX, sec. 202, the audit committee must pre-approve all audit and non-audit services provided to the company by its external auditor unless the aggregate fees for the non-audit services supplied by the auditor do not amount to more than five per cent of the total fees paid by the company to the auditor.

The responsibilities of audit committees specified in the EU's *Statutory Audit Directive* (EU, 2006) are similar to those contained in SOX. For example, Article 41 states:

The audit committee [of a public-interest entity] shall, *inter alia*:

    (a) monitor the financial reporting process;
    (b) monitor the effectiveness of the company's internal control, internal audit where applicable, and risk management systems;
    (c) monitor the statutory audit of the annual and consolidated accounts;
    (d) review and monitor the independence of the statutory auditor . . . and in particular the provision of additional [non-audit] services to the audited entity.

[T]he proposal of the [Board of Directors] . . . for the appointment of a statutory auditor . . . shall be based on a recommendation made by the audit committee.

The statutory auditor . . . shall report to the audit committee on key matters arising from the statutory audit, and in particular on material weaknesses in internal control in relation to the financial reporting process.

The provisions of the EU's *Statutory Audit Directive* apply to the audit committees of public companies and other public-interest entities in the UK as in all other EU Member States. However, listed companies in the UK must also comply with the requirements of *The UK Corporate Governance Code* (the Code: FRC, 2012a). As can be seen from the Code provisions set out below, these are somewhat broader than those contained in the EU Audit Directive:

---

[63] Management letters (now part of auditors' 'communications with those charged with governance' and schedules of unadjusted differences are explained in Chapter 14, section 14.8.

C.3.2 The main role and responsibilities of the audit committee should be set out in written terms of reference and should include:

- to monitor the integrity of the financial statements of the company and any formal announcements relating to the company's financial perform-ance, reviewing significant financial reporting judgements contained in them;
- to review the company's internal financial controls and . . . [its] internal control and risk management systems;
- to monitor and review the effectiveness of the company's internal audit function;
- to make recommendations to the board . . . in relation to the appoint-ment, re-appointment and removal of the external auditor and to approve the remuneration and terms of engagement of the external auditor;
- to review and monitor the external auditor's independence and objectiv-ity and the effectiveness of the audit process . . .;
- to develop and implement policy on the engagement of the external auditor to supply non-audit services, taking into account relevant ethical guidance regarding the provision of non-audit services by the external audit firm; . . .

C.3.5 The audit committee should review arrangements by which staff of the company may, in confidence, raise concerns about possible improprieties in matters of financial reporting or other matters. The audit committee's objective should be to ensure that arrangements are in place for the pro-portionate and independent investigation of such matters and for appro-priate follow up action.

C.3.7 The audit committee should have primary responsibility for making a rec-ommendation on the appointment, reappointment and removal of exter-nal auditors. FTSE 350 companies should put the external audit contract out to tender at least every ten years. If the board does not accept the audit committee's recommendation, it should include in the annual report, and in any papers recommending appointment or re-appointment, a state-ment from the audit committee explaining the recommendations and should set out reasons why the board has taken a different position.

C.3.8 A separate section of the annual report should describe the work of the committee in discharging its responsibilities. The report should include:

- the significant issues that the committee considered in relation to the financial statements, and how these issues were addressed;
- an explanation of how it has assessed the effectiveness of the external audit process and the approach taken to the appointment or reappoint-ment of the external auditor, and information on the length of tenure of the current audit firm and when a tender was last conducted; and
- if the external auditor provides non-audit services, an explanation of how auditor objectivity and independence is safeguarded.

Reviewing the requirements of audit committees that SOX, the *Statutory Audit Directive* and *The UK Corporate Governance Code* have introduced, it is evident that they are largely designed to distance company executives from the appointment of their company's external auditor and thus prevent them from exerting 'pressure' on the auditor to comply with their wishes; in other words, they are designed to strengthen the auditor's independence. In Chapter 18 (section 18.5.1) we discuss some further changes to the responsibilities of audit committees (also largely designed to distance auditors from their clients) which have been proposed in the wake of the 2008 global financial crisis.

4.6 SUMMARY

The issue of auditors' independence seems to be aptly summarized by Turner (2001):

> . . . [T]he independence of auditors of public companies has been and continues to be an issue of paramount importance. . . . It is a subject that cannot be a question, but rather must be a given. But all too often today, the question is being asked, "Did the auditors provide an unbiased and truly independent report on the numbers?" To maintain their value to the capital markets and regain the confidence of investors, auditors around the globe must renew their covenant with investors; a covenant that says each auditor will remain . . . free from a web of entanglements or arrangements that threaten the appearance of his or her objectivity; that with the auditor's stamp, the numbers speak the truth. (p. 7)

Maintaining auditors' independence, both in fact (or of mind) and in appearance, is clearly crucial to the credibility of the opinion expressed by auditors in their audit reports and, thus, to the future of the audit function and the smooth functioning of financial markets. However, it is equally evident that various factors serve to undermine (or threaten) this independence – in particular, auditors having a financial, business, employment or personal involvement with an audit client; their undue dependence on a client for fee income; auditors receiving gifts and hospitality from, or offering gifts and hospitality to, an audit client; a long association between auditors and their clients; auditors providing non-audit services to their audit clients; and client managements' controlling the appointment and remuneration of their company's auditor.

As we have seen in this chapter, since 2001, when Turner expressed the words cited above, regulators around the world have introduced measures designed to ensure that auditors "remain free from a web of entanglements and arrangements that threaten . . . [their] objectivity." Ethical standards have been promulgated which identify threats, or perceived threats, to auditors' independence, and require auditors to assess their exposure to such threats and, when necessary, to apply appropriate safeguards. However, shaken by well-publicised audit failures in the early years of the twenty-first century, and mindful of the importance of auditors' independence to the well-being of financial markets, regulators and legislators in many countries have introduced additional safeguards. These include the mandatory rotation of senior audit personnel away from an audit client after a specified number of years, banning auditors from providing certain services to their audit clients, and requiring public (especially listed) companies to establish audit committees to oversee the external financial reporting process and the external audit function. Nevertheless, in the view of a significant number of commentators, these measures fail to address the key problem – that of auditors being appointed and remunerated by their clients' directors who are responsible for preparing the financial statements on which the auditors are to express an opinion. To overcome this difficulty, it has been proposed that auditors be appointed by (i) the State (or a State agency or an oversight body) or (ii) a panel of representatives of the client's shareholders or stakeholders. However, both of these means of appointing auditors face implementation hurdles that are difficult to overcome and, to date, neither has gained widespread support. Another proposal, designed to distance auditors from their clients – the mandatory rotation of audit firms (rather than senior audit personnel) – has been the subject of widespread debate but, currently, the costs attaching to this proposal are generally adjudged to outweigh the benefits to be derived from the resulting increase in auditor independence. Nevertheless, as will be seen from the discussion presented in Chapter 18, this proposal is attracting new regulatory support.

SELF-REVIEW QUESTIONS

4.1 Explain briefly the importance of auditors being independent both in fact (or of mind) and in appearance.

4.2 Identify, and provide examples to illustrate, six 'threats' to auditors' independence.

4.3 Explain briefly three general safeguards that audit firms and/or audit engagement partners are required to apply to help protect the auditor's independence.

4.4 (a) Identify seven circumstances that present a threat to auditors' independence.
     (b) For each circumstance, outline one safeguard that might prevent auditors' independence from being compromised.

4.5 (a) Identify two forms of 'mandatory rotation of auditors'.
     (b) Outline five arguments in favour and five arguments against mandatory auditor rotation.
     (c) Outline the auditor rotation requirements that apply in the UK.

4.6   List seven non-audit services the Sarbanes-Oxley Act of 2002 prohibits auditors from providing to audit clients which are SEC registrants.

4.7   List seven services which the APB's Ethical Standard 5 prohibits auditors in the UK from providing to their audit clients.

4.8   (a) Explain briefly how auditors' independence might be strengthened if they were appointed by:
        (i) the State or a State agency, or
        (ii) a shareholder or stakeholder panel.
        (b) For each of (i) and (ii) above, explain briefly the obstacles to appointing auditors by this means.

4.9   Explain briefly:
        (i) what is meant by 'an audit committee'
        (ii) the usual composition of audit committees in UK public listed companies.

4.10   Explain briefly two ways in which an audit committee can help to strengthen the independence of the company's auditor.

REFERENCES

American Institute of Certified Public Accountants (AICPA). (1992). *Statement of Position Regarding Mandatory Rotation of Audit Firms of Publicly Held Companies.* New York: AICPA.

Arel, B., Brody, R., & Pany, K. (2005). Audit firm rotation and audit quality. *CPA Journal,* 75(1), 36–39.

Arens, A.A., & Loebbecke, J.K. (1980). *Auditing: An Integrated Approach*, 2nd ed. Englewood Cliffs, NJ: Prentice Hall Inc.

Arrunada, B., & Paz-Ares, C. (1995). *Economic Consequences of Mandatory Auditor Rotation* (as quoted in ICAEW, 2002).

Audit Inspection Unit (AIU). (2008, December). *2007/8 Audit Quality Inspections: An Overview*. London: Financial Reporting Council.

Audit Inspection Unit (AIU). (2010, July). *2009/10 Annual Report*. London: Financial Reporting Council.

Auditing Practices Board (APB). (1992). *Future Development of Auditing*. London: APB.

Auditing Practices Board (APB). (1994). *The Audit Agenda*. London: APB.

Auditing Practices Board (APB). (2009). Ethical Standard (ES) 3: *Long Association with the Audit Engagement*. London: Financial Reporting Council.

Auditing Practices Board (APB). (2010a). Ethical Standard (ES) 2: *Financial, Business, Employment and Personal Relationships*. London: Financial Reporting Council.

Auditing Practices Board (APB). (2010b). Ethical Standard (ES) 4: *Fees, Remuneration and Evaluation Policies, Litigation, Gifts and Hospitality*. London: Financial Reporting Council.

Auditing Practices Board (APB). (2011a). Ethical Standard (ES) 1: *Integrity, Objectivity and Independence*. London: Financial Reporting Council.

Auditing Practices Board (APB). (2011b). Ethical Standard (ES) 5: *Non-audit Services Provided to Audited Entities*. London: Financial Reporting Council.

Bazerman, M.H., Loewenstein, G., & Moore, D.A. (2002). Why good accountants do bad audits. *Harvard Business Review*, *80*(11), 97–102.

Blue Ribbon Committee on Improving the Effectiveness of Corporate Audit Committees. (1999). *Report and Final Recommendations of the Blue Ribbon Committee* (Blue Ribbon Report). New York: New York Stock Exchange and National Association of Securities Dealers.

Boyle, P. (2009, 4 November). *FRC Advised Caution on Internal/External Audit Boundary*, www.frc.org.uk/press/pub2157.html, accessed 5 November 2009.

Briloff, A.J. (1986, April). *Corporate Governance and Accountability: Whose Responsibility?* Unpublished address delivered at the University of Connecticut, Storrs, CT.

Canadian Institute of Chartered Accountants (CICA). (1981). *Audit Committees: A Research Study*. Toronto: CICA.

Christodoulou, M. (2009, 20 August). *Debate Rages Over KPMG's Cut-Price Rentokil Audit Deal*, www.accountancyage.com/aa/news/1758923/debate-rages-kpmg-s-cut -price-rentokil-audit-deal, accessed 8 May 2013.

Commission on Auditors' Responsibilities (CAR). (1978). *Report, Conclusions and Recommendations* (The Cohen Commission). New York: American Institute of Certified Public Accountants.

Committee on the Financial Aspects of Corporate Governance (CFACG, Cadbury Committee). (1992). *Report of the Committee on the Financial Aspects of Corporate Governance*. London: Gee.

Cowen, S.S. (1980). Non-audit services: How much is too much? *Journal of Accountancy*, *150*(6), 51–56.

Enron Watchdog. (2002). *Why Accountants should be Banned from Providing Consulting Services to Audit Clients*, www.enronwatchdog.org/topreforms/topreforms1, accessed 5 September 2003.

European Union (EU). (2002, May). *Recommendation: Statutory Auditors' Independence in the EU: A Set of Fundamental Principles*. Brussels: EU: 2002/590/EC.

European Union (EU). (2006). *Directive 2006/43/EC of the European Parliament and of the Council on the Statutory Audits of Annual Accounts and Consolidated Accounts (Statutory Audit Directive)*. Brussels: European Parliament and Council.

European Union (EU). (2011, November). *Proposal for a Regulation of the European Parliament and of the Council on Specific Requirements Regarding Statutory Audit of Public Interest Entities. COM(2011)0779 final 2011/0359(COD)*. Brussels: European Commission.

Fédération des Experts Comptables Européens (FEE). (2004). *Mandatory Rotation of Audit Firms*. Brussels: FEE.

Financial Director. (2010). *Audit Fees Survey 2009*, www.financialdirector.co.uk/financial-director/analysis/1744271/pounds-sense-fds-audit-fees-survey-2009, accessed 9 May 2013.

Financial Reporting Council (FRC). (2004). *Financial Reporting Council Regulatory Strategy*. London: FRC.

Financial Reporting Council (FRC). (2010). *The UK Corporate Governance Code*. London: FRC.

Financial Reporting Council (FRC). (2012a). *The UK Corporate Governance Code*. London: FRC.

Financial Reporting Council (FRC). (2012b). *FRC Structure*, www.frc.org.uk/Abount-the-FRC/FRC-structure.aspx, accessed 10 August 2012.

Financial Reporting Council (FRC). (2012c). *Guidance on Audit Committees*. London: FRC.

Financial Reporting Council (FRC). (2013a). *Scope and Authority of Audit and Assurance Pronouncements*. London: FRC.

Financial Reporting Council (FRC). (2013b). International Standard on Auditing (UK and Ireland) 610: *Using the Work of Internal Auditors*, London: FRC.

Financial Reporting Council (FRC). (2013c). *FRC Prohibits the Use of Internal Audit Staff on the External Audit Team*, www.frc.org.uk/News-and-Events/FRC-Press/Press/2013/June/FRC-prohits-the-use-of-internal-audit-staff-on-t.aspx, accessed 20 June 2013.

General Accounting Office (GAO). (2003, November). *Public Accounting Firms: Required Study on the Potential Effects of Mandatory Audit Firm Rotation*. Report to the Senate Committee on Banking, Housing, and Urban Affairs and the House Committee on Financial Services. Washington: GAO-04-216.

George, N. (2004). Auditor rotation and the quality of audits. *CPA Journal, 74*(12), 22–27.

Haber, J.R. (2005). Does being the auditor impair independence? *CPA Journal, LXXV*(6), 12.

Harian, U. (2002, 16 March). Singapore banks to rotate audit firms under new rules. *Suara Merdeka*, www.suaramerdeka.com/harian/0203/16/eng8.htm, accessed 28 March 2003.

Hatherly, D.J. (1995). The case for the shareholder panel in the U.K. *European Accounting Review, 4*(3), 535–553.

Healey, T. (2004, 12 March). The best safeguard against financial scandal. *Financial Times*. London.

Healy, P.M. & Palepu, K.G. (2003). The fall of Enron. *Journal of Economic Perspectives, 7*(2), 3–26.

Hermes. (2002). *Auditor Independence*, www.hermes.co.uk/pdf/corporate_governance/ commentary/comment_on_auditor_independence, accessed 5 April 2003.

Hirsch, J. (2002, 23 January). Enron audit fee raises some brows. *Los Angeles Times*. Los Angeles.

Institute of Chartered Accountants in England and Wales (ICAEW). (2002, July). *Mandatory Rotation of Audit Firms: Review of Current Requirements, Research and Publications*. London: ICAEW.

International Ethics Standards Board for Accountants (IESBA). (2009). *Code of Ethics for Professional Accountants (IESBA Code)*. New York: International Federation of Accountants.

International Federation of Accountants (IFAC). (2002). *Code of Ethics for Professional Accountants*. New York: IFAC.

International Federation of Accountants (IFAC). (2010). *Handbook of the Code of Ethics for Professional Accountants*. New York: IFAC.

Jeppesen, K.K. (1998). Reinventing auditing, redefining consulting and independence. *European Accounting Review*, 7(3), 517–539.

Larkin, D. (2004). Mandatory auditor rotation. *Nonprofit Alert*, 4(6). USA: BDO Seidman, LLP.

Levitt, A. (2000, 18 September). *A Profession at the Crossroads*. Speech by SEC Chairman to National Association of State Boards of Accountancy, Boston.

Metcalf, L. (1976). *The Accounting Establishment: A Staff Study*. A Report of the Senate Subcommittee on Reports, Accounting and Management of the Committee on Government Operations, Chaired by Senator Lee Metcalf, Washington: US Government Printing Office.

Mitchell, A., & Sikka, P. (1993). Accounting for change: The institutions of accountancy. *Critical Perspectives on Accounting*, 4(1), 29–52.

National Commission on Fraudulent Financial Reporting. (Treadway Commission). (1987). *Report of the National Commission on Fraudulent Financial Reporting*. New York: American Institute of Certified Public Accountants.

Pajuelo, J. (2003, 21 November). Brazil reaffirms tougher auditor rule than U.S. *The ISS Friday Report*, p. 6. USA: Maryland: Institutional Shareholders Services, Inc, va.issproxy.com/resourcecenter/publications/Governance_weekly/fridayreport11212003 .html#5, accessed 8 May 2013.

Panel on Audit Effectiveness. (2000). *Report and Recommendations*. New York: Public Oversight Board.

Porter, B.A., & Gendall, P.J. (1997), *Audit Committees in Private and Public Sector Corporates: An Empirical Investigation*. Paper presented at the 20th Annual Congress of the European Accounting Association, Graz, Austria.

PricewaterhouseCoopers. (2002, 11 November). Maintaining auditor independence. *The Edge*. PricewaterhouseCoopers International Limited.

Public Company Accounting Oversight Board (PCAOB). (2008, 24 April). *Board Adopts New Ethics and Independence Rule Concerning Communications with*

Audit Committees and an Amendment to Its Existing Tax Services Rule. Washington: PCAOB.

Raiborn, C., Schorg, C.A., & Massoud, M. (2006). *Should Auditor Rotation be Mandatory? Wiley Interscience*, www.interscience.wiley.com, 37–49.

Reed, K. (2011, 6 October). *Accountants Disciplined over Audit Governance*, www.accountancyage.com/aa/news/2114979/accountants-disciplined-audit-governance, accessed 8 May 2013.

SDA Università Bocconi (Bocconi University). (2002). *The Impact of Mandatory Audit Rotation on Audit Quality and on Audit Pricing: The Case of Italy.* Milan: SDA Università Bocconi, Corporate Finance and Real Estate Department and Administration and Control Department. (Unpublished.)

Securities and Exchange Commission (SEC). (2000a). Proposed rule: *Revision of the Commission's Auditor Independence Requirements.* Washington: SEC. Ref 34-42994.

Securities and Exchange Commission (SEC). (2000b). Final rule: *Revision of the Commission's Auditor Independence Requirements.* Washington: SEC. Ref 33-7919.

Securities and Exchange Commission (SEC). (2002, 14 January). *SEC Censures KPMG for Auditor Independence Violation.* Press Release 2002-4. Washington: SEC.

Squires, S.E., Smith, C.J., McDougall, L., & Yeack, W.R. (2003). *Inside Arthur Andersen: Shifting Values, Unexpected Consequences.* Englewood Cliffs, NJ: Prentice Hall, Financial Times.

Statutory Instrument (SI) 2005 No. 2417: *The Companies (Disclosure of Auditor Remuneration) Regulations 2005.*

Statutory Instrument (SI) 2008 No. 489: *The Companies (Disclosure of Auditor Remuneration and Liability Limitation Agreements) Regulations 2008.*

Statutory Instrument (SI) 2011 No. 2198: *The Companies (Disclosure of Auditor Remuneration and Liability Limitation Agreements) Regulations 2011.*

Turner, L.E. (2001, 28 June). *Independence: A Covenant for the Ages.* Speech by SEC Chief Accountant to International Organization of Securities Commissions, Stockholm, Sweden.

ADDITIONAL READING

Al-Najjar, B. (2011). The determinants of audit committee independence and activity: Evidence from the UK. *International Journal of Auditing, 15*(2), 191–203.

Bazerman, M.H., & Moore, D. (2011). Is it time for auditor independence yet? *Accounting, Organizations and Society, 36*(4–5), 310–312.

Beattie, V., Fearnley, S., & Hines, T. (2012). Do audit committees really engage with auditors on audit planning and performance? *Accounting and Business Research, 42*(3), 349–375.

Bedard, J., & Gendon, Y. (2010). Strengthening the financial statement reporting system: Can audit committees deliver? *International Journal of Auditing, 14*(2), 174–210.

Bierstaker, J.L., Cohen, J.R., DeZoort, F.T., & Hermanson, D.R. (2012). Audit committee compensation, fairness, and the resolution of accounting disagreements. *Auditing: A Journal of Practice & Theory, 31*(2), 131–150.

Brown-Liburd, H.L., & Wright, A.M. (2011). The effect of past client relationship and strength of the audit committee on auditor negotiations. *Auditing: A Journal of Practice & Theory, 30*(4), 51–69.

Callaghan, J., Parkash, M., & Singhal, R. (2009). Going-concern audit opinions and the provision of non-audit services: Implications for auditor independence of bankrupt firms. *Auditing: A Journal of Practice & Theory, 28*(1), 153–169.

Caskey, J., Nagar, V., & Petacchi, P. (2010). Reporting bias with an audit committee. *Accounting Review, 85*(2), 447–481.

Cohen, J.R., Gaynor, L.M., Krishnamoorthy, G., & Wright, A.M. (2011). The impact on auditor judgements of CEO influence on audit committee independence. *Auditing: A Journal of Practice & Theory, 30*(4), 129–147.

Dart, E. (2011). UK investors' perceptions of auditor independence. *British Accounting Review, 43*(3), 173–185.

De-Zoort, F.T., Holt, T., & Taylor, M.H. (2012). A test of the auditor reliability framework using lenders' judgments. *Accounting Organizations and Society, 37*(8), 519–533.

Habib, A. (2012). Non-audit service fees and financial reporting quality: A meta-analysis. *Abacus, 48*(2), 214–248.

Holland, K., & Lane, J. (2012). Perceived auditor independence and audit firm fees. *Accounting and Business Research, 42*(2), 115–141.

Hudaib, M., & Haniffa, R. (2009). Exploring auditor independence: An interpretive approach. *Accounting, Auditing & Accountability Journal, 22*(2), 221–246.

Jamal, K., & Sunder, S. (2011). Is mandated independence necessary for audit quality? *Accounting, Organizations and Society, 36*(4–5), 284–292.

Kanagaretnam, K., Krishnan, G.V., & Lobo, G.J. (2010). An empirical analysis of auditor independence in the banking industry. *Accounting Review, 85*(6), 2011–2046.

Koch, C., Weber, M., & Wustemann, J. (2012). Can auditors be independent? Experimental evidence on the effects of client type. *European Accounting Review, 21*(4), 797–823.

Magilke, M.J., Mayhew, B.W., & Pike, J.E. (2009). Are independent audit committee members objective? *Accounting Review, 84*(6), 1959–1981.

Norman, C.S., Rose, J.M., & Suh, I.S. (2011). The effects of disclosure type and audit committee expertise on chief audit executives' tolerance for financial misstatements. *Accounting, Organizations and Society, 36*(2), 102–108.

Pomeroy, B. (2010). Audit committee member investigation of significant accounting decisions. *Auditing: A Journal of Practice & Theory, 29*(1), 173–205.

Pomeroy, B., & Thornton, D.B. (2008). Meta-analysis and the accounting literature: The case of audit committee independence and financial reporting quality. *European Accounting Review, 17*(2), 305–330.

Power, M. (2011). Assurance worlds: Consumers, experts and independence. *Accounting, Organizations and Society, 36*(4–5), 324–326.

Quick, R., & Warming-Rasmussen, B. (2009). Auditor independence and the provision of non-audit services: Perceptions by German investors. *International Journal of Auditing, 13*(2), 141–162.

Robinson, D. (2008). Auditor independence and auditor-provided tax services: Evidence from going-concern audit opinions prior to bankruptcy filings. *Auditing: A Journal of Practice & Theory, 27*(2), 31–54.

Sharma, V.D., Sharma, D.S., & Ananthanarayanan, U. (2011). Client importance and earnings management: The moderating role of audit committees. *Auditing: A Journal of Practice & Theory, 30*(3), 125–156.

Wang, K.J., & Tuttle, B.M. (2009). The impact of auditor rotation on auditor–client negotiation. *Accounting, Organizations and Society, 34*(2), 222–243.

Ye, P., Carson, E., & Simnett, R. (2011). Threats to auditor independence: The impact of relationship and economic bonds. *Auditing: A Journal of Practice & Theory, 30*(1), 121–148.

5 Auditors' Legal, Regulatory and Professional Responsibilities

LEARNING OBJECTIVES

After studying the material in this chapter you should be able to:
- explain the key reports companies are required to publish annually;
- state which companies are required to have an audit;
- explain how auditors are appointed and remunerated, and how they may resign or be removed;
- describe the relationship between auditors, the client company and the company's shareholders;
- differentiate between the auditor's and the directors' responsibility for a company's audited financial statements;
- describe the rights and responsibilities of auditors under:
    - (a) legislation
    - (b) decisions of the courts
    - (c) auditing standards
    - (d) other regulatory requirements – in particular, those relating to listed companies;
- describe the purpose, and outline the content, of:
    - – audit firms' transparency reports, and
    - – the audit firm governance code.

5.1 INTRODUCTION

Broadly speaking, auditors' responsibilities are defined by three 'levels' of institution, namely:
- Parliament – in legislation (or statute law);
- the courts – in case (or common) law;
- regulators – in regulations which may have general or limited application. The regulations may, for example, apply to the auditors (and audits) of all companies (as is the case with auditing standards) or just to those of companies in a particular industry (such as the banking or mining industry) or of a particular type (for example, public listed companies).

The impact of these institutions on auditors' duties in the United Kingdom (UK) is cumulative in the sense explained below.

- *Parliament* enacts legislation (for example, the Companies Act 2006) which specifies the reports which companies must produce and the companies whose financial statements must be audited. It also sets out the administrative details of auditors' appointment, remuneration and removal, defines the criteria which determine who may be appointed as a company's auditor, and outlines auditors' rights and duties.[1]
- *The courts* create case (or common) law that expands on statute law by deciding cases that come before them. Since the late nineteenth century, by hearing cases that have involved auditors, the courts have helped to clarify the standard of work expected of auditors in the performance of their statutory duties (i.e., the duties specified in legislation).
- *Regulators* put 'flesh on the bones' of auditors' duties as defined in statute and common law. Exercising powers delegated to them in legislation, they promulgate regulations which set out detailed requirements with which auditors must comply. The Audit and Assurance Council [formerly known as the Auditing Practices Board (APB)][2] develops the Auditing and Ethical Standards with which all statutory auditors[3] in the UK and Ireland must comply. Along similar lines, regulators which are responsible for regulating particular types of companies, or companies in particular industries, specify requirements that apply to the audits and auditors of those companies. For example, the Financial Reporting Council (FRC) specifies requirements with which the auditors of public listed companies must comply, and the Financial Conduct Authority (FCA)[4] specifies the requirements that apply to the auditors of financial institutions.

---

[1] Some of the legislation enacted by the UK Parliament incorporates the provisions of European Union (EU) Regulations and Directives. EU Regulations have legal effect in all Member States, irrespective of whether they are also enacted in a Member State's legislation. Directives indicate the outcomes Member States are required to achieve but, to an extent, leave each Member State to determine how the outcomes are to be achieved. However, in the case of 'maximum harmonisation' Directives, Member States have little or no flexibility as to the manner in which the outcomes are to be achieved. Nevertheless, unlike EU Regulations, all Directives require each Member State to enact measures to implement the Directive in that State (i.e., to give the Directive legal effect).

[2] From 2004 until 2012, the APB was an 'operating body' of the Financial Reporting Council (FRC) – "UK's independent regulator responsible for promoting high quality corporate governance and reporting to foster investment" (FRC, 2012b). In 2012, the APB (renamed the Audit and Assurance Council) became an advisory committee of the Codes and Standards Committee of the FRC (FRC, 2012c). The former and current structure of the FRC are depicted on page xix at the front of this book and the composition and functions of the Audit and Assurance Council are discussed in section 5.5.4.

[3] Prior to enactment of the Companies Act (CA) 2006, auditors of UK companies were required to be *registered with* a Recognised Supervisory Body (RSB) and were referred to as *registered auditors*. Since enactment of CA 2006, auditors have been required to be *members of* an RSB and are referred to as *statutory auditors*. In this book we use the terms statutory auditor, registered auditor and company auditor interchangeably to mean an individual or firm who is appointed as a company's auditor in accordance with the CA 2006.

[4] From 1997 until April 2013, the Financial Services Authority (FSA), which was established under the Financial Services and Markets Act 2000, was responsible for regulating the financial services industry in the UK. However, in April 2013, the FSA was disbanded and its functions were transferred to the Financial Conduct Authority (FCA) and the Prudential Regulation Authority (PRA) (both of which are overseen by the Policy Committee of the Bank of England).

Until a couple of decades ago, the accounting profession was also a key player in defining auditors' responsibilities. The profession was, in general, self-regulating and the criteria for becoming an accountant (and auditor), as well as accounting, auditing and ethical standards, were set and enforced by the profession itself. Over the past 20 or so years, the profession has become increasingly regulated – a process that accelerated rapidly following the Enron, WorldCom, Tyco, HIH and similar debacles in the dawn years of the twenty-first century. Today, in the international arena, the profession is represented by the International Federation of Accountants (IFAC). This has established committees (or boards), independent of the auditing profession, to develop International Standards on Auditing (ISAs), International Accounting Education Standards and the International Code of Ethics for Professional Accountants.[5] However, as noted above, in the UK, the Audit and Assurance Council of the FRC is responsible for developing auditing and ethical standards.[6] Further, the FRC's Conduct Committee is responsible for, *inter alia*, ensuring that company auditors in the UK comply with these auditing and ethical standards. Thus, responsibility for setting and enforcing the standards which govern the work of auditors in the UK has passed from the profession to regulators. Additionally, in order to be appointed as a company auditor, an individual or firm must be registered with a Recognised Supervisory Body (RSB) and be eligible for appointment under its rules – rules which are prescribed by the Companies Act 2006. (These rules are outlined in section 5.3.1). Although the RSBs coincide with UK professional bodies [in particular, the Institute of Chartered Accountants in England and Wales (ICAEW), of Scotland (ICAS) and in Ireland (ICAI), and the Association of Chartered Certified Accountants (ACCA)], in their role as RSBs, they function as regulators rather than as professional bodies. However, each of the professional bodies produces a Code of Ethics (based on the International Ethics Standards Board for Accountants' Code of Ethics) to govern the professional conduct of its members in respect of matters not covered by the APB's Ethical Standards.

The relationship between the institutions defining auditors' duties and the aspects of auditing each institution governs are presented diagrammatically in Figure 5.1.

---

[5] These standards are developed by boards which have been established by the IFAC, namely, the International Auditing and Assurance Standards Board (IAASB), the International Accounting Education Standards Board (IAESB) and the International Ethics Standards Board for Accountants (IESBA). Although the boards are independent of the auditing profession, some members of the profession are members of and/or provide advice to the boards.

[6] It should be noted that the UK's auditing and ethical standards are based, respectively, on the IAASB's ISAs and the IESBA's Code of Ethics. Most of the current ethical and auditing standards were promulgated by the APB prior to 2012 and these are referred to as 'APB standards'. Standards issued since July 2012 are referred to as 'FRC standards'. These differences are reflected in references cited throughout this book.

Figure 5.1: Institutions defining auditors' responsibilities

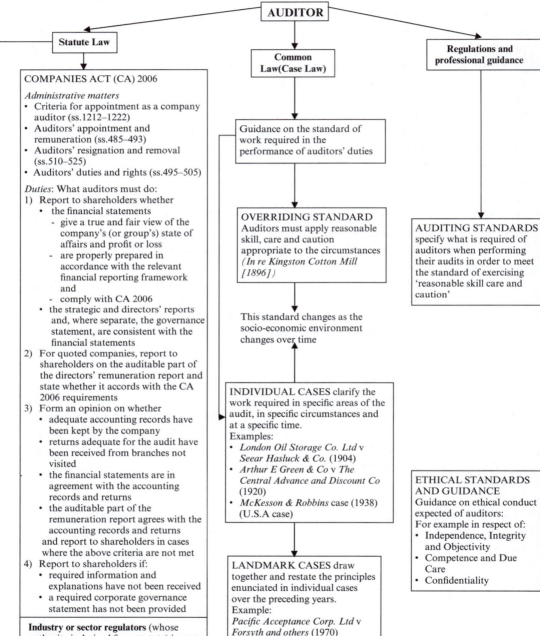

In this chapter we examine auditors' responsibilities in the context of the financial and governance reports companies are required to produce. We first outline the reporting requirements of companies and then explain how company auditors are appointed, remunerated and removed. We also explore the somewhat unusual relationship between auditors, their client companies and the companies' shareholders. Much of the chapter is devoted to discussing company auditors' responsibilities under legislation, case law and regulations; however, we defer the challenging topic of auditors' responsibility for detecting and reporting fraud until Chapter 6. Before concluding this chapter, we discuss audit firms' transparency statements and the audit firm governance code.

5.2 REPORTING AND AUDITING REQUIREMENTS OF COMPANIES[7]

5.2.1 Requirements relating to companies' audited financial statements

The main statutory provisions governing companies' financial statements are contained in the Companies Act 2006 (CA 2006). This Act distinguishes between two types of company, namely:
  (i) public companies – companies that are registered as public companies, have a certificate of incorporation which states they are a public company, and a name which ends with 'public limited company' (or p.l.c)[8] (ss. 4, 58);
  (ii) private companies – companies that are not public companies. In most cases, the name of these companies ends with the word 'limited' (or ltd.) (ss. 4, 59).
A public, but not a private, company may issue shares or loan stock (such as bonds) to the general public; private companies must raise their capital requirements by other (private) means.

CA 2006 (s. 385) also distinguishes between:
  (i) quoted companies – companies whose equity share capital is traded on a regulated market in the European Economic Area (EEA; which

---

[7] In general we restrict our discussion to companies whose financial statements are subject to audit. Other organisations such as building societies, trade unions and employer associations, housing associations, certain charities and unincorporated investment businesses, and also public sector entities, are subject to specific reporting and auditing requirements. These requirements are usually enshrined in separate legislation.

[8] Any company in which the liability of its members (shareholders) is limited by shares or by guarantee must include the word 'limited' in its name. In most companies, the liability of shareholders is limited by shares and their exposure to liability is limited to any unpaid portion of their shareholding.

includes the UK),[9] the New York Stock Exchange (NYSE) or NASDAQ;[10] and

(ii) unquoted companies – companies that are not quoted companies.

CA 2006 further distinguishes between small, medium-sized and large companies (and groups).[11] Small and medium-sized companies are companies (or groups) that meet at least two of the criteria shown in Figure 5.2. All other companies are 'large' companies. However, no company (or group) can qualify as small or medium-sized if, at any time during the financial year, it (or one of the members of the group) was a public company, a banking or insurance company, an e-money issuer, it was permitted by the Financial Services and

Figure 5.2: Qualifying criteria for small and medium-sized companies

Criteria	Small		Medium-sized	
	Company	Group	Company	Group
Company or group turnover (total sales) not more than	£6.5 million	£6.5 million net £7.8 million gross	£25.9 million	£25.9 million net £31.1 million gross
Company or group balance sheet total (total assets) not more than	£3.26 million	£3.26 million net £3.9 million gross	£12.9 million	£12.9 million net £15.5 million gross
Employees not more than	50	50	250	250
'Net' means turnover or balance sheet total (as applicable) after any set-offs or other adjustments have been made to eliminate intra-group transactions.				

---

[9] The EEA comprises the EU's Member States (with the exception of Croatia) together with Norway, Iceland and Liechtenstein. The last three countries have an agreement with the EU whereby they participate in the 'internal market' of the EU (i.e., they participate in the freedom of movement of goods, services, people and capital across all of the EEA Member States); they also adopt EU legislation relating to social policy, consumer protection, the environment, company law and statistics. (For further information see www.ec.europa.eu/external_relations/eea.)

[10] 'NASQAD' was originally the acronym for National Association of Securities Dealers Automated Quotations system. The APB (2012) defines a listed entity as: "An entity whose shares, stock or debt are quoted or listed on a recognized stock exchange, or are marketed under the regulations of a recognized stock exchange or other equivalent body". Although quoted and listed companies do not fully coincide, in this book we use the terms 'quoted companies' and 'listed companies' with an equivalent meaning.

[11] A group comprises a parent company and one or more subsidiary companies. In general, the directors of parent companies are required to prepare group (consolidated) financial statements (that is, financial statements which treat the parent company and its subsidiaries as a single entity) in addition to producing the individual financial statements for the parent company. If the parent company's financial statements meet the requirements of CA 2006, s. 408, a separate profit and loss account (income statement) for the parent company need not be prepared. In order to take advantage of this exemption, CA 2006, s. 408 stipulates:
 (i) the notes to the parent company's balance sheet must disclose the company's profit or loss, and
 (ii) the parent company's financial statements must disclose that the exemption from preparing a profit or loss account applies.

Market Act 2000 to carry on a regulated activity, or its shares were admitted to trading on a regulated market (CA 2006, ss. 382–384, 465–467).

The directors of all companies (whether public or private, quoted or unquoted, and irrespective of size) must prepare a balance sheet and profit and loss account for each financial year.[12,13] These must comply with either International Accounting (or Financial Reporting) Standards (IAS; IFRS) or Regulations issued by the Secretary of State (in effect, the Department for Business, Innovation & Skills).[14] CA 2006 refers to financial statements prepared in accordance with these two reporting frameworks as 'IAS accounts' and 'Companies Act accounts', respectively (CA 2006, ss. 395, 396, 403–405). In general, companies (and groups) have a choice of which framework they will adopt; however, in accordance with Article 4 of the EU's IAS Regulation (EU, 2002) and CA 2006, s. 403, the consolidated financial statements of a group whose securities are admitted to trading on a regulated market of any EU Member State (which includes the London Stock Exchange) *must* be prepared as 'IAS accounts'.[15] Other groups, individual companies within a group and other individual companies may prepare either 'IAS accounts' or 'Companies Act accounts'. Thus, while the consolidated financial statements of a group with securities listed on a regulated market in the EU must be prepared as 'IAS accounts', the financial statements of the parent company and each of its subsidiaries may be prepared as either 'IAS accounts' or 'Companies Act accounts'.

As noted above, 'Company's Act accounts' must be prepared in accordance with Regulations issued by the Secretary of State. However, the content of the Regulations is incorporated in (i) the *Financial Reporting Standard for Smaller*

---

[12] Most (other than small) companies (and groups) are also required by the financial reporting framework they adopt to prepare an annual cash flow statement. It should be noted that International Financial Reporting Standards use the terms 'statement of financial position' and 'income statement' in place of 'balance sheet' and 'profit and loss account', respectively.

[13] In general, the directors' responsibility for preparing the company's financial statements is required to be explained in a section within the auditor's report on the financial statements or in a Statement of Directors' Responsibilities included in the company's annual report. Companies listed on the London Stock Exchange are required by the Exchange's Listing Rules to include a Statement of Directors' Responsibilities in their annual reports. An example of such a statement is provided in Figure 5.3. We discuss this requirement in greater detail in Chapter 14, section 14.3.4.

[14] In 2009, the Department for Business, Innovation & Skills (BIS) replaced the Department for Business, Enterprise and Regulatory Reform (DBERR); in 2007 the latter replaced the Department for Trade and Industry (DTI). The Regulations are contained in Statutory Instrument (SI) 2008 No. 410: *Large and Medium-Sized Companies and Groups (Accounts and Reports) Regulations 2008* (SI 2008a) and SI 2008 No. 409: *Small Companies and Groups (Accounts and Reports) Regulations 2008* (SI 2008b).

[15] The EU has not adopted all of the IFRS promulgated by the International Accounting Standards Board (IASB). 'IAS accounts' must be prepared in compliance with the IFRS adopted by the EU. These are set out in EU Regulation (EC) No. 1606/2002 *on the application of international accounting standards* (IAS Regulation).

Entities (FRSSE) [Accounting Standards Board (ASB), 2008],[16] which applies to companies and groups that qualify as 'small', (ii) Financial Reporting Standard (FRS) 101: *Reduced Disclosure Framework* (FRC, 2012f), which applies to certain entities that apply IFRS, and (iii) FRS 102: *The Financial Reporting Standard Applicable in the UK and Republic of Ireland* (FRC, 2013c), which applies to large and medium-sized companies and groups. These three standards constitute 'UK Generally Accepted Accounting Practice' (or UK GAAP); hence, it is usual to refer to 'Company's Act accounts' as being prepared in accordance with UK GAAP.

Irrespective of the financial reporting framework adopted, the company's board of directors is required to formally approve its annual financial statements and at least one director must sign the balance sheet on behalf of the board (CA 2006, s. 414). This approval and signing signifies that the board accepts its responsibility for preparing the financial statements. However, the directors may not approve the financial statements unless they are satisfied that they give a true and fair view of the assets, liabilities, financial position and profit or loss of the company or group concerned (CA 2006, s. 393). This requirement for financial statements to give a true and fair view, in addition to complying with IFRSs or UK GAAP, is frequently referred to as the 'true and fair view override'.

CA 2006 (ss. 396, 404) explicitly requires 'Companies Act accounts' to present a true and fair view of the company's (or group's) state of affairs (that is, its financial position) as at the end of its financial year and its profit or loss for the financial year. The Act does not define 'true and fair' but recognises that financial statements prepared in accordance with UK GAAP may not give the required true and fair view. It provides that, if compliance with UK GAAP is insufficient to present a true and fair view of the company's (or group's) state of affairs and profit or loss, additional information is to be provided so that the required true and fair view is given. Further, if, in special circumstances, compliance with any GAAP provision is inconsistent with the requirement for the financial statements to give a true and fair view, the relevant provision is to be departed from to the extent necessary for a true and fair view to be presented. Reasons for, and the particulars and effect of, any such departure must be provided in a note to the financial statements (CA 2006, ss. 396, 404).

Along similar lines, 'IAS accounts' are required by IAS 1: *Presentation of Financial Statements* [International Accounting Standards Board (IASB), 2007] to:
> present fairly the financial position, financial performance and cash flows of [the company or group]. Fair presentation requires the faithful representation of the

---

[16] In 2012 the ASB was replaced by the Accounting Council of the FRC. The FRC has announced that a revised version of FRSSE will be effective from January 2015.

effects of transactions, other events and conditions in accordance with the definitions and recognition criteria for assets, liabilities, income and expenses set out in the *Framework*.[17] The application of IFRSs, with additional disclosure when necessary, is presumed to result in financial statements that achieve a fair presentation. . . . In the extremely rare circumstances in which management concludes that compliance with a requirement in an IFRS [or IAS] would be so misleading that it would conflict with the objective of financial statements set out in the *Framework*, the entity shall depart from that requirement. . . . (paras 15, 19)

As for 'Companies Act accounts', if in the preparation of 'IAS accounts' an IFRS or IAS is departed from, full details of the departure, and the reasons for and effect of the departure, must be disclosed in a note to the financial statements.[18]

Companies must not only prepare annual financial statements; CA 2006, s. 475, requires that they be audited. However, in general, this requirement does not apply to companies or groups which, during the relevant financial year, qualify as 'small'; that is, they meet any two of the three criteria set out in Figure 5.2 – for companies, a turnover of not more than £6.5 million, a balance sheet total of not more than £3.26 million and no more than 50 employees; for groups, an aggregate turnover of not more than £6.5 million net (or £7.8 million gross), an aggregate balance sheet total of not more than £3.26 million net (or £3.9 million gross) and no more than 50 employees.[19] Nevertheless, the audit exemption does not apply to a company or group if, at any time during the financial year:

- it (or one of the members of the group) was a public company, a banking or insurance company, or an e-money issuer, or
- members holding an aggregate of 10 per cent or more of the nominal value of the company's issued capital, or any class of it, request that the company's financial statements be audited (ss. 476, 478).

Where a company (or group) takes advantage of the audit exemption provisions, the company's directors are required to include in the balance sheet (above the director's signature) a statement to the effect that:

(a) the members (i.e., shareholders) have not required the company to have an audit for the year in question, and

---

[17] *Conceptual Framework for Financial Reporting* (IASB, 2010).

[18] Although neither CA 2006 nor IAS 1 explicitly refers to financial statements prepared in accordance with IAS (or IFRS) 'giving a true and fair view', the FRC (2011) has confirmed "that the true and fair requirement remains of fundamental importance in both UK GAAP and IFRS". It refers to a legal Opinion it obtained in 2008 from Martin Moore QC when the QC "confirmed the centrality of the true and fair requirement to the preparation of financial statements in the UK, whether they are prepared in accordance with international or UK accounting standards" (FRC, 2008b).

[19] The financial statements of most dormant companies are also exempt from the audit requirement, that is, companies which have not undertaken any significant accounting transactions during the financial year (CA 2006, s. 480).

(b) the directors acknowledge their responsibilities for complying with the requirements of CA 2006 with respect to accounting records[20] and the preparation of financial statements (s. 475).

A matter the directors are required to consider when preparing the financial statements is the status of their company as a going concern. Both UK GAAP and IFRS require the directors to satisfy themselves that it is appropriate for the company's financial statements to be prepared on the basis that it is a going concern.[21] The FRC explains what this entails in its publication *Going Concern and Liquidity Risk* (FRC, 2009):

> Directors should make and document a rigorous assessment of whether the company is a going concern when preparing . . . [the company's] financial statements. The process carried out by the directors should be proportionate in nature and depth to the size, level of financial risk and complexity of the company and its operations. (Principle 1, p. 6)

The assessment needs to be sufficient to enable the directors to conclude (on the date they approve the company's financial statements) that the company is (or is not) able to continue in business for at least the next 12 months. If a shorter period is considered, the directors must disclose the period considered and the reason for this being less than 12 months (FRC, 2009, para 55). When making their assessment, the directors are required to consider, among other things, the principal risks and uncertainties facing the company which, in the case of all but small companies, are to be reported in the company's strategic report (this is explained in section 5.2.2).

Both UK GAAP and IFRS provide that, in any case where the directors conclude there are material uncertainties that may cast significant doubt upon the entity's ability to continue as a going concern, they are to disclose the existence and nature of the uncertainties in a note to the financial statements (FRC, 2009, para 65). Further, for any company facing liquidity risk[22] which constitutes a material financial risk, the directors are required to make qualitative and quantitative disclosures explaining the risk. These disclosures must be sufficient to enable financial statement users to evaluate the nature and extent of the

---

[20] CA 2006, s. 386, requires all companies to keep adequate accounting records; that is:
  records that are sufficient –
  (a) to show and explain the company's transactions,
  (b) to disclose with reasonable accuracy, at any time, the financial position of the company, and
  (c) to enable the directors to ensure that any accounts required to be prepared comply with the requirements of [the Companies] Act (and, where applicable, of Article 4 of the IAS Regulation).

[21] Unless, in the unusual circumstance, that this is not the case. In such a circumstance, the company should produce a 'statement of affairs' in place of the normal financial statements.

[22] Liquidity risk is "the risk that an entity will encounter difficulty in meeting its obligations associated with financial liabilities" (FRC, 2009, para 70).

entity's exposure to liquidity risk and to understand how this risk arises in the business and is managed (FRC, 2009, paras 70, 71). The FRC (2009) notes that these companies' disclosures about going concern uncertainties and liquidity risk must be balanced, proportionate and clear in order for their financial statements to provide a true and fair view. It explains that such disclosures would, *inter alia*:

- identify the factors the directors have considered in reaching their conclusion about the company as a going concern;
- conclude with a statement as to whether adoption of the going concern basis of accounting is appropriate, explaining the basis for that conclusion (FRC, 2009, para 81).

While *all* companies are required to disclose risks and uncertainties which bring into question their status as a going concern, more is required of listed companies. The UK Listing Authority (UKLA)[23] requires companies listed on the London Stock Exchange to include in their annual reports a statement that the business is a going concern, together with supporting assumptions or qualifications as necessary. Thus, listed companies are required to make a statement about their status as a going concern each year, not just when the risks and uncertainties they face bring this into question.

The FRC (2009) notes that the disclosure requirements of CA 2006, the applicable financial reporting framework and the Listing Rules may result in companies providing information about their status as a going concern and their exposure to liquidity risk (and other risks and uncertainties) in different parts of their annual report and financial statements. It observes:

> It is helpful to investors and other stakeholders [and also auditors] if all of these disclosures are brought together in a single place in the company's financial statements. It may be necessary to provide a cross reference to that single place from other parts of the annual report. If it is not practicable to provide all of the information in a single place, it is still helpful if the key disclosures are brought together by way of a note that includes appropriate cross references to information in the financial statements and from the financial statements to information included elsewhere in the annual report. (para 80)

As may be seen from Figure 5.3, in 2012 the directors of Vodafone plc used their Directors' statement of responsibility as the 'single place' (with appropriate cross references) to report on the group's and company's status as a going concern.

---

[23] In 2001, regulatory responsibility for companies listed on the London Stock Exchange (and hence for the Listing Rules) passed from the London Stock Exchange to the Financial Services Authority (FSA). The FSA delegated its responsibility for listed companies to the UKLA. In 2013, when the FSA was disbanded, responsibility for the UKLA passed to the Financial Conduct Authority (FCA).

Figure 5.3: Example of a Statement of Directors' Responsibilities

Directors' statement of responsibility

Financial statements and accounting records

Company law of England and Wales requires the directors to prepare financial statements for each financial year which give a true and fair view of the state of affairs of the Company and of the Group at the end of the financial year and of the profit or loss of the Group for that period. In preparing those financial statements the directors are required to:

- select suitable accounting policies and apply them consistently;
- make judgements and estimates that are reasonable and prudent;
- state whether the consolidated financial statements have been prepared in accordance with International Financial Reporting Standards ('IFRS') as issued by the IASB, in accordance with IFRS as adopted for use in the EU and Article 4 of the EU IAS Regulations;
- state for the Company financial statements whether applicable UK accounting standards have been followed; and
- prepare the financial statements on a going concern basis unless it is inappropriate to presume that the Company and the Group will continue in business.

The directors are responsible for keeping proper accounting records which disclose with reasonable accuracy at any time the financial position of the Company and of the Group and to enable them to ensure that the financial statements comply with the Companies Act 2006 and Article 4 of the EU IAS Regulation. They are also responsible for the system of internal control, for safeguarding the assets of the Company and the Group and, hence, for taking reasonable steps for the prevention and detection of fraud and other irregularities.

Directors' responsibility statement

The Board confirms to the best of its knowledge:

- the consolidated financial statements, prepared in accordance with IFRS as issued by the International Accounting Standards Board ('IASB') and IFRS as adopted by the EU, give a true and fair view of the assets, liabilities, financial position and profit or loss of the Group; and
- the directors' report includes a fair review of the development and performance of the business and the position of the Group together with a description of the principal risks and uncertainties that it faces.[24]

Neither the company nor the directors accept any liability to any person in relation to the annual report except to the extent that such liability could arise under English law. Accordingly, any liability to a person who has demonstrated reliance on any untrue or misleading statement or omission shall be determined in accordance with section 90A and Schedule 10A of the Financial Services and Markets Act 2000.

Disclosure of information to auditor

Having made the requisite enquiries, so far as the directors are aware, there is no relevant audit information (as defined by Section 418(3) of the Companies Act 2006) of which the Company's auditor is unaware and the directors have taken all the steps they ought to have taken to make themselves aware of any relevant audit information and to establish that the Company's auditor is aware of that information.

Going concern

After reviewing the Group's and Company's budget for the next financial year, and other longer term plans, the directors are satisfied that, at the time of approving the financial statements, it is appropriate to adopt the going concern basis in preparing the financial statements. Further detail is included within liquidity and capital resources on pages 55 to 59 and notes 21 and 22 to the consolidated financial statements which include disclosure in relation to the Group's objectives, policies and processes for managing its capital; its financial risk management objectives; details of its financial instruments and hedging activities; and its exposures to credit risk and liquidity risk.

Source: Vodafone plc's 2012 annual repo[

---

[24] Since 1 October 2013, comment on the company's development and performance, and its risks and uncertainties, has been required to be included in the company's strategic report rather than in the directors' report.

5.2.2 Requirements relating to companies' governance reports

In addition to preparing their company's financial statements, the directors of each company are required to prepare a directors' report for each financial year.[25] This is to contain the names of persons who were directors of the company during the financial year and, unless the company is exempt from an audit, a statement to the effect that, as far as each director is aware:

- there is no relevant audit information of which the company's auditor is unaware, and
- the director has taken all the steps a director ought to take to become aware of any relevant audit information and to establish that the company's auditor is aware of that information (CA 2006, ss. 416, 418).

For large and medium-sized companies, the directors' report must also disclose, *inter alia*:[26]

(i) the amount of dividend (if any) the directors recommend should be paid;

(ii) the amount of political donations and expenditures by the company where these exceed £2,000;[27]

(iii) information relating to the use of financial instruments (if any) by the company including the company's risk management objectives and policies and its exposure to price, credit, liquidity and cash flow risks insofar as they are material to assessment of the company's assets, liabilities, financial position and its profit or loss;

(iv) particulars of any important events affecting the company since the end of the financial year and an indication of likely future developments in the company's business;

(v) information about the employment of disabled person and about the company's facilitation of employees' involvement in the company.

Further, for companies whose shares are traded on a regulated market, the directors' report must provide information about:

- the company's capital structure,
- any restrictions on trading of the company's shares or on voting rights,
- any person holding a significant proportion of the company's shares,

---

[25] In the case of groups, the directors of the parent company are required to prepare a 'group directors' report'.

[26] Apart from the requirement to disclose any recommended dividend (which is contained in CA 2006, s. 418), the disclosure requirements are specified in the *Large and Medium-Sized Companies and Groups (Accounts and Reports) Regulations* [Statutory Instrument (SI) 2008a] as amended by *The Companies Act 2006 (Strategic Report and Directors' Report) Regulations 2013* (SI 2013). For small companies, the (very limited) disclosure requirements are set out in SI 2008 No. 409 *Small Companies and Groups (Account and Reports) Regulations 2008* (SI 2008b) as amended by SI 2013.

[27] This provision does not apply to the directors' reports of wholly owned subsidiaries of companies incorporated in the UK.

- any employee share scheme,
- rules relating to the appointment and replacement of directors, and
- the powers of the directors.

Additionally, for quoted companies, the directors' report must provide details of the company's greenhouse gas emissions. In particular, it is required to report, for the current and preceding year [except in respect of (ii) below]:

  (i) the annual quantity of emissions in tonnes of carbon dioxide equivalent resulting from:
    – activities for which the company is responsible, including the combustion of fuel and the operation of any facility, and
    – the purchase of electricity, heat, steam or cooling by the company for its own use;[28]

  (ii) the methodologies used to calculate the information provided in accordance with (i) above;

  (iii) at least one ratio which expresses the company's reported annual emissions in relation to a quantifiable factor associated with its activities.

In some cases, the directors of large and medium-sized companies may consider the information specified for inclusion in the directors' report may more appropriately be disclosed in the company's strategic report (see below). Where this is the case, they are permitted to include the information in the strategic report but, in the directors' report, they must disclose that they have done so and identify the information concerned.

As indicated above, large and medium-sized companies are required to include a strategic report, as well as a directors' report, in each annual report.[29] The strategic report is to contain, *inter alia*:

  (i) a balanced and comprehensive analysis of the development and performance of the company's business during the financial year and of its position at the end of the year;[30]

  (ii) a description of its principal risks and uncertainties.[31]

---

[28] SI 2013 (para 15) provides that these requirements:

   apply only to the extent that is practical for the company to obtain the information in question; but . . . [where information is not provided, the directors'] report must state what information is not included and why.

[29] As for the directors' report, in the case of groups, the directors of the parent company are required to provide 'a group strategic report'.

[30] To the extent necessary for readers to gain an understanding of the development, performance or position of the company's business, this analysis is to include key financial and non-financial performance indicators. However, medium-sized companies are exempted from this requirement insofar as it relates to non-financial information.

[31] This description should include an explanation of "any particular economic conditions and financial difficulties that the company is facing" (FRC, 2009, para 64).

For quoted companies, the strategic report is also to include:
(a) to the extent necessary for readers to understand the development, performance and position of the company's business:
  - the main trends and factors likely to affect the future development, performance and position of the company's business,
  - information about:
    - environmental matters (including the impact of the company's business on the environment),
    - the company's employees, and
    - social, community and human rights issues,
    including information about the company's policies relating to these matters and the effectiveness of those policies;
(b) a description of the company's strategy and business model;
(c) the number of persons of each gender who were (a) directors, (b) senior managers[32] and (c) employees of the company as at the end of the financial year.

For all companies (whether medium-sized, large or quoted) which produce a strategic report, CA 2006, s. 414C, specifies that the report "must, where appropriate, include references to, and additional explanations of, amounts included in the company's annual [financial statements]", hence, the strategic report seems to be a step in the direction of integrated reporting (integrating a company's financial and non-financial information).

Another element of companies' governance on which the directors of all companies are required to report is that of the benefits provided by the company to its directors. The benefits to be disclosed include advances, credit and guarantees extended to the directors, individually and in total, as well as their remuneration (CA 2006, ss. 412, 413). For large and medium-sized companies the information to be provided in respect of the directors' remuneration is set out in the *Large and Medium-Sized Companies and Groups (Accounts and Reports) Regulations* (SI 2008a).[33] These require disclosure of, *inter alia*:
  (i) the aggregate amount of
    (a) remuneration (including salaries, fees, bonuses and expense allowances) received or receivable by the directors during the financial year,

---

[32] A 'senior manager' is defined in CA 2006, s. 414C, to mean a person who has responsibility for planning, directing or controlling the activities of the company, or a strategically significant part of the company, and is an employee of the company.

[33] For small companies, the required disclosures are set out in SI 2008 No. 409 *Small Companies and Groups (Account and Reports) Regulations 2008* (SI 2008b).

    (b) gains made by the directors on the exercise of share options,

    (c) the amounts of money, and the net value of assets (other than money and share options) received or receivable by directors under long term incentive schemes,

    (d) contributions by the company to pension schemes for the benefit of the directors;

  (ii) the number of directors (if any) to whom retirement benefits are accruing.

Further disclosure requirements depend on whether the company is quoted or unquoted. Unquoted companies are required by SI 2008a, Schedule 5, to disclose:

- in any case where the aggregate for the items shown above under (a), (b), (c) or (d) amounts to £200,000 or more for the financial year:
    - the amount attributed to the highest paid director, and
    - whether the highest paid director exercised any share options or received (or will receive) any shares under a long term incentive scheme;
- the number of directors who exercised share options and the number who received benefits under long term incentive schemes during the financial year;
- the aggregate amount of any compensation paid[34] to present or past directors for loss of office or retirement as a director (including any payment for loss of any office in connection with managing the company's or a subsidiary's affairs).

Not surprisingly, the disclosure requirements of quoted companies are considerably more extensive than those of unquoted companies. CA 2006, s. 420, requires the directors of quoted companies to prepare a directors' remuneration report which is to comply with the requirements of SI 2008a, Schedule 8. This identifies two categories of information – that which is, and is not, subject to audit. The information not subject to audit includes:

- the name of each director who was a member of any committee that considered matters relating to directors' remuneration during the financial year and the name of any person who advised the committee in its deliberations on these matters;
- a statement of the company's policy on directors' remuneration for the following and subsequent financial years. This is to include, for each director, a detailed summary of any performance conditions that must be met to entitle the director to share options or long term incentives,

---

[34] Compensation includes cash and benefits in kind. In the latter case, the estimated value of the benefit is to be estimated and its nature disclosed.

an explanation of why these performance conditions were chosen and a summary of the method to be used to determine whether or not the director's performance met the conditions.

Information that is subject to audit includes, for each person who has served as a director during the financial year:
- the total amount paid or payable in (i) salary and fees, (ii) bonuses and (iii) expenses;
- the total estimated value, and the nature, of any benefits received other than in cash;
- details of share options held at the beginning and end of, and awarded during, the financial year;
- any interest in a long term incentive scheme at the beginning and end of, and awarded during, the financial year;
- any rights under a pension scheme of the company.[35]

In addition to the reports we have already discussed, the directors of all large companies (those that do not qualify as small or medium-sized) are required to provide annually a corporate governance statement. In accordance with the EU's *Disclosure and Transparency Directive* 2006 (EU, 2006b), this is required:
(a) to refer to the corporate governance code to which the company is subject;
(b) to identify any respects in which it has departed from the code during the reporting period and provide reasons to explain the departure(s);
(c) to describe the main features of the company's internal control and risk management systems in relation to the financial reporting process;
(d) to provide information relating to its share capital structure;
(e) to describe the composition and operation of the company's administrative, management and supervisory bodies, and their committees.

The corporate governance statement may be provided as a separate section within the directors' report, as a separate section in the company's annual report, or on the company's website. If it is placed on the company's website, a cross reference to it must be made in the directors' report (CA 2006, ss. 446, 447 and UKLA Listing Rules).

The requirements of the EU's *Disclosure and Transparency Directive* (EU, 2006b) have been incorporated in the UKLA's Listing Rules. Under these rules, companies listed on the London Stock Exchange must comply with (or

---

[35] These examples are provided for illustrative purposes. The information to be disclosed in the Directors' Remuneration Report is very detailed; for comprehensive coverage, readers are referred to SI 2008a, Schedule 8.

explain their departure from) *The UK Corporate Governance Code* (FRC, 2012a; UK Code).[36] This Code incorporates many of the provisions of *The Combined Code* issued by the Committee on Corporate Governance (1998b), the FRC's *Combined Code on Corporate Governance* (2003, 2006, 2008a) and the predecessor *UK Corporate Governance Code* (FRC, 2010a). The 1998 Code was developed from a series of earlier corporate governance reports – particularly those of the Committee on the Financial Aspects of Corporate Governance (1992; Cadbury Committee), the Study Group on Directors' Remuneration (1995; Greenbury Committee), and the Committee on Corporate Governance (1998a; Hampel Committee). The FRC's 2003 Combined Code also included provisions derived from the Higgs *Review of the Role and Effectiveness of Non-Executive Directors* (Higgs, 2003) and the Smith Report (2003) on *Audit Committees: Combined Code Guidance*.

The UK Code (FRC, 2012a) comprises five parts (A to E), each of which contains main and supporting principles, and provisions. The Code's structure is shown in Figure 5.4.

Listed companies in the UK are required to include in their annual report a corporate governance statement which:
(i) explains how the company has applied the main principles of the UK Code; and
(ii) states that the company has complied with all relevant provisions of the Code throughout the reporting period or details those with which it has not complied, giving reasons for the non-compliance.

The Code also requires the directors of listed companies to provide, in their governance statement or elsewhere in their company's annual report, *inter alia*:
– a statement of how the board of directors operates, including an indication of the types of decisions to be taken by the board and those delegated to management (prov. A.1.1);
– the names of the chairman, the deputy chairman (where there is one), the chief executive, the senior and other independent directors, and the chairmen and members of the board committees (provs A.1.2, B.1.1);

---

[36] Since 6 April 2010, securities listed on the London Stock Exchange have had either a Premium or a Standard listing. According to the FSA (2012):
- Premium indicates securities that meet more stringent super-equivalent standards; and
- Standard indicates securities that meet EU minimum standards.
Premium Listed companies are eligible for inclusion in the FTSE UK Index Series. In February 2012, more than 800 companies, including all of the 350 largest companies (i.e., FTSE 350), had Premium Listed securities and a further 1,580 had Standard Listed securities. All companies with Premium Listed securities are required to comply with *The UK Corporate Governance Code* or to disclose and explain their non-compliance.

Figure 5.4:   Structure of *The UK Corporate Governance Code*

Section		Principles	No. of Provisions
A Leadership	A.1	The Role of the Board	3
	A.2	Division of Responsibilities	1
	A.3	The Chairman	1
	A.4	Non-executive Directors	3
B Effectiveness	B.1	The Composition of the Board	2
	B.2	Appointments to the Board	4
	B.3	Commitment	3
	B.4	Development	2
	B.5	Information and Support	2
	B.6	Evaluation	3
	B.7	Re-election	2
C Accountability	C.1	Financial and Business Reporting	3
	C.2	Risk Management and Internal Control	1
	C.3	Audit Committees and Auditors	8
D Remuneration	D.1	The Level and Components of Remuneration	5
	D.2	Procedure	4
E Relations with Shareholders	E.1	Dialogue with Shareholders	2
	E.2	Constructive Use of the AGM	4

- separate sections describing the work of the nomination, audit and remuneration committees (provs B.2.4, C.3.8, D.1.2[37]);
- a statement of how performance evaluation of the board, its committees and its directors has been conducted (prov. B.6.1);
- a statement explaining the directors' responsibility for preparing the company's annual report and financial statements and stating that they consider the annual report and financial statements, taken as a whole, is fair, balanced and understandable and provides the information necessary for shareholders to assess the company's performance, business model and strategy (prov. C.1.1);[38]
- a report that the board has conducted a review of the effectiveness of the company's risk management and internal control systems (prov. C.2.1);

---

[37] The UK Code (FRC, 2012a) requires the terms of reference of the Remuneration Committee "to be made available" (prov. D.2.1). However, the Code also notes that, in order to comply with the UKLA's Listing Rules, "this information will need to be included in the [relevant company's] corporate governance statement" (Appendix).

[38] As the second part of this requirement did not become effective until 1 October 2012, it does not appear in the directors' statement in Vodafone's 2012 annual report reproduced in Figure 5.3.

- where the board does not accept the audit committee's recommendation on the appointment, reappointment or removal of an external auditor, a statement from the audit committee explaining its recommendation and the reasons why the board has taken a different position (prov. C.3.6). (This requirement is discussed in section 5.3.2 below.)

We discuss the Accountability provisions of The UK Code further in section 5.5.5 where we also explain auditors' responsibility to review listed company clients' compliance with all but two of the Accountability provisions.

5.2.3 Signing and submission of companies' financial statements and governance reports

In section 5.2.1 we noted that the board of directors is required to approve the company's financial statements and at least one director is to sign the balance sheet on behalf of the board. In a similar way, CA 2006 requires the board of directors to approve, and a director or the company's secretary to sign on behalf of the board, the strategic report (s. 414D), the directors' report (s. 419), the corporate governance statement (where this is not provided in the directors' report; s. 419A) and, in the case of a quoted company, the directors' remuneration report (s. 422). If the financial statements, the strategic report, the directors' report or the directors' remuneration report do not comply with the requirements of CA 2006, every director who knew the financial statements or report did not comply (or was reckless as to whether it did or did not comply) and failed to take reasonable steps to secure compliance or prevent the financial statements or report from being approved, commits an offence. This may result in imprisonment for up to two years and/or a fine of up to the statutory maximum (£5,000).

Once properly approved and signed, the board of directors must send to the Registrar of Companies, a copy of:
- the company's (and, in applicable cases, the group's) annual financial statements,
- the directors' report,
- if not a small company, the strategic report,
- if not a small or medium-sized company,[39] the corporate governance statement (where this is not included in the directors' report),
- if a quoted company, the directors' remuneration report;
- the auditor's report (unless the company is exempt from an audit) on the financial statements, the strategic and directors' reports and, if applicable, the corporate governance statement and directors' remuneration report.

---

[39] It should be recalled from section 5.2.1 that no public company, or any banking or insurance company, can qualify as a small or medium-sized company.

Copies of the balance sheet, strategic and directors' reports, corporate governance statement and directors' remuneration report which are filed with the Registrar of Companies must state the name of the person who signed it on behalf of the company. Similarly, the copy of the auditor's report must state the name of the auditor and, if the auditor is a firm, the name of the person who signed it as senior statutory auditor.[40] The various documents must be filed with the Registrar within six or nine months (for public and private companies, respectively) of the end of the company's financial year.

A copy of the audited financial statements and other reports filed with the Registrar of Companies must be sent to the company's shareholders, debenture holders and all those entitled to receive notice of general meetings.[41] This is to be effected by a private company when the documents are filed with the Registrar of Companies and, by a public company, not less than 21 days before the general meeting at which copies of the documents are to be presented (the 'accounts meeting': see section 5.3.1) (CA ss. 423, 424, 442, 444–447). A quoted company must additionally make their audited financial statements and other reports available on a website (s. 430).

5.3 APPOINTMENT, REMUNERATION AND REMOVAL OF COMPANY AUDITORS

5.3.1 Who may be the auditor of a company?

We noted in section 5.2 that, in general, a company's financial statements are required to be audited. It is thus pertinent to consider who can be appointed as a company's auditor.

CA 2006 includes provisions designed to ensure that only people (or firms) who are appropriately qualified and properly supervised are appointed as statutory auditors[42] and that audits are carried out properly, with integrity and with the proper degree of independence (s. 1209). In order to be eligible for appointment as a statutory auditor in the UK, an individual or firm must be registered with one of the five Recognised Supervisory Bodies

---

[40] The senior statutory auditor is, in effect, the audit engagement partner – the partner in the firm who is responsible for the audit engagement and for the audit report that is issued as an outcome of the audit.

[41] However, under CA 2006, s. 426, companies are entitled to send a strategic report together with the supplementary material described in CA 2006, s. 426A, rather than the full set of audited financial statements to shareholders, debenture holders, and those entitled to receive notice of general meetings.

[42] Auditors appointed to perform the audits of financial statements required by statute (for example, CA 2006).

(RSBs)[43] and be eligible for appointment as a statutory auditor under the rules of that RSB (CA 2006, s. 1212).

In order to become an RSB, a professional body must have, *inter alia*:
(a) rules to the effect that:
  (i) no individual is eligible for appointment as a statutory auditor unless s/he holds an appropriate qualification. [In general, this means the person has qualified with one of the six Recognised Qualifying Bodies (RQBs)],[44] and
  (ii) no firm is eligible for such an appointment unless:
    – each individual in the firm who is responsible for statutory audit work is eligible for appointment as a statutory auditor, and
    – the firm is controlled by qualified persons (i.e., the majority of its members with voting rights, or who are otherwise able to direct its overall policy, must be eligible for appointment as statutory auditors in the UK or any other EU or EEA Member State);
(b) rules and practices designed to ensure that:
  • audit work is conducted properly and with integrity;
  • persons appointed as statutory auditors:
    – are not appointed in circumstances where they have an interest which is likely to conflict with the proper conduct of an audit,
    – take steps to safeguard their independence from any significant threats,
    – record any significant threats to their independence and the steps taken to safeguard the proper conduct of the audit from those threats,
    – do not receive fees for audit work that are affected by the provision of non-audit services or are on a contingent fee basis;
  • any firm appointed as a statutory auditor has arrangements:
    – to prevent any person from being able to influence the conduct of the audit in circumstances that are likely to affect the independence and integrity of the audit,

---

[43] The five RSBs are ICAEW, ICAS, ICAI, ACCA and the Association of Authorised Public Accountants (AAPA). Members of AAPA qualified under requirements that pertained prior to 1967 and they are only eligible for appointment as auditors of unquoted companies (CA 2006, s. 1222).

[44] The six RQBs are ICAEW, ICAS, ICAI, ACCA, the Association of International Accountants (AIA) and the Chartered Institute of Public Finance and Accountancy (CIPFA); however, CIPFA's status as an RQB is in abeyance (FRC, 2013a). (The requirements relating to Recognised Professional Qualifications are detailed in CA 2006, Schedule 11.) Although most individuals qualify with, and become a member of, the same professional body, they may, if they wish, qualify with one body and become a member of another. It should be noted that neither AIA nor CIPFA is an RSB.

- to ensure any law relating to the confidentiality of information obtained while performing statutory audit work is complied with, and
- to ensure any person ceasing to hold office as a statutory auditor makes available to the successor auditor all relevant information relating to the position of the client's statutory auditor;

- persons appointed as statutory auditors of listed companies report to the relevant company's audit committee at least once every calendar year. Their report is to include:
  - a written statement confirming the auditor's independence,
  - a description of any non-audit services provided to the audit client,
  - a description of any significant threats to the auditor's independence,
  - an explanation of steps taken by the auditor to mitigate those threats,
  - a description of any material weaknesses in the company's internal financial controls, and
  - any other significant issues arising from the audit;

- an individual (or, in the case of a firm, the engagement partner) does not accept appointment as the senior statutory auditor (or engagement partner) of a listed company for a continuous period of more than seven years and is not re-appointed to the position for at least two years;

(c) rules and practices regarding the technical (auditing) standards to be applied in audit work and the manner in which the standards are to be applied in practice;

(d) rules and practices for admitting, disciplining and excluding members, and for ensuring those eligible for appointment as statutory auditors maintain an appropriate level of competence;

(e) adequate arrangements for:
  - the effective monitoring, and enforcement, of compliance with the RSB's rules,
  - inspecting the performance of auditors who are registered with the RSB who do not audit public interest entities and (as noted below) participating in the arrangements for the inspection of RSB members who audit such entities;
  - investigating complaints about its members or itself (as an RSB), and meeting claims arising out of audit work (professional indemnity insurance).

The requirements for recognition as an RSB are set out in CA 2006, Schedule 10, Part 2.

Each RSB is also required to participate in arrangements for:

(i) setting technical auditing standards and standards relating to statutory auditors' integrity and independence (that is, ethical standards);

(ii) setting standards relating to the requirement for the auditors of listed companies to report to the company's audit committee [indicated in (b) above];

(iii) the independent inspection of the audits of listed companies and other entities in which there is major public interest;[45]

(iv) the independent investigation, for disciplinary purposes, of public interest cases (i.e., those which raise, or appear to raise, important issues affecting the public interest).

The Government has assigned overall responsibility for these activities to the FRC. Until July 2012, the FRC discharged this responsibility through its operating bodies, in particular, the APB, the Professional Oversight Board (POB) and the Accountancy and Actuarial Discipline Board (AADB) with input from, and working collaboratively with, the RSBs. Since July 2012, the FRC has discharged its responsibilities primarily through its Codes and Standards Committee and Conduct Committee.[46] The FRC also has responsibility for overseeing the activities of the RSBs.

5.3.2 Who is responsible for appointing, and setting the remuneration of, an auditor?

CA 2006 specifies that companies must appoint an auditor (or auditors) for each financial year unless the audit exemption provisions apply and the company's directors reasonably resolve that an auditor not be appointed on the ground that audited financial statements are unlikely to be required (ss. 485, 489).[47] The auditor(s) is/are to be appointed by the company's shareholders (by means of an ordinary resolution) before the end of the shareholders' general meeting at which the audited financial statements for the previous

---

[45] As we explain in Chapter 16, until July 2012, inspections of the audits of public interest entities were undertaken by the Audit Inspection Unit (AIU) – a component of the FRC's Professional Oversight Board (POB). In July 2012 the AIU was renamed 'the Audit Quality Review' team and became a component of FRC's Monitoring Committee (which has superseded the POB). The Monitoring Committee is an advisory committee of the FRC's Conduct Committee (FRC, 2012d).

[46] As shown in the diagram presented on page xix at the front of this book, since July 2012, the FRC Board has been supported by three committees – a Codes and Standards Committee, a Conduct Committee and an Executive Committee. The former Accounting Standards Board (renamed Accounting Council), APB (renamed Audit and Assurance Council), and Board of Actuarial Standards (renamed Actuarial Council) are advisory committees of the Codes and Standards Committee. Along similar lines, the Monitoring Committee (which has superseded the POB) and the Case Management Committee (which superseded the AADB) are advisory committees of the Conduct Committee (FRC, 2012c).

[47] It should be recalled from section 5.2.1 that the audit exemption provision does not apply to any public company.

financial year are presented (the 'accounts meeting') (s. 489).[48] If no auditor is appointed before the end of the 'accounts meeting', the shareholders may appoint an auditor during the following week by means of an ordinary resolution. However, if no auditor is appointed within the week, the company is to inform the Secretary of State who may then appoint one or more persons to fill the vacancy (ss. 486, 490).

The directors are permitted to appoint the company's first auditor any time before the company's first 'accounts meeting' and also to fill a casual vacancy which may arise if (for whatever reason) the auditor ceases to hold office before the end of his/her term of appointment (ss. 485, 489).

Auditors hold the office of auditor in accordance with the terms of their appointment agreed with the company subject to the requirement that:
  (i) they do not take office until the predecessor auditor has ceased to hold office, and
  (ii) their appointment ceases at the end of the next 'accounts meeting' unless they are re-appointed.
If auditors are to be re-appointed, this requires the shareholders to pass an ordinary resolution to this effect at the relevant 'accounts meeting'.[49]

The party who appoints the company's auditor is responsible for fixing the associated remuneration.[50] Thus, when the company's shareholders appoint the auditor they must also, by ordinary resolution, determine the auditor's remuneration or the manner in which it is to be fixed. Similarly, when the auditor is appointed by the directors or by the Secretary of State, the party concerned is also responsible for determining the auditors' remuneration (CA 2006, s. 492).

Notwithstanding the legal provisions empowering the shareholders to appoint, and fix the remuneration of, their company's auditor, in practice the company's directors usually decide who they wish to be appointed and their decision is merely ratified by the shareholders. Normally, the shareholders also

---

[48] This applies to the appointment of auditors of public companies; reference should be made to CA 2006, s. 485, for the period of appointment of auditors of private companies.

[49] In the case of a private company, if no auditor is appointed by the end of the next 'period for appointing auditors', the incumbent auditor is deemed to be re-appointed unless:
  – the company's articles require actual re-appointment,
  – the shareholders have resolved that the auditor not be re-appointed, or
  – shareholders holding at least five per cent of the shareholders' total voting rights have given notice that the auditor should not be re-appointed (CA 206, s. 487).

[50] The term 'remuneration' includes "sums paid in respect of expenses . . . [and] benefits in kind" (CA 2006, s. 492).

delegate responsibility for fixing the auditor's remuneration to the directors. However, as we note in Chapter 4 (section 4.5), for companies with an audit committee, it is usually a responsibility of that committee to make recommendations to the board of directors on the appointment, re-appointment or removal of the auditor, and to approve the auditor's remuneration and terms of engagement.[51]

Further (as noted in Chapter 4, section 4.3.1), in order to ensure transparency with respect to the remuneration paid to, and the services provided by, auditors, all but small and medium-sized companies are required to disclose, in the notes to their financial statements, details of the amounts paid to their auditor (or any associates of the auditor) for (i) the audit and (ii) all other services provided to the company, its subsidiaries and its associated pension funds (SI 2011).[52]

5.3.3 How may an auditor resign or be replaced?

Auditors may resign simply by depositing a written notice to this effect at the company's registered office. However, to be effective, it must be accompanied by a 'statement of circumstances' or of 'no circumstances' (these statements are explained below) (CA 2006, s. 516). Alternatively, the company may remove the auditor at any time by passing an ordinary resolution at a general meeting (s. 510). It may also pass a resolution at the 'accounts meeting' to appoint another auditor (a 'replacement auditor') in place of the auditor whose term of appointment is ending (the 'outgoing auditor'). However, notice of any intended resolution to remove or replace the outgoing auditor must be sent to the shareholders and the outgoing auditor (and, if the auditor is to be replaced, also to the proposed auditor), and the outgoing auditor must be given the opportunity to make written representations to the shareholders on the

---

[51] As noted in Chapter 4 (section 4.5) and indicated in section 5.2.2 above, *The UK Corporate Governance Code* requires companies listed on the London Stock Exchange to establish an audit committee and to include in its responsibilities, making recommendations to the board on the auditor's appointment, re-appointment or removal, and approving their remuneration – or to disclose that they have not done so and the reasons therefor (provisions C.3.1, C.3.2). This gives effect to the EU *Statutory Audit Directive's* (EU, 2006a) requirement that the recommendation given to the shareholders by the directors of a company listed on a regulated market in the EU regarding the appointment of the company's auditor is to be based on the recommendation of the company's audit committee or the directors must explain why they have not adopted the audit committee's recommendation. In addition to making recommendations on the appointment, re-appointment or removal of their company's external auditor, the audit committees of the largest 350 companies listed on the London Stock Exchange (FTSE 350) are required to "put the external audit contract out to tender at least every ten years" (FRC, 2012a, prov. C.3.7). We discuss proposals relating to the tendering of FTSE 350 company audits, and measures designed to enhance shareholders' participation in the appointment of their company's auditor, in Chapter 18, section 18.5.1.

[52] As noted in Chapter 4, footnote 18, most small and medium-sized companies are required to disclose only the remuneration paid to the auditor for the audit of their financial statements.

intended resolution to remove or replace him or her (ss. 511, 515). The notice of any intended resolution to remove an auditor must be sent to the shareholders and the outgoing auditor at least 28 days prior to the general meeting at which the resolution is to be proposed (s. 511). The same applies to an intended resolution to appoint a replacement auditor if:
- no 'accounts meeting' has been held since the outgoing auditor ceased to hold office, or
- no auditor was appointed during the 'accounts meeting' when an auditor should have been appointed (s. 515).[53]

The provisions enabling outgoing auditors to inform shareholders of the reasons they believe explain their removal or replacement are particularly important where company directors wish to remove auditors for the wrong reasons – for example, because they have uncovered or challenged questionable acts by, or practices of, the directors or senior managers of which the shareholders are not aware and of which they would not approve. Directors lacking integrity may wish the company to engage less diligent auditors!

Whenever auditors cease to hold office (whether it be through resignation, removal or replacement), they are required to deposit at the relevant company's registered office, a statement of the circumstances connected with their ceasing to hold office. However, in the case of unquoted companies, auditors are excused from making this statement if they consider there are no circumstances that should be brought to the attention of the company's shareholders or creditors. In this event, the auditor is required to deposit at the company's registered office a statement that there are no such circumstances. The statement of circumstances (or, in applicable cases for an unquoted company, a statement of no circumstances) must be deposited at the company's registered office:
- if the auditor resigns, with the letter of resignation;
- if the auditor does not seek re-appointment, at least 14 days before the end of the period for appointing the auditor (i.e., the 'accounts meeting' for public companies);
- in other cases, within 14 days of the auditor ceasing to hold office (CA 2006, s. 519).

When a company receives a statement of circumstances, unless it applies to the court for a judgment on whether the auditor is seeking needless publicity

---

[53] These provisions relate to the replacement or removal of an auditor of a public company. For the provisions pertaining to the replacement or removal of the auditor of a private company, reference should be made to CA 2006 (ss. 296, 297, 514).

for defamatory matter and the court decides in the company's favour, it must send a copy of the auditor's statement to all those entitled to receive copies of the company's audited financial statements. If the company makes application to the court, the auditor must be notified accordingly. In the absence of such notice, the auditor must send a copy of his/her 'statement of circumstances' or of 'no circumstances' to the Registrar of Companies (CA 2006, ss. 520, 521). An example of (i) 'a statement of circumstances' sent by KPMG to IMI plc when it ceased to be the company's auditor in 2009 and (ii) the letter sent by IMI to its shareholders in this regard are presented in Figure 5.5.

Auditors are also required to notify the 'appropriate audit authority' of their ceasing to hold office and to send with their notice a copy of the 'statement of circumstances' or (for unquoted companies) of 'no circumstances' they deposited at the relevant company's registered office. If the statement is of 'no circumstances', it is to be accompanied by a statement providing reasons for the

Figure 5.5:   Examples of a statement of circumstances and related letter sent to the company's shareholders

31 July 2009

Dear Sirs

Statement to IMI plc on ceasing to hold office as auditors pursuant to section 519 of the Companies Act 2006

The circumstances connected with our ceasing to hold office are the holding of a competitive tender for the audit, in which we were unsuccessful in retaining the audit.

We request that any correspondence in relation to this statement be sent to our registered office ... marked for the attention of the Audit Regulation Department.

Yours faithfully
KPMG Audit Plc

14 August 2009

Dear Shareholder

Change of auditor

I am writing to you further to the decision, announced on 12 June 2009, to appoint Ernst & Young LLP as auditor for the IMI group. The appointment of a new auditor follows the formal, competitive process for the selection of an audit firm as referred to in the company's 2008 Annual Report ... KPMG Audit Plc has consequently resigned as auditor and, as required by section 519(3) of the Companies Act 2006, has deposited with the company a statement of the circumstances connected with its resignation. A copy of this statement is set out [above] and is being sent to shareholders for information only as required by section 520(2) of the Companies Act 2006.

Yours faithfully
Norman B M Askew
Chairman

auditor ceasing to hold office. However, the 'appropriate audit authority' and requirement to provide a notice about their ceasing to hold office differ according to whether the audit from which the auditor has ceased to hold office is, or is not, a 'major audit'.[54]

- For major audits, the appropriate audit authority is the Secretary of State or the body to whom the Secretary of State delegates the function – in practice, the Conduct Committee of the FRC. For these audits, auditors are required to notify the authority whenever they cease to hold office – whatever the reason – and they must do this at the same time as they deposit their 'statement of circumstances' at the relevant company's registered office.
- For 'not major audits', the 'appropriate audit authority' is the RSB with which the auditor is registered but, for these audits, auditors are only required to inform the authority of their ceasing to hold office when this occurs before the end of their term of appointment. The notice (and 'statement of circumstances' or of 'no circumstances' together with the reasons for ceasing to hold office) is to be given to the relevant RSB "at such time as the appropriate audit authority may require" (CA 2006, s. 522).

When auditors cease to hold office before the end of their term of appointment, the relevant company (in addition to the auditor) is required to notify the 'appropriate audit authority'. The notice must be accompanied by:

(i) a statement of the company's reasons for the auditor ceasing to hold office, and

(ii) if the auditors' 'statement of circumstances' contains circumstances in connection with their ceasing to hold office that need to be brought to the attention of the company's shareholders or creditors, a copy of that statement (s. 523).

5.4   AUDITOR–CLIENT RELATIONSHIP

Before turning attention to auditors' responsibilities, it is helpful to reflect on the somewhat unusual legal relationship between the auditor and the client company, and the auditor and the company's shareholders. We noted in section 5.3.2 that, under the provisions of CA 2006, shareholders are responsible for appointing their company's auditor and it is implicit in the statutory provisions that the auditor is appointed primarily to protect shareholders' interests. Nevertheless, after being appointed at the company's general meeting (the 'accounts meeting'), the auditor has no contact with the shareholders until

---

[54] A 'major audit' is the audit of a company listed on the London Stock Exchange or in whose financial condition there is major public interest (CA 2006, s. 525).

the audited financial statements (together with the rest of the company's annual report) is sent to them.

Notwithstanding that the auditor is appointed by the company's shareholders (at least, technically), the contractual arrangement for the audit is between the auditor and the client company. As a result, the auditor owes a contractual responsibility to the company *per se*, not to its shareholders. Further, in conducting the audit, the auditor will develop a close working relationship with the company's management,[55] and it is the company's management (or, if it has one, its audit committee), not its shareholders, who receive details of the auditor's findings.[56] The auditor's relationship with the client company and its shareholders is represented diagrammatically in Figure 5.6.

Given auditors' dual relationship with their client companies and the companies' shareholders, it is essential that, when conducting their audits, auditors

Figure 5.6: The auditor's relationship with the client company and its shareholders

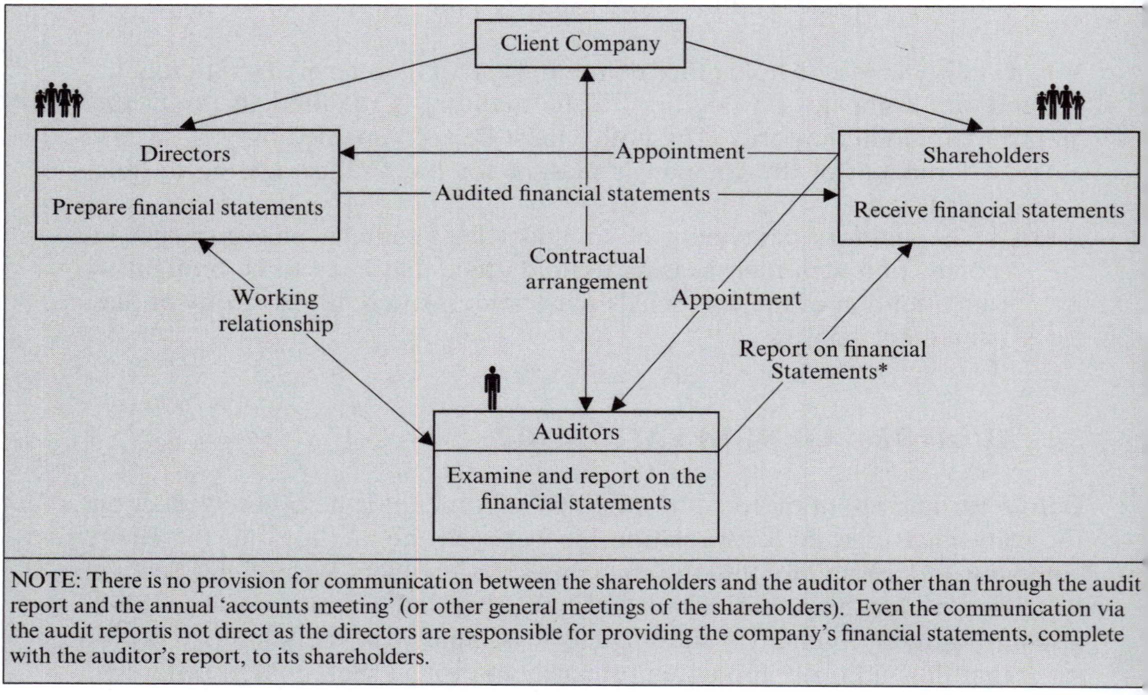

NOTE: There is no provision for communication between the shareholders and the auditor other than through the audit report and the annual 'accounts meeting' (or other general meetings of the shareholders). Even the communication via the audit report is not direct as the directors are responsible for providing the company's financial statements, complete with the auditor's report, to its shareholders.

---

[55] Readers are reminded that, in the Preface to this book, we note that the term 'management' is defined to mean a company's executive directors, non-executive directors and non-director executives (that is, all executives and directors).

[56] Auditors' 'communications of audit matters to those charged with the entity's governance' are discussed in Chapter 14, section 14.8.

adhere strictly to the fundamental ethical principle of independence – that they remain independent of the client and its management and are perceived to do so.

5.5 AUDITORS' DUTIES AND RIGHTS

5.5.1 Auditors' duties under statute law

A company auditor's primary duty is to report to the company's shareholders on the company's annual financial statements (CA 2006, s. 495). The report is to include:

(i) an introduction identifying the financial statements that have been audited and the financial reporting framework (UK GAAP or IFRS) adopted for their preparation;

(ii) a description of the scope of the audit, identifying the auditing standards applied during the audit;

(iii) a clear statement as to whether, in the auditor's opinion, the company's financial statements:
  - give a true and fair view of the company's state of affairs as at the end of the financial year and its profit or loss for the financial year;[57]
  - have been properly prepared in accordance with the relevant financial reporting framework (UK GAAP or IFRS);
  - have been prepared in accordance with the Companies Act 2006 and, in the case of the consolidated financial statements of groups with securities traded on a regulated market of an EU Member State, with the EU's IAS Regulation;[58]

(iv) a statement whether, in the auditor's opinion, the strategic and directors' reports for the financial year are consistent with the company's financial statements;

(v) for large companies which provide a corporate governance statement separate from the directors' report,[59] a statement whether, in the auditor's opinion, the information given in the corporate governance statement about (a) the company's internal controls and risk management

---

[57] In applicable cases, auditors are also required to report whether group financial statements give a true and fair view of the state of affairs and profit or loss of the undertakings included in the consolidated financial statements, so far as concerns the members of the parent company. In general, both UK GAAP and IFRS also require all but small companies to provide a statement showing the company's (or group's, if applicable) cash flows during the financial year.

[58] EU Regulation (EC) No. 1606/2002 *on the application of International Accounting Standards* (see section 5.2.1).

[59] It should be noted that, as explained in section 5.2.2, small and medium-sized companies need not provide corporate governance statements in their annual reports (in the directors' report or as a separate statement).

systems relevant to the financial reporting process and (b) share capital structures is consistent with the financial statements;

(vi) for quoted companies, a report on the auditable part of the directors' remuneration report and a statement whether, in the auditor's opinion, that part of the directors' remuneration report has been properly prepared in accordance with the Companies Act 2006.[60]

The auditor's report must be either unqualified (when the auditor is satisfied that everything is as it should be) or qualified (when the auditor is not so satisfied); it must also include a reference to any matters to which the auditor wishes to draw attention by way of emphasis without qualifying the report[61] (CA 2006, ss. 495–497A).

When determining whether the company's financial statements give a true and fair view and comply with the applicable financial reporting framework and the requirements of CA 2006, the auditor needs to consider, *inter alia*, whether the company faces material uncertainties or liquidity risk which cast significant doubt upon the ability of the company to continue as a going concern and, if so, whether adequate disclosure of the uncertainties and/or risk has been made. Similarly, for listed companies, the auditor must consider the adequacy of the directors' statement regarding the company's status as a going concern. In any case where, in the auditor's opinion, the company's going concern disclosures are not adequate, the auditor is required to qualify the audit opinion and provide reasons for so doing (FRC, 2009, para 84).

In addition to reporting to shareholders as outlined above, CA 2006 (s. 498) requires auditors to carry out investigations that enable them to form an opinion as to whether:
- adequate accounting records have been kept by the company,
- returns, adequate for their audit, have been received from branches of the company not visited by them,
- the financial statements are in agreement with the accounting records and returns, and
- in the case of a quoted company, the auditable part of the directors' remuneration report is in agreement with the accounting records and returns.

In any case where auditors consider that one or more of the above requirements has not been met, they are required to state that fact in the audit report. They are also to state in the audit report if:

---

[60] The requirements relating to corporate governance statements and the 'auditable part' of the directors' remuneration report are explained in section 5.2.2.

[61] The various types of audit report are discussed in detail in Chapter 14.4. It should be noted that, although CA 2006 refers to audit reports as being 'unqualified' or 'qualified', Auditing Standards use the terms 'unmodified' or 'modified', respectively, for these types of audit report.

- they fail to obtain all the information and explanations they considered necessary for the purposes of their audit; and/or
- a company is required to provide a corporate governance statement and, in the auditor's opinion, no such statement has been provided (CA 2006, ss. 498, 498A).

Additionally, in any case where the directors' remuneration report does not provide required information (that is, information required by SI 2008a, Schedule 8), the auditor is to provide the required particulars in the audit report, so far as reasonably able to do so.

The auditor's report must state the name of, and be signed and dated by, the auditor. If the auditor is a firm, it is to be signed by the senior statutory auditor (that is, the audit engagement partner) in his or her own name, for and on behalf of the audit firm. Every copy of the auditor's report that is published by or on behalf of the client company must state the name of the auditor and (where the auditor is a firm) the name of the person who signed it as the senior statutory auditor. A company is regarded as publishing the report if it makes it available in a manner that invites members of the public to read it (CA 2006, ss. 503–505).

5.5.2 Auditors' statutory rights

CA 2006 (ss. 499–502) provides auditors with rights that facilitate the performance of their duties. Auditors are, for example, given a right of access, at all reasonable times, to all of the auditee's books, accounts and vouchers (or source documents). They also have the right to require the directors and employees of the company, and the directors, employees and auditor of any subsidiary undertaking of the company which is incorporated in the UK, to provide any information and explanations the auditor considers necessary for the purposes of the audit. Similarly, where a parent company has subsidiary undertakings incorporated outside the UK, the auditor of the parent company can require that company to obtain relevant information and explanations from the directors, employees and auditor of those subsidiaries.

Clearly, there is the potential for ill-intentioned persons to provide inaccurate or incomplete information to the auditor. However, CA 2006 (s. 501) provides that, if any person knowingly or recklessly makes a written or oral statement to the company's auditor that:
  (i) conveys, or purports to convey, information or explanations the auditor requires, and
  (ii) is misleading, false or deceptive about a material matter,
that person is guilty of an offence. This can result in imprisonment for up to two years or a fine of up to the statutory maximum (£5,000). Along similar

lines, if a person fails to provide information or explanations requested by the auditor "without delay" (s. 501), unless it is not reasonably practical for the person to do so, s/he commits an offence that may result in a fine of up to £1,000.

Further rights provided to auditors by CA 2006 are the right to:
(i)   attend any general meeting of the company,
(ii) receive notices and other communications relating to any general meeting which a shareholder is entitled to receive, and
(iii) be heard at any general meeting on matters that concern them as auditors.

5.5.3 Auditors' duties under common law

While statute law specifies the duties auditors are to perform, it has been left to the courts to explain what is expected of auditors in fulfilment of their statutory duties.

The general standard of performance required of auditors was laid down by Lopes L J in *Re Kingston Cotton Mill Co.*(No. 2) [1896] 2 Ch 279,[62] when he said:

> It is the duty of an auditor to bring to bear on the work he has to perform that skill, care and caution which a reasonably competent, careful and cautious auditor would use. What is reasonable skill, care and caution must depend on the particular circumstances of each case.

Clearly, what is regarded as 'reasonable skill, care and caution in the circumstances' will change over time as changes occur in society, in society's attitudes and values, and in the 'technology' of auditing. As we note in Chapter 2, until the 1920s, auditors were primarily concerned with detecting fraud and error and ensuring that the solvency position of the reporting entity was fairly portrayed in the balance sheet. Accordingly, during the nineteenth century, auditors carefully checked the detailed entries in, and arithmetical accuracy of, the company's books and made sure that the amounts shown in the balance sheet corresponded with the ledger account balances. If this were all that auditors did today they would be regarded as grossly negligent. They are now expected to examine sufficient appropriate evidence, drawn from a variety of sources (from both inside and outside the entity), on which to base an opinion about the truth and fairness of the auditee's financial statements and their compliance (or otherwise) with the applicable financial reporting framework and the requirements of CA 2006.

---

[62] This case is also reported in Chapter 2, section 2.4.4. The same applies to the cases of Re London and General Bank (No 2) (1895), The London Oil Storage Co (1904) and Arthur E Green and Co (1920), which are referred to below.

Over the years, various parties who suffered a loss after relying on materially misstated audited financial statements on which the auditor expressed a 'clean' audit opinion, have taken the auditors concerned to court on claims of negligence; that is, on grounds that the auditors did not perform their duties with due skill and care. Many of these cases have helped to clarify specific duties of auditors. The following serve as examples.

- In *Leeds Estate Building and Investment Co.* v *Shepherd* (1887) 36 Ch D 787, the auditor (a bank clerk) was found to be negligent for failing to ensure that the audited balance sheet was drawn up in accordance with the company's Articles of Association (which he had, in fact, never seen). The auditor claimed his duty was to see that the balance sheet represented, and was a true result of, what appeared in the books of the company, and his certificate went no further than that. However, the judge (Sterling J) thought otherwise. He stated:

  [It is] the duty of the auditor not to confine himself merely to the task of verifying the arithmetical accuracy of the balance sheet, but to enquire into its substantial accuracy, and to ascertain that it contained the particulars specified in the articles of association . . . and was properly drawn up so as to contain a true and correct representation of the state of the company's affairs. (at 802)

- As in the *Leeds Estate* case, in *Re London and General Bank* (No. 2) (1895) 2 Ch 677, (which concerned a bank whose loans to other companies were of doubtful recoverability) the auditor, in phrasing his audit report, tried unsuccessfully to limit his duty to a comparison of the balance sheet with the books of account. Lindley L J made it clear that more was expected of auditors. He stated (at 682–3):

  [An auditor's] business is to ascertain and state the true financial position of the company at the time of the audit and his duty is confined to that. But then comes the question: How is he to ascertain such position? The answer is: By examining the books of the company. But he does not discharge his duty by doing this without enquiry, and without taking any trouble to see that the books of the company show the company's true position. He must take reasonable care to ascertain that they do. Unless he does this, his duty will be worse than a farce.

  This case is a landmark in that it established that auditors not only had to examine the auditee's books and records but they also had to form an opinion as to whether those books and records 'truly' reflected the substance of the company's financial position.

- In *The London Oil Storage Co. Ltd* v *Seear, Hasluck & Co.* (1904) Acc LR 30, it was established that auditors are required to verify the existence of assets stated in the balance sheet. In this case, the cash book balance did not agree with the physical cash balance, a fact the auditor failed to check or discover. The case is particularly significant as it is the first time that the court made it clear that auditors are expected to go beyond the books and records of the client company for evidence to support their opinion about the truth and fairness of the financial statements.

- In *Arthur E Green & Co.* v *The Central Advance and Discount Corporation Ltd* (1920) 63 Acc LR 1, an auditor was held to be negligent for accepting a schedule of bad debts provided by a responsible officer of the company when it was apparent that other debts, not included in the schedule, were also irrecoverable. The case made it clear that auditors may not blindly accept evidence given to them by officers of the auditee. They must properly relate it to other evidence gathered during the course of the audit.

- In the infamous *McKesson & Robbins* case (US, 1938), the auditor failed to uncover a massive fraud involving fictitious accounts receivable and inventory. The court held that auditors have a duty to verify the existence of these assets. This extended the *London Oil Storage Company* case ruling, making it clear that auditors must verify assets stated in the balance sheet, even when those assets are at a distant location.

Occasionally when a case comes before the court, the judge takes the opportunity to bring together the specific duties of auditors that have been settled in a number of previous cases, and to enunciate general principles. One of the most renowned cases of this type is the Australian case *Pacific Acceptance Corporation Limited* v *Forsyth and Others* (1970) 92 WN (NSW) 29. In his long judgment, Moffitt J provided comprehensive guidance on auditors' duties. The following are among the important legal principles he confirmed or established.

1. When auditors accept an engagement to conduct a statutory financial statement audit they can be taken to have promised, not only to make the report required by legislation (for example, by s. 495 of CA 2006), but also to conduct such examination as is necessary to form their opinion, and to exercise due skill and care in so doing.
2. Auditors' duties are not confined to an examination of the company's books and records at the date of the financial statements but extend to an audit of the company's financial affairs in general, and for the whole of the relevant financial reporting period.
3. The duty to audit involves a duty to pay due regard to the possibility that fraud may have occurred. The audit plan and audit tests should be structured so that the auditor has a reasonable expectation of detecting material fraud if it exists.
4. Auditors have a duty to make prompt and frank disclosure, to the appropriate level of management, of material matters discovered during the

course of an audit. This includes a duty to report promptly to the company's directors if suspicious circumstances are encountered.

5. The auditor's duty to report includes a duty to report to shareholders at their general meeting any material matters discovered during the audit. This responsibility cannot be shirked on the grounds that it involves an adverse reflection on the board, a director, or a senior executive, or on the pretext that public disclosure may damage the company.[63]

6. The auditor has a paramount duty to check material matters for him- or herself. However, reliance may be placed on enquiries from others where it is reasonable to do so. Nevertheless, reliance on others is to be regarded as an aid to, and not a substitute for, the auditor's own procedures.

7. The use of inexperienced staff, or the failure to use an adequate audit plan do not, of themselves, establish negligence. However, if audit failure occurs (that is, the auditor expresses a 'clean' audit opinion on financial statements that are materially misstated), then the use of such staff and/or the absence of a satisfactory audit plan may be taken as evidence that the failure occurred as a result of negligence.

In his judgment, Moffitt J noted that professional standards and practice must change over time to reflect changes in the economic and business environment. He further observed that the courts, in trying to ascertain what qualifies as 'reasonable skill, care and caution', are guided by professional standards and best auditing practices of the time. However, he emphasised that the courts are not bound by these standards and, if they see fit, they will go beyond them. It is the courts, not the profession, which determine, in the light of society's prevailing norms, what is reasonable skill, care and caution in the particular circumstances of the case.[64]

The relevance of these points is evident when it is realised that the duties Moffitt J attributed to auditors were frequently not practised at the time (that is, in 1970). Indeed, Kenley (1971, pp. 153–161) noted that the case brought to light key matters which required the immediate attention of auditors. These included the need for auditors:

---

[63] This principle is pertinent to the audits of some UK banks prior to the 2008–9 global financial crisis and auditors' reluctance to report doubts they had (or should have had) about the going concern status of the banks. In the subsequent House of Lords enquiry, the Lords noted: "A going concern qualification was clearly warranted in several cases, even if the auditors may understandably have been reluctant to make it . . . [because] they might fear to do so could cause a collapse of confidence and a run on the bank, to the detriment of the shareholders and, quite possibly, of the wider public interest" (House of Lords, 2011, paras 140, 147).

[64] It should be remembered that, at the time of the *Pacific Acceptance* case, all auditing and ethical standards and guidelines (such as they were) were promulgated by the professional accountancy bodies. Enshrining auditing and ethical standards in regulations is a phenomenon of the twenty-first century. However, the principle enunciated by Moffitt J remains true even in auditing's regulated environment.

1. to have an adequate written audit plan, and to correlate this with a review of the audit client's system of internal controls, and to modify it as necessary during the course of the audit to ensure that all material aspects of the entity are adequately covered;
2. to ensure that audit samples are drawn from records and events that cover the entire financial period, not just the period around the date of the financial statements;
3. to ensure that audit staff are properly supervised by both partners and managers, and that proper instructions are given to assistants who have limited qualifications and/or experience;
4. to carefully assess the level of management from which the auditor seeks information, and to record appropriate details of responses to enquiry in the audit working papers;
5. to report promptly and forthrightly to the appropriate level of the client's management, deficiencies in transactions or accounting records examined by the auditor.

Today all of these matters are regarded as 'usual practice'. Indeed, the *Pacific Acceptance* case has had a profound impact on auditing as the principles enunciated by Moffitt J underlie the Auditing Standards that were subsequently promulgated.

5.5.4 Auditors' duties under auditing standards

Until relatively recently, professional accountancy bodies around the world were responsible for setting, monitoring and amending (as appropriate) Auditing Standards that governed the work of their members who were auditors. In many, if not most, cases the 'national professional body standards' were based on, and largely replicated, the International Standards on Auditing (ISAs) issued by the International Federation of Accountants' (IFAC) Auditing Practices Committee or its replacement – the International Auditing and Assurance Standards Board (IAASB).[65]

In the UK and Ireland, rather than each of the professional bodies (or more correctly, each RSB) setting its own Auditing Standards, in 1991 the bodies established the Auditing Practices Board (APB) to perform this function on their behalf.[66] In 2004, the APB became a component (an operating body) of

---

[65] IFAC is a global organisation for the accountancy profession. It has 167 member bodies in 127 countries, including the UK. In 2002, IFAC established the IAASB as an independent standard setting body; it replaced the International Auditing Practices Committee (established by IFAC in 1978) and assumed delegated responsibility from IFAC for setting, *inter alia*, International Standards on Auditing and Quality Control (IFAC, 2012a, 2012b).

[66] Prior to 1991, Auditing Standards in the UK were set jointly by the professional bodies through the Consultative Committee of Accountancy Bodies (CCAB).

the FRC, and the status of its Auditing Standards changed from 'professional' (enforceable by the relevant professional body) to regulatory (enforceable under the law). In July 2012, the status of the APB changed once more; it was renamed 'Audit and Assurance Council' and became an advisory council of the FRC's Codes and Standards Committee.[67] The Audit and Assurance Council has an independent Chair and nine other members (unless the nominations committee approves the appointment of up to two further members); no more than half of the members may be practising members of the auditing profession (FRC, 2012e).

In its *Scope and Authority of FRC Audit and Assurance Pronouncements* (FRC, 2013b), the FRC explains that its pronouncements include:
- Quality control standards for firms that perform audits of financial statements . . . ;
- A framework of fundamental principles, 'The Auditors' Code' which the FRC expects to guide the conduct of auditors . . . ;[68]
- Ethical and engagement standards for audits of financial statements . . . ;
- Guidance for auditors of financial statements. . . . (para 1)

In relation to the UK's quality control and auditing standards, the FRC notes that the International Standards on Auditing (ISAs) (UK and Ireland) and International Standard on Quality Control (ISQC) (UK and Ireland) 1:
> . . . are based on the corresponding international standards issued by the International Auditing and Assurance Standards Board (IAASB). Where necessary, the international standards have been augmented with additional requirements to address specific UK and Irish legal and regulatory requirements; . . . This additional material is clearly differentiated from the original text of the international standards by the use of grey shading. (FRC, 2013b, para 7)

The augmentation of ISQC1 and ISAs with additional requirements to meet national regulatory requirements is recognised by IFAC. In its *Preface to the International Standards on Quality Control, Auditing, Review, Other Assurance and Related Services Pronouncements*, IFAC (2010) explains:
> IAASB members act in the common interest of the public at large and the worldwide accountancy profession. . . . The IAASB's pronouncements govern audit . . . engagements that are conducted in accordance with International Standards. They do not override the local laws or regulations that govern the audit of historical financial statements . . . in a particular country [that are] required to be followed in accordance with that country's national standards. [However, in] the

---

[67] As noted in section 5.3.1, until 2012, the APB was responsible for developing and issuing Auditing and Ethical Standards. Since 2012, the Audit and Assurance Council has been responsible for developing the Standards but they are now issued by the FRC Board not the Council.

[68] The FRC explains that *The Auditors' Code* "provides a framework of fundamental principles which encapsulate the concepts that govern the conduct of audits and underlie the ethical and engagement standards for audits of financial statements" (FRC, 2013b, para 3). The Auditors' Code is reproduced on the inside of the front cover of this book.

event that local laws or regulations differ from, or conflict with, the IAASB's Standards on a particular subject, an engagement conducted in accordance with local laws or regulations will not automatically comply with the IAASB's Standards. A professional accountant should not represent compliance with the IAASB's Standards unless the professional accountant has complied fully with all of those relevant to the engagement. (paras 2, 3)

As shown in Figure 5.7, the ISAs have been issued in a structured series. We should also note that if UK auditors comply with ISAs (UK and Ireland), they will also be in full compliance with the IAASB's ISAs.

The FRC explains the relationship between the technical (quality control and auditing) standards and the ethical standards (and differences between the International and UK approach) as follows:

The ISAs and ISQC 1 as issued by the IAASB, require compliance with 'relevant ethical requirements' which are described . . . as ordinarily comprising . . . the International Ethics Standards Board for Accountants (IESBA) *Code of Ethics for Professional Accountants* (*IESBA Code*) related to an audit of financial statements together with national requirements that are more restrictive. The ISAs (UK and Ireland) and ISQC (UK and Ireland) 1 have supplementary material that makes clear that auditors in the UK and Ireland are subject to ethical requirements from two sources: the Ethical Standards for Auditors concerning the integrity, objectivity and independence of the auditor [i.e., the APB's Ethical Standards], and the ethical pronouncements established by the auditor's relevant professional body. (FRC, 2013b, para 9)

ISQC1 and the ISAs contain basic principles and essential procedures together with related guidance. The latter, in the form of explanatory and other material (including appendices), is provided to assist auditors interpret and apply the basic principles and essential procedures. Compliance with the basic principles and essential procedures, which constitute the actual Auditing Standards,[69] is mandatory. If auditors fail to comply with these when performing company audits, disciplinary action may be taken against them by the RSB with which they are registered or, in extreme cases, by the FRC's Conduct Committee. Such disciplinary action may result in withdrawal of registration with the relevant RSB and, hence, in loss of eligibility to perform company audits (FRC, 2013b, para 18). This situation is somewhat bemusing. The ISAs are developed by the IAASB and, although it is designated an 'independent standard setting body' by IFAC, it was established by, and operates under the auspices of, IFAC – a professional body. Hence, ISQC 1 and ISAs are, in effect,

---

[69] In common parlance, entire ISAs (Auditing Standards and explanatory material) are referred to as 'Auditing Standards'. In this book we use the term 'Auditing Standard' with this meaning; that is, to refer to the relevant ISA in its entirety. In each ISA, the basic principles and essential procedures are presented in the first section of the ISA, and 'Application and other explanatory matter' is presented in a second section. The paragraphs containing the mandatory standards are numbered sequentially (1, 2, 3, etc.); the application and explanatory paragraphs are identified by the letter A (i.e., A1, A2, A3, etc.).

Figure 5.7: Structure of International Standards on Auditing

ISA No.	Title
200/299	**General Principles and Responsibilities**
200	Overall objectives of the independent auditor and the conduct of an audit in accordance with International Standards on Auditing
210	Agreeing the terms of audit engagements
220	Quality control for an audit of financial statements
230	Audit documentation
240	The auditor's responsibilities relating to fraud in an audit of financial statements
250	Consideration of laws and regulations in an audit of financial statements
260	Communication with those charged with governance
265	Communicating deficiencies in internal control to those charged with governance and management
300/499	**Risk Assessment and Response to Assessed Risks**
300	Planning an audit of financial statements
315	Identifying and assessing the risks of material misstatement through understanding the entity and its environment
320	Materiality in planning and performing an audit
330	The auditor's responses to assessed risks
402	Audit considerations relating to an entity using a service organization
450	Evaluation of misstatements identified during the audit
500/599	**Audit evidence**
500	Audit evidence
501	Audit evidence – Specific considerations for selected items
505	External confirmations
510	Initial audit engagements – Opening balances
520	Analytical procedures
530	Audit sampling
540	Auditing accounting estimates, including fair value accounting estimates, and related disclosures
550	Related parties
560	Subsequent events
570	Going concern
580	Written representations
600/699	**Using Work of Others**
600	Special considerations – Audits of group financial statements (including the work of component auditors)
610	Using the work of internal auditors
620	Using the work of an auditor's expert
700/799	**Audit conclusions and reporting**
700	Forming an opinion and reporting on financial statements
705	Modifications to the opinion in the independent auditor's report
706	Emphasis of matter paragraphs and other matter paragraphs in the independent auditor's report
710	Comparative information – Corresponding figures and comparative financial statements
720	The auditor's responsibilities in relation to other information in documents containing audited financial statements

Figure 5.7: *Continued*

ISA No.	Title
800-899	**Specialized areas**
800	Special considerations – Audits of financial statements prepared in accordance with special purpose frameworks
805	Special considerations – Audits of single financial statements and specific elements, accounts or items of a financial statement
810	Engagements to report on summary financial statements
	In addition to the ISAs issued by IAASB, the APB has issued two standards with application in the UK and Ireland. To accommodate these standards, those identified by IAASB as ISA 250 and 720 are titled 250A and 720A respectively. The additional standards are:
250B	The auditors right and duty to report to regulators in the financial sector
720B	The auditors statutory reporting responsibility in relation to directors' reports

professional standards but, through their adoption by the FRC, they have assumed the status of regulations.

In addition to the guidance on the application of particular quality control and auditing standards which is included within the relevant standard, the FRC has issued guidance to auditors in the form of Practice Notes and Bulletins. It explains:

> Practice Notes and Bulletins are persuasive rather than prescriptive and are indicative of good practice. Practice Notes assist auditors in applying engagement [i.e., auditing] standards to particular circumstances and industries and Bulletins provide timely guidance on new or emerging issues. (FRC, 2013b, para 12)

It is pertinent to observe that, although the explanatory material included in the FRC's quality control and auditing standards, like its Practice Notes and Bulletins, is persuasive rather than mandatory, the FRC notes: "All relevant FRC pronouncements are likely to be taken into account when the adequacy of the work of auditors is being considered in a court of law or in other contested situations" (FRC, 2013b, para 19).

The quality control and auditing standards serve two important purposes:
  (i) they inform individual auditors of the requirements they must meet in the performance of their audits, and
  (ii) they help to enhance the reputation of, and increase public confidence in, the profession as a whole.

As auditors' responsibilities are clearly set out in the standards, and as the standards are binding on all members of the profession in the conduct of all company audits (and any auditor falling short of the mandatory standards when performing an audit is exposed to disciplinary action), the standards help to ensure that all members of the profession perform their audits in accordance with the standards. If all auditors comply with the standards, high quality audits should result – to the benefit of users of the audited financial statements, auditees and society as a whole, as well as to the auditing profession.

We study the main provisions of ISQC 1 and many of the ISAs in the chapters which follow.

5.5.5 Auditors' duties under other regulatory requirements

Certain regulatory bodies, such as the Financial Conduct Authority (FCA), have been given authority under relevant statutes to impose requirements on entities under their jurisdiction and also on the auditors of those entities. Most of the regulatory requirements apply only to entities within the industries concerned (for example, the financial services, mining and utilities industries) and it is outside the scope of this book to discuss auditing requirements that are specific to any particular industry. However, the requirements of the UK Listing Authority (UKLA) extend widely as they apply to all companies listed on the London Stock Exchange.

As noted in section 5.2.2, the UKLA's Listing Rules require listed companies to provide, *inter alia*:
- (i) a statement that the company is a going concern, together with support-ing assumptions and qualifications as necessary; and
- (ii) a corporate governance statement which:
  - (a) explains how the company has applied the main principles of *The UK Corporate Governance Code*, and
  - (b) states that the company has complied with all relevant provisions of the Code or explains those with which it has not complied.

In respect of the directors' going concern statement, the Listing Rules require listed companies to ensure that their auditor reviews the statement prior to publication of their audited financial statements. The APB (2009, para 4) explains that the auditor's responsibility includes:
- reviewing the documentation, prepared by or for the directors, of the company's assessment of its status as a going concern;
- evaluating the consistency of the directors' going concern status with the knowledge the auditor has acquired during the audit;
- evaluating whether the directors' statement meets the disclosure require-ments. These are contained in Principle 3 of the FRC's guidance which states:

> Directors should make balanced, proportionate and clear disclosures about going concern for the financial statements to give a true and fair view. Direc-tors should disclose if the period that they have reviewed is less than twelve months from the date of approval of the . . . financial statements and explain their justification for limiting their review period. (FRC, 2009, p. 12)

Regarding the corporate governance statement, as we note in section 5.2.2, this may be included as a separate section within the directors' report or provided as a separate statement in the company's annual report or on its website. We also noted that CA 2006 (s. 446) requires the statement to include:

- reference to the corporate governance code to which the company is subject;
- a description of the main features of the company's internal control and risk management systems in relation to the financial reporting process;
- information about its share capital; and
- a description of the composition and operation of the company's administrative, management and supervisory bodies and their committees.

These four requirements are among a wide range of corporate governance disclosures listed companies are required to make: we identified some of these in section 5.2.2; others are noted below. As for the going concern statement, auditors also have responsibilities in respect of companies' corporate governance disclosures.

Irrespective of whether a listed company (or, indeed, a large unlisted company)[70] includes its corporate governance statement in the directors' report or provides it as a separate statement, the company's auditor is required to form an opinion as to whether the information given in the statement in respect of (i) the company's internal control and risk management systems that relate to the financial reporting process, and (ii) its share capital, is consistent with the financial statements.[71] The APB (2009) explains that if, in the auditor's opinion, there is an inconsistency, then the auditor must determine whether the financial statements or corporate governance statement needs revising. If there is no inconsistency and the corporate governance statement is included in the directors' report, no additional wording in the auditor's report is required; the auditor's statement that the directors' report is consistent with the financial statements is sufficient. However, if a separate corporate governance statement is provided, the auditor needs to include in the audit report a statement to the effect that the corporate governance statement (as well as the strategic and directors' reports) is consistent with the financial statements (APB, 2009, paras 22–29).

---

[70] It should be recalled from section 5.2.2 that all large companies (those that do not meet the criteria to be classified as small or medium-sized) are required to provide an annual corporate governance statement.

[71] As we explain in Chapter 13, section 13.8, ISA 720: *The Auditor's Responsibilities in Relation to Other Information in Documents Containing Audited Financial Statements* (IAASB, 2009) requires auditors to review *all* of the information in companies' annual reports to ascertain whether or not it is inconsistent with the financial statements or contains material misstatements of fact.

In addition to the above requirement, the auditors of companies listed on the London Stock Exchange are required by the UKLA's Listing Rules to review their listed company clients' corporate governance compliance statement insofar as it relates to nine of the 12 accountability provisions included in *The UK Corporate Governance Code* (see Figure 5.4).[72] The nine are as follows:

C.1.1   The directors should explain in the annual report their responsibility for preparing the annual report and accounts, and state that they consider the annual report and accounts, taken as a whole, is fair, balanced and understandable and provides the information necessary for shareholders to assess the company's performance, business model and strategy. There should also be a statement by the auditors about their reporting responsibilities.

C.2.1   The board should, at least annually, conduct a review of the effectiveness of the company's risk management and internal control systems and should report to shareholders that they have done so. The review should cover all material controls, including financial, operational and compliance controls.

C.3.1   The board should establish an audit committee of at least three, or in the case of smaller companies[73] two, independent non-executive directors. . . . The board should satisfy itself that at least one member of the audit committee has recent and relevant financial experience.

C.3.2   The main role and responsibilities of the audit committee should be set out in written terms of reference . . . [The matters to be included therein are reproduced in Chapter 4, section 4.5.3].

C.3.3   The terms of reference of the audit committee, including its role and the authority delegated to it by the board, should be made available. [This can be provided on the company's website (FRC, 2012a, footnote 7)].

C.3.5   The audit committee should review arrangements by which staff of the company may, in confidence, raise concerns about possible improprieties in matters of financial reporting or other matters. . . .

C.3.6   The audit committee should monitor and review the effectiveness of the internal audit activities. Where there is no internal audit function, the audit committee should consider annually whether there is a need for an

---

[72] Auditors also review the company's compliance with two of the other accountability provisions. These are as follows:
- The directors should include in the annual report an explanation of the basis on which the company generates or preserves value over the longer term (the business model) and the strategy for delivering the objectives of the company (prov. C.1.2).
- The directors should report in . . . [their] financial statements that the business is a going concern, with supporting assumptions or qualifications as necessary (prov. C.1.3).

Auditors assess companies' compliance with prov. C.1.2 when reviewing the company's strategic report and considering whether it is consistent with the audited financial statements and with the knowledge they have acquired during the audit. In respect of provision C.1.3, as noted above, auditors are specifically required to assess the adequacy of the directors' going concern statement. The remaining accountability provision (prov. C.3.4) (which is not subject to the auditor's review) states:

    Where requested by the board, the audit committee should provide advice on whether the annual report and [financial statements] taken as a whole, is fair, balanced and understandable and provides the information necessary for shareholders to assess the company's performance, business model and strategy.

[73] A smaller company is one that is below the FTSE 350 throughout the year immediately prior to the reporting year (FRC, 2012a, footnote 6).

internal audit function and make a recommendation to the board, and the reasons for the absence of such a function should be explained in the relevant section of the annual report.

C.3.7 The audit committee should have primary responsibility for making a recommendation on the appointment, reappointment and removal of external auditors. FTSE 350 companies should put the external audit contract out to tender at least every ten years. If the board does not accept the audit committee's recommendation, it should include in the annual report, and in any papers recommending appointment or re-appointment, a statement from the audit committee explaining the recommendations and should set out reasons why the board has taken a different position.

C.3.8 A separate section of the annual report should describe the work of the committee in discharging its responsibilities. The report should include:

- the significant issues that the committee considered in relation to the financial statements, and how these issues were addressed;[74]
- an explanation of how it has assessed the effectiveness of the external audit process and the approach taken to the appointment or reappointment of the external auditor, and information on the length of tenure of the current audit firm and when a tender was last conducted, and
- if the external auditor provides non-audit services, an explanation of how auditor objectivity and independence is safeguarded.[75]

The APB (2006) has provided guidance for auditors in respect of their review of listed company clients' corporate governance disclosures. It states:

In relation to all elements of the corporate governance disclosures relating to the provisions of the [Corporate Governance] Code that are within the scope of the auditor's review, the auditor obtains appropriate evidence to support the compliance statement made by the company. The type of procedures usually performed include:

(a) reviewing the minutes of the meetings of the board of directors, and of relevant board committees;

(b) reviewing supporting documents prepared for the board of directors or board committees . . .;

(c) making enquiries of certain directors . . . to satisfy themselves on matters relevant to those provisions of the [Corporate Governance] Code specified for review by the auditor; and

(d) attending meetings of the audit committee . . . at which the annual report and accounts, including the statement of compliance, are considered and approved for submission to the board of directors. (para 16)

---

[74] ISA (UK and Ireland) 700: *The Independent Auditor's Report on Financial Statements* (FRC, 2013d, para A18A), specifies that the audit committee report should disclose significant issues communicated to it by the external auditor and how those issues were addressed.

[75] As we explain in Chapter 18, section 18.5.1, the FRC has advanced proposals to extend the matters on which audit committees report.

If, in their compliance statement, the directors of a listed company state that the company has complied with the nine provisions of *The UK Corporate Governance Code* that are subject to the auditor's review and, in the auditor's opinion, the company has not complied with one or more of them, the auditor is required to report this fact in a section of the auditor's report headed "Matters on which we are required to report by exception".[76] ISA (UK and Ireland) 700 (FRC, 2013d, para 22B) explains that this includes reporting if the directors state "that they consider the annual report and accounts, taken as a whole, is fair, balanced and understandable and provides the information necessary for shareholders to assess the entity's performance, business model and strategy" (prov. C.1.1) but this is inconsistent with the knowledge the auditor has acquired during the audit. Along similar lines, ISA (UK and Ireland) 700 (s. 22B) notes that, if the section of the company's annual report describing the work of the audit committee does not appropriately disclose matters communicated by the auditor to the committee, which the auditor considers should have been disclosed, the auditor is to provide the relevant information in the audit report.

In a case where a listed company discloses that it has not complied with one or more of the nine provisions of *The UK Corporate Governance Code* within the scope of the auditor's review, and explains the reasons for so doing, and the auditor considers that the non-compliance is fully and properly disclosed, no reference to the non-compliance need be made in the auditor's report. However, if, in the auditor's opinion, the non-compliance is not disclosed or explained adequately, then this conclusion is to be reported in the auditor's report (APB, 2006, paras 19, 20).

5.6 AUDIT FIRMS' TRANSPARENCY REPORTS AND GOVERNANCE CODE

Some audit firms are not only required to fulfil responsibilities in relation to their audit clients' financial and governance reports, they are also required to fulfil reporting and governance responsibilities that relate to themselves. Under the requirements of the *Statutory Auditors (Transparency) Instrument 2008* (Transparency Instrument; POB, 2008), any firm which audits at least one 'public interest entity' in any financial year must publish a transparency report on its website and send a copy of the report to the FRC. This is to be done within three months of the end of the firm's financial year and the report is to remain available on the firm's website for a period of two years. A 'public

---

[76] This section of the auditor's report is explained in Chapter 14, section 14.3.5.

interest entity' includes all companies listed on the London Stock Exchange and any other entity in whose financial or business affairs the public has a particular interest. The Transparency Instrument refers to audit firms which are required to publish transparency reports as 'transparency reporting auditors'.

The information to be disclosed by a transparency reporting auditor is extensive and wide-ranging. It includes:
  – a description of the legal structure, ownership and governance structure of the firm and, if it belongs to a network, a description of the network and the network's legal and structural arrangements;
  – a description of the firm's internal quality control system and a statement by the firm's administrative or management body on its effectiveness. The FRC specifies that the description should include an indication of how the components of the firm's internal quality control system link to the drivers of audit quality identified in the FRC's Audit Quality Framework (FRC, 2008c);
  – a statement of when the audit performance of the firm was last monitored by the Audit Inspection Unit;[77]
  – a list of all of the public interest entities audited by the audit firm during its financial year;
  – a description of the firm's independence procedures and practices and confirmation that a review of its independence practices has been conducted during the year;
  – a statement on the firm's policies and procedures which are designed to ensure that all firm members who are eligible for appointment as a statutory auditor continue to maintain their theoretical knowledge, professional skills and values at a sufficiently high level;
  – the firm's financial information for the financial year; this is to show, *inter alia*, the importance of audit work to the firm;
  – information about the basis for remunerating the firm's partners.

Since June 2010, in addition to publishing a transparency report, firms which audit 20 or more companies listed on the London Stock Exchange have been required to comply with the *Audit Firm Governance Code* [Audit Firm Governance Working Group (AFGWG), 2010]. This applies to eight firms which together audit 95 per cent of such companies – Baker Tilly, BDO, Deloitte, Ernst & Young, Grant Thornton, KPMG, PKF and PricewaterhouseCoopers (FRC, 2010b). Although other audit firms are not required to comply with the Code, they are encouraged to adopt it voluntarily, in whole or in part.

---

[77] The monitoring of auditors' performance is discussed in detail in Chapter 16, section 16.4.

The Code's structure is similar to that of *The UK Corporate Governance Code* (FRC, 2012a) and, as indicated in Figure 5.8, it comprises six sections which contain 20 principles and 31 provisions. The AFGWG (2010, p. 3) explains that, in developing the Code, the Working Group was particularly cognisant of three factors, namely:

1. although the corporate governance code provides a good starting point, listed companies have to address issues arising from the separation of ownership and management interests but audit firms are generally owner-managed partnerships;
2. audit firms are professional practices which have an obligation to act in a manner that properly takes the public interest into consideration. This obligation needs to be incorporated in the Code so that it is upheld by firms' management teams and governance structures;
3. audit is subject to extensive regulation that needs to be referred to within the Code – for example, auditing, quality control and ethics standards and transparency reporting disclosure requirements.

Figure 5.8: Structure of the *Audit Firm Governance Code*

Section		Principles	No. of Provisions
A Leadership	A.1	Owner accountability	4
	A.2	Management principle	1
B Values	B.1	Professionalism	2
	B.2	Governance	1
	B.3	Openness	0
C Independent non-executives	C.1	Involvement of independent directors	2
	C.2	Characteristics of independent non-executives	1
	C.3	Rights of independent non-executives	4
D Operations	D.1	Compliance	4
	D.2	Risk management	3
	D.3	People management	2
	D.4	Whistleblowing	1
E Reporting	E.1	Internal reporting	0
	E.2	Financial statements	2
	E.3	Management commentary	1
	E.4	Governance reporting	1
	E.5	Reporting quality	1
F Dialogue	F.1	Firm dialogue	1
	F.2	Shareholder dialogue	0
	F.3	Informed voting	0

Reviewing the sections of the Code, it might seem strange that, in owner-managed audit firms, independent non-executives are an important feature. In this regard, the Working Group explains:

> One of the key features of the Code, the appointment by the firms of independent non-executives, reflects the belief that regulation is not a substitute for effective governance and that good governance complements regulation in promoting audit quality. (AFGWG, 2010, p. 3)

Similar to the reporting requirements that apply to listed companies under *The UK Corporate Governance Code* (discussed in section 5.2.2 above), the *Audit Firm Governance Code* requires the audit firms to which it applies to make certain disclosures. Principle E.4 of the *Audit Firm Code* states:

> A firm should publicly report how it has applied in practice each of the principles of the Audit Firm Governance Code excluding F.2 on shareholder dialogue and F.3 on informed voting and make a statement on its compliance with the Code's provisions or give a considered explanation for any non-compliance.

From this statement it is evident that the audit firm governance disclosures are akin to those the directors of listed companies are required to provide in their corporate governance statement. Also like *The UK Corporate Governance Code*, the *Audit Firm Code* requires audit firms to make some specific disclosures. They are to provide the following information in their transparency reports:

- an explanation of how the firm's governance structures and management team operate, their duties and the types of decisions they take (prov. A.1.2);
- the names and job titles of all members of the firm's governance structures and management team, how they are elected or appointed and their terms, length of service, meeting attendance during the year and relevant biographical details (prov. A.1.3);
- the firm's criteria for assessing the impact of independent non-executives on the firm's independence as auditors, and their independence from the firm and its owners (prov. C.2.1);
- how the firm applies policies and procedures for managing potential and actual conflicts of interest (prov. D.1.3);
- a statement that the firm has reviewed the effectiveness of its internal control system together with a summary of the process adopted for the review and confirmation that necessary actions have been (or are being) taken to remedy any significant failings or weaknesses identified by the review (prov. D.2.2, first part);
- the process the firm has applied to deal with material internal control aspects of any significant problems disclosed in its financial statements or management commentary (prov. D.2.2, second part);
- the framework the firm has applied for maintaining sound internal control and risk management systems and reviewing their effectiveness (prov. D.2.3).

The reporting and governance requirements that have been imposed on some audit firms by the Transparency Regulations and Governance Code are fairly demanding and result in transparency reports (if downloaded from the web) some 35 to 40 pages in length. Given the time and effort such reports take to compile and publish, it might be thought that the firms affected would have a negative attitude towards them. However, the comments of Ernst & Young in the introduction to its 2011 *Transparency Report* are typical of those expressed by all of the transparency reporting auditors. It states:

> We welcome the opportunity to be transparent. The audits of public companies are vital to the strength and stability of the global capital markets. As such, our stakeholders have the right to feel confident that we can deliver consistent, reliable, timely and quality audits. We firmly believe that transparency makes an important positive contribution to stakeholder confidence by increasing awareness of how we do it. (Ernst & Young, 2011)

5.7 SUMMARY

In this chapter we have noted that auditors' responsibilities are derived from statute law, case law, regulations and, to a minor and decreasing extent, the profession. However, auditors' responsibilities are inextricably linked to the reporting requirements of companies. Hence, we have examined in some detail the financial and governance reporting requirements of companies in the UK and identified the companies whose financial statements are subject to audit. We observed that many of the reporting requirements of company directors are summarised in the statement of directors' responsibilities which is included in companies' annual reports.[78]

We have also examined the provisions of CA 2006 which govern the appointment, remuneration and the resignation or replacement of auditors, and those that specify auditors' statutory responsibilities. However, CA 2006 does not explain the standard of work expected of auditors; this has been left to the courts. Case law has established that auditors must exercise due skill, care and caution appropriate to the circumstances when conducting their audits; it has also clarified some of the tasks auditors are to perform in order to properly form and express an opinion on the auditee's financial statements as required by CA 2006. Nevertheless, increasingly since the late 1970s, the requirements of auditors in fulfilment of their responsibilities have been stipulated in promulgations issued at first by the profession and more recently by regulators. Today, as reflected in the statement of auditors' responsibilities included in each audit report, auditors' duties are

---

[78] As we shall see when we examine the content of auditors' reports in Chapter 14, the auditor's report is to refer to the statement of directors' responsibilities included in the company's annual report or include a statement of directors' responsibilities for the financial statements within the auditor's report.

wide-ranging. Indeed, a theme which has emerged in this chapter is that, particularly since the turn of the twenty-first century, the statutory and regulatory requirements of both companies and auditors have become progressively more extensive and exacting.

In the final section of the chapter we have considered the reporting and governance requirements of firms that audit companies listed on the London Stock Exchange. We noted that the reporting requirements of these firms are quite extensive and that the governance requirements which apply to the eight firms which audit 20 or more listed companies are similar to those that apply to their listed company clients.

In the next chapter we turn our attention to auditors' responsibility to detect and report corporate fraud and other illegal acts. As we will see, this issue has long been very controversial and, over the years, has witnessed quite remarkable changes.

SELF-REVIEW QUESTIONS

5.1   State the institutions which define the responsibilities of auditors and the particular part played by each.

5.2   List the financial and governance reports the directors of a listed company are required to include in their company's annual report.

5.3   Explain the responsibilities of a company's:
  (i)   directors, and
  (ii) auditor,
with respect to the company's financial statements.

5.4   State the criteria to be met by:
  (i)   an individual, and
  (ii) a firm,
in order to be appointed as the auditor of a company.

5.5   List those parties who may:
  (i)   appoint the auditor,
  (ii) remove the auditor from office,
and the circumstances in which these parties can exercise their rights.

5.6   Explain the legal relationship between the auditor and (i) the client company and (ii) its shareholders.

5.7   State the fundamental standard of work required of auditors in the per-
       formance of their duties as laid down in case law [in particular, in the
       Kingston Cotton Mill case (1896)].

5.8   Explain briefly:
       (i) the purpose of Auditing Standards and the benefits they
           provide for (a) auditors, (b) financial statement users and (c) the
           auditing profession;
       (ii) how Auditing Standards differ from Practice Notes and
            Bulletins.

5.9   Explain briefly the responsibilities of auditors in respect of the following
       governance reports of companies:
       (a) the strategic and directors' reports,
       (b) the going concern statement,
       (c) the corporate governance statement, and
       (d) the directors' remuneration report.

5.10   (a) Briefly explain what is meant by:
           (i) a Transparency Report
           (ii) the Audit Firm Governance Code.
       (b) Identify which audit firms must:
           (i) publish a Transparency Report;
           (ii) comply with the Audit Firm Governance Code.

REFERENCES

Accounting Standards Board (ASB). (2008). *Financial Reporting Standard for Smaller
    Entities*. London: Financial Reporting Council.

Audit Firm Governance Working Group (AFGWG). (2010). *The Audit Firm Govern-
    ance Code: A project for the Financial Reporting Council*. London: Institute of Char-
    tered Accountants in England and Wales.

Auditing Practices Board (APB). (2006). *The Combined Code on Corporate Govern-
    ance: Requirements of Auditors under the Listing Rules of the Financial Services
    Authority and the Irish Stock Exchange*, Bulletin 2006/5. London: Financial Report-
    ing Council.

Auditing Practices Board (APB). (2009). *Developments in Corporate Governance
    Affecting the Responsibilities of Auditors of UK Companies*. Bulletin 2009/4. London:
    Financial Reporting Council.

Auditing Practices Board (APB). (2012). *Standards and Guidance 2012: Glossary of
    Terms*. London: Financial Reporting Council.

Committee on the Financial Aspects of Corporate Governance. (1992). *Report of the Committee on the Financial Aspects of Corporate Governance* (Cadbury Committee). London: Gee.

Committee on Corporate Governance. (1998a). *Final Report of the Committee on Corporate Governance* (Hampel Committee). London: London Stock Exchange Ltd.

Committee on Corporate Governance. (1998b). *The Combined Code*. London: London Stock Exchange Ltd.

Ernst & Young. (2011). *Ernst & Young LLP Transparency Report 2011*, www.ey.com/Publication/vwLUAssets/Global_Transparency_Report_2011/$FILE/Global-Transparency-report-2011.pdf, accessed 11 May 2013.

European Union (EU). (2002) Regulation (EC) No. 1606/2002 *on the application of international accounting standards* (IAS Regulation). Brussels: European Parliament and Council.

European Union (EU). (2006a). *Directive 2006/43/EC of the European Parliament and of the Council on Statutory Audits of Annual Accounts and Consolidated Accounts (Statutory Audit Directive)*. Brussels: European Parliament and Council.

European Union (EU). (2006b). *Directive 2006/46/EC of the European Parliament and of the Council Amending Council Directives 78/660/EEC on the Annual Accounts of Certain Types of Companies, 83/349/EEC on Consolidated Accounts, 86/635/EEC on the Annual Accounts and Consolidated Accounts of Banks and other Financial Institutions and 91/674/EEC on the Annual Accounts and Consolidated Accounts of Insurance Companies (Disclosure and Transparency Directive)*. Brussels: European Parliament and Council.

Financial Reporting Council (FRC). (2003; 2006, 2008a). *The Combined Code on Corporate Governance*. London: FRC.

Financial Reporting Council (FRC). (2008b). *Relevance of 'True and Fair' Concept Confirmed*. London: FRC.

Financial Reporting Council (FRC). (2008c). *The Audit Quality Framework*. London: FRC.

Financial Reporting Council (FRC). (2009). *Going Concern and Liquidity Risk*. London: FRC.

Financial Reporting Council (FRC). (2010a). *The UK Corporate Governance Code*. London: FRC.

Financial Reporting Council (FRC). (2010b). Press Release: *Audit Firm Governance Code*, www.frc.org.uk/about/auditfirm.cfm, accessed 1 July 2010.

Financial Reporting Council (FRC). (2011). *True and Fair*. London: FRC.

Financial Reporting Council (FRC). (2012a). *The UK Corporate Governance Code*. London: FRC.

Financial Reporting Council (FRC). (2012b). *About the FRC*, www.frc.org.uk/About-the-FRC, accessed 11 February 2012.

Financial Reporting Council (FRC). (2012c). *FRC Structure*, ww.frc.org.uk/About-the-FRC/FRC-structure.aspx, accessed 16 August 2012.

Financial Reporting Council (FRC). (2012d). *Audit Inspection Unit*, www.frc.org .uk/About-the-FRC/FRC-structure/Former-FRC-structure, accessed 16 August 2012.

Financial Reporting Council (FRC). (2012e). *Audit and Assurance Council Terms of Reference*, www.frc.org.uk/About-the-FRC/FRC-structure/Audit-and-Assurance, accessed 16 August 2012.

Financial Reporting Council (FRC). (2012f). Financial Reporting Standard (FRS) 101: *Reduced Disclosure Framework*. London: FRC.

Financial Reporting Council (FRC). (2013a). *Current SRBs and RQBs*, www.frc.org/ our-work/Conduct/Professional-oversight, accessed 13 January 2013.

Financial Reporting Council (FRC). (2013b). *Scope and Authority of FRC Audit and Assurance Pronouncements*. London: FRC.

Financial Reporting Council (FRC). (2013c). Financial Reporting Standard (FRS) 102: *The Financial Reporting Standard Applicable in the UK and Republic of Ireland*. London: FRC.

Financial Reporting Council (FRC). (2013d) International Standard on Auditing (ISA) (UK and Ireland) 700: *The Independent Auditor's Report on Financial Statements*. London: FRC.

Financial Services Authority (2012). *Listing Regime*, www.fsa.gov.uk/Pages/Doing/ UKLA/Regime/Index.shtml, accessed 11 February 2012.

Higgs, D. (2003). *Review of the Role and Effectiveness of Non-Executive Directors*. London: Department of Trade and Industry.

House of Lords. (2011, March). House of Lords Select Committee on Economic Affairs 2nd Report of Session 2010–2011, *Auditors: Market Concentration and Their Role, Volume 1: Report*. London: The Stationery Office Limited.

International Accounting Standards Board (IASB). (2007). International Accounting Standard (IAS) 1: *Presentation of Financial Statements*. London: IASB.

International Accounting Standards Board (IASB). (2010). *Conceptual Framework for Financial Reporting*. London: IASB.

International Auditing and Assurance Standards Board (IAASB). (2009). International Standard on Auditing (ISA): 720: *The Auditor's Responsibilities in Relation to Other Information in Documents containing Audited Financial Statements*. New York: IFAC

International Federation of Accountants (IFAC). (2010). *Handbook of International Quality Control, Auditing, Review, Other Assurance and Related Services Pronouncements 2010 Edition*. New York: IFAC.

International Federation of Accountants (IFAC). (2012a). *IFAC: Membership*, www .ifac.org/about-ifac/membership, accessed 16 February 2012.

International Federation of Accountants (IFAC). (2012b). *About IAASB*, www.ifac.org/ auditing-assurance, accessed 16 February 2012.

Kenley, W.J. (1971). Legal decisions affecting auditors. *Australian Accountant, 41*(4), 153–161.

Professional Oversight Board (POB). (2008). *The Statutory Auditors (Transparency) Instrument 2008*. London: Financial Reporting Council.

Smith, Sir R. (2003). *Audit Committees: Combined Code Guidance.* A report and proposed guidance by an FRC-appointed group chaired by Sir Robert Smith. London: Financial Reporting Council.

Statutory Instrument (SI). (2008a). No. 410: *Large and Medium-sized Companies and Groups (Accounts and Reports) Regulations 2008*. London: The Stationery Office Limited.

Statutory Instrument (SI). (2008b). No. 409: *Small Companies and Groups (Accounts and Reports) Regulations 2008*. London: The Stationery Office Limited.

Statutory Instrument (SI). (2011). No. 2198: *The Companies (Disclosure of Auditor Remuneration and Liability Limitation Agreements) Regulations 2011*. London: The Stationery Office Limited.

Statutory Instrument (SI). (2013). No. 1970: *The Companies Act 2006 (Strategic Report and Directors' Report) Regulations 2013*. London: The Stationery Office Limited.

Study Group on Directors' Remuneration. (1995). *Report of the Study Group on Directors' Remuneration* (Greenbury Committee). London: Gee.

ADDITIONAL READING

Morrison, M.A. (2004). Rush to judgment: The lynching of Arthur Andersen & Co. *Critical Perspectives on Accounting, 15*(3), 335–375.

Willekens, M., & Simunic, D.A. (2007). Precision in auditing standards: Effects on auditor and director liability and the supply and demand for audit services. *Accounting and Business Research, 37*(3), 217–232.

6 Auditors' Duties with Respect to Fraud and Non-compliance with Laws and Regulations

LEARNING OBJECTIVES

After studying the material in this chapter you should be able to:
- explain the meaning of 'fraud' and 'non-compliance with laws and regulations' in the context of an external financial statement audit;
- discuss changes in auditors' responsibility for detecting and reporting fraud acknowledged by the auditing profession between 1844 and the present;
- explain the components of 'the fraud triangle';
- outline the procedures auditors are required to perform to detect material misstatements in the financial statements due to (i) fraud and (ii) non-compliance with laws and regulations;
- describe auditors' responsibility to report discovered or suspected instances of fraud or non-compliance with laws or regulations encountered during an audit;
- discuss auditors' duty of confidentiality to their clients.

6.1 INTRODUCTION

In Chapter 5 we discuss the legal, regulatory and professional framework within which auditors' responsibilities are defined. In this chapter we explore the thorny issue of auditors' responsibility to detect and report corporate fraud – an issue which, as we shall see, has been hotly debated for many years both inside and outside of the auditing profession. We explain how – and why – the level of responsibility acknowledged by the auditing profession in this regard has changed so markedly over the period since compulsory audits were first introduced in 1844 to the present day. We also examine the current requirements relating to auditors' responsibility to detect and report corporate fraud.

We then turn our attention to a closely related issue – that of auditors' responsibility to detect and report auditees' non-compliance with laws and regulations. This matter has not had as high a profile as auditors' responsibilities in respect of fraud, nor has it been as controversial. However, misstated financial statements resulting from non-compliance with applicable laws and regulations can have an effect as equally devastating as that resulting from fraud – on the auditee and on those who invest in, are employed by, supply to, or buy from, the entity. Some laws and regulations (including accounting standards) directly affect the amounts and other disclosures made in companies' financial statements and/or the form and content of information provided elsewhere in their annual reports. Others relate more generally to companies' operations – for example, to being properly registered or holding a licence required to trade in a particular industry, or to complying with health and safety, equal opportunity and environmental regulations. Although these laws and regulations may seem far removed from the financial statements, non-compliance with any law or regulation that applies to an entity can result in financial consequences, such as fines or litigation, which are likely to impact on amounts and/or other disclosures in the entity's financial statements and, in some cases, may lead to its demise. Thus, while management[1] is responsible for ensuring that appropriate steps are taken within the entity to prevent and detect fraud and instances of non-compliance with other applicable laws and regulations, in order to express an opinion on, *inter alia*, the truth and fairness of the financial statements auditors need to ascertain whether or not the financial statements are materially misstated as a result of fraud or non-compliance with other relevant laws and regulations.

When discussing auditors' responsibility to report fraud and non-compliance with other laws and regulations detected during the audit, we observe that, in some circumstances, this includes a responsibility to report the matter in question to parties external to the entity. This involves overriding auditors' duty of confidentiality to their clients. In the final section of this chapter we discuss auditors' duty of confidentiality to their clients and the circumstances in which it may (or should) be overridden.

It should be noted that, unlike many of auditors' responsibilities which we examine in subsequent chapters of this book, their responsibility to detect fraud and non-compliance with laws and regulations is not associated with any particular part of the audit process; it extends to every aspect of the audit. Auditors must be constantly alert, throughout an audit, to the possibility that fraud or non-compliance with other laws and regulations may have caused the financial statements to be materially misstated.

6.2 DEFINITION OF FRAUD

Before considering auditors' responsibilities to detect and report fraud, we need to establish what the term 'fraud' means in the context of a financial

---

[1] Readers are reminded that in the Preface to this book we note the term 'management' is defined to mean a company's executive directors, non-executive directors and non-director executives (that is, all executives and directors).

statement audit. International Standard on Auditing (ISA) 240: *The Auditor's Responsibilities Relating to Fraud in an Audit of Financial Statements* [International Auditing and Assurance Standards Board (IAASB), 2009a] defines fraud as:

> An intentional act by one or more individuals among management, those charged with governance [i.e. the directors], employees, or third parties, involving the use of deception to obtain an unjust or illegal advantage. (para 11)

The Standard also explains:

> . . . the auditor is concerned with fraud that causes a material misstatement in the financial statements. Two types of intentional misstatements are relevant to the auditor – misstatements resulting from fraudulent financial reporting and misstatements resulting from misappropriation of assets. (para 3)

Let us examine these two types of fraud more closely:

(i) *Fraudulent financial reporting*: The International Federation of Accountants' (IFAC's) *Glossary of Terms* (2009) explains that this type of fraud: "[i]nvolves intentional misstatements, including omissions of amounts or disclosures in financial statements, to deceive financial statement users". Thus, it is intended to result in financial statements which give a misleading impression of the entity's financial affairs. It is almost always perpetrated by management but, rather than being committed for direct personal financial gain, it is usually motivated by what the individual concerned considers to be in his or her own best interests in terms of reporting the company's financial position or (more commonly) its performance in a particularly favourable (or, in some cases, unfavourable) light. Management may, for instance, feel pressured to report earnings (or net profit after tax) in line with the financial market's expectations when the 'actual' earnings figure is significantly below those expectations. This may occur, for example, when the company has announced a rather optimistic earnings forecast. It may also arise if the company plans to raise new equity or debt finance during the next financial year and the 'actual' earnings figure is unlikely to encourage further outside investment in the company.[2]

(ii) *Misappropriation of corporate assets*: According to IFAC (2009), this type of fraud:

> [i]nvolves the theft of an entity's assets and is often perpetrated by employees in relatively small and immaterial amounts. However, it can also involve management who are usually more capable of disguising or concealing misappropriations in ways that are difficult to detect.

---

[2] As explained in section 6.5, fraudulent financial reporting often develops from aggressive earnings management.

Misappropriation of assets includes such things as stealing physical assets or intellectual property (for example, items of inventory, computer hardware or software, and technological or customer data), stealing cash (through, for example, payments to fictitious employees or suppliers, and kickbacks paid by suppliers in return for inflating prices) and using entity assets for personal use (for example, using entity assets as security for a personal loan). Unlike fraudulent financial reporting, theft of a company's assets is usually undertaken for personal gain.

6.3 DEVELOPMENT OF AUDITORS' RESPONSIBILITY TO DETECT AND REPORT FRAUD[3]

6.3.1 An evolving, controversial and concerning issue

The stance of the auditing profession in relation to auditors' responsibility to detect fraud has changed markedly over the years. As noted in Chapter 2, from the time compulsory audits were first introduced in the United Kingdom (UK) in 1844 until about the 1920s, the prevention and detection of fraud and error were regarded as primary audit objectives. Nevertheless, as we also noted in Chapter 2, it was decided in the *Kingston Cotton Mill* case (1896) that auditors are not required to ferret out every fraud (auditors are "watchdogs not bloodhounds") but they are expected to exercise reasonable skill, care and caution appropriate to the particular circumstances. Further, if anything comes to their attention which arouses their suspicion, they are expected to "probe the matter to the bottom" and to report it promptly to the appropriate level of management.

Between the 1920s and 1960s, the importance of fraud detection as an audit objective was steadily eroded. During this period companies grew in size and complexity and the volume of their transactions increased very significantly. As a consequence, company managements established accounting systems, which incorporated internal controls, to capture and process accounting data. The internal controls were designed to prevent or detect both error and fraud and, thus, to protect the integrity of the accounting information. Further, with the growth in the volume of company transactions, it became impractical, within the limits of reasonable time and cost constraints, for auditors to check every entry in auditees' accounting records. Auditing procedures changed accordingly – from meticulous checking of every transaction to techniques based on testing samples of transactions combined with an evaluation of the

---

[3] A more comprehensive account of the development of auditors' responsibility to detect and report corporate fraud is provided in Porter (1997).

effectiveness of the accounting system's internal controls (see Chapter 2, section 2.5.2).

Given these developments, the auditing profession argued that management is responsible for preventing and detecting fraud, and that these are best achieved through the maintenance of an effective system of internal control. It also argued that auditing procedures are not designed, and cannot be relied upon, to detect fraud. The general attitude of the profession from the 1940s to 1960s is reflected in the American Institute of Certified Public Accountants' (AICPA) *Codification of Statements on Auditing Procedure*, published in 1951. It states:

> The ordinary examination incident to the issuance of an opinion respecting financial statements is not designed and cannot be relied upon to disclose defalcations and other similar irregularities, although their discovery frequently results. In a well-organized concern reliance for the detection of such irregularities is placed principally upon the maintenance of an adequate system of accounting records with appropriate internal control. If an auditor were to discover defalcations and similar irregularities he would have to extend his work to a point where its cost would be prohibitive. (AICPA, 1951, paras 12, 13)

Nevertheless, by the 1960s, the profession's position on detecting fraud was subject to criticism from both inside and outside the profession. Additionally, by 1970, the judiciary (i.e., the courts and judges) also seemed to be adopting a stance contrary to that reflected in the AICPA's statement (cited above). As we observe in Chapter 5 (section 5.5.3), in his long judgment on the *Pacific Acceptance* case (1970), Moffitt J noted that the duty to audit includes a duty to pay due regard to the possibility that fraud may have occurred, and the audit plan and audit tests should be structured so that the auditor has a reasonable expectation of detecting material fraud if it exists.

Notwithstanding widespread criticism and comments of judges like Moffitt J, the auditing profession continued to deny a responsibility to detect fraud. However, as the size and incidence of corporate fraud continued to grow, so dissatisfaction with the profession's stance increased. This is evident, for example, from the report of the Commission on Auditors' Responsibilities (CAR, 1978: the Cohen Commission) which noted:

> Court decisions, criticism by the financial press, actions by regulatory bodies, and surveys of users indicate dissatisfaction with the responsibility for fraud detection acknowledged by auditors. Opinion surveys . . . indicate that concerned segments of the public expect independent auditors to assume greater responsibility in this area. Significant percentages of those who use and rely on the auditor's work rank the detection of fraud among the most important objectives of an audit. (p. 31)

The level of discontent with auditors' denial of responsibility for detecting fraud in the 1970s and 1980s is also evident from the following illustrations:

- Woolf (1978) drew attention to the pertinent question raised by the investment analyst whose solo efforts were responsible for exposing the notorious *Equity Funding* fraud in the United States of America (USA) in the early 1970s:

  > If routine auditing procedures cannot detect 64,000 phony insurance policies [two-thirds of the total number], $25 million in counterfeit bonds, and $100 million in missing assets, what is the purpose of audits? (Woolf, 1978, p. 62)

- In similar vein, Carty (1985), a member of the UK's Auditing Practices Committee (predecessor of the Auditing Practices Board), observed:

  > [T]he public do not readily accept the limitations on the scope of an audit that the auditors inevitably build into their approach. Whenever there is a revelation in the press of a fraud, there is public outcry and the usual question, 'Why didn't the auditors pick this up years ago?' (Carty, 1985, p. 30)

In the UK, as in most other parts of the world, corporate fraud continues to be an increasingly worrying issue. KPMG's annual surveys of fraud cases involving £100,000 or more that reached the UK courts (i.e., serious fraud cases) found that between 1987 and 2000 there were 855 such cases, totalling £4,177 million in value (KPMG, 2006; Yirrell, 2007); between 2000 and 2009, there were 1,750 cases involving a total of £7 billion (Sims, 2010). Since 2009, the situation has continued to worsen. According to Patel (2011): "The volume of fraud cases snowballed in 2010, with 314 incidents reported (total value £1,374 bn), the highest value ever recorded in the 23-year history of KPMG's fraud [surveys]". However, this was dwarfed by the serious fraud cases reaching the UK courts in 2011. In that year, the number of cases fell to 251 but their value rose to £3,548 billion (KPMG, 2012). Notwithstanding the staggering value of these frauds, even more startling is the high proportion of frauds committed by management. In 2007, KPMG found that 34 of the serious fraud cases (totalling £129 million in value) involved companies' own managers (KPMG, 2008); in 2010, KPMG found 61 such cases, involving a total of £419 million. In 2011, the number of management fraud cases dropped to 57 but their value soared to £729 million (Patel, 2011). Although the proportion of management fraud appears to be lower in the UK than in the USA (see Turner's comments below), it accounts for more than 20 per cent of all of the serious fraud cases heard in the UK courts. This is particularly worrying, given auditors' reliance on management's responses to enquiries in relation to many aspects of the audit.

6.3.2 Increased responsibility for auditors to detect and report corporate fraud

From the early 1980s, auditors came under mounting pressure from politicians, the media and influential commentators to play a more active role in combating corporate fraud. In the mid-1980s, for example, faced by the rising wave of corporate fraud in the UK, Fletcher and Howard, successive Ministers of Corporate and Consumer Affairs, made it clear that they viewed auditors as being in the front line of the public's defences in the fight against fraud, and they called upon auditors to extend their duties in this regard. Their stance was supported by fraud investigators who stated that they considered it both practical and desirable, within the limits of cost and auditing procedures, for auditors to accept a general responsibility to detect fraud (Smith, 1985, p. 10).

Similar opinions were expressed in the USA by senior staff of the Securities and Exchange Commission (SEC). For example, Walker (1999a), former Director of the SEC's Division of Enforcement, stated:

> The Commission looks to auditors to combat fraud. . . . The Commission, with its small staff and limited resources . . . necessarily must rely heavily on the accounting profession to perform its tasks diligently and responsibly. In short, auditors are the first line of defense. (p. 2)

He also noted (1999b):

> [There] are indicators that financial fraud is still occurring at too great a pace. . . . National Economic Research Associates (NERA) issued a report on recent trends in securities litigation. NERA found that a whopping 55 percent of all securities claims actions in the first half of 1999 were based on claims of fraudulent accounting. (p. 2)

Although he did not say so directly, Walker implied that the instances of fraudulent financial reporting should have been detected by the relevant company's auditors.

Turner (1999), former Chief Accountant of the SEC, was more direct in his criticism of auditors for failing to detect fraud – in particular, fraudulent financial reporting:

> You only have to look as far as the March 1999 report sponsored by the Committee of Sponsoring Organizations of the Treadway Committee (COSO) on fraudulent financial reporting to understand the problems with today's audits. One startling fact in that report, which summarizes fraud cases from 1987-1998, is that over 80% of the fraud cases involved the highest levels of management . . . the very group responsible for ensuring the adequacy of the control environment. The irony of today's audit processes is that significant audit assurance is derived from internal controls; however, the very group . . . charged with ensuring the effectiveness of internal controls is responsible for committing fraud. (p. 4)

In Turner's (2000) view, auditors should be required to perform additional forensic-type procedures during their audits, specifically designed to detect fraudulent activities by management.

Since the 1980s, in response to the criticism levelled against it, the auditing profession (led principally by the AICPA) has progressively acknowledged greater responsibility for detecting fraud. In 1988, the AICPA issued Statement on Auditing Standards (SAS) no. 53, *The Auditor's Responsibility to Detect and*

Report Errors and Irregularities (AICPA, 1988). This adopted a new positive approach towards defining auditors' responsibility to detect fraud. In place of the former defensive tone and insistence that audits cannot be relied on to disclose irregularities, SAS no. 53 stated:

> Because of the characteristics of irregularities, particularly those involving forgery and collusion, a properly designed and executed audit may not detect a material irregularity. [However], the auditor should exercise (a) due care in planning, performing and evaluating the results of audit procedures, and (b) the proper degree of professional skepticism to achieve reasonable assurance that material errors or irregularities will be detected. (paras 7, 8)

Auditors' role in detecting fraud was strengthened in SAS no. 82: *Consideration of Fraud in a Financial Statement Audit* (AICPA, 1997). Unlike its predecessor (SAS no. 53), which embraced both errors and irregularities (i.e., fraud), SAS no. 82 dealt only with fraud in financial statement audits. Further, SAS no. 82 (unlike SAS no. 53) went beyond requiring auditors to plan and perform their audits to obtain reasonable assurance that material fraud (or errors) will be detected, to requiring them to actively consider the likelihood of fraud occurring. The Standard required auditors to assess, specifically, the risk of material misstatement in the financial statements resulting from fraud and to consider that assessment when planning and performing the audit. In making their assessment, auditors were required:

(i) to consider whether risk factors that might indicate the existence of fraud are present, and

(ii) to make enquiries of management to obtain management's understanding and assessment of the likelihood of fraud occurring within the entity.

To assist auditors in their fraud risk assessment, SAS no. 82 provided an extensive list of fraud risk factors[4] they should consider. SAS no. 82 also explicitly required auditors to respond appropriately to the risk factors they identified, and to document:

(i) the performance of their fraud risk assessment,

(ii) the specific risk factors they identified,

(iii) their response to those factors.

At the conclusion of their audits, auditors were required to re-assess, in the light of all the evidence gathered during the audit, the risk of material misstatement in the financial statements due to fraud.

In 2002, SAS no. 82 was superseded by SAS no. 99: *Consideration of Fraud in a Financial Statement Audit* (AICPA, 2002). Although it has the same name as its predecessor, the new Standard represents a major shift in the level of

---

[4] Fraud risk factors are "events or conditions that indicate an incentive or pressure to commit fraud or provide an opportunity to commit fraud" (ISA 240; IAASB, 2009a, para 11).

responsibility acknowledged by the auditing profession to detect fraud. As Ramos (2003) explains:

> [SAS no. 99 requires auditors to] enter a much expanded arena of procedures to detect fraud. . . . [They] will gather and consider much more information to assess fraud risks than . . . in the past. . . . It has the potential to be a watershed for how auditors think about and perform an audit. (pp. 1, 10)

The key elements of SAS no. 99 include:
- an emphasis on the importance of auditors exercising professional scepticism;
- the introduction of a requirement for audit team members to discuss how and where the financial statements might be susceptible to material misstatement as a result of fraud;
- an extension of auditors' responsibilities in respect of:
    (a) gathering information needed to identify risks of material misstatement due to fraud,
    (b) identifying risks (from the information gathered) that may result in material misstatement due to fraud,
    (c) assessing the identified risks, after taking into account an evaluation of the client's systems and controls that address the identified risks, and
    (d) responding to the results of their fraud risk assessment;
- highlighting the need for auditors' assessment of the risk of material misstatement due to fraud to be ongoing throughout the audit;
- specifying the requirements relating to auditors' documentation of their consideration of the risk of fraud and response thereto;
- providing guidance on auditors' communication of detected or suspected fraud to the company's management, audit committee and others.

In the international arena, ISA 240: *Fraud and Error* [International Auditing Practices Committee (IAPC), 2001][5] closely resembled the AICPA's SAS no. 82 (AICPA, 1997). The major point of difference was that ISA 240 covered both fraud and error in financial statement audits rather than being confined to auditors' responsibilities with respect to fraud. Similarly, ISA 240: *The Auditor's Responsibilities Relating to Fraud in an Audit of Financial Statements* (IAASB, 2009a), which was first published in 2006, resembles SAS no. 99 (AICPA, 2002). We will discuss the requirements of ISA 240 (IAASB, 2009a) after considering the developments in auditors' responsibility to detect and report fraud in the UK prior to the UK's adoption of ISAs in 2004.

---

[5] Until 2002, the IAPC (a committee of IFAC) was responsible for developing International Standards on Auditing. In April 2002, the IAPC was replaced by the International Auditing and Assurance Standards Boards (IAASB). (For further details see Chapter 5, footnote 65.)

In the UK, SAS 110: *Fraud and Error*, which was published by the Auditing Practices Board (APB) in 1995 (APB, 1995a), required auditors to "plan, perform and evaluate their audit work in order to have a reasonable expectation of detecting material misstatements arising from error and fraud" (para 18). Thus, like the AICPA's SAS no. 53 (AICPA, 1988), its requirements were relatively inexplicit and undemanding. However, in respect of reporting fraud discovered during an audit, SAS 110 went beyond the requirements of both SAS no. 82 (AICPA, 1997) and ISA 240 (IAPC, 2001), which were published subsequently. SAS 110 (APB, 1995a) required auditors in the UK:

- if they suspected or discovered fraud, to communicate their findings as soon as practicable to the appropriate level of management, the board of directors or the audit committee. Even if the potential effect of a fraud or suspected fraud was immaterial to the financial statements, the auditor should still report it to the appropriate level of management (para 41);
- to qualify the audit report if they formed the opinion that, as a result of fraud, the financial statements did not give a true and fair view.[6] Similarly, they were required to qualify the audit report if they disagreed with the accounting treatment, or with the extent of disclosure, of the fraud or its consequences (para 45).

Thus far, the reporting requirements of SAS 110 resemble those of SAS no. 82 (AICPA, 1997) and ISA 240 (IAPC, 2001). However, SAS 110 (APB, 1995a) went further: it recognised that there might be circumstances in which auditors should report suspected or actual instances of fraud to an appropriate external authority. More specifically, it required auditors who encountered a suspected or actual fraud during an audit to consider whether the matter ought to be reported "to a proper authority in the public interest" (para 50). In normal circumstances, the auditor's duty of confidentiality to the client[7] is paramount and SAS 110 acknowledged this by noting: "confidentiality is an implied term of the auditor's contract". Nevertheless, it went on to state: "In certain exceptional circumstances auditors are not bound by their duty of confidentiality and have the right or duty to report matters to a proper authority in the public interest" (para 53). More specifically:

> When a suspected or actual instance of fraud casts doubt on the integrity of the directors, auditors should make a report direct to a proper authority in the public interest without delay and without informing the directors in advance. (para 52)

SAS 110 explained that, providing auditors report a suspected or actual fraud encountered during an audit to a proper authority in the public interest, and

---

[6] Different types of audit report are discussed in Chapter 14, section 14.4.

[7] We discuss auditors' duty of confidentiality to their clients in section 6.7.

the disclosure is not motivated by malice, they are protected from the risk of liability for breach of their duty of confidentiality or defamation (para 55).

When deciding whether disclosure of a suspected or actual fraud to a proper authority in the public interest is justified, the auditor was required to consider factors such as:
- the extent to which the fraud is likely to affect members of the public;
- whether the directors are taking corrective action or are likely to do so;
- the extent to which non-disclosure of the fraud is likely to enable it to recur with impunity;
- the gravity of the matter;
- the weight of evidence and degree of suspicion that fraud has occurred (SAS 110, para 56).

Acceptance of a duty to report to a proper authority when it is in the public interest to do so represents a significant extension to the responsibility to report fraud previously acknowledged by auditors. Prior to issuance of SAS 110, auditing standards in the UK interpreted public interest reporting as a right rather than a duty, and the reporting of fraud to anyone outside the entity was generally considered by auditors as likely to be perceived as a breach of their duty of confidentiality.

After publication of SAS 110, the issue of auditors' responsibility for detecting and reporting fraud remained high on the APB's list of priorities. In 1998 it published a Consultation Paper: *Fraud and Audit: Choices for Society* (APB, 1998), in which it reported that research it had undertaken had shown that:
- most material frauds involve management;
- more than half of frauds involve misstated financial reporting (i.e., fraudulent financial reporting) but do not involve diversion of funds from the company (i.e., theft of company assets);
- management fraud is unlikely to be detected in a financial statement audit.

These findings support those reported by Turner in the USA, and by Patel and KPMG in the UK, noted earlier.

The APB also reported that "a review of the effectiveness of new Auditing Standards on fraud [that is, SAS 110] indicates that auditors have increased the emphasis they place on fraud in the course of their work" (APB, 1998, p. 5). However, it further noted that, despite the steps taken by both the APB and audit firms to improve performance in this regard, there was a continuing gap between society's expectations of auditors and auditors' performance. It reported that although society expects auditors to find fraud, "particularly when a fraud involves factors that threaten the entity's ability to continue in

business . . . , auditors cannot ensure that they will discover management fraud" (p. 15). It cited factors that hamper auditors in detecting fraud. These include:
- the nature of evidence available to auditors[8] which results in them rarely having sufficient evidence to resolve suspicions that fraud may have occurred;
- the ability of directors and senior managers to override internal controls;
- the focus of external financial statements – and the audit thereof – on the provision of a 'true and fair view' rather than on the incidence of fraud. Company law does not require directors or auditors to report on fraud discovered within an auditee;
- the ability of auditees to impose time constraints, by specifying the date when the audited financial statements are due to be published, to discourage auditors from seeking evidence to resolve suspicions of fraud.

Notwithstanding these and other difficulties, the APB (1998) suggested ways in which auditors' performance in detecting fraud might be better aligned with society's expectations. More specifically it suggested:
(i)   Auditing Standards might be changed, for example:
- to increase the emphasis placed on professional scepticism, and
- to introduce more specific requirements for particular types of evidence to be gathered or procedures to be performed;
(ii) the auditor's role in detecting fraud within an entity might be extended by, for example:
- requiring auditors to report to boards of directors and audit committees on the adequacy of controls within the entity to prevent and detect fraud;
- encouraging the use of forensic fraud reviews based on an assessment of the risk of fraud that are inherent in an auditee;
- considering whether it would be beneficial to extend auditors' responsibility to report fraud – including suspected fraud. In this regard the APB explains:

> Auditors of regulated entities are normally required to report frauds. Current Auditing Standards require auditors of other entities who suspect fraud to report to an appropriate authority if they consider it necessary in the public interest. There may be benefit in reviewing these arrangements to determine whether auditors should report suspicions in a wider range of circumstances . . . (APB, 1998, p. 27)

---

[8] The concept of audit evidence is discussed in Chapter 3, section 3.4.1 and further explained in Chapter 7, section 7.4.

6.4 AUDITORS' CURRENT RESPONSIBILITIES TO DETECT AND REPORT FRAUD

6.4.1 Detecting and reporting fraud

It is interesting to observe that many of the APB's suggestions have been incorporated in ISA 240: *The Auditor's Responsibilities Relating to Fraud in an Audit of Financial Statements* (IAASB, 2009a). As noted earlier, this Standard closely resembles SAS no. 99 (AICPA, 2002) and, like SAS no. 99, its key elements include:

(i)   noting the limitation of audits as a means of detecting fraud;

(ii)   identifying the conditions conducive to fraud;

(iii)   emphasising the importance of professional scepticism;

(iv)   requiring a discussion of audit engagement team members about the susceptibility of the financial statements to material misstatement due to fraud;

(v)   specifying the requirements of auditors in respect of identifying, assessing and responding to the risk of material misstatement due to fraud;

(vi)   detailing auditors' responsibilities to communicate detected or suspected fraud to management, the board of directors (or audit committee) and regulatory authorities;

(vii)   detailing the documentation required of matters relating to the detection and reporting of fraud.

We discuss each of these elements below.[9]

(i) Limitation of audits to detect fraud

Like previous auditing standards, ISA 240 states that primary responsibility for the prevention and detection of fraud rests with management. It notes that, although an auditor is responsible for obtaining reasonable assurance that the audited financial statements are free from material misstatement, whether caused by fraud or error, because of the inherent limitations of an audit [such as those identified by APB (1998) noted earlier], there is an unavoidable risk that some material misstatements may not be detected even though the audit is properly planned and performed in accordance with ISAs. The Standard also explains:

> The risk of not detecting a material misstatement resulting from fraud is higher than the risk of not detecting one resulting from error. This is because fraud may involve sophisticated and carefully organized schemes designed to conceal it, such as forgery, deliberate failure to record transactions, or intentional misrepresentations being made to the auditor. . . . Collusion may cause the auditor to believe that audit evidence is persuasive when it is, in fact, false. The auditor's

---

[9] Unless indicated otherwise, all references to ISA 240 in this section refer to ISA 240 (IAASB, 2009a).

ability to detect fraud depends on factors such as the skillfulness of the perpetrator, the frequency and extent of manipulation, the degree of collusion
involved, the relative size of individual amounts manipulated, and the seniority
of those individuals involved. . . . [T]he risk of the auditor not detecting a material misstatement resulting from management fraud is greater than for employee
fraud, because management is frequently in a position to directly or indirectly
manipulate accounting records, present fraudulent financial information or override control procedures designed to prevent similar frauds by other employees.
(paras 6, 7)

Having cautioned that a properly planned and conducted audit may not detect
material misstatement due to fraud, ISA 240 provides some exacting requirements for auditors which are designed to ensure that, if a significant fraud has
been committed within the auditee, unless it has been cleverly concealed, there
is a reasonable likelihood that the auditor will detect it.

(ii)   Conditions conducive to fraud

ISA 240 identifies three conditions which are conducive to fraud, namely:
incentive or pressure, opportunity, and rationalisation or attitude. These three
conditions, which are frequently referred to as 'the fraud triangle', are explained
as follows:

- Incentive or pressure to commit fraudulent financial reporting may exist
  when management is under pressure, from sources outside or inside the
  entity, to achieve an expected (and perhaps unrealistic) earnings target or
  financial outcome. . . . Similarly, individuals may have an incentive to misap-
  propriate assets, for example, because the individuals are living beyond their
  means.
- A perceived opportunity to commit fraud may exist when an individual
  believes internal control can be overridden, for example, because the individual is in a position of trust or has knowledge of specific deficiencies in
  internal control.
- Individuals may be able to rationalize committing a fraudulent act. Some
  individuals possess an attitude, character or set of ethical values that allow
  them knowingly and intentionally to commit a dishonest act. However, even
  otherwise honest individuals can commit fraud in an environment that
  imposes sufficient pressure on them. (ISA 240, para A1)

(iii)   Importance of professional scepticism [10]

A key theme permeating ISA 240 is the importance of auditors maintaining
an attitude of professional scepticism at every stage of the audit. The Standard
explains that this requires auditors to conduct their audits with a questioning
mind and critical assessment of audit evidence. They must not be swayed by
past experience of honesty and integrity of clients' managements and they must

---

[10] The concept of professional scepticism is discussed in Chapter 3, section 3.4.5.

continually question whether information and other audit evidence obtained indicate that a material misstatement due to fraud may have occurred. If they have cause to believe that records or other documents are not genuine or have been wrongfully modified, or if responses from management to their enquiries are inconsistent, they are required to investigate further to resolve their concerns (paras 12–14, A7, A8).

(iv) *Discussion among audit engagement team members*

A significant feature of ISA 240 is its requirement for audit engagement team members to have a discussion regarding the risk of the auditee's financial statements being materially misstated as a result of fraud. During their discussion they are to "[set] aside beliefs . . . that management and those charged with governance are honest and have integrity" (para 15). Among the matters to be discussed are the following:

- how and where the entity's financial statements may be susceptible to material misstatement due to fraud, how management could perpetrate and conceal fraudulent financial reporting, and how assets of the entity could be misappropriated;
- the circumstances that might indicate earnings management and the practices management might adopt to manage earnings that could lead to fraudulent financial reporting;
- how external and internal factors affecting the entity may create an incentive or pressure for management or others to commit fraud, provide the opportunity for fraud to be perpetrated, and indicate a culture or environment that enables management or others to rationalise committing fraud;
- management's involvement in overseeing employees with access to cash or other assets susceptible to theft;
- any unusual or unexplained changes in the behaviour or lifestyle of management or employees which have come to the attention of engagement team members (ISA 240, para A11).

Unlike ISA 240, SAS no. 99 (AICPA, 2002) refers to this discussion as "brainstorming" which, according to Ramos (2003, p. 2) "is a new concept in auditing literature". Ramos (2003) suggests that the discussion provides an opportunity "to set the proper tone at the top for conducting the engagement". He notes that it should be conducted with an attitude which "includes a questioning mind" and it should "model the proper degree of professional skepticism and set the culture for the engagement" (p. 2). He also observes:

> The mere fact that the engagement team has a serious discussion about the entity's susceptibility to fraud also serves to remind auditors that the possibility does exist in every engagement – in spite of any history or perceived biases about management's honesty and integrity. (p. 2)

(v) *Identifying, assessing and responding to the risk of material misstatement due to fraud*

(a) Gathering information to identify the risk of fraud

In order to gather the information needed to identify the risk of material misstatement due to fraud, ISA 240 requires auditors to:

- make enquiries of the entity's executives (i.e., senior manages), directors, internal audit function (if the entity has one) and other appropriate individuals within the entity (for example, operating personnel not directly involved in the financial reporting process, employees with different levels of authority, in-house legal counsel, and the person(s) responsible for dealing with allegations of fraud). Such enquiries enable auditors to determine whether those questioned have knowledge of any actual, suspected or alleged fraud affecting the auditee and, in the case of internal auditors, to ascertain their views on the risk of fraud affecting the entity;
- gain an understanding of how the directors oversee the executives' processes for identifying and responding to the risk of fraud and the internal controls established to mitigate that risk;
- evaluate whether any unusual or unexpected relationships have been identified through analytical procedures[11] or other evidence gathered during the audit which may indicate the risk of material misstatement due to fraud;
- evaluate whether information obtained from other fraud risk assessment procedures and related activities indicates that one or more fraud risk factors are present. (These factors are discussed below.)

Among these information-gathering procedures, making enquiries of the entity's executives is particularly important. ISA 240 (para 17) requires the enquiries to include the executives':

- assessment of the risk that the financial statements may be materially misstated due to fraud and the nature, extent and frequency of such assessments;
- process for identifying and responding to the risk of fraud in the entity;
- communication, if any, to the board of directors regarding their (i.e., the executives') process for identifying and responding to the risk of fraud in the entity;
- communication, if any, to employees regarding their views on business practices and ethical behaviour.

---

[11] Analytical procedures are explained in Chapter 7, section 7.4.2.

Notwithstanding the importance of these enquiries, ISA 240 also advises:

> Management is [i.e., the executives are] often in the best position to perpetrate fraud. Accordingly, when evaluating [their] responses to inquiries with an attitude of professional skepticism, the auditor may judge it necessary to corroborate responses to inquiries with other information. (para A17)

Fraud, especially management fraud, may be difficult to detect as it is usually carefully concealed; however, events or conditions may indicate an incentive or pressure, or an opportunity, to commit fraud. Such events or conditions are known as 'fraud risk factors'. Just because such factors are present does not necessarily mean that fraud exists but they often provide warning signs where it does. To help auditors consider whether fraud risks are present, an extensive list of fraud risk factors is provided in ISA 240, Appendix 1. These are arranged in two sets – one for fraudulent financial reporting, the other for misappropriation of assets; in each set, the factors are grouped under the subheadings 'Incentives/Pressure', 'Opportunities' and 'Attitudes/ Rationalisation'. As an indication of the fraud risk factors identified in ISA 240, a few examples in each category are provided in the Appendix to this chapter.

(b)   Identifying and assessing the risk of fraud

Once auditors have gathered information to assist them identify the risk of material misstatement due to fraud (including consideration of relevant fraud risk factors), they are required to identify and assess the risk at both the financial statement level and the assertion level for classes of transactions, account balances and disclosures.[12] In this context, an interesting requirement of ISA 240 (as in SAS no. 99) relates to revenue recognition. According to Ramos (2003, pp. 6–7): "The vast majority of fraudulent financial reporting schemes [reviewed] involved improper revenue recognition". Given this situation, it is not surprising that ISA 240 specifically requires auditors, when identifying and assessing the risk of material misstatement due to fraud, to evaluate which types of revenue and revenue transactions give rise to such risk, based on a presumption that there is a risk of fraud in revenue recognition. Further, if auditors conclude that this presumption is not applicable in the particular circumstances of the audit (i.e., they consider improper revenue recognition does not present a risk of material misstatement due to fraud), they are to document the reasons supporting their conclusion (paras 26, 47).

When auditors identify risks of material misstatement due to fraud, they are required to treat them as significant risks and, as a consequence, accord them

---

[12] Assertions for classes of transactions, account balances and disclosures are discussed in Chapter 11.3.1.

special audit attention. They must obtain a good understanding of the internal controls relevant to those risks in order to determine whether the controls mitigate the identified risks sufficiently to enable the auditor to conclude that fraud has not resulted in material misstatement in the financial statements. Such a conclusion makes it unnecessary for the auditor to conduct procedures that would otherwise be required.

(c) Responding to the assessed risk of fraud

Once the risks of material misstatement due to fraud have been identified and assessed, auditors need to respond to them at the financial statement level, at the assertion level for classes of transactions, account balances and disclosures, and in respect of management's ability to override internal controls.

ISA 240 (para A33) explains that auditors' responses to assessed risks of material misstatement due to fraud at the financial statement level generally include considering how the performance of the audit can reflect increased professional scepticism. This may be achieved through, for example:
  – increased sensitivity in selecting for examination documentation that supports material transactions; and
  – increased recognition of the need to corroborate management's explanations regarding material matters.

Additionally, the audit engagement partner is required:
  – when assigning work to, and supervising, audit engagement team members, to take into account:
    (a) their knowledge, skill and ability to fulfil significant audit engagement responsibilities, and
    (b) his/her (i.e., the partner's) assessment of the risk of material misstatement due to fraud;
  – to evaluate whether the selection and application of accounting policies, particularly those relating to subjective measurements and complex transactions, may indicate fraudulent financial reporting resulting from management's efforts to manage the entity's reported earnings;
  – to incorporate an element of unpredictability in the nature, timing and extent of audit procedures performed during the audit so that entity personnel cannot 'second guess' what the engagement team will examine – or when (ISA 240, para 29).

For assessed risks at the assertion level, auditors are required to design and perform audit procedures whose nature, timing and extent[13] are responsive to the assessed risks. ISA 240 provides extensive illustrative examples (in paras

---

[13] The nature, timing and extent of audit procedures are discussed in Chapter 7, section 7.4.3.

A37–A39 and Appendix 2) of ways in which the nature, timing and extent of audit procedures may be modified, and additional procedures that may be performed, in order to address, specifically, the assessed risks of material misstatement due to fraud in classes of transactions, account balances and/or financial statement disclosures.

In respect of responding to the risk of fraud arising from management's ability to override internal controls, ISA 240 (para 31) explains:

> Management is in a unique position to perpetrate fraud because of management's ability to manipulate accounting records and prepare fraudulent financial statements by overriding controls that otherwise appear to be operating effectively. . . . Due to the unpredictable way in which such override could occur, it is a risk of material misstatement due to fraud and thus a significant risk.

Following from this stance, irrespective of their assessment of the likelihood of management overriding the entity's internal controls, auditors are required to design and perform audit procedures to test, *inter alia*, journal entries, accounting estimates and significant transactions that appear unusual in the context of the auditee's business. The significance of each of these factors is discussed below.

- *Journal entries*: According to ISA 240 (para A41), material misstatement of financial statements due to fraud often involves recording inappropriate or unauthorised journal entries. As a consequence, auditors are required to design and perform audit procedures to test the appropriateness of journal entries and other adjustments. In designing these procedures auditors are, among other things, required to enquire of individuals involved in the financial reporting process about inappropriate or unusual activity relating to the processing of journal entries and other adjustments. ISA 240 (para A44) also notes:

  > . . . because fraudulent journal entries and other adjustments are often made at the end of the reporting period, . . . the auditor [is required] to select [for examination] journal entries and other adjustments made at that time. Further, because material misstatements due to fraud can occur throughout the period and may involve extensive efforts to conceal how the fraud is accomplished, . . . the auditor [is required] to consider whether there is also a need to test journal entries and other adjustments throughout the period.

- *Accounting estimates*: When preparing the financial statements, management is responsible for making a number of judgments or assumptions that affect significant accounting estimates and for monitoring the reasonableness of such estimates. However, estimates are just that – and therefore prone to bias and error. A motivated manager could use the subjective nature of accounting estimates to bias the financial statements in order to achieve, for example, a 'desired' level of earnings. As ISA 240 points out: "Fraudulent financial reporting is often accomplished through intentional misstatement of accounting estimates" (para A45). In order to uncover such actions, auditors are required to review accounting estimates for bias and to consider the reasonableness of management's judgments and assumptions underlying the estimates. If auditors find evidence of bias they are required to evaluate whether the circumstances surrounding the bias are such as to result in a risk of material misstatement due to fraud.

- *Significant transactions outside the normal course of the auditee's business*: Such transactions, like manipulated journal entries and biased accounting estimates, may signal an intent to commit fraud. For any significant transaction that appears unusual (given the auditor's understanding of the entity, its environment and other information obtained during the course of the audit), the auditor is required to evaluate whether the business reasons (or absence thereof) for the transaction suggest that it may have been entered into in order to facilitate fraudulent financial reporting or to conceal misappropriation of assets. Signals of possible ill-intent include the following examples:
    - the form of the transaction appears to be unnecessarily complex;
    - the entity's executives have not discussed the nature of, or accounting for, the transaction with the non-executive directors (or audit committee);
    - documentation supporting the transaction is inadequate;
    - the executives place greater emphasis on adopting a particular accounting treatment for the transaction than on its underlying substance (ISA 240, para A48).

In addition to responding to identified risks of material misstatement due to fraud as outlined above, auditors are required to evaluate analytical procedures performed during the 'completion and review stage' of the audit[14] to ascertain whether they indicate a previously unidentified risk of material misstatement due to fraud. If they identify a misstatement and establish that it may indicate fraud, recognising that an instance of fraud is unlikely to be an isolated event, they are required to evaluate the implications of the misstatement for other aspects of the audit, especially the reliability of management's representations. Further, irrespective of the materiality of the misstatement, if auditors believe that management is involved, they are required to re-evaluate their assessment of the risk of material misstatement due to fraud and its impact on the nature, timing and extent of audit procedures performed in response to the assessed

---

[14] The completion and review stage of an audit is the subject of Chapter 13.

risks. Additionally, when reconsidering the reliability of evidence previously obtained, they are required to "consider whether circumstances or conditions indicate possible collusion involving employees, management or third parties" (IAS 240, para 36).

During the completion and review stage of the audit, auditors obtain 'written representations' from management in which management confirms, in writing, significant representations (or statements) made to the auditor.[15] However, ISA 240 (para 39) specifically requires auditors to obtain written representations from management that confirm that it (i.e., management):

(a) acknowledges its responsibility for designing, implementing and maintaining internal controls to prevent and detect fraud;

(b) has disclosed to the auditor:

- the results of its assessment of the risk that the financial statements may be materially misstated as a result of fraud;
- its knowledge of fraud or suspected fraud affecting the entity involving:
    - members of management (executives or directors);
    - employees who have significant roles in internal control; or
    - others where the fraud could have a material effect on the financial statements;
- its knowledge of any allegations of fraud, or suspected fraud, affecting the entity's financial statements communicated by employees, former employees, analysts, regulators or others.

(vi) Communicating detected or suspected fraud

If auditors detect fraud, or have reason to believe that fraud may have occurred within an auditee, they are required to report the matter to the appropriate level of management as soon as practicable.[16] ISA 240 (para A60) explains that auditors should perform this duty: "even if the matter might be considered inconsequential (for example, a minor defalcation by an employee at a low level in the entity's organization)". What constitutes an 'appropriate level of management' is a matter for the auditor's professional judgment but, ordinarily, it is at least one level above those who appear to be involved in the detected or suspected fraud.

---

[15] Written representations are discussed in Chapter 13, section 13.5.

[16] It should be recalled from Chapter 5 (section 5.5.3) that Moffitt J, when ruling on the *Pacific Acceptance* case, established that auditors have a duty to make prompt and frank disclosure, to the appropriate level of management, of material matters discovered during the course of an audit. This includes a duty to report promptly to the company's managers and/or directors if suspicious circumstances are encountered.

In cases where a detected or suspected fraud involves:
  (i)   one or more members of management,
  (ii) employees who have a significant role in designing, implementing or maintaining the auditee's internal controls, or
  (iii) other employees (or external parties) if the fraud has resulted in material misstatement in the financial statements,
the auditor has a duty to report the matter, on a timely basis, orally or in writing, to the board of directors (or audit committee).[17] In some circumstances, auditors may consider it appropriate to report fraud involving 'other employees' to the auditee's directors (or audit committee) even if the fraud (or suspected fraud) has not resulted in a material misstatement in the financial statements. In this regard, ISA 240 (para A62) points out that it is helpful if the directors and auditor clarify, at an early stage of the audit, the nature and extent of matters relating to fraud the directors wish the auditor to communicate to the full board or its audit committee. In some cases, the directors or audit committee may indicate that they wish the auditor to report to them all matters involving detected or suspected fraud.

If auditors believe that one or more senior manager is involved in a detected or suspected fraud, they are not only required to report the matter to the directors (or audit committee); they are also required to "discuss with them the nature, timing and extent of audit procedures necessary to complete the audit" (ISA 240, para 41). This is because, if fraud involving senior managers is detected or suspected, the auditor will need to re-assess audit evidence already gathered – in particular, the reliability of the managers' responses to the auditor's enquiries – and additional audit procedures are likely to be needed. This has time and cost implications for the audit – and thus for the audit fee.

Even if fraud or suspected fraud has not been encountered, ISA 240 explains that auditors should discuss with the directors (or audit committee) concerns they have relating to fraud. These may include, for example:
  • Concerns about the nature, extent and frequency of management's [i.e., executives'] assessments of the controls in place to prevent and detect fraud and of the risk that the financial statements may be misstated.
  • A failure by management to appropriately address identified significant deficiencies in internal control, or to appropriately respond to an identified fraud.
  • The auditor's evaluation of the entity's control environment,[18] including questions regarding the competence and integrity of management.
  • Actions by management that may be indicative of fraudulent financial reporting, such as management's selection and application of accounting

---

[17] Auditors' communications with the directors (or audit committee) is discussed in Chapter 14, section 14.8.

[18] The term 'control environment' is explained in Chapter 10, section 10.3.2.

policies that may be indicative of management's effort to manage earnings in order to deceive financial statement users. . . .
- Concerns about the adequacy and completeness of the authorization of transactions that appear to be outside the normal course of business. (para A64)

In addition to reporting detected or suspected fraud to the appropriate level of management, if auditors believe that an auditee's financial statements are materially misstated as a result of fraud and, on having the matter drawn to their attention, the directors refuse to correct the misstatement(s), they must convey this to the shareholders by modifying the audit report. Similarly, if auditors are prevented by the auditee, or by circumstances beyond the auditee's control, from obtaining sufficient appropriate evidence to establish whether or not fraud which may be material to the financial statements has occurred, the position needs to be reflected in the audit report.[19]

However, (as indicated in section 6.3.2 above) auditors' reporting duties go beyond reporting detected or suspected fraud to the entity's management and, in appropriate cases, to the shareholders. In certain circumstances, notwithstanding their duty of confidentiality to their clients, auditors may have an obligation to report detected or suspected fraud to a third party such as a regulatory authority. ISA 240 (para A65) explains:

> The auditor's professional duty to maintain the confidentiality of client information may preclude reporting fraud to a party outside the client entity. However, . . . in certain circumstances, the duty of confidentiality may be overridden by statute, the law or courts of law.[20] In some countries [for example, the UK], the auditor of a financial institution has a statutory duty to report the occurrence of fraud to supervisory authorities.

Auditors' duty to report fraud to management and shareholders under ISA 240 (2009a) is not dissimilar from that embodied in earlier Standards such as ISA 240 (IAPC, 2001). However, it is interesting to observe that, as regards reporting to external parties, ISA 240 (IAASB, 2009a) seems less demanding of auditors in the UK than SAS 110 (effective in the UK from 1995 to 2004), which it has superseded. It may be recalled (from section 6.3.2) that SAS 110 (APB, 1995a) stated:

> In certain exceptional circumstances auditors are not bound by their duty of confidentiality and have the right or duty to report matters to a proper authority in the public interest. . . . When a suspected or actual instance of fraud casts doubt

---

[19] Auditors' duty to report to shareholders is discussed in Chapter 14, section 14.2.

[20] ISA (UK and Ireland) 240 (APB, 2009a) states:

In the UK and Ireland, anti-money laundering legislation imposes a duty on auditors to report suspected money laundering activity. Suspicions relating to fraud are likely to be required to be reported under this legislation. (footnote 24a) on the integrity of the directors, auditors should make a report direct to a proper authority in the public interest without delay and without informing the directors in advance. (paras 52, 53)[21]

(vii)   *Required documentation relating to detecting and reporting fraud*

One of the characteristic features of the post-2002 regulatory auditing environment is a significant increase in the documentation required of auditors. It is, therefore, no surprise that ISA 240 (IAASB, 2009a) significantly extends the requirements of previous Standards in respect of documenting audit procedures performed to detect fraud, and steps taken to report detected and/ or suspected fraud. The matters auditors are required to document include:

- significant decisions reached during the audit team's discussion about the susceptibility of the entity's financial statements to material misstatement due to fraud;
- identified and assessed risks of material misstatement due to fraud at both the financial statement and the assertion level;
- their responses to the assessed risk of material misstatement due to fraud at the financial statement level, and the nature, timing and extent of audit procedures performed in response to the assessed risk of material misstatement due to fraud at the assertion level – and the relationship between those procedures and the overall responses;
- the results of the audit procedures performed, including those designed to address the risk of management overriding the entity's internal controls;
- if they conclude that improper revenue recognition does not present a risk of material misstatement due to fraud in the particular circumstances of the audit, the reasons supporting that conclusion;
- the nature, timing and extent of communications about fraud to the entity's senior managers, directors (and/or the audit committee) and others.

Thus, auditors are required to document their compliance with all of the key provisions of ISA 240.

6.4.2   Possible withdrawal from an audit engagement

In certain exceptional circumstances, such as when an auditor detects or suspects fraud has been perpetrated by the auditee's senior managers and/or (more particularly) its directors, the auditor may have such serious doubts about the integrity and honesty of the entity's management that s/he feels unable to continue with the engagement. In such circumstances, ISA 240 (para

---

[21] As will be seen in section 6.6.4, auditors' duty to report to parties external to the entity under ISA (UK and Ireland) 250: *Section A – Consideration of Laws and Regulations in an Audit of Financial Statements* (APB, 2009b) is very similar to that set out in SAS 110. As perpetrating fraud constitutes non-compliance with law (i.e., it is an illegal act), the reporting provisions of ISA (UK and Ireland) 250 apply to auditors in the UK and Ireland reporting detected or suspected fraud.

A63) suggests the auditor may consider it appropriate to obtain legal advice to assist in determining the appropriate course of action – including possible withdrawal from the engagement. Subject to any such advice, ISA 240 (para 38) requires the auditor:

- to consider whether it is appropriate to withdraw from the engagement;
- if withdrawal is considered appropriate:
  (a) to discuss the intended withdrawal with the appropriate level of management (in the UK this is the directors or audit committee), and the reasons for the withdrawal, and
  (b) to determine whether there is a professional or legal requirement to report the withdrawal to those who appointed the auditor (in the UK, this is the shareholders) or, in some cases, to a regulatory authority,[22] and to explain the reasons for the withdrawal.

6.5 AGGRESSIVE EARNINGS MANAGEMENT

In 2001, the APB issued a Consultation Paper entitled *Aggressive Earnings Management* (APB, 2001). This seems to be closely linked to the APB's finding in the UK that "more than half of frauds involved misstated financial reporting . . ."[23] (APB, 1998, p. 5) and that of, for example, National Economic Research Associates (NERA) in the USA which reported: "55 percent of all securities claims actions in the first half of 1999 were based on claims of fraudulent accounting" (see quotation from Walker, 1999b, in section 6.3.2 above).

The APB (2001) defines aggressive earnings management as follows:

[A]ccounting practices including the selection of inappropriate accounting policies and/or unduly stretching judgments as to what is acceptable when forming accounting estimates. These practices, while presenting the financial performance of the companies in a favourable light, do not necessarily reflect the underlying reality. (paras 4, 5)

The APB explained that as a result of, and in response to, commercial pressures (for example, to report earnings in line with the market's expectations or to conform with financial thresholds or ratios requirements specified by law or

---

[22] As we note in Chapter 5 (section 5.3.3), auditors in the UK are required to notify the 'appropriate authority' when they cease to hold office as the auditor of a company (whatever the reason therefor), and to send with their notice, a 'statement of circumstances' and/or a statement explaining the reasons for them ceasing to hold office.

[23] The APB explains:

Misstatements include (1) errors, (2) other inaccuracies (whether intentional or not), and (3) with regard to estimates and amounts dependent upon an exercise of judgment, unreasonable differences between (a) the amount intended to be included in the financial statements [by the directors] and (b) the auditors' assessment of what that amount should be based on the available audit evidence. (APB, 2001, p. 9) regulations), a company may begin in a small legitimate way to ensure that it reports the 'desired results'. However, over time, manipulation of the financial statements may increase until it "crosses the border of acceptability" (APB, 2001, p. 7). Thus 'aggressive earnings management' may be seen as a rung on the ladder leading to fraudulent financial reporting. An example of how aggressive earnings management can develop into 'unacceptable financial reporting' is presented in Figure 6.1.

In its Consultation Paper, the APB (2001) asserted that it wished auditors to be alert, and responsive, to the risk of aggressive earnings management. It also reported that it would consider whether Auditing Standards needed to be enhanced in order to ensure that auditors:

- better understand the pressures on directors and management to report a specific level of earnings;
- act with greater scepticism when circumstances are encountered that may be indicative of aggressive earnings management;
- take a more robust attitude with directors when seeking adjustments for misstatements identified by the audit;
- communicate openly and frankly with the entity's directors – and, more particularly, with its audit committee (if it has one).

By tackling 'aggressive earnings management' as soon as they suspect an auditee may be engaging in it, auditors may well prevent their clients from sliding down the slippery slope to cross the boundary from 'undesirable practices' into fraudulent financial reporting.

As we have seen in this chapter, the provisions of ISA 240 incorporate the steps needed to counter aggressive earnings by management identified by the APB (2001).

6.6 AUDITORS' RESPONSIBILITY TO DETECT AND REPORT NON-COMPLIANCE WITH LAWS AND REGULATIONS[24]

6.6.1 Definition of non-compliance

Before we can examine auditors' responsibility to detect and report auditees' non-compliance with laws and regulations, we need to know what we mean by

---

[24] It should be noted that ISA (UK and Ireland) 250 (APB, 2009b) contains two sections:
- Section A – Consideration of Laws and Regulations in an Audit of Financial Statements;
- Section B – The Auditor's Right and Duty to Report to Regulators in the Financial Sector.
As it is outside the scope of this book to discuss auditing requirements that are specific to any particular sector, we do not discuss to the provisions in Section B of ISA (UK and Ireland) 250.

Figure 6.1:   Example illustrating how legitimate business practices can develop into unacceptable financial reporting

Year ended 31 December XXX1

A listed manufacturing company has thrived in an economic expansion and announced a series of record-breaking results. Analysts believe earnings will continue their strong upward trend and have forecast the results for the year and the earnings per share to the penny. Shareholders see increased earnings producing an ever-higher share price.

Management perceives a slow-down in its business and is very concerned about the impact on the share price if the analysts' forecasts are not met. Departmental heads are told to pull out all the stops; targets are set; management will see missing the target as a failure. The pressure is on.

Being a manufacturing company, earnings are based on completed items shipped and invoiced. In this instance, for the earnings target to be met, overtime is authorised and worked to accelerate completions so that the necessary shipments are made, and invoices raised before the year-end.

Year ended 31 December XXX2

The analysts, seeing their forecast met by the company at December XXX1, project a further increase in the company's earnings in line with its record-breaking past. Management, believing, or hoping, that the slow-down will be temporary, issues departments with new targets to enable it to meet the analysts' forecast for the next year-end.

Unfortunately, the business slow-down turns out not to be temporary. Not only have completions and shipments failed to increase to meet the new forecast but also some method has to be found to make up in this year for the sales and profit which were accelerated into the previous year. The pressure is now greater than at the previous year-end.

Overtime is again authorised to increase shipments but will not be enough to meet the target. To further stimulate sales the company announces a price discount that will apply to sales and shipments made in December. In addition to the continued efforts to accelerate shipments for completed goods, the provisions for bad debts, returns and warranty costs are also reduced. While individually each provision can be justified, each has been calculated on the basis of the most optimistic view of the ranges of possible outcomes. No disclosures are given in the financial statements, nor in the other information published with the financial statements, of the actions taken to stimulate sales or the fact that each provision is determined on the most optimistic basis.

Year ended 31 December XXX3

A year later the position has escalated out of control and many employees are now involved. In addition to all the actions taken in XXX2, goods are now being shipped on sale or return (without a provision for returns) and fictitious shipments are made close to the year end on the basis of false documentation, both being designed to deceive the auditors.

At some point the 'balloon goes up', the police are called in and, inevitably, the cry goes up 'what were the directors doing and where were the auditors?'

Source: Consultation Paper: *Aggressive Earnings Management* (APB, 2001) 'non-compliance'. ISA 250: *Consideration of Laws and Regulations in an Audit of Financial Statements* (APB, 2009b),[25] defines it as:

> Acts of omission or commission by the entity, either intentional or unintentional, which are contrary to the prevailing laws or regulations. Such acts include transactions entered into by, or in the name of, the entity, or on its behalf, by those charged with governance, management or employees. (para 11)

6.6.2 Nature of non-compliance with laws and regulations

As shown in Chapter 5, many laws and regulations (including the Companies Act 2006 and Accounting Standards) govern the form and content of companies' financial statements and certain other disclosures in their annual reports. Other laws and regulations, such as those governing entities' operations (including, for example, obtaining a licence to conduct business within an industry and health and safety regulations), may seem far removed from the financial statements. However, non-compliance with *any* laws and regulations that apply to an entity may result in adverse financial consequences, such as fines or litigation – consequences that impact on the entity's financial statements.

Clearly, a company's executives and directors are responsible for ensuring their company complies with all applicable laws and regulations, and that controls are in place to prevent non-compliance from occurring – or, if it does, to detect it in a timely manner. However, auditors also have a role to play: they are responsible for ensuring their audits are conducted so as to obtain reasonable assurance that their auditees' financial statements are not materially misstated as a result of non-compliance with applicable laws and regulations. Notwithstanding this responsibility, as ISA 250 points out: "there is an unavoidable risk that some material misstatements in the financial statements may not be detected, even though the audit is properly planned and performed in accordance with the ISAs" (para 5). In the case of material misstatements resulting from non-compliance with laws and regulations (like those resulting from fraud), the risk of auditors failing to detect them may be particularly high because, amongst other things:

- non-compliance may involve efforts to conceal it – for example, by collusion, forgery, deliberate failure to record transactions, management override of controls or intentionally giving erroneous responses to the auditor's enquiries;
- many laws and regulations relate principally to the operating aspects of the entity which, typically, are not captured by the accounting system or reflected in the financial statements.

---

[25] Unless indicated otherwise, all references to ISA 250 in this section refer to ISA 250: *Consideration of Laws and Regulations in an Audit of Financial Statements* (IAASB, 2009b).

6.6.3 Detection of non-compliance with laws and regulations

As for detecting fraud, the key requirements of auditors in respect of detecting non-compliance with applicable laws and regulations include:

(i) maintaining an attitude of professional scepticism throughout the audit, and

(ii) being alert to the possibility that procedures performed at any time, for any purpose, during the audit may indicate possible non-compliance with applicable laws and regulations.

In addition to these overarching requirements, auditors need to perform specific procedures directed towards detecting clients' non-compliance with laws and regulations. As we will see in Chapter 7, one of the earliest, and possibly most important, steps in the audit process is that of gaining a thorough understanding of the client, its business, industry, key personnel, and so on. As an element of obtaining this general understanding, auditors need to obtain an understanding of:

(a) the legal and regulatory framework which applies to the client and the industry or business sector within which it operates, and

(b) how the entity complies with that framework.

In order to gain this understanding, auditors may make enquiries of management (and/or, if it has one, the auditee's in-house lawyer) about, for example:

- laws and regulations which may be expected to have a significant effect on the entity's operations and its financial statements;
- the entity's policies and procedures which are designed to:
  - ensure the entity, and entity personnel, comply with applicable laws and regulations, and
  - detect any non-compliance with applicable laws and regulations;
- the entity's policies and procedures for identifying, evaluating and accounting for litigation claims.

Auditors need to be particularly alert to the possibility of non-compliance with laws and regulations that may have a fundamental effect on the operations of the business – non-compliance that may result in the entity having to cease its operations (such as an omission to obtain a required licence to operate in the industry) or call into question its ability to continue as a going concern (for example, a breach of environmental or product safety laws which is likely to result in crippling fines or other penalties).

Once auditors have gained a sound understanding of their auditees' legal and regulatory environment, they are required to perform procedures in relation to two different sets of laws and regulations:

(i) For laws and regulations which are generally recognised as having a direct effect on material amounts and other disclosures in the financial statements (for example, income tax and pension laws and regulations), auditors are to obtain sufficient appropriate evidence so as to be reasonably assured that their auditees have complied with these laws and regulations (i.e., auditors seek evidence of *compliance*).

(ii) For other laws and regulations, which generally do not have a direct effect on the amounts and other disclosures in the financial statements but compliance with which may be fundamental to auditees' ability to continue in business or avoid material penalties (for example, health and safety, employment or environmental requirements), auditors are to perform procedures designed to identify instances of non-compliance (i.e., auditors seek evidence of *non-compliance*) (ISA 250, paras 13, 14)

To help auditors detect instances of non-compliance, they should, *inter alia*:
- enquire of management whether the entity is in compliance with all applicable laws and regulations, and
- inspect correspondence between the entity and relevant regulatory authorities.

They may also be alerted to possible non-compliance by signals such as:
- an investigation by a regulatory authority into the entity's affairs;
- the payment of fines or penalties;
- payments for unspecified services or loans to consultants, related parties or employees;
- the purchasing of goods, services or assets at prices significantly above or below the market price;
- payments for goods or services made to a country other than that from which the goods or services originated;
- the failure of an information system (deliberately or accidentally) which results in an inadequate audit trail or insufficient evidence;
- unauthorised or improperly recorded transactions.

Auditors should also request auditees' management to provide written representations to the effect that all known, or suspected, instances of non-compliance with laws and regulations whose effects should be considered when preparing the financial statements have been disclosed to the auditor (ISA 250, para 16).

Once possible non-compliance with laws and/or regulations has been detected, auditors need to obtain:
(i) an understanding of the nature of the non-compliance and the reasons why it has occurred;

(ii) information to enable them to evaluate the possible effect of the non-compliance on the financial statements – in particular:
- the potential financial consequences of the non-compliance (for example, fines, penalties or litigation),
- whether the potential financial statement consequences require disclosure in the financial statements, or
- whether they are so serious as to render the financial statements misleading (for example, where the consequences of the non-compliance threaten the ability of the auditee to continue as a going concern).

Armed with the necessary understanding and information about detected or suspected non-compliance with relevant laws and/or regulations, the auditor should discuss the matter with the auditee's management with a view to obtaining evidence that the entity is, in fact, in compliance with all applicable laws and regulations. If such evidence is not forthcoming, the auditor needs to consider:
(i) the effect of the lack of evidence on the audit opinion,[26] and
(ii) the implications for other aspects of the audit, including the auditor's risk assessment[27] and the reliability of written representations obtained from management.

ISA 250 explains that the auditor may also:

consider it appropriate to consult with the entity's in-house legal counsel or external legal counsel about the application of the laws and regulations to the circumstances, including the possibility of fraud, and the possible effects on the financial statements. . . . [Alternatively] the auditor may consider it appropriate to consult [his/her] own legal counsel as to whether a contravention of a law or regulation is involved, the possible legal consequences, including the possibility of fraud, and what further action, if any, the auditor should take. (para A16)

6.6.4 Reporting non-compliance with laws and regulations

Auditors' duty to report instances of detected or suspected non-compliance with laws and regulations parallels their duty to report detected or suspected fraud. If auditors encounter or suspect non-compliance with laws and/or regulations, they should report the matter promptly to the next level of management within the entity above that at which the non-compliance appears to have occurred. If they believe that senior managers are involved in the non-compliance, they should report the matter to the audit committee or full board

---

[26] Different types of audit opinion, and the circumstances in which each should be expressed, are discussed in Chapter 14, section 14.4.

[27] Auditors' risk assessment is discussed in Chapter 8, section 8.4.

of directors. Additionally, unless they have already discussed the instances of non-compliance with the directors, auditors should communicate to the directors:

(i)   any significant matter(s) involving non-compliance with laws and regulations which have a material effect on the financial statements, and

(ii)   any other (non-inconsequential) matter(s) involving non-compliance that have come to their attention.

If auditors believe the entity's directors are involved in the detected or suspected non-compliance with applicable laws and/or regulations, or they believe the directors will not act on their (the auditors') communication about non-compliance, they should consider the need to obtain legal advice (ISA 250, paras 22, 24).

In addition to reporting to the appropriate level of management, if auditors believe that non-compliance with applicable laws and/or regulations is material to, but not properly reflected in, the financial statements, they are required to express a qualified or adverse audit opinion.[28] Similarly, if they are prevented by the auditee, or by circumstances beyond the auditee's control, from obtaining sufficient appropriate evidence to establish whether or not non-compliance with applicable laws and/or regulations, which may be material to the financial statements, has occurred, they are required to reflect the position in their audit report.

However, as for reporting fraud, auditors' duty to report detected or suspected instances of non-compliance with laws and regulations may extend beyond the auditee's management and shareholders. In certain circumstance, they may have an obligation to override their duty of confidentiality to their clients and report non-compliance with laws and/or regulations to a regulatory authority.

In the UK, a distinction is made between auditors reporting to an appropriate authority when they have a statutory responsibility, and when it is in the public interest, to do so. A statutory responsibility may arise, for example, for the auditors of financial service entities, pension schemes and charities to report "matters that are likely to be of material significance to the regulator . . . subject to compliance with legislation relating to 'tipping off' or 'prejudicing an investigation'" [ISA (UK and Ireland) 250, footnote 11b].[29] However, even in the

---

[28] These forms of audit opinion are explained in Chapter 14, section 14.4.

[29] ISA (UK and Ireland) 250, footnote 4a, explains:

    In the UK, 'tipping off' is an offence under POCA [Proceeds of Crime Act 2002] section 333A. It arises when an individual discloses:

        (a) that a report (internal or external) has already been made where the disclosure by the individual is likely to prejudice an investigation which might be conducted following the internal or external report that has been made; or absence of a statutory requirement to report, auditors may encounter circumstances in which they consider detected or suspected non-compliance with laws and/or regulations should be reported to a proper authority[30] in the public interest. When deciding whether or not disclosure in the public interest is justified, auditors should consider factors such as:

- the extent to which the actual or suspected non-compliance with laws or regulations is likely to affect members of the public;
- whether the entity's directors have taken effective corrective action or are likely to do so;
- the extent to which non-disclosure is likely to enable non-compliance with laws and/or regulations to recur with impunity;
- the gravity of the matter;
- whether there is a general ethos within the entity of disregarding laws and regulations.

It may be recalled from section 6.3.2 that these factors reflect those included in SAS 110 (APB, 1995a).

Having decided that the detected or suspected non-compliance with laws and/or regulations justifies reporting to a proper authority in the public interest, unless the circumstances have caused the auditor to lose confidence in the integrity of the company's directors,[31] s/he should first discuss the non-compliance with the audit committee and/or board of directors. If, after considering the audit committee's and/or the board's response (and any legal advice obtained), the auditor concludes the matter should be reported to a proper authority in the public interest, the directors should be given written notice of this conclusion. If the directors do not voluntarily report the matter, or do not provide evidence that the matter has been reported, the auditor should report it [ISA (UK and Ireland) 250, para A19-5].

(b) that an investigation is being contemplated or is being carried out into allegations that a money laundering offence has been committed and the disclosure by the individual is likely to prejudice that investigation.

[30] In the UK, a 'proper authority' includes the Serious Fraud Office, the Crown Prosecution Service, the police, the Financial Conduct Authority, HM Revenue & Customs, the Department for Business Innovation & Skills and the Health and Safety Executive [ISA (UK and Ireland) 250, footnote 11e]. It should be noted that ISA (UK and Ireland) 250 refers to the Financial Services Authority (FSA) rather than the Financial Conduct Authority (FCA) however, in April 2013, the FSA was disbanded and its functions were transferred to the FCA and the Prudential Regulation Authority (PRA). (The FCA and PRA are both overseen by the Policy Committee of the Bank of England.)

[31] Such loss of confidence may occur, for example, where the auditor suspects, or has evidence of, the directors' involvement in possible non-compliance with laws or regulations which could have a material effect on the financial statements, or where the auditor knows the directors are aware of such non-compliance and, contrary to regulatory requirements or the public interest, have not reported the matter to a proper authority within a reasonable period of time.

Auditors may be concerned that reporting to a party external to the entity will expose them to liability for breaching their duty of confidentiality to the client or for defamation. However, ISA (UK and Ireland) 250 (para A19-8) explains that auditors are protected from exposure to such liability providing:

(i)   the disclosure is made in the auditor's capacity as auditor of the entity,
(ii) it is made in the public interest to an appropriate authority, and
(iii) there is no malice motivating the disclosure.

ISA (UK and Ireland) 250 (APB, 2009b) further explains:

> An auditor who can demonstrate having acted reasonably and in good faith in informing an authority of a breach of law or regulations which the auditor thinks has been committed would not be held by the court to be in breach of a duty to the client even if, an investigation or prosecution having occurred, it was found that there had been no offence. (para A19-10)

6.6.5 Documentation of non-compliance with laws and regulations

As for all other aspects of an audit, auditors are required to fully document matters relating to an auditee's actual or suspected non-compliance with applicable laws and regulations. Such documentation includes detailing the instances of non-compliance detected or suspected, audit procedures performed to confirm compliance or non-compliance, copies of relevant records or documents, minutes of meetings held with executives, the board of directors (and/ or audit committee) and, in applicable cases, parties external to the entity, and the results of such meetings.

6.7 AUDITORS' DUTY OF CONFIDENTIALITY TO THEIR CLIENTS

During the course of an audit, members of the audit engagement team become very knowledgeable about the client's business, its operations and its financial affairs, and it is imperative that they respect the confidential nature of this knowledge – that is, adhere to their duty of confidentiality to their clients. In its *Code of Ethics for Professional Accountants*, section 140: *Confidentiality*,[32] the International Ethics Standards Board for Accountants (IESBA, 2010) explains this duty in the following terms:

> The principle of confidentiality imposes an obligation on all professional accountants [including auditors] to refrain from:
> (a) Disclosing outside the [audit] firm or employing organization confidential information acquired as a result of professional and business relationships without proper and specific authority or unless there is a legal or professional right or duty to disclose, and

---

[32] The Codes of Ethics of each of the professional bodies in the UK are based on, and are very similar to, the IESBA's *Code of Ethics for Professional Accountants* (2010).

(b) Using confidential information acquired as a result of professional and business relationships to their personal advantage or the advantage of third parties.

A professional accountant shall maintain confidentiality, including in a social environment, being alert to the possibility of inadvertent disclosure, particularly to a close business associate or a close or immediate family member. (paras 140.1, 140.2)

Although this duty of confidentiality is paramount, as we have noted in this chapter, there are circumstances in which auditors may (or are required to) override the duty and disclose information which would otherwise remain confidential. Such circumstances include those where the auditor has:

- the client's consent to disclose information;
- a legal responsibility to disclose information, for example, to enable documents to be located or to give evidence in legal proceedings;
- a legal responsibility to disclose information to appropriate authorities, for example, to regulators such as the Financial Conduct Authority and, in appropriate cases, issuing a 'statement of circumstances'[33] when the auditor ceases to hold office;
- a professional responsibility to disclose information to appropriate authorities of infringements of the law or regulations which come to light during an audit;
- a professional responsibility to disclose information in compliance with, for example:
  - ethical requirements (for example, disclosing information to a successor auditor);
  - auditing standards [for example, reporting when it is in the public interest to do so under ISA (UK and Ireland) 240 and ISA (UK and Ireland) 250];
  - monitoring or inspection requirements of a regulatory body such as the auditor's Recognised Supervisory Body (RSB) or the Audit Quality Review team;[34]
  - in response to an enquiry from a professional accounting or regulatory body.

In order to ensure that auditors adhere to their duty of confidentiality to the extent possible, and do not disclose information when it is inappropriate to do so, IESBA's *Code of Ethics* (para 140.8) requires auditors, before disclosing otherwise confidential information, to consider four factors, namely:

---

[33] 'Statements of circumstances' are explained in Chapter 5, section 5.3.3.

[34] Monitoring and inspection of auditors' performance by the RSBs and the Audit Quality Review team [formerly known as the Audit Inspection Unit (AIU)] are discussed in Chapter 16, section 16.4.

(i)   whether the interests of all parties, including third parties whose interests may be affected, could be harmed if the client consents to the auditor disclosing the information;

(ii)   whether all the relevant information is known and substantiated, to the extent to which this is practicable; if this is not the case, the auditor should use professional judgment to determine the type of disclosure to be made, if any;

(iii) the type of communication expected, and to whom it should be addressed;

(iv) whether the addressee(s) of the communication is/are the appropriate recipient(s).

Prior to 1990, when the Auditing Practices Committee (APC; predecessor of the APB) issued an Auditing Guideline: *The Auditor's Responsibility in Relation to Fraud, Other Irregularities and Errors* (APC, 1990), the circumstances in which auditors could go beyond their duty of confidentiality and disclose matters of concern to parties outside the auditee were extremely limited. In essence, they could only disclose otherwise confidential information when:
- they had their client's permission to do so, and
- in response to a subpoena (summons from a court of law).

However, during the 1980s, as an increasing number of cases of fraud and other illegal acts by company directors or senior executives came to light – primarily during investigations of major companies which collapsed unexpectedly – politicians, the courts, financial journalists and the public questioned why the auditors had not discovered such acts and reported them to an appropriate authority. In its defence, the auditing profession pointed out that, in the absence of a legal requirement to do so, auditors' duty of confidentiality to their clients precluded them from reporting matters of concern discovered during an audit to third parties.

It was largely in response to public and political pressure that the APB included provisions in SAS 110: *Fraud and Error* and SAS 120: *Consideration of Law and Regulations* (APB 1995a, 1995b) [and their successors, ISA (UK and Ireland) 240 and ISA (UK and Ireland) 250 (APB 2009a, 2009b)] requiring auditors, on occasion, to override their duty of confidentiality: when they have a statutory duty, or it is in the public interest, to do so, they are to report suspected or actual instances of fraud or non-compliance with other applicable laws and regulations they encounter during an audit to a proper authority.

Today, application of auditors' duty of confidentiality is a far cry from that pertaining in the 1980s and seems more in line with society's expectations. In brief, in the absence of particular circumstances, auditors are required to adhere to their duty of confidentiality but when a statutory or regulatory duty exists, or it is in the public interest to do so, they are required to subordinate this duty and disclose matters of concern to an appropriate authority. This position is reflected in the second portion of the fundamental principle of external auditing – *Integrity*:

> Confidential information obtained in the course of an audit is disclosed only when required in the public interest, or by operation of law. (Financial Reporting Council, 2013)[35]

6.8 SUMMARY

In this chapter we have examined auditors' responsibilities in relation to fraud and auditees' non-compliance with applicable laws and/or regulations. We have noted that auditors today acknowledge significantly greater responsibility to detect fraud than they did 50 years ago and that the requirements of auditors in this regard are now very exacting. We have also observed that auditors' responsibilities in respect of auditees' non-compliance with laws and regulations depend on whether the laws and regulations:

- have a direct effect on the financial statements (in this case, auditors seek evidence of auditees' compliance), or
- are related to auditees' operations but non-compliance may have consequences which impact on the financial statements (in this case, auditors seek evidence of auditees' non-compliance).

If auditors detect or suspect fraud or non-compliance with applicable laws and/or regulations, they are required to report it to an appropriate level of management within the entity. Further, if the fraud or non-compliance with laws and/or regulations is material to the financial statements, and is not reflected in those financial statements, auditors are required to report this in their report to the company's shareholders. Additionally, when auditors have a statutory duty, or it is in the public interest to do so, they are required to report the detected or suspected fraud, or non-compliance with laws and/or regulations, to an appropriate authority.

In the concluding section of the chapter, we have highlighted the confidential nature of knowledge gained by audit engagement team members and the importance of them respecting their duty of confidentiality to the client. However, we have also observed that, corresponding with the reporting duty noted above, auditors may have an overriding duty to report to an appropriate

---

[35] The fundamental principles of auditing which constitute *The Auditors' Code* are reproduced on the inside of the front cover of this book.

authority when there is a statutory duty to so report or when it is in the public interest to do so.

SELF-REVIEW QUESTIONS

6.1   Explain briefly the two types of fraud which are particularly relevant to auditors.

6.2   The importance of detecting fraud as an audit objective has changed markedly over the period from 1844 to the present time. State the significance of fraud detection as an audit objective in each of the following periods:
      (i)   1844–1920s
      (ii) 1920s–1960s
      (iii) 1960s–1980s
      (iv) 1980s–present.
      List reasons to explain the change in the importance of fraud detection as an audit objective in each of these periods.

6.3   Explain the factors that constitute 'the fraud triangle'.

6.4   In the context of detecting fraud, explain the purpose of a discussion among audit engagement team members.

6.5   Giving examples to illustrate your answer, explain what is meant by 'a fraud risk factor' and the role of such factors in auditors' detection of fraud.

6.6   Outline the procedures auditors may perform:
      (i)   to assess the risk of the financial statements being materially misstated as a result of fraud;
      (ii) to respond to the possibility of the financial statements being materially misstated as a result of management overriding the auditee's internal controls.

6.7   Explain briefly the circumstances in which auditors seek evidence of auditees':
      (i)   compliance with applicable laws and regulations;
      (ii) non-compliance with applicable laws and regulations.

6.8   Describe briefly the procedures auditors may perform to detect non-compliance with laws and regulations.

6.9   Explain the meaning of the phrase 'auditors' duty of confidentiality to their clients'.

6.10   Outline auditors' responsibility to report detected or suspected instances of fraud or non-compliance with other laws and/or regulations to:
      (i)   the auditee's management;
      (ii) the auditee's shareholders;
      (iii) parties external to the auditee.

REFERENCES

American Institute of Certified Public Accountants (AICPA). (1951). *Codification of Statements on Auditing Procedure*. New York: AICPA.

American Institute of Certified Public Accountants (AICPA). (1988). Statement on Auditing Standards (SAS) no. 53, *The Auditor's Responsibility to Detect and Report Errors and Irregularities*. New York: AICPA.

American Institute of Certified Public Accountants (AICPA). (1997). Statement on Auditing Standards (SAS) no. 82: *Consideration of Fraud in a Financial Statement Audit*. New York: AICPA.

American Institute of Certified Public Accountants (AICPA). (2002). Statement on Auditing Standards (SAS) no. 99: *Consideration of Fraud in a Financial Statement Audit*. New York: AICPA.

Auditing Practices Board (APB). (1995a). Statement of Auditing Standards (SAS) 110: *Fraud and Error*. London: APB.

Auditing Practices Board (APB). (1995b). Statement of Auditing Standards (SAS) 120: *Consideration of Law and Regulations*. London: APB.

Auditing Practices Board (APB). (1998). *Fraud and Audit: Choices for Society*. Consultation Paper. London: APB.

Auditing Practices Board (APB). (2001). *Aggressive Earnings Management*. Consultation Paper. London: APB.

Auditing Practices Board (APB). (2009a). International Standard on Auditing (ISA) (UK and Ireland) 240: *The Auditor's Responsibilities Relating to Fraud in an Audit of Financial Statements*. London: Financial Reporting Council.

Auditing Practices Board (APB). (2009b). International Standards on Auditing (ISA) (UK and Ireland) 250: *Section A: Consideration of Laws and Regulations in an Audit of Financial Statements*. London: Financial Reporting Council.

Auditing Practices Committee (APC). (1990). *The Auditor's Responsibility in Relation to Fraud, Other Irregularities and Errors*. London: Consultative Committee of Accountancy Bodies.

Carty, J. (1985, September). Fraud and other irregularities. *Certified Accountant*, p. 30.

Commission on Auditors' Responsibilities (CAR). (1978). *Report, Conclusions and Recommendations* (The Cohen Commission). New York: AICPA.

Financial Reporting Council (FRC). (2013). *Scope and Authority of FRC Audit and Assurance Pronouncements*. London: FRC.

International Auditing and Assurance Standards Board (IAASB). (2009a). International Standard on Auditing (ISA) 240: *The Auditor's Responsibilities Relating to Fraud in an Audit of Financial Statements*. New York: International Federation of Accountants.

International Auditing and Assurance Standards Board (IAASB). (2009b). International Standard on Auditing (ISA) 250: *Consideration of Laws and Regulations in an Audit of Financial Statements*. New York: International Federation of Accountants.

International Auditing Practices Committee (IAPC). (2001). International Standard on Auditing (ISA) 240: *Fraud and Error*. New York: International Federation of Accountants.

International Ethics Standards Board for Accountants (IESBA). (2010). *Code of Ethics for Professional Accountants*. New York: International Federation of Accountants.

International Federation of Accountants (IFAC). (2009). *Glossary of Terms,* included in *Handbook of International Quality Control, Auditing, Review, Other Assurance and Related Services Pronouncements 2010 Edition*. New York: IFAC.

KPMG. (2006, 30 January). *Massive Surge in Fraud in 2005*, www.kpmg.co.uk/news/detail.cfm?pr=2425, accessed 11 May 2013.

KPMG. (2008, 4 February). *Fraud Hits 12 Year High in 2007*, www.kpmg.co.uk/news/detail.cfm?pr=3028, accessed 11 May 2013.

KPMG. (2012). *Boom Time for Fraudsters as 'Austerity Bites'*, www.kpmg.com/uk/en/issuesandinsights/articlespublications/newsreleases/pages/fraud-barometer-boom-time-for-fraudsters-as-austerity-bites.aspx, accessed 11 May 2013.

Patel, H. (2011, January). *KPMG Forensic Fraud Barometer, January 2011*, www.kpmg fightingfraud.com/15390, accessed 17 March 2012.

Porter, B.A. (1997). *Auditors' Responsibilities with Respect to Corporate Fraud: A Controversial Issue*. In Sherer, M., & Turley, S., *Current Issues in Auditing*, 3rd ed., Chapter 2. London: Paul Chapman Publishing.

Ramos, M. (2003, January). Auditors' responsibility for fraud detection. *Journal of Accountancy*, Online Issues, 1–11.

Sims, B. (2010, 25 January). *Record Fraud in 2009 Closes out 'Naughty Noughties'*, www.ifsecglobal.com/document.asp?doc_id=550302&site=ifsecglobal, accessed 11 May 2013.

Smith, T. (1985, 22 August). Expectation gap trips up fraud fight's 'front line'. *Accountancy Age*, p. 10.

Turner, L.E. (1999, 7 October). *Remarks to the Panel on Audit Effectiveness*. New York

Turner, L.E. (2000, 10 July). *Remarks to the Panel on Audit Effectiveness*. New York.

Walker, R.H. (1999a, 7 December). *Behind the Numbers of the SEC's Recent Financial Fraud Cases*. Speech, 27th National AICPA Conference on Current SEC Developments.

Walker, R.H. (1999b, 9 October). *Remarks to the Panel on Audit Effectiveness*. New York.

Woolf, E. (1978). Profession in peril: Time running out for auditors. *Accountancy*, *89*(1014), 58–65.

Yirrell, S. (2007, 30 January). *Fraud Explodes in 2006*, www.channelweb.co.uk/crn-uk/news/1871467/fraud-explodes-2006, accessed 11 May 2013.

ADDITIONAL READING

Bowlin, K. (2011). Risk-based auditing, strategic prompts, and auditor sensitivity to the strategic risk of fraud. *Accounting Review*, *86*(1), 1231–1253.

Brazel, J.F., Carpenter, T.D., & Jenkins, J.G. (2010). Auditors' use of brainstorming in the consideration of fraud: Reports from the field. *Accounting Review*, *85*(4), 1273–1301.

Chen, Q., Kelly, K., & Salterio, S.E. (2012). Do changes in audit actions and attitudes consistent with increased auditor scepticism deter aggressive earnings management? An experimental investigation. *Accounting, Organizations and Society*, *37*(2), 95–115.

Dalal, C. (2008). Do the math (fraud). *Accountancy*, *141*(1373), 120–121.

Fathil, F.M., & Schmidtke, J.M. (2010). The relation between individual differences and accountants' fraud detection ability. *International Journal of Auditing*, *14*(2), 163–173.

Hammersley, J.S. (2011). A review and model of audit judgements in fraud-related planning tasks. *Auditing: A Journal of Practice & Theory*, *30*(4), 101–128.

Hammersley, J.S., Bamber, E.M., & Carpenter, T.D. (2010). The influence of documentation specificity and priming on auditors' fraud risk assessments and evidence evaluation decisions. *Accounting Review*, *85*(2), 547–571.

Hoffman, V.B., & Zimbelman, M.F. (2009). Do strategic reasoning and brainstorming help auditors change their standard audit procedures in response to fraud risk? *Accounting Review*, *84*(3), 811–837.

Hogan, C.E., Rezaee, Z., Riley Jr., R.A., & Velury, U.K. (2008). Financial statement fraud: Insights from the academic literature. *Auditing: A Journal of Practice & Theory*, *27*(2), 231–252.

Huang, Y., & Scholz, S. (2012). Evidence on the association between financial restatements and auditor resignations. *Accounting Horizons*, *26*(3), 439–464

Kaplan, S.E., Pany, K., Samuels, J.A., & Zhang, J. (2009). An examination of the effects of procedural safeguards on intentions to anonymously report fraud. *Auditing: A Journal of Practice & Theory*, *28*(2), 273–288.

Kaplan, S.E., Pope, K.R., & Samuels, J.A. (2011). An examination of the effect of inquiry and auditor type on reporting intentions for fraud. *Auditing: A Journal of Practice & Theory*, *30*(4), 29–49.

Lee, C.-C., & Walker, R.B. (2008). Identification of perceived interviewee behaviours that influence auditors' assessment of deception. *International Journal of Auditing*, *12*, 205–220.

Lin, J.W., & Hwang, M.I. (2010). Audit quality, corporate governance, and earnings management: A meta-analysis. *International Journal of Auditing*, *14*(1), 57–77.

Lynch, A.L., Murthy, U.S., & Engle, T.J. (2009). Fraud brainstorming using computer-mediated communication: The effects of brainstorming technique and facilitation. *Accounting Review*, *84*(4), 1209–1232.

Perols, J. (2011). Financial statement fraud detection: An analysis of statistical and machine learning algorithms. *Auditing: A Journal of Practice & Theory*, *30*(2), 19–50.

Sharma, V.D., Sharma, D.S., & Ananthanarayanan, U. (2011). Client importance and earnings management: The moderating role of audit committees. *Auditing: A Journal of Practice & Theory*, *30*(3), 125–156.

Simon, C. (2012). Individual auditors' identification of relevant fraud schemes. *Auditing: A Journal of Practice & Theory*, *31*(1), 1–16.

Sitorus, T., & Scott, D. (2009). Integrated fraud risk factors and robust methodology: A review and comment. *International Journal of Auditing*, *13*(3), 281–297.

Srivastava, R.A., Mock, T.J., & Turner, J.L. (2009). Bayesian fraud risk formula for financial statement audits. *Abacus*, *45*(1), 66–87.

Tremblay, M.-S., & Gendron, Y. (2011). Governance prescriptions under trial: On the interplay between the logics of resistance and compliance in audit committees. *Critical Perspectives on Accounting*, *22*(3), 259–272.

Trotman, K.T., & Wright, W.F. (2012). Triangulation of audit evidence in fraud risk assessments. *Accounting, Organizations and Society*, *37*(1), 41–53.

Wright, W.F., & Berger, L. (2011). Fraudulent management explanations and impact of alternative presentations of client business evidence. *Auditing: A Journal of Practice & Theory*, *30*(2), 153–171.

APPENDIX

EXAMPLES OF FRAUD RISK FACTORS

Risk factors relating to misstatements arising from fraudulent financial reporting

Incentives/pressures

Financial stability or profitability is threatened by economic, industry or entity operating conditions such as (or as indicated by):

- High degree of competition or market saturation, accompanied by declining margins.
- Significant declines in customer demand and increasing business failures in either the industry or overall economy.

Excessive pressure exists for management to meet the requirements or expectations of third parties due to:

- Profitability or trend level expectations of investment analysts, institutional investors, significant creditors, or other external parties (particularly expectations that are unduly aggressive or unrealistic) including expectations created by management in, for example, overly optimistic press releases or annual report messages.
- Need to obtain additional debt or equity financing to stay competitive – including financing of major research and development or capital expenditures.

Opportunities

The nature of the industry or the entity's operations provides opportunities to engage in fraudulent financial reporting that can arise from:

- A strong financial pressure or ability to dominate a certain industry sector that allows the entity to dictate terms or conditions to suppliers or customers that may result in inappropriate or non-arm's length transactions.
- Significant related-party transactions not in the ordinary course of business or with related entities not audited or audited by another firm.

Internal control components are deficient as a result of:

- Inadequate monitoring of controls, including automated controls and controls over external interim financial reporting.
- High turnover rates or employment of accounting, internal audit, or information technology staff that are not reliable.

Attitudes/rationalizations

- Communication, implementation, support, or enforcement of the entity's values or ethical standards by management that are not effective, or the communication of inappropriate values or ethical standards.
- Non-financial management's excessive participation in, or preoccupation with, the selection of accounting policies or the determination of significant estimates.
- Excessive interest by management in maintaining or increasing the entity's share price or earnings trend.
- Management failing to remedy known significant deficiencies in internal control on a timely basis.

Risk factors relating to misstatements arising from misappropriation of assets

Incentives/pressures

- Personal financial obligations that create pressure on management or other employees with access to cash or other assets susceptible to misappropriation of those assets.

- Adverse relationships between the entity and employees with access to cash or other assets susceptible to theft, for example:
  - Recent or anticipated future employee layoffs or changes to employee compensation or pension plans;
  - Promotions, compensation or other rewards inconsistent with expectations.

Opportunities

Characteristics or circumstances which increase the susceptibility of assets to misappropriation, such as:
- Large amounts of cash on hand or processed;
- Inventory items that are small, of high value, or in high demand.

Inadequate internal controls over assets which increases their susceptibility to misappropriation, for example:
- Inadequate segregation of duties or independent checks;
- Inadequate oversight of senior management's expenditures, such as travel and other re-imbursements.

Attitudes/rationalizations

- Disregard of the need for monitoring or reducing risks relating to misappropriation of assets.
- Disregard for internal control over misappropriation of assets by overriding existing controls or by failing to take appropriate remedial action on known deficiencies in internal controls.
- Changes in behaviour or lifestyle that may indicate assets have been misappropriated.
- Tolerance of petty theft.

Source: ISA 240, Appendix 1.

7 Overview of the Audit Process, Audit Evidence, Staffing and Documenting an Audit

LEARNING OBJECTIVES

After studying the material in this chapter you should be able to:

- outline the steps in the audit process from 'Pre-engagement procedures' to 'Reporting';
- describe the procedures used to gather audit evidence;
- discuss the different sources of audit evidence;
- explain the factors auditors should consider when deciding which audit evidence to seek;
- discuss the requirements with respect to auditors' capabilities and competence;
- explain the importance of carefully assigning, directing, supervising and reviewing the work of engagement team members;
- explain the responsibilities of audit engagement partners when part of the audit work is performed by experts or other auditors;
- discuss the importance of audit documentation;
- explain the importance of reviewing audit documentation and how this is accomplished;
- describe auditors' responsibilities with respect to assembling and retaining audit documentation.

7.1 INTRODUCTION

In Chapter 5 we note that the primary responsibility of auditors in the United Kingdom (UK) is to form and express an opinion on whether or not their audit clients' financial statements provide a true and fair view of the entity's financial position and performance and are properly prepared in accordance with the applicable financial reporting framework and the Companies Act (CA) 2006.[1] In order to form this opinion, auditors must gather and evaluate sufficient appropriate audit evidence – evidence which is collected through the audit process. Although the audit process is similar in all audits, audit clients differ markedly in size, nature and complexity and, therefore, in order to ensure that each audit is conducted effectively and efficiently it must be carefully planned

---

[1] See Chapter 5, section 5.5.1.

and controlled. This involves, *inter alia*, ensuring the audit is properly staffed and documented.[2]

In the next seven chapters of this book we describe and discuss the various stages of the audit process. In this chapter we 'set the scene' by providing an overview of the process and discussing important administrative aspects of an audit. In particular, we examine the required capabilities and competence of auditors, the importance of engagement partners (and other senior members of the audit team) carefully assigning, directing, supervising and reviewing the work of engagement team members, and audit engagement partners' responsibilities when they use experts or other auditors to perform part of the audit. Before concluding the chapter we consider the content and importance of audit documentation and discuss (i) working paper review and (ii) assembling and retaining audit documentation.

7.2 OVERVIEW OF THE AUDIT PROCESS

As may be seen from Figure 7.1, the audit process comprises a series of logical steps; each step has a specific objective or purpose and is performed using appropriate audit procedures. However, the steps are not as distinct as Figure 7.1 might imply: instead, each complements the others as auditors gradually accumulate evidence to enable them to form an opinion about, *inter alia*, the truth and fairness of their auditees' financial statements. In order to illustrate the relationship between the audit steps, their objectives and the procedures used to achieve those objectives, we will refer to Step 4 of the audit process, that is: 'Gain an understanding of the client, its activities, circumstances and financial affairs. Plan the audit' (Figure 7.1).

What are the objectives of this step? Why is it performed? It is performed so as to ensure the auditor gains an understanding of:
- events, transactions and practices of (or affecting) the auditee which may have a significant impact on its financial statements; and
- how the events and transactions are reflected in the financial statements and whether, based on a preliminary analysis of the financial statements, anything 'looks wrong'.

The auditor needs this understanding, among other reasons:
- to ascertain whether there are circumstances which increase (or reduce) the likelihood of the financial statements containing material misstatements;

---

[2] As note in Chapter 3, an important aspect of ensuring audits are conducted effectively and efficiently is the implementation of, and adherence to, appropriate quality control policies and procedures. This issue is discussed in Chapter 16, section 16.3.

Figure 7.1: Summary of the audit process

Audit Step	Primary Objective	Example Procedures	Discussed in Chapter
1. Pre-engagement procedures	To ensure the client has integrity and the auditor is competent and has resources and time to complete the engagement and can comply with ethical requirements	Enquiry of relevant personnel inside and outside of the entity and of the incumbent auditor (if any)	8
2. Auditor's appointment at the annual 'accounts meeting' of shareholders*			5
3. Letter of engagement sent to client	To document the audit arrangements and to clarify matters that may be misunderstood	Gathering information about the client's industry and business; observation of the entity's operations, facilities and plant; enquiry of relevant personnel; inspection of manuals and legal and other documents; application of overall analytical procedures to the financial statements.	8
4. Gain an understanding of the client, its activities, circumstances and financial affairs. Plan the audit	To understand events, transactions and practices that may have a significant impact on the financial statements; identify and assess the risk of material misstatements; develop the overall audit strategy and audit plan		9
5. Gain an understanding of the accounting system and evaluate its internal controls	To understand how the accounting system 'works'; to identify strengths and deficiencies of internal controls	Observation, enquiry, completion of: - flow charts - narrative descriptions - internal control questionnaires 'Walk through' test	10
6. Test internal control strengths through compliance testing	To ascertain whether controls on which the auditor plans to rely to reduce substantive testing are functioning properly	Compliance testing. Examples: Looking for evidence of authorisation, review, reconciliation, etc	10
7. Test transactions and account balances through substantive testing	To evaluate the completeness, accuracy and validity of data produced by the accounting system	Substantive testing: (a) specific analytical procedures (b) tests of details. Examples: Confirmation with outside parties, recomputation, tracing forwards and backwards	11
8. Completion and review	To ensure sufficient appropriate evidence has been collected on which to base an opinion	Review for contingent liabilities and subsequent events. Review and evaluate audit evidence (with assistance from analytical procedures). Form an opinion on the truth and fairness of the financial statements	13
9. Reporting to: (a) Shareholders and other parties external to the entity	To inform shareholders and other interested parties of the opinion formed about (*inter alia*) the truth and fairness of the financial statements	Auditor's report	14
(b) Those charged with the entity's governance	To inform those charged with governance about the nature, scope and findings of the audit, deficiencies found in the accounting system and any other matters of concern. To offer advice on how the accounting system and its internal controls can be improved	Communication of audit matters to those charged with governance.	8
10. Auditor's continuance procedures and (re)appointment at the company's 'accounts meeting'			5

* Auditors of public companies in the UK are appointed at the shareholders' annual 'accounts meeting': private companies may appoint their auditor without such a meeting during the 'period for appointing auditors'. (see Chapter 5 section 5.3.2.).

- to assess the likelihood that material misstatements are present in the financial statements and to identify where, within the statements, they appear most likely to have occurred;
- to plan the audit (that is, develop the overall audit strategy and audit plan);[3]
- to provide a background against which evidence gathered during the audit can be evaluated to see if it 'makes sense' and 'looks right'.

How is this objective achieved? Audit procedures used to gain this understanding of the client include the following:
- Gathering information from a wide range of sources (including, for example, the Internet, relevant trade magazines, and making enquiries of relevant knowledgeable people) about the client's industry and its operating, economic, legislative and regulatory environment.
- Observing the client's operations, facilities and plant; i.e., visiting the client, touring the premises and meeting key personnel (for example, the managing and financial directors, and the marketing, sales, production and human resources managers).
- Making enquiries of relevant personnel; i.e., discussing with key personnel matters such as the trading and financial position of the entity during the past year and any significant changes in business, accounting or personnel policies and procedures which occurred during the year.
- Inspecting the entity's manuals and legal and other documents; i.e., reviewing the organisation's legal documents, policy and procedures manuals, minutes of directors' meetings and those of significant committees (especially the audit committee), and any important commercial and financial agreements (for example, franchise and loan agreements).
- Conducting analytical procedures which enable the auditor to form an initial assessment of the likelihood of material misstatements being present in the financial statements.

This audit step is supported, in particular, by step 5, that is, 'Gain an understanding of the accounting system and evaluate its internal controls' – the audit step that focuses on gaining a thorough understanding of the auditee's financial reporting process. Audit step 5 helps the auditor gain an in-depth understanding of the client; at the same time, audit step 4 (gaining an understanding of the client and its financial affairs) assists the auditor accomplish audit step 5. The steps are complementary and mutually supportive. As auditors proceed through the audit process, they seek confirmatory – or contradictory – evidence that supports – or brings into question – the opinion they are gradually forming about their auditee's financial statements (and other matters on which they are required to express an opinion: see Chapter 5, section 5.5.1).

---

[3] Planning the audit is discussed in Chapter 9.

It should be noted that the summary of the audit process presented in Figure 7.1 is designed to give a general overview of the process. It is intended to provide a contextual setting for the detailed discussion of the individual steps in the process which are the subject of Chapters 8 to 14 of this book. The chapter in which each audit step is discussed is indicated in the extreme right column of Figure 7.1. However, before moving on to discuss the collection of audit evidence, we need to clarify the meaning of some troublesome jargon.

7.3 CLARIFICATION OF SOME JARGON

7.3.1 Audit objectives and audit procedures

There appears to be considerable confusion about the terms 'audit objectives' and 'audit procedures'. This seems to stem from three main causes:
- (i) the use of different terms to mean the same thing;
- (ii) the failure to distinguish between audit objectives and audit procedures;
- (iii) the use of the single term 'audit objective' when separate levels of objectives exist.

(i) *Use of different terms to mean the same thing:* This cause of confusion may be illustrated by reference to the use of the terms 'audit procedures' and 'audit tests' to convey the same meaning; that is, methods used to gather audit evidence. Indeed, the terms are frequently used interchangeably.

(ii) *Failure to distinguish between audit objectives and audit procedures:* The term 'compliance procedures' provides an example of this cause of misunderstanding. The term refers to audit procedures which are used to meet the objective of ascertaining whether audit client personnel have complied with identified internal controls. The audit procedures adopted (such as enquiry and observation) are not restricted to compliance testing: they are also used to meet other audit objectives. Thus, the term 'compliance procedures' does not denote a particular set of audit procedures; rather, it indicates the objective or purpose for which the procedures are employed.

(iii) *Use of the single term 'audit objective' when separate levels of objectives exist:* Notwithstanding use of the term 'audit objective', as shown in Figure 7.2, three distinct levels of audit objectives may be distinguished: overall, general and specific audit objectives.

An audit objective is what the auditor is trying to find out – the purpose for which audit procedures are performed. It is often helpful to express an audit objective in the form of a question. From Figure 7.2 it can be seen that at the highest level is the overall audit objective. This is

Figure 7.2:   Hierarchy of audit objectives

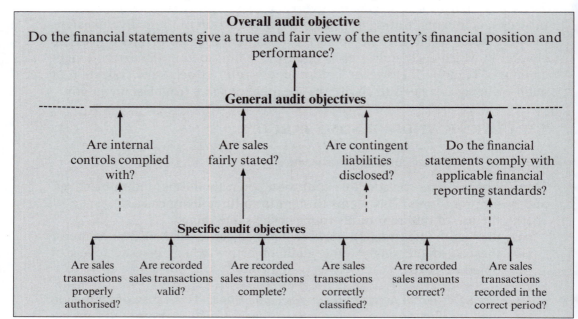

reflected in the question: Do the financial statements give a true and fair view of the entity's financial position and performance?

In order to answer this question, and thus accomplish the overall audit objective, further, more detailed, questions need to be asked. For example, do the financial statements comply with financial reporting standards? Have the entity's internal controls operated effectively throughout the reporting period? Is the amount shown in the financial statements for, say, sales or accounts receivable fairly stated? Questions of this general nature reflect general audit objectives.

To accomplish these general objectives, even more specific questions need to be asked. These are expressions of the specific audit objectives. For example, to accomplish the general objective of ascertaining whether sales are fairly stated in the financial statements, the auditor needs to determine whether:

- sales transactions have been properly authorised;
- recorded sales transactions are valid;
- all valid sales transactions have been recorded;
- sales transactions have been correctly classified;
- sales transactions have been recorded at their correct amount;

- sales transactions have been recorded in their proper accounting period.

Each of these factors constitutes a specific audit objective.[4]

7.3.2 Compliance vs substantive procedures

A further area of confusion is the distinction between compliance and substantive procedures. The relationship between these terms and some specific audit procedures is shown in Figure 7.3.

In order to form an opinion on whether or not the auditee's financial statements give a true and fair view of its financial position and performance and comply with the applicable financial reporting framework and CA 2006, the auditor needs to establish whether each financial statement amount and disclosure is fairly stated (i.e., not materially misstated).

Auditors can reduce their work in determining this if they can assure themselves that the auditee's financial reporting system incorporates internal controls that can be relied upon to prevent or detect errors and irregularities in the accounting data. If such controls are in place and working effectively, the auditor can feel reasonably assured that the accounting data passing through the system and presented in the financial statements do not contain material misstatements.

Thus, an audit includes the following three distinct steps:

(i) *Gaining an understanding of the financial reporting system* [see Figure 7.3(i)]: This enables the auditor:
- to understand how the financial reporting system captures and processes the accounting data and how it converts the data into the information which is presented in the entity's financial statements;
- to identify internal control 'strengths' and 'deficiencies' within the financial reporting system; that is, internal controls which, if operating properly, can be relied upon to prevent or detect errors and irregularities in the accounting data (strengths), and internal controls which are needed but which are absent or ineffective (deficiencies).

In order to test the 'correctness' of his/her understanding of the financial reporting system and its internal controls, the auditor conducts a 'walk

---

[4] As we explain in Chapter 11, each of these specific objectives is linked to an assertion. In its *Glossary of Terms*, the International Federation of Accountants (IFAC; 2009) defines 'assertions' as: "Representations by management, explicit or otherwise, that are embodied in the financial statements . . .".

Figure 7.3: Relationship between compliance and substantive procedures, tests of details, tests of transactions and tests of balances

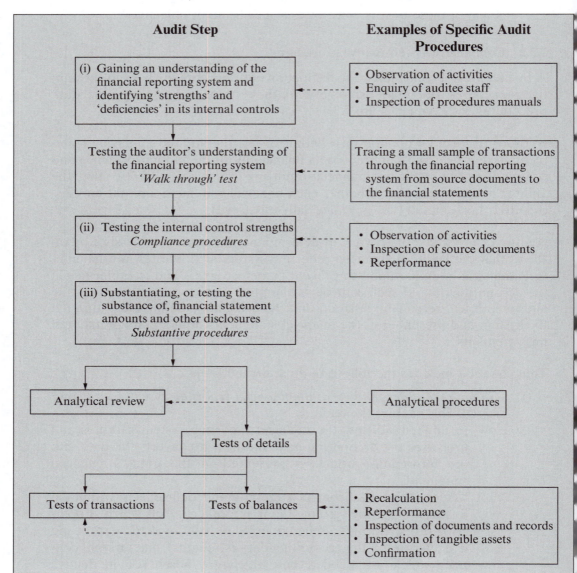

through' test. This involves following a small number of transactions through the entire financial reporting system – from their initial recording on source documents to their final inclusion in the financial statements.

(ii) *Testing internal control 'strengths'* [see Figure 7.3(ii)]: As noted above, while gaining an understanding of the financial reporting system, the auditor identifies internal control 'strengths'. These controls, if operating effectively, help to ensure that the accounting data is complete, valid, and accurate as to amount, account classification and reporting period. However, before the auditor can rely on these controls to protect the integrity of the accounting data, they must be tested to establish that they are, in fact, operating effectively and have been so operating throughout the reporting period. Such tests are referred to as compliance procedures (or tests of control): they are tests or procedures which are performed in order to ascertain whether the controls on which the auditor plans to rely to prevent or, failing this, to detect errors or irregularities in the accounting data have been complied with by personnel within the reporting entity.[5]

(iii) *Testing the financial statement amounts and other disclosures* [see Figure 7.3(iii)]: The auditor's primary responsibility is to form and express an opinion on the truth and fairness of the financial statements and their compliance (or otherwise) with the applicable financial reporting framework and CA 2006. As we explain in Chapter 10 (section 10.3.6), all systems of internal control have inherent limitations – for example, the possibility of human error and the ability of management to override the controls. Therefore, compliance procedures can never constitute sufficient appropriate audit evidence and, irrespective of how effective an entity's internal controls may appear to be, tests must always be performed to substantiate, or to test the substance of, the amounts and other disclosures in the financial statements. Such tests are referred to as substantive procedures.[6]

7.3.3 Tests of detail, tests of transactions and tests of balances

Substantive procedures constitute a further area of confusion. As indicated in Figure 7.3, these procedures fall into two broad categories:

(i) analytical procedures;
(ii) tests of details.

---

[5] Compliance procedures are discussed in detail in Chapter 10, section 10.6.

[6] Substantive procedures are discussed in detail in Chapter 11, section 11.3.

(i) *Analytical procedures:* These procedures (which include ratio, trend and comparative analysis) facilitate the examination of meaningful relationships between financial data, and between financial and non-financial data.[7] As a substantive procedure, they are used primarily to establish the reasonableness of financial statement amounts. For example, the relationship between average debt and average interest rates may provide an estimate of an entity's interest expense. If, based on this estimate, the interest expense in the draft financial statements looks 'reasonable' (i.e., not materially misstated), this may be the extent of the audit tests conducted to substantiate this balance. If, however, there is a marked discrepancy between the estimated amount and the amount shown in the draft financial statements, the discrepancy will need to be investigated. For other account balances, such as accounts receivable or inventory, analytical procedures may be used to establish whether or not the balances shown in the draft financial statements look 'reasonable' or materially misstated and, thereby, they affect the nature and extent of further tests which need to be performed to substantiate these balances.

(ii) *Tests of details:* As may be seen from Figure 7.3, two subsets of tests of details may be distinguished, namely, tests of transactions and tests of balances.

- *Tests of transactions* are audit tests (or procedures) which are applied to classes of transactions (such as credit sales or wages) or, more correctly, to the source documents which provide evidence of the transactions. Transaction testing is normally used to substantiate revenue and expense account balances in the income statement. The opening balance of these accounts is zero and all the transactions affecting the account are similar in nature – and, therefore, are relatively straightforward to test. If the transactions affecting an account during the reporting period are complete, accurate and valid, then logically the balance shown in the income statement must also be correct.

- *Tests of balances* are audit tests (or procedures) which directly test the completeness, accuracy and validity of financial statement balances (rather than testing the transactions which constitute those balances). Such tests are frequently used to substantiate the balances of accounts in the statement of financial position. An example

---

[7] Analytical procedures are used in three stages of an audit:
    (i) during the initial stages, to assess the likelihood of material misstatement in the financial statements;
    (ii) as a substantive procedure;
    (iii) during the 'completion and review' stage.
These different uses of analytical procedures are discussed in Chapters 9, 11 and 13, respectively.

is the confirmation of accounts receivable whereby the auditor writes to a sample of the auditee's accounts receivable asking them to confirm their outstanding account balance with the audit client.[8]

In relation to tests of transactions, it is pertinent to note that source documents used to substantiate the completeness, accuracy and validity of a class of transactions may also be used for compliance tests. For example, a customer order and related despatch note may be used to substantiate the validity of a sale (a substantive test). The same source documents might also be examined for evidence indicating that an internal control, designed to ensure that despatches of goods are only made against customer orders, has been complied with (that is, for compliance testing).

7.4 AUDIT EVIDENCE

7.4.1 General requirement

As auditors proceed through the audit process they accumulate audit evidence to meet specific audit objectives and thereby form conclusions about the related general audit objectives. Eventually, they will have sufficient appropriate audit evidence to meet the overall audit objective, that is, to support their opinion about the truth and fairness of the financial statements and their compliance (or otherwise) with the applicable financial reporting framework and CA 2006. The importance of auditors accumulating sufficient appropriate audit evidence is explained in International Standard on Auditing (ISA) 200: *Overall Objectives of the Independent Auditor and the Conduct of an Audit in Accordance with International Standards on Auditing* [International Auditing and Assurance Standards Board (IAASB) 2009b] which states:

> . . . the auditor [is required] to obtain reasonable assurance about whether the financial statements as a whole are free from material misstatement . . . Reasonable assurance . . . is obtained when the auditor has obtained sufficient appropriate audit evidence to reduce audit risk (that is, the risk that the auditor expresses an inappropriate opinion when the financial statements are materially misstated) to an acceptably low level. (para 5)

In Chapter 3 (section 3.4.1) we note that 'sufficiency' refers to the quantity of evidence and 'appropriateness' refers to its relevance and reliability.

7.4.2 Audit procedures

As we observe in section 7.3.1, audit procedures are the methods used to gather audit evidence. ISA 500: *Audit Evidence* (IAASB, 2009e) identifies seven audit procedures and explains them as follows:

---

[8] Confirmation of accounts receivable balances is explained in Chapter 11, section 11.8.

Inspection

Inspection involves examining records or documents, whether internal or external, in paper form, electronic form or other media, or a physical examination of an asset. Inspection of records and documents provides audit evidence of varying degrees of reliability, depending on their nature and source and, in the case of internal records and documents, on the effectiveness of the controls over their production. An example of inspection used as a test of controls is inspection of records for evidence of authorization. (para A14)

Some documents represent direct evidence of the existence of an asset, for example, a document constituting a financial instrument such as a stock [i.e., shares] or bond. Inspection of such documents may not necessarily provide audit evidence about ownership or value. In addition, inspecting an executed contract may provide audit evidence relevant to the entity's application of accounting policies, such as revenue recognition. (para A15)

Inspection of tangible assets may provide reliable audit evidence with respect to their existence, but not necessarily about the entity's rights and obligations or the valuation of the assets. Inspection of individual inventory items may accompany the observation of inventory counting. (para A16)

Observation

Observation consists of looking at a process or procedure being performed by others, for example, the auditor's observation of inventory counting by the entity's personnel, or of the performance of control activities. Observation provides audit evidence about the performance of a process or procedure, but is limited to the point in time at which the observation takes place, and by the fact that the act of being observed may affect how the process or procedure is performed. (para A17)

External Confirmation

An external confirmation represents audit evidence obtained by the auditor as a direct written response to the auditor from a third party (the confirming party), in paper form, or by electronic or other medium. External confirmation procedures frequently are relevant when addressing assertions associated with certain account balances and their elements. However, external confirmations need not be restricted to account balances only. For example, the auditor may request confirmation of the terms of agreements or transactions an entity has with third parties; the confirmation request is designed to ask if any modifications have been made to the agreement and, if so, what the relevant details are. External confirmation procedures are also used to obtain audit evidence about the absence of certain conditions, for example, the absence of a "side agreement"[9] that may influence revenue recognition. (para A18)

Recalculation

Recalculation consists of checking the mathematical accuracy of documents or records. Recalculation may be performed manually or electronically. (para A19)

---

[9] A 'side agreement' is an agreement between the audited entity and a customer which enables the entity to inflate revenue. For example, the entity may enter into a side agreement with a customer whereby a significant item is 'sold' to the customer but the entity agrees to repurchase it (at a profit to the 'customer') if the customer is unable to sell the item within a specified period.

Reperformance

Reperformance involves the auditor's independent execution of procedures or controls that were originally performed as part of the entity's internal control. (para A20)

Analytical Procedures

Analytical procedures consist of evaluations of financial information through analysis of plausible relationships among both financial and non-financial data. Analytical procedures also encompass such investigation as is necessary of identified fluctuations and relationships that are inconsistent with other relevant information or that differ from expected values by a significant amount. (para A21)

Inquiry

Inquiry consists of seeking information of knowledgeable persons, both financial and non-financial, within the entity or outside the entity. Inquiry is used extensively throughout the audit in addition to other audit procedures. Inquiries may range from formal written inquiries to informal oral inquiries. Evaluating responses to inquiries is an integral part of the inquiry process. (para A22)

Responses to inquiries may provide the auditor with information not previously possessed or with corroborative audit evidence. Alternatively, responses might provide information that differs significantly from other information that the auditor has obtained, for example, information regarding the possibility of management override of controls. In some cases, responses to inquiries provide a basis for the auditor to modify or perform additional audit procedures. (para A23)

7.4.3   Different sources and types of audit evidence

We note in Chapter 3 that auditors generally examine only part of the evidence available to them. They may select evidence from different sources and of different types. Which evidence they decide to collect depends on a number of factors, in particular, its relevance, reliability, availability, timeliness and cost.

- *Relevance* of evidence refers to how closely the evidence relates to the particular objective the auditor is trying to accomplish. For example, observation is a useful procedure for verifying the existence, but not the ownership, of tangible assets. To establish ownership, relevant purchase (or similar) documents need to be scrutinised.

- *Reliability* of evidence refers to how confident the auditor can be that the evidence reflects the facts of the matter being investigated. For example, the auditor can have greater confidence in bank reconciliations performed by a member of the audit team than in assurances from client personnel that the entity's bank statements and bank balances have been correctly reconciled. In general, audit evidence is more reliable when:
  - it is obtained directly by the auditor (that is, by a member of the audit team); for example, audit team member(s) observing

the operation of an internal control provides more reliable audit evidence than enquiring of entity personnel about the operation of the control;
- it is obtained from independent sources outside, rather than from inside, the entity;
- it exists in documentary form, whether paper, electronic or other medium; for example, written minutes of a meeting are more reliable than a subsequent oral report of the matters discussed;[10]
- it is derived from original documents rather than from photocopies or facsimiles;
- for internally generated evidence, the related internal controls are (and have been) operating effectively.

- *Availability* of evidence refers to how readily the auditor can acquire the evidence. For example, the auditor has ready access to the client's accounting records – including, for example, the balances of the entity's bank accounts. Evidence of the validity of these balances, obtained by confirming them by writing to the banks concerned, is less readily available.

- *Timeliness* of evidence refers to how quickly the evidence can be obtained. For example, the auditor may be aware that the amount of a contingent liability arising from the client breaching environmental regulations will be clarified when the case is decided in a court of law. However, if the case is to be deferred for some months, the auditor may decide to forgo that evidence and rely on an estimated amount. If audited financial statements are to be useful to external parties interested in the reporting entity, they must be made available – and hence the audit must be completed – on a timely basis.[11]

- *Cost* of evidence. The auditor generally has a choice of evidence which may be used to establish, for example, whether an internal control has been complied with or a financial statement amount is fairly stated. Therefore, the cost of obtaining particular evidence should be weighed against its benefits, that is, the contribution the evidence may make towards the auditor forming an opinion about the level of compliance with the internal control, or the truth and fairness of the financial statement amount, under investigation.

---

[10] However, it is pertinent to observe that minutes of meetings do not always portray accurately what was said during the meeting. A request can (and often is) made for certain observations and/or remarks not to be minuted!

[11] Further, as we note in Chapter 5, section 5.2.3, companies must file their audited financial statements with the Registrar of Companies within six or nine months (for public and private companies, respectively) of the end of their financial year.

Reviewing the above factors it may be seen that, with the exception of relevance, they are all affected by the source from which the evidence is derived. As shown in Figure 7.4, audit evidence may be obtained from three sources:
- (i) direct personal knowledge of members of the audit team;
- (ii) sources external to the client;
- (iii) sources internal to the client.

Evidence obtained by audit team members' direct personal knowledge is the most reliable, is generally readily available on a timely basis, but is very costly to acquire. At the other extreme, evidence obtained from sources internal to the client is the least reliable but is generally readily available on a timely basis and is the least costly to obtain. Evidence derived from sources external to the client has an intermediate placing in terms of reliability and cost but is frequently less readily available and is less timely to acquire than evidence obtained from the other two sources (see Figure 7.4).

We note in section 7.4.1 that auditors are required to obtain sufficient appropriate audit evidence to be reasonably assured that the audited financial statements do not contain an unidentified material misstatement. However, what amounts to sufficient appropriate evidence varies with the circumstances of each audit client and each audit engagement. It depends on a wide range of factors including:
- the auditor's assessment of the risk of material misstatement at the overall financial statement level and at the assertion level for classes

Figure 7.4: Sources of evidence and accompanying characteristics

	Sources of evidence		
	Direct personal knowledge	**External to the client**	**Internal to the client**
Examples / **Characteristics of evidence***	• *Observation* • *Reperformance*	• *Confirmation from third parties* • *Documents (e.g. invoices) from third parties*	• *Accounting records* • *Responses to enquiries by auditee personnel*
Reliability	High level of reliability	High to medium level of reliability	Low level of reliability
Availability	Readily available	Less readily available	Readily available
Timeliness	Available on a timely basis	May not be available on a timely basis	Available on a timely basis
Cost	High cost	High to medium cost	Low cost

* Relevance of evidence is excluded from the characteristics as it is dependent on the audit objective to be met, not the source of the evidence.

of transactions, account balances and other financial statement disclosures;[12]
- the auditor's assessment of the effectiveness of the entity's financial reporting system and its internal controls;
- the significance of the internal control, or financial statement amount or disclosure, being examined;
- the findings of audit procedures already performed, including any indication that fraud or non-compliance with other laws or regulations may have occurred;
- the source and reliability of the evidence obtained.

Factors such as those outlined above also affect the nature, timing and extent of audit procedures performed during an audit. These terms are explained as follows:

- *The nature of audit procedures* refers to the type of audit procedures to be performed. Whether, for example, emphasis should be placed on compliance or substantive tests and, in either case, which procedures from those set out in section 7.4.2 above are the most appropriate to meet the particular audit objective.

- *The timing of audit procedures* refers to when the selected procedures are to be performed. Should they be performed prior to the entity's year end in an 'interim audit', or should they be performed shortly after the end of the entity's financial year in the 'final audit'. For example, if, in previous audits, an audit client was found to have an effective system of internal control, and the auditor's initial review of the controls indicates that the system has continued to operate effectively during the current financial year, some audit procedures (particularly compliance tests) may be performed during an interim audit, two or three months before the auditee's year end.

- *The extent of audit procedures* refers to how extensive audit testing needs to be to achieve an audit objective; that is, how many different audit procedures should be performed and the extensiveness of each. For example, in order to test whether the auditee's employees have complied with an internal control, should observation and/or enquiry and/or inspection of records or documents be used? To what extent should the relevant employees be observed or questioned? How large should the sample of documents inspected be?

Notwithstanding that the factors indicated above (and other similar factors) affect what qualifies as 'sufficient appropriate evidence' in a particular audit engagement, for any given set of circumstances there is a trade-off between

---

[12] We discuss the risks at these two levels in Chapter 9, section 9.3.1.

Figure 7.5: Sufficient appropriate evidence trade-off

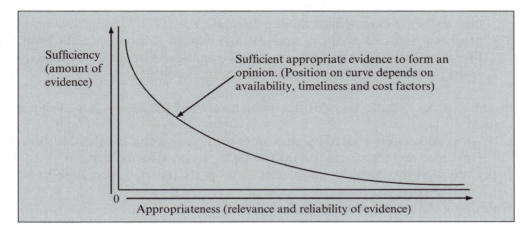

the quantity of evidence required (its sufficiency) and its relevance and reliability (its appropriateness). The greater the relevance and reliability of evidence, the less that is needed to enable the auditor to form an opinion about the truth and fairness of the financial statements (and *vice versa*). This trade-off is depicted in Figure 7.5. All points on the curve represent combinations of quantity and quality of evidence which meet the 'sufficient appropriate' requirement. The particular combination the auditor selects will be affected by consideration of factors such as the availability, timeliness and cost of the evidence. The auditor will seek the combination which will provide a sufficient amount of reliable evidence, relevant to the objective being sought, within a reasonable time – at the lowest possible total cost.

7.5 STAFFING AN AUDIT

7.5.1 Audit team personnel

Having discussed some important aspects of audit evidence, we need to consider who collects this evidence. Although the audit engagement partner has responsibility for the audit engagement, an audit engagement team (varying from two or three to 20 or more people – depending on the size, complexity and specific circumstances of the audit) is usually involved in collecting the audit evidence.

When considering audit teams we need to distinguish between three categories of audit personnel, namely:
  • *the audit engagement partner* – the person who is responsible for the audit and its performance and who signs the audit report;

- *audit staff* – the professional staff members employed by the audit firm who work on the audit. They range from new entrants to the firm (trainees) to highly experienced audit managers;
- *other auditors and experts* – auditors and experts from outside the audit firm who, for a variety of reasons, may be employed by the audit engagement partner to perform some part(s) of the audit.

In order for an audit to be performed effectively and efficiently, it is essential that:

(i) it is adequately staffed by personnel who possess the capabilities, competence and time required for the tasks to be performed, and

(ii) the work assigned to audit staff is properly directed, supervised and reviewed.

We examine these two requirements below.

7.5.2 The audit engagement team's capabilities and competence[13]

In order to perform an audit to the required standard, an audit engagement team must possess the necessary capabilities and competence. The audit firm and the engagement partner share responsibility for ensuring an audit engagement is adequately staffed by appropriate personnel.

At the firm level, International Standard on Quality Control (ISQC) 1: *Quality Control for Firms that Perform Audits and Reviews of Financial Statements . . .* (IAASB, 2009a) requires each audit firm to establish policies and procedures which are designed to provide reasonable assurance that a new or continuing audit engagement will only be accepted if the firm has the capabilities, competence, time and resources to complete the engagement to the required standard within a reasonable timeframe. In particular, the firm is to consider whether:

- firm personnel have knowledge of the client's industry (or industries) and have experience with relevant regulatory and reporting requirements or the ability to gain the necessary knowledge and skills;
- the firm has sufficient personnel with the capabilities and competence required for the audit engagement;
- experts are available, if needed;
- suitably qualified individuals to perform an engagement quality control review are available;[14]
- the firm is able to complete the engagement within the reporting deadline (paras 29, A18).

---

[13] The concepts of capabilities and competence are discussed in chapter 3, section 3.2.2.

[14] Engagement quality control reviews are explained in section 7.6.4.

The firm is also responsible for assigning responsibility for each audit engagement to an engagement partner. In so doing, the firm should ensure:
- the identity and role of the engagement partner are communicated to key members of the audit client's management;[15]
- the engagement partner has the appropriate capabilities, competence, authority and time to perform the role;
- the engagement partner's responsibilities are clearly defined and communicated to the partner concerned.

Additionally, the firm should ensure that audit staff assigned to an engagement have the necessary capabilities, competence and time to perform the audit in accordance with professional standards and regulatory and legal requirements, and to enable the engagement partner to issue an appropriate audit report (ISQC 1, paras 30, 31).

Once appointed to an audit engagement, the engagement partner is responsible for ensuring the audit team is appropriately constituted. This is reflected in the Auditing Practices Board's (APB) Ethical Standard (ES) 4: *Fees, Remuneration and Evaluation Policies, Litigation, Gifts and Hospitality* (APB, 2010), which requires an audit engagement partner:

> [to] be satisfied and able to demonstrate that the audit engagement has assigned to it sufficient partners and staff with appropriate time and skill to perform the audit in accordance with all applicable Auditing and Ethical Standards, irrespective of the audit fee to be charged. (para 5)

Along similar lines, ISA 220: *Quality Control for an Audit of Financial Statements* (IAASB, 2009c) requires the audit engagement partner to be satisfied that, collectively, the engagement team and any external experts and other auditors who are to perform part of the audit work have the appropriate capabilities and competence to perform the audit in accordance with professional standards and regulatory and legal requirements, and to enable an appropriate audit report to be issued.[16]

ISA 220 (para A11) explains that the capabilities and competence expected of the engagement team as a whole include:
- an understanding of, and practical experience with, audit engagements of a similar nature and complexity acquired through appropriate training and participation;

---

[15] Readers are reminded that in the Preface to this book we note the term 'management' is defined to mean a company's executive directors, non-executive directors and non-director executives (that is, all executives and directors).

[16] The engagement partner must also (i) be satisfied that engagement team members comply with the ethical requirements of integrity, objectivity, professional competence and due care, confidentiality and professional behaviour and (ii) remain alert to any evidence of non-compliance with these requirements (ISA 220, paras 9, A4). These ethical principles are discussed in Chapter 3.

- an understanding of professional standards and applicable legal and regulatory requirements;
- appropriate technical knowledge and expertise, including knowledge of relevant information technology and specialised areas of accounting or auditing;
- knowledge of industries in which the client operates;
- the ability to apply professional judgment;
- an understanding of the firm's quality control policies and procedures.

It should be noted that it is not necessary for all audit team members to possess all of the capabilities and competencies required for a particular audit; they need to be possessed by the team as a whole. For most audits, the engagement partner and other senior audit team members are expected to possess the capabilities and competencies outlined above but junior team members are unlikely to do so. Nevertheless, for some audits, particularly those of a highly specialised or technical nature, even senior and experienced members of the engagement team may not possess all of the required skills. In such circumstances, the engagement partner (and audit firm) should ensure that the required expertise is available, and secured, at the appropriate time. If, for example, the audit firm lacks the competence needed to perform specialised aspects of an audit, technical advice may be sought from experts such as lawyers, actuaries, engineers and valuers. External experts would probably be required to assist in the audit of – say – a company specialising in jewellery manufacture. If the audit firm lacks the competence to evaluate the company's valuation of, say, its inventory of diamonds, the auditor may (indeed, should!) seek assistance from a diamond valuation expert. If the firm does not possess, and cannot acquire, the necessary skills and/or competence to perform or complete a particular audit engagement to the required standard within a reasonable timeframe, the engagement should be declined or discontinued (as applicable).

7.5.3   Assigning, directing, supervising and reviewing the work of audit staff

(a) *Assigning audit work*

In section 7.5.2 we noted that:
- audit firms are required to ensure that staff assigned to an audit engagement have the necessary capabilities and competence to perform the audit in accordance with professional standards and regulatory and legal requirements; and
- the audit engagement partner must be satisfied that, collectively, the engagement team possesses such capabilities and competence.

However, if the audit engagement is to be conducted effectively and efficiently, not only must the audit team possess the required capabilities and competence but the work assigned to individual engagement team members must also be commensurate with their particular capabilities and competence. For example, areas of significant audit risk (aspects of the audit where the risk of material misstatement is such that they require special audit attention) should be assigned to more experienced engagement team members rather than to trainees. Nevertheless, it is also important that trainees and other junior audit team members receive 'on the job' training to enable them to develop their capabilities and competence. It is equally important that the audit is conducted to a high standard. In order to achieve these goals, engagement partners need to ensure that audit work is carefully directed, supervised and reviewed.

(b) Directing audit work

At a simple level, 'direction' means informing audit staff of their responsibilities and the tasks they are to perform. However, in the auditing context it also involves:

- ensuring engagement team members understand the need to comply with relevant ethical requirements and for the audit to be planned and performed with an attitude of professional scepticism; and
- providing engagement team members with background information about the client and the audit so they can understand the importance and context of the work they are asked to perform.

Audit staff should, for example, be provided with information about the nature of the entity's business and risk-related issues, accounting or auditing problems that may arise, details of the approach to the performance of the audit, and the objectives of the work they are to perform. ISA 220 suggests that discussion among engagement team members is particularly useful in helping more junior staff members understand what is required of them in the performance of their audit work. It states:

> Appropriate teamwork and training assist less experienced members of the engagement team to clearly understand the objectives of the assigned work. . . . Discussion among members of the engagement team allows less experienced team members to raise questions with more experienced team members so that appropriate communication can occur within the engagement team. (paras A13, A14)

Free and frank communication between audit team members is vitally important for both the performance of a high quality audit and the personal development of audit staff: it facilitates audit team members clarifying matters when they have incomplete understanding and seeking advice or guidance, when needed, on appropriate action(s) in particular circumstances. It also helps to ensure that all members of the audit team remain informed of significant matters, including unexpected results of audit procedures or other findings, relating to the auditee and the audit engagement.

(c) Supervision of audit work

Appropriately assigning audit work to engagement team members and giving them direction on the work they are to perform is not the end of the story – the work needs to be properly supervised to ensure it is performed appropriately. ISA 220 (para A15) explains that supervision by the engagement partner includes:

- monitoring the progress of the audit engagement;
- considering the capabilities and competence of individual members of the engagement team and whether they:
    - have sufficient time to carry out their work,
    - understand their instructions, and
    - are carrying out their work in accordance with the audit plan;
- ensuring engagement team members recognise matters which require consultation[17] or consideration by more experienced team members;
- addressing significant issues arising during the engagement, considering their significance and, if necessary, appropriately, modifying the audit plan.

However, supervision of audit work is not only the task of the engagement partner. More senior members of the engagement team should also be assigned responsibility for supervising the work of more junior members along similar lines to that required of the engagement partner for the engagement as a whole.

(d) Reviewing audit work

Once audit work is completed by an audit staff member, it needs to be reviewed, on a timely basis, by a more experienced engagement team member. The reviewer should consider, amongst other things, whether:

- the work has been performed in accordance with professional standards and applicable regulatory and legal requirements;
- specified audit objectives have been met by the audit procedures performed;
- the work performed and results obtained support the conclusions reached;
- unexpected findings or difficult matters encountered have been raised for further consideration and, where necessary, appropriate consultation has taken place and the resulting conclusions have been documented and implemented;
- the results of audit procedures indicate a need to revise the planned nature, timing and/or extent of audit procedures;

---

[17] The meaning and importance of 'consultation' are explained in Chapter 16, section 16.3.

- the audit work performed, results obtained and conclusions reached are adequately documented (ISA 220, para A17).

The review of audit work is, in general, not a remote and post-event process. Rather, upon its completion, those who have performed the work discuss it directly with their supervisor (a more senior audit team member). This enables the reviewer to question the more junior staff member about the work performed and results obtained – and this, in turn, enables any audit issues to be identified and followed up on a timely basis. It also facilitates developing the capabilities and competence of, and providing training for, the more junior staff member.

The provisions of ISQC 1 and ISA 220 relating to staffing an audit are clearly very important. If an audit is to be conducted effectively, efficiently and with due professional care, but most of the work is to be performed by audit staff, it is essential that care is taken to ensure that work delegated to the staff members:
- is within their capabilities and competence to perform, and
- is carefully directed, supervised and reviewed.

If these responsibilities are not discharged properly, the audit is in danger of being performed inadequately and the door may be opened to allegations of negligence.

7.5.4 Using the work of experts and other auditors

In a significant number of audits, especially those of large and complex companies, and of companies in specialised industries, experts and/or other auditors are frequently used to perform part of the audit work. However, irrespective of the assistance provided by such parties, the audit engagement partner remains responsible for all aspects of the audit and the opinion expressed in the audit report. It is, therefore, important that the engagement partner:

(i) is satisfied that the expert(s) or other auditor(s) whose work is to be used in the audit
  – possess the capabilities and competence needed to perform the relevant tasks, and
  – are independent of the audit client and conduct their work objectively;
(ii) is reasonably assured that the work is performed to the appropriate standard.

In order to meet the above requirements in respect of experts, ISA 620: *Using the Work of an Auditor's Expert* (IAASB, 2009g) requires auditors:

(a) to evaluate whether the expert has the necessary competence, capabilities and objectivity for the purposes of the audit. To achieve this, auditors may consider, *inter alia*, information derived from sources such as:
  - personal experience of previous work performed by the expert;
  - discussions with the expert, and with other auditors and others who are familiar with the expert's work;
  - knowledge of the expert's qualifications, membership of a professional body or industry association, licence to practice or other forms of external recognition;
  - published papers or books by the expert (paras 9, A15);
(b) to be satisfied that no relationship exists between the expert and the client that may create a threat to the expert's objectivity that cannot be reduced to an acceptable level by the application of available safeguards (paras 9, A19);
(c) to obtain an understanding of the expert's field of expertise including, for example:
  - whether any professional or other standards, and regulatory or legal requirements, apply;
  - the assumptions made, and methods used, by the expert, and whether these are generally accepted within the expert's field and are appropriate for financial reporting purposes;
  - the nature of internal and external data and information used by the expert (para 10, A22);
(d) to agree with the expert, usually in writing:
  - the nature, scope and objectives of the work the expert is to perform;
  - the respective roles of the auditor and the expert; for example, whether:
    - the auditor or the expert will undertake detailed testing of source data,
    - the expert consents to the auditor discussing his/her findings with the entity and other third parties, and (if appropriate) to including details of the findings in a modified audit report,[18]
    - the auditor and expert will have access to each other's working papers;
  - the nature, timing and extent of communication between the auditor and the expert so as to ensure the work done by the expert is properly integrated with other audit work;

---

[18] Anything other than a 'clean' (i.e., unmodified) audit report is termed a 'modified' audit report. Modified audit reports are discussed in Chapter 14, section 14.4.

- the form of any report to be provided by the expert (paras 11, A28–A30);
(e) to evaluate the adequacy of the expert's work for the purposes of the audit, including:
    - the relevance and reasonableness of the expert's:
        - assumptions and methods, and
        - findings and their consistency with other audit evidence;
    - if significant to the expert's work, the relevance, accuracy and completeness of source data used by the expert.

In order to evaluate the adequacy of the expert's work, the auditor may, for example:

- make enquiries of the expert;
- review the expert's working papers;
- observe the expert's work;
- confirm relevant matters with third parties;
- discuss with another expert with relevant expertise any of the expert's findings which are not consistent with other audit evidence;
- discuss the expert's report with the audit client's management (paras 12, A33).

If the engagement partner concludes the expert's work is not adequate for the purposes of the audit, s/he is required to:

(a) agree with the expert the nature and extent of further work the expert is to perform; or
(b) perform further audit procedures appropriate to the circumstances (ISA 620, para 13).

Similar conditions apply when an auditor relies on the work of another auditor. This may arise, for example, when a branch, division or subsidiary (i.e., 'a component') of the audit client is located at a distant geographical location and the auditor relies on another auditor (the 'component auditor') to gather evidence in relation to that component. ISA 600: *Special Considerations – Audits of Group Financial Statements (Including the Work of Component Auditors)* (IAASB, 2009f) requires an engagement partner in this situation to, *inter alia*:

(a) ascertain whether the component auditor understands, and will comply with, ethical requirements that are relevant to the audit, in particular, the independence requirements (para 19a);
(b) be satisfied that the component auditor possesses the necessary professional competence to perform the audit of the component in accordance with the auditing and other standards applicable to the group audit (para 19b, A38);

    (c) determine whether the engagement team and the component auditor:
- adopt similar audit methodologies,
- have common quality control policies and procedures, and
- are subject to similar external professional oversight, disciplinary procedures and quality assurance mechanisms (such as monitoring or inspections) (para A33);

    (d) perform procedures to obtain sufficient appropriate audit evidence that the work of the component auditor is adequate for the purposes of the group audit.[19] Such procedures may include:
- discussing with the component auditor:
  - the component's business activities that are significant to the group, and
  - the susceptibility of the component's financial information to material misstatement due to fraud or error;
- reviewing the component auditor's:
  - overall audit strategy and audit plan, and
  - audit documentation;
- participating in the closing and other key meetings between the component auditor and the component's management (paras 30, A55);

    (e) request the component auditor to communicate matters such as:
- whether the ethical requirements relevant to the group audit have been complied with;
- uncorrected misstatements in the component's financial information;
- any indications of management bias in the component's financial information;
- any significant deficiencies identified in the component's internal financial controls;
- other significant matters the component auditor has communicated, or expects to communicate, to the component's management, including fraud or suspected fraud involving the component's management, employees with significant roles in the component's internal control system, or others where the fraud resulted in material misstatement of the component's financial information;
- the component auditor's overall findings, conclusions and opinion (para 41).

---

[19] For significant components, the group audit engagement team is required to be involved in the component auditor's risk assessment in order to identify significant risks of material misstatement of the group financial statements. As a minimum, this 'involvement' includes performing the procedures identified under (d).

Another 'other auditor' on which the engagement partner might rely for part of the audit work is that of the client's internal auditors. Where this is the case, ISA 610: *Using the Work of Internal Auditors* (IAASB, 2013) requires the audit engagement partner to be satisfied that the auditee's internal auditors conduct their audit work with:

(i)   an appropriate level of objectivity and competence;
(ii) a systematic and disciplined approach.

ISA 610 explains these requirements as follows:

> Objectivity refers to the ability to perform [the internal audit work on which the external auditor plans to rely] without allowing bias, conflict of interest or undue influence of others to override professional judgments. (para A7)

> Competence of the internal audit function refers to the attainment and maintenance of knowledge and skills of the function as a whole at the level required to enable assigned tasks to be performed diligently and in accordance with applicable professional standards. (para A8)

> [Adoption of] a systematic and disciplined approach to planning, performing, supervising, reviewing and documenting its activities distinguishes the activities of the internal audit function from other monitoring control activities that may be performed within the entity. (para A10)

The Standard (paras A7, A8) further explains that, in evaluating the internal auditors' objectivity and competence, the audit engagement partner should consider factors such as:

- the organisational status of the internal audit function (for example, whether the internal auditors report, or have direct access, to the audit committee or board of directors or are required to report to the entity's executives);
- whether the internal auditors have conflicting responsibilities such as operational or managerial responsibilities in addition to their internal audit duties;
- whether the internal audit function is subject to constraints or restrictions imposed by management (such as limiting communication of the internal audit findings to the external auditor);
- whether the internal auditors are subject to objectivity requirements either through internal policies or through membership of a relevant professional body;
- whether the internal audit function is adequately and appropriately resourced;
- whether the internal auditors have adequate technical training, are proficient in auditing and have a thorough knowledge of the entity's financial reporting processes;
- whether the internal auditors are members of relevant professional bodies which require them to adhere to professional standards, including professional development requirements.

In respect of determining whether the auditee's internal auditors adopt a systematic and disciplined approach to their internal audit work, ISA 610 suggests external auditors should consider:

- The existence, adequacy and use of documented internal audit procedures or guidance covering such areas as risk assessments, work programs, documentation and reporting . . .;
- Whether the internal audit function has appropriate quality control policies and procedures . . . (para A11)

Although the internal auditors may possess the required competence and objectivity, and may adopt a desired approach to their work, this does not necessarily mean their work is appropriate for the purposes of the external audit or is of the required standard. Hence, the engagement partner needs to evaluate these matters. This may be achieved by, for example:

(i) reading internal audit reports that relate to the work the engagement partner plans to use for the external audit in order to gain an understanding of the nature and extent of the audit procedures performed and the related findings;

(ii) conducting sufficient audit tests on the internal audit work performed to determine its adequacy for the purposes of the external audit, including ascertaining whether:

- the internal audit work has been properly planned, performed, supervised, reviewed and documented,
- sufficient appropriate evidence has been obtained for the internal auditors to draw reasonable conclusions,
- the conclusions reached are appropriate in the circumstances and the internal audit reports are consistent with the results of the work performed (ISA 610, paras 22, 23).

Having concluded that the work of the auditee's internal auditors can be relied on for the purposes of the external audit, the audit engagement partner needs to decide the respects in which it is appropriate to use their work. This largely depends on the nature and scope of the internal audit work, its relevance to the external audit and the extent of judgment involved. Examples of internal audit work the engagement partner may decide to use for the external audit include:

- testing the effectiveness of the auditee's internal controls;
- substantive procedures where these involve limited judgment such as recalculating extensions and footings on sales or purchase invoices;
- observation of inventory counts;
- tracing transactions through the financial reporting system from source documents to financial statements or the reverse;
- testing the entity's compliance with regulatory requirements (ISA 610, para A16).

However, ISA 610 (para A19) emphasises that the external auditor should not rely on the work of internal auditors where significant judgment is involved. For example, for:

- assessing the risk of material misstatement in the financial statements;
- evaluating the sufficiency of audit tests performed;
- evaluating the appropriateness of preparing the financial statements based on the going concern assumption;
- evaluating the reasonableness of significant accounting estimates;
- evaluating the adequacy of disclosures in the financial statements.[20]

7.6 DOCUMENTING AN AUDIT

7.6.1 Definition, purpose and importance of audit documentation

We noted above that among the matters reviewers of audit work are to consider is whether the audit work performed, the results obtained and the conclusions reached thereon are adequately documented. ISA 230: *Audit Documentation* (IAASB, 2009d) defines audit documentation as:

> The record of audit procedures performed, relevant audit evidence obtained, and conclusions the auditor reached (terms such as "working papers" or "workpapers" are also sometimes used). (para 6)

It also explains: "Audit documentation may be recorded on paper or on electronic or other media" and "may include abstracts or copies of the entity's records (for example, significant and specific contracts and agreements) . . ." (para A3).

The primary purpose of audit documentation is to provide evidence that work performed during the audit, the results obtained, and the conclusions reached, all accord with ISAs and applicable legal and regulatory requirements, and that evidence resulting from audit work is sufficient and appropriate to

---

[20] The provisions of ISA 610 we outline here relate to the use by external auditors of work performed by clients' internal audit functions for their company's (not the external auditor's) purposes. In some jurisdictions, external auditors are permitted to use 'direct assistance' from their clients' internal audit staff. ISA 610 (IAASB, 2013) defines 'direct assistance' as follows:

> Direct assistance – The use of internal auditors to perform audit procedures under the direction, supervision and review of the external auditor. (para 14)

In other words, internal audit staff become members of the external audit team.

As we note in Chapter 4 (footnote 46), in the UK, ISA (UK and Ireland) 610, para 5-1, prohibits external auditors from using 'direct assistance' from their clients' internal auditors (FRC, 2013). For jurisdictions where external auditors are permitted to use such assistance, ISA 610 (IAASB, 2013; paras 26–35, 37) provides guidance on whether, in which areas, and the extent to which, they should use direct assistance from the internal auditors and, in cases where such assistance is used, the required associated documentation.

support the opinion expressed in the audit report. However, it also serves other more specific purposes. For example, it provides:

(i) *a basis for planning the audit:* Records of preliminary discussions with the client, notes relating to the assessment of audit risk and the setting of materiality limits,[21] and other similar documentation provide a basis for planning the nature, timing and extent of other procedures to be performed during the audit;

(ii) *a basis for performing the audit:* The audit plan (or programme)[22] provides directions on the audit procedures to be performed. Other documents provide evidence of procedures already completed and the conclusions reached based on the results of those procedures. Additionally, the audit documentation includes notes on any particular matters audit staff need to consider when performing certain audit procedures;

(iii) *a basis for reviewing work performed and evaluating evidence gathered and conclusions reached:* The audit documentation provides a record of work performed in relation to particular audit objectives. It thus provides a means for those responsible for directing and supervising the work of more junior engagement team members to review the work performed by their subordinates. Along similar lines, audit documentation enables the engagement partner and other senior members of the engagement team to assess the adequacy of audit work performed, the quality of the results obtained and validity of the conclusions reached;

(iv) *an aid to planning subsequent audits:* The findings of previous audits, and matters of continuing significance to future audits recorded in the audit documentation, provide a basis for the initial planning of a subsequent audit;

(v) *enabling subsequent reviews by the engagement quality control reviewer and external audit monitors [or inspectors]:* ISA 220 (IAASB, 2009c, para 19) requires a quality control reviewer to be appointed for each audit engagement of listed companies. The reviewer's primary function is to determine whether the opinion the engagement partner plans to express in the audit report is appropriate and is adequately supported by the audit procedures performed, evidence gathered, results obtained and conclusions reached, as documented in the audit working papers. In addition, all statutory auditors in the UK are subject to

---

[21] Assessment of audit risk and the setting of materiality limits are discussed in Chapter 9.

[22] In recently issued ISAs, the term 'audit plan' is used in place of the former term 'audit programme'.

monitoring by the Recognised Supervisory Body of which they are a member or inspections by the Financial Reporting Council's (FRC's) Audit Quality Review (AQR) team.[23] Audit documentation provides important evidence for the monitors/inspectors of the quality of the audits performed.

7.6.2 Form and content of audit working papers

ISA 230 (IAASB, 2009d) specifies that audit documentation must be:

sufficient to enable an experienced auditor, having no previous connection with the audit, to understand:

(a) The nature, timing and extent of the audit procedures performed to comply with the ISAs and applicable legal and regulatory requirements;

(b) The results of the audit procedures performed, and the audit evidence obtained; and

(c) Significant matters arising during the audit, the conclusions reached thereon, and significant professional judgments made in reaching those conclusions. (para 8)

We expand on these requirements when discussing the preparation of audit documentation below.

Although this general standard applies to the documentation of all audits, the form, content and extent of documentation varies from audit to audit, reflecting such things as:

- the size, nature and complexity of the client, its organisational structure and its activities;
- the nature and quality of the client's record keeping, accounting system and internal controls;
- the identified risks of material misstatement in the financial statements;
- the nature and extent of audit procedures performed;
- the extent of judgment required in performing audit procedures and in evaluating the results;
- the significance of the audit evidence obtained;
- the nature and extent of exceptions found in evidence gathered.

Although all matters of audit significance must be documented so that the requirements of the general standard for audit documentation (noted above) are met, ISA 230 observes: "it is neither necessary nor practicable for the auditor to document every matter considered, or professional judgment made, in an audit . . ." (para A7).

---

[23] We discuss audit engagement quality control reviews in section 7.6.4 and monitoring/inspections of statutory auditors in Chapter 16, section 16.4. As explained in Chapter 5, section 5.3.1, until July 2012, the AQR team was known as the Audit Inspection Unit and was an element the FRC's Professional Oversight Board. (The latter has been superseded by the FRC's Monitoring Committee.)

Notwithstanding differences in audit documentation resulting from factors like those mentioned above, certain documents (in paper or electronic form) are present in virtually every audit and, as may be seen from Figure 7.6, these are arranged logically in either the permanent or the current audit file.

(i) The permanent audit file

As indicated in Figure 7.6, the permanent audit file contains documents of a 'permanent' nature which are required in every audit of the client. Typical permanent audit file documents include the following:

(a) *Legal documents* – extracts or copies of documents such as the entity's Memorandum and Articles of Association, contracts (including, for example, pension plans and leases), agreements (such as loan agreements) and debenture deeds. A copy of the audit engagement letter[24] is also frequently kept in this section of the audit file.

Figure 7.6:   Form and content of audit working papers

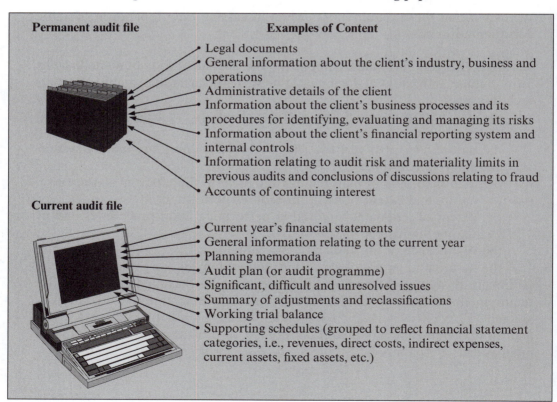

Permanent audit file

Examples of Content
- Legal documents
- General information about the client's industry, business and operations
- Administrative details of the client
- Information about the client's business processes and its procedures for identifying, evaluating and managing its risks
- Information about the client's financial reporting system and internal controls
- Information relating to audit risk and materiality limits in previous audits and conclusions of discussions relating to fraud
- Accounts of continuing interest

Current audit file

- Current year's financial statements
- General information relating to the current year
- Planning memoranda
- Audit plan (or audit programme)
- Significant, difficult and unresolved issues
- Summary of adjustments and reclassifications
- Working trial balance
- Supporting schedules (grouped to reflect financial statement categories, i.e., revenues, direct costs, indirect expenses, current assets, fixed assets, etc.)

---

[24] Engagement letters are explained in Chapter 8, section 8.3.

(b) *General information about the client's industry, business and operations* – information relating to the auditee's industry (for example, its business, economic, legislative and regulatory environment), its historical development, and its present organisational and operational structure. This information includes details of the company's board of directors and board committees (for example, its remuneration and audit committees), details of any subsidiaries, divisions or departments (their geographical location, size, principal products, etc.), and details of key suppliers, customers, competitors, bankers, solicitors, etc.

(c) *Administrative details of the client* – documents reflecting the client's administrative structure, for example, its organisation chart, chart of accounts, policies and procedures manuals, and job descriptions.

(d) *Business processes and risks* – information gathered during previous audits about the auditee's business processes and its procedures for identifying, evaluating and managing its financial, operational, compliance and other risks.

(e) *Financial reporting system and internal controls* – information relating to the client's financial reporting system and internal controls, including flowcharts, narrative descriptions and internal control evaluations obtained during previous audits. Also, notes made in previous audits about strengths and deficiencies identified in the client's internal controls, and copies of communications relating to these matters to the client's directors, audit committee and/or senior executives.[25]

(f) *Information on audit risk and materiality limits* – the results of analytical procedures and other information relating to the assessment of audit risk and the setting of materiality limits in previous audits. Also, the conclusions of audit team discussions in previous audits about the susceptibility of the client's financial statements to material misstatement due to fraudulent financial reporting or misappropriation of assets.[26]

(g) *Accounts of continuing interest* – analyses from previous audits of accounts that are of continuing importance to the auditor. These include equity accounts, non-current liabilities, and tangible and intangible non-current assets.

(ii)   The current audit file

As may be seen from Figure 7.6, the current audit file (which is usually in electronic form, accessible to all members of the engagement team) contains

---

[25] Internal controls, and audit documents relating thereto, are discussed in Chapter 10. Communication of audit matters to the entity's directors, audit committee and executives is discussed in Chapter 14.

[26] These discussions are explained in Chapter 6, section 6.4.1.

information pertaining to the current year's audit.[27] It includes records such as:

(a) *The financial statements under examination.*

(b) *General information* – information of a general nature relating to the current year's audit. This includes, for example, notes on discussions with the client about economic, financial, operational and other matters which have occurred during the reporting period; abstracts or copies of directors' (and similar) meetings; abstracts or copies of contracts or agreements that are relevant to the current year's audit; and comments on the current year's evaluation of the auditee's internal controls and risk assessment and management processes.

(c) *Planning memoranda relating to the current audit* – records of audit team planning meetings where matters such as significant features of the audit client (its industry, business, operations, and organisation), the audit strategy, matters of particular audit interest or concern, and the planned nature, timing and extent of audit tests are discussed.[28] A record of the audit team's discussion about the susceptibility of the current year's financial statements to material misstatement due to fraud, and management's assessment of the risk of the financial statements being materially misstated, may also be retained in this section of the audit file.

(d) *The audit plan (or audit programme)* – a list of the procedures to be performed during the audit. As the audit progresses, the staff member who performs a particular procedure initials and dates the audit plan to indicate the procedure has been completed; usually, a cross-reference to the relevant detailed working paper(s) is also provided.

(e) *Significant matters arising during the audit*: This section of the current audit file includes notes on, for example:
  (i) difficult issues which have arisen during the audit and how they have been resolved, and
  (ii) issues remaining to be resolved prior to completion of the audit.
  ISA 230 (para A8) explains that significant matters include:
  • matters that give rise to significant risks (i.e., risks of material misstatement in the financial statements that require special audit consideration);

---

[27] We should perhaps note that virtually all (if not all) audit firms have standard audit working papers, in electronic form (including schedules such as those shown in Figures 7.7 and 7.8), which are 'tailored' as appropriate to meet the requirements of (and audit procedures performed during) individual audit engagements.

[28] Planning the audit is the subject of Chapter 9.

- the results of audit procedures which indicate:
  - the financial statements could be materially misstated, and/or
  - the need to revise the auditor's previous assessment of the risk of the financial statements being materially misstated and the auditor's responses to those risks;
- circumstances that cause the auditor significant difficulty in applying necessary audit procedures;
- findings that could result in modification of the audit report or the inclusion of an Emphasis of Matter paragraph.[29]

ISA 230 places particular emphasis on the need to document significant professional judgments relating to significant matters arising during the audit. It notes that such documentation "serves to explain the auditor's conclusions and to reinforce the quality of the judgment" (para A9). The standard also requires documentation of discussions of significant matters with the entity's executives, directors, other entity personnel, and/or external parties such as those providing professional advice to the entity. The nature of the significant matters discussed, and those with whom and when the discussions took place, are all to be recorded. Similarly, if, having reached a conclusion about a significant matter, the auditor encounters information that is inconsistent with that conclusion, s/he is required to document how the inconsistency was resolved (ISA 230, paras 10, 11).

(f) *Summary of adjustments and reclassifications*: As the audit proceeds, engagement team members almost invariably encounter accounting entries which require correction of the amount or account classification; for example, a direct payment into the client's bank account by a credit customer on the last day of the client's financial year may not have been recorded as a receipt in the current period, or office equipment purchased during the year may have been recorded as 'repairs and maintenance' instead of 'office equipment'. All errors discovered during the audit which require adjustment or reclassification are recorded on a summary schedule (which is frequently located at, or close to, the front of the current audit file). Such a summary enables the engagement partner (or another senior member of the audit team) to assess at a glance the significance of individual errors, and the cumulative effect of errors, to the financial statements as a whole and to the affected components thereof (for example, to net or gross profit, current assets, non-current liabilities, etc.).

---

[29] Modifications of the auditor's report and Emphasis of Matter paragraphs are discussed in Chapter 14.

Although, the audit team will find and record errors as the audit progresses, no adjustments to the client's ledger accounts or financial statements can be made without the consent of the client's directors. As noted in Chapter 5, the directors are responsible for maintaining the accounting records and preparing the financial statements. The auditor will request the directors to effect adjusting entries to correct errors discovered during the audit. In many cases no difficulty is encountered and the directors make the requested changes. If the directors refuse to correct what the auditor considers to be a material misstatement, the auditor will need to express a modified opinion in the audit report.

(g) *Working trial balance*: Usually, as soon as possible after the end of the client's financial year, the auditor obtains or prepares a list of general ledger accounts and their year end balances. This is known as a working trial balance. It is frequently in the form of a list of balances which appear in the financial statements. Each line of the working trial balance is supported by a lead schedule. This lists the general ledger accounts (and their balances) which constitute the relevant financial statement balance. (For example, the 'Cash' balance in the financial statements may comprise petty cash and a number of current and deposit account balances held at one or more banks – possibly in different currencies in different countries.) Each significant account shown in the lead schedule is, in turn, supported by detailed audit working papers. These show the audit work performed in relation to the account in question, the results obtained, and the conclusion reached regarding the 'fairness' (or otherwise) of the account balance.

The relationship between the statement of financial position, working trial balance, lead schedule and supporting schedules is shown in simplified form in Figure 7.7. This shows that the cash balance presented in the statement of financial position as at 31 March 20x8, and recorded as the 'final amount' in the working trial balance, is £254,790. The composition of this balance is detailed in the 'Lead Schedule: Cash'. Audit work has revealed that a receipt from a customer of £320 was not recorded in the reporting period and, as a consequence, an adjusting entry is required.

(h) *Supporting schedules*: The supporting schedules, which provide details of audit work performed in relation to individual financial statement balances, constitute the major portion of the current audit file. Frequently they are grouped in the file in sections which reflect financial statement categories. There may, for example, be sections for revenues, direct costs, indirect expenses, current assets, tangible non-current assets, investments, intangible non-current assets, current liabilities, non-current liabilities and equity. Each of these sections may be subdivided into groups of related accounts. The amount of subdivision largely depends on the size and complexity of the particular audit client.

Each group of accounts has a lead schedule which is cross-referenced to the working trial balance, relevant 'working accounts' and supporting schedules (see Refs A-1, A-1.1 and A-1.1.1 to A-1.1.4 and A-1S in Figure 7.7). Each supporting schedule presents, in relation to an individual account balance, details of:
- the objective(s) of audit procedures performed;[30]
- the procedures performed;
- the results of the procedures;
- relevant comments;
- the conclusion reached in respect of the account balance investigated;
- comments from the audit engagement team member who reviewed the supporting schedule (and, hence, the audit work performed).

These features, and those required by ISA 230, para 9 noted below, are reflected in Figure 7.8.

7.6.3 Preparation of audit documentation

We noted in section 7.6.1 that the primary objective of audit documentation is to provide:
- (a) evidence that the audit was conducted in accordance with ISAs and applicable legal and regulatory requirements, and
- (b) support for the opinion expressed in the audit report.

In order to meet these objectives, it is essential that audit documentation is properly prepared.

Although the details of working papers vary according to the nature of the schedule concerned and the specific audit objectives being met, audit documentation should always contain certain features. These are outlined below and illustrated in Figure 7.8.

Each audit working paper should indicate:
- the name of the client;
- the audit area (or account) to which the working paper (schedule) relates;
- the relevant accounting period;
- a unique reference number which is cross-referenced to the relevant lead schedule, working trial balance and/or other related working papers;
- the audit objective(s) of the procedures performed;
- the procedures performed (these should be cross-referenced to the audit plan);

---

[30] The objectives of audit procedures, and the procedures to be performed, may be also specified in the audit plan.

Figure 7.7: Simplified representation of the relationship between the financial statements and audit working papers

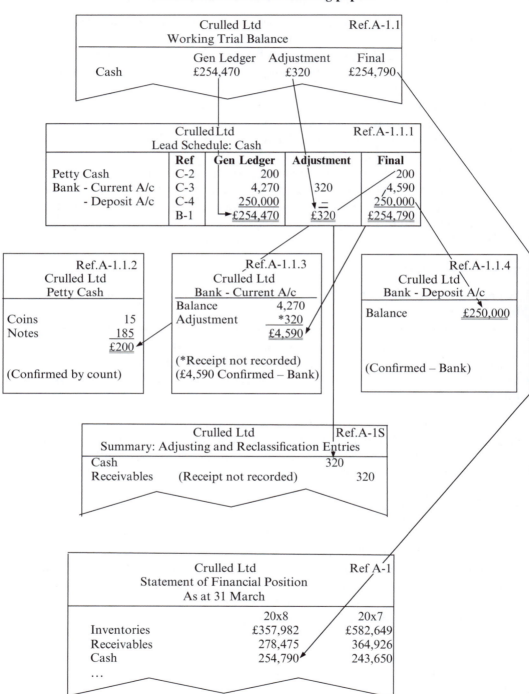

Figure 7.8: Example of a supporting schedule

Working paper reference

Name of client ——————————▶ **CRULLED LIMITED**
Audit area ——————————————▶ **Inventory Purchases and Cash Payments**
Accounting period ———————————▶ **Year to 31 March 20x8**

REF: K-2
Prepared by: RB◀
Date: 10.4.x8 ◀
Reviewed by: MC◀---┐
Date: 16.4.x8 ◀----┘

*Preparer and
Preparation date
Reviewer and
Review date*

Audit Objectives:
• To verify that merchandise is properly ordered and received and is for legitimate
   business purposes.
• To verify that expenses (purchases) and assets (inventories) are properly valued and classified
• To verify that cash payments are for legitimate liabilities and are properly valued.

Audit Procedures (and key to symbols):

\#   Traced payment to purchase invoice. Agreed invoice with amount and date of payment. As a result of cash discount
      received, each payment is 5% less than invoice amount. Recalculated all discounts. (A-6) ←*Audit plan reference*

<   Compared invoice prices with master price list. All agreed except those marked*. (A-7)

Ø   Examined purchase invoices for evidence that company employee verified prices, extensions and footings.
      Markings or initials present in all cases. (A-8)

>   Verified arithmetical accuracy of extensions and totals of invoices. (A-9)

v   Examined (electronic) payments records for payee name and bank account number. Confirmed bank account
      number with payee's details in client's database; checked for subsequent amendment of details (none found).
      Checked for authorisation. All payments made by Mears (Accounts Clerk) after authorisation by Thomas (Chief
      Accountant). (A-10)

t   Examined receiving report for agreement with purchase invoice as to description and quantity. All reports were
      properly signed by Backhouse (Receiving Officer). (A-11)

@   Examined purchase order with receiving report and invoice. Verified account code. All orders agreed with receiving
      report and were properly approved except those marked + and ❷. (A-12)

Sample selection:
Population: All purchases were from Yumslip Products, Western Corporation and Capers Ltd .
Sample: Judgmental. Selected 12 payments for merchandise from Cash Payments Journal for period 1.4.x7 to 31.3.x8
            beginning with payment no. 1690.

Results of Procedures:

		Payment				Audit Procedure			
Date	**Payee**	**No.**	**Amount**	**1**	**2**	**3**	**4**	**5**	**6**	**7**
10-4-x7	Western Corporation	1690	£1,432.67	#	<	Ø	>	v	t	@
9-5-x7	Yumslip Products	1725	£2,568.91	#	<*	Ø	>	v	t	@+
15-6-x7	Western Corporation	1744	£1,021.05	#	<	Ø	>	v	t	@
6-7-x7	Yumslip Products	1769	£456.26	#	<	Ø	>	v	t	@❷
10-8-x7	Capers Ltd	1780	£461.34	#	<	Ø	>	v	t	@❷
8-9-x7	Yumslip Products	1795	£1,263.76	#	<*	Ø	>	v	t	@
14-10-x7	western Corporation	1841	£1,246.34	#	<	Ø	>	v	t	@
17-11-x7	Yumslip Products	1860	£319.38	#	<	Ø	>	v	t	@❷
9-12-x7	Capers Ltd	1887	£248.21	#	<	Ø	>	v	t	@❷
15-1-x8	Yumslip Products	1898	£1,219.47	#	<	Ø	>	v	t	@
13-2-x8	Western Corporation	1924	£2,639.31	#	<	Ø	>	v	t	@
15-3-x8	Yumslip Products	1953	£1,632.19	#	<	Ø	>	v	t	@

NOTE: Symbols used are shown alongside relevant audit procedure.

Figure 7.8: *Continued*

Comments:

* Prices on purchases of 9-5-x7 and 8-9-x7 do not agree with master price list by £56.00 and £124.34 respectively. According to Smithson (Purchasing Officer) the differences represent special prices available in May and September which differed from price list. (Confirmed with Yumslip).

+ Purchase order does not agree with receiving report for one item. Smithson indicated that a replacement (similar) item was supplied as a result of a stock-out. (Confirmed replacement item ordered).

❷ Four orders were approved by Thomas (Chief Accountant) instead of Mates (Finance Director). According to Smithson only orders in excess of £1,000 need be approved by Mates. (Confirmed with Mates). NOTE: Need to alter flow chart to reflect this. (MC 16-4-x8) ◄— *Follow-up by audit staff member*

Conclusions:

(1) The purchases are properly ordered and received and are for legitimate purposes.
(2) Purchases are properly valued and classified.
(3) Payments are properly valued and are for legitimate liabilities.
(4) Purchases and payments transactions are fairly stated in the accounts. (K-1) ◄——— *Lead schedule reference*

Review: Review and discussion of results of audit procedures and conclusions; MC 16.4.x8. Follow up on flow chart amendment actioned: MC 17.4.x8

- the results obtained (these frequently involve the use of tick marks or symbols; all such notation must be clearly explained);
- the conclusion(s) reached in respect of the audit objectives, based on the results of the procedures performed.

If sampling is used, the relevant working paper should indicate the population from which the sample was drawn, the size of the sample and the means by which the sample was selected.

In relation to the procedures performed, ISA 230 (para 9) specifies the following are to be recorded:

(a) The identifying characteristics of the specific items or matters tested;
(b) Who performed the audit work and the date such work was completed
(c) Who reviewed the audit work performed and the date and extent of such review.

Explaining the "identifying characteristics" that are to be documented, ISA 230 (para A12) notes:

Identifying characteristics will vary with the nature of the audit procedure and the item or matter tested. For example:

- For a detailed test of entity-generated purchase orders, the auditor may identify the documents selected for testing by their dates and unique purchase order numbers. . . .
- For a procedure requiring systematic sampling from a population of documents, the auditor may identify the documents selected by recording their source, the starting point and the sampling interval (for example, a systematic sample of shipping reports selected from the shipping log for the period

from April 1 to September 30, starting with report number 12345 and selecting every 125th report).[31]

- For a procedure requiring inquiries of specific entity personnel, the auditor may record the dates of the inquiries and the names and job designations of the entity personnel.
- For an observation procedure, the auditor may record the process or matter being observed, the relevant individuals, their respective responsibilities, and where and when the observation was carried out.

The identifying characteristics of the payments selected for examination in the audit of Crulled Limited are shown in Figure 7.8.

Where any deviation from the expected result of an audit procedure is encountered, the deviation, and an explanation thereof, should be clearly recorded. In cases where some follow-up is required, the person undertaking the follow-up should initial and date the relevant working paper entry to indicate that the follow-up has been performed.

7.6.4 Working paper review

In Chapter 3 we note that a characteristic feature of all audits (and all stages of an audit) is the importance of, and necessity for, the exercise of professional judgment – a fact that will become increasingly evident as we study the steps in the audit process in more detail. This characteristic, combined with the fact that members of audit teams are human (and therefore prone to make mistakes and faulty judgments), means that reliance cannot be placed on audit staff correctly identifying audit objectives, performing appropriate audit procedures, making optimal judgments and drawing correct conclusions, on *every* occasion. If an effective audit is to be conducted, it is essential that the work of each audit team member is reviewed by a more senior member of the audit team.

Working paper review is usually effected in the following manner.

(i) As each section of the audit is completed, the working papers of the relevant audit staff member are reviewed by a more senior member of the audit team. The audit procedures performed are compared with those set down in the audit plan, and the results obtained and conclusions reached (based on those results) are evaluated by the reviewer and discussed with the staff member. The working papers are also reviewed for completeness, orderly presentation and cross-referencing to other relevant working papers. Any matters requiring follow-up are noted and either actioned by the staff member or reviewer, or referred to the appropriate member of the audit team for actioning.

---

[31] We discuss sample selection in Chapter 12, section 12.5.3.

(ii) *The reviewer* (who is usually responsible for one or more segment of the audit) prepares summary notes on each audit segment for which s/he is responsible, regarding:

  (a) the evidence gathered and conclusions reached;

  (b) any problems encountered and how they were dealt with;

  (c) the scope of, and conclusions resulting from, any consultations on difficult or contentious issues;

  (d) matters requiring the attention of the audit manager (usually the most senior member of the audit team other than the engagement partner) or the engagement partner;

  (e) matters to be considered for inclusion in the communication of audit matters to the client's directors (and/or audit committee).

(iii) *The audit manager* (or another senior member of the audit team) reviews the summary notes prepared by each reviewer and also a sample of the detailed working papers reviewed by that reviewer to ensure they contain evidence indicating they have been reviewed and to evaluate the reviewer's findings. The manager discusses with the audit team members who performed and/or reviewed the audit work:

- any matters which require clarification,
- any difficult or contentious issues,
- whether consultation occurred and how the issues in question were resolved, and
- any issues remaining to be resolved.

The audit manager prepares summary notes (similar to those prepared by the reviewers noted above) on each major segment of the audit and on the audit as a whole. The audit manager will be particularly concerned to see that:

  (a) all audit problems have been adequately dealt with;

  (b) any unresolved issues are either resolved or highlighted, by way of a working paper note, for the audit engagement partner;

  (c) the conclusions reached are supported by the evidence gathered;

  (d) sufficient appropriate audit evidence has been obtained in each audit segment and for the audit as a whole to support the audit opinion;

  (e) all significant audit matters (including all significant judgments made) are fully and properly documented.

The audit manager usually also prepares the formal communication (i.e., letter) of audit matters to the client's directors (and/or audit committee).[32]

---

[32] The communication of audit matters to the entity's directors (or audit committee) is discussed in Chapter 14, section 14.8.

(iv) *The audit engagement partner* considers, in detail, the final draft of the financial statements, and the summary notes and formal communication of audit matters to the client's directors prepared by the audit manager. The engagement partner also:
    (a) reviews the audit working papers for completeness, orderliness, adequacy, cross-referencing and evidence of review. S/he will pay particular attention to working papers that relate to:
        – critical areas of judgment, especially those relating to difficult or contentious matters identified during the audit, and
        – identified areas or matters of significant audit risk;
    (b) discusses with the audit manager and/or relevant audit team members any matters that require clarification and/or difficult or unresolved audit issues.

The engagement partner is particularly concerned to ensure:
- an appropriate opinion on the financial statements can be formed based on the evidence recorded in the audit documentation, considered in the light of his/her knowledge of the client, its operations and its financial affairs;
- if the adequacy of the audit engagement is challenged in a court of law, the audit documentation clearly shows:
    – the audit was conducted in accordance with the ISAs and applicable legal and regulatory requirements, and
    – the opinion expressed in the audit report is supported by audit evidence that is both sufficient and appropriate.

Although the audit partner reviews the audit documentation at the conclusion of the audit as outlined above, this is not the only time s/he reviews the documentation. As ISA 220, observes:

> Timely reviews of [audit documentation] by the engagement partner at appropriate stages during the engagement allow significant matters to be resolved on a timely basis to the engagement partner's satisfaction before the date of the auditor's report. (para A18)

(v) *Audit engagement quality control review*: In order to ensure the audit documentation meets the objectives outlined above, most audit firms require the audit working papers to be reviewed by a second audit partner who has not had any involvement in the audit engagement in question. Indeed, ISQC 1 (IAASB, 2009a, para 35) requires an engagement quality control review to be conducted for the audits for all listed companies and for other audits which meet criteria specified by the audit firm. ISQC 1 explains that the criteria a firm considers when determining which audit engagements should be subject to an engagement quality control review include:
- The nature of the engagement, including the extent to which it involves a matter of public interest.

- The identification of unusual circumstances or risks in an engagement or class of engagements.
- Whether laws or regulations require an engagement quality control review. (para A41)

ISA 220 (IAASB, 2009c, para 18) expands on the requirements of ISQC 1 noting that the engagement partner is responsible for:
(a) determining that an engagement quality control reviewer has been appointed;
(b) discussing with the engagement quality control reviewer significant issues arising during the audit (including those identified during the quality control review);
(c) not finalising (by signing and dating) the audit report until the engagement quality control review has been completed.

But – what is an engagement quality control review and who qualifies as a reviewer? The answers are provided in IFAC's *Glossary of Terms* (IFAC, 2009) as follows:

Engagement quality control review – A process designed to provide an objective evaluation, on or before the date of the [audit] report, of the significant judgments the engagement team made and the conclusions it reached in formulating the report.

Engagement quality control reviewer – A partner, other person in the firm, suitably qualified external person, or a team made up of such individuals, none of whom is part of the engagement team, with sufficient and appropriate experience and authority to objectively evaluate the significant judgments the engagement team made and the conclusions it reached in formulating the report.

ISA 220 expands on the above definition of an engagement quality control review by explaining that it involves:
(a) Discussion with the engagement partner;
(b) Review of the financial statements and the proposed auditor's report;
(c) Review of selected audit documentation relating to the significant judgments the engagement team made and the conclusions it reached;
(d) Evaluation of the conclusions reached in formulating the auditor's report and consideration of whether the proposed auditor's report is appropriate. (para 20)

For listed companies the engagement quality control reviewer is also required to consider:
(a) The engagement team's evaluation of the firm's independence in relation to the audit engagement;
(b) Whether appropriate consultation has taken place on matters involving differences of opinion or other difficult or contentious matters, and the conclusions arising from those consultations; and

(c) Whether audit documentation selected for review reflects the work performed in relation to the significant judgments and supports the conclusions reached. (ISA 220, para 21)

As for all other aspects of the audit, the engagement quality control review is to be documented. In particular, the engagement quality control reviewer is to note that:

- the review has been performed prior to the audit report being finalised, and
- the reviewer is not aware of any unresolved matters that would cause him/her to believe that significant judgments made, and conclusions reached, by the engagement team were not appropriate (ISA 220, para 25).

Before leaving the topic of engagement quality control reviews we should note that, notwithstanding the involvement of a quality control reviewer, the audit engagement partner remains responsible for the audit engagement and its performance.

7.6.5 Assembly, retention, ownership and safe custody of audit documentation

One of the causes of the demise of Arthur Andersen in 2002 (as part of the fallout from the Enron debacle) was the shredding of audit working papers by Andersen staff. It is, therefore, not surprising that ISA 230 (IAASB, 2009d) includes a section relating to assembling and retaining the final audit file. This requires auditors to:

... complete the administrative process of assembling the final audit file on a timely basis after the date of the auditor's report. . . . An appropriate time limit within which to complete the assembly of the final audit file is ordinarily not more than 60 days after the date of the auditor's report. (paras 14, A21)

Assembling the final audit file is an administrative process that does not involve any additional audit procedures. It involves making sure the audit documentation is complete and in good order. It includes, for example:

- deleting or discarding documentation which has been superseded;
- sorting, collating and cross-referencing working papers;
- documenting audit evidence (not yet recorded) obtained, discussed and agreed with relevant members of the audit team before the date of the auditor's report;
- signing off on completion checklists relating to the final assembly of the file.

Once the final audit file is assembled, no one is permitted to delete or discard audit documentation of any nature before the end of its retention period (ISA 230, para 15). In the UK, the retention period is ordinary not less than five years from the date of the auditor's report [ISA (UK and Ireland) 230, para A23; APB, 2009].

If auditors find it necessary to modify, or add to, existing audit documentation after assembly of the final audit file has been completed, irrespective of the nature of the modifications or additions, they are required to document:
- the specific reasons for making the modifications or additions, and
- when, and by whom, the modifications or additions were made and reviewed (ISA 230, para 16).

In general, audit documentation is owned by the auditor (that is, the audit firm) who prepared it. However ISQC 1 (IAASB, 2009a) specifies that auditors may, if they wish, make parts of, or extracts from, their audit documentation available to audit clients, "provided such disclosure does not undermine the validity of the work performed, or . . . the independence of the firm or its personnel" (para A63). Along similar lines, professional standards generally require an incumbent auditor to make its audit documentation available to a successor auditor.[33]

Notwithstanding these and a few other limited exceptions, audit documentation is normally kept confidential to the relevant audit firm. It must also be kept secure; ISQC 1 requires audit firms to "establish policies and procedures designed to maintain the confidentiality, safe custody, integrity, accessibility and retrievability of engagement documentation" (para 46). Thus, audit firms need to establish controls that will, *inter alia*:
  (i)   enable determination of when, and by whom, audit working papers were prepared, modified and reviewed;
  (ii) protect the integrity of the audit documentation at all stages of the engagement, especially when information is shared between engagement team members or transmitted to other parties via the Internet;
  (iii) prevent unauthorised changes to the documentation (ISQC 1, para A57).

7.7 SUMMARY

In this chapter we have reviewed the audit process, discussed the meaning and nature of audit evidence, and examined some important administrative aspects of auditing – in particular, staffing and documenting an audit. We have seen that the audit process comprises a series of steps through which auditors proceed, gradually gathering evidence to enable them to form an opinion on (amongst other things) whether the financial statements provide

---

[33] We discuss this requirement in Chapter 8, section 8.2.3.

a true and fair view of the entity's financial position and performance, and comply with the applicable financial reporting framework and the Companies Act 2006.

We have also drawn a distinction between audit objectives (the purpose for which audit evidence is obtained) and audit procedures (the methods by which the evidence is gathered). Additionally, we have identified three levels of audit objectives (overall, general and specific objectives), explained terms such as compliance and substantive procedures, and tests of transactions and tests of balances, and outlined some common audit procedures. We have also examined some characteristics of evidence obtained from different sources and explored factors which affect auditors' choice of evidence, namely, reliability, relevance, availability, timeliness and cost. We have observed that there is a trade-off between the quantity of evidence an auditor needs to gather (sufficiency) and its relevance and reliability (appropriateness or quality).

In relation to staffing an audit we have considered the capabilities and competence required of auditors, engagement partners' responsibilities in cases where they rely on experts or other auditors to perform part of an audit, and the need for audit engagement partners to carefully assign, direct, supervise and review audit work. As regards documenting an audit, we have discussed the purpose and importance of audit working papers and their form, content and preparation. We have also explained working paper review, and the requirements with respect to assembling and retaining the final audit file, and ownership of audit documentation.

From our examination of these topics it is evident that, in order for an audit to be conducted effectively, efficiently and with due professional care, it must be adequately staffed by personnel who possess the personal qualities of integrity, objectivity and independence, and who also have the capabilities, competence and time required to perform the tasks assigned to them. Additionally, work assigned to audit staff must be carefully directed and supervised and all audit work must be fully and properly documented and carefully reviewed. Proper documentation is also required to provide evidence that sufficient appropriate audit evidence was gathered during the audit, and the conclusions reached accord with that evidence and support the opinion expressed in the audit report.

SELF-REVIEW QUESTIONS

7.1   Identify the major steps in the audit process.

7.2   Briefly explain the objective of:
        (i)   compliance procedures, and
        (ii) substantive procedures.
        For each of these objectives give one example of an audit procedure
        which is designed to meet that objective.

7.3   State whether you agree or disagree with the following statement. Briefly
        explain your answer.
            Gathering evidence in accordance with ISAs requires the auditor
            to obtain the strongest possible evidence for each item in the
            financial statements regardless of cost or difficulties that may be
            encountered.

7.4   Outline the requirements of audit engagement partners with
        respect to:
        (i)   assigning
        (ii) directing,
        (iii) supervising, and
        (iv) reviewing
        the work of engagement team members.

7.5   Briefly explain the responsibilities of the audit engagement partner when
        relying on the work of experts to perform part of an audit.

7.6   (a) Define 'audit documentation';
        (b) List five specific purposes of audit documentation.

7.7   (a) Distinguish between information contained in:
               (i)   the permanent audit file, and
               (ii) the current audit file.
        (b) Provide two examples of the information contained in each of the
            above files.

7.8   Briefly explain the key concerns of:
        (i)   a senior member of the engagement team when reviewing the
              work of a more junior member of the team;
        (ii) the audit engagement partner when reviewing the documentation
              of the audit engagement.

7.9   (a) Define the term: 'engagement quality control review';
        (b) Explain who may be an engagement quality control reviewer;
        (c) Briefly explain how an engagement quality control review is
            conducted.

7.10   Outline the requirements of audit firms regarding:
   (i)   assembling the final audit file and subsequent modifications or additions thereto, and
   (ii) retention, ownership and custody of audit documentation.

REFERENCES

Auditing Practices Board (APB). (2009). International Standard on Auditing (ISA) (UK and Ireland) 230: *Audit Documentation*. London: Financial Reporting Council.

Auditing Practices Board (APB). (2010). Ethical Standard (ES) 4: *Fees, Remuneration and Evaluation Policies, Litigation, Gifts and Hospitality*. London: Financial Reporting Council.

Financial Reporting Council (FRC). (2013). International Standard on Auditing (UK and Ireland) 610: *Using the Work of Internal Auditors*. London: FRC

International Auditing and Assurance Standards Board (IAASB). (2009a). International Standard on Quality Control (ISQC) 1: *Quality Controls for Firms that Perform Audits and Reviews of Financial Statements, and Other Assurance and Related Services Engagements*. New York: International Federation of Accountants.

International Auditing and Assurance Standards Board (IAASB). (2009b). International Standard on Auditing (ISA) 200: *Overall Objectives of the Independent Auditor and the Conduct of an Audit in Accordance with International Standards on Auditing*. New York: International Federation of Accountants.

International Auditing and Assurance Standards Board (IAASB). (2009c). International Standard on Auditing (ISA) 220: *Quality Control for an Audit of Financial Statements*. New York: International Federation of Accountants.

International Auditing and Assurance Standards Board (IAASB). (2009d). International Standard on Auditing (ISA) 230: *Audit Documentation*. New York: International Federation of Accountants.

International Auditing and Assurance Standards Board (IAASB). (2009e). International Standard on Auditing (ISA) 500: *Audit Evidence*. New York: International Federation of Accountants.

International Auditing and Assurance Standards Board (IAASB). (2009f). International Standard on Auditing (ISA) 600: *Special Considerations – Audits of Group Financial Statements (Including the Work of Component Auditors)*. New York: International Federation of Accountants.

International Auditing and Assurance Standards Board (IAASB). (2009g). International Standard on Auditing (ISA) 620: *Using the Work of an Auditor's Expert*. New York: International Federation of Accountants.

International Auditing and Assurance Standards Board (IAASB). (2013). International Standard on Auditing (ISA) 610: *Using the Work of Internal Auditors*. New York: International Federation of Accountants.

International Federation of Accountants (IFAC). (2009). *Glossary of Terms*, included in *Handbook of International Quality Control, Auditing, Review, Other Assurance and Related Services Pronouncements 2010 Edition*. New York: IFAC.

ADDITIONAL READING

Agoglia, C.P., Brazel, J.F., Hatfield, R.C., & Jackson, S.B. (2010). How do audit work-paper reviewers cope with the conflicting pressures of detecting misstatements and balancing client workloads? *Auditing: A Journal of Practice & Theory*, *29*(2), 27–43.

Guiral, A., Ruiz, E., & Rodgers, W. (2011). To what extent are auditors' attitudes towards the evidence influenced by the self-fulfilling prophecy? *Auditing: A Journal of Practice & Theory*, *30*(1), 173–190.

Han, J., Jamal, K., & Tan, H.-T. (2011). Auditors' overconfidence in predicting the tech-nical knowledge of superiors and subordinates. *Auditing: A Journal of Practice & Theory*, *30*(1), 101–119.

Institute of Chartered Accountants of Scotland (ICAS). (2007). *Appraising Your Audi-tors: A Guide to the Assessment and Appointment of Auditors*, 2nd ed. Edinburgh: ICAS.

Kornberger, M., Justesen, L., & Mouritsen, J. (2011). "When you make manager, we put a big mountain in front of you": An ethnography of managers in a big 4 account-ing firm. *Accounting, Organizations and Society*, *36*(8), 514–533.

Payne, E.A., & Ramsey, R.J. (2008). Audit documentation methods: A path model of cognitive processing, memory, and performance. *Auditing: A Journal of Practice & Theory*, *27*(1), 151–168.

Payne, E.A., Ramsey, R.J., & Bamber, E.M. (2010). The effect of alternative types of review on auditors' procedures and performance. *Auditing: A Journal of Practice & Theory*, *29*(1), 207–220.

Peecher, M.E., Piercey, M.D., Rich, J.S., & Tubbs, R.M. (2010). The effects of a supervi-sor's active intervention in subordinates' judgments, directional goals, and perceived technical knowledge advantage on audit team judgments. *Accounting Review*, *85*(5), 1763–1786.

Shankar, P.G., & Tan, H.-T. (2006). Determinants of audit preparers' workpaper justi-fications. *Accounting Review*, *81*(2), 473–496.

Tan H.-T., & Jamal, K. (2001). Do auditors objectively evaluate their subordinates' work. *Accounting Review*, *76*(1), 99–110.

Tan, H.-T., & Shanker, P.G. (2010). Auditor reviewers' evaluation of subordinates' work quality. *Auditing: A Journal of Practice & Theory*, *29*(1), 251–266.

Tan, H.-T., & Trotman, K.T. (2003). Reviewers' responses to anticipated stylization attempts by preparers of audit workpapers. *Accounting Review*, *78*(2), 581–606.

Trotman, K.T., & Wright, W.F. (2012). Triangulation of audit evidence in fraud risk assessments. *Accounting, Organizations and Society*, *37*(1), 41–53.

8 Commencing an Audit: Engagement Procedures, Understanding the Client and Identifying Risks

LEARNING OBJECTIVES

After studying the material in this chapter you should be able to:

- outline the reasons for, and the process of, pre-engagement investigations;
- discuss the purpose and content of audit engagement letters;
- explain the importance of gaining a thorough understanding of the client, its business, industry and performance measures;
- identify external and internal environmental factors which impact on an entity and explain their relevance for the entity's external audit;
- outline the audit procedures used to gain an understanding of the client, its business, industry and performance measures;
- explain the meaning of 'analytical procedures' and their use in the initial, substantive testing and completion stages of the audit;
- discuss the importance of (a) understanding the client and (b) analytical procedures, for identifying and assessing the risk of material misstatement in the financial statements.

8.1 INTRODUCTION

In this chapter we begin our journey through the audit process. We assume that an auditor (an individual or an audit firm) has been approached by a company to accept nomination, or to submit a tender, for appointment as its auditor. We discuss the steps the auditor should take before accepting the engagement and the audit engagement letter that is prepared once the audit is accepted. We also explore the all-important audit step of the auditor gaining a thorough understanding of the client, its business, industry and performance measures and the importance of this understanding, together with the performance of analytical procedures, for identifying and assessing the risk of material misstatement in the financial statements.[1] Before concluding the chapter we discuss

---

[1] It should be noted that gaining a preliminary understanding of the client's control environment and other internal control components is an element of 'Gaining an understanding of the client'. However, we defer our discussion of internal control until Chapter 10.

the meaning of 'analytical procedures' and their use in the initial, substantive testing and completion stages of the audit.

8.2 PRE-ENGAGEMENT INVESTIGATION

8.2.1 The need for a pre-engagement investigation

In a competitive environment it is not always easy to obtain and retain audit clients. Nevertheless, when auditors are offered a new or continuing audit engagement they should consider carefully whether it is prudent to accept the offer. It is, for example, generally unwise to accept (or continue with) an audit client whose management lacks integrity or constantly argues about the proper conduct of the audit and/or the audit fee. Equally, it is important that an audit engagement is not accepted if it cannot be adequately staffed with personnel who are independent of the client and possess the required capabilities and competence. These matters are addressed in International Standard on Quality Control (ISQC) 1: *Quality Control for Firms that Perform Audits and Reviews of Financial Statements* . . . (IAASB, 2009a) which specifies that each audit firm:

> shall establish policies and procedures for the acceptance and continuance of client relationships and specific [audit] engagements, designed to provide the firm with reasonable assurance that it will only undertake or continue relationships and engagements where the firm:
>
> (a) Is competent to perform the engagement and has the capabilities, including time and resources, to do so;
> (b) Can comply with relevant ethical requirements; and
> (c) Has considered the integrity of the client, and does not have information that would lead it to conclude that the client lacks integrity. (para 26)

International Standard on Auditing (ISA) 220: *Quality Control for an Audit of Financial Statements* (IAASB, 2009c) (para 12) adds to this by requiring the engagement partner to be satisfied that appropriate acceptance or continuance procedures have been followed and the conclusions reached in this regard are appropriate.

In the light of the requirements of ISQC 1 cited above, it is convenient to discuss the elements of a pre-engagement investigation under the following headings:

* assessing the auditor's competence to perform the audit;
* complying with ethical requirements;
* evaluating the integrity of the client's owners, directors and senior managers.

8.2.2 Assessing the auditor's competence to perform the audit

In Chapters 3 and 7 we consider the importance of auditors possessing (or, in the case of specialised skills and knowledge, having available) the capabilities and competence, and also the time and resources, required to complete the audit to a high standard within a reasonable timeframe.

Our earlier discussions of these matters highlight the need for an audit firm, before accepting a new or continuing audit engagement, to consider carefully the specific requirements of the engagement and whether it (or, more pertinently, the audit engagement partner):

- possesses the level of training, experience and competence required to perform the audit satisfactorily.[2] This includes possessing:
  - technical skills and experience in auditing;
  - adequate knowledge of the (potential) client's industry (or industries);
  - adequate knowledge of the relevant regulatory and reporting requirements;
- has available, at the appropriate time, adequate audit staff who possess the capabilities, competence and time necessary to perform the work assigned to them;
- is able to direct, supervise and review the work of audit staff;
- has available, at the appropriate time, assistance from experts and/or other auditors if they are to perform part of the audit;
- if the audit is to be subject to an engagement quality control review (for example, if the potential client is a listed company), has available, at the appropriate time, an engagement quality control reviewer;
- is able to complete the audit within the reporting timeframe.

Additionally, before accepting a new audit client, an audit firm needs to consider the impact of accepting the engagement on its audit client portfolio. In particular, the firm should consider whether acceptance of the client would give rise to any conflict of interest with existing clients and/or whether it would adversely affect its ability to service existing clients properly.

---

[2] The importance of auditors possessing required capabilities and competence to conduct an audit was highlighted in July 2007 when the Securities and Exchange Commission (SEC) in the United States of America (USA) censured Ernst & Young in Dublin for failing to assign auditors with sufficient expertise to examine the financial statements of a software company, SkillSoft plc (a company based in New Hampshire which, at the time of the offence, was known as SmartForce). Ernst & Young in Dublin agreed to pay $725,000 (approximately £362,500) as settlement for its failure (Accountancy Age, 2007).

8.2.3   Complying with ethical standards

In Chapters 3 and 4 we examine in some detail the importance of auditors (engagement partners and audit staff) being independent of their audit clients and their clients' managements. We identify several threats that may endanger auditors' independence – in appearance if not in fact[3] – and various requirements the law, the Auditing Practices Board's (APB) Ethical Standards and the International Ethics Standards Board for Accountants' (IESBA) *Code of Ethics for Professional Accountants* (2009) impose on auditors in order to protect and/or strengthen their independence. Additionally, in section 8.2.2 above, we note the importance of auditors ensuring they have the necessary capabilities and competence to perform the audit before accepting a new or continuing engagement. However, the IESBA's *Code of Ethics* (2009, para 210.1) requires more than this: before accepting a new client or engagement, all professional accountants (including auditors) are to consider whether acceptance would create any threats not just to their independence and competence but to their compliance with *any* of the fundamental ethical principles – integrity, objectivity, professional competence and due care, confidentiality and professional behaviour.[4]

The *Code of Ethics* (IESBA, 2009, para 210.3) requires auditors to evaluate the significance of any identified threats and, unless they are insignificant, to apply safeguards to eliminate or reduce the threats to an acceptable level. The Code explains (para 210.7):

Examples of such safeguards include:
- Acquiring an appropriate understanding of the nature of the client's business, the complexity of its operations, the specific requirements of the engagement and the purpose, nature and scope of the work to be performed.
- Acquiring knowledge of relevant industries or subject matters.
- Possessing or obtaining experience with relevant regulatory or reporting requirements.
- Assigning sufficient staff with the necessary competencies.
- Using experts where necessary.
- Agreeing on a realistic time frame for the performance of the engagement.
- Complying with quality control policies and procedures designed to provide reasonable assurance that specific engagements are accepted only when they can be performed competently.

If auditors are unable to apply safeguards that can eliminate or reduce identified threats to an acceptable level, the engagement should be declined.

---

[3] In Chapter 3 we note that, in the United Kingdom (UK), the Auditing Practices Board has adopted the term 'independence' for independence in appearance and 'objectivity' for independence in fact (or mind). See Chapter 3, section 3.3.1b.

[4] Each of these concepts is discussed in Chapter 3.

In situations where audit firms are invited by a potential client to accept nomination, or to tender, for appointment as auditor and the audit engagement is currently held by another audit firm, in addition to evaluating the firm's ability to comply with all of the ethical principles, the IESBA's *Code of Ethics* (para 210.9) requires the prospective auditor to ascertain whether there are any professional or other reasons for not accepting the appointment. It is important that the prospective audit firm establishes all the facts and circumstances surrounding the proposed change of auditor so that it can make an informed decision about accepting nomination, or tendering, for appointment as auditor. Without knowledge of all of the pertinent facts, acceptance of the audit engagement may, for example, result in exposure to unidentified threats to the auditor's professional competence and due care; or there may be disagreements between the existing auditor and the client which, if known by the prospective auditor, may influence the latter's decision regarding acceptance of nomination, or tendering, for the audit engagement.

Ascertaining the facts and circumstances surrounding a change of auditor usually involves direct communication between the proposed and incumbent auditor. However, the incumbent is bound by his/her duty of confidentiality to the client.[5] Therefore, a prospective auditor, when first invited by a client to accept nomination, or to submit a tender, for appointment as auditor, should explain to the potential client that s/he has a professional duty to communicate with the existing auditor. S/he should also request the potential client to inform the existing auditor of the proposed change and to give the existing auditor written authority to discuss the client's affairs with the prospective auditor. If the client fails or refuses to grant the existing auditor permission to discuss its affairs with the prospective auditor (or, for other reasons, the prospective auditor is unable to communicate with the incumbent), the IESBA *Code of Ethics* requires the prospective auditor to:

> . . . take reasonable steps to obtain information about any possible threats [to compliance with the fundamental ethical principles] by other means, such as through inquiries of third parties or background investigations on senior management or those charged with governance of the client. (para 210.14)[6]

If the prospective auditor is unable to ascertain the necessary facts to make an informed decision as to whether or not to accept nomination, or tender, for the engagement, s/he should not accept nomination or submit a tender.

---

[5] This duty is discussed in Chapter 6, section 6.7.

[6] If a client refuses to give the existing auditor permission to discuss its affairs with the prospective auditor this raises questions about the information the client fears may be conveyed – and, thus, about the wisdom of accepting nomination, or tendering, for appointment as auditor for the client.

Once an existing auditor receives permission from the client to disclose information to a prospective auditor, the existing auditor should provide to the prospective auditor:

> honestly and unambiguously . . . known information on any facts or circumstances that, in the existing [auditor's] opinion, the proposed [auditor] needs to be aware of before deciding whether to accept the engagement. (IESBA, 2009, paras 210.11, 210.14)[7]

Normally the communication between the existing and prospective auditor is a matter of routine and nothing of significance needs to be reported by the former to the latter. However, occasionally, circumstances arise which are likely to affect the prospective auditor's decision to accept or reject the nomination or invitation to submit a tender. These are the matters the incumbent auditor should communicate to the proposed auditor.[8] For example:

(i) reasons for the change of auditor advanced by the client which the existing auditor is aware are not in accordance with the facts (as understood by the latter);

(ii) in the opinion of the existing auditor, the proposal to replace him/her has resulted from the auditor conducting the audit in accordance with Auditing Standards in the face of opposition or evasions by the client which have given rise to important differences of opinion with the client;

(iii) the client, its directors, or employees have deliberately withheld information required by the existing auditor for the performance of his/her duties or have limited, or attempted to limit, the scope of audit work;

(iv) the existing auditor has serious doubts regarding the integrity of the client's directors and/or senior managers. (This matter is considered below.)

From the above, it is evident that the communication between the existing and prospective auditor serves two main purposes, namely:

---

[7] In the UK, the Companies Act 2006 requires the Recognised Supervisory Bodies of which UK company auditors must be members (see Chapter 5, section 5.3.1) to "have adequate rules and practices designed to ensure that – . . . a person ceasing to hold office as a statutory auditor makes available to [the prospective auditor] all relevant information which he holds in relation to that office."

[8] However, the Institute of Chartered Accountants of Scotland's (ICAS) *Code of Ethics* (2011) warns:

> [C]are must be taken when communicating all relevant facts to a [prospective auditor] in situations where the existing [auditor] knows or suspects that their client is involved in money laundering or a terrorist activity. Under the Money Laundering Regulations 2007, the Terrorism Act 2000, and the Terrorism Act 2006 it is a criminal offence to "tip off" a money launderer or terrorist. Accordingly:
>
> • The prospective [auditor] shall not specifically enquire whether the existing [auditor] has reported suspicions of money laundering or terrorism. Such questions place the existing [auditor] in a difficult position and are likely not to be answered . . . ;
> • Disclosure of money laundering or terrorism suspicion reporting by the existing [auditor] to the potential successor shall be avoided because this information may be discussed with the client or former client. (para 210.13)

The *Codes of Ethics* of the other UK professional bodies contain similar warnings.

(i) it reduces the likelihood of the prospective auditor accepting an invitation to be nominated, or to tender, for an audit engagement in circumstances where all of the pertinent facts are not known; and

(ii) it protects the interests of the existing auditor when the proposed change arises from, or is an attempt to interfere with, the conscientious exercise of the existing auditor's duty to act as an independent professional.

8.2.4 Evaluating the integrity of the client's owners, directors and senior managers

It has been noted in earlier chapters that an auditor is required, *inter alia*, to examine financial statements which are prepared by the auditee's directors for parties external to the entity, and to form and express an opinion as to whether these financial statements present a true and fair view of the entity's financial position and performance, and comply with the applicable financial reporting framework and the Companies Act 2006.

During the past 30 to 40 years, deliberate manipulation of financial statement information has been recognised as a serious problem in many parts of the world. Indeed, the problem was perceived to be so serious in the United States of America (USA) in the mid-1980s that, in 1986, the National Commission on Fraudulent Financial Reporting (1987; the Treadway Commission) was established to investigate it. In some cases, entity managements[9] have manipulated financial statement information in order to cover up a fraud (as, for example, in the infamous *Equity Funding* and *Parmalat* cases); in other instances, management has been motivated by a desire to portray the entity's financial position and performance in a more favourable light than is warranted by the underlying facts. This has arisen from management's wish to avoid occurrences such as a decline in the value of the company's shares or public criticism of its performance; or its desire to secure outcomes such as personal bonuses which are linked to reported profits, achieving an unrealistically optimistic profit forecast, or raising new debt or equity capital in financial markets on favourable terms.

In the United Kingdom (UK) (as elsewhere in the world), deliberate but legal manipulation of financial statements (somewhat flatteringly entitled 'creative accounting') has received considerable attention. The International

---

[9] Readers are reminded that in the Preface to this book we note the term 'management' is defined to mean a company's executive directors, non-executive directors and non-director executives (that is, all executives and directors).

and UK Accounting Standards Boards have sought to eliminate so-called creative practices by issuing more tightly prescribed accounting standards. However, in recent years, aggressive earnings management, a variant of creative accounting, has emerged as a significant problem and, as noted in Chapter 6 (section 6.5), the UK's Auditing Practices Board (APB)[10] is keen for auditors to be alert to, and respond to, the risk of clients engaging in this activity – an activity which, unless checked, may progress into fraudulent financial reporting.

If an entity's management lacks integrity, there is a fairly high probability that some manipulation of financial statement information will occur whenever the management perceives it advantageous so to do. Additionally, such a management is likely to be at pains to deceive the auditor to the extent necessary to ensure the auditor does not discover the underlying situation. In this regard it is pertinent to observe that, in many of the court cases where auditors have faced charges of negligence as a result of failing to uncover management fraud, it has been revealed that the senior executives and/or directors who were responsible for the fraud had a past history of such deeds. Arens and Loebbecke (1980), amongst others, have drawn attention to this phenomenon. They state:

> An analysis of recent court cases involving management fraud shows that in most instances the individuals responsible for the fraud had also been previously involved in illegal or unethical business practices. (p. 176)

A specific example of such a case is afforded by de Angelis, instigator of the massive salad oil fraud in the 1960s at the Allied Crude Vegetable Oil Refining Corporation of New Jersey. During the court hearing it was revealed that de Angelis had a string of previous convictions for fraud and other illegal acts committed whilst acting as a company director.[11]

The importance of auditors evaluating the integrity of a potential client's management was emphasised by Pratt and Dilton-Hill (1982). They suggested that management integrity is probably the single most important factor in the

---

[10] As explained in Chapter 5 (section 5.3.1 and footnote 46), in July 2012, the APB (renamed the Audit and Assurance Council) changed from being an 'operating body' of the Financial Reporting Council (FRC) to being an advisory council to the FRC's Codes and Standards Committee. The former and current structure of the FRC is presented on page (xix) at the front of this book.

[11] It is pertinent to note that, in the UK, the Company Directors Disqualification Act 1986 provides for individuals to be disqualified from appointment as a director for a period of up to five years on grounds, among others, of "unfitness" (s. 9). According to the Act, "Unfitness" can result from the individual, when a director of a company, failing to ensure the company:
  – maintained proper accounting records, and
  – prepared financial statements that provide a true and fair view and comply with accounting standards and companies legislation (Schedule 1).

potential for (intentional) material misstatements in financial statements. They also drew attention to the extent to which an auditor relies on information and responses provided by an auditee's management. The nature of an audit is such that auditors form many judgments based on discussions with, and information provided by, management. If an auditee's management lacks integrity, information given to the auditor may be untrustworthy and, as a result, erroneous audit judgments may be made. Examples of cases in the UK where auditors have found themselves in court for alleged negligence, in which the integrity of the directors is highly questionable, include Maxwell Communications, Polly Peck and the Bank of Credit and Commerce International (BCCI).

ISQC 1 (IAASB, 2009a) explains that, in order to form an opinion about the integrity of a potential client, an audit firm should consider matters such as:
- The identity and business reputation of the [potential] client's principal owners, key management [i.e., executives], and those charged with its governance.
- The nature of the client's operations, including its business practices.
- Information concerning the attitude of the client's principal owners, key management and those charged with its governance towards such matters as aggressive interpretation of accounting standards and the internal control environment.
- Whether the client is aggressively concerned with maintaining the [audit] firm's fees as low as possible.
- Indications of an inappropriate limitation in the scope of [audit] work.
- Indications that the client might be involved in money laundering or other criminal activities.
- The reasons for the proposed appointment of the [audit] firm and non-reappointment of the previous firm.
- The identity and business reputation of related parties. (para A19)

In the case of a new audit client, if the potential client has been audited previously, as indicated in section 8.2.3, communication with the incumbent (or outgoing) auditor is an important source of information for a prospective auditor about the matters outlined above, and, more particularly, about the integrity of the entity's management. However, ISQC 1 (para A20) notes that other sources of information include others who may have relevant knowledge about the prospective client; for example, audit firm personal and third parties such as the prospective client's bankers, legal advisors and others in the same industrial sector. Additionally, the audit firm should conduct searches of relevant media databases for references to the potential client and any of its directors, senior executives or influential shareholders during the past three to five years, to ascertain whether there is any information in the public domain which indicates they may have been associated with anything untoward (in particular, with any unethical or illegal activities).

In the USA, some auditors and audit firms consider the integrity of a potential client's management to be so important that they hire professional investigators to obtain information about the reputation and background of key members of its management. In the UK, it is not usual to go to such lengths but, faced by the spate of unexpected company failures and allegations of corporate fraud which have occurred around and since the turn of the twenty-first century, audit firms in the UK have become more diligent than formerly about investigating the integrity of the directors and senior executives of potential audit clients, and more willing to refuse to accept nomination to act as auditors for companies where that integrity is in doubt.[12]

For a continuing audit engagement, the auditor should evaluate the integrity of the client's management by reviewing his/her past experience with that management. However, if significant changes have occurred among the client's senior executives and/or directors during the reporting period, further investigation may be necessary similar to that undertaken for a new audit client.

8.3 AUDIT ENGAGEMENT LETTERS

Once the pre-engagement investigation is complete and the auditor has decided to accept the engagement, an engagement letter is prepared. This is required by ISA 210: *Agreeing the Terms of Audit Engagements* (IAASB, 2009b), which states: "The auditor shall agree the terms of the audit engagement with [the directors] . . . [T]he agreed terms of the audit engagement shall be recorded in an audit engagement letter or other suitable form of written agreement" (paras 9, 10). The purpose of the letter (or other form of written agreement) is:

- to document and confirm the auditor's acceptance of the appointment
- to ensure there is no misunderstanding between the auditor and the client about
  - the auditor's and directors' respective responsibilities,
  - the scope of the audit engagement, and
  - the form of the reports the auditor is to provide at the conclusion of the audit.

It confirms the terms and conditions of the audit engagement and, in effect, is a contract for the audit engagement between the client and the auditor.

---

[12] This information was conveyed to one of the authors of this textbook during interviews with senior audit partners in the Big 4 and some mid-tier firms in London. They also intimated that, since 2002 (and the Enron and other debacles around the same time), most audit firms in the UK have introduced stringent acceptance and continuance audit engagement procedures. These include considering an extensive list of factors (including a set of factors addressing the integrity of the potential client's management) that are listed in engagement acceptance or continuance checklists.

Although the details of engagement letters vary according to the circumstances of the particular audit, certain items are almost invariably included. They usually include, for example, statements referring to:

- the objective of the audit of financial statements;
- the directors' responsibility for preparing financial statements that give a true and fair view of the entity's financial position and financial perform-ance, and comply with an applicable financial reporting framework and the Companies Act (CA) 2006;
- the directors' responsibility for establishing and maintaining an internal control system – a system that is necessary for the preparation of financial statements that are free from material misstatement, whether due to fraud or error;[13]
- the directors' responsibility for ensuring that all of the company's records and documents, and any other information requested in connection with the audit, are made available to the auditors and the auditor will have unrestricted access to those within the entity from whom it is necessary to obtain audit evidence;
- identification of the applicable financial reporting framework;
- the auditor's responsibility to form and express an opinion on the financial statements and to report, in the audit report, if the financial statements do not comply in any material respects with the applicable financial reporting framework, unless the auditor considers that non-compliance is justified in the circumstances;
- other matters the auditor must consider and may need to refer to in the audit report – for example, whether adequate accounting records have been kept by the entity, whether information given in the strategic and directors' reports is consistent with the financial statements, and whether the financial statements give the details of the directors' remuneration required by the CA 2006;
- the scope of the audit and the fact that it will be conducted in accordance with applicable legislation, regulations, ISAs and ethical requirements. Reference is also made to any additional work the auditor is to do beyond that required for a statutory audit;
- arrangements regarding the planning and performance of the audit, including the composition of the audit team;

---

[13] ISA 210, para A11, points out that the directors' assumption of this responsibility is a premise that is "fundamental to the conduct of an independent audit. To avoid misunderstanding, agreement is reached with management [the directors in the UK context] that it acknowledges and understands that it has such responsibilities as part of agreeing and recording the terms of the audit engagement." As we explain in Chapter 13, during the completion and review stage of the audit, the auditee's directors are requested to provide the auditor with written representations, *inter alia*, confirming they have fulfilled their responsibili-ties for the financial statements and financial reporting process.

- in appropriate cases, the involvement of other auditors or experts in certain aspects of the audit;
- the fact that, because of the inherent limitations of an audit, together with the inherent limitations of internal control, there is an unavoidable risk that some material misstatements in the financial statements may remain undiscovered;
- the expectation that the directors and/or executives will provide written confirmation of certain oral representations expressed by them to the auditor during the course of the audit. Attention may also be drawn to the legislative provision under which it is an offence for any person to withhold information from, or to provide misleading or false information to, the auditor in respect of any matter which is material to the audit (i.e., CA 2006, s. 501; see Chapter 5, section 5.5.2);
- the auditor's responsibility for the financial statements for the year in question ceases once the audit report has been issued; however, the auditor should be informed of any material event occurring between the issue of the audit report and the general meeting of the company's shareholders at which the financial statements are presented (i.e., the 'accounts meeting': see Chapter 5, section 5.3.2);
- the form of any reports or other communications that are to be provided by the auditor in relation to the audit;
- the basis on which fees are to be computed and billed;
- any restriction on the auditor's liability that may apply.[14]

An example of an audit engagement letter is provided in Figure 8.1. The auditor prepares two copies of the letter: they are both sent to the client for signing; one is retained by the client; the other is returned to the auditor for inclusion in the current audit file.

In cases where an auditor of a parent entity is also the auditor of a subsidiary, branch or division (i.e., a component) of the entity, ISA 210 (para A25) notes that whether or not a separate engagement letter is sent to the component depends on factors such as:
- who appoints the auditor of the component;
- whether a separate audit report is to be issued on the component's financial statements;
- legal and regulatory requirements relating to auditor appointments;
- the degree of ownership of the component by the parent entity;
- the degree of independence of the component's management from the parent entity.

---

[14] Liability limitation agreements are discussed in Chapter 16, section 16.5.4.

Figure 8.1: Example of an audit engagement letter for use in the UK
(*This specimen letter is modified to meet the needs of specific circumstances relating to the client or the engagement*)

To the directors of Foolproof plc

The objective and scope of the audit

You have requested that we audit the financial statements of Foolproof plc, which comprise the statement of financial position as at 31 March 20X2, and the income statement, statement of changes in equity and cash flow statement for the year then ended, and a summary of significant accounting policies and other explanatory information. We are pleased to confirm our acceptance and our understanding of this audit engagement by means of this letter. Our audit will be conducted with the objective of our expressing an opinion on the financial statements.

The responsibilities of the auditor

We have a statutory responsibility to report to the members of the company whether in our opinion the financial statements give a true and fair view and have been properly prepared in accordance with the Companies Act 2006. In arriving at our opinion, we are required to consider the following matters, and to report on any in respect of which we are not satisfied:
(a) Whether adequate accounting records have been kept by the company and proper returns adequate for our audit have been received from branches not visited by us;
(b) Whether the company's statement of financial position and income statement are in agreement with the accounting records and returns;
(c) Whether we have obtained all the information and explanations we consider necessary for the purpose of our audit; and
(d) Whether the information given in the strategic and directors' reports is consistent with the financial statements.

In addition, there are certain other matters which may need to be dealt with in our report. For example, where the financial statements do not give details of the directors' remuneration or of their transactions with the company, the Companies Act 2006 requires us to disclose such matters in our report.

We have a responsibility to report if the financial statements do not comply in any material respect with applicable financial reporting standards, unless in our opinion the non-compliance is justified in the circumstances. In determining whether or not the departure is justified we consider:
(a) Whether the departure is required in order for the financial statements to give a true and fair view; and
(b) Whether adequate disclosure has been made concerning the departure.

Our responsibilities also include:
• Including in our report a description of the directors' responsibilities for the financial statements; and
• Considering whether other information in documents containing the audited financial statements is consistent with those financial statements.

Once we have issued our report we have no further direct responsibility in relation to the financial statements for that financial year. However, we expect you to inform us of any material event occurring between the date of our report and that of the members' Accounts Meeting which may affect the financial statements.

We will conduct our audit in accordance with International Standards on Auditing (ISAs). Those Standards require that we comply with ethical requirements and plan and perform the audit to obtain reasonable assurance about whether the financial statements are free from material misstatement. An audit involves performing procedures to obtain audit evidence about the amounts and disclosures in the financial statements. The procedures selected depend on the auditor's judgment, including the assessment of the risks of material misstatement of the financial statements, whether due to fraud or error. An audit also includes evaluating appropriateness of accounting policies used and the reasonableness of accounting estimates made by the the directors, as well as evaluating the overall presentation of the financial statements.

Because of the inherent limitations of an audit, together with the inherent limitations of internal control, there is an unavoidable risk that some material misstatements may not be detected, even though the audit is properly planned and performed in accordance with ISAs.

Figure 8.1: *Continued*

In making our risk assessments, we consider internal control relevant to the entity's preparation of the financial statements in order to design audit procedures that are appropriate in the circumstances, but not for the purpose of expressing an opinion on the effectiveness of the entity's internal control. However, we will communicate to you in writing concerning any significant deficiencies in internal control relevant to the audit of the financial statements that we have identified during the audit.

The responsibilities of the directors

Our audit will be conducted on the basis that the directors acknowledge and understand that they have responsibility:

(a) For the preparation and presentation of financial statements that give a true and fair view and are prepared in accordance with International Financial Reporting Standards [or other financial reporting framework];

(b) For such internal control as the directors determine is necessary to enable the preparation of financial statements that are free from material misstatement, whether due to fraud or error; and

(c) To provide us with:

  (i) Access to all information of which the directors and/or executives are aware that is relevant to the preparation of the financial statements such as records, documentation and other matters;

  (ii) Additional information that we may request from the directors or executives for the purpose of the audit; and

  (iii) Unrestricted access to persons within the entity from whom we determine it necessary to obtain audit evidence.

As part of our audit process, we will request from the directors written confirmation concerning representations made to us in connection with the audit.

We look forward to full co-operation from your staff during our audit.

Fees

Our fees, which will be billed as work progresses, are based on the time required by the individuals assigned to the engagement plus out of pocket expenses. Individual hourly rates vary according to the degree of responsibility involved and the experience and skill required.

Reporting

We expect to be able to issue an unmodified audit report but the form and content of our report many need to be amended in the light of our audit findings.

Please sign and return the attached copy of this letter to indicate your acknowledgment of, and agreement with, the arrangements for our audit of the financial statements including our respective responsibilities.

Robinson & Crusoe
(Registered Auditors)

Acknowledged and agreed on behalf of Foolproof plc

....

    (Signed)

....

Name and title of person signing   Date

Source: Adapted from ISA 210 (IAASB, 2009b), Appendix 1

In the case of a continuing audit engagement (or, as ISA 210 terms it, a 'recurring audit'), the auditor may decide that an engagement letter is not needed. However, as part of the annual planning process, the auditor should consider whether a new engagement letter is required.

ISA 210 (para A28) notes that the following factors may make it appropriate to prepare a new engagement letter:

- Any indication that the entity misunderstands the objective and scope of the audit.
- Any revised or special terms of the audit engagement.
- A recent change of senior management [or directors].
- A significant change in ownership.
- A significant change in nature or size of the entity's business.
- A change in legal or regulatory requirements.
- A change in the financial reporting framework adopted in the preparation of the financial statements.
- A change in other reporting requirements.

Before leaving the subject of audit engagement letters, we should note that these letters do not absolve the auditor from any duties in relation to the audit. Their principal purpose is to clarify the objective and scope of the audit and to ensure the client's directors/management are aware of the nature of the audit engagement and of their own responsibilities with respect to the financial statements and other matters mentioned in the engagement letter.[15]

8.4 UNDERSTANDING THE CLIENT, ITS BUSINESS AND ITS INDUSTRY AND HOW IT EVALUATES ITS PERFORMANCE

8.4.1 Importance of gaining an understanding of the client and its performance measures

Once the engagement letter is signed by both the auditor and the client (thereby formalising the audit agreement), the auditor embarks on what is possibly the most important step in the audit process – that of gaining a thorough understanding of the client and the external and internal factors which

---

[15] We should also note that the Companies Act 2006, s. 493, provides for the Secretary of State to develop regulations that require the terms on which a company's auditor is appointed to be disclosed in the company's annual report.

The regulations may require disclosure of –
  (i) a copy of any terms that are in writing, and
  (ii) a written memorandum setting out any terms that are not in writing.

Although in October 2013 there was no indication that such regulations were on the horizon, should they be developed, it seems likely that they will have a significant impact on the form and content of audit engagement letters.

affect it. As indicated in section 8.2, some understanding of the client and its key personnel is necessary before the auditor can decide whether or not to accept, or tender for, the audit engagement. However, in order to plan and perform an effective audit, it is essential that the auditor possesses an in-depth understanding of the client's organisation, structure and key personnel; its business, business operations and processes; its operational, financial and compliance risks; its economic, commercial and competitive environment; the industry in which it operates; and the means by which it evaluates its financial and non-financial performance. Such an understanding is necessary for the auditor to identify and evaluate the client's business risks and, through this, the risk of its financial statements being materially misstated. Hence, gaining a thorough understanding of the client is a pre-requisite to planning the audit.

The link between a client's business risks and the risk of its financial statements being materially misstated is explained in ISA 315: *Identifying and Assessing the Risks of Material Misstatement through Understanding the Entity and its Environment* (IAASB, 2012). This states:

> Business risk is broader than the risk of material misstatement of the financial statements, though it includes the latter. . . . Business risk may arise, for example, from:
> - The development of new products or services that may fail;
> - A market which, even if successfully developed, is inadequate to support a product or service; or
> - Flaws in a product or service that may result in liabilities and reputational risk.
>
> An understanding of the business risks facing the entity increases the likelihood of identifying risks of material misstatement, since most business risks will eventually have financial consequences and, therefore, an effect on the financial statements. However, the auditor does not have a responsibility to identify or assess all business risks because not all business risks give rise to risks of material misstatement.[16] (ISA 315, paras A37, A38)

ISA 315 also explains the importance of understanding the client's business, organisation, industry, performance measures etc. to planning and performing the audit. It observes:

> . . . The understanding establishes a frame of reference within which the auditor plans the audit and exercises professional judgment throughout the audit, for example, when:
> - Assessing risks of material misstatement of the financial statements;
> - Determining materiality . . . ;

---

[16] It may be recalled from Chapter 2, section 2.7.2, that an in-depth and wide-ranging knowledge of the client underlies the business risk approach to auditing. Although an in-depth knowledge of the client is required today, it is less wide-ranging and more focused on risks affecting the financial statements than applied under the business risk approach to auditing.

- Considering the appropriateness of the selection and application of accounting policies, and the adequacy of financial statement disclosures;
- Identifying areas where special audit consideration may be necessary, for example, related party transactions, the appropriateness of management's use of the going concern assumption, or considering the business purpose of transactions;
- Developing expectations for use when performing analytical procedures;
- Responding to the assessed risks of material misstatement, including designing and performing further audit procedures to obtain sufficient appropriate audit evidence; and
- Evaluating the sufficiency and appropriateness of audit evidence obtained, such as the appropriateness of assumptions and of management's oral and written representations. (para A1)

From this it is evident that a thorough understanding of the client, and the external and internal factors which affect it, impacts on virtually every aspect of the audit. It forms the basis for planning the audit, enables the auditor to exercise "appropriate judgment throughout the audit" (ISA 315, para A1) and provides a context for evaluating the credibility of evidence gathered during the audit, including the responses given to the auditor by the client's management and employees: it enables the auditor to determine, in the light of his/her knowledge of the business, its circumstances and its external and internal environment, whether the audit evidence gathered 'makes sense' and 'rings true'.

Notwithstanding the critical importance of obtaining an in-depth understanding of the client in the initial stage of the audit, it should be recognised that this is not a 'one-off' exercise. Instead, it is "a continuous, dynamic process of gathering, updating and analyzing information throughout the audit" (ISA 315, para A1). Thus, this audit step overlaps other audit steps we identify in Chapter 7 (see Figure 7.1).

8.4.2 Environmental factors which affect the client and aspects of its performance measurement

It is all very well to assert that the auditor needs to understand the client and the external and internal environmental factors which affect it, but the question arises: What are these factors? We provide some examples below and then outline key aspects of the auditee's financial and non-financial performance measures which the auditor also needs to understand.

(i) External environmental factors

External factors that affect business entities are very wide ranging. Some are generic to the economy as a whole or to the industry in which an entity operates; others are more entity specific. They may include for example:
- economy-wide factors such as general economic conditions, interest rates, the availability of financing, inflation and foreign currency exchange rates;

- the general economic and competitive conditions of the industry within which the client operates, and the industry's vulnerability to changing economic and political factors;
- government policies affecting the entity's industry or business such as monetary (including financial exchange) controls, tax incentives, and tariffs and trade restrictions;
- legal or other regulatory requirements which affect the client and its industry such as the need to obtain a licence or registration in order to undertake business within the industry, and relevant consumer protection and employment laws and regulations;
- environmental requirements affecting the industry and/or the client's business such as those relating to water and energy supply and cost, waste disposal and pollutants;
- the presence or absence of factors which may characterise the client's industry or its strategy such as changes in product or process technology, cyclical or seasonal activity, products prone to consumer fads or to rapid obsolescence or deterioration, rapidly declining or expanding markets, and price competition;
- environmental considerations such as the availability of suitably qualified employees, and supplier and customer relations, that affect the industry in general and/or the client in particular;
- major policies and practices of the industry, and industry specific legislation, regulations and accounting policies and practices (if any) (for example, loans and investments for banks, and research and development for pharmaceutical businesses);
- reporting obligations to external parties such as shareholders, debenture-holders, regulators (in the case of clients in regulated industries), HM Revenue & Customs, the Department for Business, Innovation & Skills, the Office for National Statistics and the Companies Registrar.

(ii) Internal environmental factors

A wide range of internal factors also affect the client's business, its risk exposures and its financial statements. Those affecting an auditee may include:

- its ownership interests and relationships;
- its organisational structure, and management and governance characteristics;
- the directors' objectives, philosophy and general approach (for example, entrepreneurial or conservative, planned or haphazard, management);
- the relationship between the client's owners (shareholders), directors and non-director executives, and the influence of stakeholders other than shareholders;
- its geographical dispersion and industry segmentation;
- its major subsidiaries and associated entities (if any);
- the location of its production facilities, warehouses and inventories;

- its operational and financial strategies and their related business risks;
- its operating characteristics including its revenue sources (in particular, its products or services), markets (including involvement in electronic commerce such as Internet sales and marketing activities), stages and methods of production and distribution, and activities exposed to environmental risks;
- its key customers and important suppliers of goods and services;
- its employment arrangements, including union contracts, pensions and incentive payment arrangements;
- its financial structure and solvency, and its debt structure and related terms;
- its asset structure and capital investment activities;
- any planned or recently executed acquisitions or divestitures;
- its ethical tone or culture;
- the effectiveness of its control environment and internal controls.

(iii) Key aspects of clients' financial and non-financial performance measures

In addition to obtaining an understanding of the environmental factors which affect an auditee, the auditor needs to understand how the entity measures its financial and non-financial performance. In particular, the auditor needs to understand:
- the client's key financial and non-financial performance indicators and significant ratios, trends and operating statistics;
- how its financial and non-financial performance compares with that of its competitors and industry norms;
- the client's preparation and use of budgets and variance analyses, and of segmental, divisional and departmental information;
- the means by which it reviews its overall financial and non-financial performance and sets targets for the following year;
- the means by which it selects and applies its accounting policies – and why and how changes to the policies are effected. In this regard, the auditor needs to consider in particular: "whether the entity's accounting policies are appropriate for its business and consistent with the applicable financial reporting framework and accounting policies used in the relevant industry" (ISA 315, para 11c).

8.4.3 Obtaining an understanding of the external and internal environmental factors that affect audit clients and their performance measures

Having identified some of the external and internal environmental factors that affect auditees, and elements of their performance measures that are of importance to their external auditor, we need to consider how auditors obtain an understanding of these matters.

A variety of procedures (known as 'risk assessment procedures') are available to assist auditors with this task. They include:
- (i)   visiting the client and touring the premises;
- (ii)   having discussions with key personnel inside and outside of the entity;
- (iii) inspecting the client's documentation;
- (iv)   reviewing industry and business data and publications;
- (v)   reviewing media reports.

We consider each of these below.

(i)   Visiting the client and touring the premises

By visiting the client and touring its premises, the auditor can become familiar with the client's layout, organisation and business operations. It enables the auditor to obtain knowledge of the client's production or service provision processes, its storage facilities and its dispatching procedures. It also enables him/her to gain insight (by observation and enquiry) into the security (or otherwise) of inventories, supplies and property, plant and equipment, and the quantity and quality of these items. Additionally, it enables the auditor to obtain information (by observation and inspection of records) about the client's accounting records, information technology, preparation and use of budget, segmental and divisional information, and the expertise and work habits of its accounting and other personnel. Further, it provides the opportunity to gauge (by observation of activities) the general attitude of client personnel to the control environment and the care with which they discharge their responsibilities.

(ii)   Having discussions with key personnel inside and outside of the entity

By having discussions with key client personnel (for example, the directors and/or audit committee members, chief executive officer, finance director, sales and production managers, and chief internal auditor), the auditor is able to obtain an understanding of the environment in which the entity's financial statements are prepared. The discussions also provide an opportunity for the auditor:
- to gain insight into the objectives, philosophy, strategic plans and general approach/attitudes of key executives within the entity;
- to ascertain its operational and human resources policies and procedures and any changes to these which have occurred during the reporting period or are expected to occur in the current or future periods;
- to determine the views of key personnel about the entity's financial position and performance during the past year, and any changes in its operations, organisation, financial structure or personnel which are planned or expected to occur in the near to medium term future;
- to gain knowledge of its policies and procedures with respect to selecting and applying accounting policies and any changes thereto.

Discussions with these key personnel should cover topics such as likely changes in divisions or departments, or in premises or plant facilities; expected developments in technology, products or services, markets, and/or in production and distribution methods; and any planned or expected changes in senior accounting personnel or to the client's information technology, management information systems (including its accounting system) and/or internal controls.

ISA 315 (IAASB, 2012) explains that enquiries directed to specific entity personnel may be valuable for gaining an understanding of particular aspects of the client and its financial affairs. It notes, for example:

- Inquiries of employees involved in initiating, processing or recording complex or unusual transactions may help the auditor to evaluate the appropriateness of the selection and application of certain accounting policies.
- Inquiries directed toward in-house legal counsel may provide information about such matters as litigation, compliance with laws and regulations, knowledge of fraud or suspected fraud affecting the entity, warranties, . . . , and the meaning of contract terms.
- Inquiries directed towards marketing or sales personnel may provide information about changes in the entity's marketing strategies, sales trends, or contractual arrangements with its customers.
- Inquiries directed to the risk management function (or those performing such roles) may provide information about operational and regulatory risks that may affect financial reporting.
- Inquiries directed to information systems personnel may provide information about systems changes, system or control failure, or other information system-related risks. (para A7)
- If an entity has an internal audit function, inquiries of the appropriate individuals within the function may provide information that is useful to the auditor in obtaining an understanding of the entity and its environment, and in identifying and assessing risks of misstatement at the financial statement and assertion levels. (para A9)

Discussions with significant people outside the client, such as economists and industry regulators, as well as legal, financial (including valuation experts) and other advisors who have provided services to the client or within the industry, enables the auditor to obtain an understanding of some of the external factors affecting the client – and may also provide insight into how other external parties view the client, its directors and its senior executives.

(iii) Inspecting the client's documentation

The auditor may gain considerable knowledge about internal aspects of an auditee and its performance measures by inspecting its documentation. Such documentation includes:

- its legal documents (for example, Memorandum and Articles of Association, and any debenture trust deeds or other loan agreements, and any significant commercial agreements);

- its organisation chart, policies and procedures manuals, and job descriptions;
- its code of corporate conduct and compliance procedures;
- minutes of its directors' and other (especially board committee) meetings;
- reports to shareholders and to regulatory agencies (such as HM Revenue & Customs and, in the case of an auditee in a regulated industry, to the relevant regulator);
- promotional material (in hard copy and electronic form);
- internal financial management reports, budgets and variance reports, and chart of accounts;
- marketing, sales and production strategies and plans; and
- internal audit reports.

(iv)   Reviewing industry and business data and publications

A review of industry and business data, visiting relevant Internet sites, and reading reports by analysts and rating agencies and also trade journals, magazines and similar publications relating to the client or its industry, provides the auditor with information which is helpful in understanding the general economic, political, commercial and competitive factors and processes which are likely to affect the client's operational and financial well-being – and, hence, its financial statements.

(v)   Reviewing media reports

Along similar lines, reviewing media reports which mention the client and/or its directors or senior executives can provide the auditor with an overview of activities in which these parties have been engaged. This, in turn, enables the auditor to understand the character attributes of the client's key personnel and to gain insight into changes which have affected the client and its impact (if any) on the local or wider community.

8.5   IDENTIFYING AND ASSESSING RISKS OF MATERIAL MISSTATEMENT IN THE FINANCIAL STATEMENTS

8.5.1   Importance of identifying and assessing the risk of material misstatement

As indicated in section 8.4.1, a key objective of the auditor gaining an understanding of the client, its external and internal environment, and its financial and non-financial performance measures, is to assist the auditor identify and assess the risk of material misstatement in the financial statements. For example, obtaining knowledge about new products may help the auditor identify potential product liability and/or inventories with values lower than cost;

and knowledge of current and prospective financing arrangements may indicate a risk of loss of financing which may raise questions about the auditee's ability to continue as a going concern.

ISA 315 (para 25) requires auditors to perform procedures to identify and assess the risk of material misstatement at both:
(a) the financial statement level; and
(b) the assertion level[17] for classes of transactions, account balances and disclosures.

ISA 315 explains the relevance of these two levels of risk to auditors as follows:
Risks of material misstatement at the financial statement level refer to risks that relate pervasively to the financial statements as a whole . . . Risks of this nature are not necessarily risks identifiable with specific assertions at the class of transactions, account balance, or disclosure level. Rather, they represent circumstances that may increase the risks of material misstatement at the assertion level, for example, through management override of internal control. Financial statement level risks may be especially relevant to the auditor's consideration of the risks of material misstatement arising from fraud. (para A118)

Risks of material misstatement at the assertion level for classes of transactions, account balances, and disclosures need to be considered because such consideration directly assists in determining the nature, timing, and extent of further audit procedures at the assertion level necessary to obtain sufficient appropriate audit evidence.[18] (para A122)

In addition to identifying and assessing the risks of material misstatement at the financial statement and assertion level, auditors are required to identify and assess any significant risks, that is, risks of material misstatement which, in the auditor's judgment, require special audit attention. Such risks frequently relate to transactions that:
• are unusual because of their size, nature, infrequency of occurrence, are outside the normal course of the entity's business, or relate to recent significant economic, accounting or other developments and, through lack of established practice, are prone to error;

---

[17] Assertions are defined in ISA 315, para 4a, to mean: "Representations by management, explicit or otherwise, that are embodied in the financial statements, as used by the auditor to consider the different types of potential misstatements that may occur." The specific audit objectives referred to in Chapter 7, section 7.3.1, and shown in Figure 7.2, are assertions about sales transactions: i.e., by presenting 'sales' (or revenue) in the financial statements, management is implicitly asserting that recorded sales transactions are authorised, valid, complete and accurate as to their amount, account classification and accounting period. We discuss assertions and audit procedures designed to test them, in Chapter 11.

[18] Expressed alternatively, identification of these risks is necessary for the development of the audit plan (that is, the audit tests to be performed, and when, and by whom, they are to be conducted), which we discuss in Chapter 9.

- involve significant judgment, such as estimates, for which there is a wide range of measurement uncertainty;
- are particularly complex; or
- involve significant transactions with related parties.

Other identified areas of significant risk may relate, for example, to the possibility of fraud, non-compliance with applicable laws and regulations, or doubt about the ability of the entity to continue as a going concern. All areas of significant risk require particularly careful audit examination – examination which is usually undertaken by more senior (more experienced) members of the audit engagement team.

It is only by identifying and assessing the risk of material misstatement at the financial statement level, the assertion level for classes of transactions, account balances and disclosures, and areas of significant risk that auditors are able to plan their audit procedures so as to achieve the audit objective (that is, expressing the appropriate opinion on the financial statements) and to do so efficiently (that is, reaching the appropriate opinion on the financial statements without collecting too much or too little audit evidence).

8.5.2 Means of identifying and assessing the risk of material misstatement

Similar to gaining an understanding of the external and internal factors that affect a client and its performance measures, the question arises about the procedures the auditor needs to perform to identify and assess the risk of material misstatement in the client's financial statements. Three important procedures are as follows:

  (i)   reviewing previous years' audit working papers and past experience with the client;
  (ii) discussion among engagement team members;
  (iii) performing analytical procedures.

We discuss the first two of these procedures below but analytical procedures are the subject of section 8.6.

(i) Reviewing previous years' audit working papers and past experience with the client

Reviewing previous years' audit working papers may highlight problems encountered during previous audits which need to be followed up, or watched for, during the current audit. It may also reveal planned or expected developments which are of significance to the present year's audit – for example, plans disclosed during the previous year to expand or change production and sales, to develop new products, processes and/or markets, to amend distribution policies, or to alter the accounting system, that are likely to have an impact on this year's audit.

Along similar lines, the auditor may glean information, helpful for identifying risks of material misstatement in the current year's financial statements, from the engagement acceptance (or continuance) process and/or from previous audits of the client in which the engagement partner or other senior members of the audit team were involved. Such information may be useful, for example, in enhancing the auditor's understanding of the entity and its external and internal (including its control) environment, and in identifying significant changes the entity or its operations have undergone since the previous audit which may have ramifications for the current year's audit. However, before using information from the past (recorded in previous years' working papers or prior experience with the client), the auditor should perform audit procedures designed to identify any significant changes which have affected the client, its business or its industry since the last audit, and to determine whether the subsequent changes have affected the relevance of that information for the current audit.

(ii) Discussion among engagement team members

It is important that knowledge of the client, its business, its business processes and risks, and its industry do not remain the prerogative of the audit engagement partner and senior members of the audit team. It is essential that all members of the audit team have sufficient relevant knowledge about the client to enable them to perform effectively the audit work assigned to them. It is also important to harness the observations, expertise and thoughts of all members of the audit team in identifying risks of material misstatement in the financial statements. Hence, a key risk assessment procedure is a discussion among audit team members about the client, its business, and the external and internal factors that affect it, and the susceptibility of its financial statements to material misstatement.[19] ISA 315 notes that this discussion, among other things:

- Allows the engagement team members to exchange information about the business risks to which the entity is subject and about how and where the financial statements might be susceptible to material misstatement due to fraud or error.
- Assists the engagement team members to gain a better understanding of the potential for material misstatement of the financial statements in the specific areas assigned to them, and to understand how the results of the audit procedures that they perform may affect other aspects of the audit including the decisions about the nature, timing, and extent of further audit procedures.

---

[19] This meeting usually coincides with that discussed in Chapter 6, section 6.4.1, that is, the audit team meeting which is required by ISA 240: *The Auditor's Responsibilities Relating to Fraud in an Audit of Financial Statements* (IAASB, 2009d) in connection with identifying risks of misstatement resulting from fraud.

- Provides a basis upon which engagement team members communicate and share new information obtained throughout the audit that may affect the assessment of risks of material misstatement or the audit procedures performed to address these risks. (para A21)

ISA 315 (para A22) points out that, for practical reasons, this discussion may not include all members of the audit engagement team (for example, it may be a multi-location and/or large audit, with widely dispersed and/or many members in the audit team). Further, it may not be necessary for all members of the engagement team to be informed about all of the matters discussed or the decisions reached during the discussion. In some cases, the engagement partner may hold the discussion with key members of the engagement team including, if considered appropriate, specialists and those responsible for the audits of components (i.e., subsidiaries or divisions of the client entity), and delegate responsibility for communicating relevant information to others in the audit team to one or more key people involved in the original discussion. Where this responsibility is delegated, the engagement partner should determine the extent of the information to be provided to, and discussed with, other members of the engagement team.

It should be noted that (as highlighted in ISA 315, para A1, cited in section 8.4.1 above) acquiring knowledge and understanding of a client, its business and its industry is not a one-off event which is completed at the commencement of an audit. Rather, it is a continuous and cumulative process which proceeds as the audit progresses. Although information is gathered and assessed during the initial stage of an audit as a basis for planning the rest of the audit, it is usually refined and added to as the engagement partner and other members of the audit team learn more about the client and its business. However, the discussion among audit team members (outlined above) and analytical procedures (discussed below) are generally specific risk assessment procedures which are performed during the initial phase of the audit.

8.6 ANALYTICAL PROCEDURES

8.6.1 Meaning of analytical procedures

Analytical procedures are the means by which meaningful relationships and trends in both financial and non-financial data may be analysed, actual data may be compared with budgeted or forecast data, and the data of an entity may be compared with that of similar entities and industry averages. By this means, any unusual or unexpected characteristics in the audit client's data may be identified. ISA 520: *Analytical Procedures* (IAASB, 2009e) explains:

Analytical procedures include the consideration of comparisons of the entity's financial information with, for example:
- Comparable information for prior periods.
- Anticipated results of the entity, such as budgets or forecasts, or expectations of the auditor, such as an estimation of depreciation.
- Similar industry information, such as a comparison of the entity's ratio of sales to accounts receivable with industry averages or with other entities of comparable size in the same industry.

Analytical procedures also include consideration of relationships, for example:
- Among elements of financial information that would be expected to conform to a predictable pattern based on the entity's experience, such as gross margin percentages.
- Between financial information and relevant non-financial information, such as payroll costs to number of employees. (paras A1, A2)

Analytical procedures primarily consist of ratio, percentage, trend and comparative analyses, although they also include more sophisticated statistical techniques such as regression analysis. In financial accounting the term 'interpretation and analysis' is used to mean essentially the same thing as 'analytical procedures' in auditing. As the ratios, percentages, trends and comparisons used by financial statement users for interpreting financial statements are essentially the same as those used by auditors in analytical procedures, it follows that analytical procedures prompt consideration of the size of errors which would be material to financial statement users.[20] For example, the auditor would seek an explanation of a change in the gross profit percentage from, say, 18 to 20 per cent if such a change would cause financial analysts or other users to change their assessment of the entity's financial performance. It follows that any error in the sales and/or cost of sales account(s) which caused such a shift in the gross profit percentage would be material.

8.6.2 Importance of analytical procedures

Analytical procedures are generally regarded as highly efficient and effective audit procedures; however, it must be borne in mind that their effectiveness is always dependent on the quality of the underlying data. As indicated above, these procedures provide a useful means of establishing whether financial statement amounts display unexpected characteristics, that is, whether they deviate from the auditor's expectations, given his/her understanding of the client, its business, its industry and detailed knowledge of events which have affected the client's financial position and/or performance over the reporting period.

---

[20] Materiality, and the link between the auditor's determination of what is material and financial statement users, is discussed in Chapter 3, section 3.4.2 and Chapter 9, section 9.3.

As shown in Figure 8.2, analytical procedures are used at three different stages during an audit to achieve three different objectives.

1. *During the risk identification and assessment stage* they are used to help:
   - obtain an understanding of the client's business and, more particularly, its financial affairs;
   - assess the likelihood of material misstatements in the financial statements as a whole and in specific classes of transactions, account balances and/or disclosures;
   - identify areas of significant risk;
   - determine appropriate levels of materiality; and
   - plan the nature, timing and extent of further audit procedures.

2. *During the substantive testing stage* they are used to obtain audit evidence in relation to individual classes of transactions, account balances and other disclosures to help establish whether or not they are materially misstated.

3. *During the final review stage* they are used to help confirm (or challenge) conclusions reached by the auditor regarding the truth and fairness of the financial statements.

Figure 8.2:   The use of analytical review procedures in an audit

Stage in the Audit	Objective	Nature of Procedures Used
Risk identification and assessment	• To understand the client's business and its financial affairs • To assess the likelihood of material misstatements in the financial statements • To identify high risk audit areas (i.e., significant risks) • To set materiality limits • To plan the nature, timing and extent of further audit procedures	• Trend analysis • Ratio analysis of entity data • Comparative analysis of entity data with that of other similar entities and industry averages • Relationship between financial and non-financial data (Focus is on the entity's overall financial position and performance)
Substantive procedures	To obtain evidence to help confirm (or refute) the truth and fairness of individual classes of transactions, account balances and other disclosures	Ratio analysis based on direct relationships amongst individual accounts. (Focus is on the reasonableness of individual account balances)
Final review	To confirm (or question) conclusions reached with respect to the truth and fairness of: – income statement amounts – amounts disclosed in the statement of financial position – cash flow statement amounts – financial statement note disclosures	• Trend and percentage analysis of individual accounts • Ratio analysis of financial statement data (Focus is on the truth and fairness of the financial statements as a whole in portraying the entity's financial position, performance and cash flows)

The use of analytical procedures as substantive tests and in the final review of the financial statements is discussed in Chapters 11 and 13, respectively.

8.6.3 Analytical procedures as risk assessment procedures

ISA 315 (IAASB, 2012) para 6, specifically requires analytical procedures to be performed as risk assessment procedures. Expanding on this requirement, the Standard explains:

> Analytical procedures performed as risk assessment procedures may identify aspects of the entity of which the auditor was unaware and may assist in assessing the risks of material misstatement in order to provide a basis for designing and implementing responses to the assessed risks. (para A14)

Analytical procedures performed as risk assessment procedures frequently involve both financial and non-financial information; for example, the relationship between sales and square footage of selling space, or between sales and quantity of goods sold; however, their focus is primarily on the overall financial position and performance of the entity, in particular, its liquidity, solvency (or capital adequacy) and profitability. Analytical procedures performed at this stage of the audit frequently use highly aggregated data and, as they are usually performed only part way (often seven to eight months) into the financial year, surrogates for the end of year data need to be adopted. These may be year-to-date figures (used as they are or extrapolated to the end of the financial year), budgeted data or figures derived from a comparison of this year's figures with those of previous years. For these reasons, analytical procedures used for risk assessment purposes provide only an initial indication of whether (and where) the financial statements may be materially misstated and their results need to be interpreted in the light of information the auditor has obtained through the performance of other procedures designed to provide an understanding of the entity and its financial affairs.

On the basis of his/her understanding of the client and knowledge of events and significant transactions which have affected the client's financial position and performance during the reporting period, the auditor will have certain expectations regarding the results of the analytical procedures performed as risk assessment procedures. Where the results differ from the auditor's expectations, they raise questions about the accuracy of the financial and/or non-financial data used in the analysis (and, hence, about the accuracy of the entity's information systems as well as its financial statements) and/or about the propriety of other information the auditor has obtained on which his/her understanding of the entity and its financial affairs is based. Thus, analytical procedures performed during the initial phase of an audit are useful for confirming or challenging the auditor's understanding of the client and its financial affairs, as well as for ascertaining whether it is likely that the financial statements are materially misstated and for identifying the classes of transactions, account balances or disclosures in which material error appears most likely. Once the likelihood of errors being present in the financial statements has been established, and areas requiring particular audit consideration (i.e., significant risks) have been identified, the auditor can determine the audit segments where audit effort is to be concentrated and plan the nature, timing and extent of further audit procedures to be performed.

8.7 SUMMARY

In this chapter we have discussed the first steps in the audit process. We have considered why an auditor should conduct an investigation before accepting an audit engagement and pointed out that this investigation involves (i) evaluating the integrity of the (potential) client's management, (ii) assessing the auditor's competence to perform the audit and (iii) assessing the auditor's ability to comply with ethical (in particular, independence) requirements.

We have also discussed the purpose and content of audit engagement letters, and examined the importance of the auditor gaining a thorough understanding of the client, its business and industry, and its performance measures. We have noted, in particular, the importance of this understanding for identifying and assessing risks of misstatement in the financial statements, and therefore as a basis for planning the audit. However, we have also observed that this understanding is invaluable for providing a background (or context) against which the auditor can evaluate the credibility of evidence gathered during the audit.

For a new audit engagement, the auditor (or, more specifically, the engagement partner and senior members of the audit team) need to expend considerable time and effort in establishing a sound understanding of the client and its financial and non-financial performance. For continuing engagements, less time and effort may be devoted to this audit step but it should not be skipped altogether. The auditor needs to update and re-evaluate information gathered during previous audits to determine whether it is still valid and relevant.

In the latter part of the chapter, we have considered various means by which the auditor gains an understanding of the client and identifies the risk of material misstatement in the financial statements (i.e., risk assessment procedures). We have paid particular attention to the meaning and importance of analytical procedures and noted that, in addition to constituting risk assessment procedures performed during the initial phase of the audit, they are used in later stages of the audit as substantive and final review procedures.

SELF-REVIEW QUESTIONS

8.1 List three matters the auditor must carefully evaluate before accepting an audit engagement.

8.2 Explain briefly why it is necessary for an auditor to investigate the integrity of a (prospective) client's management before accepting an audit engagement.

8.3 Explain briefly the factors auditors should consider before concluding they are competent to accept a particular audit engagement.

8.4 (a) Explain briefly the purpose of a proposed auditor communicating with the predecessor auditor; and
(b) list three matters about which the proposed auditor should seek information.

8.5 (a) Explain briefly the purpose of audit engagement letters; and
(b) list five items which are almost invariably included in such letters.

8.6 Explain briefly the importance of an auditor gaining a thorough understanding of the client, its business operations, its risks, its industry, and its financial and non-financial performance.

8.7 List (a) five external environmental factors and (b) five internal environmental factors which are likely to affect an entity and its external audit.

8.8 Explain briefly the importance of each of the following as risk assessment procedures:
(i) touring the client's premises;
(ii) reading trade journals and magazines;
(iii) reviewing the client's documentation;
(iv) reviewing prior years' audit working papers and drawing on past experience with the client;
(v) discussion among engagement team members.

8.9 (a) Briefly explain the meaning of the term 'analytical procedures'; and
(b) outline three ways in which these procedures are used during an audit.

8.10 List four ways in which analytical procedures can assist the auditor during the initial (risk assessment) stage of an audit.

REFERENCES

Accountancy Age. (2007, 20 July). *Google Man Settles Accounting Claim at Skillsoft*, www.accountancyage.com/aa/news/1784771/google-settles-accounting-claim-skillsoft, accessed 11 May 2013.

Arens, A.A., & Loebbecke, J.K. (1980). *Auditing: An Integrated Approach*, 2nd ed. New Jersey: Prentice-Hall Inc.

International Auditing and Assurance Standards Board (IAASB) (2009a). International Standard on Quality Control (ISQC) 1: *Quality Control for Firms that Perform Audits and Reviews of Financial Statements, and Other Assurance and Related Services Engagements*. New York: International Federation of Accountants.

International Auditing and Assurance Standards Board (IAASB). (2009b). International Standard on Auditing (ISA) 210: *Agreeing the Terms of Audit Engagements*. New York: International Federation of Accountants.

International Auditing and Assurance Standards Board (IAASB). (2009c). International Standard on Auditing (ISA) 220: *Quality Control for an Audit of Financial Statements*. New York: International Federation of Accountants.

International Auditing and Assurance Standards Board (IAASB). (2009d). International Standard on Auditing (ISA) 240: *The Auditor's Responsibilities Relating to Fraud in an Audit of Financial Statements*. New York: International Federation of Accountants.

International Auditing and Assurance Standards Board (IAASB). (2009e). International Standard on Auditing (ISA) 520: *Analytical Procedures*. New York: International Federation of Accountants.

International Auditing and Assurance Standards Board (IAASB). (2012). International Standard on Auditing (ISA) 315: *Identifying and Assessing the Risks of Material Misstatement through Understanding the Entity and its Environment*. New York: International Federation of Accountants.

International Ethics Standards Board for Accountants (IESBA). (2009). *Code of Ethics for Professional Accountants*. New York: International Federation of Accountants.

Institute of Chartered Accountants of Scotland (ICAS). (2011). *Code of Ethics*. Edinburgh: ICAS.

National Commission on Fraudulent Financial Reporting. (1987). *Report of the National Commission on Fraudulent Financial Reporting* (Treadway Commission). New York: American Institute of Certified Public Accountants.

Pratt, M.J., & Dilton-Hill, K. (1982). The elements of audit risk. *The South African Chartered Accountant*, *18*(4), 137–141.

ADDITIONAL READING

Audit Quality Forum. (2005). *Shareholder Involvement – Auditor Engagement: Disclosure of Contractual Terms*. London: Institute of Chartered Accountants in England and Wales.

Bobek, D.D., Daugherty, B.E., & Radtke, R. (2012). Resolving audit engagement challenges through communication. *Auditing: A Journal of Practice & Theory*, *31*(4), 21–45.

Emby, C., & Favere-Marchesi, M. (2010). Review partners and engagement partners: The interaction process in engagement quality review. *Auditing: A Journal of Practice & Theory*, *29*(2), 215–232.

Epps, K.K., & Messier Jr., W.F. (2007). Engagement quality reviews: A comparison of audit firm practices. *Auditing: A Journal of Practice & Theory*, *26*(2), 167–181.

Gendron, Y. (2002). On the role of the organization in auditors' client-acceptance decisions. *Accounting, Organizations and Society*, *27*(7), 659–684.

Glover, S.M., Jiambalvo, J., & Kennedy, J. (2000). Analytical procedures and audit-planning decisions. *Auditing: A Journal of Practice & Theory*, *19*(2), 27–45.

Green, W. (2008). Are industry specialists more efficient and effective in performing analytical procedures? A multi-stage analysis. *International Journal of Auditing*, *12*(3), 243–260.

Khalil, S.K., Cohen J.R., & Schwartz, K.B. (2011). Client engagement risks and the auditor search period. *Accounting Horizons*, *25*(4), 685–702.

Kochetova-Kozloski, N., & Messier Jr., W.F. (2011). Strategic analysis and auditor risk judgement. *Auditing: A Journal of Practice & Theory*, *30*(4), 149–171.

Lansman, W.R., Nelson, K.K., & Roundtree, B.R. (2009). Auditor switches in the pre- and post-Enron eras: Risk or realignment? *Accounting Review*, *84*(2), 531–558.

Laux, V., & Newman, D.P. (2010). Auditor liability and client acceptance decisions. *Accounting Review*, *85*(1), 261–285.

Luippold, B.L., & Kida, T.E. (2012). The impact of initial ambiguity on the accuracy of analytical review judgments. *Auditing: A Journal of Practice & Theory*, *31*(2), 113–129.

Moroney, R. (2007). Does industry expertise improve the efficiency of audit judgment? *Auditing: A Journal of Practice & Theory*, *26*(2), 69–94.

O'Donnell, E., & Perkins, J.D. (2011). Assessing risk with analytical procedures: Do systems-thinking tools help auditors focus on diagnostic patterns? *Auditing: A Journal of Practice & Theory*, *30*(4), 273–183.

Pollins, M. (2007). Engaging behaviour. *Accountancy*, *140*(1372), 50–51.

Shah, S. (2008) Open access. *Accountancy*, *141*(1373), 122–123.

Stanley, J.D. (2011). Is the audit fee disclosure a leading indicator of clients' business risk? *Auditing: A Journal of Practice & Theory*, *30*(3), 157–179.

Vanderveide, S.D., Chen, Y., & Leitch, R.A. (2008). Auditors' cross-sectional and temporal analysis of account relations in identifying financial statement misstatements. *Auditing: A Journal of Practice & Theory*, *27*(2), 79–107.

9 Planning the Audit; Materiality and Audit Risk

LEARNING OBJECTIVES

After studying the material in this chapter you should be able to:

- discuss the importance of planning an audit;
- explain where 'planning the audit' fits into the audit process;
- differentiate between the two phases of planning an audit;
- distinguish between planning materiality, tolerable error and performance materiality;
- describe the documentation auditors are required to prepare in relation to planning an audit and materiality limits;
- explain what is meant by the auditor's desired level of audit risk (or desired level of assurance) and the factors which affect this;
- discuss the relationship between the auditor's desired level of audit risk, inherent risk, internal control risk and detection risk;
- explain the relationship between materiality limits, audit risk and planning audit procedures.

9.1 INTRODUCTION

If a task is to be accomplished effectively and efficiently it must be carefully planned. This is no less true for an audit than it is for a social event such as a party. The auditor needs to plan what evidence to collect in order to be able to express an opinion on whether the auditee's financial statements give a true and fair view of its financial position and performance and comply with the applicable financial reporting framework and Companies Act 2006 – and how and when to collect this evidence.

In this chapter we discuss the importance of planning an audit and explain where audit planning fits into the audit process. We outline the two phases of planning an audit, that is, establishing the overall audit strategy and developing the audit plan (or audit programme),[1] but, as we discuss developing the

---

[1] Current ISAs adopt the term 'audit plan' for what was formerly referred to as the 'audit programme'; similarly, current ISAs refer to the 'overall audit strategy' in place of the formerly used term: 'overall audit plan'.

audit plan in Chapter 10, we do not consider it in detail here. In this chapter we focus on developing the audit strategy and key elements of that strategy, namely, materiality limits (or thresholds) and the auditor's desired level of audit risk (or desired level of assurance). We also discuss the distinction between planning materiality, tolerable error and performance materiality, factors which affect the auditor's desired level of audit risk, and the relationship between inherent and internal control risk on the one hand and detection risk on the other. Before concluding the chapter we explore the interrelationship between materiality limits, audit risk and planning audit procedures.

9.2 PHASES OF PLANNING AN AUDIT

9.2.1 Benefits and characteristics of audit planning

International Standard on Auditing (ISA) 300: *Planning an Audit of Financial Statements* (IAASB, 2009b) states:

> The objective of the auditor is to plan the audit so that it will be performed in an effective manner [that is, it arrives at the appropriate opinion on the financial statements]. The engagement partner and other key members of the engagement team shall be involved in planning the audit. . . . (paras 4, 5)

Adequate planning provides a number of benefits for an audit. They include ensuring that:

- engagement team members with the required capabilities and competence are selected for the audit and assigned appropriately to segments of the audit;[2]
- the work to be done by experts and/or other auditors is properly integrated with the audit as a whole;
- potential problems are identified on a timely basis;
- engagement team members are adequately directed and supervised, and their work is properly reviewed in a timely manner;
- appropriate attention is given to the different segments of the audit;
- the work is completed in an efficient and timely manner;
- sufficient appropriate audit evidence is collected to enable the auditor to form the appropriate opinion on the auditee's financial statements.

ISA 300 (paras 7, 9) notes that planning an audit entails two distinct phases, namely:

(i) establishing an overall audit strategy which defines the scope, timing and direction of the audit and guides the development of the audit plan;

---

[2] Audit segments are explained in Chapter 10, section 10.2.

(ii) developing an audit plan which sets out, in detail, the expected nature, timing and extent of the audit procedures to be performed.

The Standard also emphasises that planning is not a 'one-off' event which occurs at the start of the audit but it continues throughout an audit. It explains:

> Planning is not a discreet phase of an audit, but rather a continual and iterative process that often begins shortly after (or in connection with) the completion of the previous audit and continues until the completion of the current audit engagement . . . As a result of unexpected events, changes in conditions, or the audit evidence obtained from the results of audit procedures, the auditor may need to modify the overall audit strategy and audit plan and thereby the resulting planned nature, timing and extent of further audit procedures . . . The auditor shall update and change the overall audit strategy and the audit plan as necessary during the course of the audit. (ISA 300, paras A2, A13, 10)

9.2.2 The overall audit strategy

As indicated above, for a continuing audit, planning the current audit engagement often begins as the previous year's audit is completed. For a new client, planning commences before or as soon as the audit engagement letter is signed. Whether a new or continuing audit, planning commences with planning the risk assessment procedures – procedures designed to gain an understanding of the client and its financial affairs, and to identify and assess the risk of its financial statements being materially misstated – and where, within the financial statements, material misstatement seems most likely. It is only when this risk has been assessed that the auditor is in a position to plan audit procedures to address the identified risks. Thus, planning the audit occurs prior to, concurrently with, and as an outcome of, the auditor gaining an understanding of the client and its financial affairs and performing other risk assessment procedures. Nevertheless, as noted earlier, there are two distinct phases in planning an audit – establishing the overall audit strategy (the broad approach to the audit) and developing the audit plan (the detailed audit tests to be performed).

Establishing the overall audit strategy involves setting the parameters for the audit – it defines in broad terms:
- how much and what evidence to gather;
- how, when and by whom this should be done.

It depends on a wide range of factors, including, for example:[3]
- the general economic and industry conditions affecting the entity's business, and important characteristics of the entity including its organisational structure; business operations; financial position and performance; operational, financial and compliance risks; and statutory, regulatory and reporting requirements. (These factors coincide with those identified in

---

[3] The Appendix to ISA 300 provides a comprehensive list of matters the auditor should consider when establishing the overall audit strategy.

Chapter 8, section 8.4, in relation to 'Understanding the client, its business and its industry');

- the limits beyond which errors in the financial statements as a whole, and in individual financial statement amounts or disclosures, are to be regarded as 'material'. (This factor is discussed in section 9.3 below);
- the level of risk the auditor is prepared to accept that the opinion expressed in the audit report may be inappropriate. (This factor is discussed in section 9.4 below);
- the likelihood of material errors being present in the (pre-audited) financial statements as a whole and in sections thereof (that is, the level of inherent risk and internal control risk). (This factor is discussed in section 9.5 below);
- the appropriate segments into which the audit should be divided to facilitate the conduct of audit work. (This factor is discussed in Chapter 10, section 10.2);
- the availability of audit evidence from different sources and of different types. (This factor is discussed in Chapter 7, section 7.4);
- the availability of audit staff with the appropriate level of capabilities and competence and, where applicable, other (outside) auditors and experts. (This factor is discussed in Chapter 7, section 7.5);
- the likely impact of the use of information technology by (i) the entity and (ii) the auditor. (This factor is discussed in Chapter 12, section 12.9).

Taking factors such as those outlined above into consideration, the overall audit strategy sets out in broad terms, *inter alia*:

(i) the resources (number and experience level of engagement team members and hours) expected to be allocated to the audit as a whole and to specific audit segments – for example, the use of appropriately experienced team members for areas of significant risk,[4] the involvement of experts for complex and specialised matters, and the number of team members expected to be required to observe the inventory count at various locations;

(ii) the nature of audit procedures to be performed – in particular, the expected emphasis to be placed on, respectively, compliance testing (testing the compliance of the client's employees with its internal controls) and substantive testing (substantiating the client's transactions, account balances and other financial statement disclosures);[5]

(iii) the timing of audit procedures – more particularly, the expected proportion of testing to be conducted during the interim audit (that is, two or three months before the end of the client's reporting period) and the

---

[4] Areas of significant risk are explained in Chapter 8, section 8.5.1.

[5] Compliance testing is discussed in Chapter 10; substantive testing in Chapter 11.

final audit (that is, at or shortly after the end of the client's reporting period);[6]

(iv) the extent of audit procedures – the amount of audit testing expected to be performed in respect of each audit segment;

(v) how audit team members are to be directed and supervised, when team briefing and debriefing meetings are expected to be held, and how audit working paper reviews are expected to take place (whether, for example, they are to be reviewed on-site or off-site and face-to-face or electronically).

9.2.3 The audit plan (or audit programme)

The audit plan, in effect, operationalises the overall audit strategy. It sets out, in detail, the audit procedures to be performed at each stage, and in each segment, of the audit; it also indicates those to be performed during the interim audit and those to be performed during the final audit. Frequently, it includes details of such things as the objective(s) of the procedures to be performed, the size of samples to be tested and how the samples are to be selected.

As noted in Chapter 7, the audit plan often lists audit procedures in the form of instructions audit staff can follow. As the procedures are performed, they are signed off by the staff member concerned and cross-referenced to relevant audit working papers. (Developing the audit plan is discussed further in Chapter 10, section 10.5.)

9.2.4 Audit planning documentation

In addition to developing the overall audit strategy and audit plan, auditors are required to prepare related documentation. More specifically, ISA 300 (paras 12, A16–A19) requires auditors to document:

(a) the overall audit strategy: this is to record the key decisions the auditor considered necessary for the proper planning of the audit and for communicating significant matters to the audit team. ISA 300 (para A16) notes that the audit strategy may be summarised in the form of a memorandum which records key decisions regarding the overall scope, timing and conduct of the audit;

(b) the audit plan: this is to record the planned nature, timing and extent of risk assessment procedures and the procedures performed in response

---

[6] In general, the interim audit focuses on understanding the entity's accounting system and testing entity employees' compliance with internal controls; the final audit focuses, more particularly, on substantive testing and the completion and review phase of the audit.

to the assessed risks. ISA 300 (para A17) notes that standard audit programmes or audit checklists may be used providing these are tailored appropriately for the particular circumstances of the audit engagement;

(c) any significant changes made during the audit to the overall audit strategy or audit plan, and resulting changes to the planned nature, timing and extent of audit procedures – and the reasons for the changes. As we note in section 9.2.1, planning continues throughout the audit – and changes to the overall audit strategy and audit plan are frequently required when the auditor encounters unexpected events or conditions or the results of audit procedures differ from those expected.

9.3   IMPACT OF MATERIALITY ON PLANNING AN AUDIT

9.3.1   Planning materiality and tolerable error

We note in Chapter 3 (section 3.4.2) that auditors are required to express an opinion "on whether the financial statements are prepared, in all *material* respects, in accordance with an applicable financial reporting framework[7] . . . [and] give a true and fair view in accordance with the framework" [ISA 200: *Overall Objectives of the Independent Auditor and the Conduct of an Audit* . . . (IAASB, 2009a, para 3: emphasis added)]. We also note that, according to ISA 320: *Materiality in Planning and Performing an Audit* (IAASB, 2009c):

- Misstatements, including omissions, are considered to be material if they, individually or in aggregate, could reasonably be expected to influence the economic decisions of users taken on the basis of the financial statements;
- Judgments about materiality are made in the light of the surrounding circumstances, and are affected by the size or nature of a misstatement or a combination of both. (para 2)

From these quotations it is evident that, when planning their audits, auditors need to form a judgment on what is 'material' in the context of the particular audit engagement (that is, what error(s) or omission(s) are likely to affect the economic decisions of users of the audited financial statements). In Chapter 3 we explain that auditors need to consider materiality at the level of (i) the financial statements as a whole and (ii) an individual account balance or other disclosure. As we explain below, the distinction between financial statement and account level materiality is important when planning an audit.

---

[7] As noted in Chapter 5, section 5.2.2, in the United Kingdom (UK), the Companies Act 2006 recognises two such frameworks – International Accounting (or Financial Reporting) Standards (IAS) and UK Generally Accepted Accounting Practice (UK GAAP).

(i) Planning materiality at the financial statement level

Planning materiality (or materiality at the financial statement level) is the amount of misstatement (errors and/or omissions) the auditor is prepared to accept in the financial statements as a whole while still concluding that they provide a true and fair view of the financial position and performance of the reporting entity and comply with the applicable financial reporting framework. The auditor needs to estimate this level of misstatement, or materiality limit, prior to commencing the audit based on his/her:

- understanding of the client, its business and its industry; and
- assessment of the decision needs of users of the entity's financial statements.

It is often referred to as 'planning materiality' as it affects the nature, timing and extent of procedures planned for the audit as a whole. The lower the level of planning materiality (the smaller the amount of misstatement in the financial statements as a whole which qualifies as 'material'), the greater the amount and/or the more appropriate the evidence[8] that needs to be collected in order to establish that the combined errors and/or omissions in the financial statements do not exceed it.

There are essentially three steps in determining planning materiality, namely:

- (a) selecting one or more appropriate benchmark(s);
- (b) identifying appropriate financial data for the selected benchmark(s);
- (c) determining a percentage to be applied to be selected benchmark(s).

- (a) Selecting appropriate benchmarks: ISA 320 identifies a number of factors that may affect the selection of an appropriate benchmark. These include:
  - The elements of the financial statements (for example, assets, liabilities, equity, revenue, expenses);
  - Whether there are items on which the attention of the users of the particular entity's financial statements tends to be focused (for example, for the purpose of evaluating financial performance users may tend to focus on profit, revenue or net assets);
  - The nature of the entity, where the entity is in its life cycle,[9] and the industry and economic environment in which the entity operates;
  - The entity's ownership structure and the way it is financed (for example, if an entity is financed solely by debt rather than equity, users may put more emphasis on assets, and claims on them [i.e., liabilities], than on the entity's earnings); and
  - The relative volatility of the benchmark.[10] (para A3)

---

[8] The relationship between the sufficiency and appropriateness of evidence is discussed in Chapter 7, section 7.4.

[9] During their initial years of existence, for instance, companies may (and frequently do) trade at a loss.

[10] For example, over time, profit before tax may be more variable than sales (or vice versa).

The standard cites as examples of benchmarks that may be appropriate:

> . . . categories of reported income such as profit before tax, total revenue, gross profit and total expenses, total equity or net asset value. Profit before tax from continuing operations is often used for profit-oriented entities . . . [but if this] is volatile, other benchmarks may be more appropriate, such as gross profit or total revenues. (para A4)

(b) *Identifying financial data:* Once appropriate benchmarks have been selected, financial data for the benchmark(s) need to be identified. This is not quite as straightforward as it might appear because, as we note above, materiality limits provide the basis for planning the nature, timing and extent of audit procedures to be performed during the audit and, in most cases, the audit is planned, and materiality limits are determined, part way through the client's financial year. As a consequence, the end of year financial statement figures are not usually available and alternative financial data need to be used for the selected benchmark(s). ISA 320 explains that such data:

> . . . ordinarily includes prior periods' financial results and financial positions, the period-to-date financial results and financial position, and budgets or forecasts for the current period, adjusted for significant changes in the circumstances of the entity (for example, a significant business acquisition) and relevant changes of conditions in the industry or economic environment in which the entity operates. (para A5)

(c) *Determining the percentage to apply:* The percentage to be applied to a benchmark is a matter for the auditor's professional judgment but, in general, it varies according to the benchmark in question. For example, as may be seen from Figure 9.1, a higher percentage is generally applied to profit before tax than to total revenue.

Although an estimate of planning materiality is usually determined in this way, the figure arrived at is not a fixed monetary amount which, if exceeded even by a small margin, will necessarily cause the auditor to conclude that the financial statements are materially misstated but which, if not exceeded, will lead to the contrary conclusion. When forming an opinion on the truth and fairness of a set of financial statements, the auditor considers a myriad of factors – including the size and direction of the difference between misstatements in the financial statements identified by audit procedures and planning materiality (that is, the maximum amount of error the auditor is prepared to accept while still concluding the financial statements are 'true and fair'). Planning materiality provides a starting point for the auditor's conclusion.

To emphasise the imprecise nature of planning materiality, auditors frequently express it as a range rather than a single monetary amount and, in many cases, it is derived from the 'average' of applying appropriate percentages to three or four benchmarks. Surveys in the United States of America (USA), New Zealand (NZ) and elsewhere have shown the variety of benchmarks and percentages auditors adopt when determining planning materiality. A survey conducted in the USA by Read, Mitchell and Akresh (1987), for example, found that the 97 auditors surveyed used nine different benchmarks to establish planning materiality. The most popular were pre-tax operating income (used by 45 per cent of respondents), total revenue (used by 15 per cent) and after-tax operating income (used by 10 per cent). Other benchmarks used include total assets, current assets, current liabilities and non-current liabilities. Interestingly, 12 per cent of the auditors surveyed did not use a financial statement amount to arrive at a figure (or range of figures) for planning materiality but relied instead on judgment (or 'instinct').[11] The study also showed that even where different auditors adopted the same benchmark to estimate planning materiality (such as pre-tax operating income), they applied a variety of percentages to the benchmark.

A survey conducted in NZ in 2007[12] found that the 'Big 4' accounting firms and three middle tier firms (all represented internationally) determined their planning materiality based on the benchmarks and percentages shown in Figure 9.1. From Figure 9.1, it can be seen that, as found by Read *et al.* (1987), in 2007, audit firms in NZ used a variety of benchmarks and applied different percentages to the same benchmark. However, all of the survey respondents emphasised that the results derived from applying percentages to benchmarks provide only an initial guide to planning materiality. They stressed that determining planning materiality involves considerable judgment and that a wide range of factors are taken into consideration. They observed, for example, that the size and complexity of the entity, in addition to the factors identified in ISA 320, para A3 (cited above), may affect the selection of appropriate benchmarks. Similarly, the percentage applied to a particular benchmark is affected by factors such as the expectations of users of the entity's financial statements, the measure of planning materiality adopted in prior years, the entity's concept of materiality and the risk of the engagement – in particular, the potential for fraud and the industry in which the entity operates.

---

[11] Given the requirements of ISA 320, it seems unlikely that such a finding would be obtained today. Nevertheless, as shown by the results of a survey conducted in NZ in 2007 (presented in Figure 9.1), key benchmarks used by auditors in the mid-1980s remain important in the current auditing arena.

[12] The survey was conducted by one of the authors for the purposes of this chapter. The results are not reported elsewhere.

**Figure 9.1: Planning Materiality Guidelines used in New Zealand in 2007 by the
'Big Four' and three middle-tier audit firms for profit-oriented companies**

Criteria	_Audit Firms_ 1	2	3	4	5	6	7
Net profit – before tax – after tax	5–10%	5–10%*	5–10%	-	5–10%‡	5%	5%
Sales (or turnover)	0.5%–1%	0.5–3%	0.5 %	1%	0.5–1%	0.5%††	0.5%
Gross profit	-	-	1–2% (rarely used)	-	-	-	-
Total assets	1.5%	-	0.25–0.5%	2%†	0.5–1%	0.5%††	-
Current assets	-	2%	-	-	-	-	-
Net assets	-	-	-	-	0.5–1%	-	0.5%
Shareholders' funds	5–10%	2%	1–5%	1–5%	1–2%	-	-

Notes: * Audit firm 2 uses 5–10% of net profit after tax for public companies and all four benchmarks indicated for non-public companies.
† Used by audit firm 4 for financial institutions.
‡ Audit firm 5 uses 5% of pre-tax profit for public companies and 5–10% for non-public companies.
†† Audit firm 6 uses the most appropriate of these two benchmarks when net profit before tax is not the most suitable benchmark for setting planning materiality.

(ii) Planning materiality at the account or disclosure level (tolerable error)

The monetary amount (or range) established for planning materiality defines the maximum amount of error the auditor is prepared to accept in the financial statements as a whole before concluding they are materially misstated and, therefore, not 'true and fair'. It also provides the basis for establishing the maximum amount of error the auditor will accept in an individual class of transactions, account balance or other disclosure before concluding that the relevant class of transactions, account balance or disclosure is materially misstated. Similarly, while planning materiality helps to determine the nature, timing and extent of audit procedures for the audit as a whole, materiality at the account or disclosure level helps to determine the nature, timing and extent of audit procedures to be performed in relation to the particular class of transactions, account balance or other disclosure. Use of the term 'tolerable error' for materiality at the account or disclosure level is useful for distinguishing between this level of materiality and materiality at the financial statement level (i.e., planning materiality). We therefore adopt this term for use in this book.

It should be noted that auditors are not required to determine a tolerable error for every class of transactions, account balance or other disclosure. This is only necessary for classes of transactions, account balances or other financial statement disclosures:

> . . . for which misstatements of lesser amounts than materiality for the financial statements as a whole[13] could reasonably be expected to influence the economic decisions of users taken on the basis of the financial statements, . . . (ISA 320, para 10)

In practice, most audit firms determine a tolerable error for each significant class of transactions, account balance or other financial statement disclosure. However, as for setting planning materiality, the task involves considerable professional judgment, and different audit firms approach it in different ways. Nevertheless, in general, as a starting point, tolerable error for each class of transactions, account balance or other disclosure for which a tolerable error is to be determined is set at a selected level of planning materiality (for example, 75 or 50 per cent of planning materiality, or somewhere between these limits[14]). Factors which influence the auditor's decision as to whether tolerable error should be set closer to 75 or 50 per cent of planning materiality for a particular class of transactions, account balance or other disclosure include the following:

(a) past history with the client's audits and, more especially, whether audit adjustments have usually been required. If this is the case, tolerable error will be set at a lower level, that is, closer to 50 per cent of planning materiality; if not, it is likely to be set at a higher level, that is, closer to 75 per cent;

(b) the level of risk attaching to the audit engagement, that is, whether the likelihood of the auditor failing to detect material misstatements is higher or lower than usual. The risk is higher, for example, where the industry in which the client operates is characterised by volatile revenues and/or profits, or when it is a 'first time audit' and the auditor is not familiar with the client. The riskier the audit engagement, the closer tolerable error will be to 50 per cent of planning materiality.

The monetary amount initially established as the tolerable error for a class of transactions, account balance or disclosure may be adjusted upwards or downwards for factors which are specific to the class of transactions, account balance or disclosure in question. Such factors include:

---

[13] If planning materiality is the maximum amount of error the auditor will accept in the financial statements as a whole while still concluding that they give a true and fair view of the reporting entity's financial position and performance, it is evident that tolerable error (the maximum amount of error the auditor will tolerate in a class of transactions, account balance or disclosure while concluding that the relevant balance or disclosure is true and fair) cannot exceed the monetary amount of planning materiality.

[14] These percentages reflect the bases for setting tolerable error used by firms included in the materiality survey conducted in NZ in 2007.

- the significance of the account balance to the decisions of users of the financial statements. The cash balance, for instance, with its implications for the company's liquidity and adaptability, is likely to be more important to financial statement users than – say – prepaid expenses. The more important a particular account balance or disclosure is to users, the more important its accuracy; hence, the smaller the tolerable error. In the case of cash, it may even be set at around 10 per cent of planning materiality;
- the size of the account balance. For example, if the accounts receivable balance is £1,500,000 and the inventory balance is £4,700,000, the tolerable error for accounts receivable (in monetary terms) is likely to be set at a lower level than for inventory;
- the auditability of the account. The balances of certain accounts such as cash and loans are capable of more accurate determination than others – for example, accounts receivable and depreciation where provisions (or allowances) need to be estimated. This variation is likely to be reflected in the expectations of financial statement users; the greater the expected accuracy of an account balance, the smaller the tolerable error is likely to be;
- the sensitivity of the account or disclosure and/or its susceptibility to fraud (whether in the form of misappropriation of assets, such as inventory, or fraudulent financial reporting, such as accruals). For example, a disclosure relating to loan covenants or directors' remuneration is likely to be highly sensitive and, as a consequence, the tolerable error is likely to be relatively small. In the case of disclosures about directors' remuneration that are required by law and highly sensitive, tolerable error will tend towards zero;
- the relative significance of understatement and overstatement of an account balance. In general, overstatements of assets and understatements of liabilities are likely to be more important to financial statement users than their counterparts (understatements of assets and overstatements of liabilities) and this can be reflected in the materiality limits. Tolerable error may, therefore, be set at different levels for understatements and overstatements in certain account balances.

It should be noted that tolerable error (like planning materiality) is an estimate, not a 'magic number' which, if exceeded by even a minuscule amount, will cause the auditor to require the account balance or disclosure to be adjusted before a 'clean' (unmodified) audit report can be issued but which, if not exceeded, prompts no action. It is a starting point for the auditor to investigate further the class of transactions, account balance or other financial statement disclosure to ascertain whether it is or is not materially misstated.

As for determining planning materiality, determining the tolerable error for individual classes of transactions, account balances or other disclosures is an important step in planning the audit; the magnitude of the tolerable error in each class of transactions, account balance or disclosure has a direct impact on what qualifies as 'sufficient appropriate audit evidence' (see Chapter 7, section 7.4). The smaller the tolerable error, the more relevant and reliable and/or the greater the amount of evidence the auditor needs to collect in order to be assured that misstatement of the account or disclosure in question does not exceed the pre-determined limit.

9.3.2   Performance materiality

It should be recalled that planning materiality is the amount of mistatement in the financial statements as a whole, and tolerable error is the amount of mistatement in a class of transactions, account balance or disclosure, that the auditor will accept while still concluding that the financial statements as a whole, or the class of transactions, account balance or disclosure (as applicable) are fairly stated. These levels of materiality allow for both:
  (i)   mistatements detected by the auditor, through examination of samples of audit evidence, which remain uncorrected (that is, uncorrected mistatements);[15] and
  (ii) mistatements the auditor estimates to be present in the populations of evidence which are not detected through examination of samples of evidence drawn from those populations (that is, undetected mistatements).
Clearly, the auditor's estimate of undetected mistatements (like all estimates) is prone to error. It is, therefore, useful for the auditor to specify an amount, lower than planning materiality (or tolerable error) which, if equalled or exceeded during the performance of the audit, gives warning that planning materiality (or tolerable error) may be exceeded.[16] This lower level of materiality is known as performance materiality. ISA 320 explains the term as follows:

> [P]erformance materiality means the amount or amounts set by the auditor at less than materiality for the financial statements as a whole to reduce to an appropriately low level the probability that the aggregate of uncorrected and undetected mistatements exceeds materiality for the financial statements as a whole [that is, planning materiality]. . . . [P]erformance materiality also refers to

---

[15] When mistatements are detected, unless they are clearly trivial, the auditor will request the client's management to correct them. If corrected, they are no longer mistatements. Thus, the errors of relevance to planning materiality and tolerable error are those that management refuses to correct (that is, uncorrected mistatements) together with an estimate of undetected mistatements.

[16] It needs to be remembered that the auditor is required to specify amounts for planning materiality, tolerable error and performance materiality when planning the audit, that is, before audit testing commences.

the amount or amounts set by the auditor at less than the materiality level or levels for particular classes of transactions, account balances or disclosures [i.e., tolerable error]. (para 9)

If, during the audit, the aggregate of uncorrected and undetected mistatements gets close to performance materiality, it warns the auditor that the financial statements as a whole, or an account balance or disclosure, as applicable, may be materially misstated. The auditor then needs to perform further audit procedures in order to obtain a better estimate of the mistatement in the financial statements as a whole, or in the class of transactions, account balance or disclosure under consideration.

Like determining planning materiality and tolerable error, determining performance materiality requires the exercise of the auditor's professional judgment. As ISA 320 observes:

> . . . The determination of performance materiality is not a simple mechanical calculation and involves the exercise of professional judgment. It is affected by the auditor's understanding of the entity, updated during the performance of the risk assessment procedures; and the nature and extent of misstatements identified in previous audits and thereby the auditor's expectations in relation to misstatements in the current period. (para A12)

9.3.3 Illustration of planning materiality, tolerable error and performance materiality

Planning materiality, tolerable error and performance materiality may, perhaps, be best understood if they are illustrated by an example. Let us assume that for the audit of a particular company the auditor has decided it is appropriate to determine planning materiality based on the average of the following:

- five per cent of net profit before tax; this is calculated to be £5.9 million;
- one per cent of total sales; this is calculated to be £6.4 million;
- one point five per cent of total assets; this is calculated to be £6.3 million; and
- two per cent of shareholders' funds (equity); this is calculated to be £5.4 million.

Thus, planning materiality is determined to be in the region of

$$(£5.9m + £6.4m + £6.3m + £5.4m)/4 = £6 \text{ million}.$$

During the performance of the audit, the auditor will accept an aggregate of (a) detected but uncorrected mistatements and (b) undetected mistatements (mistatements the auditor considers might be present in the population which are not detected through examination of audit samples) of up to about £6 million and still conclude that the financial statements as a whole are fairly stated (provide a true and fair view).

Let us also assume that, given the particular circumstances of the audit, the auditor considers it appropriate to initially set tolerable error for significant classes of transactions, account balances and other financial statement disclosures at between 50 and 75 per cent of planning materiality (between £3 million and £4.5 million). If the account being considered is – say – inventory, the auditor will be aware, amongst other things, of the difficulty of estimating the value of this account balance as a consequence of, for example, assessing the condition of some of the inventory, the degree of completion of manufactured goods, and possible obsolescence. Given such factors, the initial estimate of tolerable error may be close to 75 per cent of planning materiality (let us say 70 per cent; i.e., £4.2 million). On the other hand, if the account being considered is cash, the significance of this account balance to users of the financial statements and their probable expectation that the balance will be stated fairly accurately mean that it is likely that the initial estimate of tolerable error will be adjusted downwards by a significant amount – to, say, 20 per cent of planning materiality (i.e., £1.2 million). Thus when the audit is performed, the auditor will accept an aggregate of uncorrected and undetected mistatements of about £4.2 million in the inventory account balance and £1.2 million in the cash account balance and still conclude that these account balances are fairly stated.

Let us further assume that the auditor considers it is appropriate to set performance materiality (an amount lower than planning materiality and tolerable error which warns the auditor that planning materiality or tolerable may be exceeded) at 75 per cent of planning materiality and tolerable error. This means that the auditor sets performance materiality for:
- the financial statements as a whole, at £4.5 million;
- the inventory account, at £3.15 million; and
- the cash account, at £900,000.

If misstatements of this magnitude are encountered during the audit (allowing for both uncorrected and undetected mistatements) it highlights the risk that planning materiality and/or tolerable error may be exceeded and further audit procedures will need to be conducted to ascertain whether this is, or is not, the case.

9.3.4 Amending materiality estimates

When considering materiality in the auditing context it is important to remember that planning materiality, tolerable error and performance materiality are set by the auditor during the initial planning phase of the audit. Although the quantitative limits of these levels of materiality are determined as objectively as possible, this does not mean they should be regarded as fixed and immutable. As explained in Chapter 3 (section 3.4.2), qualitative characteristics of financial statement items are also important and, when the materiality (or otherwise) of a misstatement is evaluated, as much attention should be given to the nature of the misstatement as to its size.

Further, as the audit progresses, the auditor may find that the level of planning materiality, tolerable error in one or more class of transactions, account balance or disclosure, or performance materiality needs to be amended. This may occur, for instance, because:

- the financial data applied to a benchmark used to establish planning materiality (such as pre-tax profits or sales) part way through the client's financial year is found to be significantly inaccurate as more complete data for the financial year becomes available;
- the auditor's understanding of the entity and its operations is changed as a result of performing further audit procedure; and/or
- there is a change in the client's circumstances such as the disposition or acquisition of a major part of the entity's business.

In any case where new information or changed circumstances are such that, had the auditor known the facts initially, different materiality limits would have been determined, the auditor should revise them accordingly. Additionally, the implications of the revised materiality levels for the planned audit procedures – their nature, timing and extent – need to be considered and any necessary modifications made to the audit plan.

In general, auditors find it easier to adjust materiality estimates upwards. They tend to be less willing to adjust them downwards or to maintain those which are found to have been exceeded. This asymmetry arises because, the lower the level of materiality:

- the greater the amount and/or the more appropriate (relevant and/or reliable) the audit evidence that needs to be collected to make sure the limit has not, in fact, been exceeded. (The lower the materiality limit, the smaller the margin of error within which the auditor must work – and, thus, the more 'careful' the auditor must be to establish, through the collection of evidence, that the limit has not been exceeded);
- the more likely it is that the aggregate of uncorrected and undetected misstatements will exceed planning materiality or tolerable error (as applicable) and thus qualify as 'material'. Such (material) errors, if not adjusted by the reporting entity, will almost certainly result in a modified audit report.[17]

The auditor will not relish having to increase the extent, or amend the nature, of planned audit procedures, largely because such an extension or amendment

---

[17] The various types of audit report are discussed in Chapter 14, section 14.

is likely to adversely affect audit time and cost.[18] Similarly, the auditor will not welcome having to put pressure on the reporting entity's management (if this becomes necessary) to correct misstatements in the financial statements which are judged by the auditor to be material and, in the event of the auditee's directors not making the required amendments, issuing a modified audit report. Such eventualities almost invariably cause a strain in the auditor–client relationship.

Thus, when factors are encountered which raise questions about the propriety of planning materiality, tolerable error and/or performance materiality established during the planning phase of the audit, justification for amending those estimates must be considered carefully. Upward adjustments should only be made, and downward adjustments should not be resisted, when examination of the benchmarks on which planning materiality (and, hence, tolerable error and performance materiality) were determined reveals that the initial materiality estimates were inappropriate. In particular, if the auditor finds that misstatements in individual account balances, or in the financial statements as a whole, exceed the pre-set materiality limits, s/he must avoid any temptation to adopt spurious arguments to justify adjusting the relevant materiality level(s) upwards to avoid additional audit work.

9.3.5 Documenting materiality

As for other steps in the audit process, the materiality limits for each audit engagement must be fully documented. Auditors are required to document:

(a) the materiality level for the financial statements as a whole (i.e., planning materiality);

(b) the materiality level for each class of transactions, account balance or disclosure (that is, tolerable error) for which such a level was determined;

(c) the amount(s) determined for performance materiality for the financial statements as a whole and for the classes of transactions, account balances and other disclosures for which a tolerable error was established;

(d) changes made to any of the above as the audit progressed.

They are also required to document the factors they considered when determining planning materiality, tolerable error and performance materiality.

---

[18] An increase in audit time may create difficulties for scheduling the work of audit team members. If they remain on the current audit for longer than planned, they will not be available to commence work, as scheduled, on their next audit assignment. Additionally, an increase in audit time will result in increased audit cost and, thus, in an increase in the audit fee charged to the client or, if the fee charged remains the same, in a reduction in the profits of the audit firm.

9.4 DESIRED LEVEL OF AUDIT RISK (DESIRED LEVEL OF ASSURANCE)

9.4.1 Meaning of desired level of audit risk (desired level of assurance)

The Companies Act (CA) 2006 requires auditors to state in their audit reports whether, *in their opinion*, the audited financial statements give a true and fair view of the state of affairs (or financial position) of the company (and, in relevant cases, of the group) and its (or the group's) profit or loss for the reporting period and have been properly prepared in accordance with an applicable financial reporting framework (emphasis added.)

It is important to note that auditors are required to *express an opinion on*, not *to certify*, the truth and fairness of the financial statements. It seems that, when enacting the legislation, Parliament did not expect auditors to reach a state of certainty with respect to the matters on which they are required to express an opinion in the audit report. A similar idea is conveyed by ISA 200 (IAASB, 2009a) which states:

> As the basis for the auditor's opinion, ISAs require the auditor to obtain *reasonable assurance* about whether the financial statements as a whole are free from material misstatement, whether due to fraud or error. (para 5, emphasis added)

This raises the question: What is meant by 'reasonable assurance'? According to IFAC's *Glossary of Terms* (IFAC, 2009) it means: "A high, but not absolute, level of assurance". This does not seem to shed much light on the matter; ISA 200 (para A45) is more helpful. It states:

> The auditor is not expected to, and cannot reduce audit risk to zero and cannot therefor obtain absolute assurance [i.e., certainty] that the financial statements are free from material misstatement due to fraud or error. This is because there are inherent limitations of an audit, which result in most of the audit evidence on which the auditor draws conclusions and bases the auditor's opinion being persuasive rather than conclusive. The inherent limitations of an audit arise from:
> - The nature of financial reporting;
> - The nature of audit procedures; and
> - The need for the audit to be conducted within a reasonable period of time and at a reasonable cost.

ISA 200 expands on these three sources of an audit's inherent limitations as follows:

The Nature of Financial Reporting

The preparation of financial statements involves judgment by management in applying the requirements of the entity's applicable financial reporting framework to the facts and circumstances of the entity. In addition, many financial statement items involve subjective decisions or assessments or a degree of uncertainty, and there may be a range of acceptable interpretations or judgments that may be made. Consequently, some financial statement items [such as estimates] are subject to an inherent level of variability which cannot be eliminated by the application of additional auditing procedures. (para A46)

The Nature of Audit Procedures

There are practical and legal limitations on the auditor's ability to obtain audit evidence. For example:

- There is the possibility that management or others may not provide, intentionally or unintentionally, the complete information that . . . has been requested by the auditor. Accordingly, the auditor cannot be certain of the completeness of information . . . .
- Fraud may involve sophisticated and carefully organized schemes designed to conceal it. Therefore, audit procedures used to gather audit evidence may be ineffective for detecting an intentional misstatement that involves, for example, collusion to falsify documentation which may cause the auditor to believe that audit evidence is valid when it is not. (para A47)

Timeliness of Financial Reporting and the Balance between Benefit and Cost

[T]he relevance of information, and thereby its value, tends to diminish over time, and there is a balance to be struck between the reliability of information and its cost. . . . [T]here is an expectation by users of financial statements that the auditor will form an opinion on the financial statements within a reasonable period of time and at a reasonable cost. . . . Consequently, it is necessary for the auditor to:

- Plan the audit so that it will be performed in an effective manner;
- Direct audit effort to areas most expected to contain risks of material misstatement, whether due to fraud or error, with correspondingly less effort directed at other areas; and
- Use testing and other means of examining populations for misstatements. (paras A48, A49)

From the quotations cited above it is clear that auditors are not expected to – indeed cannot – be *certain* that financial statements they report as giving a true and fair view of the entity's financial position and performance and complying with an applicable financial reporting framework are not, in fact, materially misstated. However, they clearly want to be reasonably confident that the opinion they express is appropriate. The level of confidence they wish to attain about the 'correctness' of the opinion they express on the financial statements is known as their 'desired level of assurance'.

The auditor's desired level of assurance is the complement of his/her desired level of audit risk. As noted in Chapter 3 (section 3.4.3), the IFAC's *Glossary of Terms* (2009) defines audit risk as: "The risk that the auditor expresses an inappropriate audit opinion when the financial statements are materially misstated". It follows that if, for example, the auditor wishes to be 95 per cent assured (or confident) that the financial statements on which s/he expresses a 'clean' (unmodified) audit opinion are free of material misstatements, this means s/he is prepared to accept a five per cent risk that they contain such errors. ISA 200 conveys succinctly the link between the concepts of reasonable assurance and audit risk by stating:

> To obtain reasonable assurance, the auditor shall obtain sufficient appropriate audit evidence to reduce audit risk to an acceptably low level and thereby enable the auditor to draw reasonable conclusions on which to base the auditor's opinion. (para 17)

This also reflects the fact that the more assured the auditor wishes to be about the appropriateness of the opinion expressed in the audit report (the more s/he wishes to reduce the risk of expressing the 'wrong' opinion), the more the audit evidence (in terms of quantity and/or relevance and reliability) that needs to be collected and evaluated.

9.4.2 Factors affecting the auditor's desired level of audit risk (desired level of assurance)

An auditor's desired level of audit risk will always be low (i.e., his/her desired level of assurance will always be high). It is sometimes expressed in quantitative terms (a five per cent level of audit risk or 95 per cent level of assurance is often quoted as a 'rule of thumb'), but it is clearly difficult to pinpoint when a particular numeric level of risk or assurance has been reached. As a result, in practice, auditors often adopt a qualitative approach and think in terms of a 'low' or 'medium' level of audit risk (or a 'high' or 'medium' level of assurance) rather than in precise percentage terms.

In certain circumstances auditors wish to attain a particularly low level of audit risk (or high level of assurance). This applies, for example, in cases where a large number of users are likely to rely on the financial statements and/or where there is doubt about the client's ability to continue as a going concern. In each of these cases, if the auditor signifies that the financial statements give a true and fair view of the entity's financial position and performance when they are materially misstated, serious consequences may ensue for both the financial statement user(s) and for the auditor.

Generally speaking, the larger the entity (in terms of total revenues or total assets), and the more widely disbursed its ownership and/or its debts, the greater the number of users of its audited financial statements. A large listed public company such as BP, GlaxoSmithKline, HSBC or Vodafone, which has extensive economic resources and numerous shareholders, debtholders and creditors, is likely to have its audited financial statements used far more widely than companies with few shareholders and/or few debtholders and other creditors. Private companies, wholly owned subsidiaries and companies whose directors hold a large proportion of the company's equity and debt (as applies in some smaller companies) are likely to have relatively few financial statement users who are remote from the company. As Arens, Elder and Beasley (2005) point out:

> When the [financial] statements are heavily relied on, a great social harm could result if a significant error were to remain undetected. . . . The cost of additional evidence [to reduce the level of audit risk] can be more easily justified when the loss to users from material errors is [likely to be] substantial. (p. 244)

Additionally, where audited financial statements have a large number of users, each of whom may suffer loss if the auditor fails to detect a material error or omission, and inappropriately issues a 'clean' (unmodified) audit report thereon, the auditor may have wide exposure to potential liability for negligence.[19] Thus, where a large number of users rely on a particular company's financial statements, it is in the auditor's own interest to seek a particularly low level of audit risk (high level of assurance). The same is true (in countries where the *Caparo* decision does not apply) where one or more users are likely to rely on the audited financial statements when making a major investment decision (such as in a takeover situation). If potential investors decide to make the investment and the audited financial statements on which they rely subsequently prove to be materially misstated, they are likely to suffer serious financial loss. As a result, they are likely to seek redress from the auditor for the loss they sustain.[20]

Another situation in which the auditor may desire a particularly low level of audit risk is where there is some doubt about the entity's status as a going concern. This is because, if a client is forced into liquidation shortly after receiving a 'clean' audit report and the financial statements are subsequently found to contain one or more material misstatements, the auditor may be exposed to litigation by the company's liquidator or those who suffer loss as a result of the entity's collapse. When there is doubt about an auditee's status as a going concern, the auditor will generally reduce his/her desired level of audit risk by gathering more (or more relevant and/or reliable) audit evidence than

---

[19] In the UK, in 1990 the *Caparo* case limited the parties to whom auditors owe a duty of care and thus their exposure to potential liability. This is discussed in detail in Chapter 15, section 15.4.2. Other recent developments in limiting auditors' liability are discussed in Chapter 16, section 16.5.

[20] Regulators may also bring actions against auditors. For example, the Securities and Exchange Commission (SEC) in the USA has brought actions against auditors when financial statements on which a 'clean' audit report was issued were subsequently found to be materially misstated. An example is the SEC's action against KPMG LLP, two former KPMG partners, and a current partner and senior manager

> for engaging in improper professional conduct as auditors for Gemstar-TV Guide International, Inc. . . . [F]rom September 1999 through March 2002, the respondents' conduct resulted in repeated audit failures in connection with KPMG's audits of Gemstar's financial statements . . . the respondents reasonably should have known that Gemstar improperly recognized and reported . . . material amounts of licensing and advertising revenue. . . . Stephen M. Cutler, the SEC's Director of Enforcement, said, "The sanctions in this case should reinforce the message that accounting firms must assume responsibility for ensuring individual auditors properly discharge their special and critical gatekeeping responsibilities". Randall, R. Lee, Regional Director of the SEC's Pacific Regional Office, said, ". . . KPMG's auditors repeatedly relied on Gemstar management's representations even when those representations were contradicted by their audit work. The auditors thus failed to abide by one of the core principles of public accounting – to exercise professional skepticism and care".

KPMG agreed to a settlement that included censure and payment of $10 million to Gemstar's shareholders – the largest payment ever made by an accounting firm in an SEC action (SEC, 2004).

s/he would do otherwise and be particularly concerned to see that the nature of the going concern problem is adequately disclosed in the notes to the financial statements. As a result of these actions, the auditor is more likely to detect material misstatements in the financial statements (if they exist) and, failing this, will be better placed to defend the quality of the audit should a challenge arise.[21]

9.5 IMPACT OF AUDIT RISK ON PLANNING THE AUDIT

9.5.1 Risk-based approach to auditing

We noted in section 9.4.1 that audit risk (the risk of the auditor expressing an inappropriate opinion on a set of financial statements[22]) is the complement of the auditor's level of assurance (the auditor's level of confidence that the opinion expressed is 'correct'). Ultimately, to the auditor, audit risk amounts to exposure to legal liability if, as a result of issuing a 'clean' audit report on financial statements which are materially misstated, a user of the financial statements is misled and suffers a loss as a consequence. However, as we note in section 9.4.1, an auditor is required to *express an opinion* on the financial statements, not *to certify* their truth and fairness. Further, (as we also note) ISA 200, para A45, recognises that some degree of audit risk is unavoidable. Thus, legal action against an auditor should succeed only if the auditor knowingly or negligently accepts an unreasonably high level of audit risk (i.e., forms an opinion on the financial statements based on evidence s/he knows, or ought to know, is inadequate, or does not care whether or not it is adequate).

In today's highly competitive audit environment, audit firms have focused their attention on conducting cost-effective audits. This has led to them adopting a risk-based approach to auditing; that is, identifying and assessing the risk of the financial statements being materially misstated, identifying where, within the financial statements such misstatements seem most likely, and planning the nature, timing and extent of their audit procedures accordingly.

Like establishing materiality limits, the risk of misstatements occurring in the pre-audited financial statements (which we refer to as pre-audit risk) is considered at two levels, namely, the overall (financial statement) level

---

[21] Auditors' responsibilities in relation to assessing their audit clients' status as a going concern are discussed in Chapter 13, section 13.4.

[22] As we explained in Chapter 3 (section 3.4.3), because the likelihood of the auditor expressing a modified audit opinion on financial statements which are *not* materially misstated is so small, the term audit risk is usually taken to mean the risk of an auditor expressing a 'clean' (i.e., an unmodified) audit opinion on financial statements that are materially misstated.

and at the level of individual classes of transactions, account balances or disclosures.

- *Pre-audit risk at the overall level* refers to the risk of material misstatements being present in the financial statements as a whole (that is, the likelihood of planning materiality being exceeded) and, based on this, determining the amount of audit effort required for the audit as a whole. (The higher the likelihood of material misstatements being present, the greater the amount and/or the more relevant and reliable the audit evidence that needs to be collected – and, hence, the greater the amount of audit effort required).

- *Pre-audit risk at the class of transactions, account balance or disclosure level* refers to identifying high audit-risk areas; that is, identifying specific classes of transactions, account balances or disclosures where material misstatements seem most likely to occur (or, alternatively stated, tolerable error is most likely to be exceeded). Once these areas have been identified, the total audit effort may be allocated so as to ensure that high-risk areas receive greater audit attention than lower-risk areas.

The objective of risk-based auditing is to achieve maximum effectiveness and efficiency (that is, to arrive at the appropriate audit opinion whilst incurring least cost). It is designed to ensure that neither the financial statements as a whole, nor any segment thereof, are under- or over-audited; that is, that neither too little nor too much audit evidence is gathered to achieve the auditor's desired level of audit risk. Too little audit evidence leaves the auditor with greater exposure to audit risk than s/he wishes to accept; too much evidence means the auditor's exposure to risk is reduced to beyond the level s/he is prepared to accept and, as a result, represents unnecessary expenditure of audit time and cost.

The auditor assesses the overall risk of material misstatements being present in the pre-audited financial statements, and identifies high audit-risk areas, primarily through:
- gaining a thorough understanding of the client, its business, its industry and its key personnel (as discussed in Chapter 8, section 8.4),
- performing analytical procedures (as discussed in Chapter 8, section 8.6), and
- evaluating the client's system of internal control (discussed in Chapter 10, section 10.4.4).

9.5.2 Relationship between inherent risk, internal control risk and detection risk

In Chapter 3 (section 3.4.3) we note that audit risk comprises two main components:

(i) the risk that the pre-audited financial statements are materially mis-stated in one or more respects. (This is a function of inherent risk and internal control risk); and

(ii) the risk that the auditor will fail to detect a material misstatement which is present. (This is a function of sampling and quality control risk, collectively referred to as detection risk.)

The relationship between audit risk and its components may be presented (in simplified form) as an equation as follows:

Risk of the auditor expressing a 'clean' opinion on materially misstated financial statements	=	Risk of material misstatements being present in the pre-audited financial statements	+	Risk of the auditor failing to detect material misstatements
Audit risk	=	Inherent risk + internal control risk	+	Detection risk

At this point it may be helpful to recall (from Chapter 7) that audit procedures are basically of two kinds, namely, compliance and substantive procedures.

- *Compliance procedures* are designed to ascertain whether the entity's internal controls are operating effectively (that is, are being complied with by the auditee's personnel) and have been so operating throughout the reporting period. In the context of the audit risk equation, compliance procedures are particularly relevant to the evaluation of internal control risk.

- *Substantive procedures* are designed to substantiate, or to evaluate the substance (validity, completeness and accuracy) of, financial statement account balances and other disclosures. They fall into two broad categories, namely:
  - specific analytical procedures;
  - tests of details. These tests are of two types – tests of transactions and direct tests of account balances.

Substantive procedures have a direct bearing on detection risk. In general, the lower the level of inherent risk and internal control risk (that is, the lower the risk that the pre-audited financial statements contain material misstatements), the less extensive the substantive procedures that are required to confirm that the financial statements are, in fact, free of material misstatements. Expressed differently, where the auditor believes there is little likelihood of material misstatement(s) occurring in the pre-audited financial statements (inherent and internal control risk are low), the greater the risk s/he is prepared to accept that a material error, if present, will not be detected (i.e., the auditor is prepared to accept high detection risk). As a consequence, less extensive substantive procedures will be conducted. Alternatively, if the auditor considers there is a high likelihood that the pre-audited financial statements contain material misstatement(s) (i.e., inherent + control risk is high), then s/he will want to be fairly sure that if material misstatement(s) are present, they will be detected (i.e., the auditor will seek low detection risk). As a consequence, extensive substantive tests will be performed.

When considering the relationship between the components of audit risk we need to bear in mind the following four separate sets of factors.

(i) Inherent risk is the risk of material misstatements being present in the pre-audited financial statements in the absence of internal controls. Thus, conceptually, the auditor determines the likelihood of misstatements occurring in the financial statements in two stages: first inherent risk is assessed then the extent to which the entity's internal controls can be relied upon to reduce the likelihood of misstatements occurring in the financial statements is evaluated.

(ii) Gaining an understanding of the client (and its internal and external environment) and performing analytical procedures are particularly important for assessing inherent risk. Evaluating the effectiveness of the client's internal control system and performing compliance procedures are the primary means of determining internal control risk.

(iii) Inherent risk and internal control risk are beyond the direct control of the auditor. Therefore, the auditor must adjust detection risk (primarily by increasing or reducing the extent and/or appropriateness of substantive procedures) in order to achieve his/her desired level of audit risk (or desired level of assurance).

(iv) Inherent risk and internal control risk may both be assessed as high, may both be assessed as low, or one may be assessed as high and the other as low. However, whatever their combined level of assessed risk may be, it directly impacts the nature, timing and extent of the substantive procedures the auditor must conduct in order to achieve his/her desired level of audit risk.

The conceptual aspects of the relationships indicated above may be illustrated (in simplified form) by numerical examples.

Example 1: Assume the following facts:

- The auditor's desired level of audit risk is five per cent (equivalently, the auditor's desired level of assurance is 95 per cent).
- After assessing inherent risk the auditor believes there is a 60 per cent risk of material misstatements being present in the pre-audited financial statements.
- After evaluating the entity's internal controls, the auditor reduces his/her assessment of the risk of material misstatements occurring in the

---

---

pre-audited financial statements to 20 per cent (a reduction of 40 percentage points).

Given the facts outlined above, it is evident that in order to achieve a desired level of audit risk of five per cent, the auditor's audit risk needs to be reduced by a further 15 percentage points through the performance of substantive procedures.

Desired level of audit risk	=	Assessment of inherent risk	−	Reduction in assessed risk through evaluation of internal controls	−	Reduction in audit risk through substantive audit procedures
5%	=	60%	−	40%	−	15% (Detection risk = 85%)

Example 2: Assume the following facts:
- The auditor's desired level of audit risk is five per cent (equivalently, the auditor's desired level of assurance is 95 per cent).
- After assessing inherent risk, the auditor believes there is an 85 per cent risk of material misstatements being present in the pre-audited financial statements.
- After assessing the effectiveness of the entity's internal controls, the auditor assesses the risk of material misstatements occurring in the pre-audited financial statements as 75 per cent (a reduction of 10 percentage points).

Given the above facts, it is evident that in order to achieve a desired level of audit risk of five per cent, the auditor must reduce audit risk by a further 70 percentage points through the performance of substantive procedures.

Desired level of audit risk	=	Assessment of inherent risk	−	Reduction in assessed risk through evaluation of internal controls	−	Reduction in audit risk through substantive audit procedures
5%	=	85%	−	10%	−	70% (Detection risk = 30%)

In the first example the auditor plans to use substantive procedures to reduce his/her combined assessment of inherent and control risk by 15 percentage points, whereas in the second case such procedures need to reduce the assessed inherent plus control risk by 70 percentage points. It follows that, in the second case, substantive procedures need to be significantly more extensive (and/or more relevant and reliable) than in the first – and detection risk will be correspondingly lower.

The above examples convey how, conceptually, inherent risk (the likelihood of errors being present in the financial data in the absence of internal controls) is reduced to the auditor's desired level of audit risk in two stages:

(i)   evaluating (by means of compliance procedures) the likelihood of mis-statements that are present in the financial data not being detected by the auditee's internal controls and thus occurring in the pre-audited financial statements; and

(ii) performing substantive procedures to reduce the likelihood of undetec-ted misstatements remaining in the financial statements on which the auditor expresses a 'clean' audit opinion.

Although we have represented this risk reduction process as two sequential subtractions from inherent risk, a simple probability multiplication rule is more appropriate to determine the level of detection risk to which the audi-tor's planned substantive procedures need to accord in order to achieve the auditor's desired level of audit risk. In statistics, the probability of two events (A and B) both happening is the multiple of the probability of $A[p(A)]$ and the probability of $B[p(B)]$. Thus the multiple of the risk (or probability) of a material misstatement occurring in the pre-audited financial statements and the risk (or probability) of the auditor's substantive tests failing to detect it gives the risk of the auditor expressing a 'clean' opinion on materially mis-stated financial statements (that is, audit risk). This reasoning underlies what is commonly referred to as the 'audit risk model', which may be represented as follows:[23]

Desired level of audit risk	=	Risk of material error(s) occurring in the pre-audited financial statements	×	Risk of auditor failing to detect material error(s)
Audit risk	=	Inherent risk	× Control risk ×	Detection risk
AR	=	IR	× CR ×	DR

Applying this to the figures given in the examples set out above:

Example 1:

Desired level of audit risk	=	Risk of material error(s) occurring in the pre-audited financial statements	×	Risk of auditor failing to detect material error(s)
Audit risk	=	Inherent risk	× Control risk ×	Detection risk
AR	=	IR	× CR[24] ×	DR
5%		60%	× 34%	

[23] The audit risk model is widely cited in auditing literature as a useful audit planning tool. However, it is not without its critics. As indicated above, the model is grounded in probability theory and, in order for it to be valid, the probability of the events IR, CR and DR must be independent of each other. A number of commentators have raised doubt about the independence of IR, CR and DR and thus about the validity of the audit risk model. Nevertheless, the model provides useful insights into the relationship between inherent risk, internal control risk, detection risk and the auditor's desired level of audit risk.

[24] $[IR = 60\% \times CR = 34\%]$ = Risk of error occurring in pre-audited financial statements = 20% (as in previous Example 1)

Rearranging the equation to find detection risk:

$$DR = \frac{5\%}{60\% \times 34\%} = 25\%$$

Example 2:

Desired level of audit risk	=	Risk of material error(s) occurring in the pre-audited financial statements	$\times$	Risk of auditor failing to detect material error
Audit risk	=	Inherent risk $\times$ Control risk	$\times$	Detection risk
AR	=	IR $\times$ CR[25]	$\times$	DR
5%	=	85% $\times$ 88%	$\times$	DR

Rearranging the equation to find detection risk:

$$DR = \frac{5\%}{85\% \times 88\%} = 7\%$$

It may be seen that, in Example 1, in order to achieve a desired level of audit risk of five per cent, the auditor can accept a 25 per cent risk of failing to detect material error(s) which may be present in the financial statements; in Example 2, the auditor can accept detection risk of only seven per cent. These examples demonstrate that, the greater the likelihood of material misstatements occurring in the pre-audited financial statements (the greater the combined level of inherent and internal control risk), the less the risk the auditor can take of not detecting material misstatements which are present. The lower the level of detection risk the auditor can accept, the more extensive the substantive audit procedures must be.

We can use a town's water supply (as in Figure 9.2) to illustrate the inverse relationships between:
  (a) inherent risk and internal control risk on the one hand and detection risk on the other; and
  (b) detection risk and the extent of substantive testing.

For the purpose of illustration, assume:
  • the population of Jolleytown derives its water supply from Smillie Reservoir;
  • three rivers flow into Smillie Reservoir; and
  • the water from the rivers passes through a purification filter before flowing into the reservoir.

---

[25] [IR = 85% $\times$ CR = 88%] = Risk of error occurring in pre-audited financial statements = 75% (as in previous Example 2)

Figure 9.2: Jolleytown's water supply

Jolleytown's water supply	*Parallel in audit risk terms*
Situation 1	
1. The rivers (mountain streams) flowing down towards the purification filter are crystal clear.	1. Management integrity appears to be high, there are no apparent pressures likely to motivate management to manipulate the financial statement information, and business risk is low. (Inherent risk is low.)
2. The purification filter is in excellent order and can be relied upon to filter out impurities in the river water.	2. Internal controls appear to be effective in preventing and detecting errors in the financial data. (Internal control risk is low.)
3. In order for the authorities to be assured that the water in Smillie Reservoir is safe for the population of Jolleytown to drink, relatively little testing will be required.	3. The auditor, having assessed inherent risk and internal control risk, will be fairly confident that the financial statements are not materially misstated. Thus s/he will conduct relatively little substantive testing to confirm that material misstatements are not present.
Because the authorities believe the reservoir water is 'pure', they will not test it extensively. They thus run the risk of failing to detect impurities which may, in fact, have 'slipped through' the system	By conducting relatively little substantive testing, the auditor runs the risk of not detecting material misstatements which may, in fact, have 'slipped through' the system. Thus detection risk is high.
Situation 2	
1. The rivers flowing down from the hills towards the purification filter are muddy and carry lots of impurities such as rocks, stones and vegetation.	1. Management integrity appears to be fairly low and business risk is high. The risk of material misstatements occurring in the pre-audited financial statements in the absence of internal controls (i.e., inherent risk) is high.
2. The purification filter is not in a good state of repair. A number of holes have developed and the filter is in need of replacement.	2. Internal controls do not appear to be effective: they seem unlikely to prevent or detect errors which are present in the financial data. (Internal control risk is high.)
3. Before the water in the reservoir can be accepted as safe for Jolleytown residents to drink, extensive testing will be required. (A large number of water samples will need to be taken from various parts of the reservoir.)	3. Before the financial statements can be adjudged 'true and fair', account balances and disclosures will need to be tested extensively.
As a result of the extensive testing, the failure to detect impurities in the water (if they are present) will be fairly low.	As a result of the extensive (substantive) testing, the chances of failing to detect material misstatements in the financial statements is fairly low (i.e., low detection risk).

9.5.3 Audit risk at the overall and individual account (or audit segment) level

The discussion in section 9.5.2 focuses on assessing inherent risk and internal control risk at the overall (financial statement) level and considers the extent of substantive procedures required to reduce detection risk, and thus audit risk, to the desired level for the audit as a whole. However, as we note in section 9.5.1, audit risk is also considered at the level of individual classes of transactions, account balances and disclosures. The principles explained in relation to overall audit risk apply equally to audit risk at the more detailed level. Indeed, in practice, the audit risk equation and determination of the substantive procedures required to reduce detection risk to the desired level has greater application at the account balance and disclosure level (or, more pertinently, at the level of audit segments) than at the overall (financial statement) level.

9.5.4 Relationship between materiality, audit risk and audit planning

It follows from our discussion of audit risk that the relationship among the audit risk components has a significant impact on audit planning. Audits must be planned so as to ensure that:
- inherent risk is properly assessed (which largely depends on gaining an adequate knowledge of the client – and its internal and external environment – and overall analytical procedures);
- internal control risk is properly evaluated (which includes planning, performing and evaluating compliance procedures); and
- sufficient appropriate substantive procedures are performed so that detection risk – and thus audit risk – is reduced to the level desired by the auditor.

Hence, in order to reduce audit risk to the desired level, the auditor must carefully plan the nature, timing and extent of audit procedures.

Like audit risk, the level at which materiality limits (planning materiality, tolerable error and performance materiality) are set affects the planning of audit procedures – their nature, timing and extent. In section 9.3 we noted that a misstatement in the financial statements is material if it is reasonably likely to affect the economic decisions of users of the financial statements. We also noted that the level at which the auditor sets planning materiality and tolerable error affects the amount and/or appropriateness of the audit evidence the auditor needs to gather: the lower the materiality limits the more (and/or more relevant and reliable) the evidence the auditor must collect in order to ensure those limits are not exceeded.

Linking materiality to audit risk and the extent of audit procedures, we can say that, the lower the materiality limits, the more readily misstatements that exist in the pre-audited financial statements will exceed those limits and thus qualify as *material* misstatements. It follows that the lower the materiality limits, all other things remaining constant, the higher the auditor's assessment of inherent and control risk and, consequently, the more extensive the audit procedures that need to be performed in order to reduce audit risk to an acceptably low level. Additionally, the lower the materiality limits, the more careful the auditor needs to be in determining whether or not those limits are exceeded. Thus, the auditor will wish to reduce detection risk to a level lower than would otherwise be the case – and, accordingly, plan to perform more extensive substantive procedures. It can, therefore, be seen that there is an inverse relationship between materiality and audit risk and thus between materiality and the extent of substantive procedures. This relationship is depicted in Figure 9.3.

Figure 9.3: The effect of setting materiality limits at different levels on audit risk and planned audit procedures

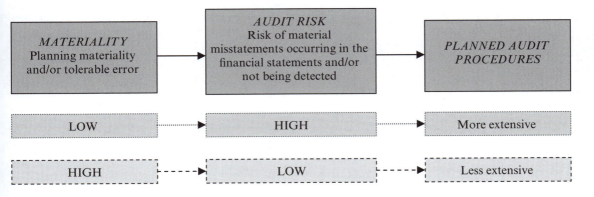

9.6 SUMMARY

In this chapter we have identified two phases in planning an audit – developing the overall audit strategy and designing the audit plan (or audit programme) – and we have examined various aspects of developing the overall audit strategy. In particular, we have discussed:

- the distinction between planning materiality, tolerable error and performance materiality;
- setting materiality limits;
- the auditor's desired level of audit risk (or desired level of assurance); and
- the relationship between inherent risk, internal control risk and detection risk.

We have also noted that, in order to achieve their desired level of audit risk, auditors need to assess inherent risk and internal control risk (over which they have no direct control) and then plan the nature, timing and extent of audit procedures so as to ensure that detection risk, and hence audit risk, is reduced to the desired level. In the final section of the chapter we highlighted the inverse relationship between materiality and audit risk – and the relationship between these factors and the extent of substantive testing.

A summary of the main ideas discussed in this chapter (and some of those considered in Chapters 3 and 7) is presented in Figure 9.4.

Figure 9.4: **Relationship between steps in the audit process,[26] planning the audit, establishing materiality limits, and assessing audit risk**

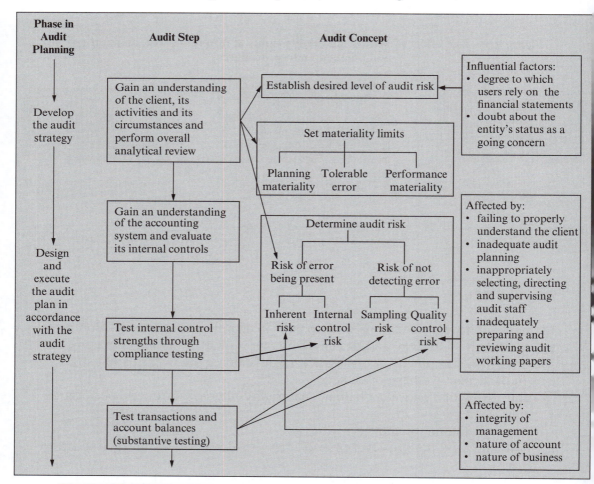

_____

[26] As shown in Chapter 7.

SELF-REVIEW QUESTIONS

9.1 State the two main phases in planning an audit and outline the main objective(s) of each.

9.2 When planning an audit, the auditor must consider:
 (i) the extent of audit procedures,
 (ii) the timing of audit procedures,
 (iii) the nature of audit procedures.
 Briefly explain the meaning of each of these terms.

9.3 Define 'materiality' and explain briefly the distinction between planning materiality and tolerable error.

9.4 Explain briefly what is meant by 'performance materiality' and how it relates to planning materiality and tolerable error.

9.5 Describe briefly the three steps in setting planning materiality.

9.6 Explain briefly how setting materiality limits at different levels affects planned audit procedures.

9.7 Explain briefly what is meant by 'the auditor's desired level of audit risk' and how it relates to the auditor's desired level of assurance.

9.8 Explain briefly the circumstances in which the auditor's desired level of audit risk is likely to be particularly low.

9.9 Explain briefly how the auditor's assessment of inherent risk and internal control risk affects the planning of substantive procedures.

9.10 Explain briefly the relationship between materiality limits, audit risk and audit planning.

REFERENCES

Arens, A.A., Elder, R.J., & Beasley, M.S. (2005). *Auditing and Assurance Services: An Integrated Approach*, 11th ed. New Jersey: Prentice-Hall Inc.

International Auditing and Assurance Standards Board (IAASB). (2009a). International Standard on Auditing (ISA) 200: *Overall Objectives of the Independent Auditor and the Conduct of an Audit in accordance with International Standards on Auditing*. New York: International Federation of Accountants.

International Auditing and Assurance Standards Board (IAASB). (2009b). International Standard on Auditing (ISA) 300: *Planning an Audit of Financial Statements*. New York: International Federation of Accountants.

International Auditing and Assurance Standards Board (IAASB). (2009c). International Standard on Auditing (ISA) 320: *Materiality in Planning and Performing an Audit*. New York: International Federation of Accountants.

International Federation of Accountants (IFAC). (2009). *Glossary of Terms*, included in *Handbook of International Quality Control, Auditing, Review, Other Assurance and Related Services Pronouncements 2010 Edition*. New York: IFAC.

Read, J.W., Mitchell, J.E., & Akresh, A.D. (1987). Planning materiality and SAS No. 47. *Journal of Accountancy*, *164*(12), 72–79.

Securities Exchange Commission (SEC). (2004, 20 October). *KPMG LLP and Four Auditors Sanctioned for Improper Professional Conduct in Connection with Gemstar-TV Guide International, Inc. Audits*. New York: SEC, Press Release.

ADDITIONAL READING

Abdullatif, M., & Al-Khadash, A. (2010). Putting audit approaches in context: The case of business risk audits in Jordan. *International Journal of Auditing*, *14*(1), 1–24.

Beattie, V., Fearnley, S., & Hines, T. (2012). Do audit committees really engage with auditors on audit planning and performance? *Accounting and Business Research*, *42*(3), 349–375.

Bedard, J.C., & Johnstone, K.M. (2010). Audit partner tenure and audit planning and pricing. *Auditing: A Journal of Practice & Theory*, *29*(2), 45–70.

Bowlin, K. (2011). Risk-based auditing, strategic prompts, and auditor sensitivity to the strategic risk of fraud. *The Accounting Review*, *86*(1), 1231–1253.

Budescu, D.V., Peecher, M.E., & Solomon, I. (2012). The joint influence of the extent and nature of audit evidence, materiality thresholds, and misstatement type on achieved audit risk. *Auditing: A Journal of Practice & Theory*, *31*(2), 19–41.

Choi, J.H., Kim, J_B., Qiu, A.A., & Zang, Y. (2012). Geographic proximity between auditor and client: How does it impact audit quality? *Auditing: A Journal of Practice & Theory*, *31*(2), 43–72.

Fukukawa, H., & Mock, T.J. (2011). Audit risk assessments using belief verses probability. *Auditing: A Journal of Practice & Theory*, *30*(1), 75–99.

Fukukawa, H., Mock, T.J., & Wright, A. (2011). Client risk factors and audit resource allocation decisions. *Abacus*, *47*(1), 85–108.

Ganguly, A.R., & Hammersley, J.S. (2009). Covariance assessments with costly information collection in audit planning: An experimental study. *Auditing: A Journal of Practice & Theory*, *28*(1), 1–27.

Hellman, N. (2011). Chief financial officer influence on audit planning. *International Journal of Auditing*, *15*(3), 247–274.

Low, K.-Y., & Tan, H.-T. (2011). Does time constraint lead to poorer audit performance? Effects of forewarning of impending time constraints and instructions. *Auditing: A Journal of Practice & Theory*, *30*(4), 173–190.

O'Donnell, E., & Perkins, J.D. (2011). Assessing risk with analytical procedures: Do systems-thinking tools help auditors focus on diagnostic patterns. *Auditing: A Journal of Practice & Theory*, *30*(4), 273–283.

O'Donnell, E., & Prather-Kinsey, J. (2010). Nationality and differences in auditor risk assessment: A research note with experimental evidence. *Accounting, Organizations and Society*, *35*(5), 558–564.

Ohta, Y. (2008). On the conditions under which audit risk increases with information. *European Accounting Review*, *17*(3), 559–585.

Owhoso, V., & Weickgenannt, A. (2009). Auditors' self-perceived abilities in conducting domain audits. *Critical Perspectives on Accounting*, *20*(1), 3–21.

Piercey, M.D. (2011). Documentation requirements and quantified verses qualitative audit risk assessments. *Auditing: A Journal of Practice & Theory*, *30*(4), 223–248.

Ruhnke, K., & Lubitzsch, K. (2010). Determinants of the maximum level of assurance for various assurance services. *International Journal of Auditing*, *14*(3), 233–255.

Schultz Jr., J.J., Bierstaker, J.L., & O'Donnell, E. (2010). Integrating business risk into auditor judgment about the risk of material misstatement: The influence of a strategic-systems-audit approach. *Accounting, Organizations and Society*, *35*(2), 238–251.

Sharma, D.S., Boo, E., & Sharma, V.D. (2008) The impact of non-mandatory corporate governance on auditors' client acceptance, risk and planning judgments. *Accounting & Business Research*, *38*(2), 105–120.

Srivastava, R.P., Mock, T.J., & Turner, J.L. (2009). Bayesian and belief-functions formulas for auditor independence risk assessment. *International Journal of Auditing*, *13*(3), 163–183.

Vandervelde, S.D., Tubbs, R.M., Schepanski, A., & Messier Jr., W.F. (2009). Experimental tests of a descriptive theory of combined auditee risk assessment. *Auditing: A Journal of Practice & Theory*, *28*(2), 145–169.

Woolf, E. (2011). A mad world, my masters. *Accountancy*, *148*(1420), 71.

10 Internal Control and the External Audit

LEARNING OBJECTIVES

After studying the material in this chapter you should be able to:

- explain what is meant by 'an accounting system';
- explain why the accounting system is divided into sub-systems for audit purposes and the basis on which this is done;
- define 'internal control' and describe its five components;
- describe the characteristics of a good system of internal accounting controls;
- describe the objectives of internal accounting controls;
- discuss the inherent limitations of all systems of internal control;
- describe the procedures used for reviewing and documenting the accounting sub-systems and for assessing the effectiveness of the related internal controls;
- explain what is meant by 'a walk through test' and why it is conducted;
- explain how an audit plan[1] is developed;
- explain the meaning of the terms 'internal control strengths' and 'internal control deficiencies';
- discuss the importance of auditors identifying internal control strengths and deficiencies;
- explain the meaning of the term 'compliance testing';
- describe the audit procedures used for compliance testing;
- discuss the factors auditors need to consider when planning to rely on the results of compliance tests performed during an interim audit or in a prior year.

10.1 INTRODUCTION

As the auditor has journeyed through the audit process to reach the present stage, s/he has performed engagement procedures, gained an understanding of the client, its activities, its circumstances and its financial affairs, made a preliminary assessment of the risk of material misstatements being present in the pre-audited financial statements as a whole and in classes of transactions,

---

[1] An audit plan was formerly referred to as an audit programme.

account balances and disclosures, defined materiality limits and established a desired level of audit risk (see Chapter 7, Figure 7.1, Audit Steps 1–4).

The auditor now needs to obtain a detailed knowledge of the client's accounting system and evaluate the effectiveness of its internal controls. Once the auditor has assessed the level of reliance s/he can place on the entity's internal controls to eliminate errors and/or irregularities from the accounting data, the audit plan can be designed; that is, the nature, timing and extent of audit procedures to be performed during the rest of the audit can be planned.

In this chapter we examine what is meant by an accounting system and how the system is segmented for audit purposes. We explore some conceptual aspects of internal control and discuss how auditors obtain knowledge of their clients' accounting system and evaluate its related internal controls. We also investigate how auditors develop an audit plan. Before concluding the chapter we consider the tests auditors conduct in order to determine whether the internal controls on which they plan to rely in order to reduce their substantive tests are operating as effectively as their preliminary evaluation suggests and the factors they need to consider when planning to rely on the results of compliance tests performed during an interim audit or an audit conducted in a prior year.

10.2   THE ACCOUNTING SYSTEM

Like all systems, an accounting system has an input, processing and output stage. As Figure 10.1 indicates:

- *the input stage* involves capturing a mass of accounting data from either:
  - source documents which are completed manually or electronically when transactions take place; or

Figure 10.1:   The accounting system

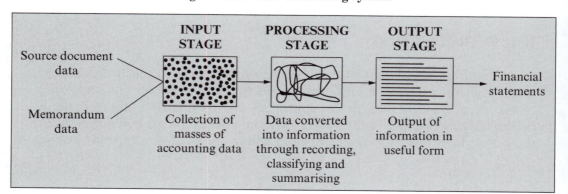

- memoranda generated by the entity's accountant. These generally record non-transactions data, for example, period end adjustments and writing off bad debts;
- *the processing stage* involves converting the mass of raw data into useful information. This is generally achieved using electronic data processing methods and is accomplished through recording, classifying and summarising the data;
- *the output stage* involves preparing the accounting information in a form useful to those who wish to use it; that is, appropriately classifying, grouping and presenting financial information in a meaningful manner.

In order to ensure that all relevant data are captured as input to the accounting system, and to ensure that the data are properly and correctly processed during their conversion into output (in the form of financial statements), special checking mechanisms or internal accounting controls are built into the system. The characteristics and objectives of internal accounting controls are discussed in sections 10.3.4 and 10.3.5, respectively.

The auditor is required, *inter alia*, to form and express an opinion on whether the entity's financial statements give a true and fair view of its financial position and performance and comply with an applicable financial reporting framework. In order to reach this opinion, the auditor needs to understand the system which generates the financial statements. If the auditor tried to gain this understanding by approaching the entity's accounting system as a single unit, s/he would find it cumbersome, inefficient and, in many cases, overwhelming. In order to facilitate the audit (or to put it on a practical footing), the auditor (conceptually) divides the accounting system into sub-systems or audit segments.

The audit segments recognised for any audit vary according to the nature, size and complexity of the audit client and its activities. However, they are almost invariably based on either classes of transaction (such as sales, purchases, administration expenses, non-current loans, etc.) or (more commonly) accounting sub-systems. When they are based on accounting sub-systems, groups of closely related accounts and associated transactions are audited as a single unit. As an example of audit segments based on accounting sub-systems in an audit of a wholesale or retail business, the following segments may be recognised:

- Sales-receivables-receipts sub-system
- Purchases-payables-payments sub-system
- Inventory and warehousing sub-system
- Payroll and personnel sub-system
- Financing and investing sub-system.

Figure 10.2: Steps in the audit process conducted on entity-wide and audit segment basis

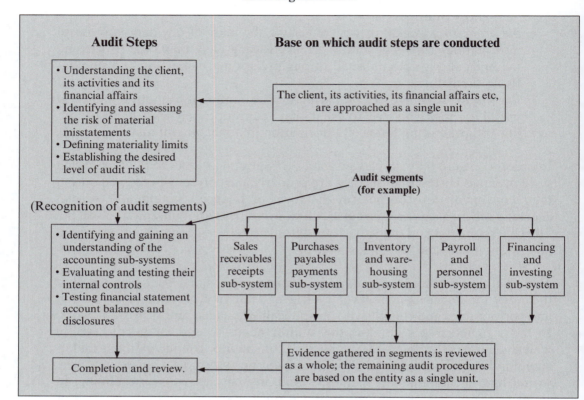

These audit segments are depicted in Figure 10.2. To illustrate related accounts which constitute audit segments, the accounts comprising the sales-receivables-receipts sub-system are shown in Figure 10.3.

It should be noted that until audit segments are identified, the audit is generally approached holistically. As shown in Figure 10.2, the auditor gains an understanding of the client, its activities and its financial affairs, makes a preliminary assessment of the likelihood of material misstatements being present in the pre-audited financial statements, determines materiality limits and establishes a desired level of audit risk, based on the client as a whole. Once audit segments have been recognised, obtaining a detailed knowledge of the accounting system, evaluating and testing its internal controls, and assessing the accuracy, validity and completeness of financial statement balances and other disclosures revolve around particular audit segments.[2] When the detailed segment-based work is

---

[2] However, we should note that, when auditors assess the risk of material misstatements being present in the pre-audited financial statements, they identify the classes of transactions, account balances or disclosures where the material misstatements appear most likely to occur. These are designated 'areas of significant risk' and are assigned special audit attention.

Figure 10.3: Accounts comprising the sales-receivables-receipts sub-system

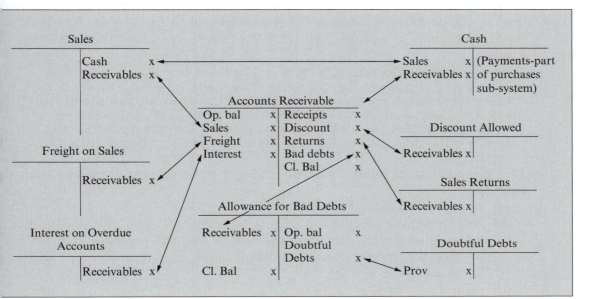

complete, the auditor reviews, as a whole, the evidence gathered in the segments, and conducts the remaining audit procedures on an entity-wide basis. These final steps of the audit process constitute the completion and review stage which is discussed in Chapter 13.

10.3   CONCEPTUAL ASPECTS OF INTERNAL CONTROL

10.3.1   Meaning and importance of internal control

When an entity is small, its owner or manager can personally perform, or directly oversee, all of the entity's functions. However, as the entity grows larger it becomes necessary to delegate functional responsibilities to employees. Once this occurs, mechanisms need to be put in place to enable the performance of the employees to be checked, to ensure they are fulfilling their responsibilities as intended. As Anderson (1977) explains:

> With the best of intentions, most people make mistakes. The mistakes may be errors in the end results of their work, needless inefficiencies in achieving those end results, or both. And sometimes, without the best of intentions, a few people deliberately falsify. Any organisation wishing to conduct its business in an orderly and efficient manner and to produce reliable financial accounting information, both for its own and for others' use, needs some controls to minimise the effects of these endemic human failings. When such controls are implemented within the organisation's systems they are described as internal controls. . . . (p. 143)

It is significant that Anderson refers to internal controls as controls within the *organisation's* systems rather than within its *accounting* system. This recognises the fact that internal controls are mechanisms designed to control *all* of an entity's functions, not just its accounting function. The wide application of the term is reflected in the definition of internal control adopted by the International Federation of Accountants' (IFAC) *Glossary of Terms* (IFAC, 2009), namely:

> Internal control – The process designed, implemented and maintained by those charged with governance [i.e., the board of directors], management and other personnel to provide reasonable assurance about the achievement of an entity's objectives with regard to reliability of financial reporting, effectiveness and efficiency of operations, and compliance with applicable laws and regulations. The term "controls" refers to any aspects of one or more of the components of internal control.

The 'components of internal control' referred to in this definition are the entity's:

(a) control environment;
(b) risk assessment process;
(c) information system, including the related business processes relevant to financial reporting, and communication of financial roles and responsibilities;
(d) control activities;
(e) monitoring of the controls.

We discuss these components, which we collectively refer to as 'an internal control system', in section 10.3.2.

Over the past couple of decades, the importance of internal control has been increasingly recognised in the United Kingdom (UK) (as elsewhere) largely as a result of its inclusion in Codes of Corporate Governance, starting with that of the Committee on the Financial Aspects of Corporate Governance (CFACG, 1992; Cadbury Committee) to the most recent – the Financial Reporting Council's (FRC) *The UK Corporate Governance Code* (2012)[3] – and the adoption of the Codes' requirements by the UK Listing Authority (UKLA). In respect of internal control, the FRC's 2012 Code states:

> **Principle C.2**: ... The board should maintain sound risk management and internal control systems.
>
> **Provision C.2.1**: The board should, at least annually, conduct a review of the effectiveness of the company's risk management and internal control systems and should report to shareholders that they have done so. The review should cover all material controls, including financial, operational and compliance controls.

---

[3] This Code essentially consolidates the recommendations of earlier reports, especially those of the Cadbury Committee (1992), the Committee on Corporate Governance (1998a; Hampel Committee), the Study Group on Directors' Remuneration (1995; Greenbury Committee), Higgs on non-executive directors (2003) and Smith on audit committees (2003). It also supersedes the FRC's *Combined Code on Corporate Governance* (FRC, 2003, 2006, 2008) and subsequent *The UK Corporate Governance Code* (FRC, 2010). The FRC's *Combined Code on Corporate Governance* (2003) replaced the *Combined Code* of the Committee on Corporate Governance (1998b).

As we note in Chapter 5 (section 5.2.2), the UKLA's rules require the directors of companies listed on the London Stock Exchange to include in their company's annual report a governance statement which:
- explains how they have applied the Code's principles (including Principle C.2, cited above); and
- states that they have complied with the Code's provisions throughout the reporting period or explains the respects in which they have not done so.

They are also required to provide a description of the main features of their company's internal control and risk management systems in relation to the financial reporting process. Additionally, the company's auditor is required to review the governance statement insofar as it relates to nine of the Code's 11 accountability provisions – including Provision C.2.1 (cited above) and to form an opinion as to whether the description of the company's internal control and risk management systems is consistent with the financial statements.

It should be noted that the FRC's 2012 Code requires:
- the directors of listed companies to *review* the effectiveness of their company's internal controls and to report to the shareholders that they have done so;
- auditors to *review* the directors' report.

Neither party is required to *report on the effectiveness* of the controls. However, managements[4] and auditors of companies subject to the Sarbanes-Oxley Act of 2002 (SOX) must go further. SOX, sec. 404, requires the managements of all companies registered with the Securities and Exchange Commission (SEC) in the United States of America (USA) or listed on a stock exchange in the USA, and any subsidiary of such a company (irrespective of where in the world the company or subsidiary is located), to include in their company's annual report:
- (i) a statement to the effect that management is responsible for establishing and maintaining an adequate internal control structure and procedures for financial reporting; and
- (ii) an assessment, as of the end of the most recent reporting period, of the effectiveness of the company's internal control structure and procedures for financial reporting.

Additionally, the company's auditor is required to "attest to, and report on, the [internal control] assessment made by the management of the [company]" (SOX, sec. 404). Thus, auditors of these companies are required to evaluate and report on the effectiveness of the company's internal controls which relate to financial reporting.

---

[4] Readers are reminded that in the Preface to this book we note the term 'management' is defined to mean a company's executive directors, non-executive directors, and non-director executives (that is, all executives and directors).

10.3.2   Internal control components

In section 10.3.1 we note that an entity's internal control system comprises five components. These are presented in Figure 10.4 and briefly described below.

(a) *The control environment* – the environment created by the entity's directors and executives through their attitudes, awareness and actions in respect of the entity's internal controls and their importance.

(b) *The risk assessment process* – the process adopted by the entity for identifying business risks relevant to financial reporting, deciding how to respond to those risks and the results of those responses.

(c) *The information system, including the related business processes, relevant to financial reporting, and communication of financial roles and responsibilities* – the financial reporting system and its procedures and records for initiating, recording, processing and reporting entity transactions, events and conditions, and accounting for related assets, liabilities and equity; also the means by which the entity communicates financial roles and responsibilities and significant matters relating to financial reporting.

(d) *Control activities* – policies and procedures designed to ensure that responsibilities delegated by management are fulfilled and performed in the intended manner. This internal control component includes control activities that relate to information technology (IT) environments which are explained below.

(e) *Monitoring of controls* – a process designed to assess the effectiveness of internal control performance over time. It includes assessing the design and operation of controls on a timely basis, taking corrective action when required and modifying the controls, as appropriate, for changed conditions.

In an information technology (IT) environment, two types of control activities are generally recognised – general IT controls and application controls.

(i)   *General IT controls*

General controls are policies and procedures designed to control the IT environment and facilitate the effective functioning of application controls. They include:

- procedures for acquiring, developing and modifying the computer system and application software;
- restricting access to computers, data, programs and files to authorised personnel;
- ensuring that duties are clearly assigned and that incompatible duties are segregated; for example, assigning systems analysis, programming, program testing, computer operation and library (storage) duties to different employees;

Figure 10.4: Relationship between the components of an internal control system

Internal Control System

Process designed, implemented and maintained by management to provide reasonable assurance about achieving the entity's objectives in respect of reliable financial reporting, effective and efficient operations and compliance with applicable laws and regulations.

Control environment

Sets the tone of the entity: the attitudes, awareness and actions of directors and managers in respect of the entity's internal controls and their importance.
Examples:
• Management philosophy and operating style;
• Organisational structure and methods of assigning authority and responsibility.

Risk assessment process

Process designed to identify business risks relevant to financial reporting objectives, responses to those risks and the results thereof.

Information system including financial reporting system

Procedures and records for initiating, recording, processing and reporting transactions, events and conditions and accounting for assets, liabilities and equity. Also the means of communicating financial roles and responsibilities.

Control activities

Policies and procedures designed to ensure responsibilities delegated by management are fulfilled as intended.
Examples:
• Approval and control of documents;
• Restricted access to assets and records;
• Authorisation of transactions;
• Segregation of incompatible duties.

Monitoring of controls

Process to assess the effectiveness of internal controls over time: includes assessing the design and operation of controls, taking corrective action and implementing changes when needed.
Examples:
• Review of documents;
• Supervision of subordinates;
• Internal audit;
• Following up customers' complaints.

Use of IT affects control activities

General (computer environment) controls

Policies and procedures that support the effective functioning of application controls and maintain the integrity and security of data.
Examples:
• Restricting access to computers, programs, data, and files to authorised personnel;
• Ensuring there are adequate backup facilities for both hardware and software;
• Ensuring all computer applications are fully documented;
• Procedures for acquiring, developing and changing system and application software.

Application controls

Procedures that apply to the processing of individual applications designed to ensure the integrity of the accounting records and financial data. Controls over the input, processing and output of accounting applications.
Examples:
• Controls to ensure that:
  - all transactions input to the system are properly authorised;
  - output is checked against input data;
  - transactions are properly and accurately recorded and processed;
  - data files are properly maintained and protected.

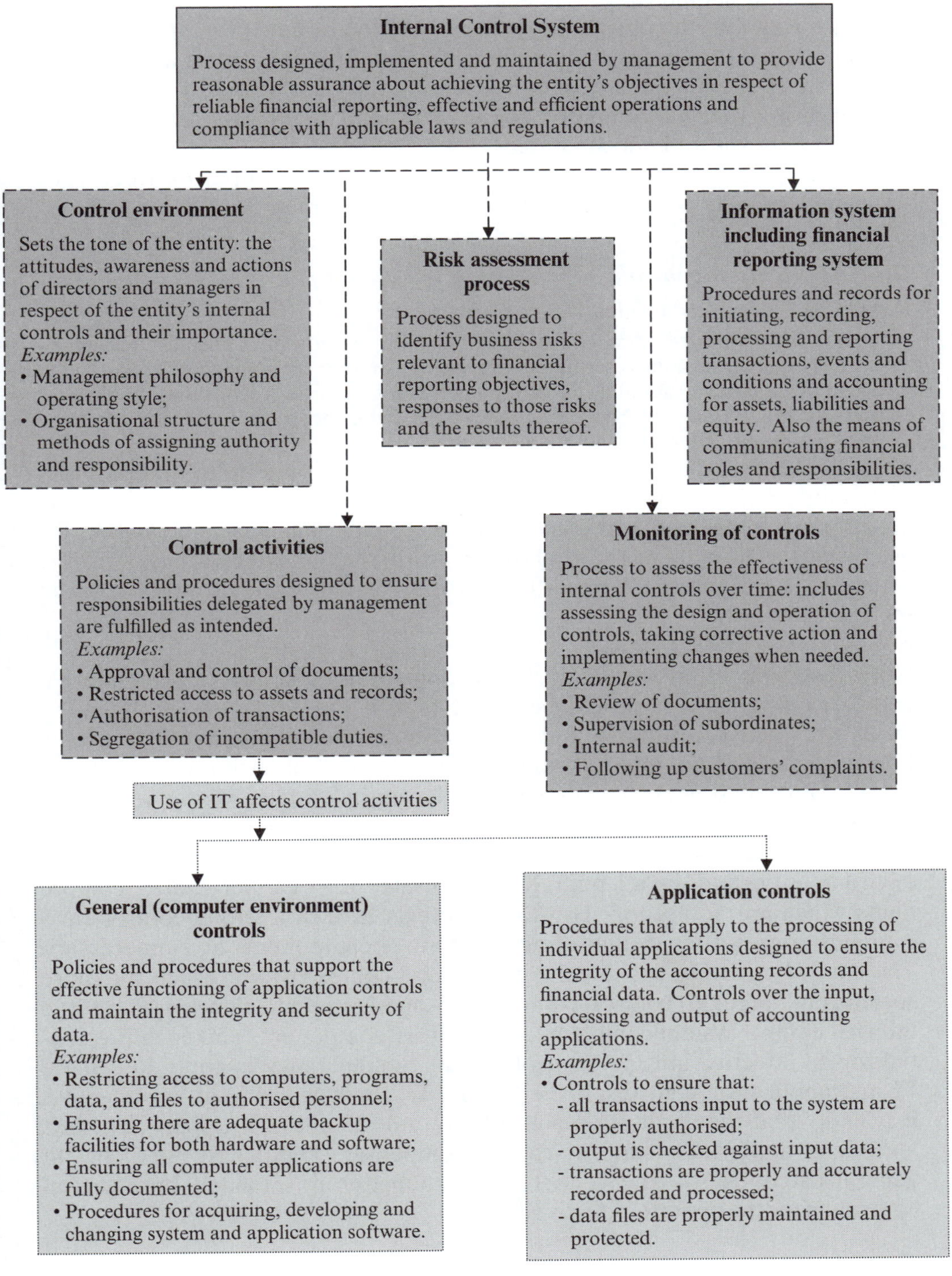

- ensuring that there are adequate back-up facilities for both software and hardware, should they be needed;
- ensuring that the development or acquisition of new programs (or packages), and the testing and implementation of new programs and program changes, are adequately planned and properly authorised;
- ensuring that all computer applications, and modifications thereof, are properly and fully documented;
- ensuring that computer systems are used only for authorised purposes, and that only authorised programs and data are used.

(ii) Application controls

IFAC (2009) defines application controls as:

> Manual or automated procedures that typically operate at a business process level. Application controls can be preventive or detective in nature and are designed to ensure the integrity of the accounting records. Accordingly, application controls relate to procedures used to initiate, record, process and report transactions or other financial data.

They include controls designed to ensure that all (but only) relevant and legitimate data are input into the accounting system and that the accounting data are properly processed and converted into reliable financial information for use by parties internal or external to the entity. The objective of these controls, which we term 'internal accounting controls', is discussed in more detail in section 10.3.5.

Notwithstanding that the control environment is just one of five internal control components, it should be noted that, if the control environment is weak or defective, it is likely that the other control components will not function properly and the internal control system as a whole will not be effective in providing reasonable assurance that the entity's objectives in respect of reliable financial reporting, effective and efficient operations, and compliance with applicable laws and regulations will be met. Deficiencies in the control environment cannot be adequately compensated for by other control components which are 'foolproof'. However, the existence of a strong control environment does not mean that the other control components are unnecessary. The control environment sets the culture and context within which the more specifically targeted control components operate: each component of the internal control system complements the other components and each is essential for an effective internal control system. Similar remarks apply to general IT and application controls. If the general IT controls are weak or defective, it is likely that the application controls will not be applied properly. Further, 'excellent' application controls cannot compensate adequately for deficient general IT controls. If the IT system is to function as intended, both sets of controls need to operate effectively.

Where entities have internal auditors, these auditors are generally responsible for implementing, monitoring and maintaining all aspects of the internal control system. External auditors need to be familiar with the system and to evaluate the quality of the control environment. However, as we explain in section 10.4, external auditors are primarily concerned with the internal controls that relate to the accounting function – in particular, those concerned with safeguarding the entity's assets and accounting records, and ensuring that the financial statements are reliable (that is, internal accounting controls); they are less concerned with the entity's operational and compliance controls.

10.3.3 Preliminary understanding of internal control components

In Chapter 8 (footnote 1) we observe that auditors are required to obtain a preliminary understanding of their audit clients' internal control system as an element of their gaining an understanding of the client, its activities and its financial affairs. We now examine the understanding auditors are required to obtain of the five components of internal control.

(a) Control environment

In order to obtain a proper understanding of the control environment, International Standard on Auditing (ISA) 315: *Identifying and Assessing the Risks of Material Misstatement* . . . (IAASB, 2012, para 14) requires auditors to evaluate, *inter alia*:
*   whether management has created and maintained a culture of honesty and ethical behaviour; and
*   whether the control environment supports the other components of internal control, and whether the other components are undermined by deficiencies in the control environment.

The Standard (para A77) identifies elements of the control environment which may be relevant to the auditor's understanding. They include the following:
(i)   the manner in which the principles of integrity and ethical values are communicated and enforced within the entity. These attributes have a major impact on the effectiveness of the design, implementation and monitoring of internal controls;
(ii)   attributes of the company's directors – in particular, their independence from executives, their experience and stature, the extent of their involvement in the entity, the completeness and relevance of information they receive, their scrutiny of the company's activities, the degree to which they raise and pursue difficult questions with executives, and their interaction with the entity's internal and external auditors;
(iii) the philosophy and operating style of senior executives, in particular, their approach to taking and managing business risks and their attitudes

towards the accounting function, information processing and financial reporting;

(iv) how authority and responsibility for operating activities are assigned, and how reporting relationships and authorisation hierarchies are established;

(v) human resource policies and practices relating to, for example, recognition of requisite skills and knowledge for particular roles and/or responsibilities, recruitment, training, evaluation, counselling, promotion, compensation and remedial actions.

(b) *Risk assessment process*

ISA 315 (IAASB, 2012, paras 15, 16) requires auditors to determine whether their auditees have established a process for:

- identifying business risks relevant to financial reporting,
- estimating the significance and the likelihood of occurrence of those risks, and
- deciding on actions to address the identified risks –

and, if so, to gain an understanding of that process. If an auditee has such a process and the auditor identifies risks of material misstatement in the financial statements which management failed to identify, the auditor needs to determine whether there is an underlying risk s/he would have expected the entity's risk assessment process to identify. If this is the case, the auditor is to obtain an understanding of why the process failed to identify the risk and evaluate whether the process is appropriate to the entity's circumstances or whether a significant deficiency exists in the entity's risk assessment process.

In cases where auditees have not established a formal risk assessment process, auditors are required to discuss with management whether business risks relevant to financial reporting have been identified and, if so, how they have been addressed. They are also required to evaluate whether the absence of a documented risk assessment processes is appropriate in the entity's circumstances or whether it represents a significant deficiency in the entity's internal control system (ISA 315, para 17).

(c) *Information system and related business processes relevant to financial reporting*

Auditors are also required to obtain an understanding of the entity's information system and the related business processes that are relevant to financial reporting. ISA 315 explains:

An entity's business processes are the activities designed to:
- Develop, purchase, produce, sell and distribute an entity's products and services;
- Ensure compliance with laws and regulations; and

- Record information, including accounting and financial reporting information.

Business processes result in the transactions that are recorded, processed and reported by the information system. Obtaining an understanding of the entity's business processes . . . assists the auditor obtain an understanding of the entity's information system relevant to financial reporting in a manner that is appropriate to the entity's circumstances. (para A92)

According to ISA 315 (para 18), the particular aspects of the information system auditors are required to understand include:

(i) the classes of transactions which are significant to the entity's financial statements;

(ii) the procedures (in both electronic and manual systems) by which those transactions are initiated, recorded, processed, corrected as necessary, transferred to the general ledger and reported in the financial statements;

(iii) how the information system captures events and conditions other than transactions that are significant to the financial statements (for example, depreciation and amortisation of assets, and changes in the recoverability of accounts receivable);

(iv) the financial reporting process used to prepare the entity's financial statements (including the determination of significant accounting estimates and the disclosures to be made);

(v) controls over journal entries, in particular, controls over non-standard journal entries which record non-recurring, unusual transactions or adjustments.

In addition to obtaining an understanding of the information system relevant to financial reporting, auditors are required to understand how financial reporting roles and responsibilities, and significant matters relating to financial reporting, are communicated within the entity. This includes understanding matters such as:

- the extent to which entity personnel understand:
  - how their responsibilities and tasks relate to those of others, and
  - the means by which exceptions (errors) should be reported to an appropriate higher level within the organisation;
- how the entity's executives and directors communicate with each other about financial reporting and related matters;
- how the entity communicates with external parties such as regulatory authorities (ISA 315, paras 19, A94).

(d) Control activities

In respect of control activities, auditors are required to obtain an understanding of those that are relevant to the audit, that is, activities they judge "it necessary to understand in order to assess the risks of material misstatement at the assertion level[5] and design further audit procedures responsive to [the] assessed risks" (ISA 315, para 20). These control activities primarily relate to controls within the accounting system, that is, to internal accounting controls which we discuss in more detail in sections 10.3.4 and 10.3.5.

(e) Monitoring of controls

Auditors need to gain an understanding of the means by which their clients monitor the internal controls relevant to financial reporting and the manner in which they effect corrective action. ISA 315 explains the monitoring activities of management and the understanding auditors are to obtain as follows:

> . . . Management accomplishes monitoring of controls through ongoing activities, separate evaluations, or a combination of the two. Ongoing monitoring activities are often built into the normal recurring activities of an entity and include regular management and supervisory activities. Management's monitoring activities may include using information from communications from external parties such as customer complaints and regulator comments that may indicate problems or highlight areas in need of improvement. . . . Much of the information used in monitoring may be produced by the entity's information system. If management assumes that data used for monitoring are accurate without having a basis for that assumption, errors may exist in the information . . . Accordingly, [auditors need] an understanding of [*inter alia*]:
> • the sources of the information related to the entity's monitoring activities; and
> • the basis upon which management considers the information to be sufficiently reliable for the purpose. (paras A106, A107, A117)

10.3.4 Characteristics of a good system of internal accounting controls

Although auditors must obtain a good understanding of each of the components of a client's internal control system, they pay particular attention to controls within the accounting and financial reporting processes, that is, to internal accounting controls. If these controls possess certain characteristics, it is likely that the entity's assets will be adequately safeguarded and its accounting data (and thus its financial statements) will be reliable. These internal control characteristics, and the internal control component of which they are an element, are presented in Figure 10.5 and explained below.

(i) Competent, reliable personnel who possess integrity

The most important factor in safeguarding an entity's assets and records, and in securing reliable financial data, is the quality of the entity's personnel. If the entity's directors, executives and other employees are competent, they are able to fulfil their responsibilities efficiently and effectively; if they are also

---

[5] Assertions relate to aspects of classes of transactions, account balances and disclosures; they are discussed in Chapter 11, section 11.3.1.

Figure 10.5: Characteristics of good system of internal accounting controls

Characteristics	Internal control system component of which the characteristic is an element
(i) Competent, reliable personnel who possess integrity	Control environment
(ii) Clearly defined areas of authority and responsibility	Control environment
(iii) Proper authorisation procedures	Control environment and control activity
(iv) Adequate records	Information system
(v) Segregation of incompatible duties	Control activity
(vi) Independent checks on performance	Control activity
(vii) Physical safeguarding of assets and records	Control activity

reliable and possess integrity, they will fulfil their responsibilities carefully and honestly. Indeed, if this control characteristic is satisfied, it is probable that the entity's assets will remain safe and its financial data will be free of material misstatements even if the other elements are weak.

(ii) Clearly defined areas of authority and responsibility

Irrespective of how competent and reliable an entity's personnel may be, in order to ensure that all necessary tasks are performed correctly – and performed in an efficient and timely manner – it is important that the authority and responsibility of each employee is clearly defined. This not only ensures that employees know what is expected of them, it also facilitates pinpointing responsibility in cases where tasks are not performed properly. Such identification of responsibility motivates employees to work carefully and also enables management to ascertain where corrective action is required.

(iii) Proper authorisation procedures

In order to safeguard its physical assets and protect the integrity of its records, an entity requires proper authorisation procedures. For example, appropriate procedures are required to ensure that all transactions are initiated, or approved, by a person who has the requisite authority. An entity may, for instance, establish procedures for approving credit sales whereby:

- all credit sales have to be authorised in writing by the credit manager before the goods are sold;
- the credit manager has discretion to extend credit to individual customers up to a maximum of, say, £8,000;
- if the £8,000 limit is to be exceeded, written authority must be obtained from the managing director.

Similarly, a purchases manager may be given authority to purchase inventory and/or supplies up to the value of a specified amount, or a departmental manager may be authorised to purchase capital equipment for his/her department up to a specified value. If the purchases or departmental manager wishes to exceed their authorised limit, they must seek approval to do so from a higher authority, such as a divisional manager, managing director or the board of directors (depending on the procedures established in the entity).

Procedures are also required to ensure that the acquisition or development of all new computer programs or packages, and their testing and implementation, are properly authorised. The same applies to all program changes. Even small errors in computer programs can cause considerable harm to an organisation. They can result in erroneous data, and, hence, in faulty decisions being made based on those data. They can also result in much wasted organisational time and effort spent in locating and correcting the errors and in rectifying the damage they have done. This may extend to faulty documents being sent to third parties and, thus, in damage to the entity's reputation.

(iv)   Adequate records

If an entity is to safeguard its assets and secure reliable financial data, it is essential that it maintains adequate records. This includes ensuring that:
- the entity's records (such as order forms, receiving reports, sales invoices, receipts, and payments vouchers – whether in paper or electronic form) are numbered consecutively and are designed so that they may be completed easily and fully at the time a transaction takes place;
- every transaction is supported by a source document in paper or electronic form;
- all accounting entries are supported by a source document (for transactions) or a memorandum generated by the entity's accountant (for non-transactions, such as period end adjustments and writing off bad debts);
- transaction authorisations are supported by appropriate and adequate evidence;
- an adequate chart of accounts is maintained to facilitate recording transactions in the correct accounts;
- adequate procedures manuals and job descriptions are maintained to ensure that employees:
  - know (or can find out) the procedures to follow when undertaking organisational activities;
  - are aware of the requirements of their own position in the entity and how this relates to the duties attaching to associated positions;
- in the IT area, the specifications and authorised application of computer programs (and any modifications thereof) are properly and fully documented.

(v) Segregation of incompatible duties

When defining areas of responsibility and assigning tasks to employees, it is essential that incompatible duties are vested in different people. In particular:

- no one person should have custody of assets and also maintain the related records. For example, the cashier (who handles money) should not record cash received or paid. If the same person performs these duties s/he is able to steal cash and cover his/her traces by making appropriate adjustments in the cash records;
- no one person should have custody of assets and also authorise transactions relating to those assets. For example, the stores manager should not be given authority to authorise purchases or sales of items under his/her control. If these tasks are vested in the same person, it enables that person to obtain assets for their own benefit by authorising fictitious transactions;
- no one person should have responsibility for:
  - software design and computer programming;
  - computer programming and computer operations;
  - computer programming and software testing.
  In each of these cases, if the responsibilities are assigned to one person, it enables that person to manipulate computer programs to his/her own advantage; it also allows unintentional errors to remain undetected;
- no one person should have responsibility for all of the entries in the accounting records. Careful allocation of accounting duties enables the work of one employee to automatically cross-check the work of another. This facilitates the detection of unintentional errors.

(vi) Independent checks on performance

Even if personnel are competent, reliable and trustworthy, and their responsibilities are clearly defined and carefully assigned so that no one person performs incompatible duties, there remains the possibility that errors will occur. All employees are humans, not robots, and humans are prone to make mistakes. Unintentional errors may occur, for example, as a result of tiredness, boredom or failure to concentrate fully on the task in hand. Occasionally, employees may become careless in following defined procedures or may deliberately fail to do so, either because they perceive an 'easier' way to accomplish the task or because they wish to defraud the entity. If financial data are to be reliable, and the entity's assets and records are to be safeguarded, it is important that there are independent checks on employees' performance.

One means of achieving these checks is to assign accounting duties so that the work of one employee automatically cross-checks that of another – a process known as 'internal check'. For example, one accounts clerk may maintain the

Accounts Receivable (or Credit Sales) Subsidiary Ledger and another, the Accounts Receivable Control account in the General Ledger. Similarly, before preparing a payment, the payments clerk may be required to match the supplier's invoice with a copy of the relevant order form (from the purchases department) and receiving note (from the receiving department), to check for authorised signatures on the order form and receiving note, and to verify and reconcile the items, quantities and monetary amounts shown on the documents. In computerised systems, the computer can be programmed so that a payment is prepared (electronically) once the purchase order, receiving report and supplier's invoice (all in electronic form) have been properly authorised and 'matched' by the computer. In other situations, two employees may be involved in a single task, so that each provides a check on the performance of the other; for example, two employees may be involved in opening the mail when it is expected to contain remittances from customers (accounts receivable).

A further means of checking employees' performance is for supervisors to review the work of subordinates; for example, the chief accountant may review journal and ledger entries and bank reconciliations completed by others in the accounts department.

(vii) *Physical safeguarding of assets and records*

As we noted earlier, one of the objectives of an internal control system is to safeguard the entity's assets and records. The most effective way to achieve this is to provide physical protection for assets and records, combined with restricted access. For example, inventory and supplies may be stored in a locked store-room to which only authorised personnel can gain access; cash, cheques, marketable securities and similar items may be kept in a fireproof safe, with few personnel having access to the safe keys or being privy to the combination lock number; the entity's land and buildings may be protected by such things as fences, locked entry doors, closed circuit television, burglar and fire alarms, smoke detectors, water sprinklers and similar devices.

An entity's legal, accounting and other documents are important components of its assets and should be protected in the same way as its other assets; that is, secure facilities should be provided for their safekeeping and access should be strictly limited to authorised personnel. The same applies to computer hardware, programs, data and files. Additionally, back-up copies should be kept (preferably at a secure, off-site location) of information generated or stored in the entity's computers, and emergency use of computer facilities should be arranged in case the entity's system should fail.

In section 10.3.1 we observed that internal controls become necessary when an entity grows beyond the size at which the owner or manager can personally perform or oversee all of the entity's functions and functional responsibilities have to be delegated to employees. It follows that the extent of an internal control system, and its degree of formalisation, are likely to vary according to the size and complexity of the entity and its operations. However, irrespective of the entity's size and complexity, if its internal accounting controls possess the seven characteristics outlined above, then it is likely that its assets and records will be adequately safeguarded and its financial data (and hence its financial statements) will be reliable.

10.3.5 Objectives of internal accounting controls

As we explained in section 10.2, an entity's accounting system is designed to capture accounting data and to convert and output this data as useful financial information. If financial information is to be useful, it must be reliable – hence, the underlying accounting data must be valid, complete and accurate. In order to generate data which meet these criteria, control activities are built into the accounting system which are designed, in particular, to ensure that transactions which give rise to the accounting data are:

(i) properly recorded: that is, all relevant details of transactions are recorded at the time the transactions take place;

(ii) properly authorised: that is, all transactions are authorised by a person with the requisite authority;

(iii) valid: that is, transactions recorded in the accounting system represent genuine exchanges with *bona fide* parties;

(iv) complete: that is, all genuine transactions are input to the accounting system; none is omitted;

(v) properly valued: that is, transactions are recorded at their correct exchange value;

(vi) properly classified: that is, transactions are recorded in the correct accounts;

(vii) recorded in the correct accounting period.

As practically all entities' accounting systems are now largely or wholly electronic, internal accounting controls which seek to ensure that all (but only) valid transactions are recorded correctly are, in essence, application controls.

In addition to control activities designed to ensure that data input to the accounting system are authorised, valid, complete and accurate as to amount, account and accounting period, controls are needed to ensure that the transactions (or input data) are properly processed. Thus, application controls are required to ensure, for example, that:

• invalid and incorrect data are rejected;

• processing errors are identified and corrected on a timely basis;

• data files are properly maintained and protected;

- output is checked against input data;
- output is provided to appropriate, authorised personnel on a timely basis;
- exception reports are acted upon promptly and appropriately;
- only the latest versions of programs and data are used for processing.

10.3.6 Inherent limitations of systems of internal control

Irrespective of how well designed an internal control system may be, and how effectively it operates, it will always possess inherent limitations. These may be illustrated by the following examples:

(i)   The extent of an entity's internal control activities depends on their cost-effectiveness. Beyond some point, the cost of instituting additional control activities will exceed the benefits to be gained from more accurate financial information or increased safeguarding of assets. For example, there is little point in installing a £75,000 surveillance system to prevent the theft of, say, one 25p biro each week!

(ii)   Internal accounting controls are designed to prevent and detect errors and irregularities in normal, frequently recurring transactions. However, errors are more likely to occur in the recording and/or processing of infrequent, unusual transactions – for the very reason that they are unusual.

(iii)   The potential for error is always present because employees are human and therefore prone to make mistakes. Similarly, there may be an error in the design of a control activity or the person responsible for performing it may not fully understand its purpose and, as a result, fails to take appropriate action. Thus, internal controls may not always operate as intended.

(iv)   There is the possibility that management will override the controls, or two or more employees will collude so as to circumvent particular controls, or a computer operator may override or disable checks within a software program. A computer operator may, for example, override or disable edit checks designed to identify and report transactions that exceed a specified amount.

(v)   Internal control procedures may become inadequate or inappropriate as a result of changes in the entity's internal and/or external environment and, as a consequence, compliance with the controls may deteriorate.

Because of the inherent limitations of all systems of internal control, irrespective of how 'perfect' a system may appear to be, auditors can never rely on it to prevent or detect *all* material errors and irregularities in the accounting data. Auditors always have to evaluate, at least to some extent, the accuracy, validity and completeness of the information presented in the financial statements; thus, some substantive testing will always be necessary.

10.3.7 Significance of internal control to the external auditor

External auditors are not responsible for establishing or maintaining an auditee's internal control system – that is the responsibility of management. Nevertheless, understanding the system and assessing its effectiveness can, and usually does, have a significant impact on the audit. More specifically, it assists the auditor to assess the risk of material misstatements being present in the pre-audited financial statements, to identify where, within the financial statements, such misstatements seem most likely, and, thus, to determine the nature, timing and extent of further audit procedures.

If the client's internal accounting controls are well designed (if they possesses the seven characteristics outlined in section 10.3.4), and the control activities operate effectively so as to achieve the internal accounting control objectives set out in section 10.3.5, then the auditor can be reasonably assured that any material errors or irregularities in the accounting data will be prevented or detected (and corrected) as the data passes through the accounting system. Thus, the auditor can be fairly confident that the financial statements are free of material misstatement. Expressed in terms of audit risk, where an entity has an internal control system that is well designed and implemented, the risk of material misstatements in the accounting data not being eliminated (that is, internal control risk) will be fairly low. However, before the auditor can rely on internal controls to eliminate material misstatements from the financial statements (and, thus, to reduce substantive testing), s/he must conduct compliance tests[6] to confirm that the controls are operating as his/her preliminary assessment suggests. Further, as a consequence of the inherent limitations of all internal control systems, internal control risk can never be reduced to zero. As explained in Chapter 9 (section 9.5), when inherent risk and internal control risk are low, the likelihood of material misstatements being present in the pre-audited financial statements is considered to be low and, as a result, substantive procedures need not be extensive. Thus, in audits where the client has effective internal controls, the auditor is likely to place greater emphasis on compliance testing than on substantive testing and more audit testing will be conducted during an interim audit than would otherwise be the case.

Conversely, if an entity's internal control system is poorly designed and implemented and, as a result, is ineffective in meeting the internal accounting control objectives, the auditor will gain little assurance that the financial statements are free of material misstatement (that is, internal control risk will be assessed as high). As a consequence, before a 'clean' audit report can be issued, the auditor will need to conduct extensive substantive testing – and to do so close to the client's year end – in order to gain sufficient assurance that the

---

[6] Compliance tests are discussed in section 10.6.

financial statements are, in fact, free of material misstatement. Thus, in audits characterised by weak or ineffective internal controls, the auditor is likely to focus on substantive testing and most testing will be conducted during the final (year end) audit.

10.4 REVIEWING THE ACCOUNTING SYSTEM AND EVALUATING ITS INTERNAL CONTROLS

10.4.1 Gaining an understanding of the accounting sub-systems and related controls

In section 10.2 we observed that, in order to facilitate the audit, the auditor (conceptually) divides the auditee's accounting system into sub-systems (or audit segments) and conducts the detailed audit examination based on these audit segments. As the starting point of the detailed examination, the auditor seeks to understand, and to document, the client's accounting sub-systems and their internal controls. In section 10.3.3, we examined the requirements of auditors as regards gaining an understanding of the components of their clients' internal control systems. We now consider how they obtain this understanding and, more particularly, how they gain an understanding of the accounting sub-systems and related internal controls.

Auditors obtain their understanding of an accounting sub-system primarily through the following audit procedures.

(i) *Enquiries of client personnel*: Auditors ask questions of relevant personnel from management, supervisory and staff levels of the client about various aspects of the sub-system. They enquire, for example, how data are captured and input to the sub-system, and how the data are recorded, classified and summarised. They also enquire about which employees are responsible for what duties, how employees know what to do, how much guidance is provided by procedures manuals and similar documents, and what reviews of employees' work take place.

(ii) *Inspection of client documents*: By inspecting relevant documents, auditors gain significant insight into the operation of an accounting sub-system. They examine, for example, the auditee's organisation chart, its chart of accounts and the guidance given on account classification of transactions, and its policies and procedures manuals insofar as they relate to the accounting sub-system. They also inspect more detailed documents such as source documents, journals, ledgers and trial balances, and discuss the various documents with client personnel to ascertain how well they are used and understood.

(iii) *Observation of client personnel*: In addition to asking client personnel about their various duties and inspecting documents which specify the duties that should be performed, auditors observe personnel at various levels of the organisation carrying out their normal accounting and review functions. (What employees *actually do* may differ from what they *say they do* and what the documents indicate they *should do*!)

10.4.2 Documenting the accounting sub-systems

Once the auditor has gained a preliminary understanding of an accounting sub-system, s/he needs to document that understanding (or, more usually, obtain relevant documents from the client and check his/her understanding against those documents). Two primary forms of documentation are used, namely:
 (a) narrative descriptions, and
 (b) flowcharts.

(a) Narrative descriptions

A narrative description is a detailed description of accounting routines which take place within an accounting sub-system. An example of part of a narrative description from the purchases-payables-payments sub-system is provided in Figure 10.6.

A narrative description should include details of:

 (i) *all of the documents (whether in paper or electronic form) which are used in the accounting routine*: For example, in a purchases routine the

Figure 10.6: Narrative description of part of a purchases-payables-payments sub-system

When the issue of a regular item of stock results in the re-order point for that stock item being reached, the staff member in the Stores Department responsible for that stock item prepares a requisition. The requisition is sent electronically to the manager or assistant manager of the Stores Department. He authorises the requisition and sends a copy to the Purchasing Department. A copy is also filed (by requisition number) in the Approved Requisitions (Pending) file. The filed copy is subsequently matched by the Stores Department with a copy of the purchases order and receiving report and moved to a Goods Received file. Discrepancies between goods requested, ordered and received are reported (by means of a computer generated exception report) to the Stores Department, Purchasing Department, Receiving Department and Accounts Payable Ledger clerk and filed with the relevant (matched) documents.

On receiving a copy of the approved requisition, the Purchasing Department prepares a purchase order. Copies are sent electronically to the supplier, the Stores Department (see above), the Receiving Department, and the Accounts Payable Ledger clerk. A copy is also filed in the Purchase Orders (Pending) file according to the purchase order number.

The Receiving Department files the purchase order (by number) pending the arrival of the goods. On arrival, the goods are inspected and counted and compared with the purchase order. A receiving report is prepared and copies are sent (electronically) to the Purchasing Department, Accounts Payable Ledger clerk and Stores Department (see above). A copy is also filed, by receiving report number, together with purchase order, in a Goods Received file...

narrative description should refer to order forms, receiving reports, suppliers' invoices and credit notes, payments vouchers, etc. The description should detail how each document is initiated, the steps through which it passes between initiation and filing, where and how it is filed (for example, the name and location of the relevant file and whether it is arranged alphabetically, by document number or by date), and who is responsible for preparing, reviewing, using and filing the document;

(ii) *all of the processes which take place within the routine*: For example, what triggers goods to be ordered, how a supplier is selected, how quantities to be ordered are determined, how price is ascertained, how goods received are checked against goods ordered, how discrepancies between goods ordered and received are handled and so on;

(iii) *internal control procedures*: The narrative also should refer to controls within the accounting routine such as the segregation of incompatible duties, authorisation procedures, independent checks on performance and safeguards for assets and records (for example, the use of locked storerooms and fireproof safes, and access being restricted to authorised personnel).

As a means of documenting the entity's accounting sub-systems, narrative descriptions are generally less time consuming and less technically demanding to prepare than flowcharts. However, they do not convey the sequence of processes or document flows as clearly as flowcharts, they are time consuming to read, they may be difficult to comprehend, and key points may not be readily apparent.

Narrative descriptions are appropriate for describing simple accounting routines or sub-systems but their use requires a careful balance between giving sufficient detail to provide an adequate description and giving too much detail which adversely affects clarity and ease of comprehension. Narrative descriptions are frequently used, and are useful, as supplements to flowcharts – to expand on elements of a flowchart where additional detail or explanation is considered necessary.

(b) Flowcharts

A flowchart is a diagrammatic representation of the flow of documents or information through an accounting routine or sub-system and the processes which take place within the routine or system. An example of a flowchart of part of a purchases-payables-payments sub-system is presented in Figure 10.7.[7]

---

[7] The narrative description in Figure 10.6 describes part of the sub-system depicted in Figure 10.7. This is for illustrative purposes only. In practice one or other method would be adopted to represent the

Figure 10.7: Flowchart of part of a purchases-payables-payments sub-system

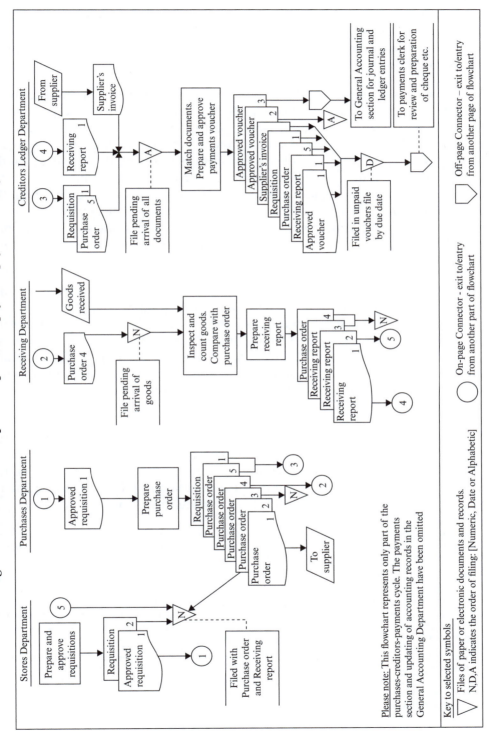

Please note: This flowchart represents only part of the purchases-creditors-payments cycle. The payments section and updating of accounting records in the General Accounting Department have been omitted

Key to selected symbols

▽ Files of paper or electronic documents and records.
N,D,A indicates the order of filing: [Numeric, Date or Alphabetic]

◯ On-page Connector - exit to/entry from another part of flowchart

⬠ Off-page Connector – exit to/entry from another page of flowchart

Although Figure 10.7 depicts the flow of paper documents through part of the purchases-payables-payments sub-system, it could equally depict the flow of information in electronic form from one department to another. The principles remain unchanged.[8]

The primary advantages of a flowchart are the clear overview of the accounting routine or sub-system it provides and the ease with which internal control strengths and deficiencies can be identified. Compared with a narrative description, a flowchart is easier to read and understand and, when changes are made to the routine or accounting sub-system, it is easier to update. However, on the downside, a flowchart is time consuming and technically demanding – and, therefore, costly – to prepare. It is largely for these reasons (together with the inefficiency of duplicating effort) that external auditors generally obtain and use (at least as a starting point) flowcharts of the accounting sub-systems prepared by their audit clients (or usually, if they have one, the internal audit function) for their own internal use.

Once auditors have documented (or checked, using the auditee's documentation) their understanding of an accounting sub-system, they test this understanding against the sub-system itself. This is achieved by means of a 'walk through test' (also known as a 'cradle to the grave test'). One or two transactions from each major class (for example, credit purchases and cash payments) are traced through the entire sub-system, from their initial recording at source to their final destination as components of account balances in the financial statements.

It should be noted that a walk through test is not an audit procedure oriented towards evaluating the truth and fairness of the auditee's financial statements: instead, it is a procedure designed to confirm (or correct) the auditor's understanding (and documentation) of the flow of data through, and the documents, processes and controls within, the client's accounting sub-systems.

---

sub-system. However, this is not to say that one form may not be used to supplement the other. For example, a narrative description may be used to clarify an element of a flowchart; similarly, a flowchart component may be used to clarify a point in a narrative description.

[8] When electronic documents are used, frequently only one document will be generated by-say-the Stores Department and this will be sent (sequentially) to the Purchasing and Receiving Departments, the Accounts Payable ledger clerk and the accounting department for each department to record relevant information on, or to take other appropriate action in relation to, the document. The document can be filed (electronically or in hard copy) by each department in the order most appropriate for its use. Should additional copies of the document be required, they can be generated readily.

When electronic documentation is used, it is important that internal controls are incorporated in the accounting system to ensure that:
(i) only authorised personnel are able to access, and record information on, the document; and
(ii) whenever changes are made to, or additional copies made of, the document, a record of those changes (or additional copies) is generated automatically so the changes can be reviewed and approved subsequently by authorised personnel.

10.4.3 Evaluating internal accounting controls

After gaining an understanding of, and documenting, an accounting sub-system, the auditor needs to identify internal controls within the sub-system that are (i) strengths and (ii) deficiencies.

(a) *Strengths* are internal controls which operate effectively to prevent or detect errors and irregularities in the accounting data which pass through the accounting sub-system. These are controls on which the auditor may plan to rely to prevent material misstatements from occurring in the relevant section of the financial statements and, thus, to reduce the related substantive testing.

(b) *Deficiencies* are controls that are needed to prevent or detect misstatements in the accounting data which pass through the accounting sub-system but are either missing or are designed, implemented or operated in such a way that they are ineffective.

In order to identify internal control strengths, the auditor needs to:
(i)   gather information about the internal controls;
(ii) assess their design in terms of their ability to prevent or detect potential misstatements in the accounting data;
(iii) establish that the controls whose design is effective in terms of preventing or detecting misstatements in the accounting data have been implemented.

(i)   Gathering information

The primary means of gathering information about internal controls within an accounting sub-system (or audit segment) is an internal control questionnaire (ICQ). This consists of a series of questions relating to control activities which are normally considered necessary to prevent or detect errors and irregularities which may occur in a particular class of transactions. The questions are usually phrased so that they require a 'yes' or 'no' response. As a result, ICQs are generally simple (and quick) to complete. A useful way to organise the questions, so as to ensure good coverage of the audit segment, is to link them to the internal accounting control objectives outlined in section 10.3.5. An example of part of an ICQ relating to purchase transactions prepared on this basis is presented in Figure 10.8.

It should be noted that, although we have presented 'gathering information about the internal controls within an accounting sub-system' as an audit step subsequent to the auditor gaining an understanding of, and documenting, the sub-system, ICQs are commonly completed at the same time as the auditor obtains an understanding of the sub-system.

**Figure 10.8:   Part of an ICQ relating to the purchases-payables-payments
sub-system**

Internal Control Questionnaire Purchases				Ref: C-4
Client: Jasper Limited Period: Year to 31 March 2014		Prepared by: RB Date: 12/12/13 Reviewed by: MC Date: 15/12/13		

Control Procedure	Yes	No	N/A	Remarks
1. Are sequentially numbered requisitions used to initiate purchase orders?	✓			
2. Are all numbered requisitions accounted for?	✓			Copies are filed numerically. Cancelled requisitions also filed (marked to indicate cancellation).
3. Are requisitions approved by a responsible official?	✓			Manager or Assistant Manager of Stores Department
4. Is initiation of requisitions limited to authorised personnel?		✓		All Stores Department employees can initiate requisitions
5. Can purchase orders be prepared without a requisition?		✓		
6. Are purchase orders sequentially numbered?	✓			
7. Are all numbers accounted for?	✓			Copies are filed numerically (including cancelled order forms)
8. Are purchase orders prepared by a responsible official?	✓			Manager or Assistant Manager of Purchasing Department
9. Is initiation of purchase orders restricted to authorised personnel?	✓			
10. Do all purchase orders show: (a) Quantities ordered? (b) Prices of goods ordered? (c) Special terms of the order? (d) Initials of preparer? (e) Date of preparation?	✓ ✓ ✓ ✓ ✓			
11. Is there a limit to the value of goods that may be ordered?	✓			Maximum order size £5,000
12. Is a copy of the purchase order sent to: (a) Stores Department? (b) Receiving Department? (c) Accounts Payable Ledger Clerk?	✓ ✓ ✓			

(ii) Assessing the design and implementation of the internal accounting controls

Once information about the controls within an accounting sub-system has been gathered, the auditor needs to evaluate their effectiveness in preventing or detecting errors in the accounting data. In performing this evaluation the auditor will consider, in particular:

- the errors and irregularities which could occur in the accounting sub-system;
- whether the controls have been appropriately designed and implemented so as to be effective in preventing or detecting such errors and irregularities;
- where effective controls appear to be absent, whether there are compensating controls which overcome the apparent internal control deficiency.

Once the auditor has identified internal controls which appear to be effective in preventing material misstatements from occurring in the relevant part of the financial statements, s/he needs to decide whether or not to rely on those controls to reduce the related substantive testing. This decision affects the nature, timing and extent of subsequent audit tests.

10.4.4 Internal control evaluation and audit planning

Irrespective of how effective internal accounting controls may appear to be in preventing material misstatements from occurring in the financial statements, before auditors can rely on them to reduce related substantive tests, they must test them. Auditors need to obtain audit evidence which demonstrates that the controls are operating as effectively as their assessment of the controls' design and implementation suggests, and that they have been so working throughout the reporting period. The greater the reliance the auditor plans to place on internal controls to eliminate material misstatements from the financial statements (and, thus, to reduce substantive tests), the more extensive the tests of those controls (i.e., compliance tests) need to be. According to ISA 330: *The Auditor's Responses to Assessed Risks* (IAASB, 2009c), extensive compliance testing is also required in situations where it is not possible:

> to design effective substantive procedures that by themselves provide sufficient appropriate audit evidence at the assertion level. This may occur when an entity conducts its business using IT and no documentation of transactions is produced or maintained, other than through the IT system. (para A24)

When the auditor believes that a client's internal accounting controls are effective, a significant proportion of the audit procedures (especially compliance tests) may be performed during an interim audit, two or three months prior to the end of the client's financial year. This enables the audit to be completed in a timely manner following the end of the client's financial year. It also facilitates efficient scheduling of audit work (and thus audit staff) over the calendar year and avoids 'bottlenecks' occurring when the year ends of a number of audit clients coincide.

From the above, it is evident that, when auditors' assessment of a client's internal accounting controls indicates they can be relied upon to prevent misstatements from occurring in the financial statements, compliance procedures will be given greater emphasis, more audit procedures will be conducted during an interim (rather than the year end) audit, and substantive testing will be less extensive[9] than would apply if the controls were assessed as weak or defective. Thus, auditors' assessment of their auditees' internal accounting controls has a direct impact on audit planning and, once the assessment is complete, the auditor proceeds to develop the audit plan.

When considering the audit procedures to be included in the audit plan, the following points need to be borne in mind:

(i) Irrespective of how effective an auditee's internal accounting controls may appear to be, auditors may not rely upon them to reduce substantive procedures until they have tested them and found them to be operating effectively – and operating in this manner throughout the reporting period. This may appear to preclude the planning of substantive procedures until compliance testing is complete. However, such a delay would introduce inefficiencies into the audit process. As a consequence, auditors proceed to develop their audit plan on the assumption that the internal controls on which they plan to rely (and thus need to test) operate as indicated by their assessment of the controls' design and implementation, and that the controls have functioned effectively throughout the reporting period. Nevertheless, auditors must remain alert to the possibility that compliance tests may reveal internal accounting controls that are not as effective as they first thought, and adjustments to the audit plan may be required as a result.

(ii) Although particular internal controls may appear to be operating effectively, auditors may decide not to rely on them to reduce substantive procedures because they consider the audit effort required to test compliance with the controls is likely to exceed the reduction in effort (in terms of reduced substantive testing) that could result. In this case, no testing of the relevant controls is undertaken and internal control

---

[9] As explained in Chapter 9, section 9.5, low internal control risk (combined with low inherent risk) results in the auditor's desired level of audit risk being attained with less substantive testing than is needed when internal control risk (and/or inherent risk) is assessed as high.

risk is assumed to be high. As a consequence, extensive substantive testing will be needed to reduce detection risk to the desired (low) level.

10.5 DEVELOPING THE AUDIT PLAN

10.5.1 Purpose and formats of audit plans

An audit plan sets out, in detail, the nature, timing and extent of audit procedures which are designed:

(i) to assess the risk of the pre-audited financial statements containing material misstatements and identifying where, within the financial statements, misstatements seem most likely. These 'risk assessment procedures' include:
- gaining an understanding of the client, its business, industry, key personnel, etc.,
- conducting overall analytical review of the financial statements,
- gaining an understanding of, and documenting, the client's accounting sub-systems (audit segments) and conducting a preliminary assessment of the design and implementation of the related internal controls;

(ii) to test the operating effectiveness of the internal controls within the accounting sub-systems on which the auditor plans to rely to reduce related substantive testing (i.e., compliance tests);

(iii) to meet the specific audit objectives of each audit segment (or, expressed differently, to test the assertions associated with classes of transactions, account balances and disclosures within the audit segment (i.e., substantive testing);

(iv) to ensure that sufficient appropriate audit evidence is collected in each audit segment and for the audit as a whole on which the auditor can base an opinion on the truth and fairness of the financial statements.

Although ISA 300: *Planning an Audit of Financial Statements* (IAASB, 2009b, para 9) requires audit plans to describe the nature, timing and extent of risk assessment procedures, it is not until these have been performed, and the risk of material misstatements in the various audit segments have been identified and assessed, that detailed planning of compliance and substantive tests can be undertaken. Consequently, the audit plan is developed as the audit progresses. However, once the risk assessment procedures have been performed, the plan for the detailed compliance and substantive testing is prepared (at least conceptually) in two stages, namely:

(i) a planning format;
(ii) a performance format.

(i) Planning format

In this stage, the audit objectives (or assertions) for each class of transactions, account balance or other financial statement disclosure within each audit segment are identified. For example, the audit objectives for purchase transactions might be:

To ascertain whether:
- purchase transactions are recorded;
- purchase transactions are authorised;
- recorded purchase transactions are valid;
- recorded purchase transactions are complete;
- purchase transactions are properly classified (recorded in the correct account);
- purchase transactions are stated at their correct value (or amount);
- purchase transactions are recorded in their correct accounting period.

Based on his/her assessment of the inherent and control risk of an audit segment, the auditor then determines how each audit objective (or assertion) for each class of transactions, account balance or other disclosure is best met through compliance and/or substantive procedures, and identifies the specific procedure(s) to be performed. Certain procedures may be identified as appropriate for meeting more than one objective.

(ii) Performance format

Once the lists of audit procedures to be performed in each audit segment have been compiled, the procedures are arranged in a logical sequence, and any overlapping procedures are eliminated. This results in a list of audit procedures which are set out in a manner suitable for their performance.

Although we can identify two stages in preparing the audit plan, where audit plans are generated electronically (which is normally the case), the two stages may occur concurrently (that is, the planning format procedures are concurrently arranged in their performance format). Further, although we describe as a sequential process, the auditor's:
- (i) risk assessment procedures (including assessment of the design and implementation of internal accounting controls),
- (ii) compliance testing of controls on which the auditor plans to rely to reduce substantive testing, and
- (iii) substantive tests of classes of transactions, account balances and other disclosures,

in practice more than one audit step may be performed concurrently. The overlapping nature of various audit procedures is described in ISA 330 as follows:

> Testing the operating effectiveness of controls is different from obtaining an understanding of and evaluating the design and implementation of controls.

However, the same types of audit procedures are used. The auditor may, therefore, decide it is efficient to test the operating effectiveness of controls at the same time as evaluating their design and determining that they have been implemented. (para A21)

Further, although some risk assessment procedures may not have been specifically designed as tests of controls, they may nevertheless provide audit evidence about the operating effectiveness of the controls and, consequently, serve as tests of controls. For example, the auditor's risk assessment procedures may have included:
- Inquiring about management's use of budgets.
- Observing management's comparison of monthly budgeted and actual expenses.
- Inspecting reports pertaining to the investigation of variances between budgeted and actual amounts.

These audit procedures provide knowledge about the design of the entity's budgeting policies and whether they have been implemented, but may also provide audit evidence about the effectiveness of the operation of budgeting policies in preventing or detecting material misstatements in the classification of expenses. (para A22)

In addition, the auditor may design a test of controls [i.e., a compliance test] to be performed concurrently with a test of details [i.e., a substantive test] on the same transaction. . . . For example, the auditor may design, and evaluate the results of, a test to examine an invoice to determine whether it has been approved [a compliance test] and to provide substantive audit evidence of a transaction [its occurrence, amount, accounting period, etc.]. (para A23)

Notwithstanding factors such as those described above, this stage of the auditor's planning process results in an audit plan (in paper or electronic form), in performance format, which specifies for each significant class of transactions, account balance or disclosure within each audit segment:
- the audit objectives to be met;
- the compliance and substantive procedures to be performed to meet the stated objectives;
- the timing of the procedures, that is, whether they are to be performed during the interim or final (year end) audit.

An example of part of an audit plan relating to purchases transactions is presented in Figure 10.9.

10.5.2 Review of the audit plan

As we explain in Chapter 9, section 9.2.1, development of the audit plan (like that of the audit strategy) is not a 'one-off' event but continues throughout the audit. Its adequacy and appropriateness are re-evaluated as audit evidence is gathered, and it is revised as and when this is found to be necessary. This usually occurs when the auditor encounters unexpected events or changes in conditions or when the results of audit tests differ from those the auditor expected.

Figure 10.9:   Part of an audit plan for purchases transactions

	Procedure	Completed by	Date	Workpaper Ref
1	*Test sequence of purchase orders.* Randomly select five purchase orders from total. Test number sequence - five forwards and five backwards.			
2	*Test purchase order approval.* (See 3(i) below)			
3	*Test adherence to authority limits and compatibility with nature of client's business.* Randomly select 25 purchase orders: (i) Vouch for initials of purchasing officer. (ii) Compare value of order with authorised limit. (iii) Evaluate compatibility of goods ordered with nature of client's business.			
4	*Test sequence of receiving reports.* Randomly select five receiving reports from total. Test number sequence - five forwards and five backwards.			
5	*Test for matching of purchase orders with receiving reports.* Randomly select 25 receiving reports: (i) Check for matching with purchase orders. (ii) Vouch for independent check of items and quantities ordered and received.			
6	*Test sequence of purchase returns records.* Randomly select three purchases returns records. Test number sequence - five forwards and five backwards.			
7	*Test for matching of purchases returns records and suppliers' credit notes.* Randomly select 15 purchases returns records: (i) Check for matching with credit notes. (ii) Vouch for independent check of items and quantities returned and credited.			

8	*Test suppliers' invoices and payments vouchers.*
	Randomly select 25 payments vouchers:
	(i) Check for matching with
	      - supplier's invoice
	      - purchase order
	      - receiving report
	      - purchase returns report
	      - supplier's credit note.
	(ii) Vouch supplier's invoice for evidence of independent check of:
	      - items, quantities and prices of goods ordered and received
	      - extensions and footings.
	(iii) Vouch payments vouchers for:
	      - account classification shown
	      - evidence of independent check of:
	        • amount of payment
	        • account codes.			

Figure 10.9: *Continued*

(iv) Test accuracy of amounts and account classifications: - recalculate extensions and footings on suppliers' invoices and credit notes - recalculate VAT on invoices and credit notes - check propriety of account codes. *Review all outstanding purchase orders at year end.* Check for goods in transit at year end. • • •			

10.6 COMPLIANCE TESTING

10.6.1 Purpose of compliance procedures

In section 10.4.4 we noted that, as auditors assess the design and implementation of their clients' internal accounting controls, they identify internal control strengths, that is, control activities which appear to be operating effectively to meet certain audit objectives. Two examples are presented in Figure 10.10.

Figure 10.10: Examples of control activities meeting audit objectives

Audit objective	Control activities meeting the audit objective
1. Sales transactions are properly authorised.	The credit manager approves all credit sales before goods leave the premises and initials the sales invoice to indicate approval.
2. Sales transactions are properly valued.	All sales invoices are checked (prices are checked against price lists, and extensions and additions are checked) by an independent person prior to a copy of the invoice being sent to the customer. The 'checker' initials the invoice to indicate it has been checked.

However, in section 10.4.5 we emphasise that, irrespective of how effective internal controls may appear to be, before auditors can rely on them to eliminate errors and irregularities from the accounting data (and, thus, to reduce their substantive testing), their operating effectiveness must be tested through compliance procedures. ISA 330 (para 10) requires auditors to establish how, by whom, and how consistently the controls have been applied during the reporting period. The Standard also notes: "inquiry alone is not sufficient" (para A26); auditors must perform other procedures in order to obtain audit evidence to support responses to their enquiries by client personnel.

10.6.2 Types of compliance procedures

Compliance procedures fall into two main categories:
(i) those performed where the control activities leave no audit trail;
(ii) those performed where the control activities leave an audit trail.

(i) Procedures where the control activities leave no audit trail

The primary compliance procedures performed where the client's control activities do not leave an audit trail are inspection of relevant documents, enquiry, observation and – for certain computer applications – reperformance. For example, in order to ascertain whether a control involving the segregation of incompatible duties is being complied with, the auditor will first establish, by reviewing relevant procedures manuals, which employees should perform the duties, and when and how they should be performed. The auditor will then ascertain, by means of enquiry and observation, who actually performs the duties and whether they do so in the intended manner. Along similar lines, in order to determine whether controls designed to protect assets and records are being complied with, the auditor will observe if access to restricted areas is limited to authorised personnel. Additionally, tests may be performed on specific computer applications or on the general control environment; for example, the auditor may check whether access to computer hardware, files and data is restricted by, for example, passwords or voice or fingerprint recognition, by trying to gain access thereto.

(ii) Procedures where the control activities leave an audit trail

Where an audit trail is available (that is, where there is tangible evidence that a control procedure has or has not been performed), the primary audit tests are inspection of relevant procedures manuals, enquiry and observation (as for where no audit trail is left), inspection of source documents and other accounting records and documents, and reperformance. For example, in addition to establishing (by inspecting relevant procedures manuals) who should perform certain duties and how and when they should do so, and ascertaining by enquiry and observation whether the 'correct' person performs the duties and does so as intended, source documents are inspected for things like evidence of compliance with authorisation procedures and independent verification of prices, quantities, extensions and additions (such as the initials of the person performing the control procedure). Similarly, other documents, such as reconciliations, journals and ledgers, may be inspected for evidence indicating that independent reviews of work performed have been carried out. Along similar lines, automated logs may be inspected to ascertain whether controls restricting access to elements of the IT system (hardware, programs, files, data, etc.) have been effective. Reperformance of control activities may take the form of, for example, trying to gain unauthorised access to storerooms or to computer hardware, programs, files and data.

10.6.3 Evaluating the results of compliance tests

If some deviations in the operation of a control are discovered by the auditor's compliance procedures (i.e., evidence is found which indicates that the control has not, on occasion, operated as intended), the auditor may still judge the relevant control to be operating effectively and able to be relied upon to reduce the related substantive testing. This may occur, for example, if the rate of deviation discovered in the sample of items examined by the compliance tests corresponds to the rate of deviation the auditor expected, based on his/her previous assessment of the design and implementation of the control. Nevertheless, if any deviations are found in the sample of items examined, the auditor needs to understand why they occurred and their potential consequences.

Further, if deviations discovered by compliance procedures are numerous (especially if they exceed the error rate expected by the auditor), or are significant in terms of their potential consequences, the auditor is likely to conclude that the control in question is not operating effectively and, therefore, cannot be relied upon to reduce substantive testing. The same applies if misstatements the auditor would have expected to be prevented by internal accounting controls are detected by substantive procedures. In either case, the auditor will need to re-assess his/her conclusion about the operating effectiveness of the control(s) in question and to adjust the planned nature, timing and extent of further audit procedures – and, therefore, the audit plan – accordingly.

It should be noted that deviations from the proper operation of controls may occur as a result of changes of personnel in key control functions (for example, a change of credit manager). Such personnel changes may be permanent or temporary; they may occur, for example, when the person responsible for the control activity is on holiday or ill. It is important that the auditor's compliance procedures cover any periods of change in relevant personnel so as to ensure that deviations from the controls have not occurred, or have not occurred more frequently than expected, during or since the change.

10.6.4 Using audit evidence from an interim audit or audits conducted in prior years

In section 10.4.5 we noted that, when the auditor's evaluation of the effectiveness of a client's internal accounting controls indicates they can be relied upon to prevent or detect errors and irregularities in the accounting data, a significant portion of the compliance testing is likely to be performed during an interim audit. In cases where auditors test the operating effectiveness of controls in an interim audit, they need to assure themselves that the controls they found to be operating effectively at that time continued to so operate between the interim audit and the end of the client's financial year. More specifically, auditors need to establish whether any significant changes have been made to the controls since they were tested, and determine what additional audit evidence needs to be obtained regarding the controls' continued effective operation.

When deciding what additional evidence needs to be obtained, auditors consider factors such as:

- the significance of the assessed risks of material misstatement at the assertion level for classes of transactions, account balances and disclosures within the audit segment in question;
- the significance of changes to the controls that were tested during the interim audit, including changes within the accounting sub-system and in relevant personnel;
- the length of the period between the interim audit and the client's year end;
- the extent to which it is planned to reduce substantive procedures based on reliance of the effective operation of the controls;
- the strength of the client's control environment.

The additional audit evidence may be obtained by performing further compliance tests and/or by testing the effectiveness of the client's monitoring of controls and its responses to the findings of the monitoring activities.

In similar vein, auditors may wish to use audit evidence about the operating effectiveness of internal accounting controls obtained during audits conducted in prior years. However, before relying on such evidence, ISA 330 requires auditors to consider:

(a) The effectiveness of other elements of internal control, including the control environment, the entity's monitoring of controls, and the entity's risk assessment process;

(b) The risks arising from the characteristics of the control, including whether it is manual or automated;[10]

(c) The effectiveness of general IT controls;

(d) The effectiveness of the control and its application by the entity, including the nature and extent of deviations in the application of the control [i.e., instances when the control was not complied with] noted in previous audits, and whether there have been personnel changes that significantly affect the application of the control;

(e) Whether the lack of a change in a particular control poses a risk due to changing circumstances; and

(f) The risks of material misstatement [in the relevant section(s) of the financial statements] and the extent of reliance [to be placed] on the control [to reduce substantive testing in the current period]. (para 13)

---

[10] In relation to automated controls, ISA 330, para A29, notes:

An automated control can be expected to function consistently unless the program (including the tables, files, or other permanent data used by the program) is changed. Once the auditor determines that an automated control is functioning as intended . . . the auditor may consider performing tests to determine that the control continues to function effectively. Such tests might include determining that:
- Changes to the program are not made without being subject to the appropriate program change controls,
- The authorized version of the program is used for processing transactions, and
- Other relevant general controls are effective.

In addition to considering the factors outlined above, auditors are required to establish whether changes to the controls on which they plan to rely have rendered evidence obtained in previous years' audits irrelevant. In this case, the controls in question are to be tested during the current period (ISA 330, para 14). ISA 330 (para 14) also specifies that, irrespective of the relevance of evidence obtained during previous years' audits, controls on which auditors plan to rely to reduce substantive tests must be tested at least once every three years, but some controls are to be tested during each period so that not all of the testing occurs in one period, followed by two periods in which no testing takes place. Further, some controls may be tested more frequently than every third year. This is appropriate, for example, when:

- the client's control environment, general IT controls, and/or monitoring of controls is weak;
- the relevant controls include a significant manual element and are, therefore, prone to human error or manipulation (factors which do not characterise automated controls);
- personnel changes have occurred that may significantly affect the application of the control; and
- changed circumstances indicate a need for changes in the control.

10.7 REPORTING INTERNAL CONTROL DEFICIENCIES TO MANAGEMENT

In section 10.4.4 we observed that, when evaluating the internal accounting controls, auditors seek to identify internal control strengths and deficiencies. The internal control strengths on which the auditor plans to rely to reduce substantive procedures are tested by means of compliance tests. However, the deficiencies are internal controls that are needed to prevent or detect errors or irregularities in the accounting data but are either absent or not operating effectively. Clearly, the auditor cannot rely on these controls to reduce substantive tests and, therefore, does not subject them to compliance testing. However, they are not ignored.

ISA 265: *Communicating Deficiencies in Internal Control to Those Charged with Governance and Management* (IAASB, 2009a) requires auditors to report deficiencies they have identified in the design, implementation or operating effectiveness of controls (unless the deficiencies are clearly trivial) at the earliest opportunity, preferably in writing, to managers at the appropriate level of responsibility and to the board of directors (or, more usually, if it has one, to the audit committee). This enables appropriate corrective action to be taken on a timely basis. Similarly, deficiencies in internal controls discovered during compliance testing, and errors in the financial statements discovered during substantive testing which indicate internal control deficiencies, are to be reported to an appropriate level of management and/or to the directors (or audit committee). Suitable action to correct internal control deficiencies is usually suggested by the auditor at the same time as the deficiencies are reported. Additionally, at the conclusion of the audit, significant internal deficiencies identified by the auditor, together with other audit matters, are communicated to the directors or audit committee. (This communication is discussed in Chapter 14, section 14.8.)

10.8 SUMMARY

In this chapter we have discussed what is meant by 'an accounting system' and considered why and how a client's accounting system is divided into sub-systems (or audit segments) for audit purposes. We have also examined the process by which an auditor gains a detailed understanding of each audit segment, and documents and tests this understanding.

Additionally, we have explored the topic of internal control. We have noted that an internal control system comprises five elements, namely: (i) the control environment, (ii) the risk assessment process, (iii) the information system relevant to financial reporting, (iv) the control activities and (v) the monitoring of controls. We have also observed that the control activities include both general IT controls and application controls.

An entity's management frequently delegates responsibility for establishing and maintaining the organisation's internal control system to the internal audit function (if the entity has one). However, the external auditor is particularly interested in the controls that are designed to safeguard the entity's assets and to ensure that its accounting data are free of material errors and irregularities (that is, internal accounting controls). We have discussed the seven characteristics of a good system of internal accounting controls, identified the objectives of these controls and observed that, irrespective of how effective a system of internal control may appear to be, it will always possess some inherent limitations.

We have also examined why and how the auditor conducts a preliminary evaluation of the internal controls in each audit segment. Once the auditor has identified internal control strengths (controls which appear to be effective in preventing or detecting errors and irregularities in the accounting data) and deficiencies (controls which are required to prevent or detect errors and irregularities but which are absent or ineffective), the auditor is in a position to plan the detailed compliance and substantive procedures. These are usually planned (at least on a conceptual level) in two stages, a planning and a performance stage. The resulting audit plan comprises a list of audit procedures set out in a format which audit staff can follow.

We have emphasised throughout the chapter that, although certain internal controls may appear to be operating effectively, the auditor may not rely on them to prevent material misstatements from occurring in the financial statements until their operating effectiveness has been tested, that is, until the auditor has conducted compliance procedures. If the compliance procedures confirm that the internal accounting controls are operating effectively, this will result in reduced substantive testing – the topic of the next chapter.

SELF-REVIEW QUESTIONS

10.1   Explain briefly what is meant by 'an accounting system'.

10.2   Explain briefly why a client's accounting system is divided into sub-systems (or audit segments)   for audit purposes. State two bases on which this sub-division may be based.

10.3   Explain briefly the meaning of each of the following terms:
    (i)   internal control system;
    (ii)   control environment;
    (iii) risk assessment process;
    (iv) control activities;
    (v)   monitoring of controls;
    (vi) general IT controls;
    (vii) application controls.

10.4   Outline the seven characteristics of a good system of internal accounting controls.

10.5   Describe briefly two procedures which are used to document auditees' accounting sub-systems.

10.6   Explain briefly the purpose of a 'walk through test' and how it is conducted.

10.7   In relation to internal controls, define:
    (i) a strength;
    (ii) a deficiency.

10.8   List five examples of inherent limitations of internal control systems.

10.9   (a) Explain briefly the purpose of 'compliance procedures'.
        (b) Give two examples of compliance procedures and link each to the audit objective it is designed to test.

10.10   Describe briefly what is meant by 'an audit plan' and how and when it is prepared.

REFERENCES

Anderson, R.J. (1977). *The External Audit*. Toronto: Cropp Clark Pitman.

Committee on the Financial Aspects of Corporate Governance (CFACG). (1992). *Report of the Committee on the Financial Aspects of Corporate Governance* (Cadbury Committee). London: Gee.

Committee on Corporate Governance. (1998a). *Final Report of the Committee on Corporate Governance* (Hampel Committee). London: The London Stock Exchange Ltd.

Committee on Corporate Governance. (1998b). *The Combined Code*. London: The London Stock Exchange Ltd.

Financial Reporting Council (FRC). (2003, 2006, 2008). *The Combined Code on Corporate Governance*. London: FRC

Financial Reporting Council (FRC). (2010, 2012). *The UK Corporate Governance Code*. London: FRC.

Higgs, D. (2003). *Review of the Role and Effectiveness of Non-Executive Directors*. London: Department of Trade and Industry.

International Auditing and Assurance Standards Board (IAASB). (2009a). International Standard on Auditing (ISA) 265: *Communicating Deficiencies in Internal Control to Those Charged with Governance and Management*. New York: International Federation of Accountants.

International Auditing and Assurance Standards Board (IAASB). (2009b). International Standard on Auditing (ISA) 300: *Planning an Audit of Financial Statements*. New York: International Federation of Accountants.

International Auditing and Assurance Standards Board (IAASB). (2009c). International Standard on Auditing (ISA) 330: *The Auditor's Responses to Assessed Risks*. New York: International Federation of Accountants.

International Auditing and Assurance Standards Board (IAASB). (2012). International Standard on Auditing (ISA) 315: *Identifying and Assessing the Risks of Material Misstatement through Understanding the Entity and Its Environment*. New York: International Federation of Accountants.

International Federation of Accountants (IFAC). (2009). *Glossary of Terms*, included in *Handbook of International Quality Control, Auditing, Review, Other Assurance and Related Services Pronouncements 2010 Edition*. New York: IFAC.

Smith, Sir Robert. (2003). *Audit Committees: Combined Guidance.* A report and proposed guidance by an FRC-appointed group chaired by Sir Robert Smith. London: Financial Reporting Council.

Study Group on Directors' Remuneration. (1995). *Report of the Study Group on Directors' Remuneration (Greenbury Committee).* London: Gee.

ADDITIONAL READING

Bedard, J.C., Hoitash, R., Hoitash, U., & Westermann, K. (2012). Material weakness remediation and earnings quality: A detailed examination by type of control deficiency. *Auditing: A Journal of Practice & Theory, 31*(1), 57–78.

Beneish, M.D., Billings, M.B., & Hodder, L.D. (2008). Internal control weaknesses and information uncertainty. *Accounting Review, 83*(3), 665–703.

Bierstaker, J.L., Hunton, J.E., & Thilbodeau, J.C. (2009). Do client-prepared internal control documentation and business process flowcharts help or hinder and auditor's ability to identify missing controls. *Auditing: A Journal of Practice & Theory, 28*(1), 79–94.

Brandon, D.M. (2010). External auditor evaluations of outsourced internal auditors. *Auditing: A Journal of Practice & Theory, 29*(2), 159–173.

Chan, K.C., Farrell, B., & Lee, P. (2008). Earnings management of firms reporting material internal control weaknesses under Section 404 of the Sabannes-Oxley Act. *Auditing: A Journal of Practice & Theory, 27*(2), 161–179.

Desai, N.K., Gerard, G.J., & Tripathy, A. (2011). Internal audit sourcing arrangements and reliance by external auditors. *Auditing: A Journal of Practice & Theory, 30*(1), 149–171.

Deumes, R., & Knechel, W.R. (2008). Economic incentives for voluntary reporting on internal risk management and control systems. *Auditing: A Journal of Practice & Theory, 27*(1), 35–66.

Earley, C.E., Hoffman, V.B., & Joe, J.R. (2008). Reducing management's influence on auditors' judgments: An experimental investigation of SOX 404 assessments. *Accounting Review, 83*(6), 1461–1485.

Goh, B.W., & Li, D. (2011). Internal controls and conditional conservatism. *Accounting Review, 86*(3), 975–1005.

Gordon, L.A., & Wilford, A.L. (2012). An analysis of multiple consecutive years of material weaknesses in internal control. *Accounting Review, 87*(6), 2027–2060.

Hammersley, J.S., Myers, L.A., & Zhou, J. (2012). The failure to remediate previously disclosed material weaknesses in internal controls. *Auditing: A Journal of Practice & Theory, 31*(2), 73–111.

Hoitash, U., Hoitash, R., & Bedard, J.C. (2009). Corporate governance and internal control over financial reporting: A comparison of regulatory regimes. *Accounting Review, 84*(3), 839–867.

Krishnan, G.V., & Wu, W. (2012). Do small firms benefit from auditor attestation of internal control effectiveness? *Auditing: A Journal of Practice & Theory*, *31*(4), 115–137.

Mohamed, Z., Zain, M.M., Subramaniam, N., & Yusoff, W.F.W. (2012). Internal audit attributes and external audit's reliance on internal audit: Implications for audit fees. *International Journal of Auditing*, *16*(3), 268–285.

Rose-Green, E., Huang, H.-W., & Lee, C.-C. (2011). The association between auditor industry specialization and firms' disclosure of internal control weaknesses. *International Journal of Auditing*, *15*(2), 204–216.

Shapiro, B., & Matson, D. (2008). Strategies of resistance to internal control regulation. *Accounting, Organizations and Society*, *33*(2–3), 199–228.

Stefaniak, C.M., Houston, R.W., & Cornell, R.M. (2012). The effects of employer and client identification of internal and external auditors' evaluations of internal control deficiencies. *Auditing: A Journal of Practice & Theory*, *31*(1), 39–56.

Van de Poel, K., & Vanstraelen, A. (2011). Management reporting on internal control and accruals quality: Insights from a 'comply-or-explain' internal control regime. *Auditing: A Journal of Practice & Theory*, *30*(3), 181–209.

Wolfe, C.J., Mauldin, E.G., & Diaz, M.C. (2009). Concede or deny: Do management persuasion tactics affect auditor evaluation of internal control deviations? *Accounting Review*, *84*(6), 2013–2037.

11 Testing Financial Statement Assertions: Substantive Testing

LEARNING OBJECTIVES

After studying the material in this chapter you should be able to:

- explain the significance of substantive testing in the audit process;
- explain the terms 'misstatement' and 'financial statement assertions';
- state the objectives of substantive procedures;
- discuss the purpose and importance of analytical procedures as substantive tests (substantive analytical procedures);
- explain what is meant by 'testing the details' of financial statement balances;
- distinguish between the two approaches to testing the details – testing classes of transactions which generate account balances and directly testing account balances;
- describe common audit procedures used to test the details of financial statement balances;
- explain the actions auditors are required to take in respect of misstatements identified during the audit;
- discuss the importance of, and procedures used for, confirming the existence, ownership and value of inventory;
- discuss the importance, and performance, of confirmations as a substantive test of accounts receivable;
- explain the factors the auditor should consider when assessing the adequacy of the client's allowance for bad debts (alternatively known as provision for doubtful debts);
- outline the 'incoming auditor's' responsibilities in respect of financial statements' 'opening balances' when there has been a change of auditor.

11.1 INTRODUCTION

A company's financial statements comprise a set of statements by its directors which, taken together, provide a picture of the company's financial position, the results of its operations and (in applicable cases) its cash flows. These statements are presented as account balances (appropriately grouped and classified in the statement of financial position, income statement and, in applicable cases, statement of cash flow), a statement of accounting policies and notes to the financial statements. In presenting the financial statement balances (and accompanying notes), the entity's directors are making implicit assertions about the balances and the items they represent. More particularly, they are implicitly asserting that the balances (and accompanying notes) are valid, complete and accurate.

The auditor is required, *inter alia*, to form and express an opinion on whether or not the financial statements give a true and fair view of the entity's financial position and performance and comply with an applicable financial reporting framework. To accomplish this, the auditor conducts substantive tests – tests which examine the substance of the financial statement balances and note disclosures (or, more correctly, the assertions embodied therein).

In this chapter we examine the significance of substantive testing in the audit process and discuss the objectives of substantive procedures. We also explore the different approaches which may be taken to test the financial statement disclosures and explain the audit procedures commonly adopted for each approach. More particularly, we discuss substantive analytical procedures and procedures used for testing the details of financial statement balances – whether this be through testing the classes of transactions which generate account balances or testing the balances directly. We also explain the actions auditors are required to take in respect of misstatements they identify during the audit. After studying the principles of substantive testing, we examine in more detail the application of substantive procedures in auditing the inventory and accounts receivable accounts. Before concluding the chapter, we consider the responsibilities of an 'incoming auditor' (following a change of auditor) with respect to financial statements' 'opening balances'.

11.2 SIGNIFICANCE OF SUBSTANTIVE TESTING IN THE AUDIT PROCESS

When considering the significance of substantive testing in the audit process, it is important to appreciate the integrative character of an audit. The nature, timing and extent of substantive procedures are essentially determined by the audit steps we have discussed in previous chapters, in particular:

- understanding the client, its industry, its business, its activities and its risks;
- assessing the likelihood of material misstatements being present in the pre-audited financial statements;
- setting materiality limits (planning materiality, tolerable error and performance materiality);
- establishing the desired level of audit risk (or desired level of assurance);
- for each audit segment, assessing inherent risk (the likelihood of material misstatements being present in the relevant financial statement account balances in the absence of internal controls);

- understanding and documenting each accounting sub-system (or audit segment) and assessing the effectiveness of its internal controls in preventing or detecting errors and irregularities in the accounting data;
- testing the internal controls on which the auditor plans to rely to prevent material misstatements from occurring in each significant class of transactions, account balance or disclosure within the audit segment.

From the above, it is evident that both:
- the auditor's assessment of the effectiveness of internal controls within an accounting sub-system, and
- the results of testing the controls on which the auditor plans to rely,

have a significant impact on the nature, timing and extent of substantive testing. This is reflected in Figure 11.1.

If, based on an assessment of the internal controls within a particular audit segment, the auditor concludes that the controls are not effective in preventing material misstatements from occurring in the relevant account balances in the financial statements or, alternatively, having initially concluded that the controls appear to be effective but the results of compliance tests prove this

Figure 11.1: Impact of internal control evaluation and testing on substantive testing

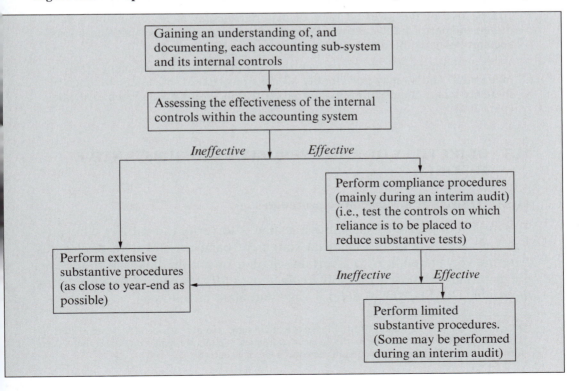

not to be the case, the auditor will need to perform extensive substantive procedures before attaining his/her desired level of assurance that the account balances in question are not materially misstated. Further, this testing will need to take place as close as possible to the end of the accounting period.

Conversely, if the auditor's assessment of the internal controls indicates that they are effective, and this finding is supported by the results of compliance tests, the auditor will be reasonably confident that the relevant balances in the financial statements are valid, complete and accurate. As a result, the auditor will perform more limited substantive testing than would otherwise be the case. However, substantive tests may not be omitted altogether. The auditor is required to form and express an opinion about the truth and fairness of the financial statements *per se* – not about the effectiveness of the internal controls.[1] Further, as we note in Chapter 10 (section 10.3.6), no internal control system is perfect; they all possess some inherent limitations. Therefore, irrespective of how confident the auditor may be that the financial statements are not materially misstated, in order to form and express the required opinion, some substantive testing of the financial statement balances and note disclosures is always necessary.

These ideas are conveyed in International Standard on Auditing (ISA) 330: *The Auditor's Responses to Assessed Risks* (IAASB, 2009a), which states:

> Irrespective of the assessed risks of material misstatement, the auditor shall design and perform substantive procedures for each material class of transactions, account balance, and disclosure. (para 8)

> . . . This requirement reflects the facts that: (a) the auditor's assessment of risk is judgmental and so may not identify all risks of material misstatement; and (b) there are inherent limitations to internal control, including management override. (para A42)

11.3 OBJECTIVES OF, AND APPROACHES TO, SUBSTANTIVE TESTING

11.3.1 Objectives of substantive procedures

The overall objective of substantive testing is to verify the validity, completeness and accuracy of the financial statement balances and note disclosures. Alternatively stated, it is to ascertain whether or not the financial statements are materially misstated. ISA 450: *Evaluation of Misstatements Identified during the Audit* (IAASB, 2009b) defines a misstatement as follows:

---

[1] As noted in Chapter 10, section 10.3.1, for clients that are subject to the Sarbanes-Oxley Act of 2002, in addition to expressing an opinion on the financial statements, auditors are required to attest to the directors' statement about the effectiveness of the entity's internal controls.

Misstatement – A difference between the amount, classification, presentation, or disclosure of a reported financial statement item and the amount, classification, presentation, or disclosure that is required for the item to be in accordance with the applicable financial reporting framework. (para 4)

The Standard also explains that misstatements may result from:

(a) An inaccuracy in gathering or processing data from which the financial statements are prepared;

(b) An omission of an amount or disclosure;

(c) An incorrect accounting estimate arising from overlooking, or clear misinterpretation of, facts; and

(d) Judgments of management concerning accounting estimates that the auditor considers unreasonable or the selection and application of accounting policies that the auditor considers inappropriate. (para A1)

Each financial statement amount or disclosure embodies a number of assertions and, if any of the assertions are invalid, then the amount or disclosure is misstated. ISA 315: *Identifying and Assessing the Risks of Material Misstatement through Understanding the Entity and its Environment* (IAASB, 2012) defines 'assertions' to mean: "Representations by management, explicit or otherwise, that are embodied in the financial statements, as used by the auditor to consider the different types of potential misstatements that may occur" (para 4a). The Standard distinguishes three categories of assertions as follows:

(a) Assertions about classes of transactions and events for the period under audit:

    (i) Occurrence – transactions and events that have been recorded have occurred and pertain to the entity.

    (ii) Completeness – all transactions and events that should have been recorded have been recorded.

    (iii) Accuracy – amounts and other data relating to recorded transactions and events have been recorded appropriately.

    (iv) Cut-off – transactions and events have been recorded in the correct accounting period.

    (v) Classification – transactions and events have been recorded in the proper accounts.

(b) Assertions about account balances at the period end:

    (i) Existence – assets, liabilities and equity interests exist.

    (ii) Rights and obligations – the entity holds or controls the right to assets, and liabilities are the obligations of the entity.

    (iii) Completeness – all assets, liabilities and equity interests that should have been recorded have been recorded.

    (iv) Valuation and allocation – assets, liabilities, and equity interests are included in the financial statements at appropriate amounts and any resulting valuation or allocation adjustments are appropriately recorded.

(c) Assertions about presentation and disclosure:

    (i) Occurrence and rights and obligations – disclosed events, transactions, and other matters have occurred and pertain to the entity.

(ii) Completeness – all disclosures that should have been included in the financial statements have been included.

(iii) Classification and understandability – financial information is appropriately presented and described, and disclosures are clearly expressed.

(iv) Accuracy and valuation – financial and other information are disclosed fairly and at appropriate amounts. (para A124)

Verifying each assertion relating to a class of transactions, account balance or note disclosure constitutes a specific audit objective.[2] If the specific audit objectives are met, the overall objective of confirming the validity, completeness and accuracy of the financial statement balances and disclosures will also be met.

11.3.2   Alternative approaches to substantive testing

Although all substantive testing has as its objective determining the validity, completeness and accuracy of financial statement balances and disclosures, two basic approaches may be adopted, namely:

(i) substantive analytical procedures;

(ii) tests of details.

(i) *Substantive analytical procedures*: Where this approach is adopted, meaningful relationships between account balances, or between financial and non-financial information, are examined to ascertain the reasonableness (or otherwise) of the related financial statement amounts.

(ii) *Tests of details*: This approach may take one of two forms:

    (a) testing the classes of transactions which give rise to account balances, and

    (b) testing the account balances directly.

Where the transactions approach is adopted, attention is focused on the opening balance of the account in question and the transactions which affect the account during the reporting period. If the opening balance and the transactions are recorded and totalled correctly, the closing balance must, of necessity, be correct.[3]

Where account balances are tested directly, components of the balance are usually tested. For example, individual accounts receivable account

---

[2] Readers may find it helpful to refer to Chapter 7, section 7.3 (and Figure 7.2), where we introduce the notion of specific audit objectives.

[3] In the case of accounts in the statement of financial position, the opening balance is established from the audited closing balances of the previous period; for income statement accounts, the opening balance is, of course, zero.

balances are tested as a means of substantiating the accounts receivable account balance in the statement of financial position.

Regarding the selection of the appropriate approach to substantive testing, ISA 330 (IAASB, 2009a) explains:

Depending on the circumstances, the auditor may determine that:
- Performing only substantive analytical procedures will be sufficient to reduce audit risk to an acceptably low level. . . .
- Only tests of details are appropriate.
- A combination of substantive analytical procedures and tests of details are most responsive to the assessed risks. (para A43)

ISA 520: *Analytical Procedures* (IAASB, 2009f) adds to this by noting:

. . . The decision about which audit procedures to perform, including whether to use substantive analytical procedures, is based on the auditor's judgment about the expected effectiveness and efficiency of the available audit procedures to reduce audit risk at the assertion level to an acceptably low level. (para A4)

Although different approaches to substantive testing may be adopted, auditors frequently use a combination of substantive analytical procedures and tests of details, and the two approaches interlock in a mutually supportive manner. This may be illustrated by reference to the sales-receivables-receipts audit segment, as shown in Figure 11.2.

Substantive analytical procedures may be used to ascertain the reasonableness of the accounts receivable closing balance. If it appears to be reasonable, the extent of further detailed testing may be reduced. Conversely, if substantive analytical procedures indicate that the balance may be materially misstated,

Figure 11.2:   Substantive testing of accounts receivable and related accounts

Verified by	Accounts Receivable			Verified by
Previous year's audit ⟶	Opening bal	x	Receipts x Discount x	Testing cash receipts transactions
Testing sales transactions ⟶	Sales	x		
Substantive analytical procedures or testing transactions (depending on materiality)	Freight Interest	x x	Returns x Bad debts x Closing bal x	Substantive analytical procedures or testing transactions (depending on materiality)
		=	=	
Substantive analytical procedures (for reasonableness) and direct tests of balance	Balance b/d	x		

NB: Verification of complementary account balances (such as sales) simultaneously helps to confirm the accounts receivable account balance.
Verification of the accounts receivable account balance (through direct testing) simultaneously helps to confirm the balances of related accounts (such as sales).

more extensive detailed testing will be required in order to identify the nature and extent of any misstatement(s). Substantive analytical procedures may also be used to substantiate less material account balances such as 'interest on overdue accounts' and 'freight charged to credit customers'. (Substantive analytical procedures are discussed in section 11.4 below.)

In order to determine the validity, completeness and accuracy of the sales account balance, the period's sales transactions are tested. Similarly cash receipts, discount received and sales returns transactions may be tested to substantiate their respective account balances. It should be noted that testing these transactions serves two purposes: it confirms the relevant account balance in the income statement and simultaneously provides support for an element of the accounts receivable account balance in the statement of financial position. If the balance of the accounts receivable account is also confirmed through direct testing this, by implication, provides support for the accuracy of the related accounts (such as sales). By obtaining mutually supportive evidence in this manner, the auditor can be confident that all of the accounts constituting the sales-receivables-receipts audit segment are fairly stated.

We should emphasise that substantive testing is concerned with verifying the validity, completeness and accuracy of information presented in the financial statements. Its objective is very different from that of compliance testing. Compliance testing is concerned with confirming that the internal controls on which the auditor plans to rely to prevent material misstatements from occurring in the financial statements are operating effectively, and have been so operating throughout the reporting period. Thus, compliance procedures conducted in relation to, for example, sales transactions, seek evidence which indicates, *inter alia*, that credit sales transactions have been authorised, and that extensions, additions, and account codes shown on sales invoices have been independently checked. By contrast, substantive procedures are concerned with examining the monetary amounts and the correctness with which transactions are recorded in terms of their validity, completeness and accuracy as to amount, account classification and reporting period.

Confusion between the two types of procedures frequently arises in relation to testing transactions. This is because the source documents recording transactions are used for both types of tests. For example, copies of sales invoices may be inspected to see if initials are present which indicate that extensions, additions and account classifications have been checked by an independent person. In this case, evidence of compliance with an internal control procedure (independent review of performance) is sought. The same document may be used for substantive testing; that is, for checking that the extensions and additions are arithmetically correct, and that the transaction has been recorded in the correct accounts. The same source document (and transaction) is used for two entirely different purposes.[4]

11.4 SUBSTANTIVE AUDIT PROCEDURES

11.4.1 Overview of substantive audit procedures

We noted above that there are two broad types of substantive tests – substantive analytical procedures and tests of details. We also noted that tests of details may be either tests of classes of transactions or direct tests of account balances. The relationship between these types of substantive tests, and the procedures used for each, are depicted in Figure 11.3.

During the initial stages of an audit, analytical procedures are used as risk assessment procedures – more specifically, as procedures to assist the auditor:
- understand the client's financial and non-financial information,
- identify unusual transactions or events,

Figure 11.3: Overview of substantive audit procedures

Objective: To verify the validity, completeness and accuracy (as to amount, account classification and reporting period) of financial statement account balances and note disclosures.

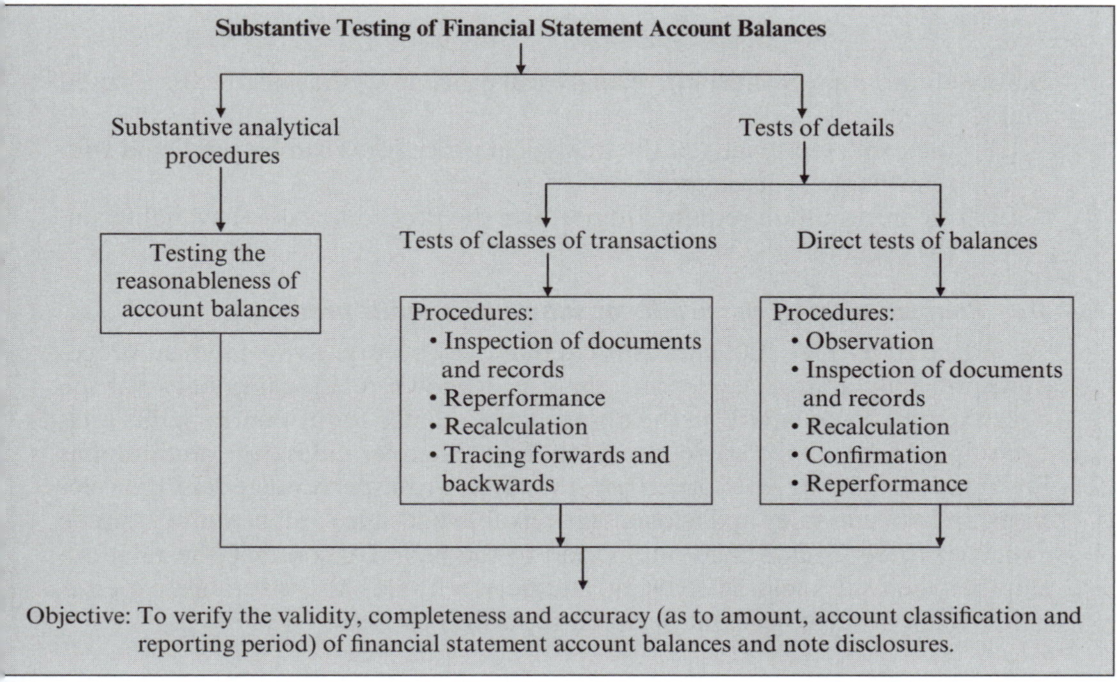

[4] We refer to the overlapping nature of audit procedures in Chapter 10, section 10.5, when discussing the performance format of audit plans.

- assess the likelihood of material misstatements being present in the (pre-audited) financial statements, and
- identify areas or items of significant audit risk.[5]

At this stage, broad entity-wide measures are important such as the current ratio, debt to equity ratio, gross profit percentage, return on assets, and return on shareholders' funds. During the substantive testing stage, auditors focus on individual classes of transactions, account balances and disclosures. To distinguish between these two uses of analytical procedures, the term 'overall analytical procedures' is frequently applied to the broad risk assessment procedures and 'substantive analytical procedures' to the account focused substantive tests.

11.4.2 Requirements for substantive analytical procedures

ISA 520 explains:

> . . . The application of planned analytical procedures is based on the expectation that relationships among data exist and continue in the absence of known conditions to the contrary. However, the suitability of a particular analytical procedure will depend upon the auditor's assessment of how effective it will be in detecting a misstatement that, individually or when aggregated with other misstatements, may cause the financial statements to be materially misstated. (para A6)

Before auditors apply substantive analytical procedures they need to be assured that:
(i) the expected results of the analytical procedures can be predicted with reasonable accuracy, and
(ii) the information required to perform the procedures is (a) available and (b) reliable.

(i) Predictability of the results of substantive audit procedures

As indicated by ISA 520, para A6 (cited above), substantive analytical procedures are only appropriate where there is a known relationship between the data examined and where, in the absence of evidence to the contrary, this relationship can be expected to continue. For example, unless the auditor has information that suggests otherwise, the gross profit percentage and the relationship between sales and accounts receivable and sales and inventory can be expected to be similar from one period to the next. By contrast, the relationship between sales and advertising, and between sales and insurance expense, is less likely to be consistent between reporting periods.

---

[5] The use of analytical procedures as risk assessment procedures is explained in Chapter 8, section 8.6.3 and a general discussion of analytical procedures is provided in section 8.6.

(ii) Availability and reliability of required information

Regarding the availability and reliability of required information, ISA 520 observes:

> The auditor may inquire of management as to the availability and reliability of information needed to apply substantive analytical procedures, and the results of any such analytical procedures performed by the entity. It may be efficient to use analytical data prepared by management, provided the auditor is satisfied that such data is properly prepared. (para A5)

In order to perform substantive analytical procedures, in addition to financial statement data, auditors generally require financial information such as budgets or forecasts, and non-financial information such as the number of units produced and/or sold. They also need to consider the degree to which the information can be disaggregated, for example, whether information is available for individual components of a diversified entity. Further, if auditors plan to use budgeted information, they need to establish whether the budgets have been prepared based on expected results or as goals (or targets) to be achieved.

However, having access to required information is not sufficient for auditors to perform substantive analytical procedures; they must also satisfy themselves that the information is reliable. Where information is obtained from independent sources outside of the entity it is generally considered to be reliable. However, for internally generated information, auditors will seek evidence that controls over the preparation of the relevant data are effective. ISA 520 observes:

> . . . When such controls are effective, the auditor generally has greater confidence in the reliability of the information and, therefore, in the results of analytical procedures. The operating effectiveness of controls over non-financial information may often be tested in conjunction with other tests of controls. For example, in establishing controls over the processing of sales invoices, an entity may include controls over the recording of unit sales. In these circumstances, the auditor may test the operating effectiveness of controls over the recording of unit sales in conjunction with tests of the operating effectiveness of controls over the processing of sales invoices. (para A13)

11.4.3 Application of substantive analytical procedures

During the substantive testing phase of an audit, substantive analytical procedures are usually used in two different ways, namely:
(i)   as preliminary tests which are to be followed by tests of details, and
(ii) as complete tests when no subsequent tests of details are planned.

(i) Substantive analytical procedures as preliminary tests

For material classes of transactions and account balances which are to be subjected to tests of details (for example, accounts receivable and inventory), substantive analytical procedures are frequently used as preliminary tests – to test the reasonableness of the account balance as a basis for deciding the extent to which tests of details are required. If an account balance appears to be reasonable (i.e., close to that expected by the auditor based on his/her risk assessment procedures), material misstatement may be considered unlikely and, as a result, less extensive tests of details are needed to confirm the absence of material misstatements than in situations where material misstatement seems more likely. (Use of substantive analytical procedures as a preliminary test in auditing the inventory account balance is illustrated in section 11.7 below.)

Substantive analytical procedures may also be used in combination with tests of details. For example, when auditing the collectability of amounts owed by accounts receivable, the auditor may apply substantive analytical procedures to an ageing of customers' accounts in addition to performing tests of details on subsequent cash receipts.

(ii) Specific analytical procedures as complete tests

For less significant classes of transactions and account balances (for which less substantive testing is usually required), substantive analytical procedures are commonly used to test the reasonableness of the account balances. If they appear to be reasonable, no further testing is undertaken. However, if misstatement appears likely, then the class of transactions or account balance concerned is subjected to detailed testing.

The following two examples illustrate the ways in which substantive analytical procedures may constitute complete substantive tests.

1. Historically, a fairly stable relationship may exist between sales returns and sales. Therefore, assuming that nothing has come to the auditor's attention which suggests the relationship may not hold in the current year, if the sales returns account balance is calculated as a percentage of sales, the result should be similar to that for previous years. If it is, the account balance will probably be considered reasonable and accepted as 'true and fair'.

2. The balance of the interest paid account may be estimated by using a known relationship between debt and interest rates. More specifically, the average debt and the average interest rate for the reporting period may be ascertained, and then the average interest rate applied to the average debt to provide an estimate of the interest paid account balance. In the absence of exceptional circumstances known to the auditor, if the interest paid account balance is close to the estimated amount, it will probably be judged to be reasonable and accepted as 'true and fair'.

11.4.4 Tests of details

As noted in section 11.3, substantive tests of details may involve testing the transactions which give rise to an account balance or directly testing the balance itself. The approach adopted is generally that which provides the most efficient means of determining the validity, completeness and accuracy of the account balance in question.

(i) Testing transactions

Income statement accounts (i.e., revenue and expense accounts) commence the accounting period with a zero balance and the transactions comprising the account are generally of a similar type (belong to the same class of transactions). For example, entries in sales and purchases accounts are usually confined to cash and credit sales and purchases, respectively. The similarity of the transactions facilitates selecting and testing a representative sample and, as a result, testing the transactions which constitute the account balance is generally more efficient than directly testing the account balance *per se*.

Some accounts in the statement of financial position (such as property, plant and equipment) are frequently affected by a relatively small number of transactions during the reporting period relative to the size of the account balance. In these cases, it may be more efficient to test the transactions which generate the account balance than directly testing the balance itself. An example is afforded by the motor vehicle account in entities which have large fleets of vehicles but relatively few additions and disposals during any one financial year (such as British Telecom). The opening balance of accounts in the statement of financial position were verified during the previous year's audit and, if the opening balance and the transactions affecting the account are recorded and totalled correctly, the closing balance must be correct.

As shown in Figure 11.3, the principal procedures for testing the accuracy, validity and completeness of transactions are inspection of documents and records, reperformance, recalculation, and tracing forwards and backwards. Other than tracing forwards and backwards, these procedures are directed towards examining the accuracy of financial statement account balances – their accuracy as to amount, account and reporting period. These audit procedures may be illustrated as follows:

- *Inspection of documents and records*: Source documents may be inspected to determine whether transactions are *bona fide* and have been recorded in the correct account and reporting period. The auditor checks the account codes used for recording the transactions and, particularly for transactions near the year end, examines the dates and terms of the transactions to ascertain the accounting period to which they relate. Other documents, such as price lists, may be also be inspected to check that correct prices have been applied to goods and services bought and sold.

- *Reperformance*: The auditor may, for example, match purchase orders with receiving reports, suppliers' invoices and payments vouchers to ensure that the quantities and prices of goods ordered and received, invoiced and paid for are in agreement. Similarly, source document totals may be matched with journal entries, and journal entries with ledger records.

- *Recalculation*: The auditor may recalculate extensions (quantity multiplied by the price of goods bought or sold) and additions on source documents in order to check that transactions have been recorded at their correct amount.

Tracing backwards and forwards are substantive procedures designed to test the validity and completeness, respectively, of recorded transactions, rather than their accuracy.

- *Tracing backwards* involves tracing selected entries back through the accounting records, from the financial statements, through the ledgers and journals, to the source documents. This procedure is designed to check that the amounts recorded in the financial statements represent valid transactions and that financial statement account balances are not overstated. Because of the (usual) desirability of having more rather than less assets and revenue, auditees may have an incentive to inflate asset and revenue accounts. Thus, tracing backwards has particular application for testing the validity of transactions involving asset and revenue accounts and for ensuring that the account balances are not overstated.

- *Tracing forwards* involves tracing selected transactions forwards through the accounting records, from source documents, through the journals and ledgers, to the financial statements. This procedure is designed to check that financial statement account balances include all relevant transactions and are not understated. Because of the desirability of having less rather than more liabilities and expenses, auditees may have an incentive to understate liability and expense accounts. Tracing forwards has particular application for testing the completeness of transactions involving liabilities and expenses and ensuring that the account balances are not understated.

(ii) Direct tests of balances

For some accounts it is more efficient to audit the closing balance directly than to examine the transactions which generate the balance. This applies to many accounts in the statement of financial position such as cash, inventory, accounts receivable, accounts payable and loans.

The principal audit procedures used to directly test the validity, completeness and accuracy of account balances are observation, inspection of documents and records, recalculation, confirmation and reperformance. These may be illustrated as follows:

- *Observation*: The auditor will, for example, observe the existence, quantity and quality of inventory and of non-current assets such as plant, equipment and motor vehicles. In some cases, observation extends to observing identification numbers of some non-current assets, for example, the engine and chassis numbers of motor vehicles.
- *Inspection of documents and records*: Documents such as marketable securities and loan, lease and hire purchase contracts are inspected to confirm the existence of the items concerned and to ascertain their terms and conditions.
- *Recalculation*: Accounts such as depreciation and accumulated depreciation, doubtful debts and allowance for bad debts, are usually recalculated to confirm the arithmetical accuracy of their balances.
- *Confirmation*: The auditor will confirm certain information with parties outside the audit client. For example, the auditor is likely to confirm the balance of accounts receivable and bank accounts, and also items such as contingent liabilities and commitments, by communicating with the client's customers, bank(s) and legal counsel, respectively. (Confirmation of accounts receivable is discussed in detail in section 11.8 below and confirmation of contingent liabilities and commitments is considered in Chapter 13, section 13.2).
- *Reperformance*: The auditor will, for example, compare the general ledger bank account balance with the confirmation letter received from the bank, and the subsidiary ledger totals with the relevant general ledger control account to ensure they are in agreement.

With reference to auditees' year-end closing process, ISA 330 (IAASB, 2009a) specifically requires auditors to perform substantive procedures that include:

(a) Agreeing or reconciling the financial statements with the underlying accounting records; and

(b) Examining material journal entries and other adjustments made during the course of preparing the financial statements. (para 20)

Checking the journal entries and other adjustments made by the client at the end of the reporting period (including such things as writing off bad debts, adjusting the allowance for bad debts, and recognising accrued expenses and income) is particularly important as these accounting entries involve the exercise of considerable judgment[6] and affect both the income statement (an income or expense account) and the statement of financial position (an asset or a liability account).

---

[6] As a result, these entries provide an opportunity for manipulation of the financial statements by dishonest directors.

11.4.5 Substantive procedures performed during an interim audit

In certain circumstances, auditors may perform some substantive procedures during an interim audit.[7] However, if they do so, they are required to obtain sufficient appropriate audit evidence to provide a reasonable basis for extending the conclusions they reached during the interim audit about the validity, completeness and accuracy of classes of transactions or account balances to the end of the reporting period. More particularly, ISA 330 requires auditors:

> . . . to compare and reconcile information concerning the balance [of the relevant account] at the period end with the comparable information at the interim date to:
>
> (a) Identify amounts that appear unusual;
> (b) Investigate any such amounts; and
> (c) Perform substantive analytical procedures or tests of details to test the intervening period. (para A55)

When deciding whether or not it is cost-effective to perform substantive procedures during an interim audit, auditors need to consider factors such as the following:

- the effectiveness of the auditee's control environment and other relevant controls – the more effective the internal controls, the more likely it is that it will be cost-effective to perform substantive tests during an interim audit;
- the availability and reliability of information required to perform substantive tests at the period end compared with its availability at an interim date;
- the assessed risk of material misstatement in the classes of transactions or account balances to be tested during an interim audit – the greater the risk, the less likely it is that it will be cost-effective to perform substantive procedures during an interim audit;
- the auditor's ability to perform appropriate substantive procedures, or substantive procedures combined with tests of the controls (compliance procedures), for the period between the interim audit and period end, that will reduce to an acceptably low level the risk of failing to detect misstatements that exist in the relevant classes of transactions or account balances at the period end.

When auditors conduct substantive tests during an interim audit and they encounter misstatements which, based on their assessment of the risk of material misstatements being present in the relevant account(s), they did not expect,

---

[7] In Chapter 10, section 10.4.5, we note that compliance procedures are frequently performed during an interim audit; in certain circumstances, some substantive procedures may be performed at the same time.

they are required to evaluate whether (i) their assessment of risk and (ii) the planned nature, timing and extent of substantive procedures covering the period between the interim audit and period end need to be modified. Such modification may include extending, or repeating at the period end, procedures performed during the interim audit (ISA 330, paras 23, A58).

11.5 REQUIREMENTS OF AUDITORS WHEN MISSTATEMENTS ARE DETECTED

As the audit proceeds, but particularly during the substantive testing process, auditors invariably identify misstatements in various account balances and other financial statement disclosures. Having discovered them, what are they required to do about them? As we explain below, identified misstatements must be:

(i) accumulated;
(ii) evaluated to determine whether the audit strategy and audit plan require revision; and
(iii) communicated to management.

(i) Accumulation of misstatements

ISA 450 (IAASB, 2009b, para 5) specifies that auditors are to accumulate misstatements identified during the audit, other than those that are clearly trivial. It explains:

> "Clearly trivial" is not another expression for "not material". Matters that are clearly trivial will be of a wholly different (smaller) order of magnitude than materiality [used in planning and performing the audit], . . . and will be matters that are clearly inconsequential, whether taken individually or in aggregate and whether judged by any criteria of size, nature or circumstances. When there is any uncertainty about whether one or more items are clearly trivial, the matter is considered not to be clearly trivial. (para A2)[8]

(ii) Evaluation to determine whether the audit strategy and audit plan require revision

As misstatements are accumulated, auditors are required to consider whether their size and/or nature are such that the overall audit strategy and audit plan need to be revised. This is particularly likely in situations where:

- the nature of misstatements, and the circumstances of their occurrence, indicate that other (undetected) misstatements may exist which, when aggregated with the misstatements accumulated during the audit, could be material. This may be the case, for example, if a misstatement arose

---

[8] For one of the firms included in the materiality survey reported in Chapter 9, the 'clearly trivial' threshold is two per cent of planning materiality.

from a breakdown in internal control or from inappropriate assumptions or valuations that have been applied widely by the entity; or
- the aggregate of the accumulated misstatements approaches performance materiality.[9] In this event, once allowance is made for undetected misstatements resulting from sampling risk and quality control risk,[10] if auditors do not revise the overall audit strategy and audit plan, they run the risk of unknowingly exceeding their planning materiality and/or tolerable error and thus expressing an inappropriate audit opinion on the financial statements (ISA 450, paras 6, A4, A5).

ISA 450 (para A3) notes that when evaluating the effect on the financial statements of misstatements accumulated during the audit, and communicating them to management, auditors may find it useful to distinguish between:
- factual misstatements, that is, misstatements about which there is no doubt;
- judgmental misstatements, that is, misstatements resulting from what the auditor considers to be incorrect judgments by management about accounting estimates which, in the auditor's opinion, are unreasonable, or the selection or application of accounting policies which, in the auditor's opinion, are inappropriate; and
- projected misstatements, that is, the auditor's best estimate of misstatements in populations (that is, classes of transactions or account balances) determined by projecting (or extrapolating) misstatements identified in the samples examined by the auditor to the populations from which the samples were drawn.[11]

(iii) Communication with management
Once auditors have accumulated misstatements, they are required to communicate them, on a timely basis, to the appropriate level of management and request management to correct them. Referring to this communication, ISA 450 explains:

> Timely communication of misstatements to the appropriate level of management is important as it enables management to evaluate whether the items are misstatements, inform the auditor if it disagrees, and take action as necessary. Ordinarily, the appropriate level of management is the one that has responsibility and authority to evaluate the misstatements and to take the necessary action. (para A7)

If management (or, more usually, the finance director) refuses to correct some or all of the misstatements communicated by the auditor, the auditor is required

---

[9] Performance materiality, planning materiality and tolerable error are discussed in Chapter 9, section 9.3.

[10] Sampling risk is the risk of misstatements not being detected as they are in the portion of populations not examined by the auditor. Quality control risk is the risk of misstatements not being detected as a result of failings by the audit team. These risks are explained further in Chapter 3, section 3.4.3.

[11] Audit sampling is discussed in Chapter 12.

to obtain an understanding of their reasons for so doing and to consider that understanding when evaluating whether the financial statements as a whole are free from material misstatement. If management refuses to correct identified misstatements on the grounds that their effect on the financial statements is immaterial, the auditor is to obtain written representations from management stating that they believe the effects of the uncorrected misstatements are immaterial, individually and in aggregate, to the financial statements as a whole. A summary of the uncorrected misstatements is to be included in, or attached to, the written representations provided to the auditor[12] (ISA 450, paras 9, 14).

In some circumstances (such as when, in the light of the auditor's estimation of misstatements in a population based on the audit sample examined, it is considered desirable), the auditor may request management (or, more usually, the finance director) to examine a class of transactions, account balance or disclosure in order to ascertain the cause of misstatements identified by the auditor, determine the extent of the actual misstatement in the class of transactions, account balance or disclosure, and make appropriate adjustments to the financial statements (ISA 450, para A6). If management takes this action, the auditor is required to perform additional audit procedures to determine whether misstatements remain (ISA 450, para 7).

11.6 INTRODUCTION TO SUBSTANTIVE TESTING OF INVENTORY AND ACCOUNTS RECEIVABLE

To illustrate the application of substantive procedures, some aspects of auditing inventory and accounts receivable account balances are discussed in sections 11.7 and 11.8, respectively. These accounts frequently constitute the largest proportion of a company's current assets[13] and represent its primary sources of short term cash. They are also accounts which are prone to misstatement. In the case of inventory, this largely arises from its possible over-valuation resulting from obsolescence, damage or deterioration and/or some of the recorded inventory not being owned by the client. For accounts receivable, it results primarily from the subjectivity involved in estimating the allowance for bad debts. As a consequence of these factors, the inventory and accounts receivable account balances almost invariably attract considerable audit attention. Particular interest in these accounts initially arose as a result of the infamous *McKesson & Robbins* case in the United States of America (USA) in the 1930s which involved many millions of dollars' worth of fictitious inventory and accounts receivable.

---

[12] We discuss written representations, and the actions auditors are required to take in respect of uncorrected misstatements, in Chapter 13 (sections 13.5 and 13.6.1, respectively) and we also explain auditors' responsibility to report uncorrected misstatements to the directors in Chapter 14, section 14.8.

[13] In companies that sell services rather than goods, inventory is frequently immaterial but, as for companies selling goods, accounts receivable almost always constitute a material financial statement amount.

Subsequent to this case, in all audits where these items are material (which, as noted above, is usually the case), auditors have generally attended their client's year-end inventory count and confirmed their accounts receivable balances.

11.7 SIGNIFICANT ASPECTS OF AUDITING INVENTORY

11.7.1 Overview of auditing inventory

When auditing inventory, the auditor is particularly concerned to confirm its existence, ownership and value. As shown in Figure 11.4, each of these audit objectives requires a different set of audit procedures.

Figure 11.4: Procedures for auditing inventory

Assertion/Audit Objective	Audit Procedures
Existence – Does inventory exist?	Observation (attendance at the inventory count)
Ownership – Is inventory owned?	Inspection of source documents and other documents for dates and terms of inventory purchases and sales
Valuation – Is inventory correctly valued?[14]	• Observation of the quality of inventory and the degree of completion of work-in-progress; • Evaluation of the method used to value inventory and its conformity to accounting standards; • Inspection of source documents and price lists for the cost of inventory; • Recalculation of the value of inventory

Before testing the details of the inventory account balance, in order to ascertain whether misstatement seems likely, substantive analytical procedures may be performed. For example, the ratio of inventory to cost of goods sold (COGS) may be calculated for each significant type of inventory, at each material location. The trend for the current and past years may then be plotted and the resultant 'picture' evaluated in the light of the auditor's understanding of the client's business and its operations. Some possible scenarios (where no change in the ratio in the current year was expected) are presented in Figure 11.5.

When assessing the results of substantive analytical procedures it is essential that they are not viewed in isolation. The auditor must evaluate the results within the context of his/her understanding of the client and its operations, and must give due consideration to all relevant external and internal environmental factors. Additionally, graphs such as those presented in Figure 11.5 need to be

---

[14] This includes ascertaining the condition of the inventory which is accomplished at the same time as ascertaining its existence.

Figure 11.5:   Scenarios of the ratio between inventory and cost of goods sold over time

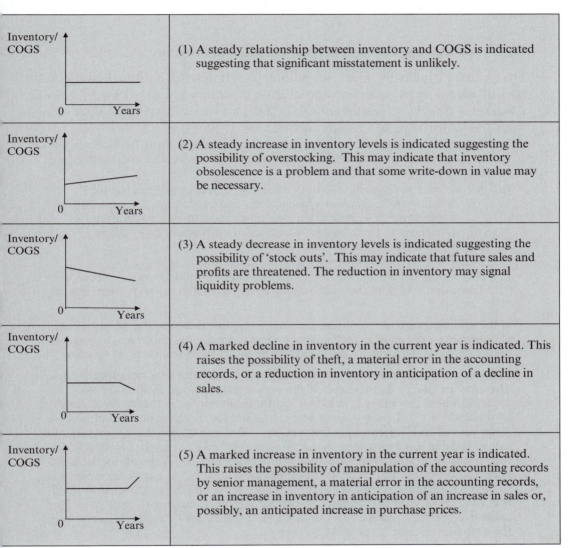

assessed on the basis of the inventory item(s) and/or location(s) to which they relate and how they compare with the graphs of other inventory items and/or locations. Consideration must also be given to pertinent policy decisions of management, such as planned changes in product mix, changes in target market(s) and/or changes in purchases and sales policies. Similarly, due allowance needs to be given to local and national economic, competitive and other factors which may have a bearing on sales and, therefore, on inventory levels.

It is important that substantive analytical procedures be regarded, not as a source of answers, but as a means of identifying questions which need to be asked.

11.7.2   Ascertaining the existence and condition of inventory

The primary means by which an auditor ascertains the existence and condition of inventory is attending the client's inventory count.[15] ISA 501: *Audit Evidence – Specific Considerations for Selected Items* (IAASB, 2009c) recognises the importance of this audit procedure. It states:

> If inventory is material to the financial statements, the auditor shall obtain sufficient appropriate audit evidence regarding the existence and condition of the inventory by:
> (a) Attendance at physical inventory counting, unless impracticable, to:
>   (i)   Evaluate management's instructions and procedures for recording and controlling the results of the entity's physical inventory counting;
>   (ii) Observe the performance of management's count procedures;
>   (iii) Inspect the inventory; and
>   (iv) Perform test counts; and
> (b) Performing audit procedures over the entity's final inventory records to determine whether they accurately reflect actual inventory count results. (para 4)

> If the auditor is unable to attend physical inventory counting due to unforeseen circumstances, the auditor shall make or observe some physical counts on an alternative date and perform audit procedures on intervening transactions. (para 6)

> In some cases, attendance at physical inventory counting may be impracticable. This may be due to factors such as the nature and location of the inventory, for example where inventory is held in a location that may pose threats to the safety of the auditor. . . . In some cases where attendance is impracticable, alternative audit procedures, for example, inspection of documentation of the subsequent sale of specific inventory items acquired or purchased prior to the physical inventory counting, may provide sufficient appropriate audit evidence about the existence and condition of inventory. In other cases, however, it may not be possible to obtain sufficient appropriate audit evidence regarding the existence and condition of inventory by performing alternative audit procedures. In such cases [the auditor is required] to modify the opinion in the auditor's report as a result of the scope limitation.[16] (paras A12–A14)

Audit procedures relating to physical inventory counting fall into three main groups:
  (i)   those conducted prior to the commencement of the inventory counting;
  (ii) those conducted while the counting is in progress;
  (iii) those conducted when the inventory counting is complete.

---

[15] It should be noted that this applies whether the client employs a periodic or a perpetual system for recording inventory. However, where a perpetual recording system is used, the auditor may attend inventory counts one or more times during the year.

[16] This form of audit opinion is explained in Chapter 14, section 14.5.2.

(i) Procedures conducted prior to inventory counting

Before attending their clients' inventory counts, auditors need to consider factors that are likely to affect their planned attendance and procedures at the counts. For example:

- the assessed risks of material misstatement relating to inventory;
- the effectiveness of internal controls relevant to the safeguarding and recording of inventory;
- whether adequate procedures are expected to be established, and proper instructions given to client staff, for the physical counting of inventory;
- the locations at which inventory is held;
- whether the specialised nature of the inventory is such that an expert's assistance is required.

Before the inventory count is due to begin, auditors should review their clients' inventory counting procedures to ensure they are adequate. They need to establish, *inter alia*:

- when the inventory counting is to take place and whether sufficient time has been allowed to enable the task to be completed satisfactorily;
- which personnel are to be involved in the counting, their seniority and experience, and whether they are to work in pairs;
- how the counting is to be performed; whether, for example, electronic recording devices are to be used;
- whether the instructions given to the inventory counting teams are clear, easily understood and complete;
- whether management's control procedures are adequate; whether, for example, appropriate procedures have been established to facilitate accurate counting and, if necessary, recounting of inventory, and to prevent inventory from being counted twice or omitted from the count;
- whether management has established adequate procedures for identifying the stage of completion of work-in-progress, obsolete or damaged items and/or inventory owned by a third party (such as goods held on consignment);
- whether appropriate arrangements have been made for counting inventory moved between locations (or within one location) just prior to, during or shortly after the inventory count, and the despatch and receipt of inventory before and after the cut-off date.[17]

If, having reviewed their clients' inventory counting procedures, auditors are of the opinion that they are inadequate, they should discuss their concerns with

---

[17] 'Cut-off' date is the end of the accounting period. It defines (or 'cuts-off') the inventory (and other assets and liabilities) controlled – and those not controlled – by the entity at the date of the financial statements. Only (but all) inventory owned or controlled by the entity at the end of the accounting period should be included in the inventory count.

management so the deficiencies can be rectified before the inventory counting begins.

Where inventory is held at several locations, auditors need to decide at which locations audit attendance is appropriate. In making this decision, they should consider (amongst other things) the materiality of the inventory held, and their assessment of inherent and internal control risk relating to inventory, at each location. Audit staff should attend the inventory count at each location where the inventory held is material and/or inherent risk and internal control risk are assessed as high.

(ii) Procedures conducted during inventory counting

During the inventory counting, auditors should observe whether their clients' employees adhere to the procedures prescribed by management and they should also perform test counts. ISA 501 explains:

> Observing the performance of management's count procedures, for example those relating to control over the movement of inventory before, during and after the count, assists the auditor in obtaining audit evidence that management's instructions and count procedures are adequately designed and implemented. (para A5)

> Performing test counts, for example by tracing items selected from management's count records to the physical inventory and tracing items selected from the physical inventory to management's count records, provides audit evidence about the completeness and the accuracy of those records. (para A7)

> In addition to recording the auditor's test counts, obtaining copies of management's completed physical inventory count records assists the auditor in performing subsequent audit procedures to determine whether the entity's final inventory records accurately reflect actual inventory count results. (para A8)

Many companies use hand-held electronic recording devices as aids to their inventory counting. An effective counting system, assisted by such devices, proceeds along the following lines:

- The person responsible for the inventory count at a particular location (the inventory count supervisor or manager) prepares a location inventory listing which shows the identity and quantity of all inventory items held at the location. This is usually extracted from the company's perpetual inventory records but also has columns to record, for each inventory item:
  - the result of the physical count,
  - the variance between the physical count and the quantity recorded in the perpetual inventory records,
  - the result of a second physical count if this is required,
  - the 'correct' quantity of the item, and

- any relevant notes (for example, comments on the age or condition of the inventory item concerned).
- Counting of the inventory items is assigned to pairs of counters, and the items for which each pair of counters is responsible are recorded on the location inventory list.
- For each inventory item they are assigned to count, the counters scan its bar code (to identify the item concerned) and count and record its quantity. They also record any relevant information about the item – for example, if it appears to be obsolete or damaged. The information is electronically transferred to the location inventory listing and the variance between the physical count and the quantity of the item recorded in the perpetual inventory records is automatically calculated and recorded.
- Once the items of inventory have been counted, the inventory count manager (or supervisor) reviews the variances between the physical count and quantity reflected in the perpetual inventory records. Where the variance is significant (for example, it is close to, or greater than, ten per cent), the item concerned is recounted, usually by a different pair of counters.
- Any significant variances remaining after the second count are investigated to establish the correct quantity of the inventory item concerned and the reasons for the differences.

(iii) Procedures following completion of inventory counting

When the inventory counting is complete, the auditor reviews the inventory listing and determines whether it accurately reflects the inventory count. As indicated above, this involves tracing a selection of items from the inventory listing to the physical inventory and tracing a sample of other items from the physical inventory to the inventory listing. The auditor will also verify that the inventory counts at the various locations have been correctly combined to produce a master inventory listing for the company. Further, where the physical count revealed the need to adjust the inventory records, the auditor inspects the accounting and perpetual inventory records to ascertain whether they have been adjusted appropriately.

Because the balance of the inventory account in the financial statements reflects the value of inventory owned by the entity at the date of the financial statements, inventory counting is usually undertaken at, or as close as possible to, the end of the accounting period. However, ISA 501 recognises that this may not be practical. It observes:

> For practical reasons, the physical inventory counting may be conducted at a date, or dates, other than the date of the financial statements. This may be done irrespective of whether management determines inventory quantities by an annual physical inventory counting or maintains a perpetual inventory system. In either

case, the effectiveness of the design, implementation and maintenance of controls over changes in inventory determines whether the conduct of physical inventory counting at a date, or dates, other than the date of the financial statements is appropriate for audit purposes. (para A9)

If the auditor concludes that the controls over changes in inventory are adequate for a counting of inventory to take place at a date other than that of the financial statements, s/he is required to perform procedures to establish that changes in inventory between the date of the count and that of the financial statements are properly recorded (ISA 501, para 5).

11.7.3   Ascertaining ownership of inventory

Inventory recorded as a current asset in the financial statements should reflect the value of inventory owned by the entity at the date of the financial statements. It should not include inventory which is not owned by the entity: neither should it exclude inventory which is owned. Therefore, as part of the audit of inventory, the auditor inspects source documents and other relevant documents in order to determine inventory ownership. The two following situations are of particular concern to the auditor:

(i)   Ownership of goods bought and sold near year end

The auditor needs to determine whether legal title to (i.e., ownership of) goods purchased, but in transit on the date of the financial statements, had passed to the client by that date. [This usually depends on whether the terms of the contract are f.o.b. (free on board) at shipping point or destination.] The auditor must also ascertain whether the goods in question have been properly included in, or excluded from, the client's master inventory list at the date of the financial statements.

Similarly, the auditor needs to ensure that where goods have been sold (and legal title has passed to the customer), but are still on the client's premises awaiting delivery on the date of the financial statements, these goods have not been recorded as part of the client's inventory.

(ii)   Goods on consignment

The auditor needs to ascertain whether any inventory included in the client's master inventory list is held on consignment, or under a franchise agreement, whereby title to the goods does not pass to the client until a specified condition is met; for example, title may not pass to the client until the goods are sold to a third party. Such goods are not owned by the client and, therefore, do not form part of the client's inventory.

By the same token, the auditor needs to ensure that inventory owned by the client which is held by a third party on consignment or under a franchise agreement is included as part of the client's inventory. ISA 501 explains auditors' responsibilities in this situation. It states:

> If inventory under the custody and control of a third party is material to the financial statements, the auditor shall obtain sufficient appropriate audit evidence regarding the existence and condition of that inventory by performing one or both of the following:
>
> (a) Request confirmation from the third party as to the quantities and condition of inventory held on behalf of the entity.
>
> (b) Perform inspection or other audit procedures appropriate in the circumstances. (para 8)

> Depending on the circumstances, for example, where information is obtained that raises doubt about the integrity and independence of the third party, the auditor may consider it appropriate to perform other audit procedures instead of, or in addition to, confirmation with the third party. Examples of other audit procedures include:
> - Attending, or arranging for another auditor to attend, the third party's physical counting of inventory, if practicable.
> - Obtaining another auditor's report . . . on the adequacy of the third party's internal control for ensuring that inventory is properly counted and adequately safeguarded.
> - Inspecting documentation regarding inventory held by third parties, for example, warehouse receipts.
> - Requesting confirmation from other parties when inventory has been pledged as collateral. (para A16)

11.7.4 Ascertaining that inventory is correctly valued

In addition to establishing the quantity and ownership of inventory, auditors must verify that it is correctly valued. To accomplish this, they perform procedures such as the following:

- determining the valuation method adopted by the client and confirming that this method:
  - is in accordance with International Accounting Standard (IAS) 2: *Inventories* (International Accounting Standards Board, 2011),
  - has been applied consistently across all inventory items, and
  - is consistent with previous years;
- inspecting suppliers' invoices, price lists and other relevant documents to determine the cost of items held as inventory;
- recalculating the value of inventory based on its quantity (from the master inventory list), cost information, and the valuation method adopted;
- establishing that the degree of completion of work-in-progress has been determined appropriately, and that raw materials, work-in-progress and finished goods inventory are properly classified;
- assessing the quality, condition and possible obsolescence of inventory items, and determining whether the net realisable value of inventory is lower than its cost;

- determine whether 'the lower of cost or net realisable value' rule has been applied correctly.

In relation to assessing the value of inventory, it is important that the auditor evaluates his/her competence to estimate its value and, if necessary, seeks assistance from an appropriate expert. A commonly cited example to illustrate this point is the auditor's inability, in general, to distinguish between diamonds and glass. The following case, reported in a BBC news broadcast in 1983, also provides a pertinent example. In this case the problem was an inability to distinguish between brass and gold.

> A North Wales jeweller committed suicide when it was discovered that his company's stock of gold was really brass. The Chester coroner was told that the jeweller had instructed his staff not to use the stock of what he said was gold wire, but when the bank sent investigators around, he admitted to a friend that the stock had been over-valued by £1 million. He then drove to a hotel where he drank a solution of cyanide poison. (BBC *News about Britain*, August 1983)

11.8 SIGNIFICANT ASPECTS OF AUDITING ACCOUNTS RECEIVABLE

11.8.1 Overview of auditing accounts receivable

The accounts receivable account balance is frequently audited as an element of the sales-receivables-receipts accounting sub-system. Substantive testing of this sub-system involves, *inter alia*:
- performing substantive analytical procedures to test the reasonableness of relevant accounts in the income statement and statement of financial position (for example, sales, sales returns, doubtful debts, allowance for bad debts, and accounts receivable);
- verifying the validity, completeness and accuracy of sales and cash receipts transactions;
- directly testing the accounts receivable account balance.

In this section, our focus of attention is the accounts receivable account balance. When auditing this balance the auditor is concerned, in particular, to verify the existence, ownership and value of accounts receivable. As for auditing inventory, each of these audit objectives (or assertions) requires a different set of audit procedures. These are shown in Figure 11.6.

11.8.2 Confirmation of accounts receivable

As noted in section 11.6, confirmation of accounts receivable became a standard audit procedure as a result of the *McKesson & Robbins* case in the USA

Figure 11.6: Procedures for auditing accounts receivable

Assertion/Audit Objective	Audit Procedures
Existence – Do accounts receivable exist?	Confirmation
Ownership – Are accounts receivable owned?	Enquiry and inspection of documents for possible factoring of accounts receivable
Valuation – Are accounts receivable correctly valued?	• Confirmation • Recalculation of allowance for bad debts

in the 1930s. ISA 505: *External Confirmations* (IAASB, 2009d) defines external confirmations as follows:

> External confirmation – Audit evidence obtained as a direct written response to the auditor from a third party (the confirming party), in paper form, or by electronic or other medium. (para 6)

From our discussion of the reliability and relevance of audit evidence in Chapter 7 (section 7.4.3), it is evident that audit evidence obtained directly by the auditor from an external source in documentary form (whether paper, electronic or other medium) is generally regarded as reliable. Hence, in general, external confirmations are considered to provide reliable audit evidence. However, the relevance of confirmations as evidence to support specific assertions varies. For example, they are relevant for establishing the existence of accounts receivable but are less relevant for ascertaining their recoverability and, hence, the value of accounts receivable.

External confirmations constitute the most widely used, and most reliable, audit procedure available for verifying the existence and accuracy of accounts receivable. Nevertheless, as will become evident as we examine the steps involved in the confirmation process, the extent of auditors' reliance on confirmations as a procedure for auditing the accounts receivable account balance is affected by characteristics of the environment in which the auditee operates and the practice of potential respondents in dealing with requests for direct confirmation. Thus, it varies from audit to audit.

The process of confirming accounts receivable balances involves the following seven steps.

(i)   Designing the confirmation request.
(ii) Deciding on the timing of confirmations.
(iii) Selecting a sample of accounts receivable.
(iv) Preparing and despatching the confirmation requests.
(v)   Following-up non-responses.
(vi) Analysing discrepancies.

(vii) Drawing conclusions about the accuracy of the accounts receivable account balance.

We discuss each of these steps below.

(i) Designing the confirmation request

As ISA 505 explains:

> The design of a confirmation request may directly affect the confirmation response rate, and the reliability and the nature of the audit evidence obtained from responses. (para A3)

> Factors to consider when designing confirmation requests include:
> • The assertions [or specific audit objectives] being addressed.
> • Specific identified risks of material misstatement, including fraud risks.
> • The layout and presentation of the confirmation request.
> • Prior experience on the audit or similar engagements.
> • The method of communication (for example, in paper form, or by electronic or other medium).
> • Management's authorization or encouragement to the confirming parties to respond to the auditor. . . .
> • The ability of the intended confirming party to confirm or provide the requested information (for example, individual invoice amount versus total balance). (para A4)

Confirmations may be of two types, positive and negative.

- A *positive confirmation* requests the confirming party to reply to the auditor signifying agreement or disagreement with the information provided (for example, on a given date the respondent owed the auditee a specified amount) or to provide requested information (for example, how much the respondent owed the client on a given date).

- A *negative confirmation* requests the confirming party to reply to the auditor only if s/he disagrees with the information provided.

Positive confirmations are generally considered to provide more reliable evidence as the confirming party is requested to respond whether the amount stated in the confirmation request is correct or incorrect. This enables the auditor to perform follow-up procedures in cases where responses are not received. However, the auditor also needs to bear in mind the possibility that a confirming party may reply to a confirmation request without actually verifying the information. Where the auditor considers this is likely, instead of stating an amount in the confirmation request, the confirming party may be asked to provide the relevant amount. The problem with this type of 'blank' confirmation request is that it may result in a reduced response rate because more is required of the confirming party.

Where negative confirmations are used, recipients of a confirmation request are asked to respond only if the amount stated is incorrect. Thus, all non-responses are treated as if the amount stated in the confirmation request is correct – even though its recipient may merely have ignored it. However, negative confirmations are less expensive than positive confirmations (because there are no follow-up procedures for non-responses) and, therefore, for a given total cost, more negative than positive confirmation requests may be sent. Nevertheless, because negative confirmations provide less reliable evidence than positive confirmations, the auditor needs to consider whether other substantive procedures are required to supplement the negative confirmations.

Determining which type of confirmation to use in any given audit engagement is a matter of judgment. Nevertheless, it is generally accepted that positive confirmations are appropriate when the following circumstances apply:
- A small number of large accounts represent a significant proportion of the total accounts receivable account balance.
- The auditor has reason to believe that there may be disputed or inaccurate accounts (for example, when internal controls are weak).
- The auditor has good reason to expect that recipients of confirmation requests will not give them reasonable consideration. (For example, low response rates have been experienced in previous years. In this circumstance, negative confirmations are not appropriate.)

By way of contrast, it is generally accepted that negative confirmations are appropriate when:
- the auditor considers that internal controls are reliable and, as a result, material misstatement in accounts receivable accounts is unlikely;
- the auditor has no reason to believe that recipients will disregard the confirmation request or fail to treat it seriously; and/or
- a large number of small account balances is involved.

In some audits, a combination of positive and negative confirmations are used. For example, where the total accounts receivable account balance comprises a small number of large balances and a large number of small balances, positive confirmations may be used for all, or a sample of, the large balances and negative confirmations for a sample of the small balances.

A further factor auditors should consider when designing confirmation requests is the type of information respondents will be able to confirm readily. For example, certain respondents' accounting systems may facilitate the confirmation of single transactions rather than account balances. Where this is the case, the confirmation request should contain details of one or more transactions rather than the total account balance. If information is sought in confirmations that is not readily available to the recipient, it is likely to result in a reduced response rate.

(ii) Deciding on the timing of confirmations

Confirmations provide the most reliable evidence when confirmation requests are sent close to the end of the auditee's reporting period. When this occurs, the accounts receivable account balances are tested directly, without any inferences having to be made about transactions which take place between the confirmation date and the period end. However, in order to complete the audit on a timely basis, and to facilitate the scheduling of audit staff workloads, it is often convenient to confirm accounts receivable at an interim date (generally, two or three months prior to the period end). This practice is acceptable if (but only if) the auditee's internal controls over accounts receivable are evaluated as effective and the auditor can be reasonably assured that sales, sales returns and cash receipts transactions are properly recorded between the confirmation date and the period end.

(iii) Selecting a sample of accounts receivable

In order to select a sample of accounts receivable to be confirmed, two separate decisions need to be made, namely:

(a) how large the sample is to be;
(b) how the sample is to be selected.[18]

The auditor also needs to consider the characteristics of intended respondents.

(a) *The size of the sample* will depend on a number of factors, including:
- the materiality of the total accounts receivable account balance. (The more material the balance, the larger the sample size);
- the number of accounts which constitute the total accounts receivable balance;
- the size distribution of individual accounts receivable account balances;
- the results of the auditor's evaluation of the related internal controls, and of substantive analytical procedures, which indicate the likelihood (or otherwise) of the total accounts receivable account balance being materially misstated;
- the results of confirmations in previous years;
- the type of confirmation being used.

(b) *The sample selection* usually involves some stratification of the total population of accounts receivable. In most audits where confirmation is used as an audit procedure, the population is stratified based on (i) size and (ii) age of outstanding balances. Emphasis is given to testing large and old accounts as these accounts are the most likely to contain a material error. (Old accounts may indicate a dispute between the company

---

[18] Determining sample size and selecting samples are discussed in detail in Chapter 12.

and customer about the amount or even the existence of the debt, or may raise other questions about its collectability.) However, it is important that the auditor's sample includes some items from every material stratum of the population.

In most cases, the auditor confirms all balances which exceed some designated monetary amount and all accounts beyond a specified age limit (for example, 90 days), and selects a random sample from the remainder.

(c) *Characteristics of respondents*: Responses to confirmation requests are more likely to provide reliable audit evidence if the confirmation requests are sent to recipients who are:
- knowledgeable about the information to be confirmed;
- able and willing to respond to the request. (The confirming party may, for instance, be disinclined to respond if doing so is costly or time consuming);
- independent of the client entity. (If the confirming party is not independent of the auditee, his/her response to a confirmation request may not be reliable).

The auditor needs to take these factors into account when deciding whether to rely on confirmation procedures to verify individual accounts receivable balances and, more particularly, when selecting those to whom confirmation requests are to be sent.

(iv) *Preparing and despatching the confirmation requests*

Once the auditor has decided on the type of confirmation to be used and selected the sample of accounts receivable to be confirmed, the confirmation requests are prepared.

A confirmation request is usually in the form of a letter (in paper or electronic form). It is frequently prepared on the client's letterhead but, in any event, should include an authorisation from the client to the customer to disclose the requested information to the auditor. As noted earlier, the confirmation request generally sets out the amount owed by the customer to the client as shown in the client's accounts on a specified date (confirmation date) but, in some circumstances, the respondent is asked, instead, to fill in the amount owed on confirmation date. If a positive confirmation is used, the customer is requested to confirm whether the amount stated in the letter is correct or incorrect (or to provide requested information); if a negative confirmation is used, the recipient is asked to respond only if the amount stated is not correct. However, irrespective of the type of confirmation used, if the confirming party indicates the amount stated in the confirmation request is incorrect, s/he is asked to indicate what s/he believes is the correct amount.

Notwithstanding the use of the client's letterhead to prepare confirmation requests, it is essential that all aspects of the confirmation process remain under the control of the auditor. This includes preparing the confirmation requests, placing them in envelopes, and stamping and mailing the envelopes. In order to ensure that any undelivered requests are returned to the audit firm, the audit firm's address should be shown as the return address on the outside of the envelope. A stamped envelope, addressed to the audit firm, should be enclosed with the confirmation request.

If a confirmation request is returned to the audit firm as undelivered mail, the reason for the non-delivery needs to be carefully evaluated. In most cases it represents a customer who has moved away without settling his/her account, but there is always the possibility that it represents a fictitious customer. Further, even if the customer is valid, a large number of undelivered confirmation requests could highlight errors in the client's customers' address records. This could signal a collectability problem which will need to be reflected in the allowance for bad debts.

(v) Following-up non-responses

As noted above, when negative confirmations are used it is assumed that amounts stated in confirmation requests which are not returned are correct. Non-responses are not followed-up. However, when positive confirmations are used, no assumption is made as to the correctness or otherwise of amounts stated in confirmation requests which receive no response. Instead, second, and in some cases even third, confirmation requests are sent.

If the customer still fails to respond, the auditor has to rely on alternative audit procedures to confirm the amount in question. The auditor will, for example, examine the cash receipts records to ascertain whether the customer paid an amount subsequent to the confirmation date. However, receipt of cash from the customer does not necessarily establish that the amount being investigated was owed at confirmation date; it could relate to a subsequent sale. Therefore, in addition to examining the cash receipts records, the auditor needs to examine copies of:

- sales invoices – to confirm that the customer was billed for the relevant goods or services;
- despatch records – to confirm that the goods were despatched to the customer;
- sales returns records – to confirm that the goods were not returned by the customer.

In each case, careful attention must be paid to the dates and details of the records to ensure they all relate to the same transaction(s).

Inspection of correspondence in a disputed accounts file may also provide evidence that a customer who failed to respond to a confirmation request owed the amount in question at the confirmation date but, if the amount is in dispute, it may indicate a collectability problem.

The nature and extent of alternative audit procedures performed to verify accounts receivable balances for which no response to a positive confirmation request is received largely depend upon the materiality of the account balances in question, the types of errors discovered from the confirmation responses received, subsequent cash receipts from accounts receivable who have not responded to positive confirmation requests, and the auditor's evaluation of the quality of the client's internal controls over accounts receivable. However, in order for valid conclusions to be drawn about the population of accounts receivable from the sample of accounts examined, *all* of the unconfirmed balances (following positive confirmation requests) should be investigated using alternative procedures, even if the amounts involved are small.

Although not a 'non-response' in the usually understood meaning of the term, ISA 505 observes:

> On its own, an oral response to a confirmation request does not meet the definition of an external confirmation because it is not a direct written response to the auditor. However, upon obtaining an oral response to a confirmation request, the auditor may, depending on the circumstances, request the confirming party to respond in writing directly to the auditor. If no such response is received, . . . the auditor seeks other audit evidence to support the information in the oral response. (para A15)

Notwithstanding that external confirmations are usually considered to provide reliable audit evidence, ISA 505 points out that:

> . . . circumstances may exist that affect [a confirmation's] reliability. All responses carry some risk of interception, alteration or fraud. . . . Factors that may indicate doubts about the reliability of a response include that it:
> - Was received by the auditor indirectly; or
> - Appeared not to come from the originally intended confirming party. (para A11)
>
> Responses received electronically, for example by facsimile or electronic mail, involve risks as to reliability because proof of origin and authority of the respondent may be difficult to establish, and alterations may be difficult to detect. A process used by the auditor and the respondent that creates a secure environment for responses received electronically may mitigate these risks. If the auditor is satisfied that such a process is secure and properly controlled, the reliability of the related responses is enhanced. . . . (para A12)

In any case where the auditor concludes that a response to a confirmation request is not reliable, the auditor is required to evaluate the implications for, and if appropriate amend:

- the assessment of the relevant risks of misstatement, including the risk of fraud;
- the nature, timing and extent of other audit procedures (ISA 505, paras 11, A17).

(vi) Analysing discrepancies

When confirmations are returned to the auditor, any disagreements with amounts stated in the confirmation requests must be analysed carefully. In many cases these will result from timing differences between the customer's and the client's records (for example, a payment by a customer may not have been recorded in the client's records by the confirmation date). However, in other cases, disagreements may signal errors in the auditee's accounts. These may arise, for example, from incorrect recording of amounts (that is, clerical errors) or from failure to record certain transactions, such as goods returned by the customer. Alternatively, they may reflect disputed amounts where the customer claims, for instance, that the wrong price has been charged, incorrect quantities or items were received, or the goods arrived in a damaged condition.

All disagreements with amounts in confirmation requests should be investigated to determine whether the client's records are in error and, if this is the case, by how much. Generally, the auditor asks the client to perform the necessary reconciliation but, if necessary, will communicate with the customer to settle discrepancies which have come to light.

(vii) Drawing conclusions about the accuracy of the accounts receivable account balance

When all discrepancies found in the sample of accounts receivable have been explained, including those discovered as a result of procedures performed as follow-ups to non-responses, the auditor needs to:

- re-evaluate the internal controls over accounts receivable and determine whether detected errors are consistent with the auditor's original assessment of the controls;
- generalise from the sample of accounts receivable examined to the total population of accounts receivable;
- draw conclusions as to whether sufficient appropriate evidence has been gathered regarding the assertions being tested (i.e., the existence and accuracy of accounts receivable as recorded in the client's accounts).

If the auditor concludes that the confirmation process, together with any alternative or additional procedures, has not provided sufficient appropriate audit evidence regarding the assertions tested, additional procedures will need to be performed.

11.8.3 Adjusting accounts receivable for doubtful debts

Based on evidence gathered by the confirmation process and any additional procedures performed, the auditor may conclude that the accounts receivable balances recorded in the client's accounts are accurate. However, before concluding that the value of the accounts receivable balance in the financial statements is 'true and fair', the auditor must assess the adequacy of the auditee's allowance for bad debts. To make this assessment, the auditor (if s/he has not already done so) usually prepares, or more commonly, obtains from the client, an 'aged accounts receivable schedule'; that is, a listing of all of the accounts receivable account balances classified according to the length of time they have been outstanding. Frequently they are grouped into balances that have been outstanding for less than 30 days, 31 to 60 days, 61 to 90 days, and over 90 days. Based on the premise that the longer accounts receivable balances are outstanding the greater the probability that they will never be paid, it is usually appropriate to apply a sliding scale of percentages to each group of accounts receivable balances to establish an allowance for bad debts (with a large percentage being applied to the 'old' balances and progressively smaller percentages being applied to more recent balances). When assessing the propriety of the percentages applied to the accounts receivable balances by the client when estimating the allowance for bad debts, the auditor will consider whether, compared with previous years, there has been any change in factors such as:

- the client's credit policy;
- the client's credit approval procedures;
- the level of compliance by employees with the credit approval procedures;
- the volume of credit sales;
- general economic conditions which are likely to affect customers' ability to meet their financial obligations.

The auditor will also reperform the calculation to determine whether the client's estimate of the allowance for bad debts is reasonable.

11.8.4 Ownership of accounts receivable

In most cases ownership of accounts receivable does not give rise to problems; the amounts owed by customers are owed to the client. However, particularly where there is evidence that the auditee has cash flow problems, the auditor must remain alert to the possibility that all, or part of, the client's accounts receivable may have been factored, that is, sold to a financial institution at a discount. When this occurs, customers are frequently not aware of the change in the ownership of their debt because they continue to make payments to the client. As a consequence, factoring does not, in general, come to light through the confirmation process. The most common means by which the auditor discovers that factoring has occurred is through discussions with management and inspection of documents such as minutes of directors' meetings and correspondence.

11.9 INITIAL ENGAGEMENTS

A less frequently occurring example of substantive testing than those discussed in previous sections of this chapter involves an incoming auditor substantiating the 'opening balances' presented in the current period's financial statements following a change of auditor. In this regard, ISA 510: *Initial Audit Engagements – Opening Balances* (IAASB, 2009e) requires auditors to:

> . . . obtain sufficient appropriate evidence about whether the opening balances contain misstatements that materially affect the current period's financial statements by:
>
> (a) Determining whether the prior period's closing balances have been correctly brought forward to the current period or, when appropriate, have been restated;
> (b) Determining whether the opening balances reflect the application of appropriate accounting policies; and
> (c) Performing one or more of the following:
>   (i) Where the prior year's financial statements were audited, reviewing the predecessor auditor's working papers to obtain evidence regarding the opening balances;
>   (ii) Evaluating whether audit procedures performed in the current period provide evidence relevant to the opening balances; or
>   (iii) Performing specific audit procedures to obtain evidence regarding the opening balances. (para 6)

In respect of reviewing a predecessor auditor's working papers, ISA 510 states:

> . . . Whether such a review provides sufficient appropriate audit evidence [regarding the opening balances] is influenced by the professional competence and independence of the predecessor auditor. (para A4)

If, after performing audit procedures to obtain sufficient appropriate audit evidence to establish whether the opening balances contain misstatements that cause the current period's financial statements to be materially misstated, the auditor concludes that this is the case, the auditor is to inform an appropriate level of management and the client's directors, and request that the misstatements in the current period's financial statements be corrected (ISA 510, para 7).

ISA 510 (para 8) also requires incoming auditors to obtain sufficient appropriate audit evidence to determine whether:

> (i) the accounting policies reflected in the opening balances have been consistently applied in the current period's financial statements;

(ii) any changes in the accounting policies have been properly accounted for and adequately disclosed in the statement of accounting policies which accompanies the financial statements.

11.10 SUMMARY

In this chapter we have discussed substantive testing, that is, testing the substance of the financial statement account balances and note disclosures (or, more correctly, the assertions embodied therein). It is these balances and disclosures about which the auditor is required to form and express an opinion and, irrespective of how 'perfect' a client's internal control system may appear to be, some substantive testing is always necessary.

We have noted that there are two forms of substantive testing – substantive analytical procedures and tests of details – and that tests of details may involve testing the classes of transactions which give rise to a financial statement account balance or testing the balance directly. However, whichever form of substantive testing is used, the objective is always the same, namely, to test the validity, completeness and accuracy of the financial statement amounts and other disclosures.

In addition to discussing the general principles of substantive testing, we have considered the application of commonly used substantive audit procedures (observation, inspection, recalculation, tracing, confirmation and reperformance) and examined, in some detail, significant aspects of auditing the inventory and accounts receivable accounts. In the final section of the chapter we have outlined the requirements of the incoming auditor (following a change of auditor) with respect to the opening balances presented in the current year's financial statements.

SELF-REVIEW QUESTIONS

11.1 State the overall audit objective of substantive testing.

11.2 Explain briefly why some substantive testing is required in every audit engagement.

11.3 Explain the meaning of the term 'assertion' and list four assertions about classes of transactions and four relating to account balances.

11.4 Explain briefly two ways in which substantive analytical procedures may be used as substantive tests.

11.5   (a) Explain briefly two ways in which the details of account balances may be tested; and

(b) for each of these ways, explain the circumstances in which its use is particularly appropriate.

11.6   (a) Describe briefly how the following audit procedures are performed:
    (i) tracing forwards
    (ii) tracing backwards.

(b) Using a specific example to illustrate your answer, explain the purpose of each of the above audit procedures.

11.7   Explain briefly the procedures the auditor may use to test the specific audit objectives:
    (i) Does the inventory exist?
    (ii) Is the inventory owned by the client?

11.8   In relation to auditing accounts receivable, distinguish between a positive and a negative confirmation request.

11.9   (a) List five elements of the process of confirming accounts receivable which must remain under the auditor's control.

(b) Explain briefly why it is important that the auditee is not permitted to assist the auditor in the process of confirming accounts receivable.

11.10   Explain briefly the responsibilities of an 'incoming auditor' (following a change of auditor) in respect of the 'opening balances' in the current period's financial statements.

REFERENCES

International Accounting Standards Board (IASB). (2011). International Accounting Standard (IAS) 2: *Inventories*. London: International Financial Reporting Standards Foundation.

International Auditing and Assurance Standards Board (IAASB). (2009a). International Standard on Auditing (ISA) 330: *The Auditor's Responses to Assessed Risks*. New York: International Federation of Accountants.

International Auditing and Assurance Standards Board (IAASB). (2009b). International Standard on Auditing (ISA) 450: *Evaluation of Misstatements Identified during the Audit*. New York: International Federation of Accountants.

International Auditing and Assurance Standards Board (IAASB). (2009c). International Standard on Auditing (ISA) 501: *Audit Evidence – Specific Considerations for Selected Items*. New York: International Federation of Accountants.

International Auditing and Assurance Standards Board (IAASB). (2009d). International Standard on Auditing (ISA) 505: *External Confirmations*. New York: International Federation of Accountants.

International Auditing and Assurance Standards Board (IAASB). (2009e). International Standard on Auditing (ISA) 510: *Initial Audit Engagements: Opening Balances*. New York: International Federation of Accountants.

International Auditing and Assurance Standards Board (IAASB). (2009f). International Standard on Auditing (ISA) 520: *Analytical Procedures*. New York: International Federation of Accountants.

International Auditing and Assurance Standards Board (IAASB). (2012). International Standard on Auditing (ISA) 315: *Identifying and Assessing the Risks of Material Misstatement through Understanding the Entity and its Environment*. New York: International Federation of Accountants.

ADDITIONAL READING

Asare, S.K., Cianci, A.M., & Tsakumis, G.T. (2009). The impact of competing goals, experience, and litigation consciousness on auditors' judgments. *International Journal of Auditing*, *13*(3), 223–236.

Auditing Practices Board (APB). (2011). *Practice Note 25 (Revised): Attendance at Stocktaking*. London: Financial Reporting Council.

Bell, T.B., & Griffin, J.B. (2012). Commentary on auditing high-uncertainty fair value estimates. *Auditing: A Journal of Practice & Theory*, *31*(1), 147–155.

Canadian Institute of Chartered Accountants (CICA). (2000). *Use of Specialists in Assurance Engagements*. Toronto: CICA.

Canadian Institute of Chartered Accountants (CICA). (2003). *Electronic Audit Evidence*. Toronto: CICA.

Christensen, B.E., Glover, S.M., & Wood, D.A. (2012). Extreme estimation uncertainty in fair value estimates: Implications for audit assurance. *Auditing: A Journal of Practice & Theory*, *31*(1), 127–146.

Chung, J.O.Y., Cohen, J.R., & Monroe, G.S. (2008). The effect of moods on auditors' inventory valuation decisions. *Auditing: A Journal of Practice & Theory*, *27*(2), 137–159.

Gramling, A.A., O'Donnell, E., & Vanderelde, S.D. (2010). Audit partner evaluation of compensating controls: A focus on design effectiveness and extent of audit testing. *Auditing: A Journal of Practice & Theory*, *29*(2), 175–187.

Green, W.J., & Trotman, K.T. (2003). An examination of different performance outcomes in an analytical procedures task. *Auditing: A Journal of Practice & Theory*, *22*(2), 219–235.

Hoffman, V.B., Joe, J.R., & Moser, D.V. (2003). The effect of constrained processing on auditors' judgments. *Accounting, Organizations and Society*, *28*(7–8), 699–714.

Hoitash, R., Kogan, A., & Vasarhelyi, M.A. (2006). Peer-based approach for analytical procedures. *Auditing: A Journal of Practice & Theory*, *25*(2), 53–84.

Lin, K.Z., Fraser, I.A.M., & Hatherly, D.J. (2003). Auditor analytical review judgement: A performance evaluation. *British Accounting Review*, *35*(1), 19–34.

McDaniel, L.S., & Simmons, L.E. (2007). Auditors' assessment and incorporation of expectation precision in evidential analytical procedures. *Auditing: A Journal of Practice & Theory*, *26*(1), 1–18.

12 Audit Sampling and Computer Assisted Auditing Techniques (CAATs)

LEARNING OBJECTIVES

After studying the material in this chapter you should be able to:
- explain what is meant by 'sampling' and why this technique is important in auditing;
- explain the meaning of the basic terminology used in sampling;
- distinguish between judgmental and statistical sampling and explain the advantages and disadvantages of each;
- distinguish between attributes and variables sampling and identify the type of audit procedures to which each is most applicable;
- describe the methods commonly used for selecting samples;
- within the context of statistical sampling, explain:
  - the process of attributes sampling,
  - the basic principles of sampling with probability proportional to size (monetary unit sampling);
- discuss how auditors follow up the results obtained from testing samples of items;
- explain what is meant by 'computer assisted auditing techniques' (CAATs);
- distinguish between 'test data' and 'audit software' and explain how each technique may be used in audit testing;
- discuss the use and control of CAATs in auditing.

12.1 INTRODUCTION

In this chapter we consider two audit techniques that traverse both compliance and substantive testing, namely, audit sampling and computer assisted auditing techniques (CAATs). We explain the meaning and importance of sampling in auditing, the meaning of basic terminology related to sampling, and the differences between, and advantages and disadvantages of, judgmental and statistical sampling. We also explain the difference between attributes and variables sampling and identify the types of audit tests to which each is most applicable. Additionally, we discuss factors that affect the size of samples and describe some commonly used methods of selecting samples. Within the context of statistical sampling, we provide detailed examples of the application of (a) attributes sampling to compliance testing and (b) sampling with probability proportioned to size (PPS, or monetary unit sampling) to substantive testing. Before concluding this part of the chapter we discuss the ways in which the auditor follows up the results obtained from testing samples of items.

In the second part of the chapter we explain what is meant by CAATs and discuss the meaning and use of 'test data' and 'audit software' in relation to audit procedures. We also examine the use and control of CAATs during an audit engagement.

12.2 MEANING AND IMPORTANCE OF SAMPLING IN AUDITING

International Standard on Auditing (ISA) 530: *Audit Sampling* (IAASB, 2009b) defines audit sampling as follows:

> Audit sampling (sampling) – The application of audit procedures to less than 100% of items within a population of audit relevance such that all sampling units have a chance of selection in order to provide the auditor with a reasonable basis on which to draw conclusions about the entire population. (para 5a)

Expressed in more general terms, sampling is the examination of a few items (or sampling units) drawn from a defined mass of data (or population), with a view to inferring characteristics found in the sample to the population as a whole. This may be illustrated by a simple example.

Example: Assume that an auditee has 800,000 suppliers' invoices and that the auditor wishes to ascertain:
  (i)   whether, before payment, the invoices were:
        • matched with purchase orders and receiving reports;
        • checked for correct extensions and additions;
        • checked for correct account classifications; and
  (ii) whether:
        • the extensions and additions are arithmetically correct;
        • the transactions have been coded to the correct accounts;
        • the correct amounts have been recorded in the correct accounts;
        • the transactions have been recorded in the correct accounting period.

Reviewing these audit objectives, it should be noted that the first group relates to the client's internal control procedures. In order to test the level of compliance by client personnel with these control procedures, the auditor performs compliance tests. The second group of objectives relates to the accuracy of the recorded amounts, account classifications and accounting periods of the transactions. To test these, the auditor performs substantive tests (or, more precisely, tests of details).

Clearly, it is not economically feasible for the auditor to apply the seven tests to all 800,000 invoices. Instead, a sample of, say, 40 invoices will be selected and the seven tests will be applied to these. Based on the results of the tests, the auditor will draw conclusions about the population of suppliers' invoices with respect to each of the characteristics tested. (That is, for each characteristic tested, the results obtained from testing 40 invoices will be accepted as applying to the population as a whole.)

Sampling has been an accepted auditing technique since the early part of the twentieth century and today is recognised as an essential feature of most audits. Three main reasons account for its importance, namely:
- in the modern business environment it is not economically feasible for the auditor to examine the details of all of the client's transactions and account balances;
- testing a sample of transactions is faster and less costly than testing the whole population and all audits must be completed within a reasonable period of time and at reasonable cost;
- auditors are required to form an opinion (not reach a position of certainty) about the truth and fairness of the financial statements and their compliance (or otherwise) with an applicable financial reporting framework. This can usually be accomplished by testing samples of evidence; there is no need to test the whole population.

Notwithstanding its undoubted advantages, reliance on audit sampling introduces a concern for auditors. It exposes them to sampling risk, that is, the risk of reaching a conclusion about the population based on the sample of items examined that may differ from that which would have been reached had the entire population been tested. Expressed in different terms, it is the risk that auditors will draw an inappropriate conclusion about the population because the sample examined is not representative of the population.

ISA 530 notes that sampling risk can lead to two types of erroneous conclusion, namely:
  (i) In the case of a test of controls, that controls are more effective than they actually are, or in the case of a test of details, that a material misstatement does not exist when in fact it does. The auditor is primarily concerned with this type of erroneous conclusion because it affects audit effectiveness and is more likely to lead to an inappropriate audit opinion.
  (ii) In the case of a test of controls, that controls are less effective than they actually are, or in the case of a test of details, that a material misstatement

exists when in fact it does not. This type of erroneous conclusion affects audit efficiency as it would usually lead to additional work to establish that initial conclusions were incorrect. (para 5c)

If sampling procedures are used, sampling risk cannot be avoided altogether but it can be reduced by increasing the size of the sample and by selecting sampling units at random. (Random sample selection is discussed in section 12.5.3.) Additionally, sampling risk may be quantified and controlled through the use of statistical sampling techniques.

12.3 BASIC TERMINOLOGY RELATING TO SAMPLING

In order to understand the fundamental principles of audit sampling, it is necessary to have a good grasp of a few terms which are commonly used. These include the following:

- *Population*: This refers to all of the items which possess a particular characteristic about which the auditor wishes to draw a conclusion. For example, if the auditor wishes to determine whether all credit sales were authorised, and the auditee's control procedures require the credit manager to initial sales invoices to signal authorisation, the population would comprise the credit manager's initials.

- *Frame*: This is the physical representation of the population. In the above example, duplicates of sales invoices[1] (which should contain the credit manager's initials) are the frame. If the auditor is interested in the accuracy of accounts receivable account balances, accounts receivable subsidiary ledger records may be the frame.

- *Sampling unit*: This is a unit which is selected from the population and included in the sample to be examined.

- *Characteristic of interest*: This term refers to the characteristic the auditor wishes to test. There are two basic characteristics of interest – an attribute and a variable.
  - *An attribute* is a characteristic of the population which is either present or absent. Attributes sampling measures how frequently the characteristic is present (or, more usually, absent); for example, how frequently the credit manager's initials, signalling approval of a credit sale, are absent on duplicates of the auditee's sales invoices.
  - *A variable* is a measurement which is possessed by every member of the population but which can take any one of a wide range of values.

---

[1] The original sales invoice is given to the customer; one or more duplicates is/are retained by the company.

An example of a variable is the monetary amount of a transaction or account balance. In variables sampling the auditor is concerned with estimating a monetary value – for example, the balance of the inventory account, or the amount by which this balance may be in error.

- *Stratification*: This refers to dividing a single population into sub-populations, or strata, of sampling units with a similar characteristic. It is undertaken to improve audit efficiency and effectiveness. As ISA 530 (Appendix 1) explains:
    1. Audit efficiency may be improved if the auditor stratifies a population by dividing it into discrete sub-populations which have an identifying characteristic. The objective of stratification is to reduce the variability of items within each stratum and therefore allow sample size to be reduced without increasing sampling risk.
    2. When performing tests of details, the population is often stratified by monetary value. This allows greater audit effort to be directed to the larger value items, as these items may contain the greatest potential misstatement in terms of overstatement. Similarly, a population may be stratified according to a particular characteristic that indicates a higher risk of misstatement, for example, when testing the allowance for doubtful debts in the valuation of accounts receivable, balances may be stratified by age.

An important advantage of stratification is that it permits the auditor to allow for variations in the risk attaching to identifiable components of a population. For example, as we note in Chapter 11, section 11.8, accounts receivable account balances are frequently stratified according to size and/or age. Balances exceeding some monetary amount (which may be overstated), and balances beyond some age limit (say, 90 days) (which raise questions about their collectability) may be subjected to 100 per cent testing (no sample will be selected and the entire population will be tested). The remaining balances will be treated as a homogenous population from which a sample may be selected and tested.

- *Precision limits*: This term refers to how closely the results obtained from the sample of items examined match the results that would have been obtained had the entire population been tested. For example, in attributes sampling, if the sample shows that a particular characteristic occurs in two per cent of cases, how closely this reflects the rate of occurrence of the characteristic which would have been found had every item in the population been checked. Alternatively, in variables sampling, if, based on testing a sample of items, the auditor estimates the balance of the inventory account is £1,250,000, how close this is to the amount that would have been arrived at had the value of every individual item of inventory been ascertained and totalled.

- *Level of assurance (or confidence) (or level of sampling risk)*: This term refers to how confident the auditor wishes to be that the sampling units examined will produce a result for the population with the desired precision. For example, if the auditor wishes to estimate the balance of the inventory account and specifies a precision limit of £20,000 with a 95 per cent level of confidence, this means that the auditor wishes his/her estimate of the balance of the inventory account to be within £20,000 of the actual value of the account balance at least 95 times out of every 100. By inference, it also means that the auditor is prepared to accept that, on five occasions out of 100, his/her estimate of the inventory account balance (based on the sample units examined) may differ from its actual value by more than £20,000. Expressed alternatively, there is a five per cent risk that the sample selected will not be representative of the population from which it is drawn and will result in the auditor reaching an inappropriate conclusion about the population based on the sample.

- ISA 530 defines two further important terms related to precision limits and assurance levels. These are as follows:
  - Tolerable misstatement – A monetary amount set by the auditor in respect of which the auditor seeks to obtain an appropriate level of assurance that [the amount] . . . is not exceeded by the actual misstatement in the population. (para 5i)
  - Tolerable rate of deviation – A rate of deviation from prescribed internal control procedures set by the auditor in respect of which the auditor seeks to obtain an appropriate level of assurance that [the rate] . . . is not exceeded by the actual rate of deviation in the population. (para 5j)

In effect, these terms refer to the amount of misstatement in a class of transactions or account balance the auditor is prepared to tolerate (or accept) while still concluding that the class of transactions or account balance is not materially misstated,[2] or the rate of deviation from the correct operation of an internal control the auditor is prepared to accept while still concluding that the control is operating effectively.

12.4 JUDGMENTAL SAMPLING vs STATISTICAL SAMPLING AND SAMPLING METHODS

When discussing audit sampling, it is important to distinguish between judgmental and statistical sampling.

12.4.1 Judgmental sampling

Judgmental sampling refers to the use of sampling where the auditor relies on his/her own judgment to decide:

---

[2] This coincides with the definition of tolerable error provided in Chapter 9, section 9.3.1.

- how large the sample should be;
- which items from the population should be selected;
- whether to accept or reject the population as reliable[3] based on the results obtained from the sampling units examined.

This sampling method has the advantages over statistical sampling that it is generally faster, and therefore less costly, to apply. Additionally, it enables the auditor to incorporate in the sampling procedures, allowance for factors of which s/he is aware as a result of earlier steps in the audit process such as gaining an understanding of the client and its business, and evaluating the effectiveness of its internal controls; for example, the size of samples can be increased for areas identified as 'significant risks' (i.e., prone to misstatement). However, unlike statistical sampling, judgmental sampling provides no measure of sampling risk and, should the auditor's judgment be challenged (particularly in a court of law), the conclusions reached with respect to the sample may be difficult to defend. Further, when using judgmental sampling it is difficult not to introduce bias – whether in relation to sample size, the items selected or the conclusions reached about the population from which the sample was drawn.

12.4.2 Statistical sampling

Statistical sampling refers to the use of sampling techniques which rely on probability theory to help determine:
- how large the sample should be;
- whether to accept or reject the population as reliable based on the results obtained from the sampling units examined.

We should note that, when statistical sampling is used, the sampling units *must* be selected at random.

Statistical sampling has three important advantages over judgmental sampling, namely:
- it is unbiased;
- should aspects of the sampling be challenged, because it is based on probability theory and, therefore, considered to be objective (rather than based on the auditor's subjective judgment), it is readily defensible;
- it permits quantification of sampling risk (i.e., the risk that the sample is not representative of the population and, as a result, inappropriate conclusions are reached about the population).

However, statistical sampling has the disadvantage of being more complex and costly to apply than judgmental sampling. Further, in general, small and many

---

[3] If it is a compliance test, 'reliable' signifies the internal control concerned is operating effectively; if a test of details, the class of transactions or account balance is not materially misstated.

medium-sized companies do not have populations which are sufficiently large and homogeneous for full application of statistical sampling. As a consequence, in the audits of small and medium-sized clients where statistical sampling is applied, it tends to be applied in a modified form.

In relation to statistical sampling it is pertinent to note that, notwithstanding the distinction between statistical and judgmental sampling, significant elements of judgment are involved in the application of statistical sampling techniques. This will be evident from our discussion of attributes sampling and probability proportional to size (PPS) sampling in section 12.7.

Irrespective of whether judgmental or statistical sampling is used, the characteristic of interest in the population the auditor wishes to test will be either:

- an attribute (a characteristic which is present or absent; the relevant question in this case is usually 'how many times is the characteristic absent'?); or
- a variable (a characteristic which can take on a range of values; the relevant question in this case is 'how much'? – what is the estimated value of an account balance or of a misstatement in a class of transactions or account balance?).

Because evidence of compliance with internal control procedures (such as the credit manager's initials appearing on duplicates of sales invoices signifying authorisation of credit sales) is generally either present or absent, attributes sampling has particular application in compliance testing. Along similar lines, because variables sampling focuses on monetary amounts, it has particular application in tests of details.

Although we can recognise these two basic methods of sampling, as may be seen from Figure 12.1, there are variations of both attributes and variables sampling. We discuss these variations when we examine examples of statistical sampling in section 12.7.

12.5 DESIGNING AND SELECTING SAMPLES

12.5.1 Designing a sample

When designing a sample the auditor must consider:

- the audit objective(s) to be met by testing a sample of items,
- the frame which represents the population, and
- the characteristic of interest to be examined.

As we have observed in previous chapters, the audit objective largely determines the audit procedure(s) to be applied. In applying the audit procedure(s),

Figure 12.1:   Relationship between sampling methods

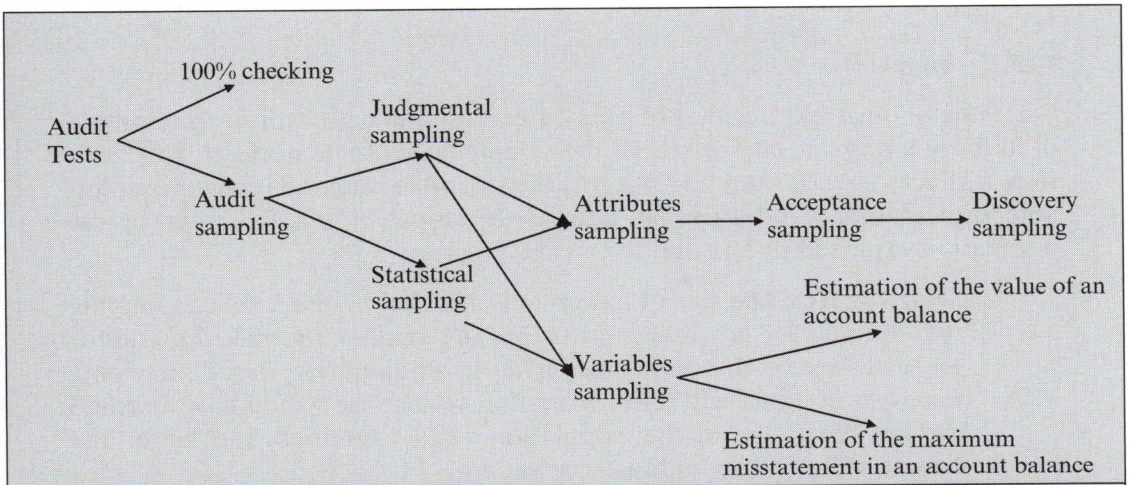

Note: Probability proportional to size (PPS), or monetary unit, sampling is a hybrid of attributes and variables sampling. It is variables sampling in the sense that it measures monetary amounts but attributes sampling techniques are employed to determine sample size and evaluate the sample results.

Source: Adapted from McRae (1971, p. 376)

the auditor needs to define what constitutes an error and this, in turn, affects the population from which the sample is to be drawn. For example, if the objective of a compliance test relating to credit sales is to ascertain whether credit sales are properly authorised, and the client's control procedures require the credit manager to initial sales invoices to signify approval of the sales, an appropriate audit procedure is to inspect a sample of duplicates of sales invoices for the credit manager's initials. In this case:

- the population comprises the credit manager's initials,
- the frame is the duplicates of all sales invoices issued during the accounting period, and
- the characteristic of interest is the presence or absence of the credit manager's initials (each absence constitutes an error or deviation).

However, if the objective of a test of details is to ascertain whether sales invoices have been properly extended (price per item multiplied by the quantity sold) and totalled, an appropriate audit test is to recalculate the extensions and additions on a sample of duplicates of sales invoices. In this case:

- the population comprises the extensions and totals shown on duplicates of sales invoices,
- the frame is, once again, the duplicates of all sales invoices issued during the accounting period, and

- the characteristic of interest is the accuracy of the extensions and totals shown on the invoices (an error is an arithmetic error on any invoice).

12.5.2 Sample size

Once the auditor has decided to apply a certain audit procedure to a sample of items in a population, the size of the sample needs to be decided. This decision is affected by: (i) sampling risk, (ii) the tolerable rate of deviation or tolerable misstatement and (iii) the rate of deviation or misstatement in the population expected by the auditor.[4]

(i) *Sampling risk*: The size of a sample is affected by the level of sampling risk the auditor is willing to accept. The smaller the risk the auditor wishes to accept that a conclusion about a population, based on testing a sample of items, will differ from that which s/he would have reached had all the items in the population been examined, the larger the sample will need to be (and vice versa).

(ii) *Tolerable error*: Sample size is also affected by the maximum rate of deviation or misstatement (for a test of controls or a test of details, respectively) in the population the auditor is willing to accept (or tolerate), while still concluding the audit objective has been reached.[5] The smaller the tolerable error, the larger the sample the auditor needs to select.

(iii) *Expected rate of deviation or misstatement in the population*: The size of samples is also affected by the rate of deviation or misstatement the auditor expects to find in the population. If deviations or misstatements are expected, a larger sample of items will need to be examined to enable the auditor to conclude that the actual rate of deviation or misstatement in the population does not exceed tolerable error. When no deviations or misstatements (as applicable) are expected in the population, sample sizes may be smaller.

As we demonstrate in section 12.7, when statistical sampling is used, sampling risk, tolerable error, and the expected rate of deviation or misstatement in the population are incorporated in the sampling method. However, when judgmental sampling is used, the auditor needs to consider the factors outlined above when determining sample size.

---

[4] These and other factors influencing sample size for tests of controls and tests of details are explained in detail in ISA 530, Appendix 2 and 3, respectively.

[5] For tests of details, as noted in Chapter 9, section 9.3.1, tolerable error is the amount of error in a class of transactions, account balance or disclosure that, in the auditor's judgment, is material to users of the audited financial statements.

12.5.3 Sample selection

Once the auditor has determined the size of the sample, the method of selecting the sampling units needs to be decided. ISA 530 specifies:

> The auditor shall select items for the sample in such a way that each sampling unit in the population has a chance of selection. . . . With statistical sampling, sample items are selected in a way that each sampling unit has a known probability of being selected. With non-statistical sampling, judgment is used to select the sample items. Because the purpose of sampling is to provide a reasonable basis for the auditor to draw conclusions about the population from which the sample is selected, it is important that the auditor selects a representative sample so that bias is avoided, by choosing sample items which have characteristics typical of the population. (paras 8, A12)

There are many methods of selecting audit samples but those used most commonly fall into two groups. These are shown in Figure 12.2 and discussed below.

Figure 12.2: Methods of selecting audit samples

Broad groups of sample selection methods	Sub-groups of methods of sample selection
(a) Random selection	• Unrestricted random selection • Systematic sampling - Cluster sampling (a variation of systematic sampling) • Selection with probability proportional to size
(b) Non-random selection	• Haphazard selection • Judgmental selection

(a) *Random selection*

The key feature of random sample selection is that each item in the population has an equal chance of selection. Whilst retaining this characteristic, three variations of random selection may be recognised, namely:
  (i)   unrestricted random selection;
  (ii) systematic selection;
  (iii) selection with probability proportional to size.

(i)   *Unrestricted random selection*

For this method of selection, the population is regarded as comprising homogeneous (but sequentially numbered) items, and computer generated random numbers or random number tables are used to identify the sampling units to be selected.

(ii) *Systematic selection*

For systematic selection, a sampling interval is first determined by dividing the population to be tested by the required sample size. For example, if the population comprises 12,625 sales invoices and the sample size is 125, the selection interval is: 12,625/125 = 101.

A number between 0 and 101 is selected at random by the auditor or (preferably, if the sample is to be truly random) by means of a computer generated random number or a random number table, and this gives the starting point. Every 101st item in the population is then selected, beginning with that point.

Systematic selection is simple to use, and is generally quicker, and therefore less costly, than unrestricted random selection. However, it has the disadvantage that it can introduce bias into the sample if the characteristic of interest is not randomly distributed through the population. The use of systematic selection to select a sample of duplicates of sales invoices to test for authorisation of credit sales will not generally cause a problem; however, if every 40th person on the payroll is fictitious, systematic selection using a sampling interval of 40 could result in a sample consisting entirely of fictitious employees. Alternatively, by selecting a different starting point and using a sampling interval of 40, the sample may fail to include any of the fictitious employees (a situation which is potentially more serious for the auditor).

Cluster selection: As indicated in Figure 12.2, cluster selection is a variant of systematic selection. It involves selecting clusters of items in the population (or groups of contiguous items or records) rather than individual items. For example, if a sample of 150 units is required, 30 clusters of five units may be selected. If the first unit in each cluster is selected using a computer generated random number or a random number table, then the sample is regarded as a random sample.

This method of selection provides a straightforward and relatively quick means of selecting a sample. However, in some circumstances it may be less efficient than selecting samples of individually selected items as it may result in a larger sample size. For example, if a sample of duplicates of sales invoices is to be checked for the credit manager's initials, a sample of 125 units selected individually may provide good coverage of invoices issued during the accounting period. However, 25 clusters of five units may not give adequate coverage of invoices issued during the accounting period and the number of clusters may need to be increased. In other cases, cluster selection may be particularly appropriate, for example, when testing for completeness of records. If the auditor wishes to check that all sales invoices, purchase orders, inventory recording sheets, and similar documents which are numbered sequentially are accounted for, it may be more effective to check the number sequence of 125 documents in 25 clusters of five than to check 125 documents selected separately.

(iii)   Selection with probability proportional to size (PPS selection)

When PPS selection is used, each individual monetary unit (that is, each individual £1) in a population is regarded as a separate unit within the population and each has an equal chance of selection. This method may be explained by reference to the following simple example.

Example: Assume that the accounts receivable account balance in an auditee's financial statements comprises ten individual accounts receivable accounts and that the balances of these accounts at the end of the accounting period are as presented in Figure 12.3. Also assume that a sample of six units is required for testing.

Figure 12.3:   PPS selection: population of pounds in the accounts receivable account balance

Account	Recorded balance	Cumulative total (pounds units)	Location of sample units
	£	£	
1	276	276	√
2	1,194	1,470	√
3	683	2,153	√
4	25	2,178	
5	1,221	3,399	√
6	94	3,493	
7	76	3,569	
8	684	4,253	√ √
9	135	4,388	
10	302	4,690	

The accounts are recorded in the order in which they appear in the accounts receivable subsidiary ledger and the cumulative pounds (£s) in the accounts are calculated (see Figure 12.3, column 3). These cumulative pounds constitute a population of 4,690 individual pounds. Pounds 1 to 276 are contained in account 1, pounds 277 to 1,470 in account 2, and so on. Unrestricted random sampling or systematic sampling is used to select the required number of sampling units, that is, individual identified pounds.

With reference to Figure 12.3, assume that unrestricted random sampling generated the random numbers: 2,997; 3,595; 3,762; 2,003; 0023; 0444. These random numbers correspond to individual pounds in the cumulative total and result in accounts 5, 8, 8, 3, 1 and 2 being selected for examination. Account 8 is a 'double hit' but is, of course, only examined once.

The advantage of PPS selection is that larger account balances have a greater chance of selection and it is these balances which are more likely to contain a misstatement which is material – in particular, a material overstatement.[6] However, this method of selection also has the disadvantage that small balances have a low probability of being included in the sample, yet a small balance may be small because it is significantly understated; additionally, a series of errors in small balances may together constitute a material misstatement. These concerns may be overcome by stratifying the population and treating balances which are smaller than a specified limit as a separate population. A sample may then be selected from this (sub)population of small balances using, for example, unrestricted random sampling.

Another problem of PPS selection is the inability to include negative balances, for example, accounts receivable accounts with credit balances. A possible approach to this difficulty is to treat negative balances as if they were positive and to include them in the cumulative total on that basis.

(b) Non-random selection[7]

As shown in Figure 12.2, there are two main methods of non-random sample selection, namely:
  (i) haphazard selection;
  (ii) judgmental selection.

(i) Haphazard selection

When using haphazard selection, the auditor attempts to replicate random sample selection by selecting items from the population haphazardly, without regard to the size, source, date or any other distinguishing feature of the items constituting the population.

This method of sample selection is simple and quick but has the disadvantage that unintended bias may be introduced into the sample. Certain items in the population tend to have a greater chance of selection than others; for example, the auditor may have a propensity to select (or avoid) items at the top, bottom or middle of a page; known (or unknown) persons; names which attract attention for some reason, and so on.

(ii) Judgmental sample selection

When using judgmental selection, the auditor deliberately tries to select a sample which is representative of the population and/or includes those items which require close attention (i.e., items of significant risk).[8]

---

[6] It should be recalled from Chapter 11, section 11.4.4, that auditees may have an incentive to overstate assets (including accounts receivable) and revenue. Because PPS sample selection increases the likelihood of larger (and possibly overstated) accounts being selected, PPS sampling is particularly useful for detecting overstatements in asset and revenue accounts.

[7] It should be remembered that non-random sample selection is not appropriate when using statistical sampling methods.

[8] Significant risks are explained in Chapter 8, section 8.5.1.

When attempting to select a representative sample, the auditor will be concerned to include, for example:
- a selection of items representing transactions occurring in each month (or even in each week) of the accounting period, and for each employee who has been involved in handling the transactionsthe period;
- a selection of account balances or transactions which are representative of those in the population. Thus, the proportion of large and small account balances included in the sample will reflect the proportion of these balances in the population.

When the auditor wishes to select a sample which includes items of significant risk, care will be taken to include:
- a high proportion of large transactions or account balances (which may be overstated and/or contain one or more misstatement(s) that is/are material);
- items representative of period(s) when internal control procedures may have been functioning less effectively than normal; for example, when the key control person (such as the credit manager, or supervisor responsible for reviewing bank reconciliations and journal entries) was on holiday or absent through illness.

The major advantage of judgmental sample selection is that it enables the auditor to tailor the sample to the unique circumstances of the client. However, it also has the significant disadvantage (which it shares with haphazard sampling) that, should the sample be challenged (for example, in a court of law), it may be more difficult to defend than random sample selection.

12.5.4 Documentation of sample selection

Before leaving the subject of sample selection, we should note that all aspects of selecting a sample should be clearly and fully documented in the audit working papers. The documentation should include details of:
- the size of the sample selected – and how this was determined;
- the method of sample selection.

Additionally, when random sampling is used, a note should be made of the source of the random numbers (for example, the computer program or random number table used), and when a population is stratified, the basis of, and rationale for, the stratification should be noted. Similarly, when judgmental sample selection is used, factors the auditor took into consideration when exercising his/her judgment should be recorded.

12.6 JUDGMENTAL SAMPLING

As we note in section 12.2, sampling involves applying an audit procedure (a compliance test or test of details) to a sample of items selected from a population and extrapolating the results obtained from the sample to the population as a whole. When judgmental sampling is adopted, the sampling process rests on the exercise of the auditor's judgment. The steps in the process are as follows:

(i)   the sample size is determined judgmentally;

(ii) the sampling units are selected using a random or non-random selection method;

(iii) the sample is examined for the characteristic being tested; that is, compliance with a specific internal control procedure, or the validity, completeness and/or accuracy of a monetary amount in a class of transactions or account balance;

(iv) the sample results are extrapolated to the population and, based on these results, the population is accepted – or rejected – as 'satisfactory'; that is, exercising judgment, the auditor concludes that the control being tested has (or has not) operated effectively throughout the reporting period, or the class of transactions or account balance is (or is not) free of material misstatement (or, more correctly, errors in the population do not exceed the auditor's tolerable rate of deviation or tolerable misstatement).

As will be seen in the next section, when statistical sampling is used, steps (i) and (iv) above are determined by applying probability theory, and step (ii) must be performed using random selection methods.

12.7   STATISTICAL SAMPLING OF ATTRIBUTES AND VARIABLES, AND PPS SAMPLING

12.7.1   Attributes sampling

In section 12.4 we observed that attributes sampling is concerned with ascertaining whether a characteristic of interest is present or absent and that it has particular application in compliance testing. As shown in Figure 12.1, two variations of attributes sampling are acceptance sampling and discovery sampling. We explain each of these below in the context of statistical sampling.

• *Acceptance sampling*: As a pre-requisite to using statistical methods for acceptance sampling, the auditor needs to specify:

1. the tolerable rate of deviation in the population (i.e., the rate of deviation in the population the auditor will accept whilst still concluding the control activity is effective);

2. the expected rate of deviation in the population (i.e., the rate of deviation the auditor expects to exist in the population, given his/her

assessment of inherent audit risk and preliminary evaluation of the client's internal control system); and

3. the desired level of sampling risk (i.e., the level of risk the auditor is prepared to accept that the conclusion reached about the deviation rate in the population, based on the results of examining a sample of items, is not valid). Alternatively stated, the level of confidence the auditor wishes to attain that the conclusion reached about the deviation rate in the population, based on the sample results, is valid.

As shown in the detailed example of attributes sampling provided below, using this information, the auditor can use statistical sampling tables to determine the appropriate size of the sample of items to be tested.

The sample is then selected using a random selection method and examined for the characteristic being tested. Based on the presence (or more usually the absence) of the characteristic in the sample, statistical sampling tables are used to determine the estimated maximum rate of deviation in the population. This sampling method gives rise to a statement such as: "There is a five per cent risk that the rate of sales invoices not carrying the credit manager's initials exceeds two per cent". (Alternatively stated: "I am 95 per cent confident that the proportion of sales invoices without the credit manager's initials does not exceed two per cent".)

The estimated maximum rate of deviation in the population is compared with the tolerable rate of deviation, and if the former does not exceed the latter, the auditor will probably accept the population as reliable (that is, the auditor will conclude that the internal control procedure is effective and can be relied upon).

- *Discovery sampling*: This is a subset of acceptance sampling where the expected rate of deviation in the population is set at zero. This gives the smallest sample size possible under acceptance sampling but, if a single deviation is found in the sample of items examined, then the tolerable rate of deviation will be exceeded and the population cannot be accepted (or the relevant internal control procedure cannot be relied upon) without further investigation.

As the discovery of a single deviation in a sample of items examined results in the population not being accepted by the auditor (at least, not without further investigation), discovery sampling reduces the number of populations which are accepted on the basis of the sample examined. However, discovery sampling is useful to the auditor as it involves small samples, and deviations which are discovered in the sample examined provide guidance as to the nature and cause of deviations in the population: discovery sampling is thus useful in directing the auditor's attention to areas which require more detailed investigation.

12.7.2 Illustration of attributes sampling

To provide an overview of attributes sampling, the procedure for acceptance sampling is presented in Figure 12.4. For purposes of illustration, it is assumed that the auditee has 20,000 sales invoices and that the auditor wishes to establish whether or not the control procedure for authorising credit sales is effective.

Figure 12.4: Steps involved in acceptance sampling

Steps in acceptance sampling	Illustration
1. Define the objective of the audit procedure.	To ascertain whether credit sales are properly authorised.
2. Define the attribute of interest.	Initials of the credit manager on duplicates of sales invoices signalling authorisation of credit sales.
3. Define the population (or, more pertinently, the frame).	Sales invoices issued during the accounting period. These are numbered from 24,494 to 44,494.
4. Specify the tolerable rate of deviation in the population.	4% tolerable rate of deviation. The auditor will tolerate up to 4% of the duplicates of sales invoices not showing the credit manager's initials and still conclude the control has operated effectively.
5. Specify the desired level of sampling risk (alternatively, the desired level of confidence).	A 5% sampling risk is required. The auditor is prepared to accept a 5% risk that the deviation rate in the population may, in fact, exceed the tolerable rate of 4% and thus, based on the sample, may incorrectly conclude that the control procedure is effective. (This is equivalent to the auditor wishing to be 95% confident that if, based on the results of the sample, s/he concludes the rate of deviation in the population does not exceed 4%, this conclusion is valid).
6. Estimate the rate of deviation in the population. (This is the auditor's estimate of the deviation rate based on a preliminary evaluation of the client's compliance with control procedures.)	The auditor estimates that 1% of duplicates of sales invoices in the population do not contain the credit manager's initials.
7. Use the relevant table to determine the required sample size.	See Figure 12.5 for the table entitled *Sample size for attributes sampling*. [A different table exists for each desired level of sampling risk. The lower the level of sampling risk (or the higher the desired level of confidence), other things being held constant, the larger the sample size.]

Figure 12.4: *Continued*

Steps in acceptance sampling	Illustration
8. Using the table and the parameters established by judgment noted above, ascertain the sample size.	The tolerable rate of deviation is 4% (see step 4 above). This identifies the relevant column in the table. The estimated population deviation rate is 1% (see step 6 above). This identifies the relevant row in the table. The required sample size is located at the intercept of the relevant column and row. It is seen to be 156.
9. Randomly select a sample of the required size.	Using computer generated random numbers, identify and select a sample of 156 duplicates of sales invoices.
10. Perform the relevant audit procedure and record deviations.	Inspect the 156 duplicates of sales invoices and record all those which do not show the credit manager's initials. Assume one such sales invoice is found.
11. Generalise from the sample to the population using the relevant table for evaluating attributes sampling results.	See Figure 12.6 for the table entitled *Evaluating attributes sampling results*. (A different table exists for each desired level of sampling risk/desired level of confidence.) The actual number of deviations found identifies the relevant column in the table. (In our example, one deviation is assumed: see step 10.) The sample size identifies the relevant row in the table. (In our example 150; this is the closest to 156: see step 8.) From the table it is seen that (given our assumptions) the maximum rate of deviation in the population (% of sales invoices without the sales manager's initials) is 3.1%. (This is not the most likely deviation rate but the 'worst case', or upper limit, of the deviation rate.)
12. Analyse detected deviations to ascertain whether they result from 'one-off' situations or are indicative of a more widespread problem, for example, the control procedure failing to function effectively when the key control person is absent.	Investigate the cause of the deviation detected. Assume this is found to be an isolated incident of control failure. [For example, two sales invoices were presented to the credit manager at one time for approval. Both invoices were reviewed but only one was initialled.]
13 Apply the decision rule for acceptance sampling. If the estimated maximum rate of deviation in the population (as shown in the sample results evaluation table) exceeds the tolerable rate of deviation, conclude that the control procedure may not be effective. If the estimated maximum rate of deviation in the population is less than the tolerable rate, subject to analysis of detected deviations (see step 12), conclude the control procedure is effective and can be relied upon.	The projected maximum rate of deviation in the population is 3.1%. This is less than the 4% tolerable rate of deviation specified as acceptable by the auditor (see step 4). Additionally, the deviation detected has been found to be an isolated incident of control failure (see step 12). As a consequence of these findings, the auditor concludes that the control procedure is effective and can be relied upon.

Figure 12.5:   Sample size for attributes sampling

5% Sampling Risk (95% Confidence Level)											
Expected Population Deviation Rate (in percentage)	Tolerable Deviation Rate (in percentage)										
	2	3	4	5	6	7	8	9	10	11	12
0.00	149	99	74	59	49	42	36	32	29	19	14
0.25	236	157	117	93	78	66	58	51	46	30	22
0.50	*	157	117	93	78	66	58	51	46	30	22
0.75	*	208	117	93	78	66	58	51	46	30	22
1.00	*	*	156	93	78	66	58	51	46	30	22
1.25	*	*	156	124	78	66	58	51	46	30	22
1.50	*	*	192	124	103	66	58	51	46	30	22
1.75	*	*	227	153	103	88	77	51	46	30	22
2.00	*	*	*	181	127	88	77	68	46	30	22
2.25	*	*	*	208	127	88	77	68	61	30	22
2.50	*	*	*	*	150	109	77	68	61	30	22
2.75	*	*	*	*	173	109	95	68	61	30	22
3.00	*	*	*	*	195	129	95	84	61	30	22
3.25	*	*	*	*	*	148	112	84	61	30	22
3.50	*	*	*	*	*	167	112	84	76	40	22
3.75	*	*	*	*	*	185	129	100	76	40	22
4.00	*	*	*	*	*	*	146	100	89	40	22
5.00	*	*	*	*	*	*	*	158	116	40	30
6.00	*	*	*	*	*	*	*	*	179	50	30
7.00	*	*	*	*	*	*	*	*	*	68	37

Figure 12.6:   Evaluating attributes sampling results

95% Confidence Level (5% sampling risk)											
Sample Size	Actual Number of Deviations Found										
	0	1	2	3	4	5	6	7	8	9	10
25	11.3	17.6	*	*	*	*	*	*	*	*	*
30	9.5	14.9	19.5	*	*	*	*	*	*	*	*
35	8.2	12.9	16.9	*	*	*	*	*	*	*	*
40	7.2	11.3	14.9	18.3	*	*	*	*	*	*	*
45	6.4	10.1	13.3	16.3	19.2	*	*	*	*	*	*
50	5.8	9.1	12.1	14.8	17.4	19.9	*	*	*	*	*
55	5.3	8.3	11.0	13.5	15.9	18.1	*	*	*	*	*
60	4.9	7.7	10.1	12.4	14.6	16.7	18.8	*	*	*	*
65	4.5	7.1	9.4	11.5	13.5	15.5	17.4	19.3	*	*	*
70	4.2	6.6	8.7	10.7	12.6	14.4	16.2	18.0	19.7	*	*
75	3.9	6.2	8.2	10.0	11.8	13.5	15.2	16.9	18.4	20.0	*
80	3.7	5.8	7.7	9.4	11.1	12.7	14.3	15.8	17.3	18.8	*
90	3.3	5.2	6.8	8.4	9.9	11.3	12.7	14.1	15.5	16.8	18.1
100	3.0	4.6	6.2	7.6	8.9	10.2	11.5	12.7	14.0	15.2	16.4
125	2.4	3.7	4.9	6.1	7.2	8.2	9.3	10.3	11.3	12.2	13.2
150	2.0	3.1	4.1	5.1	6.0	6.9	7.7	8.6	9.4	10.2	11.0
200	1.5	2.3	3.1	3.8	4.5	5.2	5.8	6.5	7.1	7.7	8.3

12.7.3 Variables sampling

As noted in section 12.4, variables sampling is concerned with monetary values. It includes estimation sampling which may take the form of estimating an account balance or estimating the maximum misstatement in an account balance (see Figure 12.1).

- *Estimating an account balance*: In this form of variables sampling, the auditor selects a sample of items (a sample of items from a class of transactions or components of an account balance, such as items of inventory) and, based on this sample, estimates the range of values (between upper and lower limits) within which the financial statement account balance should fall. This form of estimation sampling might give rise to a statement such as: "From the items of inventory examined, there is a five per cent risk that the value of the inventory account balance exceeds £765,000 or is less than £683,000". (Alternatively stated: "I am 95 per cent confident that the value of the inventory account balance lies between an upper limit of £765,000 and a lower limit of £683,000".)

- *Estimating the maximum error in an account balance*: In this case, rather than estimating the value of an account balance, the auditor estimates the maximum amount of error which may exist in the balance. It might give rise to a statement such as: "From the items of inventory examined, there is a five per cent risk that the amount of error in the inventory account balance is greater than £50,000". (Alternatively stated: "I am 95 per cent confident that the amount of error in the inventory account balance does not exceed £50,000".)

Although variables sampling is a useful auditing technique, for many populations the application of variables sampling results in a sample size which is impractically large. As a result, PPS (or monetary unit) sampling is often preferred to variables sampling.

12.7.4 Probability proportional to size (PPS) or monetary unit sampling

As noted in Figure 12.3, PPS (or monetary unit) sampling is a hybrid of variables and attributes sampling. It is a technique which is based on monetary values in a population and therefore possesses elements of variables sampling, but attributes sampling techniques are employed in determining the sample size and evaluating the sample results.

To provide an overview of PPS sampling, the steps in the process are explained in Figure 12.7. For purposes of illustration, it is assumed that the value of the accounts receivable balance in the auditee's pre-audited financial statements is £3,198,426. The auditor wishes to confirm that this balance is not materially misstated.

Figure 12.7: Steps involved in PPS (monetary unit) sampling

Steps involved in PPS sampling	Illustration
1. Define the objective of the audit procedure.	To reach a conclusion as to whether the accounts receivable balance of £3,198,426 is materially misstated.
2. Define the population.	3,198,426 individual £1 monetary units. (Each pound in the population is treated as equivalent to a physical unit in attributes sampling.)
3. Specify the tolerable deviation rate in the population.	The auditor has a tolerable deviation rate of 4%, i.e., an upper and lower materiality limit of £128,000 (4% of £3,198,426). *Prima facie*, the auditor will accept the accounts receivable balance is not materially misstated if it lies between £3,070,426 and £3,326,426.
4. Specify the desired level of sampling risk (or, alternatively, the desired level of confidence).	The auditor is willing to accept a sampling risk of 5% (or wishes to attain a confidence level of 95%).
5. Estimate the expected deviation rate in the population. This is the auditor's estimation of the deviation rate in pounds in the population (based on prior audit work). It is equivalent to the expected population deviation rate in attributes sampling.	The expected deviation rate in the population is 1%; i.e., the auditor expects the population to contain a misstatement of £32,000 (1% of £3,198,426) above or below the stated balance £3,198,426 (that the accounts receivable balance lies between £3,166,426 and £3,230,426).
6. Use the relevant table to determine the required sample size.	See Figure 12.5 for the table entitled *Sample size for attributes sampling*.
7. Using the table and the parameters noted above, ascertain the sample size.	The tolerable deviation rate is 4% (see step 3 above). This identifies the relevant column in the table. The estimated population deviation rate is 1% (see step 5 above). This identifies the relevant row in the table. The required sample size is located at the intercept of the relevant column and row. It is seen to be 156.
8. Randomly select a sample of the required size.	Using PPS selection, select a sample of 156 pounds and identify the individual accounts receivable account balances in which they are contained (see section 12.5.3).
9. Perform the relevant audit procedure and record deviations.	Confirm the accounts receivable balances containing the 156 sample pounds using confirmations or alternative procedures in the normal way (see Chapter 11, section 11.8). Assume that one accounts receivable account balance shown in the auditee's records as £20,000 should be £10,000 and that no other errors are found.
10. Generalise from the sample to the population using the relevant table for evaluating attributes sampling results.	See Figure 12.6 for the table entitled *Evaluating attributes sampling results*.

Figure 12.7: *Continued*

Steps involved in PPS sampling	Illustration
	The actual number of deviations found identifies the relevant column in the table. (In our example, one deviation is assumed. Although the accounts receivable balance of £20,000 is examined, only one of these 20,000 pounds was included in the sample. This one pound is in error) (see step 9).
	The sample size identifies the relevant row in the table. (In our example 150; this is the closest to 156: see step 7). From the table it is seen that (given our assumptions) the estimated maximum rate of deviation in the population (percentage of pounds misstated) is 3.1% (that is £99,151; this means the actual balance of accounts receivable is estimated to lie between £3,099,275 and £3,297,577).
11. Analyse detected deviations to ascertain whether they result from 'one-off' situations or are indicative of a more widespread problem, for example, a control failing to function properly when the key control person is absent.	Investigate the cause of the deviation detected. Assume it is found to be an isolated incident of control failure. (For example, two sales invoices of £10,000 were paid but only one was recorded in the cash receipts journal (and, thus, in the accounts receivable subsidiary ledger and the accounts receivable control account in the general ledger.)
12. Apply the decision rule for acceptance sampling. If the estimated maximum deviation rate in the population (as shown in the sample results evaluation table) exceeds the tolerable deviation rate, conclude that the account may be materially misstated. If the estimated maximum deviation rate in the population is less than the tolerable deviation rate, subject to analysis of the detected errors (see step 11), conclude the account is not materially misstated.	The estimated maximum deviation rate in the population of 3.1% is less than the 4% tolerable deviation rate specified as acceptable by the auditor (see step 3). Additionally, the deviation detected has been found to be an isolated incident of control failure (see step 11). As a consequence of these findings, the auditor concludes that the accounts receivable balance of £3,198,426 is not materially misstated.

Two points need to be noted in respect of this illustration, namely:

1. In section 12.5.3 we observe that PPS selection gives small balances a low probability of inclusion in the sample of items selected. In order to investigate the possibility of small balances being significantly understated, it might be necessary to supplement the sample of 156 account balances with a selection of small account balances.

2. The deviation found in the illustration was an accounts receivable balance shown in the auditee's records as £20,000 instead of £10,000. This was treated as one deviation, being one accounts receivable pound

included in the sample which was in error (step 10). Thus, to ascertain the estimated maximum deviation rate in the population, the relevant column in Figure 12.6 is that for the one deviation actually found. In reality the accounts receivable balance is not entirely misstated; it is misstated by 50 per cent since the £20,000 recorded should not be zero but £10,000. This is known as a partial error. For a misstatement of 50 per cent (or a misstatement of 0.5) it is possible to interpolate between the columns in Figure 12.6 for zero errors and for one error, giving an estimated maximum deviation rate in the population of 2.55 per cent [that is, half way between the estimated deviation rate for zero errors (2 per cent) and for one deviation (3.1 per cent).] Such a refinement in respect of partial errors can reduce the projected maximum population error rate (from 3.1 per cent to 2.55 per cent in our example). This can affect the auditor's conclusion with respect to the acceptability of the population.

12.8 FOLLOWING UP SAMPLE RESULTS

Irrespective of whether judgmental or statistical sampling techniques are used, the auditor does not slavishly follow the sampling method's accept/reject rule. For example, if the estimated maximum deviation rate in the population in acceptance sampling is less than the auditor's tolerable deviation rate, this does not mean the auditor will automatically accept the control activity as functioning effectively throughout the reporting period. Similarly, if the estimated value of an account balance falls within the auditor's specified range of tolerable misstatement, this does not automatically result in the conclusion that it is fairly stated. Instead, the auditor remains alert to the possibility that the control activity under investigation may not have functioned effectively throughout the reporting period, or the account balance being examined may be materially misstated. As indicated in Figures 12.4 and 12.7, *all* deviations detected during the examination of sampling units must be analysed to ascertain their cause, irrespective of whether the auditor's tolerable deviation rate is, or is not, exceeded.

However, assuming that nothing has come to the auditor's attention which results in a contrary conclusion, if the examination of a sample of items produces results which accord with the sampling method's 'accept' rule, the auditor will generally conclude that the internal control activity on which s/he plans to rely to prevent material misstatements from occurring in the financial statements is functioning effectively, or that the account balance examined is not materially misstated. Nevertheless, the auditor remains aware of his/her exposure to sampling risk and continues to watch for evidence which suggests that the conclusion reached about the internal control activity or account balance concerned may be invalid.

Where the results of an examination of a sample of items indicate that an internal control activity has not been operating effectively, or that an account balance may be materially misstated, this finding must be followed up by alternative auditing procedures. In the case of a control activity which is found not to be operating effectively, other control activities might be found and tested to see if reliance can be placed on them to detect or prevent the relevant (potential) misstatement(s), or substantive tests may be extended. If examination of the sample of items indicates that an account balance might be materially misstated, alternative auditing procedures must be employed to ascertain whether this is, or is not, the case.

12.9 COMPUTER ASSISTED AUDIT TECHNIQUES

12.9.1 Meaning and types of Computer Assisted Audit Techniques (CAATs)

Like audit sampling, CAATs are audit techniques that apply to both compliance and substantive procedures. In brief, they are audit procedures which use computer facilities to investigate the reliability (or otherwise) of the client's accounting system and the information it generates. The two best known CAATs are:
  (i) test data (or test decks or test packs), and
  (ii) audit software.

(i) Test data

The test data technique is principally designed to test the effectiveness of internal controls which are incorporated in the client's computer programs. Thus, it is essentially a compliance procedure.

The technique involves inputting data (such as a sample of transactions) into, and having the data processed by, the client's accounting system, and comparing the output with pre-determined results. The data may be used to test the effectiveness of general IT controls[9] such as online passwords which are designed to restrict access to specified data and programs to authorised personnel. Alternatively, the data may comprise a set of transactions which represent all of the types of transactions normally processed by the client's programs, and incorporating a variety of errors. These transactions (and errors) are designed to ascertain whether application controls are operating effectively;

---

[9] General IT controls and application controls are discussed in Chapter 10, section 10.3.2.

for example, whether exception reports are generated in appropriate cases, and whether transaction dates and amounts lying outside specified parameters are rejected.

Use of the test data technique is generally straightforward and does not require the auditor to possess a sophisticated knowledge of computer processes. Further, the tests are usually fairly quick to perform and generally cause little or no disruption to the client's normal processing schedules. However, a major disadvantage is that the test data are usually processed separately from the normal processing of the client's transactions. Although the auditor can establish whether the controls are, or are not, operating effectively at the time the audit procedure is performed, s/he does not know whether the controls operate effectively at other times.

In order to overcome this disadvantage, the test data technique can be extended into an integrated test facility (ITF). This involves establishing a dummy department, employee, or other unit appropriate for audit testing. Transactions affecting the dummy unit are interspersed among, and processed with, the client's ordinary transactions. The resultant output, relating to the dummy unit, is compared with pre-determined results.

When the ITF technique is used, the auditor must be alert to the danger of contaminating the client's files and care must be taken to reverse out all of the audit test transactions.

(ii) Audit software

In contrast to the test data technique, which requires the auditor to input test data to be processed by the client's computer programs, the audit software technique involves the auditor using audit software to process the client's accounting data. Audit software is of three main types. These are as follows:

(a) *Utility programs and existing programs used by the entity*: In this case, general (non-audit specific) application programs, or enquiry facilities available within a software package, are used to perform common data processing functions such as sorting, retrieving and printing computer files. These programs may assist the auditor perform a variety of audit procedures but they are not specifically designed for audit purposes and, in general, their audit application is limited. They are used principally to extend or to speed up procedures which would otherwise be performed manually (for example, accessing and printing all or some of the accounts receivable balances or items comprising the inventory account balance).

(b) *General audit software*: This software consists of generally available computer packages which have been specially designed to perform a variety of functions for audit purposes. These include reading computer files, selecting and retrieving desired information and/or samples, performing various calculations, making comparisons and printing required reports.

(c) *Specialised audit software*: This software comprises specially developed programs which are designed to perform audit tests in specific circumstances – usually those pertaining to a particular entity or, possibly, to an industry. These programs may be prepared by the auditor's firm, an outside programmer engaged by the auditor (or audit firm), or (less desirably because of independence considerations) by the entity's computer (IT) personnel.

Although the development of specialised audit software may be appropriate for certain clients (for example, those in specialised industries such as banking or mining), and may be a desired ideal in other cases, developing such software is extremely expensive and is often beyond the expertise of auditors and their firms. Nevertheless, whenever specialised audit software is to be developed for use in certain audits, it is essential that the auditor is actively involved in designing and testing the program(s). This is necessary to ensure that the auditor fully understands the operation (and limitations) of the software and also to ensure that it meets the requirements of the audit.

During recent years, the availability of general audit software has increased significantly and these packages are now used extensively to assist auditors perform a wide range of audit procedures and most audit firms also develop, or use commercially available, general audit software for the preparation (and amendment) of their audit plans.

In the current auditing environment, audit software is an invaluable audit tool as computers are used to process accounting data in virtually all audit clients. However, its use may be resisted by an auditee's management or IT personnel because running additional programs for audit purposes may interrupt and cause delays to the normal processing of the client's transactions. Be that as it may, where an entity's accounting system involves extensive use of computer processing (as is normally the case), manual audit procedures may well be inappropriate and application of audit software may be the only means by which an effective audit can be conducted. In such circumstances, if the auditee restricts the use of audit software, this could amount to a limitation on the scope of the audit and give rise to a modified audit report.[10]

---

[10] Limitation on the scope of an audit, and its impact on the audit report, is discussed in Chapter 14, section 14.5.2.

12.9.2   Use and control of CAATs

From the above discussion, it is evident that CAATs may be used to assist the auditor with a variety of audit procedures. They may, for example, assist the auditor perform:

- compliance tests of general IT controls – for example, to analyse processing or access logs, or to review the effectiveness of procedures to limit access to the library (or other storage facility);
- compliance tests of application controls – for example, using test data to test the effectiveness of programmed controls such as the rejection of data outside specified parameters;
- analytical procedures – for example, using audit software to calculate specified financial statement ratios and to identify unusual fluctuations or items;
- detailed tests of transactions and balances – for example, using audit software to test all (or a sample of) transactions in a computer file, or to perform statistical sampling routines to estimate account balances or the maximum misstatement in account balances or classes of transactions.

CAATs are generally user-friendly so auditors do not require specialised computer knowledge in order to apply them. Although this is an advantage to many auditors, it also carries the danger that auditors may be lulled into a false sense of security. This danger is particularly high when, in order to use CAATs, auditors require co-operation from client IT personnel (who have an extensive and detailed knowledge of the client's system). The same applies where auditors use their clients' software enquiry facilities. Such a facility could, for example, be programmed by client personnel not to reveal certain records when accessed by means of the auditor's password.

Before using test data or audit software, the auditor must ensure that s/he understands the process by which the computer performs the relevant audit procedures and the limitations of, or pitfalls related to, the process. If the auditor has limited computer knowledge, s/he should obtain assistance from, or have ready access to, specialists within the audit firm who have computer expertise, or suitable experts from outside the firm. The auditor should guard against the temptation to rely upon the auditee's IT personnel for explanations in circumstances which render it inappropriate to do so. As for all audit procedures, the auditor must ensure that the performance of CAATs remains under his/her control and that client personnel are not able to influence improperly the results obtained therefrom.

When planning an audit in which CAATs are to be used, the auditor must be cognisant of the fact that certain computer files, such as transaction files, may be retained by the client for only a short period of time. In such cases, the auditor may need to make arrangements for certain data to be retained, or to alter the timing of audit work, in order to facilitate the testing of data while it is still available.

An interesting result of the advent of CAATs is that, for some audit tests, an examination of *all* accounting data, instead of just samples thereof, is once again possible.[11] This, as in the nineteenth and early twentieth centuries, when detailed checking of all transactions was the norm, may increase the likelihood of detecting certain types of corporate fraud (although not necessarily computer fraud). Further, the change has occurred at a time when, as we observed in Chapter 6, auditors are subject to pressure from the courts, politicians, the media and the public to assume greater responsibility for detecting fraud, and ISA 240: *The Auditor's Responsibilities Relating to Fraud in an Audit of Financial Statements* (IAASB, 2009a) has imposed more stringent requirements on auditors in this regard. Nevertheless, the increasing sophistication of computer networks is opening up new possibilities for computer fraud; these present new challenges – and difficulties – for auditors.

We noted in Chapter 2 that history reveals that changes in the audit environment, changes in audit techniques, and changes in audit objectives go hand in hand. It seems possible that this is being demonstrated at the present time in relation to corporate fraud and that, in the not-too-distant future, fraud detection will re-emerge as a very significant audit objective.

12.10 SUMMARY

This chapter has provided an introduction to audit sampling and CAATs – two somewhat specialised techniques that traverse both compliance and substantive procedures. The first part of the chapter focused on audit sampling. We explained the meaning and importance of sampling and the meaning of terms associated with this technique. We also considered the distinction between judgmental and statistical sampling, and the advantages and disadvantages of each. Additionally, we distinguished between attributes and variables sampling, identified factors that affect the size of audit samples and described some commonly used methods of sample selection. Further, in the context of statistical sampling, we provided an overview of the application of attributes sampling to compliance testing and of PPS (monetary unit)

---

[11] This can happen whenever the audit procedure does not require reference to information held outside the computer system. For example, a CAAT can check calculations of the value of all inventory items but cannot check the condition or ownership of the inventory.

sampling to tests of details, and discussed the auditor's follow-up to sample results.

In the second part of the chapter we turned our attention to CAATs. We briefly explored the meaning and use of CAATs and explained that these techniques are of two main types – test data and audit software. We also noted that CAATs are equally applicable to compliance and substantive testing and mentioned some of the ways in which CAATs can assist auditors. In the concluding section of the chapter we discussed the importance of auditors fully understanding the application of CAATs and the dangers of relying on clients' IT personnel for assistance.

SELF-REVIEW QUESTIONS

12.1   Explain briefly what is meant by 'audit sampling'.

12.2   In relation to audit sampling, explain briefly what is meant by:
    (i)   sampling risk (and levels of assurance);
    (ii)   stratification;
    (iii) precision limits;
    (iv)   tolerable error.

12.3   Distinguish between judgmental sampling and statistical sampling and list two advantages and two disadvantages of each approach.

12.4   Explain briefly the essential difference between attributes sampling and variables sampling.

12.5   State the characteristic feature of random sample selection and list three variations of random sample selection.

12.6   Distinguish between:
    (i)   haphazard sample selection, and
    (ii)   judgmental sample selection.

12.7   Explain briefly why probability proportional to size (PPS or monetary unit) sampling can be referred to as a hybrid of attributes and variables sampling.

12.8   With reference to CAATs, explain briefly:
    (i)   the test data technique,
    (ii)   three types of audit software.

12.9   List five ways in which CAATs may assist the auditor during an audit engagement.

12.10   Identify, and explain briefly, two pitfalls or difficulties of which auditors should be aware when planning to use CAATs during an audit engagement.

REFERENCES

International Auditing and Assurance Standards Board (IAASB). (2009a). International Standard on Auditing (ISA) 240: *The Auditor's Responsibilities Relating to Fraud in an Audit of Financial Statements*. New York: International Federation of Accountants.

International Auditing and Assurance Standards Board (IAASB). (2009b). International Standard on Auditing (ISA) 530: *Audit Sampling*. New York: International Federation of Accountants.

McRae, T.W. (1971). Applying statistical sampling in auditing: Some practical problems. *The Accountant's Magazine*, *LXXV*(781), 369–377.

ADDITIONAL READING

Chang, H., Chen, J., Duh, R.-R., & Li, S.-H. (2011). Productivity growth in the public accounting industry: The roles of information technology and human capital. *Auditing: A Journal of Practice & Theory*, *30*(1), 21–48.

Debreceny, R.S. (2011). Data mining of electronic mail and auditing: A research agenda. *Journal of Information Systems*, *25*(2), 195–226.

Dowling, C. (2009). Appropriate audit support system use: The influence of auditor, audit team, and firm factors. *Accounting Review*, *84*(3), 771–810.

Elder, R.J., & Allen, R.D. (2003). A longitudinal field investigation of auditor risk assessments and sample size decisions. *Accounting Review*, *78*(4), 983–1003.

Hoogduin, L.A., Hall, T.W., & Tsay, J.J. (2010). Modified sieve sampling: A method for single- and multi-stage probability-proportional-to-size sampling. *Auditing: A Journal of Practice & Theory*, *29*(1), 125–148.

Hunton, J.E., & Rose, J.M. (2010). 21st century auditing: Advancing decision support systems to achieve continuous auditing. *Accounting Horizons*, *24*(2), 297–312.

Kotb, A., & Roberts, C. (2011) The impact of E-Business on the audit process: An investigation of the factors leading to change. *International Journal of Auditing*, *15*(2), 150–175.

Kriel, E.J. (Principal Author). (2007). *Application of Computer-Assisted Audit Techniques*, 2nd ed. Toronto: Canadian Institute of Chartered Accountants.

Lymer, A., & Debreceny, R. (2003). The auditor and corporate reporting on the internet: Challenges and institutional responses. *International Journal of Auditing*, 7(2), 103–120.

Masli, A., Peters, G.F., Richardson, V.J., & Sanchez, J.M. (2010). Examining the potential benefits of internal control monitoring technology. *Accounting Review*, 85(3), 1001–1034.

Messier Jr., W.F., Eilifsen, A., & Austen, L.A. (2004). Auditor detected misstatements and the effect of information technology. *International Journal of Auditing*, 8(3), 223–235.

Ponemon, L.A., & Wendell, J.P. (1995). Judgment versus random sampling in auditing: An experimental investigation. *Auditing: A Journal of Practice & Theory*, 14(2), 17–34.

Omoteso, K., Patel, A., & Scott, P. (2010). Information and communications technology and auditing: Current implications and future directions. *International Journal of Auditing*, 14(2), 147–162.

13 Completion and Review

LEARNING OBJECTIVES

After studying the material in this chapter you should be able to:

- explain the position and importance of completion and review procedures within the audit process;
- discuss the importance of, and audit procedures used for:
  - the review for contingent liabilities and commitments, and
  - the review for subsequent events;
- distinguish between subsequent events which necessitate adjustments to the financial statements and those which require note disclosure;
- discuss the actions auditors should take if significant events come to light after the audit report is signed;
- explain the auditor's responsibilities, during the completion stage of the audit, in respect of re-assessing the validity of the auditee preparing its financial statements based on the going concern assumption;
- explain the nature and importance of written representations;
- explain the key objectives of the final review of (i) the auditee's financial statements and (ii) the audit documentation, and how these are accomplished;
- explain what is meant by an 'engagement quality control review', when it is required and what it involves;
- discuss the auditor's responsibilities for unaudited information which accompanies the audited financial statements;
- explain the significance of dating the audit report.

13.1   INTRODUCTION

As we explain in Chapter 10, in order to conduct the detailed work of evaluating and testing the effectiveness of the client's internal controls and verifying the validity, completeness and accuracy of significant classes of transactions, account balances and disclosures, the auditor divides the client's accounting system into sub-systems, or audit segments. Once the detailed audit work is complete, the auditor approaches the audit holistically (as is the case for the early part of the audit), and the completion and review stage is conducted on an entity-wide basis.

As shown in Figure 13.1, the completion and review phase of an audit comprises the following seven main steps:

(i)   a review for contingent liabilities and commitments;

(ii)   a review for subsequent events before and after the audit report is signed;

(iii)   re-assessment of the validity of the auditee preparing its financial statements based on the going concern assumption;

(iv)   obtaining written representations from management;[1]

(v)   a final review of the financial statements,

(vi)   evaluation of the evidence gathered during the audit (which includes, for listed and some other companies, an engagement quality control review[2]) and formation of the audit opinion;

(vii)   a review of the unaudited information accompanying the audited financial statements.

In this chapter we discuss each of these important audit steps.

Figure 13.1:   Place of completion and review in the audit process

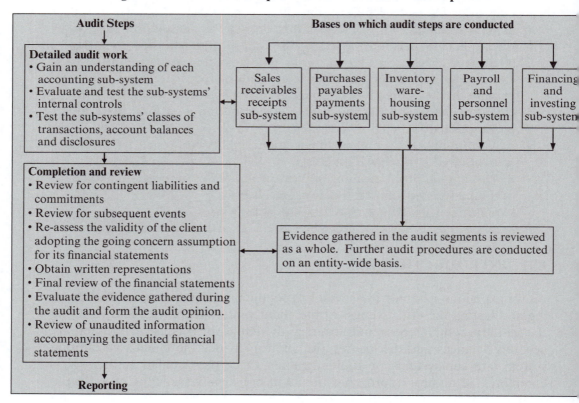

___

[1] Readers are reminded that in the Preface to this book we note that the term 'management' is defined to mean a company's executive directors, non-executive directors and non-director executives (that is, all executives and directors).

[2] We explain engagement quality control reviews in Chapter 7, section 7.6.4.

13.2 REVIEW FOR CONTINGENT LIABILITIES AND COMMITMENTS

Before considering the importance of the auditor's review for contingent liabilities and commitments, we need to clarify the meaning of these terms.

- *Contingent liabilities* are possible obligations which arise from past events but whose existence or amount is uncertain at the date of the financial statements. Their existence or amount is contingent upon the occurrence or non-occurrence of some uncertain future event(s) not wholly within the entity's control. Examples include taxation in dispute and pending litigation for infringement of, for instance, product safety or description or environmental regulations.[3]

- *Commitments* are contractual undertakings. Examples include bonus and profit sharing schemes, and agreements to purchase (or sell) inventory at an agreed price on an agreed date in the future, or to lease or buy property, plant or equipment at an agreed price on a specified future date.

The auditor faces two major problems in relation to the review for contingent liabilities and commitments, namely:
  (i) management may be reluctant to disclose them in the financial statements;
  (ii) they do not involve transactions which are recorded in the accounting system and it is generally more difficult for the auditor to discover events and agreements which lie outside the accounting records.

Nevertheless, the existence of contingent liabilities and commitments may have a significant impact on financial statement users' assessment of the auditee's financial position and performance. Therefore, in order to conclude that the financial statements provide a true and fair view of the auditee's financial affairs, the auditor must be assured that any material contingent liabilities and commitments are properly disclosed in the financial statements.

Auditors usually ascertain the existence of contingent liabilities and commitments by means of the following procedures:
  - making enquiries of management and (if applicable) the auditee's in-house lawyers;[4]
  - reviewing the minutes of directors' meetings;

---

[3] A full definition of contingent liabilities may be found in the International Federation of Accountants' (IFAC) *Glossary of Terms* (IFAC, 2009).

[4] Some (especially larger) companies have 'in-house' as well as external lawyers to advise them. When the auditor wishes to establish the position regarding actual or potential litigation and claims against the client, it is appropriate to seek confirmation from the entity's external (i.e., independent) lawyers.

- reviewing correspondence files (in particular, correspondence between the client and its external lawyers);
- reviewing current and previous years' tax returns;
- reviewing the current year's audit documentation for any information that may indicate a potential contingent liability;
- obtaining confirmation from the auditee's external lawyers of known existing, pending or expected contingent liabilities (especially arising from litigation) and/or commitments.

In respect of the last procedure noted above, International Standard on Auditing (ISA) 501: *Audit Evidence – Specific Considerations for Selected Items* (IAASB, 2009f) states:

> If the auditor assesses a risk of material misstatement regarding litigation or claims that have been identified, or when audit procedures performed indicate that other material litigation or claims may exist, the auditor shall . . . seek direct communication with the entity's external legal counsel [i.e., lawyers]. The auditor shall do so through a letter of inquiry, prepared by management and sent by the auditor, requesting the entity's external legal counsel to communicate directly with the auditor. (para 10)

Although ISA 501 (para 10) indicates the letter is "prepared by management", in practice, it is usually prepared by the auditor and signed by management. A letter of general enquiry is usually sent to the auditee's external lawyers requesting them to inform the auditor of any litigation and claims of which they are aware, their likely outcome, and the expected financial implications for the client. However, if the auditor considers the lawyers are unlikely to respond appropriately to a letter of general enquiry, a letter of specific enquiry is usually sent. ISA 501 explains that such a letter includes:

    (a) A list of litigation and claims;

    (b) Where available, management's assessment of the outcome of each of the identified litigation and claims and its estimate of the financial implications, including costs involved; and

    (c) A request that the entity's legal counsel confirm the reasonableness of management's assessments and provide the auditor with further information if the list is considered . . . to be incomplete or incorrect. (para A23)

In some circumstances (for example, where the auditor believes the matter is a significant risk[5] or the client's management and lawyers are in disagreement), the auditor may decide it is necessary to meet with the client's external lawyers to discuss the likely outcome of litigation and claims. Ordinarily, the auditor will seek management's permission to engage in such a meeting and a management representative will be in attendance (ISA 501, para A24).

---

[5] 'Significant risks' are explained in Chapter 8, section 8.5.1.

13.3 REVIEW FOR SUBSEQUENT EVENTS

13.3.1 Events between the date of the financial statements and the date of the audit report

The auditor has a responsibility to form and express an opinion as to whether the auditee's financial statements give a true and fair view of its financial position and performance as at the end of its reporting period. Consequently, the auditor needs to consider events that occur after the end of the reporting period but before the audit report is signed which might affect financial statement users' assessment of the entity's financial position and/or performance as at the date of its financial statements. These events are termed 'subsequent events'.

The auditor's review for subsequent events usually takes place during the final two to three weeks before the audit report is signed. The timing of the subsequent events review is depicted in Figure 13.2.

Figure 13.2: Timing of the subsequent events review

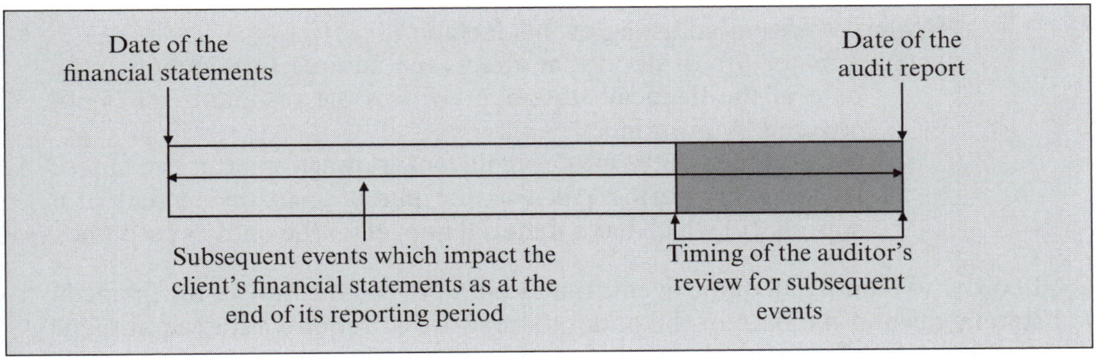

Subsequent events may be of two types, namely:
(i) adjusting events;
(ii) non-adjusting events.

(i) Adjusting events are events that clarify conditions which existed, and/ or permit a more accurate valuation of an account balance or other disclosure, as at the date of the financial statements. These events require the financial statements to be adjusted so that they reflect, as accurately as possible, the auditee's financial position and performance as at the end of its reporting period.

Examples of adjusting events include:
(i) the resolution of tax disputes and litigation which existed at the date of the financial statements but the amount involved was then uncertain;

     (ii) the unexpected collapse of a customer who constitutes a material account receivable which was regarded as 'good' at the end of the reporting period. This is an adjusting event if the conditions which caused the customer's collapse existed at the date of the financial statements.[6] If the conditions causing the customer's collapse arose after the end of the auditee's reporting period, the event is a 'non-adjusting event'.

(ii) *Non-adjusting events* are events that occur subsequent to the date of the financial statements. They do not affect the auditee's situation as it existed at the end of its reporting period and, therefore, should not be incorporated in the financial statements as adjustments to account balances or other disclosures. However, if these events are considered to be material to financial statement users (i.e., they are likely to affect users' evaluation of the entity's financial position and/or future prospects), the events should be disclosed by way of a note to the financial statements.

Examples of non-adjusting events include:
    (i) a major fire or flood that affects the auditee subsequent to the date of the financial statements where the resultant loss is not covered by insurance;
   (ii) the auditee's entry into a significant transaction after the end of its reporting period (such as the purchase or divestment of a subsidiary) which has a material impact on the entity's resources.

In order to identify all of the events that occur between the date of the financial statements and the date of the auditor's report that require adjustment of, or disclosure in, the financial statements, ISA 560: *Subsequent Events* (IAASB, 2009j) requires auditors to perform audit procedures which include:
   (a) Obtaining an understanding of any procedures management has established to ensure that subsequent events are identified.
   (b) Inquiring of management . . . as to whether any subsequent events have occurred which might affect the financial statements.
   (c) Reading minutes, if any, of the meetings, of the entity's [shareholders, managers and directors], that have been held after the date of the financial statements and inquiring about matters discussed at any such meetings for which minutes are not yet available.
   (d) Reading the entity's latest subsequent interim financial statements, if any. (para 7)

---

[6] It should be noted that, as the customer's collapse arose subsequent to the date of the financial statements, the debt was not 'bad', and therefore should not be written off at the client's year end. However, if the relevant conditions causing the collapse existed at the date of the financial statements, the debt was under threat at that time and an adjustment should be made to the allowance for bad debts.

The Standard notes that auditors may additionally:

> . . . consider it necessary and appropriate to:
> - Read the entity's latest available budgets, cash flow forecasts and other related management reports for periods after the date of the financial statements;
> - Inquire, or extend previous oral or written inquiries, of the entity's legal counsel concerning litigation and claims; or
> - Consider whether written representations covering particular subsequent events may be necessary to support other audit evidence and thereby obtain sufficient appropriate audit evidence.[7] (para A8)

ISA 560 also explains the matters on which auditors might make enquiries from management. It states:

> In inquiring of management . . . as to whether any subsequent events have occurred that might affect the financial statements, the auditor may inquire as to the current status of items that were accounted for on the basis of preliminary or inconclusive data and may make specific inquiries about the following matters:
> - Whether new commitments, borrowings or guarantees have been entered into.
> - Whether sales or acquisitions of assets have occurred or are planned.
> - Whether there have been increases in capital or issuance of debt instruments, such as the issue of new shares or debentures, or an agreement to merge or liquidate has been made or is planned.
> - Whether any assets have been appropriated by government or destroyed, for example, by fire or flood.
> - Whether there have been any developments regarding contingencies.
> - Whether any unusual accounting adjustments have been made or are contemplated.
> - Whether any events have occurred or are likely to occur that will bring into question the appropriateness of accounting policies used in the financial statements, as would be the case, for example, if such events call into question the validity of the going concern assumption.
> - Whether any events have occurred that are relevant to the measurement of estimates or provisions made in the financial statements.
> - Whether any events have occurred that are relevant to the recoverability of assets. (para A9)

13.3.2 Events subsequent to the date of the audit report

(i) *Prior to issuance of the financial statements to the entity's shareholders*

The auditor has an obligation to seek out events which occur between the date of the financial statements and the date of the audit report which might require adjustment of, or disclosure in, the financial statements. The auditor

---

[7] As we explain in section 13.5, when auditors need to rely on management's responses to enquiries (because alternative audit evidence is not available), they seek to have any significant responses (or representations) confirmed in writing. However, whenever possible, they endeavour to substantiate significant responses from management by seeking information from alternative sources.

does not have a responsibility to perform procedures to identify events after the audit report has been signed. However, events may come to the auditor's attention after the audit report is signed but before the financial statements are issued to the entity's shareholders, which the auditor considers should be reflected in the financial statements. In this circumstance, the auditor should discuss possible amendment of the financial statements with the auditee's directors. If the financial statements are amended, the subsequent period is, in effect, extended to a later date. The auditor needs to perform appropriate subsequent events procedures for the extended period and issue a new audit report as if an earlier report had not been prepared.

If, contrary to the auditor's request, management refuses to amend the financial statements, the auditor's future action depends on whether the audit report has been provided to the client.

(i)   If it has not been given to the client and the auditor considers the circumstances warrant a modified audit opinion,[8] such an opinion should be expressed in the audit report which is provided to the client.

(ii) If the audit report has been given to the client but the financial statements have not been issued to its shareholders, the auditor is required to request the directors:

> . . . not to issue the financial statements to third parties before the necessary amendments have been made. If the financial statements are nevertheless subsequently issued without the necessary amendments, the auditor shall take appropriate action, to seek to prevent reliance on the auditor's report. (ISA 560, para 13b)

The 'appropriate action' may be informing the shareholders of the position at the shareholders' meeting at which the financial statements are presented (i.e., the 'accounts meeting'; see Chapter 5, section 5.3).

(ii)   Subsequent to the issue of the financial statements to the entity's shareholders

Very occasionally a matter comes to the auditor's attention after the financial statements have been issued to the auditee's shareholders which materially affects the truth and fairness of those financial statements. If this occurs, the auditor is required to discuss the situation with the client's directors, determine whether the financial statements need to be amended, and consider the implications for the audit report. If the financial statements have been issued but the shareholders' 'accounts meeting' has not yet been held, the auditor may request the directors to make an appropriate statement at the accounts meeting and/or make a statement him/herself. Alternatively, or additionally, the directors may decide to issue a revised set of financial statements. If this happens, the auditor is required to:

---

[8] Modified audit opinions are discussed in Chapter 14, section 14.5.

- carry out the audit procedures which are necessary in the circumstances; such procedures may be limited to verifying the amendment to the financial statements but, if a new audit report is issued on the amended financial statements, the subsequent events procedures (outlined in section 13.3.1) need to be extended to the date of the new audit report;
- review the steps taken by the directors to ensure that anyone in receipt of the previously issued financial statements and auditor's report thereon is informed of the situation;
- if warranted by the circumstances, amend the auditor's report on the previously issued financial statements to cover the amendment, or issue a new report on the revised financial statements;
- for listed companies, consider whether Stock Exchange regulations require the revision of the financial statements to be publicised;
- for companies in regulated industries, consider whether there is any requirement to inform the relevant regulator.

When a new audit report is issued on revised financial statements, auditors are required to:
- (a) include an 'Emphasis of Matter' paragraph[9] in the audit report, which refers to a note to the financial statements which discusses the reason for the revision of the previously issued financial statements, or to provide such reason in the (new) audit report;
- (b) refer to the earlier audit report which was issued on the financial statements; and
- (c) date the new audit report no earlier than the date on which the revised financial statements are approved by the auditee's directors.

If the auditee's directors do not take adequate steps to ensure that those who have received the (original) financial statements are notified that they have been superseded (whether by issuing revised financial statements, or otherwise), the auditor should notify the directors that s/he will take action to try to prevent reliance on the auditor's report and then take such action (ISA 560, para 17).

The 2000 financial statements of Wiggins Group plc provide an example of revised financial statements accompanied by a revised audit report. These financial statements are the last in a series of revisions which commenced with the 1995 financial statements. As the Wiggins Group Chairman explains:

> The Financial Reporting Review Panel ("the Panel") opened an enquiry following the publication in August 2000 of our accounts for the year ended March 2000. The Panel had previously opened an enquiry into our accounts for the year ended March 1999 and had, by a letter of 27 June 2000, extended its enquiry in

---

[9] An 'Emphasis of Matter paragraph' is explained in Chapter 14, section, 14.6.

respect of the treatment of revenue from contracts for the sale of land to our accounts for the years ended March 1996 to 1998. . . . The Company announced on 22 December 2000 that it had decided to accept the Panel's position with respect to all the matters in dispute and that it was going to issue restated accounts for the years 1996 to 2000. On March 6 2001, the Company issued restated accounts for the years 1996 to 2000.

In respect of the revised financial statements for the year to 31 March 2000, the Wiggins Group directors, in an explanatory note,[10] provide details of the issues to which the Panel took exception. They explain the company's reasons for its treatment of the items in the original financial statements, the grounds for the Panel's objection and the remedial action taken by the company in the revised financial statements. They also explain, in the following words, the manner in which they have revised the Group's 2000 financial statements and the effect of the revisions on profit:

> The directors are, by this [supplementary] note, revising the directors' report and accounts in accordance with Statutory Instrument 2570 Companies (Revision of Defective Accounts and Report) Regulations 1990, which permits revision by way of supplementary note. . . . As a result of the revisions, the profit on ordinary activities before taxation originally stated of £25,077,000 (1999: £12,113,000) is changed to a loss of £9,898,000 (1999: revised loss of £5,127,000). The original tax charge of £2,066,000 (1999: £3,295,000) has been revised to a credit of £24,000.

The auditors (HLB Kidsons) issued a revised audit report that complies with the requirements of ISA 560. This is reproduced in Figure 13.3.

13.4 (RE)ASSESSMENT OF THE GOING CONCERN ASSUMPTION

An important element of the completion and review stage of the audit is (re) assessing the propriety of the auditee preparing its financial statements based on the going concern assumption. Regulatory interest in this issue, and auditors' role therein, has risen sharply in recent years as a result of the 2008–9 global financial crisis. For example, in the United Kingdom (UK), the Financial Reporting Council (FRC)[11] introduced new going concern requirements for both company directors and auditors in October 2009[12] (FRC, 2009) and, in March 2011, it established the Panel of Inquiry into Going Concern

---

[10] The explanatory note precedes the formal 'Supplementary note' to the 2000 financial statements. The latter supplements the original 2000 financial statements and comprises the revised 2000 financial statements (including the related notes) and an amended paragraph of the Directors' Report.

[11] The FRC is the "UK's independent regulator responsible for promoting high quality corporate governance and reporting to foster investment" (FRC, 2012b). It is responsible for the oversight of financial reporting by, and auditing and governance of, all companies in the UK.

[12] The requirements became effective for reporting periods ending on or after 31 December 2009 (FRC, 2009, para 2)

Figure 13.3:   Auditors' report on Wiggins Group plc's 2000 revised financial statements

Report of the auditors to the shareholders of Wiggins Group plc

We have audited the revised accounts of Wiggins Group plc for the year to 31 March 2000 which have been prepared under the historical cost convention and accounting policies set out on pages 38 to 40 in the original accounts and on page 10 of these revised accounts. The revised accounts replace the original accounts approved by the directors on 26 July 2000 and consist of the attached supplementary note together with the original accounts, which were dated 26 July 2000.

Respective responsibilities of directors and auditors

The directors are responsible for preparing the Annual Report, including, as described on page 27 of the original accounts, the accounts. Our responsibilities, as independent auditors, are established by statute, the Auditing Practices Board, the Listing Rules of the Financial Services Authority, and by our profession's ethical guidance.

We report to you our opinion as to whether the accounts give a true and fair view and are properly prepared in accordance with the Companies Act. We also report to you if, in our opinion, the directors' report is not consistent with the accounts, if the Company has not kept proper accounting records, if we have not received all the information and explanations we require for our audit, or if information specified by law or the Listing Rules regarding directors' remuneration and transactions with the Group and the Company is not disclosed. We are also required to report whether in our opinion the original accounts failed to comply with the requirements of the Companies Act in the respects identified by the directors.

We review whether the corporate governance statement on pages 24 to 26 of the original accounts reflects the Company's compliance with those provisions of the Combined Code specified for our review by the Financial Services Authority, and we report if it does not. We are not required to consider whether the Board's statements on internal control cover all the risks and controls, or form an opinion on the effectiveness of the Company's corporate governance procedures or its risk and control procedures.

We read the other information contained in the annual report, including the corporate governance statement, and consider whether it is consistent with the audited accounts. We consider the implications for our report if we become aware of any apparent misstatements or material inconsistencies with the accounts.

Basis of opinion

We conducted our audit in accordance with Auditing Standards issued by the Auditing Practices Board. An audit includes examination, on a test basis, of evidence relevant to the amounts and disclosures in the accounts. It also includes an assessment of the significant estimates and judgements made by the directors in the preparation of the accounts, and of whether the accounting policies are appropriate to the Group's and the Company's circumstances, consistently applied and adequately disclosed. The audit of the revised accounts includes the performance of additional procedures to assess whether the revisions made by the directors are appropriate and have been properly made.

We planned and performed our audit so as to obtain all the information and explanations which we considered necessary in order to provide us with sufficient evidence to give reasonable assurance that the revised accounts are free from material misstatement, whether caused by fraud or other irregularity or error. In forming our opinion we also evaluated the overall presentation of information in the revised accounts.

Opinion

In our opinion the revised accounts give a true and fair view, seen as at 26 July 2000, the date the original accounts were approved, of the state of the Group's and the Company's affairs as at 31 March 2000 and of the Group's loss and cash flows for the year then ended and have been properly prepared in accordance with the provisions of the Companies Act 1985 as they have effect under The Companies (Revision of Defective Accounts and Report) Regulations 1990.

Figure 13.3: *Continued*

In our opinion the original accounts for the year ended 31 March 2000 failed to comply with the requirements of the Companies Act 1985 for the reasons identified by the directors on pages 1 to 4 of the supplementary note.

Ocean House	HLB Kidsons
Waterloo Lane	Registered Auditors
Chelmsford	Chartered Accountants
Essex CM1 1BD	
Date: 6 March 2001	

Assessments chaired by Lord Sharman (the Sharman Inquiry). The Inquiry published its final report and recommendations in June 2012 (Sharman, 2012). We explain some of the FRC's requirements and the Sharman Inquiry's recommendations below. However, first we need to consider what is meant by 'the going concern assumption'.

ISA 570: *Going Concern* (IAASB, 2009k) provides the following explanation of the concept:

> Under the going concern assumption, an entity is viewed as continuing in business for the foreseeable future. General purpose financial statements are prepared on a going concern basis, unless management either intends to liquidate the entity or to cease operations, or has no realistic alternative but to do so. . . . When the use of the going concern assumption is appropriate, assets and liabilities are recorded on the basis that the entity will be able to realize its assets and discharge its liabilities in the normal course of business. (para 2)

The amounts at which assets can reasonably be expected to realise, and liabilities to be discharged, in the ordinary course of business may differ quite significantly from those that would apply in the event of the entity's liquidation. Thus, when forming an opinion about the truth and fairness (or otherwise) of the entity's financial statements, the auditor must consider whether adherence to the going concern assumption is justified.

Until the mid-1990s, during the planning and evidence gathering stages of an audit, auditors were merely required to remain alert to the possibility that an auditee may not be able to continue as a going concern. In the absence of anything which raised doubt in auditors' minds, formal evaluation of the propriety of auditees preparing their financial statements on a going concern basis was left until the completion and review stage of the audit. If, during the course of the audit, or through their completion and review procedures, something came to light which raised doubt in auditors' minds about the ability of an auditee to continue in operation, they were required to perform specific audit procedures to resolve those doubts. If, after conducting those procedures and evaluating management's plans for future action, auditors still had doubts about an auditee's status as a going concern, they were required to express those doubts in their audit report. This duty was unequivocal. However, during the 1980s and early 1990s (particularly following the stock market crash in October 1987), auditors in the UK, the United States of America (USA) and elsewhere were severely criticised for not fulfilling this duty adequately.[13]

In response to the criticism, the auditing profession developed more stringent and explicit 'going concern' auditing requirements and auditors are now required to perform specific audit procedures at each stage of the audit to address the issue. However, both auditing standards and regulators have also placed increased emphasis on management's responsibility to properly assess the appropriateness of preparing the entity's financial statements on a going concern basis and to disclose any related material uncertainties. For example, ISA 570 states:

> ... [S]ince the going concern assumption is a fundamental principle in the prepa-
> ration of financial statements . . . , the preparation of the financial statements
> requires management to assess the entity's ability to continue as a going concern
> ... [This] involves making a judgment, at a particular point in time, about inher-
> ently uncertain future outcomes of events or conditions. The following factors
> are relevant to that judgment:
> - The degree of uncertainty associated with the outcome of an event or condi-
>   tion increases significantly the further into the future an event or condition or
>   the outcome occurs. . . .
> - The size and complexity of the entity, the nature and condition of its business
>   and the degree to which it is affected by external factors affect the judgment
>   regarding the outcome of events or conditions.
> - Any judgment about the future is based on information available at the time
>   at which the judgment is made. Subsequent events may result in outcomes that
>   are inconsistent with judgments that were reasonable at the time they were
>   made. (paras 4, 5)

As we explain in Chapter 5 (section 5.2.2), the FRC requires the directors of all UK companies (irrespective of their size and whether or not they are listed on a stock exchange), when preparing their company's financial statements, "to make and document a rigorous assessment of whether the company is a going concern" (FRC, 2009; Principle 1, p. 6). This assessment is to be sufficient to enable the directors to conclude (on the date they approve the company's financial statements) that the company is (or is not) able to continue in business for at least the next 12 months. In any case where the directors conclude there are material uncertainties that may cast significant doubt upon the entity's ability to continue as a going concern, they are to disclose the existence

---

[13] Research investigating the audit expectation-performance gap in New Zealand in 1989 found that auditors were more severely criticised for not performing adequately their responsibility to report doubts (or doubts they should have had) about the going concern status of their auditees than for any other of their responsibilities. Even the auditors included in the survey were highly critical of auditors' performance in this regard (see Porter, 1993).

and nature of the uncertainties in a note to the financial statements[14] (FRC, 2009, para 65). Further, for any company facing liquidity risk[15] which constitutes a material financial risk, the directors are required to make qualitative and quantitative disclosures explaining the nature and extent of the risk, how it arises in the business and how it is managed (FRC, 2009, paras 70, 71).

While *all* UK companies are required to disclose risks and uncertainties which bring into question their status as a going concern, the UK Listing Authority (UKLA)[16] requires the directors of companies listed on the London Stock Exchange to include in their company's annual report a statement that the business is a going concern, together with supporting assumptions or qualifications as necessary. Thus, listed companies are required to make a statement about their status as a going concern each year, not just when the risks and uncertainties they face bring this into question.

Sharman (2012) has recommended that the FRC's and UKLA's requirements be extended. In respect of the directors' 'going concern assessment', it proposes that this be integrated with the company's business planning and risk management and that it focus on both solvency and liquidity risks that could threaten the company's survival. As regards the reporting of going concern uncertainties, Sharman recommends that, rather than companies disclosing going concern risks only when there are significant doubts about the company's survival (as currently applies to non-listed companies), they be required to integrate a report on their status as a going concern with a fuller description than is currently required of the principal risks the company is taking and facing in pursuit of its business model and strategy. Sharman additionally recommends that companies' audit committees be required to:

   (i) evaluate the effectiveness of the directors' going concern assessment; and
   (ii) include in the audit committee's report (which is included in the company's annual report):
         – confirmation that "a robust risk assessment" has been made, and
         – comment on, or cross-reference to, information on the material risks to going concern the directors have considered and, where applicable, how they have been addressed (p. 11).

---

[14] Such disclosure is also required under UK Generally Accepted Accounting Practice and International Financial Reporting Standards. Additionally, the Companies Act 2006, s. 414C, requires the directors of all but small companies to include in the company's strategic report a description of the company's principal risks and uncertainties. The FRC (2009) specifies that this description is to include an explanation of "any particular economic conditions and financial difficulties that the company is facing" (para 64).

[15] The risk that the company may not be able to meet its financial obligations.

[16] In 2001, regulatory responsibility for companies listed on the London Stock Exchange (and hence for the Listing Rules) passed from the London Stock Exchange to the Financial Services Authority (FSA). The FSA delegated its responsibility for listed companies to the UKLA. In 2013, when the FSA was disbanded, responsibility for the UKLA passed to the Financial Conduct Authority (FCA).

While it is management's (or, more precisely in the UK context, the directors') responsibility, when preparing the company's financial statements, to establish whether or not the company is a going concern, auditors are responsible for determining whether their conclusion is justified. ISA 570 explains:

> The auditor's responsibility is to obtain sufficient appropriate audit evidence about the appropriateness of management's use of the going concern assumption in the preparation and presentation of the financial statements and to conclude whether there is a material uncertainty about the entity's ability to continue as a going concern. (para 6)

As indicated in Figure 13.4, rather than deferring detailed consideration of the propriety of management's adherence to the going concern assumption until the completion and review stage of the audit (as formerly), auditors are required to perform relevant procedures during the risk assessment, evidence gathering, completion and review and reporting phases of the audit. We examine the requirements for each of these phases below.

(i) Risk assessment phase of the audit

It may be recalled from Chapter 8 that, once the audit engagement procedures are completed, the auditor performs 'risk assessment procedures' – gaining a thorough understanding of the client and its financial affairs and assessing the risk of material misstatement of its (pre-audited) financial statements. One risk to be considered is whether the entity is, and will remain for the foreseeable future, a going concern. In order to make a preliminary assessment of the auditee's status as a going concern, the auditor is required to:

(i) ascertain whether management has performed a preliminary assessment of the entity's ability to continue as a going concern and, if so, to discuss the assessment with management;

(ii) if an assessment has not yet been performed, ascertain the basis for management's adoption of the going concern assumption for its financial statements.

The auditor is also to determine whether management has identified events or conditions that may cast significant doubt on the entity's ability to continue as a going concern and, if so, its plans to address them. According to ISA 570, taking these steps at this early stage of the audit assists:

> . . . the auditor to determine whether management's use of the going concern assumption is likely to be an important issue and its impact on planning the audit.
> . . . [They] also allow for more timely discussions with management, including a discussion of management's plans and resolution of any identified going concern issues. (para A3)

Auditors of companies in the UK are assisted in the performance of these procedures by the FRC's (2009) requirements and, if implemented, by the Sharman (2012) recommendations outlined above.

Irrespective of auditors' preliminary conclusion about the going concern status of an auditee, they are required to: "remain alert throughout the audit for audit

Figure 13.4: Assessing the propriety of auditees' adoption of the going concern assumption

Audit Steps	Audit Phase
Preliminary assessment of the risk that the auditee may be unable to continue as a going concern based on understanding its business, assessing risk factors, discussions with management, and establishing how management plans to support its adoption of the going concern assumption	Risk assessment phase of the audit
Perform specific procedures to evaluate management's assessment of the entity's going concern status and to identify signs of going concern difficulties Perform other routine audit procedures. Decide on the need for a meeting with, or confirmation from, the client's bankers	Evidence gathering phase
Consider and, if necessary, revise the preliminary going concern assessment. Determine and document the extent of concern (if any) Decide on the need for formal representations from management Assess the need for, and adequacy of, disclosures relating to the auditee's going concern status	Completion and review phase
Express the appropriate opinion in the audit report, if necessary making relevant disclosures about going concern uncertainties	Reporting phase

evidence of events or conditions that may cast significant doubt on the entity's ability to continue as a going concern" (ISA 570, para 11).

(ii) Evidence gathering phase

During the evidence gathering phase of the audit, auditors are primarily concerned with evaluating the appropriateness of management's assessment of their company's ability to continue as a going concern. ISA 570 explains that, in some circumstances, this evaluation need not be detailed. It states:

> ... [W]hen there is a history of profitable operations and a ready access to financial resources, management may make its assessment without detailed analysis. In this case, the auditor's evaluation of the appropriateness of management's assessment may be made without performing detailed evaluation procedures if the auditor's other audit procedures are sufficient to enable the auditor to conclude whether management's use of the going concern assumption in the preparation of the financial statements is appropriate in the circumstances. (para A8)

Nevertheless, in evaluating management's going concern assessment, auditors generally consider factors such as the following:

- the assessment process adopted by management;
- factors management considered when making its assessment and the sources and reliability of the information used;
- the reasonableness of assumptions which underlie the assessment process;
- systems the entity has in place for identifying, in a timely manner, warnings of future risks and uncertainties it might face;
- any events or conditions that raise questions about the future viability of the entity that were identified during the assessment process and the extent to which they were incorporated therein;
- in appropriate cases, management's plans for future action and whether they are feasible in the circumstances. Such plans may include, for example, liquidating assets, borrowing money or restructuring debt, reducing or delaying expenditures, or increasing capital.

When making their evaluation of management's going concern assessment, auditors should use the same period as that used by management but, if this is less than 12 months from the date of the financial statements, they are to request management to extend its assessment period to at least 12 months from that date[17] (ISA 570, para 13).

In addition to evaluating the appropriateness of management's going concern assessment, auditors are required, when performing other audit procedures, to be alert to events or conditions which may cast significant doubt on the auditee's ability to continue as a going concern. To assist auditors identify such events and conditions, ISA 570 (para A2) provides a list of examples which, individually or collectively, may cast significant doubt about the continuing viability of an auditee. They are grouped under three headings: Financial, Operating and Other, and include the following:

---

[17] In the UK, the FRC (2009) requires the going concern assessment period to be at least 12 months from the date on which the directors approve the financial statements (Principle 2, p. 11). If their assessment period is for a shorter period, the directors are to disclose that a shorter period has been assessed and their reasons for limiting the review period (Principle 3, p. 12).

Financial
- Net liability or net current liability position.
- Fixed-term borrowings approaching maturity without realistic prospects of renewal or repayment; or excessive reliance on short-term borrowings to finance long-term assets.
- Adverse key financial ratios.
- Substantial operating losses or significant deterioration in the value of assets used to generate cash flows.
- Inability to pay creditors on due dates.

Operating
- Loss of key management without replacement.
- Loss of a major market, key customer(s), franchise, licence, or principal supplier(s).
- Labour difficulties.
- Shortages of important supplies.

Other
- Non-compliance with capital or other statutory requirements.
- Pending legal or regulatory proceedings against the entity that may, if successful, result in claims that the entity is unlikely to be able to satisfy.
- Changes in law or regulation or government policy expected to adversely affect the entity.

Suppose an auditor identifies events or conditions such as those outlined above – what then? In this circumstance, the auditor is to:

> . . . obtain sufficient appropriate audit evidence to determine whether or not a material uncertainty exists through performing additional audit procedures . . . . These procedures shall include:

(a) Where management has not performed an assessment of the entity's ability to continue as a going concern, requesting management to make its assessment.

(b) Evaluating management's plans for future actions in relation to its going concern assessment, whether the outcome of these plans is likely to improve the situation and whether management's plans are feasible in the circumstances.

(c) Where the entity has prepared a cash flow forecast, and analysis of the forecast is a significant factor in considering the future outcome of events or conditions in the evaluation of management's plans for future action:
(i) evaluating the reliability of the underlying data generated to prepare the forecast; and
(ii) determining whether there is adequate support for the assumptions underlying the forecast.

(d) Considering whether any additional facts or information have become available since the date on which management made its assessment.

(e) Requesting written representations from management . . . regarding their plans for future action and the feasibility of these plans. (ISA 570, para 16)

Further more specific procedures auditors may perform if they encounter events or conditions that cast significant doubt on the ability of the entity to continue as a going concern are identified in ISA 570 (para A15). These include:

- analysing cash flow, profit and other relevant forecasts, and also the entity's latest available interim financial statements, and discussing these forecasts and statements with management;
- reading the terms of debentures and loan agreements, and determining whether any of the terms have been breached;
- reading the minutes of shareholders' and directors' meetings, and those of other relevant committees (such as the audit committee), for any reference to financing difficulties;
- enquiring of the entity's lawyers about the existence of litigation and claims against the client and the reasonableness of management's assessments of their outcome and estimate of their financial implications;[18]
- confirming the existence, legality and enforceability of arrangements to provide financial support to, or receive financial support from, related and third parties, and assessing the financial position of these parties;
- evaluating the entity's plans in respect of unfilled customer orders;
- confirming the existence, terms and adequacy of borrowing facilities and supplier credit.

In respect of borrowing facilities, the auditor needs to assess the bank's intentions (or otherwise) to extend borrowing facilities to the auditee and the terms thereof. More particularly, the auditor should examine written evidence, or make notes of discussions with the directors, regarding bank lending facilities. In some circumstances, an auditor may seek written confirmation from, or meet with, an auditee's bankers about the existence and terms of borrowing facilities available to the client. This is particularly likely when:
- financial resources available to the auditee are limited;
- the auditee is dependent on borrowing facilities shortly due for renewal;
- correspondence between the bank and the auditee shows that the last renewal of borrowing facilities was agreed with difficulty;
- a significant deterioration in the auditee's cash flow is expected;
- the value of assets granted as security by the auditee to the bank is declining;
- the auditee has breached, or seems likely to breach, the terms of borrowing.

(iii) Completion and review phase

During the completion and review phase of the audit, the auditor needs to reconsider, and if necessary revise, his/her preliminary assessment of the auditee's status as a going concern. If the auditor has concerns in this regard, s/he should document the extent of, and reasons for, his/her concerns. The auditor also needs to decide whether to obtain formal written representations

---

[18] As we note in section 13.2, the auditor also needs to perform this procedure in relation to the auditee's contingent liabilities.

from the client's directors confirming that, in their considered view, the entity is a going concern, together with supporting assumptions or qualifications, as necessary.[19] In any case where the auditor considers there is uncertainty about events or conditions that, individually or collectively, may cast significant doubt on the entity's ability to continue as a going concern, s/he needs to ensure that appropriate disclosure of the nature and implications of the uncertainty is provided in the entity's financial statements (ISA 570, para 17).

For auditees that are listed companies in the UK, auditors must also review the directors' going concern statement in the company's annual report. The Auditing Practices Board (APB; 2009) explains that the auditors' responsibility includes:

- reviewing the documentation, prepared by or for the directors, which explains the basis for the directors' conclusion that the company is a going concern;
- evaluating the consistency of the directors' going concern status with knowledge they have acquired during the audit;
- evaluating whether the directors' statement meets the disclosure requirements. These are contained in the FRC's (2009) guidance which states:

  Directors should make balanced, proportionate and clear disclosures about going concern for the financial statements to give a true and fair view. Directors should disclose if the period that they have reviewed is less than twelve months from the date of approval of the . . . financial statements and explain their justification for limiting their review period. (Principle 3, p. 12)

(iv) Reporting phase

If, after examining sufficient appropriate audit evidence, the auditor concludes that an auditee's adherence to the going concern assumption is justified but a material uncertainty exists, the auditor is required to:

 . . . determine whether the financial statements:

(a) Adequately describe the principal events or conditions that may cast significant doubt on the entity's ability to continue as a going concern and management's plans to deal with these events or conditions; and

(b) Disclose clearly that there is a material uncertainty related to events or conditions that may cast significant doubt on the entity's ability to continue as a going concern and, therefore, that it may be unable to realize its assets and discharge its liabilities in the normal course of business. (ISA 570, para 18)

The various reporting options available to auditors in relation to a going concern uncertainty are depicted in Figure 13.5. This shows that, when the

---

[19] It should be recalled from earlier in this section that the directors of listed companies in the UK are required to provide such a statement in the company's annual report, thus, for these companies, auditors will not need to obtain written representations about the matter from the directors.

Figure 13.5:   Auditors' reporting options in relation to a going concern uncertainty

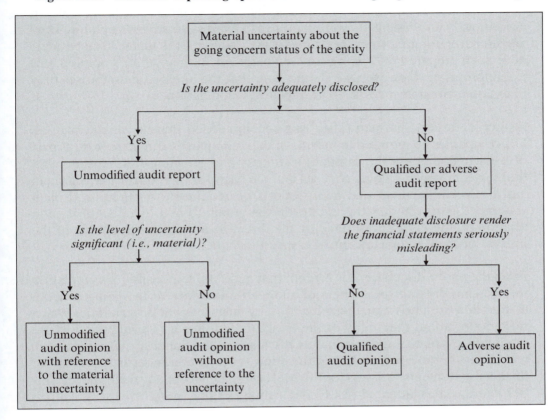

auditor considers the uncertainty is adequately disclosed, an unmodified audit opinion is appropriate. However, if the uncertainty is significant, the auditor is required to highlight in an 'Emphasis of Matter' paragraph[20] in the audit report:

(a) the existence of a material uncertainty relating to the events or conditions that raise significant doubt about the entity's ability to continue as a going concern;

(b) the note in the financial statements that discloses the relevant matters.

If the auditor considers that the going concern uncertainty is not adequately disclosed in the financial statements, this will usually result in a qualified audit opinion which specifically refers to the fact that there is a material uncertainty which gives rise to significant doubt about the entity's ability to continue as a going concern.

---

[20] The various types of audit report and 'Emphasis of Matter' paragraphs are discussed in Chapter 14, sections 14.5 and 14.6, respectively.

In circumstances where auditors conclude that financial statement disclosures about a material uncertainty regarding the entity's status as a going concern are seriously misleading, they are required to express an adverse opinion. They are similarly required to express an adverse opinion if the financial statements have been prepared on a going concern basis but, in the auditor's opinion, this is inappropriate. However, we should note that the latter situation arises only in extreme circumstances, such as impending liquidation.

As noted earlier, Sharman (2012) has recommended that the directors of all UK companies be required to include in their company's annual report (as part of a discussion about the company's strategy and principal risks) a statement that the company is a going concern and the basis for this conclusion. Sharman has also recommended that audit reports be required to include an explicit statement as to whether the auditor has anything to add to, or emphasise in relation to, the disclosures made by the directors about the robustness of the process of their going concern assessment or its outcome.[21]

From the above discussion it is evident that auditors' responsibilities in relation to assessing the appropriateness of auditees' adherence to the going concern assumption are fairly exacting. However, by ensuring that uncertainties which raise doubt about the ability of the entity to continue as a going concern are identified, evaluated and adequately disclosed in the financial statements and, where appropriate, referred to in the audit report, auditors assist users of the financial statements to assess for themselves the impact of any major uncertainties and the consequential risk to the viability of the entity.

13.5 WRITTEN REPRESENTATIONS

13.5.1 Importance of written representations

When conducting an audit, auditors frequently have cause to rely on information given to them by management – especially when audit evidence from alternative sources is not available. Examples include management's responses to auditors' enquiries about instances of fraud or other illegal acts known to

---

[21] As we explain in Chapter 18, section 18.4, in the aftermath of the global financial crisis, proposed changes to the auditor's report include requiring the auditor to include in the audit report clear statements of:
- the auditor's conclusion about the appropriateness of the company preparing its financial statements based on the going concern assumption, and
- any material uncertainties or events that may cast doubt on the ability of the entity to continue as a going concern (or that there are none).

We also explain that the FRC (2013b) has proposed that the auditors of companies that are required, or choose, to comply (or explain their non-compliance) with *The UK Corporate Governance Code* (2012a) be required to provide the company's audit committee with information relevant to the directors' responsibility to report in the financial statements that the company is a going concern; this is to include the auditor's views on the robustness of the directors' going concern assessment and its outcome.

management, and management's intentions with respect to holding or disposing of a long term investment. As part of the completion and review stage of the audit, auditors seek to have significant representations made by management and other relevant parties within the auditee recorded in writing. These are known as 'written representations'.

Technically, these representations are written by the client's directors (with input from other relevant parties) but, in practice, they are normally prepared by the auditor and signed by the directors. They have two primary purposes, namely:

- to obtain evidence that the client's directors acknowledge their responsibility for the entity's financial statements and for making available complete information to the auditor;[22] and
- to place on record management's (and other relevant parties') responses to enquiries by the auditor that relate to significant classes of transactions, account balances or other financial statement disclosures. Written representations ensure there is no misunderstanding between management and the auditor as to what was said – and they provide management with an opportunity to correct any response the auditor has misinterpreted. They also ensure that management assumes responsibility for representations made to the auditor.

13.5.2 From whom, and about what, should written representations be requested?

In order for written representations to have value for the auditor, they must be requested from an appropriate party. Accordingly, ISA 580: *Written Representations* (IAASB, 2009l) requires auditors to "request written representations from management with appropriate responsibilities for the financial statements and knowledge of the matters concerned" (para 9). In practice, the directors (or, more correctly, if the company has one, members of its audit committee) generally sign written representations but they usually seek input (or information) from senior executives or other employees who are

---

[22] We note in Chapter 5 (sections 5.5.2 and 5.2.2, respectively) that the Companies Act 2006 (CA 2006) requires the directors of companies to:
  (i) provide complete information and explanations to the auditor as and when they are requested to do so (s. 499); and
  (ii) state in their directors' report that, as far as each director is aware:
    – there is no relevant information of which the company's auditor is unaware, and
    – all necessary steps have been taken by the director to become aware of any relevant audit information, and to establish that the auditor is aware of that information (s. 418).
Additionally, under the CA 2006, s. 501, if any person knowingly or recklessly makes a written or oral statement to the auditor that is misleading, false or deceptive in a material particular, they are guilty of an offence which can result in imprisonment for up to two years or a fine of up to £5,000. Therefore, under the provisions of CA 2006, company directors are legally bound to provide complete and truthful information to the company's auditor.

particularly knowledgeable about the preparation of the financial statements and the assertions therein, and individuals who have specialised knowledge about matters for which written representations are requested. ISA 580, para A4, explains:

> . . . Such individuals may include:
> - An actuary responsible for actuarially determined accounting measurements.
> - Staff engineers who may have responsibility for and specialized knowledge about environmental liability measurements.
> - Internal counsel [i.e., 'in-house' lawyers] who may provide information essential to provisions for legal claims.

While some matters included in written representations are unique to the particular client and audit engagement, others are required by auditing standards and are, therefore, invariably included. These include written representations confirming that management:

- has fulfilled its responsibility, as set out in the terms of the audit engagement (or audit engagement letter[23]), for preparing and presenting financial statements that give a true and fair view of the company's financial performance and position and comply with the applicable financial reporting framework (ISA 580, para 10);
- has provided the auditor with all relevant information and access as agreed in the audit engagement letter and, in the UK, as required by the Companies Act 2006 (ISA 580, para 11a);
- all of the company's transactions have been recorded and are reflected in the financial statements (ISA 580, para 11b).

ISA 580 explains that auditors need to obtain written representations on these matters:

> . . . because the auditor is not able to judge solely on other audit evidence whether management has prepared and presented the financial statements and provided information to the auditor on the basis of the agreed acknowledgement and understanding of its responsibilities [i.e., as spelt out in the audit engagement letter]. For example, the auditor could not conclude that management has provided the auditor with all relevant information . . . without asking it whether, and receiving confirmation that, such information has been provided. (para A7)

ISA 580 (para A10) notes that auditors may also consider it necessary to request written representations from the directors confirming that:

- the selection and application of accounting policies are appropriate;
- the following matters, where relevant, have been recognised, measured and/or disclosed in the financial statements in accordance with the applicable financial reporting framework:

---

[23] These letters are discussed in Chapter 8, section 8.3. The directors' responsibilities should be described in the written representations in the same manner as they are described in the audit engagement letter (ISA 580, IAASB, 2009l, para 12).

- plans or intentions that may affect the value or classification of assets and liabilities;
- actual and contingent liabilities;
- title to, or control over, assets, liens or encumbrances on assets, and assets pledged as collateral;
- aspects of laws, regulations and contractual agreements that may affect the financial statements, including any instances of non-compliance therewith.

In some circumstances auditors may additionally consider it necessary to obtain written representations about specific financial statement assertions in order to corroborate their understanding, obtained from other audit evidence, about management's intentions. For example, if management's intentions affect the valuation basis for investments, auditors may not be able to obtain sufficient appropriate audit evidence about the value of the investments without a written representation from management about its intentions (ISA 580, para A13).

In addition to meeting the requirements of ISA 580, other auditing standards require auditors to obtain written representations. For example, auditors are required to request auditees' directors to provide written representations confirming:

- they are responsible for the design, implementation and maintenance of internal control to prevent and detect fraud, and they have disclosed to the auditor:
  - the results of their assessment of the risk that the financial statements may be materially misstated as a result of fraud;
  - any known, or suspected, fraud involving the company's executives, employees who have significant roles in designing or implementing internal control, or others where the fraud could have a material effect on the financial statements;
  - any known allegations of fraud, or suspected fraud, that affect the entity's financial statements which have been communicated by employees, former employees, analysts, regulators or others (ISA 240: *The Auditor's Responsibilities Relating to Fraud ...*, IAASB, 2009b, para 39);
  - any known, or suspected, instances of non-compliance with laws and regulations whose effects may impact the financial statements (ISA 250: *Consideration of Laws and Regulations in an Audit of Financial Statements*, IAASB, 2009c, para 16);
- their belief that:
  - the effects of misstatements identified by the auditor which the directors have refused to correct (as set out in, or attached to, the written representations) are immaterial, individually and in aggregate, to the

financial statements as a whole (ISA 450: *Evaluation of Misstatements Identified during the Audit*, IAASB, 2009e, para 14);[24]
- significant assumptions underlying accounting estimates included in the financial statements are reasonable (ISA 540: *Auditing Accounting Estimates. . .*, IAASB, 2009h, para 22);
• they have provided the auditor with complete information about the auditee's related parties and related party relationships and transactions, and all related party relationships and transactions have been properly accounted for and disclosed (ISA 550: *Related Parties*, IAASB, 2009i, para 26);
• all events subsequent to the date of the financial statements, for which the applicable financial reporting framework requires adjustment or disclosure, have been adjusted or disclosed (ISA 560: *Subsequent Events*, IAASB, 2009j, para 9).

Despite the acknowledged need for auditors to obtain written representations from management about significant matters for which alternative audit evidence is not available, it is important to note that auditors cannot just accept them without question. Written representations do not, by themselves, provide sufficient appropriate audit evidence; they serve to corroborate, not provide a substitute for, evidence the auditor should obtain through other audit procedures.[25] For example, a written response to a specific enquiry about the cost of an asset is not a substitute for audit evidence relating to the cost of the asset the auditor would ordinarily be expected to obtain by other means (for example, by examining the purchase invoice). In other cases, auditors may obtain audit evidence that is inconsistent with written representations provided by management. They cannot merely accept the written representation as 'correct'; as we explain below, they must perform alternative procedures to resolve the inconsistency.

13.5.3   Problematic, or the non-provision of, written representations

If written representations from management appear to be inconsistent with other audit evidence, auditors need to perform additional audit procedures to

---

[24] As we explain in Chapter 14, section 14.8, as an element of the auditor's communication to the directors, the auditor reports misstatements identified during the audit which the senior executives have refused to correct. The directors have responsibility for the financial statements so it is their prerogative to decide which, if any, of the uncorrected misstatements are to be corrected. The directors' written representation to the auditor confirms their belief that any misstatements that remain uncorrected are immaterial to the financial statements.

[25] This corresponds to one of the principles enunciated by Moffitt J in the *Pacific Acceptance* case discussed in Chapter 5, section 5.5.3, namely, an auditor has a paramount duty to check material matters for him/herself. However, reliance may be placed on enquiries from others where it is reasonable to do so. Nevertheless, reliance on others is to be regarded as an aid to, and not a substitute for, the auditor's own procedures.

determine the reasons for the inconsistency. If, after performing those procedures, they have reason to doubt the reliability of the written representations, they are required to reconsider their assessment of the competence, integrity, ethical values and/or diligence of management, or its commitment to or enforcement of these, and determine the effect this may have on the reliability of other representations (oral and written) made to the auditor, evidence obtained during the audit in general, and their assessment of the risk of material misstatements in the financial statements. If the reconsideration of their risk assessment results in its revision, additional audit procedures will need to be planned and performed in response to the new level of assessed risk (ISA 580, IAASB, 2009l, paras 17, A23).

In some cases, management may fail to provide one or more of the written representations requested by the auditor. If this occurs, the auditor is required to:

(a) discuss the matter with management [or, more precisely in the UK context, the directors or audit committee];

(b) re-evaluate his/her assessment of the integrity of management and determine the effect this may have on the reliability of representations (oral or written) and other audit evidence obtained during the audit;

(c) consider the possible effect on the opinion expressed in the audit report.

However, in the special case of management failing to provide representations confirming that:

(i) it has fulfilled its responsibilities for preparing and presenting financial statements that give a true and fair view of the entity's financial position and performance and comply with the applicable financial reporting framework, and

(ii) it has provided the auditor with all relevant information and access as agreed in the terms of the audit engagement, and

(iii) all of the entity's transactions have been recorded and are reflected in the financial statements,

or the auditor concludes that the written representations provided on these matters are unreliable, ISA 580, para 20, specifies that the auditor should take the extreme step of disclaiming an opinion on the financial statements.[26]

13.5.4 Form and content of representation letters

Figure 13.6 provides an example of a letter containing written representations in circumstances where neither the company's going concern status nor the completeness and reliability of the written representations is in question. It should be noticed that the letter is prepared on the client's letterhead, addressed to the auditor and dated. The date should be the same as, or as close as possible to, the end of the period during which the auditor has considered subsequent events (this usually coincides with the date of the audit report).

---

[26] Disclaimers of audit opinion are explained in Chapter 14, section 14.5.

Figure 13.6:   Example of a representation letter

(Company letterhead)

(To Auditor)   (Date)

This representation letter is provided in connection with your audit of the financial statements of ABC Company for the year ended 31 December 20XX for the purpose of expressing an opinion as to whether the financial statement give a true and fair view and are prepared in accordance with International Financial Reporting Standards.

We confirm that, to the best of our knowledge and belief, having made such enquiries as we considered necessary for the purpose of appropriately informing ourselves:

Financial Statements
- We have fulfilled our responsibilities, as set out in the terms of the audit engagement dated 6 March 20XX, for the preparation of the financial statements in accordance with International Financial Reporting Standards; in particular, the financial statements give a true and fair view in accordance therewith.
- Significant assumptions used by us in making accounting estimates, including those measured at fair value, are reasonable.
- Related party relationships and transactions have been appropriately accounted for and disclosed in accordance with the requirements of International Financial Reporting Standards.
- All events subsequent to the date of the financial statements and for which International Financial Reporting Standards require adjustment or disclosure have been adjusted or disclosed.
- The effects of uncorrected misstatements are immaterial, both individually and in the aggregate, to the financial statements as a whole. A list of the uncorrected misstatements is attached to this letter.
- We confirm that:
  - Our selection and application of accounting policies is appropriate.
  - All plans or intentions that may materially alter the carrying value or classification of assets and liabilities in the financial statements have been accounted for or disclosed in accordance with International Financial Reporting Standards.
  - All liabilities, actual and contingent, have been recorded and, where appropriate, disclosed in accordance with International Financial Reporting Standards.
  - The entity has satisfactory title to, or control over, all assets disclosed in the financial statements and, where appropriate, all liens or encumbrances on these assets have been disclosed in accordance with International Financial Reporting Standards.
  - We have complied with the aspects of contractual agreements that could have a material effect on the financial statements and instances of non-compliance have been disclosed in accordance with International Financial Reporting Standards.

Information provided
- We have provided you with:
  - Access to all information of which we are aware that is relevant to the preparation of the financial statements, such as records, documentation, and other matters;
  - Additional information that you have requested from us for the purpose of the audit; and
  - Unrestricted access to persons within the entity from whom you determined it necessary to obtain audit evidence.
- All transactions have been recorded in the accounting records and are reflected in the financial statements.
- We have disclosed to you the results of our assessment of the risk that the financial statements may be materiall misstated as a result of fraud.
- We have disclosed to you all information in relation to fraud or suspected fraud that we are aware of and that affects the entity and involves:
  - Management;
  - Employees who have significant roles in internal control; or
  - Others where the fraud could have a material effect on the financial statements.

Figure 13.6: *Continued*

We have disclosed to you all information in relation to allegations of fraud, or suspected fraud, affecting the entity's financial statements communicated by employees, former employees, analysts, regulators or others.
We have disclosed to you all known instances of non-compliance, or suspected non-compliance with laws and regulations whose effects should be considered when preparing financial statements.
We have disclosed to you the identity of the entity's related parties and all the related party relationships and transactions of which we are aware.

─────────────────────────────   ─────────────────────────────

irector   Director

Source: ISA 580 (IAASB, 2009l, Appendix 2)

13.6 FINAL REVIEW OF THE FINANCIAL STATEMENTS

13.6.1 Objectives of the final review of the financial statements

The final review of the financial statements is designed to:
- identify previously unrecognised misstatements;
- evaluate identified misstatements which remain uncorrected;
- ensure that the overall presentation of the financial statements complies with the applicable financial reporting framework.

We discuss each of these objectives below.

13.6.2 Identifying previously unrecognised misstatements

We note in Chapter 8, section 8.6, that analytical procedures are used in three stages of the audit – as risk assessment procedures, substantive tests and in the final review of the financial statements.[27] During the final review of the financial statements, analytical procedures are used to corroborate (or challenge) conclusions reached from the results of tests of significant classes of transactions, account balances and disclosures in the various audit segments and, thereby, to assist the auditor to form a conclusion as to whether the financial statements are consistent with the auditor's understanding of the entity and its financial affairs; expressed alternatively, they help the auditor to identify previously unrecognised misstatements in the financial statements.

Analytical procedures performed as final review procedures are similar to those performed as risk assessment procedures near the start of the audit. They include ratios to determine, for example, the gross and net profit margins, return on assets and on equity, inventory and accounts receivable to sales, rate of inventory turnover, the working capital ratio and debt to equity ratio. In calculating these and similar ratios, and comparing the results with those from

---

[27] A summary of the use, objective and nature of analytical procedures is provided in Chapter 8, Figure 8.2.

previous years, the auditor is particularly concerned to identify any relationships or fluctuations which, in the light of knowledge gained and evidence gathered during the audit, are unexpected. Such a finding may indicate a risk of misstatement not previously recognised; such a misstatement, individually or when aggregated with other misstatements, may cause the financial statements to be materially misstated.

When a previously unrecognised risk of misstatement is identified, the auditor is required to discuss the finding with management and to evaluate management's explanation in the light of the auditor's understanding of the entity and the evidence gathered during the audit. If management is unable to provide an adequate explanation of the finding, the auditor is required to perform additional audit procedures to resolve the matter (ISA 520: *Analytical Procedures*, IAASB, 2009g, paras 7, A20, A21).

13.6.3 Evaluation of uncorrected misstatements

In Chapter 11, section 11.5, we note that, as the audit progresses, the auditor is required to accumulate all identified misstatements (other than those that are clearly trivial). These misstatements (categorised into those that are factual, judgmental and projected) are to be communicated to the appropriate level of management (i.e., senior executives) on a timely basis and request that they be corrected. In the event that the senior executives refuse to correct some or all of the misstatements, the auditor is required to obtain an understanding of their reasons for so doing and to consider that understanding when evaluating whether the financial statements as a whole are free from material misstatement. They are also to notify the directors of any uncorrected misstatements and the effect these may have, individually and in aggregate, on the opinion expressed in the audit report (ISA 450, IAASB, 2009e, paras 5, 8, 9, 12).

As the auditee's directors are responsible for the entity's financial statements, it is their prerogative to decide which, if any, of the misstatements the senior executives have refused to correct are to be corrected. However, as we observed in section 13.5, if the directors partially or fully support their executives' stance, and misstatements remain uncorrected, the auditor is required to obtain written representations from the directors stating that, in their considered opinion, the uncorrected misstatements are immaterial to the financial statements. Nevertheless, the story does not end here for the auditor.

Although the directors may consider uncorrected misstatements are immaterial to the financial statements, it is the auditor's responsibility to decide whether this is, or is not, the case. However, before making this decision, the auditor is required to re-assess the levels (or amounts) determined for planning materiality and tolerable error to ascertain whether they remain appropriate in the context of the entity's actual financial results.[28] Once this is accomplished, the auditor is to evaluate whether the uncorrected misstatements are material, individually or in aggregate, to the financial statements as a whole. The size and nature of each misstatement is to be considered separately in order to evaluate its effect on relevant classes of transactions, account balances or disclosures. This includes ascertaining whether the tolerable error of the particular class of transactions, account balance or disclosure, if any, has been exceeded (ISA 450, paras 10, 11). ISA 450 further explains:

> If an individual misstatement is judged to be material, it is unlikely that it can be offset by other misstatements. For example, if revenue has been materially overstated, the financial statements as a whole will be materially misstated, even if the effect of the misstatement on earnings is completely offset by an equivalent overstatement of expenses. It may be appropriate to offset misstatements within the same account balance or class of transactions; however, the risk that further undetected misstatements may exist is [to be] considered before concluding that offsetting even immaterial misstatements is appropriate. (para A14)

In some circumstances, the auditor may judge misstatements to be material, individually or when considered together with other misstatements, even when they fall below planning materiality or the tolerable error for a particular class of transactions, account balance or disclosure. Such circumstances include the extent to which the misstatement:

- affects compliance with regulatory requirements, debt covenants or other contractual requirements;
- relates to the incorrect selection or application of an accounting policy that has an immaterial effect on the current period's financial statements but is likely to have a material effect on future periods' financial statements;
- masks a change in earnings or other trends, especially in the context of general economic and industry conditions;
- affects ratios used to evaluate the entity's financial position, results of operations or cash flows;

---

[28] In Chapter 9, section 9.3.1, we explain that, during the planning stage of the audit, planning materiality and tolerable error are usually determined on the basis of estimates of the entity's financial results because its actual financial results are not then known. As the audit progresses, the auditor is required to revise planning materiality and/or tolerable error for classes of transactions, account balances or disclosures if the audit evidence gathered indicates that such revision is appropriate. Therefore, any significant revision of planning materiality and tolerable error is likely to have been effected before reaching the closing stages of the audit. Nevertheless, when evaluating the effect of uncorrected misstatements on the financial statements, the auditor may consider it appropriate (given the findings of the audit) to lower planning materiality and/or tolerable error for certain classes of transactions, account balances or disclosures and, in this event, further audit procedures may need to be performed to ensure that sufficient appropriate audit evidence is obtained on which to base the audit opinion.

- has the effect of increasing management compensation, for example, by ensuring that the requirements for the award of bonuses or other incentives are satisfied;
- is significant in the light of previous communications to users of the financial statements such as earnings forecasts;
- is an omission of information not specifically required by the applicable financial reporting framework but which, in the auditor's judgment, is important to the financial statement users' understanding of the financial position, financial performance or cash flows of the entity;
- affects other information the auditee will communicate in documents containing the audited financial statements (such as the company's annual report) that may reasonably be expected to influence the economic decisions of users of the financial statements.

The cumulative effect of immaterial uncorrected misstatements in prior periods may have a material effect on the current period's financial statements. As a result, auditors' consideration of uncorrected misstatements is not limited to the current period. As indicated above, they must be conscious of the effect uncorrected errors in the current year may have on future periods; similarly, they are required to consider the effect of uncorrected misstatements in prior periods on relevant classes of transactions, account balances or disclosures, and the financial statements as a whole, in the current period (ISA 450, para A18).

13.6.4 Review of the overall presentation of the financial statements

During their final review of the financial statements, auditors are required to evaluate the overall presentation of the financial statements and their conformity (or otherwise) with the applicable financial reporting framework. This involves, *inter alia*, evaluating whether the information presented in the individual financial statements and the notes thereto is properly classified and described, and whether the form, arrangement and content of the financial statements and related notes are appropriate. The evaluation includes consideration of the terminology used, the amount of detail provided and the clarity with which the measurement bases are disclosed (ISA 330: *The Auditor's Responses to Assessed Risks*, IAASB, 2009d, paras 24, A59).

13.7 EVALUATION OF AUDIT EVIDENCE GATHERED AND FORMATION OF THE AUDIT OPINION

Before reaching a final opinion on the truth and fairness of the financial statements and their compliance (or otherwise) with the applicable financial reporting framework, auditors are required to determine:

(a) whether their assessment of the risk of material misstatement at the assertion level for classes of transactions, account balances and other disclosures remains appropriate, and

(b) whether sufficient appropriate audit evidence has been gathered in relation to each assertion in each significant class of transactions, account balance and disclosure in each audit segment (ISA 330, paras 25, 26).

Let us examine the reasons for these requirements a little more closely.

(a) Re-evaluation of risk assessment

The auditor needs to re-evaluate his/her assessment of the risk of material misstatement at the assertion level during the final stage of the audit because, as the audit has progressed and audit evidence has been gathered, information may have come to light that differs from the information on which the auditor's risk assessment was based. For example:

- the results of substantive tests may indicate an unexpected significant deficiency in the auditee's internal controls;
- discrepancies in, or omissions from, the accounting records or other documents, or conflicting audit evidence, may have been found; and/or
- the analytical procedures performed for the final review of the financial statements may indicate a previously unrecognised material misstatement.

If these or similar factors prompt a revision of the auditor's risk of material misstatement at the assertion level for classes of transactions, account balances or other disclosures, this will result in the performance of additional audit procedures to address the newly assessed risk(s) (ISA 330, para A60).

(b) Sufficient appropriate audit evidence

Before concluding the audit, the auditor (i.e., the audit engagement partner) needs to be assured that sufficient appropriate evidence has been gathered during the audit on which to base an audit opinion. ISA 330 (para A62) explains that the auditor's judgment about what constitutes sufficient appropriate audit evidence will be affected by a number of factors including the following:

- the significance of any potential misstatement identified in an assertion and the likelihood of it having a material effect, individually or when aggregated with other misstatements, on the financial statements;
- the results of audit procedures performed, including whether they have identified specific instances of fraud or error;
- the source and reliability (and hence the persuasiveness) of the audit evidence obtained;
- the auditor's understanding of the auditee and its environment (including the effectiveness of its internal controls).

In order to determine that sufficient appropriate audit evidence has been obtained, bearing in mind factors such as those outlined above, the engagement partner reviews the work performed during the audit, as documented in the audit working papers, and has discussions with audit team members as s/he thinks appropriate. The review of the audit documentation is designed to achieve a number of objectives. These include ensuring that:

- conclusions reached in relation to specific audit objectives are consistent with the results obtained from the audit procedures performed;
- all questions and difficulties arising during the course of the audit have been resolved;
- all audit work has been properly performed, documented and reviewed;
- the information presented in the financial statements complies with relevant statutory and regulatory requirements;
- the accounting policies adopted are in accordance with the financial reporting framework adopted by the entity, and are appropriate to the entity, properly disclosed and consistently applied;
- the financial statements as a whole, and the assertions contained therein, are consistent with the auditor's knowledge of the entity's business and the results of audit procedures performed;
- the presentation of the financial statements (including their form, content and manner of disclosure) is appropriate.

Audit engagement partners frequently use checklists to ensure that all aspects of the financial statements are properly covered.

On the basis of his/her review of the audit documentation, together with knowledge gained during the audit, the audit engagement partner forms an opinion as to whether the financial statements give a true and fair view of the auditee's financial position and performance and comply with the applicable financial reporting framework. However, for all but small audits, a second audit partner, who has not been involved in the audit, usually reviews the audit documentation with similar objectives to those of the audit engagement partner. Indeed, as we note in Chapter 7, section 7.6.4, for all listed companies and other companies that meet the audit firm's criteria for an engagement quality control review, ISA 220: *Quality Control for an Audit of Financial Statements* (IAASB, 2009a) requires an engagement quality control review to be performed.

ISA 220 (para 7b) explains that an engagement quality control review is a process designed to provide an objective evaluation of the significant judgments made by the audit engagement team and the conclusions it reached in forming the opinion to be expressed in the auditor's report. It involves, *inter alia*:

- discussing with the audit engagement partner significant matters arising during, and in relation to, the audit;

COMPLETION AND REVIEW _____

- reviewing the financial statements and considering the appropriateness of the opinion proposed to be expressed in the auditor's report;
- reviewing selected audit working papers relating to the significant judgments made by the audit team and the conclusions it reached;
- considering whether proper consultation has taken place on matters involving differences of opinion or difficult or contentious issues, and the conclusions reached as an outcome of the consultations;
- (for listed company audits) considering the audit team's evaluation of the audit firm's independence in relation to the audit engagement (ISA 220, paras 20, 21).

In respect of what amounts to 'significant judgments', ISA 220 (para A28) explains that these include:

- Significant risks identified during the engagement . . . and the responses to those risks . . . , including the engagement team's assessment of, and response to, the risk of fraud. . . .
- Judgments made, particularly with respect to materiality and significant risks.
- The significance and disposition of corrected and uncorrected misstatements identified during the audit.
- The matters to be communicated to [the directors] and, where applicable, other parties such as regulatory bodies.[29,30]

13.8 REVIEW OF UNAUDITED INFORMATION

Even if the financial statements are found to be in order, before the auditor can complete the audit one further procedure needs to be performed. ISA 720: *The Auditor's Responsibilities Relating to Other Information in Documents Containing Audited Financial Statements* (IAASB, 2009m, paras 6, 14) requires auditors to review any unaudited information which accompanies the audited financial statements (known as 'other information') to determine whether it contains information that is materially inconsistent with the financial statements and to identify any material statement that is factually incorrect. This requirement accords with the fundamental principle of external auditing – *Association* which states:

> Auditors allow their reports to be included in documents containing other information only if they consider that the additional information is not in conflict with the matters covered by their report and they have no cause to believe it to be misleading. (FRC, 2013a, Appendix 2)

---

[29] Further details about engagement quality control reviews are provided in Chapter 7, section 7.6.4.

[30] Auditors' communication with their auditees' directors are discussed in Chapter 14, section 14.8.

ISA 720 defines 'other information', 'inconsistency' and 'misstatement of fact' as follows:

> Other information – Financial and non-financial information (other than the financial statements and the auditor's report thereon) which is included, either by law, regulation or custom, in a document containing audited financial statements and the auditor's report thereon. (para 5a)

> Inconsistency – Other information that contradicts information contained in the audited financial statements. A material inconsistency may raise doubt about the audit conclusions drawn from audit evidence previously obtained and, possibly, about the basis for the auditor's opinion on the financial statements. (para 5b)

> Misstatement of fact – Other information that is unrelated to matters appearing in the audited financial statements that is incorrectly stated or presented. A material misstatement of fact may undermine the credibility of the document containing audited financial statements. (para 5c)

In their review of other information (which includes information presented in the unaudited portion of companies' annual reports), ISA 720 requires auditors to:

(a) actively search for any material inconsistencies between the other information and the audited financial statements; and

(b) while searching for inconsistencies, to remain alert for any material misstatements of fact.

ISA (UK and Ireland) 720: Section A – *The Auditor's Responsibilities Relating to Other Information in Documents Containing Audited Financial Statements* (FRC, 2012c) requires auditors in the UK and Ireland to go further. In addition to identifying material inconsistencies between the other information and the audited financial statements, these auditors are required:

> to identify any information that is apparently materially incorrect based on, or inconsistent with, the knowledge [they] acquired . . . in the course of performing the audit or that is otherwise misleading. (para 6-1)

ISA (UK and Ireland) 720 also explains:

> A material misstatement of fact in other information would potentially include an inconsistency between information obtained by the auditor during the audit (such as information obtained as part of the planning process or analytical procedures, or as written representations) and information which is included in the other information. (para A10-1)

The auditor's action(s) on discovering a material inconsistency or material misstatement of fact depends on which of these eventualities has occurred.[31]

---

[31] Although the requirements of auditors in respect of identifying material inconsistencies and material misstatements of fact in other information differ between ISA 720 (IAASB, 2009m) and ISA (UK and Ireland) 720 (FRC, 2012c), the actions of auditors on finding such matters are the same under both versions of the Standard.

(a) Material inconsistency

If auditors discover a material inconsistency, they need to ascertain whether the financial statements or the other information needs revision. However, in either case, they should seek to resolve the matter through discussion with the auditee's senior executives and, if necessary, with its directors (or, more usually, its audit committee). If the financial statements are in error and the directors refuse to make the required amendment, the auditor is to express a modified opinion in the audit report (ISA 720, IAASB, 2009m, para 9). However, if the other information is incorrect and the directors refuse to amend it as requested by the auditor, ISA 720, para 10, provides the auditor with three options, namely:

- to describe the material inconsistency in an 'Other Matter' paragraph in the audit report,
- to withhold the audit report until the required correction is made, or
- to withdraw from the engagement. Although ISA 720 provides this option, it is almost inconceivable that an auditor would exercise it at this late stage of an audit – they would have realised there were serious difficulties with the audit very much earlier and, if they thought it appropriate, they would have resigned at that stage.

Two other options may apply to auditors in the UK under the Companies Act (CA) 2006.

1. If the company's strategic report or the directors' report is materially inconsistent with the financial statements,[32] the auditor is legally obliged to refer to the inconsistency in the audit report (CA 2006, s. 496). Such inconsistencies may include, for example, contradictions between amounts or narrative appearing in the financial statements and statements made about the company's financial position or performance in the directors' report or about the risks and uncertainties the company faces in the strategic report.

2. The CA 2006, s. 502, provides auditors with the right to be heard at any general meeting of the company's shareholders on matters that concern them as auditors. Thus, they have an opportunity to highlight any material inconsistency between the other information in the company's annual report and the audited financial statements. Similarly, they can use this opportunity to draw members' attention to a misstatement of fact in the other information.

---

[32] As explained in Chapter 5, section 5.2.2, the directors of all UK companies are required to prepare a directors' report, and those of all but small companies (which are generally also exempt from having an audit) are required to prepare a strategic report, for each financial year of the company. These reports are included in the company's annual report along with the audited financial statements and other information the company wishes to provide.

(b) Material misstatements of fact in other information

If auditors should discover an apparent material misstatement of fact in the other information, they are required to discuss the matter with the auditee's senior executives and, if necessary, with the directors (or, more usually, the audit committee). ISA 720 (para A10) observes that auditors may not be in a position to evaluate the validity of some of the statements included in the other information or the directors'/senior executives' responses to their enquiries. In such circumstances, the auditor may conclude that the matter in question reflects a valid difference of judgment or opinion rather than a misstatement of fact. However, if, after discussing the matter with the senior executives/directors, the auditor still considers there is a material misstatement of fact, s/he is required to request the directors to consult with a qualified third party, such as the company's lawyer(s), and the auditor is to consider the advice the directors receive from the third party. In the event that the directors continue to refuse to effect a correction the auditor considers necessary, "the auditor shall notify [the directors] of the auditor's concern regarding the other information and take any further appropriate action" (ISA 720, para 16). Such action may include describing the material misstatement of fact in an 'Other Matter' paragraph in the audit report, reporting the matter at a general meeting of the company's shareholders and/or obtaining advice from the audit firm's lawyer.

A special situation arises in the UK for the auditors of companies listed on the London Stock Exchange which are required (or choose) to comply with *The UK Corporate Governance Code* (FRC, 2012a) or to explain the respects in which they have not done so.[33] As we shall see in Chapter 14 when we examine audit reports prepared by auditors in the UK and Ireland in accordance with ISA (UK and Ireland) 700: *The Independent Auditor's Report on Financial Statements* (FRC, 2013c), these auditors are required to include in their audit reports a section headed "Matters on which we are required to report by exception" in which they explain such matters and provide an appropriate conclusion thereon. These matters include statements made by a listed company's directors about their application of *The UK Corporate Governance Code* (FRC, 2012a) which the auditor considers to be materially inconsistent with, or materially incorrect based on, knowledge the auditor has acquired during the performance of the audit or which, in the auditor's opinion, are otherwise misleading.[34]

---

[33] As explained in Chapter 5, section 5.2.2, companies with a Premium Listing on the London Stock Exchange are required to comply with the Code or explain the respects in which they have not done so but other listed and non-listed public companies are encouraged to do likewise.

[34] Examples of matters on which auditors in the UK and Ireland are required to report by exception are provided in Chapter 5, section 5.5.5 and Chapter 14, section 14.3.5.

13.9 FINAL CONFERENCE

Once all audit matters have been resolved and the audit engagement partner (in consultation with senior audit team members and, in applicable cases, the engagement quality control reviewer) has formed an opinion about the financial statements and prepared the audit report, a final conference is held between the client's directors (or its audit committee), the audit engagement partner and (usually) the audit manager. The conduct and findings of the audit are discussed, the financial statements are signed by one or more directors[35] (if this has not already been done at a previous directors' meeting) and, finally, the audit report is signed and dated by the audit engagement partner.[36] It is important that the engagement partner does not sign the audit report prior to the directors signing the financial statements. By signing the financial statements, the directors signal their responsibility for, and acceptance of, the statements as presented. The auditor's report expresses an opinion on the financial statements prepared, presented and approved by the directors.[37] The date of the audit report is of the utmost importance because it signifies the end of the period considered by the auditor when expressing an opinion on the financial statements. It marks the end of the 'subsequent events period' in which events may have occurred that affect the truth and fairness of the financial statements as at the date of the financial statements.

13.10 SUMMARY

In this chapter we have discussed the steps which constitute the completion and review phase of the audit. More specifically, we have examined the importance of, and procedures used for, the review for contingent liabilities and commitments, and the review for events (adjusting and non-adjusting) occurring subsequent to the date of the financial statements. We have also discussed the auditor's responsibilities with respect to the going concern assumption and the meaning and significance of written representations. Additionally, we have reviewed the steps involved in the final review of the financial statements and in evaluating the evidence gathered during the audit and forming an opinion about the truth and fairness of the financial statements and their compliance (or otherwise) with the applicable financial reporting framework. In the concluding

---

[35] The statutory requirement for one or more directors to sign the auditee's balance sheet (statement of financial position) is referred to in Chapter 5, section 5.2.3.

[36] As noted in Chapter 5 (section 5.5.1), the CA 2006, s. 505, requires the audit report to state the name of the auditor and, where the auditor is a firm, the name of the person who signed it as senior statutory auditor (in effect, the audit engagement partner).

[37] Cuthbert (1982) reports some salutary tales about what can happen if the auditor signs the audit report before the directors sign the financial statements.

sections of the chapter, we have drawn attention to the need for auditors to review unaudited information in their clients' annual reports (or other documents containing the audited financial statements), noted the importance of auditors signing their audit reports after the directors have signed the financial statements and explained the significance of the date of the audit report.

SELF-REVIEW QUESTIONS

13.1 Define (a) contingent liabilities and (b) commitments and explain briefly why contingent liabilities and commitments may present problems for the auditor.

13.2 List five procedures auditors commonly use during their review for contingent liabilities and commitments.

13.3 (a) Briefly distinguish between (i) adjusting and (ii) non-adjusting subsequent events.
(b) Give one specific example to illustrate each of these types of subsequent events.

13.4 (a) State the period which is subject to the auditor's review for subsequent events.
(b) List three procedures auditors commonly use during their review for subsequent events.

13.5 Explain briefly what is meant by the going concern assumption.

13.6 Explain briefly the auditor's responsibility for assessing the propriety of the auditee adopting the going concern assumption during:
(i) the ' risk assessment' phase of the audit;
(ii) the 'evidence gathering' phase of the audit;
(iii) the 'completion and review' phase of the audit.

13.7 Explain briefly what is meant by written representations and outline five matters for which auditors are required to obtain such representations.

13.8 List four objectives of the audit engagement partner's final review of the audit documentation.

13.9 Explain briefly the purpose of an engagement quality control review and how it is conducted.

13.10 Explain the significance of dating the audit report.

REFERENCES

Auditing Practices Board (APB). (2009). *Developments in Corporate Governance Affecting the Responsibilities of Auditors of UK Companies.* Bulletin 2009/4. London: Financial Reporting Council.

Cuthbert, S. (1982). How easy to hoodwink the auditor! *Accountancy, 93*(1063), 136.

Financial Reporting Council (FRC). (2009). *Going Concern and Liquidity Risk.* London: FRC.

Financial Reporting Council (FRC). (2012a). *The UK Code of Corporate Governance.* London: FRC.

Financial Reporting Council (FRC). (2012b). *About the FRC,* www.frc.org.uk/About -the-FRC.aspx, accessed 14 May 2013.

Financial Reporting Council (FRC). (2012c). International Standard on Auditing (ISA) (UK and Ireland) 720 Section A – *The Auditor's Responsibilities Relating to Other Information in Documents Containing Audited Financial Statements.* London: FRC.

Financial Reporting Council (FRC). (2013a). *Scope and Authority of Audit and Assurance Pronouncements.* London: FRC.

Financial Reporting Council (FRC). (2013b). *Consultation Paper: Implementing the Recommendations of the Sharman Panel.* London: FRC.

Financial Reporting Council (FRC). (2013c). International Standard on Auditing (ISA) (UK and Ireland) 700: *The Independent Auditor's Report on Financial Statements.* London: FRC

International Auditing and Assurance Standards Board (IAASB). (2009a). International Standard on Auditing (ISA) 220: *Quality Control for an Audit of Financial Statements* New York: International Federation of Accountants.

International Auditing and Assurance Standards Board (IAASB). (2009b). International Standard on Auditing (ISA) 240: *The Auditor's Responsibilities Relating to Fraud in an Audit of Financial Statements.* New York: International Federation of Accountants.

International Auditing and Assurance Standards Board (IAASB). (2009c). International Standard on Auditing (ISA) 250: *Consideration of Laws and Regulations in an Audit of Financial Statements.* New York: International Federation of Accountants.

International Auditing and Assurance Standards Board (IAASB). (2009d). International Standard on Auditing (ISA) 330: *The Auditor's Responses to Assessed Risks.* New York: International Federation of Accountants.

International Auditing and Assurance Standards Board (IAASB). (2009e). International Standard on Auditing (ISA) 450: *Evaluation of Misstatements Identified during the Audit.* New York: International Federation of Accountants.

International Auditing and Assurance Standards Board (IAASB). (2009f). International Standard on Auditing (ISA) 501: *Audit Evidence – Specific Considerations for Selected Items.* New York: International Federation of Accountants.

International Auditing and Assurance Standards Board (IAASB). (2009g). International Standard on Auditing (ISA) 520: *Analytical Procedures.* New York: International Federation of Accountants.

International Auditing and Assurance Standards Board (IAASB). (2009h). International Standard on Auditing (ISA) 540: *Auditing Accounting Estimates, Including Fair Value Accounting Estimates, and Related Disclosures*. New York: International Federation of Accountants.

International Auditing and Assurance Standards Board (IAASB). (2009i). International Standard on Auditing (ISA) 550: *Related Parties*. New York: International Federation of Accountants.

International Auditing and Assurance Standards Board (IAASB). (2009j). International Standard on Auditing (ISA) 560: *Subsequent Events*. New York: International Federation of Accountants.

International Auditing and Assurance Standards Board (IAASB). (2009k). International Standard on Auditing (ISA) 570: *Going Concern*. New York: International Federation of Accountants.

International Auditing and Assurance Standards Board (IAASB). (2009l). International Standard on Auditing (ISA) 580: *Written Representations*. New York: International Federation of Accountants.

International Auditing and Assurance Standards Board (IAASB). (2009m). International Standard on Auditing (ISA) 720: *The Auditor's Responsibilities Relating to Other Information in Documents Containing Audited Financial Statements*. New York: International Federation of Accountants.

International Federation of Accountants (IFAC). (2009). *Glossary of Terms*, included in *Handbook of International Quality Control, Auditing, Review, Other Assurance and Related Services Pronouncements 2010 Edition*. New York: IFAC.

Porter, B.A. (1993). An empirical study of the audit expectation-performance gap. *Accounting and Business Research*, 24(93), 49–68.

Sharman, Lord. (2012, June). *The Sharman Inquiry: Going Concern and Liquidity Risks: Lessons for Companies and Auditors*. Final Report and Recommendations of the Panel of Inquiry. London: Financial Reporting Council.

ADDITIONAL READING

Arnedo, L., Lizarraga, F., & Sanchez, S. (2008). Going-concern uncertainties in pre-bankrupt audit reports: New evidence regarding discretionary accruals and wording ambiguity. *International Journal of Auditing*, 12(1), 25–44.

Basioudis, I.G., Papakonstantinou, E., & Geiger, M.A. (2008). Audit fees, non-audit fees and auditor going-concern reporting decisions in the United Kingdom. *Abacus*, 44(3), 284–309.

Beattie, V., Fearnley, S., & Hines, T. (2011). *Reaching Key Financial Reporting Decisions: How Directors and Auditors Interact*. Chichester: John Wiley & Sons, Ltd.

Blay, A.D., Geiger, M.A., & North, D.S. (2011). The auditor's going-concern opinion as a communication of risk, *Auditing: A Journal of Practice & Theory*, 30(2), 77–102.

Brown, H.L., & Johnstone, K.M. (2009). Resolving disputed financial reporting issues: Effects of auditor negotiation experience and engagement risk on negotiation process and outcome. *Auditing: A Journal of Practice & Theory*, *28*(2), 65–92.

Callaghan, J., Parkash, M., & Singhal, R. (2009). Going-concern audit opinions and the provision of non-audit services: Implications for auditor independence of bankrupt firms. *Auditing: A Journal of Practice & Theory*, *28*(1), 153–169.

Carcello, J.V., Vanstaelen, A., & Willenborg, M. (2009). Rules rather than discretion in audit standards: Going concern opinions in Belgium. *Accounting Review*, *84*(5), 1395–1428.

Coyne, M.P., Biggs, S.F., & Rich, J.S. (2010, Priming/reaction-time evidence of the structure of auditors' knowledge of financial statement errors. *Auditing: A Journal of Practice & Theory*, *29*(1), 99–123.

Fargher, N.L., & Jiang, L. (2008). Changes in the audit environment and auditors' propensity to issue going-concern opinions. *Auditing: A Journal of Practice & Theory*, *27*(2), 55–77.

Fu, H., Tan, H.-T., & Zhang, J. (2011). Effect of auditor negotiation experience and client negotiating style on auditors' judgements in an auditor–client negotiation context. *Auditing: A Journal of Practice & Theory*, *30*(3), 225–237.

Gibbins, M., McCracken, S., & Salterio, S.E. (2010). The auditor's strategy selection for negotiation with management: Flexibility of initial accounting position and nature of the relationship. *Accounting, Organizations and Society*, *35*(6), 579–595.

Hatfield, R.C., Houston, R.W., Stefaniak, C.M., & Usrey, S. (2010). The effect of magnitude of audit difference and prior client concessions on negotiations of proposed adjustments. *Accounting Review*, *85*(5), 1647–1668.

Hollindale, J., Kent, P., & McNamara, R. (2011). Auditor tactics in negotiations: A research note. *International Journal of Auditing*, *15*(3), 288–300.

Joe, J., Wright, A., & Wright, S. (2011). The impact of client and misstatement characteristics on the disposition of proposed audit adjustments. *Auditing: A Journal of Practice & Theory*, *30*(2), 103–124.

Kaplan, S.E., O'Donnell, E.F., & Arel, B.M. (2008). The influence of auditor experience on the persuasiveness of information provided by management. *Auditing: A Journal of Practice & Theory*, *27*(1), 67–83.

Kaplan, S.E., & Williams, D.D. (2012) The changing relationship between audit firm size and going concern reporting. *Accounting, Organizations and Society*, *37*(5), 322–341.

Krishnan, G.V., & Sengupta, P. (2011). How do auditors perceive recognized vs. disclosed lease and pension obligations? Evidence from fees and going-concern opinions. *International Journal of Auditing*, *15*(2), 127–149.

Lee, T.A., Clarke, F., & Dean, G. (2008). The dominant senior manager and the reasonably careful, skilful, and cautious auditor. *Critical Perspectives on Accounting*, *19*(5), 677–711.

McCraken, S., Salterio, S.E., & Gibbins, M. (2008). Auditor–client management relationships and roles in negotiating financial reporting. *Accounting, Organizations and Society*, *33*(4–5), 362–383.

Menon, K., & Williams, D.D. (2010). Investor reaction to going concern audit reports. *Accounting Review*, *85*(6), 2075–2105.

Rennie, M.D., Kopp, L.S., & Lemon, W.M. (2010). Exploring trust and the audit–client relationship: Factors influencing the auditor's trust of a client representative. *Auditing: A Journal of Practice & Theory*, *29*(1), 279–293.

Robinson, D. (2008). Auditor independence and auditor-provided tax services: Evidence from going-concern audit opinions prior to bankruptcy filings. *Auditing: A Journal of Practice & Theory*, *27*(2), 31–54.

Shah, S. (2009) In the spotlight (going concern). *Accountancy*, *143*(1386), 64–65.

14 Auditors' Reports to Users of Financial Statements and to Management

LEARNING OBJECTIVES

After studying the material in this chapter you should be able to:
- state the auditor's statutory reporting obligations;
- explain what is required in order for financial statements to provide a 'true and fair view';
- explain what is meant by 'adequate accounting records';
- describe the format of a standard audit report;
- explain the various types of audit opinion expressed in audit reports and the circumstances in which each is appropriate;
- describe significant differences between the standard 'expanded' (or 'long form') audit report and the former 'short form' report;
- discuss the advantages and disadvantages of (i) the 'expanded' and (ii) the 'short form' audit report;
- discuss the advantages and disadvantages of (i) a standardised and (ii) a 'free form' audit report;
- explain the purpose, form, content and timing of auditors' communication of significant audit matters to those charged with the auditee's governance.

14.1 INTRODUCTION

During the last few chapters we have journeyed through the various stages of the audit process and we have reached the point where the auditor is ready to report his/her audit findings to shareholders, and other users of the audited financial statements, and also to those charged with the auditee's governance. The report to financial statement users communicates the auditor's conclusions about, amongst other things, the truth and fairness with which the financial statements portray the entity's financial position and performance and their compliance (or otherwise) with the applicable financial reporting framework and relevant legislation. The auditor's report to those charged with the company's governance (i.e., the board of directors) is a private communication between the auditor and the directors which addresses various aspects of the audit and the entity's financial reporting process; it highlights, in particular, any significant deficiencies in the company's internal control discovered during the audit and recommends ways in which these might be rectified.

In this chapter we discuss the auditor's reporting obligations to financial statement users and to those charged with the auditee's governance. We explore the issue of what is required for financial statements to be adjudged 'true and fair' and examine the format of a standard audit report. We also consider the various types of audit opinion the auditor may express and the circumstances in which each is appropriate. Observing that the audit report is frequently the auditor's only opportunity to communicate with users of the audited financial statements, we discuss the differences between, and the advantages and disadvantages of, the 'expanded' (or 'long form') audit report currently in use and the former 'short form' report. We also consider the advantages and disadvantages of using a standardised audit report rather than one in which the auditor uses whatever format and wording s/he likes. Before concluding the chapter we address the topic of auditors' communications with those charged with governance, focusing in particular on their purpose, form, content and timing.

14.2 AUDITORS' REPORTING OBLIGATIONS UNDER THE COMPANIES ACT 2006

As we note in Chapter 5, the Companies Act 2006 (CA 2006) places a major responsibility on auditors. First, it specifies that the directors of every company must prepare financial statements comprising a balance sheet and a profit or loss account for each financial year and, in the case of a company with subsidiaries, group financial statements.[1] These financial statements are required to:
- give a true and fair view of the company's (or group's) state of affairs as at the end of the financial year and of its profit or loss for the financial year;
- comply with the applicable financial reporting framework;[2]

---

[1] As we note in Chapter 5, footnote 11, in general, the directors of parent companies within a group are required to prepare group (consolidated) financial statements (that is, financial statements which treat the parent company and its subsidiaries as a single entity) in addition to producing financial statements for the parent company. However, if the financial statements meet the requirements of CA 2006, s. 408, a separate profit and loss account for the parent company need not be prepared. CA 2006, s. 408 requires:

    (i) the notes to the parent company's balance sheet to disclose the parent company's profit or loss, and

    (ii) the parent company's financial statements to disclose that the exemption from preparing a profit or loss account applies.

Although CA 2006 refers to companies preparing 'a balance sheet' and 'profit and loss account', International Accounting Standards refer to these documents as, respectively, "a statement of financial position" and "income statement".

[2] International Financial Reporting Standards (IFRS: 'IAS accounts') or United Kingdom Generally Accepted Accounting Practice (UK GAAP: 'Companies Act accounts'). The requirements relating to these financial reporting frameworks are explained in Chapter 5, section 5.2.1.

- be properly prepared in accordance with CA 2006; and
- for the consolidated financial statements of groups whose securities are traded on a regulated market in any European Union (EU) Member State, comply with the EU's IAS Regulation (EU, 2002).

The company's directors are responsible for preparing financial statements which meet the statutory requirements outlined above. However, except in the case of companies which are exempt from having an audit,[3] CA 2006 gives auditors the responsibility of examining the financial statements and forming and expressing an opinion on whether or not they meet the statutory requirements. Additionally, auditors are required to form an opinion on whether:

- adequate accounting records have been kept by the company;
- returns, adequate for their audit, have been received from branches (or components) of the company they have not visited;
- the financial statements are in agreement with the underlying accounting records and returns;
- for a quoted company,[4] the auditable part of the directors' remuneration report is in agreement with the accounting records and returns;
- they have received all the information and explanations they required for the purposes of their audit.

In cases where auditors are of the opinion that any of these requirements have *not* been met, they are required to say so in their audit report (CA 2006, s. 498). Additionally, auditors are required to state whether, in their opinion:

- the information given in the strategic report and directors' report is consistent with the financial statements, and
- for quoted companies, that part of the directors' remuneration report that is subject to audit has been properly prepared in accordance with CA 2006.[5]

Two of the matters on which auditors must form an opinion require some explanation, namely:

(i) adequate accounting records;
(ii) a true and fair view.

(i) Adequate accounting records

CA 2006 (s. 386) requires all companies to maintain adequate accounting records. The Act explains that such records must be sufficient to show and explain the company's transactions and, amongst other things:

---

[3] An explanation of companies exempted from an audit is provided in Chapter 5, section 5.2.1.

[4] A quoted company is one whose equity share capital is traded on a regulated market in a Member State of the EEA (that is, any Member State of the EU, with the exception of Croatia, together with Norway, Iceland and Liechtenstein) or on the New York Stock Exchange or NASDAQ (CA 2006, s. 385).

[5] The requirements relating to strategic, directors' and directors' remuneration reports are explained in Chapter 5, section 5.2.2.

- disclose the company's financial position, with reasonable accuracy, at any time;
- enable the directors to prepare a balance sheet (statement of financial position) and profit and loss account (income statement) which comply with the applicable reporting framework;
- record the day-to-day details of all receipts and payments of cash;
- provide details of the company's assets and liabilities.

Additionally for companies dealing in goods:

- provide details of stock (inventory) held by the company at the end of each financial year and the related stocktaking (inventory counting) records;
- provide details of trading goods bought and sold (other than goods sold by way of ordinary retail trade). The records must be in sufficient detail to enable the goods, and the buyers and the sellers to be identified.

It can be seen from these requirements that CA 2006 is both specific and strict as regards the criteria to be met in order for a company's accounting records to be considered adequate. It does not, however, lay down any detailed requirements for particular procedures or controls to be incorporated in companies' accounting systems.

It is important to appreciate that auditors must form an opinion as to whether or not the auditee has maintained adequate accounting records in *every* audit. However, CA 2006 requires them to state their opinion in the audit report only when they consider that adequate accounting records have *not* been kept. This is an example of 'exception reporting'.

(ii) A true and fair view

Although the directors of companies are required to prepare annual financial statements which give a true and fair view of their company's financial position and performance, what is meant by a 'true and fair view' has not been explained in legislation or by the courts. This has led to conflicting interpretations of the phrase. As Johnston, Edgar and Hays (1982) observed:

> It is clear that the interpretation applied by most accountants is that the words 'true and fair' have a technical meaning. It is also clear that many lawyers (as well as investors) are of the opinion that these words have a popular meaning which should be followed by those responsible for their application. (p. 259)

The following quotations serve to illustrate the opposing viewpoints of lawyers and accountants. First the lawyers:

> [I]t is probably not an exaggeration to assert that company accounts remain almost unintelligible to the general public, including shareholders and intending investors, and that practices continue which are difficult to reconcile with the statutory obligations that balance sheets give a true and fair view of the company's affairs and that the auditors certify that the accounts give a true and fair

view of the company's affairs. . . . Essentially, the question is: are the accounts where there has been an undervaluation of assets[6] 'true'? . . . 'True and fair' are unambiguous words. Practice needs to conform to the legal obligation. (Northey, 1965, pp. 41–42)

Although this view may have intuitive appeal, it does not provide guidance on how it may be operationalised. It does not recognise, for example, that a range of possible 'true values' exist – historical cost, net realisable value, current replacement cost, deprival value and net present value. Which should be used to give a true and fair view of asset values?

Recognising such difficulties, accountants assert that criteria are needed to provide benchmarks against which the 'true and fair' requirement can be judged. This has resulted in accountants giving the phrase a technical interpretation. The Inflation Accounting Committee (1975; Sandilands Committee) explained this as follows:

> Accounts drawn up in accordance with generally accepted accounting principles, consistently applied, are in practice regarded as showing a 'true and fair view'. . . . The [Companies] Acts . . . give only limited guidance to the accountancy profession in interpreting the phrase 'true and fair' and it has been traditionally left to the profession to develop accounting practices which are regarded as leading to a 'true and fair view' being shown. (paras 50, 52)

The above quotation indicates that the Sandilands Committee was of the opinion that financial statements prepared in accordance with accounting standards will provide a true and fair view. This stance was supported by legal counsel, whose opinion on the matter was sought by the United Kingdom's (UK) Accounting Standards Board. Counsel stated:

> Accounts which meet the true and fair requirement will in general follow rather than depart from standards and [any] departure is sufficiently abnormal to require to be justified. . . . [It is likely] that the Courts will hold that in general compliance with accounting standards is necessary to meet the true and fair requirement. (Arden, 1993, para 7)

However, Counsel went on to observe:

> . . . true and fair is a dynamic concept. Thus what is required to show a true and fair view is subject to continuous rebirth. (Arden, 1993, para 14)

It is interesting to note that some commentators have expressed the view that the legislature deliberately delegated to the accountancy profession the task of defining what qualifies as 'true and fair' financial statements at any point of time. For example, Ryan (1974) (Commissioner for Corporate Affairs in New South Wales) observed that, if a court were called upon to determine whether a

---

[6] Undervaluation as a result of adherence to historical cost principles. The introduction of 'fair value accounting' in IFRS has, to an extent, overcome Northey's difficulty of the undervaluation of assets. However, the fact remains that a number of values may be identified as 'true'.

particular set of financial statements presented a true and fair view, the fact that they had or had not been prepared in accordance with the principles embodied in professional pronouncements would be very persuasive. He continued:

> I have come to the conclusion . . . that in selecting the phrase 'true and fair view' as the standard by which the profit or loss of a company and the state of its affairs are to be judged, the Legislature in effect conferred a legislative function on the accountancy profession. It is a legislative function of an ambulatory nature: what is 'true and fair' at any particular point of time will correspond with what professional accountants as a body conceive to be proper accounting principles. The evolution, development and general acceptance of those principles will cause the concept of what is 'true and fair' to shift accordingly. (p. 14)

Although accountants have applied a technical interpretation to the phrase 'true and fair', they nevertheless acknowledge that financial statements prepared in conformity with accounting standards may not, in all circumstances, provide the required true and fair view. This point was emphasised by Flint (1980) when he observed:

> [P]rescription by legislation and professional standards and guidance statements . . . [is] necessary in the interests of good order and effective communication. . . . But giving a 'true and fair view' must always be a standard of a higher order. Whatever may be the extent of prescription, an overriding requirement to give a 'true and fair view' is, at the lowest level of its utility, a safety valve protecting users from bias, inadequacy or deficiency in the rules; a fail-safe device for the unavoidable shortcomings of prescription. More positively, its real utility is in establishing an enduring conceptual standard for disclosure in accounting and reporting to ensure that there is always relevant disclosure – where necessary beyond the prescription – based on an independent professional judgement. (p. 9)

Similarly, as we note in Chapter 5 (section 5.2.1), CA 2006 recognises that compliance with the applicable financial reporting framework may not always result in the provision of a true and fair view. In respect of 'Companies Act accounts', the Act provides that, if compliance with UK Generally Accepted Accounting Practice (UK GAAP) results in financial statements that are "not sufficient to give a true and fair view", additional information is to be provided [CA 2006, s. 396(4)]. The Act also provides that where compliance with the reporting framework would result in financial statements not giving a true and fair view, accounting standards should be departed from to the extent necessary to give a true and fair view. In this situation, the departure, its effect and the reasons for the departure are to be disclosed in a note to the financial statements [CA 2006, s. 396(5)]. Similar departures from International Financial Reporting Standards (IFRS) are permitted in order for 'IAS accounts' to present a true and fair view.[7]

---

[7] Departures are permitted under IAS 1: *Presentation of Financial Statements* (International Accounting Standards Board, 2007), paras 13 and 17. It should be noted that IAS 1 refers to 'fair presentation' rather than 'true and fair view' but the Financial Reporting Council (FRC) has confirmed "that the true and fair requirement remains of fundamental importance in both UK GAAP and IFRS" (FRC, 2011).

Given the recognition that compliance with accounting standards does not always result in financial statements that give a true and fair view, we suggest that the most appropriate interpretation of the phrase lies somewhere between the literal and the technical viewpoints. This interpretation was explained by Porter (1990) when she drew a parallel with a good landscape painting. Such a painting portrays the landscape so 'truly and fairly' that anyone seeing the picture will gain an impression of the scene depicted, similar to the one they would have gained had they been present when the picture was painted. In similar vein, in order to meet the 'true and fair' requirement, financial statements must portray the financial affairs of the reporting entity in such a way that anyone reading the statements can gain an impression of the entity's financial position and performance similar to the one they would have obtained had they personally monitored the recording of the entity's transactions.

Many of the items presented in financial statements are subject to judgment.[8] As a consequence, in order to provide a good reproduction of the entity's financial picture (and to avoid the impressionist artist's creativity) some conventions or rules are needed to guide and direct the exercise of that judgment. Such 'rules' are embodied in accounting standards (or, more correctly in the UK context, UK GAAP and IFRS). For financial statements to meet the required standard, they must be presented in such a way as to create the 'correct impression' of the entity's financial affairs (Porter, 1990). In most circumstances this will be achieved through judgmental application of UK GAAP or IFRS, as applicable, to the particular circumstances of the entity.

14.3 FORMAT AND CONTENT OF AUDIT REPORTS

14.3.1 Example of a standard audit report containing an unmodified opinion

In the UK, the format and content of audit reports are prescribed by CA 2006 and International Standard on Auditing (ISA) (UK and Ireland) 700: *The Independent Auditor's Report on Financial Statements* [Financial Reporting Council (FRC), 2013b]. The latter is based on, and is very similar to, ISA 700: *Forming an Opinion and Reporting on Financial Statements* [International Auditing and Assurance Standards Board (IAASB), 2009i].[9] The audit

---

[8] For example, the allowance to be made for debts which might prove to be 'bad'; the number of accounting periods in which non-current assets are likely to generate income; the appropriate basis for recognising revenue and valuing non-current assets.

[9] It is important to note that ISA 700, as issued by the IAASB, has not been adopted for use in the UK. Further, it is unclear whether the European Commission will adopt ISA 700 (IAASB, 2009i) or exercise its right under Article 28 of the EU's Statutory Audit Directive (EU, 2006a) to require all Member States to adopt a standard audit report different from that prescribed by ISA 700.

Figure 14.1: Example of an audit report containing an unmodified opinion

---

Independent auditor's report to the members of Vodafone Group Plc

We have audited the consolidated financial statements of Vodafone Group Plc for the year ended 31 March 201 which comprise the consolidated income statement, the consolidated statement of comprehensive income, the consolidated statement of financial position, the consolidated statement of changes in equity, the consolidated statement of cash flows, and the related notes 1-33. The financial reporting framework that has been applied in their preparation is applicable law and International Financial Reporting Standards ('IFRSs') as adopted by the European Union.

This report is made solely to the Company's members, as a body, in accordance with Chapter 3 of Part 16 of the Companies Act 2006. Our audit work has been undertaken so that we might state to the Company's members those matters we are required to state to them in an auditor's report and for no other purpose. To the fullest extent permitted by law, we do not accept or assume responsibility to anyone other than the Company and the Company's members as a body, for our audit work, for this report, or for the opinions we have formed.[10]

Respective responsibilities of directors and auditor
As explained more fully in the directors' statement of responsibilities, the directors are responsible for the preparation of the consolidated financial statements and for being satisfied that they give a true and fair view.

Our responsibility is to audit and express an opinion on the consolidated financial statements in accordance with applicable law and International Standards on Auditing (UK and Ireland). Those standards require us to comply with the Auditing Practices Board's Ethical Standards for Auditors.

Scope of the audit of the financial statements
An audit involves obtaining evidence about the amounts and disclosures in the financial statements sufficient to give reasonable assurance that the financial statements are free from material misstatement, whether caused by fraud or error. This includes an assessment of whether the accounting policies are appropriate to the Group's circumstances and have been consistently applied and adequately disclosed; the reasonableness of significant accounting estimates made by the directors; and the overall presentation of the financial statements. In addition we have read all the financial and non-financial information in the annual report to identify material inconsistencies with the audited financial statements. If we become aware of any apparent material misstatements or inconsistencies we consider the implications for our report.

Opinion on financial statements
In our opinion the consolidated financial statements:

- give a true and fair view of the state of the Group's affairs as at 31 March 2012 and of its profit for the year then ended;
- have been properly prepared in accordance with IFRSs as adopted by the European Union; and
- have been prepared in accordance with the requirements of the Companies Act 2006 and Article 4 of the IAS Regulation.

Separate opinion in relation to IFRS as issued by the IASB
As explained in note 1 to the consolidated financial statements, the Group in addition to complying with its legal obligation to apply IFRSs as adopted by the European Union, has also applied IFRS as issued by the International Accounting Standards Board ('IASB').

---

[10] This paragraph is not required (or encouraged) by legislation, regulation or auditing standards. It is an attempt by Deloitte to limit the parties to whom the firm may be liable should these financial statements, on which an unmodified opinion has been expressed, subsequently prove to be materially misstated. Since 2005, such paragraphs (known as Bannerman clauses after the case of *Royal Bank of Scotland* v *Bannerman, Johnstone, Maclay* [2003] OHSC 125; [2005] CSIH 39) have been routinely included in audit reports issued by each of the Big 4 and a number of the mid-tier audit firms. From Figure 14.12 it may be seen that such a clause was included in Ernst & Young's audit report on BP Group plc's 2006 financial statements. The Institute of Chartered Accountants in England and Wales (ICAEW) actively encourage its registered auditors to use such clauses. In contrast, the Association of Chartered Certified Accountants (ACCA) suggests they should be used only in exceptional circumstances so as not to undermine confidence in audit work (Howard, 2013). We discuss the *Bannerman* case in Chapter 15, section 15.4.3.

Figure 14.1: (Continued)

Opinion on other matter prescribed by the Companies Act 2006

In our opinion the information given in the directors' report for the financial year for which the consolidated financial statements are prepared is consistent with the group financial statements.

In our opinion the consolidated financial statements comply with IFRSs as issued by the IASB

Matters on which we are required to report by exception

We have nothing to report in respect of the following:

Under the Companies Act 2006 we are required to report to you if, in our opinion:
* certain disclosures of directors' remuneration specified by law are not made; or
* we have not received all the information and explanations we require for our audit.

Under the listing rules we are required to review:
* the directors' statement contained within the directors' report in relation to going concern;
* the part of the Corporate Governance Statement relating to the Company's compliance with the nine provisions of the UK Corporate Governance Code specified for our review; and
* certain elements of the report to shareholders by the Board on directors' remuneration.

Other matter

We have reported separately on the parent company financial statements of Vodafone Group Plc for the year ended 31 March 2012 and on the information in the Directors' Remuneration Report that is described as having been audited.

Panos Kakoullis FCA (Senior Statutory Auditor)
for and on behalf of Deloitte LLP
Chartered Accountants and Statutory Auditor
London
United Kingdom
22 May 2012

Source: 2012 Annual Report Vodafone Group Plc

report on Vodafone Group Plc's 2012 financial statements, presented in Figure 14.1, provides an example of an unmodified audit report that complies with the requirements of CA 2006 and ISA (UK and Ireland) 700. In the 'Other matter' paragraph close to the end of Figure 14.1, reference is made to a separate audit report issued on Vodafone's parent company's financial statements. As some of the matters on which CA 2006 requires auditors to report, or to report by exception, are included in Vodafone's parent company's audit report, but not its Group audit report, we have reproduced part of the former in Figure 14.2.[11]

---

[11] We should note that Vodafone's audit reports (as presented in Figures 14.1 and 14.2) do not include the requirements introduced into ISA 700 (UK) which became effective for reporting periods beginning on or after 1 October 2012. These are described in sections 14.3.3 and 14.3.5. Similarly, they do not refer to the consistency of the company's strategic report (as well as that of its directors' report) with the company's financial statements as this requirement (which is explained in Chapter 5, sections 5.2.2 and 5.5.1) did not become effective until 1 October 2013.

Figure 14.2: **Extract from the audit report on Vodafone's parent company's 2012 financial statements**

Opinion on other matters prescribed by the Companies Act 2006

In our opinion:
- the part of the directors' remuneration report to be audited has been properly prepared in accordance with the Companies Act 2006; and
- the information given in the directors' report for the financial year for which the financial statements are prepared is consistent with the parent company financial statements.

Matters on which we are required to report by exception

We have nothing to report in respect of the following matters where the Companies Act 2006 requires us to report to you if, in our opinion:

- adequate accounting records have not been kept by the parent company, or returns adequate for our audit have not been received from branches not visited by us; or
- the parent company financial statements and the part of the directors' remuneration report to be audited are not in agreement with the accounting records and returns; or
- certain disclosures of directors' remuneration specified by law are not made; or
- we have not received all the information and explanations we require for our audit.

Other matter

We have reported separately on the consolidated financial statements of Vodafone Group Plc for the year ended 31 March 2012.

Source: 2012 Annual Report Vodafone Group Plc

14.3.2 Companies Act 2006 requirements regarding the format and content of audit reports

The CA 2006 (ss. 495–497A) specifies that the auditor's report is to include:
(i) an introduction identifying the financial statements that have been audited and the financial reporting framework (UK GAAP or IFRS) adopted for their preparation;
(ii) a description of the scope of the audit, identifying the auditing standards applied during the audit;
(iii) the auditor's opinion as to whether:
  (a) the financial statements:
  - give a true and fair view of the company's (and, in applicable cases, the group's) state of affairs (in essence, its financial position) as at the end of the financial year and its profit or loss for the financial year,
  - have been properly prepared in accordance with the relevant financial reporting framework, and
  - have been prepared in accordance with CA 2006 and, in applicable cases, the EU's IAS regulation;[12]

---

[12] It may be seen that CA 2006 requires the auditor to express an opinion on three distinct matters. As a consequence, it has come to be termed a 'three part opinion' (APB, 2007, para 3.6).

(b) the information given in the strategic report and directors' report is consistent with the financial statements;

(c) for large companies which prepare a corporate governance statement separate from the directors' report,[13] the information given in the corporate governance statement about (i) the company's internal control and risk management systems relevant to the financial reporting process, and (ii) share capital structures [as required by the EU's Disclosure and Transparency Directive, (EU, 2006b)] is consistent with the financial statements;

(d) for a quoted company, that part of the directors' remuneration report which is subject to audit has been prepared in accordance with CA 2006.

CA 2006 also requires the auditor's report:

- to be qualified or unqualified, and
- to refer to any matters to which the auditor wishes to draw attention by way of emphasis without qualifying the report. (Paragraphs drawing attention to such matters are known as 'Emphasis of Matter paragraphs' and are explained in section 14.6.)

14.3.3 Requirements of ISA (UK and Ireland) 700 and ISA 700 regarding the format and content of audit reports

ISA (UK and Ireland) 700 (FRC, 2013b) and ISA 700 (IAASB, 2009i) which, for ease of reference, we designate ISA 700 (UK) and ISA 700 (International), respectively, provide more detailed requirements than CA 2006 regarding the format and content of auditors' reports.[14] As shown in Figure 14.3 and explained below, although the requirements of the two Standards are similar, there are some notable differences; this applies, in particular, to the statements of the directors' and the auditor's responsibility for the financial statements, the description of the scope of the audit (what the audit involves) and the matters on which auditors in the UK are required to report by exception.

---

[13] As explained in Chapter 5, section 5.2.2, small and medium-sized companies need not provide corporate governance statements (in the directors' report or as a separate statement in their annual report). Most large companies include their corporate governance statement within their strategic or directors' report and, in these cases, the auditors' confirmation that the strategic report and the directors' report are consistent with the financial statements, as required by point (b) above, is all that is needed.

[14] In July 2013, the IAASB issued a suite of Exposure Drafts (EDs) of new and revised ISAs relating to auditors reporting on audited financial statements, namely: ISA 260 (Revised): *Communication with Those Charged with Governance* (IAASB, 2013a); ISA 570 (Revised): *Going Concern* (IAASB, 2013b); ISA 700 (Revised): *Forming an Opinion and Reporting on Financial Statements* (IAASB, 2013c); ISA 701: *Communicating Key Audit Matters in the Independent Auditor's Report* (IAASB, 2013d); ISA 705 (Revised): *Modifications to the Opinion in the Independent Auditor's Report* (IAASB, 2013e); and ISA 706 (Revised): *Emphasis of Matter Paragraphs and Other Matter Paragraphs in the Independent Auditor's Report* (IAASB, 2013f). In this chapter, we explain the current reporting requirements of auditors but we also highlight important changes proposed in these EDs. In Chapter 18, section 18.4.1 we discuss the background to the proposed changes – in particular, those originally proposed by the IAASB in its publication *Improving the Auditor's Report* (IAASB, 2012).

**Figure 14.3:   Elements of audit reports required by ISA 700 (UK)
and ISA 700 (International)**

	ISA 700 (UK)	ISA 700 (International)
(i)	Report title	Report title
(ii)	Addressee	Addressee
(iii)		Sub-heading 'Report on the financial statements'
(iv)	Introductory paragraph	Introductory paragraph
(v)	Statement of the directors' and the auditor's responsibilities for the financial statements	Statement of management's (or the directors') responsibility for the financial statements
(vi)	Scope of the audit of the financial statements	Statement of the auditor's responsibility for the financial statements
(vii)	Opinion on the financial statements	Opinion on the financial statements
(viii)	Opinion in respect of an additional financial reporting framework	
(ix)	Additional reporting requirements for the auditors of companies that apply *The UK Corporate Governance Code*	
(x)	Opinion on other matters Sub-heading 'Matters on which we are required to report by exception'	Sub-heading 'Report on other legal and regulatory requirements' and the associated report
(xi)	Auditor's signature	Auditor's signature
(xii)	Date of the auditor's report	Date of the auditor's report
(xiii)	Auditor's address	Auditor's address

As indicated in Figure 14.3, ISA 700 (UK) and/or ISA 700 (International) requires the auditor's report to include the following elements:

(i) *A title:* ISA 700 (UK) requires the report to have "an appropriate title" (para 12) but notes that this usually includes the term 'independent auditor'; ISA 700 (International) specifically requires the title "to clearly indicate that it is the report of an independent auditor" (para 21).

(ii) *An addressee:* Both versions of ISA 700 require the report to be addressed appropriately to its intended recipients according to the circumstances of the audit. (For the audits of companies' financial statements, the auditor's report is addressed to the company's members or shareholders.)

(iii) *Sub-heading 'Report on the financial statements':* ISA 700 (International), but not ISA 700 (UK), requires this sub-heading to be provided if the auditor's report also contains a section on 'other legal and regulatory requirements' (see below).

(iv) *An introductory paragraph:* Both versions of ISA 700 require the auditor's report to include an introductory paragraph which identifies the entity whose financial statements have been audited, the statements that constitute the audited financial statements and the date of, or period covered by, the statements. ISA 700 (International) also requires the paragraph to refer to the entity's summary of significant accounting policies and other explanatory information (i.e., notes to the financial statements).[15] In the UK, the FRC seems to assume that, as the statement of accounting policies and other notes to the financial statements form an integral part of the statements, there is no need for the auditor to specifically refer to them.

(v)&(vi) *Statement(s) of the directors' and the auditor's responsibilities for the financial statements and description of the scope of the audit:* Although ISA 700 (International) requires two separate sections to be included in the auditor's report to describe, respectively, the directors' and the auditor's responsibilities for the financial statements, ISA 700 (UK) requires both sets of responsibilities to be described in one section. However, as indicated in Figure 14.3, ISA 700 (UK) requires the auditor's report to include a section describing 'the generic scope of an audit'; the content of this section overlaps that of the statement of the auditor's responsibility prescribed by ISA 700 (International). We explain these elements of the auditor's report in section 14.3.4.

(vii) *The auditor's opinion on the financial statements:*[16] Both versions of ISA 700 require the auditor's opinion on the financial statements to be presented in a separate section in the auditor's report; ISA 700 (International) also requires this section to be headed 'Opinion'. Both versions of the Standard specify that, if the auditor's opinion is

---

[15] Proposed ISA 700 (Revised) (IAASB, 2013c) does not require the auditor's report to contain 'an introductory paragraph' but it does require the information currently included in this paragraph to be provided in the auditor's report. In its illustrative example, proposed ISA 700 presents the information in the 'Opinion paragraph' – thus clearly linking the auditor's opinion with the information on which that opinion is expressed.

[16] At present, unless the auditor's opinion is modified, there is no requirement to include a 'Basis of opinion' paragraph in the auditor's report. (We discuss modified audit opinions in section 14.5.3.) The ED of ISA 700 (Revised) proposes that audit reports containing unmodified audit opinions should also include a 'Basis of Opinion' paragraph. This is to:
  (i)   state that the audit was conducted in accordance with ISAs,
  (ii) refer to the section in the audit report that describes the auditor's responsibilities,
  (iii) include a statement that the auditor was independent of the reporting entity and complied with ethical requirements, and
  (iv) state the auditor believes the evidence obtained during the audit is sufficient and appropriate for the formation of an audit opinion.
As may be seen by reference to section 14.3.3, ISA 700 (International) currently requires all but (ii) above to be included in the auditor's responsibilities section of the auditor's report.

unmodified, it is to convey that the financial statements give a true and fair view of the reporting entity's financial position and performance in accordance with the applicable financial reporting framework. ISA 700 (International) further specifies that, if the applicable financial reporting framework is not IFRS, then the jurisdiction of the framework's origin is to be identified. An example of this situation is when the applicable framework is UK GAAP.

ISA 700 (UK) requires the auditor's report to "clearly state the auditor's opinion as required by the relevant financial reporting framework used to prepare the financial statements, including applicable law" (para 17). As we noted in section 14.3.2, CA 2006 (the "applicable law" for UK companies) requires the auditor to state whether, in his/her opinion, the financial statements:
- give a true and fair view of the company's (and, in applicable cases, the group's) state of affairs and its profit or loss,
- have been properly prepared in accordance with the relevant financial reporting framework, and
- have been prepared in accordance with CA 2006 and, in applicable cases, the EU's IAS regulation.

(viii) *Opinion in respect of an additional financial reporting framework:* ISA 700 (UK), but not ISA 700 (International), recognises that there may be occasions when an auditee requests the auditor to express an opinion about the compliance of the financial statements with an additional financial reporting framework. In such a case, ISA 700 (UK) requires the auditor to provide an appropriate heading to clearly separate the second opinion from the first. Reference to Figure 14.1 reveals that this applied in the case of Vodafone Group's 2012 financial statements.

(ix) *Additional reporting requirements for the auditors of companies that apply The UK Corporate Governance Code:* ISA 700 (UK), para 19A, specifies that, for reporting periods beginning on or after 1 October 2012, the audit reports of companies that are required, or choose, to comply (or explain their non-compliance) with *The UK Corporate Governance Code* (companies we term 'Code companies'[17]) are to:
(a) describe the risks of material misstatement assessed by the auditor which had the greatest effect on:

---

[17] While companies with Premium Listed securities on the London Stock Exchange (which includes the largest 350 listed companies) are *required* to comply with the UK Code (or to disclose and explain their non-compliance), other listed and non-listed public companies are *encouraged* to do so. Further details of Premium and Standard Listed securities are provided in Chapter 5, footnote 36.

          – the overall audit strategy,

          – the allocation of resources in the audit, and

          – directing the efforts of the audit team;

(b) explain how the auditor applied the concept of materiality in planning and performing the audit. ISA 700, para A13B, explains that the auditor's explanation should be tailored to the particular circumstances of the audit and, in addition to specifying the materiality limit or threshold used for the financial statements as a whole (that is, planning materiality), the auditor might report, for example, the level(s) of materiality applied to classes of transactions, account balances and other disclosures (that is, tolerable error), performance materiality, any significant revisions of materiality limits made during the audit and also the threshold used for reporting unadjusted misstatements to the audit committee;

(c) provide an overview of the scope of the audit which includes an explanation of how the audit scope was affected by the assessed risks of material misstatement and the application of the concept of materiality reported in (a) and (b) above. ISA 700, para A13C, indicates that the auditor might also report matters such as the audit coverage of revenue, total assets and profit before tax, the number of locations, the auditor visited as a proportion of the auditee's total locations and the nature and extent of the group engagement partner's involvement in the work of the auditors responsible for auditing the group's components.

ISA 700 (UK) further specifies (in para 19B) that the matters reported in accordance with para 19A (above) are to be described in a manner that:

- enables financial statement users to understand their significance in the context of the financial statements as a whole rather than in relation to separate elements therein;
- enables users to relate them to the specific circumstances of the audited entity (thus they should be written in the auditor's own words and not in standardised language);
- complements the audit committee's report which is included in the entity's annual report.[18]

(x) *Sub-heading 'Report on other legal and regulatory requirements and the related report/Opinion on other matters:* Where the auditor reports on other (non-financial statement) responsibilities in the audit report, both the UK and International versions of ISA 700 require those

---

[18] Further requirements relating to the auditor's responsibility in respect of the audit committee's report in the company's annual report are described in section 14.3.5.

responsibilities, and any opinion thereon, to be presented in a separate section of the audit report after the auditor's opinion on the financial statements. ISA 700 (International) requires the section to be headed 'Report on other legal and regulatory responsibilities'. ISA 700 (UK) does not require such a heading but specifies that, if the auditor is required to report on certain matters by exception, the relevant responsibilities are to be set out under the heading 'Matters on which we are required to report by exception' and to provide a suitable conclusion thereon. We discuss the requirements relating to this section of UK auditors' reports in section 14.3.5.

(xi)   *The auditor's signature:* Both versions of ISA 700 require the auditor's report to be signed. ISA 700 (UK) specifies that, where the auditor is an individual, the report is to be signed by that individual but where the auditor is a firm, it is to be signed by the senior statutory auditor[19] in his/her own name for and on behalf of the audit firm.[20]

(xii) *The date of the auditor's report:* Both versions of ISA 700 require the auditor's report to be dated. ISA 700 (International) specifies that this is to be:

> . . . no earlier than the date on which the auditor has obtained sufficient appropriate evidence on which to base the auditor's opinion on the financial statements, including evidence that: . . . [t]hose with the recognized authority [such as the board of directors] have asserted that they have taken responsibility for those financial statements. (para 41)

ISA 700 (UK) is rather more stringent in its requirements. It specifies that:

- the date of the audit report is to be the same as that on which the auditor signs the report expressing an opinion on the audited financial statements;
- the auditor is not to sign, and hence not to date, the report earlier than the date on which:
  - the directors approve not only the financial statements but all of the information in the document containing the financial statements (for example, the company's annual report), and
  - the auditor has considered all necessary available evidence (paras 23, 24, A21).

In Chapter 13 (section 13.9) we note that the date of the audit report marks the end of the period during which the auditor collects and

---

[19] The senior statutory auditor is, in effect, the audit engagement partner – the partner in the audit firm who is responsible for the audit engagement and also for the audit report that is issued on behalf of the firm.

[20] The ED of ISA 700 (Revised) proposes that the name of the audit engagement partner should be included in the audit reports on the financial statements of all listed companies.

evaluates evidence (including events and transactions that occur in the subsequent events period) which enables the expression of an opinion on the financial statements.

(xiii) *The auditor's address:* Both versions of ISA 700 require the auditor's report to show the location of the office from which the audit was conducted (that is, where the engagement partner is based).[21]

Referring to Figure 14.1, we can see that the auditor's report on Vodafone's 2012 financial statements complies with the requirements of CA 2006 and ISA 700 (UK) (other than those that became effective on 1 October 2012). The report has a title indicating it is the report of an independent auditor and it identifies those to whom the report is addressed (the members of Vodafone Group Plc). It also identifies the financial statements on which the auditor's opinion is expressed, and contains separate, suitably headed, sections which explain the responsibilities of the directors and the auditor for the financial statements and the scope of the audit. It provides a clear statement of the auditor's opinion on the financial statements and a separate opinion on the financial statements' compliance with IFRS. The report also sets out some of the matters on which the auditor is required to report by exception (others are set out in the parent company's audit report: see Figure 14.2), is signed by the auditor (the senior statutory auditor for and on behalf of Deloitte LLP) and identifies the office of the auditor (London, United Kingdom). The report is also dated (22 May 2012).

14.3.4 Responsibilities of the directors and auditor for the financial statements and the scope of the audit

We indicated earlier that ISA 700 (UK) and ISA 700 (International) differ markedly in respect of the statements of the directors' and the auditor's responsibility for the financial statements and the explanation of the scope of the audit. However, as will become evident, the differences are primarily in format

---

[21] Further notable proposed changes to the current requirements of ISA 700 (International) include the following:
  (i) The inclusion of additional sections in the auditor's report which report on, respectively:
    (a) (for listed entities) key audit matters, that is, matters the auditor considers were of greatest significance in the audit. These are to be selected from the matters the auditor reports to those charged with the entity's governance and the auditor is to state in the audit report that they have been so selected. Proposed ISA 701 (IAASB, 2013d) provides guidance to auditors on identifying and reporting on these matters;
    (b) the appropriateness of preparing the entity's financial statements on the basis that it is a going concern;
    (c) other information in the entity's annual report the auditor has read and considered in the light of the audited financial statements and knowledge acquired during the audit.
  (ii) The absence of prescription regarding the location of various sections within the auditor's report. Nevertheless, the ED of ISA 700 (Revised) encourages the 'Opinion paragraph' to constitute the first item in the auditor's report followed by the 'Basis for Opinion' paragraph.
We discuss each of these matters in Chapter 18, section 18.4.1.

rather than content. Both versions of ISA 700 require the auditor's report to state that the directors are responsible for the financial statements and the auditor is responsible for auditing and expressing an opinion on those financial statements. ISA 700 (International), but not ISA 700 (UK), also requires the statement of the directors' responsibilities to explain that:

- the financial statements for which the directors are responsible are required to comply with the applicable financial reporting framework and give a true and fair view, and
- the directors are also responsible for "such internal control as [they] determine is necessary to enable the preparation of financial statements that are free from material misstatement, whether due to fraud or error" (para 26).[22]

It is evident that ISA 700 (International) requires greater detail about the directors' responsibility for the financial statements than ISA 700 (UK). The reason for this probably lies in the fact that, as we explain in Chapter 5 (section 5.2.2), the directors of all UK listed companies are required to include in their company's annual report a detailed statement of their responsibilities for the financial statements. An example of such a statement is provided in Chapter 5, Figure 5.3, which reproduces the directors' statement of responsibility included in Vodafone Group Plc's 2012 annual report.

Regarding the statement explaining the auditor's responsibility for the financial statements, both versions of ISA 700 specify that this is to refer to the fact that the audit is conducted in accordance with International Standards on Auditing [or, in the case of ISA 700 (UK), International Standards on Auditing (UK and Ireland)] and those standards require the auditor to comply with ethical requirements. ISA 700 (International) further requires the statement:

- to explain that the auditor is required to plan and perform the audit so as to obtain reasonable assurance as to whether or not the financial statements are free from material misstatement (para 30);
- to state whether the auditor believes the audit evidence obtained is sufficient and appropriate to provide a basis for the auditor's opinion (para 33);
- to explain that an audit involves:
  - performing procedures to obtain audit evidence about the amounts and disclosures in the financial statements. The procedures applied

---

[22] The proposed ISA 700 (Revised) suggests that when responsibility for (a) preparing the financial statements (including the related internal controls – those necessary for the preparation of financial statements that are free from material misstatements) and (b) overseeing the financial reporting process lie with different individuals or groups of people, each set of responsibilities should be separately described in a section of the auditor's report (suitably titled) that explains the responsibilities for the financial statements.

depend on the auditor's judgment, including his/her assessment of the risks of material misstatement in the financial statements, whether due to fraud or error. In making those risk assessments, the auditor considers internal control relevant to the preparation of the financial statements in order to design audit procedures that are appropriate in the circumstances but not for the purpose of expressing an opinion on the effectiveness of the entity's internal control;[23]

- evaluating the appropriateness of the accounting policies adopted by the entity and the reasonableness of accounting estimates made by the directors, as well as the overall presentation of the financial statements (para 31).

ISA 700 (UK) adopts a different approach to explaining what an audit involves. Rather than including an explanation in the statement of the auditor's responsibilities, it requires a separate section to be included in the auditor's report that describes the generic scope of an audit. UK auditors are then given the option of providing in this section either:

- a cross-reference to the applicable version of a 'Statement of the Scope of an Audit' that is maintained on the FRC's website, or to a similarly headed statement elsewhere in the company's annual report, which describes what an audit involves; or
- the following statement:

> An audit involves obtaining evidence about the amounts and disclosures in the financial statements sufficient to give reasonable assurance that the financial statements are free from material misstatement, whether caused by fraud or error. This includes an assessment of: whether the accounting policies are appropriate to the [entity's] circumstances and have been consistently applied and adequately disclosed; the reasonableness of significant accounting estimates made by the directors; and the overall presentation of the financial statements. In addition, we read all the financial and non-financial information in the annual report to identify material inconsistencies with the audited financial statements and to identify any information that is apparently materially incorrect based on, or materially inconsistent with, the knowledge acquired by us in the course of performing the audit. If we become aware of any apparent material misstatements or inconsistencies we consider the implications for our report. (para 16)[24]

---

[23] For companies that are subject to the Sarbanes-Oxley Act of 2002, auditors are to omit reference to their consideration of internal control not being for the purpose of expressing an opinion on the effectiveness of internal control.

[24] The IAASB (2013c) proposes that the statement of auditor's responsibilities for the audit should include, *inter alia*, the following three statements:

(a) The objectives of the audit are to obtain reasonable assurance as to whether the financial statements as a whole are free of material misstatement, whether caused by fraud error, and to issue an audit report that includes that opinion;

Reference to Figure 14.1 reveals that the audit report on Vodafone's 2012 financial statements includes most of this statement. The part of the penultimate sentence which refers to "information that is apparently materially incorrect based on, or materially inconsistent with" became effective for financial reporting periods beginning on or after 1 October 2012. Hence, it was not required when the audit report on Vodafone's 2012 financial statements was issued.

14.3.5 Matters on which UK auditors are required to report by exception

As indicated in section 14.3.3, ISA 700 (UK), but not ISA 700 (International), specifies that when auditors are required to report on certain matters by exception, they are to identify these matters, and provide a suitable conclusion thereon, in a section in the auditor's report headed "Matters on which we are required to report by exception" (para 22). If, after examining the relevant matters, auditors conclude they have nothing to report, they are to express their conclusion using the phrase: "We have nothing to report in respect of the following:" (para A17).

CA 2006, s. 498, requires the auditors of UK companies to report by exception if they are of the opinion that:
- the company has not kept adequate accounting records;
- returns, adequate for their audit, have not been received from branches of the company not visited by them;
- the financial statements are not in agreement with the underlying accounting records and returns;
- in the case of a quoted company, the auditable part of the directors' remuneration report is not in agreement with the accounting records and returns;
- they have not obtained all the information and explanations they considered necessary for the purposes of their audit.

(b) Reasonable assurance is a high level of assurance but not a guarantee that the audit has detected all material misstatements in the financial statements, if they exist;

(c) Misstatements can arise from fraud or error and are considered to be material if, individually or in aggregate, they could reasonably be expected to affect the economic decisions of users of the financial statements based on these financial statements.

It also requires the auditor's report to state that the auditor is required to report to those charged with the entity's governance, *inter alia*, the planned scope and timing of the audit and significant audit findings and, for listed entities, to provide those charged with governance with a statement that the auditor has complied with relevant independence requirements. Additionally, in the case of group audits, the auditor's report is to explain that the engagement partner for the group audit is responsible for directing, controlling and supervising the group audit and for expressing the opinion on the consolidated financial statements. The IAASB (2013c) further notes that, apart from the statements indicated in (a) to (c) above, the description of the auditor's responsibilities for the audit may be located within, or annexed to, the audit report or, in jurisdictions where it is permitted (as in the UK), on the website of an appropriate authority.

Additional exception reporting is required of the auditors of Code companies [companies that are required, or choose, to comply (or explain their non-compliance) with *The UK Corporate Governance Code* (FRC, 2012a; UK Code)]. These are as follows:

(a) As we explain in Chapter 5 (section 5.5.5), the UK Listing Authority's (UKLA) Rules require the auditors of Code companies to review their clients' corporate governance compliance statement insofar as it relates to nine of the UK Code's 12 accountability provisions.[25] If a company states that it has complied with these provisions but, in the auditor's opinion, it has not complied with one or more of them, the auditor is to report this fact in the 'reporting by exception' section of the auditor's report. The same applies if a company discloses that it has not complied with one or more of the nine provisions but, in the auditor's opinion, the non-compliance is not fully and properly disclosed and explained.

(b) ISA 700 (UK) also requires the auditors of Code companies to report by exception if, when reading information in the company's annual report,[26] they identify information:

> . . . that is materially inconsistent with the information in the audited financial statements or is apparently materially incorrect based on, or materially inconsistent with, the knowledge acquired by the auditor in the course of performing the audit or that is otherwise misleading. (para 22A)

The Standard explains that this includes reporting an inconsistency between (i) the directors' statement that they consider the annual report and financial statements, taken as a whole, is fair, balanced and understandable and provides the information necessary for shareholders to assess the entity's performance, business model and strategy (required by UK Code prov. C.1.1) and (ii) the knowledge the auditor acquired during the audit [ISA 700 (UK), para 22B]. Along similar lines, the standard (para 22B) notes that, if the section in the company's annual report which describes the work of the audit committee (as required by UK Code prov. C.3.8) does not appropriately disclose matters the auditor has communicated to the committee, which the auditor considers should have been disclosed, the auditor is to provide the relevant information in the 'exception reporting' section of the audit report.

In the audit reports on Vodafone's 2012 Group and parent company financial statements presented in Figures 14.1 and 14.2, reference is made to most of the

---

[25] These provisions are set out in detail in Chapter 5, section 5.5.5.

[26] As explained in Chapter 13, section 13.8, and as indicated in the description describing the scope of an audit in section 14.3.4, auditors are required to read *all* of the information in documents containing the audited financial statements. Hence, they read all of the information in companies' annual reports.

matters on which CA 2006 and the Listing Rules require the auditor to report by exception. It also reveals that the auditor concluded he has nothing to report by exception. However, as the requirements of ISA 700 (UK), paras 22A and 22B, (outlined above) only became effective for reporting periods beginning on or after 1 October 2012, they are not referred to in the audit reports on Vodafone Group's or its parent company's 2012 financial statements.

14.4 TYPES OF AUDIT OPINION

14.4.1 Overview of types of audit opinion

Having examined the format and content of auditors' reports, we need to consider the types of opinion auditors may express on the financial statements they have audited. There are basically two types of audit opinion:
- an unmodified (or unqualified) opinion; and
- a modified opinion.[27]

However, there are three types of modified opinion, namely:
- a qualified opinion;
- an adverse opinion;
- a disclaimer of opinion.

We explain below the circumstances in which each type of opinion is appropriate.

Irrespective of the type of audit opinion expressed, it should be expressed clearly so that readers are in no doubt about the auditor's meaning. The fundamental principle of external auditing in *The Auditors' Code – Clear Communication* observes that the audit report should also contain sufficient information for readers to gain a proper understanding of the auditor's opinion. In the words of the principle:

> Auditors' reports contain clear expressions of opinion and set out information necessary for a proper understanding of that opinion. (FRC, 2013a)

14.4.2 Unmodified ('clean') audit opinions

In order to express an unmodified opinion on the auditee's financial statements, the auditor must have gathered and evaluated sufficient appropriate audit evidence to form a conclusion as to whether the financial statements:

---

[27] While CA 2006, s. 495, requires auditors' opinions to be 'unqualified' or 'qualified', ISA 705: *Modifications to the Opinion in the Independent Auditor's Report* (IAASB, 2009j) refers to auditors' opinions being 'unmodified' or 'modified'. In this chapter we adopt the terminology of ISA 705. The FRC has issued ISA (UK and Ireland) 705 (FRC, 2012c) but in most respects this is identical to ISA 705 (IAASB, 2009j). Nevertheless, there are some minor differences and we draw attention to these in section 14.5.3. For ease of reference, where we need to distinguish between the two version of the Standard, as for ISA 700, we refer to ISA 705 (IAASB, 2009j) as ISA 705 (International), and ISA (UK and Ireland) 705 as ISA 705 (UK).

- give a true and fair view of the company's (and, in applicable cases, the group's) financial position as at the end of the financial year and its profit or loss and cash flows for the financial year;[28] and
- comply with the applicable financial reporting framework (UK GAAP or IFRS); and
- are properly prepared in accordance with CA 2006 and, in applicable cases, the EU's IAS Regulation.

In reaching a conclusion about the truth and fairness of the financial statements and their compliance with the applicable financial reporting framework, the auditor is required to consider, *inter alia*, whether:
- the financial statements have been prepared using appropriate accounting policies which have been consistently applied;
- estimated amounts in the financial statements are reasonable;
- the amounts and disclosures in the financial statements are presented so as to enable users to gain a proper understanding of the entity's financial position, profit or loss, and cash flow.

It should be noted that these elements coincide with those referred to in the explanation of the scope of the audit required by both ISA 700 (UK) and ISA 700 (International).

The audit report on Vodafone's 2012 financial statements presented in Figure 14.1 contains an unmodified audit opinion.

14.4.3 Modified audit opinions

ISA 705: *Modifications to the Opinion in the Independent Auditor's Report* (para 6)[29] explains that a modified audit opinion is expressed when the auditor:
  (i) concludes that the financial statements as a whole are not free from material misstatement, or
 (ii) is unable to obtain sufficient appropriate audit evidence to conclude that the financial statements as a whole are free from material misstatement.

Although each of these circumstances will give rise to a modified opinion, as indicated in Figure 14.4, which of the three forms of modification is appropriate (qualified, adverse or disclaimer) depends on the pervasiveness of the effects, or possible effects, of the matter(s) in question on the financial statements.

---

[28] As noted in Chapter 5, footnote 12, in the UK all but small companies are generally required to produce a cash flow statement for each financial year, in addition to an income statement and statement of financial position.

[29] As indicated in footnote 27, unless indicated otherwise, references to ISA 705 refer to both ISA 705 (UK) and ISA 705 (International).

Figure 14.4: Circumstances giving rise to different types of modified audit opinions

Nature of matter giving rise to the modification	Auditor's judgment about the pervasiveness of the effects, or possible effects, on the financial statements	
	Material[30] but not pervasive	**Material and pervasive**
Financial statements are materially misstated	Qualified opinion	Adverse opinion
Inability to obtain sufficient appropriate audit evidence	Qualified opinion	Disclaimer of opinion

Source: ISA 705 (para A1)

A misstatement or an inability to obtain sufficient appropriate audit evidence is considered to be pervasive if, in the auditor's judgment, the effects, or possible effects, of the matter:

    (i)   Are not confined to specific elements, accounts or items of the financial statements,

    (ii) If so confined, represent or could represent a substantial proportion of the financial statements, or

    (iii) In relation to disclosures, are fundamental to users' understanding of the financial statements. (ISA 705, para 5a)

14.5 DIFFERENT FORMS OF MODIFIED AUDIT OPINION

14.5.1 Modifications resulting from material misstatement

ISA 705, para A3, explains that a material misstatement of the financial statements may arise in relation to:

    (a) The appropriateness of the selected accounting policies;

    (b) The application of the selected accounting policies; or

    (c) The appropriateness or adequacy of disclosures in the financial statements.

The standard expands on the circumstances in which each of these factors may result in material misstatement of the financial statements:

    (a) In relation to the appropriateness of the selected accounting policies, ISA 705 (para A4) notes that the policies selected:

        – may not be consistent with the applicable financial reporting framework, or

        – may result in the financial statements, including the related notes, not fairly reflecting the underlying transactions and events.

---

[30] The concept of materiality is explained in Chapter 3, section 3.4.2.

(b) In relation to the application of the selected accounting policies, ISA 705 (para A6) observes that material misstatement may result from:
  - the accounting policies not being applied consistently in different reporting periods and/or to similar transactions and events in the same period, or
  - the method of applying the selected policies (for example, an unintentional error in the application of an accounting policy).

(c) In relation to the appropriateness or adequacy of disclosures in the financial statements, ISA 705 (para A7) states that material misstatement may arise when the financial statements:
  - do not include all of the disclosures required by, or the disclosures are not presented in accordance with, the applicable financial reporting framework, or
  - do not provide the disclosures necessary for the financial statements to give a true and fair view.

If, in the auditor's opinion, any of the situations outlined above are material to the financial statements, they will result in a modified audit opinion. However, as indicated in section 14.4.3, the type of modification depends on the pervasiveness of the effect(s) of the misstatement(s) on the financial statements. If, in the auditor's opinion the effects of the misstatements, individually or in aggregate, on the financial statements are:
- material but not pervasive, a qualified opinion is expressed. [That is, the auditor states that, in his/her opinion, the financial statements give a true and fair view of the reporting entity's financial position and performance except for the matter(s) identified in the audit report];
- material and pervasive and, as a consequence, the financial statements are seriously misleading, an adverse opinion is expressed. (That is, the auditor states that, in his/her opinion, the financial statements do not give a true and fair view.)

14.5.2 Inability to obtain sufficient appropriate audit evidence

ISA 705, para A8, explains that the auditor may not be able to obtain sufficient appropriate audit evidence (or, alternatively expressed, the scope of the audit is limited) as a result of:
  (a) Circumstances beyond the control of the entity;
  (b) Circumstances relating to the nature or timing of the auditor's work; or
  (c) Limitations imposed by management.[31]

---

[31] Readers are reminded that in the Preface to this book we note that the term 'management' includes the reporting entity's non-executive directors, executive directors and non-director executives (that is, all directors and executives).

The Standard illustrates each of the above situations by means of examples.

(a) Examples of circumstances beyond the control of the entity include:
   - the destruction of the entity's accounting records (for example, through a fire or flood);
   - governmental authorities seizing indefinitely the accounting records of a significant component of the reporting entity (para A10).

(b) Examples of circumstances relating to the nature or timing of the auditor's work include:
   - the auditee is required to use the equity method of accounting for an associated entity and the auditor is unable to obtain sufficient appropriate audit evidence about an associated entity's financial affairs to evaluate whether the equity method has been applied appropriately;
   - the timing of the auditor's appointment precludes observing the counting of the auditee's physical inventories;
   - the auditor determines that performing only substantive procedures is not sufficient but the auditee's internal controls are not effective (para A11).

(c) Examples of limitations on the scope of the audit imposed by management include the latter preventing the auditor from:
   - observing the counting of the entity's physical inventory, or
   - sending external confirmation requests to specific customers (accounts receivable).

   The auditor's actions in cases where management limits the scope of the audit after the engagement is accepted are explained in section 14.5.4.

When any of the above matters are material to the financial statements, the auditor will express a modified opinion in the audit report. However, like modifications resulting from misstatements, and as shown in Figure 14.4, the type of modification depends on the pervasiveness of the effect(s) or, in this case, the possible effect(s) of the limitation on the auditor's evaluation of the financial statements. If, in the auditor's opinion, the effects, or possible effects, of the limitation are:
   • material but not pervasive, a qualified opinion will be expressed. [That is, the auditor states that, in his/her opinion, the financial statements give a true and fair view of the reporting entity's financial position and performance except for the matter(s) specified in the audit report];
   • material and pervasive and, as a consequence, the auditor is unable to form an opinion on the financial statements, the auditor disclaims an opinion. (That is, the auditor states that s/he is unable to form an opinion on the financial statements.)

14.5.3 Format of audit reports containing a modified opinion

Whenever material misstatement of the financial statements results in a qualified or adverse opinion, or the auditor's inability to obtain sufficient appropriate audit evidence results in a qualified or disclaimer of opinion, changes are made to the standard audit report we describe in section 14.3.3.[32] These are as follows:

(i)   A suitably headed paragraph is inserted prior to the paragraph containing the auditor's opinion which explains the reason(s) for the modified audit opinion.

(ii) A modified audit opinion is expressed in a suitably headed paragraph.

(iii) When a disclaimer of opinion is expressed, minor changes are made to the wording of the introductory paragraph, and, for audit reports prepared in accordance with ISA 705 (International), the explanation of the scope of the audit is omitted from the paragraph describing the auditor's responsibilities.

(iv) For audit reports prepared in accordance with ISA 705 (UK), some modification may be made to the wording of the "Matters on which we are required to report by exception" and also to the "Opinion on other matter(s) prescribed by the Companies Act 2006".

We discuss below the changes indicated in (i) to (iii) above and illustrate those indicated in (iv) in the example audit reports provided in Figures 4.6 to 4.8.

(i)   *Paragraph explaining the basis for the modified opinion*: Whenever a modified opinion is expressed, an additional paragraph, headed 'Basis for Qualified Opinion', 'Basis for Adverse Opinion' or 'Basis for Disclaimer of Opinion', as applicable,[33] is included in the audit report immediately before the Opinion paragraph. It describes the matter(s) giving rise to the modified audit opinion.

   • If there is a material misstatement which relates to specific amounts in the financial statements (including quantitative note disclosures), unless it is impracticable to do so, the auditor is to describe and quantify the financial effects of the misstatement (for example, the effect of an overstatement of inventory on income tax, net profit before tax, net profit after tax and equity). If it is impracticable to quantify the effects of the misstatement, the auditor is to state that this is the case (ISA 705, para 17).

---

[32] The general changes in the format and content of auditors' reports proposed in the ED of ISA 700 (Revised) and described in footnotes 15, 16, 20–22 and 24 (of this chapter) also apply, insofar as they are applicable, to auditors' reports which contain a modified audit opinion.

[33] For audit reports prepared in accordance with ISA 705 (UK), the words 'on Financial Statements' are added after 'Opinion' to each of these headings; for example, Basis for Qualified Opinion on Financial Statements.

- If a material misstatement relates to narrative disclosures, the auditor is to explain how the disclosures are misstated. If the misstatement relates to the non-disclosure of required information, the auditor is to describe the nature of the omitted information and, if it is practicable to do so and sufficient appropriate audit evidence about the omitted information has been obtained, provide the omitted information (ISA 705, paras 18, 19). Examples of situations where it would be impracticable for the auditor to include the omitted information are where:

    (a) the disclosures have not been prepared by management or are otherwise not readily available to the auditor;

    (b) in the auditor's opinion, the disclosures would be unduly voluminous in the auditor's report (ISA 705, para A19).

- If the modification of the auditor's opinion results from an inability to obtain sufficient appropriate audit evidence, the auditor is to explain the reasons for this inability (ISA 705, para 20).

In the event that the auditor expresses an adverse or disclaimer of opinion, the paragraph explaining the basis for the modified audit opinion is to contain a description of any other matter(s) that would have given rise to a qualified audit opinion (in the absence of the adverse, or disclaimer of, opinion) along with the financial effects of the matter(s) in question (ISA 705, para 21).

(ii) *The opinion paragraph*: When a modified audit opinion is expressed, the opinion paragraph is to be headed 'Qualified Opinion', 'Adverse Opinion' or 'Disclaimer of Opinion', as applicable.[34] As explained below, the wording of the paragraph depends on the type of modified opinion expressed.

(a) *A qualified opinion* is to state that, in the auditor's opinion, except for the effects of the matter(s) described in the Basis for Qualified Opinion paragraph, the financial statements give a true and fair view in accordance with the applicable financial reporting framework (ISA 705, para 23).[35] Figures 14.5 and 14.6 illustrate qualified

---

[34] As for the heading of the 'basis for the modified opinion' paragraph, for audit reports prepared in accordance with ISA 705 (UK), the words 'on Financial Statements' are added after the word 'Opinion'; for example, Qualified Opinion on Financial Statements.

[35] If the qualified opinion arises from the auditor's inability to obtain sufficient appropriate audit evidence, the statement is to begin with: "in the auditor's opinion, except for the possible effects of the matter(s) described in the Basis for Qualified Opinion paragraph . . .". Because qualified opinions state that, in the auditor's opinion, the financial statements give a true and fair view and comply with the applicable financial reporting framework and relevant legislation *except for* the matter(s) identified, these audit opinions are frequently referred to as 'except for' opinions.

audit opinions prepared in accordance with ISA 705 (UK). The qualified audit opinion in Figure 14.5 has resulted from material misstatement of accounts receivable; that in Figure 14.6 has resulted from the directors not preparing cash flow forecasts sufficiently far into the future for the auditor to be able to assess the going concern status of the company. (Thus, the scope of the auditor's examination of relevant evidence has been limited by the company's directors.) In both of these cases, the auditor is of the opinion that the matter is material but not pervasive to the financial statements.[36]

(b) *An adverse opinion* is to state that, in the auditor's opinion, because of the significance of the matter(s) described in the Basis for Adverse Opinion paragraph, the financial statements do not give a true and fair view in accordance with the applicable financial reporting framework (ISA 705, para 24). Figure 14.7 illustrates an adverse opinion which has resulted from the auditee failing to make provision for losses that are expected to arise on long term contracts. In the auditor's opinion, this misstatement is material and pervasive to the financial statements.

(c) *A disclaimer of opinion* results in additional changes to the standard auditor's report:
   - The introductory paragraph is amended to state that the auditor was engaged to audit the financial statements.
   - For audit reports prepared in accordance with ISA 705 (International), the description of the auditor's responsibilities for the financial statements is limited to stating:

   > Our responsibility is to express an opinion on the financial statements based on conducting the audit in accordance with International Standards on Auditing. Because of the matter(s) described in the Basis for Disclaimer of Opinion paragraph, however, we were not able to obtain sufficient appropriate audit evidence to provide a basis for an audit opinion. (para 27)[37]

---

[36] The illustrative examples of modified audit opinions presented in Figures 14.5 to 14.8 are derived from APB Bulletin 2010/2 (Revised) (APB, 2012). We are not able to provide examples of actual qualified, adverse or disclaimed opinions in audit reports issued on UK companies' financial statements as, at the time of writing, the authors are not aware of any that have been issued since ISA 705 (International) and APB Bulletin 2010/2 became effective; that is, for reporting periods ending on or after 15 December 2010.

[37] The ED of ISA 705 (Revised) proposes replacing this requirement with one that requires auditors to state that:
   (i) the auditor's responsibility is to conduct the audit in accordance with ISAs;
   (ii) because of the matters described in the Basis for Disclaimer of Opinion paragraph, the auditor has not been able to obtain sufficient appropriate audit evidence to provide an opinion on the financial statements.

In these audit reports, no description of what an audit involves is provided. However, audit reports prepared in accordance with ISA 705 (UK) which contain a disclaimer of opinion include a paragraph describing the scope of the audit with the same wording as that described in section 14.3.4.

- In the opinion paragraph, the auditor is to state: Because of the significance of the matter(s) described in the Basis for Disclaimer of Opinion paragraph, the auditor has not been able to obtain sufficient appropriate audit evidence to provide a basis for an audit opinion; accordingly, the auditor does not express an opinion on the financial statements (ISA 705, para 25).

Figure 14.8 illustrates a disclaimer of opinion which has resulted from the auditor's inability to attend the auditee's inventory count and to confirm accounts receivable. In the auditor's opinion, the effects or possible effects of these matters are material and pervasive to the financial statements.

Figure 14.5:   A qualified opinion on the financial statements of BHD plc resulting from a material misstatement of accounts receivable

---

(The first part of the report is as described in section 14.3.3)

Basis for Qualified Opinion on Financial Statements

Included in the accounts receivable shown in the statement of financial position is an amount of £1,579,000 due from a company which has ceased trading. BHD plc has no security for this debt. In our opinion the company is unlikely to receive any payment and full provision of £1,579,000 should have been made. Accordingly, accounts receivable should be reduced by £1,579,000, the deferred tax liability should be reduced by £362,000, and profit for the year and retained earnings by £1,217,000.

Qualified Opinion on Financial Statements

In our opinion, except for the effects of the matter described in the Basis for Qualified Opinion paragraph, the financial statements:
- give a true and fair view of the state of the group's affairs as at 31 March 20XX and of its profit for the year then ended;
- have been properly prepared in accordance with IFRS as adopted by the European Union; and
- have been prepared in accordance with the requirements of the Companies Act 2006 and Article 4 of the IAS Regulation.

(The rest of the report is as described in section 14.3.3)

Source: Adapted from APB (2012) Example 37

The ED also proposes that, when the auditor disclaims an opinion, the auditor's report should not contain sections reporting on (a) key audit matters, (b) the entity as a going concern or (c) other information in the entity's annual report the auditor has read and considered. (These sections are explained in footnote 21.)

Figure 14.6:   A qualified opinion on MSN's financial statements arising from the auditor being unable to assess the going concern status of MSN plc

(The first part of the report is as described in section 14.3.3)

Basis for Qualified Opinion on Financial Statements

The audit evidence available to us was limited because the directors of the company have prepared cash flow forecasts and other information needed for the assessment of the appropriateness of the going concern basis of preparation of the financial statements for a period of only nine months from the date of approval of these financial statements. We consider that the directors have not taken adequate steps to satisfy themselves that it is appropriate for them to adopt the going concern basis because the circumstances of the company and the nature of the business require that such information be prepared, and reviewed by the directors and ourselves, for a period of at least twelve months from the date of approval of the financial statements. Had this information been available to us we might have formed a different opinion on the financial statements.

Qualified Opinion on Financial Statements

In our opinion, except for the possible effects of the matter described in the Basis for Qualified Opinion paragraph, the financial statements:

• give a true and fair view of the company's affairs as at 30 June 20XX and of its profit for the year then ended;
• have been properly prepared in accordance with IFRS as adopted by the European Union; and
• have been prepared in accordance with the requirements of the Companies Act 2006 and Article 4 of the IAS regulation.

Opinion on other matter prescribed by the Companies Act 2006

In our opinion the information given in the Strategic Report and the Directors' Report for the financial year for which the financial statements are prepared is consistent with the financial statements.

Matter on which we are required to report by exception

In respect solely of the limitation on our work relating to the assessment of the appropriateness of the going concern basis of preparation of the financial statements, described above, we have not obtained all the information and explanations that we considered necessary for the purpose of the audit.

(The rest of the report is as described in section 14.3.3.)

Source: Adapted from APB (2012) Example 41

Figure 14.7:   An adverse opinion on the financial statements of DJB plc resulting from DJB not making provision for losses expected to arise on long term contracts

(The first part of the report is as described in section 14.3.3)

Basis for Adverse Opinion on Financial Statements

As more fully explained in note 17 to the financial statements, no provision has been made for losses expected to arise on certain long-term contracts currently in progress as the directors consider that such losses should be offset against amounts recoverable on other long-term contracts. In our opinion, provision should be made for foreseeable losses on individual contracts as required by Statement of Standard Accounting Practice 9: *Stocks and long-term contracts*. If losses had been so recognised the effect would have been to reduce the carrying amount of contract work in progress by £4,673,000, the deferred tax liability by £876,000 and the profit for the year and retained earnings at 31 December 20XX by £3,797,000.

Adverse Opinion on Financial Statements

In our opinion, because of the significance of the matter described in the Basis for Adverse Opinion paragraph, the financial statements:

• do not give a true and fair view of the state of the group's affairs as at 31 December 20XX and of its
  profit for the year then ended; and
• have not been properly prepared in accordance with IFRS as adopted by the European Union.

In all other respects, in our opinion, the financial statements have been prepared in accordance with the requirements of the Companies Act 2006 and Article 4 of the IAS Regulation.

Opinion on other matter prescribed by the Companies Act 2006

Notwithstanding our adverse opinion on the financial statements, in our opinion the information given in the Strategic Report and the Directors' Report for the financial year for which the financial statements are prepared is consistent with the financial statements.

(The rest of the report is as described in section 14.3.3)

Source: Adapted from APB (2012) Example

Figure 14.8:   A disclaimer of opinion on the financial statements of NDT plc as a result of the auditor's inability to attend its inventory count and to confirm its accounts receivable

INDEPENDENT AUDITOR'S REPORT TO THE MEMBERS OF NDT plc

We were engaged to audit the financial statements of NDT plc for the year ended 30 June 20XX which comprise the company's income statement, statement of comprehensive income, the statement of financial position, the statement of changes in equity, the statement of cash flows and the related notes. The financial reporting framework that has been applied in their preparation is applicable law and International Financial Reporting Standards (IFRS) as adopted by the European Union.

Respective responsibilities of directors and the auditor

As explained more fully in the Directors' Responsibilities Statement set out on page 95, the directors are responsible for the preparation of the financial statements and for being satisfied that they give a true and fair view. Our responsibility is to audit and express an opinion on the financial statements in accordance with applicable law and International Standards on Auditing. Those standards require us to comply with ethical requirements. Because of the matter described in the Basis for Disclaimer of Opinion paragraph, however, we were not able to obtain sufficient appropriate audit evidence to provide a basis for an audit opinion.

Figure 14.8:   (Continued)

Scope of the audit

(This paragraph is the same as that described in section 4.3.3.)

Basis for Disclaimer of Opinion on Financial Statements
The audit evidence available to us was limited because we were unable to observe the counting of physical inventory having a carrying amount of £8,793,000 and send confirmation letters to accounts receivable having a carrying amount of £6,436,000 due to limitations placed on the scope of our work by the directors of the company. As a result of this we have been unable to obtain sufficient appropriate audit evidence concerning both inventory and accounts receivable.

Disclaimer of Opinion on Financial Statements
Because of the significance of the matter described in the Basis for Disclaimer of Opinion paragraph, we have not been able to obtain sufficient appropriate audit evidence to provide a basis for an audit opinion. Accordingly, we do not express an opinion on the financial statements.

Opinion on other matter prescribed by the Companies Act 2006
Notwithstanding our disclaimer of an opinion on the financial statements, in our opinion the information given in the Strategic Report and the Directors' Report for the financial year for which the financial statements are prepared is consistent with the financial statements.

Matters on which we are required to report by exception
Arising from the limitation of our work referred to above:
• we have not obtained all the information and explanations that we considered necessary for the purpose of our audit; and
• we were unable to determine whether adequate accounting records have been kept.

We have nothing to report in respect of the following matters where the Companies Act 2006 requires us to report to you if, in our opinion:
• returns adequate for our audit have not been received from branches not visited by us; or
• the financial statements are not in agreement with the accounting records and returns; or
• certain disclosures of directors' remuneration specified by law are not made.

(The rest of the report is as described in section 14.3.3)

Source: Adapted from APB (2012) Example 44

14.5.4   Auditors' actions when the scope of the audit is limited after the engagement is accepted

If, after an audit engagement has been accepted, the auditee's senior executives or directors impose a limitation on the scope of the audit which the auditor considers is likely to result in the expression of a qualified or disclaimer of opinion, the auditor is to request that the limitation be removed. If it was imposed by senior executives and they refuse to remove it, the auditor should communicate with the directors (or, if the entity has one, the audit committee) about the matter (ISA 705, paras 11, 12).

If the limitation is still not removed, the auditor is required to determine whether alternative procedures can be performed to obtain sufficient appropriate audit evidence on which to base an unmodified opinion. If such procedures cannot be performed and, as a result, the auditor is unable to obtain sufficient appropriate audit evidence, the auditor is to determine whether the possible effects on the financial statements of undetected misstatements, if any, are:

(i) material but not pervasive, in which case a qualified audit opinion is to be expressed; or

(ii) material and pervasive. In this case, the auditor is to:
  (a) resign from the audit, or
  (b) if resignation prior to issuing the auditor's report is not practicable, express a disclaimer of opinion (ISA 705, para 13).

If the auditor resigns from the audit, before doing so, s/he is to communicate to the directors any misstatements identified during the portion of the audit conducted that would, in the auditor's opinion, have given rise to a qualified or adverse opinion.

ISA 705 (para A13) explains that, if the limitation on the scope of the audit is imposed when the audit is substantially complete, the auditor may decide to complete the audit to the extent possible and disclaim an opinion. In this event, the auditor should explain the limitation on the scope of the audit in the Basis for Disclaimer of Opinion paragraph.

In the event that the auditor resigns from the audit, the Companies Act 2006 provisions relating to the resignation of auditors apply, including the need to deposit a written notice of resignation at the company's registered office together with a statement of circumstances connected with the auditor ceasing to hold office, and to notify the appropriate audit authority, that is, the FRC's Conduct Committee or the auditor's Recognised Supervisory Body, depending on whether it is a 'major' or 'not major' audit (see Chapter 5, section 5.3.3).

14.6 EMPHASIS OF MATTER AND OTHER MATTER PARAGRAPHS

Occasionally, auditors may wish to draw financial statement users' attention to, or elaborate on, certain matters within the financial statements or elsewhere in the entity's annual report which, in the auditors' opinion, are particularly important to users' understanding of the financial statements.[38] Auditors refer

---

[38] As we note in section 14.3.2, the UK Companies Act 2006 specifically recognises that these situations can arise.

to such matters in an 'Emphasis of Matter' paragraph if they relate to disclosures within the financial statements or in an 'Other Matter' paragraph if they relate to disclosures other than within the financial statements. We discuss each of these types of paragraphs below.

(a) Emphasis of Matter paragraphs

ISA 706: *Emphasis of Matter Paragraphs and Other Matter Paragraphs in the Independent Auditor's Report* (IAASB, 2009k) explains the use of an Emphasis of Matter paragraph as follows:

> If the auditor considers it necessary to draw users' attention to a matter presented or disclosed in the financial statements that, in the auditor's judgment, is of such importance that it is fundamental to users' understanding of the financial statements, the auditor shall include an Emphasis of Matter paragraph in the auditor's report provided the auditor has obtained sufficient appropriate audit evidence that the matter is not materially misstated in the financial statements. Such a paragraph shall refer only to information presented or disclosed in the financial statements. (para 6)[39]

Examples of situations when an Emphasis of Matter paragraph is appropriate include the following:

- when the auditor has doubt about the ability of the entity to continue as a going concern but the matter is adequately disclosed in the financial statements;[40]
- when there is uncertainty relating to the outcome of an exceptional litigation or regulatory action that will significantly affect the auditee's financial position and profit or loss;
- when application of a new accounting standard (for example, a new IFRS) has had a pervasive effect on the audited financial statements in advance of its effective date (i.e., where early application is permitted);
- when a major catastrophe has had, or continues to have, a significant effect on the entity's financial position;
- when it is necessary for the auditor to issue a new auditor's report on amended financial statements as a result of the auditor becoming aware of a fact that existed on the date the auditor's report was signed which, if known then, would have caused the auditor to request the financial

---

[39] In its ED of ISA 706 (Revised) (IAASB, 2013f), the IAASB notes that a matter should not be included in an Emphasis of Matter paragraph if it is described as a key audit matter. However, for matters that are addressed in an Emphasis of Matter paragraph, the auditor is to explain that the matter(s) in question are separate from those discussed as key audit matters.

[40] ISA (UK and Ireland) 706 (FRC, 2012d), footnote 1a, notes that, in the UK, when auditees make adequate disclosure of a going concern uncertainty, the auditor should *always* include an Emphasis of Matter paragraph in the auditor's report to highlight the existence of an event or condition that might cast significant doubt on the entity's ability to continue as a going concern. Going concern uncertainties are explained in Chapter 13, section 13.4.

statements to be amended or to modify the auditor's opinion on the financial statements.[41]

When auditors include an Emphasis of Matter paragraph in their audit reports, they are required to:
- use the heading 'Emphasis of Matter' (or other appropriate heading) and place the paragraph immediately after the paragraph containing the auditor's opinion on the financial statements;[42]
- clearly explain the matter being emphasised and refer to where, within the financial statements, the disclosures that fully describe the matter are to be found; and
- indicate that the auditor's report is not modified in respect of the matter emphasised.

An abstract from the auditor's report on BP Group plc's 2012 financial statements, which includes an Emphasis of Matter paragraph relating to BP's oil spill in the Gulf of Mexico, is provided in Figure 14.9.

ISA 706 encourages auditors to use Emphasis of Matter paragraphs sparingly. It observes: "A widespread use of emphasis of matter paragraphs diminishes the effectiveness of the auditor's communication of such matters" (para A2).

(b) Other Matter paragraphs

In addition to drawing attention to particular matters in the financial statements, auditors may consider it appropriate to use the auditor's report to communicate information to users of the financial statements about matters disclosed other than in the financial statements that may assist or affect their understanding of the financial statements, the auditor's responsibilities for the financial statements, the scope of the audit or the auditor's report. Such information is to be provided in a paragraph headed 'Other Matter' (or another appropriate heading), which is to be placed after the paragraph containing the auditor's opinion on the financial statements and any Emphasis of Matter paragraph or, if the content of the Other Matter paragraph is relevant to other responsibilities of the auditor, it may be located elsewhere in the auditor's

Reference to Figures 14.1 and 14.9 reveals that the auditors of Vodafone Group plc's and BP Group plc's 2012 financial statements have used an 'Other Matter' paragraph to draw attention to the fact that they have reported separately on

---

[41] This 'subsequent event' circumstance is explained in Chapter 13, section 13.3.2.

[42] In accordance with the removal of prescription regarding the location of sections within the auditor's report (noted in footnote 21), the ED of ISA 706 proposes removing the requirement for an Emphasis of Matter paragraph to be placed immediately after the Opinion paragraph. Similarly, the ED removes any requirement governing the placement of 'Other matter' paragraphs, which we discuss below.

Figure 14.9: An unqualified audit opinion with an Emphasis of Matter paragraph

---

INDEPENDENT AUDITOR'S REPORT TO THE MEMBERS OF BP p.l.c

The introductory paragraph, statement of respective responsibilities of directors and auditor, and the explanation of the scope of the audit of the financial statements, are the same as those provided in the auditor's report on Vodafone's 2012 financial statements presented in Figure 14.1.

Opinion on financial statements

In our opinion the consolidated financial statements:
- give a true and fair view of the state of the group's affairs as at 31 December 2012 and of its profit for the year then ended;
- have been properly prepared in accordance with IFRS as adopted by the European Union; and
- have been prepared in accordance with the requirements of the Companies Act 2006 and Article 4 of the IAS Regulation.

Separate opinion in relation to IFRS as issued by the International Accounting Standards Board

As explained in Note 1 to the consolidated financial statements, the group in addition to applying IFRS as adopted by the European Union, has also applied IFRS as issued by the International Accounting Standards Board (IASB). In our opinion the consolidated financial statements comply with IFRS as issued by the IASB.

Emphasis of matter – significant uncertainty over provisions and contingencies related to the Gulf of Mexico oil spill

In forming our opinion we have considered the adequacy of the disclosures made in Notes 2, 36 and 43 to the financial statements concerning the provisions, future expenditures for which reliable estimates cannot be made and other contingencies related to the Gulf of Mexico oil spill significant event. The total amounts that will ultimately be paid by BP in relation to all obligations relating to the incident are subject to significant uncertainty and the ultimate exposure and cost to BP will be dependent on many factors. Furthermore, significant uncertainty exists in relation to the amounts of claims that may become payable by BP, the amount of fines that will ultimately be levied on BP (including any determination of BP's culpability based on any findings of negligence, gross negligence or willful misconduct), the outcome of litigation and arbitration proceedings, and any costs arising from any longer-term environmental consequences of the oil spill, which will also impact upon the ultimate cost for BP. Our opinion is not qualified in respect of these matters.

Opinion on other matter prescribed by the Companies Act 2006

In our opinion the information given in the Directors' Report for the financial year for which the consolidated financial statements are prepared is consistent with the consolidated financial statements.

Matters on which we are required to report by exception

We have nothing to report in respect of the following:

Under the Companies Act 2006 we are required to report to you if, in our opinion:
- certain disclosures of directors' remuneration specified by law are not made; or
- we have not received all the information and explanations we require for our audit.

Under the Listing Rules we are required to review:
- the directors' statement, set out on page 178, in relation to going concern;
- the part of the Governance and Risk section of the Annual Report relating to the company's compliance with the nine provisions of the UK Corporate Governance Code specified for our review; and
- certain elements of the report to shareholders by the Board on directors' remuneration.

Other matter

We have reported separately on the parent company financial statements of BP p.l.c. for the year ended 31 December 2012 and on the information in the Directors' Remuneration Report that is described as having been audited.

Figure 14.9: (Continued)

Ernst & Young LLP Allister Wilson (Senior Statutory Auditor) for and on behalf of Ernst & Young LLP, Statutory Auditor London 6 March 2013

Source: BP Group's 2012 Annual Report

the respective parent company's financial statements. Other matters for which an 'Other Matter' paragraph might be used include the following situations:

- information in a document containing the audited financial statements (such as the annual report) is materially inconsistent with the financial statements or, in the auditor's opinion, is materially misleading;[43]
- a predecessor auditor audited the prior period's financial statements (and, hence, the opening balances for the current financial period). In such a case, the auditor should draw attention to this fact, state the type of opinion the predecessor auditor expressed in the audit report (and, if it was modified, the reasons for the modification) and the date of that report.

It should be noted that Other Matter paragraphs provide information which may assist or affect users' understanding of the audited financial statements, the audit thereof or the report thereon, but they do not refer to matters within the current year's financial statements. Further, they do not deal with legal and regulatory responsibilities which are additional to the auditor's responsibility to express an opinion on the financial statements. These additional responsibilities do not impact financial statement users' understanding of the audit of the financial statements or the auditor's report thereon. In the UK, neither the CA 2006 requirement for auditors to report on the consistency of the strategic and directors' reports with the financial statements nor the matters on which auditors are required to report by exception (reflected in in Figures 14.1 and 14.7–14.9), are Other Matter paragraphs within the meaning of ISA 706; they report on additional legal and regulatory responsibilities.

14.7 THE AUDIT REPORT – THE AUDITOR'S CHANCE TO COMMUNICATE

When considering the standard auditor's report, we should remember that this is the auditor's primary means of communicating with users of the audited financial statements. If the auditor's opinion is to achieve its objective of providing credibility to the financial statements (statements prepared by the

---

[43] The auditor's responsibilities in relation to unaudited information which accompanies the audited financial statements are explained in Chapter 13, section 13.8.

entity's directors, which essentially report on their own performance), it is essential that financial statement users read and understand the auditor's report. Yet, as shown below, evidence from many parts of the English-speaking world suggests that, particularly until the 'expanded' (or 'long form')[44] audit report was adopted two decades ago, this was not the case. Indeed, it was principally as a result of concern about the apparent ineffectiveness of the audit report as a means of communication that the former 'short form' standard audit report was replaced by an 'expanded' form of report.

Figure 14.10 provides an example of the short form audit report that was used in the UK (as elsewhere) prior to adoption of the expanded report (in 1993 in the UK).[45] From this, it is evident that the report is characterised by its brevity. It merely states that the accounts have been audited in accordance with auditing standards, they give a true and fair view of the company's and group's state of affairs at 31 December 1991 and the group's profit and cash flows for the year then ended, and they comply with the Companies Act 1985.

Figure 14.10: Example of standard unqualified audit report used in the UK until 1993

Report of the auditors

To the members of The Peninsular and Oriental Steam Navigation Company

We have audited the accounts on pages 27 to 49 in accordance with Auditing Standards.

In our opinion the accounts give a true and fair view of the state of affairs of the Company and the Group at 31 December 1991 and of the profit and cash flows of the Group for the year then ended and have been properly prepared in accordance with the Companies Act 1985.

KPMG Peat Marwick
Chartered Accountants
London   Registered Auditor
24 March 1992

From the early 1970s, apparent deficiencies in the short form audit report attracted considerable attention particularly in the United States of America (USA), Canada, the UK, New Zealand (NZ) and Australia. Studies by, for example, Lee and Tweedie (1975) in the UK and Wilton and Tabb (1978) in NZ found that little more than 50 per cent of financial statement users read audit reports. Further, in the USA, the Commission on Auditors' Responsibilities (CAR, 1978; the Cohen Commission) found that the standard short form audit report (then in use) served to confuse rather than inform financial statement users. The Commission noted, for example, that "users are unaware of the limitations of the audit function and are confused about the distinction

---

[45] The expanded audit report was adopted first, in the United States of America, in 1988.

[44] What is commonly referred to as the 'expanded' audit report in the UK is referred to as the 'long form' report in countries such as the United States of America, Australia and New Zealand.

between the responsibilities of management and those of the auditor" (p. 71). Surveys conducted by researchers such as Lee (1970) in the UK, Beck (1973) in Australia, the Canadian Institute of Chartered Accountants (CICA, 1988) in Canada, and Porter (1993) in NZ, provide support for the Cohen Commission's conclusions. These surveys found that a significant number of auditee representatives (directors, senior executives, chief accountants and internal auditors of companies), as well as financial statement users, believed that auditors are responsible for preparing auditees' financial statements, that they verify *every* transaction of the entity, and that a 'clean' audit report signifies the auditor *guarantees* that the financial statements are accurate and/or the reporting entity is financially secure.

Concerned about the apparent shortcomings of the short form audit report, and stimulated by the Cohen Commission's observation that "the auditor's standard report is almost the only formal means used both to educate and inform users of financial statements concerning the audit function" (CAR, 1978, p. 71), professional accountancy bodies throughout the English-speaking world adopted the expanded form of audit report. More specifically, between 1988 and 1993, new auditing standards prescribing the use of an expanded audit report were promulgated by the American Institute of Certified Public Accountants (AICPA), the CICA, the UK's Auditing Practices Board (APB), the Australian Accounting Research Foundation (AARF), the New Zealand Society of Accountants (NZSA)[46] and the International Federation of Accountants (IFAC). In each case, unlike its predecessor short form report, the new expanded report included, *inter alia*:
- a statement explaining the respective responsibilities of the directors and the auditor for the financial statements;
- a brief description of the audit process;
- a statement that an audit is planned and performed so as to obtain sufficient evidence to provide reasonable assurance that the financial statements are free (or not free, as the case may be) of material misstatement, whether caused by fraud, other irregularity or error.

An example of the expanded form of audit report adopted in the UK in 1993 is presented in Figure 14.11. This shows the unmodified audit report issued by Ernst & Young on the 1995 financial statements of British Airways Plc.

The primary motive for the professional accountancy bodies adopting the expanded audit report was the education of financial statement users about the respective responsibilities of the directors and the auditor for the financial statements, the audit process and the level of assurance provided by the auditor's opinion. Studies by Kelly and Mohrweis (1989), Hatherly, Innes and

---

[46] The NZSA is now known as the New Zealand Institute of Chartered Accountants (NZICA).

Figure 14.11: Example of the standard unqualified audit report adopted for use in the UK in 1993

Report of the auditors to the members of British Airways Plc

We have audited the accounts on Pages 16 to 47, which have been prepared under the historical cost convention as modified by the revaluation of certain fixed assets and on the basis of the accounting policies set out on Pages 20 to 22.

Respective responsibilities of Directors and auditors

As described above, the Company's Directors are responsible for the preparation of the accounts. It is our responsibility to form an independent opinion, based on our audit, on those accounts and to report our opinion to you.

Basis of opinion

We conducted our audit in accordance with Auditing Standards issued by the Auditing Practices Board. An audit includes examination, on a test basis, of evidence relevant to the amounts and disclosures in the accounts. It also includes an assessment of the significant estimates and judgements made by the Directors in the preparation of the accounts and of whether the accounting policies are appropriate to the Group's circumstances, consistently applied and adequately disclosed.

We planned and performed our audit so as to obtain all the information and explanations which we considered necessary in order to provide us with sufficient evidence to give reasonable assurance that the accounts are free from material misstatement, whether caused by fraud or other irregularity or error. In forming our opinion we also evaluated the overall adequacy of the presentation of information in the accounts.

Opinion

In our opinion the accounts give a true and fair view of the state of affairs of the Company and of the Group as at 31 March 1995 and of the profit of the Group for the year then ended and have been properly prepared in accordance with the Companies Act 1985.

Ernst & Young
Chartered Accountants
Registered Auditor
London
11 May 1995

Brown (1991), and Zachry (1991), among others, suggest that the expanded report achieved some success in meeting its objective. However, this has been at the cost of changing the audit report into a longer and more complex document. Further, questions were raised, for example by Alfano (1979), about the ease with which a financial statement user can determine whether the auditor has reservations about the financial statements, and the value of explaining the responsibilities of the directors and the auditor for the financial statements *in the audit report*. To Alfano, this merely enables financial statement users to allocate blame if something is wrong. Additionally, commentators such as Elliott and Jacobson (1987) questioned the ability of a few sentences in the audit report to convey adequately the essence of the audit process, and Epstein (1976) and Alfano (1979) suggested that users are not interested in such information but primarily want to know if, in the auditor's opinion, the financial statements "are right or wrong" (Alfano, 1979, p. 39) – a fact they could glean by merely glancing at the former short form report. Certainly it seems pertinent to ask whether financial statement users require details of the auditor's and the directors' responsibilities for the financial statements, and a standard description of the audit process, in *every* audit report. According to critics of the expanded audit report (such as those named above), including such information in the audit report detracts from fulfilment of the report's primary function, that is, conveying the auditor's opinion on the audited financial statements.

Notwithstanding the criticism levelled against the expanded audit report, since 1993 its wording has been amended to provide even more information. More specifically, unlike the standard audit report adopted for use in the UK in 1993 (reflected in Figure 14.11), the standard long form report adopted in 2004 (reflected in Figure 14.12[47]) includes information explaining:

(i) the matters on which auditors are required to express an opinion, including the truth and fairness of the financial statements and their compliance with the Companies Act and IAS Regulation, and also the consistency of the directors' report (including the business review)[48] with the financial statements;

(ii) the matters on which auditors are required to report if the entity has not complied with relevant statutory and/or regulatory requirements (for example, if the entity has not disclosed required information on directors' remuneration and other transactions) and if they have not received the information and explanations they required for the purpose of the audit;

(iii) auditors' responsibility with respect to the nine provisions of *The Combined Code on Corporate Governance*[49] the Listing Rules require them to review. It also highlights certain corporate governance matters that lie outside of auditors' responsibilities (for example, forming an opinion on the effectiveness of the group's corporate governance procedures and its risk and control procedures);

(iv) that auditors read specified other information in the annual report to identify any apparent misstatements or material inconsistencies with the financial statements, but their responsibilities do not extend beyond

---

[47] This report complies with the Companies Act 1985 and ISA 700: *The Auditor's Report on Financial Statements* (IAASB, 2004) and, other than the inclusion of the third paragraph in the introductory section, follows the wording recommended by the APB in Bulletin 2006/6, Appendix 1, Example 7 (APB, 2006). The additional third paragraph (known as a Bannerman clause) is explained in footnote 11 in relation to the auditor's report on Vodafone's 2012 financial statements.

[48] In 2013, *The Companies Act 2006 (Strategic Report and Directors' Report) Regulations 2013* [Statutory Instrument (SI) 2013], in essence, transferred the business review from the directors' report to a newly introduced strategic report.

[49] *The Combined Code on Corporate Governance* was renamed *The UK Corporate Governance Code* when the Code was revised in 2010.

Figure 14.12:   Example of the standard unqualified audit report adopted for use in the UK in 2004

Independent auditor's report to the members of BP p.l.c.

We have audited the consolidated financial statements of BP p.l.c. for the year ended 31 December 2006 which comprise the group income statement, the group balance sheet, the group cash flow statement, the group statement of recognized income and expense and the related notes 1 to 51. These consolidated financial statements have been prepared under the accounting policies set out therein.

We have reported separately on the parent company financial statements of BP p.l.c. for the year ended 31 December 2006 and on the information in the Directors' Remuneration Report that is described as having been audited.

This report is made solely to the company's members, as a body, in accordance with Section 235 of the Companies Act 1985. Our audit work has been undertaken so that we might state to the company's members those matters we are required to state to them in an auditors' report and for no other purpose. To the fullest extent permitted by law, we do not accept or assume responsibility to anyone other than the company and the company's members as a body, for our audit work, for this report, or for the opinions we have formed.

Respective responsibilities of directors and auditors
The directors are responsible for preparing the Annual Report and the consolidated financial statements in accordance with applicable United Kingdom law and International Financial Reporting Standards (IFRS) as adopted by the European Union as set out in the Statement of directors' responsibilities in respect of the consolidated financial statements.

Our responsibility is to audit the consolidated financial statements in accordance with relevant legal and regulatory requirements and International Standards on Auditing (UK and Ireland).

We report to you our opinion as to whether the consolidated financial statements give a true and fair view and whether the consolidated financial statements have been properly prepared in accordance with the Companies Act 1985 and Article 4 of the IAS Regulation. We also report to you whether in our opinion the information given in the directors' report, including the business review, is consistent with the financial statements.

In addition we report to you if, in our opinion, we have not received all the information and explanations we require for our audit, or if information specified by law regarding directors' remuneration and other transactions is not disclosed.

We review whether the governance board performance report reflects the company's compliance with the nine provisions of the 2006 Combined Code Principles of Good Governance and Code of Best Practice specified for our review by the Listing Rules of the Financial Services Authority, and we report if it does not. We are not required to consider whether the board's statements on internal control cover all risks and controls, or form an opinion on the effectiveness of the group's corporate governance procedures or its risk and control procedures.

We read other information contained in the Annual Report and consider whether it is consistent with the audited consolidated financial statements. The other information comprises the Additional information for US reporting, the Supplementary information on oil and natural gas, the Directors' Report and the Governance: Board performance report. We consider the implications for our report if we become aware of any apparent misstatements or material inconsistencies with the consolidated financial statements. Our responsibilities do not extend to any other information.

Figure 14.12:   (Continued)

Basis of audit opinion

We conducted our audit in accordance with International Standards on Auditing (UK and Ireland) issued by the Auditing Practices Board. An audit includes examination, on a test basis, of evidence relevant to the amounts and disclosures in the consolidated financial statements. It also includes an assessment of the significant estimates and judgements made by the directors in the preparation of the consolidated financial statements, and of whether the accounting policies are appropriate to the group's circumstances, consistently applied and adequately disclosed.

We planned and performed our audit so as to obtain all the information and explanations which we considered necessary in order to provide us with sufficient evidence to give reasonable assurance that the consolidated financial statements are free from material misstatement, whether caused by fraud or other irregularity or error. In forming our opinion we also evaluated the overall adequacy of the presentation of information in the consolidated financial statements.

Opinion

In our opinion:

- The consolidated financial statements give a true and fair view, in accordance with IFRS as adopted by the European Union, of the state of the group's affairs as at 31 December 2006 and of its profit for the year then ended.
- The group financial statements have been properly prepared in accordance with the Companies Act 1985 and Article 4 of the IAS Regulation.
- The information given in the directors' report is consistent with the consolidated financial statements.

Separate opinion in relation to IFRS

As explained in Note 1 to the consolidated financial statements, the group, in addition to complying with its legal obligation to comply with IFRS as adopted by the European Union, has also complied with IFRS as issued by the International Accounting Standards Board.

In our opinion the consolidated financial statements give a true and fair view, in accordance with IFRS, of the state of the group's affairs as at 31 December 2006 and of its profit for the year then ended.

Ernst & Young LLP
Registered auditor
London
23 February 2007

Source: BP Group's 2006 Annual Report

the information specified. (In BP's case, Ernst & Young reported it had read the additional information provided by BP for US reporting purposes, supplementary information relating to oil and natural gas, the directors' report, and the company's corporate governance report.)[50]

The additional information provided by Ernst & Young in the Opinion paragraph on BP's 2006 financial statements, compared with that it provided on

---

[50] As noted in footnote 26 (and Chapter 13, section 13.8), auditors are now required to read all of the information auditees provide in their annual reports.

British Airways' 1995 financial statements, reflects the additional matters on which auditors were legally required to express an opinion in 2006 compared with 1995. Similarly, much of the additional information provided in the auditor's responsibilities section of the standard audit report adopted for use in the UK in 2004, reflects the additional responsibilities placed on auditors by the law, regulations or auditing standards between 1993 (when, as we noted earlier, the expanded form of audit report was first adopted for use in the UK) and 2004.

From Figure 14.12 we can see that the audit report in use in the UK in 2004 is long and complex. Nevertheless, it informs readers about the auditor's responsibilities and the basis for the auditor's opinion. It should give users of the audited financial statements some understanding of what the audit entailed and the reliance they may (justifiably) place on the auditor's opinion. Further, the section headings reduce the report's complexity by providing guidance to readers about the content of the various sections; similarly, the heading for the Opinion paragraph signals whether the auditor's opinion is unmodified, qualified, adverse or disclaimed. However, we should perhaps note that, while qualified, adverse, and disclaimers of opinion are clearly signalled in the heading of the Opinion paragraph, the same does not apply to an unmodified opinion; in this case, the heading is limited to 'Opinion' or 'Opinion on the financial statements'. In our view, financial statements users would benefit from an equally clear signal in the case of an unmodified audit opinion.

The latest version of ISA 700 issued by the IAASB (IAASB, 2009i) is an attempt by the standard setter to clarify the information content of the standard audit report and to highlight the auditor's opinion on the financial statements. It has introduced a two-part structure to the report – the first relates to the audited financial statements and the second to auditors' other legal and regulatory responsibilities.[51] Comparing Ernst & Young's audit report on BP's 2006 financial statements with Deloitte's audit report on Vodafone's 2012 financial statements presented in Figure 14.1, we can see that the content is fairly similar but the 2012 report separates information about the audit of Vodafone's financial statements from the auditor's other legal and regulatory responsibilities.

Although the information provided in the current standard auditor's report should aid users' understanding of an audit and the reliance they may place on the auditor's opinion, research conducted in the UK by the Audit Quality Forum's (AQF) Working Group on Auditor Reporting (AQF, 2007) found

---

[51] Although ISA 700 (IAASB, 2009i) has not been adopted for use in the UK, as reflected in section 14.3.3, ISA (UK and Ireland) 700 (FRC, 2013b) is similar to ISA 700 (IAASB, 2009i) and audit reports prepared in accordance with the UK and Ireland standard have the same two-part structure as those which comply with ISA 700 (IAASB, 2009i).

that financial statement users were very critical of the report.[52] The users stated that the standard audit report is:

> too boilerplate and overly standardised and . . . shareholders can feel excluded from what they perceive to be the "real" findings of the audit. [T]he report is too long . . . [and] reports are virtually identical from one company to another and, consequently, most of the information [is] too generic to be of real use. . . . [D]espite the existence of wording within the audit report that provides the assurance that the annual accounts have been prepared in accordance with the relevant standards and show a true and fair view, the report does not clearly identify the key areas of audit focus that were addressed to arrive at these conclusions. (AQF, 2007, paras 25, 46)

The research found that financial statement users wanted audit reports to be less standardised, more company-specific and more discursive. Specifically, they would like audit reports to provide:
- more information about emphases of matter and refer to uncertainties and future risks;
- a discussion of material issues encountered during the audit and how they were resolved;
- a discussion of alternative accounting treatments considered, and the reasons for selecting the treatment adopted, where material;
- more information on material areas of judgment and difficult, sensitive or contentious issues (AQF, 2007).

It is pertinent to observe that, as we explain in section 14.8, much of this information is reported by the auditor to the company's directors (or its audit committee) but, as yet, auditors are not required to report it to shareholders and other users of the company's audited financial statements.[53]

The AQF Working Group found that financial statement users acknowledge that much of the standardised wording in the audit report "is necessary in order to provide clarification as to what auditors' responsibilities are and perhaps more importantly, in order to clarify what auditors both can and cannot do" (AQF, 2007, para 25). However, the other information they would like to see included in the audit report, outlined above, brings us into the realm of 'free form' reporting whereby each audit report is specifically prepared for the audit that has been performed. A move away from 'boilerplate, standardised wording' is likely to encourage financial statement users to read the audit report and to better understand the context and meaning of the

---

[52] The standard audit report reflected in Figure 14.12 was the subject of the research.

[53] However, the FRC has taken steps in this direction. As we explain in Chapter 5, section 5.5.5, the FRC requires the audit committees of companies that are required, or choose, to comply with *The UK Corporate Governance Code* to disclose in their company's annual report significant issues the auditor has reported to the committee and how it has addressed them. Further, as we note in section 14.3.5, the FRC (2013b, para 22B) also specifies that, if, in the auditor's opinion, the audit committee has not appropriately disclosed matters the auditor considers should have been disclosed, the auditor is to provide the relevant information in the audit report. This issue is discussed further in Chapter 18, section 18.4.

auditor's opinion. However, free form reporting also has some significant disadvantages. These include the following:

- The absence of standardised wording may cause confusion for financial statement users regarding the auditor's precise meaning; it may "give rise to misunderstandings, unrealistic expectations, misplaced concerns and other problems derived from a lack of knowledge on the part of shareholders as compared to directors who have in depth knowledge as a result of running the business" (AQF, 2007, para 47).
- Preparing each audit report individually would be time consuming and costly for auditors and may result in their inadvertent failure to meet all of the statutory and regulatory requirements.
- Auditors are bound by their duty of confidentiality and this may prevent them from disclosing their discussions about company matters to anyone other than the directors (or audit committee).
- Provision of additional information within the audit report, beyond that which is required by legislation, regulation or auditing standards, could extend auditors' exposure to liability.
- Much of the information obtained by auditors may be commercially sensitive 'insider information' and, if such information were inappropriately made more widely available, it could affect the market value of the company.

According to the AQF working group, considerations of auditor's duty of confidentiality, 'insider trading' implications and potential extension of their exposure to liability result in auditors tending to be circumspect in what they say and how they say it (AQF, 2007, paras 22, 28).

By comparing the requirements of ISA 700 (International) with those of ISA 700 (UK) (discussed in sections 14.3.3 to 14.3.5), it may be discerned that the FRC has addressed some of the criticisms levelled against the standard auditor's report. More specifically, the statements of directors' and auditors' responsibilities have been significantly reduced from those required by ISA 700 (International). From Figures 14.1 and 14.13 it may be seen that, in the statement of directors' responsibilities section of the audit report, reference is made to a detailed statement of the directors' responsibilities located elsewhere in the company's annual report. Additionally, the statement of the auditor's responsibility for the financial statements is very brief and the explanation of the scope of the audit, if this is included in the audit report (as in Vodafone's case; see Figure 14.1), is far briefer than that prescribed by ISA 700 (International). Further, as shown in Figure 14.13, the explanation can be reduced to a simple cross reference to the APB's (or, from 1 October 2012, the FRC's) website.

Although some of the criticisms of the extended form of auditor's report have been addressed in the UK (in particular, its length), research by the IAASB (2009l, 2011), among others, has found continued widespread dissatisfaction

Figure 14.13:   Extract from KPMG's audit report on Diageo plc's 2012 financial statements

Respective responsibilities of directors and auditor
As explained more fully in the Directors' Responsibilities Statement set out in the corporate governance report, the directors are responsible for the preparation of the group financial statements and for being satisfied that they give a true and fair view. Our responsibility is to audit, and express an opinion on, the group financial statements in accordance with applicable law and International Standards on Auditing (UK and Ireland). Those standards require us to comply with the Auditing Practices Board's (APB's) Ethical Standards for Auditors.

Scope of the audit of the financial statements
A description of the scope of an audit of financial statements is provided on the APB's website at http://www.frc.org.uk/apb/scope/private.cfm.

Opinion on financial statements

(The rest of the report is the same as for the auditor's report on Vodafone's 2012 financial statements other than the signatory).

Ian Starkey (Senior Statutory Auditor)
for and on behalf of KPMG Audit Plc, Statutory Auditor

Chartered Accountants
15 Canada Square
London
E14 5GL
22 August 2012

Source: Diageo plc 2012 Annual Report

with the auditor's report among financial statement users. In Chapter 18 (section 18.4) we discuss some radical proposed changes to the standard auditor's report which were advanced in the wake of the 2008 global financial crisis. As indicated in footnotes to this chapter, many of the proposals have been advanced to the stage of inclusion in proposed new or revised ISAs. If they are adopted in final ISAs, auditors' reports should go some way towards better meeting the information needs of users of audited financial statements.

14.8   AUDITORS' COMMUNICATION WITH THOSE CHARGED WITH GOVERNANCE

14.8.1   Importance and purpose of governance communications

Traditionally, auditors have routinely reported to auditees' directors and senior executives significant deficiencies in internal control detected during the audit, and how they might be rectified, in what were known as 'management letters'. These letters were sent on a voluntary basis by auditors as a service to management. In general they were a 'one-way' communication from the auditor to management and were sent at the conclusion of both the interim and final audit. The interim letter, which reported internal control deficiencies discovered during the interim audit, was sent to senior executives (such as the chief executive and/or the finance director) and/or to the audit committee as soon as possible after the interim audit so that the deficiencies could be rectified on a timely basis. The final management letter was frequently broader in nature and usually included comments on the conduct and findings of the audit as a whole. However, the main focus was generally on matters relating to the entity's accounting and internal control systems and/or its financial affairs where the auditor considered improvements could be made.

Today, reporting by auditors to auditees' directors is no longer voluntary. It is now required by ISA 260: *Communication with Those Charged with Governance* (IAASB, 2009d). Further, compared with the former management letters, these 'governance communications' are broader in scope, they involve two-way communication between the auditor and the directors, and are ongoing throughout the audit. Nevertheless, as we shall see, a major component of governance communications comprises the auditor reporting significant internal control deficiencies detected during the audit and how they might be rectified. The benefits of these communications are reflected in the fundamental principle of external auditing included in *The Auditors' Code* (FRC, 2013a) – Providing Value. This states:

> Auditors add to the reliability and quality of financial reporting; they provide to directors and officers constructive observations arising from the audit process; and thereby contribute to the effective operation of business capital markets and the public sector.

In cases where auditees have an audit committee, auditors usually communicate with that committee rather than with the full board of directors.[54] In this regard, ISA 260 observes:

> . . . communication with the audit committee, where one exists, has become a key element in the auditor's communication with those charged with governance. Good governance principles suggest that:
> - The auditor will be invited to regularly attend meetings of the audit committee.
> - The chair of the audit committee and, when relevant, the other members of the audit committee, will liaise with the auditor periodically.
> - The audit committee will meet the auditor without management [i.e., senior executives] present at least annually. (para A7)

---

[54] In this section, wherever we use the term 'the directors', it should be read as 'the directors or, if the entity has one, the audit committee'. In this connection, it should be recalled that *The UK Corporate Governance Code* requires listed companies in the UK to have an audit committee or to disclose that they do not have one and the reasons therefor.

However, the Standard (para A6) also notes that when auditors communicate with an audit committee (or other subgroup of the board of directors), they should determine whether and, if so, the extent to which they also need to communicate with the full board. Factors affecting their decision include their assessment of how effectively and appropriately the audit committee communicates relevant information to the full board.

14.8.2 Matters to be communicated in governance communications

ISA 260 identifies four categories of matters to be included in governance communications, namely:

(i) the auditor's responsibilities in relation to the financial statement audit;
(ii) the planned scope and timing of the audit;
(iii) significant audit findings;
(iv) for listed companies, auditor independence.

We discuss each of these below.

(i) The auditor's responsibilities in relation to the financial statement audit

The auditor is required to communicate to the directors that:

- the auditor is responsible for forming and expressing an opinion on the financial statements that have been prepared by, or whose preparation has been overseen, by the directors;
- the auditor is required to communicate to the directors significant matters arising from the audit of the financial statements that are relevant to their responsibility for overseeing the financial reporting process;
- the audit of the financial statements does not relieve the directors of their responsibility for the financial statements and the financial reporting process (ISA 260, paras 14, A9).

ISA 260, para A9, notes that if these matters are included in an audit engagement letter,[55] providing the directors with a copy of that letter is an appropriate way to communicate the auditor's responsibilities in relation to the financial statements (i.e., to meet this requirement of ISA 260).

(ii) Planned scope and timing of the audit

The auditor is also required to communicate with the directors about the planned scope and timing of the audit.[56] According to ISA 260 (para A11), this may assist:

---

[55] Audit engagement letters are discussed in Chapter 8, section 8.3.

[56] The ED of ISA 260 (Revised) (IAASB, 2013a) proposes that this communication should include informing those charged with governance (i.e., in the UK, the company's directors) of significant risks the auditor identified during the audit.

(a) the directors to:
- better understand the consequences of the auditor's work,
- discuss issues of risk and materiality with the auditor,
- identify areas where they wish the auditor to undertake additional work; and

(b) the auditor to better understand the entity and its environment. The auditor may, for example, discuss with the directors matters such as the impact of changes in regulations or general economic conditions that have affected the entity, or changes in trading conditions, key personnel, markets, products and processes and so on.

However, ISA 260 warns that the auditor needs to be careful not to provide too much detail about, for example, the nature and timing of audit procedures as this may compromise the effectiveness of the audit (para A12).

The auditor's communication to the directors about the planned scope and timing of the audit generally includes the auditor informing the directors about matters such as:

- how the auditor proposes to address significant risks of material misstatement in the financial statements, whether due to fraud or error;
- the auditor's approach to internal control relevant to the audit;
- application of the concept of materiality in the context of the audit;
- if the entity has an internal audit function, the extent to which the auditor will use the work of the internal auditors, and how the external and internal auditors can best work together in a constructive and complementary manner (paras A13, A14).

However, the communication should not be limited to the auditor providing information to the directors; it should be a two-way process between the auditor and the directors. The auditor may, for instance, find it useful to discuss with the directors matters such as:

- the directors' views about the entity's objectives and strategies, and related business risks that may result in material misstatements in the financial statements;
- matters the directors consider warrant particular attention during the audit;
- any significant communications the entity has with regulators;
- the attitudes, awareness and actions of the directors concerning:
  - the entity's internal control, its importance, and how the directors oversee its effectiveness, and
  - the detection or possibility of fraud within the entity;
- the directors' response to developments in, for example, legislation, accounting standards, corporate governance practices, listing rules, and other matters relevant to the entity's financial statements and annual report;

- the directors' response to previous communications from the auditor. If significant matters raised previously have not been dealt with effectively, the auditor needs to enquire why appropriate action has not been taken – and, if still valid, the matter(s) need to be raised again in the current communication so the directors are aware that they are still significant.

Like informing the directors about the auditor's responsibilities for the financial statements, communicating with them about the planned scope and timing of the audit is usually most appropriately undertaken near the commencement of the audit.

(iii) Significant audit findings

A major component of governance communications comprises the auditor reporting key audit findings to the directors. ISA 260 (para 16) requires the auditor to communicate any audit findings that are significant to the directors' responsibility to oversee the financial reporting process. However, both ISA 260 and various other ISAs also identify specific matters about which the auditor is to communicate with the directors. These include the following:

    (a) qualitative aspects of the entity's accounting practices (ISA 260, para 16a);

    (b) significant difficulties, if any, encountered during the audit (ISA 260, para 16b);

    (c) uncorrected misstatements [ISA 450: *Evaluation of Misstatements Identified During the Audit* (IAASB, 2009f, paras 12, 13)];

    (d) significant deficiencies in internal control identified during the audit [ISA 265: *Communicating Deficiencies in Internal Control to Those Charged with Governance and Management* (IAASB, 2009e)];

We discuss each of the above matters in more detail below.

    (e) significant matters, if any, arising from the audit that were discussed, or were the subject of correspondence, with senior executives. These may include, for example, business conditions affecting the entity, the entity's business plans and strategies that may affect the risk of material misstatement in the financial statements, and concerns about senior executives' consultations with other accountants on accounting or auditing matters (ISA 260, paras 16c, A19);

    (f) any matters relating to fraud which, in the auditor's judgment, are relevant to the directors' responsibility to oversee the financial reporting process. More specifically, ISA 240: *The Auditor's Responsibilities Relating to Fraud in an Audit of Financial Statements* (IAASB, 2009b), para A64, suggests the matters communicated may include:
- Concerns about the nature, extent and frequency of management's assessments of the controls in place to prevent and detect fraud and of the risk that the financial statements may be misstated.

- A failure by management to appropriately address identified significant deficiencies in internal control, or to appropriately respond to an identified fraud.
- The auditor's evaluation of the entity's control environment, including questions regarding the competence and integrity of management.
- Actions by management [i.e., senior executives] that may be indicative of fraudulent financial reporting, such as management's selection and application of accounting policies that may be indicative of management's effort to manage earnings in order to deceive financial statement users. . . .
- Concerns about the adequacy and completeness of the authorization of transactions that appear to be outside the normal course of business;

(g) any matters (other than those which are clearly inconsequential) involving non-compliance with laws and regulations that come to the auditor's attention during the course of the audit [ISA 250: *Consideration of Laws and Regulations in an Audit of Financial Statements* (IAASB, 2009c, para 22)];

(h) events and conditions identified during the audit that may cast significant doubt on the entity's ability to continue as a going concern [ISA 570: *Going Concern* (IAASB, 2009h, para 23)];

(i) significant matters identified during the audit regarding the entity's related party relationships and transactions [ISA 550: *Related Parties* (IAASB, 2009g)]. Examples of such matters include:

- any non-disclosure to the auditor by senior executives (whether intentional or not) of related parties or significant related party transactions;
- significant related party transactions that have not been appropriately authorised and approved, which may give rise to suspected fraud;
- disagreement with senior executives about the accounting for, and disclosure of, significant related party transactions required by the applicable financial reporting framework (ISA 550, para A50).[57]

We now return to examine in more detail the first four significant audit findings listed above [(a) to (d)] about which auditors are to communicate with the directors.

(a) *Qualitative aspects of accounting practices and financial reporting*: ISA 260 states that the auditor is to communicate to the directors:

> The auditor's views about significant qualitative aspects of the entity's accounting practices, including accounting policies, accounting estimates

---

[57] The ED of ISA 260 (Revised) proposes that auditors should also communicate to those charged with governance any circumstances that resulted in significant modification of the auditor's planned approach to the audit. These may arise, for example, as a result of unexpected events or changes in the client's circumstances, identification of significant internal control deficiencies, or results of audit procedures differing significantly from those expected.

and financial statement disclosures. When applicable, the auditor shall explain to [the directors] why the auditor considers a significant accounting practice, that is acceptable under the applicable financial reporting framework, not to be the most appropriate to the particular circumstances of the entity. (para 16a)

The Standard (Appendix 2) suggests that other aspects of accounting and financial reporting practices the auditor may discuss with the directors include:

- the appropriateness of accounting policies adopted for the preparation of the entity's financial statements to its particular circumstances. Where acceptable alternative policies exist, the auditor may identify the financial statement items that are affected by the choice of significant accounting policies and inform the directors of accounting policies used by similar entities;
- changes in significant accounting policies (including the application of new accounting standards) that have, or could have, a material effect on the entity's financial statements;
- the items for which accounting estimates are significant, the entity's process for making such estimates, the reasonableness of (and possible bias in) accounting estimates included in the financial statements, and the disclosure of estimation uncertainty in the financial statements;
- factors affecting asset and liability carrying values, including the entity's bases for determining the useful economic lives of tangible and intangible assets. The auditor may explain how senior executives (usually the finance director or equivalent) selected the factors that affect the carrying values and how the selection of alternative factors would have affected the financial statements;
- if applicable, the selective correction of misstatements by senior executives – for example, correcting those which have the effect of increasing reporting earnings but not those which have the opposite effect.

(b) *Significant difficulties encountered during the audit*: ISA 260 (para A18) observes that the auditor should communicate to the directors significant difficulties encountered during the audit such as:

- significant delays in entity personnel providing the auditor with requested information;
- the unavailability of expected information and/or the auditor having to expend unexpected effort to obtain sufficient appropriate audit evidence;
- the unwillingness of senior executives to make or extend their assessment of the entity's ability to continue as a going concern when requested to do so;

- attempts by senior executives to place restrictions on the auditor; this may include providing the auditor with an unnecessarily brief time to complete the audit.

In some circumstances, difficulties such as those outlined above may constitute a limitation on the scope of the audit that would result in the auditor expressing a modified opinion in the auditor's report.

(c) *Uncorrected misstatements*: As we explain in Chapter 11, section 11.5, as the audit progresses, the auditor accumulates identified misstatements and communicates them to senior executives (usually the finance director or equivalent) and requests that they be corrected. If the senior executives refuse to correct some or all of the misstatements on the grounds that their effect is immaterial, individually or in aggregate, to the financial statements as a whole, the auditor is to obtain written representations from the senior executives to this effect, together with a summary of the misstatements which remain uncorrected.

As an element of the governance communication, the auditor is to inform the directors of the misstatements the senior executives have refused to correct and may discuss with them the executives' reasons for, and the implications of, their refusal. The auditor is to provide the directors with a copy of the executives' written representations, together with the summary of the uncorrected misstatements which is attached to, or included in, the written representations. All material misstatements are to be identified individually but, for a large number of individually immaterial uncorrected misstatements, the number and overall monetary effect of the misstatements may be reported. The auditor is to:

- request the directors to correct the uncorrected misstatements;
- explain to them:
  - the effect the uncorrected misstatements, individually and in aggregate, may have on the opinion expressed in the auditor's report and their possible implications for future financial statements, and
  - the effect of uncorrected misstatements related to prior periods on (i) elements in the current period's financial statements and (ii) the financial statements as a whole (ISA 450, paras 12, 13, A22, A23).

As we explain earlier in this chapter, an auditor cannot express an unmodified audit opinion on financial statements which, in the auditor's judgment, are materially misstated. So, if the directors decline to correct such misstatements, the auditor has no choice but to express a modified opinion.

(d) *Significant deficiencies in internal control identified during the audit*: We note in section 14.8.1 that auditors' voluntary reports to management on various aspects of the audit but, primarily, on internal control deficiencies detected during the audit, were forerunners of the current mandated governance communications. Publication of ISA 265: *Communicating Deficiencies in Internal Control* (IAASB, 2009e) reflects the importance the auditing profession accords to auditors reporting internal control deficiencies to management, and the requirements of auditors in this regard are now explicit.

ISA 265 defines a deficiency, and a significant deficiency, in internal control as follows:

(a) Deficiency in internal control – This exists when:
  (i) A control is designed, implemented or operated in such a way that it is unable to prevent, or detect and correct, misstatements in the financial statements on a timely basis; or
  (ii) A control necessary to prevent, or detect and correct, misstatements in the financial statements on a timely basis is missing. (para 6a)

(b) Significant deficiency in internal control – A deficiency or combination of deficiencies in internal control that, in the auditor's professional judgment, is of sufficient importance to merit the attention of those charged with governance [i.e., the board of directors]. (para 6b)

The Standard (para A7) provides a list of factors that may indicate the existence of significant deficiencies in the internal controls. These include:
- Evidence of ineffective aspects of the control environment, such as:
  - Indications that significant transactions in which management [i.e., senior executives] is financially interested are not being properly scrutinized by those charged with governance [i.e., the directors].
  - Identification of management fraud, whether or not material, that was not prevented by the entity's internal control.
  - Management's failure to implement appropriate remedial action on significant deficiencies previously communicated. . . .
- Evidence of an ineffective entity risk assessment process, such as management's failure to identify a risk of material misstatement that the auditor would expect the entity's risk assessment process to have identified.
- Evidence of an ineffective response to identified significant risks (for example, absence of controls over such a risk).
- Misstatements detected by the auditor's procedures that were not prevented, or detected and corrected, by the entity's internal control. . . .

All significant deficiencies in internal control identified during the audit are to be reported on a timely basis, in writing, to the directors and also to

an appropriate level of management, that is, a level of management able to effect corrective action (for example, the finance director and/or the chief executive officer).[58] The written communication to both the directors and to senior executives is to include:
- a description of the deficiencies and an explanation of their potential effects on the financial statements;
- sufficient information to enable the directors and senior executives to understand the context of the communication of internal control deficiencies. In particular, the auditor is to explain that:
  - the purpose of the audit was to enable the auditor to express an opinion on the financial statements;
  - as part of the audit, internal control relevant to the preparation of the financial statements was considered in order to design audit procedures appropriate in the circumstances but not for the purpose of expressing an opinion on the effectiveness of the entity's internal control;
  - the deficiencies reported are limited to those identified during the audit that the auditor considers are sufficiently important to warrant being reported to the directors (ISA 265, paras 9–11).

Although auditors usually indicate ways in which the reported significant internal control deficiencies may be rectified, ISA 265 notes:

> Management and those charged with governance may already be aware of significant deficiencies that the auditor has identified during the audit and may have chosen not to remedy them because of cost or other considerations. The responsibility for evaluating the costs and benefits of implementing remedial action rests with management and those charged with governance. Accordingly, the requirement [for the auditor to communicate deficiencies to those charged with governance] applies regardless of cost or other considerations that management and those charged with governance may consider relevant in determining whether to remedy such deficiencies. (para A16).

Auditors in the UK who audit companies that are required, or choose, to comply (or explain their non-compliance) with *The UK Corporate Governance Code* (Code companies) have further matters they are to communicate to those charged with governance. ISA (UK and Ireland) 260: *Communication with Those Charged with Governance* (FRC, 2012b, para 16-1) requires these auditors to communicate to the company's audit committee, information the auditor believes to be relevant to:

---

[58] Although ISA 265 requires auditors to report significant internal control deficiencies to the directors and senior executives in writing, it also notes that, initially, they may be communicated orally so that timely remedial action may be taken to minimise the risk of material misstatement occurring in the financial statements (para A14).

- the board's responsibility to:
  - state that it considers the annual report and financial statements, taken as a whole, is fair, balanced and understandable and provides the information necessary for shareholders to assess the company's performance, business model and strategy (Code prov. C.1.1);
  - conduct an annual review of the effectiveness of the company's risk management and internal control systems (Code prov. C.2.1.);
- the audit committee's responsibility to:
  - provide advice to the board (when requested to do so) on whether the annual accounts and financial statements, taken as a whole, is fair, balanced and understandable. . . (Code prov. C.3.4);
  - review the company's internal financial controls and internal control and risk management systems, and to monitor and review the effectiveness of the company's internal control function (Code prov. C.3.2).

The information the auditors of Code companies may provide in these regards include the auditor's views on:
- business risks relevant to financial reporting objectives, the application of materiality and the implications of the auditor's judgments in relation to these matters for the overall audit strategy, the audit plan and the evaluation of identified misstatements;
- management's valuations of the entity's material assets and liabilities and its related disclosures;
- risks identified by the auditor during the audit that may affect financial reporting, and other risks arising from the entity's business model, and the effectiveness of the related internal controls.

(iv) Auditor independence

For listed companies, ISA 260 (IAASB, 2009d and FRC, 2012b, para 17) requires the auditor's governance communication to:
- confirm to the directors that members of the audit engagement team, the audit firm and, if applicable, its related firms have complied with relevant ethical requirements regarding independence;[59]
- inform the directors of:
  - all relationships between the audit firm (and its related firms) and the company (and its related entities) that, in the auditor's professional judgment, may reasonably be thought to bear on independence. This is to include the total fees the audit firm (and its related entities) has charged the company (and its related entities) for the

---

[59] The ethical requirements relating to independence are discussed in detail in Chapter 4.

provision of audit and non-audit services during the reporting period, analysed into appropriate categories, so as to enable the directors to assess the effect of the provision of non-audit services on the auditor's independence;
– the related safeguards that have been applied to eliminate, or reduce to an acceptable level, identified threats to independence.

The Standard explains:

> The relationships and other matters, and safeguards to be communicated, vary with the circumstances of the [audit] engagement, but generally address:
>
> (a) Threats to independence, which may be categorized as: self-interest threats, self-review threats, advocacy threats, familiarity threats, and intimidation threats; and
>
> (b) Safeguards created by the profession, legislation or regulation, safeguards within the [company], and safeguards within the [audit] firm's own systems and procedures. (ISA 260, para A22)

These requirements underline the importance the auditing profession places on auditors being, and being seen to be, independent of their audit clients. They also accord with ISA 220: *Quality Control for an Audit of Financial Statements* (IAASB, 2009a, para 11), which requires audit engagement partners to form a conclusion on compliance with the independence requirements that apply to the audit engagement. This includes identifying circumstances and relationships that create threats to independence and applying safeguards to eliminate such threats or to reduce them to an acceptable level. They similarly accord with provision C.3.2 of *The UK Corporate Governance Code* which requires the audit committees of Code companies, *inter alia*, to review and monitor the independence and objectivity of the company's external auditor and the audit process.

14.8.3 Timing and form of governance communications

Although auditors are required to communicate with their auditees' directors as an element of each audit, the frequency, form and content of the communication vary widely – reflecting variations in the size, complexity, organisation and nature of auditees, as well as in the judgment of individual auditors about the importance of the matters communicated. The larger and more complex the organisation, the more formal the governance communication is likely to be. To ensure there is no misunderstanding between the auditor and the directors regarding the governance communication(s), ISA 260 (para 18) requires auditors to communicate with the directors about the timing, form and expected general content of the communications.

Unlike the auditor's report to the company's shareholders, which is a single report produced at the conclusion of the audit, governance communications are ongoing throughout an audit. Indeed, ISA 260 requires auditors to communicate with the directors "on a timely basis" (para 21). In general, auditors communicate their responsibility for the financial statements, and provide an outline of the scope and timing of the audit, near the commencement of the audit. However, they report significant findings of the audit which require the directors' prompt attention as the audit progresses. This applies, for example, when auditors encounter significant internal control deficiencies which require prompt corrective action, or if they experience difficulties with the audit which the directors may help to resolve. At the conclusion of the audit, auditors usually provide the directors with a summary of the significant audit findings (those previously reported as well as those not yet reported) and also, in the case of listed companies, a statement on the auditor's independence.

Also unlike auditors' reports to financial statements users, for which the format and wording is prescribed, the form and wording of governance communications are matters for auditors' judgment. In general, they may be oral or in writing but ISA 260 (para 19) notes that, when the auditor considers an oral communication would not be adequate, it is to be in writing.[60] Further, when the auditor communicates matters orally, the matters concerned, and when and to whom they were communicated, are to be fully documented in the audit working papers. Where matters are communicated in writing, a copy of the communication is to be included in the audit documentation (ISA 260, para 23).

ISA 260 (para 38) explains that, when deciding on the appropriate form of communication (whether it should be oral or in writing) and on the extent of the detail or summarisation to provide, the auditor should consider factors such as:
- the significance of the particular matter being communicated;
- whether the matter has been satisfactorily resolved;
- whether the matter has been communicated previously to the directors by senior executives;
- the expectations of the directors, and the frequency and nature of ongoing contact and dialogue between the auditor and the directors;
- whether there have been significant changes in the membership of the board of directors or, more particularly, the audit committee.

The auditor's task is not complete when all relevant matters have been communicated – the auditor is also to evaluate whether the two-way communication between the auditor and the directors has been adequate for the purpose of the audit (ISA 260, para 22). When making this evaluation, the auditor is to consider factors such as the following:

---

[60] Additionally, as noted in section 14.8.2, all significant deficiencies in internal control detected during the audit are to be reported to the directors and senior executives in writing.

- the appropriateness and timeliness of actions taken by the directors in response to matters raised by the auditor;
- the apparent openness of the directors in their communications with the auditor;
- the willingness and ability of the directors to meet with the auditor without senior executives present;
- the apparent ability of the directors to fully comprehend matters raised by the auditor. This may be reflected, for example, in the extent to which the directors ask probing questions and question the auditor's recommendations;
- the difficulty the auditor experiences in reaching a mutual understanding with the directors about the form, timing and expected general content of the governance communications (para A42).

If, in the auditor's opinion, the two-way communication has not been adequate for the purpose of the audit, the auditor is to evaluate the effect, if any, on his/her:
- assessment of the risk of material misstatements in the financial statements, and
- ability to obtain sufficient appropriate audit evidence to express an audit opinion.

Having made the evaluation, the auditor is required to "take appropriate action" (ISA 260, para 22).

Governance communications, like the predecessor management letters, are private communications between the auditor and the directors of the client entity. They constitute a valuable service to the client which, amongst other things, assists those responsible to improve the entity's internal control system and financial reporting process. With improvements in these regards, the auditor's confidence about the completeness, accuracy and validity of the accounting data may well increase, and thus the audit work required to form an opinion about the financial statements (and hence audit fees) may, in subsequent years, be reduced.

14.9 SUMMARY

In this chapter we have discussed the reports auditors provide for users of audited financial statements and for those charged with the governance of reporting entities. We have examined the standard form of audit report used for companies in the UK as well as that required by ISA 700. We have also explained the various types of audit opinion which may be expressed, and the circumstances in which each is appropriate. Additionally, we have considered differences between the expanded form of audit report and its short form predecessor. We have noted that the expanded report was introduced to reduce misconceptions about the auditor's (*vis-à-vis* the directors') responsibility for the financial statements, the audit process, and the level of assurance provided by the audit report. But we have also seen that the result is a long and complex document which some commentators maintain is less effective than the former short form report in communicating the auditor's key message about the financial statements. Nevertheless, notwithstanding criticisms of the expanded audit report, in recent years, additional information has been included in the report. However, we have also noted that, in the UK, means have been found to reduce the information provided in the auditor's report about the directors' and auditor's responsibilities for the financial statements, and also about the scope of the audit, by cross-referencing to more detailed information about these matters located elsewhere.

In the final section of the chapter we have considered auditors' communications to those charged with the governance of auditees. We have noted that, unlike auditors' reports to users of financial statements, these governance communications vary widely in form and content according to the client and the circumstances of the audit engagement. They are designed to assist the directors fulfil their responsibility to oversee the financial reporting process. In virtually all cases, a key component of the communication concerns the existence and effect of significant deficiencies in the auditee's internal control and financial reporting systems discovered during the audit and how these might be rectified. In reporting such matters to the directors, auditors provide them with a valuable service. However, governance communications are private between the auditor and the directors and, as we explain in greater detail in Chapter 18, many financial statement users consider that they too should have access to information about significant findings of the audit.

SELF-REVIEW QUESTIONS

14.1   List the elements the Companies Act 2006 requires auditors to refer to in their audit reports.

14.2   The auditor of a company is required to form and express an opinion on the truth and fairness of the company's financial statements. Explain briefly:
    (i)   the meaning frequently given to the phrase 'true and fair' by lawyers;
    (ii)   why the lawyers' interpretation is not useful for preparers and auditors of financial statements;
    (iii) the interpretation of the phrase 'true and fair' which is generally adopted by the accounting profession.

14.3   Describe briefly the format of the standard audit report currently in use in the United Kingdom (as required by ISA (UK and Ireland) 700 (FRC, 2013b) and how it differs from the standard audit report prepared in accordance with ISA 700 (IAASB, 2009i).

14.4   State the criteria which need to be met before the auditor may express an unmodified audit opinion.

14.5   List three types of modified audit opinion and briefly explain the circumstances in which each is appropriate.

14.6   Explain briefly the difference between an 'Emphasis of Matter' paragraph and an 'Other Matter' paragraph.

14.7   Explain briefly:
        (a) the ways in which the expanded (or long form) audit report differs from its short form predecessor;
        (b) the advantages and disadvantages of each of these forms of audit report.

14.8   Discuss briefly the advantages and disadvantages of a standard form of audit report compared with a free-flow form of report;

14.9   Explain briefly the purpose, form and timing of auditors' communications of significant audit matters to those charged with auditees' governance.

14.10   Outline the matters to be included in auditors' communications with those charged with auditees' governance.

REFERENCES

Alfano, J.B. (1979). Making auditor's reports pure and simple. *CPA Journal*, *46*(6), 37–41.

Arden QC, M. (1993). *The True and Fair Requirement* (Counsel's opinion). London: Accounting Standards Board [Also reprinted in Institute of Chartered Accountants in England and Wales. (1994). *Members' Handbook: Volume 2*. Appendix to the Foreword (pp. 14–20)].

Auditing Practices Board (APB). (2006). *Auditor's Reports on Financial Statements in the United Kingdom*, Bulletin 2006/6. London: Financial Reporting Council.

Auditing Practices Board (APB). (2007). *The Auditor's Report: A Time for Change*. London: Financial Reporting Council.

Auditing Practices Board (APB). (2012). *Compendium of Illustrative Auditor's Reports on United Kingdom Private Sector Financial Statements for Periods Ended on or after 15 December 2010*. Bulletin 2010/2 (Revised). London: Financial Reporting Council.

Audit Quality Forum (AQF). (2007). *Fundamentals: Auditor Reporting* (Report of the working group on auditor reporting). London: Institute of Chartered Accountants in England and Wales (ICAEW).

Beck, C.W. (1973). The role of the auditor in modern society: An empirical appraisal. *Accounting and Business Research*, *3*(10), 117–122.

Canadian Institute of Chartered Accountants (CICA). (1988). *Report of the Commission to Study the Public's Expectations of Audits* (Macdonald Commission). Toronto: CICA.

Commission on Auditors' Responsibilities (CAR). (1978). *Report, Conclusions and Recommendations* (The Cohen Commission). New York: AICPA.

Elliott, R.K., & Jacobson, P.D. (1987). The auditor's standard report: The last word or in need of change? *Journal of Accountancy*, *164*(2), 72–78.

Epstein, M.J. (1976). The Corporate Shareholders' View of the Auditor's Report, in Commission on Auditors' Responsibilities. Report, Conclusions and Recommendations. New York: AICPA, p. 164.

European Union (EU). (2002). *Regulation (EC) No. 1606/2002 on the Application of International Accounting Standards* (IAS Regulation). Brussels: European Parliament and Council.

European Union (EU). (2006a). *Directive 2006/43/EC of the European Parliament and of the Council on Statutory Audits of Annual Accounts and Consolidated Accounts* (Statutory Audit Directive). Brussels: European Parliament and Council.

European Union (EU). (2006b). *Directive 2006/46/EC of the European Parliament and of the Council amending Council Directives 78/660/EEC on the Annual Accounts of Certain Types of Companies, 83/349/EEC on Consolidated Accounts, 86/635/EEC on the Annual Accounts and Consolidated Accounts of Banks and other Financial Institutions and 91/674/EEC on the Annual Accounts and Consolidated Accounts of Insurance Companies* (Disclosure and Transparency Directive). Brussels: European Parliament and Council.

Financial Reporting Council (FRC). (2011). *True and Fair*. London: FRC.

Financial Reporting Council (FRC). (2012a). *The UK Corporate Governance Code*. London: FRC.

Financial Reporting Council (FRC). (2012b). International Standard on Auditing (ISA) (UK and Ireland) 260: *Communication with Those Charged with Governance*. London: FRC.

Financial Reporting Council (FRC). (2012c). International Standard on Auditing (ISA) (UK and Ireland) 705: *Modifications to the Opinion in the Independent Auditor's Report*. London: FRC.

Financial Reporting Council (FRC). (2012d). International Standard on Auditing (ISA) (UK and Ireland) 706: *Emphasis of Matter Paragraphs and Other Matter Paragraphs in the Independent Auditor's Report*. London: FRC.

Financial Reporting Council (FRC). (2013a). *Scope and Authority of Audit and Assurance Pronouncements*. London: FRC.

Financial Reporting Council (FRC). (2013b). International Standard on Auditing (ISA) (UK and Ireland) 700: *The Independent Auditor's Report on Financial Statements*. London: FRC.

Flint, D. (1980). *The Significance of the Standard True and Fair View*. Invitation Research Lecture. New Zealand: New Zealand Society of Accountants.

Hatherly, D., Innes, J., & Brown, T. (1991). The expanded audit report: An empirical investigation. *Accounting and Business Research*, *21*(84), 311–319.

Howard, J. (2013, 31 July). *Auditors' Duties: The Burden of Expectation*, www.accountancyage.com/aa/feature/2286005/auditors-duties-the-burden-of-expectation, accessed 5 August 2013.

Inflation Accounting Committee. (1975). *Report of the Inflation Accounting Committee (Sandilands Committee)*. London: HMSO, CMND 6225.

International Accounting Standards Board (IASB). (2007). International Accounting Standards (IAS) 1: *Presentation of Financial Statements*. London: IASB.

International Auditing and Assurance Standards Board (IAASB). (2004). International Standard on Auditing (ISA) 700: *The Auditor's Report on Financial Statements*. New York: International Federation of Accountants.

International Auditing and Assurance Standards Board (IAASB). (2009a). International Standard on Auditing (ISA) 220: *Quality Control for an Audit of Financial Statements*. New York: International Federation of Accountants.

International Auditing and Assurance Standards Board (IAASB). (2009b). International Standard on Auditing (ISA) 240: *The Auditor's Responsibilities Relating to Fraud in an Audit of Financial Statements*. New York: International Federation of Accountants.

International Auditing and Assurance Standards Board (IAASB). (2009c). International Standard on Auditing (ISA) 250: *Consideration of Laws and Regulations in an Audit of Financial Statements*. New York: International Federation of Accountants.

International Auditing and Assurance Standards Board (IAASB). (2009d). International Standard on Auditing (ISA) 260: *Communication with Those Charged with Governance*. New York: International Federation of Accountants.

International Auditing and Assurance Standards Board (IAASB). (2009e). International Standard on Auditing (ISA) 265: *Communicating Deficiencies in Internal Control to Those Charged with Governance and Management*. New York: International Federation of Accountants.

International Auditing and Assurance Standards Board (IAASB). (2009f). International Standard on Auditing (ISA) 450: *Evaluation of Misstatements Identified During the Audit*. New York: International Federation of Accountants.

International Auditing and Assurance Standards Board (IAASB). (2009g). International Standard on Auditing (ISA) 550: *Related Parties*. New York: International Federation of Accountants.

International Auditing and Assurance Standards Board (IAASB). (2009h). International Standard on Auditing (ISA) 570: *Going Concern*. New York: International Federation of Accountants.

International Auditing and Assurance Standards Board (IAASB). (2009i). International Standard on Auditing (ISA) 700: *Forming an Opinion and Reporting on Financial Statements*. New York: International Federation of Accountants.

International Auditing and Assurance Standards Board (IAASB). (2009j). International Standard on Auditing (ISA) 705: *Modifications to the Opinion in the Independent Auditor's Report*. New York: International Federation of Accountants.

International Auditing and Assurance Standards Board (IAASB). (2009k). International Standard on Auditing (ISA) 706: *Emphasis of Matter Paragraphs and Other Matter Paragraphs in the Independent Auditor's Report*. New York: International Federation of Accountants.

International Auditing and Assurance Standards Board (IAASB). (2009l). *Auditor's Report Research Project*. Unpublished. Distributed to the IAASB/AICPA ASB Joint Working Group for the meeting held on 8–9 October 2009.

International Auditing and Assurance Standards Board (IAASB). (2011). *Draft Consultation Paper: Enhancing Auditor Reporting and Evolving the Standard Auditor's Report*. Unpublished. IAASB Main Agenda Item 4-A, meeting held March 2011.

International Auditing and Assurance Standards Board (IAASB). (2012). *Improving the Auditor's Report*. New York: International Federation of Accountants.

International Auditing and Assurance Standards Board (IAASB). (2013a). Proposed International Standard on Auditing (ISA) 260 (Revised): *Communication with Those Charged with Governance*. New York: International Federation of Accountants.

International Auditing and Assurance Standards Board (IAASB). (2013b). Proposed International Standard on Auditing (ISA) 570 (Revised): *Going Concern*. New York: International Federation of Accountants.

International Auditing and Assurance Standards Board (IAASB). (2013c). Proposed International Standard on Auditing (ISA) 700 (Revised): *Forming an Opinion and Reporting on Financial Statements*. New York: International Federation of Accountants.

International Auditing and Assurance Standards Board (IAASB). (2013d). Proposed International Standard on Auditing (ISA) 701: *Communicating Key Audit Matters in the Independent Auditor's Report*. New York: International Federation of Accountants.

International Auditing and Assurance Standards Board (IAASB). (2013e). Proposed International Standard on Auditing (ISA) 705 (Revised): *Modifications to the Opinion in the Independent Auditor's Report*. New York: International Federation of Accountants.

International Auditing and Assurance Standards Board (IAASB). (2013f). International Standard on Auditing (ISA) 706 (Revised): *Emphasis of Matter Paragraphs and Other Matter Paragraphs in the Independent Auditor's Report*. New York: International Federation of Accountants.

Johnston, T.R., Edgar, G.C., & Hays, P.L. (1982). *The Law and Practice of Company Accounting in New Zealand*, 6th ed. Wellington: Butterworths.

Kelly, A.S., & Mohrweis, L.C. (1989). Bankers' and investors' perceptions of the auditor's role in financial statement reporting: the impact of SAS No. 58. Auditing: A Journal of Practice & Theory, Fall.

Lee, T.A. (1970). The nature of auditing and its objectives. *Accountancy*, *81*(920), 292–296.

Lee, T.A., & Tweedie, D.P. (1975). Accounting information: An investigation of private shareholder usage. *Accounting and Business Research*, *5*(20), 280–291.

Northey, J. (1965). *Recommendations for Company Law Reform*. Business Law Symposium.

Porter, B.A. (1990). True and fair view: An elusive concept, *Accountants' Journal*, *69*(110), Editorial.

Porter, B.A. (1993). An empirical study of the audit expectation-performance gap. *Accounting and Business Research*, *24*(93), 49–68.

Ryan, S.J.O. (1974). A true and fair view revisited. *Australian Accountant*, *44*(1), 8–10, 14–16, (Commissioner for Corporate Affairs in New South Wales).

Statutory Instrument (SI). (2013) No. 1970: *The Companies Act 2006 (Strategic Report and Directors' Report) Regulations 2013*. London: The Stationery Office Limited.

Wilton, R.L., & Tabb, J.B. (1978, May). An investigation into private shareholder usage of financial statements in New Zealand. *Accounting Education*, *18*, 83–101.

Zachry, B.R. (1991). Who understands audit reports? *The Woman CPA*, *53*(2), 9–11.

ADDITIONAL READING

Alexander, D. (2010). Material misstatement of what? A comment on Smieliauskas *et al.*, 'A proposal to replace "True and Fair View" with "Acceptable Risk of Material Misstatement"'. *Abacus*, *46*(4), 447–454.

Alexander, D., & Eberhartinger, E. (2009). The true and fair view in the European Union. *European Accounting Review*, *18*(3), 571–594.

Alexander, D., & Jermakowicz, E. (2006). A true and fair view of the principles/rules debate. *Abacus 42*(2), 132–164.

Bruynseels, L., & Willekens, M. (2012). The effect of strategic and operating turnaround initiatives on audit reporting for distressed companies. *Accounting, Organizations and Society*, *37*(4), 223–241.

Bruynseels, L., Knechnel, W.R., & Willekens, M. (2011). Auditor differentiation, mitigating management actions, and audit-reporting accuracy for distressed firms. *Auditing: A Journal of Practice & Theory*, *30*(1), 1–20.

Carey, P.J., Geiger, M.A., & O'Connell, B.T. (2008). Costs associated with going-concern-modified audit opinions: An analysis of the Australian audit market. *Abacus*, *44*(1), 61–81.

610 _____ PRINCIPLES OF EXTERNAL AUDITING

Chong, K.-M., & Pflugarth, G. (2008). Do different audit report formats affect share-holders' and auditors' perceptions? *International Journal of Auditing 12*(3), 221–241.

Clarke, F.L. (2006). Introduction: True and fair - *Anachronism or Quality Criterion* par excellence? *Abacus, 42*(2), 129–131.

Dean, G., & Clarke, F. (2005). 'True and fair' and 'fair value': Accounting and legal will-o'-the-wisps. *Abacus, 41*(2), i–vii.

Evans, L. (2003). The true and fair view and the 'fair presentation' override of IAS1. *Accounting and Business Research, 33*(4), 311–325.

Grant, J. (2008). The auditor's report: A time for change, *Accountancy, 141*(1375), 76–77.

Kirk, N. (2006). Perceptions of the true and fair view concept: An empirical investigation. *Abacus, 42*(2), 205–235.

Laitinen, E.K., & Laitinen, T. (2009). Audit report in payment default prediction: A contingency approach. *International Journal of Auditing, 13*(3), 259–280.

Lee, H.-Y., Mande, V., & Son, M. (2009). Do lengthy auditor tenure and the provision of non-audit services by the external auditor reduce audit report lags? *International Journal of Auditing, 13*(2), 87–104.

Leonard, S. (2008) Cutting back. *Accountancy, 142*(1374), 70–71.

Low, K.-Y., & Boo, E. (2012). Do contrasting statements improve users' understanding of different assurance levels conveyed in assurance reports? *International Journal of Auditing, 16*(1), 19–34.

Menon, K., & Williams, D.D. (2010). Investor reaction to going concern audit reports. *Accounting Review, 85*(6), 2075–2105.

Munsif, V., Raghunanddan, K., & Rama, D.V. (2012). Internal control reporting and audit report lags: Further evidence. *Auditing: A Journal of Practice & Theory, 31*(3), 203–218.

Seidler, L.J. (1976). Symbolism and communication in the auditor's report. In Stettler, H.F., (ed.). *Auditing Symposium III*. University of Kansas: Touche Ross/University of Kansas Symposium on Auditing Problems.

Smieliauskas, W., Craig, R., & Amernic, J. (2008). A proposal to replace 'True and Fair View' with 'Acceptable Risk of Material Misstatement'. *Abacus, 44*(3), 225–250.

Sundgren, S. (2009). Perceived audit quality, modified audit opinions and the likelihood of liquidating bankruptcy among financially weak firms. *International Journal of Auditing, 13*(3), 203–221.

Vanstraelen, A., Schelleman, C., Meuwissen, R., & Hoffmann, I. (2012). The audit reporting debate: Seemingly intractable problems and feasible solutions. *European Accounting Review, 21*(2), 193–215.

15 Legal Liability of Auditors

LEARNING OBJECTIVES

After studying the material in this chapter you should be able to:
- **distinguish between auditors' exposure to liability as a result of breaching their (a) statutory duties and (b) common law duties;**
- **state three facts a plaintiff must prove before damages will be awarded against an auditor;**
- **discuss auditors' exposure to liability should they fail to fulfil their contractual obligations;**
- **explain how auditors' duty of care to third parties was extended by a series of cases between 1931 (*Ultramares* v *Touche*) and the late 1980s (*Jeb Fasteners* and *Twomax Ltd*);**
- **explain the significance of the House of Lords' decision in the *Caparo* case (1990);**
- **describe how the law relating to auditors' liability to third parties has developed since the *Caparo* judgment;**
- **discuss the effect of out-of-court settlements.**

15.1 INTRODUCTION

When an auditor[1] accepts an audit engagement, it gives rise to the assumption that the auditor undertakes to perform the audit in accordance with certain statutory and common law obligations. If these obligations are not met, in general, the auditor is liable to parties who suffer loss as a result. These parties

---

[1] As we note in Chapter 5, section 5.3.1, under the Companies Act 2006 (CA 2006), s. 1212, an individual or an audit firm may be appointed as 'the auditor'. The principles of legal liability apply equally in either case. If the audit firm is constituted as an ordinary partnership, the partners are jointly and severally liable. This means they are liable jointly with the other partners of the firm for any damages awarded by a court against any of the firm's partners; they are also liable individually to meet damages awarded against a partner of the firm, should that partner not be able to pay. Where firms are constituted as limited liability partnerships (LLPs), which have been permitted in the United Kingdom since 2001, apart from the partner who is guilty of the negligence for which damages have been awarded, the liability of the firm's partners is limited to the amount of capital they have invested in the partnership. The personal assets of the partner guilty of negligence can be called upon to meet a claim for damages but not those of the other partners. We should perhaps note that international audit firms arrange their affairs so that the firm in any one country (or, sometimes a region) constitutes a separate entity. As a consequence, any damages awarded against a partner in a firm which is an ordinary partnership, or against an LLP, is enforceable only against the other partners of the firm concerned, or the LLP, (as applicable) in that country – not those in other countries. LLPs are discussed in detail in Chapter 16, section 16.5.3.

include the client entity with which the auditor has a contractual relationship and may also include third parties who do not have a contract with the auditor but who, nevertheless, rely on the proper performance of the auditor's duties or, more particularly, on the opinion expressed in the auditor's report.

In this chapter we address the issue of auditors' legal liability. More specifically, we examine auditors' contractual liability to their clients and trace the development of their liability to third parties. We also discuss the House of Lords' decision in the *Caparo* case (1990) which remains the most influential case in the United Kingdom (UK) with respect to auditors' liability; it is notable for reversing the trend towards extending auditors' liability to third parties and returning the law to where it stood some 30 years earlier. Additionally, we consider some cases decided since *Caparo* and note that, although the courts are once again gradually widening auditors' liability to third parties, they are anxious to keep auditors' liability within reasonable bounds. Before closing the chapter we explore the effect of out-of-court settlements on the development of the law relating to auditors' liability.

15.2 OVERVIEW OF AUDITORS' LEGAL LIABILITY

15.2.1 Auditors' exposure to legal liability

When an auditor accepts an audit engagement, it is understood that s/he undertakes to perform the applicable statutory and common (or case) law duties and to perform them with due skill and care. Should the auditor fail to perform any of these duties, or fail to perform them with due skill and care, s/he will be exposed to liability. The causes of auditors' exposure to liability are depicted in Figure 15.1 and discussed below.

15.2.2 Breach of statutory duties

Some of the auditor's duties are specified in statute law, for example, in the Companies Act 2006 (CA 2006) and the Theft Act 1968. If the auditor fails to perform these duties, the breach may constitute either:

- *a civil wrong*: in this case the client entity or an individual who suffers loss as a result of the auditor failing to meet his/her statutory obligations may sue the auditor; or
- *a criminal act*: in this case the State may sue the auditor. An example of a criminal act is an auditor "knowingly or recklessly" including "any matter that is misleading, false or deceptive in a material particular" in the audit report on a company's financial statements, [CA 2006, s. 507(1)].

The penalty for a civil wrong or criminal act (in the form of a fine and/or imprisonment) is specified in the statute the auditor breaches. For example,

Figure 15.1: Auditors' exposure to legal liability

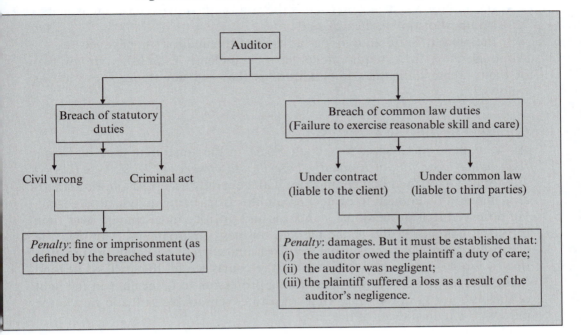

CA 2006, s. 507(4), specifies that an auditor who knowingly or recklessly signs an audit report which contains a misleading audit opinion is liable:

(a) on conviction on indictment, to a fine;

(b) on summary conviction, to a fine not exceeding the statutory maximum.[2]

15.2.3 Breach of common law duties

In addition to the statutory obligations which arise when an auditor agrees to audit a company's financial statements, a common law duty to perform the audit with reasonable skill and care arises. Any auditor who fails to exercise reasonable skill and care when performing an audit is liable to make good any resultant loss suffered by those to whom the auditor owes a duty of care. Such a duty may arise under a contractual relationship with the client or under the common law to third parties (that is, those with whom the auditor does not have a contractual arrangement).

The penalty for proven negligence (that is, failure to exercise due skill and care) is the award of damages. However, in order for damages to be awarded against an auditor, the plaintiff (an entity or an individual) must prove three facts, namely:

---

[2] The statutory maximum in the UK has been £5,000 since 1992.

- the auditor owed the plaintiff a duty of care,
- the auditor was negligent (that is, the auditor did not exercise a reasonable standard of skill and care), and
- the plaintiff suffered a loss as a result of the auditor's negligence.

Although these three requirements have been clearly established in law, two of them create difficulties for auditors as they are not static. These are as follows.

(i)   What qualifies as negligence?[3]

As we explain in Chapter 5 (section 5.5.3), in the Australian case of *Pacific Acceptance Corporation Limited* v *Forsyth and Others* (1970) 92 WN (NSW) 29 Moffitt J explained that compliance with generally accepted auditing standards may not be enough to protect an auditor from being adjudged negligent. He observed that professional standards and practice must change over time to reflect changes in the economic and business environment. Although the courts are guided by professional standards and current best auditing practice, they will not be bound by them and, if the courts see fit, they will go beyond them. It is for the courts not the auditing profession to determine, in the light of society's norms of the time, what constitutes reasonable skill and care in the particular circumstances of the case.

This leaves auditors in a difficult and unenviable position. Not only do they lack a clear standard to which they are expected to work (the required standard of skill and care varies over time and between different sets of circumstances) but, additionally, when the courts evaluate whether or not they have exercised the required standard of skill and care in the particular circumstances of the case, it is with the wisdom of hindsight.

(ii)   The parties to whom auditors owe a duty of care

As indicated in Figure 15.1, a duty of care may arise under either:
  (a) *contract*, that is, as part of the contractual arrangement between the auditor and the client. In general, this duty is clear-cut and does not give rise to uncertainty; or

---

[3] Negligence applies to situations in which auditors fail to exercise due care. The concept of Due Care is discussed in Chapter 3, section 3.6.1. There we note that two significant characteristics of the concept are as follows:

  (i) the standard of 'reasonable skill and care' has become more exacting over the past 100 or so years, as society and, more particularly, the commercial and corporate worlds, have become more complex and dynamic;

  (ii) although auditing standards and other professional promulgations provide guidance to the court on what may reasonably be expected of auditors, it is up to the court, not the auditing profession, to determine whether an auditor has exercised due care in any particular audit.

(b) *common law*. This duty of care to third parties (a party other than the auditee) is imposed on auditors when the courts consider it reasonable and equitable to do so. As is shown in section 15.4, between the early 1960s and the end of the 1980s, the parties to whom auditors were held to owe a duty of care were extended progressively. Then, as a result of the *Caparo* case, they were reduced significantly only to be broadened once more, at least to an extent, in post-*Caparo* cases. The various changes leave auditors unsure as to whom they are liable should they fail to exercise a reasonable standard of skill and care in the particular circumstances of the audit.[4]

15.3 AUDITORS' CONTRACTUAL LIABILITY TO THEIR CLIENTS

By accepting an audit engagement, the auditor contracts with the client to perform certain duties. Some of these are specified in legislation (such as CA 2006); others have been determined over the years by the courts as a result of various cases being brought against auditors (some of which are discussed in Chapter 5, section 5.5.3). If the auditor fails to perform the applicable statutory and common law duties (and any other duties agreed with the client),[5] or to perform them with reasonable skill and care, and the client entity suffers a loss as a result, then the auditor is liable to make good that loss.

Three examples of cases brought against auditors for breaching their contractual obligations are provided below – the *AWA*, *Sasea* and *Equitable Life* cases. In general, cases of this type focus on the question of whether the auditor was negligent. Once this is decided, the question of whether the auditor's negligence caused the plaintiff's loss is addressed. As indicated in section 15.2.3, the question of whether the auditor owes the client a duty of care is not usually an issue. However, as the *Equitable Life* case bears witness, it may arise in particular circumstances.

In the Australian case of *AWA Limited* v *Daniels, trading as Deloitte Haskins & Sells & Others* (1992) 10 ACLC 933; 14 May 1995, (NSW) CA, AWA's

---

[4] As we explain in Chapter 14, footnote 11, the inclusion of 'Bannerman clauses' in audit reports is an attempt by auditors to restrict their exposure to liability to the client company and its shareholders as a body and, thus, to ensure they cannot be sued by individual shareholders or by any other third party.

[5] Many of these duties are set out in the audit engagement letter which, as we explain in Chapter 8, section 8.3, International Standard on Auditing (ISA) 210: *Agreeing the Terms of Audit Engagements* (IAASB, 2009a), requires auditors to prepare when they accept an audit engagement. This letter (which constitutes a contract) cannot excuse the auditor from performing the applicable statutory or common law duties, or from performing them with reasonable skill and care, but it minimises any misunderstanding between the client and the auditor about the duties to be performed – and thus helps the auditor to avoid being sued for failing to perform duties which lie outside the contractual agreement.

manager of foreign exchange operations, whilst appearing to trade profitability in foreign exchange dealings, caused AWA to incur a loss of A$50 million. The manager concealed the losses by various means, including unauthorised borrowing from a number of banks, allegedly on behalf of AWA. AWA sued the auditor for damages in breach of contract, claiming that the loss suffered was caused by Deloitte's failure to draw attention to serious deficiencies in the company's internal controls and accounting records, and for failing to qualify their audit reports.

Rogers C J found that Deloitte failed to perform its contractual duties in the following ways:

(i)   It was clear that the books and records relevant to AWA's foreign exchange transactions were "inaccurate and inadequate" and "the auditors should have formed the opinion that proper accounting records had not been kept" (Rogers, C J at 959). They failed to fulfil this duty.

(ii) The auditors had doubts about the extent of the foreign exchange manager's authority to enter into foreign exchange transactions on behalf of AWA. In such circumstances, the auditors had a duty to make enquiries from an appropriate level of management. This, Deloitte failed to do.

(iii) Notwithstanding that the auditors discussed the inadequate system of recording foreign exchange transactions with AWA's general manager, they did nothing to ensure the matter was dealt with urgently and effectively, nor did they ensure it was referred to AWA's board of directors. Rogers C J held that simply identifying shortcomings and bringing them to the attention of managers below board level is an insufficient discharge of an auditor's duty in cases where the auditor is aware that the managers fail to respond adequately. Managers' failure to take action to rectify the position imposes on the auditor an obligation to inform the board. Further, this obligation is not discharged by relying on the possibility that the chief executive officer will have already informed the board.[6]

The court decided that Deloitte was negligent in the performance of its duties and that its negligence had contributed to the loss suffered by AWA. However, AWA's senior management was also found to have contributed to the company's loss by virtue of deficiencies in its system of internal controls and record keeping.

---

[6] As we explain in Chapter 14, section 14.8, this responsibility is now explicitly required by ISA 260: *Communication with Those Charged with Governance* (IAASB, 2009b).

Deloitte appealed the trial judge's ruling but it was upheld by the Court of Appeal. Nevertheless, the Appeal Court gave greater weight than the trial judge to the part played by AWA's management in the loss suffered by the company. Recognising the contributory negligence of AWA's management, the Court of Appeal reduced the damages awarded against Deloitte from A\$17 million to A\$6 million. In the Court of Appeal's view, the crux of Deloitte's negligence lay in its failure to give appropriate advice to the board of directors regarding:

(i) the absence of controls over the foreign exchange operations, and

(ii) the failure of senior managers to respond to their (the auditors') warnings regarding the absence of controls (Shanahan, 1995, p. 214).

As regards auditors' contractual liability to their clients, the AWA case is particularly interesting as it illustrates both:

- a breach of auditors' statutory duties [that is, their failure to qualify their audit reports for the company's failure to maintain proper accounting records as required by section 331E(2) of the Australian Corporations Law[7]]; and
- a breach of their common law duties [that is, their failure to make the necessary enquiries of AWA's senior managers about matters of which they were uncertain (for example, the extent of the foreign exchange manager's authority), and their failure to report to the appropriate level of the entity's management (namely, the board of directors) serious deficiencies they discovered in the entity's internal controls and record keeping].

The case is also interesting in that it illustrates the exercise by the court of the principle of contributory negligence which we discuss in Chapter 16, section 16.5.6.

In the English case of *Sasea Finance Ltd* v *KPMG* [2000] 1 All ER 676; [2000] 1 BCLC 236; [2001] 1 All ER (D) 127 (May), Sasea Finance Limited (SFL), an English-registered company which was part of the Swiss-based Sasea group of companies, sued its auditor, KPMG, for the negligent performance of its audit for the year ending 31 December 1989. The audit was completed and the audit report signed in November 1990.

In 1992, the Sasea group collapsed and SFL went into liquidation. The group's affairs were subject to a criminal investigation which revealed that the companies in the group had been vehicles for a massive fraud. SFL claimed that, had

---

[7] This section contains the same provisions as section 498(2) of the UK Companies Act 2006.

KPMG acted with reasonable skill and care, it would have taken such action that would have allowed SFL to avoid suffering four losses which resulted from fraud (£2.4m, £113,000, £458,000 and £8m, respectively) between September 1990 and early 1991. KPMG contended that none of the losses was caused by any breach of contract or negligence on its part.

The High Court held that SFL's claims in respect of two of the losses (those of £2.4m and £8m) had insufficient grounds to proceed to trial but it refused to strike out the other two claims. SFL appealed the Court's decision and KPMG cross-appealed. KPMG contended, amongst other things, that any negligence on its part was not the cause of the alleged losses (the third of the three facts a plaintiff must prove: see section 15.2.3).

The Court of Appeal overturned the High Court's decision and SFL's claim against KPMG for all four losses was reinstated. During the Court of Appeal hearing, Kennedy L J explained some aspects of auditors' duties. He stated:

> Where a firm of accountants accepts instructions to audit the accounts of a company for a fiscal year, its primary obligation is, within a reasonable time, to exercise an appropriate level of skill and care in reporting to the company's members on the accounts of the company stating, in their opinion, whether the accounts . . . give a true and fair view of the company's financial affairs.

He went on to clarify auditors' duty to report significant facts to their client's management,[8] and to do so in a timely fashion. He said:

> If, for example, the auditors discover that a senior employee of the company has been defrauding the company on a grand scale and is in the position to go on doing so, then it would normally be the duty of the auditors to report what had been discovered to the management of the company at once, not simply when rendering the auditor's report weeks or months later.

He concluded that *Sasea's* losses resulted from fraud or irregularities, the risk of which KPMG ought to have apprehended and reported. KPMG had a duty to warn the company's directors as soon as the fraud or irregularities had been detected.

Our third example of a case brought against auditors for a breach of their contractual obligations is that of *Equitable Life Assurance Society* v *Ernst & Young* [2003] EWHC 804 (Comm); [2003] 2 BCLC 603; [2003] EWCA (Civ) 114. This case is of particular interest for the following reasons:

    (i)   it involves one of the largest claims ever brought against a firm of auditors (£3.75 billion);

    (ii)   a question to be addressed by the court was whether, in the particular circumstances, the auditor owed its client a duty of care;

---

[8] Readers are reminded that in the Preface to this book we note that we use the term 'management' to include the reporting entity's non-executive directors, executive directors and non-director executives (that is, all directors and executives).

(iii) it indicates that the courts are concerned to keep claims lodged against auditors within reasonable bounds;

(iv) the court drew attention to the fact that, in the area of professional advisors' duty of care, the law is in a state of development and flux and is facts-sensitive.

The case has its origins in an earlier case – *Equitable Life Assurance* v *Hyman* [2000] 3 All ER 961; [2000] 3 WLR 529, HL; [2000] 2 WLR 798, CA; [2002] 1 AC 408. In 1999, Equitable was unable to meet its obligation to pay holders of guaranteed annuity policies their guaranteed bonuses and it sought leave from the court to reduce the bonuses of non-guaranteed annuity policyholders in order to meet the shortfall of £1.5 billion. The court of first instance found in Equitable's favour but disaffected policyholders (including Hyman) appealed the decision. The Court of Appeal reversed the lower court's ruling. Equitable appealed the Appeal Court's decision but it was upheld by the House of Lords. The Law Lords ruled that Equitable was not entitled to distinguish between policyholders holding guaranteed and those holding non-guaranteed annuity policies.

During its audit of Equitable's 1999 financial statements, E&Y (inadvisably) accepted the assurance of Equitable's lawyers (without seeking further advice) that the company's "chances of losing the case were remote" (Christodoulou, 2010). As a consequence, E&Y did not require the company to disclose the contingent liability and uncertainties associated with the case in its financial statements. However, the Lords' decision left Equitable exposed to additional liabilities of £1.5 billion and, unable to meet them, it put itself up for sale. When no sale was achieved, Equitable sued its auditor, E&Y, (in the case in which we are interested) alleging that E&Y had breached its duty of care in the following ways:

(i) Equitable's 1998 and 1999 audited financial statements should have included substantial provisions in respect of the guaranteed annuity liability; and

(ii) its 1999 financial statements should have disclosed contingent liabilities and uncertainties in respect of the *Hyman* litigation.

Equitable claimed that E&Y's failure to exercise due care had resulted in it suffering:

(a) a diminution in the value of the business of £2.6 billion between 1998 and 2001; or

(b) alternatively, a lost opportunity (valued at £1.7 billion) to sell the business; and

(c) losses of £1.6 billion in 1997, tapering to £0.8 billion in 1999, through declaring unwarranted bonuses to policyholders (Simmons & Simmons, 2003b, pp. 1–2).

Not surprisingly, E&Y sought to have the claims struck out. In the High Court, Langley J struck out the first two claims on the grounds that, based on both the facts and the law, they were unlikely to succeed. Equitable appealed the ruling and the Court of Appeal found in Equitable's favour. Brooke L J concluded there were no grounds in the facts to dismiss the claims. He also noted that the legal issues involved in the case concern "the concepts which are used to limit the scope of the legal consequences of negligence or of legal responsibility for negligence" and, as these "continue to be in a state of development and flux, and sensitive to the facts", the court "had to show extra caution before disposing of them summarily" (Simmons & Simmons, 2003b, p. 2).

The key issue was whether E&Y owed Equitable a duty to protect it from the losses claimed. E&Y argued that it did not owe a duty of care in this regard as Equitable had never sought its advice about the desirability of selling the business or about its bonus declarations. Equitable, on the other hand, argued that it should have been protected from making inappropriate decisions (or from failing to make appropriate decisions) when it relied on its audited financial statements in the belief that they were free from material error. Brooke L J, after considering a number of decided cases (including *Caparo* and others we discuss in section 15.4), concluded that the issue is one that turns on the particular facts of the case and it could not be said that Equitable had no real prospect of persuading a court that E&Y owed it the duty to protect it from the harm Equitable had identified. He observed:

> When auditors undertake for a reward to perform services and are found to be negligent in the way they perform those services, the law does not require the client to ask for specific advice before it can recover damages for the foreseeable losses it later suffered. (as cited in Simmons & Simmons, 2003b, p. 2)

Thus, the Court of Appeal allowed Equitable's claims to proceed to trial although the claims relating to the lost sale of the business were restricted to damages for the loss of an opportunity of achieving a sale. The Court of Appeal expressed sympathy with E&Y's submission that the size of Equitable's claim (of £3.75 billion) was an unwarranted burden for a litigant to carry to trial but, having concluded that the claims could not be struck out, the Court of Appeal could not see how the claims could be limited to a certain amount (Simmons & Simmons, 2003b, p. 3).

The case went to trial in April 2005 but, in September 2005, Equitable suddenly dropped its claim against E&Y. Its counsel, Milligan QC, informed the court: "the claim by the Society [i.e., Equitable] against Ernst & Young has been settled on terms of the claim being discontinued and each party bearing its own costs" – costs reputed to be in the region of £30 million for each side (Pearson, 2005). Hopgood QC, counsel for E&Y stated:

At the end of this very long and costly and utterly pointless piece of litigation, which has culminated in the biggest climb-down in English legal history, there is a salutary lesson to be learned for those thinking of suing auditors. It is simply this: bringing a hugely inflated claim for blood-curdling amounts of money in the hope that the sheer scale of the claim will force the defendant into making a substantial cash payment is misconceived. It has not worked against Ernst & Young in this claim and it will not work against Ernst & Young in the future. (as quoted in Pearson, 2005, p. 1)[9]

This statement has relevance to out-of-court settlements, which we discuss in section 15.5.

It should be noted that, in order for contractual liability to be invoked, the aggrieved party must be a party to the contract. In the case of auditors appointed to perform a statutory audit under CA 2006, the contract is between the auditor and the company *per se*, not the company's shareholders as individuals. As the *AWA*, *Sasea* and *Equitable* cases illustrate, if an auditor fails to perform the applicable statutory and common law duties, or fails to exercise due skill and care in so doing, the client may sue for breach of contract. Should a shareholder wish to take action against the auditor, s/he can only do so by exercising his/her rights as a third party under the common law (see section 15.4 below). However – worse news yet for a company's shareholders: as a result of the House of Lords' decision in the *Caparo* case (1990), even this avenue of relief for them as individuals is of doubtful availability (see section 15.4.2).

---

[9] In addition to the case brought against E&Y by Equitable, the UK profession's Joint Disciplinary Scheme (JDS) investigated complaints about E&Y's audits of the company's financial statements – complaints which alleged, *inter alia*, that:

   (i) Equitable's 1999 financial statements on which E&Y expressed an unqualified opinion were not true and fair; and
   (ii) E&Y was not objective and independent when conducting its audit.

The JDS convened a Tribunal (JDT) which found that E&Y was incompetent in its audit of Equitable's 1999 financial statements (for failing to take independent advice on the likely outcome of the *Hyman* case) and that it was not properly objective and independent when conducting the audit. Fines and costs of nearly £10 million were imposed on E&Y. E&Y successfully appealed the JDT's finding in respect of its lack of independence and objectivity, but did not challenge the JDT's finding in respect of (i) its failure to warn shareholders of the consequences of losing the *Hyman* case and (ii) not disclosing that Equitable's 1999 financial statements did not show a true and fair view because of the inadequate provision for bonus payments. The Appeal Tribunal reduced the fines and costs awarded against E&Y to a little under £3 million (Reed, 2010).

In 2004, when the FRC became "UK's independent regulator responsible for promoting high quality corporate governance and reporting to foster investment", the JDS was replaced by the FRC's Accounting Investigation and Discipline Board. In 2007, when actuarial discipline was added to its remit, it became the Accounting and Actuarial Discipline Board (AADB). In 2012, when the FRC was restructured, the AADB was replaced by Case Management Committee, an advisory Committee of the FRC's Conduct Committee (FRC, 2012b). The former and current structure of the FRC is presented in diagrammatic form on page xix at the front of this book.

15.4 LIABILITY TO THIRD PARTIES UNDER THE COMMON LAW

15.4.1 Development of auditors' duty of care to third parties – until the *Caparo* decision

In addition to potential liability for breaching their contractual obligations, auditors may be exposed to liability to third parties if they fail to perform their duties with due skill and care. In these cases, the central issue for the court to decide is whether the auditor owed the plaintiff a duty of care (the first of the three facts a plaintiff must prove before damages will be awarded against an auditor: see section 15.2.3).

Through a series of cases, beginning in 1931 in the United States of America (USA), when it was held that auditors' liability should be restricted to contractual relationships, and not extended to third parties, the parties to whom auditors have been held to owe a duty of care were widened progressively until the decision in the *Caparo* case in 1990. The relevant cases are summarised in Figure 15.2.

In 1931, in the USA case of *Ultramares Corporation* v *Touche* (1931) 255 NY 170, it was held that auditors' liability can arise only under a contractual relationship. Cardozo J decided it would be too much to impose on accountants a liability to third parties for financial loss as this may expose them to liability out of all proportion to the gravity of their actions. As Cardozo J expressed it (at 179):

> [it] may expose accountants to liability in an indeterminate amount for an indeterminate time to an indeterminate class.

In 1932, the English case of *Donoghue* v *Stevenson* (1932) AC 562 started the process of recognising a liability to parties outside a contractual relationship. The case involved the purchase of a bottle of ginger beer, complete with decomposed snail, by a young man who gave it to his girlfriend to drink. Not surprisingly, the girlfriend (who was not a party to the contract between her boyfriend and the seller of the ginger beer) became ill. The court held that a duty of care is owed to third parties in circumstances where it can reasonably be foreseen that failure to take care may result in physical injury.

Nearly 20 years later, in *Candler* v *Crane Christmas & Co.* [1951] 2 KB 164, the court confirmed that no duty of care is owed to third parties in the case of financial loss. In this case, the defendant firm of chartered accountants negligently prepared a set of financial statements for their clients, knowing they would be shown to the third party plaintiff for the purpose of making an investment decision. The investment failed and the plaintiff sued the accountants. The majority of the court, re-iterating the fears expressed by Cardozo J in the

Figure 15.2: Summary of significant cases relating to auditors' liability to third parties up to and including *Caparo* v *Dickman* (1990)

Case	Key finding(s) of the case
Ultramares Corporation v *Touche* (1931) 255 NY 170 [USA case]	Accountants' liability can only arise under a contractual relationship; it should not be extended to third parties.
Donoghue v *Stevenson*(1932) AC 562 [UK case]	A duty of care is owed to third parties in circumstances where it can reasonably be foreseen that failure to take care may result in physical injury.
Candler v *Crane Christmas & Co.* [1951] 2 KB 164 [UK case]	No duty of care is owed to third parties in the case of financial loss. Lord Denning's dissenting judgment indicated things to come. He considered that accountants owe a duty of care to any third party to whom they know the financial statements are to be shown in order to induce him/her to invest money or to take some other action on them. He did not think the duty could be extended to strangers (i.e., persons of whom the auditor knows nothing at the time of the audit).
Hedley Byrne & Co. Ltd v *Heller and Partners* [1963] 2 All ER 575; [1964] AC 465 [UK case]	A duty of care is owed to third parties for financial loss where it can be shown that a 'special relationship' exists: i.e., where the provider of information knows, or ought to know, that a particular person is going to rely on the information for some specific purpose. The duty of care does not extend to strangers.
Diamond Manufacturing Company v *Hamilton*[1969] NZLR 609 [NZ case]	A 'special relationship' was said to exist because one of the auditors had been involved in negotiations with the investor; a duty of care therefore existed.
MLC v *Evatt* [1971] AC 793 [Australian case]	A 'special relationship' can arise only where the person giving financial advice holds him- or herself out to be an expert. (The *Hedley Byrne* principle was effectively narrowed.)
Haig v *Bamford* [1976] 3WW R331 (SC Can) [Canadian case]	No duty of care is owed to strangers. Auditors do not owe a duty of care to those who, at the time of the audit, they are not aware will rely on the audited financial statements for a particular purpose.
Anns v *Merton London Borough Council* [1977] 2 All ER. 492, [1978] AC 728 [UK case]	The requirement for a 'special relationship' was replaced by a 'relationship of proximity or neighbourhood', and the test of 'knowledge' that someone would rely on advice given and may suffer loss as a result of a failure to take care was replaced by one of 'reasonable foreseeability'. This case extended quite considerably the third parties to whom a duty of care is owed in cases involving non-physical injury.
Scott Group Ltd v *McFarlane* [1978] 1 NZLR 553 [NZ case]	A duty of care is owed by auditors who could, or should, reasonably foresee that a particular person or group of persons will rely on the audited financial statements for a particular type of investment decision. The *Hedley Byrne* principle of knowledge of reliance on the audited financial statements was replaced by a test of reasonable foreseeability. Attention was drawn to the fact that the audited financial statements of companies become a matter of public record through filing with the Companies Office.
Jeb Fasteners Ltd v *Marks, Bloom & Co.* [1981] 3 All ER 289 [UK case]	Auditors owe a duty of care to any person or class of persons whom they do not know but should reasonably foresee might rely on the audited financial statements when making an investment decision in respect of the company. The case extended the *Scott Group* case from circumstances in which a takeover is reasonably foreseeable to circumstances in which any form of financial support seems likely to be needed and reliance on audited financial statements could or should be expected.
Twomax Ltd v *Dickson McFarlane and Robinson* [1982] SC 113, [1983] SLT 98 [UK - Scottish case]	The duty of care owed by auditors to third parties established in the *Scott Group* case was extended to virtually anyone who can prove they relied on negligently audited financial statements when making an investment decision and suffered a loss as a consequence.

Figure 15.2: *Continued*

12. *Caparo Industries plc* v *Dickman and Others* [1990] 1 All ER 568; [1990] 2 AC605; [1990] 2 WLR 358, HL [UK case]	In the absence of special circumstances, auditors owe a duty of care only to: (i) the audit-client company, and (ii) the company's shareholders as a body. A duty of care is owed to third parties only when the three-part test of reasonable foreseeability of damage, proximity of relationship and fairness of imposing a duty is satisfied.

Ultramares case, held that a duty of care is not owed to third parties in the case of financial loss. However, the dissenting judgment of Lord Denning signalled the way the law would develop. He said:

> [Accountants] owe a duty, of course, to their employer and client and also, I think, to any third party to whom they themselves show the accounts or to whom they know their employer is going to show the accounts so as to induce him to invest money or to take some other action on them. But I do not think the duty can be extended still further so as to include strangers of whom they have heard nothing. . . .

Twelve years later, in *Hedley Byrne & Co Ltd* v *Heller and Partners* [1963] 2 All ER 575, [1964] AC 465, the court accepted as correct the reasoning of Lord Denning in the *Crane Christmas* case. The *Hedley Byrne* case involved a telephone enquiry by a bank to a merchant bank (Heller & Partners) regarding the credit worthiness of a company for which Heller was banker. The bank communicated Heller's reply – that the company was "considered good for its normal business engagements" and, in particular, for a proposed advertising contract – to one of its customers (Hedley Byrne & Co). The court held that a duty of care is owed to third parties where it can be shown that a 'special relationship' exists. Such a relationship will exist when the person giving the information knows, or ought to know, that another particular person is going to rely on the information for a specific purpose. However, the court emphasised that a duty of care does not extend to strangers; that is, persons of whom the person giving the information knows nothing at the time.

Hedley Byrne is a landmark decision in that it recognised third-party liability in a case involving financial loss. Until then, liability to third parties had been limited to situations involving physical injury.

The next two cases in the series helped to clarify the meaning of a 'special relationship'. In the New Zealand (NZ) case of *Diamond Manufacturing Company* v *Hamilton* [1969] NZLR 609, a member of an audit firm showed the financial statements the firm had audited to another party, knowing that they would be used for an investment decision. The court held that the auditors were liable to the third party as a special relationship existed and, therefore, a duty of care was owed. The special relationship arose because one of the auditors was involved in the negotiations with the investor. However, the court confirmed that a duty of care did not extend to strangers.

In 1971, in the Australian case of *Mutual Life & Citizens' Assurance Co. Ltd* v *Evatt* [1971] AC 793, the circumstances in which a special relationship could arise were somewhat narrowed. This case involved an insurance agent who was negligent in giving financial advice at a social function. It was held that, in order for a special relationship to exist, the person giving the financial advice must not only know that a particular person is going to rely on the financial advice proffered but, further, he [or she] must be giving the advice in a professional capacity. The special relationship can only arise in circumstances where the person giving the advice holds him- or herself out to be an expert.

Five years later (and 12 years after the *Hedley Byrne* principle was established) a Canadian court, in *Haig* v *Bamford* [1976] 3WW R331 (SC Can), confirmed that in cases involving financial loss, no duty of care is owed to a stranger: liability to third parties cannot arise in the absence of knowledge that a particular person will rely on the financial advice given (or the audited financial statements) for a specific purpose. This principle was to be tested in the UK just one year later.

The case of *Anns* v *Merton London Borough Council* [1977] 2 All ER 492, [1978] AC 728 involved the failure of a local authority to inspect a faulty building. The court held that the authority owed a duty of care to the occupants of the building. Although not involving auditors or accountants, this case is of singular importance to the extension of auditors' liability to third parties. It introduced the concept of a 'relationship of proximity or neighbourhood' in place of a 'special relationship', and also replaced the test of 'knowledge' that someone would rely on advice given and may suffer damage or loss as a result of failure to take care, with one of 'reasonable foreseeability'. The court provided a two-step approach as a guideline for determining whether or not a duty of care exists in particular circumstances. In the words of Lord Wilberforce:

> In order to establish whether a duty of care arises in a particular situation, two questions must be asked:
> 1. As between the alleged wrongdoer and the injured party there must be a relationship of proximity or neighbourhood, such that in the reasonable contemplation of the former, carelessness on his part may be likely to cause damage to the latter, in which case a *prima facie* duty of care arises.
> 2. If the question is answered affirmatively, it is necessary to consider whether there are any considerations which ought to negative, or to reduce or limit the scope of the duty or class of person to whom it is owed.

The principles enunciated in this case extended quite considerably the third parties to whom a duty of care is owed in circumstances involving non-physical injury. However, it is pertinent to note that it also brought the law in such cases into line with that obtaining in situations involving physical injury: the reasonable foreseeability test was established in circumstances involving physical injury in *Donoghue* v *Stevenson* in 1932 (supra).

The courts did not have long to wait before the *Anns* case principles were applied in a case involving auditors. In the NZ case of *Scott Group Ltd* v *McFarlane* [1978] 1 NZLR 553, auditors failed to detect a basic double counting error which resulted in a significant overvaluation of the entity's assets. At the time of the audit, the defendant auditor had no knowledge that the plaintiff had any intention of making a takeover offer. However, the court held that the company's rich assets and low profits situation made it a prime target for a takeover or merger and, therefore, the auditor should have foreseen that some person or group of persons was likely to rely on the audited financial statements to make such an offer.

This case extended the *Hedley Byrne* test of knowledge to one of reasonable foreseeability in situations involving audited financial statements. It established that a duty of care is owed by auditors who can, or should, reasonably foresee that a particular person or group of persons will rely on the audited financial statements when deciding whether to make a takeover (or similar) offer. Applying the two-part *Anns* test for a duty of care to be recognised, Woodhouse J identified four factors which give rise to a *prima facie* duty of care in the case of auditors. These are as follows:
1. Auditors are professionals in the business of providing expert advice for reward. If they did not intend the financial statements they audited to be relied upon, their work would be pointless.
2. Confidence in the ability of a company to handle its commercial arrangements would disappear if the auditor's report authenticating the company's financial statements could not be relied upon.
3. In ordinary circumstances there is no opportunity for a person to make any intermediate examination of the company's financial statements, nor is it practicable for many persons to do so.
4. Auditors are aware that the audited financial statements will be filed with the Companies Office and therefore become a matter of public record; they are available to the public, and anyone interested in the company has direct access to them.

Considering whether there are any factors which might negate or limit the scope of auditors' duty of care or the persons to whom it is owed, Woodhouse J found the only argument in favour of negating liability was that raised by Cardozo J in *Ultramares* v *Touche* (supra) over 45 years earlier, namely, the fear that auditors may be exposed "to liability in an indeterminate amount for an indeterminate time to an indeterminate class". However, his Honour considered that this need not be a matter of concern because of the difficulty of bringing a successful action against auditors for negligence. To succeed in such an action, the plaintiff must prove:

- it is reasonable to expect the auditors to have anticipated that the plaintiff would act on the audited financial information;
- the plaintiff actually relied on the audited financial information; and
- the auditors' failure to take care when auditing the financial information was the cause of the plaintiff's loss.

Woodhouse J concluded:

> [The auditors] must be taken to have accepted . . . a duty to those persons whom they can reasonably foresee will need to use and rely on [the audited financial statements] when dealing with the Company in significant matters affecting the Company's assets and business.

The *Scott Group* decision was applied and extended in the UK case of *Jeb Fasteners Ltd* v *Marks Bloom & Co.* [1981] 3 All ER 289. In this case, the defendants conducted an audit for a company which they were aware was undergoing a liquidity crisis and needed to raise finance. The company's financial statements included assets that were seriously overvalued, a fact that the auditors failed to detect. The plaintiffs had reservations about the assets figure but nevertheless proceeded with the takeover. The court re-affirmed that the auditor owes a duty of care to any person or class of persons whom they do not know but should reasonably be able to foresee might rely on the audited financial statements when making an investment decision relating to the company. Woolf J, citing the *Scott Group* decision with approval, stated:

> When he audited the accounts, Mr Marks would not know precisely who would provide the financial support, or what form the financial support would take, and he certainly had no reason to know that it would be by way of takeover by the plaintiffs. However, this was certainly one foreseeable method, and it does not seem to me that it would be right to exclude the duty of care merely because it was not possible to say with precision what machinery would be used to achieve the necessary financial support. Clearly, any form of loan would have been foreseeable, . . . and, while some methods of raising money were more obvious than others, and a takeover was not the most obvious method, it was certainly one method which was within the contemplation of Mr Marks.

Woolf J concluded that the auditor should have foreseen that a person might rely on the audited financial statements for the purpose of making an investment decision and that the person could, therefore, suffer loss if the financial statements were inaccurate.

Analysing Mr Justice Woolf's judgment (above) it appears that, although the case involved a takeover, he extended the *Scott Group* decision from circumstances in which a takeover is reasonably foreseeable to circumstances in which any form of financial support seems likely to be needed and reliance on audited financial statements can (or should) be expected.

In the Scottish case of *Twomax Ltd* v *Dickson, McFarlane & Robinson* [1982] SC 113, [1983] SLT 98, the facts are similar to those of the *Jeb Fasteners* case and Lord Stewart had little hesitation in applying Woolf J's judgment. He held that, although the auditors did not know the plaintiffs would rely on the audited financial statements to make an investment decision, they were aware that the auditee company (Kintyre Knitwear) needed capital. Given these circumstances, the auditors should reasonably have foreseen that some person (or group of persons) would rely on the audited financial statements and would suffer loss if they were inaccurate.

This case is significant because it confirmed the *Scott Group's* and *Jeb Fasteners'* extension of auditors' duty of care to third parties whom they do not know but should reasonably foresee might rely on the audited financial statements when making an investment decision relating to the reporting entity. But, unlike the plaintiffs in the *Scott Group* and *Jeb Fasteners* cases, the plaintiffs in the *Twomax* case were able to prove to the satisfaction of the court that they not only relied on the financial statements when making their investment decision, they also suffered a loss as a result of relying on those statements which had been audited negligently. As a consequence, damages were awarded against the defendant auditors.

Reviewing the cases outlined above, it is evident that between 1931 and 1983 the auditor's duty of care to third parties evolved from nothing to a very wide duty. Prior to 1963, influenced by the *Ultramares* case, auditors' liability was restricted to that arising under a contractual relationship. By the mid-1980s, auditors' duty of care extended to virtually anyone whom the auditors could, or should, reasonably foresee might rely on the audited financial statements when making an investment decision in respect of the reporting entity. When it is remembered that the audited financial statements of companies are filed with the Registrar of Companies and are readily available for public scrutiny, auditors' duty of care and their exposure to potential liability had become very wide indeed.

In this regard it is interesting to note the remarks of Savage (1981), made after the *Jeb Fasteners*, but before the *Twomax*, decision:

> [I]t is not beyond the bounds of possibility that a British Court might hold that an auditor owes a duty of care to anyone who consults audited accounts at the Companies Registry and sustains a loss as a result of a negligent audit. To that extent the Jeb decision only brings the law into line with the public's expectations. If the auditor carries out his work with reasonable care and competence . . . he

has nothing to fear.[10] If he fails to do so then, rightly, justice and equity demand that the law give remedy to those who have suffered as a direct result of his negligence. (p. 341)

Nevertheless, as is shown below, Savage's views were not shared by the House of Lords in the case of *Caparo Industries plc* v *Dickman & Others* [1990] 1 All ER 568; [1990] 2 AC 605; [1990] 2 WLR 358, HL. The Law Lords apparently felt the law had gone too far.

15.4.2 The *Caparo* decision

The facts of this case are briefly as follows. In June 1984, Caparo Industries plc (Caparo) purchased shares in Fidelity plc. Prior to the purchase (in May 1984), Fidelity's directors announced that the company's profits for the year were £1.3 million – well short of the forecast profit of £2.2 million. Nevertheless, relying on the audited financial statements, Caparo purchased more shares in Fidelity and, later in the year, made a successful takeover bid for the company.

Subsequent to the takeover, Caparo brought an action against the auditor (Touche Ross)[11] alleging that, notwithstanding the unqualified audit report, Fidelity's financial statements were inaccurate; the reported pre-tax profit of £1.3 million should, in fact, have been a reported loss of £0.46 million. In bringing its action, Caparo claimed that Touche Ross, as auditor of Fidelity, owed a duty of care to investors and potential investors and, in particular, to Caparo, in respect of the audit of Fidelity's financial statements. More particularly, Caparo asserted that:

- Touche Ross knew or ought to have known that:
  - (a) in March 1984 a press release had been issued stating that Fidelity's profits for the financial year would fall significantly short of £2.2 million;
  - (b) Fidelity's share price fell from 143 pence per share on 1 March 1984 to 75 pence per share on 2 April 1984; and
  - (c) Fidelity required financial assistance.

---

[10] This has been demonstrated in the case of *Lloyd Cheyham & Co. Ltd* v *Littlejohn & Co*. [1987] BCLC 303 which established that:
  (i) Auditors are not required to do any more than a person can or should do for himself. A person is not entitled to place unwarranted reliance on the financial statements.
  (ii) Auditors who have performed good-quality audits, and who have good defensible working papers which show their conclusions were justified on the basis of the evidence gathered, are able to defend themselves.

[11] A 'former Big 8' auditing firm that merged with Deloitte in 1996 to become one of the current 'Big 4' firms. After the merger, the merged firm was known as Deloitte & Touche for a number of years in many parts of the world.

- Touche Ross therefore ought to have foreseen that Fidelity was vulnerable to a takeover bid and that persons such as Caparo might well rely on the audited financial statements for the purpose of deciding whether to take over Fidelity and might well suffer loss if the financial statements were inaccurate.

The Law Lords were unanimous in their decision that, in general, auditors do not owe a duty of care to individual shareholders or to potential investors. Rather, a duty of care is owed to the company's shareholders as a body. In reaching this decision, the Lords held that *Scott Group Ltd* v *McFarlane & Others* (supra), and the subsequent English and Scottish decisions which had relied on *Scott Group*, namely, *Jeb Fasteners Ltd* v *Marks Bloom & Co.* (supra) and *Twomax Ltd* v *Dickson, McFarlane & Robinson* (supra), had been decided wrongly.

Analysis of the House of Lords' decision in the *Caparo* case reveals that the Law Lords were concerned to ensure that the scope of liability arising in professional negligence cases is not extended beyond reasonable limits. They referred with considerable respect to Cardozo J's statement in the *Ultramares* case, namely, that auditors' liability should not be extended to the point where it may exist "in an indeterminate amount for an indeterminate time to an indeterminate class". Their concern is reflected in Lord Oliver's statement:

> To apply as a test of liability only the foreseeability of possible damage without some further control would be to create a liability wholly indefinite in area, duration and amount and would open up a limitless vista of uninsurable risk for the professional man.

Lord Bridge indicated what "further control" might be imposed before the court would find that auditors (and other professional advisors) owe a duty of care to those who rely upon their statements. He stated:

> [T]here should exist between the party owing the duty and the party to whom it is owed a relationship characterised by the law as one of proximity or neighbourhood and the situation should be one in which the court considers it fair, just and reasonable that the law should impose a duty of a given scope upon the one party for the benefit of the other.

Following from these and other similar lines of reasoning, the Law Lords considered that, in order to establish that a duty of care exists, a three-part test needs to be satisfied, namely:

(i) *Reasonable foreseeability of damage*: when a person (A) makes a statement for another (B) (either an individual or a member of an identifiable class) to rely upon, A should be able to reasonably foresee that B might suffer loss if the statement is incorrect.

(ii) *Relationship of proximity*: with respect to the statement made, there must be a relationship of proximity between A and B. Such a relationship will exist if, when making the statement, A knew:
- the statement would be communicated to B;
- the statement would be communicated in relation to a particular transaction or a transaction of a particular kind;
- B would be very likely to rely on the statement when making a decision with respect to the transaction in question; and
- B acted on the statement to his or her detriment.

In determining whether there is a relationship of proximity between the parties, the court will determine whether the particular damage suffered by B is the kind of damage A was under a duty to prevent and whether there are circumstances from which the court can pragmatically conclude that a duty of care existed.

(iii) *Fairness*: the court must consider it fair, just and reasonable to impose a duty of care on A for the benefit of B.

While recognising that audited financial statements might be used for a variety of purposes, including the making of investment decisions, the Lords were of the view that their primary purpose is to protect the interests of the company *per se*, and to enable the company's shareholders and debenture holders to evaluate the quality of the stewardship exercised by the company's directors and "to exercise such powers as are vested in them by virtue of their respective propriety interests" (per Lord Oliver).[12] Their purpose is not to protect the interests of the general public or investors in particular who choose to use the financial statements for a particular purpose. The Law Lords saw the auditor's function within the context of this purpose of financial statements. Lord Oliver, for example, stated:

> It is the auditor's function to ensure, so far as possible, that the financial information as to the company's affairs prepared by the directors accurately reflects the company's position in order, first, to protect the company itself from the consequences of undetected errors . . . and, secondly, to provide shareholders with reliable intelligence for the purpose of enabling them to scrutinise the conduct

---

[12] It is interesting to compare this conclusion of the Law Lords with the objective of (audited) financial statements stated by the International Accounting Standards Board (IASB) in its *Conceptual Framework for Financial Reporting* (IASB, 2010):

> The objective of general purpose financial reporting is to provide financial information about the reporting entity that is useful to existing and potential investors, lenders and other creditors in making decisions about providing resources to the entity. . . . To assess an entity's prospects of future cash inflows, existing and potential investors, lenders and other creditors need information about the resources of the entity, claims against the entity, and how efficiently and effectively the entity's management and governing board have discharged their responsibilities to use the entity's resources. . . . Information about management's discharge of its responsibilities is also useful for decisions by existing investors, lenders and other creditors who have the right to vote on or otherwise influence management's actions. (OB3, OB4)

It is clear that the IASB envisages (audited) financial statements are for the use of individual shareholders (and other users) for making economic decisions related to the entity rather than for the shareholders as a body.

of the company's affairs and to exercise their collective powers to reward or control or remove those to whom that conduct has been confided.

Following from this view of the auditor's function, the Law Lords concluded that, in the absence of special circumstances, auditors owe a duty of care only to:

(i) the company *per se*, and

(ii) the company's shareholders as a body.

More particularly, in general, auditors do not owe a duty of care to individual shareholders or potential investors, irrespective of any reliance they may place on the audited financial statements for their investment decision(s). In order for a duty of care to arise, other than to the company or its shareholders as a body, the three-part test of reasonable foreseeability of damage, proximity of relationship and fairness of imposing a duty of care must be satisfied.

This returned the law roughly to where it stood nearly 30 years earlier at the time of *Hedley Byrne* v *Heller and Partners* (supra). However, many commentators consider the reversal of the law is unfortunate. Baxt (1990) for example notes that, as a result of the *Caparo* decision, both professional investors, such as Caparo, and ordinary individual investors are denied a possible avenue for relief when they suffer loss as a result of negligence on the part of auditors. He states:

> Clearly, we do not wish to see the prophecy come true of Chief Justice Cardozo, nor do we wish to identify any particular group of professionals as being more subject to liabilities than others. But some protection is needed for the investor in circumstances such as [Caparo], assuming (and this is important and tends to be overlooked in cases of this kind) that liability can be established. (Baxt, 1990, p. 18)

Picking up on the last point made by Baxt in the above quotation, he (Baxt, 1990), Gwilliam (1988) and others (including Woodhouse J in the *Scott Group* case) have emphasised the difficulty of an investor bringing a successful action against auditors. As noted in section 15.2, in order to do so, the investor must satisfy the court that:

(i) the auditor owed him/her a duty of care;

(ii) the auditor was negligent in the performance of his/her duties; and

(iii) the investor suffered a loss as a result of relying on the negligently audited financial statements.

It seems that in the *Caparo* case, the House of Lords, in seeking to ensure that auditors are not exposed to unbounded liability, focused on the first requirement (above); they appear to have given little attention to the third factor. Yet, as cases such as *Scott Group* and *Jeb Fasteners* have demonstrated, this is the most difficult factor to prove. Most investors would find it difficult to prove to the satisfaction of the court that audited financial statements provided the sole or main basis for an investment decision. As Baxt (1990) observes:

There must be a number of factors that will influence a shareholder to buy more shares in a company for investment purposes – a comparative analysis of other companies' performances, the market reaction to the information about those companies, the individual shareholder's financial position, his/her interests and needs, and a myriad of other individual factors. Each case will see different shareholders having to prove different things in order to show that the particular investment decision taken was based on the auditor's report, and that any loss is linked to the report, assuming further, that the report was negligent. (p. 9)

In the case of a large investor such as Caparo, it must surely be extremely difficult to prove reliance on negligently prepared audited financial statements. A large investor would almost certainly be expected to seek additional information from the company and elsewhere (that is, to undertake due diligence) before committing significant resources to the investment, such as occurs when a takeover offer is made.

15.4.3 Development of auditors' duty of care to third parties since *Caparo*

As may be seen from Figure 15.3, since *Caparo* a number of cases relevant to auditors' duty of care to third parties have been decided in the UK.[13] Some of these, such as *Al-Saudi Banque and Others* v *Clark Pixley* [1990] Ch 313, have clarified aspects of the *Caparo* three-part test for a duty of care to be established; others, especially those in more recent years, such as *Independent Advantage Insurance Co Ltd* v *Representatives of Michael Cook (deceased)* [2002] All ER (D) 151 (Nov); [2003] EWCA Civ 1103; [2003] All ER (D) 423 (Jul), have served to widen once more the parties to whom auditors may be held to owe a duty of care. In a number of the cases, the judges have emphasised that the law in this area remains 'transitional', 'developing', 'in a state of flux' and 'facts-sensitive'.

The *Al-Saudi Banque* case (supra) helped to clarify what is required for a 'special relationship' to exist, such as to give rise to auditors owing a duty of care to third parties. The case concerned a company whose business involved providing finance to overseas customers in exchange for bills of exchange. The company then used the bills of exchange (which constituted virtually all of its assets) to negotiate advances from the ten plaintiff banks. In 1983 the company was compulsorily wound up and the bills of exchange were found to be worthless. The banks sued the auditor for negligence, alleging that it ought reasonably to have foreseen that the banks would rely on the auditor's reports when deciding whether to continue, renew or increase loans to the company, that they did so rely on the reports and were misled thereby. At the time of the relevant audit reports (1981 and 1982), seven of the plaintiff banks were existing creditors of the company but three were not.

---

[13] A number of cases have also been decided overseas. However, in the interests of keeping our discussion within reasonable bounds, we limit the cases discussed in section 15.4.3 to significant cases decided in the UK.

Figure 15.3: Summary of significant UK cases since the *Caparo* ruling relating to auditors' liability to third parties

Case	Key finding(s) of the case
1. *Al-Saudi Banque & Others* v *Clark Pixley* [1990] Ch 313	The court applied *Caparo* and held that, in order for auditors to owe a duty of care to a third party, they must have given the third party a copy of their audit report, or know or intend that their audit report will be supplied to the third party.
2. *James McNaughton Papers Group Ltd.* v *Hicks Anderson* [1991] 1 All ER 134; [1990] BCC 891; (1991) 9 ACLC 3091	The court applied *Caparo* and held that when deciding whether a 'special relationship' exists, such as to give rise to a duty of care to a third party, the following need to be considered: 1. the purpose for which a statement is made, 2. the purpose for which it is communicated to the third party, 3. the relationship between the maker of the statement and the third party, 4. the size of the class to which the third party belongs, 5. the knowledge of the maker of the statement, and 6. the extent to which the third party relies on the statement or advice.
3. *Morgan Crucible Co plc* v *Hill Samuel Bank Ltd* [1991] Ch 295; [1991] 1 All ER 148; [1991] 2 WLR 655; [1991] BCLC 178; [1991] BCC 82; [1990] NLJR 1605	Applying *Caparo* the court held that if, during a contested takeover bid, financial advisors of the target company make express representations after an identified bidder has emerged, intending the bidder to rely on those representations, a relationship of proximity exists such that the financial advisors owe the bidder a duty of care not to be negligent in making representations which might mislead him.
4. *Berg Sons & Co. Ltd.* v *Mervyn Hampton Adams* [1993] BCLC 1045	The court applied, but effectively narrowed, the *Caparo* decision. It held: 1. For a company to succeed in an action against its auditor, it must show the company or its shareholders were misled. 2. To establish that auditors owe a duty of care to a third party, it must be shown that: (a) a specific relationship exists between the audit function and the transaction in relation to which reliance was placed on the audit report, and (b) the case is brought within the period in which it is reasonably foreseeable that reliance may be placed on the audited financial statements.
5. *Galoo Ltd* v *Bright Grahame Murray* [1995] 1 All ER 16; [1994] 1 WLR 1360; [1994] 2 BCLC 492; [1994] BCC 319	Applying *Caparo* the court held that: 1. A plaintiff can claim damages for breach of contract by an auditor only when the breach is the effective or dominant cause of his loss – not when the breach merely provides the opportunity to sustain a loss. 2. If an auditor is aware that a particular investor will rely on the audited financial statements for a particular lending or share purchase decision, and intends the lender or bidder to rely on them for this purpose, a duty of care to the lender or bidder will arise.
6. *Henderson* v *Merrett Syndicates* [1995] 2 AC 145; [1994] 3 All ER 506; [1994] 3 WLR 761; [1994] NLJR 1204; [1994] 4 LRC 355	The House of Lords introduced 'assumption of responsibility' as an alternative to the three-part *Caparo* test for determining whether a professional advisor owed a duty of care to a third party. It also established that a professional advisor may owe a common law duty of care to: (i) a party to whom the advisor has assumed responsibility, notwithstanding any contractual relationship between the parties, and (ii) to one party under a contractual relationship and also, simultaneously, to a third party.
7. *ADT Ltd* v *BDO Binder Hamlyn* [1996] BCC 808	Binder Hamlyn was held to have assumed responsibility to a third party (ADT), and thus owed it a duty of care, because a Binder Hamlyn partner made (negligently prepared) oral representations to ADT, knowing the purpose for which the information was required and knowing that ADT would rely on it without independent enquiry.
8. *Coulthard & Ors* v *Neville Russell* (1998) PNLR 276; (1998) 1 BCLC 143; (1998) BCC 359	As a matter of principle, accountants can owe a duty of care to a client company's directors. However, whether a duty is owed depends on the facts of the particular case and, more especially, on whether the accountants can be shown to have assumed responsibility to the directors.

Figure 15.3: *Continued*

9. *Siddell* v *Sydney Cooper & Partners* (1999) PNLR 511	The Court of Appeal emphasised that: 1. in the area of the liability of professional advisors, the law is in a state of transition or development; 2. professional advisors can owe a duty of care to shareholders or directors as third parties at the same time as they owe those shareholders or directors a duty of care under a contractual arrangement; 3. there is a distinction between breaches of duty by professional advisors that cause another's loss and those that merely provide the opportunity to sustain a loss. The type of loss sustained, and whether it was caused by the advisor's breach of duty, are questions to be decided based on the facts of the case; 4. whether or not professional advisors owe a company's individual shareholders and directors a duty of care depends on the circumstances of the particular case.

0. *Bank of Credit & Commerce International (Overseas) Ltd, BCCI Holdings (Luxembourg) SA, and BCCI SA* v *Price Waterhouse, and Ernst & Whinney* [1998] BCC 617, [1998] 15 LS Gaz R 32, 142 Sol Jo LB 86, [1998] 5 PNLR 564	A duty of care may be owed by the auditors of one company to another (third party) company where the business of the two companies is conducted as a single business.
	
	Leading decided cases considering the liability of professional advisors to third parties for financial loss have adopted two approaches
	1. the 'threefold test' – for a duty of care to be owed by an advisor to an advisee:
	    (a) it must be reasonably foreseeable that, if negligent advice is given, the recipient is likely to suffer damage;
	    (b) there is a sufficient proximate relationship between the parties; and
	    (c) it is just and reasonable to impose the liability;
	2. the 'voluntary assumption of responsibility test'.
	
	Factors to be taken into account when deciding whether these tests have been met, include:
	(i) the precise relationship between the advisor and advisee;
	(ii) the precise circumstances in which the advice was given and in which it was communicated to the advisee;
	(iii) the degree of reliance the advisor intended or should reasonably have anticipated would be placed on the accuracy of the advice by the advisee, and the reliance in fact placed on it;
	(iv) the presence or absence of other advisors on whom the advisee would or could rely;
	(v) the opportunity, if any, given to the advisor to issue a disclaimer of responsibility.

1. *Electra Private Equity Partners* v *KPMG Peat Marwick & Ors* [1999] All ER (D) 415; [2000] BCC 368; [2001] 1 BCLC 589	The Court of Appeal's decision indicates that:
	1. when deciding whether auditors owe a duty of care to a third party, the court will consider factors such as:
	    (a) the auditor's knowledge or foreseeability that the third party will rely on the audited financial statements for a particular decision;
	    (b) any direct communications between the auditor and the third party;
	    (c) whether the auditor believed the third party would receive independent advice and, if so,
	    (d) whether the auditor appreciated the advisor would rely on the audited financial statements when giving the advice;
	2. the law in relation to the liability of professional advisors to third parties is in a state of development and transition.

2. *Barings plc* v *Coopers & Lybrand & Ors, Barings Futures (Singapore) Pte Ltd* v *Mattar & Ors* [2002] EWHC 461 (Ch); [2002] All ER (D) 309 (Mar); [2003] Lloyd's Rep IR 566	In circumstances where the auditor of a subsidiary forwards information to the parent company and its auditor for use in the preparation and audit of the group's consolidated financial statements, a duty of care may be owed by the auditor of the subsidiary to the parent company and its auditor.

Figure 15.3: *Continued*

13. *Andrew* v *Kounnis Freeman* [1999] 2 BCLC 641 (CA); [1999] All ER (D) 553; [2000] Lloyd's PN 263	As a result of a letter from the Civil Aviation Authority (CAA) to Kounnis Freeman (KF), the latter knew or ought to have known that the CAA would rely on F plc's audited financial statements when deciding whether or not to renew F plc's licence to organise air travel. As a result, KF had assumed responsibility to the CAA and thus owed it a duty of care.
14. *Independent Advantage Insurance Co Ltd* v *Representatives of Michael Cook (deceased)* [2002] All ER (D) 151 (Nov); [2003] EWCA Civ 1103; [2003] All ER (D) 423 (Jul); [2004] PNLR 3 CA	The auditors did not know the identity of the party seeking to rely on their work or the purpose for which it would be relied upon; nor did they have any direct contact with the third party. Nevertheless, they were considered to owe a duty of care to the third party on the grounds that they knew, or ought to have known, that Swift's audited financial statements would be relied upon when Swift applied to "one of a possible class of providers" for bonds and/or other securities. This case marks a distinct broadening of auditors' potential liability to third parties.
15. *Royal Bank of Scotland* v *Bannerman, Johnstone, Maclay* [2003] OHSC 125; [2005] CSIH 39	A duty of care to a third party may exist when the provider of information or advice knows that it will be passed to the third party for a specific purpose and the recipient is likely to rely on it for that purpose. The intention of the advisor that the recipient should rely on the information may support the existence of proximity between the auditor and the third party but it is not essential in every case. The absence of a disclaimer may indicate an assumption of responsibility by the auditor.
16. *Man Nutzfahzeuge AG and Ors* v *Freightliner Ltd and Ors* [2003] EWHC 2245; [2005] EWHC 2347 (Comm); [2007] EWCA (Civ) 910	Cases involving auditor's liability to third parties are facts-sensitive and the law in the area "is in development and not without difficulty". The Caparo ruling was applied and E&Y were held not to owe a duty of care to (third party) Freightliner. The case seems to have stemmed the gradual extension of parties to whom auditors will be held to owe a duty of care evident in cases decided since Caparo.
17. *Moore Stephens* v *Stone & Rolls (in liquidation)* [2007] EWHC 1826 (Comm); [2007] All ER (D) 448 (Jul); [2008] EWCA Civ 644; [2009] UKHL39.	The case against Moore Stephens (MS), auditor of Stone & Rolls (S&R), for performing its audits negligently and failing to detect fraud, was struck out because: (i) the fraud was perpetrated by S&R's sole shareholder and director who was indistinguishable from the company (i.e., the company perpetrated the fraud against itself); (ii) following *Caparo*, auditors do not owe a duty of care to the company's creditors (on whose behalf the action against MS was brought); (iii) in the circumstances of the case, it would not be fair, just and reasonable to impose liability on MS. The final point seems to be the principle the courts are now seeking to apply in cases brought against auditors.

Millet J held that the auditor did not owe the banks a duty of care:

- In respect of the three banks which were not existing creditors at the dates of the audit reports, the judge noted that the auditor had not reported directly to the banks and had not intended or known that its reports would be communicated to them. Even though it was foreseeable that a bank might ask a company for copies of its audited financial statements as a basis for making relevant loan decisions, the element of proximity necessary to find a duty of care was lacking.[14]
- Regarding the other seven banks, Millet J observed that, although their identities and amounts of exposure were known to the auditor when the

---

[14] As we shall see, this ruling is diametrically opposed to that of Chadwick L J, 13 years later in the *Independent Advantage* case.

auditor's reports were signed, their position was not comparable to that of the company's shareholders to whom the auditor owed a statutory duty to report. As the auditor had not sent copies of its reports directly to the banks, or sent copies to the company with the intention or knowledge that they would be supplied to the banks, the auditor owed no duty of care to the plaintiffs.

This case suggested that, in order for auditors to owe a duty of care to a third party (or, more particularly, to the audit client's bankers), they must either give a copy of their audit report to the third party or intend or know that their report will be supplied to that party. The case of *James McNaughton Papers Group Ltd* v *Hicks Anderson & Co* [1991] 1 All ER 134; [1990] BCC 891; (1991) ACLC 3091 indicated other factors the court will consider when deciding whether or not auditors owe a duty of care to a third party. In this case, James McNaughton Ltd was involved in the takeover of another company (MK). Draft financial statements for use in the negotiations were prepared by Hicks Anderson and, at a meeting of the negotiators, a representative of that firm stated that MK was breaking even. After the takeover was completed, discrepancies were found in the draft financial statements, and MK was found to be insolvent. McNaughtons sued the accountants for negligent preparation of the financial statements and stated that, in proceeding with the takeover, they had relied on the financial statements and the statement made at the negotiating meeting by the accountants' representative.

The court of first instance found that the accountants owed McNaughton Ltd a duty of care, but this decision was reversed on appeal. The Court of Appeal, applying *Caparo*, held that when a statement or advice is acted upon by a person [C], other than the person intended by the giver of the statement or advice [A] to act on it, the factors to be considered in determining whether A owes C a duty of care include:
- the purpose for which the statement is made;
- the purpose for which the statement is communicated;
- the relationship between A, C and any relevant third party;
- the size of any class to which C belongs;
- the state of knowledge of A;
- the reliance by C on A's statement or advice.

Considering these factors, the court found that the accountants owed no duty of care to McNaughton Ltd in respect of the draft financial statements because:
- the financial statements were produced for MK and not McNaughton;
- the financial statements were merely draft financial statements and the accountants could not reasonably have foreseen that McNaughton would treat them as final financial statements;

- the accountants did not take part in the negotiations;
- McNaughton was aware that MK was in a poor financial state and, thus, could have been expected to consult its own accountants;
- the statement made at the negotiating meeting was very general and did not affect the figures in the financial statements. The accountants could not reasonably have foreseen that McNaughton would rely on the statement without further enquiry or advice.

The *McNaughton* case added to the *Al-Saudi* decision in that it provided guidance on the matters (other than the auditor's knowledge, or intention, of a particular person's reliance on the auditor's report) the court would consider when deciding whether or not auditors owe a duty of care to a third party. These include the purpose for which an audit report is prepared, the purpose for which it is communicated to a third party, and the extent to which the third party relies (or sensibly should rely) on it.

Unlike the two cases cited above, *Morgan Crucible Co plc* v *Hill Samuel Bank Ltd* [1991] Ch 295; [1991] 1 All ER 148; [1991] 2 WLR 655; [1991] BCLC 178; [1991] BCC 82; [1990] NLJR 1605 provides an example of a case in which the auditor (and another financial advisor) was held to owe a duty of care to a third party. On 6 December 1985, Morgan Crucible (MC) announced a takeover bid for First Castle Electronics plc (FCE). On 19 December 1985, FCE's chairman sent the company's shareholders the first of a number of circulars recommending that the takeover offer be rejected. Each circular, which was also issued as a press release by Hill Samuel Bank Ltd (HSB, the merchant bank advising FCE), referred to the company's audited financial statements for the years to 31 January 1984 and 1985 and its unaudited interim statements for the six months to 31 July 1985. A circular from FCE's chairman, dated 24 January 1986, forecast a 38 per cent increase in the company's pre-tax profits for the year to 31 January 1986. The circular also contained:
  (i)   a letter from FCE's auditor stating that the profit forecast had been properly compiled in accordance with FCE's stated accounting policies, and
  (ii) a letter from HSB expressing the opinion that the forecast had been made after due and careful enquiry.

On 29 January 1986, MC increased its offer for FCE and this was accepted. MC subsequently found that FCE was worthless. MC sued the bank, the auditor and FCE's directors, alleging it was foreseeable that it would rely on the representations contained in the pre-bid financial statements and the profit forecast. MC claimed that FCE's accounting policies were flawed, its pre-bid financial statements were prepared negligently, and its profit had been grossly overstated. It asserted that, had it known the true facts, it would not have made the takeover bid, let alone increase it.

The court of first instance, relying on *Caparo*, held that neither the financial advisors (in this case, HSB and the auditor) nor the directors of a target company in a contested takeover bid owe a duty of care to a known takeover bidder regarding the accuracy of profit forecasts, financial statements, and defence documents prepared for the purpose of contesting the bid. Such documents are prepared for the purpose of advising shareholders whether or not to accept the bid, not for the guidance of the bidder. Hence, there is insufficient proximity between the financial advisors and directors of the target company and the bidder to give rise to a duty of care.

The Court of Appeal reversed this decision. It held that if, during the course of a contested takeover bid, the financial advisors and directors of the target company make express representations after an identified bidder has emerged, intending the bidder to rely on those representations, they owe the bidder a duty of care not to be negligent in making representations which might mislead him. In the instant case, the defendants intended the plaintiff to rely on the pre-bid financial statements and profit forecast for the purpose of deciding whether to make an increased bid and the plaintiff did so rely. There was, therefore, a relationship of proximity between each of the defendants (HSB, the auditor and FCE's directors) and the plaintiff (MC) such as to give rise to a duty of care.

The next case in the series, *Berg Sons & Co. Ltd* v *Mervyn Hampton Adams* [1993] BCLC 1045, focused primarily on auditors' duty of care to the auditee (that is, auditors' contractual duties) but it also explored, and to an extent further narrowed, auditors' duty of care to third parties. The case involved a small company all of whose shares were held by the sole executive director, his wife and his son. In 1985 the company was put into liquidation and the company's liquidator, together with a discount house which had provided Berg Sons & Co. with finance, sued the auditor for negligence. It was alleged that, as a consequence of the auditor's unqualified audit report on the company's 1982 financial statements:
   (i)   the company was able to continue in business and borrow money which it had no prospect of repaying, and
   (ii) the discount house discounted bills receivable which should have been shown in the financial statements as irrecoverable.

Hobhouse J found the auditors were not negligent even though they had received unsatisfactory assurances from both the acceptor of certain bills and Mr Berg and that this should have prompted an auditor's report qualified on grounds of uncertainty. His Honour, following the reasoning of the Law Lords in *Caparo*, stated:
   [T]he purpose of the statutory audit is to provide a mechanism to enable those having a proprietary interest in the company . . . to have access to accurate

financial information about the company. Provided that those persons have that information, the statutory purpose is exhausted . . . In the present case the . . . plaintiffs have based their case not upon any lack of information on the part of the company's executive director but rather upon the opportunity that the possession of the auditor's certificate is said to have given for the company to continue to carry on business and borrow money from third parties. Such matters do not fall within the scope of the duty of the statutory auditor.

With respect to the auditor owing the company a duty of care, the court held that, in order for a company to bring a successful action against its auditor, it must show "that the company or its members were in some way misled or left in ignorance of some material fact" (per Hobhouse J). A 'one-man' company such as Berg Sons & Co. could never prove that it had been misled because its controlling director and shareholder would always know better than anyone else the true position of the company and its business.

The court also held that the auditor owed no duty of care to the discount house. Hobhouse J reaffirmed, but went beyond, the *Caparo* decision. He stated that, before a duty of care to third parties will arise, the following two criteria must be satisfied.
1. There must be a specific relationship between the function the defendant has been requested to perform and the transaction for which the plaintiff relied on the proper performance of that function; (in this case, between the statutory audit and the discounting of bills receivable).
2. The case must be brought within a limited period of the alleged negligence. There is only a limited period of time within which it would be reasonably foreseeable that a bank or discount house would rely upon a given set of audited financial statements.

Commenting on this decision of Hobhouse J, Davies (1992) pointed out:
> The effect of these additional limitations is to place such stringent restrictions on the circumstances in which the creditors of a company can sue its auditors that it is now difficult to imagine any circumstances when such a claim could succeed arising out of the statutory audit function. (p. 4)

He also noted that, as a result of the *Berg Sons & Co.* judgment, it is most unlikely that a successful case can be brought in the UK against auditors by their small company audit clients.

The case of *Galoo Ltd* v *Bright Grahame Murray* [1995] 1 All ER 16; [1994] 1 WLR 1360; [1994 2 BCLC 492; [1994] BCC 319 served to confirm the difficulty a company's creditors will experience in trying to establish that the company's auditor owes them a duty of care. It also helped to clarify what the UK courts will accept (in the wake of the *Caparo* decision) as a 'special relationship' which may give rise to auditors owing a duty of care to a third party.

The facts of this case are briefly as follows. In 1987, Hillsdown Holdings (HD) purchased 51 per cent of the shares in GM; Galoo Ltd (GL) was a wholly owned subsidiary of GM. The acquisition agreement stated that the purchase price of the shares in GM was to be 5.2 times the net profit of GM, as reflected in the audited financial statements of GM and GL for the year ending December 1986. The financial statements were audited by Bright Grahame Murray who delivered them to HD for the specific purpose of establishing the share price. Between 1987 and 1992, HD advanced £30 million in loans to GM and GL and, in 1991, purchased a further 44 per cent of shares in GM on terms set out in a supplemental share purchase agreement.

In 1992, HD, GM and GL sued the auditors claiming that GM's and GL's audited financial statements for the years 1985 to 1989, and the draft audited financial statements for 1990, contained substantial inaccuracies. In failing to discover or report the inaccuracies, the auditors had been negligent and in breach of the duties they owed to the plaintiffs. Had the auditors performed their duties with reasonable skill and care, the insolvency of GM and GL would have been revealed and they would have ceased trading immediately. They would not have accepted advances from HD, and HD would not have purchased shares in GM or made loans to GM and GL.

The Court of Appeal was asked to rule on whether there was a sustainable cause of action against the auditors. It found there was – but only in respect of HD's initial 51 per cent investment. The court held:
1. A plaintiff's claim that it had suffered a loss by entering into a loan agreement did not give rise to any damages since the mere acceptance of a loan could not be described as a loss giving rise to damages. The mere acceptance by GM and GL of loans from HD in reliance on the audit reports did not give rise to any cause of action against the auditors.
2. A plaintiff is entitled to claim damages for breach of contract by the defendants where the breach is the effective or dominant cause of his loss – rather than merely providing him with the opportunity to sustain loss. Based on the facts in this case, the auditors' breach of duty provided GM and GL with the opportunity to incur, and to continue to incur, trading losses, but it could not be said to have caused those losses.
3. The fact that it is foreseeable that a potential investor in a company might rely on the company's audited financial statements is not of itself sufficient to impose on the auditors a duty of care to the investor. However, if the auditors have been made aware that a particular identified lender or bidder for shares will rely on the audited financial statements, and the auditors intend the party to so rely, the auditors owe a duty of care to the identified party and may be liable in the event of any breach of this duty. In respect of the 1987 acquisition of shares in

GM by HD, it is clear that the auditors knew the audited financial statements for the year to December 1986 would be relied upon by HD for calculating the purchase price of the shares and they were required to submit the audited financial statements to HD for that specific purpose. Thus, the auditors owed a duty of care to HD in that regard. However, with respect to HD's loans to GM and GL and additional shares purchased in GM, it was not alleged that the auditors either knew or intended that HD would rely on GM's and GL's audited financial statements when deciding whether to make the loans or when calculating the purchase price of shares in GM under the supplemental share price agreement. Hence, no duty of care was owed by the auditors to HD in respect of the loans or the additional shares purchased.

From the post-*Caparo* cases reviewed above, it is evident that, subsequent to the *Caparo* judgment, it was (and, indeed remains) difficult for third parties to establish that auditors owed them a duty of care. However, as the cases outlined below bear witness, in more recent years, the courts have modified the *Caparo* decision to some extent and have recognised a duty of care to third parties in situations where strict application of the three-part *Caparo* test (reasonable foreseeability of damage, relationship of proximity, and fairness of imposing a duty) would have precluded such a duty being owed. The most significant modification of the *Caparo* ruling is the court's recognition of a duty of care arising when auditors (or other professional advisors) 'assume responsibility' to a third party. This principle was enunciated by the House of Lords in *Henderson* v *Merrett Syndicates* [1995] 2 AC 145; [1994] 3 All ER 506; [1994] 3 WLR 761; [1994] NLJR 1204; [1994] 4 LRC 355.

In the *Henderson* case the plaintiffs were Lloyd's Names[15] who were members of syndicates that were managed by the defendants.[16] The plaintiffs fell into two groups:
   (i)   direct Names – Names who belonged to syndicates that were managed by the members' agents. Thus, the agents were both the members' and managing agents;
   (ii) indirect Names – Names who were placed by their members' agents with syndicates that were managed by other agents. The members' agents

---

[15] Names are persons who underwrite (or accept the risks, and hence the financial consequences, attaching to) insurance contracts within the Lloyd's insurance market. As the potential liability attaching to an insurance contract can run into many millions of pounds sterling, the Names are organised in syndicates which operate as single entities to underwrite one or more insurance contracts and also, in appropriate circumstances, to re-insure the syndicate against the risks attaching to insurance contracts it has accepted.

[16] Names are members of Lloyd's; each member (or Name) has an agent (which, almost invariably, is a firm of professional insurance underwriters) who looks after his/her interests within the Lloyd's insurance market. Additionally, each syndicate has a managing agent (also a firm of professional insurance underwriters) who conducts the business of the syndicate.

entered into sub-agency agreements with the managing agents of those syndicates.

The relationship between the Names, members' agents and managing agents was regulated by agency and sub-agency agreements. An implied term of the agreements with the managing agents was that the managing agents would exercise due care and skill in their managing activities.

Following poor performance in the Lloyd's insurance market, the plaintiffs sued the defendants alleging they had been negligent in their management of the plaintiffs' syndicates. The key issues for the court to decide included the following:

(i)   whether the members' (and managing) agents owed a common law duty of care to the direct Names, notwithstanding that a contractual relationship existed between them;

(ii) whether the managing agents who were appointed as sub-agents by the members' agents owed a duty of care to the indirect Names (who were third parties in respect of the sub-agency agreements);

(iii) whether the members' agents were responsible to the indirect Names for any failure on the part of the managing agents to whom they had delegated insurance underwriting duties under the sub-agency agreements.

The court of first instance found in the plaintiffs' favour on all three questions. When the defendants appealed the decision, the Court of Appeal dismissed their appeal. When the defendants appealed to the House of Lords, the Law Lords did likewise. The Lords explained their reasons as follows:

1. Where a person assumes responsibility to perform professional services for another who relies on those services, the relationship between the parties is sufficient, in itself, to give rise to a duty by the person providing the services to exercise reasonable skill and care in so doing. By holding themselves out as possessing special expertise to advise the Names on insurance transactions in which to engage, the managing agents clearly assumed responsibility towards the Names in the syndicates they managed. Accordingly, they owed a duty of care to the Names who were members of those syndicates.

2. An assumption of responsibility by a person rendering professional services, coupled with reliance on those services by the person for whom they are rendered, can give rise to a common law duty of care irrespective of any contractual relationship between the parties. The contractual relationship between the direct Names and their members' (and managing) agents included an implied term to exercise due skill and care in their managing activities. This duty to exercise due skill and care is no different from that arising under the common law.

3. For the indirect Names, the chain of contracts in the agency and sub-agency agreements did not prevent them from suing the managing agents as third parties under the common law. The managing agents' assumption of responsibility in respect of their managing activities to the members' agents under sub-agency agreements (thus, under contract) did not prevent them from also assuming responsibility in respect of the same activities to the indirect Names as third parties to those agreements.

Thus, in *Henderson* v *Merrett Syndicates*, the House of Lords recognised the criterion of 'assumption of responsibility' as an alternative to the three-part *Caparo* test to apply when determining whether or not a professional advisor (or professional services provider) owed a duty of care to a third party who relied on his/her advice (or services). It also established that a professional advisor may owe a common law duty of care:

(i) to a person to whom the advisor has assumed responsibility and who relies on the advice (or services) provided by the advisor, notwithstanding any contractual relationship between the parties; and

(ii) to a party with whom the advisor has a contractual relationship and also, simultaneously, to a third party.

The court applied the criterion of 'assumption of responsibility' in *ADT Ltd* v *BDO Binder Hamlyn* [1996] BCC 808 to determine whether a professional advisor (in this case the auditor) owed a duty of care to a third party. Binder Hamlyn issued an unqualified audit report on the 1989 financial statements of Britannia Securities Group (BSG) – a company ADT Ltd was contemplating purchasing. In January 1990, a partner of Binder Hamlyn attended a meeting with a director of ADT and confirmed that BSG's 1989 audited financial statements showed a true and fair view of BSG's state of affairs. On the strength of this representation ADT purchased BSG for £105 million. It was subsequently found that BSG's true value was £40 million.

The question to be decided by the court was whether, as a result of the oral assurance given by Binder Hamlyn's partner to the ADT director in respect of BSG's audited financial statements, Binder Hamlyn had assumed responsibility to ADT and thus owed it a duty of care. May J held that Binder Hamlyn had assumed responsibility to ADT (in January 1990) when its partner gave (negligently prepared) information or advice directly to ADT, knowing the purpose for which it was required and knowing ADT would place reliance on it without further enquiry. The judge also noted that the defendants were negligent when conducting the 1989 audit; their standard of professional competence did not achieve that of ordinarily skilled auditors. The judge awarded damages against Binder Hamlyn of £65 million, the difference in the amount paid for BSG (£105 million) and its true value (£40 million).

Like the *ADT* case, those of *Coulthard & Ors* v *Neville Russell* (1998) PNLR 276; (1998) 1 BCLC 143; (1998) BCC 359, and *Siddell* v *Sydney Cooper & Partners* (1999) PNLR 511, extended the *Caparo* decision by recognising that an accountant's duty of care is not limited to the company *per se* and the company's shareholders as a body, but may also be owed to the company's directors and shareholders as individuals. However, in each case, the court emphasised that whether or not a duty of care is owed by a professional advisor to a third party depends upon the particular circumstances of the case.

The *Coulthard* case involved the failure by Neville Russell (a firm of accountants) to advise its client company's directors that loan payments to a shell company to pay for shares the company was purchasing in the parent company might infringe the Companies Act 1985, s. 151. The High Court judge refused to uphold Neville Russell's assertion that the plaintiff's action against it had insufficient legal grounds to proceed. Neville Russell appealed the decision but the Court of Appeal confirmed the lower court's ruling. The Court of Appeal held that, as a matter of principle, accountants can owe a duty of care to a client company's directors but whether or not a duty is owed in a particular case depends upon the facts of the case and, in particular, on whether it can be shown that the accountants had assumed responsibility to the directors.

In *Siddell* v *Sydney Cooper & Partners* (supra), the defendants (SCP) were the auditors and management accountants of a small family-run company with four shareholders and directors (Mr and Mrs Siddell and Mr and Mrs Fellows). In 1992, following the departure of the company's finance director (the only 'outside' director), irregularities were found in the accounting records. Soon afterwards the company, which had been thought to be profitable, went into receivership with a deficit of more than £1 million.

The plaintiffs sued SCP for breach of their duty of care to them as shareholders and directors. The court of first instance held that the plaintiffs' claim had insufficient legal grounds to proceed. Following the *Caparo* ruling, the judge held that auditors do not normally owe a duty of care to a company's shareholders (as individuals). The plaintiffs appealed the decision and the Court of Appeal overturned the lower court's ruling. Mummery L J and Clarke L J explained their reasons as follows:

1. Where, as in the case of the liability of professional advisors, the law is in a state of transition or development, an order to disallow an action to proceed should not be made unless the court can properly be persuaded that the claim is bound to fail. That is not the position in this case.
2. The judge (in the court of first instance), relying on *Caparo* v *Dickman* (1990) and *Galoo Ltd* v *Bright Grahame Murray* (1994), disallowed the appellants' action to proceed on the basis that SCP owed them, as third parties, no duty of care. The judge also submitted that, as in *Caparo*,

liability did not arise unless it could be shown that the advisors intended or knew the third parties were personally relying on the services being provided to the company and there was actual reliance. Whilst accepting these requirements for liability to arise (although noting that the law is in a state of transition or development), the facts in this case are very different from those in *Caparo*. SCP was not simply acting as auditor but was providing broader services to the company, including the preparation of quarterly and annual financial statements and the giving of advice. Following *Henderson* v *Merrett Syndicates Ltd* (1995) 2 AC 145, it cannot be maintained that the existence of a contract between the parties necessarily precludes a co-extensive duty of care at common law.

3. The judge in the first court also disallowed the appellants' action to proceed, on the basis that the alleged breaches of duty did not cause the appellants' loss but merely provided an opportunity to sustain loss. Only the former kind of loss is recoverable. It is for the court to decide, by applying common sense, which type of loss has been suffered. However, the question of whether a particular loss has been caused by a breach of duty is a question of fact and, as such, an action should not be prevented from proceeding on this ground unless it is bound to fail. That is not the position in this case.

In the course of its judgment, the Court of Appeal noted:

> The principles upon which *Caparo* was based cannot be restricted to large companies [but] whether a duty of care [to third parties] exists depends upon all the circumstances of the particular case. Those circumstances will include the size of the company and the number and type of shareholders (or indeed directors) to whom the duty is said to be owed. (as quoted in Scott, 1999)

By recognising that auditors (or accountants) may owe a duty of care to their client company's shareholders and/or directors as individuals, *Coulthard* v *Neville Russell* and *Siddell* v *Sydney Cooper & Partners* clearly extended the *Caparo* decision. However, the story does not end here. In the case of *Bank of Credit & Commerce International (Overseas) Ltd, BCCI Holdings (Luxembourg) SA*, and *BCCI SA* v *Price Waterhouse and Ors*, and *Ernst & Whinney and Ors* [1998] BCC 617, [1998] 15 LS Gaz R 32, 142 Sol Jo LB 86, [1998] 5 PNLR 564, the Court of Appeal held that the auditor of one company may owe a duty of care to another (third-party) company. In this case, the court also took the opportunity to summarise the approaches to the liability of professional advisors for financial loss which had been adopted in leading cases where the issue had been considered.

The facts of the case are briefly as follows. On 5 July 1991, after evidence emerged of a long-standing, large scale, global fraud, an international swoop (co-ordinated by the Bank of England) closed down the Bank of Credit & Commerce International (BCCI) group of companies. Until 1987, when BCCI was persuaded to engage Price Waterhouse (PW) as its sole auditor, it was able to obscure its fraudulent operations by engaging different auditors for its different banking subsidiaries. While Ernst & Whinney (E&W) acted as the auditor of BCCI Holdings (Luxembourg) SA and BCCI SA (located in Luxembourg), PW acted as the auditor of BCCI (Overseas) (located in the Cayman Islands).[17]

The liquidators of all three banks brought proceedings against PW [as auditor of BCCI (Overseas) prior to 1987 and of all three banks for the years 1987, 1988 and 1989] and E&W [as auditor of BCCI (Holdings) and BCCI SA prior to 1987] for negligently performed audits – audits that failed to detect massive frauds perpetrated on BCCI's creditors and shareholders. In addition to suing PW for breach of its contractual duties, BCCI (Overseas) alleged that E&W also owed it a duty of care on the grounds that the business and operations of BCCI (Overseas) and BCCI SA were managed as if they were the business and operations of a single bank (Lascelles & Donkin, 1991).

In the trial court, Laddie J held that BCCI (Overseas)'s claim against E&W could not proceed. To do so, BCCI (Overseas) had to show that E&W had provided it with information, knowing or intending that it would rely on the information for a particular purpose, and that BCCI (Overseas) had in fact relied on it for that purpose. (Expressed in terms of the *Caparo* ruling, it had to meet the requirements for a relationship of proximity to be established.) Laddie J ruled that BCCI (Overseas) had not established the presence of the required elements.

Upon appeal, the Court of Appeal overturned the decision. During its judgment, the court noted:

> The liability of accountants and of other professional advisors for economic loss caused by reason of their alleged negligence to persons other than their clients has been the subject of a substantial number of leading cases. In *Smith* v *Eric S Bush* (1990) 1 AC 83 "the threefold test" as to whether a duty of care is owed by an advisor to those who act on his advice was stated to be: (a) it must be foreseeable that if the advice is negligent the recipient is likely to suffer the kind of damage that has occurred; (b) there is a sufficient proximate relationship between the parties and (c) it is just and reasonable to impose the liability (Lord Griffiths at (1990) 1 AC 864H). To this test has been added "the voluntary assumption of responsibility test" referred to in *Henderson* v *Merrett Syndicate Ltd* (1995) 2 AC 145 by Lord Goff and extended from the principle underlying the decision in *Hedley Bryne* v *Heller and Partners Ltd* (1964) AC 465.

The court pointed out that the "threefold test" and the "assumption of responsibility test" indicated the criteria that had to be satisfied in order for liability to be attached to the appellants. It also noted that the authorities had provided

---

[17] In 1989, Ernst & Whinney merged with Arthur Young to become Ernst & Young; in 1998, Price Waterhouse merged with Coopers & Lybrand to become PricewaterhouseCoopers.

guidance on factors to be taken into account in deciding whether these criteria had been met. These include:

(i)   the precise relationship between the advisor and advisee;
(ii) the precise circumstances in which the advice was given and in which it was communicated to the advisee, and whether the communication was made by the advisor or by a third party;
(iii) the degree of reliance the advisor intended or should reasonably have anticipated would be placed on the accuracy of the advice by the advisee and the reliance in fact placed on it;
(iv) the presence or absence of other advisors on whom the advisee would or could rely;
(v)   the opportunity, if any, given to the advisor to issue a disclaimer of responsibility.

The court also observed that decided cases concerning the liability of professional advisors to third parties had established that any development in the law in this area ought only to be made incrementally (i.e., in small steps). It further noted:

> It needs to be borne in mind that . . . a barrier exists between an advisor and any person who is not his immediate client [i.e., a third party] which has to be overcome before the advisor can be said to owe a duty to that person, a barrier which will be all the stronger if that person is in receipt of independent advice. However, the reality in the present case is that any barrier between Ernst & Whinney and BCCI (Overseas) was a mere shadow. Overseas' and BCCI SA's banking activities were conducted as those of a single bank, such was the intermingling of their operations and the constant exchange of information between them. Ernst & Whinney were, in effect, the supervising auditors of both banks, as well as the auditors of BCCI Holdings (Luxembourg) SA.

The court held that, if the threefold test or the assumption of responsibility test were applied to the facts of the case, it would be quite wrong to dismiss the claims of BCCI (Overseas) against E&W on the grounds that they had no legal foundation.[18] However, the court noted that the facts of the case were very unusual and, therefore, the case ought not to be regarded as setting a precedent. Nevertheless, the court's decision is very significant in terms of auditors' liability to third parties as it shows that, in certain circumstances (such as where the business of two companies is conducted as if it were a single business), the court will recognise that the auditors of one company may owe a duty of care to another (third party) company.

Since the Court of Appeal's summary of the law relating to the liability of professional advisors (including auditors) to third parties for financial loss

---

[18] BCCI's liquidators originally filed claims against PW and E&W for US$11 billion (approximately £6.5 billion). However, PW and E&W agreed an out-of-court settlement with the liquidators for an amount reputed to be in the region of US$95–100 million (Nisse, 1999).

suffered as a result of negligence by the professional advisor, a number of other cases of note have reached the courts. We discuss seven of these below.[19]

The first case is *Electra Private Equity Partners* v *KPMG Peat Marwick & Ors* [1999] All ER (D) 415; [2000] BCC 368; [2001] 1 BCLC 589. It concerned venture capital fund managers (Electra) who, in May 1992, invested (Irish)£10 million in unquoted convertible loan stock and thereby acquired effective control of C plc, an Irish leasing company. Eighteen months later, C plc went into receivership and the plaintiffs lost all of their investment. The plaintiffs sought to recover their losses from two firms of accountants:

(i) KPMG – which the plaintiffs had instructed to investigate and report on the suitability of the investment in C plc, and

(ii) SKC (an Irish partnership which was part of the KPMG International firm) – which, as auditor of C plc had provided, or concurred in C plc providing to the plaintiffs prior to the investment, C's audited financial statements (complete with unqualified audit report) for the year ending 29 February 1992.

Carnwath J disallowed Electra's claim against SKC from proceeding on the basis that, in order for a duty of care to arise to a third party, the claimant would need to show that the auditor had consciously assumed responsibility to the third party.[20] The plaintiffs appealed the ruling and the Court of Appeal found in their favour. Reasons advanced by the Appeal Court for its decision included the following:

1. The court's determination in a case such as the present (i.e., the Electra case) might depend, in particular, on:

   (i) knowledge or foreseeability by the auditor that the potential investor would rely on the accuracy of the audited financial statements in deciding whether to invest – as distinct from insisting on audited financial statements and an unqualified auditor's report as a condition of investment;

   (ii) the fact and nature of any direct communications between the auditor and the potential investor;

   (iii) whether the auditor reasonably believed that the potential investor would obtain independent advice on the suitability of the investment; and

---

[19] We do not discuss the case of Ernst & Young's (E&Y's) alleged negligence in the case of Lehman Brothers as (i) the case has not been referred to a UK court and (ii) in June 2012, the Accountancy and Actuarial Discipline Board (AADB) of the Financial Reporting Council (FRC) concluded: "There is no realistic prospect that a Tribunal would make an adverse finding against Ernst & Young LLP in the UK [that is, the UK arm of E&Y; E&Y UK]" (FRC, 2012a). Given this conclusion, it seems unlikely that a case brought against E&Y UK for negligence would succeed. However, in the light of the significance of this case, and as many cases have been filed against E&Y in the USA (that is, the USA arm of E&Y), we provide an outline of its key points in Appendix 2 to this chapter.

[20] There was no problem with Electra's claim against KPMG as these parties had a contractual relationship.

    (iv) if the auditor did so believe, whether he appreciated that the independent advisor would rely on his (the auditor's) figures for the purpose of advising the potential investor.

The Appeal Court held that Carnwath J had wrongly focused on a 'conscious assumption of responsibility' as the test for the existence of a duty of care and this could have resulted in too high a threshold for the plaintiffs. Electra's claim against SKC gave rise to a triable issue, namely, whether SKC knew or foresaw the purpose for which the plaintiffs required the audited financial statements, and whether they assumed responsibility for their accuracy by providing them to the plaintiffs in the alleged circumstances (i.e., for the purpose of deciding whether to invest in C plc).

2. The court should proceed with great caution in exercising its power to disallow cases from proceeding on the basis of the facts presented when:
    (i)   all the facts are not known by the court,
    (ii) the facts, and the legal principles turning on them, are complex, and
    (iii) the law, as in the instant case, is in a state of development.

Actions by a third party against auditors and other professional advisors for negligence are notable examples of facts-sensitive cases where the law is still in a state of transition.

3. Carnwath J wrongly held that the involvement of KPMG as independent advisors was fatal to the duty of care the plaintiffs claimed they were owed by SKC. There had been considerable direct contact between Electra and SKC. At the very least, it was arguable that such a tripartite relationship, particularly having regard to the close professional association between KPMG and SKC, created a 'special relationship' between the plaintiffs and SKC.

The *Electra* case appears to signal a loosening by the court of the strict principles enunciated in the *Caparo*, *Galoo* and *Merrett Syndicates* cases and seems to indicate that, when the court considers it just and equitable to do so (the third of *Caparo's* three-part test), it will find a way to hold that auditors (or other professional advisors) owe a duty of care to a third party. Such a process can be discerned in *Barings plc* v *Coopers & Lybrand & Ors, Barings Futures (Singapore) Pte Ltd* v *Mattar & Ors* [2002] EWHC 461 (Ch); [2002] All ER (D) 309 (Mar); [2003] Lloyd's Rep IR 566.

The *Barings* case (or, more correctly, the portion which is relevant to the theme of this section of the chapter, namely, auditors' liability to third parties) essentially turned on the question of whether Coopers & Lybrand Singapore (C&LS) owed a duty of care to Barings plc. During 1992 and 1993, Deloitte & Touche (D&T) was the auditor of Barings Futures (Singapore) Pte Ltd (BFS) – a subsidiary of Barings Securities Ltd (BSL) which, in turn, was an indirect subsidiary of Barings plc, a non-trading group holding company based in London. In 1994, D&T was replaced by C&LS as auditor of BFS. Coopers & Lybrand (C&L) was the auditor of both BSL and Barings plc throughout the relevant period. As auditors of BFS, D&T and C&LS were required to provide consolidated schedules (and a copy of BFS's audit report) to the directors of Barings plc for use in the preparation of the group's consolidated financial statements.

The Barings Group collapsed in February 1995 as a result of unauthorised, and heavily loss-making, speculative trading on the Singaporean and Japanese stock markets by Leeson, general manager of BFS. In 1996, the liquidators of the Barings Group sued C&L, C&LS, and the Singapore partners of D&T for £1 billion (Perry, 2001b), claiming that their negligent auditing of the consolidated financial statements (by C&L) and of BFS's financial statements (by D&T and C&LS) was responsible for the collapse of the Barings Group in 1995. C&L, C&LS and D&T maintained that the collapse of the group was due to management failings and fraud, not to the work of the auditors (Perry, 2001a). Irrespective of the outcome of that fundamental argument, at a more detailed level, C&LS challenged the claims brought against it by Barings plc (a third party).[21]

C&LS sought to have Barings plc's claim against it dismissed as having no legal foundation. The firm submitted that it owed a duty of care to BFS (its audit client) but not to Barings plc: any claim for damage suffered as a consequence of its negligence could only be claimed by the subsidiary that had suffered damage (i.e., BFS) and not by its shareholder (Barings plc). The information C&LS was required to supply to Barings plc was simply so that Barings plc's directors could comply with their legal obligation to prepare consolidated financial statements. The High Court found in favour of C&LS but Barings plc appealed its ruling.

Unlike the High Court, the Court of Appeal did not accept C&LS's arguments. Leggatt L J pointed out that at no time during the audit of BFS's consolidation schedules, prepared for the purpose of the group's consolidated financial statements, did the auditors detect or report the unauthorised trading of Leeson or the losses which resulted. On the contrary, those schedules showed BFS to be profitable. Leggatt L J noted that C&LS could not have supposed that the only

---

[21] D&T also challenged the case brought against it by BFS but that portion of the case does not concern auditors' liability to third parties. The question for the court to decide was whether D&T had sufficient grounds to negate claims brought against it by BFS. As this question centred on the reliance auditors may place on written representations, a topic we discuss in Chapter 13 (section 13.5), that portion of the case is reported in Appendix 1 to this chapter.

responsibility it assumed to Barings plc was to submit BFS's schedules in a form suitable for incorporation in the consolidated financial statements, and that it did not matter whether or not they showed a true and fair view of BFS's financial affairs. His Honour observed that an auditor's task is to conduct the audit so as to make it probable that material misstatements in financial documents will be detected. That did not occur and C&LS had a case to answer. The Court of Appeal concluded that C&LS must have appreciated that its audit report and consolidated schedules would be used for the purpose of producing the consolidated financial statements. That was enough to establish that C&LS owed a duty of care to Barings plc in addition to that owed to BFS.[22]

According to Leggat L J, a critical point in this case was that Barings plc pleaded a direct relationship between it and C&LS arising from the circumstance in which work was done for, and information was supplied by, C&LS to Barings plc and its auditor in England (C&L) for the preparation and audit of the group's consolidated financial statements. This seems to limit future application of the decision to cases in which the facts are fairly similar. Nevertheless, as a result of the court's ruling in this case, it seems likely that where the auditor of a subsidiary forwards information to the parent company (and its auditor) for use in the preparation and audit of the group's consolidated financial statements, a duty of care will be owed, more or less routinely, by the auditor of the subsidiary to the parent company and to the parent company's auditor.

Auditors were similarly held to owe a duty of care to a third party in *Andrew v Kounnis Freeman* [1999] 2 BCLC 641, CA; [1999] All ER (D) 553; [2000] Lloyd's PN 263, a case involving F plc, a company which organised air travel. Prior to renewing F's licence to organise air travel, the Civil Aviation Authority (CAA), in a letter dated 15 March 1996, notified F plc that it required, amongst other things, a copy of F plc's 1995 audited financial statements. The CAA also notified F plc's auditor, Kounnis Freeman (KF), of this requirement and that it required the auditor to confirm certain matters. Following its audit of F plc's 1995 financial statements, KF wrote to the CAA confirming the relevant matters. Relying on F's 1995 audited financial statements and KF's confirmations, the CAA renewed F plc's licence. However, the company collapsed suddenly a few months later and the CAA was left to pay the return flights of

---

[22] Rather than pursue their case through the courts, in October 2001, C&L and C&LS (now part of PwC) reached an out-of-court settlement with the liquidators of the Barings Group for £65 million (Schlesinger, 2003). By that time, legal costs in the cases brought by the Barings Group against C&L, C&LS and D&T exceeded £100 million (Perry, 2002a). In addition to its out-of-court settlement, C&L was to have been fined £1 million by the Accountants' Joint Disciplinary Scheme (JDS) which, at the time, conducted independent disciplinary enquiries into cases referred to it by the Institutes of Chartered Accountants in England and Wales, and of Scotland. Upon appeal by C&L, the Appeal Tribunal reduced the fine to £250,000 but stated that C&L's belief that Leeson's trading activities "posed little (or no) risk to the Barings group, but yielded very good returns, is implausible and in our view, demonstrates a degree of ignorance of market reality that totally lacks credibility" (Perry, 2002b).

stranded passengers. The CAA sued KF claiming that KF owed it a duty of care, that it was negligent in its audit of F plc's 1995 financial statements and, as a consequence of that negligence, the CAA had suffered a loss.

KF sought to have the claim struck out on the basis that it did not owe the CAA a duty of care. However, the court of first instance refused to strike out the claim – a decision upheld by the Court of Appeal. Notwithstanding that there was no contractual relationship between the CAA and KF, the court held that, as a result of the CAA's letter of 15 March 1995, KF knew, or ought to have known, that the CAA would rely on F plc's 1995 audited financial statements for the purpose of deciding whether to renew F plc's licence to organise air travel. In these circumstances, KF had assumed responsibility to CAA and thus owed it a duty of care.

The facts of *Independent Advantage Insurance Company Ltd* v *Representatives of Michael Cook (deceased)* [2002] All ER (D) 151 (Nov); [2003] EWCA Civ 1103; [2003] All ER (D) 423 (Jul); [2004] PNLR 3 CA are similar to those of *Kounnis Freeman* (above) but, while the latter followed the ruling in *Henderson* v *Merrett Syndicates*, and thus applied existing law, the *Independent* case extended auditors' duty of care to third parties.

Swift Travel was a member of the Association of British Travel Agents (ABTA) and the International Air Transport Association (IATA). The rules of these Associations require members to have in place a bond or other form of security in the Associations' favour. Independent Advantage Insurance Co Ltd provides bond facilities to travel agents to enable them to satisfy ABTA's and IATA's requirements.

Michael Cook (deceased) was a partner in the firm which audited Swift's financial statements from 1995 to 1998. The audited financial statements were sent by Swift to ABTA and IATA, and also to Independent, in support of its applications to renew its membership of the Associations and bond facilities, respectively. Placing reliance on the audited financial statements, Independent provided and renewed bonds to Swift between 1996 and 1999 and, in late 1999, also provided Swift with a loan. In March 2000, Swift went bankrupt and Independent lost £32,000 in respect of the bond and all of its loan. Independent sued the audit firm, arguing that its audits had been conducted negligently and that, but for the audited financial statements, it would not have provided finance to Swift. The audit firm sought to have the claim struck out on the grounds that it did not owe Independent a duty of care. However, both the court of first instance and the Appeal Court refused to support its position.

In the Court of Appeal, Chadwick L J relied heavily on the court's decision in the *Kounnis Freeman* case (supra). He was swayed by Independent's argument that, as a result of the audit firm's experience in providing accountancy and audit services to travel agents (as well as several alleged conversations between Swift and an employee of the audit firm), the auditor knew, or ought to have known, that:

(i) Swift obtained bond facilities from institutions such as Independent to satisfy the bond requirements of ABTA and IATA; and

(ii) Swift's audited financial statements were provided to institutions such as Independent (and would be relied upon by them) to support applications for bond facilities and other financial support.

The judge concluded that it was arguable that the auditor owed Independent a duty of care when auditing Swift's financial statements.

Commenting on the *Independent* case, Simmons and Simmons (2003a) note that, although the Court of Appeal relied on the judgment in the *Kounnis Freeman* case, there are significant differences between the two cases. They note, in particular, the following differences:

1. In the *Kounnis Freeman* case, the auditors knew the identity of the party seeking to rely on their work, that is, the CAA. In contrast, the auditors in the *Independent* case did not know the identity of the provider of the bond facilities.

2. In the *Kounnis Freeman* case, there was direct contact between the CAA and the auditors. The CAA wrote a letter pointing out that it would be relying on the financial statements which Kounnis Freeman was auditing. In the *Independent* case, there was no such contact between the auditors and Independent.

3. In the *Kounnis Freeman* case, the auditors knew precisely why the CAA required input from them; the CAA had stated it would only renew the company's licence on confirmation of certain matters by the company's auditors. In the *Independent* case, the auditors had no idea of the precise use Independent would make of their work; Independent's requirements had not been communicated to them.

Simmons and Simmons (2003a) conclude that, given the facts of the case, it is not surprising that Kounnis Freeman was found to have assumed a responsibility and, thus, a duty of care to the CAA, but the same cannot be said of the *Independent* case.

Considering the implications of the ruling in the *Independent* case Simmons and Simmons (2003a) observe:

> Of particular interest (and, to a degree, concern) is the Judge's statement that, although the auditors did not know the identity of Independent, it was arguably sufficient that Independent was one of a "possible class of providers" of bonds and other securities on behalf of Swift to the Associations [ABTA and IATA] . . . for Independent to be within the range of proximity so as to give rise to a duty of care to them. Auditors often know, for example, that audited . . . financial

statements may be provided to banks financing the company being audited. Even without knowing the identity of the bank involved, could it be said, following the Judge's conclusions in this case, that auditors owe a duty of care to a bank relying on their audit just because the auditors know that "banks" might rely on their work? (p. 2)

These observations seem to indicate that, as an outcome of the judgment in the *Independent* case, auditors' exposure to liability to third parties was edging towards that which existed prior to *Caparo*. However, a potential avenue of relief for auditors was indicated in the judgment in *Royal Bank of Scotland* v *Bannerman Johnstone Maclay* [2003] OHSC 125; [2005] CSIH 39.

The *Bannerman* case concerns overdraft facilities and term loans provided by the Royal Bank of Scotland (RBS) to APC Ltd. When APC failed the bank asserted:

(i) it made the loans after relying on the company's audited financial statements;

(ii) the auditors (Bannerman's firm) failed to exercise reasonable care when auditing the financial statements;

(iii) had the financial statements not contained the errors in question, the bank would not have provided the loans;

(iv) the auditors were closely involved in the financial affairs of APC Ltd and were well aware of the bank's role in providing financial support;

(v) because of the terms of the company's overdraft facility letters, the auditors knew the audited financial statements would be passed to the bank and relied upon for the purpose of making lending decisions.

In these circumstances, the auditors owed RBS a duty of care in respect of the audited financial statements and were liable to it for the loss sustained.

The auditors sought to have the case struck out on the grounds that RBS had to show that:

- an advisor knows the identity of the person to whom advice or information is to be communicated, the purpose for which the information is communicated, and the person to whom it is given is likely to rely on it for the known purpose, and
- it must be the advisor's intention that the recipient should rely upon the information (i.e., the audited financial statements).

In the Outer House of the Scottish Court of Session, Lord Macfadyen held, *inter alia*:

(i) the authorities established that proximity in relation to a duty of care in circumstances such as the present was determined by whether there had been an assumption of responsibility by the party sought to be made liable (i.e., the auditors);

(ii) no disclaimer of responsibility had been made to the bank by the auditors such that an assumption of responsibly was denied.

As a consequence, it could not be argued that the auditors did not owe RBS a duty of care.

The auditors appealed Lord Macfayden's decision but it was upheld by the Inner House of the Scottish Court of Session. The court noted that in some circumstances, in order to establish a duty of care, it may be sufficient for the provider of information or advice to know that it will be passed to a known third party for a specific purpose and that the recipient is likely to rely on it for that purpose. Although intention, if present, may support the existence of proximity between the auditor and the third party, it should not be seen as essential in every case. Following *Caparo*, what really matters is not the intention of the auditor but the auditor's actual or presumed knowledge that the information or advice is likely to be relied on by the third party. The Court also confirmed that a failure to disclaim responsibility to a third party can, in appropriate circumstances, be a factor pointing to an assumption of responsibility on the part of the provider of information or advice (i.e., the auditor).

It is interesting to observe that in the *BCCI* case (supra), one of the factors the court noted as needing to be taken into consideration when determining whether or not the threefold *Caparo* test or the 'assumption of responsibility' test had been met is whether the advisor (in this case, the auditor) has been given the opportunity to disclaim responsibility. It is as a result of the ruling in the *Bannerman* case that, as we explain in Chapter 14 (footnote 11), audit reports issued on companies' financial statements by the Big 4 and many mid-tier firms in the UK (as elsewhere) now generally include a paragraph disclaiming responsibility to anyone other than the company *per se* and its shareholders as a body.

The next significant case to explore the issue of auditors' liability to third parties is that of *Man Nutzfahzeuge AG and Ors* v *Freightliner Ltd and Ors* [2003] EWHC 2245; [2005] EWHC 2347 (Comm); [2007] EWCA (Civ) 910. This case involved the sale by Western Star Truck (a Canadian company) of its wholly owned subsidiary, ERF plc (a British truck maker), to Man (a German company) in March 2000. The settlement price of approximately £100 million was based on financial statements audited by Ernst & Young (E&Y) which indicated that ERF was making a small profit and had net assets of around £25 million.

In July 2001, Man discovered that ERF's financial controller, Ellis (who was heavily involved in the sale negotiations on behalf of Western Star), had been fraudulently manipulating ERF's financial statements since 1996 and had also made fraudulent misrepresentations during the due diligence process prior to the sale. Rather than making profits and holding net assets, ERF was making losses and had net liabilities of around £75 million. After the fraud was discovered, Man successfully sued Freightliner (the then owner of Western Star) for £350 million for breaches of warranties given in the sale agreement and for fraudulent misrepresentations by Western Star's agent (i.e., Ellis) which allegedly had induced the sale (Sukhraj, 2007; Simmons & Simmons, 2003c).

Freightliner then sought to recoup its losses from E&Y. It alleged that E&Y had been negligent and, due to its negligence, had failed to detect the falsification of accounting records by Ellis with the result that the audited financial statements for 1998 and 1999 did not give a true and fair view of ERF's affairs. E&Y applied to the High Court to have the claim struck out on the grounds that it could not succeed because of the *Caparo* ruling (i.e., they owed no duty of care to Freightliner as a third party). They asserted that, in order for auditors' duty of care to be extended beyond *Caparo*, there had to be a clear assumption of responsibility by the auditors to the third party concerned and, in this case, there had been no such assumption (Simmons & Simmons, 2003d). However, Cooke J was not persuaded by E&Y's argument. He observed:

> the issues of duty and causation which [arise in this case] are fact sensitive and inappropriate for determination on a summary basis. . . . [Further] the areas of law [involved] are areas which are not only developing but also not free from difficulty. (at p. 2259).

He concluded there were real issues to be tried and that Freightliner had a real prospect of success.

The case was heard in the High Court in 2005. The trial judge (Moore Bick L J) accepted E&Y's argument that the *Caparo* ruling applied and found that, although E&Y admitted to making errors in aspects of its audit of ERF's financial statements in the late 1990s, Freightliner's claims went far beyond the scope of E&Y's duties as auditor. E&Y did not owe Freightliner a duty of care and was not liable for the losses claimed. He noted that E&Y could not be held responsible for the use Ellis, acting as Western Star's agent, made of the audited financial statements in the negotiations surrounding ERF's sale to Man.

Freightliner appealed the court's decision but it was upheld by the Court of Appeal. It seemed that the case was at an end. E&Y claimed not to be surprised by the Appeal Court's decision. Cameron, E&Y's lawyer, explained:

> We have stressed consistently since the beginning of this action that the case brought by Freightliner against Ernst & Young was unsustainable because it attempted to extend the recognised boundaries of an auditor's duties and responsibilities. (as quoted in Sukhraj, 2007)

However, E&Y was not quite 'out of the woods'. In December 2007, Freightliner petitioned the House of Lords seeking leave to appeal the Court of Appeal's ruling. In January 2008, the House of Lords rejected Freightliner's petition and E&Y could breathe a sigh of relief; it was now assured of avoiding liability, possibly, of £350 million (Sukhraj, 2008). Other auditors may also breathe a sigh of relief as the court's decision in this case appears to have stemmed (at least for the time being) the steady extension of auditors' duty of care to third parties evident (as we have seen) in a number of cases in the UK since *Caparo*.[23]

Our final case, *Moore Stephens* v *Stone & Rolls Ltd (in liquidation)* [2007] EWHC 1826 (Comm); [2007] All ER (D) 448 (Jul); [2008] EWCA Civ 644; [2009] UKHL 39, is particularly important as it encapsulates the principle the courts now seem to be seeking to apply in cases brought against auditors for negligence, namely, to impose a liability on auditors only when it is fair, just and reasonable to do so in the particular circumstances.

This case centres on the use of Stone & Rolls (S&R) by Mr Stojevic, the company's sole shareholder and director, to defraud a number of banks. The fraud was discovered and, in 1999, both Mr Stojevic and S&R were successfully sued by the principal victim, Komercni Bank SA. Substantial damages were awarded against S&R and Mr Stojevic but, unable to pay, S&R went into liquidation. Acting on behalf of S&R's creditors, its liquidators sued the company's auditor, Moore Stephens (MS), for auditing negligently the company's 1996, 1997 and 1998 financial statements and, as a result, failing to detect the fraud. MS accepted it owed S&R a duty to exercise reasonable skill and care when performing its audits and that it was in breach of that duty. However, it argued that a claim against it could not succeed because of the principle of *ex turpi causa non oritur acto* (*ex turpi causa*: a court will not assist a plaintiff whose cause of action is founded on his own illegal or immoral act).

In the court of first instance, Langley J acknowledged that there was no real distinction between Stojevic and S&R and, as a result, it was artificial to describe the company as a 'victim' of fraud. However, because detecting fraud was what auditors were engaged to do, MS could not rely on the defence of *ex turpi causa* to protect it from the negligence claim against it. MS appealed the judge's ruling. The Court of Appeal reversed Langley J's decision holding that

---

[23] It is perhaps surprising that (unlike the *Equitable Life* case in which E&Y also admitted negligent auditing), in this case, despite:

    (i) E&Y admitting it had been negligent in a number of respects in its audit of ERF's financial statements, and

    (ii) its issuance of unqualified opinions on ERF's 1997, 1998 and 1999 financial statements which did not give a true and fair view,

the profession's disciplinary bodies [in particular, the Recognised Supervisory Body (The Institute of Chartered Accountants in England and Wales (ICAEW) with which E&Y was registered, and the Joint Monitoring Unit which, at the time, was responsible for monitoring the performance of auditors registered with, *inter alia*, the ICAEW] did not, apparently, ask the JDS to take disciplinary action against E&Y for its deficient auditing of this listed company's financial statements (Gwilliam, 2010).

the fact that the company (in the form of Stojevic) had caused its own loss through illegal acts (*ex turpi causa*) could not be discarded just because detecting fraud is what auditors are meant to do.

S&R appealed to the House of Lords and, by a three to two majority decision, the Law Lords upheld the Appeal Court's ruling. Lord Philips explained that it was "a matter of common sense that [S&R's claim] could not succeed" (2009, UKHL, 39, para 5) and gave three reasons for this conclusion:

1. S&R was representing itself as a victim of fraud when it was, in fact, the perpetrator of the fraud. The true victims of the fraud were the banks.
2. MS was also a victim of S&R's fraud. It was induced to act as S&R's auditor by a fictitious and fraudulent account of S&R's business by Mr Stojevic and it was deceived by financial statements that were fraudulently prepared. Although MS has accepted it was negligent in not detecting the fraud, "[i]t does not seem just that, in these circumstances, S&R should be able to bring a claim in respect of the very conduct that S&R had set about inducing" (ibid.).
3. The reality of this claim is that it is brought for the benefit of the defrauded banks (the creditors on whose behalf S&R's liquidators sued MS) on the grounds that MS should have prevented S&R from perpetrating the fraud. One reason why the banks could not bring an action against MS for themselves is because:

   > a duty of care in negligence will only arise where this is fair, just and reasonable. It would not be considered fair, just and reasonable for auditors of a company to owe a duty of care to an indeterminate class of potential victims in respect of unlimited losses that they might sustain as a result of the fraud of the company. If it would not be fair, just and reasonable for the banks to have a direct claim [against MS] then it would not seem fair, just and reasonable that they should achieve the same result through a claim brought by the company's liquidators for their benefit. (ibid.)

The House of Lords, applying the *Caparo* ruling, concluded that, although auditors owed a duty of care to the client company and its shareholders as a body, this duty does not extend to its creditors. Mr Stojevic was the only shareholder and, as he was responsible for the company's illegal conduct, the fraud was properly attributable to the company. Therefore, S&R could not rely on the fraud to claim that MS had breached its duty; *ex turpi causa* was a legitimate defence for MS and the claim against it was struck out.

15.4.4 Synopsis of auditors' liability to third parties

From our review of cases decided in the post-*Caparo* era, it is evident that since the House of Lords' momentous decision in the *Caparo* case in 1990, which essentially returned the law relating to auditors' liability to third parties to where it had stood nearly 30 years earlier at the time of *Hedley Bryne* v

Heller and Partners (supra), the courts have tended towards extending once again the parties to whom auditors may be held to owe a duty of care. However, judgments in the *Bannerman*, *Freightliner* and *Stone & Rolls* cases suggest that the tide may have turned once more in auditors' favour but, in any event, the law in the area remains uncertain and in a state of development and transition.

Whilst acknowledging this characteristic of the law in the area, some key principles relating to auditors' duty of care to third parties – and also to their clients – can be distilled from the cases we have reviewed. These are as follows:

1. In addition to the 'three-part *Caparo* test', the courts may apply the 'assumption of responsibility test' to determine whether or not an auditor owed a duty of care to a third party plaintiff in a particular case. The same may apply in cases involving the provision of information or advice by an auditor to a client on matters not directly related to the audit of the financial statements (or other duties agreed with the client in the terms of the audit engagement).

2. When a third party has received independent advice, this will serve to strengthen the barrier between the auditor and the third party which will need to be overcome before the auditor will be held to owe a duty of care to the third party. Nevertheless, the fact that a third party has received independent advice will not necessarily negate the auditor's duty of care to that party. The same principle applies in cases where a client claims to rely on information or advice provided by the auditor about a matter not directly related to the audit of the financial statements (or other duty agreed with the client) but also receives independent advice.

3. When a third party or a client claims to have suffered financial loss as a consequence of the auditor's negligence, the court will evaluate the facts of the case to determine whether the auditor's negligence was the cause of the loss or whether it merely provided an opportunity for the plaintiff to sustain a loss. Only the former type of loss will give rise to damages.

4. In order to succeed in a case alleging financial loss caused by an auditor's negligence, a third party or a client must commence proceedings within the period in which it is reasonably foreseeable that reliance may be placed on the audited financial statements.

5. Whether or not an auditor will be held to owe a duty of care to a third party in a particular case depends upon the facts of that case. The courts have demonstrated that, notwithstanding the *Caparo* decision, auditors may, in principle, be held to owe a duty of care to, *inter alia*, individual shareholders and directors of auditee companies, a 'sister' subsidiary and/ or parent company of the auditee and the auditor of the parent company, and also to financial institutions who provide financial support to the auditee. However, in virtually all cases where the auditor has been held

to owe a duty of care to a third party, the court has emphasised that its decision is case specific; that is, it applies only in the circumstances of the particular case considered by the court.

6. It may be possible for auditors to disclaim responsibility to third parties by conveying that fact to relevant third parties.

Although we can identify these and other elements of the law relating to auditors' liability to third parties (and to their clients), a more general principle may be discerned from the cases we have reviewed. This was given explicit recognition by the NZ Court of Appeal in *South Pacific Manufacturing Co Ltd v New Zealand Security Consultants & Investigations Ltd* [1992] 2 NZLR 282.[24] The court held that proper standards of care should be imposed on professionals who undertake tasks (for financial reward) which require skill and judgment and on whom others are dependent. However, this must be balanced by the need to preserve a proper balance between the differing interests of people (such as the plaintiffs and defendants) going about their business or daily lives. The court concluded that, irrespective of whether judges follow the *Anns* rule (cited in section 15.4.1 above) or adopt a more conservative approach (such as that enunciated in *Caparo*), they essentially seek to decide whether it is fair, just and reasonable that a duty of care should be imposed on one party (the auditor) for the benefit of another (a third party or the client entity) in the particular circumstances of the case. The *Equitable Life* case we considered in section 15.3 also seems to indicate that the courts are concerned to ensure that successful claims for damages brought against auditors are kept within reasonable bounds.

15.5 THE EFFECT OF OUT-OF-COURT SETTLEMENTS

Three decades ago, Woolf (1983) observed that the development of the law relating to auditors' liability and, more particularly, auditors' common law liability to third parties was being hampered by the auditing profession's predisposition to settle out-of-court – a predisposition which remains evident today. However, the issue is complex and worthy of further examination.

As we noted in section 15.2.3, a major difficulty for auditors in respect of their liability for a breach of their common law duties is that neither the parties to whom they owe a duty of care nor the requirements which constitute a reasonable standard of skill and care are static. This leaves auditors uncertain as

---

[24] The case involved insurance assessors who reported suspected arson in two separate incidents of suspicious fires preceding insurance claims. The insured sued the assessors for preparing their reports negligently. The Court of Appeal was asked to decide whether a duty of care was owed by insurance assessors to an insured.

to their legal obligations and may incline them towards going on the defensive, 'playing safe' and agreeing an out-of-court settlement with those who bring an action against them. Added to this are the enormous costs involved in lengthy court hearings – costs that are not limited to hefty legal fees;[25] they also include the lost earnings of partners who spend days, if not weeks or months, in court, and the costs associated with damaged reputations resulting from allegations (whether justified or not) of negligent auditing. Given the legal uncertainties and high costs involved, it is not surprising that auditors are predisposed to settle out-of-court – even in circumstances where they believe they may be able to defend successfully a case brought against them. This action is often encouraged by their indemnity insurers who frequently pressure them to settle out-of-court as they consider this to be the least costly option.[26]

Nevertheless, auditors' propensity to settle out of court has some serious adverse consequences for the profession. For example, it prevents the underlying legal issues with respect to auditors' liability from being resolved and, as a result, stifles clarification and development of the law in this area – an area which, as we have observed, is in a state of transition and flux. It also causes indemnity insurance premiums to rise to unnecessarily high levels. A further damaging outcome is that, when news of a significant out-of-court settlement reaches the media headlines (which it inevitably does), it seems to convey to interested parties, and to the public at large, that the auditors concerned accept they are in the wrong and are unable to defend successfully the claims brought against them. It is arguable that, in general, this is more damaging to the reputation of the auditors involved, and to the auditing profession as a whole, than having the facts of the case exposed in court – and the possibility that the case will be decided in the relevant auditor's favour.

It may be that E&Y's success in the *Equitable Life* and *Freightliner* cases, and Moore Stephens' success in *Stone & Rolls*, will encourage other auditors not to settle out of court. Whatever the advantages and disadvantages of auditors settling out of court, decided cases have demonstrated that the courts will not impose an unfair burden on auditors. *Caparo*, and subsequent cases, show that

---

[25] As noted in footnote 22, by the time PwC reached an out-of-court settlement with the liquidators of the Barings Group, legal fees alone exceeded £100 million.

[26] A senior audit partner in one of the 'Big 4' firms observed to one of the authors of this book that out-of-court settlements are analogous to proportional liability. He said:

> Audit firms are prepared to pay for harm they cause when they get it wrong [are negligent] but they are not prepared to foot the total bill for the harm suffered by a plaintiff when the auditee's management is also culpable. The amount paid by an audit firm in an out-of-court settlement usually represents the amount of harm for which the audit firm accepts responsibility.

We discuss proportional liability in Chapter 16, section 16.5.6.

the courts have been concerned to limit the parties to whom auditors owe a duty of care so as not to leave them exposed to liability which is indeterminate in amount for an indeterminate time to an indeterminate class (Cardozo, *Ultramares* case, 1931). The guiding principle the courts seem anxious to apply in cases involving auditors' breach of their duty of care (i.e., negligence) is to impose liability only when, and to the extent that, it is fair, just and reasonable to do so in the circumstance of a particular case.

15.6 SUMMARY

In this chapter we have addressed the issue of auditors' legal liability. We have distinguished between a breach of auditors' statutory duties and a breach of their common law duties, and between auditors' contractual and third-party liability. We have also traced the development of auditors' duty of care to third parties and noted the effect of the *Caparo* ruling. We have additionally noted that, since *Caparo*, the law relating to auditors' liability to third parties has continued to evolve but the courts have been concerned to ensure that auditors are not exposed to a liability burden that is unreasonable.

In the final section of the chapter we have considered the effect of out-of-court settlements on the development of the law relating to auditors' liability, on auditors' indemnity insurance, and on auditors' (and the profession's) reputation. In the next chapter we discuss measures the auditing profession and regulators have taken (and are taking) to try to reduce auditors' exposure to liability through the performance of high quality audits and other means.

SELF-REVIEW QUESTIONS

15.1   Distinguish briefly between a breach of auditors' statutory duties and a breach of their common law duties.

15.2   Distinguish briefly between auditors' contractual liability and their liability to third parties.

15.3   List the three facts a plaintiff must prove before a court will award damages against an auditor for negligence.

15.4   Explain the position adopted in the case of *Ultramares* v *Touche* (1931) with respect to auditors' liability to third parties. What reason did the judge give for his decision in this case?

15.5   Explain briefly the significance of the decision in *Hedley Byrne & Co. Ltd* v *Heller and Partners* (1963) to the development of auditors' liability to third parties.

15.6   Explain briefly the position adopted in the cases of *Jeb Fasteners* (1981) and *Twomax Ltd* (1983) with respect to auditors' liability to third parties.

15.7   Explain briefly the principles enunciated in the *Caparo* decision (1990) with respect to the parties to whom auditors are liable.

15.8   Identify the parties to whom auditors may be held to owe a duty of care as a result of the *Coulthard, Siddell, BCCI, Barings* and *Independent Advantage* cases.

15.9   Briefly state the general principle that may be distilled from the post-*Caparo* cases reported in this chapter which the courts appear to seek to apply in cases involving auditors' breach of their duty of care.

15.10   Explain briefly the impact of out-of-court settlements on:
         (i)   the development of the law as it relates to auditors' liability;
         (ii)   auditors' professional indemnity insurance;
         (iii) the reputation of the auditors concerned and, more generally, the auditing profession.

REFERENCES

Baxt, R. (1990). Shutting the gate on shareholders in actions for negligence – the Caparo decision in the House of Lords. *Companies and Securities Forum*, pp. 2–12. CCH Australia Ltd.

Christodoulou, M. (2010, 10 June). Equitable Life: E&Y spared the worst. *Accountancy Age*, www.accountancyage.com/aa/news/1808520/equitable-life-e-y-spared-worst, accessed 21 November 2012.

Davies, J. (1992). *Auditors' Liabilities: Who Can Sue Now?* Unpublished paper written for Reynolds Porter Chamberlain, UK.

Financial Reporting Council (FRC). (2012a, 22 June). *Lehman Brothers International (Europe)*, www.frc.org.uk/News-and-Events/FRC-Press/Press/2012/June/Lehman -Brothers-International-(Europe), accessed 5 November 2012.

Financial Reporting Council (FRC). (2012b). *About the FRC*, www.frc.org.uk/About -the-FRC, accessed 11 February 2012.

Gwilliam, D. (1988). Making mountains out of molehills. *Accountancy*, *101*(1135), 22–23.

Gwilliam, D. (2010, April). *Trucking On – Audit in the Real World*. Unpublished paper presented at the National Auditing Conference, Aston Business School.

International Accounting Standards Board (IASB). (2010). *Conceptual Framework for Financial Reporting*. London: IASB.

International Auditing and Assurance Standards Board. (2009a). International Standard on Auditing (ISA) 210: *Agreeing the Terms of Audit Engagements*. New York: International Federation of Accountants.

International Auditing and Assurance Standards Board. (2009b). International Standard on Auditing (ISA) 260: *Communication with Those Charged with Governance*. New York: International Federation of Accountants.

Lascelles, D., & Donkin, R. (1991, 8 July). The bank that liked to say yes. *Financial Times*, p. 10.

Nisse, J. (1999, 29 September). Pots of money appear on the horizon for BCCI's creditors. *The Times*.

Pearson, R. (2005, 22 September). Collapsed claim against Ernst & Young was 'blood-curdling'. *Accountancy Age*, www.accountancyage.com/aa/news/1770913/collapsed-claim-e-y-blood-curdling, accessed 21 November 2012.

Perry, M. (2001a, 31 July). Coopers' Barings settlement collapses. *Accountancy Age*.

Perry, M. (2001b, 11 October). Analysis – Battle of Barings rages on. *Accountancy Age*, www.accountancyage.com/aa/news/1783240/analysis-battle-barings-rages, accessed 21 November 2012.

Perry, M. (2002a, 21 March). Barings' case against Deloitte set for May. *Accountancy Age*, www.accountancyage.com/aa/news/1767141/barings-deloitte-set-may, accessed 21 November 2012.

Perry, M. (2002b, 29 April). Coopers fined in Barings Disciplinary. *Accountancy Age*, www.accountancyage.com/aa/news/1774559/coopers-fiined-barings-disciplinary, accessed 21 November 2012.

Reed, K. (2010, 4 June). E&Y wins appeal over Equitable Life audit objectivity. *Accountancy Age*, www.accountancyage.com/aa/analysis/1807959/e-y-wins-appeal-equitable-life-audit-objectivity, accessed 21 November 2012.

Savage, N. (1981). The auditor's legal responsibility to strangers? *The Accountant's Magazine*, 85(904), 338–341.

Schlesinger, L. (2003, 18 June). Coopers paid £65m in Barings case. *Accountancy Age*, www.accountancyage.com/aa/news/1786952/coopers-paid-gbp65m-barings, accessed 21 November 2012.

Scott, A. (1999). Another Year in Court: 1998's key liability cases, *Accountancy*, 123(1266), 106.

Shanahan, J. (1995, 19 May). The AWA case: An auditor's view, reported in *Butterworths Corporation Law Bulletin* (Australian Corporation Law), No. 10, 213–214.

Simmons & Simmons. (2003a, January). *Professional Liability, Issue No. 31. Case Focus Audit Negligence: Another Third Party Claim*, www.simmons-simmons.com/docs/plb_11Jan03, accessed 11 November 2012.

Simmons & Simmons. (2003b, August). *Auditors – Duty of care: Equitable Life Assurance Society v Ernst & Young*, www.elexica.com/en/legal-topics/dispute-resolution -financial-markets-/20-auditors-duty-of-care-equitable-life-assurace-society-v-ernst -young, accessed 11 November 2012.

Simmons & Simmons. (2003c, October). *Case Summary of Man Nutzfahrzeuge Aktiengesellschaft and others v Freightliner Ltd*, www.elexica.com/en/legal-topics/ dispute-resolution-financial-markets-/31-auditors-negligence, accessed 11 November 2012.

Simmons & Simmons. (2003d, November). *Professional Liability, Issue No. 42. Recent Cases, Auditors' Negligence*, www.simmons-simmons.com/docs/plb_42_Nov03, accessed 11 November 2012.

Sukhraj, P. (2007, 12 September). E&Y heads off £350m Freightliner claim. *Accountancy Age*, www.accountancyage.com/aa/news/1767858/e-y-heads-gbp350m -freightliner-claim, accessed 21 November 2012.

Sukhraj, P. (2008, 24 January). E&Y claims victory in £350m case. *Accountancy Age*, www.accountancyage.com/aa/news/1757415/e-y-claims-victory-gbp350m, accessed 21 November 2012.

Woolf, E. (1983). Auditing and staying out of court. *Accountancy*, *94*(1074), 65–66.

ADDITIONAL READING

Casterella, J.R., Jensen, K.L., & Knechel, W.R. (2010). Litigation risk and audit firm characteristics. *Auditing: A Journal of Practice & Theory*, *29*(2), 71–82.

Cornell, R.M., Eining, M.M., & Warne, R.C. (2012). Practitioner summary of can auditors reduce negligence verdicts? An examination of remedial tactics. *Current Issues in Auditing*, *6*(2), 1–6.

Erickson, M., Mayhew, B.W., & Felix Jr, W.L. (2000). Why do audits fail? Evidence from Lincoln Savings and Loan. *Journal of Accounting Research*, *38*(1), 165–194.

Grenier, J., Pomeroy, B., & Reffett, A. (2012). Speak up or shut up? The moderating role of credibility on auditor remedial defense tactics. *Auditing: A Journal of Practice & Theory*, *31*(4), 65–83.

Khurana, I.K., & Raman, K.K. (2004). Litigation risk and the financial reporting credibility of Big 4 verses Non-Big 4 audits: Evidence from Anglo-American countries. *Accounting Review*, *79*(2), 473–496.

Lowe, D.J., Reckers, P.M.J., & Whitecotton, S.M. (2002). The effects of decision-aid use and reliability on jurors' evaluations of auditor liability. *Accounting Review* *77*(1), 185–203.

Venkataraman, R., Weber, J.P., & Willenborg, M. (2008). Litigation risk, audit quality, and audit fees: Evidence from initial public offerings. *Accounting Review*, *83*(5), 1315–1345.

APPENDIX 1

Barings plc (in liquidation) v Coopers & Lybrand & Ors, Barings Futures (Singapore) Pte Ltd (in liquidation) v *Mattar & Ors* [2002] EWHC 461 (Ch); [2002] ALL ER (D) 309 (Mar); [2003] EWHC 1319 (Ch); [2003] All ER (D) 142 (Jun).

The facts of this case are as set out in section 15.4.3. The part of the case reported here concerns the action brought by Barings Futures (Singapore) (BFS) against Deloitte & Touche (D&T) for negligent auditing in 1992 and 1993.

D&T sought to have BFS's action dismissed on the grounds that Jones, a qualified accountant and finance director of BFS at the relevant time, signed letters of representation addressed to D&T prior to the 1992 and 1993 audit reports being signed. D&T claimed that, when signing the audit reports, it relied on statements in the letters, namely:

- there had been no irregularities involving employees that could have a material effect on the financial statements;
- the financial statements were free of material errors and omissions;
- transactions with related parties, and losses on sale and purchase commitments, had been properly recorded;
- BFS had recorded or disclosed all of its liabilities;
- there had been no post-balance-sheet events requiring adjustment to the financial statements.

D&T informed the court that it routinely requires audit clients to provide a representation letter, signed by a suitably knowledgeable director or senior employee, before it will sign an unqualified audit report on audited financial statements; the same requirement applied in this case before it signed its unqualified report on the consolidated schedules.[27]

It was undisputed that Jones had signed the letters but, unknown to D&T, his contact with BFS during the 1992 and 1993 accounting periods was so small that he had no relevant knowledge which would render him properly able to sign the letters. D&T claimed that, had Jones not signed the letters, it would not have issued an unqualified audit report and, had it refused to issue an unqualified report, the subsequent damage to BFS would have been averted. Therefore, Jones' reckless signature was a cause of D&T's exposure to the

---

[27] As we note in Chapter 13, section 13.5, ISA 580: *Written Representations* (IAASB, 2009) now requires auditors to obtain written representations from their auditee's directors prior to completion of the audit.

claims of negligence made against it. Jones signed the letters as a director of BFS in the course of acting as a director. It followed that BFS was vicariously liable for the consequences. It also followed that D&T had a claim against BFS for the consequences of Jones' fraud. That claim, mirrored the claim against D&T and so gave them an absolute defence of circuity.

The court held that Jones' action in signing the letters was not recklessly fraudulent. D&T had not proved to the court's satisfaction that, when he signed the representation letters, he did so:

(i)   knowing that the statements in the letters were untrue, without honest belief in their truth, or with indifference as to whether or not they were true; or

(ii)   knowing that he had no reasonable grounds for making the statements, without an honest belief that he had such grounds, or with indifference as to whether he had or not.

Hence, Evans-Lombe J ruled that, although the letters signed by Jones were inaccurate, D&T's claim should be dismissed and BFS's negligence claim against D&T for £200 million could proceed.

In June 2003, when BFS's case against D&T was heard, Evans-Lombe J found that the audits conducted by D&T in 1992 and 1993 were negligent. However, the losses suffered by BFS as a result of Leeson's fraudulent trading on the Singaporean and Japanese financial markets were largely brought about by BFS's lack of control over Leeson. Indeed, so serious was BFS's contributory negligence that the damages to which BFS was entitled from D&T for the period from November 1992 to April 1994 was reduced to between 20 and 50 per cent,[28] but, beyond April 1994, BFS alone was responsible for the losses it suffered as a result of Leeson's actions (Milner, 2003). Evans-Lombe J held that D&T was responsible for about "£1.5m, a tiny fraction of the £200m claimed by the bank [BFS]" (Accountancy Age, 2003). Both parties appealed Evans-Lombe J's ruling but, in April 2004, shortly before the appeals were to be heard, the parties reached a final agreement whereby BFS would not enforce its claim against D&T and each party would bear its own cost of the appeals (Deloitte, 2004).

REFERENCES

Accountancy Age. (2003, 17 October). Deloitte fined £1.5m over Barings. *Accountancy Age*. www.accountancyage.com/aa/news/1773969/deloitte-fined-gbp15m-barings, accessed 21 November 2012.

---

[28] The precise damages were to be settled between D&T and Barings' liquidator, KPMG (Milner, 2003).

Deloitte. (2004, 27 April). *Statement on Behalf of Deloitte & Touche Singapore*. www
.deloitte.com/dtt/press_release/0,1014, accessed 15 November 2005.

International Auditing and Assurance Standards Board (IAASB). (2009). International Standard on Auditing (ISA) 580: *Written Representations*. New York: International Federation of Accountants.

Milner, M. (2003, 12 June). Deloitte & Touche negligent in Barings audit, rules judge.
The Guardian, www.guardian.co.uk/business/2003/jun/12/10, accessed 1 November
2012.

APPENDIX 2

People of the State of New York v *Ernst & Young LLP*, 11-cv-00384, US District
Court, Southern District of New York (Manhattan).[29] When filing this case in
December 2010, and claiming $150 million – the amount Ernst & Young (E&Y)
earned as auditor of Lehman Brothers from 2001 to 2008 – plus damages,
Cuomo (then New York's Attorney General) asserted:

> E&Y substantially assisted Lehman Brothers Holdings Inc. . . . to engage in a
> massive accounting fraud, involving the surreptitious removal of tens of billions
> of dollars of securities from Lehman's balance sheet in order to create a false
> impression of Lehman's liquidity, thereby defrauding the investing public. (as
> quoted in Reed, 2010)

When Cuomo became Governor of New York, the case was taken over by the
new Attorney General, Schneiderman. Following an unsuccessful attempt to
transfer the case to the Federal Court, it was returned to the New York District
Court in February 2012. [In addition to this case, at least 47 cases have been
filed against E&Y in the United States of America (USA) by shareholder
groups (Watkins, 2010).]

Following Lehman Brothers' bankruptcy in September 2008 – a bankruptcy
that was larger than those of Enron, WorldCom, General Motors and Washington Mutual combined (CBS, 2012) – the New York bankruptcy court
appointed Valukas (chairman of the Chicago law firm of Jenner & Block) to
investigate and report on the causes of Lehman's bankruptcy. In his 2,200-page
report, Valukas suggested that E&Y may be guilty of "malpractice", "negligence" and "failure to exercise professional care". He was critical, in particular,
of E&Y failing to question Lehman's failure to disclose in its financial

---

[29] Although this case does not specifically involve the legal matters we discuss in this chapter, its key points
are outlined here because many cases have been filed against E&Y alleging it was negligent in its audits
of Lehman's financial statements and because of its significance. According to CBS News (2012):

> It's hard to overstate the enormity of the 2008 collapse of Lehman Brothers. It was the largest bankruptcy in history;
> 26,000 employees lost their jobs; millions of investors lost all or most of their money; and it triggered a chain reac-
> tion that produced the worst financial crisis and economic downturn in 70 years.

statements the timing and volume of its Repo transactions (Valukas, 2010). In response to Valukas' allegations, E&Y stated: "We stand behind our work on the Lehman audit and our opinion that Lehman's financial statements were fairly stated in accordance with US GAAP, applying the rules that existed at the time" (as quoted in International Accounting Bulletin, 2011).

The case hinges on Lehman's use of Repo transactions to improve its apparent liquidity position in its 2007 annual financial statements and quarterly statements for the first two quarters of 2008. In essence, Repo (or repurchase) transactions are short term financing agreements whereby cash is exchanged for assets but the assets are re-purchased a few days later. In the USA, such transactions (which are commonly used by financial institutions) cannot be accounted for as sales. However, Linklaters, a large law firm based in London, advised Lehman that, under British law, if two parties exchange assets for cash, and "equivalent assets (such as securities of the same series and nominal value) rather than the very assets that were originally delivered" (as quoted in De La Merced & Werdigier, 2010) are re-purchased by the assets' original owner, that amounts to a sale as the 'seller' has lost control of the (precise) assets in question.

Based on Linklaters' advice, Lehman used Repo 105 and 108 transactions (whereby the assets exchanged for cash are valued at 105 or 108 per cent, as applicable, more than the cash received) and its subsidiary, Lehman Brothers International (Europe) (LBIE), to 'sell' assets (primarily mortgages and bonds) to banks in Britain a few days before its financial statements for 2007 and the first two quarters of 2008 were published. The cash received ($8.3 billion in December 2007, and $14.9 and $13.5 billion in March and June 2008, respectively) was used to reduce the company's liabilities, thereby improving its debt to equity ratio.[30] A few days later, the transaction was reversed; further cash was borrowed and the assets (or virtually identical assets) were (re) purchased and returned to the USA (De La Merced and Werdigier, 2010). Lehman's financial statements did not disclose its commitment to (re)purchase the assets.

In May 2008, Lee (a senior vice president of Lehman's finance division) informed Lehman's financial controller and audit committee of his concerns about possible accounting improprieties. The audit committee requested Schlich, the audit engagement partner, and his colleague, Hansen, to investigate every aspect of Lee's claims and to report to the committee. In June 2008 (a

---

[30] The ratio was changed from 17.8 to 16.1 in December 2007, and from 17.3 to 15.4 and 13.9 to 12.1 in March and June 2008, respectively (Christodoulou, 2010).

day after discussing the matter with Lee), Schilich and Hansen met with the audit committee but did not mention's Lee's allegations. Similarly, in July 2008, when E&Y staff met with the audit committee to discuss the second quarter's figures, E&Y did not mention the Repo transactions or Lee's concerns (Watkins, 2010, p. 2).

When questioned by Valukas about its failure to report on its investigation to the audit committee, E&Y explained:

> Lehman conducted an investigation of the allegations. . . . In July 2008 Lehman's management reported to the audit committee and concluded the allegations were unfounded and that there were no material issues identified. We never concluded our review of the matter because Lehman went into bankruptcy before we completed our audit. (as quoted in Watkins, 2010, p. 2)

In the UK in June 2010, the Financial Reporting Council's (FRC) Accountancy and Actuarial Discipline Board (AADB),[31] after considering Valukas' report, began an investigation into the audit by E&Y in the UK (E&Y UK) of LBIE and the Repo transactions that were conducted through LBIE. E&Y UK audited LBIE's trial balance, which was prepared under US GAAP for incorporation in Lehman's consolidated financial statements. In February 2012, following a detailed investigation, Executive Counsel (Gareth Rees, QC) concluded: "There is no realistic prospect that a Tribunal would make an adverse finding against Ernst & Young LLP in the UK or Members within that firm". As a result, the investigation is closed and no further action will be taken (FRC, 2012a). However, while E&Y UK seems to be in the clear, the firm in the USA faces years of legal battles in the New York and other American courts.

REFERENCES

CBSNews.Com (2012, 22 April). *The Case Against Lehman Brothers*, www.cbsnews .com/8301-18560_162-57417397/the-case-against-lehman-brothers/?pageNum= 2&tag=content Main;contentBody, accessed 5 May 2013.

Christodoulou, M. (2010, 18 March). Lehman smoking gun leaves E&Y facing questions. *Accountancy Age*, www.accountancyage.com/aa/news/1808180/lehman -smoking-gun-leaves-e-y-facing-questions, accessed 21 November 2012.

De La Merced, M.J., & Werdigier, J. (2010, 12 March). The origins of Lehman's 'Repo 105'. *New York Times*, dealbook.nytimes.com/2010/03/12/the-british-origins-of -lehmans-accounting-gimmick, accessed 21 November 2012.

---

[31] As noted in footnote 9 of this chapter, until July 2012, the AADB was one of its operating bodies. In July 2012, when the FRC was restructured, the AADB was replaced by Case Management Committee, an advisory Committee of the Conduct Committee (FRC, 2012b).

Financial Reporting Council (FRC). (2012a, 22 June). *Lehman Brothers International (Europe)*, www.frc.org.uk/News-and-Events/FRC-Press/Press/2012/June/Lehman -Brothers-International-(Europe).aspx, accessed 5 November 2012.

Financial Reporting Council (FRC). (2012b). *About the FRC*, www.frc.org.uk/About -the-FRC, accessed 11 February 2012.

International Accounting Bulletin (AIB). (2011, 28 July). Investor suit against lehmans gets go ahead. Editorial. *The Accountant*, www.vrl-financial-news.com/accounting/ intl-accounting-bulletin/issues-2011/iab-493-494/investor-suit-against-lehman-g, accessed 5 May 2013.

Reed, K. (2010, 21 December). E&Y sued over Lehmans audit. *Accountancy Age*, www.accountancyage.com/aa/news/1934026/-sued-lehmans-audit, accessed 21 November 2012.

Valukas, A. (2010). *Lehman Brothers Holdings Inc. Chapter 11 Proceedings*, www .lehmanreport.jenner.com, accessed 6 November 2012.

Watkins, S. (2010, 13 March). Will Lehman Brothers and Repo 105 allegations bring down Ernst & Young? Mail Online, www.dailymail.co.uk/money/article-1255524/ Will-Lehaman-Brothers-Repo-105-allegations-bring-Ernst–Young, accessed 5 November 2012.

16 Avoiding and Limiting Auditors' Liability

LEARNING OBJECTIVES

After studying the material in this chapter you should be able to:

- discuss the adverse consequences auditors may suffer if they perform their audits deficiently;
- describe and evaluate the measures (a) audit firms and (b) engagement partners are required to implement in order to ensure that high quality audits are performed;
- explain the objectives, process and outcomes of the monitoring/inspection of auditors' performance in the United Kingdom (UK);
- discuss the advantages and disadvantages of the following means of limiting auditors' liability:
  - the formation of audit firms as limited liability companies,
  - the formation of audit firms as limited liability partnerships,
  - auditors' liability limitation agreements,
  - liability caps,
  - proportionate liability;
- in the context of the UK, evaluate the effectiveness of the above means of limiting auditors' liability.

16.1 INTRODUCTION

In Chapter 15 we review a number of cases in which auditors were sued by their clients and/or by third parties for (allegedly) performing their audits negligently (that is, without due skill and care). The damages claimed against the auditors in some of these cases are staggering. For example, Price Waterhouse (PW) and Ernst & Whinney (E&W) faced a claim of US$11 billion (about £6.5 billion) as a result of their (allegedly) negligent auditing of the Bank of Credit and Commerce International (BCCI) Group,[1] and Ernst & Young (E&Y) faced a claim for £3.75 billion for (allegedly) failing to exercise due skill and care in its audits of Equitable Life Assurance Society.[2]

Not only are some of the damages *claimed* against auditors astounding, in some cases the amounts *awarded* against them have been enormous. For instance, in

---

[1] We note in Chapter 15 (footnote 18) that PW and E&W agreed a settlement with the liquidators of the BCCI Group for an amount reputed to be in the region of US$95–100 million.

[2] As we note in Chapter 15, section 15.3, in September 2005, Equitable Life dropped its claim against E&Y.

2004, US$10 million (about £6 million) was awarded against KPMG in the United States of America (USA) in an enforcement action by the Securities and Exchange Commission (SEC) for "repeated audit failures in connection with audits of Gemstar's financial statements . . . from 1999 through 2002" (SEC, 2004b).[3] Along similar lines, in February 2007, Deloitte & Touche's (D&T) Italian firm was ordered to pay US$130 million (£66 million) as:

> part of the $149m that [D&T] . . . agreed to pay to settle lawsuits accusing it of helping former Parmalat management hide debt and inflate results that led to it [i.e., Parmalat] filing for bankruptcy in December 2003. (Accountancy Age, 2007)

Further, in July 2007, PricewaterhouseCoopers (PwC) agreed to pay US$225 million (£120 million) to the shareholders of Tyco International as settlement for its (alleged) failure to uncover the massive fraud perpetrated by Tyco's chief executive and chief financial officer (Kozlowski and Swartz, respectively) during its audits of Tyco's financial statements in the late 1990s and early 2000s (Norris, 2007).[4]

In some cases, deficient auditing has not only resulted in hefty financial penalties for the audit firms concerned; it has also resulted in curtailment of their activities. For example, in April 2004, E&Y in the USA was barred from accepting any new audit clients for six months as a result of engaging in a business venture with an audit client, PeopleSoft Inc. In her judgment, the SEC's Chief Administrative Judge referred to E&Y's "repeated violations of the auditor independence standards by conduct that was reckless, highly unreasonable, and negligent" (SEC, 2004a, p. 62). In addition to the ban, E&Y was ordered to return nearly $1.7 million in audit fees, plus interest, it had received from PeopleSoft Inc. between 1994 and 1999 and to hire an outside consultant to improve its independence policies which the judge called a "sham" (SEC, 2004a).

---

[3] An SEC press release (SEC, 2004b) reported the following statement by its Director of Enforcement, Stephen Cutler:

> Our action today holds KPMG as a firm accountable for the audit failures of its partners. Sanctions in this case should reinforce the message that accounting firms must assume responsibility for ensuring that individual auditors properly discharge their special and critical gatekeeping duties. (p. 1)

The same press release reported that Randall Lee, Regional Director of the SEC's Pacific Regional office, said:

> This case illustrates the dangers of auditors who rely excessively on the honesty of management. KPMG's auditors repeatedly relied on Gemstar management's representations even when those representations were contradicted by their audit work. The auditors thus failed to abide by one of the core principles of public accounting – to exercise professional skepticism and care. (p. 1)

[4] PwC argued that the plaintiffs could not show that its conduct had led to the losses of the company's shareholders. In agreeing the settlement, a spokesman for PwC explained: "while PwC was prepared to continue to defend all aspects of its work in the litigation process, the cost of that defense and the size of the securities class action made settlement the sensible choice for the firm". However, the SEC banned PwC's engagement partner for the Tyco audits (Richard Scalzo) from auditing public companies. The SEC stated: "from 1999 onwards Mr Scalzo had good reason to doubt the honesty of Mr Kozlowski and Mr Swartz . . . but did not pursue auditing procedures that could have uncovered the fraud" (Norris, 2007).

Likewise, in May 2006, following the collapse of cosmetics company Kanebo Ltd, the Japanese Financial Services Agency suspended ChuoAoyama Audit Corporation, the Japanese affiliate of PwC, from providing some statutory audit services. The Agency found that three of the audit firm's partners had assisted in an accounting fraud which, over the course of five years, boosted Kanebo's earnings by about $1.9 billion (Answers.com, 2006, p. 4).

In other cases, the adverse consequences of poor auditing have been so severe that the audit firm concerned collapsed. Probably the most dramatic demise is that of Arthur Andersen in 2002, which resulted from its misdeeds (and consequential loss of reputation) in relation to its energy giant client, Enron. However, in 1990, Laventhol & Horwath, then the seventh-largest accounting firm in the USA, was forced into bankruptcy. At the time, this sent shockwaves throughout the accounting profession similar to those resulting from Andersen's collapse 12 years later. According to Richards (2002):

> In the years leading up to 1990, Laventhol was frequently hauled into court to settle allegations of sloppy work. At its end, the firm had 115 legal actions against it [almost entirely related to failed savings and loan institutions], seeking a total of $362 million. (p. 1)

Notwithstanding the severe sanctions auditors may suffer if they perform deficient audits, as we observe in Chapter 15 (section 15.4.4), the courts have demonstrated a reluctance to impose on auditors a standard of skill and care which is higher than that generally regarded as appropriate by the auditing profession. It seems to follow that the most effective way for auditors to address their exposure to liability and other sanctions is to avoid them by performing high quality audits. Nevertheless, auditors, fearing the imposition of punitive damages have called for, and adopted, ways to limit their liability.

In this chapter we explore ways in which auditors may avoid or limit their exposure to liability and other sanctions. More specifically, we discuss measures implemented by the auditing profession and by regulators which are designed to ensure that auditors perform consistently high quality audits. We also examine moves by audit firms to form limited liability companies (LLCs) or limited liability partnerships (LLPs) and/or to enter into liability limitation agreements with their audit clients. Additionally, we discuss proposals to limit auditors' liability by means of imposing a liability cap or enshrining the principle of proportionate liability in legislation.

16.2 IMPORTANCE OF, AND RESPONSIBILITY FOR, QUALITY CONTROL OF AUDITS

The performance of high quality audits is essential not only to enable auditors to avoid exposure to liability and other sanctions but also, and more importantly, so they fulfil their function in society and satisfy the needs of those who depend on their work. In order to ensure that high quality audits are performed, quality control is needed. In Chapter 3 (section 3.6.2), we note that Flint (1988) explained the importance of quality control as follows:

> Auditors have both a legal duty and a professional obligation to work to the highest standards which can reasonably be expected to discharge the responsibility that is placed on them. . . . In a profession whose authority is dependent among other things on public confidence . . . a demonstrable concern, individually and collectively on the part of the members of the profession, to control and maintain the highest quality in its work, is a matter of basic principle. The basis of continuing public confidence and trust in professional competence is a belief that the standards of the members of the profession will be maintained and can be relied on. (pp. 159, 161)

The key issue is minimising the prospect of audit failure; that is, auditors failing to detect material misstatements in the financial statements, or failing to report those they detect but are not corrected by the auditee's directors. Flint explains, "this is what society in general, and those who rely on audit in particular, expect". He adds, "this is what the professional accountancy bodies as the regulatory authority[5] have an obligation to pursue in the public interest" (Flint, 1980, p. 64).

Whether prompted by a concern for the public interest, the interests of users of audited financial statements, the potential damage to the profession's reputation if poor quality audits are performed, or the possible extent of auditors' exposure to liability (or a mixture of these factors), both the auditing profession and regulators have taken steps designed to ensure that all audits are performed to a high standard. We examine the steps taken by the profession in section 16.3 and those taken by regulators in 16.4.

16.3   THE PROFESSION'S MEASURES TO SECURE HIGH QUALITY AUDITS

16.3.1   Overview of quality control standards

International Standard on Quality Control (ISQC) 1: *Quality Control for Firms that Perform Audits and Reviews of Financial Statements* . . . (IAASB, 2009a)

---

[5] As we explain in Chapter 5 (section 5.3.1), in order to be eligible for appointment as a company auditor in the UK, persons or firms must be registered with one of the five Recognised Supervisory Bodies [RSBs – the Institutes of Chartered Accountants in England and Wales (ICAEW), of Scotland (ICAS), and in Ireland (ICAI) and the Associations of Chartered Certified Accountants (ACCA) and of Authorised Public Accountants (AAPA)]. The Financial Reporting Council (FRC) has overall responsibility for ensuring that the audits of companies' financial statements in the UK are performed to a high standard; part of its role is to oversee the regulatory activities of the RSBs. Hence, strictly speaking, the RSBs and FRC, rather than the professional accountancy bodies *per se*, constitute the 'regulatory authority' for auditing in the UK.

and International Standard on Auditing (ISA) 220: *Quality Control for an Audit of Financial Statements* (IAASB, 2009b) place responsibility on audit firms and engagement partners, respectively, for ensuring that high quality audits are performed. More specifically, ISQC 1 states (paras 18, A4):

> The [audit] firm shall establish policies and procedures designed to promote an internal culture recognizing that quality is essential in performing engagements . . . The promotion of a quality-oriented internal culture depends on clear, consistent and frequent actions and messages from all levels of the firm's management that emphasize the firm's quality control policies and procedures, and the requirement to:
>
> (a) Perform work that complies with professional standards and applicable legal and regulatory requirements; and
> (b) Issue reports that are appropriate in the circumstances.

Along similar lines, ISA 220 notes (paras 8, A3):

> The engagement partner shall take responsibility for the overall quality on each audit engagement to which that partner is assigned. . . . The actions of the engagement partner and appropriate messages to the other members of the engagement team . . . emphasize:
>
> (a) The importance to audit quality of:
>   (i) Performing work that complies with professional standards and applicable legal and regulatory requirements;
>   (ii) Complying with the firm's quality control policies and procedures as applicable;
>   (iii) Issuing auditor's reports that are appropriate in the circumstances; and
>   (iv) The engagement team's ability to raise concerns without fear of reprisals; and
> (b) The fact that quality is essential in performing audit engagements.

In the next two sub-sections, we first examine the quality control requirements applying to audit firms and then those that apply to audit engagement partners.

16.3.2 Audit firms' responsibility for ensuring high quality audits are performed

ISQC 1, para 16, requires audit firms to:

> establish and maintain a system of quality control that includes policies and procedures that address each of the following elements:
>
> (a) Leadership responsibilities for quality within the firm.
> (b) Relevant ethical requirements.
> (c) Acceptance and continuance of client relationships and specific engagements.
> (d) Human resources.
> (e) Engagement performance.
> (f) Monitoring.

Audit firms are also required to document their quality control policies and procedures and ensure they are communicated to the firm's personnel. The Standard explains that the communication should, in general, include:

> . . . a description of the quality control policies and procedures and the objectives they are designed to achieve, and the message that each individual has a personal responsibility for quality and is expected to comply with these policies and procedures. (para A2)

As may be seen from Figure 16.1, each of the elements to be addressed by audit firms' quality control policies and procedures (which are discussed below) makes a unique but complementary contribution towards ensuring high quality audit work is performed.

Figure 16.1:   Elements to be addressed by an audit firm's quality control system

Element	Contribution to securing high-quality audit work
Leadership responsibilities for quality within the audit firm	The firm's chief executive officer or managing board of partners is responsible for the firm's quality control system. The firm's commitment to quality should be reflected in performance evaluation, promotion and reward. Personnel with operational responsibility for developing and implementing quality control policies and procedures should have appropriate experience, ability and authority.
Relevant ethical requirements	The firm's policies and procedures should include those designed to ensure the firm and its personnel comply with relevant ethical requirements – especially those relating to independence.
Acceptance and continuance of client relationships and specific engagements	The firm's policies and procedures should include those designed to provide reasonable assurance that only appropriate clients and audit engagements are accepted.
Human resources	Responsibility for the quality of audit work performed during an engagement lies with the engagement partner but firms need to ensure that audit staff have the necessary capabilities, competence and time to perform work assigned to them.
Engagement performance	The firm's policies and procedures should include those designed to ensure audit team members are properly briefed, comply with ethical and technical standards, and receive adequate supervision and training. In appropriate cases, engagement quality control reviews of audits and their documentation should be undertaken, including reviews of the audit team's significant judgments and conclusions.
Monitoring	The firm's policies and procedures should include those designed to provide reasonable assurance that the firm's quality control system is relevant, adequate, operating effectively and complied with in practice. Monitoring the firm's quality control system includes inspection of a selection of completed engagements, the reporting of deficiencies uncovered and instigating corrective action.

(a) Leadership responsibilities for quality within the firm

ISQC 1 places ultimate responsibility for an audit firm's quality control system with its chief executive officer or managing board of partners, depending on the firm's organisational structure. It also notes that promoting a culture based on quality within the firm may be achieved by measures such as:

(i) ensuring performance evaluation, compensation and promotion of firm personnel reflect the firm's overriding commitment to quality, and

(ii) assigning responsibility for developing and implementing the firm's quality control policies and procedures (including their documentation and communication to relevant people) to a senior audit quality control partner. This partner needs to have sufficient and appropriate ability and experience, and the necessary authority, to fulfil the responsibility. Such ability, experience and authority enable the partner to identify and understand relevant quality control issues and to develop and implement appropriate policies and procedures (ISQC 1, paras 18, 19).

(b) Relevant ethical requirements

Each audit firm is required to: "establish policies and procedures designed to provide it with reasonable assurance that the firm and its personnel comply with relevant ethical requirements" (ISQC 1, para 20). ISQC 1 notes that these requirements are specified in the International Ethics Standards Board for Accountants' (IESBA) *Code of Ethics for Professional Accountants* (*IESBA Code*; IESBA, 2009). However, independence is so crucial to audit engagements that ISQC 1 addresses this issue separately.[6] It requires each audit firm to:

> establish policies and procedures designed to provide it with reasonable assurance that the firm, its personnel and, where applicable, others subject to independence requirements[7] . . . maintain [their] independence. . . (para 21)

In order to achieve this objective, the firms' policies and procedures are required to ensure that:

(a) the firm's independence requirements are communicated to all relevant personnel within and outside the firm, and relevant information is provided to these people to enable them to determine whether or not they satisfy those requirements;

(b) the firm identifies and evaluates circumstances and relationships that create threats to its, and its personnel's, independence, and applies appropriate safeguards to eliminate identified threats or reduce them to

---

[6] In respect of independence, as we observe in Chapter 4, auditors in the UK are subject to the Auditing Practices Board's Ethical Standards.

[7] For example, external experts used during the audit, and auditors of components (such as subsidiaries) of the audit client (see Chapter 7, section 7.5.4).

an acceptable level. To assist in this regard, the firm's policies and procedures are to require:

(i) engagement partners to provide the firm with relevant information about client engagements (including the scope of services provided to the client) to enable the firm to evaluate the impact, if any, on its independence requirements;

(ii) firm personnel to notify the firm promptly of circumstances and relationships of which they become aware that create a threat to the firm's (or a member of the firm's) independence;

(iii) all personnel within or associated with the firm to provide, at least annually, written confirmation of their compliance with the firm's independence policies and procedures.

Further details of the independence requirements that apply to audit firms are provided in Chapter 4.

(c) Acceptance and continuance of client relationships and specific engagements

ISQC 1 (para 26) requires audit firms to establish policies and procedures designed to ensure that the propriety of accepting a new or continuing client relationship, and specific audit engagements, is properly evaluated. Such policies and procedures are to be designed to provide the firm with reasonable assurance that it only accepts, or continues with, clients and engagements if the firm:

(i) is competent to perform the engagement, paying due regard to factors such as the firm's knowledge and experience of the (potential) audit client's business sector, any potential conflict with another client in the same sector, and the availability of audit staff with the required capabilities, experience and time to conduct the audit;

(ii) can comply with relevant ethical (especially independence) requirements;

(iii) has considered the integrity of the (potential) client and the identity and reputation of its owners, directors and senior managers.

Pre-engagement investigations and procedures for accepting new and continuing audit engagements are discussed in detail in Chapter 8, section 8.2.

(d) Human resources

Clearly, it is fundamental to the performance of high quality audits that audit firms have sufficient audit engagement partners and staff with the required capabilities, competence and commitment to the profession's ethical principles to perform such audits. In order to achieve this, audit firms need to have effective recruitment procedures that help to identify individuals with integrity and the ability to develop the capabilities and competence needed to perform the firm's work. Audit firms also require appropriate policies and procedures for staff members' performance evaluation, career development, promotion and reward (ISQC 1, para 29, A24).[8]

In addition to ensuring suitable personnel are recruited and nurtured (so as to ensure the proper development of their capabilities and competence), care is needed to ensure that appropriate engagement partners and audit staff are assigned to particular audit engagements. However, it is not just a case of assigning engagement partners to particular audits. ISQC 1 (para 30) requires audit firms to establish policies and procedures that ensure:

(a) the identity and role of the engagement partner is communicated to key members of the client's senior executives and directors;

(b) the engagement partner has the appropriate competence, capabilities and authority to perform the role;

(c) the responsibilities of the engagement partner are clearly defined and communicated to that partner.

Given that audit engagement partners are responsible for the audit work performed during the engagements to which they are assigned, they clearly have a pivotal role in securing high quality audits. The requirements cited above that apply to audit firms are designed to enable these partners to discharge their responsibilities satisfactorily. (We discuss the responsibilities of audit engagement partners for securing high quality audit work in section 16.3.3 below.) However, it is not only engagement partners who need to be appropriately assigned to audit engagements; it is equally important to assign to each engagement, staff who have the capabilities, competence and time required to perform the audit work expected of them. More specifically, when assigning staff to audit engagements, audit firms need to consider staff members':

- understanding of, and practical experience with, engagements of a similar nature and complexity;
- understanding of professional standards and legal and regulatory requirements;
- technical knowledge and expertise, including knowledge of relevant information technology;
- knowledge of the industry (or industries) in which the client operates;
- ability to apply professional judgment; and
- understanding of the firm's quality control policies and procedures (ISQC 1, para A31).

---

[8] The importance of staffing audits with personnel who possess high ethical standards (especially integrity and objectivity), who are intelligent, and who have the ability and willingness to learn, is discussed in Chapter 7, section 7.5.2. We discuss the concept of competence and how it may be acquired in Chapter 3, section 3.3.2.

(e) Engagement performance

In order to be reasonably assured that their audits are of a consistently high standard, audit firms require policies and procedures that address issues such as:

- how audit teams are briefed about audit engagements so as to ensure they understand the objectives of the work assigned to them;
- the means of ensuring that audit team members comply with applicable ethical and auditing standards;
- how the supervision and training of audit team members is effected;
- the documentation of audit work performed;
- the method, timing and extent of reviews of audit work performed, and of significant judgments made, and the documentation thereof (ISQC 1, Para A32).[9]

Audits are invariably conducted by audit teams and, in order to secure high quality audits, it is essential that more junior audit team members refer matters of which they are uncertain to more experienced members. It is similarly essential for senior audit team members to consult with each other and/or with specialists from within (or, when appropriate, outside) the audit firm whenever they encounter difficult or contentious issues. Recognising the importance of appropriate consultation to high quality audits, ISQC 1 requires audit firms to establish policies and procedures designed to provide them with reasonable assurance that:

(a) Appropriate consultation takes place on difficult or contentious matters;
(b) Sufficient resources are available to enable appropriate consultation to take place;
(c) The nature and scope of, and conclusions resulting from, such consultations are documented and are agreed by both the individual seeking consultation and the individual consulted; and
(d) Conclusions resulting from consultations are implemented. (para 34)

Another element of engagement performance that contributes to high quality audits is an independent review of each completed audit engagement (and related documentation) prior to the audit report being signed and dated. As noted in Chapter 7 (section 7.6.4), the audits of all listed company clients, and those of other clients that meet the criteria specified by the audit firm, are required to be reviewed by an engagement quality control reviewer.[10] ISQC 1 (para 38) specifies that such a review is to include:

(a) Discussion of significant matters with the engagement partner;

---

[9] Requirements relating to the review of audit work are discussed in Chapter 7, section 7.5.3.

[10] Factors to be considered when audit firms establish criteria for audits to be subject to engagement quality control reviews are explained in Chapter 7, section 7.6.4. Definitions of 'engagement quality control review' and 'engagement quality control reviewer' are also provided in Chapter 7, section 7.6.4.

    (b) Review of the financial statements or other subject matter information and the proposed [audit] report;

    (c) Review of selected engagement documentation relating to significant judgments the engagement team made and the conclusions it reached; and

    (d) Evaluation of the conclusions reached in formulating the [audit] report and consideration of whether the proposed report is appropriate. (para 37)

For listed entities, the review is also to consider:

    (a) The engagement team's evaluation of the firm's independence in relation to the specific engagement;

    (b) Whether appropriate consultation has taken place on matters involving differences of opinion or other difficult or contentious matters, and the conclusions arising from those consultations; and

    (c) Whether documentation selected for review reflects the work performed in relation to the significant judgments and supports the conclusions reached.

With reference to the engagement quality control reviewer's evaluation of the audit team's significant judgments, ISQC 1 (para A45) explains that relevant matters include:

- Significant risks identified during the engagement and the responses to those risks.
- Judgments made, particularly with respect to materiality and significant risks.
- The significance and disposition of corrected and uncorrected misstatements identified during the engagement.
- The matters to be communicated to management and those charged with governance [or, more usually, the audit committee] and, where applicable, other parties such as regulatory bodies.

Audit firms are required to establish policies and procedures governing the nature, timing and extent of engagement quality control reviews and their documentation. The policies and procedures are to be designed so as to ensure the reviews are conducted in a timely manner at appropriate stages during the engagement so that significant matters can be resolved promptly to the reviewer's satisfaction. They should also ensure that the extent of a review is appropriate to the circumstances – whether, for example, the auditee is a listed company, the engagement is complex and/or there is a risk that the audit report might not be appropriate in the circumstances; in such cases a more extensive review will be required. Additionally, the policies and procedures should ensure that the documentation of a review includes confirmation that:

    (i) the firm's procedures for engagement quality control reviews have been followed;

    (ii) the review was completed before the audit report was signed and dated; and

    (iii) the reviewer is not aware of any unresolved matters that would cause him/her to believe that significant judgments made by the engagement team, or the conclusions it reached, were not appropriate (ISQC 1, para 42).

(f) Monitoring

As indicated in Figure 16.1, an audit firm's quality control system should include policies and procedures designed to provide it with reasonable assurance that the system is relevant, adequate, operating effectively and complied with in practice. ISQC 1 (paras 48–55) specifies that such policies and procedures should include requiring:

(i) one or more partners, or other person(s), with sufficient, appropriate experience and authority to be responsible for monitoring the firm's quality controls on an ongoing basis. (For convenience, we refer to a such person as the firm's audit quality control compliance partner[11];

(ii) ongoing monitoring of the firm's quality control system which includes, on a cyclical basis, the inspection of at least one completed audit engagement for each engagement partner;

(iii) evaluation of the effect of any deficiencies uncovered by the monitoring process and determination of whether they are:
  - 'one-off' in nature (hence, not indicating a fundamental failing of the firms' quality control system), or
  - systemic, repetitive or otherwise significant (thus necessitating prompt corrective action);

(iv) communication of deficiencies uncovered by the monitoring process, together with recommended corrective action(s), to the engagement partner(s) concerned, and other relevant personnel. The corrective action(s) may include:
  - taking remedial action in relation to a particular audit engagement and/or one or more members of the relevant audit team;
  - communicating the findings to those responsible for the firm's training and professional development;
  - effecting changes to the firm's quality control policies and procedures;
  - taking disciplinary action against those who fail to comply with the firm's policies and procedures – especially those who repeatedly do so;

(v) communication, at least annually, of the monitoring procedures performed and the results obtained to the relevant engagement partners and other appropriate individuals within the firm (including the firm's chief executive officer or its managing board of partners) so as to enable those responsible, if the circumstances warrant it, to instigate corrective action.

---

[11] A firm's audit quality control compliance partner is usually (but not necessarily) the partner with responsibility for developing and implementing the firm's quality control system referred to in sub-section (a) above in connection with leadership responsibilities for quality in audit firms.

Audit firms are additionally required to establish policies and procedures (including the provision of clearly defined channels for firm personnel to raise concerns without fear of reprisals) so as to provide them with reasonable assurance that they deal appropriately with:

(i) complaints and allegations that work performed by the firm fails to comply with professional standards and/or legal and regulatory requirements; and/or

(ii) allegations of non-compliance with the firm's quality controls.

Although not specifically identified in Figure 16.1, as might be expected, documentation of the quality control system is important. ISQC 1 (paras 57, 58) requires audit firms to establish policies and procedures designed to ensure that the operation of each element of the quality control system is appropriately documented and that the documentation is retained for a sufficient period to enable those responsible for monitoring activities to evaluate the firm's compliance with its quality control system.

16.3.3 Engagement partners' responsibility for securing high quality audits

Although the six elements of an audit firm's quality control system outlined above provide a framework for ensuring that high quality audits are performed by the firm, responsibility for the quality of an individual audit engagement is that of the engagement partner. The responsibility of this partner is limited in scope in that it is restricted to the particular audit engagement but, in respect of that engagement, it is all embracing. The engagement partner is responsible for the quality of all the audit work performed during the engagement, for ensuring compliance with the firm's quality control policies and procedures throughout the engagement, and for finalising and signing the audit report on behalf of the firm. Whilst acknowledging this overall responsibility for the audit engagement, ISA 220 (IAASB, 2009b) identifies six duties relating to audit quality for which the engagement partner is responsible, namely:

(a) providing leadership for quality throughout the audit engagement;

(b) ensuring audit team members comply with relevant ethical requirements;

(c) ensuring appropriate acceptance or continuance procedures are followed;

(d) ensuring that, collectively, the audit team has the appropriate capabilities, competence and time to complete the audit to the required standard;

(e) the performance of audit work throughout the engagement;

(f) documentation of the engagement.

These responsibilities are summarised in Figure 16.2 and discussed below. By comparing Figures 16.1 and 16.2 it may be seen that the quality control responsibilities of the engagement partner reflect those of the audit firm.

Figure 16.2: Engagement partner's responsibilities for securing a high quality audit

Responsibility	Contribution to securing a high quality audit engagement
	The engagement partner should:
Leadership responsibilities for quality during the audit engagement	emphasise to audit team members, the importance of, *inter alia*, the audit engagement being conducted in accordance with professional standards, applicable legal and regulatory requirements, and the firm's quality control policies and procedures;
Compliance with relevant ethical requirements	ensure audit team members comply with ethical standards, and any threats to independence are identified and appropriate safeguards are applied;
Performance of acceptance or continuance procedures	ensure the firm's procedures for accepting the audit engagement have been followed;
Adequacy of the audit team's capabilities, competence and time	ensure that, collectively, the audit team and any external experts to be used on the audit have the capabilities, competence and time required to complete a high quality audit;
Performance of audit work during the engagement	ensure audit work is appropriately directed, supervised and reviewed and that audit team members consult appropriate personnel when difficult or contentious issues are encountered;
Documentation of the engagement	ensure there is proper documentation of audit work performed, issues relating to compliance with ethical standards, conclusions on compliance with independence and engagement acceptance requirements, and audit team consultations.

(a) *Leadership responsibilities for quality of the audit engagement*

As noted above, the audit engagement partner is responsible for all aspects of the audit engagement. In order to ensure that a high quality audit is performed, the engagement partner is required to convey to members of the audit team, by setting an example and through communication, the importance of:
  (i)   performing work that complies with professional standards and applicable legal and regulatory requirements;
  (ii) complying with the firm's quality control policies and procedures;
  (iii) issuing an audit report that is appropriate in the circumstances;
  (iv) audit team members' ability to raise concerns without fear of reprisals;
  (v)   quality as an essential element in performing the audit (ISA 220, para A3).

(b) *Compliance with relevant ethical requirements*

A key responsibility of the audit engagement partner is ensuring that all members of the audit team comply with the profession's ethical requirements; that is, the fundamental principles of integrity, objectivity, professional competence and due care, confidentiality and professional behaviour.[12] However ISA

---

[12] These principles, which are specified and explained in the *IESBA Code* (IESBA, 2009) and the Auditing Practices Board's Ethical Standards, are discussed in Chapter 3.

220 highlights, in particular, the engagement partner's responsibility for forming a conclusion about the compliance of the audit engagement with independence requirements. In order to form this conclusion, the engagement partner is to:

(a) Obtain relevant information from the firm and, where applicable, network firms,[13] to identify and evaluate circumstances and relationships that create threats to independence;

(b) Evaluate information on identified breaches, if any, of the firm's independence policies and procedures to determine whether they create a threat to independence for the audit engagement; and

(c) Take appropriate action to eliminate such threats or reduce them to an acceptable level by applying safeguards,[14]. . . (para 11)

If the firm's independence is in doubt, the engagement should not be accepted or, if already accepted and appropriate safeguards cannot be applied, the firm should withdraw from the engagement. If the independence of the (proposed) engagement partner, or that of a member of the engagement team, is open to question, the person(s) concerned should not be involved in the audit engagement.

(c) Performance of acceptance or continuance procedures

We note in section 16.3.2(c) that audit firms are required to establish policies and procedures designed to ensure that the propriety of accepting new or continuing audit clients, and specific audit engagements, is properly evaluated. However, ISA 220, para 12, requires each audit engagement partner to be satisfied that their firm's procedures have been followed, and its conclusion about accepting the audit engagement is appropriate. If the engagement partner becomes aware of information which, had it been known earlier, the firm would have declined the engagement, s/he is required to communicate the information to the firm promptly so that appropriate action may be taken.

(d) Adequacy of the audit team's capabilities, competence and time

While assignment of the engagement partner and audit team members to an audit engagement is the responsibility of the audit firm, ISA 220, para 14, requires the engagement partner to be satisfied that, collectively, the engagement team and any external experts to be used during the audit have the appropriate capabilities, competence and time to perform the engagement in accordance with professional standards and applicable legal and regulatory requirements, and to enable an appropriate audit report to be issued.

---

[13] A network firm is defined as a firm that belongs to a network. A network is:
  A larger structure:
  (i) That is aimed at cooperation, and
  (ii) That is clearly aimed at profit or cost-sharing or shares common ownership, control or management, common quality control policies and procedures, common business strategy, the use of a common brand name, or a significant part of professional resources. (ISA 220, para 7j)

[14] Independence threats and safeguards are discussed in detail in Chapter 4.

(e) Performance of audit work

Given that the engagement partner is responsible for the quality of work performed during the audit, it is evident that s/he is responsible for ensuring the work is properly directed, supervised and reviewed. As these aspects of an audit engagement are discussed in detail in Chapter 7, section 7.5.3, we do not elaborate on them here. However, in addition to ensuring that audit work is properly directed, supervised and reviewed, the audit engagement partner is required to be satisfied, particularly in relation to difficult or contentious issues, that:

    (i)   audit team members have undertaken appropriate consultation with other members of the audit team and, when required by the circumstances, with appropriate people within or, if necessary, outside the audit firm;

   (ii)   the nature and scope of, and conclusions resulting from, such consultations are agreed between the consulting and consulted party;

  (iii)   the conclusions resulting from such consultations have been implemented (ISA 220, para 18).

A further element of the engagement partner's responsibility for the quality of work performed during the audit of listed company clients, and of other clients where the audit firm considers it appropriate, is ensuring that the audit engagement is subject to an independent quality control review. This requirement is discussed in section 16.3.2(e) above.

(f) Documentation

In earlier chapters we have emphasised that auditing standards require each step of the audit process to be fully and properly documented. However, in addition to ensuring that all audit work performed is properly documented, the engagement partner (and/or other appropriate members of the audit team) is required to document matters relating to the quality control responsibilities outlined above. More specifically, ISA 220 requires the audit documentation to include:

    (a) Issues identified with respect to compliance with relevant ethical requirements and how they were resolved.

    (b) Conclusions on compliance with independence requirements that apply to the audit engagement, and any relevant discussions with the firm that support these conclusions.

    (c) Conclusions reached regarding the acceptance and continuance of client relationships and audit engagements.

    (d) The nature and scope of, and conclusions resulting from, consultations undertaken during the course of the audit engagement. (para 24)

16.3.4 Firms' oversight of the quality of audit engagements

In order for audit firms to be assured that audits conducted by their firm are of a high quality, they need to ensure that all of the quality controls outlined above are adhered to during every audit engagement. As indicated in section 16.3.2(f), each audit firm is expected to appoint an audit quality control compliance partner. In multi-office firms, these senior audit partners need to satisfy themselves (usually by visiting each office of their firm) that each office of the firm (and each audit engagement partner in that office) is adhering to the firm's quality control policies and procedures and performing high quality audits.

Where audit firms have a number of offices internationally, intra-firm quality control reviews may be conducted, usually on a regular basis (every three to five years). These involve a team of about five senior audit quality control compliance partners (drawn from different countries where the firm has offices) visiting various offices of the firm around the world to review the adequacy of, and level of compliance with, the firm's quality control procedures. Such reviews are internal to the firms concerned and are designed to ensure that all offices of the firm (internationally) maintain an adequate and effective system of quality control. This helps to reduce to a minimum the risk of poor quality audits being performed by the firm and, thus, to maintain, or enhance, the reputation of the firm for high quality professional audit work.

16.4 REGULATORS' MEASURES FOR SECURING HIGH QUALITY AUDITS[15]

16.4.1 Overview of monitoring of auditors' performance

In addition to audit firms developing, implementing and monitoring systems of quality control, in the UK, as in countries such as the USA, Canada, Australia and New Zealand and in all European Union (EU) Member States, 'quality control monitoring mechanisms' have been implemented. Although different countries use varying titles for their monitoring schemes, they all have two key objectives, namely:

---

[15] This section contains the acronyms of a large number of regulatory bodies. As these can be rather confusing, although each acronym is defined in the text when first used, it is also included in the Glossary of Terms provided in the front of this book on page xxi.

- to ensure auditors meet their obligation to society to perform audits in accordance with the profession's standards and with regulatory and legal requirements;
- to sustain public confidence in the auditing profession (and the audit function) by demonstrating a concern for maintaining a high standard of audit work.

We explain in Chapter 5 (section 5.3.1) that, in the UK and Ireland, only individuals and firms who are registered with a Recognised Supervisory Body (RSB) are eligible for appointment as a company's auditor.[16] In order to become an RSB, a professional body must have rules and practices regarding, *inter alia*:

(i) auditors performing audit work properly and with integrity;
(ii) persons not being appointed as auditors in circumstances where their independence may be compromised;
(iii) auditors taking steps to safeguard their independence from significant threats, and documenting identified threats and the safeguards applied;
(iv) technical standards to be applied in audit work;
(v) admitting, disciplining and excluding members;
(vi) monitoring and enforcing compliance with the RSB's rules.

Thus, monitoring registered auditors' compliance with ethical and auditing standards is a condition of a professional body gaining RSB status – and has been since the RSBs were established in 1991.[17] Monitoring fulfils both a 'carrot' and a 'stick' function. It provides the opportunity for auditors to receive constructive advice on best practice, compliance issues and/or training needs; however, if an auditor is found not to be complying with auditing and ethical

---

[16] It should be recalled from Chapter 5, footnote 3, that in this book we use the terms company auditor, statutory auditor and registered auditor to mean an individual or firm who is appointed as a company's auditor in accordance with the Companies Act (CA) 2006.

[17] Although monitoring of auditors' performance has been required in the UK and Ireland since 1991, it was not required in all EU Member States until the *Statutory Audit Directive* (EU, 2006) became effective in 2008. This Directive requires all Member States to ensure that:

   . . . all statutory auditors and audit firms are subject to a system of quality assurance which meets at least the following criteria:

   (a) the quality assurance system shall be . . . independent of the reviewed statutory auditors and audit firms and subject to public oversight . . . ; . . .
   (b) the persons who carry out quality assurance reviews shall have appropriate professional education and relevant experience in statutory audit and financial reporting combined with specific training on quality assurance reviews; . . .
   (c) the scope of the quality assurance review, supported by adequate testing of selected audit files, shall include an assessment of compliance with applicable auditing standards and independence requirements, of the quantity and quality of resources spent, of the audit fees charged and of the internal quality control system of the audit firm; . . .
   (d) quality assurance reviews shall take place at least every six years;
   (e) the overall results of the quality assurance system shall be published annually;
   (f) recommendations of quality reviews shall be followed up by the statutory auditor or audit firm within a reasonable period. (art. 29, para 1)

standards and other audit regulations, sanctions may result – including the ultimate sanction of loss of audit registration.

A further requirement for recognition as an RSB is participation in arrangements for:
  (i)   setting technical auditing standards and standards relating to auditors' integrity and independence;
  (ii) independent monitoring of the audits of listed companies and other entities in which there is major public interest; and
  (iii) independent investigation, for disciplinary purposes, of public interest cases (i.e., those which raise, or appear to raise, important issues affecting the public interest).

Since April 2004 (following the UK Government's post-Enron review of regulation of the accountancy profession in the UK), the Financial Reporting Council (FRC) has held overall responsibility for these activities. Until July 2012, it discharged this responsibility through its operating bodies, specifically, the Auditing Practices Board (APB), the Professional Oversight Board (POB) and the Accountancy and Actuarial Discipline Board (AADB), with input from, and working collaboratively with, the RSBs. Since July 2012 (when the FRC was restructured), the APB has been replaced by the Audit and Assurance Council (an advisory council of the FRC's Codes and Standards Committee), the AADB and POB have been superseded by the Case Management Committee and Monitoring Committee, respectively. (The former and current structure of the FRC is presented diagrammatically on page xix at the front of this book.)

From 1991, when monitoring of auditors' performance commenced, until 2004, the monitoring function of the RSBs was discharged by two units:
  (i) the Joint Monitoring Unit (JMU), which monitored auditors registered with the Institutes of Chartered Accountants in England and Wales (ICAEW), of Scotland (ICAS) and in Ireland (ICAI); and
  (ii) the ACCA monitoring unit, which monitored auditors registered with the Associations of Chartered Certified Accountants (ACCA) and of Authorised Public Accountants (AAPA).

The JMU was established as a limited company, jointly owned by the ICAEW (with an 80 per cent ownership share) and ICAS and ICAI (each with a ten per cent ownership share). However, all JMU staff were ICAEW employees. The ACCA monitoring unit was established as a component of the ACCA's Regulation and Monitoring Department.

In 2005, in order to meet the requirements of the *Statutory Audit Directive* (EU, 2006), each of the three Institutes established its own system for monitoring its registered auditors. In the UK, the ICAEW established a Quality Assurance

Directorate (QAD) to monitor the work of all of its members, including its registered auditors, and the former JMU staff transferred to the QAD. Similarly, ICAS established its own audit monitoring unit. Auditors registered with the two Associations have continued to be monitored by the ACCA's monitoring unit. In compliance with the *Statutory Audit Directive*, the activities of these three monitoring units in the UK are overseen by the FRC's Conduct Committee.[18]

In Ireland, company auditors may be registered with any one of six RSBs – ACCA, ICAEW, ICAS, ICAI, the Institute of Certified Public Accountants in Ireland (ICPAI) and the Institute of Incorporated Public Accountants (IIPA). Auditors registered with the ACCA, ICAEW and ICAS are monitored by the monitoring units mentioned above. The ICAI has established an independent Chartered Accountants' Regulatory Board (CARB) with responsibility for regulating ICAI members (including the monitoring of ICAI registered auditors). The monitoring activities of the six RSBs recognised in Ireland are overseen by the Irish Auditing & Accounting Supervisory Authority (IAASA) – an independent body established in January 2006 with responsibility for overseeing the accountancy profession in Ireland. In effect, it is the Irish equivalent of the FRC in the UK.

In addition to the changes noted above, between 2004 and 2012, monitoring (or, more correctly, inspections) of the audits of companies listed on the London Stock Exchange, and other entities in whose financial condition there is a major public interest, were conducted by the Audit Inspection Unit (AIU) of the POB. In July 2012, the AIU was renamed the Audit Quality Review (AQR) team and, as noted earlier, the POB was superseded by the FRC's monitoring Committee. These inspections (or quality reviews) complement the monitoring activities of the RSBs.

16.4.2   Monitoring by the RSBs

The remit of the RSBs' monitoring units is to ascertain whether auditors registered with the RSB in question are complying with the audit regulations.[19]

---

[18] The *Statutory Audit Directive* (art. 32) provides:
    (2) All statutory auditors shall be subject to public oversight.
    (3) The system of public oversight shall be governed by non-practitioners who are knowledgeable in the areas relevant to statutory audit.... Persons involved in the governance of the public oversight system shall be selected in accordance with an independent and transparent nomination procedure.
    (4) The system for public oversight shall have the ultimate responsibility for the oversight of:
      (a) the approval and registration of statutory auditors and audit firms;
      (b) the adoption of standards on professional ethics, internal quality control of audit firms and auditing, and
      (c) continuing education, quality assurance and investigative and disciplinary systems.

[19] The audit regulations are primarily derived from the criteria specified in the CA 2006 (Schedule 10, Part 2) which RSBs must meet in order to be recognised as RSBs. However, each RSB may impose additional requirements, as it sees fit, on its members.

Thus, their monitoring activities embrace registered auditors' compliance with, *inter alia*, auditing, ethical and quality control standards, and regulations relating to independence, maintaining professional competence and professional indemnity insurance.[20] The focus of monitoring is generally the audit firm rather than individual auditors. At 31 December 2011, there were 7,738 registered audit firms in the UK and Ireland (excluding auditors registered with the IIPA)[21] and a further 107 individuals and firms were registered with the IIPA. However, the number and profile of firms registered with the ICAEW, ICAS and ICAI on the one hand, and the ACCA[22] and ICPAI on the other, differ markedly. In December 2011, 5,095 firms were registered with three Institutes of Chartered Accountants; about 47 per cent were sole practitioners, some 50 per cent had between two and ten principals, and nearly three per cent had more than ten principals. The Institutes' registered audit firms audited all of the companies listed on the London and Irish Stock Exchanges.[23] In contrast, 2,643 firms were registered with the ACCA and ICPAI; approximately 63 per cent were sole practitioners, nearly 37 per cent had between two and ten principals, and only seven firms (all registered with ACCA) had more than ten principals. No ACCA or ICPAI registered auditors had listed company clients (POB, 2012; IAASA, 2011).

In general, the monitoring process, which is depicted in Figure 16.3, involves both desktop reviews and firm visits; however, monitoring by the ACCA and IIPA tends to rely primarily on firm visits. The *Statutory Audit Directive* requires all statutory auditors to be subject to monitoring visits at least once every six years[24] but, where a firm is identified as possessing a number of risk factors, monitoring visits occur more frequently (generally between one and three years depending on the firm's level of risk). According to the IAASA (2006, p. 108), the risk factors that increase the likelihood of more frequent monitoring visits include the following:

---

[20] As reflected in Figure 16.5, the AQR team (and its predecessor, AIU) is responsible for reviewing the 'firm-wide' quality control policies and procedures of any firm which audits ten or more major public interest entities and also a sample of the audits of such entities conducted by these firms. Monitoring these firms' audits of non-major public interest entities remains the responsibility of the RSB with which the firm is registered.

[21] Unlike the other RSBs (which register only audit firms), the IIPA registers both individuals and firms as auditors (IAASA, 2011, p. 100).

[22] Auditors registered with the AAPA are included with those registered with the ACCA.

[23] In 2011, 99 of the largest 100 companies listed on the London Stock Exchange (FTSE 100 companies) were audited by the Big Four audit firms (Deloitte, Ernst & Young, KPMG and PricewaterhouseCoopers); these firms also audited 95.6 per cent of the 250 next largest companies listed on the London Stock Exchange (FTSE 250 companies). The remainder of these large companies were audited by BDO (one FTSE 100 and five FTSE 250 companies) and Grant Thornton (five FTSE 250 companies) (POB, 2011a, p. 60)

[24] The *Statutory Audit Directive* refers to 'quality assurance reviews' rather than monitoring visits: see footnote 17.

Figure 16.3: Generalised outline of the RSBs' monitoring process

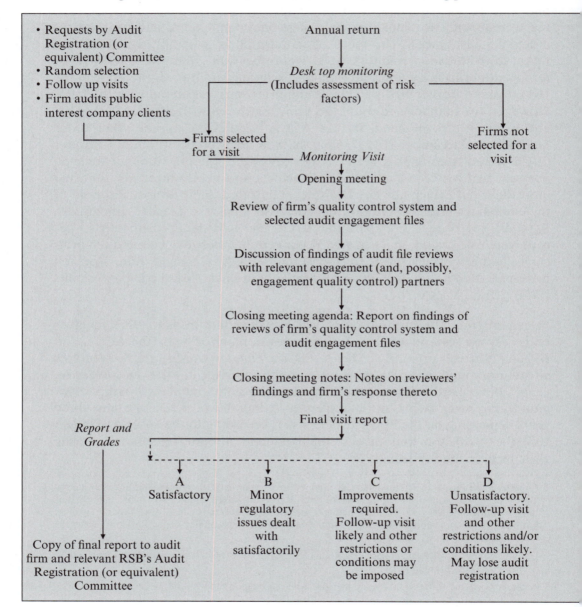

- the number of audit clients;
- the type of audit clients; specifically, specialist or public interest clients and clients in regulated industries such as credit institutions, pension funds, insurance brokers and investment firms;
- deficiencies detected during the last monitoring visit;
- an indication of quality control problems within the firm;

- a history of complaints against the firm;
- failure to make an annual return (as required) to the relevant RSB;
- length of time since the last visit.

(a) *Desktop reviews:* In general, registered audit firms are required to submit (electronically) completed annual returns to their RSB. With the aid of computer software, these are reviewed for any inconsistencies or omitted information and subjected to a risk assessment. Some monitoring units, such as the ICAEW's QAD, have an extensive list of risk factors in addition to those noted above – for example, checking whether the firm conducts an annual audit compliance review, updates its accounting disclosure checklist and standard audit plan, and/or has an audit manual or similar document which is updated regularly. Where significant risk factors are identified a risk report may be generated.

(b) *Monitoring visits:* In the year to 31 December 2011, a total of 1,246 monitoring visits were made to registered auditors in the UK and Ireland.[25] In general, audit firms are selected for visits in one of the following four ways:
- At the request of the Audit Registration (or equivalent) Committee of the RSB with which the firm is registered. These visits are usually prompted by complaints lodged against the firm in question. In the year to 31 December 2011, 94 firms (nearly 8 per cent) were selected for visits on this basis.
- Random selection. In the year to 31 December 2011, 923 firms (about 74 per cent of the total) were selected for visits at random – without reference to risk factors identified by desktop monitoring.
- As a result of heightened risk (identified from the assessment of risk factors). This applied to 179 firms (approximately 14 per cent of visits) in the year to 31 December 2011. This category includes follow-up visits which occur when a previous monitoring visit to the firm in question identified deficiencies and the firm undertook to implement improvements.
- Firms have public interest company clients which are not subject to inspections by the AIU (or AQR team). In the year to 31 December 2011, this basis of selection applied to 50 firms (4 per cent of visits) – 49 ICAEW audit registrants and one ICAS registrant.[26]

As may be seen from Figure 16.3, a monitoring visit begins with an opening meeting. At this meeting, the visiting reviewers discuss with the audit quality control compliance partner (and other audit partners who wish, or are requested

---

[25] In the year to 31 December 2011, 373 visits were made to ACCA audit registrants, 716 to ICAEW registrants, 56 to ICAS registrants, 22 to ICAI registrants, 62 to ICPAI registrants and 17 to IIPA registrants (IAASA, 2011; POB, 2012).

[26] The statistics reported in this paragraph are sourced from IAASA (2011) and POB (2012).

by the reviewers or the firm, to be present), the firm's quality control policies and procedures and their adequacy for ensuring compliance with auditing, ethical and quality control standards and other audit regulations. As noted in section 16.3.2(f), a key component of an audit firm's quality control system is 'monitoring' – internal monitoring by the firm to ensure, amongst other things, that the firm, its audit engagement partners and its audit staff are complying with auditing, ethical and quality control standards and other audit regulations. It is not, therefore, surprising that a significant element of a monitoring visit involves reviewing the firm's quality control monitoring process, deficiencies detected by the process and the remedial actions the firm has implemented.

During the opening meeting, the reviewers also discuss other elements of the firm's quality control system – including its policies and procedures relating to client and engagement acceptance and continuance, the capabilities and competence of audit personnel, and audit engagement performance. The reviewers also identify the individual audit engagement files and other records they wish to review.

The reviewers then conduct a detailed review of the firm's quality control system and the selected audit engagement files. When reviewing the files, the reviewers discuss their findings with the relevant engagement partner(s), and any minor issues are clarified and resolved. Major points arising from the reviews, together with deficiencies the reviewers have found in the firm's quality control policies and procedures – and/or compliance therewith – are summarised in a closing meeting agenda. These points are usually expressed as actual or potential instances of non-compliance with auditing, ethical or quality control standards, or other audit regulations, resulting in risks to the firm's audit work.

At the conclusion of the visit, the reviewers meet with the audit quality control compliance partner and other partners who wish, or are requested, to be present at a closing meeting. The partners give the firm's initial response to the issues identified by the reviewers and the reviewers' suggestions for improvement. The firm is usually requested to send notes of the closing meeting ('the closing meeting notes') to the reviewers noting, in particular, its response to matters raised during the visit and how it plans to address them.

Upon receipt of the firm's closing meeting notes, the reviewers finalise their visit report. A copy of the final report is sent to both the audit firm and the relevant RSB's Audit Registration (or equivalent) Committee. As indicated in Figure 16.3, monitoring visits result in one of the outcomes we have designated Grades A to D. The grades signify the following outcomes:
- *Grade A* – there are no compliance or regulatory issues that require attention.

- *Grade B* – any regulatory issues have been dealt with adequately in the firm's closing meeting notes and no further RSB action is required. [However, information on the implementation of remedial action(s) agreed at the closing meeting may be required];
- *Grade C* – the review findings are less than satisfactory and improvements are required. Depending on the severity of non-compliance with auditing, ethical or quality control standards, or other audit regulations, the audit firm may be required to provide information on the implementation of agreed improvements or follow-up visits may be arranged to ensure required remedial action has been taken. Additional restrictions or conditions may also be imposed; for example, the imposition of continuing education/training requirements for audit staff and/or partners, or a prohibition on the firm accepting new audit clients until required improvements have been made;
- *Grade D* – the review findings are unsatisfactory and the relevant RSB's Audit Registration (or equivalent) Committee may take one of the following regulatory actions:
  - impose conditions such as requiring a follow-up visit to confirm that remedial action has been taken;
  - impose restrictions or conditions on the firm's registration such as prohibiting the acceptance of new audit clients for a specified period and/or until specified improvements have been made, or specifying that identified audit engagement partners are not to be given responsibility for audit engagements until they have undertaken further training;
  - in very serious cases, the suspension or withdrawal of audit registration.

The results of monitoring visits by (or on behalf of) the RSBs for the years 1992 to 2011 are presented in Figure 16.4.

As might be expected, the size of the team of reviewers and the time taken for monitoring visits varies with the size of audit firms. Some teams of reviewers may comprise just a couple of members, while others may have nine or ten (or more) reviewers; similarly, while visits to single office practitioners may be completed within one day, full monitoring visits to large firms may take 15 to 20 (or more) days. Additionally, as we noted earlier, audit firms with public interest clients may be subject to inspections by the FRC's Audit Quality Review (AQR) team in addition to monitoring by their RSB.

16.4.3 Monitoring by the AQR team (and predecessor Audit Inspection Unit)

As noted in section 16.4.1, in April 2004 the FRC was assigned responsibility for, *inter alia*, overseeing the independent monitoring of the audits of UK listed

Figure 16.4:   Results of visits by the RSB's monitoring units 1992 to 2011[27]

Years: 1992–2011		92	93	94	95	96	97	98	99	00	01	02	03	04	05	06	07	08	09	10	11
ICAEW, ICAS and ICAI monitoring visits Total visits	No.	291	312	793	1087	1098	1033	937	1066	880	957	1081	1030	1099	1023	826	1058	1130	897	907	794
Outcomes	%	%	%	%	%	%	%	%	%	%	%	%	%	%	%	%	%	%	%	%	%
A & B Satisfactory		40	31	38	63	60	63	65	56	57	63	66	65	66	69	61	58	57	61	59	53
C Appropriate plans for improvement		—	58	48	22	24	26	28	33	32	25	25	22	21	24	27	30	25	22	21	22
D Restriction on audit registration		—	5	7	9	10	7	4	8	9	8	6	10	10		9	9	12	12	11	9
D Audit registration · withdrawn		—	4	4	3	3	2	1	1	1	2	1	2	2	7	3	3	2	2	3	3
· surrendered			2	3	3	3	2	2	2	1	2	2	1	1							
Concerns about audit work or non-compliance with regulations				—	—	—	—	—	—	—	—	—	—	—	—			—	—		—
Not graded*		60																4	3	6	13
ACCA unit visits Total visits	No.	297	409	517	394	833	717	475	535	468	605	695	456	432	462	371	285	401	425	351	373
Outcomes	%	%	%	%	%	%	%	%	%	%	%	%	%	%	%	%	%	%	%	%	%
A & B Satisfactory		45	44	49	54	54	56	53	52	46	46	45	55	57	59	49	56	52	56	62	56
C Not satisfactory:																					
C+ Revisit a low priority		27	27	21	16	17	12	12	13	15	18	13	10	13	14	17	23	24	15	11	12
C- Early revisit required		20	19	12	14	17	14	16	19	22	19	21	13	11	6	9	7	8	5	3	4
D Referred to Authorisation Committee		8	10	18	16	12	18	19	16	17	17	21	22	19	21	25	14	16	24	24	28

*Situations where grading cannot be applied in accordance with specified criteria, for example, where the firm wishes to maintain its audit registration but has no audit clients

Source: ICAEW, ICAS and ICAI Reports, and ACCA Reports, to the Department of Trade and Industry 1992 to 2004; POB, 2005 to 2010, 2011b, 2012; IAASA, 2006 to 2011

---

[27] As may be deduced from Figure 16.4, the grading system of the Institutes' and the ACCA's monitoring units differ slightly. Monitoring visits referred to the ACCA's Authorisation Committee are subject to regulatory action but details are not disclosed by the ACCA.

companies and other entities in which there is a major public interest. Between April 2004 and July 2012, it delegated this responsibility to its Professional Oversight Board (POB); the POB fulfilled the function by means of its Audit Inspection Unit (AIU). In July 2012, the AIU was replaced by the AQR team and the POB was superseded by the FRC's Monitoring Committee. The scope of AQR is determined annually by the FRC's Conduct Committee[28] but, since 2004, it has included the following entities:

- all UK incorporated companies with listed securities (equity or debt);
- UK unquoted companies, groups of companies and limited liability partnerships whose group turnover exceeds £500 million;
- UK incorporated building societies; (until 1 April 2011, only building societies with assets exceeding £1,000 million were included);
- private sector pension schemes with more than £1,000 million of assets or more than 20,000 members;
- charities with incoming resources exceeding £100 million;
- UK Open-ended Investment Companies and UK Unit Trusts managed by a fund manager with more than £1,000 million of UK funds under management;
- from 1 April 2010, all UK incorporated banks not included in another category.

The FRC (2013) explains the remit of AQR as follows:

> The Audit Quality Review (AQR) team monitors the quality of the audits of listed and other major public interest entities and the policies and procedures supporting audit quality at the major audit firms in the UK. The overall objective of our work is to monitor and promote improvements in the quality of auditing of listed and other major public interest entities. . . .
>
> There are currently ten audit firms undertaking more than ten audits within our scope ('major firms'). These firms are subject to inspections which include a review of their policies and procedures supporting audit quality. The largest four of these audit firms [Deloitte, Ernst & Young, KPMG and PricewaterhouseCoopers] are subject to inspection on an annual basis and the other major firms on an extended cycle of up to three years. Our work at other firms [which audit between one and ten major public interest entities] is limited to periodic reviews of one or more audits within our scope (with the review of these firms' policies and procedures being delegated to the professional body [i.e., RSB] with which they are registered for audit purposes). (FRC, 2013, p. 1)[29]

A summary of the scope of the AQR team and RSB monitoring units is presented in Figure 16.5.

---

[28] Prior to July 2012, the scope of AIU inspections was determined annually by the POB. The scope of inspections for the subsequent year was reported in an appendix to each of the AIU's annual reports (AIU, 2005 to 2012 inclusive).

[29] The remit of the AIU was explained in almost identical terms (see, for example, POB, 2012, pp. 31–32). In 2012 there were approximately 40 'other firms' (which audit between one and ten major public interest entities).

Figure 16.5:   Summary of scope of the AQR team and RSB monitoring units

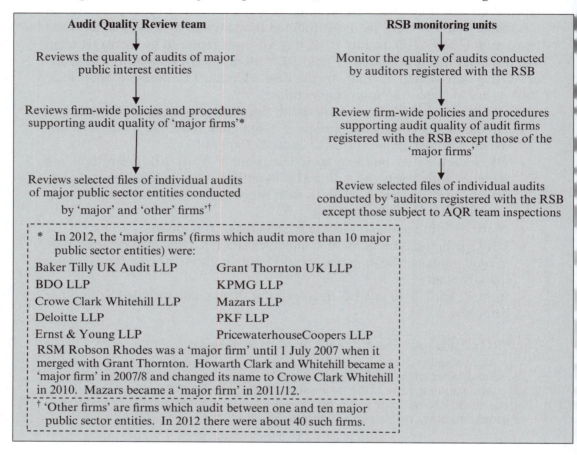

As indicated in Figure 16.5, the AQR team (like its predecessor AIU) reviews both firm-wide policies and procedures that support audit quality and the quality of the audits of major public interest entities. The FRC notes that the reviews cover but are not restricted to:

> . . . compliance with the requirements of relevant standards and other aspects of the regulatory framework for auditing. This includes the Auditing Standards, Ethical Standards and Quality Control Standards for auditors issued by the FRC and the Audit Regulations issued by the relevant professional bodies [that is, the RSBs]. . . . [The] reviews of firm-wide procedures are wide-ranging in nature and include an assessment of how the culture within firms impacts on audit quality. (FRC, 2013, p. 1)

More specifically, the firm-wide reviews of policies and procedures cover:

- the quality of leadership within the firm;
- independence and ethics;
- performance evaluation and other human resources matters;

- audit methodology, training and guidance;
- client risk assessment and acceptance/continuance procedures and decisions;
- consultation during the audit and the review of completed audit work;
- audit quality monitoring (AIU, 2012, p. 18).

Like the RSB monitoring units, the AQR team applies a risk-based approach to selecting individual audits for review. The FRC explains:

> [The] reviews of individual audits place emphasis on the appropriateness of key audit judgements made in reaching the audit opinion and the sufficiency and appropriateness of the audit evidence obtained. (FRC, 2013, p. 1)

The AQR team's visits to the 'major firms' follow the same general process as those of the RSBs' monitoring units. They include an opening meeting, a detailed review of the firm's system of quality control and selected engagement files, discussions with key audit partners (including the firm's audit quality control compliance partner, relevant engagement partners and engagement quality control reviewers), a closing meeting and the preparation of review reports. The reviewers:

> . . . seek to identify areas where improvements are . . . needed in order to safeguard audit quality and/or comply with regulatory requirements and to agree action plans with the firms designed to achieve these improvements. . . . [They] also assess the extent to which each firm has addressed the findings arising from [its] previous inspection. (AIU, 2012, p. 18)

At the conclusion of a visit, the AQR team sends a private report to the Audit Registration (or equivalent) Committee of the RSB with which the firm is registered. For a 'major firm', the report contains the key findings of the AQR team's review of the firm's quality control policies and procedures and its review of individual audits, together with an overall recommendation on whether the audit registration of the firm should be continued. For 'other firms' (those which audit less than ten major public interest entities), the report sets out significant findings of the reviews of individual audits undertaken by the firm together with an overall assessment of the firm's audit quality. In each case, the reports are discussed with senior partners of the relevant firm before they are finalised (AIU, 2012; FRC, 2013). The FRC (2013, p. 2) notes: "A key element of our reporting arrangements is that firms are expected to provide copies of [the] reports to the directors of the audited entities concerned and confirm to us [that is, the AQR team] that they have done so."

In addition to the private reports, the FRC publishes an annual report on Audit Quality Reviews conducted during the year. This provides an overview of the findings of the AQR team and a summary of its activities. It also publishes annually an individual report on each 'major firm', and a summary report on 'other firms', reviewed during the year.

Figure 16.6: **Number of audit files reviewed, and results of inspections of the audits of FTSE 350 companies, by the AIU 2005–2012**

Year to 31 March	2005	2006	2007	2008	2009		2010		2011		2012	
No. of audit files reviewed	27	77	103	90	92		93		92		94	
No. of audits of FTSE 350 companies reviewed	N/A	38	47	N/A	25		38		35		36	
Results of reviews of FTSE 350 company reviews					No.	%	No.	%	No.	%	No.	%
Good with minor improvements required	Information not available				11	44	19	50	22	63	20	56
Acceptable but with improvements required					10	40	15	39	12	34	13	36
Significant improvements required					4	16	4	11	1	3	3	8

Source: AIU, 2006 to 201?

As may be seen from Figure 16.6, during each year between 2008 and 2012, inclusive, the AIU inspected the audits of about 92 major public interest entities. In the year to 31 March 2009, only 25 (27 per cent) of the 92 audits examined were of FTSE 350 companies[30] but, in subsequent years about 36 (40 per cent) of the audits examined were of these companies. Figure 16.6 also reveals that, in most years, less than 60 per cent of the audits of FTSE 350 companies were found to be 'good with minor improvements required' and, although the number judged to be 'requiring significant improvements' has fallen since 2009, in the year to 31 March 2012, three such audits were identified.

16.4.4 Effectiveness of monitoring auditors' performance

The results of RSB monitoring visits and AIU inspections presented in Figures 16.4 and 16.6, respectively, suggest that, in general, auditors' performance has improved since monitoring/inspections commenced. Perhaps not surprisingly, greatest improvement was noted in the early years, as audit firms became more acquainted with the standard of work required and more accustomed to having their performance monitored. However, the proportion of RSB monitoring visits resulting in a satisfactory outcome (Grades A and B) has remained fairly stable since the turn of the twenty-first century. Nevertheless, the AIU has noted continuing improvement. In its 2011 report, the AIU observed:

---

[30] FTSE is an abbreviation of 'Financial Times Stock Exchange'. It is an independent company that originated as a joint venture between the *Financial Times* newspaper (FT) and the London Stock Exchange (LSE). FTSE has developed a wide array of share indices including the FTSE 100 (the 100 largest companies by market capitalisation listed on the LSE; these represent more than 80 per cent of the entire market capitalisation of the LSE) and the FTSE 250 (comprising the next 250 largest companies on the LSE; these companies represent about 15 per cent of the market capitalisation of the LSE).

The actions taken by firms in response to the AIU's inspection findings continue to contribute to an improvement in the overall quality of audit work in the UK. . . . [T]he proportion of audits assessed as good with limited improvements required has been approximately 50% of all audits reviewed in the last two years. The number of major listed company audits assessed as requiring significant improvement has declined this year, with only one FTSE 350 audit in this category compared with four in each of the previous two years. (AIU, 2011, p. 8)

In 2012 the AIU did not refer to the increase in FTSE 350 company audits requiring significant improvement but, with reference to all of the inspections it conducted in the year to 31 March 2012, it reported:

We have seen an improvement in overall inspection results, with a further reduction in the proportion of audits requiring significant improvements. These now account for less than 10% of the audits reviewed. (AIU, 2012, p. 4)

In recent years, the RSB monitoring units have found that the majority of audit firms conduct their audits in accordance with auditing, ethical and quality control standards and audit regulations (see, for example, ICAEW, 2011, p. 4). Similarly, the AIU "considers the overall quality of major public company audit work to be fundamentally sound" (AIU, 2009, p. 2). Nevertheless, the monitoring/inspection units have identified some commonly occurring deficiencies. Those found in recent years include the following:[31]

1. The failure to exercise sufficient scepticism when conducting audits – especially in key areas requiring judgment. This applies, for example, to auditors' failure to challenge clients':
   - estimates of the fair value of investment property, financial assets and liabilities (for example, pension fund assets and liabilities) and of provisions for losses (including loan losses by banks);
   - key assumptions which underpin determination of impairment of goodwill and other intangible assets;
   - key assumptions, financial projections and the time period used to support the conclusion that the entity is a going concern;
   - bases for recognising revenue, especially on long term contracts.
2. Inadequate identification, assessment and/or documentation of audit risk. This includes a failure to:
   - gain a proper understanding of the client, its business and its industry and/or to document that understanding;
   - identify relevant laws and regulations with which the client must comply;

---

[31] Most of the deficiencies we report here were identified in audits conducted by the full range of audit firms – including each of the Big Four firms. Further details of these and other deficiencies identified by the monitoring/inspection units may be found in the AIU's annual reports (AIU, 2009 to 2012), the ICAEW monitoring reports (ICAEW, 2010, 2011) and the ICAS monitoring reports (ICAS, 2009, 2010, 2011).

- give adequate consideration to fraud risks and/or to discuss these risks in audit team meetings; also to document the team meeting discussions and the fraud risks identified;
- identify significant risks (such as revenue recognition).

These failures result, in turn, in a failure to plan an adequate response to audit risks which exist.

3. Inadequate evaluation of the effectiveness of internal controls on which reliance is placed in order to reduce substantive testing – this includes giving inadequate consideration to the possibility of management overriding internal controls.

4. Inadequate planning for specific audit engagements; some firms rely on standard checklists for planning the audit, and on standard audit plans, without tailoring them to the circumstances of particular audit engagements.

5. Using experts, internal or external to the audit firm, without giving adequate consideration to the qualifications and experience of the experts, failing to test the robustness and reasonableness of the assumptions they applied, and failing to form a conclusion about the appropriateness of their work as audit evidence.

6. The failure to calculate performance materiality and/or setting planning materiality limits too high or inappropriately raising materiality limits during the audit. (The audit monitors/inspectors noted the last two deficiencies, in particular, after the 2008–2009 financial crisis and ensuing 'credit crunch'. They attribute them to cost-cutting measures by audit firms;[32] see, for example, AIU, 2010, pp. 20–1; 2012, p. 8).

7. Gathering insufficient audit evidence. This includes audit firms' failure to:

   - attend inventory counts when inventory is material to the financial statements, or to attend counts at locations where material amounts of inventory are held;
   - confirm cash, short-term investment and accounts receivable balances directly with relevant third parties;
   - obtain sufficient appropriate audit evidence to support revenue balances, despite revenue being identified as a significant risk;
   - identify and/or adequately challenge the completeness and veracity of related party transactions;
   - corroborate management representations with other audit evidence, especially those relating to the existence, ownership and condition of long-term assets, ownership of inventory, and collectability of accounts receivable;

---

[32] The AIU found that, for a PricewaterhouseCoopers audit it inspected, the audit team had been instructed to reduce the hours worked by five per cent (Christodoulou, 2009).

- test adequately the propriety of unusual and end-of-period journal entries (particularly those prone to manipulation or falsification by management).
8. The failure to use overall analytical procedures when assessing the risk of material misstatement as a basis for planning the audit and/or as a final check on the truth and fairness of the financial statements during the concluding stage of the audit.
9. Inappropriate use of substantive analytical procedures – including:
   - the use of inappropriate ratios to obtain substantive audit evidence,
   - failure to specify expected results prior to applying analytical procedures,
   - inadequately investigating variances between expected and actual results, and
   - failure to corroborate variances with other audit evidence.
10. Inadequate documentation of the rationale underlying key audit judgments, of audit procedures performed and of evidence gathered, especially in respect of:
    - identifying and assessing risks as a basis for planning the nature and extent of other audit procedures;
    - analytical procedures performed during the planning and/or overall review stage of the audit;
    - determination of sample sizes and methods used to select sample units;
    - review of audit work and, more particularly, how significant issues raised during the review were dealt with.
11. Inadequate documentation of engagement quality control reviews – in particular, the absence of documentation to indicate:
    - the audit team's key judgments, and the extent to which professional scepticism had been applied, were appropriately challenged, and
    - audit work papers had been reviewed and any issues raised had been properly addressed.
12. Deficient auditing of financial statement disclosures. This includes the failure to:
    - consider the adequacy of disclosures relating to going concern uncertainties and related party transactions;
    - identify omissions of required disclosures – for example, the omission of auditors' remuneration, or the separate reporting of fees for audit and non-audit services;
    - identify inconsistencies between the front part of companies' annual reports and their financial statements – for example, in relation to reportable segments.

13. Audit reports being signed before completion of all audit work and/or by someone other than the engagement partner (or another Responsible Individual with authority to sign the audit report on behalf of the firm).

14. Inadequate reporting to clients' audit committees of, for example:
    - significant matters relating to the audit firms' independence (including significant threats that were identified and the safeguards applied);
    - how key risk areas communicated at the planning stage were addressed and the conclusions reached in relation thereto;
    - significant findings of the audit, including areas of disagreement with management;
    - identified unadjusted misstatements.

15. Breaches of independence requirements, including:
    - engagement (and/or other key) partners being involved in the audit of listed clients in excess of the permitted period (normally five years); instances of periods of 15 to 20 years were encountered by the AIU (see, for example, AIU, 2009, p. 19);
    - more than ten per cent of fee income being derived from a particular client;
    - the provision of non-audit services that are prohibited by Ethical Standards – for example:
        • the provision of prohibited legal and IT consulting services;
        • preparation of the audit client's:
            ◦ statutory financial statements, or
            ◦ taxation calculations for inclusion in the financial statements;
        • involvement in the compilation of financial policies and procedures manuals which impact on the preparation of the client's financial statements.

16. Inadequate (or no) documentary evidence to indicate that audit quality is an overriding requirement within the firm or that audit quality constitutes an important element in partner and staff appraisals (but, contrary to Ethical Standards, evidence to indicate that the selling of non-audit services to audit clients contributes to partner promotion; see, for example, AIU, 2011, pp. 7, 29).

It is clear from their monitoring/inspection reports that the RSB monitoring units and the AIU have uncovered numerous instances of non-compliance with auditing, ethical and quality control standards – and generated innumerable suggestions for improvement. It also seems likely that the 'threat' of monitoring visits has motivated at least some practitioners to effect improvements in their quality control systems and auditing procedures. Further, when reporting on the impact of their monitoring processes, the RSBs and AIU have drawn attention to the large number of audit firms which received a less than satisfactory grade as the outcome of their initial monitoring visit (and hence were subject to a re-visit) but which had 'cleaned up their act' before the follow-up visit. The RSBs have also noted that registered auditors who persist with defective performance are disciplined and, if appropriate, lose their auditor registration. In this regard it is pertinent to note that monitoring has resulted in the removal of a significant number of 'bad eggs' from the profession's nest and restricted the auditing activities of others. Between 1992 and 2004, 223 auditors registered with the ICAEW, ICAS or ICAI had their audit registration withdrawn, another 244 surrendered their registration following a monitoring visit, and a further 932 had restrictions imposed on them until required training and/or improvements in their performance had been effected (and verified through a follow-up visit). Examples of restrictions include prohibition on accepting new audit clients and precluding certain partners from appointment as audit engagement partners or, in some cases, from engaging in audit work (ICAEW *et al.*, 1992 to 2004).[33]

Given the improvement in auditors' compliance with auditing, ethical and quality control standards which monitoring appears to have brought, it may be asked why instances of auditor negligence still occur. In answer, commentators such as Wood and Sommer (1985) note that monitoring cannot detect *all* deficiencies in audit work and thus cannot prevent *all* undesirable events from occurring. Woodley echoed this theme when, on the eve of monitoring being introduced in the UK, he stated:

> It would be foolish to believe that there will be no audit failures in the future. No amount of monitoring can eliminate the possibility of errors of judgement or failures to follow laid down procedures. But . . . the extra emphasis on quality control procedures, the possibility of a [monitoring] visit, and the dire consequences of failing to comply with the regulations [should] result in fewer audit failures in the future. (Woodley, 1991, p. 61)

Additionally, as Wood and Sommer (1985), amongst others, have observed, although monitoring cannot prevent all audit errors from occurring, society has other checks in place to ensure that those responsible for causing harm to others as a result of sub-standard professional work do not go

---

[33] Since 2004, a further 799 audit firms registered with the ICAEW, ICAS or ICAI have received a 'D' grade as the outcome of a monitoring visit. For 2005, details are not available as to whether this resulted in the withdrawal or surrender of the firms' audit registration or the imposition of restrictions. However, between 2006 and 2011, 141 ICAEW, ICAS or ICAI registered firms lost their audit registration (through withdrawal or surrender) and a further 592 had restrictions placed on them (POB, 2006 to 2010, 2011b, 2012; IAASA, 2006 to 2011).

unpunished. For example, when questions of audit failure arise, authorities such as the Department for Business, Innovation & Skills in the UK and the Securities and Exchange Commission (SEC) in the USA investigate and, if justified, impose appropriate sanctions on the culprits. Further, as evidenced by cases such as those discussed in Chapter 15, in some instances, those harmed as a result of auditors' sub-standard work may seek redress through the courts.

16.5 PROPOSALS FOR LIMITING AUDITORS' LIABILITY

16.5.1 The case for limiting auditors' liability

When investors and others suffer loss as a consequence of a company collapsing unexpectedly they may seek to recover their loss from any hopeful avenue. Although a company's failure is frequently the result of mismanagement by (and, sometimes, the dishonesty of) its directors and/or senior executives, when a company fails, the fortunes of its directors often go with it. As a consequence, suing the directors is usually perceived as an option which is unlikely to bear fruit in the form of monetary recompense. However, auditors are known to carry indemnity insurance and, if any fault can be found with the way in which they performed their duties, they are often regarded as a potential source from which losses may be recouped. It is generally accepted that this 'deep pocket' syndrome has been a prime motivator in the large and increasing number of suits brought against auditors in recent decades in English-speaking countries, particularly in the USA, the UK and Australia.

In some cases, as is noted in the Introduction to this chapter, auditors have faced enormous claims for damages. Further, the damages awarded against auditors frequently bear no relation to the size of the audit fee or the extent of the auditor's negligence. The extent of such potential liability has caused some commentators, such as Hardcastle (1988), to conclude there is a very real risk that it will result in a shortage of suitable people prepared to enter the auditing profession. Hardcastle states, for example:

> There is no doubt that, if current trends in litigation continue without check, the flow of people prepared to enter the professions will slow up and professional standards will fall, as the most able people come to regard a professional career as too risky. (Hardcastle, 1988, p. 15)

Similar concerns were expressed by Pasricha (2002) when commenting on Ernst & Young (E&Y) becoming a limited liability partnership (LLP: such partnerships are discussed below). He observed:

> Without our conversion to an LLP, I could have seen a time in the future where it would have become difficult to attract the high calibre of person needed to become a partner in a professional services firm.

The potential liability auditors face has given rise to calls by auditing firms and others for their liability to be limited. Five main proposals for limiting auditors' liability have been adopted or suggested. These are as follows:

(i)   permitting auditors to form limited liability companies;
(ii) permitting auditors to form limited liability partnerships;
(iii) permitting auditors to enter into liability limitation agreements with their clients;
(iv) establishing a statutory or regulatory cap on auditors' liability;
(v)   enshrining proportional liability (or contributory negligence) in statute law.

We discuss each of these options below.

16.5.2   Limited Liability Companies (LLCs)

Prior to enactment of the Companies Act 1989 audit firms were not permitted to form companies; they had to exist as sole practitioners or partnerships. As noted in Chapter 15, under partnership law (which does not cover LLPs), all partners within a firm have joint and several liability. If a court awards damages against a partner in a non-LLP audit firm (or the firm reaches an out-of-court settlement with the plaintiff) for any amount that exceeds the firm's insurance cover, the personal assets of the errant partner are used to make good the deficit. If there is still a shortfall, the personal assets of the other partners in the firm are called upon to rectify the deficiency. Thus, a particular partner may lose his/her personal assets as a consequence of negligence by another partner in the firm – a partner whom s/he may not even know if the firm is large and has many offices.

The Companies Act 1989 changed the law to permit audit firms to form limited liability companies (LLCs).[34] In cases where firms take advantage of this option, to the extent that any damages awarded against the audit company exceed the company's insurance cover, the assets of the company are called upon to meet the damages claim. Additionally, the personal assets of the individual 'partner' (or, more correctly, shareholder/director) responsible for the negligence giving rise to the damages may be pursued through the corporate front and used to meet any deficiency. However, the personal assets of 'partners' not associated with the defective audit cannot be called upon.

---

[34] When an audit firm exists as a (non-LLP) partnership, each partner (and not the partnership) is a separate legal entity. When a firm exists as a company, the company is a separate legal entity; the partners become shareholders and/or directors of the company. In general, the company, not the individual partners, can be sued; the partners are protected by the 'corporate front' (the existence of the audit firm as a company).

Thus, incorporation benefits audit 'partners' (shareholder/directors) who are not themselves guilty of negligence in that their personal assets are safe from seizure to meet damages awarded to a successful plaintiff. However, if the damages awarded against the audit company exceed the company's indemnity insurance cover, the damages (or settlement) might result in the company losing all of its assets (forcing the auditors out of business) and the successful plaintiffs not recovering all of their losses.[35]

Another argument raised against auditors forming LLCs is that auditors are members of a profession and, as such, they are accorded certain rights and privileges in society. As a consequence, they should not be permitted to hide behind a corporate front while retaining their professional status. One of the recognised hallmarks of a member of a profession is a preparedness to stand by the quality of his/her work and reputation as an individual. Although this argument has merit, as indicated above, incorporation does not result in the identity of the professional responsible for the negligence being lost. An individual can still be traced through the corporate front in the event of failing to perform an audit without due skill and care.

Notwithstanding the apparent benefits of changing from a partnership to an LLC (in terms of reduced exposure to liability), audit firms have demonstrated some reluctance to take advantage of this option. Only about 200 audit firms[36] have formed companies – including just one of the Big Four firms, namely, the audit section of KPMG which became KPMG Audit plc in 1996. The reasons for audit firms' reluctance to form companies appear to be associated with company (compared with individual) tax and, more particularly, National Insurance rules[37] and the need to comply with the provisions of the Companies Act 2006, including producing an annual report complete with audited financial statements. It is also possible that some firms have reservations about the propriety of professional services being provided by an incorporated entity. Another (likely) reason is the emergence of an attractive alternative – LLPs – which, in the words of Davies (2001, p. 24) are:

> a modern hybrid combining the internal flexibility of the partnership with the legal protection provided by the limited company.

---

[35] It should be recalled that, in order to be successful, plaintiffs must prove to the satisfaction of the court that, *inter alia*, they have suffered loss as a result of the auditor's negligence (i.e., they made an economic decision based on financial statements which the auditor audited without exercising due skill and care). The damages awarded by the court make good that loss suffered.

[36] Only six of the 60 largest accounting firms in the UK have become LLCs (Fisher, 2007). The six excludes KPMG Audit plc which is a component of KPMG LLP. With the formation of LLPs now available as an option, audit firms are not likely to form LLCs.

[37] These rules result in the 'partners' (shareholders/directors) being subject to significantly higher taxes (or, more particularly, National Insurance contributions) than those to which they would be subject in a partnership in which they would be taxed and pay National Insurance contributions as individuals.

16.5.3 Limited Liability Partnerships (LLPs)

LLPs were first accorded serious consideration as a possible means of reducing auditors' exposure to liability in 1996 – the year the auditing section of KPMG incorporated as KPMG Audit plc. E&Y and Price Waterhouse (PW),[38] perceiving the disadvantages of LLCs to outweigh their benefits, emerged as stalwart proponents of LLPs. As it seemed that the UK Government could not be persuaded to embrace the LLP notion, the two firms lobbied the Jersey Parliament. Their efforts were rewarded and, in May 1998, the Jersey Parliament enacted LLP law making it possible to establish LLPs in Jersey from September 1998.

Not surprisingly, the UK Government became concerned about the prospect of many UK professional firms (particularly accounting and legal firms) moving their 'Head Offices' to Jersey and setting up as LLPs there and, in 1999, an LLP Bill was drafted. Howells, the then Minister of Consumer and Corporate Affairs, explained:

> One of the functions [of LLPs] will be to help partnerships attract new partners who have been fearful of taking up leadership roles because of unlimited liability.[39] . . . [However], in return for LLP status firms will be expected to offer greater disclosure in the form of filed audited annual accounts. If you have limited liability you have disclosure so that someone who deals with the firm can make an informed decision. (as quoted, Kemeny, 1999)

The Limited Liability Partnerships Act was enacted by the UK Parliament in 2000. Under this Act, businesses could register as LLPs from 6 April 2001; on that date, E&Y became the first organisation in the UK to be issued with an LLP certificate (Hinks, 2001b). Welcoming moves by E&Y to become an LLP, Howells (Minister of Consumer and Corporate Affairs) stated:

> I know this new Act [Limited Liability Partnerships Act 2000] will be welcomed by many firms. . . . It gives members the freedom to arrange their internal relationships as they wish while retaining the benefit of limited liability . . . I am confident that the Act and [associated] Regulations strike the right balance between the interests of those who want to become Limited Liability Partnerships and those who will do business with them. (as quoted, Hinks, 2001a)

Compared with ordinary partnerships and LLCs, LLPs provide accounting (and other professional services) firms with four main advantages. These are as follows:

---

[38] Price Waterhouse merged with Coopers & Lybrand in 1998 to form PricewaterhouseCoopers.

[39] When Wilkins Kennedy (the twenty-first largest accountancy firm in the UK) became an LLP in 2012, Fenn (the managing partner) acknowledged that a key reason for converting from an ordinary partnership to an LLP was to attract potential partners and others of high calibre who would not accept unlimited liability. Fenn stated: ". . .the younger partners and the high calibre people we're after . . . want their risk left to a minimum" (as quoted, Reed, 2012).

(a) *Limited Liability*: As indicated earlier, under partnership law, all partners are jointly and severally liable for losses caused by the negligence (or other wrongful acts or omissions) of any partner acting in the ordinary course of the partnership's business. Under the Limited Liability Partnerships Act 2000, partners (who are referred to as members) are able to limit their liability to the capital they agree to invest in their firm.[40] The importance of this advantage is reflected in two comments by Land, when Chairman of E&Y:

- I think it is easy for people to forget that in our profession . . . there was real concern that, in an increasingly litigious environment, the law was unfair to us. The doctrine of joint and several liability is a pretty harsh doctrine. (as quoted, Hinks, 2001b)
- The introduction of LLPs is an important step forward in beginning to provide a fair and reasonable measure of protection for businesses such as ours in an increasingly litigious society. (as quoted, Smith, 2001)

(b) *The firm has a separate legal personality*: Under partnership law, a partnership does not have a legal personality; it exists as a network of relationships between individual partners. Each partner is an agent, not of the firm, but of the other partners. Under LLP law, the firm is a separate legal entity similar to an LLC. Each partner is an agent of the LLP in the same way as a director is an agent of his/her company.

(c) *Taxation*: As we observed earlier, incorporation as an LLC is tax disadvantageous to the shareholder/directors of the company (partners of the 'converted' partnership). However, under LLP law, members continue to be taxed as individuals. Thus, while gaining the advantages resulting from existing as a separate legal entity, LLPs have an advantage not available to LLCs in that, for tax and National Insurance purposes, they are treated as businesses conducted by partners.

(d) *Internal flexibility*: Unlike LLCs, which are required to elect a Board of Directors and comply with other organisational requirements attaching to companies, LLPs are able to organise their management structure and internal affairs in any way they wish. As in ordinary partnerships, all 'partners' (members) are able to participate in the management of their LLP.

Although there are distinct advantages to be gained by audit firms converting to LLPs, there are also some disadvantages. These include the following:

---

[40] However, as for LLCs, the personal assets of a partner (member) found guilty of negligence may be called upon to make good the loss suffered by a plaintiff as a result of that negligence.

(a) *Preparation of audited financial statements*: One of the 'costs' of becoming an LLP is that the provisions of the Companies Act 2006 regarding the preparation, audit and filing of annual financial statements apply to LLPs. Like LLCs, all LLPs are required to prepare annually, and to file with the Registrar of Companies, audited financial statements that give a true and fair view of the LLP's financial position and its profit or loss for the year. Additionally, where an LLP's profit exceeds £200,000 in any year, it must report the profit attributable to the member entitled to the largest share thereof. However, just as the Companies Act's provisions relating to the preparation, audit and filing of financial statements apply to LLPs, so too do the exemptions. Thus, an LLP which meets the Companies Act 2006's criteria to qualify as 'small'[41] is entitled to take advantage of the Act's limited reporting requirements and audit exemption provisions.

The reporting requirements applying to LLPs are viewed by some (for example, Davies, 2001) as onerous and as an obstacle to some firms becoming LLPs (especially smaller firms which, in general, have more limited exposure to liability and, thus, less to gain from LLP formation, than their larger counterparts). However, it is pertinent to observe that most audit firm clients are companies and these entities (which are probably less familiar with financial reporting and auditing requirements than audit firms) do not seem to find the reporting obligations too burdensome.

(b) *Consent of third parties may be required to transfer partnership loans and leases*: Where an existing (ordinary) partnership has, for example, a bank loan and/or overdraft, the partnership will require the bank's consent before the loan and/or overdraft can be transferred to an LLP. Further, because the liability of LLP members is limited, the bank's security is reduced when a partnership (with joint and several liability) converts to an LLP. Thus, the bank may require personal guarantees for the loan and/or overdraft from the LLP's members (former partners) before granting its consent to the transfer. Similarly, if a partnership wishes to transfer a lease to an LLP, the landlord's consent will be required. As for the bank, because the landlord's security is reduced by the transfer of the lease to an LLP, the LLP's members may be required to give personal guarantees in respect of the lease (Tutty, 2001).

(c) *Creditor safeguards are included in the Limited Liability Partnerships Act 2000*: The provisions of the Insolvency Act 1986 relating to a business

---

[41] To qualify as 'small', an LLP must meet any two of the following criteria: turnover of no more than £6.5 million, a balance sheet total (i.e., total assets) of no more than £3.26 million, and no more than 50 employees (see Chapter 5, section 5.3.1).

trading when insolvent apply to LLPs. This means that, if an LLP goes into liquidation as a result of insolvency, its members may be personally liable for the debts of the LLP if they knew, or ought to have known, that their firm was heading for insolvency and did not take appropriate action (Davies, 2001). However, the 'bad news' for LLPs does not end here. As Davies (2001, p. 25) explains:

> [The Limited Liability Partnerships Act 2000 includes] a brand new provision for a liquidator to 'claw back' any withdrawal of funds made by a member of an LLP in the two-year period leading up to the firm's liquidation if, at the time of the withdrawal or as a result of it, he knew, or should have concluded that the firm could no longer pay its debts.

In addition to these disadvantages of LLPs for audit firms, there is the (potential) disadvantage for innocent parties who suffer loss as a result of negligence (or other wrongdoing) by a member ('partner') of an LLP. If the loss suffered by a successful plaintiff exceeds the LLP's insurance cover, the capital the members agreed to contribute to the LLP and the personal assets of the member responsible for the wrongdoing, then, to the extent of the shortfall, the consequences of the member's wrongdoing are borne by the plaintiff.[42] When it is remembered that the evidence suggests that plaintiffs do not succeed easily in actions brought against auditors (see Chapter 15, section 15.4), preventing those who are successful from recovering the full amount lost as a result of the negligence of the auditor concerned seems to be somewhat inequitable.

We noted earlier that, on 6 April 2001, E&Y became the first firm in the UK to become an LLP. KPMG followed its example on 3 May 2002. As we have seen, the audit section of KPMG was incorporated as KPMG Audit plc in 1996 but the LLP covers all of KPMG's operations in the UK and embraces KPMG Audit plc as an element of the LLP. At first, the conversion of audit firms to LLPs was slow (Lee, 2002) but, as predicted by Land (speaking as chairman of E&Y) in 2001: "LLP status [has] become commonplace for professional services firms . . ." (as quoted, Smith, 2001). According to Huber (2012), in March 2012: "LLPs [were] the norm – at least for the larger accountancy firms. Around three in five [60 per cent] of firms in Accountancy Age's top 50 league table for 2011 . . . were LLPs". This compares with 25 of the 60 largest accountancy firms in the UK (42 per cent) which had formed LLPs by July 2007 (Fisher, 2007).

---

[42] Unlike in an ordinary partnership, the plaintiff does not have a right to call on the personal assets of members of an LLP who were not, themselves, involved in the negligent audit (or other wrongdoing).

16.5.4 Liability Limitation Agreements

The Companies Act (CA) 2006 introduced provisions enabling auditors to enter into liability limitation agreements with their audit clients.[43] The Act explains that such an agreement:

> purports to limit the amount of a liability owed to a company by its auditor in respect of any negligence, default, breach of duty or breach of trust, occurring in the course of the audit of [financial statements], of which the auditor may be guilty in relation to the company. (s. 534)

However, in order to be valid, the agreement must meet three criteria. It must:

(i) relate to only one financial year and specify the year in which it applies;

(ii) be authorised by a resolution of the members (i.e., shareholders) of the company, which approves the agreement's principal terms.[44] The shareholders may also withdraw their authorisation by passing a resolution to that effect before the company enters into the agreement with its auditor or, if the agreement has been entered into, before the beginning of the financial year to which it relates;

(iii) not limit the auditor's liability to less than an amount which is:

> fair and reasonable in all the circumstances of the case having regard (in particular) to –
>
> (a) the auditor's responsibilities under [CA 2006],
>
> (b) the nature and purpose of the auditor's contractual obligations to the company, and
>
> (c) the professional standards expected of him [or her]. [CA 2006, s. 537(1)]

When determining what is "fair and reasonable in all the circumstances of the case" no account is to be taken of:

(a) matters arising after the loss or damage in question has been incurred, or

(b) matters (whenever arising) affecting the possibility of recovering compensation from other persons liable in respect of the same loss or damage. [s. 537(3)]

Additionally, the company must disclose in a note to its financial statements for the year in which the agreement applies the fact that it has entered into

---

[43] In June 2008 the European Commission (EC) issued a Recommendation which states that EU Member States should be able, under national law, to:
- determine a cap in respect of auditors' liability, or
- establish a system of proportional liability according to which statutory auditors and audit firms are liable only to the extent of their contribution to the damage caused, or
- allow the company, its shareholders and the auditor to determine the limitation of the auditor's liability, subject to appropriate safeguards for investors in the company audited,

except in cases of intentional breach of their duties (EC, 2008).

[44] According to CA 2006, s. 536(4):
The "principal terms" of an agreement are terms specifying, or relevant to the determination of –
(a) the kind (or kinds) of acts or omissions covered,
(b) the financial year to which the agreement relates, or
(c) the limit to which the auditor's liability is subject.

a liability limitation agreement with its auditor, the principal terms of the agreement, and the date of the members' resolution approving it (Statutory Instrument, 2008).

The CA 2006, s. 535(4), specifies:

> . . . it is immaterial how a liability limitation agreement is framed. In particular, the limit on the amount of the auditor's liability need not be a sum of money, or a formula, specified in the agreement.

However, the Act does not provide guidance on how a "fair and reasonable" amount to which the auditor's liability is to be limited should be determined. Even before the CA 2006 provisions became effective in April 2008, discussions took place between companies and their auditors on how to determine the limit of the auditor's liability (Sukhraj, 2007a). Initially, it seems that two options were favoured – limiting the auditor's liability:

- to a multiple of the audit fee (an option favoured by auditors), or
- to the proportion of the loss suffered by the company which resulted from the auditor's deficient performance (i.e., proportional liability) (Simmons & Simmons, 2007).

However, the pendulum then swung in favour of proportional liability. In October 2007, Haddrill, then the Director General of the Association of British Insurers (ABI), stated:

> Government has proposed that the limit on auditors' liability should be proportionate to their responsibility. We agree with that. The Companies Act didn't enact the limit in these terms and some [in particular, the audit firms] are still talking of a fixed financial cap [or limit] on a liability. We can't support that and we will red top any company[45] that agrees such a cap with their auditor. (as reported, Sukhraj, 2007b).

The National Association of Pension Funds (NAPF) supported the ABI's position. Sukhraj (2007b) reports that an NAPF spokesman asserted: "We are not in favour of capped liability. We are in favour of . . . proportional liability. We need a party to be liable for their portion of any loss". Conveying the significance of the ABI's and NAPF's stance on the issue, Sukhraj (2007b) notes that, between them, members of these associations control investment funds of more than £2,000 billion.

If the shareholders agree to limit the liability of their company's auditor by means of a proportional liability arrangement, the auditor remains liable for the proportion of a loss suffered by the company as a result of deficient audit work; the auditor thus has an incentive to perform a high quality audit – and thereby avoid any liability. However, a question remains: what would motivate shareholders to agree to limit the liability of their company's auditor? If the company suffered a serious loss (or, worse, collapsed), and the auditor was

---

[45] A 'red top' is a serious governance warning given by the ABI (Sukhraj, 2007b).

found to have performed a deficient audit, it seems likely that the shareholders would wish the company to be able to sue the auditor for the maximum amount possible. It is perhaps for this reason that, at least until September 2010, "no major company [had] ever entered into [a liability limitation agreement]" (Christodoulou, 2010).

It should also be noted that the CA 2006 provisions only relate to limiting auditors' liability to their client companies. It does not affect the ability of third parties to recover damages from an auditor under the common law if they can prove: (i) the auditor owed them a duty of care, (ii) the auditor was negligent, and (iii) they suffered a loss as a result of that negligence.

Unlike the statutory provisions enabling auditors to form LLCs and LLPs, those enabling auditors to enter into liability limitation agreements appear to have had little effect in practice. In the UK, the remaining two proposals for limiting auditors' liability remain just that (i.e., proposals): neither imposing a 'cap' on their liability, nor providing for their proportional liability, has (yet) been enacted in UK legislation. However, as we shall see below, both of these measures have been incorporated in the legislation of other countries.

16.5.5 Statutory or regulatory fixed cap on auditors' liability

Capping auditors' liability to a known amount is a means of limiting auditors' liability which is favoured by audit firms (EU, 2007). The 'capped' amount may be stated as a formula, such as a multiple of the audit fee (for example, ten times the fee) or as a fixed amount (for example, in Germany the limit of auditors' liability for the audits of quoted companies is €4 million and for other clients it is €1 million).

This means of limiting auditors' liability possesses the advantages of:
- simplicity,
- preventing (or reducing) the likelihood of auditors being forced out of business by a single negligently performed audit, and
- where the cap is set as a multiple of the audit fee, linking the size of the sanction associated with a negligently performed audit to the size of the reward (i.e., fee) resulting from the audit.

However, like the other means of limiting auditors' liability, it also has some disadvantages. These include the following:

(a) *A decline in audit quality:* As the adverse financial consequences which may result from sub-standard audit work are capped at a known level, auditors may be motivated to perform less audit work – thereby reducing audit quality and increasing the risk of allegations of negligence.

(b) *Minimising the audit fee*: If the liability cap is set at a multiple of the audit fee, auditors may be encouraged to minimise the fee in order to limit their exposure to liability. If cost-cutting measures are then adopted in an attempt to adjust the audit work to the (minimal) audit fee, this may result in less audit work and, hence, in reduced audit quality.

(c) *Inequity*: As the auditor's liability is limited to a particular amount, an innocent client or third party who suffers a loss as a consequence of the auditor failing to perform the audit with reasonable skill and care may be prevented from recovering the full amount of the loss they have suffered.

In relation to the last disadvantage, Pratt (1990, p. 78) suggests that, rather than an innocent party, who relies on an auditor's expertise and professional judgment in good faith, bearing the cost of the auditor's negligence (to the extent that it exceeds the liability cap), the audit firm should carry the burden. Indeed, to Pratt, a particularly strong argument against any form of limitation of auditors' liability is the ability of an audit firm to spread the risk of potential damages for negligence through professional indemnity insurance and/or increased audit fees. Pratt cites a Federal judge in the American case of *Rusch Factors* v *Levin* [1968] 284 F Supp. 85 in support of his argument. The judge asked:

> Why should an innocent reliant party be forced to carry the weighty burden of an accountant's professional malpractice? Isn't the risk of loss more easily distributed and fairly spread by imposing it on the accounting profession, which can pass the cost on to the entire consuming public? (as reported, Pratt, 1990, p. 79)

Countering this opinion, audit firms would point to the decline in the capacity of the insurance market and their inability (particularly for the large firms) to secure – at any cost – the level of professional indemnity insurance they desire and need. Further, since the 2008 global financial crisis and ensuing 'credit crunch', auditors have faced severe downward pressure on their audit fees which has reduced their ability to "pass on the cost [of their] professional malpractice". To us, what seems more appropriate is putting pressure on auditors to perform high quality audits – making questions of who should carry the burden of their malpractice redundant.

16.5.6 Enshrining contributory negligence (or proportional liability) in statute law

An alternative suggestion for limiting auditors' liability is that of giving statutory recognition to the principle of contributory negligence (also known as proportional liability). Under this principle, damages are awarded against those responsible for a plaintiff's loss in proportion to their responsibility for (or contribution to) that loss. For example, if a court held that a plaintiff's loss was caused equally by negligence by of the company's auditor and its directors, then the auditor and the directors would each be responsible for meeting half of the damages awarded.

In the UK, the law relating to negligence generally falls within the ambit of common (that is, court) law rather than statute law. The principle of contributory negligence (proportional liability) already exists within the common law but, to date, no judge in the UK has applied it in a case involving auditors. It has been proposed that legislation be enacted requiring the courts, in any case involving auditors (or other professional groups to which it applies), to ascertain the extent of the auditor's negligence *vis-à-vis* that of any other party, for example, the auditee's directors, and apportioning blame, and hence damages, accordingly. Such legislation already exists in the USA and, as the AWA case discussed in Chapter 15 (section 15.3) shows, it is also in place in Australia.[46] Further, research conducted in the EU (which investigated the preferences of various interest groups for alternative means of limiting auditors' liability) found that respondents from the investor, banker and company groups favoured proportional liability (EU, 2007).[47]

Proportionate liability offers significant advantages for auditors and plaintiffs alike. For example, in most cases, auditors are called upon to meet only part, rather than the full amount, of the damages awarded to a successful plaintiff. As a result, there is less likelihood of audit firms being forced out of business as a consequence of meeting large damages settlements. Similarly, because damages awarded to a successful plaintiff are derived from more than one source (for example, errant auditors and company directors), there is greater likelihood than under the alternative means of limiting auditors' liability, of him/her recouping the full amount of the loss suffered. Although these benefits are clearly important, probably the single most important advantage of the principle of contributory negligence (proportional liability) is the equity it introduces; it attempts to apportion damages against errant parties according to their proportion of (or contribution towards) the cause of the loss suffered by the plaintiff.

---

[46] Proportional liability was also applied in the portion of the *Barings* case discussed in Appendix 1 to Chapter 15.

[47] As we note in Chapter 15, footnote 26, out-of-court settlements are, in effect, applications of the principle of proportional liability. In reaching the agreed settlement, the auditors implicitly acknowledge their portion of the 'blame' for losses suffered by a client or third party and agree the settlement on this basis. Notwithstanding the finding of the EU study (EU, 2007), that audit firms favour the statutory cap option for limiting their liability, in discussions with one of the authors, senior audit partners in a number of large and middle tier firms expressed the view that proportional liability is the most equitable means of limiting auditors' liability.

16.6 · SUMMARY

Although some auditors have attracted criticism – and penalties – as a result of shoddy audit work, and the reputation of, and the public's confidence in, the auditing profession has suffered as a consequence, it should be remembered that:

> Commentary in the media tends to focus on the few, high profile audit failures, rather than the huge number of successful audits. . . . The overwhelming majority of audits conducted by the major accounting firms are highly professional, effective and valuable. (Accountancy Age, 2005, p. 1)

This conclusion is supported by the findings of Francis (2004) who reviewed empirical research conducted during the last quarter of the twentieth century. His findings suggest that audit failure is infrequent, although there is some indication of a decline in audit quality during the 1990s – a decline which, as we have seen, at least in the UK, the monitoring/inspection of auditors' performance appears to have reversed.

In this chapter we have explored the issue of how auditors' exposure to legal liability may be avoided or limited. More particularly, we have discussed measures individual audit firms may implement in order to ensure that audits conducted by the firm are of a consistently high standard. We have also examined the activities of the RSBs and the AIU in monitoring the performance of registered auditors and the audits of public interest entities, respectively. Such monitoring seeks to ensure that audits are conducted in accordance with auditing, ethical and quality control standards and other audit regulations, and that audit judgments are appropriate.

Additionally, we have discussed five means by which auditors' exposure to liability may be limited, namely, the incorporation of audit firms as LLCs or LLPs, liability limitation agreements between companies and their auditors, the introduction of a statutory or regulatory cap on auditors' liability, and statutory recognition of the principle of contributory negligence (or proportionate liability). We have observed that, although the law has been changed to enable audit firms to form LLCs, relatively few firms have taken advantage of this opportunity. Similarly, the legal provisions enabling companies to agree to limit the liability of their auditor appear to have had little effect. However, many audit firms have converted their businesses from ordinary partnerships into LLPs and, as we have noted, proportional liability has much to recommend it as a means of limiting auditors' liability. However, apart from its possible use as a basis for auditor liability limitation agreements, this option has not (yet) found favour with the UK Government.

SELF-REVIEW QUESTIONS

16.1.   List six elements of a good system of quality control for audit firms.

16.2   List six specific quality control responsibilities of audit engagement partners.

16.3.   Explain briefly the rationale underlying the introduction of mechanisms designed to monitor auditors' performance.

16.4.   Outline the key features of the general process of monitoring auditors' performance.

16.5.   Evaluate briefly the effectiveness of monitoring auditors' performance in the United Kingdom.

16.6.   Given that systems of quality control have been established in audit firms and that auditors' performance is monitored by the RSBs, audit failures should be a thing of the past.
   Explain briefly:
   (a) why audit failures still occur, and
   (b) the checks which society has in place to ensure that auditors responsible for causing harm to others as a result of substandard work do not go unpunished.

16.7.   List two advantages and two disadvantages of audit firms forming:
   (a) limited liability companies (LLCs);
   (b) limited liability partnerships (LLPs).

16.8   Outline the criteria that must be met in order for a liability limitation agreement between a company and its auditor to be effective.

16.9.   List two advantages and two disadvantages of the introduction of:
   (a) a 'cap' on auditors' liability, and
   (b) contributory negligence (proportional liability) as a means of limiting auditors' liability.

16.10.   Evaluate the relative effectiveness of the five means of limiting auditors' liability discussed in this chapter.

REFERENCES

Accountancy Age.com. (2005, 5 August). *Audit Failure? Don't Blame Us*, www .accountancyage.com/aa/opinion/1787180/audit-failure-dont-blame, accessed 28 January 2013.

Accountancy Age. (2007, 21 February). Deloitte ordered to pay £66m in Parmalat settlement. *Accountancy Age*, www.accountancyage.com/aa/news/1767443/deloitte-pay -gbp66m-parmalat-settlement, accessed 30 November 2012.

Answers.com. (2006). *PricewaterhouseCoopers* (sub-headed: *ChuoAoyama Suspension*), www.answers.com/topic/pricewaterhousecoopers, accessed 30 November 2012.

Association of Chartered Certified Accountants (ACCA). (1992 to 2004 inclusive). *Annual Reports on Audit Regulation to the Secretary of State for Trade and Industry*. London: ACCA.

Audit Inspection Unit (AIU). (2005, 2006, 2007). *2004/5, 2005/6, 2006/7 Audit Quality Inspections: Public Report*. London: Financial Reporting Council.

Audit Inspection Unit (AIU). (2008). *2007/8 Audit Quality Inspections: An Overview* London: Financial Reporting Council.

Audit Inspection Unit (AIU). (2009). *2008/9 Audit Quality Inspections: An Overview* London: Financial Reporting Council.

Audit Inspection Unit (AIU). (2010). *2009/10 Annual Report*. London: Financial Reporting Council.

Audit Inspection Unit (AIU). (2011). *2010/11 Audit Quality Inspections: Annual Report*. London: Financial Reporting Council.

Audit Inspection Unit (AIU). (2012). *2011/12 Audit Quality Inspections: Annual Report*. London: Financial Reporting Council.

Christodoulou, M. (2009, 12 November). *Audit Quality under Pressure as Firms Cut Costs*, www.accountancyage.com/aa/news/1747827/audit-quality-pressure-firms-cut-costs, accessed 6 May 2013.

Christodoulou, M. (2010, 16 September). *FRC Chief Sees No "Rapid Change" to Auditor Liability Rules*, www.accountancyage.com/aa/news/1809232/frc-chief-rapid-change-auditor-liability-rules, accessed 23 January 2012.

Davies, J. (2001, 27 March). Insight: LLPs – Safety in numbers. *Accountancy Age*, 24–25.

European Commission (EC). (2008). *Commission Recommendation of 5 June 2008 Concerning the Limitation of the Civil Liability of Statutory Auditors and Audit Firms*. Brussels: EC.

European Union (EU). (2006). *Directive 2006/43/EC of the European Parliament and of the Council on Statutory Audits of Annual Accounts and Consolidated Accounts amending Council Directives 78/660/EEC and 83/349/EEC and repealing Council Directive 84/253/EEC* (Statutory Audit Directive). Brussels: European Parliament and Council.

European Union (EU). (2007). *Summary Report, Consultation on Auditors' Liability*. Brussels: EU Directorate General for Internal Market and Services.

Financial Reporting Council (FRC). (2013). *Audit Quality Review*, www.frc.org.uk/ Our-Work/Conduct/Audit-Quality-Review, accessed 21 January 2013.

Fisher, L. (2007). Boom boom. Firms are enjoying a second year of inflation-busting growth. *Accountancy 140*(1367), 22–24.

Flint, D. (1980). Quality control policies and procedures: The prospect for peer review. *The Accountant's Magazine, 84*(884), 63–66.

Flint, D. (1988). *Philosophy and Principles of Auditing.* London: MacMillan.

Francis, J.R. (2004). What do we know about audit quality? *British Accounting Review,* 36(4), 345–368.

Hardcastle, A. (1988). Going to the Government, cap in hand. *Accountancy, 101*(1133), 15–16.

Hinks, G. (2001a, 5 April). *Howells Welcomes E&Y into LLP Fold,* www. accountancyage.com/aa/news/1765101/howells-welcomes-e-y-llp-fold, accessed 28 January 2013.

Hinks, G. (2001b, 12 April). Ernst & Young is first LLP. *Accountancy Age,* p. 3.

Huber, N. (2012, 22 March). *Has LLP Status Worked?,* www.accountancyage. com/aa/ feature/2162794/llp-status, accessed 24 January 2013.

Institute of Chartered Accountants in England and Wales (ICAEW), Institute of Chartered Accountants of Scotland (ICAS), Institute of Chartered Accountants in Ireland (ICAI). (1992 to 2004 inclusive). *Audit Regulation: Annual Reports to the DTI.* London: ICAEW, ICAS, ICAI.

Institute of Chartered Accountants in England and Wales (ICAEW). (2010). *Audit Monitoring 2010,* www.icaew.com/~/media/Files/Technical/Audit-and-assurance/ audit/ working-in-the-regulated-area-of-audit/audit-news/4005-audit-report-web, accessed 21 January 2013.

Institute of Chartered Accountants in England and Wales (ICAEW). (2011). *Audit Monitoring 2011,* www.icaew.com/~/media/Files/Technical/Audit-and-assurance/ audit/working-in-the-regulated-area-of-audit/audit-news/report-on-audit-monitoring, accessed 21 January 2013.

Institute of Chartered Accountants of Scotland (ICAS). (2009, 2010, 2011). *ICAS Audit Monitoring Findings for the Year(s) Ended 31 December 2009 to 2011.* Edinburgh: ICAS.

International Auditing and Assurance Standards Board (IAASB). (2009a). International Standard on Quality Control (ISQC) 1: *Quality Control for Firms that Perform Audits and Reviews of Financial Statements, and Other Assurance and Related Services Engagements.* New York: International Federation of Accountants.

International Auditing and Assurance Standards Board (IAASB). (2009b). International Standard on Auditing (ISA) 220: *Quality Control for an Audit of Financial Statements.* New York: International Federation of Accountants.

International Ethics Standards Board for Accountants (IESBA). (2009). *Code of Ethics for Professional Accountants (IESBA Code).* New York: International Federation of Accountants.

Irish Auditing & Accounting Supervisory Authority (IAASA). (2006). *Annual Reports 2006 to 2010.* Dublin: IAASA.

Irish Auditing & Accounting Supervisory Authority (IAASA). (2007 to 2010 inclusive). *Annual Report(s) 2007 to 2010*. Dublin: IAASA.

Irish Auditing & Accounting Supervisory Authority (IAASA). (2011). *Annual Report 2011*. Dublin: IAASA.

Kemeny, L. (1999, 2 December). LLPs set for fast track through Parliament. *Accountancy Age*, p. 6.

Lee, M. (2002, 2 May). The debate: LLPs – Just delaying the inevitable. *Accountancy Age*, p. 12.

Norris, F. (2007, 7 July). PricewaterhouseCoopers to pay Tyco investors $225 million. *New York Times*, www.nytimes.com/2007/07/07/business/07tyco.html?_r=0, accessed 6 May 2013.

Pasricha, N. (2002, 1 May). The debate: LLPs – Changing nature of our business. *Accountancy Age*, p. 12.

Professional Oversight Board (POB). (2005, 2006). *Report(s) to the Secretary of State for Trade and Industry. Year to 31 March 2005 and to 31 March 2006*. London: Financial Reporting Council.

Professional Oversight Board (POB). (2007, 2008). *Report(s) to the Secretary of State for Business, Enterprise & Regulatory Reform. Year to 31 March 2007 and to 31 March 2008*. London: Financial Reporting Council.

Professional Oversight Board (POB). (2009). *Report to the Secretary of State for Business, Innovation & Skills. Year to 31 March 2009*. London: Financial Reporting Council.

Professional Oversight Board (POB). (2010). *Report to the Secretary of State for Business, Innovation & Skills. Year to 31 March 2010*. London: Financial Reporting Council.

Professional Oversight Board (POB). (2011a). *Key Facts and Trends in the Accountancy Profession*. London: Financial Reporting Council.

Professional Oversight Board (POB). (2011b). *Report to the Secretary of State for Business, Innovation & Skills. Year to 31 March 2011*. London: Financial Reporting Council.

Professional Oversight Board (POB). (2012). *Report to the Secretary of State for Business, Innovation & Skills. Year to 31 March 2012*. London: Financial Reporting Council.

Pratt, M.J. (1990). *External Auditing: Theory and Practice in New Zealand*. New Zealand: Longman Paul.

Reed, K. (2012, 11 May). *Best Practice: Wilkins Kennedy's David Fenn*, www.accountancyage.com/aa/analysis/2173949/practice-wilkins-kennedys-david-fenn, accessed 24 January 2012.

Richards, G. (2002, 2 August). *1990: The other Big Accounting Firm Meltdown Laventhal & Horwath's Final Days: A 'Sad Tragedy to Watch'*, www.bizjournals.com/philadelphia/stories/2002/08/05/focus9.html?page=all, accessed 30 November 2012.

Securities and Exchange Commission (SEC). (2004a, 16 April). *Initial Decision Release No. 249 Administrative Proceeding File No. 3-10933: In the Matter of Ernst & Young*

LLP. Washington D.C. SEC, www.sec.gov/litigation/aljdec/id249bpm.htm, accessed 30 November 2012.

Securities and Exchange Commission (SEC). (2004b, 20 Oct). *KPMG LLP and Four Auditors Sanctioned for Improper Professional Conduct in Connection with Gemstar-TV Guide International Inc. audits*. Washington DC, SEC, Press Release 2004-147.

Simmons & Simmons. (2007, 22 August). *Audit Liability*, www.elexica.com/en/legal-topics/dispute-resolution-commercial/22-audit-liablity, accessed 23 January 2013.

Smith, P. (2001, 27 June). *E&Y Reaches LLP Landmark*, www.accountancyage. com/aa/news/1773178/e-y-reaches-llp-landmark, accessed 28 January 2013.

Statutory Instrument (SI). (2008). No.489: *The Companies (Disclosure of Auditor Remuneration and Liability Limitation Agreements) Regulations 2008*.

Sukhraj, P. (2007a, 28 June). *FTSE Giants Confirm Audit Liability Cap Discussions*, www.accountancyage.com/aa/news/1778848/ftse-giants-confirm-audit-liability-cap-discussions, accessed 28 January 2013.

Sukhraj, P. (2007b, 11 October). *Investors Lay Down Law on Liability Caps*, www.accountancyage.com/aa/news/1776270/investors-lay-law-liability-caps, accessed 28 January 2013.

Tutty, R. (2001, 29 March). Headstart: LLPs – Is an LLP the right choice for you? *Accountancy Age*, p. 26.

Wood, A.M., & Sommer Jr, A.A. (1985). Statements in quotes. *Journal of Accountancy*, *156*(5), 122–131.

Woodley, K. (1991). Introducing audit regulation. *Accountancy*, *107*(1159), 60–61.

ADDITIONAL READING

Allen, A., & Woodland, A. (2010). Education requirements, audit fees, and audit quality. *Auditing: A Journal of Practice & Theory*, *29*(2), 1–25.

Babiak, J. (2008). Putting the principles into practice. *Accountancy*, *142*(1382), 70–71.

Beattie, V., Fearnley, S., & Hines, T. (2013). Perceptions of factors affecting audit quality in the post-SOX UK regulatory environment. *Accounting and Business Research*, *43*(1), 56–81.

Casterella, J.R., Jensen, K.L., & Knechel, W.R. (2009). Is self-regulated peer review effective at signalling audit quality? *Accounting Review*, *84*(3), 713–735.

Causholli, M., & Knechel, R. (2012). An examination of the credence attributes of an audit. *Accounting Horizons*, *26*(4), 631–656.

Chen, C.J.P., Su, X., & Wu, X. (2009). Forced audit firm change, continued partner-client relationship, and financial reporting quality. *Auditing: A Journal of Practice & Theory*, *28*(2), 227–246.

Choi, J.-H., Kim, C.F., Kim, J.-B., & Zang, Y. (2010). Audit office size, audit quality, and audit pricing. *Auditing: A Journal of Practice & Theory*, *29*(1), 73–97.

Choi, J.-H., Kim, C.F., Kim, J.-B., & Zang. Y. (2010). Do abnormally high audit fees impair audit quality? *Auditing: A Journal of Practice & Theory*, *29*(2), 115–140.

Church, B.K., & Shefchik, L.B. (2012). PCAOB inspections and large accounting firms. *Accounting Horizons*, *26*(1), 43–63.

Coram, P., Glavovic, A., Ng, J., & Woodliff, D.R. (2008). The moral intensity of reduced audit quality acts. *Auditing: A Journal of Practice & Theory*, *27*(1), 127–149.

Dao, M., Raghunandan, K., & Rama, D.V. (2012). Shareholder voting on auditor selection, audit fees, and audit quality. *Accounting Review*, *87*(1), 149–171.

Francis, J.R. (2011). A framework for understanding and researching audit quality. *Auditing: A Journal of Practice & Theory*, *30*(2), 125–152.

Houston, R.W., & Stefaniak, C.M. (2013). Audit partner perceptions of post-audit review mechanisms: An examination of internal quality reviews and PCAOB inspections. *Accounting Horizons*, *27*(1), 23–49.

International Auditing and Assurance Standards Board (IAASB). (2103, January). *A Framework for Audit Quality: A Consultation Paper*. New York: International Federation of Accountants.

Raffett, A.B. (2010). Can identifying and investigating fraud risks increase auditors' liability? *Accounting Review*, *85*(6), 2145–2167.

Richards, I. (2004). *Bringing Audit Back from the Brink (Auditor Liability and the Need to Overhaul a Key Investor Protection Framework)*. London: Morley Fund Management.

Stefaniak, C., & Robertson, J.C. (2010). When auditors err: How mistake significance and superiors' historical reactions influence auditors' likelihood to admit a mistake. *International Journal of Auditing*, *14*(1), 41–55.

17 Corporate Responsibility Reporting and Assurance

LEARNING OBJECTIVES

After studying the material in this chapter you should be able to:
- explain briefly the development of corporate responsibility reporting since the early 1990s;
- discuss reasons which explain why some companies report on their corporate responsibility performance;
- explain the meaning of the term 'assurance engagements';
- discuss the professional requirements for performing assurance engagements and identify the professional groups who are equipped to undertake such work;
- describe the objective and process of assuring corporate responsibility information;
- outline the content of corporate responsibility assurance statements;
- discuss reasons which explain why some companies have their corporate responsibility information independently assured;
- discuss reasons which explain why some companies choose not to have their corporate responsibility information independently assured;
- explain the relevance of corporate responsibility issues to external financial statement audits.

17.1 INTRODUCTION

During the past 30 or so years, societies throughout the world have become increasingly concerned about the environmental and social impact of companies' activities and outputs. The current level of concern is reflected in the almost daily media reports about such issues. These cover, for example, industrial plants' chimneys belching forth clouds of unsightly, odorous and potentially hazardous gaseous wastes; reputedly harmful radioactive emissions from radio and mobile telephone masts; the devastation of coastal areas by oil spills from stricken tankers (or other ships) or leaking oil-wells; illnesses (or deaths) caused by harmful products; deaths resulting from the collapse of poorly constructed buildings and/or from locked doors preventing escape from burning buildings; the exploitation of labour (especially of children and other disadvantaged groups); and dire warnings about the harmful effects of green-house gas emissions.

During the 1980s and 1990s, political, media and public concern in developed countries[1] focused on environmental degradation resulting from the operations and/or products of businesses – particularly those in the extractive, manufacturing and chemicals sectors. In an attempt to demonstrate their responsible attitude towards the environment, some companies in the United Kingdom (UK), as elsewhere, voluntarily published information explaining the environmental impact of their activities and their commitment to manage (and reduce) it.

Since the turn of the twenty-first century, political, media and public concern has become more widespread and vocal, and has broadened to include issues such as the exploitation of labour (especially 'sweat shops' and child labour), unfair trade practices, and ethical and governance issues. This has prompted an increasing number of companies (especially major public companies) to report on the social and economic, as well as the environmental, impact of their activities. Today many (if not most) major companies around the globe publish wide-ranging 'corporate responsibility' (CR) (or 'sustainability') reports.[2] In general, companies provide such reports voluntarily and this, combined with the absence of universally accepted standards for reporting CR information, results in a wide variation in the quality and quantity of the information provided. Additionally, while some companies have their CR reports (or parts thereof) independently assured (or 'audited'), others do not do so. Further, without generally accepted reporting and assurance standards, the level of assurance given on the reliability of the CR information (and thus its credibility) differs markedly.

In this chapter we explore CR reporting and assurance. First, we discuss the development of CR reporting and then consider what motivates companies to engage in this activity. We also examine assurance engagements – engagements

---

[1] In developing countries, concern about the environmental and social impact of companies' activities did not, in general, emerge until the twenty-first century.

[2] 'Corporate social responsibility' (which is now commonly abbreviated to 'corporate responsibility') has been defined as:

[T]he commitment of business to contribute to sustainable economic development, working with employees, their families, the local community and society at large to improve their quality of life. (World Business Council for Sustainable Development, 2000, p. 10)

As we explain in section 17.2, a wide variety of titles have been used for reports which provide information on companies' environmental, social, economic and similar non-financial performance. The terms 'corporate responsibility' and 'sustainability' reports are now commonly used – and this applies whether the information is provided in a separate report or included in the relevant company's annual report. In this chapter, we use the terms 'corporate responsibility' and 'sustainability' reporting to mean the same thing.

designed to provide credibility to companies' CR information – and explore reasons why some companies do, and others do not, have their CR information assured. Before concluding the chapter we consider the relevance of CR issues and information to external financial statement audits.

17.2 DEVELOPMENT OF CORPORATE RESPONSIBILITY REPORTING

Since the 1980s, the number and geographical spread of companies reporting on their CR activities has grown rapidly. The extent of the growth is reflected in KPMG's triennial *International Surveys of Corporate Responsibility Reporting*. Starting in 1993 (when the reports of 670 companies in ten countries were examined), the surveys analyse trends in CR reporting by the world's largest companies. Since 1999, the surveys have examined the reports of the largest 250 (by market capitalisation) of the Fortune Global 500 companies (denoted G250 by KPMG) as well as those of the largest 100 companies in each of a number of countries (denoted N100) – increasing from 11 countries in 1999 to 34 in 2011; see Figure 17.1). The increase in the number of countries covered by the surveys is indicative of the global extension of CR reporting by major companies.

From Figure 17.1 it may be seen that, while just 35 per cent of the G250 companies published CR reports in 1999,[3] this increased sharply to reach 95 per cent in 2011. Referring to the extent of CR reporting by major companies in 2011, KPMG notes:

> Around the world, corporate responsibility reporting has become a fundamental imperative for businesses. . . . Indeed, where CR reporting was once merely considered an 'optional but nice' activity, it now seems to have become virtually mandatory for most multinational companies, almost regardless of where they operate around the world. (KPMG, 2011, p. 6)

Figure 17.1 also shows that, in 1999, 24 per cent of the N100 companies published CR information but, by 2011, this had risen to 64 per cent – notwithstanding the marked increase in the number of countries whose largest 100 companies were included in KPMG's surveys. Commenting on the global spread of CR reporting in 2011, KPMG observes:

> While Europe has traditionally been ahead in its propensity to report on CR activities, our 2011 survey shows that other regions are quickly catching up.

---

[3] It should be noted that, in 1999, KPMG's survey only examined companies' separate (or 'stand-alone') environmental reports and, in 2002, it only examined separate CR reports. However, KPMG explains:
Due to the increasing trend in integrated reporting, the figures published after [and including] 2005 represent total [CR] reports, separate and published as part of annual reports. (KPMG, 2011, p. 7)

Figure 17.1: Changes in corporate responsibility reporting 1999 to 2011[4]

Corporate responsibility reporting	1999	2002	2005	2008	2011
	%	%	%	%	%
Proportion of world's 250 largest companies (G250)[5] that published CR reports	35	45	64	83	95
Proportion of CR reports provided by G250 companies that are accompanied by a formal assurance statement	19	29	30	40	46
UK's largest 100 companies that published CR reports	32	49	71	91	100
Proportion of CR reports provided by UK's largest 100 companies that are accompanied by a formal assurance statement	53	53	53	55	56
No. of countries with the largest 100 companies included in KPMG's survey	11	19	16	22	34
Proportion of the largest 100 companies in countries surveyed by KPMG (N100) which published CR reports	% 24	% 23	% 41	% 53	% 64
Proportion of the largest 100 companies publishing CR reports in countries where, in 2011, the proportions were greatest	%	%	%	%	%
Japan	-	72	81	99	99
South Africa	-	1	81	86	97
France	4	21	43	83	94
Denmark	29	20	29	40	91
Brazil	-	-	-	86	88
Spain	-	11	32	67	88
Finland	15	32	43	65	85
United States of America	30	36	42	79	83
Netherlands	25	26	39	79	82
Assurance of CR information	%	%	%	%	%
Proportion of CR reports provided by N100 companies that are accompanied by a formal assurance statement	18	27	33	39	38
Proportion of CR reports provided by the largest 100 companies in countries shown above that are accompanied by a formal assurance statement		%	%	%	%
Japan	-	26	31	24	23
South Africa	-	100*	22	36	31
France	25	14	40	73	60
Denmark	21	45	31	46	65
Brazil	-	-	-	27	40
Spain	-	27	44	70	65
Finland	33	29	19	30	29
United States of America	3	2	3	14	13
Netherlands	16	38	40	44	82
Titles given to CR reports by G250 companies		%	%		
Sustainability or corporate responsibility (environmental, social and economic) reports	Only environmental reports examined	14	68	No information Available	
Environmental and social reports		10	17		
Environmental and health and safety reports		73	13		
Social reports		3	2		

* Only one CR report was provided by the 100 largest South African companies and the information it contained was assured

Source: KPMG, 1999, 2002, 2005, 2008, 2011

---

[4] See footnote 3 regarding the reports examined in 1999 and 2002.

[5] The largest 250 companies in the Fortune Global 500 ranking (KPMG, 2011).

European companies continue to lead the pack, with 71 percent of companies reporting on CR, but the Americas [are] gaining ground with 69 percent, as is the Middle East and Africa region, where 61 percent of companies now report CR initiatives. However, Asia Pacific continues to trail behind as a region, with just ... 49 percent now disclosing CR data to the markets. (KPMG, 2011, p. 8)

As Figure 17.1 indicates, of the ten countries where more than 80 per cent of the largest 100 companies publish CR information (including the UK), six are European.[6] However, after the UK, where all of the largest 100 companies publish CR reports, Japan and South Africa have the greatest proportion of the largest 100 companies providing CR information (99 and 97 per cent, respectively).

Given the dramatic increase in the number of major companies around the globe providing CR reports, a similar increase in the number of companies having their CR information independently assured might be expected. Without such assurance, the reliability of the CR information remains open to question. Nevertheless, as Figure 17.1 shows, in 2011, only 46 per cent of the G250 companies who provided CR reports had the information formally assured and only 38 per cent of the N100 companies did so. Commenting on these findings, KPMG states:

> As CR reporting begins to play a larger role in the way stakeholders and investors perceive corporate value, companies should increasingly want to demonstrate the quality and reliability of their CR data. It is surprising, therefore, that only 46 percent of G250 and 38 percent of N100 companies currently use assurance ... to verify and assess their CR data. (KPMG, 2011, p. 28)

KPMG does not comment on the decline in the proportion of N100 companies which have their CR reports formally assured – a decline from 39 per cent in 2008 to 38 per cent in 2011. This may result from a change in the number of companies surveyed in the two years (2200 in 2008 but 3400 in 2011) rather than from an actual change but a similar decline is evident in most of the countries where more than 80 per cent of the largest 100 companies publish CR reports (the UK, Denmark, Brazil and the Netherlands are exceptions). This decline may result from cost-cutting measures by major companies in the face of the difficult economic conditions which have prevailed since the 2008 global financial crisis. (We discuss the assurance of CR reports in detail in section 17.5).

Since the early days of CR reporting, not only has the practice of such reporting become more prevalent but the content and form of CR reports have also

---

[6] In 1999, nine of the 11 countries included in KPMG's survey were European – Belgium, Denmark, Finland, France, Germany, the Netherlands, Norway, Sweden and the UK. The other two countries were the United States of America (USA) and Australia (KPMG, 1999).

changed markedly. As indicated in the Introduction to this chapter, during the late 1980s and 1990s, political, media and public attention focused on the environmental impact of major companies. In response, companies began to provide information on the environmental impact of their operations and products. However, as societal concern widened to embrace companies' social impact (for example, their use of child labour, 'sweat shops', equal employment opportunities, health and safety in the workplace and of products, and similar matters), companies broadened their purely 'environmental reports' into 'environmental and social' reports. Within a few years, societal concern widened further to embrace companies' total impact – environmental, social and economic. In order to demonstrate they were acting in a socially responsible manner and as good corporate citizens, companies began to publish wide-ranging 'corporate responsibility' or 'sustainability' reports. The change is reflected in KPMG's observation that, until 1999, "CR reporting [was] purely environmental [but, by 2005] sustainability (social, environmental and economic) reporting [had] become mainstream among G250 companies" (KPMG, 2005, p. 4). As shown in Figure 17.1, it is also reflected in a change in the title of CR reports published by the G250 companies between 1999 and 2005. Since 2005, the use of the title 'sustainability' (or 'corporate responsibility') report has become so commonplace that KPMG has not provided information on report titles. In the UK, the change in CR report content is similarly reflected in the change in report titles used by major UK companies. For example, between 1998 and 2000, BP plc published *Environmental and Social Reports* (termed *Update* in 1999 and *Review* in 2000). In 2001 it produced a report entitled *Performance for All of Our Futures* but, in 2002, returned to *Environmental and Social Review*. Between 2003 and 2007 it used the title *Sustainability Report* and, since 2008, *Sustainability Review*. Along similar lines, from 2003 to 2006 BT plc produced *Social and Environmental Reports* but, between 2007 and 2011, it used the title *Sustainability Report* (or *Review*). However, its 2012 report is entitled *Better Future Report*.

At the same time as the content of CR reports has changed, so too has their form. During the 1980s, CR information was frequently confined to a few brief statements in companies' annual reports. However, during the 1990s, separate CR reports (however titled) became the norm. Over time, these developed into very extensive reports, often exceeding 100 pages in length, complete with photographs, graphs and other diagrammatic and pictorial representations of relevant information.[7] As shown in Figure 17.2, in 2011, 96 (72 + 24) per cent of the G250 and 84 (69 + 15) per cent of the N100 companies

---

[7] Since 2010, many companies have provided their (very extensive) CR reports on the Internet rather than in hard copy.

Figure 17.2: Extent of 'integrating' CR information in the annual reports of companies surveyed by KPMG in 2011

	G250 companies		N100 companies	
	No.	%	No.	%
Companies whose CR reports were analysed	238	100	2189	100
- with a separate CR report only (no integrated reporting)	171	72	1505	69
- with CR information integrated in the annual report and a separate CR report	57	24	344	16
- with CR information integrated in the annual report only	10	4	340	15
Companies with CR information integrated in annual report:	67	100	684	100
- with separate CR section in annual report only	42	63	465	68
- CR information integrated throughout the directors' report only	8	12	48	7
- separate CR section in annual report and integrated throughout the directors ' report	17	25	171	25

Source: KPMG, 2011, p. 25

surveyed by KPMG produced separate CR reports, but KMPG noted a growing trend towards companies combining CR and financial information in their annual reports. In this regard, KPMG observes: "The concept of integrated reporting has exploded onto the CR agenda over the past three years" (KPMG, 2011, p. 23). However, as can be seen from Figure 17.2, only 28 (24 + 4) and 31 (16 + 15) per cent of G250 and N100 companies, respectively, 'integrate' CR information in their annual reports and, of these, 63 and 68 per cent of G250 and N100 companies, respectively, provide CR information in a separate section of their annual reports rather than integrating it with other non-CR information.[8]

17.3 WHY DO COMPANIES PUBLISH CORPORATE RESPONSIBILITY REPORTS?

Given the prevalence and rapid growth of CR reporting, and bearing in mind that much, if not most, of this reporting is undertaken voluntarily, the question arises as to why companies engage in this activity. Three key reasons may be identified, namely, (i) regulatory requirements, (ii) business drivers and (iii) investor preferences. We discuss each of these below.

---

[8] KPMG does not consider CR information in companies' annual reports to be 'integrated' if it does not include "the quality and depth of metrics to be classed as a true CR report" (KPMG, 2011, p. 24). Mere reference to CR information in the annual report does not qualify.

17.3.1 Regulatory requirements

During the past 30 or so years, non-natural environmental catastrophes have caused immense harm to humans, the environment and property. The following are among the most notorious:

- the escape of tons of toxic gas from the Union Carbide plant in Bhopal (India) in 1984;
- the release of radioactive material from the nuclear power station at Chernobyl (Ukraine) in 1986;
- the spillage of 10.9 million tons of crude oil from the supertanker *Exxon Valdez* when it ran aground in Prince William Sound (South Alaska) in 1989;
- the explosion and loss of 210 million gallons of oil from BP's Deepwater Horizon well in the Gulf of Mexico in 2010.

Disasters such as these result in a global outcry and demands that corporate activities be regulated so that those responsible are held accountable and made to suffer severe financial penalties or other sanction. Governments, first in the United States of America (USA) but rapidly followed by those in the UK, Continental Europe, Australia, New Zealand and elsewhere, have responded to society's concerns by introducing a plethora of laws and regulations designed to protect the environment. Such laws and regulations have had a major impact on businesses and how they conduct their activities. This has been noted by, for example, Roussey (1992) who explains:

> Entities operating in this country [the US] are now subject to a growing number of environmental laws and regulations. As a result, these entities may be responsible for significant clean-up costs and liabilities if they have not appropriately disposed of hazardous wastes. They may also be liable for personal injury claims from employees and customers if there are toxic problems in the workplace or associated with their products. These concerns relate not only to the original owners, operators, or users of waste disposal sites, but they also relate to other third parties not originally associated with a contaminated site, or disposal at such a site. (pp. 47–48)

In the European Union (EU), the key legislative provision was enacted in the Single European Act (SEA; European Communities, 1987) which became effective in July 1987. Art. 130R of this Act states:

1. Action by the [European] Community relating to the environment shall have the following objectives:
   (i) to preserve, protect and improve the quality of the environment;
   (ii) to contribute towards protecting human health;
   (iii) to ensure a prudent rational utilization of natural resources.
2. Action by the Community relating to the environment shall be based on the principles that preventive action should be taken, that environmental

> damage should as a priority be rectified at source, and that the polluter should pay. Environmental protection requirements shall be a component of the Community's other policies.

Guided by this Article, EU Member States enacted their own body of laws and regulations. In the UK, probably the most far-reaching legislation is that of the Environmental Protection Act 1990. This introduced the notion of integrated pollution control and the principle that the polluter must pay. As Vinten (1996) explains:

> Previously each component of the environment – air, land and water – had its own separate laws and systems of control. Now Her Majesty's Inspectorate of Pollution will control the releases [into the] air, water and land from most polluting industrial processes. . . . [and, companies will] have to . . . pay penalties for breaking the specified emission limits. . . . Attempting to avoid compliance is a high risk strategy, with serious consequences for the company and those within it. (pp. 15–16)

Although the various environmental laws and regulations introduced at this time did not require companies to provide information about their environmental impact in their annual reports, their effect on corporate activities often rendered it beneficial for companies to do so. For example, companies, especially in the USA, but increasingly in the UK and in many other countries in the world, could face enormous actual or potential liabilities as a result of breaching environmental laws or regulations, or from 'inheriting' such breaches (for example by 'acquiring' land contaminated by mercury, asbestos or other harmful substances) through transactions such as acquisitions. The extent of such liabilities may be gleaned from Beets and Souther's (1999) report on the extent of such liabilities in the USA in 1993:

> The overall known environmental liability in the United States is . . . estimated to be between 2 and 5 percent of the gross national product. Environmental cleanup costs under the Comprehensive Environmental Response, Compensation and Liability Act of 1980, or "Superfund", are approximately \$500 billion and will take 40 to 50 years to complete. (p. 130)

Against this background, it is understandable that shareholders, investors and other stakeholders put pressure on companies to disclose their environmental policy and performance in their annual report – and, in general, it is in the companies' interests to do so.

As we noted earlier, during the late 1990s and, more particularly, in the 2000s, societal concern increased and broadened from companies' environmental impact to embrace their social and economic impact. This wider concern is reflected in enactment of the EU Accounts Modernisation Directive (AMD; EU, 2003a). This Directive, which became effective in April 2005, requires all large and medium-sized companies in EU Member States to provide a business review in their annual reports; for quoted companies[9] the review is to include, to the extent necessary for an understanding of the development, performance and position of the company's business, information about, *inter alia*, environmental and social matters. In the UK, the AMD requirements were originally incorporated in the Companies Act (CA) 2006, s. 417. However, as we explain in more detail in Chapter 5, section 5.2.2, *The Companies Act 2006 (Strategic Report and Directors' Report) Regulations 2013* [Statutory Instrument (SI) 2013] removed section 417 from CA 2006 and inserted new sections (ss. 414A, 414B, 414C, 414D) in its place. These require all UK large and medium-sized companies[10] to include a strategic report within their annual reports. This is to contain, *inter alia*:

   (i)   a balanced and comprehensive analysis of the development and performance of the company's business during the financial year and of its position at the end of the year. The analysis is to include, to the extent necessary for readers to gain an understanding of the development, performance or position of the company's business, key financial and non-financial performance indicators. However, medium-sized companies need not include key performance indicators insofar as they relate to non-financial information;[11]

   (ii) a description of its principal risks and uncertainties.

The strategic reports of quoted companies must also include, to the extent necessary for readers to understand the development, performance and position of the company's business, information about:

   (i)   environmental matters (including the impact of the company's business on the environment),

   (ii) the company's employees, and

   (iii) social, community and human rights issues,

including information about the company's policies relating to these matters and the effectiveness of those policies (CA 2006, s. 414C).

The directors of companies listed on the London Stock Exchange are additionally required by *The UK Corporate Governance Code* (FRC, 2012a, prov. C.1.1) to explain in the company's annual report their responsibility for preparing the annual report and financial statements and to state that they consider the

---

[9] Quoted companies are companies whose equity securities are traded on a regulated market in the European Economic Area [EEA: the EEA comprises the EU's Member States (with the exception of Croatia) together with Norway, Iceland and Liechtenstein] or on the New York Stock Exchange or NASDAQ (CA 2006, s. 385).

[10] See Chapter 5, section 5.2.1, for the criteria companies must meet in order to qualify as small and thus fall outside of the requirement to include a strategic report within their annual reports. Also note that no public, banking or insurance company, or an e-money issuer, can qualify as a 'small company'.

[11] 'Key performance indicators' are defined in CA 2006, s. 414C, to mean: "factors by reference to which the development, performance or position of the company's business can be measured effectively".

company's annual report, together with its financial statements, is fair, balanced and understandable, and provides the information necessary for shareholders to assess the company's performance, business model and strategy (including, presumably, information that enables shareholders to assess the nature and significance of CR issues in the company's performance, business model and strategy). The UK Listing Authority's (UKLA) Listing Rules require the auditors of these companies to assess the validity of the directors' statement and, if they are of the opinion that it is not justified, to say so in their audit reports (see Chapter 5, section 5.5.5).

In recent years, as the effects of climate change have become all too evident (in the form of severe droughts and floods, melting glaciers and ice caps, a rise in sea level, and changing – or disappearing – habitats for flora and fauna, etc.) societal concern has, once again, centred on the environmental impact of companies – and, more particularly, on their greenhouse gas (GHG) emissions. In the EU, the politicians responded to this concern by establishing the EU Emissions Trading Scheme (EU ETS) (EU, 2003b). Launched in 2005, the scheme requires intensive energy-using industrial undertakings like power stations, oil refineries, iron and steel works, factories making cement, glass, bricks, and pulp and paper, to monitor and report their GHG emissions. By January 2013, the scheme covered more than 11,000 industrial installations in 31 countries (27 EU Member States, Norway, Lichtenstein, Iceland and Croatia). Between them, these industrial installations accounted for some 45 per cent of the EU's GHG emissions [European Commission (EC), 2013a].[12]

The scheme works on a 'cap and trade' principle. Each industrial installation is allocated an annual 'cap' (or limit) on the GHG it is permitted to emit. It is also given, or is able to purchase, 'allowances'[13] up to the total of its cap. At the end of each year, each installation is required to surrender sufficient allowances to cover the GHG it has emitted during the year – or face hefty fines. The scheme has three trading periods: 2005 to 2007, 2008 to 2012 and 2013 to 2020. In each period the GHG emission cap allocated to each installation is reduced so that, by December 2020, the GHG emissions of the installations covered by the scheme will be 21 per cent lower than in 2005 (EC, 2013a). In each period the 'free' allowances given to the installations is also reduced; during the first period, they received almost all of their allowances free of charge but, by 2013, this had been reduced to an average of less

---

[12] In 2012, flights to and from the 31 countries (other than Croatia which was included in 2014) were brought into the EU ETS (EC, 2013a).

[13] An 'allowance' is defined to mean: "an allowance to emit one tonne of carbon dioxide equivalent during a specified period" (EU, 2003b, art. 3).

than 60 per cent (EC, 2013a; 2013b). The remaining allowances have to be purchased – thus encouraging installations to further reduce their GHG emissions.

Since April 2010, the EU ETS has been supplemented in the UK by the Carbon Reduction Commitment (CRC) Energy Efficiency Scheme. This aims to improve energy efficiency and to reduce carbon emissions in the UK by 2050 to at least 80 per cent below the 1990 level (CarbonCredentials, 2013). The scheme which, like the EU ETS, is mandatory, applies to all large non-energy-intensive public and private sector organisations in the UK which spend more than £500,000 annually on energy bills, excluding those included in the EU ETS. In 2013, it applied to approximately 3,000 organisations (Carbon Footprint, 2013). Like the EU ETS, the CRC scheme operates on a 'cap and trade' principle and requires the affected organisations to monitor and report their GHG emissions annually. However, unlike the EU ETS, the CRC scheme does not provide 'free' allowances; since April 2011 the organisations concerned have been required to purchase an 'allowance' for each tonne of carbon emitted from energy use in buildings and some on-site fuel use (CarbonCredentials, 2013).

Although both the EU ETS and CRC scheme require affected companies to monitor and report their annual GHG emissions, this reporting is to a 'competent authority'; in the UK, this is the Department for Environment, Food and Rural Affairs (Defra). Neither scheme requires companies to report their GHG emissions in their annual reports. However, such reporting has been encouraged by Defra and, in 2009, it provided guidance to organisations on measuring and reporting their GHG emissions. Defra (2009) explains.

> . . . This guidance aims to support UK organisations in reducing their contribution to climate change. It explains how to measure greenhouse gas (GHG) emissions and set targets to reduce them. It is intended for all sizes of business and for public and voluntary sector organisations. There are direct benefits to organisations from measuring and reporting as they will benefit from lower energy and resource costs, [and] a better understanding of their exposure to the risks of climate change . . . A number of organisations are seeking information from their suppliers on greenhouse gas emissions and so many small businesses will increasingly be expected to measure and report on their emissions. (p. 2)

However, a year after the guidance was published, a survey of 100 UK listed companies by Deloitte found that "only nine per cent of the companies reported their carbon footprint in line with government guidelines" (Hinks, 2010). Further, Harrison (Deloitte's Head of Carbon Reporting) observed:

> The wide variety of both formal and informal carbon reporting practices identified does not facilitate comparison between companies or industry sectors, making it difficult to evaluate the relative performance of companies in

monitoring and reducing their carbon footprint, a primary goal of the government in publishing the Defra guidance. (as quoted, Hinks, 2010)

Perhaps not surprisingly, given the apparent failure by companies to follow voluntarily the Defra guidance, *The Companies Act 2006 (Strategic Report and Directors' Report) Regulations 2013* introduced a requirement for all UK quoted companies to report their GHG emissions in the directors' report (SI 2013).[14,15] In particular they are required to report, for the current and preceding year [except in respect of (ii) below]:

(i)   the annual quantity of emissions in tonnes of carbon dioxide equivalent resulting from:
  – activities for which the company is responsible, including the combustion of fuel and the operation of any facility, and
  – the purchase of electricity, heat, steam or cooling by the company for its own use;[16]

(ii) the methodologies used to calculate the information provided in accordance with (i) above;

(iii) at least one ratio which expresses the company's reported annual emissions in relation to a quantifiable factor associated with its activities.

Commenting on the planned introduction of the Regulations, Spelman (the then Secretary of State for Environment, Food and Rural Affairs) explained:

Mandatory reporting of GHG emissions by all quoted companies will provide transparency enabling investors to see how listed companies are managing their carbon liabilities. This is essential information for investors who wish to assess medium to long-term risks. Business groups have called for regulation to create a common standard on GHG reporting and a level playing field, and to create transparency for investors and wider stakeholders. (Spelman, 2012)

These regulations complement the CA 2006 (s. 414C) requirement for all UK quoted companies to provide environmental and social information in their strategic reports. Currently, there is no requirement for this information (including GHG information) to be audited. However, as we noted earlier, the auditors of companies listed on the London Stock Exchange (all of which are

---

[14] Greenhouse gases are defined to include the six Kyoto gases (carbon dioxide, methane, nitrous oxide, hydrofluorocarbons, perfluorocarbons and sulfur hexofloride) (SI 2013, para 20).

[15] Where they consider it appropriate to do so, companies may include their GHG emission information in their strategic report, rather than in the directors' report. But, if they do so, they must disclose in the directors' report that they have done so.

[16] SI 2013 (para 15) provides that these requirements:
apply only to the extent that is practical for the company to obtain the information in question; but . . . [where information is not provided, the directors'] report must state what information is not included and why.

quoted companies) are required to consider whether the information provided in their clients' annual reports is fair, balanced and understandable and provides the information necessary for readers to assess the company's performance, business model and strategy – and to report in their audit reports if, in their opinion, the information provided does not meet these criteria. Further, as we note in Chapter 14, section 14.2, the auditors of all companies are required to state in their audit reports whether the information provided in the directors' report and (for all but small companies) the strategic report is consistent with the company's financial statements – including information about liabilities that may have arisen as a result of breaching CR related laws and regulations.

17.3.2 Business drivers

Notwithstanding the reporting requirements noted above, much environmental, social and other CR information provided by UK companies goes well beyond the requirements and is provided voluntarily – either in stand-alone reports or (as noted in section 17.2) increasingly, within their annual reports. So, there must be reasons, other than regulatory requirements, that motivate companies to report CR information. According to Ethical Investment Research Services (EIRiS; 2007), business reasons are strong drivers of CR reporting. They state:

> For certain companies there is undoubtedly a positive financial case for adopting and enhancing responsible business practices. Companies may increase sales and profitability by increasing their appeal in the ethical consumer market. The numbers of consumers making ethical purchases is on the rise . . . In addition, responsible business has the potential to improve financial performance by delivering improvements in staff attitudes and productivity and enhancements to internal processes. Lowering operating costs can also be achieved alongside environmental performance improvements. (EIRiS, 2007, p. 17)

EIRiS' assertions are supported by the findings of KPMG's triennial surveys. As can be seen from Figure 17.3, business drivers figure prominently among the reasons for publishing CR information cited by the G250 and N100 companies.

A striking feature of Figure 17.3 is the importance of 'reputation or brand' and 'ethical considerations' as reasons for G250 and N100 companies publishing CR information. In an environment characterised by public and political concern about the environmental impact of companies' operations and outputs, the health and safety of their products and workplaces, fair trade, employment practices and so on, and increasing consumer demand for 'green' and 'sustainable' products, companies may enhance their image and reputation, and increase their sales and market share, by publishing positive CR

Figure 17.3: Reasons for publishing corporate responsibility reports cited G250 and N100 companies surveyed by KPMG

Reasons for publishing CR reports	G250 companies			N100 companies		
	2005	2008	2011	2005	2008	2011
	%	%	%	%	%	%
Reputation or brand	27	55	67	Inform-ation not avail-able	67	59
Ethical considerations	53	69	58		73	48
Employees' motivation	47	52	44		48	35
Innovation and learning	53	55	44		41	32
Risk management or risk reduction	47	35	35		38	28
Access to capital or increased shareholder value	39	29	32		26	20
Economic considerations	74	68	32		64	33
Strengthened supplier relationships	13	32	22		27	16
Market position (market share) improvement	21	22	22		36	21
Improved relationships with governmental authorities	9	21	18		19	14
Cost savings	9	17	10		14	10

Source: KPMG, 2005, 2008, 2011

information.[17] Further, combined with 'employees' motivation' and 'innovation and learning' (which are likely to increase output but lower production costs) and 'cost savings', reporting CR information seems likely to translate into improved financial performance. This conclusion is supported by KPMG's observation:

> Where Corporate Responsibility (CR) reporting was once seen as fulfilling a moral obligation to society, many companies are now recognizing it as a business imperative. Today, companies are increasingly demonstrating that CR reporting provides financial value and drives innovation. . . . Close to half of the G250 companies (47 percent) reported gaining financial value [as a result of publishing CR reports]. (KPMG, 2011, p. 18)

17.3.3 Investor preferences

Like management decisions, investors' decisions are based on available information and, all other things being equal, the more comprehensive and the higher the quality of the information, the better the decisions made. Thus, where companies publish CR reports – particularly if these are externally assured – investors have additional information on which to base their investment decisions.

---

[17] It should, however, be recalled from section 17.3.1 that, in the UK, if CR information is provided in the annual report of a listed company, it is required to be fair and balanced and, therefore, unbiased.

Globally, investor pressure on companies to provide CR information has resulted from, and been strengthened by, increased public awareness of CR issues through wider (and more probing) media coverage of corporate activities and access to information on the Internet. Further, since the 1990s, investors in the UK (particularly institutional investors) have been urged by influential bodies such as the Association of British Insurers (ABI) to pay regard to companies' environmental, social and similar performance, in addition to financial indicators, when making their investment decisions. Such developments seem to have influenced investors' decisions; the results of a number of studies of investor preferences show that many investors seek to invest in companies with a good track record for acting in an environmentally, socially and/or ethically responsible manner (see, for example, Investors Chronicle, 1998; Krumsiek, 1998; Gilmour & Caplan, 2001). If companies are to access funds from the growing pool of such investors, they need to disclose information that shows they conduct their business in an environmentally, socially and ethically responsible manner. Indeed, given investor preferences, such reporting may result in a rise in their share price (as demand for their shares increases) and enhanced ability to attract new capital. The importance of the last factor is reflected in KPMG's finding that, in 2011, 32 per cent of G250 companies cited 'access to capital or increased shareholder value' as a key reason for publishing CR information (see Figure 17.3).

The rapid growth of 'responsible' investment funds and indices (for example, FTSE4Good, Dow Jones Sustainability Index and Carbon Disclosure Leadership Index[18]) since the turn of the twenty-first century provides further evidence of the importance to investors of 'ethical' or 'responsible' investments – and the importance to companies of being accepted as providing opportunities for such investment. In this regard, EIRiS (2007) observes:

> The value of responsible investment funds under management has grown rapidly in the past ten years. . . . In addition, increasing numbers of mainstream investors are beginning to incorporate consideration of ESG [environmental, social and governance] factors into their investment decisions. Consequently, companies are motivated to behave responsibly [and report on their behaviour] in order to access this growing volume of investment funds. [Further], there is increasing evidence that considering ESG issues in investment analyses can improve the performance of funds. (p. 19)

The amounts invested in – and growth of – responsible investment funds are staggering. FTSE4Good reports that, in 2010, \$10.1 trillion (approximately, £6.4 trillion) was invested in professionally managed responsible investment funds – compared with \$6.8 trillion (£4.3 trillion) in 2008, \$3.6 trillion in 2006

---

[18] Information about these indices is provided in the Appendix to this chapter.

and \$2.6 trillion in 2002 (FTSE4Good, 2011, pp. 4–5). The Global Sustainable Investment Alliance (GSIA)[19] similarly reports that, as at 31 December 2011, "the estimated size of the global sustainable investment market . . . is at least US\$13.6 trillion"; of this, Europe accounted for nearly US\$8.8 trillion, followed by the USA with US\$3.7 trillion and Canada with US\$0.6 trillion (GSIA, 2012, p. 9).

17.4 CORPORATE RESPONSIBILITY REPORTING GUIDELINES

Given the significance of 'responsible' and 'sustainable' investments around the world, it is evident that companies need to ensure investors are aware of their CR policies and performance – hence, they need to report on these matters. However, unless they report according to a standard set of guidelines, the quantity and quality of the information provided is likely to vary widely. KPMG has highlighted the importance of companies adopting a common set of standards or guidelines for measuring and reporting their CR information. It explains:

> Developing a standard set of metrics and reporting principles is critical to the ongoing development of CR. For one, the market must be able to compare the value and relative impact of CR initiatives against the wider industry and sector competitors. Executives will also find that standard CR metrics provide a consistent method for benchmarking progress, both against internal objectives and external competitors. (KPMG, 2011, p. 20)

Notwithstanding its importance, at present, there is no universally accepted set of reporting guidelines. Nevertheless, over the past 15 or so years, CR reporting guidelines have been developed and, as shown in Figure 17.4, one set – the Global Reporting Initiative (GRI) Guidelines – seems to be gaining acceptance by major companies around the world. Indeed, KPMG has referred to the GRI Guidelines as: "the *de facto* global standard for CR reporting" (KPMG, 2011, p. 20). However, it should be noted that a significant proportion of major companies adopt the GRI Guidelines in combination with other guidance (see Figure 17.4).

The GRI is "a non-profit organisation that promotes economic, environmental and social sustainability" (GRI, 2013). The Fédération des Experts Comptables Européens (FEE; 2001, p. 2) explains its origins and objectives as follows:

> The GRI was originally convened in 1997 by CERES (Coalition for Environmentally Responsible Economies) in partnership with UNEP (United Nations

---

Figure 17.4: Guidelines adopted by G250 and N100 companies surveyed by KPMG

	G250 companies			N100 companies		
	2005	2008	2011	2005	2008	2011
No. of companies included in KPMG's survey	250	250	250	1600	2200	3400
CR reporting guidelines adopted	%	%	%	%	%	%
GRI guidelines	70	77	80	Inform-ation not avail-able	69	69
National reporting standards	13	19	21		17	10
Company developed criteria	3	20	21		19	13
Other (including stakeholder consultation)	21	13	17		13	28

Source: KPMG, 2005, 2008, 2011

Environment Programme) and has been developed by a steering committee representing a mix of stakeholders. . . . The GRI seeks to make sustainability reporting as routine and credible as financial reporting in terms of compatibility, rigour, and verifiability. . . . In June 2000 GRI published its [first] *Sustainability Reporting Guidelines* which have already formed the basis for a number of sustainability reports.

Version 2 of the Guidelines (G2) was published in 2002, version 3 (G3) in 2006 and version 3.1 (G3.1) in 2011. In G3.1, the GRI (2011, p. 3) explains:

The GRI Reporting Framework is intended to serve as a generally accepted framework for reporting on an organization's economic, environmental, and social performance. It is designed for use by organizations of any size, sector, or location. It . . . contains general and sector-specific content that has been agreed by a wide range of stakeholders around the world to be generally applicable for reporting an organization's sustainability performance.

The Sustainability Reporting Guidelines (the Guidelines) consist of Principles for defining report content and ensuring the quality of reported information. It also includes Standard Disclosures made up of Performance Indicators and other disclosure items, as well as guidance on specific technical topics in reporting.

The Guidelines (GRI, 2011) identify four principles which define the content of a CR report, namely:
- *Materiality* – the report should include topics and performance indicators that reflect the organisation's significant economic, environmental and social impacts, or are likely to substantially influence the assessments and decisions of stakeholders (p. 8).
- *Stakeholder inclusiveness* – the reporting organisation should identify its stakeholders and explain in the report how it has responded to their reasonable expectations and interests (p. 10).
- *Sustainability context* – the organisation's performance should be reported in the wider context of sustainability (that is, meeting society's current

needs without compromising the ability of future generations to meet their needs) (pp. 2, 11).

- *Completeness* – coverage of the material topics and performance indicators, and identification of the organisation's components (i.e., subsidiaries, divisions, departments, etc.) that are covered by the report, should be sufficient to reflect the reporting organisation's significant economic, environmental and social impacts, and enable stakeholders to assess its performance during the reporting period (p. 12).

The GRI (2011) explains: "Application of these Principles with the Standard Disclosures, determines the topics and [Performance] Indicators to be reported" (p. 4).

From the GRI's principles outlined above, it is evident that the content of a CR report should reflect the information needs and preferences of the company's stakeholders. In order to determine those needs and preferences, companies frequently engage in stakeholder dialogue.[20] FEE explains that such dialogue enables companies to ascertain:

- what matters stakeholders want in a sustainability report (and whether past reports have met their needs)
- the levels at which matters become significant enough to be included [that is, materiality levels]
- what imprecision in measurement or degree of approximation is acceptable [that is, the tolerable error][21]
- what assurance, if any, stakeholders value. (FEE, 2002, para 160)

In addition to identifying principles for determining the content of CR reports, the GRI Guidelines specify the following six principles which define the quality of the information:

- *Balance* – both positive and negative aspects of the organisation's performance should be reported to enable a reasoned assessment of its overall performance (p. 13).
- *Comparability* – issues and information should be selected, compiled and reported consistently; the information should also be presented in a manner that enables stakeholders to analyse changes in the organisation's performance over time and make comparisons of its performance with that of other organisations (p. 14).

---

[20] FEE (2002) defines stakeholders and stakeholder dialogue as follows:

Stakeholders: Individuals or organisations that have, or could have, a non-trivial interest in a sustainable development decision of a company. The interest could be in influencing the decision or simply through being affected by the outcomes of a decision. For a company, stakeholders include: investors, government agencies, workers, suppliers, customers, and those potentially affected by environmental and other impacts. (para 155)

Stakeholder dialogue: Interaction between a company and its stakeholders to ascertain stakeholder views and communicate information relevant to stakeholders. (Glossary)

[21] Materiality levels and tolerable error are discussed in the context of external financial statement audits in Chapter 9, section 9.3.1.

- *Accuracy* – reported information should be sufficiently accurate and detailed to enable stakeholders to assess the organisation's performance (p. 15).
- *Timeliness* – reporting should occur on a regular schedule that enables information to be available in time for stakeholders to make informed decisions (p. 16).
- *Clarity* – information should be presented in a manner that renders it understandable and accessible to stakeholders (p. 16).
- *Reliability* – information should be gathered, recorded, compiled, analysed and disclosed in a manner that facilitates its independent examination (p. 17).[22]

The principle of reliability brings us to assurance engagements.

17.5 CORPORATE RESPONSIBILITY ASSURANCE ENGAGEMENTS

17.5.1 Meaning of 'assurance engagements'

In section 17.2 we note that a significant proportion of major companies in the UK (and, indeed, around the globe) choose not only to publish CR information but also to have the information independently assured. In 2011, KPMG found that this applied to 46 per cent of the G250 and 56 per cent of the N100 companies it surveyed which published CR reports; this compares with 40 and 55 per cent, respectively, of the G250 and N100 companies that published CR reports in 2008 (see Figure 17.1). Given the marked increase over the past decade in the proportion of the world's major companies that publish CR reports, it might be expected that more of these companies would want the credibility of their reports to be enhanced by having them independently assured.

It is pertinent to note that in relation to providing credibility to CR information we use the word 'assured' rather than 'audited'. According to the International Framework for Assurance Engagements [International Auditing and Assurance Standards Board (IAASB), 2004a)] an 'assurance engagement' is:

---

[22] All sustainability reports prepared in accordance with GRI G3.1 are required to declare the level, according to the 'GRI's Application Levels' system, to which they have applied the GRI Reporting Framework. GRI (2011, p. 5) explains:

> . . . [T]here are three levels in the system. They are titled C, B, and A. The reporting criteria found in each level reflects an increasing application or coverage [from C at the lowest level to A at the highest] of the GRI Reporting Framework. An organization can self-declare a "plus" (+) at each level (ex., C+, B+, A+) if they have utilized external assurance [i.e. + signifies that the report has been independently assured].

From Ernst & Young's Assurance Statement on BP's 2011 *Sustainability Report* presented in Figure 17.7, it may be seen that BP declared an Application Level of A+.

. . . an engagement in which a practitioner expresses a conclusion designed to enhance the degree of confidence of the intended users [of information about a subject matter] other than the responsible party [for the subject matter] about the outcome of the evaluation or measurement of a subject matter against criteria. (para 7)

It can be seen that an external audit falls within this definition. Indeed, audits constitute a subset of assurance engagements but the terms 'audit' and 'assurance engagement' are usually distinguished by the level of assurance they are designed to give the information on which the auditor/assuror expresses an opinion. This difference is usually reflected in the form in which the opinion is expressed.

- *An audit* is designed to give what the IAASB (2004a, para 2) refers to as a 'reasonable' level of assurance about the credibility of the information the auditor has examined (such as a company's financial statements) and on which the auditor expresses an opinion. The opinion is expressed in a positive form – along the lines of: "In my opinion the information I have examined (which is identified) is a fair reflection of the underlying data or performance".

- *An assurance engagement* (which covers all assurance engagements other than an audit) is usually designed to give what the IAASB (2004b, para 2) refers to as 'limited assurance'. This is a lower level of assurance than that provided by an audit about the credibility of the information the assuror has examined (such as a company's CR information) and on which the assuror expresses an opinion. The opinion is usually expressed in a negative form – along the lines of: "In examining the information (which is identified) I have not encountered evidence which indicates the information is not a fair reflection of the underlying data or performance".

Similar to the IAASB, AccountAbility (AA),[23] in its assurance standard AA1000AS (2008) (AA, 2008), distinguishes between assurance engagements that provide a 'high' and a 'moderate' level of assurance. These equate to what the IAASB refers to as 'reasonable' and 'limited assurance' engagements. The nature of an assurance engagement conducted to provide credibility to CR information is almost invariably a 'limited assurance' engagement, designed to give a 'moderate' level of assurance.[24]

---

[23] The Institute of Social and Ethical Accountability refers to itself, in its publications, as AccountAbility.

[24] However, it should be noted that the assurance provided by Lloyd's Register Quality Assurance (LRQA) on BT's 2012 *Better Future* report is stated as a 'high level' of assurance. Nevertheless, LRQA also provides the following negative opinion: "It is also our conclusion that the specified performance information is reliable as nothing has come to our attention that would cause us to believe otherwise" (see Figure 17.8).

17.5.2 Development of assurance standards

Just as the GRI Guidelines emerged to assist organisations report their CR performance, so an Assurance Standard (AA1000AS) was developed by AA in 2003 (AA, 2003) to assist assurance providers assure the reported information. According to AA, AA1000AS was "the world's first sustainability standard. It was developed to assure the credibility and quality of sustainability performance reporting. . ." (AA, 2008, p. 5). In 2008, AA1000AS was superseded by AA1000AS (2008). Referring to this standard, AA explains:

> . . . [It] provides a comprehensive way of holding an organisation to account for its management, performance and reporting on sustainability issues by evaluating the adherence of an organisation to the AA1000 AccountAbility Principles and the quality of the disclosed information on sustainability performance. (AA, 2008, p. 6)

There are three AA1000 Principles, namely:

> **Inclusivity:** For an organisation that accepts its accountability to those on whom it has an impact and who have an impact on it, inclusivity is the participation of stakeholders in developing and achieving an accountable and strategic response to sustainability.
>
> **Materiality:** Materiality is determining the relevance and significance of an issue to an organisation and its stakeholders. A material issue is an issue that will influence the decisions, actions and performance of an organisation or its stakeholders.
>
> **Responsiveness:** Responsiveness is an organisation's response to stakeholder issues that affect its sustainability performance and is realised through decisions, actions and performance, as well as communication with its stakeholders. (AA, 2013)

It can be seen that these principles are closely aligned to those defining the content of CR reports specified in the GRI's Guidelines (see section 17.4). AA (2013) explains that the value of its principles

> . . . lies in their comprehensive coverage and the flexibility of their application. They demand that an organisation actively engages with its stakeholders, fully identifies and understands sustainability issues that will have an impact on its performance, including economic, environmental, social and longer term financial performance, and then uses this understanding to develop responsible business strategies and performance objectives. (AA, 2013)

It should be noted that AA1000AS (2008) has a broader focus than its predecessor [AA1000AS (2003)]; in addition to providing guidance on assuring entities' published sustainability reports, it provides guidance on assuring the adherence of their sustainability management and performance to the three principles indicated above. Indeed, it distinguishes between two types of engagements.

- *Type 1 engagements* focus on the organisation's adherence to the three AA1000 Principles. AA (2008) explains that these engagements are "intended to give stakeholders assurance on the way an organisation manages [its] sustainability performance, and how it communicates this in its sustainability reporting, without verifying the reliability of the reported information" (p. 9). Type 1 engagements are primarily concerned with examining the entity's sustainability systems and processes, and evaluating their adherence to the AA1000 Principles. The manner in which the entity reports on its sustainability performance is reviewed but the information is not examined for completeness or accuracy.

- *Type 2 engagements* have a dual focus – they require the assuror not only to evaluate the adherence of the entity's sustainability management and performance to the three AA1000 Principles (as for a Type 1 engagement) but also to evaluate the reliability of specified sustainability performance information (information the reporting organisation and the assuror agree to include within the assurance engagement). AA (2008) explains:

  ... Specified information is selected based on the materiality determination and needs to be meaningful to the intended users of the assurance statement. . . . The evaluation of the reliability of specified sustainability performance information is based on explicit management assertions about sustainability performance and includes a review of their completeness and accuracy. (p. 10)

  The outcome of a Type 2 engagement is a formal assurance statement in which the assuror reports the engagement's findings and conclusions about the reliability of the sustainability performance information. Examples of such statements are provided in Figures 17.7 and 17.8.

Another assurance standard with general application to published CR reports, and one with which all qualified accountants (including auditors) in the UK must comply if they undertake assurance engagements, is the International Standard on Assurance Engagements (ISAE) 3000: *Assurance Engagements other than Audits or Reviews of Historical Financial Information* (IAASB, 2004b).[25] This provides guidance for assurance engagements that are similar in nature to AA1000AS (2008) Type 2 engagements but focuses on assuring reported CR information. The Standard encapsulates the key elements of the International Standards on Auditing (ISAs) and has sections addressing: ethical requirements, quality control, engagement acceptance and continuance, agreeing the terms of the engagement, planning and performing the engagement, using the work of an expert, obtaining evidence, considering subsequent events, documentation, and preparing the assurance report.

---

[25] The IAASB has issued a separate assurance standard for assuring published GHG information, namely, ISAE 3410: *Assurance Engagements on Greenhouse Gas Statements* (IAASB, 2012). This is a detailed and technical standard focusing, as its name suggests, on providing assurance on information provided by organizations on their GHG emissions. In order to comply with ISAE 3410, assurance providers must also comply with ISAE 3000 (ISAE 3410, para 15).

It might be thought that those undertaking engagements to assure externally reported CR information would choose to adopt either AA1000AA (2008) or ISAE 3000. However, according to Focus Report (2005, p. 6):

> [A joint study] by AccountAbility (a standards developer) and KPMG Sustainability B.V. in the Netherlands (an assurance practitioner) . . . concluded that the two international assurance standards are not in conflict and are not substitutes, but rather are complementary. As such, sustainability assurance based on the combined use of AA1000AS[26] and ISAE 3000 is likely to deliver enhanced results in approach, methodology, and conclusion, their communication, credibility, and ultimately the outcome in relation to stakeholder trust and behavior.

The standards used to assure the CR reports of the G250 and N100 companies surveyed by KPMG are shown in Figure 17.5. From a review of the figures, it can be seen that some assurance providers apply more than one standard. The dominance of ISAE 3000 may be explained by the requirement for all qualified accountants to adhere to this standard, irrespective of whether they also comply with AA1000AS (2008) or some other assurance standard. Ernst & Young, for example, applied both ISAE 3000 and AA1000AS (2008) in its assurance of BP plc's 2011 sustainability report (see Figure 17.7).

Figure 17.5: Assurance standards used to assure the CR reports of the G250 and N100 companies surveyed by KPMG

	G250 companies			N100 companies		
	2005	2008	2011	2005	2008	2011
No. of companies with independently assured CR reports	48	80	108	171	454	759
Assurance standards applied	%	%	%	%	%	%
ISAE 3000	24	62	65	10	36	59
AA1000AS	18	33	29	14	54	29
Other*	—	19	0	21	21	21
Information not provided by KPMG survey participants	Information not available		12	Information not available		13
* 'Other' standards are frequently national standards that apply in a particular country						

Source: KPMG, 2005, 2008, 2011

17.5.3   Providers of assurance services

From Figure 17.6 it may be seen that there are three main providers of assurance services – accounting firms, technical specialists and certification bodies.[27] Figure 17.6 also indicates that, rather than (or, in a few cases, as well as) having their CR information formally assured, a number of major companies rely on

---

[26] The study examined AA1000AS (2003) rather than AA1000AS (2008).

[27] The assurance provided by certification bodies in the context of a CR report is limited to assessing whether the reporting entity's report complies with the relevant certification body's requirements. It should be

commentary from third parties which they include in their CR reports. In this regard, KPMG (2008) explains:

> The commentary may be from influential stakeholder groups or reputable experts in a specialist corporate responsibility field. Some companies opt for a panel of stakeholders or experts to provide broader insight into their activities and performance. (p. 60)

Figure 17.6: Assurance providers for the G250 and N100 companies surveyed by KPMG

	G250 companies			N100 companies		
	2005	2008	2011	2005	2008	2011
No. of companies with independently assured CR reports	48	80	108	171	452	759
Assurance providers	%	%	%	%	%	%
Accounting/auditing firms	58	70	71	60	65	64
Certification bodies	21	13	16	8	18	15
Technical specialists and experts	2	17	14	25	22	18
Other (including third party commentary)	19	6	0	7	4	3

Source: KPMG, 2005, 2008, 2011

Commenting on the relative merits of the major accounting firms and technical specialists as providers of assurance services, MacKay (2000, p. 2) observes:

> The Big Five[28] trade on their audit experience, their sophisticated audit methodologies and their global brands. The consultants trade on their specialisation in environmental consultancy and their environmental expertise. The Big Five employ environmental specialists and the consultants employ auditors.[29]

> They both poach each other's staff and KPMG's environmental audit division was augmented some years ago by a mass defection of environmental audit experts from a client – The Body Shop. . . .The consultants can . . . be relied on to use words such as correct, accurate and complete in their reports; auditors generally balk at saying anything stronger than "properly collated".

Clearly, if assurance is to provide credibility to companies' CR reports, those providing assurance services must possess the attributes of independence, impartiality and competence. If accounting firms (or, indeed, any qualified accountants) provide assurance services, they are required by ISAE 3000, para 4, to comply with the International Ethics Standards Board for Accountants' (IESBA) *Code of Ethics for Professional Accountants* (2009). As a

---

noted that Lloyd's Register Quality Assurance (LRQA) is the certification body for BT's certification with the International Organization for Standardization (ISO) standards ISO 9001 (Quality management); ISO 14001 (Environmental management); ISO 27001 (Information technology – security techniques) and ISO 20000 (Information technology – service management) (see Figure 17.8).

[28] Arthur Andersen, Deloitte, Ernst & Young, KPMG, and PricewaterhouseCoopers. Andersen's collapsed in 2002 – after MacKay's statement.

[29] As we note in section 17.2, in 2000, CR reporting was still largely confined to environmental reporting.

consequence, they must meet the ethical requirements relating to independence, objectivity, ethical conduct, competence and due care, confidentiality and professional behaviour which we discuss in earlier chapters of this book (in particular, in Chapter 3).

For others who provide assurance services, AA1000AS (2008) spells out relevant requirements. The standard distinguishes between firms and individuals who provide assurance services, using the terms 'assurance providers' and 'assurance practitioners', respectively.[30] It specifies that an assurance provider is not to accept an assurance engagement "if it will be unduly limited by its relationship with the organisation or its stakeholders in reaching and publishing an independent and impartial assurance statement" (p. 14). It also stipulates that the assurance provider is to include, in its assurance statement, a statement regarding its independence and impartiality. This is to disclose:

- any relationships (including financial, commercial, preparation of the [CR] report, governance and ownership positions) that could be perceived to affect the assurance provider's ability to provide an independent and impartial statement, and
- any mechanisms or professional codes of practice designed to ensure independence to which the assurance provider or assurance practitioner are bound. (p. 14)

AA1000AS (2008) also specifies that an assurance provider is not to accept an assurance engagement unless it possesses the necessary competence. The firm is to ensure that its engagement teams (individual assurance practitioners and any external experts who, together, constitute an engagement team) are:

demonstrably competent in the following areas as a minimum:
- the AccountAbility Principles [outlined in section 17.5.2 above];
- application of reporting and assurance practices and standards;
- sustainability subject matter (including the specific subject matter of the engagement) [this includes environmental, economic, social and ethical matters], and
- stakeholder engagement. (p. 15)

Assurance providers are also required to "demonstrate adequate institutional competencies" (p. 15). These include possessing:

- infrastructure and systems designed to ensure that assurance engagements conducted by the firm are performed to a high standard;
- oversight mechanisms to ensure practitioners and experts conducting the firm's assurance engagements comply with assurance standards, the terms of the engagements, and any quality control policies and procedures the firm has developed;
- an adequate understanding of the legal aspects of the assurance process.

---

[30] We use the term 'assuror' to apply to either an assurance provider or an assurance practitioner.

17.5.4 Assuring corporate responsibility information

Having discussed the meaning of an assurance engagement, the standards that may be applied therein, the professional groups who conduct such engagements and the attributes they need to possess, we now need to consider how an assurance engagement is performed. As might be expected from our explanation of the difference between an audit and an assurance engagement in section 17.5.1, it proceeds in much the same way as an external financial statement audit. The engagement must be planned and conducted so as to enable the assuror to obtain sufficient appropriate evidence to support a conclusion about the reliability and completeness of the CR information examined. Like an external financial statement audit, it proceeds in a series of logically ordered steps that include the following.

(i) Pre-engagement procedures

Before accepting an assurance engagement, the potential assurance provider needs to consider, *inter alia*, whether:

- the assurance team possesses the necessary capabilities (including multi-disciplinary skills), competence and resources to complete the engagement to the required professional standard within a reasonable period of time;
- assurance team members (practitioners and, if applicable, external experts) possess the necessary degree of independence from the reporting entity;
- the subject matter to be assured is appropriate for assurance, and suitable criteria exist to enable the intended level of assurance to be achieved. The *International Framework for Assurance Engagements* (IAASB, 2004a) explains the characteristics of 'appropriate subject matter' and 'suitable criteria' as follows:

> An appropriate subject matter is:
> (a) Identifiable, and capable of consistent evaluation or measurement against the identified criteria; and
> (b) Such that the information about it can be subjected to procedures for gathering sufficient appropriate evidence to support . . . [an] assurance conclusion . . . (para 33)

> Suitable criteria exhibit the following characteristics:
> (a) Relevance: relevant criteria contribute to conclusions that assist decision-making by the intended users [of the assured information].
> (b) Completeness: criteria are sufficiently complete when relevant factors that could affect the conclusions in the context of the engagement circumstances are not omitted. Complete criteria include, where relevant, benchmarks for presentation and disclosure.

(c) Reliability: reliable criteria allow reasonably consistent evaluation or measurement of the subject matter . . . when used in similar circumstances by similarly qualified [assurance] practitioners.

(d) Neutrality: neutral criteria contribute to conclusions that are fee from bias.

(e) Understandability: understandable criteria contribute to conclusions that are clear, comprehensive, and not subject to significantly different interpretations. (para 36)

(ii) Agreeing the terms of the engagement

Unlike an external financial statement audit, where the objectives and scope are defined by statute and the level of assurance to be provided must, by definition, be high (or, more correctly, 'reasonable'), the objectives, scope[31] and level of assurance[32] to be provided by a CR assurance engagement need to be agreed by the reporting entity and the assurance provider. In many companies where such engagements take place, the directors reach a decision about these matters as an outcome of stakeholder dialogue.

The scope of a particular engagement may be limited to less than the whole of the entity's CR report. As FEE (2002) explains:

> This may be because the company does not want assurance on all of the report (perhaps because of cost or other assurance providers being involved), or because there are limitations through lack of suitable criteria or evidence that preclude some matters being included. [Additionally], for a given set of subject matter, the objectives of the assurance engagement may be restricted. For example: assurance may be given on the implementation of a policy, but not its enforcement; . . . [Further], for a given objective, a company may request in advance that the assurance provider does not employ the full range of possible evidence-gathering procedures. For example, visits to sites may be restricted or stakeholder dialogue prevented. (paras 117–119)

When considering the assurance of CR reports, we need to remember that, unlike statutory financial statement audits, in general, companies both publish CR information and have it independently assured voluntarily. Nevertheless, where the evidence-gathering procedures to be performed are restricted in some way, or the scope of the engagement is limited to less than the full CR report, the assuror needs to assess whether sufficient appropriate evidence can be collected to support a conclusion, and whether the parts of the report that

---

[31] The scope of the engagement refers to the aspects of the reporting entity's CR management, performance and reports that are to be covered by the assurance engagement.

[32] The entity and assuror may agree on a 'high' or 'moderate' level of assurance in terms of AA1000AS (2008) or on a 'reasonable' or 'limited' level in terms of ISAE 3000. Both Standards emphasise that, once the level of assurance to be provided has been agreed and the engagement has commenced, the assuror should not agree to a request by the entity to lower the level unless the entity provides reasonable justification for the change. Nevertheless, it is pertinent to note that, when the terms of the engagement are agreed, different levels of assurance may be agreed for different portions of the subject matter to be assured.

have (and have not) been independently assured can be defined sufficiently clearly for the report's users.

(iii) Planning the engagement

Both AA1000AS (2008) and ISAE 3000 require assurance practitioners to adopt an attitude of professional scepticism[33] when planning and performing an assurance engagement. They also require the engagement to be planned so that it will be performed effectively. This involves developing:

- an overall strategy for the scope, timing and performance of the engagement, and
- an engagement plan which sets out the nature, timing and extent of the evidence-gathering procedures to be performed and the reasons for selecting them.

The nature and extent of the planning process will vary depending on factors such as:

- the size and complexity of the reporting entity;
- the subject matter to be assured, and the identified criteria against which the subject matter is to be evaluated and/or measured;
- the assuror's understanding of the entity and its internal and external environment;
- the assuror's assessment of the risk of the CR information that is subject to assurance being materially misstated;
- the information needs of intended users of the CR report (and assurance statement thereon) and, hence, considerations of materiality;
- the level of assurance to be provided, as agreed with the reporting entity.

As for planning an audit, the process of planning an assurance engagement is iterative and, as the engagement proceeds, evidence may come to light that requires the assuror to change the overall strategy and/or the planned nature, timing and extent of further evidence-gathering procedures.

(iv) Performing the engagement

As we noted earlier, the engagement must be performed in a manner that enables the assuror to obtain sufficient appropriate evidence to support the conclusion expressed in the assurance statement about the reliability and completeness of the CR information examined. This requires the assuror to perform, *inter alia*, the following procedures:

- Obtain an in-depth understanding of the reporting entity's systems and processes for managing and collecting data about its CR performance. This may be achieved by, for example, inspecting relevant documentation, observing the operation of the management and data collection processes, and making enquiries of client personnel who are responsible for, or involved in, the systems and processes.

---

[33] The concept of professional scepticism is explained in Chapter 3, section 3.4.5.

- Assess the risk of the CR information containing material misstatements. This may be achieved by, for example, reviewing the design of the entity's systems and processes (and their related internal controls) for managing and assembling CR information, and by performing analytical procedures such as trend analysis.
- Test the effectiveness of the internal controls within the entity's CR information systems and processes on which the assuror plans to rely to reduce substantive testing of the reported CR information that is subject to assurance.
- Perform substantive procedures such as inspecting relevant documents and records, recalculating important performance data and confirming specific information with external third parties to corroborate its validity.
- Obtain written representations from the reporting entity's management, or other responsible individuals within or outside of the entity, where this is necessary to enable the assuror to obtain sufficient appropriate evidence on which to base a conclusion about the reliability and completeness (or otherwise) of the CR information on which assurance is provided.

(v)   Issuing the assurance report

As for an audit report, an assurance statement should be in writing and should contain a clear statement of the assuror's conclusion about the reliability and completeness (or otherwise) of the information in the CR report which is assured. More specifically, an assurance statement should contain:

(a)   a title that clearly indicates the statement is an independent assurance statement;

(b)   the addressee – that is, the intended users of the assurance statement;

(c)   identification and description of the information being assured. This includes reference to the period covered by the assurance statement and, where the assured information is limited to less than all of the CR report or the report does not apply to all of the reporting entity, the parts of the report or the reporting entity covered by the assurance statement;

(d)   identification of the criteria against which the subject matter was evaluated or measured;

(e)   an explanation of the characteristics of the subject matter underlying the assured information and how these characteristics may influence the precision of the evaluation or measurement of the subject matter against the identified criteria;

(f)   any limitations which apply to the scope of the CR information on which assurance is provided, the assurance engagement or the gathering of evidence;

(g) a statement explaining the respective responsibilities of the reporting entity and the assurance provider in respect of the information to which the assurance statement relates;

(h) identification of the assurance standard(s) applied in the performance of the engagement. As noted earlier, this is commonly ISAE 3000 and/ or AA1000AS (2008); where AA1000AS1000 (2008) has been adopted, the Type of engagement (Type 1 or 2) should also be indicated;

(i) a summary of the work performed. This helps intended users to understand the nature of the assurance provided. Due to the absence of generally accepted standards for reporting CR information, and because much of the information is subjective and qualitative in nature, assurors of CR information are generally only able to provide a 'limited' or 'moderate' level of assurance. ISAE 3000 (para 49) suggests that the assurance provider should explain, in the assurance statement, limitations on the nature, timing and extent of the evidence-gathering procedures employed and state that the evidence-gathering procedures are more limited than for a reasonable assurance engagement (such as an audit of financial statements);

(j) the assurance provider's conclusion. Where the assured CR information covers a number of different aspects, separate conclusions may be provided on each aspect. Where the engagement provides 'limited' or 'moderate' assurance, the assurer's conclusion should be expressed in the negative form: for example, "We are not aware of any matters that would lead us to conclude that BP has not applied the inclusivity principle in developing its approach to sustainability" (Ernst & Young, Assurance Statement 2011; see Figure 17.7). If the assurance provider expresses other than an unqualified conclusion, the report should contain a clear description of the reasons therefor;

(k) the name of the assurance provider and the location of the office of the practitioner responsible for the engagement;

(l) the date on which the assurance statement was signed. As for an audit report, the date informs intended users that the assurance provider has considered the effect of events that occurred up to that date on the assured CR information and on the assurance statement;

(m) any comments, observations or recommendations of which, in the assurance provider's opinion, the intended users of the CR information should be aware;

(n) notes on the competencies and independence of the assurance provider.[34]

---

[34] If the assurance statement contains the elements shown here, it will comply with the requirements of both ISAE 3000 and AA1000AS (2008). However, the requirements shown in points (m) and (n) are required by AA1000AS (2008) but not by ISAE 3000.

Reference to Figure 17.7 and Figure 17.8 reveals that the assurance engagements conducted by Ernst & Young (E&Y) on BP's 2011 *Sustainability Report* and by Lloyd's Register Quality Assurance (LRQA) on BT's 2012 *Better Future Report* both complied with AA1000AS (2008). It may also be seen that E&Y, but not LRQA, also complied with ISAE 3000. E&Y, but not LRQA, is an accounting firm and, as such, is required to comply with ISAE 3000.

Figure 17.7: Ernst & Young LLP's Assurance statement on BP's 2011 Sustainability Report

E&Y assurance statement
BP's sustainability web content 2011 (the Report) has been prepared by the management of BP p.l.c., who are responsible for the collection and presentation of information within it. Our responsibility, in accordance with BP management's instructions, is to carry out a limited assurance engagement on the Report and to include specific observations from our work in relevant sections of the Report. We do not accept or assume any responsibility for any other purpose or to any other person or organisation. Any reliance any such third party may place on the Report is entirely at its own risk.

What we did to form our conclusions
Our assurance engagement has been planned and performed in accordance with ISAE3000[1] and to meet the requirements of a Type 2 assurance engagement as defined by AA1000AS (2008)[2]. The AA1000AS (2008) assurance principles of Inclusivity, Materiality and Responsiveness have been used as criteria against which to evaluate the Report.

In order to form our conclusions we undertook the steps outlined below:

1. **Interviewed a selection of BP executives and senior managers** to understand the current status of safety, social, ethical and environmental activities, and progress made during the reporting period.

2. **Reviewed selected group level documents** relating to safety, social, ethical and environmental aspects of BP's performance to understand progress made across the organisation and test the coverage of topics within the Report.

3. **Reviewed BP's approach to stakeholder engagement** through interviews with employees at group and four local businesses, and reviewed selected associated documentation.

4. **Carried out the following activities to review health, safety and environment (HSE), community investment, leadership diversity and ethics dismissals data samples and processes:**
   • Reviewed disaggregated HSE data reported by a sample of five businesses to assess whether the data had been collected, consolidated and reported accurately.
   • Reviewed and challenged supporting evidence from the sample of businesses.
   • Tested whether HSE data had been collected, consolidated and reported appropriately at group level.
   • Reviewed leadership diversity, community investment and ethics dismissal data at group level.

5. **Reviewed BP's processes for determining material issues to be included in the Report.** As part of our work, we attended two independently facilitated Roundtables on Transparency and Reporting held in London and Washington (the Roundtables) and reviewed BP's processes for responding to material issues raised through its reporting.

6. **Reviewed the coverage of material issues within the report** against the key issues raised in the Roundtables, material issues and areas of performance covered in external media reports and the environmental and social reports of BP's peers and the topics discussed by BP's board level committee on sustainability.

7. **Reviewed information or explanations about selected data, statements and assertions** regarding BP's sustainability performance.

Figure 17.7: (*Continued*)

8. **Reviewed whether BP's reporting has applied the GRI G3 Guidelines** to a level consistent with the A+ application level.

Level of assurance
Our evidence gathering procedures were designed to obtain a limited level of assurance (as set out in ISAE3000) on which to base our conclusions. The extent of evidence gathering procedures performed is less than that of a reasonable assurance engagement (such as a financial audit) and therefore a lower level of assurance is provided.

The limitations of our review
Our work did not include physical inspections of any of BP's operating assets.
Only the pages of the Report that are marked with the attestation footnote formed part of our review.

Our conclusions
Based on the scope of our review our conclusions are outlined below:

Inclusivity
Has BP been engaging with stakeholders across the business to develop its approach to sustainability?
- We are not aware of any key stakeholder groups that have been excluded from dialogue.
- We are not aware of any matters that would lead us to conclude that BP has not applied the inclusivity principle in developing its approach to sustainability.

Materiality
Has BP provided a balanced representation of material issues concerning BP's sustainability performance?
- With the exception of the subject area listed below, we are not aware of any material aspects concerning BP's sustainability performance which have been excluded from the Report.
- We consider that BP could have covered the following subject area in more depth in the Report:
  ○ Disclosure of future environmental performance targets.
  ○ Additional results of studies gathering data on the impacts on natural resources in the Gulf of Mexico.
- Nothing has come to our attention that causes us to believe that BP management has not applied its processes for determining material issues to be included in the Report.

Responsiveness
Has BP responded to stakeholder concerns?
- We are not aware of any matters that would lead us to conclude that BP has not applied the responsiveness principle in considering the matters to be reported.

Completeness and accuracy of Performance Information
How complete and accurate is the HSE, community investment, leadership diversity data and ethics dismissals data in the Report?
- With the exception of TNK-BP's GHG emissions and the volume of oil spilled as a result of the Deepwater Horizon accident, we are not aware of any material reporting units that have been excluded from the group wide datarelating to HSE, community investment, leadership diversity data and ethics dismissals data.
- Nothing has come to our attention that causes us to believe that the data relating to the above topics has not been collated properly from group-wide systems.
- We are not aware of any errors that would materially affect the data as presented in the Report.

How plausible are the statements and claims within the Report?
- We have reviewed information or explanation on selected statements on BP's sustainability activities presented in the Report and we are not aware of any misstatements in the assertions made.

GRI
Does the Report meet the requirements of the A+ application level of the GRI G3 Guidelines?
- Based on our review, including consideration of the Report, BP's sustainability web content and elements of the BP Annual Report and Accounts, nothing has come to our attention that causes us to believe that BP management's assertion that their sustainability reporting meets the requirements of the A+ application level of the Guidelines is not fairly stated.

Observations and areas for improvement
Our observations and areas for improvement will be raised in a report to BP management. Selected observations are provided below. For more information on our observations, please go to www.bp.com/sustainabilityobservations.

Figure 17.7: (*Continued*)

These observations do not affect our conclusions on the Report set out above.

- During our interviews we discussed activities to support diversity within BP. Although there has been some success in increasing female representation in recent years, women remain under-represented at executive management and Board level. We note that the BP Board wrote in October to Lord Davies (in response to his report on gender diversity) setting out a goal to increase the number of women on the Board by two by 2013. BP will need to provide an update on progress made in future reporting.
- BP reports five-year performance data for total GHG emissions. During our interviews we discussed the requirements for businesses to report on forecast GHG emissions for the year ahead and new developments to model emissions over the life of the project. As BP faces calls for greater transparency in its sustainability reporting, there is an opportunity to highlight projected trends for its GHG emissions, for example explaining the impact that investments in Canadian oil sands are likely to have and projected changes from operational efficiency.
- During our work we interviewed staff responsible for engaging with external stakeholders and reviewed evidence of how information from these dialogues is captured. We have also attended a selection of briefings to investors and two of the roundtable discussions held in 2011 to understand the perspectives of various thought leaders on how BP should evolve its reporting and communications. We noted that stakeholders welcome this dialogue but there remains a desire for more comprehensive reporting on how BP is changing
- BP refers to studies that have been undertaken to help understand the impact on habitats in the Gulf of Mexico. Whilst it is clear that a wide range of activities are underway or have been completed, the full analysis of the various studies is pending and BP should provide updates in due course.
- BP sets out an overview of its programme of action on climate change but there is limited explanation of the difference that this is making to decisions or practices. For example, BP has incorporated carbon pricing into its projects but it is not clear to what extent this process has impacted project plans; or whether BP can explain how targets set for energy efficiency through the local operating management system can be linked to real sustainable reductions reported.
- One of the areas where stakeholders continue to request increased transparency in BP's sustainability reporting is the value that is delivered to society as a whole. Different stakeholder groups take an interest in different elements of the value chain, and economic impacts may either be direct or indirect. This report has attempted to capture these explicitly but BP will need to seek feedback on how it has described the contribution that it is making and consider incorporating additional socio-economic metrics in future.

Our Independence

As auditors to BP p.l.c., Ernst & Young are required to comply with the requirements set out in the Auditing Practices Board's (APB) Ethical Standards for Auditors. Ernst & Young's independence policies, apply to the firm, partners and professional staff. These policies prohibit any financial interests in our clients that would or might be seen to impair independence. Each year, partners and staff are required to confirm their compliance with the firm's policies.

We confirm annually to BP whether there have been any events including the provision of prohibited services that could impair our independence or objectivity. There were no such events or services in 2011.

Our Assurance Team

Our assurance team has been drawn from our global Climate Change and Sustainability Services Practice, which undertakes engagements similar to this with a number of significant UK and international businesses. The work has been led and reviewed by Lead Sustainability Assurance Practitioners.

Ernst & Young LLP, London
21 March 2012

Footnotes

[1] International Federation of the Accountants' International Standard for Assurance Engagements Other Than Audits or Reviews of Historical Financial Information (ISAE3000).

[2] AA1000AS (2008) – The second edition of the AA1000 assurance standard from the Institute of Social and Ethical Accountability.

Figure 17.8:   LRQA's Assurance statement on BT's 2012 Better Future Report

LRQA Assurance Statement

Terms of Engagement

This Assurance Statement has been prepared for BT Group plc.
Lloyd's Register Quality Assurance Ltd. (LRQA) was commissioned by BT Group plc (BT) to assure its web-based 'Better Future Report 2012' for the financial year ending 31st March 2012 (hereafter referred to as "the Report"). The Report relates to the sustainability performance data and information for BT's global operations.

Our terms of engagement exclude data and information:
• Accessed through links that take the reader out of this Report, including video streams.
• Presented by BT but originates from a second party. Here LRQA corroborated only that data and information
  was transcribed accurately or the correct reference was provided.
• Communicated via social networks.

Management Responsibility

BT's management was responsible for preparing the Report and for maintaining effective internal controls over the data and information disclosed. LRQA's responsibility was to carry out an assurance engagement on the Report in accordance with our contract with BT.
Ultimately, the Report has been approved by, and remains the responsibility of BT.

LRQA's Approach

Our verification has been conducted against AA1000 Assurance Standard 2008 (AA1000 AS), where the scope was a Type 2 engagement.
The objective of the assurance engagement was to review adherence to the AA1000 AS Accountability Principles of Inclusivity, Materiality and Responsiveness and evaluate the reliability of the specified sustainability performance information.

To form our conclusions the assurance was undertaken as a sampling exercise and covered the following activities:
  • Reviewing BT's stakeholder engagement process and related information collected from these various
    stakeholder forums.
  • Evaluating BT's material issues against our own independent analysis of stakeholder issues.
  • Carrying out a benchmarking exercise of material issues by reviewing sustainability reports written by BT and
    its peers.
  • Understanding how BT determine, respond and report on their material issues.
  • Interviewing senior management to understand BT's reporting processes and use of sustainability performance
    data within their business decision-making processes.
  • Interviewing key personnel to understand BT's processes for setting performance indicators and for monitoring
    progress made during the reporting period.
  • Auditing BT's data management systems and reviewing supporting evidence made available by BT's section
    owners.

Note 1: With the exception of telephone interviews with selected personnel in UK offices, our verification was
           undertaken at BT's headquarters in London, UK. LRQA did not visit any international locations.
Note 2: Economic performance data was taken direct from the audited financial accounts.

We also used BT's Internal Audit Division (IAD) to review the validity of data and information in some sections of the Report. IAD reviewed the following sections and specific contents disclosed within:
  • Better connected – Customer experience; Safe connections & Connections for all
  • Better business – Innovation; Procurement and supply chain; Sales and marketing practice & Great place to work
  • BT and sustainability - Our economic impacts

Level of Assurance & Materiality

The opinion expressed in this Assurance Statement has been formed on the basis of a high level of assurance and applying professional judgement for materiality.

Figure 17.8: *(Continued)*

LRQA's Opinion

Based on LRQA's approach, BT has adhered to the AA1000 AS Accountability Principles. It should be noted that for the principles of:

Inclusivity - BT has effective processes in place to identify stakeholder groups and actively encourages them to participate in the determination of material sustainability issues.

Materiality - The process for determining materiality is robust, dynamic and the evaluation criteria are aligned with both business and stakeholder needs. BT uses the results of its materiality evaluation and feedback from peer reviews to present information on the most relevant and significant sustainability issues in the Report.

Responsiveness - BT has developed a comprehensive and balanced business response, in the form of strategies, plans and actions, for addressing their material sustainability issues. BT is also involved in public forums developing policies which will influence evolving sustainability issues.

It is also our opinion that the specified performance information is reliable as nothing has come to our attention that would cause us to believe otherwise.

LRQA's recommendations
BT should

- Ensure as it progresses organizational change and builds its new governance structure that sufficient attention is given to the management of sustainability performance data and information. This includes the planning of resource to ensure report content and associated evidence is provided to LRQA in a timely manner.
- Review whether their long-term plan to reduce the carbon dioxide equivalent intensity of its worldwide business by 80% is still realistic; provide annual updates of progress against the key milestones and, if applicable, explain any obstacles identified.

It is LRQA's opinion that our recommendations made in 2011 have been addressed as BT has improved the collection, version control and checking of non-UK environmental data.

Dated: 9th May 2012

S M Fletcher, LRQA Lead Verifier
G Farmer, LRQA Verifer
On behalf of Lloyd's Register Quality Assurance
Hiramford, Middlemarch Office Village, Siskin Drive, Coventry, UK.
LRQA Reference: LRQ0772591

LRQA's Competence and Independence
LRQA ensures the selection of appropriately qualified individuals based on a rigorous appraisal of their training, qualifications and experience. The team conducting the assurance of the Report was multi-disciplinary and has been involved in numerous assurance engagements. LRQA's internal systems have been designed to manage and review verification and certification assessments. This involves independent review by senior management of the outcome derived from the process applied to the assurance of sustainability reports.

Independence of LRQA from BT
LRQA is BT's ISO9001, ISO14001, ISO27001 and ISO20000 certification body. We also provide BT with a range of training services primarily related to Management Systems. The assurance and certification assessments, together with the training are the only work undertaken by LRQA for BT.

Independence of BT's Internal Audit Division
The role of Internal Audit (IA) is to provide independent and objective assurance to senior management and the Board, via the Board Audit & Risk Committee (BARC), as to the adequacy and effectiveness of key controls and of risk management activities across the organisation. The Director IA reports to the Group Finance Director and has access at all times to the Chair of the BARC and the Chief Executive. The Director IA has a responsibility to report to the BARC on the quality of the assurance, internal controls and risk management operating within BT, independently of the influence of management.

17.6 WHY DO SOME COMPANIES HAVE THEIR CORPORATE RESPONSIBILITY REPORTS INDEPENDENTLY ASSURED WHILE OTHERS DO NOT?

17.6.1 Reasons for having corporate responsibility reports independently assured

In section 17.5.4 we note that a significant number of companies have their CR information independently assured voluntarily. This raises the question – why do they do so? According to the results of KPMG's 2008 and 2011 surveys presented in Figure 17.9, the main reasons are to increase the credibility, and improve the quality, of the CR information. Increasing the credibility of the information is particularly important as, without independent assurance, some users may consider the information to be biased or otherwise unreliable. Some may even go so far as to regard the provision of the information to be an exercise in public relations rather than reporting on environmentally, socially and ethically responsible performance.

Figure 17.9: Reasons cited by G250 and N100 companies surveyed by KPMG for having their CR information independently assured

	G250 companies		N100 companies	
	2008	**2011**	**2008**	**2011**
No. of companies with independently assured CR reports	80	108	452	759
Reasons for having CR information assured	%	%	%	%
Increasing the credibility of the CR information	18	23	20	29
Improving the quality of reported information	21	21	18	22
Improving the reporting processes	16	7	14	10
Improving CR performance	4	1	6	2
Primarily responding to legal requirements	2	0	2	4
Other reasons	3	0	5	3
No reasons provided	N/A	54	N/A	50

N/A denotes information not available

Source: KPMG, 2008, 2011

Another reason reflected in Figure 17.9 for having CR information independently assured is the benefit it can provide in improving the company's underlying CR performance and its CR data collection and reporting processes. During the assurance engagement, competent knowledgeable professionals, divorced from the day-to-day operation of the company's CR management and reporting systems and processes, review the elements of these systems and processes, identify weaknesses or opportunities for improvement and make recommendations. As we observe in section 17.5.4, making recommendations is a requirement for assurance engagements conducted in accordance with AA1000AS (2008).

A further benefit for companies which have their CR information independently assured is reduced risk of litigation resulting from misrepresentation. Where companies publish (non-assured) CR information, they may believe it is complete and unbiased and that it fairly represents the underlying facts. However, unless the information is independently assured, they run the risk of inadvertently disclosing inaccurate or misleading information – and, hence, of being sued by parties who act in reliance on the company's published CR information and thereby suffer loss.

17.6.2 Reasons for not having corporate responsibility reports independently assured

Earlier in this chapter we observed that, in 2011, 54 per cent of the G250 and 62 per cent of the N100 companies surveyed by KPMG who published CR reports did not have the reports independently assured. The same applied to 44 per cent of the largest 100 companies in the UK, all of whom publish CR reports (see Figure 17.1). The question arises – Why do so many companies choose not to have their CR reports independently assured? Three key reasons may be identified, namely:
  (i) the high cost of publishing CR reports and having them independently assured;
  (ii) the absence of generally accepted CR reporting and assurance standards;
  (iii) the possible adverse consequences of publishing assured CR information.
We discuss each of these below.

(i) High cost of publishing CR information and having it assured

A significant obstacle to publishing CR information and having it independently assured is the cost involved. Many companies which publish separate CR reports produce a document that is nearly as 'thick' as their annual report and one which contains significantly more photographs, graphs and diagrams. Such reports are extremely expensive to compile in terms of gathering relevant information and data, deciding what to include and what to leave out, and how to present the material to be included. They are also expensive to publish, whether in hard copy or electronic form.[35] Companies

---

[35] In recent years, many companies (including, for example, BP and BT) have sought to reduce the cost of reporting assured CR information – as well as the use of resources such as paper and ink – by publishing their reports only on the Internet. However, although this reduces the cost of publishing the reports, it does not affect the cost of compiling them.

that have these reports independently assured also incur the costly professional fees of the assurance providers. It may be for reasons of cost that, in general, there is a lack of external pressure (from stakeholders, regulators and peers) on companies to have their CR information independently assured.[36]

(ii) Absence of generally accepted CR reporting and assurance standards

In the absence of generally accepted standards prescribing the information to be included in CR reports and defining how quantitative items are to be identified, measured and reported, the content, format and quality (in terms of completeness, accuracy and validity) of companies' reports varies widely. Similarly, without generally accepted assurance standards, the rigour of the assurance process to which the reports are subject varies markedly. This prevents meaningful evaluation of the relative CR performance of different companies which publish assured CR information in the same, or in other, industrial sectors.

A further difficulty for companies resulting from the absence of a universally accepted set of CR reporting standards is the potential for report users to misinterpret the information provided. Such misunderstanding may result in adverse consequences for the company concerned; it may, for example, result in unjustified negative publicity or even in a court action alleging misrepresentation. Similarly, in the absence of generally accepted assurance standards, there is a danger that users of assured CR reports may not properly understand the nature and level of the assurance provided. If informed users are familiar with audited financial statements, they may mistakenly conclude that a higher level of assurance is provided by the assurance statements attached to CR reports than is justified.

While the absence of generally accepted reporting and assurance standards remains an obstacle to CR reporting and assurance, its significance is declining. As we have seen in earlier sections of this chapter, the GRI's CR reporting guidelines and AccountAbililty's AA1000AS (2008) assurance standard are gaining acceptance by major companies around the globe and this trend seems likely to continue (KPMG, 2011). Further, as we note in section 17.5.2, for companies that engage a professional accountant to assure their CR information, the assurance engagement is required to be conducted in accordance with ISAE 3000.

---

[36] Bartels, the KPMG partner who oversees KPMG's triennial corporate responsibility surveys, informed the authors of this book that, in his experience, the lack of external pressure is an important reason for companies not having their CR information independently assured.

(iii) Possible adverse consequences of providing assured CR information

A disadvantage accruing to companies that publish information about their CR performance is that their reports need to be, and need to be accepted by users as, complete and balanced (that is, reporting both 'good' and 'bad' performance). Such reporting is essential for CR reports which are assured as the assuror will draw attention to any deficiency in these regards. However, if a company's report discloses previously unknown detrimental environmental effects resulting from its activities, products or services, or employment of child or 'sweat shop' labour, and/or other similar untoward outcomes or aspects of its activities, this may generate negative publicity and/or prompt an adverse reaction by customers, investors and/or regulators. It may, for example, trigger a regulatory investigation of a previously unknown breach of environmental or labour laws and, possibly, litigation.

17.6.3 Cost-effectiveness of publishing independently assured corporate responsibility reports

Notwithstanding the financial resources that are consumed by publishing independently assured CR reports and other obstacles which discourage companies from doing so, as we have seen, a significant proportion of the world's major companies provide such reports voluntarily. These companies will only engage in this activity if they believe the 'downside' is outweighed by the 'upside'. In other words, they will only publish independently assured CR reports if they believe it makes good business sense to do so.

17.7 RELEVANCE OF CORPORATE RESPONSIBILITY ISSUES TO EXTERNAL FINANCIAL STATEMENT AUDITS

17.7.1 General relevance of corporate responsibility issues to the external auditor

Although this chapter is concerned with the reporting and assurance of CR information, the focus of this book is external financial statement auditing. It is therefore appropriate to consider the relevance of CR issues to external financial statement audits. That environmental matters are relevant to financial statement audits has been noted by commentators such as Owen (1992) and Collison (1996).[37] Owen (1992), for example, observes:

---

[37] Given the extension of environmental reports, which were common in the 1990s, into wide-ranging CR reports which are more usually produced by major companies today, it seems likely that, if Owen and Collison were commenting a little more than a decade later, their remarks would have been extended to 'sustainability' or 'corporate responsibility' issues rather than being limited to environmental matters.

[T]he fact that environmental issues, and particularly company shortcomings in response to these issues, have ever-increasing financial consequences for business means that the financial auditor must pay due regard to them now in the conduct of current statutory audits.

Collison (1996) further explains:

A company's environmental policy and obligations and its reaction to environmental developments, such as the changing attitudes of consumers are clearly a concern to the financial auditor to the extent that they are material to the financial statements. (p. 328)

However, during the last decade, the relevance of CR issues and reports to financial statement audits has been made more explicit. As we note in section 17.3.1, the Companies Act (CA) 2006, s. 414A, requires the directors of all large and medium-sized companies to include a strategic report within their annual reports. For quoted companies this is to include, to the extent necessary for a reader to understand the development and performance of the company during the financial year and its position at the end of the year, information about environmental matters (including the impact of the company's business on the environment), the company's employees and social, community and human rights issues. Additionally, *The Large and Medium-sized Companies and Groups (Accounts and Reports) Regulations 2008* (SI 2008, as amended by SI 2013) require the directors of all quoted companies to include information about the company's GHG emissions in their directors' report. We also noted that *The UK Corporate Governance Code* (FRC, 2012a, prov. C.1.1) requires the directors of companies listed on the London Stock Exchange to explain their responsibility for preparing the company's annual report and financial statements and to state that they consider the annual report (together with the financial statements) is fair, balanced and understandable, and provides the information necessary for shareholders to assess the company's performance, business model and strategy – including, presumably, information on the company's CR performance and on the nature and extent to which CR considerations are incorporated in the company's business model and strategy.

The auditors of all companies are specifically required (by CA 2006, s. 496) to state whether, in their opinion, the directors' report and, for all but small companies, the strategic report is consistent with the company's audited financial statements. Additionally, they are required to review all of the information in the company's annual report (including any CR information contained therein) and, if they encounter statements about any material matter that are inconsistent with the audited financial statements, or are misstatements of fact, they are required to request the directors to effect corrections. If the directors fail to do so, the auditor is to draw attention to the matter(s) concerned in the audit report (IAASB, 2009b). The auditors of companies listed on the London Stock Exchange are further required (by the UK Listing Authority's Listing Rules) to form an opinion as to whether the information contained in these companies' annual reports is fair, balanced and understandable. If, in their opinion, it is not, they are to say so in their audit reports (FRC, 2012b).[38]

It can thus be seen that external financial statement auditors have a general responsibility to review CR information provided by companies in their strategic and directors' reports, or elsewhere in their annual report,[39] to ascertain whether the information provided about any material matter is misstated or is inconsistent with the company's audited financial statements – and, for listed companies, to determine whether the information is presented in a manner that is fair, balanced and understandable. However, as we shall see below, there are other, more specific aspects of a financial statement audit where CR issues have a significant impact.

17.7.2 Gaining an understanding of the client's business and assessing its risks

Earlier in this chapter we drew attention to:
  (i)   society's increasing awareness of companies' environmental impact, health and safety aspects of products and workplaces, employment practices and other similar issues;
  (ii) the increasing volume and complexity of laws and regulations relating to these issues; and
  (iii) the increasing importance of incorporating CR considerations into business decisions.
Given these factors, it is clearly important that, when gaining an understanding of a client's business as a basis for conducting its financial statement audit, the auditor obtains a thorough understanding of:
  – the company's environmental, social and ethical policies and related management and information systems and processes;
  – the environmental, economic and social impact of the company's operations and outputs; and
  – related legal and regulatory obligations.
However, in addition to gaining an understanding of these matters, the auditor needs to consider their significance and effect when assessing the client's financial, operational, compliance and other risks, and the impact of these risks on the financial statements.

---

[38] The auditor's responsibilities in respect of non-audited information in documents containing the audited financial statements are explained in Chapter 13, section 13.8.

[39] As we note in section 17.2, major companies are increasingly moving towards integrated reporting. As a consequence, in the future, the CR information content of companies' annual reports is likely to increase.

17.7.3 Ascertaining audit clients' compliance with corporate responsibility related laws and regulations

As part of gaining an understanding of the client, International Standard on Auditing (ISA) 250: *Consideration of Laws and Regulations in an Audit of Financial Statements* (IAASB, 2009a) requires the auditor to obtain a general understanding of:

(a) The legal and regulatory framework applicable to the entity and the industry or sector in which the entity operates; and

(b) How the entity is complying with that framework. (para 12)

Virtually all companies are, to a greater or lesser extent, subject to environmental, health and safety, employee and other CR related laws and regulations. Such laws and regulations are components of the entity's 'legal and regulatory framework' and, therefore, must be understood by the auditor. In order to obtain the required understanding, auditors may, for example, ascertain from the entity's directors and/or senior executives:

- the entity's policies and procedures for ensuring its, and its employees', compliance with applicable laws and regulations,
- the laws and regulations that may be expected to have a fundamental effect on the operations of the entity and its financial statements, and
- the policies and procedures adopted by the entity for identifying, evaluating and accounting for litigation claims.

Although auditors are required to obtain a general understanding of their clients' legal and regulatory framework and their compliance therewith, ISA 250, para 6, distinguishes the auditor's responsibilities in relation to the entity's compliance with:

(a) The provisions of those laws and regulations generally recognized to have a direct effect on material amounts and disclosures in the financial statements . . . ; and

(b) Other laws and regulations that do not have a direct effect on . . . the financial statements, but compliance with which may be fundamental to the operating aspects of the business, to an entity's ability to continue its business, or to avoid material penalties . . . ; non-compliance with such laws and regulations may therefore have a material effect on the financial statements.

Environmental, health and safety, employment practices and other CR related laws and regulations fall within the latter category.

For organisations in industrial sectors such as chemicals, manufacturing and the extractive industries, environmental laws and regulations may well be "fundamental to the operating aspects of the business, to [the] entity's ability to continue its business, or to avoid material penalties"[40] (ISA 250, para 6). For audit clients for which environmental and other CR laws and regulations are significant, auditors are required to make enquiries of the directors and/or senior executives about the entity's compliance with the laws and regulations, and inspect correspondence with relevant licensing or regulatory authorities to identify instances of non-compliance that may have a material effect on the financial statements. They are also required to request the directors and/or senior executives to provide written representations confirming that all known actual or possible non-compliance with applicable laws and regulations, whose effect should be considered when the preparing financial statements, have been disclosed to the auditor (ISA 250, paras 14, 16).

17.7.4 Evaluating the adequacy of provisions and disclosures relating to contingent liabilities

If a company breaches environmental and/or other CR related laws and regulations it may be exposed to liabilities in the form of, for example, fines, damages and remediation costs (that is, costs to remedy any harm to the environment, property or people that result from the breach). In some cases the liabilities may be minor in relation to the company's financial affairs but in others they may be material to the company's financial statements.

ISA 250 explains auditors' responsibilities when they encounter, or suspect, instances of non-compliance with applicable laws and regulations. They are to obtain:

(a) An understanding of the nature of the act and the circumstances in which it has occurred; and

(b) Further information to evaluate the possible effect [of the non-compliance] on the financial statements. (ISA 250, para 18)

The Standard also identifies matters the auditor should consider when evaluating the possible effect of the non-compliance on the financial statements, namely:

- The potential financial consequences . . . including, for example, the imposition of fines, penalties, damages, threat of expropriation of assets, enforced discontinuance of operations, and litigation.
- Whether the potential financial consequences require disclosure.
- Whether the potential financial consequences are so serious as to call into question the fair presentation of the financial statements [in particular,

---

[40] For example, in a waste disposal company, the terms of licences under which the company is allowed to dispose of hazardous waste are central to its ability to conduct its business. If the company should breach the terms of the licences, it is likely that it will be unable to continue in business. Similarly, if companies breach the permitted limit of their GHG emissions, they may face significant financial penalties. In some cases, these may be sufficiently severe to threaten the emitting company's survival.

whether adherence to the going concern assumption is justified], or otherwise make the financial statements misleading. (ISA 250, para A14)

Where the potential financial consequences of one or more violations of CR related legal or regulatory requirements are material to the client's financial statements, the auditor needs to evaluate the adequacy of disclosures relating to the associated contingent liability, in terms of both the likely amount involved and the explanation of the relevant circumstances.[41]

Additionally, for audit clients whose activities, processes, products or services have (or may have) a significant impact on the environment, employees, customers or others, the auditor needs to evaluate the adequacy of the client's insurance cover for the possible consequences of breaching relevant laws or regulations (including the associated legal costs) and for potential environment-related emergencies and disasters. Similarly, they need to evaluate the adequacy of their provisions in respect of these matters.

17.7.5 Reviewing the valuation of non-current assets and inventory

Among other matters to which external auditors need to pay special attention for auditees for which environmental matters are particularly significant is the value of non-current assets (especially land and buildings) and inventory. The value of land may be altered dramatically by factors such as the discovery of hazardous waste, or contaminated soil or underground water, at any of the client's locations (anywhere in the world) irrespective of whether the hazardous waste was dumped, or the soil or water was contaminated, by the client or a previous occupier of the site(s) concerned.

Similarly, the value of buildings and of manufacturing or processing plant may be affected by, for instance, the discovery that they breach health and safety or environmental regulations. This may apply, for example, if it is discovered that the current arrangement for storing waste poses a fire or health hazard, or radioactive or gaseous emissions exceed permitted levels. In some cases, violation of regulations may be caused by changes in the regulations themselves: for example, permitted levels of emissions may be reduced as a result of a regulatory change.[42] Whatever their cause, where buildings or plant (or, indeed, any other productive asset) breaks current or soon-to-be-implemented

---

[41] It should be remembered that when an audit client has been prosecuted for non-compliance with laws or regulations and the resultant fine, damages, remediation costs, etc. have been settled by the regulatory authority or the court but are not yet paid, an actual liability exists and should be recorded as such in the financial statements. Contingent liabilities relate, amongst other things, to breaches of environmental laws or regulations which have been discovered but the resultant financial consequences remain uncertain.

[42] A pertinent example is afforded by the reduction in permitted GHG emissions noted in section 17.3.1.

regulations, considerable capital expenditure may be required to bring existing assets into line with the required standards. Apart from affecting the value of the assets as stated in the statement of financial position, planned capital expenditure may give rise to commitments that need to be disclosed in the financial statements. The external auditor will need to review the adequacy of any such disclosures.

Along similar lines, for clients with products that have a significant influence on the environment or have health and safety implications, auditors need to be alert to the fact that the value of inventory may be diminished, or items of inventory may be rendered obsolete (or even give rise to costs rather than revenues). This may arise, for example, from 'health hazard' issues,[43] or through "environmental concerns, storage and disposal costs of environmentally-maligned materials and recycling commitments" (Collison, 1996, p. 32). The value of inventory stated in the statement of financial position may need to be adjusted accordingly.

17.8 SUMMARY

In this chapter we have explored aspects of CR reporting – wide-ranging reports that provide information on entities' environmental, social, economic and similar non-financial performance – and their independent assurance. We have also discussed some reasons why many major companies engage in such reporting – in particular, the influence of regulatory requirements, business drivers and investor preferences. In relation to the last factor, we noted the emergence and rapid growth of 'ethical' or 'responsible' investments and indices such as the FTSE4Good, Dow Jones Sustainability Index and the Carbon Disclosure Leadership Index. These indices appear to be equally important to investors seeking to invest in such equity and to companies seeking inclusion therein.

Much of the chapter is concerned with the independent assurance of CR reports – the objectives of such engagements, their performance and their outcome in the form of assurance statements. We have observed that companies which have their CR reports assured do so primarily to enhance their credibility. However, we have also noted that some companies may be deterred from publishing independently assured CR reports because of the

---

[43] A pertinent example of inventory rendered obsolete, and also giving rise to costs, is provided by the return of many millions of toys manufactured in China during 2007 which contained lead paint that exceeded permitted levels in the USA, EU, Australia, New Zealand and elsewhere.

cost involved, the absence of universally accepted reporting and assurance standards and/or the risk of disclosing hitherto unknown untoward activities or events. Despite these apparent obstacles to companies engaging in CR reporting and assurance activities, the majority of major companies in the UK and elsewhere appear to find that publishing such reports makes good business sense.

In the final section of the chapter we have discussed some of the ways in which CR issues may impact on the statutory audit of companies' financial statements – in particular, their impact on the auditor's understanding of the client and its compliance with applicable CR related laws and regulations, the adequacy of provisions and disclosures of contingent liabilities and commitments, and the value of non-current assets and inventory reported in the company's financial statements.

SELF-REVIEW QUESTIONS

17.1   Distinguish between:
    (a) an environmental report and a corporate responsibility report;
    (b) a 'reasonable assurance' engagement and a 'limited assurance' engagement.

17.2   Explain briefly three motivations for companies to engage in corporate responsibility reporting.

17.3   Outline the principles identified in the Global Reporting Initiative's Sustainability Reporting Guidelines (G3.1) that define the *content* of corporate responsibility reports.

17.4   Outline the principles identified in the Global Reporting Initiative's Sustainability Reporting Guidelines (G3.1) that define the *quality* of the information provided.

17.5   (a) Identify the main professional groups who assure companies' corporate responsibility reports;
    (b) Outline the professional requirements for assurance providers and assurance practitioners.

17.6   Outline the three principles that underpin assurance engagements conducted in accordance with AccountAbility's AA1000AS (2008).

17.7   Outline the content of an assurance statement.

17.8   Briefly explain two factors which may motivate companies to have their corporate responsibility reports independently assured.

17.9   Briefly explain three factors that may deter companies from publishing independently assured corporate responsibility reports.

17.10   Briefly explain four ways in which corporate responsibility issues may impact the statutory audit of companies' financial statements.

REFERENCES

AccountAbility (AA). (2003). *AA 1000 Assurance Standard*. London: Institute of Social and Ethical Accountability.

AccountAbility (AA). (2008). *AA 1000 Assurance Standard* 2008. London: Institute of Social and Ethical Accountability.

AccountAbility (AA). (2013). *AA 1000 Assurance Principles Standard (2008)*, www.accountability.org/standards/aa1000aps.html, accessed 8 February 2013.

Beets, S.D., & Souther, C.C. (1999). Corporate environmental reports: The need for standards and an environmental assurance service. *Accounting Horizons*, *13*(2), 129–145.

CarbonCredentials. (2013). *CRC*, www.carboncredentials.com/crc, accessed 4 February 2013.

Carbon Footprint. (2013). *Carbon Reduction Commitment (CRC)*. www.carbonfoot print.com/ carbonreductioncommitment.html, accessed 4 February 2013.

Collison, D.J. (1996). The response of statutory financial auditors in the UK to environmental issues: A descriptive and exploratory case study. *British Accounting Review*, *28*, 325–349.

Department for Environment, Food and Rural Affairs (Defra). (2009, September). *Guidance on How to Measure and Report Your Greenhouse Gas Emissions*, www .defra.gov.uk /environment/business/reporting/index.htm, accessed 3 February 2013.

Ethical Investment Research Services (EIRiS). (2007). *The State of Responsible Business: Global Corporate Response to Environmental, Social and Governance (ESG) Challenges*. London: EIRiS Ltd.

European Communities. (1987). *Single European Act: Official Journal (OJ) No. L 169 (29.6.87)*. Brussels: European Communities

European Commission (EC). (2013a). *Climate Action: The EU Emissions Trading Scheme (EU ETS)*. ec.europa.eu/clima/policies/ets/index_en.htm, accessed 16 February 2013.

European Commission (EC). (2013b). *Climate Action: EU ETS 2005–2012*. ec.europa.eu/ clima/ policies/ets/pre2013/index_en.htm, accessed 16 February 2013.

European Union (EU). (2003a). *Directive 2003/51/EC of the European Parliament and of the Council of 18 June 2003 Amending Directives 78/660/EEC, 83/349/EEC, 86/635/*

EEC and 91/674/EEC on the Annual and Consolidated Accounts of Certain Types of Companies, Banks and other Financial Institutions and Insurance Undertakings (Accounts Modernisation Directive). Brussels: European Parliament and Council.

European Union (EU). (2003b). *Directive 2003/87/EC of the European Parliament and of the Council of 13 October 2002 Establishing a Scheme for Greenhouse Gas Emission Allowance Trading within the Community and Amending Council Directive 96/61/EC*. Brussels: European Parliament and Council.

Fédération des Experts Comptables Européens (FEE). (2001, November). *FEE Update on Sustainability Issues*. Brussels: FEE.

Fédération des Experts Comptables Européens (FEE). (2002, April). *FEE Discussion Paper Providing Assurance on Sustainability Reports*. Brussels: FEE.

Financial Reporting Council (FRC). (2012a). *The UK Corporate Governance Code*. London: FRC.

Financial Reporting Council (FRC). (2012b). International Standard on Auditing (ISA) (UK and Ireland) 720 *Section A – The Auditor's Responsibilities Relating to Other Information in Documents Containing Audited Financial Statements*. London: FRC.

Focus Report. (2005). Focus Report: Comparing sustainability reporting assurance standards. *Business and the Environment, XVI*(6), 6–7.

FTSE4Good. (2011). *FTSE4Good 10 Years of Impact & Investment*. London: FTSE.

Gilmour, G., & Caplan, A. (2001). Who cares? *Accountancy, 128*(1297), 44–45.

Global Reporting Initiative (GRI). (2011). *Sustainability Reporting Guidelines (version 3.1)*. Amsterdam: GRI.

Global Reporting Initiative (GRI). (2013). *About GRI*. www.globalreporting.org/ Information/ about-gri/Pages/default.aspx, accessed 13 February 2013.

Global Sustainable Investment Alliance (GSIA). 2012 *Global Sustainable Investment Review*. gsiareview2012.gsi-alliance.org/#/1, accessed 16 February 2013.

Hinks, G. (2010, 8 November). *Companies Failing on Carbon Reporting*. www.account ancyage.com/aa/news/1885579/companies-failing-carbon-reporting, accessed 3 February, 2013.

International Auditing and Assurance Standards Board (IAASB). (2004a). *International Framework for Assurance Engagements*. New York: International Federation of Accountants.

International Auditing and Assurance Standards Board (IAASB). (2004b). International Standard on Assurance Engagements (ISAE) 3000: *Assurance Engagements other than Audits or Reviews of Historical Financial Information*. New York: International Federation of Accountants.

International Auditing and Assurance Standards Board (IAASB). (2009a). International Standard on Auditing (ISA) 250: *Consideration of Laws and Regulations in an Audit of Financial Statements*. New York: International Federation of Accountants.

International Auditing and Assurance Standards Board (IAASB). (2009b). International Standard on Auditing (ISA) 720: *The Auditor's Responsibilities Relating to*

Other Information in Documents Containing Audited Financial Statements. New York: International Federation of Accountants.

International Auditing and Assurance Standards Board (IAASB). (2012). International Standard on Assurance Engagements (ISAE) 3410: *Assurance Engagements on Greenhouse Gas Statements*. New York: International Federation of Accountants.

International Ethics Standards Board for Accountants (IESBA). (2009). *Code of Ethics for Professional Accountants (IESBA Code)*. New York: International Federation of Accountants.

Investors Chronicle. (1998). Survey – ethical investment: Pensions with principles. *Investors Chronicle*, (17 July). 44.

KPMG. (1999). *KPMG International Survey of Corporate Responsibility Reporting 1999*. Amsterdam: KPMG Global Sustainability Services. (Unpublished; provided by KPMG upon request.)

KPMG. (2002). *KPMG International Survey of Corporate Responsibility Reporting 2002*. Amsterdam: KPMG Global Sustainability Services.

KPMG. (2005). *KPMG International Survey of Corporate Responsibility Reporting 2005*. Amsterdam: KPMG Global Sustainability Services.

KPMG. (2008). *KPMG International Survey of Corporate Responsibility Reporting 2008*. Amsterdam: KPMG Global Sustainability Services.

KPMG. (2011). *KPMG International Survey of Corporate Responsibility Reporting 2011*. Amsterdam: KPMG Global Sustainability Services.

Krumsiek, B.J. (1998). The emergence of a new era in mutual fund investing: Socially responsible investing comes of age. *Journal of Investing, Winter*, 84–99.

MacKay, E. (2000, 13 June). *Environmental Reporting: Creating the Right Environment*, www.accountancyage.com/aa/news/1785782/environmental-reporting-creating-en vironment, accessed 22 February 2013.

Owen, D. (1992). *Green Reporting: Accountancy and the Challenge of the Nineties*. London: Chapman and Hall.

Roussey, R.S. (1992). Auditing environmental liabilities. *Auditing: A Journal of Practice & Theory, 11*(1), 47–57.

Spelman, C. (2012, 12 June). *Company Reporting of Greenhouse Gas Emissions by Quoted Companies*. Written Ministerial Statement, Department for Environment, Food and Rural Affairs. www.parliament.uk/documents/commons-vote-office/June2012/20-06-12/3. DEFRA-Company-reporting-greenhouse-gas-emissions-by -quoted-companies.pdf, accessed 4 February 2013).

Statutory Instrument (SI). (2008). No. 410: *Large and Medium-sized Companies and Groups (Accounts and Reports) Regulations 2008*. London: The Stationery Office Limited.

Statutory Instrument (SI). (2013). No. 1970: *The Companies Act 2006 (Strategic Report and Directors' Report) Regulations 2013*. London: The Stationery Office Limited.

Vinten, G. (1996). The objectives of the environmental audit. *Environmental Management and Health*, 7(3), 12–21.

World Business Council for Sustainable Development (WBCSD). (2000). *Corporate Social Responsibility: Making good Business Sense*. Geneva: WBCSD.

ADDITIONAL READING

Adams, C.A., & McNicholas, P. (2007). Making a difference: Sustainability reporting, accountability and organisational change. *Accounting, Auditing & Accountability Journal, 20*(3), 382–402.

Darnall, N., Seol, I., & Sarkis, J. (2009). Perceived stakeholder influences and organizations' use of environmental audits. *Accounting, Organizations and Society, 34*(2), 170–187.

Fédération des Experts Comptables Européens. (FEE). (2006). *Key Issues in Sustainability Assurance: An Overview*. Brussels: FEE

Green, W., & Li, Q. (2012). Evidence of an expectation gap for gas emissions assurance. *Accounting, Auditing & Accountability Journal, 25*(1), 146–173.

Huggins, A., Green, W.J., & Simnett, R. (2011). The competitive market for assurance engagements on greenhouse gas statements: Is there a role for assurers from the accounting profession? *Current Issues in Auditing, 5*(2), A1–A12.

O'Dwyer, B., Owen, D., & Unerman, J. (2011). Seeking legitimacy for new assurance forms: The case of assurance on sustainability reporting. *Accounting, Organizations and Society, 36*(1), 31–52.

Pflugarth, G., Roebuck, P., & Simnett, R. (2011). Impact of assurance and assurer's professional affiliation on financial analyst's assessment of credibility of corporate social responsibility information. *Auditing: A Journal of Practice & Theory, 30*(3), 239–254.

Simnett, R., Nugent, M., & Huggins, A.L. (2009). Developing an international assurance standard on greenhouse gas statements. *Accounting Horizons, 23*(4), 347–363.

Simnett, R., Vanstraeian, A., & Wai, F.C. (2009). Assurance on sustainability reports: An international comparison. *The Accounting Review, 84*(3), 337–367.

Smith, J.L. (2012). Investors' perceptions of audit quality: Effects of regulatory changes. *Auditing: A Journal of Practice & Theory, 31*(1), 17–38.

APPENDIX

BRIEF DESCRIPTIONS OF 'RESPONSIBLE INVESTMENT' INDICES

1. FTSE4GOOD

FTSE is an abbreviation of 'Financial Times Stock Exchange'. It is an independent company that originated as a joint venture between the *Financial Times* newspaper (FT) and the London Stock Exchange (LSE). The FTSE Group has developed 200,000 indices "which cover over 7,400 securities in 47 countries and capture 98 per cent of the world's investable market capitalisation" (FTSE, 2010). Among its indices are the FTSE4Good benchmark series – including the FTSE4Good Global, FTSE4Good UK, FTSE4Good USA, FTSE4Good Europe and FTSE4Good Japan Indexes.

The FTSE4Good Index series was launched in 2001 "in response to the growing interest in socially responsible investment around the world" (FTSE, 2012a, p.3); it is a series of indices for investors interested in environmental, social and governance (ESG) equity investments (FTSE, 2012b). In order to qualify for inclusion in a FTSE4Good index, companies must meet prescribed criteria in six areas, namely:
(i) environmental management;
(ii) mitigating climate change;
(iii) human and labour rights;
(iv) supply chain labour standards;
(v) countering bribery;
(vi) corporate governance (FTSE, 2013).
With reference to the criteria, FTSE explains:

> To remain consistent with market expectations and developments in ESG practice, the [FTSE4Good] inclusion criteria are revised regularly. Since [FTSE4Good was launched in 2001] this has included tougher environmental and human rights criteria as well as new supply chain labour standards and countering bribery requirements. (FTSE, 2012b, p.1)

Companies with business interests in the tobacco and weapons industries are unable to qualify for inclusion in FTSE4Good indexes (FTSE, 2011, p.9) but any other company in any of the FTSE indices which meets the prescribed criteria is included in the relevant FTSE4Good Benchmark index. These companies' compliance with the criteria is reviewed in March and September each year and those found not to be complying are excluded (FTSE, 2012a, p.7). Since the launch of the FTSE4Good indices in 2001, 288 companies have been removed for failing to meet the criteria (FTSE, 2011, p.9); however, many others that have met the criteria have been added. According to a study by Nottingham University Business School, companies that meet the inclusion criteria ". . . value and promote their inclusion in the FTSE4Good index to demonstrate good environmental, social, and governance (ESG) practices to customers, investors, employees and other stakeholders" (FTSE, 2011, p.11). The number of companies in the FTSE4Good Global and UK indices is shown in Figure 17A. It is interesting to observe the decline in the number of UK companies in both indices. This may be a result of the more demanding criteria (referred to by FTSE in the quotation cited above) companies now need to meet in order to be included in a FTSE4Good index.

Figure 17A: Number of UK companies in FTSE4Good Global and UK indices and those also in the FTSE100 and FTSE 250[44]

	November 2007	March 2013
FTSE4Good Global Index	No.	No.
Companies in the index	697	735
UK companies in the index	99	82
UK companies also in the FTSE100	75	70
UK companies also in the FTSE250	24	12
Proportion of market capitalisation of companies in Index from:	%	%
USA	46	39
UK	14	14
Next highest contributor – Japan	8	9
FTSE4Good UK Index		
Companies in the index	289	237
Companies also in the FTSE100	79	71
Companies also in the FTSE250	117	109

2. DOW JONES SUSTAINABILITY INDEX (DJSI)

The Dow Jones Sustainability Index (DJSI) was launched in 1999 to track the financial performance of the top 10 per cent of the world's largest 2,500 companies (by market capitalisation) which lead the way in corporate sustainability (that is, economic, environmental and social performance) (DJSI, 2013a; 2013b). The DJSI, which was the world's first sustainability index, is a collaboration of the S&P Dow Jones Indices and RobecoSAM and thus "combine[s] the experience of an established index provider with the experience of a specialist in Sustainability Investing . . ." (DJSI, 2013a, p.1). Today, like FTSE4Good, today, the DJSI comprises a 'family' of indices; these include the main global index (DJSI World), DJSI Europe, DJSI North America, DJSI Asia Pacific, DJSI Korea, DJSI Australia and DJSI Emerging Markets (DJSI, 2013b). The constituents of DJSI World and the DJSI regional indices are shown in Figure 17B.

---

[44] The data presented in Figure 17A were provided by the FTSE Group's Responsible Investment Unit.

Figure 17B: Composition of DJSI World and DJSI regional indices[45]

Index title	No. of companies in relevant S&P Global or Regional Index	No. of countries represented	No. of industrial sectors represented	% of companies from each industrial sector selected as leaders in sustainability	No. of companies in the relevant DJSI
DJSI World	2500	45	59	10%	333
DJSI Europe	600	17*	57	20%	177
DJSI North America	600	2	59	20%	140
DJSI Asia Pacific	600	6†	53	20%	152
DJSI Korea	200	1	45	20%	53
DJSI Australia	200	1	45	30%	55
DJSI Emerging Markets	800	20‡	57	10%	81

* Austria, Belgium, Finland, France, Germany, Greece, Iceland, Ireland, Italy, Luxembourg, Netherlands, Norway, Portugal, Spain, Sweden, Switzerland the United Kingdom
† Australia, Japan, Hong Kong, New Zealand, Singapore and South Korea
‡ Brazil, Chile, China, Colombia, the Czech Republic, Egypt, Hungary, India, Indonesia, Malaysia, Mexico, Morocco, Peru, the Philippines, Poland, Russia, South Africa, Taiwan, Thailand and Turkey

Source: DJSI, 2013b

Companies are selected for inclusion in the DJSI by RobecoSAM based on an annual Corporate Sustainability Assessment (CSA). The CSA evaluates companies' performance against financially relevant general and industry-specific sustainability criteria covering economic, environmental and social dimensions. The criteria are wide-ranging and include, for example, climate change strategies, energy consumption, human resources development, knowledge management, stakeholder relations and corporate governance (DJSI, 2013a).

In September 2013, DJSI World included 333 companies; of the ten leading companies, five were from the USA (including the top company – Microsoft), three were from Switzerland, and one was from each of South Korea and France (DJSI, 2013c). In the same month, DJSI Europe included 117 companies; the ten leading companies included four from Switzerland (including the top company – Nestlé), two were from each of Germany and the UK, and one was from each of France and Spain (DJSI, 2013d).

---

[45] The constituents of DJSI World and the DJSI regional indices reported here are as at September 2013 (DJSI, 2013b).

3. CARBON DISCLOSURE LEADERSHIP INDEX (CDLI)

The Carbon Disclosure Project (CDP) is an independent not-for-profit organisation centred in the UK. It was launched in 2002 with a view to reducing greenhouse gas (GHG) emissions and water usage around the world (CDP, 2013a). It provides information to institutional investors about companies' greenhouse gas (GHG) emissions and energy use, and their climate change related risks and opportunities (CDP, 2013c). In 2012, CDP provided information to 722 investors (with total assets under management of US\$87 trillion); it obtained the information from more than 5000 of the world's largest companies (CDP, 2013b; 2013c). In addition to sourcing information from companies, CDP works with them to help them improve the measurement, management and disclosure of their GHG emissions, and their climate change and water strategies (CDP, 2013a).

In addition to the activities outlined above, since 2004, CDP has requested, annually, the Fortune Global 500 companies to respond to a questionnaire which addresses the companies' carbon disclosures and performance. The responses are reviewed, analysed and scored according to a set of criteria "developed by CDP, with advice from [their] global advisor, PwC" (CDP, 2012a). Companies which achieve a score within the top 10 per cent of the scores gained by the Fortune Global 500 companies qualify for inclusion in the Carbon Disclosure Leadership Index (CDLI). In 2012, 81 per cent of the Global 500 companies responded to the CDP's questionnaire and 52 qualified for inclusion in the CDLI. All of these companies gained a score of 94 or more and two companies, Nestlé and Bayer, gained the maximum score of 100 (CDP, 2012b).

REFERENCES

Carbon Disclosure Project (CDP). (2012a). *Leadership Indexes and the CDP Disclosure and Performance Scores*. www.cdproject.net/en-US/results/pages/leadership-index.aspx, accessed, 29 January 2013.

Carbon Disclosure Project (CDP). (2012b). *Business Resilience in an Uncertain, Resource-Constrained World: CDP Global 500 Climate Change Report 2012*. www.cdproject.net/CDPresults/CDP-Global-500-Climate-Change-Report-2012.pdf, accessed, 15 February 2013.

Carbon Disclosure Project (CDP). (2013a). *Reducing Risk and Driving Business Value*. www.cdproject.net/en-US/pages/homepage.aspx, accessed, 15 February 2013.

Carbon Disclosure Project (CDP). (2013b). *A Third of World's Invested Capital Calls for Corporate Environmental Data through the Carbon Disclosure Project*. www.cdproject .net/en-US/News/CDP News Article Pages/a-third-of-worlds-invested-capital-calls-for-corporate-environmental-data.aspx, accessed, 15 February 2013.

Carbon Disclosure Project (CDP). (2013c). *Climate Change Programs*. www.cdproject. net/en-US/Programmes/Pages/climate-change-programs.aspx, accessed, 15 February 2013.

Dow Jones Sustainability Indexes (DJSI). (2013a, 30 August). *Dow Jones Sustainability World Index Guide, Version 12.2*. www.sustainability-indices.com/images/djsi-world-guidebook_tcm1071-337244.pdf, accessed, 23 October 2013.

Dow Jones Sustainability Index (DJSI). (2013b). *Sustainability Indexes – DJSI Family Overview*. www.sustainability-indices.com/index-family-overview/djsi-family.jsp, accessed, 23 October 2013.

Dow Jones Sustainability Index (DJSI). (2013c). *Dow Jones Sustainability World Index Fact Sheet*. http://djindexes.com/mdsidx/downloads/fact_info/Dow_Jones_Sustainability_World_Index_Fact_Sheet.pdf, accessed, 23 October 2013.

Dow Jones Sustainability Index (DJSI). (2013d). *Dow Jones Sustainability Europe Index Fact Sheet*. http://djindexes.com/mdsidx/downloads/fact_info/Dow_Jones_Sustainability_Europe_Index_Fact_Sheet.pdf, accessed, 23 October 2013.

FTSE. (2010). *About us*. www.ftse.co.uk/about_us/index.jsp, accessed, 7 February 2013.

FTSE. (2011). *Responsible Investment FTSE Publications: FTSE4Good 10 years of Impact and Investment*. London: FTSE.

FTSE. (2012a, May). *FTSE4Good Ground Rules for the Management of the FTSE-4Good Index Series (Version 1.6)*. www.ftse.co.uk/Indices/FTSE4Good_Index_Series/Downloads/FTSE4Good_Index_Rules.pdf. (Accessed, 22 February 2013)

FTSE. (2012b, 31 December). *Fact Sheet: FTSE4Good Index Series*. www.ftse.co.uk / Indices/FTSE4Good_Index_Series/Downloads/4GL1.pdf. (Accessed, 12 February 2013)

FTSE. (2013, 8 March). *FTSE4Good Semi–Annual March 2013, Review Admits 20 New Companies to the FTSE4Good Index Series*. www.ftse.com/Media_Centre/Press_Releases/index.jsp (click on 2013 and scroll down to 8.3.13), accessed 12 November 2013.

18 The Audit Expectation-Performance Gap and Proposals for Reforming the External Audit Function

LEARNING OBJECTIVES

After studying the material in this chapter you should be able to:

- discuss the meaning, structure and importance of the audit expectation-performance gap and changes in the gap in the United Kingdom between 1999 and 2008;
- explain the process of change in the audit expectation-performance gap identified as an outcome of reviewing changes in the gap in New Zealand and the United Kingdom between 1989 and 2008;
- discuss changes to external auditors' reporting responsibilities to (a) financial statement users, (b) audit committees and (c) regulators, proposed (or implemented) since the 2008 global financial crisis;
- discuss the strengths and weaknesses of measures to reduce the Big Four firms' dominance in the large company audit market, and to strengthen auditors' independence, proposed (or implemented) since the 2008 global financial crisis;
- evaluate the ability of the reforms, proposed in the wake of the 2008 global financial crisis, to narrow the audit expectation-performance gap;
- discuss the conflicts which are inherent in the current external audit model and suggest ways in which they might be resolved.

18.1 INTRODUCTION

In earlier chapters of this book[1] we observe that external auditors play a key role in society by helping to secure the smooth functioning of capital markets and the accountability of company directors. They fulfil their role by examining and expressing an opinion on the reliability (or otherwise) of the financial, and some of the non-financial, information in companies' annual reports. However, the findings of research investigating the extent to which society's expectations

---

[1] In particular, in Chapters 1 and 2.

of auditors are fulfilled, together with expressions of disquiet by politicians and in the media about auditors' failure to give warning of impending crises such as the 1987 stock market crash, the Enron, WorldCom and similar debacles shortly after the turn of the twenty-first century, and the 2008 global financial crisis, have revealed considerable dissatisfaction with auditors' fulfilment of (or, more pertinently, their inadequacy in fulfilling) their societal role. Unsurprisingly, given the importance of the external audit function to society, each major crisis has resulted in a plethora of legislative, regulatory and professional body reviews of, and reports on, the role and responsibilities of external auditors followed by changes in laws and/or regulations designed to extend auditors' responsibilities and/or enhance their independence and competence.

As we examined the legal and regulatory changes which followed the 1987 stock market crash and the 2001–2 corporate debacles in earlier chapters of this book, we do not address them here.[2] In this chapter we first discuss the findings of research investigating the structure and extent of the audit expectation-performance gap – the gap between society's expectations of auditors and what it perceives they deliver – and changes in the gap in the United Kingdom (UK) between 1999 and 2008. We also explore a process of change in the audit expectation-performance gap identified as an outcome of studying the gap in New Zealand (NZ) and the UK between 1989 and 2008. This is followed by a discussion of the reforms to external auditing that have been proposed or implemented since the 2008 global financial crisis. They fall into two broad groups – those designed to:

(a) extend auditors' reporting responsibilities;
(b) reduce the dominance of the Big Four firms in the large company audit market and/or strengthen the independence and competence of external auditors.

We also examine the likely impact of the entry of Chinese firms into the large company audit market. In the final section of the chapter we identify two conflicts which are inherent in the current external audit model and consider how they might be resolved.

18.2 THE AUDIT EXPECTATION-PERFORMANCE GAP

18.2.1 Importance, definition and structure of the audit expectation-performance gap

When corporate debacles occur, such as those of Enron, WorldCom and Lehman Brothers in the United States of America (USA), Barings Bank and

---

[2] In particular, in Chapter 2 and, in respect of strengthening auditors' independence, in Chapter 4.

Equitable Life in the UK, Parmalat in Italy, HIH in Australia and Satyam in India, those who suffer loss (investors, employees, creditors, suppliers, customers and others), as well as politicians and the general public ,ask: "Why didn't the auditors warn us?". Such questions reflect the failure of the auditors in question to deliver the services expected of them – a failure which results not only in criticism of, and often litigation against, the auditors concerned but also in criticism of the auditing profession as a whole and a loss of confidence in its work.

More than 80 years ago, Limperg (1932) asserted:

> The [audit] function is rooted in the confidence that society places in the effectiveness of the audit and in the opinion of the accountant [i.e., auditor] . . . [I]f the confidence is betrayed, the function, too, is destroyed, since it becomes useless. (as reproduced by the Limperg Instituut, 1985 p. 16)

He went on to explain that auditors have a dual responsibility: not to arouse "in the sensible layman" greater expectations than can be fulfilled by the work done, and to carry out the work in a manner that does not betray the expectations evoked (p. 18). In other words, auditors have a responsibility to ensure that society does not have unreasonable expectations of them and to satisfy those it reasonably expects. However, widespread criticism of, and litigation against, auditors bear witness to the fact that they fail to fulfil this dual responsibility – that there is a gap between what society expects from auditors and what it perceives they deliver – a phenomenon known as the audit expectation gap.

Research conducted during the past four or so decades has shown that the audit expectation gap is not limited geographically – that it exists in, for example, Australia, Canada, China, Finland, Lebanon, NZ, Saudi Arabia, Singapore, South Africa, Spain, the UK and the USA.[3] Most of the studies were designed to ascertain whether an audit expectation gap exists in the country where the research was conducted and to identify its contributing factors. They universally found that financial statement users (in some cases, a broad range of interest groups) have little understanding of the role and responsibilities of external auditors and, in general, expect far more of them than is feasible for them to provide. Adopting a different approach to other studies, Porter (1993), Porter and Gowthorpe (2004), and Porter, Ó hÓgartaigh and Baskerville (2012) investigated the structure, composition and extent of the audit expectation gap in, respectively, NZ in 1989, and NZ and the UK in 1999 and 2008. The findings of the UK studies are reported below but first we define the gap that serves to undermine society's confidence in the audit function.

---

[3] Details of studies which investigated the audit expectation gap in a wide range of countries between 1970 and 2008 are reported in Porter, Ó hÓgartaigh and Baskerville (2012), Part 1.

The term 'expectation gap' was first applied in the context of auditing by Liggio (1974) who defined it as the difference in the level of expected performance "as envisioned by both the user of financial statements and the independent accountant" (p. 27). This definition was extended in the terms of reference of the Commission on Auditors' Responsibilities (CAR, 1978) from "users of financial statements" to "the public", and from "expected performance" to "what auditors can and should reasonably expect to accomplish". The Commission was required to consider "whether a gap may exist between what the public expects or needs and what auditors can and should reasonably expect to accomplish" (CAR 1978, p. xi). Porter (1993) contended that even this definition is too narrow to encapsulate the gap which results in criticism of auditors and a loss of confidence in their work as it fails to recognise that auditors may not accomplish "expected performance" (Liggio) or what they "can and reasonably should" (CAR). Accordingly, she suggested that the gap (more appropriately termed the 'audit expectation-performance gap'[4]) should be defined as the gap between society's expectations of auditors and its perception of the services auditors deliver. Following from this definition, Porter proposed that the gap has two major components:

(i) *a reasonableness gap* – the gap between the responsibilities society expects auditors to perform and those it is reasonable to expect of them;

(ii) *a performance gap* – the gap between the responsibilities society reasonably expects of auditors and those it perceives they deliver (or, more precisely, those it perceives they perform deficiently). This component comprises:

(a) *a deficient standards gap* – the gap between the responsibilities reasonably expected of auditors and those auditors are required to perform by law, regulations or professional promulgations (and are performed to the expected standard); and

(b) *a deficient performance gap* – the gap between the expected standard of performance of auditors' actual responsibilities, and the standard perceived to be delivered, as expected and perceived by society.

This structure of the audit expectation-performance gap, which is depicted in Figure 18.1, captures the dual responsibility of auditors identified by Limperg.

Studies of the audit expectation-performance gap in NZ and the UK by Porter (1993), Porter and Gowthorpe (2004) and Porter *et al.* (2012) were conducted by means of surveys of randomly selected members of four broad interest

---

[4] Traditionally, the gap has been termed the 'audit expectation(s) gap' and defined as the gap between the responsibilities society expects auditors to perform and those auditors acknowledge as theirs. While recognising that this ignores the contribution of auditors' sub-standard performance to their failure to meet society's expectations of them, in this chapter we use the terms 'audit expectation gap' and 'audit expectation-performance gap' interchangeably.

Figure 18.1:   Structure of the audit expectation-performance gap

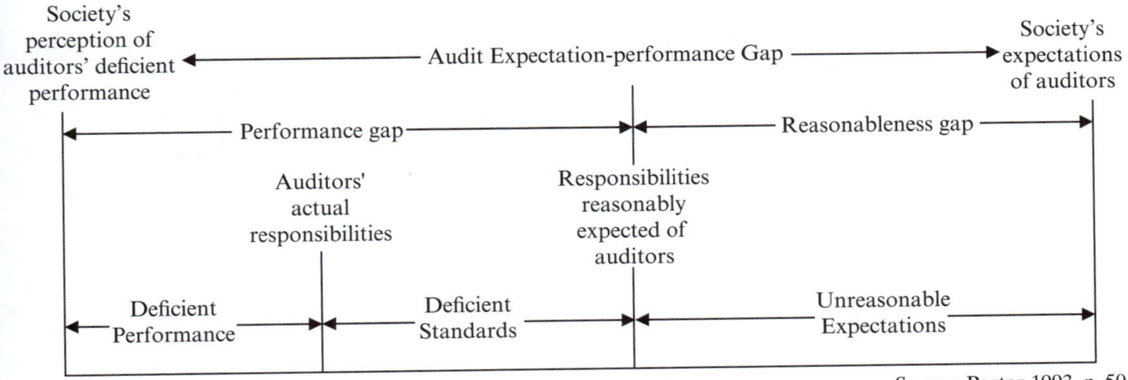

Source: Porter 1993, p. 50

groups – auditors, auditees and audit beneficiaries from both the financial and non-financial community. A list of suggested responsibilities of auditors was provided in the research instrument and, for each, respondents were asked to indicate, in their opinion (i) whether the responsibility is an existing responsibility of auditors, (ii) if so, how well it is performed, and (iii) whether the responsibility should be a responsibility of auditors. The results of the surveys are summarised in Figure 18.2.

18.2.2   Composition of the audit expectation-performance gap in the UK 1999–2008

Having identified the structure of the audit expectation-performance gap, we now examine the composition of the gap in the UK in 1999 and 2008 and changes in the gap over the decade.

(i)   Society's expectations of auditors and the reasonableness gap

From the expectation gap studies conducted around the world, it is evident that society expects auditors to perform a wide range of responsibilities. These constitute the right end of the audit expectation-performance gap depicted in Figure 18.1 and include auditors' actual responsibilities, responsibilities that are reasonably expected of them (although their performance is not required by law, regulations or professional promulgations) and those that are unreasonably expected of them.[5]

---

[5] In the Porter studies, the responsibilities constituting 'society's expectations of auditors' are those that 20 per cent or more of a 'society group' (that is, a non-auditor interest group – auditees or audit beneficiaries from the financial or non-financial community) indicated they expect auditors to perform. Details of how each boundary of the audit expectation-performance gap was determined, and the surrogate for cost-benefit analysis, are explained in Porter (1993).

Figure 18.2: Changes in the audit expectation-performance gap in the UK 1999–2008 and in NZ 1989–2008

United Kingdom

No. of constituent responsibilities

Year of Survey	Responsibilities performed OK	Deficient performance gap	Actual responsibilities	Deficient standards gap	Reasonably expected responsibilities	Reasonableness gap	Responsibilities expected by society	Responsibilities in survey instrument
1989	–	–	–	–	–	–	–	–
1999	6	8	14	9	23	24	47	51
2008	13	6	19	9	28	21	49	55

Contribution of components to the audit expectation-performance gap

Year of Survey	Deficient performance gap	Deficient standards gap	Reasonableness gap
1989	–	–	–
1999	9%	39%	52%
2008	4%	41%	55%

Measure of unfulfilled expectations[1]

Year of Survey	Deficient performance gap	Deficient standards gap	Reasonableness gap
1989	–	–	–
1999	144 units	591 units	804 units
2008	41 units	415 units	557 units

Total extent of audit expectation gap[2]

Year of Survey	
1989	
1999	1539 units
2008	1013 units

New Zealand

No. of constituent responsibilities

Year of Survey	Responsibilities performed OK	Deficient performance gap	Actual responsibilities	Deficient standards gap	Reasonably expected responsibilities	Reasonableness gap	Responsibilities expected by society	Responsibilities in survey instrument
1989	3	5	8	10	18	9	27	30
1999	4	5	9	14	23	23	46	49
2008	7	7	14	11	25	28	53	53

Contribution of components to the audit expectation-performance gap

Year of Survey	Deficient performance gap	Deficient standards gap	Reasonableness gap
1989	11%	58%	31%
1999	6%	51%	43%
2008	7%	43%	50%

Measure of unfulfilled expectations[1]

Year of Survey	Deficient performance gap	Deficient standards gap	Reasonableness gap
1989	125 units	667 units	348 units
1999	94 units	832 units	713 units
2008	116 units	725 units	834 units

Total extent of audit expectation gap[2]

Year of Survey	
1989	1140 units
1999	1639 units
2008	1675 units

1 Determined by totalling the proportion of the society group who indicated, for each responsibility constituting the gap, that they expect auditors to perform the responsibility (for the deficient standards and reasonableness gaps) or they perceive auditors perform the responsibility poorly (for the deficient performance gap). The 'society group' comprises the three non-auditor interest groups (auditees and financial and non-financial community audit beneficiaries). In order to avoid bias resulting from differential sample sizes, the opinion of 'the society group' was derived from the average of the opinions expressed by respondents in each of the non-auditor interest groups.

2 Determined by totalling the measures of unfulfilled expectations attaching to each of the three constituent gaps

It seems logical that, in order for responsibilities to be reasonably expected of auditors, they should be cost-beneficial for auditors to perform: the benefits derived by financial statement users, auditees and society as a whole from auditors performing a responsibility should be equal to or greater than the cost of them doing so. It follows that those responsibilities which society expects auditors to perform but are not cost-effective for them to do so are unreasonably expected of auditors; these responsibilities constitute the reasonableness gap component of the audit expectation-performance gap. Figure 18.2 shows that, in 1999, UK society expected auditors to perform 47 of the 51 responsibilities listed in the survey instrument but 24 of the 47 were unreasonably expected of auditors. These 24 responsibilities (which constitute the reasonableness gap) accounted for 52 per cent of the audit expectation gap and resulted in 804 units of UK society's unfilled expectations.[6]

These findings need to be considered in the light of developments in auditing's external environment during the previous decade – developments that resulted in a marked increase in society's expectations of auditors. They include growth in the size and incidence of corporate fraud, development of corporate governance requirements for UK listed companies, increasing societal concern about the environmental and social impact of major companies, expansion in the quantity and range of information in companies' annual reports,[7] and emergence of the Internet as an effective means of communication. Between 1999 and 2008, these developments continued but at a slower pace. Additionally, stimulated by well-publicised corporate failures around the turn of the twenty-first century and the global financial crisis which commenced in early 2008,[8] there was more public discussion than previously about corporate and financial matters and related auditing issues. Such discussion was promoted in the UK by publications on relevant topics by the Financial Reporting Council (FRC; for example, FRC, 2006b, 2007, 2008b) and the Auditing Practices Board (APB; for example, APB, 2007) and by regular updates of *The Combined Code on Corporate Governance* (FRC, 2003, 2006a, 2008a). As a consequence, although the contribution of the reasonableness gap to the overall audit expectation gap increased from 52 to 55 per cent between 1999 and 2008, this resulted from changes in the other components of the gap (particularly the dramatic narrowing of the deficient performance gap) rather than from an expansion of UK society's unreasonable expectations of auditors. As shown in Figure 18.2, despite the number of responsibilities listed in the questionnaire increasing from 51 to 55, and those UK society

---

[6] Expectations not fulfilled as a consequence of auditors not performing these responsibilities. Calculation of society's unfulfilled expectations of auditors is explained in Porter (1993).

[7] These changes are discussed in earlier chapters of this book – in particular, in Chapters 5, 6 and 17.

[8] The 2008 expectation gap survey was conducted in November and December 2008.

expected auditors to perform rising from 47 to 49, the number of responsibilities constituting the reasonableness gap fell from 24 to 21, and the level of society's unfulfilled expectations resulting from auditors not performing these (unreasonably) expected responsibilities decreased from 804 to 557 units (a decline of nearly 31 per cent).

Analysis of the responsibilities comprising the reasonableness gap reveals that they fall into two broad groups:

(a) Those that are not economically feasible for auditors to perform – for example, *guaranteeing* the accuracy of the company's financial statements and/or its solvency; detecting and reporting minor theft[9] of the company's assets by non-managerial employees or by the directors/senior managers, and other illegal acts by the directors/senior managers which only indirectly impact on the financial statements. Society's (unreasonable) expectation of auditors performing this group of responsibilities was a feature of the reasonableness gap in the UK in both 1999 and 2008. (They were also a persistent feature of the reasonableness gap in NZ throughout the period from 1989 to 2008.)

(b) Those relating to relatively 'new' issues in the corporate arena – for example, examining and reporting (in the auditor's report) on:
  - the effectiveness of the company's operating and information technology systems and its internal non-financial controls;
  - the adequacy of the company's procedures for identifying operational risks;
  - the efficiency and effectiveness of the company's management;
  - the company's non-financial performance.

Changes in the second group of responsibilities largely account for the narrowing of the reasonableness gap in the UK between 1999 and 2008. During this period, many of the developments in auditing's external environment which characterised the previous decade, became more commonplace and there was greater public discussion of relevant issues. Gradually, UK society gained some appreciation of the costs and benefits associated with auditors performing certain responsibilities. As a consequence:

• some of the responsibilities which contributed to the reasonableness gap in 1999 did not feature in 'society's expectations of auditors' in 2008 (for example, examining and reporting on auditees' policies and procedures for equal employment opportunities, product safety and occupational health and safety);

---

[9] 'Minor' theft was defined in the survey instrument as more than 'petty' but less than 'material' theft, that is, less than five per cent of the auditee's turnover or assets.

- others (such as reporting on the reliability of information provided in companies' entire annual reports and the adequacy of their procedures for identifying financial risks) met the cost-benefit criterion in 2008 and thus featured in the deficient standards, rather than the reasonableness, gap in that year.

(ii) Deficient standards gap and changes to auditors' actual responsibilities

As we noted earlier, the deficient standards gap comprises responsibilities that are reasonable to expect of auditors but auditors are not required to perform them by law, regulations or professional promulgations. Figure 18.2 shows that, between 1999 and 2008, the number of 'reasonably expected' responsibilities increased from 23 to 28 but nine responsibilities (not the identical nine) constituted the deficient standards gap in both years. As indicated above, some of the responsibilities which failed to meet the cost-benefit criterion in 1999 did so in 2008 and, thus, featured in the deficient standards gap in that year; other responsibilities that contributed to the deficient standards gap in 1999 did not do so in 2008 as by then they were actual responsibilities of auditors (we discuss these responsibilities below).

Like the responsibilities comprising the reasonableness gap, those constituting the deficient standards gap largely fall into two broad groups, namely:

  (a) Those that involve disclosing in the audit report, and/or to an appropriate authority, matters of concern uncovered during the audit. Such matters include the theft of a material amount of the company's assets by non-managerial employees or by the directors/senior managers, other illegal acts by the directors/senior managers which directly impact on the financial statements, deliberate distortion of the financial statements and doubts about the entity's continued existence.[10] Given that the information is already within the auditor's knowledge, it does not seem too great a step (or involve much cost) to convert these 'reasonably expected' into actual responsibilities of auditors. As we shall see below, in some cases, the standard setters appear to have agreed with this notion.

  (b) Those that relate to corporate governance issues; for example, examining and reporting (to the company's directors) on the adequacy of the company's procedures for identifying financial risks, and examining and reporting (in the audit report) on the reliability of information provided

---

[10] In most cases, in 1999 and to a lesser extent in 2008, UK auditors had an actual responsibility to report the particular 'matter of concern' discovered during the audit *either* in the audit report *or* to an appropriate authority (that is, to a 'proper authority' when it is 'in the public interest to do so'). The aspect of reporting that was not an actual responsibility of auditors met the cost-benefit criterion to be reasonably expected of them.

in the company's entire annual report,[11] in particular, on the effectiveness of its internal financial controls and, for listed company clients, their compliance (rather than instances of non-compliance) with the UK Listing Authority's corporate governance requirements.[12]

The increase in auditors' actual responsibilities between 1999 and 2008 (from 14 to 19: see Figure 18.2) resulted primarily from the 'conversion' of 'reasonably expected' into 'actual' responsibilities of auditors. This, in turn, resulted from the APB's adoption of International Standards on Auditing (ISAs) (in place of national auditing standards) in 2004[13] and the International Auditing and Assurance Standards Board's (IAASB) 'clarity project' (which extended from 2004 to 2009). The latter involved a review of all of the ISAs and produced, *inter alia*: "One new standard . . . [and] 16 standards containing new and revised requirements . . ." (IAASB, 2010). As a result of changes to ISA 240: *The Auditor's Responsibilities Relating to Fraud in an Audit of Financial Statements* (IAASB, 2009a), three responsibilities changed from being 'reasonably expected' to 'required' of auditors. These involve auditors reporting in the audit

---

[11] In respect of this 'reasonably expected' responsibility, the Institute of Chartered Accountants of Scotland (ICAS) observes:

> The external auditor has a unique and privileged access to a business during the course of the audit of the financial statements . . . [which] provides the ideal basis for providing . . . assurance . . . that the Board has presented a balanced and reasonable view of the business [in the company's annual report]. . . . [Providing such assurance] will involve additional work and . . . will come with a cost – but we believe that the benefits of this assurance will far outweigh any additional costs. (ICAS, 2010, p. 26)

[12] In the post-Enron era some of these responsibilities, such as reporting on the effectiveness of auditees' internal financial controls, have become required by law or regulation in some jurisdictions (for example, under the Sarbanes-Oxley Act in the USA). In the UK, some preliminary steps have been taken towards extending auditors' responsibilities (especially for listed companies) in some of these regards. For example, as we note in Chapter 5 (section 5.2.2), the directors of companies listed in the London Stock Exchange are required to include:

- in their strategic report, *inter alia*:
  - a description of the company's principal risks and uncertainties, and
  - to the extent necessary for readers to understand the development, performance and position of the company's business, information about environmental matters (including the impact of the company's business on the environment), its employees and social, community and human rights issues;
- in the statement of their responsibilities or elsewhere in the annual report, a statement that they consider the company's annual report (together with its financial statements) is fair, balanced and understandable and provides the information necessary for shareholders to assess the company's performance, business model and strategy.

We also note in Chapter 5 (section 5.5.5) that auditors are required to:

- review the strategic and directors' reports and state whether, in their opinion, they are consistent with the financial statements, and
- assess the directors' statement about the annual report being fair, balanced and understandable, etc. and, if they do not think the statement is justified, to say so in the audit report.

[13] As ICAS explains: "In the UK audits are performed against ISAs (UK and Ireland) as issued by the Auditing Practices Board (APB) – which are effectively the ISAs applied alongside UK legislation" (ICAS, 2010, Footnote 40).

report and/or to an appropriate authority if, during the audit, the auditor discovers material theft of the company's assets, deliberate distortion of the financial statements, or other illegal acts by the directors/senior managers that directly impact on the financial statements. Similarly, changes to ISA 260: *Communication with Those Charged with Governance* (IAASB, 2009b) resulted in auditors being required to report to the directors, material deficiencies in the company's procedures for identifying financial risks and significant difficulties encountered during an audit.

(iii) Deficient performance gap

From Figure 18.2 it may be seen that, in 1999, UK society adjudged auditors' performance of eight of their 14 actual responsibilities to be sub-standard but, in 2008, notwithstanding the addition of five actual responsibilities, just six of auditors' responsibilities were perceived to be performed deficiently. Analysis of the responsibilities comprising the deficient performance gap reveals that, in both 1999 and 2008, they relate almost entirely to auditors detecting and/or reporting (in the audit report) material theft of company assets by non-managerial employees or by the directors/senior managers, and other illegal acts by the directors/senior managers that directly impact on the financial statements.

Figure 18.2 also reveals a sharp decline in UK society's unfulfilled expectations resulting from perceived deficient performance by auditors between 1999 and 2008 (from 144 to 41 units: a drop of 72 per cent). This equates to a sharp improvement in auditors' performance (as perceived by society) which may, at least in part, be an outcome of clearer specification of their responsibilities in the IAASB's 'clarified and revised' auditing standards. However, it seems likely that the monitoring of auditors' performance, and recommendations by the monitors on how identified defective performance might be rectified, are primarily responsible. As we explain in Chapter 16 (section 16.4), monitoring was introduced in the UK in 1991 when the Recognised Supervisory Bodies (RSBs)[14] became responsible, *inter alia*, for monitoring the performance of their registrant auditors. Since its inception, the rigour of monitoring has increased and, since 2004, it has been supplemented by inspections of the audits of major public interest entities by the Audit Inspection Unit (AIU).[15] Further, the FRC publishes annual reports on the conduct and outcome of the monitoring/inspection process so they are a matter of public record. Additionally, when

---

[14] The RSBs are the Institutes of Chartered Accountants in England and Wales, of Scotland, and in Ireland, and the Associations of Chartered Certified Accountants and Authorised Public Accountants (see Chapter 5, section 5.3.1).

[15] Since July 2012, the AIU has been known as the Audit Quality Review team.

disciplinary action is taken against an errant auditor, the matter is publicised in the financial press. Hence, UK society is in a position to be aware of the monitoring of auditors' performance and may, as a consequence, assume improved performance.

18.2.3 Extent of the audit expectation-performance gap in the UK 1999–2008

Whenever auditors fail to perform a responsibility expected of them, or fail to perform an actual responsibility to the expected standard, the expectations of some members of society are not fulfilled. A measure of 'society's unfulfilled expectations' attaching to each component of the audit expectation-performance gap may be obtained by totalling the proportion of the 'society group'[16] who signified that they expect auditors to perform a responsibility that is not required of them (for responsibilities contributing to the reasonableness and deficient standards gaps) or that auditors perform a responsibility deficiently (for responsibilities constituting the deficient performance gap). The extent of the audit expectation-performance gap may then be determined by summing the totals of society's unfulfilled expectations attaching to each of the gap's components.

Reference to Figure 18.2 shows that, in the UK in 1999, the audit expectation-performance gap comprised 1,539 units of UK society's unfulfilled expectations. Between 1999 and 2008, the extent of society's unfulfilled expectations attaching to each component of the audit expectation gap declined – by nearly 31 per cent for the reasonableness gap, 30 per cent for the deficient standards gap and, most notably, by 72 per cent for the deficient performance gap. As a consequence, between 1999 and 2008 the audit expectation-performance gap in the UK narrowed by some 34 per cent (from 1,539 to 1,013 units of unfulfilled expectations). As we shall see in the next section, this differs quite markedly from events in NZ.

18.2.4 A process of change in the audit expectation-performance gap

As we note in section 18.2.1, 'expectation gap' surveys were conducted in NZ in 1989 and in both NZ and the UK in 1999 and 2008. Although no equivalent survey was undertaken in the UK in 1989, the findings of a study by Humphrey, Moizer and Turley (1993) indicate that, in 1990, the structure and composition of the audit expectation gap in the UK was similar to that in NZ in 1989, and

---

[16] The 'society group' consists of the three non-auditor interest groups (auditees and financial and non-financial community audit beneficiaries). In order to avoid bias resulting from differential sample sizes, the opinion of the 'society group' was derived from the mean of the opinions expressed by respondents in each of the three non-auditor interest groups.

that changes in the gap in the UK between 1989 and 1999 reflect those that occurred in NZ over the decade. By examining changes in the audit expectation gap in the UK and NZ between 1989 and 2008 a four-stage process of change may be identified. We outline this process below.

(i) When significant developments occur in the corporate arena (such as corporate governance requirements and societal concern about the environmental and social impact of major companies), as happened in NZ and the UK between 1989 and 1999, society seems to expect auditors to perform a wide range of new responsibilities to help ensure that corporate managements respond appropriately to the developments. Initially, little thought appears to be given to the cost of auditors performing these responsibilities and most serve to widen the reasonableness gap. This is reflected in the widening of the reasonableness gap in NZ between 1989 and 1999 – by 105 per cent (see Figure 18.2). Using the results of Humphrey *et al.*'s study, we postulate that a similar widening of the reasonableness gap occurred in the UK.

(ii) Gradually, as the environmental developments become more commonplace and, usually, regulatory action is taken in relation thereto, so society gains an appreciation of the costs and benefits attaching to auditors performing the 'newly expected' responsibilities. As this occurs, some of the 'unreasonably expected' responsibilities disappear from society's expectations of auditors and others cross the cost-benefit threshold to be reasonably expected of them. This process is reflected in the differential changes which affected the audit expectation gap in the UK and NZ between 1999 and 2008. During this decade, the regulatory response to developments in the corporate arena was more muted in NZ than in the UK. For example, in the UK, the Companies Act 2006 requires quoted companies to provide environmental and social information in their strategic report but there is no equivalent legislative provision in NZ. Further, although corporate governance requirements were enhanced in both countries, those in NZ are far less demanding.[17] Additionally, the 2001–02 corporate debacles and 2008 global financial crisis were widely reported in the media in both countries but, while in the UK public discussion about corporate and financial matters and related auditing issues was stimulated by, for example, FRC publications, there was no equivalent stimulus in NZ. These differences appear to have enabled UK society to gain a better appreciation than its NZ

---

[17] In NZ, NZX (the NZ Stock Exchange) published the *NZX Corporate Governance Best Practice Code* in 2003 (NZX, 2003), and the NZ Securities Commission (NZSC) published its *Corporate Governance in New Zealand Principles and Guidelines* in 2004 (NZSC, 2004) but, unlike the UK, where listed companies are required to comply (or explain their non-compliance) with *The UK Corporate Governance Code* (FRC, 2012a), listed companies in NZ are merely encouraged to comply with the NZX and NZSC guidance.

counterpart of the costs and benefits attaching to auditors performing the 'newly expected' responsibilities: while the number of responsibilities constituting the reasonableness gap in the UK decreased from 24 to 21 between 1999 and 2008 (as some responsibilities were ejected from society's expectations of auditors and others moved to the deficient standards gap), they increased in NZ from 23 to 28. Similarly, while the reasonableness gap in the UK narrowed by nearly 31 per cent over the decade, it widened in NZ by 17 per cent.

(iii) Similar changes occur in the deficient standards gap. Gradually, as society's familiarity with developments in auditing's external environment evolves, its recognition of the benefits to be gained from auditors performing responsibilities that are reasonably expected but not required of them increases until, through a change in legislation, regulations or auditing standards, some of the responsibilities become actual responsibilities of auditors. Most often this occurs as an outcome of a major crisis which prompts politicians, regulators and the auditing profession to investigate the part played by auditors in – or, more frequently, not played by them in preventing – the crisis, and in regulatory reform designed to correct the perceived deficiencies. This process is evident, for example, in enactment of the Sarbanes-Oxley Act (SOX) in 2002 in the USA and in the establishment of the Co-ordinating Group on Audit and Accounting Issues (CGAA) in 2003 in the UK following the Enron and WorldCom debacles.[18] The CGAA's report (2003) resulted in the FRC becoming the UK's "unified regulator [of auditing and accounting] with a wide range of functions" (FRC, 2006c, p. 1); in effect, the FRC became the UK's equivalent of the Public Company Accounting Oversight Board established by SOX in the USA.

As politicians become involved in the profession's affairs, the profession responds by strengthening its standard setting bodies and revising its auditing standards. This is reflected in replacement of the International Federation of Accountants' International Auditing Practices Committee with an independent standard-setting body (that is, the IAASB) in 2002, the APB's adoption of ISAs in 2004, and in the IAASB's 'clarity project' (2004 to 2009). As indicated in section 18.2.2, the clarity project's "new and revised requirements" are primarily responsible for 'converting' reasonably expected into actual responsibilities of auditors between 1999 and 2008 – and, hence, for narrowing the deficient standards gap in

---

[18] The CGAA was established by the Chancellor of the Exchequer and Secretary for State for Trade and Industry to, *inter alia*, "ensure that there is a coordinated work programme by individual regulators to review the UK's current regulatory arrangements for statutory audit and financial reporting in the light of the collapse of Enron" (CGAA, 2003).

both NZ and the UK (by 30 per cent in the UK and 13 per cent in NZ). However, in 2008, NZ society's unfulfilled expectations, resulting from auditors not performing 'reasonably expected' responsibilities, were significantly greater than those of its UK counterpart (generating 725 units of unfulfilled expectations compared with 415 units). Analysis of the responsibilities constituting the deficient standards gap in the two countries reveals that this difference largely stems from auditors in the UK, but not in NZ (where auditors' duty to their clients is paramount), being required to report untoward matters they encounter during their audits to a 'proper authority' when it is in the public interest to do so. The responsibilities involving such reporting contribute to the deficient standards gap in NZ but are actual responsibilities of auditors in the UK.

(iv) As the number of auditors' actual responsibilities increases, society's perception of their performance may, at least initially, deteriorate (particularly if the changes are prompted by a major crisis for which auditors are perceived to be, at least partially, responsible). Nevertheless, history suggests that legislative and regulatory changes like those mentioned above usually include enhanced requirements for auditors' performance. For instance, following the 1987 stock market crash, the UK's Companies Act 1989 introduced the requirement for UK company auditors to be registered with an RSB which was responsible, *inter alia*, for monitoring its registrants' performance. Further, as noted earlier, in 2004 (following the Enron debacle), monitoring by the RSBs was supplemented by AIU inspections of major public interest entity audits. Along similar lines, SOX introduced the inspection of auditors' performance in the USA in 2002.

In the UK, and to a lesser extent in NZ, auditors' performance (or society's perception thereof) improved markedly between 1989 and 2008 and it seems likely that the introduction of monitoring of auditors' performance is primarily responsible. In NZ, Practice Review was introduced in 1990 by the New Zealand Institute of Chartered Accountants (NZICA). It involved a Practice Review Panel (appointed by NZICA) reviewing the performance of all NZICA members with a Public Practice Certificate (which included all company auditors). From its inception, until it was replaced in 2012 with a monitoring system more like that in the UK,[19] Practice Review remained relatively unchanged; additionally, no information was placed in the public domain about its process or outcomes. This is in marked contrast to the UK where the monitoring of auditors' performance by the RSBs was introduced in

---

[19] In July 2012, the Auditor Regulation Act 2011 introduced a system of regulating company auditors in NZ similar to that operating in the UK.

1991 as an element of a governmental regulatory system which focused solely on company auditors and audits, the rigour of monitoring has been steadily strengthened and, since 2004, it has been supplemented by AIU inspections. Furthermore, information on the monitoring/ inspection process is placed in the public domain. These differences are reflected in changes in the deficient performance gap in NZ and the UK. In NZ between 1989 and 1999, following the introduction of monitoring, the deficient performance gap narrowed by 25 per cent but, between 1999 and 2008, while the gap in UK narrowed by 72 per cent, it widened in NZ by 23 per cent (see Figure 18.2).

In 1999, the audit expectation-performance gap was just six per cent narrower in the UK than in NZ. However, between 1999 and 2008, with more widespread public discussion of corporate and financial matters and related auditing issues, more demanding auditing standards, and more rigorous monitoring of auditors' performance, the gap in the UK narrowed by 34 per cent (from 1,539 to 1,013 units of unfulfilled expectations) but widened in NZ by two per cent (from 1,639 to 1,675 units of unfulfilled expectations: a result that is not statistically significant). In 2008, the gap in the UK was nearly 40 per cent narrower than that in NZ. It is evident that, between 1989 and 2008 in the UK, the gap between society's expectations of auditors and what it perceives they deliver narrowed markedly. In the next sections we examine some of the reforms proposed in the UK and wider European Union (EU) in the wake of the 2008 global financial crisis and consider their likely impact on the audit expectation gap.

18.3 OVERVIEW OF PROPOSED REFORMS FOLLOWING THE GLOBAL FINANCIAL CRISIS

Following the 2008 global financial crisis auditors were widely criticised for failing to give warning of the impending crisis. For example, during an enquiry by the House of Lords Select Committee on Economic Affairs (HoL; 2011), Lord Lawson referred to auditors as "one of the dogs that didn't bark" and Lord Forsyth observed: "I find it difficult to understand, given what auditors are meant to do, that on looking at these expanding balance sheets [of the banks] and the makings of a crisis they did not sound the alarm" (as reported, Christodoulou, 2010d). Along similar lines, the FRC (2010) noted that many people queried:

> . . . how a bank could have received an unqualified audit report, only to collapse a few months later. . . . In considering the role of audit in the financial crisis, the critical point is that audit . . . did not give a sufficiently early warning. (paras 3.2, 3.4) Alternatively expressed, auditors did not meet society's expectations of them.

As for past crises, the 2008 global financial crisis prompted a plethora of investigations of the role and responsibilities of external auditors and numerous recommendations for reform. In general, the investigators endorsed the view expressed by Pitt-Watson (Hermes Investments), namely that: "Audit and accountancy are absolutely fundamental to the integrity of our capital markets and the good governance of our companies" (HoL, 2011, para 2). However, they also identified deficiencies in the current audit model. Among the most significant are the following:

(i) inadequate reporting by external auditors;

(ii) domination of the large company audit market by the Big Four firms [Deloitte, Ernst & Young (E&Y), KPMG and PricewaterhouseCoopers (PwC)];

(iii) inappropriately long audit tenure;

(iv) inappropriate provision of non-audit services by auditors to audit clients.

Perhaps not surprisingly, given their common stimulus and their contemporaneousness, the various investigations proposed similar reforms to rectify the perceived deficiencies. These fall into two broad groups, each of which has sub-themes:

1. Enhancing auditors' reporting responsibilities to:
   (i)   users of companies' annual reports,
   (ii) audit committees, and
   (iii) regulators;

2. Reducing audit market concentration and strengthening auditors' independence:
   (i) through more frequent changes of auditor (mandatory rotation and tendering),
   (ii) by other means – joint audits, placing restrictions on the Big Four firms and removing barriers of entry to the large company audit market.

We discuss each of these groups of proposed reforms below.

18.4 ENHANCING AUDITORS' REPORTING RESPONSIBILITIES

18.4.1 Reporting to users of companies' annual reports

In the wake of the 2008 global financial crisis the auditor's report was severely criticised for failing to provide useful information for financial statement users. For example, the House of Commons Treasury Select Committee (HCTC) which investigated the 2007–8 banking crisis in the UK (HCTC, 2009) reported: "We are perturbed that the [audit] process results in 'tunnel vision', where the big picture that shareholders want to see is lost in a sea of detail and regulatory disclosures" (para 221). Along similar lines, the FRC (2011) acknowledged:

> There has long been a general recognition that the audit process is opaque, that the pro forma audit report is wholly uninformative about the matters that interest . . . users of financial statements . . . As a result, stakeholders, and in particular investors, have called for greater transparency about the key issues that arose in the course of the audit, how they were addressed and any other matters bearing on whether the financial statements give a true and fair view. (p. 16)

The IAASB (2012) expressed similar conclusions when explaining the rationale for its proposed (significantly different) standard auditor's report.[20] It stated:

> . . . users of audited financial statements are calling for more pertinent information for their decision-making in today's global business environment with increasingly complex financial reporting requirements. The global financial crisis has also spurred users, in particular institutional investors and financial analysts, to want to know more about individual audits and to gain further insights into the audited entity and its financial statements. . . . [They] are looking to auditors to . . . point out the areas on which the auditor's work effort was focused – particularly on the most subjective matters within the financial statements. (pp. 1, 3)

Following from this reasoning, the IAASB proposed some radical changes to the format and content of the standard auditor's report. The most significant changes are as follows:

1. Placement of:
   (i) the auditor's opinion on the financial statements in the opening paragraph of the 'Report on the Financial Statements' section of the auditor's report, and
   (ii) the description of the directors' and auditor's responsibilities for the financial statements in the concluding paragraphs in this section of the report;
2. The inclusion of:
   (a) a Basis for Opinion paragraph, following the Opinion paragraph, for unmodified, audit opinions;[21]
   (b) clear statements of:
       - the auditor's conclusion about the appropriateness of preparing the financial statements based on the going concern assumption,
       - any material uncertainties or events that may cast doubt on the company's ability to continue as a going concern the auditor considers should be disclosed in the financial statements (or that there are no such matters);

---

[20] The (current) standard auditor's report, prepared in accordance with ISA 700: *Forming an Opinion and Reporting on Financial Statements* (IAASB, 2009d) is explained in Chapter 14, section 14.3.

[21] It should be recalled from Chapter 14, sections 4.3 and 14.5, that ISA 700 (2009d) only requires the auditor's report to include a 'Basis of Opinion' paragraph when the audit opinion is modified.

    (c) for the audits of public interest entities (and of other entities where the auditor chooses to provide it), an 'auditor commentary' on entity-specific matters the auditor considers are the most important to users' understanding of the audited financial statements or the audit. Auditors are expected to provide commentary on between two and ten matters and to write it in the form they consider most appropriate;

    (d) a statement identifying:

        (i) the 'other information' (information other than the audited financial statements) in the company's annual report the auditor has read,[22] and

        (ii) any material inconsistencies between that information and the audited financial statements (or a statement that none have been identified).

The inclusion of an auditor commentary in the auditor's report is the most innovative change proposed by the IAASB and is a response to calls by investors, financial analysts, and other users of company's financial statements, such as those by Jubb (Standard Life Investments, UK) in his submission to the IAASB:

> A concern of investors is that the judgments made and processes followed during the preparation of the [financial statements] and their audit are often opaque. . . . Moreover, many of the concerns investors have about the quality of audits[23] are a product of the fact that they feel excluded from the audit process and real findings. This includes evaluating: risks and controls; valuation judgments, and write downs and impairments. But currently the only communication auditors have with investors is through an audit report which is of limited use with its . . . boilerplate, technical language. (as cited, FRC, 2013a, para 16)

That the proposed 'auditor commentary' is a response to such concerns is reflected in the matters addressed in the illustrative commentary provided by the IAASB in its proposed auditor's report, namely: Outstanding litigation; Goodwill; Valuation of financial instruments; Audit strategy relating to the recording of revenue, accounts receivable and cash receipts; and Involvement of other auditors for the audit of certain subsidiaries (IAASB, 2012, p. 10). Some of these matters illuminate events or conditions disclosed in the financial statements and/or the audit thereof (for example, outstanding litigation, goodwill and the valuation of financial instruments). However, others are less directly related to disclosures in the financial statements and explain specific

---

[22] It should be recalled from Chapter 14, section 14.3.4, that, in the UK, ISA (UK and Ireland) 700: *The Independent Auditor's Report on Financial Statements* (FRC, 2013d) requires auditors to read *all* of the information in companies' annual reports.

[23] Such concerns result in criticism of auditors and hence in widening the audit expectation-performance gap.

factors that have impacted the performance of the audit (for example, the involvement of other auditors in the audit of certain subsidiaries and the effect of certain of the entity's systems, for example, for the recording of revenue, on the audit strategy). The IAASB (2012, para 43) explains that the matters addressed in the 'auditor commentary' "are likely those about which the auditor and TCWG [those charged with governance] had the most robust dialogue as part of the two-way communication required by ISA 260" [*Communication with Those Charged with Governance*; IAASB, 2009b].[24]

Notwithstanding the radical changes to the auditor's report proposed by the IAASB, they do not go far enough for some. For example, the Association of Chartered Certified Accountants (ACCA) informed the HoL that the audit should be extended from financial statements to embrace risk management, corporate governance and the company's business model. Similarly the Chartered Institute of Management Accountants (CIMA) suggested that auditors should provide assurance on the narrative operating and financial review (HoL, 2011, para 76). However, in its Green Paper, *Audit Policy: Lessons from the Crisis* (2010), the European Commission (EC) noted that equity analysts and credit rating agencies provide forward looking analysis, at least for large listed companies and "[t]he role of the auditor should thus be extended in this direction only if there is real value added to the stakeholders" (p. 9).

In accordance with this viewpoint, the audit report provided in *A Proposal for a Regulation of the European Parliament and of Council [EU] on Specific Requirements Regarding Statutory Audit of Public-Interest Entities* (EU Reg;

---

[24] Reference to the footnotes in Chapter 14, section 14.3, reveals that, in essence, the changes to the auditor's report proposed by the IAASB (outlined above) have been incorporated in its Exposure Drafts (EDs) relating to reporting by auditors on audited financial statements (see Chapter 14, footnote 14), in particular, in proposed ISA 700 (Revised): *Forming an Opinion and Reporting on Financial Statements* (IAASB, 2013b). However, two notable differences are evident, namely:

    (i) The absence of any requirement in proposed ISA 700 (Revised) regarding the placement of sections within the auditor's report (for example, those containing the auditor's opinion on the financial statements and those explaining the auditor's and the directors' responsibilities for the financial statements). Nevertheless, proposed ISA 700 (Revised) encourages placement of the auditor's opinion in the opening paragraph of the auditor's report.

    (ii) The replacement, in the auditor's report on listed companies' financial statements, of the proposed 'auditor commentary' with a section explaining 'key audit matters', that is, matters the auditor considers to have been of greatest significance in the audit. Proposed ISA 700 (Revised) also specifies that these matters are to be selected from those the auditor communicated to those charged with the entity's governance (or, in most cases, to its audit committee) and that the auditor's report is to state that the key audit matters have been so selected. Notwithstanding these differences, the proposed 'key audit matters' section of listed companies' audit reports is similar in nature to the IAASB's forerunner 'auditor commentary' proposal. The fact that the IAASB has produced an ED of ISA 701: *Communicating Key Audit Matters in the Independent Auditor's Report* (IAASB, 2013c) makes it clear that it envisages its proposals in respect of key audit matters will be advanced to the financial version of ISA 700.

EU, 2011a)[25] contains significantly more detail about the conduct of the audit than the IAASB's proposal but no forward looking company information. EU Reg (art. 22) specifies, for example, that the audit report is (among other things) to:

- describe the audit methodology, including how much of the balance sheet has been directly verified and how much has been based on system and compliance testing;
- explain any variance in the weighting of substantive and compliance testing compared with the previous year, even if there has been a change of auditor;
- provide details of the level of materiality applied to perform the audit;
- identify key areas of risk of material misstatement of the financial statements including critical accounting estimates or areas of measurement uncertainty.

As may be deduced from these limited examples, the audit reports proposed by EU Reg and the IAASB differ markedly.[26] However, changes to EU Reg suggested by the European Parliament's Legal Affairs Committee (Juri),[27] if adopted, would more closely align the EU's audit report with that of the IAASB. The key changes proposed by Juri (EU, 2012) are as follows:

1. Replacing seven items which EU Reg specifies are to be included in the audit report (including those shown above) with a single statement which provides details of the most important assessed risks of material misstatement identified during the audit, the auditor's response to those risks and key observations from that audit work.
2. Replacing EU Reg's proposed statement by the auditor "on the situation of the audited entity including an assessment of [its] ability to meet its obligation in the foreseeable future and therefore continue as a going concern" (art. 22) with the same two-part (going concern and material uncertainties) statement proposed by the IAASB noted in point 2(b) above.
3. Combining two separate items proposed in EU Reg on the scope of the auditor's review of 'other information' and the auditor's conclusion about

---

[25] EU Reg, and the accompanying *Proposal for a Directive of the European Parliament and Council . . .* (2011b), is based on the EC's Green Paper (EC, 2010) and submissions received thereon. It should be recalled from Chapter 5, footnote 1, that EU Regulations have legal effect in all Member States, irrespective of whether they are also enacted in a Member State's legislation and that Directives indicate the outcomes Member States are required to achieve but, to an extent, leave each Member State to determine how to achieve the outcomes.

[26] It is pertinent to note that, while the IAASB's proposed audit report would apply to the audits of all entities, irrespective of their size, nature or jurisdiction, that proposed by EU Reg would apply only to the audits of public interest entities in the EU.

[27] Juri is responsible for reviewing and commenting on EU Reg. Under the EU legislative process, EU Reg remains 'on the table', together with Juri's suggested amendments until the final text of a Regulation or Directive is agreed by the EU's Parliament, Council and Commission (Hooper, 2013).

the consistency (or otherwise) of 'other information' in the entity's annual report with its audited financial statements in a two-part statement like that proposed by the IAASB [see point 2(d) above].

A further similarity of the IAASB's and the EU's proposed audit report is its length – IAASB, EU Reg and Juri all envisage a report that is significantly longer than one prepared in accordance with ISA 700: *Forming an Opinion and Reporting on Financial Statements* (IAASB, 2009d). While EU Reg and Juri specify that the report is not to exceed "four pages or 10000 characters (without spaces)" (art. 22), the IAASB's illustrative report covers four A4 pages. The question remains as to how much of a report extending over four pages financial statement users will read.

Notwithstanding the broad similarity of the IAASB's and Juri's (i.e., the EU's) proposed audit report, there are four notable differences, namely:

1. The EU's audit report is to contain prescribed details about:
   - how the audit was performed (including the extent to which the audit was designed to detect irregularities, including fraud), and
   - the outcome of audit work relating to:
     - assessment of the entity's internal controls and identification of significant deficiencies therein,
     - detecting violations of accounting rules, and
     - other matters of significance for the governance of the entity.

   The IAASB's proposed report is to contain prescribed details about the auditor's responsibility for the financial statements similar to, but a little more detailed than, those required by ISA 700 (IAASB, 2009d). Details of the performance and outcomes of the audit are to be communicated to those charged with the entity's governance. However, unlike the EU's proposed audit report, that proposed by the IAASB is to contain, at least for public interest entities, an 'auditor commentary' which provides the information, and be written in the form, the auditor thinks appropriate.

2. The EU's audit report is to contain details of any non-audit services the auditor provides to the audit client; however, the IAASB proposal merely requires auditors to inform readers that they are required to comply with relevant ethical standards, including those relating to independence.

3. The EU's audit report is to include confirmation that the opinion expressed in the audit report is consistent with the auditor's report to the entity's audit committee (i.e., those charged with the entity's governance). Such a provision is absent from the IAASB's proposed report.

4. The EU's audit report is to provide details of: by whom, and when, the auditor was appointed and the length of the auditor's tenure (unless the information is disclosed elsewhere in the company's annual report). Such a requirement is absent from the IAASB's proposed report but, as we

note below, at least in the UK, this information is likely to be included in the audit committee's report within the company's annual report.

From the illustrative example of an 'auditor commentary' provided by the IAASB, it appears that the IAASB envisages auditors will (or will have the opportunity to) report company-specific information. However, commentators have cautioned against auditors commentating on management's assumptions and judgments rather than merely signing off on the financial statements. Montgomery (Deputy Chair, IAASB), for example, has pointed out that confidentiality and liability issues could arise if auditors disclose information that has not been disclosed by the company's management. He also noted the danger of some information being provided by both management and the auditor resulting in, what Montgomery terms, 'duelling information' – providing two versions of 'the truth' (Crump, 2012). In similar vein, Hodgkinson [Executive Director, technical strategy department of the Institute of Chartered Accountants in England and Wales (ICAEW)] observed:

> It is the responsibility of the company's directors to share information with investors and other stakeholders on the company's finances. The auditor is there to assess whether the company has done so appropriately. . . . While auditors are there to point out any shortcomings in the company's financial reporting, they should not provide original information on the company apart from in exceptional circumstances. (as reported, Orlik, 2011f)

The FRC went further in distinguishing between reporting by the company and by the auditor. It stated:

> [W]e believe that the responsibility for increasing the transparency of the audit should rest with the company and that the most appropriate way to transmit it to investors is via the report of the audit committee. We believe that the auditor should then be required to make a positive statement on the completeness and fairness of the audit committee report or provide additional information where the auditor considers it necessary. (FRC, 2010, para 3.10)

The FRC gave effect to these beliefs in proposed changes to the auditor's report for entities that are required, or choose voluntarily, to comply (or explain their non-compliance) with *The UK Corporate Governance Code* (Code entities; FRC, 2012a). The proposed changes affect just two sections of the auditor's report – those which explain:

(a) the scope of the audit of the financial statements, and
(b) the auditor's opinion on 'other legal and regulatory matters'.

(a) Scope of the audit of the financial statements

The first part of this section of the auditor's report is unchanged from ISA (UK and Ireland) 700: *The Auditor's Report on Financial Statements* (FRC, 2012d).[28]

---

[28] The standard auditor's report prepared in accordance with ISA (UK and Ireland) 700 is explained in Chapter 14, section 14.3.

However, the FRC (2013a) proposed that for Code entities this section should also provide:

(i) a description of the assessed risks of material misstatement identified by the auditor which had the greatest effect on the overall audit strategy, the allocation of resources in the audit, and directing the efforts of the audit team;

(ii) an explanation of how the auditor applied the concept of materiality in planning and performing the audit; this is to specify the threshold used by the auditor as materiality for the financial statements as a whole [the amount for each of (a) planning and (b) performance materiality is to be specified];[29]

(iii) a summary of the scope of the audit which, *inter alia*, explains how the scope was responsive to the assessed risks and application of materiality disclosed in accordance with (i) and (ii) above.[30]

(b) Auditor's opinion on 'other legal and regulatory matters'

In 2012, the FRC added requirements to this section of the auditor's report for Code entities to correspond with changes made to *The UK Corporate Governance Code*. In brief, these require the auditors of Code entities to report by exception if they identify 'other information' in the company's annual report that is materially inconsistent with, or materially incorrect based on, knowledge the auditor acquired during the audit.[31] In 2013, the FRC proposed that the auditors of Code entities also be required to state in this section of the audit report, whether they have anything to add, or wish to draw attention to, in relation to the directors' statement about the company's going concern assessment and its outcome[32] (FRC, 2013a).

From the proposed changes to the auditor's report outlined above, it is evident that they focus primarily on additional information auditors are to provide

---

[29] The concept of materiality, and planning and performance materiality, is explained in Chapter 9, section 9.3.

[30] As noted in Chapter 14, section 14.3.3, these proposals have been converted into requirements through promulgation of ISA (UK and Ireland) 700 (FRC, 2013d). However, the latter has introduced the requirements as a separate section of the audit report for Code entities following the opinion paragraphs. Further, while the limit (or threshold) of planning materiality is to be disclosed, the Standard suggests (rather than requires) performance materiality to be disclosed as one of a number of aspects of the application of the concept of materiality.

[31] Details of these requirements are provided in Chapter 14, section 14.3.5.

[32] The Sharman Panel Inquiry into *Going Concern and Liquidity Risks . . .* (Sharman, 2012) was prompted by the HoL finding that auditors in the UK failed to provide adequate warning of the 2007–8 banking crisis (HoL, 2011, para 142). As we note in Chapter 13 (section 13. 4), Sharman (2012) recommended that the directors of all UK companies be required to include in their company's annual report (as part of a discussion about the company's strategy and principal risks) a statement that the company is a going concern and the basis for this conclusion.

about their audit of the financial statements. However, as we alluded to earlier, investors and other users of companies' annual reports have called on auditors to provide assurance on a wide range of issues, in addition to the financial statements. The HoL (2011) noted, for example:

> Investors and others demand that audit should provide broader, more up-to-date, assurance on such matters as risk management, the firm's business model and the business review.[33] This additional assurance would help the audit to meet the current expectations of investors and the wider public [and thus narrow the audit expectation gap]. (para 79)

Along similar lines, ICAS (2010) reported:

> Stakeholders are increasingly relying on the narrative reporting in the "front half" of the annual report to enhance their understanding of the financial statements and the company's performance and future prospects. The narrative includes many different types of information – including discussion of the future prospects of the business; reporting against Key Performance Indicators; and sustainability reporting – and presents a different challenge to the assurance provider. . . . We believe that the external auditor can meet this challenge and deliver assurance on the "front half" of the annual report. (p. 25)

Following from this statement, ICAS recommended that auditors be required to provide assurance on whether the narrative portion of the annual report provides a "balanced and reasonable" review of the business. It explains that "balanced" refers to the absence of "spin" and "reasonable" refers to a situation where, "based on the information available at the time . . . , a similarly skilled professional would have reached the same conclusion" (p. 26). It also recommended that, given their importance to users of company's annual reports, the following should be provided at the front of each company's annual report:

1. A statement by the directors that they believe their company's annual report is balanced and reasonable and that the financial statements are true and fair.
2. An audit and assurance report by the external auditor which includes:
   (i) the auditor's opinion on whether:
   - the financial statements are true and fair and properly prepared;
   - the annual report is consistent with the audited financial statements;
   - based on the auditor's review of the assumptions underlying the board's going concern assessment, the board's conclusion is considered reasonable;

---

[33] The requirement for all but small companies to include a strategic report (which includes the former business review section of the director's report) in their annual report is explained in Chapter 5, section 5.2.2.

- the annual report (excluding the financial statements) is balanced and reasonable;[34]

(ii) confirmation that the audit committee's report within the annual
report is an appropriate reflection of the key issues the auditor discussed with the committee (ICAS, 2010, p. 28).

Given ICAS's recommendations, it is not surprising that it expressed disap-
pointment with the FRC's requirement for auditors only to report by exception if they identify 'other information' in the company's annual report that
is materially inconsistent with, or materially incorrect based on, knowledge
the auditor acquired during the audit (noted above). As Barbour (Director of
Technical Policy, ICAS) explained, requiring auditors to "only report by exception – in circumstances where they believe that the content of [annual] reports
is not fair, balanced and reasonable – fails to properly fill the assurance
vacuum in this area" (as reported, Singh, 2012).

From the proposals outlined above, it seems likely that, in the not-too-distant
future, auditors will be required (as a minimum) to provide greater transparency about key issues that arose during the audit, factors they relied on when
exercising their judgement during the audit and, more particularly, material
matters they considered when forming their opinion on the financial statements. They may be required to report this information directly to financial
statement users in their audit reports (as proposed by EU Reg and Juri) or
indirectly through the audit committee report (as envisaged by the FRC and
ICAS).

18.4.2   Reporting to audit committees

According to the Chief Executive of the FRC, Haddrill (2011):

> We must give users [of companies' annual reports] more information about the
> prospects of the company and a better picture of the future of the business
> and of the judgements made in the course of the preparation of the financial
> statements. We must give more insight into whether the preparation of these

---

[34] In 2013, ICAS (2013) reiterated its recommendation that auditors be required to confirm (or otherwise)
that the narrative information in companies' annual reports (that is, information other than the audited
financial statements) is balanced and reasonable. It also set out its view on how auditors (or other providers of the assurance engagement) can determine whether or not the narrative information is balanced
and reasonable. ICAS envisages that:

> a 'balanced and reasonable' opinion will take the form of a 'medium assurance' engagement, which would provide
> a lower level of assurance than that provided by an audit engagement, but greater than that provided by a review
> engagement. (ICAS, 2013, p. 4)

A review engagement results in a negative form of opinion – a form of opinion we explain in relation to
'assurance engagements' in Chapter 17, section 17.5.

statements was contentious and subject to debate within the organisation or with the auditors. (p. 3)

As we have seen, in general, commentators and reformers agree with Haddrill's viewpoint but opinion differs as to whether the information should be provided by the auditor or by the audit committee. Nevertheless, there is also general agreement that the role of audit committees (at least in listed companies) in evaluating the external auditor and external audit work should be enhanced. To enable audit committees fulfil this responsibility, auditors need to provide them with relevant information.

As we explain in Chapter 14, section 14.8, ISA 260 (IAASB, 2009b) requires auditors to provide information to audit committees about, *inter alia*:

(i)   the auditor's responsibility in relation to the financial statement audit;
(ii) the planned scope and timing of the audit;
(iii) significant findings of the audit; and
(iv) for listed companies, information relating to the auditor's independence.[35]

EU Reg and Juri (art. 23) propose that auditors of public interest entities be required to provide these entities' audit committee with information on an extensive list of matters.[36] However, analysis of the proposed requirements reveals that, in general, they do not go beyond those of ISA 260 indicated above but, in respect of (i) independence, (ii) consolidated financial statements and (iii) going concern they do so.

(i)   *Independence:* ISA 260 requires the auditors of listed companies (all of which are public interest entities) to inform the audit committee:
      - that all of the audit engagement team members and others in the audit firm, have complied with relevant ethical requirements,

---

[35] In Chapter 14, section 14.8, we note that the ED of Proposed ISA 260 (Revised): *Communication with Those Charged with Governance* (IAASB, 2013a) proposes that, in addition to the current requirements contained in ISA 260, auditors should be required to communicate to their auditees' audit committee, *inter alia*:
    (i) significant risks identified during the audit, and
    (ii) circumstances that resulted in significant modification of the planned approach to the audit.

[36] In general, Juri proposes changes to the format but not the content of EU Reg (art. 23). Nevertheless, it suggests omitting from the matters EU Reg proposes auditors should be required to report to audit committees:
    (i) dates of the auditor's meetings with the audit committee and management board;
    (ii) information about the auditor appointment process.
Information about these matters is likely to be within the committee's knowledge without the auditor reporting thereon.
    (iii) Confirmation of attendance at inventory counts and other instances of physical verification.
It is unclear why auditors should report on these aspects of the audit when other aspects could be equally or more critical to the formation of the auditor's opinion on the financial statements.

including independence; (the EU proposals contain a similar requirement[37];

- of all relationships that may be thought to bear on the auditor's independence, and safeguards applied to eliminate (or reduce to an acceptable level) identified threats to the auditor's independence. The information provided is to include details of fees charged during the period covered by the financial statements for audit and non-audit services.

The second requirement above is absent from the EU's proposals; instead, auditors are to declare in their reports to the audit committee that prohibited non-audit services have not been provided to the entity and that non-prohibited non-audit services have been provided only with the involvement or approval of the audit committee.

(ii) *Consolidated financial statements:* EU Reg and Juri specify that auditors should report to the audit committee on:
- the principles of consolidation adopted by the entity, and
- work performed during the audit by other auditors (including third country auditors; that is, auditors in countries outside the EU).

Although not explicitly required by ISA 260, it is likely that auditors will discuss these matters with the audit committee when communicating about the scope and timing, and/or significant findings, of the audit.

(iii) *Going concern:* EU Reg and Juri propose that, in their report to the audit committee, auditors be required to:
- identify and explain judgments about events or conditions identified during the audit that may cast doubt on the ability of the entity to continue as a going concern, and
- provide details of information of all guarantees, comfort letters, understandings of public intervention and other support measures relied on by the auditor when making a going concern assessment.

ISA 260 does not include any equivalent provisions; however, it is likely that 'going concern and uncertainties' will be high on the agenda of auditor–audit committee discussions.[38]

---

[37] EU Reg (art. 23) also proposes that all members of the audit engagement team be named but Juri suggests that this requirement be removed.

[38] We should also note that, as indicated in section 18.4.1, the IAASB has proposed that auditors be required to make specific disclosures in their audit reports about:
  (i) the appropriateness of the auditee's financial statements being prepared on the basis that it is a going concern, and
  (ii) the adequacy of disclosures of material events or circumstances that may cast doubt on the auditee's ability to continue as a going concern.

In the UK, ISA (UK and Ireland) 260: *Communication with Those Charged with Governance* (FRC, 2012c, paras 16-1, A20-1) requires the auditors of Code entities to communicate to the audit committee information they believe is relevant to:

(a) the directors' responsibility:
- to state, in the annual report, that they consider the annual report and financial statements, taken as a whole, is fair, balanced and understandable, and provides the information necessary for shareholders to assess the entity's performance, business model and strategy;
- to review, at least annually, the effectiveness of the company's risk management and internal control systems;

(b) the audit committee's understanding of the rationale and supporting evidence the auditor relied on when making significant audit judgments and forming an opinion on the financial statements.

In 2013, the FRC proposed that the auditors of Code entities should also be required to provide the audit committee with information they believe is relevant to the directors' responsibility to report in the financial statements that the entity is a going concern, with supporting assumptions or qualifications. The information to be provided should include the auditor's views on the robustness of the directors' going concern assessment and outcome, including the related disclosures in the financial statements and annual report (FRC, 2013b, pp. 17–18).

It is interesting to observe that the FRC's (actual and proposed) requirements go beyond those proposed by EU Reg and Juri. However, the UK's Competition Commission (CC)[39] considers that more is needed to strengthen the accountability of the external auditor to the audit committee. It observes:

> We have found that currently the Finance Director . . . has an influential role in the conduct of the company's relationship with external auditors . . . The Finance Director . . . has a key role in dialogue regarding the scope of audit, fees, reappointment and resolution of audit issues and normally requires a 'no surprises' policy in items taken to the AC [audit committee]. . . . We consider that in practice external auditors appear to have a strong reporting line to the Finance Director and a more distant, often, mediated, reporting line to the ACC [audit committee chair]. (CC, 2013a, paras 46, 47)

In order to remedy this situation, and enhance the accountability of the external auditor to the audit committee, the Commission recommended (2013b) that:

(i) the audit engagement partner should be required to report directly to the audit committee chair;

---

[39] The CC was appointed in October 2011 to investigate the apparent lack of competition in the large company audit market in the UK. 'Large companies' are defined to mean the largest 350 companies listed on the London Stock Exchange, that is the FTSE 100 and FTSE 250 companies (CC, 2011, para 1).

(ii) only the audit committee and audit committee chair should be authorised to negotiate audit fees, initiate tenders for audit work, require an audit engagement partner to be replaced, and approve the audit firm's provision of non-audit services or any other major aspect of the external audit relationship;

(iii) the audit committee chair should be the first point of contact if a material issue arises during the audit (rather than being contacted after the finance director);

(iv) the finance director's role in the selection and (re)appointment of the external auditor should be limited to the minimum necessary (para 48).[40]

The FRC (2013c) responded to the Competition Commission's proposals by noting:

> . . . [R]ecent changes to the Corporate Governance Code have increased the responsibility of the audit committee in respect of reporting to shareholders on its oversight of the external auditor. . . . To assist the audit committee in their reporting to investors and to reduce the risk that issues are resolved between the finance director and auditor without reference to the audit committee, we have recently introduced extended reporting requirements for both auditors [to audit committees] and audit committees [to investors].[41] In particular we have made it clear that both should address the issues that arose in the course of the audit and how those issues have been resolved. (para 5)

18.4.3   Reporting to regulators

In the aftermath of the UK's banking crisis, auditors of the failing banks were severely criticised for not reporting the impending crisis to the banks' regulator – then the Financial Services Authority (FSA).[42] The HoL (2011), for example, observed that although:

> There was no single cause of the banking meltdown . . . the complacency of bank auditors was a significant contributory factor. Either they were culpably unaware of the mounting dangers, or, if they were aware of them, they equally culpably failed to alert the supervisory authority of their concerns. (para 167)

However, the HoL was just as scathing in its criticism of the FSA for failing to have regular dialogue with the banks' auditors. It stated that it considered the

---

[40] In October 2013, the Competition Commission (CC) announced its "package of measures . . . to open up the UK audit market to greater competition" (CC 2013c). These include:

> a stipulation that only the Audit Committee is permitted to negotiate audit fees and influence the scope of audit work, initiate tender processes, make recommendations for appointment of auditors and authorize the external audit firm to carry out non-audit services. (CC, 2013c)

[41] We discuss audit committee reports to investors in section 18.5.1.

[42] In April 2013 the FSA was disbanded and its responsibilities were transferred to the Financial Conduct Authority (FCA) and the Prudential Regulation Authority (PRA) – both of which are overseen by the Policy Committee of the Bank of England.

"paucity of meetings between bank auditors and regulators, particularly in a period of looming financial crisis as a dereliction of duty by both auditors and regulators" (para 161).

The UK's Banking Act 1987 explicitly provided for regular confidential dialogue between bank auditors and the Bank of England (the then regulator of UK banks) and, between 1987 until supervision of the banks passed to the FSA in 1997, regular meetings took place. When supervision of the banks passed to the FSA, the relevant legislative provision was re-enacted so that confidential dialogue between the banks' auditors and regulator could continue. However, between 1997 and the banking crisis, meetings between the parties occurred infrequently and irregularly. In the FSA's view, this was due to the auditors' reluctance to report matters of concern. This is reflected in Thorpe's (Accounting and Auditing Leader, FSA) submission to the HoL in which he stated:

> Auditors rarely report to us under their whistleblowing obligation. They argue that this is because they get their clients to inform us of problems, but we believe it would be better for the auditor to inform us himself. (as reported, Christodoulou, 2010a)

Wherever the blame might lie, according to the HoL: "Adequate and timely dialogue between bank auditors and supervisors is . . . essential . . . to enable the auditors to audit more effectively and the supervisors to supervise more effectively . . ." (HoL, 2011, para 155).

Following the banking crisis, the FSA introduced a Supervisory Enhancement Programme which mandated annual meetings between the FSA and auditors of the financial institutions it regulated (FSA, 2011a). This was followed, in 2011, by publication of the FSA and the Bank of England's draft Code of Practice for the relationship between the external auditor and the supervisor of regulated financial institutions (FSA, 2011b).[43] The Code sets out the following four principles to guide this relationship:

1. *Supervisors and auditors shall seek an open, co-operative and constructive relationship at all levels.* Communication should be through formal

---

[43] It is pertinent to note that, in the UK, ISA (UK and Ireland) 250 Section B: *The Auditor's Right and Duty to Report to Regulators in the Financial Sector* (FRC, 2009) provides guidance to auditors on two existing reporting responsibilities to regulators in the financial sector, namely:

    (a) *A responsibility to provide a report on matters specified in legislation or by a regulator.* This form of report is often made on an annual or other routine basis and does not derive from another set of reporting responsibilities. . . .

    (b) *A statutory duty to report certain information, relevant to the regulators' functions, that come to the auditor's attention in the course of audit work.* . . . This form of report is derivative in nature, arising only in the context of another set of reporting responsibilities, and is initiated by the auditor on discovery of a reportable matter. (para 2)

The Standard also notes:

The auditor may [also] have a statutory right to bring information to the attention of the regulator in particular circumstances which lie outside those giving rise to a statutory duty to initiate a report. Where this is so, the auditor may use that right to make a direct report relevant to the regulator on a specific matter which comes to the auditor's channels, such as scheduled meetings between the FSA and the auditor (bilateral meetings) and between the FSA, auditor and the regulated entity (trilateral meetings), and also through informal channels, such as telephone calls and meetings as appropriate.

2. *There should be regular dialogue between the supervisor and auditor.* Communication between these parties should be as frequent as necessary and in whatever form is most appropriate. As a minimum, there should be one routine bilateral and trilateral meeting each year for banks, building societies and insurance companies that are categorised as 'high impact'.[44] Additional bilateral meetings for 'very high impact' entities should be held when the auditor is (i) planning and (ii) concluding the annual audit. A meeting should also be held during the preparation phase of formal supervisory risk assessments of these entities; the draft findings of the assessments should be "shared with the lead audit partner ahead of finalisation" (p. 3)

3. *Supervisors and auditors shall share all information relevant to carrying out their respective statutory duties in a timely fashion.* The Financial Services and Markets Act 2000 (FSMA) permits auditors to communicate information to the FSA which the auditor reasonably believes would assist the FSA fulfil its responsibilities. The information is to be disclosed directly to the FSA in timely fashion – the auditor is not to rely on the regulated entity notifying the FSA of the matter concerned. Similarly, the FSA is to disclose information to the auditor that it judges to be relevant to fulfilment of the auditor's duties.

4. *Auditors and supervisors shall respect their duty to treat information shared between the two parties or received from regulated entities confidentially.* In relation to this principle, the Code notes:

> There is specific provision within FSMA for the FSA to share confidential information with auditors for enabling or assisting either the FSA or the auditor to perform their functions. FSMA also provides for auditors to communicate in good faith with supervisors without contravening other duties they are subject to [specifically, their duty of confidentiality to their client]. (FSA, 2011b, p. 4)[45]

---

attention when the auditor concludes that doing so is necessary to protect the interests of those for whose benefit the regulator is required to act. (para 5)

Where auditors have a duty or right to report matters to regulators in the financial sector, they have legal protection from breaching their duty of confidentiality to their client when they report matters in good faith and on reasonable grounds.

[44] In broad terms, a 'high impact' entity is one that has 400,000 or more customers. 'Very high impact' entities "are a subset of [high impact entities and] are determined discretionally and communicated to the [entities] concerned" (FSA, 2011b, footnote 5).

[45] When the FSA's functions were transferred to the PRA and FCA, these bodies adopted the FCA's Code of Practice to guide their relationships with relevant auditors.

The HoL welcomed the Code of Practice but considered it to be insufficient. It explained: "in the light of the regrettable backsliding of the years 1997–2007, and of the manifest importance of this issue, we believe that a Code of Practice does not go far enough. A statutory obligation is required" (para 164). However, the Government disagrees with the HoL asserting that regular dialogue between the parties will result from the Code. Nevertheless, in the view of Lord MacGregor, the Code "lacks teeth" and, without statutory backing, regular dialogue is not assured (Orlik, 2011c).

The view of the HoL has, to an extent, been endorsed by the Parliamentary Commission on Banking Standards (PCBS) which was established by the Government following the findings of the HoL (among others) that, prior to the UK's 2007 banking crisis, bankers, regulators, investors and external auditors failed to understand the risks building up in the banking system. As an outcome of its enquiry, the PCBS recommended that the Bank of England should commission a "periodic report on the quality of the dialogue between [the banks'] auditors and supervisors" (as cited, Crump, 2013c). It also noted that, in order for the dialogue to be effective, a bank's external auditor and the banks' supervisors (that is, the PRA and FCA) need to meet regularly – and more than once a year as specified by the Code of Practice (Crump, 2013c).

Further support for the HoL's position has been provided by EU Reg and Juri which propose the introduction of mandatory reporting by auditors – not only to the regulators of financial institutions but to the regulators of any regulated public interest entity. This includes all quoted companies which are regulated by their national Listing Authority. Article 25 of EU Reg (with some minor changes suggested by Juri) specifies:
1. The auditor of a regulated public interest entity is to report promptly to the regulator information which comes to the auditor's attention during the audit which has resulted, or is likely to result, in:
   – a material breach of the laws, regulations or administrative provisions which govern the entity's activities,
   – a material threat to, or material doubt about, the ability of the entity to continue as a going concern,
   – a refusal to issue an audit opinion on the entity's financial statements or the issuance of a modified opinion;
2. Regular dialogue is to be established between (i) the auditors of credit institutions and insurance undertakings, (ii) the regulators of these entities and (iii) the body(ies) responsible for the Member State's financial stability.

Like the FSA's Code of Practice, the EU proposals provide protection for auditors who report information, or an opinion, arising from the audit of a regulated entity, or emerges from the dialogue provided for in (2) above, in good faith.

EU Reg provides that such disclosure "shall not constitute a breach of any contractual or legal restriction on disclosure of information and shall not involve such persons in liability of any kind" art. 25).

18.5 AUDIT MARKET CONCENTRATION AND STRENGTHENING AUDITORS' INDEPENDENCE

18.5.1 Reducing audit market concentration and strengthening auditors' independence through more frequent changes of auditor

The dominance of the Big Four firms [Deloitte, Ernst & Young (E&Y), KPMG and PricewaterhouseCoopers (PwC)] in the large company audit market is reflected in the fact that these firms audit 99 of the FTSE 100 and 95 per cent of the FTSE 250 companies[46] (HoL, 2011, para 14). In most EU Member States the Big Four firms similarly account for more than 90 per cent of the listed company market (EC, 2010, p. 15). The various post-global financial crisis investigations (for example, EC, 2010; HoL, 2011; CC, 2011) identified a number of adverse consequences of this audit market concentration. They include the following:

1. It limits the choice of auditors for large companies – especially those in the banking, mining and utilities sectors where not all of the Big Four firms are represented (CC, 2011, para 9). For example, E&Y does not participate in the large banks sector and, should a large bank (X) wish to change its Big Four (or, more correctly, Big Three) auditor for another, it may find it difficult to do so. One of the two alternative firms may be providing bank X with non-audit services of a kind that auditors are prohibited from supplying to audit clients, and the other firm may be the auditor of a major competitor and, thus, its appointment as auditor of bank X would be inappropriate.

2. It limits competition in the large company audit market which, according to the Competition Commission (CC, 2011), results in higher prices, lower quality and less innovation – allegations strenuously denied by the Big Four firms. Powell (PwC), for example, assured the HoL (2011) that the large company market is "fiercely competitive" (HoL, 2011, para 19), and Barnes (Deloitte) informed the Lords that his firm does not "believe the evidence supports the contention that current market conditions have led to unnecessarily higher prices, lower quality or less innovation" (as reported, Abel, 2013). Some large companies agree with the audit firms, asserting that competition exists in their audit market and that price and

---

[46] The FTSE 100 and FTSE 250 are the 100 largest, and next 250 largest, companies listed on the London Stock Exchange, respectively.

quality are thus protected. Almanza (Chairman, Hundred Group of Finance Directors),[47] for example, informed the HoL: "Audit firms know that we have a choice and that very often is all you need to keep their pricing and the quality of their service honest" (HoL, 2011, para 19). The FRC supports this viewpoint, noting: "Market theory would suggest that a market with four participants would see participants competing against each other on price, quality and innovation" (FRC, 2010, para 2.18). Nevertheless, other commentators, particularly institutional investors, have expressed a contrary view. For example, Lee (Director of Hermes) identified "lack of competition" as a "major concern" (HoL, 2011, para 21).

3. The Big Four firms are able to secure high profile audit engagements at the expense of mid-tier firms due to their reputation, international networks and many partners with relevant experience (EC, 2010, p. 15). In this regard, Michaels (Managing Partner, BDO – the only non-Big Four auditor of a FTSE 100 company) informed the HoL that some mid-tier firms have the knowledge, reach, service quality and expertise appropriate for auditing FTSE 350 companies but they lose out as "size and revenue is seen as quality" (as reported, Goundar, 2010).

4. Threats to auditor independence result from long audit tenure. According to the HoL (2011, para 28): "A FTSE 100 auditor remains in place for about 48 years on average; for the FTSE 250 the average is 36 years". Such extended tenure is perceived to create a familiarity threat to auditors' independence – a 'cosy relationship' develops between the auditor and the client such that the auditor fails to exercise an appropriate degree of professional scepticism when planning and performing the audit. If the audit is lucrative, it is also likely to create a self-interest threat which, the Competition Commission alleges, results in auditors seeking to satisfy the interests of management (so as to retain the audit) rather than those of the shareholders (CC, 2013a, para 5). The Big Four firms, however, emphasise that they focus on shareholders' not management's interests. Barnes (Deloitte), for example, stated: "We categorically disagree that auditors typically place the interests of management over those of shareholders" (as reported, Crump, 2013a).

5. The risk that financial markets will be destabilised if a Big Four firm fails or otherwise exits the audit market. According to the FRC (2010), such an event would undermine "public and investor confidence in the financial statements of the failed firm's clients . . . and equity, bond and lending markets would fall significantly as a result" (para 2.3). The HoL (2011) also noted: "Loss of one of the Big Four would restrict competition and choice to an unacceptable extent" (para 27).

---

[47] The finance directors of the FTSE 100 companies.

There is general agreement that the Big Four firms' dominance in the large company audit market generates undesirable consequences and needs to be curtailed. However, there is considerable disagreement about how this should be achieved. A particularly controversial suggestion is that of mandatory audit firm rotation – a system whereby companies are required by legislation or regulation to change their auditor after a fixed period of time. As we note in Chapter 4, such a system has been in place in some countries for some years. For example, in Italy, three year mandatory audit firm rotation (with a maximum of two re-appointments) has applied to public listed companies since 1974 and, in Brazil, "following the bankruptcy of two major banks", a five year mandatory rotation requirement was introduced in 1999 for all listed companies (ICAEW, 2002 p. 10). In other countries, the system was introduced for some years and then abolished. For example, it was adopted in the Czech and Slovak Republics in 1989 (with a four and three year maximum period of audit tenure, respectively) but was abolished in the Czech Republic in 1992 and in the Slovak Republic in 2000.[48]

Since the idea of mandatory audit firm rotation was first mooted as a means of strengthening auditors' independence in 1976, by a Senate Subcommittee in the USA chaired by Metcalf,[49] its pros and cons have been hotly debated in professional and regulatory circles. The arguments are explored in Chapter 4 (section 4.3.3) but, to enable us to consider this proposed reform in context, we identify the key arguments advanced for and against it below. Interestingly both its proponents and opponents centre their arguments on audit quality and cost.

1. Proponents of mandatory audit firm rotation assert that it results in:
    (a) Improved audit quality. This results because it:
        • prevents auditors from becoming over-familiar with their clients and, hence, from failing to exercise a proper degree of professional scepticism and making unjustified assumptions based on past experience;
        • prevents close personal relationships from developing between auditors and their clients which result in auditors associating too closely with management;
        • reduces the self-interest incentive for audit firms to accommodate management's wishes (for example, by not challenging

---

[48] Further details of countries which have, or have had, a system of mandatory audit firm rotation are provided in Chapter 4, section 4.3.3(vi).

[49] In 1976, with eight large firms (Arthur Andersen, Arthur Young, Coopers & Lybrand, Deloitte Haskins and Sells, Ernst & Whinney, KMG, Peat Marwick and Price Waterhouse), lack of auditors' independence was perceived to be the foremost problem, not audit market concentration. The Metcalf committee was highly critical of the accounting profession and, in a 1,769 page report, made numerous recommendations on how the accounting (including auditing) profession should be regulated (see, for example, Arens and Loebbecke, 1980, p. 26). Many of the Committee's recommendations were enacted, nearly three decades later, in 2002, in the Sarbanes-Oxley Act.

questionable accounting estimates and other practices) in order to retain the audit;

- introduces a fresh approach and 'fresh eyes' to the audit periodically which may result in errors or irregularities (overlooked by the previous auditor) being detected;
- increases competition in the audit market which provides an incentive for audit firms to focus on building a reputation as a supplier of high quality audit services.

(b) Reduced audit fees. These result from companies needing to change their auditor at the end of each rotation period thereby increasing competition in the market.

2. Opponents of mandatory audit firm rotation use counter arguments, noting that it causes:
(a) Reduced audit quality. This results from:
  - the loss of institutional knowledge of the audit client with each enforced change of auditor at the end of each rotation period;
  - the auditor's inability to benefit fully from a co-operative relationship with the client which takes time to build but is essential for an effective and efficient audit to be conducted;
  - a lack of incentive for audit firms to invest in training and technologies designed to enhance the effectiveness and/or efficiency of their audits for clients for whom their tenure is limited;
  - firms nearing the end of a rotation period transferring competent and experienced audit personnel to clients for which a tenure period is commencing;
  - in some audit markets (for example, large listed company and specialised industry markets) the supply of firms with the requisite capabilities and competence to conduct high quality audits is limited: companies in these markets, when forced to change auditor, may have no alternative but to appoint a sub-optimal audit firm.
(b) Increased costs for both auditees and auditors. As each rotation period ends, the auditee needs to expend time and resources investigating and selecting a new auditor. During the initial years of the audit, auditee personnel also need to spend considerable time 'educating' the auditor about the entity's business, operations and systems; likewise, the auditor needs to expend considerable time and resources on gaining a thorough knowledge of the client. Additionally, if a rotation period ends at a time when the auditee is engaged in a major transaction or restructuring, the change of auditor will cause undesirable disruption.

Opponents of mandatory audit firm rotation also note that it is ineffective as a means of reducing audit market concentration. The evidence suggests that, at least in the large company audit market, rotation results in the replacement of one Big Four firm with another. As Sexton (2013) points out: "In the last eleven years there has been one change of auditor in the FTSE 350 every month – that's more than 130 changes" yet the dominance of the Big Four firms has not been lessened. The failure of mid-tier firms to be appointed as auditors of FTSE 350 companies "simply means that the buyers of audit services are exercising their right to choose their preferred auditor" (Sexton, 2013). The cost-effectiveness of mandatory rotation as a means of strengthening auditors' independence has also been questioned. The Ramsay Committee (Ramsay, 2001), which investigated the independence of Australian company auditors, concluded: "the anticipated cost, disruption and loss of experience to companies [resulting from mandatory rotation] is considered unacceptably high, as is the unwarranted restriction on the freedom of companies to choose their own auditors [as and when they please]" (para 6.100).

Adopting a stance contrary to that of the Ramsay Committee, the European Commission (EC) maintains that mandatory rotation is not only a means of enhancing auditors' independence; it is also "a catalyst to introduce more dynamism and capacity into the audit market" (EC, 2010, p. 16). This view was initially shared by the UK's Competition Commission (CC) and it proposed that mandatory audit firm rotation be introduced for FTSE 350 companies with:

> ...[an] optimal time frame ...based on a judgement which weighs up the benefits of independence and a new firm providing a fresh approach against the potential costs of switching from a firm that has built up experience of auditing a particular company. (CC, 2013a, para 28)

Following from this reasoning, the Commission suggested a rotation period of seven, ten or 14 years (para 29).[50] This compares with the EU Reg's proposal (EU, 2011, art. 3) of a six-year rotation period (extended to nine years for entities that appoint joint auditors – a proposal we examine in section 18.5.2). However, Juri suggests that this be changed to a rotation period of 14 years which may be extended to 25 years if certain criteria are met. These include tendering the audit, a comprehensive assessment of audit quality and independence by the audit committee, or the appointment of joint auditors (Crump, 2013b).[51]

---

[50] However, following further consultation and deliberation, the Competition Commission concluded that mandatory rotation of audit firms should not be adopted as a means of enhancing competition in the large company audit market in the UK (CC, 2013b, paras 17, 18).

[51] Juri (EU, 2012) initially recommended a 25 year rotation period with no extension for the appointment of joint auditors. Given that Juri and EU Reg envisage mandatory tendering of audits at the end of a rotation period, in effect, Juri still suggests a 25 year mandatory rotation period.

In addition to recommending the mandatory rotation of audit firms, the various authorities propose that key audit partners should be subject to mandatory rotation.[52] The Competition Commission considered that the audit firm and key audit partners should be rotated at the same time in order to "avoid costs and disruption of [audit partner] rotation mid-term [of the firm's tenure]" (CC, 2013a, para 25). However, the European authorities appear not to have considered such matters: while the EC's Green Paper (which, as we noted earlier, formed the basis for EU Reg) observes that the rotation of key audit partners is necessary "[t]o prevent partners from changing firms to "take along" certain clients with them" (EC, 2010, p. 16), EU Reg (art. 33) specifies a rotation period of six years for audit firms but seven years for key audit partners.

Unlike the European authorities mentioned above (and, initially the Competition Commission), the FRC is opposed to mandatory firm rotation because it believes that companies should be free to select the best auditor for their business and not have their choice artificially constrained. This applies particularly in circumstances when audit firms with the requisite knowledge, skills and experience for a company's business may not be available. The FRC also points out that mandatory audit firm rotation risks undermining "the authority of the audit committee [to operate] in the best interests of investors by taking the question of reappointment [of the incumbent auditor] out of their hands" (FRC, 2013c, p. 3).

Although there is a lack of consensus regarding mandatory audit firm rotation, the authorities are generally agreed that a change of auditor should be effected through a mandatory tender process for which the audit committee is responsible. Sexton (PwC) explains: "Tendering is fundamentally different to rotation . . . as it does not automatically rule the incumbent [auditor] out of the process, nor dilute the critical governance principle that allows companies and shareholders to appoint the best provider in their eyes". He also suggests that regular tendering should "help counter any misconception that long audit tenure reflects a lack of competition by showing that the quality of the audit is periodically subject to challenge" (as reported, Reed, 2012b).

The European Parliament's Economic and Monetary Affairs committee (Econ) (which, like Juri, has the task of commenting on EU Reg[53]) was swayed

---

[52] As we note in Chapter 4, section 4.3.3, in most jurisdictions, professional ethical guidance/standards require key audit partners to be rotated after a specified number of years. In the UK, Ethical Standard (ES) 3 *Long Association with the Audit Engagement* (APB, 2009) requires audit engagement partners to be rotated after a period of five years (in special circumstances this may be extended to seven years), and engagement quality control reviewers and other key audit partners to be rotated after seven years (paras 12, 19).

[53] Juri has the primary role in reviewing and reporting on EU Reg but Econ is responsible for issuing an Opinion on it which feeds into Juri's final report thereon (Hooper, 2013).

by "concerns about the negative effects of mandatory rotation" but supports the notion of mandatory tendering of public interest entity audits every seven years (Woolfe, 2013). Similarly, the HoL rejected the idea of mandatory rotation but recommended that "FTSE 350 companies [be required to] carry out a mandatory tender of their audit contract every 5 years" (HoL, 2011, para 44). The Competition Commission (CC) initially suggested that FTSE 350 companies should be required to put their audits out to tender every five or seven years but noted that it was "open to considering other periods" (CC, 2013a, para 20). When it published its "provisional decision on remedies" to dilute audit market concentration in the UK, the CC proposed that a mandatory five year tender period be adopted (CC, 2013b, para 4). It supported this proposal by noting that the FRC requires audit engagement partners to be rotated every five years and that benefits may be gained from aligning the tender process with the engagement partner rotation.[54] It noted, in particular, that the change of engagement partner results in a break in the existing auditor–client relationship and this provides the company with an opportunity to switch audit firms if it so wishes without incurring undue disruption. It also limits the advantage of the incumbent firm in the tender process resulting from it being able to offer an engagement partner who has an existing relationship with the company (CC, 2013b, para 7).

In 2012, the FRC introduced a requirement for all Code companies (those that are required, or choose voluntarily, to comply, or explain their non-compliance, with *The UK Corporate Governance Code*) to "put the external audit contract out to tender at least every ten years" (Code prov. C.3.7). In its *Guidance on Audit Committees* (FRC, 2012b), the FRC explains that regular tendering enables "the audit committee to compare the quality and effectiveness of the services provided by the incumbent auditor with those of other firms" (para 4.23). The FRC is opposed to mandated audit tendering as, in its view:

> . . . a mandatory regime, removing the flexibility of "comply or explain", could lead to retendering in an inappropriate year, contrary to investors' interests, for example when the challenges facing a business, such as a major restructuring or take-over defence, make audit continuity important. (FRC, 2013c, p. 2)

However, the Competition Commission is opposed to the FRC's 'comply or explain' approach to audit tendering on the grounds that it "may undermine compliance" (CC, 2013a, para 21). Initially it was also opposed to the FRC's ten-year retendering period. It asserted that ten years is too long for the audit engagement of a FTSE 350 company not to be subject to the high level of scrutiny and competition that occurs in a rigorous tender process (CC, 2013b, para 8). After considering various alternatives, it concluded that:

---

[54] In order to facilitate this alignment, the Competition Commission (2013b) envisaged a five year transition period before its tendering requirements become fully effective.

Five years is an appropriate interval at which to subject the audit relationship to scrutiny and challenge, and that going out to tender at this interval will increase company bargaining power and ensure a competitive service between tender processes. (CC, 2013b, para 9)

Perhaps not surprisingly given its Code provision, the FRC vehemently opposed a five year audit tendering period, asserting:

... there is a very real risk that tendering at five yearly intervals will not be taken seriously either by companies or by [audit] firms and hence become a sham process which will infect the serious approach already being shown to ten year retendering. (FRC, 2013e, p. 3)

It supported its assertion by highlighting, for example, that:

- participating in an audit tender process involves high expenditure of time and money for both the companies and prospective auditors involved – particularly in the case of large and complex companies;
- audit firms may take the view that, after only five years of the incumbent firm being in office, the company is unlikely to replace the firm and, therefore, it is not worth their while to participate in the tender process;
- audit quality may suffer because, during the initial period of an audit appointment, the incoming auditor may not have sufficient understanding of the company and the risks it faces. This is of particular concern in the case of large, complex companies (which applies to most of the FTSE 100 companies if not to the next largest 250 companies) and, in particular, to large financial institutions.

The FRC noted that, before it adopted a ten year tendering period for its Corporate Governance Code, it consulted widely in order to determine the most appropriate period. It then concluded that: "tendering every ten years balanced the benefits with the costs and risks associated with regular tendering" (FRC, 2013e).

The large audit firms echoed the FRC's concern about the high costs of requiring the UK's largest 350 companies to put their audits out to tender every five years – costs they claimed the Competition Commission has grossly underestimated. According to PwC, for example, "tendering every five years, as compared with the ten year regime introduced by the FRC, would cost auditors and FTSE 350 companies around £52m more per year, significantly higher than the Commission's estimate of between £10 to £20m" (as reported, Crump, 2013e). However, not all interested parties shared the view of the FRC and the large audit firms. For example, Carstensen (Chair of the Audit Market Investigation Group) contended that "[m]ore frequent tendering will ensure that companies make regular and well informed assessments of whether their incumbent auditor is competitive and [it] will [also] open up more opportunities for other firms to compete [in the large company audit market" (as cited, Crump, 2013d).

After further consideration of arguments advanced for and against a five-year mandatory tendering period, in its "package of measures . . . to open up the audit market to greater competition" the Competition Commission has opted for a ten-year period (CC; 2013c). It states:

> FTSE 350 companies must put their statutory audit engagement out to tender at least every ten years. . . . No [FTSE 350] company will be able to delay beyond ten years, and the CC believes that many companies would benefit from going out to tender more frequently at every five years. If companies choose not to go out to tender this frequently [i.e., every five years], the Audit Committee will be required to report in which financial year it plans to put the audit engagement out to tender and why this is in the best interests of shareholders. (CC, 2013c)

Thus, although the CC has adopted the ten-year tender period supported by the FRC, it has not accepted its 'comply or explain approach'; audit tendering is to be mandatory for all FTSE 350 companies.

One way to ensure that tendering results in more audit firms competing in the large company audit market is to facilitate the participation of non-Big Four firms in the tender process. To this end, the HoL (2011) recommended that FTSE 350 companies be required to invite a non-Big Four firm to participate in their tender process. It observed that this "should promote greater competition to the benefit of both cost and quality" (para 44). Along similar lines, EU Reg specifies that audit tendering by public interest entities is to include at least two firms, at least one of which must not have received more than 15 per cent of its total audit fees during the previous year from large public interest entities[55] in the Member State concerned. To ensure that all firms participating in the tender process are put on an equal footing, EU Reg also specifies that the auditee is to prepare tender documents which will allow the tendering firms "to understand the business of the audited entity and the type of statutory audit that is to be carried out" (art. 32). The tender documents are also to "contain transparent and non-discriminatory selection criteria" which the entity is to apply when evaluating proposals submitted by the tendering firms (art. 32). The Competition Commission has similarly advocated an 'open book' approach to the tender process contending that this would provide tendering firms with:

> . . . access to relevant information from the company and the files of the incumbent auditor[56] to enable the [tendering] firms to have an accurate understanding

---

[55] A large public interest entity is defined as one of the ten largest issuers of shares in a Member State measured by market capitalisation at the end of the year or an issuer of shares which, on average over the previous three calendar years, had an average market capitalisation of more than €1 billion (EU, 2011a, art. 4).

[56] EU Reg's proposal for an 'open book' tender process does not include providing tendering firms with access to the incumbent's audit files. However, if there is a change of auditor following the tender process then the incumbent is required to provide the incoming auditor with a 'handover file'. This is to contain the information necessary to enable the incoming auditor to understand the nature of the business and the internal organization of the audited entity (art. 33). As we note in Chapter 5, section 5.3.1, company auditors in the UK are required to provide access to their audit files to a successor auditor.

of the company's control environment and all significant audit issues. . . . [This approach] should reduce the risks of switching following a tender and may also reduce the costs of tendering. (CC, 2013a, para 22)

Although the Commission does not recommend that FTSE 350 companies be required to include a non-Big Four firm in their tendering process, it notes that an 'open book' approach to tendering provides "greater opportunities for non-Big-4 audit firms to tender for FTSE 350 audits and [reduces] current barriers to entry and expansion" (CC, 2013a, para 23).

During its enquiry, the HoL noted that shareholders normally approve, without discussion or challenge, the appointment of the auditor recommended to them by the directors.[57] Based on the evidence presented to it, the HoL concluded that "most shareholders appear to care little about a company's choice of auditor" (para 50) but it acknowledged that a small number of institutional investors play an active role in the auditor's appointment in companies where they hold shares. Richards (Head of Governance, Aviva) informed the Lords that his company "did vote against a number of [auditor] appointments. . . . The difficulty is not enough of us do so" (HoL, 2011, para 46). According to the HoL, shareholders' apparent lack of interest in the auditor's appointment is, at least partially, due to a lack of information. To rectify this deficiency it recommended, *inter alia*, that:

(i) audit committees should hold discussions about the auditor and the audit service provided with the principal shareholders every five years;

(ii) the audit committee's report within the company's annual report should:
 – provide details of significant financial reporting issues raised during the course of the audit, and
 – explain the basis of the committee's decision on audit tendering and auditor choice.

The FRC has also sought to increase shareholder involvement in the auditor appointment process. In its *Guidance on Audit Committees* (2012b), it recommends that FTSE 350 companies should announce their intention to put their audits out to tender prior to commencement of the tendering process in order "to allow shareholders to provide input into the process should they wish" (para 4.23). Although this falls short of the shareholder engagement envisaged by the HoL, the FRC goes beyond the HoL's recommendations as regards audit committees reporting to shareholders on the auditor's appointment and the

---

[57] As we note in Chapter 5, footnote 51, for companies that are required, or choose to comply (or explain their non-compliance) with *The UK Corporate Governance Code*, the directors' must recommend the auditor selected for appointment by the audit committee or explain their reasons for not adopting the audit committee's recommendation.

external audit process. In its *UK Corporate Governance Code* (2012a, prov. C.3.8), the FRC requires the audit committees of Code companies to include in their audit committee reports to shareholders an explanation of:

(i)   the significant issues the committee considered in relation to the financial statements and how these were addressed;

(ii)   how the committee assessed the effectiveness of the external audit process and the approach it took to the (re)appointment of the external auditor, together with information on the length of tenure of the current audit firm and when a tender was last conducted.

In order to assess the effectiveness of the audit process, the FRC requires the audit committee of Code companies to "annually assess, and report to the board on, the qualification, expertise and resources, and independence of the external auditors and the effectiveness of the audit process, with a recommendation on whether . . . the external auditor be reappointed" (2012b, para 4.22).

ICAS (2010) contends that audit committees' reporting responsibilities should be extended still further. It proposes that they be required to disclose their retendering policy in their audit committee report (in the company's annual report) along with the date when the incumbent auditor was appointed and the date of the last full retendering of the audit appointment. In order to secure increased shareholder engagement in the external audit process, ICAS also recommends that, in addition to conducting the annual review of the effectiveness of the auditor and audit process as required by the FRC (see above), audit committees should be required to undertake a more in-depth review every five years, and involve shareholders in this review (ICAS, 2010, p. 19). ICAS further suggests that, rather than merely reporting to the board on its reviews, audit committees should be required to explain in their audit committee reports: "the process by which the committee concluded that the external auditor was effective or otherwise [and for the five yearly review] . . . how it engaged with shareholders during this process; and the conclusions of [its] review process" (p. 22).

ICAS believes that by increasing the transparency of the audit committee's review of the audit process, and also of the matters discussed with (and challenged by) the auditor, shareholders will be able "to ask more targeted questions at the Annual General Meeting (AGM)". It also believes that both the audit committee chair and the audit engagement partner should attend the company's AGM to answer questions arising from the audit committee's report (ICAS, 2010, p. 20) – a suggestion that has been endorsed by both the Competition Commission (2013a, para 54) and the FRC (2013c, p. 6). Additional transparency about the auditor's appointment and audit process should help to address the HoL's concern (noted earlier) about the disinterest of shareholders "about a company's choice of auditor" (para 50). According to the Investment

Management Association, "if audit committees increased disclosure about the tender process, shareholders would be more motivated and able to engage [thereby] boosting choice and competition in the market" (as reported, Orlik, 2011a).

The Competition Commission has gone beyond even the ICAS proposals to secure greater shareholder involvement (at least in FTSE 350 Companies) – and also to increase the accountability of audit committees to shareholders. Its "package of measures . . . to open up the audit market to greater competition" includes a requirement for the shareholders of FTSE 350 companies to vote "at the AGM on whether Audit Committee Reports in company annual reports are satisfactory" (CC, 2013c). Although this vote is to be advisory, rather than binding, in nature, it will provide shareholders with a means by which to convey to the board of directors their satisfaction (or otherwise) with the adequacy of the information provided to them by the audit committee in its report (CC, 2013b, para 11).

18.5.2   Other means of reducing audit market concentration

Four further hotly debated proposals designed to reduce audit market concentration are those which involve:
  (i)   joint audits;
  (ii) 'audit only' firms;
  (iii) limiting the size of audit firms; and
  (iv) enhancing mid-tier firms' competitiveness.
We discuss each of these proposals below.

(i)   Joint audits

A joint audit is an audit conducted by two (or more) auditors who perform the audit and sign the audit report jointly. Such audits have been required in France since 1966 for listed companies that publish consolidated financial statements. The French experience indicates that, as a means of diminishing audit market concentration, joints audits are fairly effective: while 27 per cent of the joint auditors appointed to the 120 largest companies listed on the Paris Stock Exchange are non-Big Four firms, such firms audit just one per cent of the largest 100 companies listed on the London Stock Exchange (Billard, Ivaldi & Mitraille, 2011).

In its Green Paper, the EC proposed that large public interest entities throughout the EU be required to appoint joint auditors which include at least one non-Big Four firm. The Commission viewed the latter provision as necessary "to "dynamise" the market to allow mid-tier . . . firms to become active players in the [large company audit market]" (EC, 2010, pp. 15–16). Not surprisingly, most mid-tier firms support the EC's proposal. This is reflected in the advantages they have highlighted. For example:

- Herbinet (Mazars[58]) notes that joint audits allow companies to "always have one firm in place that really understands the business. It is a nice way to maintain continuity" (as reported, Orlik, 2011g).

- Raynor (RSM Tenon) observes that joint audits can "provide a springboard for mid-tier firms, helping those growing into the [large company] market to invest as needed. It could also raise their profile among major clients [currently] unwilling to dabble outside the Big Four, and give firms the experience necessary to take on FTSE-leading clients of their own" (as reported, Orlik, 2011e).

- Raynor also points out that joint audits could improve audit quality through having "two pairs of eyes" and by having complementary and combined expertise (Orlik, 2011g).

- Herbinet (supporting Raynor's observation of joint audits employing combined expertise) notes that joint audits are "well suited to banks because of their systematic risks, complexity and the inherent subjectivity in their financial statements" (HoL, 2011, para 38). With their combined expertise, joint auditors may be better placed than a sole auditor to challenge the value banks place on their complex financial instruments, with no exact method of valuation, and thus reduce the potential for the value to be materially misstated in the financial statements.

A further advantage of joint audits identified by the EC is that, when one auditor is a non-Big Four firm, they are a means of mitigating disruption in the audit market should one of the Big Four firms fail (EC, 2010, p. 16).

Those opposing mandated joint audits draw attention to their disadvantages. For example:

- The FRC maintains that joint audits create "a risk that some matters fail to be addressed effectively as they . . . fall between the two firms. Client management may also engage in arbitrage between the two firms, particularly when it comes to difficult or contentious judgements" (FRC, 2010, para 1.8).

- A Big Four firm senior partner (who wishes to remain anonymous) notes that joint audits offer greater opportunities for fraud to be perpetrated and also to remain undetected. He observes that "the biggest fraud that ever took place in the UK, namely BCCI [Bank of Credit and Commerce International], had joint auditors" (as reported, Christodoulou, 2010c).

- Tilley (Chief Executive, CIMA) contends that joint audits "can become a bureaucratic nightmare" and Haddrill (Chief Executive, FRC) reports that some French companies informed the FRC that joint audits are a

---

[58] Mazars is a joint auditor of BNP Parabas, Europe's third largest bank (Goundar, 2010).

"nightmare [because] auditors spend all their time passing the buck" (HoL, 2011, para 39). Joint audits require the audit firms to agree on the proportion of audit work each will perform, how the work will be divided between them and how disagreements about audit issues will be settled. Indeed, when launching its joint audit proposal, the EC acknowledged that "clear lines of responsibility for the overall audit opinion as well as a resolution/disclosure mechanism for differences of opinion" would need to be established (EC, 2010, p. 16).

- Michaels (BDO) draws attention to the danger of non-Big Four firms being regarded as inferior partners in joint audits with Big Four firms. He informed the HoL that his firm feared being seen as "the poor relation of the Big Four to make up the numbers" (para 39). However, Raynor (RSM Tenon), adopting a contrary stance, asserts: "We may be smaller, but we can't be junior. We are there to play a very significant role. No one will go in and allow themselves to be dictated to" (as reported, Orlik, 2011e).

A further perceived disadvantage of joint audits is that of increased costs: the EC estimated that they are likely to result in a ten per cent increase in audit fees. Some claim this is a "huge underestimation" but Raynor challenges the idea of any fee increase; he observes: "We are operating in a competitive market, whether for sole or joint audit. No one will take this as an excuse to inflate costs" (as reported, Orlik, 2011e).

Based on his experience of joint audits, Herbinet (Mazars) concludes that they have more advantages than disadvantages. In his view, "It encourages new players to come into the market by offering visibility, and facilitates any change in auditor [by removing the risk of appointing a new sole auditor]. . . . There is no evidence that . . . it is expensive or that it means a 'race to the bottom' in terms of audit quality" (as reported, Goundar, 2010). However, the HoL, after considering the evidence presented to it, was "not convinced that [joint audits] would deliver better [financial statements but they] would certainly add bureaucracy and cost" (para 40). It seems that the drafters of EU Reg reached a similar conclusion as it does not contain a joint audit requirement. Nevertheless, as we note in section 18.5.1, both EU Reg and Juri 'encourage' the adoption of joint audits by extending the audit rotation period for companies that appoint joint auditors.

(ii) 'Audit only' firms

The creation of 'audit only' firms is another of the EC's contentious proposals. The Commission notes that the *Statutory Audit Directive* (EU, 2006) prohibits auditors from supplying audit services in circumstances where "an objective, reasonable and informed third party would conclude that the statutory auditor's . . . independence is compromised" (EC, 2010, pp. 11–12). It also observes that this provision is implemented unevenly across the EU: while in France there is a total ban on audit firms providing non-audit services to audit clients, in other Member States "the rules are much less restrictive" (p. 12). The EC concludes: "Since auditors provide an independent opinion on the financial health of companies, ideally they should not have any business interest in the company being audited" (p. 12).

The UK's House of Commons Treasury Select Committee (HCTC) shared the EC's view that auditors should be prohibited from providing non-audit services to audit clients. It weighed opposing arguments from the auditing profession and from investors. Representing the profession's stance, Hodgkinson (Executive Director of the ICAEW's technical strategy department) explained that, during its 2002–3 investigations, the Co-ordinating Group on Audit and Accounting Issues (2003) examined the issue thoroughly and concluded that a total ban on auditors providing non-audit services to their audit clients would be inappropriate. He also observed that audit quality goes well beyond auditors' independence (HCTC, 2009, para 236). Representing the investors' viewpoint, the Pensions Investment Research Company (PIRC) noted:

> . . . It did not believe audit firms could be employed to provide consultancy services for management at the same time as undertaking an independent audit on behalf of the shareholders. "We firmly believe that other commercial interests can compromise auditors in their ability to confront directors on difficult issues . . . and would wish to see a prohibition on non-audit services being provided". (HCTC, 2009, para 234)

After considering the opposing arguments, the HCTC concluded:

> Although independence is just one of several determinants of audit quality, we believe that, as economic agents, audit firms will face strong incentives to temper critical opinions of [financial statements] prepared by [management], if there is a perceived risk that non-audit work could be jeopardised. . . . We strongly believe that investor confidence, and trust in audit would be enhanced by a prohibition on audit firms conducting non-audit work for the same company . . . . (para 237)

EU Reg (EU, 2011a) gives partial effect to the EC's and HCTC's conclusions. It provides that any firm which generates more than one-third of its annual audit revenues from large public interest entities and belongs to a network whose members have combined annual audit revenues which exceed €1,500 million within the EU may not provide, directly or indirectly, non-audit services to any public interest entity or belong to a network which provides such services within the EU (art. 10). In effect, this bans all (but only) the Big Four firms from providing any non-audit services to public interest entities within the EU.

This proposal has attracted strong criticism. The FRC, for example, opposes a wholesale ban on the provision of non-audit services by auditors, observing that its consultation on the issue (which followed publication of the HCTC's report) indicated that "investors and other market participants are not in favour of such a ban" (FRC, 2010, para 1.8). The FRC also drew attention to the negative impact 'audit only' firms would have on the quality of audit staff. It explains:

> Such firms would be unable to offer their staff a wide range of work experiences and compensation packages are likely to be lower than firms can offer currently, making it more difficult to recruit and retain high quality personnel and hence impacting negatively on audit quality. (para 1.8)

Along related lines, Powell (PwC) informed the HoL that audit staff who spend some time working in non-audit parts of the firm are much better auditors when they return to audit practice "because of the quality of the training and experience that they've had" (HoL, 2011, para 85).

Other commentators emphasise the adverse effect of 'audit only' firms on audit quality. Griffith-Jones (KPMG), for example, maintains that a decline in audit quality would result if auditors were separated from the wide-ranging advisory expertise available to them in their firms – including actuary, risk management and similar expertise. However, a mid-tier firm partner counters this argument by noting that his prior Big Four firm experience suggests that the division between audit and non-audit service practices within the Big Four firms is "so sharp that there is little crossover" (as reported, Orlik, 2011d). Further, Moore (Crowe Clark Whitehall) suggests that 'audit only' firms may be more inclined to invest in audit training and technologies and, as a result, the quality of their audits may be enhanced (Orlik, 2011d).

In terms of reducing the Big Four firms' dominance in the large company audit market, an advantage of prohibiting these firms from providing non-audit services to their large company clients is that non-Big Four firms are able to fill the void – and, while providing non-audit services to large companies, they can acquire knowledge and experience of these companies and, at the same time, raise their visibility and enhance their reputation as suppliers of high quality services. This, in turn, should increase their chance of competing successfully with the Big Four firms in the large company audit market. In this regard the Competition Commission (2013a) concluded: "providing non-audit services [is] a key means by which non-incumbent audit firms [can] provide company management with experience of their expertise and obtain insight to support potential switching of the audit assignment" (para 72). However, as Newman (BDO) points out, given EU Reg's size limit on firms that are able to provide both audit and non-audit services, there is little incentive for a mid-tier firm to invest in developing its expertise and experience to the point where it can compete with the Big Four in the large company audit market "only to be bisected by Brussels" (Orlik, 2011d).

Notwithstanding the arguments for and against the creation of 'audit only' firms, if EU Reg's provision is enacted, the Big Four firms will need to choose between supplying non-audit or audit services. If one or two opt for discontinuing their supply of audit services, greater not less concentration in the large company audit market may result – as may a shortage of firms with the knowledge, expertise and experience required to audit large multi-national companies. Further, given that EU Reg specifies the ban on providing non-audit services applies to firms that derive more than one-third of their annual audit revenues from large public interest entities, the Big Four firms may be incentivised to boost their audit revenues from non-large public interest entities to the point where they account for more than two-thirds of their annual audit revenues. If the Big Four firms choose this course of action, the EU Reg's provision may result in these firms dominating not only the large company audit market but the total audit market in the EU.

In general, the notion of 'audit only' firms has been unpopular with both large companies and senior members of the auditing profession. They appear to agree with Tracey's (Senior Non-Executive Director, Chloride Group) contention that responsibility for determining whether, and if so what, non-audit services should be provided to a company by its external auditor should rest with the audit committee. Tracey noted that "Audit committees will normally ban services such as tax planning and internal audit and IT services but it may be OK for an auditor to provide services such as due diligence" (as reported, Huber, 2009). The HoL (2011) similarly concluded that a complete ban on audit firms carrying out non-audit work for audit clients is not justified but it recommended "that a [company's] external auditors should be banned from providing internal audit, tax advisory services and advice to [the company's] risk committee" (para 87). The EU's Juri and Econ Committees support the notion that a company's audit committee should be responsible for deciding on the non-audit services to be provided by the company's external auditor. However, the Econ Committee also recommends that the audit committee be required to put non-audit services out to tender (Woolfe, 2013).

In the UK, following the FRC's consultation on the HCTC's recommendation that audit firms be banned from providing non-audit services to their audit clients (referred to earlier), the APB strengthened its Ethical Standards (ES) – particularly, ES5: *Non-Audit Services Provided to Audited Entities* (APB, 2011). In essence, auditors in the UK are prohibited from providing non-audit services that would, or are likely to, impact on the company's financial statements. Additionally, amendments to the FRC's *UK Corporate Governance Code* and *Guidance on Audit Committees* in 2012 extended the responsibilities and disclosure requirements of audit committees of Code companies in respect of monitoring the independence of the company's external auditor and the auditor's provision of non-audit services.[59] Regarding the latter, the audit committee is required to:

- develop and implement policy in respect of engaging the external auditor to supply non-audit services, and to provide details of this policy in the audit committee report (in the company's annual report);
- if the external auditor provides non-audit services, the committee is to explain in its report:
  - what non-audit services the auditor has provided and why the committee concluded it was in the interests of the company to purchase these services from the auditor rather than from another provider, and
  - how the auditor's independence and objectivity have been safeguarded.

Against the background, and other evidence presented to it, the Competition Commission reported that it is "not currently minded to consider significant additional restrictions on the provision of non-audit services by auditors" (CC, 2013a, para 73).

(iii) Limiting the size of audit firms

Another proposal to reduce the Big Four firms' dominance in the large company audit market is that of limiting the number of listed companies any one firm can audit. Maslin (Grant Thornton), for example, informed the HoL that, if the Big Four firms were forced to shed 20 per cent of their FTSE 250 company audits, "the size of that audit market would be £25m to £30m [which] our firm – and some others – we believe . . . [could serve] straight away" (as reported, Goundar, 2010).

A variant of this proposal advanced by, for example, McMeeking and Niels (two academics) is that the Big Four firms be forcibly broken up (HoL, 2011, para 36). However, Craft (partner in law firm Wedlake Bell) observes that, although the Office of Fair Trading (OFT) could require the Big Four to divest some of their business to mid-tier firms, this relies on the OFT finding that the Big Four are collectively abusing their dominant position. In Craft's view, this outcome is unlikely (Huber, 2011). Craft's view seems to have merit as, after examining the issue, neither the OFT nor the Competition Commission, recommended such action. Nevertheless, large UK companies have made it clear that they would welcome more competition in the audit market. Jubb (Standard Life Investments), for example, informed the HoL that eight firms would be a "comfortable number" from which to select an auditor (Huber, 2011), and

---

[59] The provisions of the Ethical Standards, and those of *The UK Corporate Governance Code* that relate to auditors' independence, are discussed in Chapter 4.

Almanza (BG Group) stated that he would "certainly welcome a Big Five" (Huber, 2010). Nevertheless, neither of these corporate leaders would support intervention in the market. Instead, Almanza suggested that mid-tier firms could help increase competition in the large company audit market by merging or forming networks of firms.[60] Davey (when Minister for Employment) also pointed out to the HoL that "any forced break-up of the Big Four firms . . . would have to take place on a global scale and could risk unintended consequences" (Huber, 2011).

(iv)   *Enhancing mid-tier firms' competitiveness*

The three proposals outlined above (joint audits, 'audit only' firms and limiting audit firm size) focus on reducing the strength of the Big Four firms. Two other proposals – licensing firms which audit major public interest entities and relaxing audit firm ownership rules – seek to enhance the ability of mid-tier firms to compete with the 'big' firms on a more equal footing.

In the UK, the notion of licensing firms that audit major public interest entities (including FTSE 350 companies) arose from the Audit Inspection Unit's (AIU)[61] finding that around 50 per cent of the audits of major public interest entities conducted by firms that audit between one and ten of such entities "required significant improvement"[62] – and that this applied to most of the audits of multinational groups conducted by these firms (AIU, 2011). In the light of these findings, the FRC proposed that firms wishing to audit major public interest entities should be licensed by, or registered with, the FRC (Christodoulou, 2010b). At present (as we explain in Chapter 5, section 5.3.1) company auditors in the UK are required to register with one of five Recognised Supervisory Bodies (RSBs) which are overseen by the FRC. However, the FRC is not empowered to impose sanctions on auditors which perform defective audits; instead, it must report its findings to the relevant RSB and the latter can take whatever action it thinks appropriate. The HoL decried the current system of regulating auditors, stating:

> The regulation of . . . auditing is fragmented and unwieldy with manifold overlapping organisations and functions. This is neither productive nor necessary. Other professions have only one regulator – medicine for example under the General Medical Council. (HoL, 2011, para 110)

---

[60] It seems, from their merger in April 2013, that BDO and PKF heeded Almanza's advice!

[61] Details of inspections by the AIU (known as the Audit Quality Review team since July 2012) are provided in Chapter 16, section 16.4.3. In 2012, there were 40 firms that audited between one and ten major public interest entities.

[62] This finding applied to four of the nine audits of major public interest entities conducted by these firms the AIU inspected in 2010/11, six of the 11 audits inspected in 2009/10, and five of 11 audits inspected in 2008/9 (AIU, 2011, p. 6).

This statement indicates that the HoL envisages the FRC being the sole regulator of the auditing profession (without the involvement of the RSBs). However, the FRC has a narrower vision. George (Executive Director, FRC Conduct Division) suggests an approach whereby audit firms would nominate individuals to be licensed as engagement partners for the audits of major public interest entities and the FRC would grant (or refuse) a licence to nominees as it sees fit – and, in some cases, attach conditions to licences in the interests of securing high quality audits (Orlik, 2011b).

Proposals from the EU go even further than those envisaged by the HoL. In its Green Paper, the EC launched the idea of a 'European passport' for the auditors of public interest entities. It explained that this would involve "creating a European-wide registration with common professional qualification requirements and common governance, ownership and independence rules applicable across the European Union" (EC, 2010, p. 18). EU Reg (art. 50) gives effect to this proposal. It provides for the European Securities and Markets Authority (ESMA) to establish a European quality certificate for auditors that audit public interest entities within the EU and to maintain a register of individuals and firms gaining the certificate.

Most of the large firms support the notion of a European passport. E&Y, for example, considered that it would "increase choice and enhance quality" (Orlik, 2011g). However, although the FRC is not opposed to the introduction of an EU passport, it is against a single European qualification. In its view, such a qualification could undermine national practices which, in some cases, could be detrimental to audit quality. It noted that, in the UK, "graduates from all disciplines, as well as suitably qualified non-graduates [are able] to enter the profession [with a] positive effect on the recruitment of high quality staff and in turn on audit quality" (FRC, 2010, para 4.17). Juri (EU, 2012) appears to agree with the FRC as it suggests deleting the proposal (that is, art. 50) from the proposed Regulation.

Putting aside the question of a single EU qualification, a system of licensing firms that can demonstrate they have the resources, expertise and other capabilities needed to audit major public interest entities would provide aspirant mid-tier firms with tangible evidence of their ability to audit large listed companies and, thus, to compete with the Big Four firms in this market. Further, while acknowledging that most multinational companies operate on a global, rather than a European, stage, if a single licensing system extended across the EU, it would extend quite significantly the large listed company audit market in which mid-tier firms could, potentially, be active participants.

Another proposal that may assist mid-tier firms to compete on a more equal footing with their Big Four counterparts – and also, if the situation should arise, assist a financially challenged Big Four firm to ward off failure – is that of relaxing restrictions on audit firm ownership. Under existing requirements, audit firms must be controlled by registered auditors[63] but the EC suggested liberalising the rules – with the caveat that any alternative to the current structure would need to incorporate safeguards to prevent external owners from interfering with audit work. The EU's draft Directive (EU, 2011b)[64] gives effect to the Commission's proposal; if enacted, it would amend Article 3(4) of the *Statutory Audit Directive* (EU, 2006) to prohibit Member States from requiring a minimum of capital or voting rights in audit firms be held by statutory (or registered) auditors. However, the requirement for statutory auditors to constitute a majority of the firm's management body would be retained (EU, 2011b, p. 6).

When advancing its proposal, the EC explained that relaxation of the ownership rules would help non-Big Four firms "to gain access to more capital and allow them to ramp up capacities and grow more rapidly" (2010, p. 13). However, to the surprise of the HoL, BDO and Grant Thornton (the fifth and sixth largest UK audit firms) stated that they did not need to raise additional capital to expand in order to audit FTSE 250 companies (HoL, 2011, para 62). Following such submissions, the HoL stated that it could "see no immediate grounds to change the law to lift limits on shareholdings by non-auditors in audit firms, especially since such a change would carry the risk that auditors might become less independent" (para 64).

It is pertinent to note that BDO and Grant Thornton referred to auditing FTSE 250, not FTSE 350, companies. On a number of occasions, mid-tier firms have signalled that they are not interested in competing with the Big Four firms in the FTSE 100 audit market. For example, McBurnie (RSM Tenon) informed the HoL that his firm would "be wary of taking on any of the top hundred" (as reported, Goundar, 2010). Indeed, some mid-tier firms have indicated that they are reluctant to invest to enable them to compete with the Big Four firms even in the FTSE 250 audit market: they take the view that "unless there [is] real competition in the market – and an erosion of institutional prejudice against non-Big Four firms – investing in the business with the . . . aim of winning Big Four clients would be inadvisable" (as reported, Goundar, 2010).

---

[63] More precisely, as we explain in Chapter 5, section 5.3.1, the majority of its members with voting rights, or who are otherwise able to direct its overall policy, must be eligible for appointment as statutory auditors in any EU or other EEA Member State.

[64] The draft Directive was launched at the same time as EU Reg and contains proposed amendments to the *Statutory Audit Directive* (EU, 2006).

One proposal that seeks to address the perceived "institutional prejudice against non-Big Four firms", and one that has gained universal support (see, for example, CC, 2013a, para 42; FRC, 2013c, p. 4), is that of outlawing "Big Four only" covenants – clauses traditionally included in loan agreements by banks and other financial institutions restricting the auditors a large company borrower may appoint. If the EU's draft Directive is adopted, article 37 of the *Statutory Audit Directive* will be amended to prohibit such clauses.

18.6 EMERGENCE OF COMPETITION FROM CHINA

As we have seen, in the wake of the global financial crisis, a number of reforms have been proposed with the goal of changing, *inter alia*, the structure of the audit market. However, despite observations by, for example, Tweedie that Chinese firms are likely to be competitors of the Big Four firms within the next ten years (Reed, 2012a), the potential impact of Chinese firms entering the large company audit market on competition and choice appears to have been ignored.

During recent years, the Chinese Government has made a concerted effort to raise the standard of accounting and auditing in China to the level pertaining internationally. China's accounting and auditing standards have converged with international standards and (with Government 'encouragement') the Chinese Institute of Certified Public Accountants has established a Code of Ethics equivalent to that applying in Hong Kong and introduced a system of monitoring auditors' performance similar to that in the EU (Barnes, 2012). Additionally, in 2010, China's Ministry of Finance and its Securities and Regulatory Commission jointly announced an ambitious plan to develop ten 'super audit firms' which are able to compete on the international stage, 200 medium-sized firms and 7,000 specialised and small audit firms (Deng & Macve, 2012).[65] The plan has two strands – localisation and internationalisation.

(a) The 'localisation' element requires all audit firms in China (including the Big Four firms which, until 2012,[66] operated in China as joint ventures), to have at least 60 per cent of their partners domestically (mainland Chinese) qualified by the end of 2015; this increases to 80 per cent by 31 December 2017. Further, the senior partner in each firm is to be a Chinese national with a domestic qualification and eight years' experience in a Chinese accounting firm (Wang, 2012).

---

[65] The Chinese Government has also actively encouraged Chinese audit firms to merge to form larger firms or to form networks of firms.

[66] Except for PwC whose joint venture licence expires in 2017.

(b) The 'internationalisation' strand involves licensing selected mainland Chinese firms to audit Hong Kong listed companies (known as H-share companies). In order to be considered for selection, audit firms must have:

    (i)   operating revenue of at least 300 million Yuan (two-thirds of which must be derived from auditing);

    (ii)   at least 400 qualified accountants;

    (iii) a member firm in Hong Kong, or belong to an international network with a Hong Kong based firm.

Twelve of the 16 firms which applied for selection were successful (Luk, 2010) – the Big Four firms (which can only remain in China if they meet the localisation requirements[67]) and BDO China Shu Lun Pan, Grant Thornton China, Crowe Horwath China, Da Hua (a member of the BDO international network), RSM China, Shine Wing, Pan-China and Daxin (Deng & Macve, 2012). As is evident from their names, most of these firms are related to (or associated with) firms in the UK.

As we note above, the Chinese Government's goal is for ten Chinese 'super audit firms' to participate in the global large company audit market. It will be assisted in this regard by the phenomenal growth of foreign-backed enterprises in China and Chinese-backed businesses elsewhere[68] – enterprises that require external auditors. If Chinese audit firms are selected, these firms will gain visibility, have the opportunity to build their reputations as a suppliers of high quality services, and be able to invest to obtain the capacity to compete in the global large company audit market. Evidence of this process already exists: in 2009, an Australian audit firm was taken over by the Chinese firm Shine Wing (one of the 12 firms identified above), in a "move driven by a major [Chinese] industrial and resources company that was establishing a presence in Australia but preferred to work with a Chinese audit firm" (Barnes, 2012). In terms of Chinese firms competing with the Big Four Anglo-American firms on the world stage, Barnes observes: "The main thing Chinese firms still lag behind on is brand image but this will change as their businesses expand globally. The rise of the Chinese accounting profession is inexorable – the only questions that remain are . . . how fast and how far" (2012). Given recent developments, it is

---

[67] They have all signalled their intention of doing so and each is investing heavily in its Chinese firms. For example, Lu (Chief Executive of Deloitte China) has reported that Deloitte plans to invest $160m in China between 2013 and 2015, increasing its staff numbers to 15,000 by 2015. He also noted that Deloitte has invested $250m in China since 2004 (as reported, Smith, 2013).

[68] In respect of this growth, Barnes (2012) reports:

    In 2011, inward investment in excess of $116bn (£72.3bn) fuelled the creation of more than 27,000 new foreign-backed enterprises in China. In the same year domestic [Chinese] investors made accumulated direct investments totalling $60bn to more than 3,400 foreign enterprises in 132 countries and regions throughout the world.

possible that the presence of Chinese audit firms in the global large company audit market will render redundant many of the UK and EU based proposed reforms designed to weaken the dominance of the Big Four firms in this market.

18.7   INHERENT CONFLICTS IN THE CURRENT AUDIT MODEL

Reviewing the reforms which have been proposed in the aftermath of the 2008 global financial crisis, questions arise about their likely impact on the audit expectation-performance gap. Will they result in the services auditors are perceived to deliver being better aligned to those expected of them by society? It seems likely that the proposed extended reporting requirements of auditors and audit committees (outlined in sections 18.4 and 18.5.1, respectively), if implemented, will result in the provision of clear, company-specific information about, *inter alia*, key audit judgments and significant audit findings. This may enhance users' understanding of the audit function – and its potential benefits and limitations which may, in turn, help to reduce society's unreasonable expectations of auditors.

But, what of the 'performance gap' component of the audit expectation-performance gap? A key finding of the HCTC and HoL enquiries is that, in 2007 and 2008, bank auditors in the UK failed to exercise the proper degree of professional scepticism (Reed, 2011). According to the Competition Commission, such failings may be attributed to auditors' interests being more closely aligned to those of management than to those of shareholders (CC, 2013a, para 5). The Big Four firms protest this conclusion, claiming that clients' audit committees ensure that shareholders' interests are protected (Abel, 2013). However, this ignores the fact that a company's audit committee comprises (usually non-executive) directors who, together with the rest of the board, are responsible for the company's financial statements – and, like the rest of the board, are duty bound to act in a manner that is most likely to promote the success of the company (CA 2006, s. 172). Should the auditor wish to disclose information which, in the directors' opinion, might endanger the company's success, they are duty bound to oppose the auditor's disclosure of the information. This situation may have arisen during the 2007–8 banking crisis when many UK banks were in a precarious financial condition. During the HoL enquiry it emerged that the Government assured the banks' auditors that it would do "all that it took" to prevent a collapse of the UK's banking sector (HoL, 2011, para 150). Given this assurance, the auditors did not draw attention to material uncertainties relating to the banks' viability – yet, ISA 570: *Going Concern* (IAASB, 2009c) requires them to do so in an Emphasis of Matter paragraph in the audit report. As Lord Lipsey explained to the errant bank auditors:

Your duty is to report to investors the true state of the company. You were giving a statement that was deliberately timed to mislead the company and mislead markets and investors about the true state of those banks. . . . (Christodoulou, 2010e)

As noted earlier, the auditors should also have reported their findings to the Financial Services Authority (then the bank regulator).

Auditing Standards provide auditors with clear guidance on what is required of them in the performance of their audits. Yet, like the HoL, during its inspections of audits conducted by the Big Four and mid-tier firms, the Audit Quality Review team (formerly the AIU) routinely finds evidence of sub-standard auditing. As we note above, the Competition Commission attributes auditors' failure to fulfil their duties to the misalignment of auditors' and shareholders' interests. In our view, this misalignment is the outcome of two fundamental, mutually reinforcing conflicts within the current audit model. Briefly, these are as follows:

(i) Although auditing is "absolutely fundamental to the integrity of our capital markets and the good governance of our companies" (HoL, 2011, para 2) and, thus, is conducted in the public interest (as well as in the interests of investors), it is undertaken by private profit-oriented firms.

(ii) In practice, auditors are appointed by their clients' directors – by "those they are appointed to scrutinise rather than those they are meant to serve" (Haddrill, 2011, p. 5).

These inherent conflicts combine to incentivise auditors to protect their self-interest at the expense of shareholders' and the public interest. In an era in which audit firms prioritise profits ahead of professionalism (Tweedie, 2012), it seems unlikely that they will wish to endanger a lucrative audit contract by disclosing information in the audit report in the interests of "those they are meant to serve" against the wishes of the client's directors.

A possible remedy to these inherent conflicts is to assign responsibility for appointing the auditors of major public interest entities (including FTSE 350 companies) to an independent body such as the FRC[69] and requiring that their selection be based on a full, 'open book' tender process. The Competition Commission (2013a) concluded that appointment by the FRC would "ensure that shareholder interests [are] more appropriately represented and/or auditor-management familiarity [is] not a factor in auditor appointment decisions" (para 83). However, it also observed that the FRC's lack of familiarity with the particular circumstances of public interest entities "might result in ineffective appointments" (para 84). The Commission did not, apparently, entertain the

---

[69] Given the FRC's existing responsibility to inspect the quality of the audits of major public interest entities, to assign it responsibility for appointing the auditors concerned seems entirely logical.

notion of overcoming this perceived deficiency by including a small number of directors from the relevant auditee in the auditor appointment tender process, thus ensuring that the appointee possessed a proper understanding of the company's business and other attributes deemed essential by the auditee. Instead, the Commission concluded that strengthening the auditors' account-ability to the auditee's audit committee is a "more effective" remedy to the flaws in the current audit model (para 85). It appears not to have appreciated that this would leave auditors seeking to "satisfy those they are appointed to scrutinize rather than those they are meant to serve" (FRC, 2011, p. 5).

History suggests that, until the inherent conflicts in the current audit model are resolved, auditors will fail to fulfil their function in society and, each financial crisis and major corporate debacle will result in additional, more stringent audit regulation (primarily focused on strengthening auditors' independence). Numerous reforms have been proposed in the wake of the 2008 global financial crisis but none of those accorded serious consideration gets to the heart of the problem. Further, any suggestion designed to remedy the defects in the current model, such as assigning responsibility for appointing the auditors of major public interest entities to an independent body like the FRC, will face fierce opposition from those whose vested interests would be threatened – primarily the Big Four firms. Nevertheless, while the conflicts remain, as portrayed on the front cover of this book, the 'audit house' will be supported by shaky pillars – and the next crisis will not be too far away.

18.8 SUMMARY

In this chapter we have discussed the audit expectation-performance gap – the gap between what society expects from auditors and what it perceives they deliver – and identified its structure. We have also explored changes in the gap in the UK between 1999 and 2008 – and reasons for these changes. Further, we have examined a four-stage process of change in the audit expectation-performance gap identified by reviewing changes in the gap in NZ and the UK between 1989 and 2008. Additionally, we have discussed proposed changes to auditors' reporting responsibilities to shareholders, audit committees and regu-lators and noted that, if implemented, these may help to narrow the gap between society's expectations of auditors and its perception of auditors' performance.

A significant portion of the chapter is devoted to the adverse consequences of the Big Four firms' dominance in the large company audit market identified in the wake of the global financial crisis and proposed reforms to address these consequences and also perceived deficiencies in auditors' independence. The proposals include mandatory audit firm rotation, mandatory tendering of auditor appointments, joint audits, prohibition (in the EU) on the Big Four firms providing non-audit services to public interest entities, and limiting the size of audit firms – proposals primarily designed to reduce the strength of the Big Four firms; others aim to reduce the dominance of these firms in the large company audit market by enhancing the ability of mid-tier firms to compete with them in this market. These proposals centre on licensing the auditors of public interest entities and relaxing audit firms' ownership rules. However, notwithstanding the comprehensive nature of the proposed reforms, the reformers appear to have overlooked the likely impact of the entry of Chinese 'super audit firms' into the global large company audit market which may render many of the proposed reforms redundant.

In the final section of the chapter we have discussed other fundamental factors the reformers appear to have overlooked, namely, inherent conflicts in the current audit model – conflicts that arise because the audit model fails to align the profit-seeking motives of auditors with the best interests of those they are appointed to serve. Yet, until or unless these conflicts are resolved, the 'auditing house' will rest on unsteady supports and the auditing function will not fulfil properly its vitally important role in society.

SELF-REVIEW QUESTIONS

18.1   (a) Define the audit expectation-performance gap and briefly describe its structure;

         (b) Explain why the audit expectation-performance gap is of concern to the auditing profession.

18.2   Explain briefly changes in the audit expectation-performance gap in the United Kingdom between 1999 and 2008 and provide reasons for these changes.

18.3   Outline the four-stage process of change in the audit expectation-performance gap identified as an outcome of reviewing changes in the gap in New Zealand and the UK between 1989 and 2008.

18.4   Identify four adverse consequences of the Big Four firms' dominance in the large company audit market.

18.5   Outline changes to the standard auditor's report proposed in the wake of the global financial crises and provide reasons for the proposed changes.

18.6 (a) Distinguish between mandatory audit firm rotation and mandatory tendering;

(b) Explain what is meant by an 'open book' approach to tendering and outline the advantages of this approach for those wishing to participate in the tender process.

18.7 (a) Briefly explain what is meant by a 'joint audit';

(b) Outline three advantages and three disadvantages of joint audits.

18.8 Explain briefly two reforms proposed to assist mid-tier audit firms compete with the Big Four firms in the large company audit market.

18.9 Explain briefly recent developments in auditing in China which may make proposals to reduce the Big Four firms' dominance in the large company audit market redundant.

18.10 Identify two inherent conflicts in the current audit model and explain:

(a) why these conflicts threaten the future of the audit function;

(b) how they might be resolved.

REFERENCES

Abel, B. (2013, 22 February). *Big Four Dismiss Claims They are Failing Shareholders*, www.accountancyage.com/aa/news/2250149/big-four-dismiss-claims-they-are-failing-shareholders, accessed 24 April 2013.

Arens, A.A., & Loebbecke, J.K. (1980). *Auditing: An Integrated Approach*, 2nd ed. Englewood Cliffs, NJ: Prentice Hall Inc.

Audit Inspection Unit (AIU). (2011). *Public Report on the 2010/11 Inspections of Firms Auditing Ten or Fewer Entities Within AIU Scope*. London: Financial Reporting Council.

Auditing Practices Board (APB). (2007). *The Auditor's Report: A Time for Change?* London: Financial Reporting Council.

Auditing Practices Board (APB). (2009). Ethical Standard (ES) 3: *Long Association with the Audit Engagement*. London: Financial Reporting Council.

Auditing Practices Board (APB). (2011). Ethical Standard (ES) 5: *Non-audit Services Provided to Audited Entities*. London: Financial Reporting Council.

Barnes, G. (2012, 2 November). *Chinese Audit Firms Set to Challenge the World*, www.accountancyage.com/aa/feature/2222143/chinese-audit-firms-set-to-challenge-the-world, accessed 30 April 2013.

Billard, O., Ivaldi, M., & Mitraille, S. (2011). *Evaluation of the Risks of Collective Dominance in the Audit Industry in France*, www.cresse.info/uploadfiles/2011_ivaldi, billard&mitraille.pdf, accessed 29 April 2013.

Christodoulou, M. (2010a, 8 July). *New FSA Powers will Force Auditors to Speak Out*, www.accountancyage.com/aa/news/1807940/new-fsa-powers-force-auditors-speak, accessed 24 April 2013.

Christodoulou, M. (2010b, 7 October). *Small Firms Threatened with Licence Reform. Accountancy Age*, www.accountancyage.com/aa/analysis/1808542/small-firms -threaten-licence-reform, accessed 25 November 2012.

Christodoulou, M. (2010c, 15 October). *Joint Audits Will Increase Fraud: Big Four Partner*, www.accountancyage.com/aa/news/1809014/joint-audits-increase-fraud-big-four-partner, accessed 29 April 2013.

Christodoulou, M. (2010d, 16 November). *Big Four Expect a Grilling from Lords Audit Inquiry*, www.accountancyage.com/print_article/aa/analysis/1898295/expect-grilling -lords-auidt-inquiry, accessed 31 May 2012.

Christodoulou, M. (2010e, 24 November). *Lords Accuse Auditors of Deceiving Investors*, www.accountancyage.com/aa/news/1900246/lords-accuse-auditors-deceiving -investors, accessed 30 April 2013.

Commission on Auditors' Responsibilities (CAR). (1978). *Report, Conclusions and Recommendations*. American Institute of Certified Public Accountants, New York.

Competition Commission's (CC). (2012, January). *Audit Market Investigation Issues Statement*. London: The Stationery Office Limited.

Competition Commission's (CC). (2013a, February). *Statutory Audit Services Market Investigation: Notice of Possible Remedies under Rule 11 of the Competition Commission Rules of Procedure*. London: The Stationery Office Limited.

Competition Commission's (CC). (2013b, July). *Statutory Audit Services Market Investigation: Summary of Provisional Decision on Remedies*. London: The Stationery Office Limited.

Co-ordinating Group on Audit and Accounting Issues (CGAA). (2003, January). *Final Report to the Secretary of State for Trade and Industry and the Chancellor of the Exchequer*. London: The Stationery Office Limited.

Crump, R. (2012, 1 August). *Audit Reporting Rules could See Duel Accounting*, www.accountancyage.com/aa/analysis/2195678/audit-reporting-rules-could-see-duel -accounting, accessed 23 April 2013.

Crump, R. (2013a, 26 February). *Investor Power at Core of Competition Commission Remedies*, www.accountancyage.com/aa/analysis/2250485/investor-power-at-core-of -competition-commission-remedies, accessed 24 April 2013.

Crump, R. (2013b, 26 April). *Audit Reforms "Nudge" in Right Direction but Leave Many Unsatisfied*, www.accountancyage.com/aa/analysis/2264380/audit-reforms-nudge-in-right-direction-but-leave-many-unsatisifed, accessed 29 April 2013.

Crump, R. (2013c, 19 June). *Auditors Acted as "Cheerleaders" for Questionable Bank Reporting*, www.accountancyage.com/aa/news/2275987/auditors-acted-as -cheerleaders-for-questionable-bank-reporting, accessed 23 June 2013.

Crump, R. (2013d, 22 July). *Competition Commission Outlines Five-Year Audit Tenders*, www.accountancyage.com/aa/news/22838240/competition-commission-outlines -fiveyear-audit-tenders, accessed 29 July 2013.

Crump, R. (2013e, 16 August). *Tendering Changes will Cost Audit Market £100M a Year*, www.accountancyage.com/aa/news/2289430/tendering-changes-will-cost-audit-market-gbp100m-a-year, accessed 19 August 2013.

Deng, S. & Macve, R. (2012). *The Origination and Development of China's Audit Firms.* Unpublished paper presented at the American Accounting Association Conference, Washington, August.

European Commission (EC). (2010, October). *European Commission Green Paper Audit Policy: Lessons from the Crisis.* Brussels: European Commission.

European Parliament and Council (EU). (2011a, November). *Proposal for a Regulation of the European Parliament and of the Council on Specific Requirements Regarding Statutory Audit of Public Interest Entities.* COM(2011)0779 final 2011/0359(COD). (EU Reg). Brussels: European Commission.

European Parliament and Council (EU). (2011b, November). *Proposal for a Directive of the European Parliament and of the Council Amending Directive 2006/43/EC on Statutory Audits of Annual Accounts and Consolidated Accounts.* COM(2011)0778 final 2011/0389(COD). (EU Dir). Brussels: European Commission.

European Parliament Committee (EU) on Legal Affairs (Juri). (2012, September). *Draft Report on Proposal for a Regulation of the European Parliament and of the Council on Specific Requirements Regarding Statutory Audit of Public Interest Entities.* COM(2011) 0779 final 2011/0359(COD). Brussels: European Commission.

European Union (EU). (2006). *Directive 2006/43/EC of the European Parliament and of the Council on Statutory Audits of Annual Accounts and Consolidated Accounts* (Statutory Audit Directive). Brussels: European Parliament and Council.

Financial Reporting Council (FRC). (2003, 2006a, 2008a). *The Combined Code on Corporate Governance.* London: FRC.

Financial Reporting Council (FRC). (2006b, 2007). *A Report on the Main Findings of the Review of the Combined Code on Corporate Governance.* London: FRC.

Financial Reporting Council (FRC). (2006c). *Regulatory Strategy (Version 2.1).* London: Financial Reporting Council.

Financial Reporting Council (FRC). (2008b). *Consultation Paper: Going Concern and Financial Reporting.* London: FRC.

Financial Reporting Council (FRC). (2009). International Standard on Auditing (ISA) (UK and Ireland) 250 Section B: *The Auditor's Right and Duty to Report to Regulators in the Financial Sector.* London: FRC.

Financial Reporting Council (FRC). (2010). *Response to Green Paper "Audit Policy: Lessons from the Crisis".* London: FRC.

Financial Reporting Council (FRC). (2011). *Effective Company Stewardship: Next Steps.* London: FRC.

Financial Reporting Council (FRC). (2012a). *The UK Corporate Governance Code.* London: FRC.

Financial Reporting Council (FRC). (2012b). *Guidance on Audit Committees.* London: FRC.

Financial Reporting Council (FRC). (2012c). *International Standard on Auditing (ISA) (UK and Ireland) 260: Communication with Those Charged with Governance.* London: FRC.

Financial Reporting Council (FRC). (2012d). *International Standard on Auditing (ISA) (UK and Ireland) 700: The Auditor's Report on Financial Statements.* London: FRC.

Financial Reporting Council (FRC). (2013a). *Consultation Paper: Revision to ISA (UK and Ireland) 700 Requiring the Auditor's Report to Address Risks of Material Misstatement, Materiality and a Summary of the Audit Scope.* London: FRC.

Financial Reporting Council (FRC). (2013b). *Consultation Paper: Implementing the Recommendations of the Sharman Panel.* London: FRC.

Financial Reporting Council (FRC). (2013c). *FRC Responds to Competition Commission's Preliminary Report on the Statutory Audit Services Market,* www.frc.org.uk/News-and-Events/FRC-Press/Press/2013/March/FRC-responds-to-Competition-Commissions-prelimina.aspx, accessed 23 April 2013.

Financial Reporting Council (FRC). (2013d). *International Standard on Auditing (ISA) (UK and Ireland) 700: The Independent Auditor's Report on Financial Statements.* London: FRC.

Financial Reporting Council (FRC). (2013e). *FRC Response to Competition Commission's Summary of Provisional Decision on Remedies for the Statutory Audit Market,* www.frc.org.uk/News-and-Events/FRC-Press/Press/2013/August/FRC-responds-to-Competition-Commission-s-Provision.aspx, accessed 20 August 2013.

Financial Services Authority (FSA). (2011a). *Code of Practice for the Relationship between the External Auditor and the Supervisor: Introductory explanation.* www.fsa.gov.uk/ pages/Library/Policy/Guidance_consultations/2011/11_05.shtml, accessed 14 February 2013.

Financial Services Authority (FSA). (2011b). *Code of Practice for the Relationship between the External Auditor and the Supervisor.* www.fsa.gov.uk/pages/Library/Policy/ Guidance_consultations/2011/11_05.shtml, accessed 14 February 2013.

Goundar, S. (2010, 3 November). *'Institutional Prejudice' Restricting Audit Market,* www.accountancyage.com/aa/news/1867640/institutonal-prejudice-restricting-audit-market, accessed 24 April 2013.

Haddrill, S. (2011, 10 February). Speech to the European Commission Conference on Financial Reporting and Auditing, www.frc.org.uk/press/pub2508.html, accessed 14 February 2011.

Hooper, J. (2013, 5 April). Private e-mail to one of the authors of this book explaining the European Union's Legislative process.

House of Commons Treasury Select Committee (HCTC). (2009, May). *Banking Crisis: Reforming Corporate Governance and Pay in the City. Ninth Report of Session 2008–09.* London: The Stationery Office Limited

House of Lords (HoL). (2011, March). *House of Lords Select Committee on Economic Affairs 2nd Report of Session 2010–2011, Auditors: Market Concentration and their role, Volume 1: Report.* London: The Stationery Office Limited.

Huber, N. (2009, 3 June). *Former FD Attacks 'Silly' Audit Reform*, www.accountancyage.com/aa/news/1784342/former-fd-attacks-silly-audit-reform, accessed 30 April 2013.

Huber, N. (2010, 8 December). *Contingency Needed Against Big Four Collapse, Say FDs*, www.accountancyage.com/aa/news/1930703/contingency-collapse-fds, accessed 30 April 2013.

Huber, N. (2011, 27 January). *Big Four Break-Up Threat*, www.accountancyage.com/aa/analysis/1939751/break-threat, accessed 30 April 2013.

Humphrey, C. G., Moizer, P., & Turley, S. (1993). The audit expectations gap in Britain: An empirical investigation. *Accounting and Business Research*, *23*(91A), 395–411.

Institute of Chartered Accountants in England and Wales (ICAEW). (2002, July). *Mandatory Rotation of Audit Firms: Review of Current Requirements, Research and Publications*. London: ICAEW.

Institute of Chartered Accountants of Scotland (ICAS). (2010, July). *The Future of Assurance*. Edinburgh: ICAS.

Institute of Chartered Accountants of Scotland (ICAS). (2013, April). *Balanced and Reasonable*. Edinburgh: ICAS.

International Auditing and Assurance Standards Board (IAASB). (2009a). International Standard on Auditing (ISA) 240: *The Auditor's Responsibilities Relating to Fraud in an Audit of Financial Statements*. New York: International Federation of Accountants.

International Auditing and Assurance Standards Board (IAASB). (2009b). International Standard on Auditing (ISA) 260: *Communication with Those Charged with Governance*. New York: International Federation of Accountants.

International Auditing and Assurance Standards Board (IAASB). (2009c). International Standard on Auditing (ISA) 570: *Going Concern*. New York: International Federation of Accountants.

International Auditing and Assurance Standards Board (IAASB). (2009d). International Standard on Auditing (ISA) 700: *Forming an Opinion and Reporting on Financial Statements*. New York: International Federation of Accountants.

International Auditing and Assurance Board (IAASB). (2010). *IAASB Clarity Center: The Clarified Standards*, www.ifac.org/clarity-center/the-clarified-standards, accessed 24 November 2012.

International Auditing and Assurance Standards Board (IAASB). (2012). *Improving the Auditor's Report*. New York: International Federation of Accountants.

International Auditing and Assurance Standards Board (IAASB). (2013a). Proposed International Standard on Auditing (ISA) 260 (Revised): *Communication with Those Charged with Governance*. New York: International Federation of Accountants.

International Auditing and Assurance Standards Board (IAASB). (2013b). Proposed International Standard on Auditing (ISA) 700 (Revised): *Forming an Opinion and Reporting on Financial Statements*. New York: International Federation of Accountants.

International Auditing and Assurance Standards Board (IAASB). (2013c). Proposed International Standard on Auditing (ISA) 701: *Communicating Key Audit Matters in the Independent Auditor's Report*. New York: International Federation of Accountants.

Liggio, C.D. (1974). The expectation gap: The accountant's legal Waterloo. *Journal of Contemporary Business, 3*, 27–44.

Limperg, T. (1932). *The Social Responsibility of the Auditor*, reproduced by Limperg Instituut, (1985). The Netherlands: Limperg Institute.

Luk, H. (2010, 14 June). *China's New Accounting Epoch*, app1.hkicpa.org.hk/APLUS/ 1006/APLUS1006_14-18_mainland_accnt.pdf, accessed 30 April 2013.

New Zealand Securities Commission (NZSC). (2004). *Corporate Governance in New Zealand Principles and Guidelines*. Wellington. Securities Commission.

NZX. (2003). *NZX Corporate Governance Best Practice Code*. Wellington: NZX.

Orlik, R. (2011a, 26 April). *Investors Do Care about Competition*, www.accountancyage . com/aa/news/2045986/investors-care-audit-competition, accessed 29 April 2013.

Orlik, R. (2011b, 13 May). *Licensed to Audit*? www.accountancyage.com/aa/analysis/ 2070827/licensed-audit, accessed 30 April 2013.

Orlik, R. (2011c, 16 June). *Government Rejects Lords' Call for Mandatory Audit Dialogue*, www.accountancyage.com/aa/news/2079301/government-rejects-lords-manda tory-audit-dialogue, accessed 23 April 2013.

Orlik, R. (2011d, 28 September). *Untold Consequences Loom in Audit-Only Landscape*, www.accountancyage.com/aa/analysis/2112842/untold-consequences-loom-audit-landscape, accessed 30 April 2013.

Orlik, R. (2011e, 30 September). *RSM Tenon: Audit Reform is Inevitable*, www .accountancyage.com/aa/analysis/2113314/rsm-tenon-audit-reform-inevitable, accessed 29 April 2013.

Orlik, R. (2011f, 13 October). *ICAEW: Pass/Fail Audit Report is Best*, www.accountancy age .com/aa/news/2117086/icaew-pass-fail-audit-report, accessed 23 April 2013.

Orlik, R. (2011g, 30 November). *Softer Audit Reforms Provoke Hard Response*, www .accountancyage.com/aa/analysis/2129062/softer-audit-reforms-provoke-hard -response, accessed 29 April 2013.

Porter, B.A. (1993). An empirical study of the audit expectation-performance gap. *Accounting and Business Research, 24*(93), 49–68.

Porter, B.A., & Gowthorpe, C. (2004). *Audit Expectation-Performance Gap in the United Kingdom in 1999 and Comparison with the Gap in New Zealand in 1989 and 1999*.Edinburgh: Institute of Chartered Accountants of Scotland.

Porter, B.A., Ó hÓgartaigh, C., & Baskerville, R. (2012). Audit expectation-performance gap in New Zealand and the United Kingdom and changes to the gap in New Zealand 1989–2008 and the United Kingdom 1999–2008. *International Journal of Auditing, 16*(2), 101–129, and *16*(3), 215–247.

Ramsay, I. (2001, 21 October). *Independence of Australian Company Auditors: Review of Current Australian Requirements and Proposals for Reform*. Report to the Minister from Financial Services and Regulation. Australia, Canberra: Treasury.

Reed, K. (2011, 15 March). *Firms 'Doubt' FRC's Audit Direction*, www.accountancyage .com/aa/analysis/2034200/firms-doubt-frcs-audit-direction, accessed 30 April 2013.

Reed, K. (2012a, 5 April). *China will Help Create Big Six*, www.accountancyage.com/ aa/ news/2166267/china-help-create, accessed 30 April 2013.

Reed, K. (2012b, 28 September). *Mandatory Audit Tendering Introduced in UK Governance Code*, www.accountancyage.com/aa/news/2208914/mandatory-audit-tendering-introduced-in-uk-governance-code, accessed 25 April 2013.

Sexton, R. (2013, 25 February). *PwC: Don't Change Auditor for Change's Sake*, www.accountancyage.com/aa/opinion/2250367/pwc-dont-change-auditor-for -changes-sake, accessed 25 April 2013.

Sharman, Lord. (2012, June). *The Sharman Inquiry: Going Concern and Liquidity Risks: Lessons for Companies and Auditors. Final Report and Recommendations of the Panel of Inquiry*. London: Financial Reporting Council.

Singh, R. (2012, 20 April). *ICAS says FRC Audit Reforms Don't Go Far Enough*, www .accountancyage.com/aa/news/2169225/icas-frc-audit-reforms-don-t, accessed 23 April 2013.

Smith, P. (2013, 8 July). *Top 35 Networks 2013: New Markets, Opportunities, Threats*, www.accountancyage.com/aa/feature/2280064/top-35-networks-2013-new-markets -opportunities-threats, accessed 20 August 2013.

Tweedie, Sir D. (2012, 28 August). *President's Comment: Rediscovering Professionalism*, icas.org.uk/News/Latest_News/President_s_Comment_Rediscovering_Profession-alism, accessed 18 May 2013.

Wang, Y. (2012, 5 October). *Big Four Auditors Get Rules for Restructuring*, english. caixin.com/2012-05-10/100388784_all.html, accessed 27 March 2013.

Woolfe, J. (2013, 18 March). *EU Committee Votes for Seven-Year Tendering*, www .accountancyage.com/aa/news/2255328/eu-committee-votes-for-sevenyear-auditor -rotation, accessed 25 April, 2013.

ADDITIONAL READING

Bedard, J.C., Sutton, S.G., Arnold, V., & Philips, J.R. (2012). Another piece of the 'Expectations Gap': What do investors know about auditor involvement with information in the annual report? *Current Issues in Auditing, 6*(1), A17–A30.

Chen, C.J.P., Su, X., & Wu, X. (2010). Auditor changes following a big 4 merger with a local Chinese firm: A case study. *Auditing: A Journal of Practice & Theory, 29*(1), 41–72.

Daugherty, B.E., & Tervo, W.A. (2008). Auditor changes and audit satisfaction: Client perceptions in the Sarbanes-Oxley era of legislative restrictions and involuntary auditor change. *Critical Perspectives on Accounting, 19*(7), 931–951.

Dennis, I. (2010). What do you expect? A reconfiguration of the audit expectations gap. *International Journal of Auditing, 14*(2), 130–146.

Gold, A., Gronewold, U., & Pott, C. (2012). The ISA 700 auditor's report and the audit expectation gap – do explanations matter? *International Journal of Auditing*, *16*(3), 286–307.

Gray, G.L., Turner, J.L., Coram, P.J., & Mock, T.J. (2011). Perceptions and misperceptions regarding the unqualified auditor's report by financial statement preparers, users and auditors, *Accounting Horizons*, *25*(4), 659–684.

Humphrey, C., Kausar, A., Loft., A., & Woods, M. (2011). Regulating audit beyond the crisis: A critical discussion of the EU Green Paper. *European Accounting Review*, *20*(3), 431–457.

Malsch, B., & Gendron, Y. (2011). Reining in auditors: On the dynamics of power surrounding an "innovation" in the regulatory space. *Accounting, Organizations and Society*, *36*(7), 456–476.

Sikka, P. (2009). Financial crisis and the silence of the auditors. *Accounting, Organizations and Society*, *34*(6–7), 868–873.

Zerni, M., Haapamaki, E., Jarvinen, T., & Niemi, L. (2012). Do joint audits improve audit quality? Evidence from voluntary joint audits. *European Accounting Review*, *21*(4), 731–765.

Index